The Nonprofit Handbook: Fund Raising

The AFP/Wiley Fund Development Series

Beyond Fund Raising: New Strategies for Nonprofit Innovation and Investment by Kay Sprinkel Grace

The Complete Guide to Fund-Raising Management by Stanley Weinstein

Critical Issues in Fund Raising edited by Dwight F. Burlingame

Direct Response Fund Raising by Michael Johnston

The Fund Raiser's Guide to the Internet by Michael Johnston

Ethical Decision Making in Fund Raising by Marilyn Fischer

Fund Raising: Evaluating and Managing the Fund Development Process, Second Edition by James M. Greenfield

Fund-Raising Cost Effectiveness: A Self-Assessment Workbook by James M. Greenfield

International Fund Raising for Not-for-Profits: A Country by Country Profile by Thomas Harris

The Nonprofit Handbook: Fund Raising, Third Edition edited by James M. Greenfield

Nonprofit Investment Policies: A Practical Guide to Creation and Implementation by Robert P. Fry, Jr.

The NSFRE Fundraising Dictionary by National Society of Fund Raising Executives

Planned Giving Simplified: The Gift, the Giver, and the Gift Planner by Robert F. Sharpe, Sr.

The Universal Benefits of Volunteering: A Practical Workbook for Nonprofit Organizations, Volunteers, and Corporations by Walter Pidgeon

The Nonprofit Handbook: Fund Raising

Third Edition

**Edited by
James M. Greenfield, ACFRE, FAHP**

JOHN WILEY & SONS, INC.

This publication is designed to provide accurate and authoritative information in regard to the subject matter covered. It is sold with the understanding that the pub-lisher is not engaged in rendering legal, accounting, or other professional services. If legal advice or other expert assistance is required, the serices of a competent profes-sional person should be sought.

Library of Congress Cataloging-in-Publication Data:

The nonprofit handbook. Fund raising / edited by James M. Greenfield.—3rd ed.
    p. cm. — (The NSFRE/Wiley fund development series)
  Includes bibliographical references and index.
  ISBN 978-0-471-40304-3
    1. Nonprofit organizations—Management—Handbooks, manuals, etc.   2. Non-profit organizations—Finance—Handbooks, manuals, etc.   3. Total quality manage-ment—Handbooks, manuals, etc.   4. Fund raising—Handbooks, manuals, etc.
  I. Title: Fund raising.   II. Greenfield, James M., 1936-   III. Series.

HD62.6 .N662 2001
658.15'224—dc21

00-061962

The AFP/Wiley Fund Development Series

The AFP/Wiley Fund Development Series is intended to provide fund development professionals and volunteers, including board members (and others interested in the nonprofit sector), with top-quality publications that help advance philanthropy as voluntary action for the public good. Our goal is to provide practical, timely guidance and information on fund raising, charitable giving, and related subjects. AFP and Wiley each bring to this innovative collaboration unique and important resources that result in a whole greater than the sum of its parts.

The Association of Fundraising Professionals

The AFP is a professional association of fund-raising executives that advances philanthropy through its more than 25,000 members in over 158 chapters throughout the United States, Canada, and Mexico. Through its advocacy, research, education, and certification programs, the Society fosters development and growth of fund-raising professionals, works to advance philanthropy and volunteerism, and promotes high ethical standards in the fund-raising profession.

1999–2000 AFP Publishing Advisory Council

**Subscriber
Update
Service**

BECOME A SUBSCRIBER!
Did you purchase this product from a bookstore?

If you did, it's important for you to become a subscriber. John Wiley & Sons, Inc. may publish, on a periodic basis, supplements and new editions to reflect the latest changes in the subject matter that you *need to know* in order to stay competitive in this ever-changing industry. By contacting the Wiley office nearest you, you'll receive any current update at no additional charge. In addition, you'll receive future updates and revised or related volumes on a 30-day examination review.

If you purchased this product directly from John Wiley & Sons, Inc., we have already recorded your subscription for this update service.

To become a subscriber, please call **1-800-225-5945** or send your name, company name (if applicable), address, and the title of the product to:

mailing address: **Supplement Department
John Wiley & Sons, Inc.
One Wiley Drive
Somerset, NJ 08875**

e-mail: **subscriber@wiley.com**
fax: **1-732-302-2300**
online: **www.wiley.com**

For customers outside the United States, please contact the Wiley office nearest you:

Professional & Reference Division
John Wiley & Sons Canada, Ltd.
22 Worcester Road
Rexdale, Ontario M9W 1L1
CANADA
(416) 675-3580
Phone: 1-800-567-4797
Fax: 1-800-565-6802
canada@jwiley.com

Jacaranda Wiley Ltd.
PRT Division
P.O. Box 174
North Ryde, NSW 2113
AUSTRALIA
Phone: (02) 805-1100
Fax: (02) 805-1597
headoffice@jacwiley.com.au

John Wiley & Sons, Ltd.
Baffins Lane
Chichester
West Sussex, PO19 1UD
ENGLAND
Phone: (44) 1243 779777
Fax: (44) 1243 770638
cs-books@wiley.co.uk

John Wiley & Sons (SEA) Pte. Ltd.
2 Clementi Loop #02-01
SINGAPORE 129809
Phone: 65 463 2400
Fax: 65 463 4605; 65 463 4604
wiley@singnet.com.sg

About the Editor

James M. Greenfield, ACFRE, FAHP, is a veteran fund-raising professional with 38 years' experience as a development officer at three universities and five hospitals on both the East and West Coasts and in between. He has served AFP as a chapter officer and national board member. He remains active in support of AFP as a member of the AFP Foundation for Philanthropy. Jim is a frequent speaker at AFP conferences, a trainer for AFP's First Course and Survey Course, and author of six books and more than 35 articles on fund-raising practices. He was selected as the 1994 fund-raising professional of the year by AFP's Orange County Chapter and was honored by the Association of Healthcare Philanthropy (AHP) with its Harold J. (Si) Seymour International Honors Award in 1993. Another high honor, the AFP Outstanding Fund-Raising Executive Award, was conferred in March, 2000.

▼ Contributors

Sylvia Allen, MA, is president of Allen Consulting, Inc., a nationally known sports and events marketing company located in New Jersey. She is a published author, publisher of *The Sponsorship Newsletter,* and teaches sponsorship and sports marketing at New York University and at roughly one hundred conferences annually.

Albert Anderson has over twenty-five years of experience at executive levels of management and development in private and public higher education. He has served as vice president for planning/administration at the University of Minnesota Foundation, and as consultant to a broad range of not-for-profit and government organizations. Currently he is serving as consultant to and President of College Misericordia in Dallas, Pennsylvania; previously, he served for nearly seven years as President of Lenoir Rhyne College in Hickory, North Carolina. He has published in *The Harvard Theological Review* and *The Review of Metaphysics,* and is a contributor to *The Responsibilities of Wealth.*

Ted D. Bayley, ACFRE, is an Associate Vice President with the Alford Group, Inc. His 39 years of fund-raising experience included 18 years with the Boy Scouts of America, 11 years with a large Public University, and 10 years with a healthcare system. He has authored two books on fund raising.

George A. Brakeley Jr., CFRE, has been a fund-raising consultant since 1938 to more than 350 U.S., Canadian, international, and overseas not-for-profit institutions, organizations, and associations, in raising some $9 billion. He personally directed Canada's original capital campaigns in 1948 and 1950 and established the first consulting firm in San Francisco in 1956, with Stanford University as his first client.

Dwight F. Burlingame, PhD, CFRE is associate executive director at the Indiana University Center on Philanthropy, Indianapolis, and professor of philanthropic studies.

Diane M. Carlson, president of IDC in Henderson, Nevada, has led the nation in telephone fund raising. In 1977, IDC developed the PHONE/MAIL® Telecommunications Program for Yale University and, as a result, pioneered telephone wrap-up for capital campaigns. Ms. Carlson has served as an officer of the National Society of Fund Raising Executives, as well as chapter president of New Jersey. She currently chairs the American Association of Fund Raising Counsel.

Richard D. Cheshire, Ph.D., was the president of the University of Tampa, as well as the chief development officer at the Center for Strategic & International Studies, Chapman University, Colgate University, Dickinson College, and Drew University. Most recently, he is co-founder and director of the Institute for Voluntary Leadership in Orange County, California, where he has pioneered quantum civics, a new field of leadership science that applies core principles of quantum physics to the dynamics of civic action.

James E. Connell, M.Ed., FAHP, has an active 24-year involvement in fund raising and planned giving with colleges and health care organizations. Prior to establishing his own fund-raising and consulting firm, he served such distinguished institutions as Duke University Medical Center, Medical College of Pennsylvania, Robert Packer Hospital/Guthrie Clinic, the Donald Guthrie Foundation, and Presbyterian-University of Pennsylvania Medical Center. He is the author of more than 40 articles and a frequent speaker on current opportunities to build endowments for American charities.

Tracy Daniel Connors, MA, is President of the BelleAire Institute a management communications and publishing organization (http://www.belleaire.com). For the past 20 years, he has served as executive editor of six best-selling handbooks for leaders and managers of nonprofit organizations. In addition, he has served in a variety of management positions in business, government, and philanthropy.

Barbara M. Cox, partner, Doty & Cox, Darien, Connecticut, has been a development professional for 30 years. She has created innovative annual giving, building, and endowment campaigns and established fund-raising offices for human service, educational, and cultural organizations in Connecticut and New York.

Jean Crawford, FAHP, is the President of Jean Crawford & Company, Ltd. A 20-year veteran in professional fund raising, she provides philanthropic counsel in specialized services in strategic and change management planning, developing annual and capital campaigns, conducting development audits, and preparing boards for their fund raising role.

Nan D. Doty, partner, Doty & Cox, Darien, Connecticut, has held senior staff positions with United Ways in Connecticut, New York, and North Carolina. She was the first director of marketing for the Connecticut practice of Deloitte & Touche and is an experienced trainer on board development, strategic planning, and major gift solicitation.

John P. Dreves, MPA, CFRE, is managing partner for the Washington, D.C., offices of Staley/Robeson/Ryan/St. Lawrence, Inc. During a 30-year fund-raising career, he has been chief development executive with four medical centers and a consultant serving national social service organizations, colleges, and universities, religious groups, and cultural institutions. A focus of his consulting work is fund-raising assessments; he has directed or been instrumental in assessing programs for 32 not-for-profit organizations.

Erik D. Dryburgh, JD, CPA, Silk, Adler & Colvin, specializes in the charitable giving area, where he works with both donors and donees. His work with donee organizations includes consulting and legal work regarding the establishment of a planned giving program and advising donee organizations regarding gift proposals, gift structuring, and gift administration. Mr. Dryburgh works with donors to structure gifts that meet their charitable, financial, tax, and family goals.

William Freyd, chairman of IDC in Henderson, Nevada, has led the nation in telephone fund raising. In 1977, IDC developed the PHONE/MAIL® Telecommunications Program for Yale University and, as a result, pioneered telephone wrap-up for capital campaigns. Mr. Freyd has served as an officer of the National Society of Fund Raising Executives, as well as chapter president of the Greater New York chapter.

Dwain N. Fullerton is formerly the senior associate dean for external relations in the Stanford School of Engineering. Prior to this, he was vice president for institute relations at the California Institute of Technology and associate vice president for development at Stanford University Medical Center.

Tom Gaffny has been a member of the Epsilon team since 1980 and is currently a director of Creative Services and senior creative director for the Fund Raising and Membership Services Division. In this capacity, he directs strategy, concept, and copy for more than 20 clients. He currently works with such client accounts as Covenant House, American Cancer Society, National Multiple Sclerosis Society, and Disabled American Veterans. Mr. Gaffny has received several regional and national awards for his creative work and has spoken widely in the United States as well as in Europe.

Susan L. Golden, PhD, CFRE, President of the Golden Group in Cleveland, Ohio, is a consultant specializing in grant-seeking and capital campaigns, has participated in raising more than $700 million for more than 100 not-for-profit organizations. She is an officer of the NSFRE Greater Cleveland chapter and a member of the NSFRE National Research Council. Her book on the relationship model of grant-seeking, *Secrets of Successful Grantsmanship,* was published by Jossey-Bass in 1997.

Henry Goldstein, CFRE, is president and CEO of The Oram Group, Inc. Founded in 1980, his firm renders a broad spectrum of fund-raising and not-for-profit services to the not-for-profit community.

Robert E. Gregg, MA, CFRE, is the territorial financial development (major gifts) director for The Salvation Army Western Territory. He joined The Salvation Army as a professional staff member in 1995 with the specific mandate to build a coordinated major gifts program across the Western Territory from the ground up. To date, the program is responsible for raising over $30 million in current and deferred gifts in less than five years. In addition, Mr. Gregg developed and manages the professional training and development and revitalization programs. He also managed the process to research and select the current donor management system. This process led to the growing independence of the Army in the West from specific direct-mail vendors to internal decision making, which is part of the drive for significantly increased professionalism in each division. Prior to joining The Salvation Army professionally, he was associated with Boys Town (Father Flanagan's Boys' Home). There, he served as a planned giving representative, development director, and national director for major and planned gifts.

Patrick Guzman, CPA, CFP, is a founding partner (1988) of the accounting firm of Guzman & Gray, CPAs in Long Beach, California. Mr. Guzman has been servicing not-for-profit organizations for 30 years in the areas of auditing, analysis of internal controls, consulting, accounting, and tax planning. He has served on committees and lectured at various not-for-profit conferences on the state and local level, and served as president for the Orange County/Long Beach chapter of the California Society of CPA's.

Thomas L. Harris is the founder of The Virtual Consulting Firm, a group of multidisciplinary experts in the not-for-profit sector from various cultures. He is the author of various works in German and English, most notably of International Fund Raising: A Country-by-Country Profile, published in 1999 by John Wiley. He may be reached at *virtualhar@aol.com.*

Kimberly Hawkins, CFRE, is a partner in the New York-based fund raising and management consulting firm of Raybin Associates, Inc. Prior to joining the firm in 1987, she spent 15 years as a senior development officer with a variety of educational, cultural, and health care organizations.

John W. Hicks is vice president of J.C. Greever, Inc. He frequently consults with emerging not-for-profit organizations on fund-raising and management issues and is active as an author and speaker. He is a member of the board of directors of the AAFRC Trust for Philanthropy and of the National Society of Fund Raising Executives.

Bruce R. Hopkins, JD, LLM, is a lawyer with Polsinelli, Shalton & White in Kansas City, MO, where he specializes in the representation of not-for-profit organizations. He served as the chair of the Committee on Exempt Organizations, American Bar Association; chair of the Section of Taxation, National Association of College and University Attorneys; and president of the Planned Giving Study Group of Greater Washington, DC.

Fisher Howe, CFRE, Lavender, Howe & Associates, is a Washington, D.C., consultant on not-for-profit management and fund raising. He is a trustee of several national and local not-for-profit organizations. A former foreign service officer, he has served as assistant dean, Johns Hopkins School of Advanced International Studies, and director of Institutional Relations, Resources for the Future. His publications include *The Board Member's Guide to Fund Raising* (1991) and *Welcome to the Board: Your Guide to Effective Participation* (1996).

Michael Johnston is the President of Hewitt and Johnston Consultants, a full service fund raising consulting firm in Toronto, Canada. He is an author, speaker, and consultant to scores of not-for-profit organizations around the world on a variety of topics, especially the Internet.

Ronald R. Jordan, JD, is the former director of Planned Giving at Boston University and is currently assistant vice president for University Development at New Mexico State University in Las Cruces, New Mexico. A member of the bar since 1975, he is a graduate of the New England School of Law and Salem State College. Mr. Jordan is also an assistant professor at New Mexico State University, where he teaches courses in financial planning and consumer economics and has previously taught federal income taxation and estate planning.

Andrea Kaminski is a co-founder and executive director of the Women's Philanthropy Institute, a not-for-profit organization that educates, encourages, and inspires women to effect positive change in the world through philanthropy. She has spoken in cities across North America and has written on women and philanthropy for such publications as Advancing Philanthropy, Currents, and the Association of Healthcare Philanthropy Journal.

Kathleen S. Kelly, Ph.D., CFRE, APR, Fellow PRSA, is professor of communication and public relations at the University of Louisiana, Lafayette, where she also holds the Hubert J. Bourgeois Endowed Research Professorship. She is the author of two books on fund raising, including the field's first academic text, *Effective Fund-Raising Management* (1998).

Richard F. Larkin, MBA, CPA, is Technical Director in the Not-for-Profit Industry Services Group in the national office of PricewaterhouseCoopers LLP, with responsibility for assisting firm partners and staff worldwide with accounting and auditing issues involving not-for-profit organizations. He is a certified public accountant with thirty-one years of experience serving a wide variety of not-for-profit organizations as independent accountant, board member, treasurer, and consultant. He teaches, speaks and writes extensively on not-for-profit industry matters and is active in many professional and industry organizations. He was the chair of the AICPA's Not-for-Profit Audit Guide task force and has been a member of FASB Not-for-Profit Advisory Task Force, the AICPA Not-for-Profit Organizations Committee. He is a co-author of the sixth edition of *Financial and Accounting Guide for Not-for-Profit Organizations*, author of *Financial Statement Presentation and Disclosure Practices for Not-for-Profit Organizations* (published by the AICPA), and a contributor to *The Accountants' Handbook*. He is an adjunct professor of not-for-profit management at Georgetown University, and as a member of the Peace Corps taught business administration at Haile Sellassie I University in Addis Ababa, Ethiopia.

Kay Partney Lautman, CFRE, president, Lautman & Company, Washington, D.C., and New York City. Prior to founding Lautman & Company in 1992, she was, for 17 years, director of Oram Group Marketing, the direct mail division of The Oram Group, Inc. She is the coauthor of *Dear Friend: Mastering the Art of Direct Mail Fund Raising*, published by the Taft Corporation. Chosen Outstanding Fund Raising Executive by the Washington Chapter of NSFRE in 1985 and Woman of the Year in 1994 by the Women's Direct Response Group, Ms. Lautman serves on the NSFRE Foundation Board, on the board of the Association of Direct Response Fundraising Council, and on several not-for-profit boards.

Charles E. Lawson, MPC, Brakeley, John Price Jones Inc., is one of the leading figures in the not-for-profit field. He is the author of the *NSFRE Glossary of Fund-Raising Terms*, founder of the AAFRC Trust for Philanthropy, and a frequent lecturer and contributor to books and periodicals. In 1990 he was honored as Fund-Raiser of the Year by the NSFRE Connecticut Chapter.

Jerry A. Linzy, MA, AAHP, is senior managing partner of Jerold Panas, Linzy & Partners. Linzy has 25 years of fund-raising experience in higher education, health care, and community organizations.

Elizabeth M. Lowell is a partner at Raybin Associates, Inc., a Greenwich, Connecticut-based consulting firm assisting clients with fund raising, strategic planning, and board development. She has helped many smell and medium-sized organizations to engage their trustees in the fund-raising process.

George F. Maynard III, FAHP, Senior Partner, Jerold Panas, Linzy & Partners, Inc., was president of the Orlando Regional Healthcare Foundation in Orlando, Florida, from 1987 to 1998 and chaired the 1997 AHP Think Tank Project. He has more than 20 years of experience in health care public relations and philanthropy.

Barry J. McLeish is vice president of McConkey/Johnston, Inc., a marketing and management consulting firm based in Woodland Park, Colorado. Previously, he was the director of marketing for a nonprofit with more than 800 employees and an annual budget of $27 million. He is also the author of *Successful Marketing Strategies for Nonprofit Organizations*, published by John Wiley & Sons.

Lynda S. Moerschbaecher, JD, is an attorney and consultant in San Francisco and counsel to Freeman, Freeman and Smiley, a law firm in Los Angeles, Orange County, and San Francisco. Her practice focuses on planned giving, and she advises donors, donees, and trustees. She has written a series of books, manuals, and audio and video tapes, the *Plain English Planned Giving* series, and has produced document assemble software for all charitable gift vehicles, "Docs in a Box." Other software in production includes planned gift office management products.

August A. Napoli Jr. is president of the Catholic Charities Corporation, the fund-raising arm of the Catholic Charities system of 43 human service agencies in the Diocese of Cleveland. Prior to arriving at Catholic Charities in 1992, he was Cleveland State University's vice president for University Relations and Development. He also served as director of development at two other Cleveland area colleges. Mr. Napoli is a past president of the Ohio Council of Fund Raising Executives and is a member of the Business Volunteerism Council of Cleveland and the National Catholic Stewardship Council.

Cheryl Carter New is the President of Polaris Corporation. She is the founder of the company which was incorporated in 1984. Her background includes many years of academic instruction, and grant proposal writing.

Judith E. Nichols, MBA, PhD, CFRE, is a development consultant with a variety of not-for-profit clients across the USA, Canada, the United Kingdom, and Europe. A popular trainer and presenter, she specializes in helping organizations understand the implications of our changing demographics and psychographics on fund raising, marketing, and membership. Dr. Nichols has been a featured speaker and trainer at numerous conferences, workshops, and symposia around the world. An active member of the Association of Fundraising Professionals, Judy Nichols has served on both the Michigan and Oregon boards. She is listed in *Who's Who of American Women* and *Who's Who in Education*. She has written several well-received books on fund raising, most recently including *Global Demographics* and *Growing from Good to Great*.

Barry T. O'Hare is managing director of Brakeley, John Price Jones Inc. A professional fund raiser for 27 years, he offers special expertise in designing and conducting development programs for religious communities, churches, dioceses, and facilities for disabled persons. He has served as a featured speaker at regional seminars and national conventions on a broad range of subjects in the fund-raising field.

Edith M. Pearson is a senior consultant with Raybin Associates, Inc., a fund-raising consulting firm based in Greenwich, Connecticut. Prior to becoming a consultant, she spent 20 years working with arts-related and youth organizations to begin full-service development programs.

Seth Perlman BS, JD, is a senior partner of Perlman and Perlman. He has litigated in numerous state and federal jurisdictions on issues relevant to the philanthropic community and is special counsel for the Association of Fundraising Professionals, and the American Association of Fundraising Consultants. Mr. Perlman is a frequent commentator and lecturer on issues affecting the nonprofit sector. Along with Betsy Hills Bush, he is the author of *Fund-Raising Regulation*, the definitive handbook on charitable solicitations.

Lester A. Picker, EdD, Picker & Associates, was a syndicated columnist on not-for-profits for four years in *The Baltimore Sun*. He is a features writer for national business magazines and is a regular commentator for National Public Radio's *Marketplace*. Mr. Picker is a former director of and consultant to not-for-profit organizations.

Walter P. Pidgeon Jr., PhD, CFRE, CAE, currently serves as major gifts officer for the National Society of Fund Raising Executives and is a recognized authority on the worth of volunteering in enriching the community and returning value to the individual who volunteers. He is a published author and consultant on fund-raising, volunteering, strategic planning, membership development, and health-related issues. Mr. Pidgeon is a former CEO of the National Rural Health Association and the American Council on Alcoholism, as well as former president of the Maryland Society of Association Executives.

Jason Potts, BA, has worked in direct response for 8 years, in both business-to-business and business-to-consumer. Jason also speaks regularly at conferences about the future of new media for the sector, writes articles for several industry journals, and is regularly quoted in the English press. He has recently had a chapter published in a Wiley book, *New Trends in Direct Response Fundraising*, dealing with the use of new media by not-for-profits on a global level.

James A. Quick is the Chief Exective Officer for Polaris, a South Carolina Corporation. He has served in this capacity since 1989. As the Senior Instructional Specialist for Polaris, he has spoken before thousands of potential grant seekers and written successful grant proposals for over ten years.

Katelyn L. Quynn, JD, is currently the associate director of development at Massachusetts General Hospital and manages its planned giving program. She is on the board of the National Committee on Planned Giving and is 1994–1995 president of the Planned Giving Group of New England. Ms. Quynn is a graduate of Tufts University and Boston University School of Law.

Nancy L. Raybin, MBA, is managing partner of Raybin Associates, Inc., a consulting firm that works with not-for-profit and grant-making organizations on fund-raising and strategic planning projects. Prior to joining the firm, she was a consultant with McKinsey & Co. Currently, Ms. Raybin is president of the AAFRC Trust for Philanthropy.

James A. Rice, PhD, is President of the Governance Institute in La Jolla, California, which helps boards and physician leaders improve the performance of their health systems. Mr. Rice has 25 years of experience in integrated system development, managed care, and HMOs, and has worked as a teacher, author, speaker, and consultant to physician groups, boards of directors, and industry leaders nationwide.

Arthur H. Roach, DD, specializes in full-service fund raising for church-related and arts organizations for Brakeley, John Price Jones Inc. He has served on the boards of the Washington Shakespeare Company, the Opera Camerata of Washington, and the Famine Relief Fund and is also a Business Volunteer for the Arts for the Cultural Alliance of Greater Washington (D.C.).

John J. Schwartz, CFRE, has been in the fields of fund raising and philanthropy since 1946. He is the founding president of the National Center for Charitable Statistics, the AAFRC Trust for Philanthropy, and the New York Chapter of NSFRE. Mr. Schwartz was president of the American Association of Fund Raising Counsel for 21 years.

R. Glen Smiley, FAHP, CFRE, is corporate vice president for philanthropy at Henry Ford Health System in Detroit, MI. Smiley previously served as vice president for development at Baylor College of Medicine in Houston, TX (1990–1995), and as senior vice president for external affairs and president of the Children's Hospital Los Angeles Foundation (1988–1990). His career in not-for-profit development began at Duke University in 1971, when he assumed the position of field secretary for the Duke Annual Fund in the office of Alumni Affairs. In 1973, he became assistant director of medical center development at the Duke University Medical Center. Smiley has been an AHP Fellow since 1978, and is co-author of AHP's *A New Environment for Health Care Philanthropy* (1996).

Sally J. Smith, CFRE, has been in the fund raising field for 25 years in the Washington, D.C. area. In that time, she has served both local and national organizations, including: the American Cancer Society, the Corcoran Gallery of Art, the Hospital for Sick Children and Grafton School. While maintaining her fund raising responsibilities, Sally has also taken on additional assignments, such as facilitating strategic planning initiatives, guiding quality improvement efforts, teaching dialogue techniques and co-leading a leadership development program. In May, 2000, she joined the consulting firm of Coviello & Associates, where she continues to serve not-for-profit clients. In addition to her work assignments, Sally has held leadership roles on local and national boards of the National Society of Fund Raising Executives as well as the NSFRE Foundation. In 1996, she helped found a new NSFRE Chapter in the northwest-

ern area of Virginia. She is currently a member of both the Greater Washington D.C. Chapter and the Tri-State Chapter in Virginia.

Bobbie Strand is a principal in the Minneapolis office of Bentz Whaley Flessner. She is a nationally recognized leader in prospect development, including prospect research and management, cultivation and solicitation strategy development, and capital campaign support systems. Her professional background includes teaching English at the high-school level and broad editorial experience. She is a frequent speaker and has chaired conferences on major donor research for the Council for the Advancement and Support of Education (CASE).

Peter Swords is the former President of the Nonprofit Coordinating Committee of New York, an umbrella group of New York Section 501(c)(3) organizations, devoted to improving and protecting the City's nonprofit sector. Mr. Swords teaches courses at Columbia University on not-for-profit institutions at the School of Law and at Teachers College. He is currently working on a project designed to help people understand the Form 990.

Daniel Turse Jr., CFRE, is associate director of planned and major gifts at Wayne State University School of Medicine. His 15 years of fund-raising experience include corporate/foundation relations, the annual fund, special events, and prospect research. His fund-raising articles appear in several prominent journals.

Susan B. Ulin, MS, has been a fund-raising executive since 1975. She entered into a special events partnership in 1985 and opened her own firm in 1990. Susan Ulin Associates, Ltd., located in New York City, specializes in events management and special projects for not-for-profit organizations, political groups, and corporations.

Gail L. Warden, MHCM, is president and chief executive officer of Henry Ford Health System in Detroit, one of the nation's leading vertically integrated health care systems. He is also immediate past chairman of the American Hospital Association Board of Trustees and vice chairman of the Hospital Research and Educational Trust. He is an elected member of the Institute of Medicine of the National Academy of Sciences and serves on the Institute's Governing Council. At Henry Ford Health System, Mr. Warden has spearheaded affiliations to optimize health care delivery services and insurance programs for Detroit area residents. A graduate of Dartmouth College with a master's degree in health care management from the University of Michigan, Mr. Warden is a member of the Pew Health Professional's Commission. He also served as an advisor to President Bill Clinton's Health Care Delivery Task Force. He received the CEO Award in 1993 from the American Hospital Association's Society for Healthcare Planning and Marketing.

Douglas E. White is director of client relations at Kaspick & Co., a planned investment firm in Boston, Massachusetts. He assists not-for-profit organizations with establishing planned giving policies and donor relations. He has served as Ethics Chair for the National Committee of Planned Giving (NCPG) and as president of the Planned Giving Group of New England. Currently a board member of NCPG, Mr. White is also the technical consultant for Paragon, the planned giving software created by Blackbaud, Inc.

M. Jane Williams, MBA, MEd, is a partner in the Philadelphia-based development, marketing, and management consulting firm of Schultz & Williams, Inc. Ms. Williams was a development officer for 23 years in higher education, including positions at the University of Pennsylvania and New York University. As a consultant, she has worked with public broadcasting and health care, educational, and cultural organizations in capital campaign planning, major gift programs, board and staff training, and development program restructuring.

David A. Woodruff is director of institutional advancement at the Massachusetts Institute of Technology in Cambridge, Massachusetts. He has over 15 years of experience in international and domestic fund raising from corporations, individuals, and government organizations.

Contents

CONTENTS

▼ Preface

In 2000, for the first time ever, the American charitable impulse to assist others will exceed $200 billion. Our nation and others around the world have experienced continuous economic growth and prosperity. To paraphrase, "Never before have so many enjoyed so much so soon." More men and women have realized extraordinary wealth in the past decade than ever before in history. In 1982, in the United States, there were 13 billionaires and 1.3 million millionaires. By 1999, their numbers had swelled to 267 billionaires and 5 million millionaires. While philanthropy also enjoyed the benefits of this growth in wealth and appreciated assets, giving as a percentage of annual household income remains at 2 percent, a statistic that cannot be explained. Can this apparent slump be due to a lack of better answers to the question "Why give?"

The number of not-for-profit organizations in America is now estimated at 1.3 million. Of that number, 750,000 are public benefit corporations within Internal Revenue Code 501(c)(3). The solicitation tools in use for fund raising remain the same as they have been for years, with one exception—fund raising on the Internet, highly touted as a boon to all yet unproven for its effectiveness to significantly increase funds raised for charitable purposes. More substantive evidence is the report estimating that the forthcoming transfer of wealth (from all adults alive today to heirs, charities, taxes, and other recipients) for the period from 1998 to 2052 will be between $41 trillion and $136 trillion.[1] Charitable organizations around the world must be included among the designated beneficiaries of some of this extraordinary sum.

Fund-raising practice is the means to many ends. First and foremost, it helps to satisfy the needs and desires of its donors. Second, it aids in fulfilling the mission and vision of its recipients whose good works benefit the communities they serve. Third, it provides the opportunity for citizens to be involved in the causes of their choice through voluntary leadership and support roles. Volunteers, who are the arms and legs of all fund-raising activity, also must be recruited, trained, and rewarded for the valuable gifts of their time, talent, and treasure. However, enabling organizations to do more good works takes more than money. Fund-raising professionals must expand the commitment and support of those already involved while inviting others to join in. When everyone is working together toward a common community benefit, progress can be made. Problems can be solved. Needs can be met. There is no better cause than people helping people.

The practice of philanthropy requires proper legal form, duly elected and active boards of directors, managers and staff with professional training and certified competence, astute fiscal management, dedicated employees who deliver quality programs and services, and more, all dedicated to provide for others in need. The standard of performance called for in these daily operations is not "good enough," or even "be the best you can," but a commitment to excellence. To be a part of any not-for-profit organization is to give your best to achieve excellence in serving others, a goal worthy for each of us. It also is a goal that attracts others to work as volunteers.

This handbook is dedicated to all the elements of successful fund-raising practice. With its companion volume, *The Nonprofit Handbook: Management, Third Edition*, it pro-

---

[1]Paul G. Shervish and John J. Havens, *Millionaires and the Millennium: New Estimates of the Forthcoming Wealth Transfer and the Prospects for a Golden Age of Philanthropy* (Boston: Report of The Boston College Social Welfare Research Institute, 1999).

vides a rich resource toward the achievement of excellence. Together, they represent as complete a summary as possible of current knowledge and instruction for those who lead and serve not-for-profit organizations everywhere.

This handbook is designed to assist fund development work by fund-raising professionals and their volunteers and staff. Chapters cover all the related knowledge areas essential to application of the design and management of a successful fund development program. On behalf of our more than 60 author contributors, we believe the contents will answer questions, provide guidance and direction, and aid in the delivery of successful results.

Part I addresses elements of managing the fund development process. These chapters are essential to understanding what is required to enjoy success. A short history of the past 50 years outlines how we have achieved our current status of competency. Organizations must undertake strategic planning; without sound plans, they cannot explain their requests as a precise vision with clear direction. Marketing translates vision and plans into messages that inspire people to participate in improving their community and the quality of life of all its residents. Budgeting for fund raising is a skill area to be mastered along with understanding how research, programming, evaluation, and stewardship (ROPES) presents a well-organized plan that donors, acting as investors, can study and decide on the merits of the cause. A variety of performance assessments are required to be able to demonstrate effectiveness and efficiency along with accountability in delivering benefits to the community in exchange for its support. And that's only the beginning.

Part II introduces ethics and professionalism. Not-for-profit organizations and their fund-raising practices are called to the highest standards of conduct. Volunteer boards of directors are challenged to act above self in their governance in order to assure the public their contributions are used well for the most urgent needs. The working roles of the board chair, chief executive officer, and fund development executive are described along with a prescription of the board's role in fund raising. In instances where reengineering of the organization is necessary, guidance for transformation and revitalization is provided.

Part III addresses readiness. No organization should ask for public support without knowledge of the demographics of its community. In our more complex society, a clear understanding and appreciation of why people donate to charity is required. Add the requirement that every organization must engage more women in philanthropy in order to succeed in the future. Finally, organizations must look to themselves as progressive enterprises, skillful as well as flexible in adapting to new styles of management and leadership. The twenty-first century brings with it the need to become a learning community that can succeed in the new economy and measure up to the demands of accountability for its leadership.

Part IV begins instruction of fund-raising practice with annual giving programs. Every not-for-profit organization and its fund-raising staff must excel in annual giving because the programs depend on support from the community. These services must be carried out, evaluated, planned, and executed successfully year after year. The art and science of annual giving rests firmly on time-tested, proven methods and techniques that work. Beginning with direct mail communications and progressing to engage and involve people through benefit event participation, communication among donors, volunteers, and organizations is enhanced on the Internet and other media options to help get the message heard. Improved results are achieved with direct conversation on the telephone and culminate in personal, volunteer-led solicitations. Mastery of each of these techniques and their effective deployment utilizing the entire 12 months of the year assures the organization of a reliable and an expanding resource of public support.

Part V focuses on the highly selective area of major gift solicitation. Major giving is a focus on selected individuals as donors and prospects for the organizations they admire most. It is a plan to work together for maximum benefit of both parties. Here too a focus on corporate and foundation giving is applied, but it is more complex and must answer more substantive questions since significant funds are involved, whether in the form of sponsorship and underwriting or multiyear grants. Succeeding in major gift solicitation requires commitment and expertise that begins with prospect research followed by a sensitive understanding of why donors make major gifts. Capital campaigns are fund-raising strategies that can transform organizations. They also are where fund-raising practice is most challenged to succeed at its highest levels. Planned giving is designed to serve donors and organizations with permanent gifts—estate decisions made today mature in the future to become endowments to sustain organizations in perpetuity. Major gifts come in many forms, are more complex, require more expertise, and often depend on alliances with professional advisors to meet donors' final aspirations.

Part VI adds to all the previous chapters an understanding of select audiences and environments. Religious communities are the most successful of all fund-raising enterprises. They excel using all the same skills, methods, and techniques described earlier but have distinct advantages that need to be appreciated. National organizations also carry out philanthropic efforts, delivering their programs and services through local affiliates. They combine public solicitation through local affiliates with national and international solicitation. Another example is the special challenge of grass-roots organizations, where local needs can be addressed without leaving the community. The expanding world of international solicitation practices also is included.

Part VII addresses the essential support areas required for maximum success in any fund-raising effort. These services use fund-raising consultants and appropriate donor recognition followed by applications of today's technology. Proper accounting of all funds raised is essential to public credibility and trust. Disclosure of operating details, including fiscal performance by all not-for-profit organizations, is now publicly available on the Internet in IRS Form 990, a complex tax return that requires understanding of its contents and interpretation of the data revealed. A host of federal and state regulations for public solicitation must be observed by all not-for-profit organizations. Last, the ever-present need for self-renewal requires organizations to pay constant attention to themselves. They need a relevant mission and an aspiring vision plus sound strategic plans and financial management to continue to succeed in delivering valued services to their communities.

This handbook has attempted to address the best in professional fund-raising practice. With the companion volume on management practice, the entire spectrum of philanthropic practice is available. Fund raising is highly dependent on the organizations it serves to provide leadership to its mission and quality application of the contributions it receives. Fund raising is much more than the business of asking for money. Properly understood as a profit center with the means to inspire greater public confidence and trust in organizations serving community needs, these volunteer-led professional practices depend on the recruitment, solicitation, recognition, and communication of all those who would join the cause in order to make a difference to others. In the end, what the money does for others is the real answer to the question "Why give?"

Jim Greenfield
Fundrazer@aol.com
Newport Beach, CA
October 2000

Acknowledgments

Fund-raising professionals are busy people. The contributions of these 62 authors who volunteered their time to write about their areas of expertise are an invaluable resource to you, the reader. We each owe them a large measure of gratitude for sharing so much of themselves. I respect each of them for their friendship as well as their quality work and thank them again for their participation.

No text of this size and magnitude is the work of any one individual. The team of authors provided the content. The team of professionals at John Wiley & Sons assembled it, edited it, designed it, printed it, and now are marketing its use. This team includes Martha Cooley, editor of Wiley's Law, Finance and Management Series. The AFP Publications Advisory Council reviewed the text and approved its entry in the AFP/Wiley Fund Development Series. The balance of work to complete the handbook was performed by Debra Manette, copy editor, Alexia Meyers, Associate Managing Editor, and Jill Lynch, Joanne McIlvaine, and Lisa Fickinger at North Market Street Graphics, for production.

To all of you who made this handbook a reality, thank you on behalf of those who will use its contents to benefit their organizations and improve the lives of those living in their communities.

PART I ▼ Managing Fund Development

Fund-raising Overview

JOHN J. SCHWARTZ, CFRE
Former President, American Association of Fund Raising
Counsel (AAFRC)

1.1 Historical Perspective: The Growth of Credibility and Professionalism of Fund-raising Management

(A) THE STARTING POINT

Upon entering the new century, much needs to be reviewed about the burgeoning field of fund-raising management. *The Nonprofit Handbook: Fund Raising, Third Edition,* will place in perspective the history of the fund-raising field, the major developments of its progress, and the issues requiring solutions. More than 60 seasoned experts in the field of fund-raising management will identify the important developments we are now working with. All will provide further evidence of the fund-raising verities that should never be ignored or forgotten by the true professional.

(B)   WHAT IS PHILANTHROPY?

Much understanding of philanthropy's current state can be gained by reviewing its key developments and placing them in historical perspective. A succinct definition by Robert L. Payton, former director of the University Center of Philanthropy, states, "Philanthropy is voluntary action for public good." It is important to remember the role of fund raising in this context. We will be talking about the philanthropic process because we are a critical element of the larger picture. *All* philanthropy is made possible by these essential ingredients:

The charitable cause
A strong case (bigger than the institution)
The potential donors—individuals, foundations, and corporations
A marketing and communications program to generate a cultivated audience
Volunteer leaders and solicitors for face-to-face solicitation to achieve pace-setting
    gifts
Supplemented by other methods for reaching out for contributions: direct mail,
    phone mail, telemarketing, planned giving, and the burgeoning Internet
The voluntary spirit—the basic motivation for philanthropy
Last but not least, the enablers—the fund-raising managers

Today, any not-for-profit organization needs some measure of all these elements to achieve maximum success.

(C)   THE PROBLEMS AND PROMISE OF PHILANTHROPY

A review of major developments and activities in philanthropy and the fund-raising profession since World War II helps to clarify how far we have come and how prepared we are for the new century.

Although the last 55 years is only 1 percent of recorded history, it has proven to be a seminal period in the development of fund-raising management. It has been a time of establishing ethical practices, professional standards for accreditation, courses on philanthropic studies, training programs, and building intercommunications.

As defined in *Webster's New World Dictionary*, "a profession is a vocation, requiring advanced education and training, and involving intellectual skills." We are now on the brink of becoming a true profession.

(D)   THE CLIMATE FOR FUND RAISING IMMEDIATELY
AFTER WORLD WAR II

In the early 1940s, much of America's resources were absorbed by wartime efforts. As the war ended, many not-for-profits, colleges and universities, hospitals and medical centers, social services, museums, and health causes were establishing development offices and wanted to immediately organize fund-raising campaigns to make up for the years lost by the Great Depression and the war. Competition for the philanthropic dollar was soaring. Although postwar jobs were scarce, the established fund-raising counseling firms such as

Ketchum, Kersting and Brown, John Price Jones, Ward Dreshman & Rheinhart, American City Bureau, and Marts and Lundy could all provide senior campaign directors imbued with deep experience gained in prewar efforts. Their established techniques were proven, and now they were providing a frontline experience for the new generation of returning war veterans. This created a trend of too much, too fast, for several years.

In 1946, my first assignment was with the New York Metropolitan Museum of Art for its seventy-fifth anniversary campaign for $7.5 million, conducted by the John Price Jones Co. Inc. (JPJ). Thomas J. Watson, founder of IBM, was the campaign chair. Top government leadership, including the governor and the mayor, and a distinguished array of volunteers supported this effort. JPJ had assigned its most experienced professionals to conduct interviews and develop a campaign plan that anticipated most contingencies. However, the one issue not given enough attention was the state of the economy immediately after peace was won. By the end of 1946, only $4 million of the $7.5 million goal had been raised. Most fund-raising professionals involved agreed in hindsight that the campaign would have had a much greater chance to succeed if it had been conducted a year later.

Although the situation has improved considerably since, at that time there was little public understanding of the role of professional fund raisers, whether they work for a firm or a not-for-profit organization. Some felt that we were exploiting the philanthropic process and that successful campaigns could be accomplished by voluntary effort without the expensive services of fund raisers, paid out of donated funds. Many leaders seemed confident that the talent and skills that made them successful in their fields would be all they needed to plan and implement a successful fund-raising campaign.

(E) THE FABULOUS 1950s: REACHING FOR THE AMERICAN DREAM

With the demands for the services of not-for-profit organizations far exceeding the resources, the field of fund raising continued to grow at an accelerated rate. Many charities had set up development departments and had conducted successful capital campaigns. The seasoned professionals were ready to link up with any efforts that could improve their professionalism, share experiences, attract new talent, and increase public understanding of the field. Informal meetings in small groups to explore these needs became more commonplace. By the end of the 1950s, people in the field were comparing experiences and sharing lessons learned. Another gain was the stabilization of society and better-developed career paths with an economy recovered from the war years.

(F) THE 1960s: COMPETITION AND PROFESSIONALISM GROW APACE

In 1960, $11.5 billion was given by individuals, corporations, and foundations, an increase of 9 percent from the preceding year. Yet the needs were growing at a faster rate.

1.2 The Combining of Forces

The American Association of Fund-Raising Counsel (AAFRC), incorporated in 1935, had 30 of the leading professional fund-raising counseling firms as members. From the start, members had agreed that ethical and standard practices should guide their conduct when serving their clients. The Fair Practice Code that they established emphasized ethical practices; it was soon emulated by most in the profession.

In 1960 the National Society of Fund Raisers, now the Association of Fundraising Professionals (AFP), was established with the objectives of guiding the fund-raising field into greater professionalism, setting ethical standards, encouraging exchange of ideas and discussions of experiences between agencies, building intercommunications, and aiding the general public to understand the contributions being made by this budding profession. Similar organizations in specific fields—higher education, hospitals and medical centers, and private foundations—were forming today's Council for Advancement and Support of Education (CASE), Association of Healthcare Philanthropy (AHP), National Catholic Development Council, Council on Foundations (COF), and the Foundation Center.

Donors and donees began to communicate with each other and become aware that they shared many problems and challenges. These groups recognized the most pressing needs and the limited resources available, and encouraged a combined effort to allocate funds where they were most needed.

1.3 *Major Milestones*

(A) THE 1970s: PHILANTHROPY BEGINS TO GET ITS ACT TOGETHER

John D. Rockefeller 3rd was an extraordinary factor in improving public awareness and understanding of American philanthropy. Foundations and charitable giving were under scrutiny by Congress as it deliberated on the Tax Reform Act of 1969. JDR 3rd enlisted Peter G. Peterson, chairman of Bell & Howell, to form a commission, known as the Peterson Commission, to study American philanthropy and foundations. Its members were 15 private citizens representing education, the arts, the legal profession, former government officials, labor, publishing, and corporate executives.

In the course of the legislative process, some of the provisions harmful to philanthropy were eased or eliminated in the final version of the bill. Yet the experience as a whole raised an uneasy question: Who spoke for philanthropy when the chips were down?

The Peterson Commission identified more of philanthropy's problems than its solutions. However, it had tremendous influence on the formation and deliberations on future studies embodied by the Filer Commission formed three years later.

In November 1973, JDR 3rd once again responded to his strong conviction that the role of philanthropy in our society was little understood or appreciated, and organized the Commission on Private Philanthropy and Public Needs. He appointed John H. Filer, chairman of Aetna Life & Casualty, as chairman. He also made a start-up grant of $25,000 with the caveat that the commission was now "on its own" to raise the necessary funds.

The Filer Commission's membership included 27 leaders from the fields of religion, labor, government, education, foundations, corporations, and ethnic groups. The commission's activities reached a scope never before obtained: "An Advisory Committee was formed of more than 100 experts from the fields of economics, law, sociology, and taxation, plus representatives of many philanthropic and nonprofit areas. . . . It sponsored in the course of two years of operation no fewer than 85 studies of various aspects of philanthropy and nonprofit activity; extensive analysis of laws and precedents of philanthropy."[1] On November 7, 1975, Filer and JDR 3rd presented the final report to George Shultz, and William Simon, assistant secretary and secretary of the U.S. Treasury, respectively, and the chairs of the House Ways and Means and the Senate Finance committees. The *Wall Street Journal* characterized it as "two & one half cheers for philanthropy." The report had a powerful and lasting impact. It established the continuing need to expand research, it emphasized that in our pluralistic society, strengthening the partnership between the private and public sector is essential; it enhanced a continuing dialogue between donors and donees; and most important to the fund-raising field, AAFRC agreed to donate its professional services to raise the more than $2 million needed to fund its programs, as a public service, waiving all fees. (AAFRC received glowing recognition of this voluntary action.) The final total achieved was $2,311,584 from 738 donors at a cost of less than 2 percent. I was very proud that our member firms agreed to donate their professional services to make this a most successful campaign. This was a major and lasting step to increase both understanding of and respect for our profession by many top leaders and government officials. All combined to, at last, give the field of fund-raising management the credit and respect so well earned over the years.

Included in the report's recommendations was the establishment of a permanent, quasi-governmental commission. Many in our field strongly agreed that a permanent commission was needed but it should be *private*, above and beyond political pressures. Further, a private commission could perform research and advocate action in many important areas that would never be undertaken by government because of political restraints. Key national not-for-profit organizations were stimulated to combine resources to try to put a commission together. In July 1976 the Coalition of National Voluntary Organizations (CONVO) was formed. Soon it had enlisted 47 national not-for-profit organizations, among them the American Cancer Society, the Council for Aid to Education, the Council of Jewish Federations and Welfare Funds, the AAFRC, and the United Way. CONVO's program was formed in order to:

- Maximize the contributions of the voluntary sector in meeting America's human needs
- Increase public understanding of the history, accomplishments, and rich capacity of the voluntary sector to improve the quality of American life
- Gather and disseminate data on the scope and nature of the philanthropic process
- Study public policies that impact on the private sector
- Promote the accountability and accessibility to the public of both donor and donee organizations.

(B) THE GENESIS OF THE INDEPENDENT SECTOR

CONVO's progress was slow in the 1970s because its leadership did not have enough movers and shakers. In fact, there was concern that the energy expended on the Filer Commission had exhausted the interest of many of the sector's leaders.

---

[1]Report of the Commission on Private Philanthropy and Public Needs, *Giving in America, Toward a Stronger Voluntary Sector* (1975), Commission on Private Philanthropy and Public Needs, p. 1

The National Council of Philanthropy (NCOP)—an organization of not-for-profit executives and corporate giving officers that organized annual conferences of donors and donees—began meeting with CONVO representatives to explore the possibility of combining the two organizations to establish a new organization that would be greater than the sum of the two parts. Brian O'Connell, seeking a new change in his career, had just resigned as executive director of the National Institute of Mental Health. We approached him to do a feasibility study on this merger.

The study report was encouraging, and John W. Gardner, founding chair of Common Cause, agreed to chair an organizing committee. After 18 months of deliberations, the organizing committee, with the approval of both CONVO and NCOP boards, recommended the formation of the Independent Sector in early 1980. Its board would have 45 members representing a full spectrum of major leaders from the private sector, including corporations and foundations. Its programs would address:

- Public education to improve understanding of the sector's role
- Communications within the sector so that shared problems and opportunities may be identified and pursued
- Improved relationships with the government
- Research to provide a body of knowledge about the sector
- Encouragement of effective operation to maximize the sector's capacity to serve society.

Today IS members consist of over 700 major foundations, corporations, and leading national not-for-profit organizations. While it is not quite a commission for philanthropy, it has been a highly successful coalition for representing donors, donees, and the best interests of American philanthropy. However, its programs are inevitably influenced by the combined interests of its members. A true commission would have a broader program base, using its resources to improve such problems as elitism; gender and ethnic prejudices; finding sufficient funding; and providing mentoring resources to new, controversial not-for-profit organizations.

1.4 The Maturing of the Philanthropic Process

(A) THE 1980s

Led by the example of Independent Sector, the historical schism between donors and donees was fast disappearing. Most elements in our field began to work together in earnest. One successful example was the formation of the National Center for Charitable Statistics in the fall of 1980, under the aegis of the National Charities Information Bureau. Its purpose is to aid states to put reports from charitable organizations on computer to improve data gathering and (it was hoped) establish a uniform state report, saving thousands of dollars in preparation costs. Two years later IS took full responsibility for its operation. Today all states have the reports of their not-for-profit-organizations on computer, facilitating statistics gathering.

Bimonthly consortium meetings began with the chief executive officers of the AFP, AAFRC, CASE, IS, AHP, and the United Way to identify the field's most pressing needs, to bring each other up-to-date on their respective programs, and to begin to share resources to deal with common problems.

In 1984 the AAFRC Trust for Philanthropy was established to foster programs to promote more effective philanthropy. This enabled the professional firms to deal with issues that are beyond their self-interest. Funding for its programs comes from contributions from corporations, member firms, and selected foundations.

The AAFRC Trust for Philanthropy began working with the Association of American Colleges in 1986 to raise funds to establish courses on philanthropic studies in 15 liberal arts colleges. By the end of the 1980s more than 20 institutes of higher education offered courses on philanthropic studies, ranging from Duke and Boston College to the University of Maryland and Seton Hall; two programs were based overseas—York University and Stockholm Universitet. Several colleges also set up centers on philanthropy. They are collaborating with each other and national not-for-profit organizations on the development of a core curriculum and sponsoring research programs to build the much-needed body of knowledge a true profession requires. These activities are well received by students and are producing enthusiasm in the new generation to pursue careers in the nonprofit world.

In 1986 Indiana University established its Center on Philanthropy after consulting with an eclectic group of academic scholars and fund-raising management practitioners. Bringing to its campus The Fund-Raising School that had been based in California and organized by Henry Rosso strengthened this bond. Academicians and practitioners collaborating on a joint project? A few years earlier this would never have even been considered. The center's courses on philanthropic studies are a fine example for other academic institutions.

National Philanthropy Day (NPD) was organized in 1981 by Douglas Freeman, a Los Angeles attorney specializing in estate, tax, and charitable planning, to promote and celebrate the philanthropic process nationally. Annually, National Philanthropy Day gives recognition and awards to the local community's top volunteers, donees, and fund-raising managers. In 1986, after the AFP Foundation assumed responsibility for this program, 32 of its chapters held NPD celebrations.

(B)   THE 1990s

The 1990s were a decade of dramatic changes. Stimulated by a tremendous growth in our economy, giving has not only multiplied but outpaced a modest inflation.

The AAFRC Trust for Philanthropy estimated that the total giving in 1999 totaled $190.16 billion—an increase of 9.1 percent.

According to the Foundation Center, there are 37,765 active grant-making foundations. Growth in the 1990s exceeded growth in the 1980s. And, more than ever, foundation giving includes providing not-for-profits with initial funds to enable them to develop self-help programs to broaden their giving base. Their giving in 1999 totaled $19.81 billion, an increase of 16.5 percent.

Susan V. Beresford, president of the Ford Foundation, highlighted in the July 15, 1999, *Chronicle of Philanthropy* developing trends in foundation management. New donors have a global philanthropic vision; a growing number of high-technology entrepreneurs bring an investment approach to grant making with a more businesslike approach to be clear about desired returns; the multiplicity of grant-making organizations is likely to generate greater concern about what constitutes good philanthropic practice; and the changing landscape means that there will be greater need for working alliances that do not now exist between foundations.

The growth and influence of community foundations are a major factor of giving. In 1998, 555 community foundations had assets of $25 billion, gifts to them exceeded $2.8 billion, and grants were over $1.5 billion.

The 1999 totals for corporations reflected gains and the stock market surge. Their giving totaled $11.02 billion, an increase of 16.5 percent.

A true reflection of growing individual assets, bequests in 1998 were $13.62 billion, up 7.8 percent.

A 7.2 percent growth to $143.71 billion from individuals showed, once again, that giving is a people business. Adding totals from bequests, individuals accounted for over 87 percent of all giving. Philanthropy is and always will be a "people business" flourishing when committed volunteers approach cultivated prospects face-to-face. Si Seymour said it best:

> No campaign ever fails because too many people say no. They fail when not enough people are asked.
>
> Every cause . . . needs people more than money. For when the people are with you and are giving your cause their attention, interest, confidence, advocacy and service, financial support should just about take care of itself. Whereas without them—in the right quality and quantity, in the right places, and in the right states of mind and spirit—you might as well go and get lost.[2]

1.5 The Current State

(A) KEY ORGANIZATIONS

Organized in 1960, AFP now has over 25,000 members and 157 chapters in the United States, Canada, and Mexico. Its membership is the most eclectic of fund-raising organizations as it includes development officers from all fields of charity—hospitals and medical centers, museums, colleges and universities, social services, research groups, and the like. And today, over 64 percent of its members are women—the male bastion keeps dwindling.

More than 4,000 development executives have qualified for its CFRE program (Certified Fund Raising Executive). This accreditation has these partner organizations: the Association for Healthcare Philanthropy, Association of Lutheran Development Executives (ALDE), Council for Resource Development (CRD), and National Catholic Development Conference (NCDVC).

National Philanthropy Day is now celebrated by 110 AFP chapters involving nearly 40,000 participants. As these events honor the volunteer, donor, and fund-raising manager of the year, the local community increases its understanding of and appreciation of the philanthropic process.

The Council for Advancement and Support of Education is the largest association of educational institutions. Its membership includes more than 2,900 colleges, universities, and independent elementary and secondary schools in the United States, Canada, Mexico, the United Kingdom, and 27 other countries. Representing these institutions are over 20,000 advancement professionals.

---

[2]Seymour, Harold J. *Designs for Fund Raising: Principles, Patterns, Techniques.* New York: McGraw-Hill, 1966, p. ix). (Paperback edition: Ambler, PA: Fund Raising Institute, 1988.)

In 1999 the Association of Healthcare Philanthropy had 2,807 members representing over 1,600 healthcare organizations in North America.

(B) WHAT MAKES A GOOD AND SUCCESSFUL FUND-RAISING MANAGER?

In addition to having professional skills and related experience, managers must care about our society. Since managers are dealing with contributed funds, they must be like Caesar's wife, with a deep and durable integrity. Selective integrity is no more effective than open dishonesty.

Managers must take the time and effort to earn (not demand) the respect of others. Fund-raising managers are like coaches helping to guide the team—a task that requires mutual respect.

Managers must develop enthusiasm for the mission of the organization. This can be contagious and always rubs off on those whom the managers are working with.

Fund-raising managers must be alert and prepared to deal with some common misconceptions:

- Members of a nonprofit board and its key leaders often believe that the skills that made them successful in their careers equip them to plan and organize a fund-raising campaign—without any professional guidance.
- Potential donors must be cultivated prior to any solicitations. This is best accomplished by a good marketing program. But marketing, as such, never should be used for fund raising. No charity can begin to reach its fund-raising potential without an organized fund-raising campaign set up with professional guidance.
- Cause-related marketing is *not* philanthropy. Corporations charge their promotional expenses to business expenses, not their contribution budget. And only a select few charities with national constituencies are eligible to participate.

(C) A BURGEONING FIELD HAS A BROADENING BASE

We have made some remarkable strides in opening this field to ethnic groups and have diminished male preponderance. The rapidly growing number of women in the field demonstrates that the ready presence of female intuition seems to make women particularly equipped to flourish in a "people business." AFP, the Council on Foundations, United Way, the Foundation Center, Independent Sector, and the Ford Foundation are just a few major national philanthropic organizations that are now headed by women who are well paid for their skills.

The glass ceiling is beginning to become pretty lofty. However, the salary gap between men and women remains an unsolved problem. Solving this will take patience, persistence, and coordinated effort by board members and executives in the nonprofit sector, but it must be high on everyone's agenda.

Thirty years ago a remarkable thing happened in Canada. Charlotte Whitton was elected mayor of Ottawa. In her campaign she said, "In today's world, a woman must do twice as well as a man to be perceived half as good." "Luckily," she went on to say, "this isn't very difficult."[3]

(D) THE ALL-IMPORTANT VOLUNTEERS

Just about every campaign relies on pace-setting gifts made possible by face-to-face solicitation—peers to peers who are enthusiastic, affluent, and influential. Over the years, volunteers have become much more sophisticated with high expectations for good organization, planning, and staff support from fund-raising managers. The trauma created by the United Way and New Era scandals have deeply increased their awareness of the extent of their responsibilities. They take their commitments and assignments more seriously. Our field's progress has engendered much more of their respect. The toughest road is to find ways to lure the newly wealthy entrepreneurs into devoting more time and funds to philanthropy. (The older generation is culturally more geared to give back something to society.)

This fact is borne out further by some pertinent statistics compiled recently by Jerold Panas, Linzy & Partners, an established reputable fund-raising counseling firm in Chicago, Illinois: To raise a dollar from special events, it costs $0.50 to $1.00; from phonathons, $0.20 to $0.40; from direct mail, $0.30 to $1.20; from personal involvement of volunteers, $0.07 to $0.15.

(E) FORM 990

Federal and state laws now require public disclosure by way of the uniform federal/state Forms 990. All not-for-profit organizations with income of over $25,000 must have their 990 report available on the Internet. Active and potential contributors can determine a not-for-profit organization's program and fund-raising costs as well as executive salaries and actual funds spent on programs. Managers must deal with the filing of these reports with clarity, documentation, and integrity.

Development directors are used to acting as coaches, and it is important that they work with the executives, board members, and certified public accountants to ensure that the organization's 990 form is filled out with accuracy, full documentation, and integrity. New not-for-profit organizations must expect negative reactions to their high fund-raising costs, but the 990 form can point out that these costs will reduce over the next few years.

The Nonprofit Accountability Collaborates (990-NAC Activities) has been formed under the co-sponsorship of the National Center for Charitable Statistics at the Urban Institute and the Independent Sector. Thirty national groups, ranging from the American Institute of Certified Public Accountants to United Way of America, also support the 990-NAC, established in 1998.

---

[3]John J. Schwartz, Quoted in "The Dwindling Male Bastion," *Fund-Raising Management* (December 1994).

1.6   Where Are We Today?

Even the most cynical person would agree that fund-raising management has made phenomenal progress. Most fund raisers are proud to be a member of this near profession. We are proving that we care about society and are willing to accept lower compensation and fewer benefits usually available in similar positions in the for-profit sector. We can take heart in the fact that our careers, even in a small way, are helping to make a difference in improving society. Our efforts are helping the next generation to acquire better values. Collectively, we may be reducing the prevailing public cynicism about what America stands for.

1.7   How Well Are We Prepared for the Twenty-first Century?

Philanthropy's critical issues are many and complex. A list of items that need urgent attention was presented in a recent book on our field.[4] Solving these problems would foster a much greater capacity by the philanthropic process to deal with society's accelerating needs as we enter the twenty-first century. We need to develop more effective ways to:

- Reduce parochialism and open up wider communications between donors and donees and the varied philanthropic causes.
- Set up and adopt a universal code of ethics.
- Persuade more able young people to make philanthropy their career.
- Apply the principles of our pluralistic society to improve the partnership between the public and the private sectors.
- Educate state and federal legislators and their administrative staffs on the importance of making philanthropy more effective—which cannot be accomplished with punitive legislation and reduced tax incentives.
- Help board members to better understand and accept increased responsibility for their stewardship.
- Increase the interest and development of philanthropic studies at all levels of education.
- Establish a single generic certification process for all professionals.
- Increase the level of professionalism of fund raisers, foundation and corporate program officers, and trustees.
- Increase the public's understanding of philanthropy and fund raising.
- Attract, train, and retain more minorities.
- Identify and train leaders from the new generation.
- Preserve for posterity the wisdom and experience of the older generation.
- Increase accountability.
- Establish guidelines and ranges for executive salaries and benefits to ensure the principle that the mission of all philanthropic organizations is never secondary to personal gain.

---

[4]John J. Schwartz, *Modern American Philanthropy: A Personal Account* (New York: John Wiley & Sons, 1994).

- Compensate all staff on the basis of skill, responsibilities, and real seniority, regardless of gender or ethnic background.
- Reduce the commercialization of the field and strengthen the essential values of voluntarism.

Your own experiences will help you identify other critical issues. What is important is that each of us should bear in mind that fostering more effective philanthropy requires the energy of all of us in the field. A constant goal is to help the key local and national organizations to work together using their combined resources to improve our effectiveness. And each of us should be prepared to give our time and talents to aid these organizations.

Suggested Readings

Burlingame, Dwight F., ed. *Critical Issues in Fund Raising*. San Francisco: Jossey-Bass, 1996.

Foundations, Private Giving, and Public Policy, Report and Recommendations of the Commission on Foundations and Private Philanthropy, 1970. The University of Chicago Press.

Report of the Commission on Private Philanthropy and Public Needs, *Giving in America, Toward a Stronger Voluntary Sector* (1975), Commission on Private Philanthropy and Public Needs.

Glaser, John S. *The United Way Scandal*. New York: John Wiley & Sons, 1994.

Greenfield, James M. *Fund-Raising—Evaluating and Managing The Development Process*. 2nd ed. New York: John Wiley & Sons, 1999.

Greenfield, James M. *Fund-Raising Fundamentals*. New York: John Wiley & Sons, 1994.

Hopkins, Bruce R. *Law of Tax-Exempt Organizations*, 7th edition. New York: John Wiley & Sons, 1998.

———. *A Legal Guide to Starting and Managing a Nonprofit Organization*. New York: John Wiley & Sons, 1993.

———. *The Tax Law of Charitable Giving*. New York. John Wiley & Sons, 1993.

Levis, Wilson C., & Sumariwalla Russy. *Unified Financial Reporting for Not-for-Profit Organizations*. New York: John Wiley & Sons, 2000.

Panas, Jerold. *Born to Raise*. Chicago: Precept Press, 1996.

———. *Finders Keepers*. Chicago: Precept Press, 1999.

Rosso, Henry A. *Achieving Excellence in Fund Raising*. San Francisco: Jossey-Bass, 1991.

Sharpe, Robert F., Sr. *Planned Giving Simplified: The Gift, the Giver, and the Gift Planner*. New York: John Wiley & Sons, 1999.

White, Douglas E. *The Art of Planned Giving: Understanding Donors and the Culture of Giving*. New York: John Wiley & Son, 1995.

▼2 Strategic Planning for Fund Raising

KIMBERLY HAWKINS, CFRE
Raybin Associates, Inc.

2.1 Introduction

(A) WHAT IS STRATEGIC PLANNING FOR FUND RAISING?

Strategic planning for fund raising is driven by the same impetus that drives organizational strategic planning: the need to define a preferred future and figure out how to get there. Strategic planning for fund raising uses many of the same types of analyses and projections as does institutional planning, but focuses on a single function—resource development.

The process of strategic planning for fund raising looks at an organization's current mix of income sources and the methods it uses to generate philanthropic support. It examines all of an organization's assets that support fund raising:

- Case for support
- Potential giving constituencies
- Volunteer and staff resources
- Fund-raising programs
- Budget

Then, given the organization's assets, the process encourages leaders to make thoughtful judgments about:

- The fund-raising strategies most likely to be productive
- Priorities for new or enhanced fund-raising activities
- Additional investment that may be needed
- Incremental income projections
- A realistic implementation plan and budget

(B) WHY DO STRATEGIC PLANNING FOR FUND RAISING?

There are many good reasons for an organization to engage in strategic planning for fund raising:

- The organization is in the process of developing a full strategic plan, and it has become evident that substantially greater resources will be required to implement the plan.
- The organization desires to develop new programs or to put more money into existing programs.
- The organization has experienced the loss of a major contributor whose longtime support has undergirded the development program and, indeed, the organization's operating budget.
- The vulnerability of existing streams of income—contributed or earned—is recognized.
- The organization has a new chief executive officer (CEO) or director of development.
- New members, who have an interest in fund raising, are added to the board.
- The organization observes that competitors are beginning to receive a larger share of the philanthropic pie.
- The organization experiences changes in the demographics of its constituency or in the community's economic well-being.
- It has been four or five years since the organization has looked at where its money comes from and the methods it uses to foster giving.

2.2 *Who Does Strategic Planning for Fund Raising?*

Good planning of any kind builds consensus and commitment among board and staff members and gets everyone working toward the same goals. It requires the participation of the organization's decision makers—most especially, those who will be involved in carrying out the plan. Therefore, at minimum, the following should be part of the process:

Board Development Committee
CEO
Director of development
All other professional development staff (and the value of insights from support
  staff should not be underestimated)

At some point, the plan will be presented to the entire board for approval or endorsement. However, it is usually neither necessary nor efficient to try to engage all trustees in the process of developing the plan.

An experienced director of development—particularly one who has worked in a variety of gift-supported institutions—often can successfully develop a fund-raising strategic plan without outside assistance. More commonly, organizations find it helpful to engage a fund-raising consultant to structure and guide the effort. In this case, the director of development coordinates the process.

The word "guide" is important here. Because significant amounts of time and effort are involved and everyone already has too much to do, there may be a temptation to ask counsel to "just give us a fund-raising plan." Such an approach is almost always short-sighted, for no one but the consultant is then invested in making the plan work. The plan is the consultant's plan, not the organization's, and may join many other such documents in gathering dust on someone's bookshelves.

Counsel can, however, bring the discipline and focus necessary to work through the steps required to develop the plan. And because they work with many different organizations, consultants have a broad perspective on what works, what does not, and what, realistically, is required to implement certain fund-raising programs. (See Chapter 46, "Fund-raising Consultants," for detailed advice on hiring consultants.)

2.3 Planning Steps: An Overview

The process of developing a strategic plan for fund raising involves four principal steps:

1. Understand the current situation.
2. Identify the potential fund-raising building blocks.
3. Assemble the building blocks into strategic options.
4. Select the best strategy.

Each of these steps and its components is discussed in detail, using a fictitious library called "Metropolis Public Library" for illustration. The planning steps described for Metropolis Public Library can be adapted to fit gift-supported organizations of all types.

Metropolis Public Library serves a middle- and upper-middle-income suburban community of 70,000. Most of its operating budget is provided by the town. Additional funding is generated by the Friends of Metropolis Library and the Metropolis Public Library Foundation, both separately incorporated entities (a common arrangement for public libraries). Both organizations conduct a variety of fund-raising activities throughout the year, largely managed by volunteers but with part-time support from a director of development and a secretary.

Metropolis Library expects that municipal funding will continue to provide most of its operating budget for the foreseeable future. Nevertheless, under citizen pressure to moderate property taxes, the town council has been considering how it should allocate a budget that is not growing as fast as the budget requests of town departments. The town council has, in fact, recently ranked all municipal services according to how critical they are to the community. The library is in the lowest-priority group. In addition, there has been some discussion among members of the town council about reducing appropriations to those town agencies that have the capacity to raise money to support at least part of their operating budgets.

The Library Board is anticipating that town funding as a percentage of its operating budget may decline somewhat over the next few years. Board members and other library supporters are developing a plan to educate town council members about the critical role of the library in the educational and cultural life of the community. They are also gathering statistics to show that communities with strong cultural institutions such as libraries have higher property values. At the same time, however, they recognize that the library may have to raise more of its budget from private sources and have decided that a fund-raising strategic plan will help them in this effort.

2.4   Planning Steps: Situation Analysis

(A)   SOURCES OF REVENUE

Working with internal information (financial statements and reports and Development Office records), an organization should analyze, for at least three years, the sources of revenue that make up the operating budget. Most organizations will have earned income (programs and fees), contributions (which should be broken down by source), and interest and dividends. For Metropolis Public Library, municipal funding is an important component of the budget. Other organizations may have sources particular to their type or community, such as United Way, fraternal organizations (Kiwanis, Rotary), church groups, and federal grants.

Exhibit 2.1 shows Metropolis Public Library's revenue sources for the past three years. Several trends can be observed in taking a three-year look at Metropolis Public Library's revenue sources:

- Although town funding increased each year, the rate of increase is slowing, and this source constitutes a declining percentage of the total budget. This trend is likely to continue. Thus, for services and programs to keep pace with demand, contributed and investment income must grow.
- Earned income has remained a stable percentage of the budget. Although revenue from user fees and fines is largely beyond the library's control, there may be some opportunities to increase facility rentals by more aggressive promotion.
- Contributed income has grown from 13 percent to 14 percent of the budget. Significant growth occurred in the most recent fiscal year when the Friends of the Library put more effort into organizing and promoting their used book sale and their major fund-raising event—a book and author luncheon.
- Revenue from Library Foundation activities has kept pace with budget increases, but no new approaches have been tried. The dramatic increase in memorial gifts in 1995 resulted when the family of a beloved longtime mayor, who died during that year, requested that contributions in his memory be made to the library.
- Two bequests totaling $1.5 million were received in fiscal years 98 and 99, bringing the total endowment to $2 million. Interest and dividends, as a percentage of the total budget, therefore grew from less than 1 percent to 2 percent. Metropolis Public Library will almost certainly want to consider ways to encourage more people to remember the library in their wills.

EXHIBIT 2.1 Sources of Operating Revenue

	FY98		FY99		FY00	
	$ Amount	% of Budget	$ Amount	% of Budget	$ Amount	% of Budget
1. Town Funding	$3,825,000	85%	$3,978,000	84%	$4,057,560	81%
2. Earned Income						
User fees (e.g., copier)	30,000	<1%	32,000	<1%	35,000	<1%
Late fees	15,000	<1%	16,000	<1%	17,500	<1%
Facility rental	50,000	1%	55,000	1%	50,000	1%
	95,000	2%	103,000	2%	102,500	2%
3. Contributed Income*						
Friends of the Library						
Memberships	45,000	1%	48,000	1%	55,000	1%
Used book sale	12,000	<1%	12,000	<1%	20,000	<1%
Fund-raising events	65,000	1%	72,000	2%	100,000	2%
Library Foundation						
Major gifts	200,000	4%	225,000	5%	230,000	5%
Foundations	60,000	1%	60,000	1%	75,000	2%
Corporations	40,000	<1%	45,000	1%	48,000	1%
Direct mail appeals	113,000	3%	125,000	3%	140,000	3%
Memorial gifts	20,000	<1%	15,000	<1%	35,000	<1%
	555,000	13%	602,000	13%	703,000	14%
4. Interest and Dividends	25,000	<1%	50,000	1%	100,000	2%
TOTAL	**$4,500,000**	**100%**	**$4,733,000**	**100%**	**$4,963,060**	**100%**

Note that although Metropolis Library received bequests in each of the three years, these funds do not show as a separate source of contributed funds. They were added to the endowment; therefore, only the income appears on the Interest and Dividends line.

(B) COMPARISON WITH SIMILAR ORGANIZATIONS

Although no organization is exactly like any other, it can be illuminating to examine the pattern of revenue sources of similar or competing organizations. Many publish annual reports, and almost all make their audited financial statements available on request. Colleagues at other institutions may be willing to share information, especially if they do not compete directly for donors.

Exhibit 2.2 compares Metropolis Public Library's revenue sources with four other community libraries in the state and with an out-of-state library recently featured in an American Library Association publication for its successful and innovative fund-raising programs. As compared with other institutions in this sample, Metropolis Public Library generates the second smallest percentage of its operating budget from contributions. Only Village Community Library, 90 percent of whose revenue comes from the town, raises less of its budget.

Those libraries with the highest percentages of gift income—Suburban and Out-of-State—have responded to major cuts in their municipal budget allocations by hiring full-time development staff and increasing their fund-raising efforts dramatically. Suburban

EXHIBIT 2.2 Sources of Revenue as a Percentage of Total Operating Budget (FY99 figures)

| | Municipal Funding | Earned Income | Contributions | | | | | Int. & Div. | Total Revenue |
			Indiv.	Corps.	Found.	Events	Total		
Metropolis Public Library	84%	2%	9%	1%	1%	2%	13%	1%	$4,733,000
Small City Library	73%	4%	12%	3%	2%	5%	22%	1%	$7,000,000
Village Community Library	90%	1%	2%	<1%	<1%	6%	9%	<1%	$1,500,000
Donor Memorial Library	76%	3%	6%	1%	4%	6%	15%	4%	$2,800,000
Suburban Public Library	65%	5%	8%	5%	4%	10%	27%	3%	$6,000,000
Out-of-State Public Library	70%	3%	10%	10%	2%	4%	26%	1%	$10,000,000

has emphasized special events. The annual Suburban Library benefit dinner dance and auction is *the* fund-raising event in the community, and there is a waiting list for tickets each year. Out-of-State, on the other hand, has focused on personal solicitation of individual major gifts, which generates $1 million annually. It has also taken advantage of its location in a city that is home to a number of corporations by building a very productive corporate membership program. There may be lessons here for Metropolis.

Donor Memorial appears to be something of an anomaly for a library of its size, with 4 percent of its budget coming from foundation support and 4 percent from interest and dividends. Closer examination reveals, however, that the founder, for whom the library was named, left a substantial bequest in his will. In addition, there is a family foundation, run by his children who all live in the community, that provides a major operating grant each year. This is a unique situation. At some point, though, Metropolis staff may want to research the library's founders, determine whether any of their descendants remain in town, and identify those who control family foundations.

Some not-for-profits may also deem it helpful to compare themselves to all others of their type in the country by obtaining data from national organizations or governing bodies. Even if the information is available, this particular analysis may be of limited usefulness—especially to smaller organizations. Planning time may be more productively spent on other tasks.

(C) DEVELOPMENT PROGRAM AND OPERATIONS ASSESSMENT

A concurrent step in the situation analysis is to examine current fund-raising programs and operations. (See Exhibit 2.3.) This task is most objectively done by a consultant, though development staff can conduct at least some elements of the audit themselves.

EXHIBIT 2.3　Fund-raising Assets

1. The Organization
   - Well managed
   - Defined mission and goals
   - Needed programs and services
   - Strong management

2. Board Leadership
   - Committed
   - Well informed
   - Knowledgeable about responsibilities
   - Active Development Committee

3. Public Image
   - Well regarded
   - No major PR problems
   - Regular media coverage
   - Contributes to community

4. Organizational Vision and Plan
   - Related to mission
   - Endorsed by board
   - Put in writing

5. Case for Support
   - Evolved from vision and plan
   - Articulates how funding will make a difference
   - Is compelling

6. Prospects
   - Who could be interested
   - With some connections
   - Who have resources
   - Who are involved

7. Volunteers
   - Make own commitments
   - Responsible for asking
   - Trained in asking

8. Fund-Raising Resources
   - Professional staff
   - Support staff
   - Adequate budget
   - Computers

9. Attention to Detail
   - Names correct
   - Accurate giving records
   - Timely, appropriate thank-you's
   - Donor stewardship

10. Supportive Organizational Culture
    - Nice people can talk about money
    - Director of Development reports to CEO
    - Director of Development has access to board
    - Everyone understands fund raising to be a long-term *process*

If consultants do the assessment, they will spend some time reviewing materials:

- Mission and vision statements
- Case statements
- Fund-raising plans and timetables
- Fund-raising letters, brochures, phonathon scripts, volunteer training packets
- Records, reports, and analyses
- Publications
- Public relations materials
- Representative prospect research files
- Cultivation and solicitation plans
- Gift acknowledgment letters

Through individual interviews with professional and support staff, they will inquire into Development Office operations:

- Processes for updating and maintaining donor records
- Processes for identifying new prospects

- Gift-processing procedures
- Turn-around time for gift acknowledgment
- Quality and relevance of donor and prospect research
- Staff ability to manage the computer system
- Intraoffice communications as well as communications with other departments

Consultants may also want to interview the CEO, the board chair, and key fund-raising volunteers to get their perspectives on:

- What works well in fund raising
- What could work better
- How well the board works
- What the institution does to support and recognize volunteers
- Helpful insights and experiences they may have gained from other not-for-profit involvements

(See Chapter 6 for a detailed approach to conducting a fund-raising assessment.)

At the end of this step in the planning process, the organization should have a clear picture of what its fund-raising assets are and how it currently uses them to encourage contributed income.

2.5   Planning Process: Creating the Building Blocks

(A)   IDENTIFYING THE FUND-RAISING OPPORTUNITIES

The next step in creating a strategic plan for fund raising is to match all segments of the organization's constituency with the fund-raising vehicles available to it (whether they are currently used or not). It is useful to create at least three matrices for this purpose: individuals, corporations, and foundations. Other categories of contributors—such as churches or fraternal organizations—can usually be included in the foundations matrix.

Exhibits 2.4, 2.5, and 2.6 show the three matrices created by Metropolis Public Library. The shaded blocks are the primary fund-raising opportunities identified by the planning group for further exploration.

(B)   ELABORATING THE FUND-RAISING OPPORTUNITIES

It is important to determine which fund-raising vehicle, or "cell," will offer each source a primary fund-raising opportunity and begin to detail specific programs and approaches. For Metropolis Public Library, the primary opportunities appear to be those listed in Exhibit 2.7. Some of these activities have been tried in the past, but they may be worth trying again with additional commitment of time and resources.

EXHIBIT 2.4 Individuals as Potential Contributors

Market Segments	*Fund-raising Vehicles*				
	Major Gifts	Direct Mail	Planned Gifts	Events	Memorial Gifts
Board of directors					
Former board members					
Friends of the Library					
Donors					
Event attendees					
Community at large/cardholders					
Staff					

EXHIBIT 2.5 Corporations as Potential Contributors

Market Segments	*Fund-raising Vehicles*			
	Annual Giving	Special Programs and Proposals	Events	Corporate Membership Program
Major corporations				
Small–medium-size companies				
Local merchants				

EXHIBIT 2.6 Foundations as Potential Contributors

Market Segments	*Fund-raising Vehicles*		
	Annual Giving	Project Proposals	Events
Large private foundations			
Small family foundations			
Community foundations			

EXHIBIT 2.7 Matching Fund-raising Programs to Market Segments

Fund-raising Program	Market Segment
BOARD GIVING • Explicit expectation of 100% participation every year • Personal solicitation by board chair or Development Committee chair early in the year	• Board
FORMER BOARD SOLICITATION • Reception for former board members before annual meeting • Follow-up solicitation letter from board chair • Personal solicitation of $1,000+ prospects	• Former board
PATRONS PROGRAM • Development Committee solicits by phone for specific gifts • 1–2 special patrons' events • Listing in annual report • Consider cultivation dinners hosted by board members	• Friends of the Library capable of $1,000 annually • Donors capable of $1,000 annually
DIRECT MAIL ANNUAL GIVING SOLICITATION • Solicitation letter in fall for specific project (separate from Friends membership mailing) • Follow-up in spring • Staff solicitation by letter signed by staff Annual Giving chair	• Friends of the Library • Donors • Event attendees • Community/library cardholders • Staff
PLANNED GIFTS • Planned giving brochure • Annual mailings • Personal follow-up of interested prospects • Articles in newsletter	• Board and former board • Donors • Cardholders
MEMORIAL GIFTS PROGRAM • Memorial gifts listed in newsletter and annual report • Memorial gift envelopes placed at information and check-out desks • New envelopes included with thank you's for all memorial gifts	• Board and former board • Friends of the Library • Donors • Event attendees • Community/cardholders • Staff
EVENTS Friends' Book and Author Luncheon • Promote widely through mailings and media • Consider more than one per year Friends' Used Book Sale • Promote widely • Consider expanding beyond used library books to include books donated by others	• Board and former board • Friends of the Library • Donors • Events attendees • Community/cardholders • Staff

EXHIBIT 2.7 *(Continued)*

Fund-raising Program	*Market Segment*
ANNUAL BENEFIT EVENT • Black tie • Tickets priced to net significant income • Corporate underwriting	• Board and former board • Friends of the Library • Event attendees • Community/cardholders • Staff • Corporations • Local merchants • Family foundations • Community foundations
FOUNDATION STRATEGY Annual Fund mailing • Solicitation letter/proposal and follow-up • Use board/volunteer contacts (some may be approached in major gifts program)	• Small family foundations • Community foundations
Program/Project Proposals • Priority prospect list • Use board/volunteer contacts	• Large private foundations • Small family foundations • Community foundations
CORPORATE STRATEGY Corporate Membership Program • Benefits/Perks • Priority prospect list • Use board contacts	• Major corporations • Small–medium-size companies
Annual Fund Mailing	• Local merchants
Program/project proposals • Priority prospect list • Use board/volunteer contacts	• Major corporations • Small–medium-size companies

2.6 *Planning Process: Identifying Strategic Options*

(A) STRATEGIC OPTIONS

Metropolis Public Library's fund-raising strategic plan should include a variety of fund-raising programs—the building blocks—designed to appeal to the various segments of its constituency in different ways. These building blocks can be assembled in an almost infinite number of combinations, depending on the planning group's decisions about fit and style with the community as well as projected return on investment.

The Metropolis Library's planning group combined the building blocks it had identified into two strategic options. Exhibits 2.8 and 2.9 show the strategic options—with advantages and disadvantages—they decided to present to the board.

EXHIBIT 2.8 Strategy 1: Comprehensive Development Program, with Major Gift Focus

This strategy includes a comprehensive program, with emphasis on identifying, cultivating, and soliciting major gifts ($1,000+). Its secondary elements are designed to "feed" the major gifts program.

Key Elements	• Personal solicitation of board and former board • Patrons' program for donors of $1,000 or more • Corporate membership program for donors of $5,000 or more • Planned giving program • Solicitation of corporations and foundations for special projects
Secondary Elements	• Direct mail annual appeal to all cardholders and Friends of the Library, with eventual expansion to all households • Expanded Friends' events • Memorial gifts program
Advantages	• Should significantly increase gift income fairly quickly • Takes advantage of special talents of Library director in meeting with and cultivating prospects and donors
Disadvantages	• Requires board to make significant commitment to fund raising
Key Factors for Success	• Larger board, including members with high-level business and social contacts and willingness to use them • Experienced full-time director of development and secretary

(B) SUPPORTING BUDGET AND INCOME PROJECTIONS

The library's planning group then asked the director of development to project an implementation budget and incremental income for each of the two strategic options. Exhibits 2.10 and 2.11 compare projected budgets; Exhibits 2.12 and 2.13 compare projected incremental income.

The planning group then compared the library's projected net incremental income for the two strategies, as shown in Exhibit 2.14.

2.7 *Planning Process: Selecting the Best Strategic Option*

The library's planning group presented both strategic options to the board, with a recommendation that Metropolis Public Library pursue Strategy 2: High-Visibility Strategy. Board members were reluctant to commit themselves to the amount of personal solicitation required in Strategy 1. They also felt that building a broad base of support, rather than a group of elite donors, better fit the style of the library and the community.

The board accepted the planning group's recommendation, and the director of development will now prepare a detailed work plan to help her realistically implement the library's new fund-raising strategy.

EXHIBIT 2.9 Strategy 2: High-Visibility Strategy

Visibility, leading to heightened community awareness and development of a broader donor base, is the focus of this strategy. There is less emphasis on major gifts from individuals, corporations, and foundations.

Key Elements	• Direct mail annual appeal to all householders and cardholders • Corporate Membership program, including corporate event • Major benefit event • Planned Giving program • Trustee giving
Secondary Elements	• Major Donor program • Corporate and foundation solicitations • Memorial Gifts program
Advantages	• Builds broad base of donors to feed major gifts and planned giving programs as part of longer-term strategy • Builds broad community awareness of library, its programs, and its needs • Does not require reluctant board to make major commitment to personal solicitation • Maintains "democratic" vs. "exclusive" image of library
Disadvantages	• Implementation dependent on outside consultants (events consultant and direct mail house); board does not "own" program • Full impact of program will not be felt for several years • Successful corporate event requires board with more corporate connections • Major benefit event may require more volunteers than Library has available
Key Factors for Success	• Highly skilled direct mail and event consultants (and/or many volunteers) • Development staff skilled at managing outside consultants • Board members with high-level corporate connections

EXHIBIT 2.10 Strategy 1: Comprehensive Development Program with a Focus on Major Gifts

DRAFT 3-YEAR IMPLEMENTATION BUDGET

	Year 1	Year 2	Year 3
Operations			
Staff			
Director of Development	$50,000	$52,000	$55,000
Administrative Assistant	$25,000	$26,000	$27,600
Fringes 30%	$22,500	$23,400	$24,600
Development Office Operating Budget			
(Phone, postage, memberships, stationery)	$30,000	$35,000	$38,000
Fund-raising Program			
Trustee Giving	$0	$0	$0
Patrons Program			
(Event and mailings)	$15,000	$15,000	$15,000
Corporate Membership Program			
(Materials; meeting expenses)	$6,000	$7,000	$8,000
Corporate and Foundation Solicitation Program	$0	$0	$0
Planned Giving Program			
(Brochure; mailings; estate planning			
workshops)	$15,000	$12,000	$12,000
Direct Mail Annual Appeal	$5,000	$6,000	$10,000
Memorial Gifts Program	$500	$500	$500
Friends' Events (3/year)	$10,000	$12,000	$15,000
TOTALS	**$179,000**	**$188,900**	**$205,700**

EXHIBIT 2.11 Strategy 2: High-Visibility Strategy

DRAFT 3-YEAR IMPLEMENTATION BUDGET

	Year 1	Year 2	Year 3
Operations			
Staff			
Director of Development	$50,000	$52,000	$55,000
Administrative Assistant	$25,000	$26,000	$27,600
Fringes 30%	$22,500	$23,400	$24,600
Development Office Operating Budget			
(Phone, postage, memberships, stationery)	$30,000	$35,000	$38,000
Fund-raising Program			
Direct Mail Annual Appeal			
(All households)	$10,000	$12,000	$15,000
Corporate Membership Program			
(Materials; event)	$6,000	$7,000	$8,000
Major Benefit Event	$40,000	$50,000	$60,000
Planned Giving Program			
(Brochure; mailings; estate planning			
workshops)	$15,000	$12,000	$12,000
Trustee Giving	$0	$0	$0
Major Donor Program			
(Personal solicitation)	$0	$0	$0
Corporate and Foundation Solicitation Program	$0	$0	$0
Memorial Gifts Program	$500	$500	$500
TOTALS	**$199,000**	**$217,900**	**$240,700**

EXHIBIT 2.12 Strategy 1: Comprehensive Development Program with a Focus on Major Gifts

PROJECTED INCREMENTAL INCOME

	Year 1	Year 2	Year 3
Trustee Giving	$50,000	$75,000	$100,000
Patrons' Program	$100,000	$150,000	$200,000
Corporate Membership Program	$30,000	$40,000	$60,000
Planned Giving	$0*	$0*	$0*
Direct Mail Annual Appeal	$20,000	$25,000	$30,000
Expanded Friend's Events	$40,000	$50,000	$60,000
Corporate and Foundation Solicitation			
for Special Projects	$40,000	$50,000	$75,000
Memorial Gifts	$5,000	$8,000	$10,000
TOTALS	**$285,000**	**$398,000**	**$535,000**

Payback not before 3 years. Long-term payback could be substantial.

EXHIBIT 2.13 Strategy 2: High-Visibility Strategy

PROJECTED INCREMENTAL INCOME

	Year 1	Year 2	Year 3
Trustee Giving	$50,000	$75,000	$100,000
Major Donor Program	$30,000	$40,000	$50,000
Corporate Membership Program	$30,000	$40,000	$60,000
Planned Giving	$0*	$0*	$0*
Direct Mail Annual Appeal	$75,000	$100,000	$125,000
Major Benefit Event	$100,000	$125,000	$175,000
Corporate and Foundation Solicitation (for special projects)	$20,000	$30,000	$35,000
Memorial Gifts	$5,000	$8,000	$10,000
TOTALS	**$310,000**	**$418,000**	**$555,000**

Payback not before 3 years. Long-term payback could be substantial.

EXHIBIT 2.14 Summary Incremental Income and Expense Projection

	Strategy 1	Strategy 2
Year 1		
Incremental Income	$285,000	$310,000
Expense	$179,000	$199,000
Net Gain	$106,000	$111,000
Year 2		
Incremental Income	$398,000	$418,000
Expense	$188,900	$217,900
Net Gain	$209,100	$200,100
Year 3		
Incremental Income	$535,000	$555,000
Expense	$205,700	$240,000
Net Gain	$329,300	$315,000

Marketing Strategies in Development

BARRY J. MCLEISH, VICE PRESIDENT
McConkey/Johnston, Inc.

Significant portions of this chapter are adapted from the author's book *Successful Marketing Strategies for Nonprofit Organizations* (New York: John Wiley & Sons, 1995).

3.1 Introduction

Could anyone have predicted the changes that have occurred in the not-for-profit marketplace in the last 15 years? Not-for-profit practitioners today face social, governmental, and economic changes of unprecedented magnitude and variety. Such changes are based on the following factors:

- A global donor community has become a reality for many not-for-profit organizations.
- Increased media sophistication has led donors to force not-for-profit organizations to change their methods of communication.
- The growth in the number of not-for-profit organizations has caused competition for the same audiences.
- Fund raising has become a battlefield as not-for-profit organizations compete for scarce resources.
- Database fund raising has changed the way not-for-profit organizations conduct business.
- An organizational presence on the Internet is increasingly becoming competitively important for some not-for-profit agencies.

These changes forever alter the way not-for-profit organizations must operate in the future, requiring innovative responses that past practices simply cannot accommodate.

3.2 Need for a Marketing Orientation

Traditionally, marketing has not been a popular subject in not-for-profit circles, and competition even less so. Today not-for-profit organizations are operating under more changes and pressures than ever before. Without closely monitored and implemented marketing strategies designed to take the organization through a particular course of action, and without the ability to change that course should the need arise, an organization risks being lost in the throes of internal and economic upheaval.

3.3 Dealing with Not-for-Profit Organizations in Flux

Consider the state of most not-for-profit organizations in operation today. Many are experiencing both internal and external turbulence. Internally they may be weighed down by a top-heavy hierarchy of executives, little opportunity for subordinate employee advancement, or a variety of other human resource inequities. Externally these same organizations are dealing with the need to reorganize, cut costs, improve communications, and involve their constituencies in more profitable ways.

(A) A CHANGING DOMAIN: CONSTITUENTS AND SUPPORTERS WANT MORE CONTROL

In today's climate of change, not-for-profit organizations must serve four distinct groups: *clients, constituents, volunteers,* and *donors.* Clients are the individuals whom the not-for-profit organization serves directly and who are the immediate beneficiaries of its output. Constituents represent the consuming public that purchases some output from the organization—perhaps a book. Volunteers and donors (also called *supporters* by some organizations) supply or lend the not-for-profit organization various types of resources: time, money, energy, knowledge, encouragement, or facilities.

Each of these groups is distinct, yet it is not unusual to observe some overlapping of the roles. Friends of a not-for-profit organization may take on the role of donor, volunteer, constituent, or client by receiving benefits from the organization while providing a volunteer service at the same time.

The problems encountered in serving these groups include their increasing lack of sustained loyalty to a cause as well as an increasing concern about how not-for-profit organizations run their day-to-day operations. Given the sea of worthy causes an individual can choose to support, volunteer for, or seek services from, not-for-profit organizations can no longer assume that today's constituent, volunteer, or donor will be theirs forever.

(B) EXTERNAL CHANGES

Among the more important changes are the federal and state governments' new restrictive policies concerning tax deductions, postal subsidies, and what constitutes appropriate not-for-profit activity. But the change that affects marketing most is the growing competition between not-for-profit organizations for charitable dollars and time. Clearly, this new environment in which not-for-profits now operate must be taken into consideration before implementing any new plan. Some organizations are confronting these changes with long-range planning, innovation, and a renewed marketing spirit; others are floundering, as work patterns and communication styles used for years no longer seem to fit.

(C) THE NEED FOR A PHILOSOPHY OF CHANGE

"Today, the idea of modest change everywhere in the corporation is becoming orthodoxy," states author and former editor of the *Harvard Business Review* Rosabeth Moss Kanter.[1] No sooner do you digest one new change than another appears. This is true in the not-for-profit field as well. Much of the way not-for-profits work today, as compared with 10 years ago, must be revitalized. This is no more apparent than in the way a not-for-profit organization develops, evaluates, and implements strategies of solicitation and service.

Today the typical not-for-profit has some measure of momentum. It is going somewhere, and its mission has been decided implicitly, through organizational drift, or by individuals inside or outside the cause. A marketing strategy can play a significant role in transforming that momentum into an organization's productive direction. To accomplish this, an organization's marketing strategies must be related to the surrounding competitive environment, melding the external world into the organization's internal operations, rather than waiting for new programs and new donors to solve all ills. Addressing market and competitive realities can no longer be viewed as an embarrassing undertaking or an unfortunate consequence. Strategy must be set through purposeful research and planning, to take the organization to the next level.

---

[1]Rosabeth Moss Kanter, *The Change Masters* (New York: Simon and Schuster, 1984), p. 17.

The organization should build its programmatic, volunteer, and solicitation strategies by assessing and evaluating constituencies and markets, and then build its marketing strategies. This procedure allows the organization to align its programs with the values and interests of its natural constituencies, creating a mutual bond.[2] This kind of competitive marketing strategy is a broad formula for:

- Determining how a not-for-profit organization will undertake its business
- Deciding how it will deliver its services in such a way that the organization is positively noticed and supported
- Considering how it will identify its goals
- Outlining the systems and policies to reach its goals

In this effort, not-for-profit organizations cannot afford to forget the point of view of their intended audiences. Successful not-for-profit organizations should be able to bring resources together quickly upon recognizing new audience needs or values. Constituent, volunteer, and donors' wants, expectations, and perceptions, taken seriously, can create a competitive edge in the field in which the not-for-profit organization operates. Not-for-profit organization directors will do well to prepare for the pressures of the future by taking these competitive advantages and more. The first three steps in such preparation are to:

1. Define a marketing strategy.
2. Define how it operates.
3. Ask why a not-for-profit organization needs a marketing strategy.

3.4 *"Marketing" Defined*

Those who have been involved in not-for-profit marketing no doubt realize that as little as 15 years ago, the word "marketing" was barely uttered aloud at "fund-raising" conferences. Not-for-profit organizations could afford to adopt this attitude as long as there were adequate resources. However, as institutions experienced a decline in funds, students, and members, the word "marketing," according to Philip Kotler, "was heard with increasing frequency and organizations suddenly discovered marketing or reasonable facsimiles thereof."[3] Philip Kotler, author of *Strategic Marketing for Nonprofit Organizations* as well as many other books on marketing, is an internationally renowned expert on marketing and the S.C. Johnson & Son Distinguished Professor of International Marketing at Northwestern University. In Kotler's text, the definition of not-for-profit marketing is: "the function of a not-for-profit whose goal is to plan, price, promote and distribute the organization's programs and products by keeping in constant touch with the organization's various constituencies, uncovering their needs and expectations for the organization and themselves, and building a program of communication to not only express the organization's purpose and goals, but also their mutually beneficial want-satisfying products."[4]

---

[2]Barry McLeish, *The Donor Bond* (Rockville, Md.: The Taft Group, 1991).
[3]Philip Kotler, "Strategies for Introducing Marketing into Nonprofit Organizations," in *Strategic Marketing for Nonprofit Organizations: Cases and Readings*, 3d ed., edited by Philip Kotler, O. C. Ferrell, and Charles Lamb (Englewood Cliffs, N.J.: Prentice-Hall, 1987), p. 5.
[4]*Ibid.*

Unfortunately, the notion of marketing for some has come to mean aggressive promotion, as opposed to aggressive listening to constituent needs. There has been a concentration of effort to communicate the not-for-profit's needs to the public rather than first listening to its constituents. Although promotional programs are part of a marketing strategy, the strategy must first move away from the point of sale and address this question: *Who are our constituents and what are their needs and wants?*

(A) DEFINING CONSTITUENTS' NEEDS

Today's not-for-profit supporters are more aware of what good performance means, are more aware of what they want from an organization, and are more concerned about their own values. It is here that marketing must function as the organization's "ear" in an ever-changing environment. As such, the organization moves from a "we need" philosophy to a "they need and we can provide" philosophy based on both groups' participation in working toward a commonly agreed-on end.

Exhibit 3.1 contains a list of questions that can help to define "marketing" as it relates to all aspects of a not-for-profit organization.

Research, in the form of listening to constituents, donors, and clients, allows the organization to uncover what is perceived to be special about its constituents, both in how they think and in the values they hold, as well as in the benefits they want in relation to the not-for-profit organization. In addition, listening to constituents produces more than just information on promotional tactics. Organizations discover whether their

---

EXHIBIT 3.1 Defining Marketing Tasks

The not-for-profit organization's marketing plan should answer the following questions:

1. What are the targeted markets?
2. What are the key segments within these markets?
3. What are the needs of each market segment?
4. What "business" do constituents think the not-for-profit is in?
5. How much interest or awareness do the organization's activities generate?
6. How satisfied are current constituents with output?

Concerning resources:

1. What are the major strengths or weaknesses that could either enable or limit expansion?
2. What opportunities are presented that will enable an expanded resource base?

Concerning business orientation:

1. What is the organization's mission?
2. What are the organization's values?
3. Who are the key constituents?
4. Who are the major competitors?
5. What are the benefits of the organization that will allow a position different from competitors'?
6. Are there market segments "open" for competition that would allow the organization to excel?

"product mix," comprising their causes, style of activity or ministry, and "hard" product offerings, such as literature, should be maintained, increased, or phased out.

The *product mix* of an organization is the sum total of all of the organization's service outputs on behalf of particular constituencies. Market research allows an organization to discover trends affecting its constituents (and ultimately, the not-for-profit organization itself), the values of different market segments, whether constituents are satisfied with the organization's goals, and the benefits they are seeking. Market research allows an organization to:

- Assess new or emerging marketing opportunities.
- Furnish information for developing marketing plans, both short- and long-term.
- Provide information needed to solve problems that arise within an organization's constituencies.
- Know which marketing decisions have been correct and which are in need of change.
- Develop new promotional appeals.
- Assess where it stands vis-à-vis its competitors in the light of marketplace activities.

3.5   *Developing an Outline of Marketing Strategies*

Most not-for-profit directors will agree that marketing must become as intrinsic to the not-for-profit sector as it is to the for-profit sector. However, we find ourselves in a marketing "preculture," where we have adapted the terminology of for-profit marketers without any of their commensurate systems of evaluation and procedure. This preculture often negatively impacts the following five arenas of thought and action in the not-for-profit world:

1. The *business* or *mission* the not-for-profit organization is in and the corporate values and philosophy that are transmitted through its mission
2. *Exchange theory:* The notion that each party in a transaction should sense that he or she is receiving more than each is giving up—the notion of *self-interest* as it relates to the exchange
3. The actual *marketing task* itself, which stresses the importance of meeting consumer needs
4. The *tools* the not-for-profit marketer uses (sometimes called the *marketing mix*), such as advertising, fund raising, pricing, and channels of communication and distribution
5. The not-for-profit organization's *distinctive competencies,* through which the organization concentrates on doing what it does best in order to minimize any weaknesses it might have[5]

---

[5]This section is adapted from the following articles: Benson S. Shapiro, "Marketing for Nonprofit Organizations," *Harvard Business Review* (September/October, 1973): 123–132; and Siri N. Espy, "Corporate Identity and Directions," in *The Nonprofit Organization,* edited by David L. Gies, J. Steven Ott, and Jay M. Shafritz (Pacific Grove, Calif.: Brooks/Cole Publishing, 1990), pp. 143–155.

The marketing task is fundamentally a transaction in which the self-interest of both parties is key. The promotional tools and marketing mix available to the not-for-profit practitioner has only one purpose: to satisfy efficiently and effectively the not-for-profit's half of the transaction. By further identifying the areas in which it excels, a not-for-profit can then strive to better serve individuals seeking competence in those same areas. Each of the five elements listed is explained in the sections that follow.

(A) ORGANIZATIONAL MISSION

The marketing process begins with a definition of the mission, or "business," of the not-for-profit organization. The mission is important for a variety of reasons, not the least of which is the foundation on which all other marketing planning is built. An organization's mission is its purpose and reasons for being and may also serve to determine accurately the types of service it can provide.

Although "mission" can be hard to define, it must be addressed in order to properly develop all of a not-for-profit's marketing goals and its plan to meet those goals. Ultimately, mission has ramifications in three important areas:

1. *Definition of the constituent groups (sometimes called "stakeholder groups") that will be served.* If there is agreement on the organization's mission through an analysis of constituent perceptions and feelings, the effect can be a powerful catalyst for the organization to achieve its goals.
2. *Identification of the needs of the constituents and the community that will be satisfied by the not-for-profit organization.* The organization must know what criteria individual and multiple stakeholders are using to judge the success of its performance.
3. *The ultimate strategy by which the needs of the constituency will be satisfied.* The strategies and philosophies used by the not-for-profit must be in keeping with its core set of values; otherwise, there is little chance of achieving stakeholder satisfaction.

(B) SELF-INTEREST ASPECT: EXCHANGE THEORY

A not-for-profit organization is often consumed with its need for more outside involvement in order to harvest the additional resources it constantly requires. Marketing must answer the problem of how to get the desired response from those groups the organization has targeted for involvement.

The key to success is to ensure a certain level of satisfaction for the not-for-profit's various constituents. This can be accomplished surreptitiously through what is commonly called an "exchange." Under the *exchange theory,* an individual gives up something (e.g., time, money) in exchange for something else. The individual should perceive the return to be of greater value than that which he or she has given up. *The receiving is thus the motivation for the giving.*

A sense of prestige often plays a major role in convincing people to serve on boards. Similarly, donors are often motivated not only by the feeling that they are part of an exclusive group, but by being made to feel generous, important, and central to an organization's success or failure. For a volunteer, the self-image of being essential, being needed, and belonging often explains why they work hard for no compensation.[6] Successful exchanges often comprise several factors:

- Activities
- Markets
- Prospects
- Costs
- Benefits
- Associated costs
- Nonfinancial benefits

Exchanges are activities that are engaged in by at least two parties. Each party has a goal. The organization initiating the exchange is the *marketer,* and the individual likely to be involved with the exchange is the *prospect.* Together they constitute a *market,* a group of sellers and buyers bargaining in terms of exchanges for goods and services.

(C) MARKETING TASK

The marketing function in the for-profit sector assumes that good marketing management results in truly satisfied consumers and, ultimately, company profitability. This world assumes a profit motive, a primary constituency (donors, clients, etc.) for the company to work with, and the ability to allocate resources based on the viability of a product or service and its acceptance within a constituency. There are, however, intrinsic characteristics that are unique to not-for-profit marketing.

First, not-for-profit organizations do not seek to make a "profit" yet often find it necessary to generate surpluses over expenses to fund unpopular or unfundable parts of their operating budgets.

Second, some causes do not lend themselves easily to performance evaluation. For example, a university may want to provide education for all classes of people. Although these organizations may create a psychological or social "profit," actual performance measurement is difficult.

Third, it is difficult to determine how a not-for-profit manager allocates resources without an accurate assessment of previous performance levels. Many not-for-profits do not charge for services rendered. How does a not-for-profit director gauge the correctness of decisions to enhance some programs and curtail others?

Finally, if the essence of the marketing task is meeting the needs of the constituent, how does a not-for-profit organization do so if its mission is inconsistent with the desires of at least some of its constituents, as in the case of an antidrug or antitobacco organization?

The differences between for-profit and not-for-profit organizations as they relate to marketing are most pronounced in three areas:

1. The profit motive
2. The nature of a not-for-profit organization's constituency
3. Resource attraction

---

[6]Thomas Wolf, *Managing a Nonprofit Organization* (New York: Simon and Schuster, 1990), p. 126.

(i) Profit Motive

A not-for-profit organization does not operate to produce a profit. In other words, not-for-profit organizations do not have a *profit motive.* However, the profit motive gives for-profit managers a control tool that is far superior to most not-for-profit control tools. The nature of the profit motive allows managers to better measure the efficiency and effectiveness in reaching their objectives. On the other hand, the not-for-profit director must deal in "services rendered," which, in most not-for-profit organizations, is a nebulous concept not easily defined.

(ii) Nature of a Not-for-Profit's Constituency

To further complicate matters, a not-for-profit organization usually deals with two principal constituencies:

1. Clients for whom the not-for-profit exists and to whom goods and services are provided.
2. Donors (and volunteers) who provide a portion of the resources allowing the not-for-profit organization's service to take place.

The profit-motivated company has one marketing function, namely, to facilitate direct two-way exchanges that simultaneously include both resource allocation (providing goods and services) and resource attraction (obtaining revenue). In contrast, the not-for-profit organization must approach each of these two tasks separately because they involve separate constituencies.[7] (See Exhibit 3.2.)

(iii) Resource Attraction

Resource attraction is the attraction of funding and other resources to not-for-profit organizations. A not-for-profit organization's resources typically have been obtained

---

[7]Shapiro, "Marketing for Nonprofit Organizations," p. 263.

EXHIBIT 3.2 Not-for-Profit Exchanges

Exchange Partners	Type of Exchange Sought
a. Board Member	Significant contribution, access to leadership
Organization	Wisdom, leadership, access to knowledge
b. Client	Personal benefits, services, friendship
Organization	Fulfillment of mission, success, contribution
c. Volunteer	Service, community worthiness
Organization	Cheap labor, lowering of costs
d. Donor	Recognition, involvement, gratitude
Organization	Resources, growth potential, service

by communication of its needs through one or a combination of the following four paths:

1. A "keep quiet about our needs" approach
2. An advertising and public relations approach
3. A mass media solicitation approach whereby the need is made known, along with a "hard ask"
4. A strong personal selling approach

Each path, or combination of paths, requires a different marketing strategy, and each leads to a different outcome.

There are typically five issues a not-for-profit marketer must consider in planning for resource attraction:

1. *Demographic research.* The not-for-profit marketer must seek information concerning the demographic nature of either the not-for-profit's clients or its supportive constituency.
2. *Articulating the mission.* Not-for-profit strategy must address "donor fatigue" resulting from excessive competition in some philanthropic causes. The strategy must also specify the mix of resources needed to carry out the organization's marketing task.
3. *Targeting audiences.* Not-for-profit organizations are constantly under pressure to be "democratic" in their approach. Internal politics and the fact that a not-for-profit organization often deals with multiple constituencies must be set aside in order to target the most appropriate audiences for solicitation or service.
4. *Pricing.* Typically, not-for-profit organizations have less pricing flexibility than their for-profit cousins. The problem is amplified in those not-for-profit organizations that rely solely on contributions and give their services away for free. The not-for-profit organization must determine realistically how much money can be raised and how much money can be charged for services.
5. *Resource allocation.* The not-for-profit organization should develop a resource allocation strategy. The way funds are distributed in an organization ultimately helps to define its mission. Some not-for-profit organizations undertake causes that are tangential to their own mission; others undertake causes that constituencies will not support or are perceived as being "outside" the organization's scope of expertise. A clear definition of what is and what is not in keeping with its mission will positively affect the organization's ability to raise funds and solicit volunteers.

(D) MARKETING TOOLS

The marketing tools (or *marketing mix*) with which a not-for-profit attracts resources, accomplishes constituent persuasion, and executes appropriate program allocation encompass the following:

The not-for-profit organization's communications program
Its pricing policy
Its causes or products and
Its distribution channels

Houston Elam, a professor of marketing at Metropolitan State College of Denver, and Norton Paley, president of Alexander-Norton, Inc., authors of the book *Marketing for Nonmarketers,* believe marketing can be viewed as a *systematic philosophy and approach to doing business.* It is equally important to recognize that marketing requires interacting business activities, reinforcing the premise that each area of management has a stake in the successful operation of the company and depends on every other area if it is to do its part properly.[8]

The not-for-profit organization's marketing mix can be expressed in two different organizational formats. First, marketing can take the form of a *marketing campaign,* an extended effort by an organization to reach specific financial, membership, or other resource goals within a particular time period.

This specific effort on behalf of a unique organizational goal is in contrast to the second type of marketing, which has to do with an agency's *day-to-day marketing operations* and its ongoing relationship with its donors, customers, volunteers, and clients in their joint undertakings and interactions. Marketing, in this sense, is the attempt by the organization to accomplish its short-term goals.

A not-for-profit organization's marketing campaign and daily marketing operations depend on its *communications program.* Most communication efforts by not-for-profit organizations rely heavily on advertising media (direct mail, space advertising, electronic advertising, etc.) to accomplish specific marketing mix goals. These goals typically range from fund raising to client recruitment to volunteer enrollment.

Elements of a typical communications program include:

- An annual report designed for donors, volunteers, and friends
- A fact and/or photo book to provide a midyear update on the organization's operation
- A quarterly (minimum) newsletter to discuss subjects of importance to the constituency
- Press releases to communicate fast-breaking news of significance
- Specialty brochures to promote various aspects of a not-for-profit organization's program
- Public meetings or gatherings to give management and supportive constituents a chance to interact
- Mass marketing efforts, such as direct mail, advertising, space ads, telemarketing, television and radio specials
- Highly targeted events for purposes of conveying special information to preselected audiences

One of the principal goals of a communications program is to relay information about the not-for-profit organization's *pricing* policies. Pricing is the cost of resources demanded by the seller. In a for-profit company, price is the direct link between resource allocation and resource attraction. A company's product price allows it to attract more resources than expended for the product's production. Some not-for-profit organizations seek to emulate this system by charging fees for services. In undertaking such a move, a not-for-profit organization often relies on a single constituency—its clients—to ensure financial viability through the price it charges for its services.

---

[8]Houston G. Elam and Norton Paley, *Marketing for Nonmarketers* (New York: AMACOM, 1992), p. 7.

3

Other not-for-profit organizations use more than one constituency—donors and clients—in their day-to-day operations. The use of two constituencies usually implies two pricing considerations. Donors provide various dollar amounts—some are asked for higher amounts and others for lesser amounts. (Technically, donors in this situation are paying different *fees*.) For example, a halfway house for drug abusers may offer walk-in treatment at one price, a methadone program at another, and ongoing care at still another. Other not-for-profit organizations may not charge a fee; nevertheless, a psychological "fee" is extracted through a "commitment" to the organization and its goals.

Finally, how does a not-for-profit organization *deliver or distribute its programs or products* to the right audiences? Usually the following four questions are key to a not-for-profit organization's distribution system:

1. Where is the best place for a not-for-profit organization to sell its services?
2. Where and how will the not-for-profit organization collect its donations?
3. Will the not-for-profit organization place its programs in the same areas from which it is raising funds, or in different areas?
4. How will the not-for-profit organization access information from its distribution channels in order to improve its services?

(E) USING DISTINCTIVE COMPETENCIES TO ASSESS COMPETITION

In another approach to defining not-for-profit marketing practices in terms that relate to the for-profit world, the term "distinctive competencies" arises. Basically, a distinctive competency is an area of operation in which a not-for-profit organization delivers better quality than its competitors. The fundamental reason to look at a not-for-profit organization's distinctive competencies is to assess the presence of "competitors" offering the same or similar services to the same constituency.

In the for-profit world, competition theoretically forces an organization to better serve its customers. How, then, does a not-for-profit organization distinguish itself from competitors in order to be rewarded by strong consumer confidence and financial viability? The not-for-profit organization accomplishes this by evaluating its role in terms of how it serves its clients and donors and measuring the programs and services it offers against those of other not-for-profit organizations. In this way, an organization can begin to pinpoint the tasks it performs best.

3.6 *Building a Competitive Marketing Strategy*

A not-for-profit organization needs a marketing strategy so as to provide itself, its volunteers and philanthropic supporters, and those directly benefiting from its work with a substantial sense of purpose and movement toward the achievement of the organization's goals. A marketing strategy provides a way for all parties to see effective goal and resource attainment; it also offers a way to ensure that limited resources are used wisely in pursuit of those goals.

(A)   DISCIPLINED EFFORT TO ESTABLISH "WHO WE ARE"

A marketing strategy is a disciplined process enacted through a management system, whose goal is to develop and produce actions that help the organization to understand what is needed and determine the marketing strategy to attain its goal. The process consists of four steps:

1. A not-for-profit organization's management system.
2. The system develops and produces actions to understand what is needed.
3. Not-for-profit organization develops marketing strategies.
4. Marketing strategy attains goals.

The ensuing strategy includes a look at the not-for-profit organization's *outputs*—programs, products, and the "markets" available to the organization—to determine within which the organization should compete, as well as a look at its *inputs*—from supporters and from those it serves—to help initiate sustainable competitive advantages for each market.

A marketing strategy helps reinforce internally and externally the answers to such fundamental organizational questions as:

- What is the purpose of the organization?
- Who are the people we support and serve, and what are the methods of service we value?
- What are our goals in shaping the environment?
- How are we funded and resourced?
- What business are we in?
- What are our goals in shaping the surrounding conditions and influences on our organization?

Such a strategy builds cooperation between the organization's funding and volunteer base, the constituency it serves, and those who lead and influence the organization. The process and presence of a marketing strategy builds a common framework of assumptions and information and helps differentiate those who support the organization from those who support or use the programs and services of competing organizations. This sense of purpose, embodied in strategy, is especially important as this nation redefines its national and community strategies. As the editors of *The Nonprofit Organization* put it: "This is a time of unparalleled opportunity and danger. . . . Without a clear sense of identity and a strategic plan, non-profit organizations flounder in a sea of competing sorrows, always at the whim of whatever well-articulated hard luck story motivates action."[9]

3.7   *Defining and Building a Strategy: First Steps*

How would your organization define a marketing strategy? John Bryson, in his book *Strategic Planning for Public and Nonprofit Organizations*, states: "First, [not-for-profit]

---

[9]Geis, Ott, and Shafritz, *The Nonprofit Organization*, p. 138.

organizations must think strategically as never before. Second, they must translate their insights into effective strategies to cope with changed circumstances. And third, they must develop the rationales necessary to lay groundwork for the adoption and implementation of their strategies."[10]

Many find it helpful to build a marketing strategy by first defining six elements:

1. *Mission.* A not-for-profit organization may have (or may be able to develop) competitive advantages, but these do not matter unless there are specific organizational objectives toward which the advantage can be directed. A not-for-profit organization must compete for a purpose, and the purpose should be its mission. Without a purpose or mission, competitive advantages are meaningless.

2. *Market and services.* The services provided by a not-for-profit and the market in which it operates define the scope of its competitive environment and, in turn, impose limits on what and for whom it provides.

3. *Competition.* The knowledge of other not-for-profit organizations with similar missions, the approach they take with their constituents, and an approximation of the amount they spend on promotions allows a not-for-profit organization to evaluate its own program and eliminate duplication. The process starts by asking how a not-for-profit competes:
   - What actions are our competitors taking?
   - How does our not-for-profit develop a strategic position within our field?
   - What will our not-for-profit industry look like 10 years from now?

4. *Competitive advantages.* Competitive advantages are those qualities of programs or services offered that distinguish a not-for-profit organization from other organizations offering similar programs or services. These advantages come in a variety of forms:
   - Services or programs of the highest quality available
   - The most reasonably priced services or programs
   - The most experienced staff
   - The greater variety of services offered
   - The most highly endorsed services or programs

5. *Marketing and fund-raising budget.* The resources allocated to marketing and the fund-raising effort contributes significantly to the success or failure of a strategy. These include not just money but time, volunteers, and services provided.

6. *Commitment.* Without the means and organization commitment to support a strategy, the not-for-profit organization is hamstrung when it comes to necessary activities like coordination of resources, providing a forum to work together organizationally, hiring staff, and developing a direction.

(A)   OPERATING ENVIRONMENT'S EFFECTS ON MARKETING AND FUND-RAISING STRATEGY

In beginning to develop a strategy, an organization must first look at the donor, constituent, and supporter environment within which it operates to determine how to pro-

---

[10]John M. Bryson, *Strategic Planning for Public and Nonprofit Organizations* (San Francisco: Jossey-Bass, 1988), p. 4.

ceed. Individual lifestyles, the situations and organizations the donors are involved in, and the resulting effect on those organizations they may (or may not) support are all being assaulted by massive forces of change. George Barna, in his book *The Frog in the Kettle*, contends that an individual's beliefs and values can undermine institutional loyalty.[11] A lack of individual support clearly poses a problem for the future of some not-for-profit organizations that assume they will get public support for their programs as long as they continue "doing what they have done for years."

There are other trends that signal individuals' loosening sense of commitment:

- The divorce rate is climbing.
- Studies show that adults feel they have fewer close friends.
- Brand loyalty has dropped in most product categories.
- The proportion of people willing to join an organization as formal members is declining.
- Fewer people are willing to make long-term commitments.
- The percentage of adults who consider it their duty to fight for their country, regardless of the cause, has dropped.
- The percentage of people who commit to attending events but fail to show is on the rise.

American culture has also become increasingly fragmented, and factors such as double-income families and higher divorce rates have blurred demographic lines and forced new thinking on the part of not-for-profit marketers.

These changes in audience mean that a not-for-profit must *throw away any preconceived notions of who it is marketing to* and instead must *constantly monitor* its constituencies in order to match their interests to the services and programs the organization provides.

Five operating conditions have arisen to constrain not-for-profit marketers today, which should be considered as operational "givens" in planning a competitive strategy:

1. *More competition exists.* Because of an increase in competition, principally in the last 35 years, not-for-profit organizations today encounter operating conditions that may have not been in effect when they were first incorporated.
2. *New experts have arisen.* Many not-for-profits now experience many competitors that offer the same or similar services. As a consequence, there is an increase in the number of not-for-profit organizations that offer the same functions or are *expert organizations* in the same area. This leads to a market condition known as a *parity situation*, whereby the products or services being produced by different organizations are similar in nature.
3. *Not-for-profit organizations are businesses.* Many not-for-profit organizations are similar to businesses in respect to *product lines, customer and donor convenience,* and *marketing.*
4. *Not-for-profit organizations are no longer culturally favored.* Not-for-profit organizations formerly harbored a sense of being "safe" because, in respect to their donors and each other, they did not view themselves in direct competition. They could expect a certain number of donors and clients each year. Because of this complacency, many not-for-profits have not cultivated a *performance mentality,*

---

[11]George Barna, *The Frog in the Kettle* (Ventura: Regal Books, 1990).

never having to define formally where they are going, what they are doing, and what results they are achieving.

5. *Not-for-profits must get rid of the blinders.* Not-for-profit organizations must view themselves as serving different constituencies and not a single group. Their concepts of markets for services must change. The constituency (or lack of one) will define what other markets are available to or appropriate for a not-for-profit.

3.8 Building an Effective Marketing Strategy

There are many ways to build an effective marketing strategy. One approach is to divide the task into six phases so that concerns are dealt with in a sequential manner:

1. The external analysis phase
2. The internal or self-analysis phase
3. The market development phase
4. The strategy selection phase
5. The presentation of the plan to stakeholders
6. The evaluation phase

(A) EXTERNAL ANALYSIS PHASE

In not-for-profit marketing, a practitioner must consider how the external environment impacts the organization's cause, its products, and its services, either positively or negatively. By understanding this action first, a not-for-profit organization will comprehend clearly the societal segments represented by its clients, its constituents, its volunteers, and its donors. From this analysis, a not-for-profit organization can develop a plan to appeal to the motivational needs of each.

(i) Client, Donor, Constituent, and Volunteer Analysis
As stated previously, not-for-profits principally serve four distinct groups: clients, constituents, volunteers, and donors. Two critical issues are basic in analyzing these four groups:

1. Who are the major audience segments involved with the not-for-profit?
2. What are their motivations and unfelt needs?

To understand why these points are important, consider the following trends the United States is currently experiencing and how they might impact the clients, constituents, volunteers, and donors of a not-for-profit organization:

- We are becoming older, and, fortunately, we seem to be getting healthier.
- Most Americans are single for longer periods of their lives, and there are more single people than ever before. People are delaying marriage and children.
- As of 2000, more than 66 percent of women were in the workforce.
- Childbirth is being delayed, and we are having fewer children. In fact, demographers tell us that, without immigration, the United States would have zero population growth.

- We are now the sixth largest Spanish-speaking country in the world, after Mexico, Spain, Argentina, Colombia, and Peru.
- There has been a huge growth in environmental consciousness in the last 15 years.
- Sociologists are seeing an increased willingness to trade our incomes and material possessions for meaning in our lives.

The process of defining the not-for-profit's audience and the trends affecting them should help produce client, donor, volunteer, and constituent profiles. The purpose of these profiles is to determine the characteristics a not-for-profit organization thinks will help it define its targeted markets. The following factors are also important in putting such profiles together:

Sex
Age
Race
Education
Family income
Geographic residence
Employment
Buying behavior

Once an organization develops a profile for each group, it can then begin to look at its competitors and determine how they fit into this market. To this end, a competitor profile must be developed.

(ii) Defining Competitors
Today not-for-profit organizations must *assume* they have competition and must get to know their competitors. In developing a competitor profile, the not-for-profit industry is addressed as a whole. It can serve to identify the strengths and weaknesses of those that are a part of the same industry.

The critical questions underlying a competitor analysis are as follows:

- Who are the competitors of the not-for-profit organization today?
- Who will they be tomorrow?
- Can the not-for-profit organization identify the strengths and weaknesses of each competitor?
- What are their competitive strategies?
- How many people does the competitor serve? How much money is it raising?

(iii) Defining the Industry
As part of a competitor analysis, a not-for-profit organization should assess the likelihood that other not-for-profit organizations could provide the same services. In an industry analysis, it should ask these questions:

- How attractive is this industry to other potential competitors?
- What trends does this industry exhibit?
- Are there key success factors that a marketing strategy will have to take into account in order for the organization to compete effectively?

- Is there an option to collaborate with another not-for-profit to accomplish its mission?
- Does the industry have a history of stability? (This analysis should consider the general trends in the industry—use of technology, changes in leadership, and changes in service delivery—to help a marketing manager anticipate industry changes.)

(B) INTERNAL ANALYSIS PHASE

Having begun the process of looking internally through a competitor profile, a not-for-profit organization must take the next step in this process by determining how others view its own work. In particular, the organization must assess how its constituency defines what it does. This type of *image survey* seeks to determine constituent answers to the following questions: What work do constituents think the organization is engaged in? Can they describe it in detail?

An internal analysis must begin by addressing the following questions:

- Does the organization keep track of its current performance levels, particularly in the service it delivers to individuals and the community?
- If the organization has a strategy, can it identify it for itself and others, along with a sense of how it has performed as an organization? Can its strategy's strengths and weaknesses be identified, as compared with those of its competitors' strategies?
- What is the self-image of the not-for-profit organization? How does the organization describe its culture, structure, key stakeholders, and operational systems?
- How will these perceptions affect the organization's strategy?
- Does the not-for-profit know its costs of doing business?
- Does it know what its competitors are spending to enact the same services and the same service support?
- Is there any advantage in one cost structure over another?
- What internal factors constrain the organization and keep it from having a great success in its market?

These questions are designed to assess the internal context from which the not-for-profit organization can operate. The market development phase goes one step further and forces the institution to develop a direction for its services.

(C) MARKET DEVELOPMENT PHASE

In this phase, competitive advantages are studied in relation to the organization's ability to deliver these benefits to clients, constituents, and donors alike. Decisions about growth or maintenance of its current marketing position also are made in this phase, as are decisions about the types of strategies that are compatible with the organization's objectives.

Critical issues in the market development phase are as follows:

- What is the not-for-profit organization's business mission vs. what it should be?
- What areas of growth should the organization consider that are not currently pursued?
- What strategies should the organization consider for each area of current service?
- What level of investment should the organization consider for each area of current service?
- What competitive strategy options are available to the not-for-profit organization given its service portfolio and product line, particularly those services and products that are deemed weaker in the marketplace?
- Given the different strategic options available to the organization, which best suit its strengths and weaknesses and, particularly, its culture and stakeholder expectations?

(D) STRATEGY SELECTION PHASE

The strategy selection phase is a synthesis of the previous three phases. This phase combines all of the strategic options that have been discussed and, taking into account the not-for-profit institution's identity, goals, and its abilities to fulfill its vision, presents the best choices for a strategy. There are usually two or three "best" strategic options from which one is selected by asking questions like the following:

- Looking at all of the key performance measures—clients served, sales, investment, dollars raised, donors acquired—which strategy will deliver the best performance in each area?

(E) PRESENTATION OF THE PLAN

The presentation of the plan offers a selected, refined marketing strategy listing all of the programs and support services, plus client and financial projections for the strategy's performance for the coming year. The presentation of the plan to all levels of management and, ultimately, all levels of employees lists all the programs and support services, plus client and financial projections for the strategy's performance for the coming year.

(F) EVALUATION PHASE

There are increasingly better ways to run an organization and produce its services and products. In the 1990s the concept of *benchmarking* (the technique of searching out the best in competitor processes and systems and then emulating them) expanded beyond the bounds of the for-profit industries.

Identifying superior performance in particular functions is just one way not-for-profit organizations can engage their various environments strategically and build systems of evaluation. Many not-for-profits today must stop assuming that they do not have to evaluate their performance. In a great number of for-profit organizations, a worker's pay is directly dependent on performance. Evaluations of results that measure benefits delivered back to the community will become required, possibly to retain tax-exempt status. This will be hard medicine for most not-for-profit organizations. Many nonprofit organizations still believe that good intentions are more important than good results. The presence of this attitude means that many not-for-profits do not consider themselves to be accountable for their results.

3.9 Implementing Strategic Marketing Choices

Bringing a marketing strategy into a not-for-profit organization, especially an organization that has operated without one, is hard work. In "Managing Change in Nonprofit Organizations," Jacquelyn Wolf offers these practical suggestions for remembering how organizations tend to change:

- Organizational change must be seen as a process, not an event.
- Change must be approached as a people-centered process. It may involve physical alterations in site, technology, and structure, but the managers' concern ultimately should be with the involvement, commitment, resistance, and acceptance of those involved as stakeholders.
- Support from the top—someone very senior in the organization must have a vision of what life will be like after the change effort is undertaken.
- Change and its outcome must be flexible—it is not possible to anticipate all of the steps and potential outcomes.
- Beware of emulating too closely the success of other nonprofit organizations. Effective change is highly contextual.
- Persuasion and participation are far stronger tools than brute force in implementing change.[12]

(A) SIX BARRIERS TO IMPLEMENTATION

There are six major barriers not-for-profit organizations generally must cross to begin the process of putting a strategy in place:

1. The not-for-profit culture
2. The large scale of their goals and purpose statements
3. The environment
4. Their staff and volunteer interaction
5. The mixing of revenue- and nonrevenue-generating activities
6. The need for a strong performance culture

(i) Not-for-Profit Culture
The typical not-for-profit organization is made up of a highly committed office that is somewhat underpaid and understaffed. The office furniture is often old or used. Sayings

---

[12]Jacquelyn Wolf, "Managing Change in Nonprofit Organizations," in *The Nonprofit Organization*, edited by Geis, Ott, and Shafritz, pp. 246–247.

related to the not-for-profit organization's mission adorn the wall. The office leaders are typically articulate, highly educated, and motivated, especially in areas of the core mission relating to the organization. And because most not-for-profit organizations produce services, most office staffers can talk in detail about the types of services the not-for-profit provides.

In addition, the policies and programs the not-for-profit organization generates, and the corresponding values that evolve within the organization, are often more important to the organization's personnel than achieving the end results or goals of the organization. Workers are dedicated to the cause, not necessarily to the bottom line.

A performance-predicated marketing strategy whose goal is to take the organization "somewhere" to accomplish some end result is often unsuccessful, not because it is the wrong strategy, but because it is simply *not accepted as one of the core values of the organization.*

(ii) Goals and Purpose Statements

The unfortunate truth is that many not-for-profit organizations set goals for themselves that they can never accomplish (i.e., to eliminate all smoking from the State of Wisconsin). Such organizational purpose statements, too sweeping in their breadth, are self-defeating for two reasons: First, they cannot reach everyone (all smokers), and, second, the missions (or goals) they define are not sufficiently specific.

In addition, such broad and overreaching goals make personnel and programmatical performance evaluation by the board and senior organizational directors almost impossible.

(iii) Dealing with the Environment

Some perceive working in the not-for-profit world as working in a fishbowl—not only can everyone see what people are doing inside the bowl, but everyone also has an opinion on what they are doing. Consider the not-for-profit executive director's pressures today:

- The demand for not-for-profit services has increased.
- Contributions in some sectors are down.
- Operating grants are on a decline.
- There is a need for not-for-profit organizations to operate in a "businesslike" fashion.
- The public becomes worried if a not-for-profit organization operates in a way that seems too "businesslike."
- Donors expect efficiency and demonstrated competence.
- Competition is increasing.

(iv) Staff and Volunteers

There is often a tremendous advantage to having volunteers within the organization when the task that needs to be accomplished can be handled by them adequately. On the other hand, the needs of volunteers in relation to the organization are not the same as the needs of a paid, full-time staff. The two are sometimes at odds with each other. An operating strategy can serve to enhance integration, or it can completely stymie cooperation by positioning the groups—paid staff and volunteers—with no common ground.

(v) Revenue and Nonrevenue Activities

As not-for-profit organizations seek to improve the bottom line, an increasing number are venturing into for-profit activities; making a profit in one area allows the organization to fund and provide services in another. This organizational duality in purpose and methodology, however, can be problematic.

To tackle the problem means that the organization must build strong, shared values and attitudes for each group and build a shared strategy for the two groups.

(vi) Performance Culture

Robert Waterman, author of *The Renewal Factor*, relates an interesting experience with the San Francisco Symphony. Having volunteered his time to introduce this West Coast symphony to the concept of long-range planning, he discovered that to do so, he first had to help the symphony measure its own performance as compared with other great orchestras. This was accomplished through looking at attributes that made other symphonies great.

> *We measured as many parameters as we could find. First we tackled the financial state of the orchestra, then our own past and that of some of the world's "great" orchestras. We looked at things like the long tenure of great conductors with great orchestras. . . . We compared the average weekly salary of our musicians with the great orchestras. . . . We contrasted the utilization of our symphony hall (83 percent at the time) with that of the others (all running in excess of 90 percent) . . . we measured out subscription ticket sales (70 percent) against those of the others (most running over 85 percent). . . . We evaluated factors like average ticket revenues and income from broadcasting and recording.*[13]

By benchmarking themselves against other orchestras, the San Francisco Symphony developed a list of key indicators from which to evaluate itself by. This enabled the symphony to strengthen areas it was strong in and to begin the process of upgrading performance in areas that needed work. To build a great not-for-profit organization means to move away from a short-term preoccupation to a long-term approach in every aspect, with multiple goals and measurement systems.

3.10 Conclusion

The increased uncertainty in our culture and the constant change and flux in organizational environments requires not-for-profit directors to think and act as never before. For some not-for-profit organizations, this means using strategies to help reach their institutional end goals that produce certain fundamental decisions and actions new to the institution that ultimately guide them into becoming the organization they envision.

A good marketing strategy not only matters but is the essential, or critical, ingredient to an organization's goal completion. A marketing strategy incorporates an organization's mission, policies, and action sequences and guides the not-for-profit organization in allocating resources—time, money, and people—to achieve its goals.

---

[13]Robert H. Waterman, Jr., *The Renewal Factor* (New York: Bantam Books, 1988), p. 125.

Budgeting for Fund Raising

James E. Connell, M.Ed., FAHP
James E. Connell & Associates

4.1 Introduction

(A) THE BUDGET

A budget is one of the most important planning tools in the development function. A budget reflects the philosophy and values of an organization. Developing the budget can be a time-consuming process; it should involve the coordination of the organization's administration, staff, volunteers, and board of directors. Because of the wide variety of programs and the infinitely varied circumstances under which these programs are conducted, a budget must be developed in many stages.

The end results of proper budgeting are the realization of the anticipated revenue and the control of expenses. Budgeting is a major leadership task of fund-raising professionals, an essential process that consumes the time and talents of staff and volunteers. Budgets are both evaluation and planning tools, designed to measure the fiscal performance of fund-raising efforts. A budget may be an important part of other administrative tasks, such as the formulation of grant proposals, determining program support, and establishing new programs and campaign efforts. A budget may also serve as an occasional reference on program progress or as a step-by-step guide for financial development.

Budgeting is used to both plan and control fund-raising efforts. Budgeting forces the fund-raising director to evaluate past program results and to make decisions on future activities. It is not an isolated function, and to be successful it must be based on realistic institutional planning. The budgeting activity must be a well conceived process that forms a fiscal plan of action for future fund-raising efforts. At the beginning of a new program, as well as during periods of intense campaign activity, a budget takes on new importance. Do not view budget development as a routine chore. If your organization does not have plans, it does not need support and you would not be undertaking a fund-raising or budget development plan. The budget development process is an opportunity to plan, evaluate current activities, and change directions.

(B) BUDGET ENVIRONMENT—LEVEL ONE

Budget development is dependent on several factors. No fund-raising program exists in a vacuum. Organizations change, and, to be effective, fund-raising programs must also change. It is the risky program that assumes a static fund-raising environment and endorses repetition of the previous year's program. For many organizations, public support will be the principal source for keeping programs operating. Therefore, proper attention should be given to the current fund-raising climate.

Each program is affected in some way by both national and local trends and influences. The nature and configuration of the fund-raising program determines the direction and general nature of the program's budget. There are general factors that affect every fund-raising program and program-specific factors that have a direct impact on charities' development efforts.

The status of the fund-raising environment greatly affects the accomplishment of realistic financial goals. When developing a budget, reflect on the following seven issues and decide how they affect fund-raising activities. Self-examination and self-assessment establishes a foundation for developing a preliminary budget audit.

When developing a budget:

1. Examine your current fund-raising constituency. Is your constituency local, statewide, or national? What are the size, nature, and scope of the current constituency?
2. Examine the nature of the volunteer cadre. Are there sufficient volunteers to accomplish fund-raising goals? Will new volunteers have to be recruited? Is there a need to establish a new way for volunteers to connect with or establish ownership in the success of the fund-raising program?
3. Establish an understanding of the current stage of the fund-raising program. Is this a new or almost new fund-raising program? What is the current level of fund-raising expertise? What is the experience level of the current staff?
4. Review status of all fund-raising programs. Are any new programs being proposed? Are there programs that should be eliminated during the current year? What resources must be allocated to establish new programs?
5. Establish awareness of the fund-raising need and the reputation of the charity as perceived by the public. Does the public know about the mission and services performed by the charity? If the public is aware of the mission and objectives, what activities are being used to connect the public with the organization beyond financial support? Should new public awareness efforts be established to make the public more aware of new or expanded fund-raising needs?
6. Establish the short- and long-range goals of the organization that would make the public want to support the charity. If the charity enjoys public awareness, what is the level of public understanding of the success of the charity in meeting its goals? Can the internal volunteer leadership and external community leadership articulate the activities of the charity in meeting community needs?
7. Assess the commitment of the organization's internal leadership to the fund-raising process. Do internal leaders participate in fund-raising activity? Is fund-raising activity viewed as a primary or secondary function of the executive staff? Does the board of directors or external leadership have a fund-raising champion who articulates the role and responsibilities of leadership in the fund-raising process?

Program analysis is necessary to establish the direction that will determine the financial expectations and the resources necessary to accomplish programmatic goals.

(C)   BUDGET ENVIRONMENT—LEVEL TWO

Several well-documented environmental factors affect an organization's fund-raising program. The seven key environmental factors that determine both program and budget objectives include the following:

1. Size of the program: How many donors have supported the organization within the last year; the last two years; the last three years? What is the financial capacity of the current donor pool? What is the size of the potential constituency that would support the charity if properly motivated?

2. How long has the charity had a fund-raising program? Older, more stable programs tend to produce results quite cost-effectively, whereas new programs may be very expensive to initiate.
3. What type of charity does the organization represent? Is it an education, social service, arts, museum, or hospital charity? Does the organization have a special mission that sets it apart from other worthy charitable organizations?
4. Does the charity have a list of current and future needs? Does the list of needs include program, capital, or endowment projects that are consistent with its mission and objectives? Are the projects capable of attracting public interest and support?
5. What is the reach of the charity's service area? Can the charity expand its fund-raising program into new geographic areas? Does the charity have a local or national constituency? What factors affect the ability of the charity to engage its donors in its fund-raising program?
6. Does the charity have access to prospects with demonstrated wealth or high net worth? If the charity does not have access to wealth, what steps are necessary to create access? Does access to wealth in the service area determine fund-raising success for similar organizations?
7. What is the current corporate and foundation view of the organization's mission and fund-raising program? What do opinion leaders think of the organization's leadership and administrative ability, and services provided by the charity?

An examination of the environmental factors that affect all fund raising can assist a charity in forming financial objectives, which will help in determining the resource allocations necessary to meet its goals.

(D) BUDGET OBJECTIVES

All budgeting should begin with a clear statement of the budget assumptions and objectives. Budget assumptions are the result of institutional planning. A budget assumption is a major institutional directive about how the fiscal planning will be accomplished. Developed by the senior administration, a budget assumption affects each operating department within a charity. Typical assumptions can be stated as follows:

Assumption 1. Personnel salaries will increase no more than 3 percent for each operating department.

Assumption 2. Benefit expenses will increase 8 percent for each department, based on increased retirement and healthcare costs.

Assumption 3. There will be a cost reduction of 5 percent of variable expenses in all departments during fiscal year 20__ __.

Budget objectives are specific objectives of each operating department. Objectives are targets to be achieved within the budget period. They are expressed in statements about the end result of program planning and reflect the choices made concerning a department's activity for the upcoming year. The chief development officer is responsible for the development of both planning and budget objectives. In larger departments with staff members assigned specific programmatic responsibilities, each staff member should be responsible for developing his or her programmatic and budget objectives. As the budget is developed, goals may change. The chief development officer is then responsible for the refinement of the staff's objectives, consistent with good judgment as to development and institutional planning.

(E) WRITING A BUDGET OBJECTIVE

Objectives are not easy to write. They force directors to make decisions on appropriate programs and on the fiscal behavior of the staff in their management of the fund-raising program. The clearer and more specific the objective, the greater the likelihood of its achievement.

Budget objectives are a commitment of fiscal resources to achieve desired program objectives. No department has unlimited resources, so choices must be made as to how to achieve both departmental and institutional goals. Having a clear sense of the productivity of each development program element helps the chief development officer to focus the available resources.

Well-defined budget objectives have certain characteristics: They are written, relevant, specific, verifiable, clear, quantified, oriented toward results, challenging, and prioritized. A budget goal should also indicate the person responsible for the objective and the time period allocated for the accomplishment of the objective. A budget objective is an indicator of change, results, and responsibility, all accomplished within a defined time period. For an overall program to be successful, all of these elements must be included in both planning and budget objectives.

An example of a weak objective might be: "The annual fund shall raise $300,000 next year." A more comprehensive objective would be: "The annual fund-raising direct mail spring and fall solicitation program shall increase unrestricted revenue from $250,000 to $300,000, and its net dollar return, after allocation of direct expenses, from $125,000 to $140,000 during fiscal year 20__ __. Person Responsible: Director #1."

This budget objective states the desired goal to be accomplished, both in terms of gross revenue ($300,000) to be generated and net revenue returned ($140,000) to the organization. The expense budget for all of the program's direct costs can be calculated ($160,000). The objective targets the final end product of the activity and assigns specific responsibility for achieving the objective to the appropriate director.

(F) UTILIZING A BUDGET QUESTIONNAIRE

One of the best methods to focus staff and volunteer activity on major budget issues is to develop a budget questionnaire. The director should design the questionnaire to uncover both program concerns and program opportunities. The budget questionnaire can be used as a mini–planning activity. All questions should be tailored to the charity's fund-raising situation. A review of historical information can prompt many questions that might be covered in the survey. The staff can view the questionnaire as their opportunity for significant input into the budget process.

The following is a sample of budget review questions:

1. List your number-one major program objective.
2. List program changes you would like to implement within the next year.

3. Review the five most expensive items in your budget for the last fiscal year. Are these items the same as the previous years? If not, what are the changes and why did they occur?
4. Review and list the five major activities in your budget.
5. Do your budget expenditures match your major activity area? If not, why not?
6. List and review the five least expensive items in your budget? Can any of these items be eliminated in the next fiscal year?
7. If you could change one item in your budget, as either an increase or a decrease, which would you choose to change and why?
8. List five major budget items that you can completely control that affect your program performance.
9. List five major budget items you cannot control that affect your program performance.

(G) FIVE STAGES OF THE BUDGET PROCESS

There are five stages in the typical budget process:

1. Preparation
2. Building
3. Reaction, questioning, and analysis
4. Comparison
5. Approval

The stages are interrelated and form a continuum of action steps. In the preparation stage, facts are gathered on previous years' performance. Information is obtained on the performance of the existing budget to date at the time of preliminary preparation. A list of key objective and financial assumptions for the upcoming budget year is used as a guideline for the development of any major changes in the existing budget. What changes must be anticipated, what new programs are to be implemented, what opportunities exist for change and expansion of existing efforts—these are key questions to be answered as budget preparation begins.

The building stage is characterized by the assembling of financial information and documentation. A budget worksheet is prepared. In addition, this is the stage where budget and program planning merge. When the budget is the primary planning tool of the development operation, this is the stage where all the what-if? questions are asked. Continued questioning often changes the initial budget assumptions and has a profound effect on the final budget projections.

Information obtained from reliable sources on changes to the budget are incorporated in the budget projections. The financial assumptions of the budget are verified. Information on changes to salaries and benefits that affect the entire organization are incorporated into the budget projections.

A budget is a financial document in preparation. In the reaction stage, the financial projections are challenged by senior administration and revised to conform to budget assumptions, and a financial analysis is performed. A director seeking to expand the development function during a period of shrinking resources may meet strong resistance during this stage. To succeed in increasing a budget, the director would be wise to have strong documentation on the return on investment that successful fund raising can produce.

Research and national surveys have produced historical data that indicates the productivity of selected fund-raising activities. Information is also available on selected not-for-profit industry groups such as healthcare, education, social service, and the arts. As a development program grows, so does the body of available information to compare and contrast fund-raising results. The director should begin to compare the current budget projections with previous financial results. There is a strong tendency to examine only last year's financial results. It would be wise to chart a five-year history of both income and expenses for the fund-raising operation in presenting a case for the current-year budget. Budget and performance comparisons provide solid business arguments for future investment in fund-raising resources.

In the approval stage, the final budget is presented to the administrative and volunteer leadership for approval. If the development operation has a separate finance committee, it is the responsibility of this committee to present the budget to the full board of directors for final approval. If the development function is an operating department within a larger organization, the administration is responsible for presenting and receiving approval for the larger institutional budget, which will include a development department budget allocation.

(H) TIMING OF THE BUDGET ACTIVITY

The budget process should not be a last-minute activity. Each department or program should review its monthly or quarterly operational results and have a good idea of its current financial status. In developing the new fiscal year budget, begin early. Budget development can be a lengthy process, especially when the development budget must be incorporated into the organization's final operational budget. Program planning should precede budget development. Planning makes budgeting considerably easier. Planning provides answers to program directions that help to determine the financial resources.

(I) PRIMARY AND SECONDARY FUNCTIONS OF THE BUDGET

The first primary function of a budget is to record in financial terms the program plans for the fund-raising function. Budget development forces an organization to decide what it wants to create and accomplish within the next budget or financial planning period. The second primary function of a budget is to monitor and control the financial income and expenses of the fund-raising function. Budgets can provide an early warning of difficulty in reaching revenue or expense targets.

A secondary function of the budget is that the process may force the organization to plan its short- and long-range future. The budget development process may educate volunteers about the many segments and activities that form a successful fund-raising program. A budget forces everyone to look at the business basics of the fund-raising process: Where is the organization spending its fund-raising resources? What is it costing the charity to raise private support, and what is the return on investment? Budget development provides an opportunity for the fund-raising leadership to compare and contrast their results with those of similar organizations. Moreover, the budget serves as a resource document to track individual staff and program performance.

The budget cycle provides a convenient opportunity to conduct an annual review of fund-raising activities. Budget development offers an opportunity to audit current program activities and forces the issues of fund-raising efficiency and effectiveness in regard to both staff and programs.

(J) BUDGET MASTER PLAN

The budget master plan should cover a five-year projection of income and expenses. This is a summary budget projection based on the institutional master plan objectives. The goals and objectives may change, resulting in a change in the budget projections. These projections help the organization plan for changes in fund-raising production designed to support institutional goals. The purpose of the five-year projection is to force the board, fund-raising staff, and volunteers to look ahead and anticipate potential problems and opportunities.

The master plan involves estimating the nature and scope of the fund-raising program for the next five years, stating the amount of change in fund-raising revenue and expenses, estimating staff additions, and anticipating program changes. The development of the five-year master plan requires considerable participation by staff and leadership. A few knowledgeable volunteers, the fund-raising staff, and selected leadership members should be sufficient to develop the plan. The institutional goals should be clearly stated and the fund-raising plan based on these objectives. The master plan is the result of stating objectives and making decisions about how the fund-raising program will support the organizational plan. The plan is a guideline that must be sufficiently flexible to change when the environment presents fund-raising opportunities that will enhance the total return to the charity.

The development of the master plan requires development of a plan for revenue and expense projections, which should be reviewed every year. A change in organizational goals will require a revision of the master plan projections. The financial projections should be general in nature and represent summary categories of the major expense and revenue sources. As each year passes the five-year plan should be updated and revised as appropriate. Exhibit 4.1 is a sample five-year master plan budget projection.

(K) BUDGET AND INSTITUTION'S VIEW OF THE DEVELOPMENT PROCESS

Fund raising is conducted either as an operational department within the charitable organization or as an external, separate support foundation. Each of these organizational arrangements has advantages and disadvantages, which are beyond the scope of this chapter. However, each organizational structure may have a different view of the role of fund raising in the development of the charity. One structure may see fund raising as an absolute necessity because generation of revenue is vital to the survival of the charity. Another view may be that fund raising is designed to capture the existing potential support from interested supporters, which, when added to the existing endowment, will greatly aid in the long-range development of the charity by allowing it to address cur-

EXHIBIT 4.1 Sample Worksheet for Five-Year Master Plan Budget

Goals	Year One	Year Two	Year Three	Year Four	Year Five
Revenue Program Area					
Annual					
Major Gifts					
Corporate Grants					
Foundation Grants					
Planned Gifts and Estates					
Special Events					
Future Endowments					
Revenue Total					
Expenses Categories					
Salary					
Benefits					
Overhead Expenses					
Expense Total					
Net Fund-raising Revenue					

rent priority programs and enhance other existing programs. Both views may be present to a greater or lesser degree in all fund-raising functions.

The institution's desired financial revenue outcome will dictate the nature, structure, and budget of the current and future fund-raising programs. Fund raising produces two types of institutional financial revenue, (1) unrestricted revenue and (2) restricted revenue. Fund-raising revenue is typically allocated to three functional financial areas: (1) program support, (2) capital purchases, and (3) endowment investments. Thus, there are six planning possibilities for the revenue generated by fund-raising programs. Fund raising may produce unrestricted revenue, which, when allocated, could be used to support operational programs, capital programs, or endowment investments. The restricted revenue produced through fund-raising programs must be allocated according to the directions of the donor. Restricted revenue may be given to the charity to support existing or new operational program efforts, existing or new capital programs, or existing or new endowment funds. Applying the revenue support to new or existing programs expands the budgeting possibilities to 12, as listed in Exhibit 4.2.

EXHIBIT 4.2 Budget Planning Possibilities Based on Fund-raising Revenue Objectives

Program Quality	Program Type	Fund-raising Support
New	Program	Unrestricted
		Restricted
	Capital	Unrestricted
		Restricted
	Endowment	Unrestricted
		Restricted
Existing	Program	Unrestricted
		Restricted
	Capital	Unrestricted
		Restricted
	Endowment	Unrestricted
		Restricted

For example, a *New, Endowment, Restricted* budgeting format would be used by a charity desiring to start a new endowment fund, with the income from the endowment restricted to support its five-year old Rape Crisis Intervention Center. An *Existing, Program, Unrestricted* budgeting format would be used by an organization raising annual unrestricted revenue and applying the revenue to one or more existing programs that need support; perhaps a social service agency with multiple delivery sites would have an areawide appeal to generate unrestricted support that it would apply to one of its operating divisions and its program that has financial need.

It is risky for most organizations to use fund-raising support to balance an operating budget. Only organizations with a history of successful annual unrestricted support, such as colleges and universities with successful alumni fund-raising activities, should attempt to balance a current operating budget with annual fund-raising support. A budgeting alternative to using the current year's annual support is for the organization to segregate the annual unrestricted support received in one year and apply the funds for unrestricted institutional operating support in the following budget year. This method provides adequate planning time when revenues change drastically.

A charity committed to using fund-raising revenue to build its asset base and capital will have a totally different fund-raising budget configuration from one committed to using every available revenue dollar to support current program efforts. The more time allowed to reach the goal of the fund-raising effort, the more flexibility the staff has in structuring a comprehensive program designed to raise maximum support from all sources over time. Long-range budget and planning goals also require constant evaluation to ensure the effectiveness of and growth in the fund-raising activities. Periodic fund-raising revenue, expense, and budget reports contribute greatly to providing adequate information to plan for program changes and evaluate fund-raising success.

4.2   Budget Planning Process

(A)   FACTORS TO CONSIDER IN BUDGET PLANNING

Presentation and layout are important in the development of a budget. Forms for operating departments of larger organizations often do not reflect the program activity components of the development function. If the budget forms are organized according to institutional objectives, they may be difficult to use in creating a comprehensive development budget. The director may wish to create specific development budget forms. Once developed, completed, and approved, the information may be transferred to the institutional budget format. Directors with separate operating foundations should be able to tailor the budget reporting format and subsequent accounting summaries to specific fund-raising needs.

An organization required to submit Internal Revenue Service (IRS) Form 990 might consider using its statement of functional expenses as a suggested budget format. This format separates financial details into three functional reporting areas: (1) program services, (2) management and general, and (3) fund-raising costs.

(B)   DEVELOPING A BUDGET PLANNING CALENDAR/TIMETABLE

What does a typical budget calendar represent? How long should it take to develop an adequate budget? Exhibit 4.3 is a typical 10-week schedule for budget development. It is important that the budget process involve staff, administration, and volunteer leadership. Involving others can lengthen the budget development process, but it provides valuable information from business leaders experienced in financial matters and builds ownership of the budget and program objectives.

(C)   DEVELOPING THE BUDGET WITH ADMINISTRATIVE LEADERSHIP

The administration of a charity is involved in budget development on several levels. The administration is responsible for setting challenging but realistic goals for the fund-raising effort. Whereas the charity's chief executive officer (CEO) must hold the fund-raising director accountable for producing fund-raising revenue, the director must depend on administrative leadership for strategic and planning objectives. The CEO, responsible to the board for the accomplishment of the charity's mission, must be involved in developing and approving the goals of the fund-raising process. Strategy, goals, and objectives for fund raising must be clearly understood by the fund-raising staff and volunteers and endorsed at all administrative levels. This is truly a process in which everyone involved is "marching in the same direction." It is important for administration to understand that fund-raising programs cannot change their objectives monthly. Long-range fund-raising success is built on a consistent pattern of activity that requires several steps in planning and execution. Altering fund-raising objectives several times during a year is a prescription for failure. Because fund raising involves vol-

EXHIBIT 4.3 Sample Calendar of Budget Development Activity

Week	Activity
Week 1	Gather all documents, historical reports, previous planning information, program status reports, etc. necessary to begin budget planning process.
Week 2	Analyze historical information. Begin development of the budget assumptions. Review environmental factors affecting future year fund-raising program. Prepare budget questionnaire. Develop budget narrative on program strategy.
Week 3	Begin budget planning process; staff and leadership to complete budget questionnaire. Complete the budget assumptions affecting salaries, benefits, and other administrative objectives.
Week 4	Begin development of program objectives. Begin to assemble financial information necessary to carry out program objectives. Meet with employees to review personnel performances and assign salary changes to personnel budget.
Week 5	Finalize program and budget objectives for next year. Present program objectives to leadership for reaction and review.
Week 6	Present draft budget to the finance committee for review. Revise budget and program objectives based on further staff and volunteer comments. Complete all financial information that affects program accomplishment.
Week 7	Review, compare, and contrast current budget information with historical data, local financial information, and national trends. Continue development of budget documents.
Week 8	Finalize all budget information.
Week 9	Prepare final documents for presentation and approval.
Week 10	Present final budget documents to administration, finance committee, or board of directors for final approval.

unteers, constant change affects the integrity of the program in the minds and hearts of community leaders, who conduct their own businesses in a different manner.

The development of the fund-raising budget with administration should be a participatory process whereby the CEO and fund-raising director share ideas, opportunities, and aspirations for the impact of private support on the accomplishment of the charitable mission. If the CEO's management style is directive, whereby goals are handed down without the participation of other key players, the budget and program planning process may be at risk. Although directive-style management may be successful with administrative activities that are internal to the organization's functioning, it places the fund-raising program at risk, because fund raising involves external community leadership for the accomplishment of its objectives.

The development of the fund-raising budget will involve the organization's finance director or controller. It is important for the director to understand the financial operation of the charity and how fund raising makes its impact on financial results. It is also important for the director to speak "controllerese," which means understanding and articulating the financial objectives of the organization to ensure that the finance department is not dictating fund-raising activities because of strictly financial needs. Every organization needs private support, but organizations that seek only one type of support, such as unrestricted income, must appreciate this constraint and how it results in lost financial opportunities. Sometimes called the "opportunity cost" of fund raising, this is the direct result of restrictive financial needs that ultimately translate into single-focus solicitation activities.

Long-range planning, environmental influences, new or revised program planning, and economic and social influences on an organization may dictate a change in its mission, goals, and objectives during any planning or budget period. It is important for the CEO to address the impact of these changes on the fund-raising program. Through a participatory process the director and the CEO probably can devise an appropriate strategy resulting in maximum private support for the charity.

(D)   DEVELOPING THE BUDGET WITH STAFF

The organizational structure of each development office will determine the extent of participation and authority assigned to each staff person for budget development. If staff members are responsible for the accomplishment of specific program objectives, they should be responsible for deciding the revenue and expense components of those objectives. Individual program directors who are in close contact with vendors should be responsible for the detailed expense budget for each program component. The director is responsible for determining the salary, benefits, and overhead costs of the budget assigned to him or her to each program component.

An experienced director will guide staff in the development of realistic and productive budget projections. Staff budget assignments are an opportunity to identify and assign dollar values to specific program items needed to accomplish fund-raising objectives. Staff budget preparation should have two stages: (1) preliminary preparation and (2) final refinement. In the preliminary preparation stage, every activity should be examined to decide its suitability for the next budget year. Those programs and projects that were productive should be retained, and unproductive programs should be ended. If an unproductive program is not discontinued but needs another year to be evaluated, the complete rationale for its continuance should be documented in the budget narrative. This procedure ensures that the program is examined and reviewed as the budget projections are reviewed regularly. In the final refinement stage, the director is required to make judgments on the specific allocation of available resources to each program area. Institutional and administrative concerns may affect the amount of available resources for the fund-raising effort. After the final budget has been determined, the director should present the budget to staff, explaining the extent of changes required because of administrative, environmental, or program factors. By developing a two-stage system for budget development with the staff, the director creates staff ownership and responsibility while generating an environment of independent growth in staff capabilities.

(E)　DEVELOPING THE BUDGET WITH VOLUNTEERS

Volunteers with strong administrative and financial skills can be very helpful during the budget process. Volunteers can be advocates for change and can also be critical of the effectiveness of current programs. Those serving on the finance committee can provide assistance in shaping the budget assumptions. Volunteer input is essential when new programs are being proposed or there is a significant shift in current program efforts. It is also important to have a strong budget advocate on the finance or executive committee who can speak on issues raised by peers. The budget process may be the only planning opportunity available to change program formats with volunteer input.

Important principals in fund raising can be communicated during the budget process. "Investment in new program" and "return on investment" are common terms and evaluation methods in business and industry. There is always a natural tendency to focus on fund-raising expenses. Every expense dollar saved drops to the bottom line, increasing the net income available for program support. Yet concentration on expenses can ultimately erode fund-raising effectiveness by assuming expense dollars are not necessary to achieve fund-raising revenues. Fund raising should be viewed as an investment process wherein success is measured by the number of dollars returned to the organization for each dollar spent. This business orientation should focus on the key question: "How many dollars are returned to our charity if I invest another dollar in my fund-raising budget?"

The variable direct expenses of fund raising must be controlled. Historical information is helpful in spotting expense trends. The majority of fund-raising expenses are investments in the salaries and personnel benefits of staff. Eliminating staff positions to save expense dollars may jeopardize the program.

4.3　Budget Implementation

(A)　TYPES OF BUDGETS

There are several types of budgets. The strategic budget is the financial plan resulting from the long-range planning process and master plan for the organization. The program budget represents the financial revenue and expense incurred by the organization in its efforts to deliver services. The development department's operational budget represents the revenue and expenses of the fund-raising program. The cash-flow budget presents a listing of the monthly cash available from revenue sources and the expenses incurred during the budget year. The capital budget represents the funds available for extraordinary purchases of property, plant, equipment, and other fixed assets.

(B)　STRATEGIC BUDGET

The strategic budget is vastly different from the annual operating budget. The strategic budget is the direct result of the organization's long-range planning process and is part of the organization's master plan. The strategic budget takes the three- to five-year objectives of the organization and translates them into fiscal and fund-raising goals. It is important for the organization to have a clear vision of the services it renders; without a clear vision and an articulated mission, development of a strategic budget is not possible. Fund-raising staff should be involved in the process of developing the strategic budget.

Achieving strategic goals requires a fiscal and fund-raising plan. The strategic plan helps the fund-raising program by committing the organization to specific long-range objectives. The development department must translate the long-range goals into an operational and fund-raising plan. This plan may include significant change in direction for the fund-raising activities. It may include significant increases in the financial resources devoted to the fund-raising process; it may include a significant and intensive fund-raising effort. It may require the development function to change its current operational plans to achieve a larger and more significant objective some time in the future.

It is important for the board to realize that the fund-raising process needs time to produce significant results. Additional fiscal goals are achievable for an organization when there is a partnership between the strategic plan and the annual operational plan. It is extremely important for the chief development officer to establish appropriate expectations about the ability of the fund-raising process to deliver fiscal results. This would include stating the staff and fiscal requirement necessary to achieve the long-range goals. If the expectations of the administrative and volunteer leadership far exceed the professional judgment of the chief development officer as to the program's ability to produce results, the board may wish to revise the objectives or expand its commitment to fund raising.

(C) PROGRAM BUDGET

The fund-raising budget is only one component of the charity's program budget. The program budget represents the financial plan for the delivery of services. Developed by administration and approved by the board, it reflects all anticipated revenue and expenses of the organization. It lists investments in new plant and facilities, new program initiatives, expansion of existing activities, anticipated income from endowments, and changes in the capital structure of the organization. It truly represents the organization's financial "big picture." It also provides a monthly check on how the staff and services are using available financial resources.

(D) OPERATIONAL BUDGET—THE FUND-RAISING PROGRAM BUDGET

The development budget represents funds appropriated on an ongoing basis to sustain a development effort. The organization of a development budget takes planning and a systematic approach. The most successful system to use in assembling budget information is the cost center approach.

The first step in developing the cost center approach is to define the cost center program areas. A program area is a set of activities designed to produce a desired financial return. In development and institutional advancement these activities have traditionally been divided into the following general areas: Public Relations, Annual Giving, Corporate Giving, Foundation Grants, Special Events, Planned Giving, Capital Campaign, and New Program Efforts. Divisions of the cost centers are possible when discrete activities within the major activities dictate separation. This can aid in an examination of the cost-benefit return of the activities. Thus, Annual Giving may be divided into membership activities, direct mail appeals, memorial and tribute programs, telemarketing programs, and so on. Once a title is assigned to an activity, the person responsible for the execution of the program, generation of revenue, and expenses must be identified.

Each program can be budgeted and the return on investment identified for each program and subprogram area. This procedure is beneficial in identifying the size and trend of the financial return from each program area. Knowing such trends can be helpful in identifying problem areas. Recording the trend of a program's financial return is a good management evaluation technique and may lead to changing program efforts to achieve greater returns from more highly productive programs. A sample budget planning worksheet by program area is shown in Exhibit 4.4.

The sources of revenue should be defined on separate worksheets listing revenue by source and program activity. There are various methods for estimating the financial revenue for each fund-raising activity. The best technique is to review the prior year's performance and, using informed judgment about the current fund-raising environment, estimate the financial revenue. The more homogeneous the environment from year to year, the more accurate and reliable the revenue estimates. The expenses to conduct the program should be defined similarly to those listed in Exhibit 4.16 on page 82.

(i) Budgets for Annual Funds

Annual support programs represent the ongoing gift activities of the charity to acquire small gifts on a sustainable basis. An annual gift program may take many forms and have several components. Direct mail, memorial gifts, donor club solicitations, telemarketing activity, and annual special events may all be part of an annual gift program.

To develop the annual giving budget, the revenue and expenses of each component should be determined. Developing the final budget may require budgets for several sub-budget components. For example, the direct mail program may have three all-constituency mailings and two target-constituency mailings per year. The total of each of these subaccount activities forms the total budgeted in the direct mail budget category. (See Exhibit 4.5.)

Each of the subcomponent budgets will contain different budget categories. For example, telephone expenses for the telemarketing program conducted by paid staff,

EXHIBIT 4.4 Sample Budget Planning Worksheet by Program Area

Category	Activity				Total
	Program Area 1	Program Area 2	Program Area 3	Program Area 4	
Revenue					

Expenses
  Direct Expense
  Overhead Expense					

Total Expenses					
Net Revenue					

EXHIBIT 4.5 Subaccount Budget Worksheet

Program: Annual Giving

Activity	Type	Number Mailed	Cost/Package	Estimated Cost	Projected Revenue	Return on Investment
Mailing 1						
Mailing 2						
Mailing 3						
Mailing 4						
Mailing 5						
Totals						

R = Renewal, A = Acquisition

professional firms, or volunteers would not exist in the direct mail budget where postage, material preparation, and creative fees would appear. See Exhibit 4.6 for a sample of an annual budget worksheet including direct expenses.

(ii) Budgets for Grants

Grants budgets operate on two levels. The director must budget for the personnel and expenses of the functional activity of developing grant solicitations from corporations and foundations. In addition, the development office must be skilled in developing grant requests for capital and program projects, which may take many years to complete.

EXHIBIT 4.6 Annual Giving Budget Worksheet

Direct Expenses

Activity	Projected Revenue	Projected Budget	Return on Investment
Direct Mail			
Memorial Gifts			
Donor Clubs			
Telemarketing			
Annual Events			
Unsolicited Gifts			
Other			
Totals			

The expenses of developing grants fall into three categories:

1. *Grant preparation.* This stage involves research on potential sources of support, obtaining administrative endorsement for the grant request, writing of the grant request, and obtaining or creating supporting documentation.
2. *Grant presentation.* This stage involves meeting with the potential funding source, cultivation activities with related parties, and on-site review of grant materials by the potential grantor.
3. *Grant stewardship.* This stage occurs after the grant is funded. It involves creating periodic reports on the grant's progress, on-site meetings with administration and/or those funded from the grant, courtesy invitations to special events, and plaques or other materials honoring the grantor. (See Exhibit 4.7.)

EXHIBIT 4.7 Grants Budget Worksheet

Direct Expenses

Activity	Prior Year Expenses	Projected Expenses
Grant Preparation		
Research material		
On-line research services		
Proposal preparation and supplies		
Consultant expenses		
Grant Presentation		
Local travel		
Local cultivation		
Long-distance travel		
Long-distance cultivation		
Grant Stewardship		
Plaques		
Reports		
On-site events		
Miscellaneous Expenses (List)		
Total Expenses		
Actual/Projected Revenue		

In submitting grant applications, the organization should list all of the direct expenses requested. Some grant guidelines for foundations and corporations allow for the inclusion of organizational overhead as an organizational expense. The guidelines should be reviewed, and if overhead allocations are not mentioned, a personal phone call to the grant agency can clarify this important issue.

(iii) Budgets for Events

The planning, production, and analysis of events are critical components of many fund-raising budgets. The director should be concerned with both the budget impact of all events' direct and overhead costs incurred and the financial results of each event. The financial management of events is important in estimating both the revenue and expense projections. The traditional industry standard, that events should produce a minimum 50 percent return of revenue over direct costs, applies to all fund-raising events. The standard may be adjusted to fit newly established events, but an event that does not meet this standard within three years should be ended.

The event budget should be prepared with both staff and volunteers. The determination of revenue and expense projections should be based on reasonable cost guidelines. The nature of the event will determine available revenue sources and expense categories. There are many possible sources of income for events, including revenue from ticket sales, sponsorships, donations, in-kind support, and advertising revenue. The expense categories should include event promotion, event production, and event stewardship activities. In addition to the direct cost of conducting an event, the budget should include an allocation for the indirect costs and overhead, which will help the director to determine the true cost of the event. Indirect costs include salaries for employees and costs of training, consultants, temporary staff, and travel not allocated as direct costs of the event. Overhead costs include the allocated costs of operating the fund-raising office to produce the event.

Events are very time-intensive, and if the activity is not well managed and well executed, it raises questions about the ability of both staff and volunteers. The budget becomes the guiding management document for the event and should be evaluated frequently. Any deviations or unexpected costs should be recorded immediately and a new pro forma budget statement prepared. Events are valuable in many ways, both qualitatively and quantitatively. The budget will project the financial results of the entire event. A sample budget format is shown in Exhibit 4.8.

(iv) Budgets for Major and Planned Gifts

Major and planned gift programs have become increasingly important for the financial success of fund-raising programs. Demographic changes and the need to obtain significant support with minimal expense have focused increasing attention on major and planned gift fund-raising efforts. Establishing a financial return from a planned gift or charitable estate planning program may take many years. However, historical evidence shows charitable estate planning programs are the most cost-effective means of raising long-term support. Major gift efforts that focus on the accomplishment of a program or project with a few but significant major gifts are also quite cost effective.

Budgeting for planned and major gift activity depends on the status of the fund-raising program and the time it has been committed to this effort. A newly established program will require more support than an established program. The initial costs may be high, but the total return from the substantially increased cash flow should become evi-

EXHIBIT 4.8 Budget Worksheet for an Event

Activity	Estimated Budget	Actual Budget
Revenue		
Ticket sales		
Sponsorships		
Underwriter fees		
Event receipts		
Other revenue		
In-kind donations		
Contributions in lieu of event		
Total Revenue		
Expenses		
Promotion		
Materials		
Advertising		
Postage and handling		
Event management		
Rental fees and licenses		
Food and beverage		
Entertainment		
Temporary staff		
Consultant fees		
Stewardship		
Recognition materials		
Miscellaneous expenses and contingency fund		
Total Expenses		
Projected Net Revenue		
Revenue Return Per Expense Dollar		

dent within five to seven years. Planning activities with senior Americans who are preparing for the distribution of their estates often results in larger current contributions. In establishing a planned gift budget, it is important to be realistic and commit budget resources for at least five years. Long-term staff involvement and time are required for success. A planned and major gifts effort launched without a realistic budget will not succeed.

Budget support for the major and planned gift effort must come from other operating income of the fund-raising program and/or from an organizational subsidy. Some programs have received start-up grants from foundations or individuals committed to this type of fund raising. Some costs may be shared with other departments or programs; for example, legal fees may be part of the retainer fee the organization pays for legal advice. Planned and major gift costs involve three components:

1. *The cultivation and solicitation costs incurred to obtain the agreement or pledge of support.* Cultivation often involves assembling a group of local or national professional advisors to assist with prospect identification, policy development, and professional education. The signing of the agreement means that the cultivation and solicitation costs incurred in obtaining the gift were invested productively.
2. *The costs incurred to administer, maintain, and service the planned gift arrangements after they are established.* Gift administration will continue to exist for all agreements. As gifts increase, there should be many cost efficiencies to be achieved. In some agreements, such as a charitable remainder trust, the agreement may sustain annual costs, freeing the charity from this continuing expense. Many charities administer life income agreements at no costs to the donor/beneficiary as an incentive to participate in their program.
3. *The investment costs to provide professional investment management for the agreement.* Agreements need professional oversight by skilled investment professionals. If the charity does not have investment expertise, it must be obtained and the costs incurred. The board of directors and/or the investment or finance committee of the board must become skilled in the oversight of planned gift agreements when they are managed and invested by the charity's internal staff. Administration of planned gift arrangements means that the charity is committed to the dual responsibility of maintaining the corpus of the agreement for the current benefit of the donor and the future benefit of the charity.

To evaluate the real future economic effectiveness of the program and the impact of each agreement, the net present value of the future benefit to the charity should be calculated and reported. The net present value represents the true economic impact of the future inflow of dollars measured in today's dollars. The calculations take into account inflation and the time value of the earning power of money. This data is readily available in planned gift computer software programs. The calculation should be performed yearly on existing annuities, trusts, and pooled life income fund contracts and on each newly established agreement.

In many prospect solicitations, charitable estate planning arrangements and life income contracts are the only suitable means to obtain a major gift. Major gifts result when donors contribute a portion of their assets, not their current income. The contribution of assets is enhanced when the charity can show the prospect the current income, capital gains, and estate tax benefits of a life income arrangement. In many situations it is possible to increase a donor's income and decrease the donor's taxes, thereby enhancing his or her living standard during retirement years.

In providing an estimate of the budget success of a major and planned gifts program, a score sheet including both qualitative and quantitative measurements should be established. It is possible to estimate with reasonable assurance the historical costs of obtaining a pool of charitable life income arrangements that may be in existence today. Using such historical results, it is possible to estimate future results and costs with some reliability.

What kind of budget is needed to sustain a major and planned gifts effort? It is difficult to generalize, but sometimes a planner may not want to stay within budget. If a donor offers a charity property worth $200,000 at a bargain sale price of $100,000, the charity may deem the investment worthy of additional budget support. The charity may be required to sell the property, thus incurring selling costs, but the net result after direct, indirect, and overhead costs may be a significant gift to the charity. A charity should maintain a gift acceptance committee to evaluate any gift situation that does not meet the standards preapproved in the planned gift policies and procedures. A sample major and planned gift budget is shown in Exhibit 4.9.

(E) BUDGETING FOR SPECIAL PROJECTS AND CONTINGENCIES

There are occasions when every development program must launch a time-limited project or program in response to a special fund-raising opportunity or organizational need. It is important for the budget to reflect the nature and scope of the one-time effort. The special project should be noted wherever appropriate in the budget. If the program is of some significance and the budget has already been developed and approved, the director, with board approval, should revise the original budget projections.

The budget should track both the budgeted and planned revenue and expenses of the special project for the current and, if appropriate, future budget years. When future comparisons are made with this budget, notations about the special project will assure valid comparisons.

When experience indicates that annual special project opportunities may materialize, the program developer may wish to plan more formally by budgeting for contingencies. A set contingency budget amount of 3 percent, 5 percent, or even 10 percent of the projected budget might be set aside to respond to new fund-raising opportunities and needs. Special projects can take many forms. For example, a new corporation may open a store or begin doing business in a not-for-profit organization's area and would like to conduct an open house at which it will match the donations of other visitors up to a stipulated amount. The corporation may request the organization to help publicize the event by mailings, at the organization's expense, to its major donors.

In some development budgets the special project category may reflect the costs of the project with the highest priority for the coming fiscal year. Each year a development program may select one program, project, or capital need to receive focused development effort. In this case the more formal procedure of listing expense categories should be used. The focused fund-raising effort, which may involve major gift solicitations by selected volunteers, may be compared to conducting a mini–annual capital campaign. For example, suppose a social service agency wishes to move into a new market by remodeling and upgrading a donated building. The project includes capital and program needs for the current year and operational needs for the next two years. A sample budget for a focused special project is shown in Exhibit 4.10.

EXHIBIT 4.9 Budget Worksheet for Major and Planned Gift Program

Activity	Estimated Budget	Actual Expenses
Prospect Research and Identification		
Research materials, directories, etc.		
Research data bank connections		
Research newsletters		
Professional Advisor Activities		
Meeting expenses		
Directory expenses		
Educational expenses		
Outside speakers		
Conference fees		
Professional newsletter purchase and mailings		
Prospect Promotional Activities		
Donor newsletters and mailing expenses		
Brochure purchases		
Estate planning seminars		
Promotional expenses		
Speaker fees		
Facility and meal costs		
Handout materials		
Prospect Cultivation		
Travel and entertainment (local and national)		
Agreement Management		
Bank and trust fees		
Computer software (acquisition and maintenance)		
Legal and appraisal fees		
Accounting and audit fees		
Investment Management		
Donor Relations		
Donor recognition		
Special gifts and recognition		
Travel for continuing donor contact		
Annual society recognition event		
Total Expenses		

EXHIBIT 4.10 Sample Budget Worksheet for Special Project Campaign

Campaign Goal	
Revenue	
Projected first-year revenue	
Projected second-year revenue	
Projected third-year revenue	
Revenue Total	
Expenses	
Prospect research costs	
Case statement development	
Case statement production and supporting material	
Special staffing personnel needs	
Committee meetings	
Prospect cultivation and solicitation, meals and travel	
Donor recognition awards and signs	
Contingency at 3%	
Expense Total	

(F) ESTABLISHING REALISTIC FINANCIAL TARGETS

Establishing a realistic budget requires proper estimation of future financial results. In determining future financial performance, several factors should be considered. The budget is built step by step as information on the anticipated revenue and expenses is assembled. Prior fund-raising history and an assessment of program performance measures are very important in estimating future financial results.

Solid development management is essential in projecting financial targets. It is important not to overestimate fund-raising revenue unless there is a sufficiently solid reason to make projections grossly different from prior year results. Abstract from prior year results successful activities and areas of major concern. Determine the activities that led to successful results and those that led to fund-raising failures. Were the results affected by the costs of fund raising, timing of the activity, number of available prospects, receptiveness of the prospects to the fund-raising project, volunteer involvement, or lack of involvement by key leadership? What caused prior year changes? Will staff continue to be responsible for the program area? Do staff members have added responsibilities that will detract from future results? Establishing the nature of the fund-raising activities and their effect on financial performance can provide baseline information to use in future program enhancements.

The sources of revenue and expenses within each program area should be scrutinized. In examining prior history, the program performance analysis must consider and measure more than gross revenue and expenses. The nature of the organization, timing of the solicitations, solicitation methods, staff capabilities, and prospect availability all affect fund-raising results. The Nine-Point Performance Index developed by James M. Greenfield and shown in Exhibit 4.11 provides a way to analyze fund-raising performance and thus can assist in budget development. Each of the nine elements can be used as an indicator to estimate budget figures. How each element is used for budget development and the mix of elements will depend on the particular program budget under development.

Applying the performance index to budget development requires the tracking of results. Comparison of results over many years reveals trends of fund raising. When significant change takes place, the reasons should be listed and examined. Use of historical data greatly aids in budget development.

The goal of increasing net income can be achieved several ways. Net income is a function of gross income minus expenses. Net income can be increased if expenses are held constant and gross income is increased. Net income can be increased if gross income is held constant and expenses are reduced. Gross income can be increased while expenses are held constant if the percentage of participation is increased. Gross income can be increased while expenses are held constant and the percentage of participation remains constant if the average gift size is increased. Net income can be increased if both gross income and expenses are increased at a constant rate. Once it is determined how much revenue is produced per expense dollar, and if all other factors in the fund-raising

EXHIBIT 4.11 Nine-Point Performance Index

Basic Data

1. Participants	Number of donors responding with gifts.
2. Income	Gross contributions.
3. Expense	Fund-raising costs.

Performance Measures

4. Percent Participation	Divide number of participants by total solicitations made.
5. Average Gift Size	Divide income received by number of participants.
6. Net Income	Subtract expenses from income received.
7. Average Cost Per Gift	Divide expenses by number of participants.
8. Cost of Fund Raising	Divide expenses by income received; multiply by 100 for percentage.
9. Return	Divide net income by expenses; multiply by 100 for percentage.

Source: James M. Greenfield, *Fund-Raising Cost Effectiveness: A Self-Assessment Workbook,* John Wiley & Sons, 1996, p. 31. Used with permission.

mix remain constant (a significant assumption, given the nature of the fund-raising process), then investing more expense dollars should produce more gross revenue and greater net income to the organization.

Exhibit 4.12 presents an example of how using performance information can aid in budget development. The example uses two assumptions to project results and compares them with prior-year results. Assumption 1: Increase the participation rate to 25 percent, holding expenses and average gift size constant. Assumption 2: Increase expenses by 25 percent, holding the participation rate constant but soliciting 25 percent more prospects, who will contribute an average gift of 10 percent less than current donors.

As the budget is developed, it may be appropriate to review local, regional, or national fund-raising data. Such data may provide helpful information, but it should not be used to develop budget standards. Summary data represents a mix of program types with various ages, configurations, volunteer involvement, and program components. A fund-raising program's statistical results may vary greatly from year to year. Individual program comparisons to statistical data may also vary significantly, giving the false impression that a fund-raising program is not productive when performance measures indicate otherwise. Outstanding or poor performance comparisons should be examined in detail. Volunteers may focus on the cost per dollar raised as a major budget or performance requirement. The use of a single statistic to represent program effectiveness is detrimental. Performance and budget indicators must be used in combination to present an accurate picture of budget performance.

EXHIBIT 4.12 Nine-Point Performance Index

Applied to Budget Development

PROGRAM: DIRECT MAIL INDIVIDUAL GIVING

Basic Data	Actual Last Year	Budget Projection 1	Budget Projection 2
1. Participants	1,000	1,250	1,250
2. Income	$60,000	$75,000	$67,500
3. Expense	$15,000	$15,000	$18,750
Performance Measures			
4. Percent Participation	20%	25%	20%
5. Average Gift Size	$60.00	$60.00	$54.00
6. Net Income	$45,000	$60,000	$48,750
7. Average Cost per Gift	$15.00	$12.00	$15.00
8. Cost of Fund Raising	$0.25	$0.20	$0.28
9. Return	$3.00	$4.00	$2.60

(G) REVENUE PROJECTIONS—SOURCE BUDGET

Predicting or forecasting fund-raising revenue can be a difficult and tricky process. This is especially true when a charity is just beginning its fund-raising efforts and little historical information is available.

Revenue projections are determined by what is counted. Fund-raising results for accounting purposes may be vastly different from results provided by the program gifts and future commitments received during the fund-raising year. The gift-reporting standards created by the Council for Advancement and Support of Education (CASE) and the National Association of College and University Business Officers (NACUBO) and the applicable guidelines set by authorities such as the Financial Accounting Standards Board (FASB) should be used in year-by-year forecasting and reports of funds received. Although the accounting function tracks and reports on the status of the cash received and expenses incurred, the success of the fund-raising activity is reflected not only in the cash received but also in pledges of future support. A foundation grant committed within one year is viewed as a fund-raising success by staff and volunteers, even if no current cash is received. The expenses to secure the grant are recorded in one reporting year even though the cash may be paid over several years. In future-year budgets it will be necessary to estimate the amount of pledges payable so that the current activity properly reflects that period's fund-raising activity.

It would be appropriate to have the fund-raising program not only estimate the current cash flow anticipated but also forecast future pledge commitments. During periods of intense capital campaigning the amount of future pledge payments grows significantly. Most donor-reporting software produces a future pledge flow schedule that can be incorporated into current budget projections.

Each fund-raising functional area should produce a revenue estimate. The sum of all the revenue estimates form the revenue section of the final budget submission. In-kind support should be determined and included with an estimated dollar value. It is important that the revenue estimations be realistic and reflective of the program plan for the upcoming budget year. A sudden and significant shortfall can impact the organization's ability to conduct its programs. Consistent overestimation of fund-raising revenue can lead to problems with staff morale and/or damage the credibility of the fund-raising function as perceived by key volunteer leadership.

The most successful estimating technique is to examine the historical pattern of support for the particular program area. The pattern and amount of yearly support should be determined. The anticipated future cash flow resulting from pledges for the budget period should be determined. Next, the director should determine the modifications to the current program that are anticipated. What new programs will be accomplished? What is the anticipated new cash flow from the current and/or new programs? A good estimate for the future can be made if previous data and programs were fairly consistent. If previous programs have been changed significantly, prediction is difficult. In the final analysis, it is the informed judgment of fund-raising professionals and volunteers that will form the basis of the current revenue projections.

It is important to consider the impact of staff changes on fund-raising results. The goal of adding new fund-raising staff is to increase fund-raising revenue. The impact of adding new staff members will be evident over time, and the full financial impact should be apparent by the end of the third fund-raising year.

Forecasting fund-raising performance involves a careful review of several areas of prior activity, including individual solicitation programs and sources, and projecting likely results based on actual experience. (See Exhibits 4.13, 4.14, and 4.15.) To begin, program and source categories should be developed first, reflecting the type and style of the current fund-raising programs. These categories should be those that lead easily to financial comparisons, including the budget format, which should be similar to the monthly reports currently in use.

(H)　EXPENSE PROJECTIONS—EXPENSE BUDGET

(i)　Direct Costs—Start with Salaries

When developing an expense budget, begin with the direct costs. After all direct costs are considered, add the indirect costs attributable to the fund-raising operation. It may be necessary to develop subcategories of expenses for each fund-raising program area.

Direct fund-raising costs start with people, the staff of the fund-raising operation, normally the single largest cost in the fund-raising budget. To project fund-raising salaries, use full-time equivalents (FTEs) so as to provide for any personnel who do not work full time. The use of FTE costs also allows for the inclusion of volunteer support and any changes in the categories of current personnel and adjusts for any personnel hired during the year.

To project next year's direct salary costs, begin with the current salary of all existing staff and add any increases in salary for the next year. Budgeting may use a set percentage of all FTEs to determine the impact of salary increases or may be adjusted for the actual salary increase for each FTE. The director may be given a do-not-exceed salary amount to distribute among the staff, which may be capped at a maximum set percentage for any one staff member. The director may distribute the salary increase to staff, based on merit or exceptional performance. Any recategorization of a position responsibility would dictate a change in base salary, either an increase or decrease, and a salary adjustment based on longevity in the position, special expertise, exceptional performance, or some other agreed-on measure. It is important that whatever measure used to determine salary increases be communicated to each employee.

EXHIBIT 4.13　Revenue Forecasting for Fund-raising Program

Program Area	Prior Period Results	Anticipated Pledge Payments	Forecasted Cash Flow	Total	% Change
Annual					
Major Gifts					
Corporate Grants					
Foundation Grants					
Planned Gifts					
Special Events					
Total of Forecasted Revenue					

EXHIBIT 4.14 Revenue Forecasting for Program Area by Source of Support

Program Area

Source	Prior Year Results	Projected Current Year	Prior Year Budget	Current Year Budget
Individuals				
Groups				
Business and Industry				
Foundation Grants				
Events				
Estates and Trusts				
Total				

To budget new positions, use the midpoint of a salary range. Because few positions are filled the first day of the fiscal year, using the midpoint will provide for the adjustment to the actual salary paid. Check the employment classification of local fund-raising groups, associations, state or regional agencies, or national statistics to determine an appropriate salary range. If local salary ranges are not used, some adjustment for local economic conditions and the availability of skilled personnel may have to be budgeted.

If a position responsibility is split, as exemplified by a staff director responsible for individual giving who spends 25 percent of her time on planned giving, then divide the

EXHIBIT 4.15 Revenue Forecasting for Program Area by Source of Support

Program Area

Source	Next Year Projected Pledge Payments	Next Year Forecasted Cash Flow	Total Cash	% Change from Prior Year
Individuals				
Groups				
Business and Industry				
Foundation Grants				
Events				
Estates and Trusts				
Total				

salary costs between the program budgets based on the amount of time spent on each responsibility. Some adjustment in salary may be necessary to compensate for the increased technical responsibilities or increased skills required for staff who function with two program responsibilities.

Temporary employees should also be included in the direct cost budget. Temporary employees may or may not be eligible for the organization's benefit package. Volunteer hours should be included in the budget as well. Volunteers who perform needed office and/or staff responsibilities must be accounted for. If a volunteer is not available or can no longer function in his or her position, the director may need to fill the position with paid staff. If volunteer hours are accounted for, the board and the administration are made aware of both the cost savings the free-service volunteers provide and the additional costs that may have to be incurred if positions must be filled with paid personnel in a future budget period. The use of volunteers can be budgeted as a noncash in-kind expense, using the relative salary value of personnel and the replacement value of donated time. Volunteers who serve as board members or committee members should not be included in the budget unless they work as an essential part of providing fund raising or program services.

(ii) Direct Costs—Benefit Budget

Direct costs associated with the benefits program of the organization are driven by institutional policies adopted and approved by the board. A move up in position responsibilities may dictate a different level of benefits, such as an increase in allowable vacation time. Certain part-time positions may receive a prorated package of allowable benefits. In preparing the benefits package, the financial director's office normally supplies a set figure to apply to all budgeted salaries, both full and part time. Other benefits may be granted to an employee as part of the direct expenses of the program, for example, granting an employee attendance at one or more conferences or paying the fees for a conference, travel, and other expenses, or for professional certifications. (See Exhibit 4.16.)

Direct benefits include worker's compensation, Federal Insurance Contributions Act (FICA), payroll taxes, unemployment compensation, pension benefits, healthcare benefits, accident and life insurance premiums, and disability insurance coverage. The offering of specific institutional benefits is common and may include a tuition reimbursement plan for college or professional courses, long-term-care insurance, and supplemental retirement benefits beyond the pension program whereby the organization matches all or a portion of an employee's contribution. The costs of direct employee benefits, which are increasing, are normally within the range of 15 percent to 25 percent of direct salary expenses.

(iii) Direct Costs—Nonpersonnel and Direct Program Expenses

Every staff member needs essential supplies and equipment to perform his or her professional functions. Essential staff supplies may include space, furniture, computers, telephone, and general office supplies.

The staff member responsible for specific fund-raising functions needs financial resources to carry out the activities of the program. In addition to office essentials, direct fund-raising program expenses may include the production of materials, travel and entertainment, consulting resources, purchased materials, conducting events, recognition and stewardship materials, and so on. The exact nature of the direct program expenses can vary greatly, depending on the nature of the program, the type and quality of goods and services purchased, the history of the fund-raising activity, and the scope and intensity of the fund-raising activity. Technological changes are having an increasing impact on fund-raising budgets. (See Exhibits 4.17 and 4.18.)

EXHIBIT 4.16 Departmental Budget Worksheet—Personnel and Benefits

	Current Fiscal Year		Budget Year
Category	Budget Year to Date	Actual Year to Date	Estimate
Salaries and Benefits			
Director of Development			
Director of Individual Giving			
Director of Corporate Giving			
Director of Foundation Giving			
Director of Special Events			
Support Staff #1			
Support Staff #2			
Part-time Staff #1			
Part-time Staff #2			
Temporary Staff #1			
Temporary Staff #2			
Volunteer Staff In-Kind Service (non add)			
Subtotal Salaries			
Fringe Benefits (_____%)			
Pay Increase (_____%)			
Subtotal Benefits			
Total Salaries and Benefits			

If direct program expenses benefit two or more fund-raising functions, it may be appropriate to allocate the expenses across several budgets. It is important to consider potential price increases in specific program areas. If a major special event is to be expanded, using a new venue, the increased rent for the new facility should be noted. Exhibit 4.19 provides a sample budget development worksheet that may be used to estimate the costs of new activities.

(iv) Indirect Costs—Overhead Budget

Fund-raising budgets may have to include the indirect costs associated with the overhead of operating the charitable organization. Indirect expenses include occupancy costs such as heat, light, electricity, rent, parking fees, and general liability and property insurance. Depreciation and general administrative costs not assigned to specific programs may also be included as overhead allocations to the fund-raising budget.

EXHIBIT 4.17 Departmental Budget Worksheet—Direct Expenses

Category	Current Fiscal Year		Budget Year
	Budget Year to Date	Actual Year to Date	Estimate
Office Operations*			
Books, Subscriptions			
Computer Equipment			
Conferences and Staff Education			
Consultant Fees			
Donor Recognition			
Dues and Memberships			
Entertainment			
Equipment Maintenance			
Insurance			
List Fees			
Office Supplies			
Office Rental			
Printing Costs			
Postage and Mailing			
Purchased Services			
Rental Equipment			
Telephone Equipment			
Telephone Charges			
Travel Nationwide			
Travel Local			
Total Office Expense			

May include indirect and overhead costs, along with direct expense areas.

EXHIBIT 4.18 Departmental Budget Worksheet—Budget Summary

	Current Fiscal Year		Budget Year
Category	Budget Year to Date	Actual Year to Date	Estimate
Salaries and Benefits			
Office Operations			
Total Budget			

EXHIBIT 4.19 Sample Budget Development Worksheet (to Estimate Cost of New Activities)

PROGRAM CATEGORY: PLANNED GIVING

SUPPORT ACTIVITY: WILLS EMPHASIS

OBJECTIVE: During fiscal year 20__ __ establish wills awareness direct mail program to 2,500 qualified prospects and donors, with the goal of identifying 50 individuals who have included and/or would be willing to include the charity in their estate plans. Identify the type and amount of future expectancy. Supporting comments on the nature and timing of these expenses to support the accomplishment of the objective also can be added.

PERSON RESPONSIBLE: DIRECTOR #1

Expense Item	Expense Amount	Month of Expenditure
Spring newsletter—2,500	$1,500	March
Summer newsletter—2,500	$1,500	June
Fall newsletter—2,600	$1,600	September
Winter newsletter—2,600	$1,600	December
Envelopes—10,200 @ $.05	$510	March
Brochures—5 topics, 100 copies @ $.60	$300	March
Mailing fees—9,800 @ $.33	$3,234	M,J,S,D
Total Expense	$10,244	

Depreciation is the lost value of an item over time. The purpose of depreciation is to set aside funds to replace worn-out items. The alternative is to budget for the replacement of large items in one budget year. Depreciation is considered a noncash expense. The amount of depreciation to be budgeted is determined by multiplying the original cost of the item by its estimated useful life (prorated over 20 or 30 years); the result should be budgeted as a depreciation expense.

General administrative overhead includes the direct costs associated with running the organization. Program budgets that fail to include general administrative overhead may not reflect the actual cost of providing fund-raising service. Depending on the organization's view of fund raising as part of the total organizational budget, the finance department may take the position that fund-raising costs are general administrative expenses and allocate them proportionably to other departmental program budgets.

(I) CAPITAL EXPENDITURES

The capital budget represents expenditures for new plant, property, and equipment. The capital budget may not be under the control of the fund-raising director. The fund-raising program may have to compete with other departments within the organization for the dollars available for capital expenses. The purchase limit for capital expenses is an established policy of the organization. The director may not be able to expend funds for capital purchases in excess of $500 at any time without prior administrative approval.

As the fund-raising departments establish the program budgets, items suitable for capital purchases may be identified. For example, computer software with a useful life of three years or more and a cost of $500 or more is often considered a capital purchase. Replacement or updating of a donor gift accounting system may be defined as a capital purchase and not included in the fund-raising operations budget request.

If the fund-raising program is a free-standing division or foundation, it may have the ability to develop and fund its own capital budget. When capital items are part of the fund-raising budget, it is important to list the items separately, as they may distort program comparisons. This is especially likely when significantly large outlays are made at any one time for capital items or for any other major fixed asset. An organization may establish a funded depreciation account in anticipation of a capital purchase or may establish a depreciation account after a major purchase if the useful life of the purchase is such that it may become outdated or in need of replacement within a short period of time. A detailed budget narrative should accompany any request for capital purchases.

(J) COST ALLOCATIONS

As the fund-raising budget is being developed, it may be appropriate to consider how other budgets affect fund-raising results. A case could be made that many activities of an organization have a direct impact on its fund raising and the fund-raising environment. The budgets of the public relations, alumni, volunteer, support group, membership, and other departments may include activities important to the fulfillment of the fund-raising goals. To the extent reasonable, the fund-raising director may look to these other budgets for support. Often these budgets will be beyond the control of the director, which presents a problem in coordination and control. When the budgets are within the control of the director, it is appropriate to shift costs to additional budgets while keeping the entire budget development process within the organization's working guidelines. If the director allocates expenses to other budgets, it is important to maintain a consistent approach over time in order to make valid cost comparisons and to analyze the return on investment.

4.4 Budget Evaluation

(A) BUDGET REVIEW PROCESS

The budget review process is critical, must be completed on a timely basis, and should be performed on two levels. There should be a staff review of results to date and a board review of the budget and progress toward fund-raising and program goals.

The staff should examine the financial results to date, both income and expenses. Expenses should be reviewed for accuracy and completeness. Variances from revenue and expense budgets should be examined to determine whether any changes are necessary. The staff should use the current data to prepare a forecast of future results. Any changes in program content or the mix of program components, as well as any delay in implementing any program objective, should be noted and a narrative prepared to provide information to the finance committee or board.

The board of directors or the finance committee of the board should receive a periodic update of fund-raising results, budget performance, and forecasts for end-of-period results. The board, after receiving the financial performance update, should provide its input on the results. If there are any significant variances that require program changes, the board should evaluate the new directions and provide its endorsement. This process ensures that major program changes with financial consequences are made in consultation with the volunteer leadership responsible for financial policies and for monitoring financial performance. It often is possible to refine current fund-raising program efforts without making major budget changes.

If there are particular areas in which budget reports are chronically at variance, explanations must be well documented. Changes in the fund-raising environment or the emergence of new priorities will necessitate major budget revisions. Budget revisions may require substantial time commitments by staff, and the seriousness of the impact of the changes on the budget should be considered before major revisions are undertaken.

(B) BUDGETING AND FINANCIAL MANAGEMENT: ADMINISTERING THE BUDGET—REVISIONS, REPORTS, AND COMPARISONS

In addition to helping an organization plan its financial future, a budget is also a tool for financial management and analysis. A budget provides information about financial progress and can be used by the administration and the fund-raising director to guide management decisions. Fund-raising programs are being called upon to accomplish ever-increasing financial goals with fewer resources. The budget is one important tool in the process of examining the effectiveness of fund-raising activities.

It is important that budget reports, information on revenue, and expenses by category be consistent over time. Comparisons are impossible if significant changes are made between years or during one budget period. Budgets are most commonly reported monthly, quarterly, or yearly. Comparisons provide a reference point to determine how well the organization's fund-raising program is performing at any point in time.

Budget results must be compared and analyzed throughout the year. Comparisons of month to month with prior-year data for the same period are best, but quarterly comparisons may be more reflective of actual results. Fund-raising activities are often cyclical, and the timing of events, direct mail solicitations, or major gifts may skew the financial results during any one reporting period. It is important that the financial reports showing budget comparisons be produced on a timely basis. Dated or stale statements that do not properly reflect current performance are difficult for staff to use and to interpret to volunteer committees. If the length of time it takes to produce meaningful reports is too great and the information deviates too much from actual results, the decision-making ability of the entire fund-raising organization is affected.

The director should compare current and prior-period income and expenses to both the actual income and expenses and the budgeted projections. Budgeted items and expenses often do not coincide in timing throughout the year. Any major variances, both underages and overages, should be explained in a budget review narrative. Variances are clear indicators that budget evaluation is necessary and should be reported in both percentages and actual dollar amounts. The remaining budget amounts should provide an indication of any significant anticipated variances at fiscal year end. In addition to reporting on the variances and remaining budget, the director should forecast the status of the budget as to income and expenses at fiscal year end. To project the forecasted year-end results, the director must review the monthly projections and anticipate how the program will perform during the remaining time period. Some income and expenses are simple to anticipate, but the possibility of unexpected expenses or income variances should also be considered in determining the forecast. The response to significant negative variances in projected income and expenses should be to increase fund-raising efforts or limit expenses, or some combination of the two.

The accounting report for the budget may be produced using either a cash or an accrual method. Cash-basis accounting results in recognition of revenue and expenses when received or paid. In accrual-basis accounting, revenues are recognized when received and expenses are recognized when incurred but not paid. Differences in reporting may occur when accrual-basis accounting, normally required for most not-for-profits, is used. A sample budget information comparison is shown in Exhibit 4.20.

One of the first concerns in budget comparisons is whether the accounting reports for the budget provide categories similar to those of the fund-raising program documents. If this is not the case, then the fund-raising staff should translate the accounting information into a fund-raising report by program category. All accounting reports use a chart of accounts to define the elements to be included within one financial area. Often the organization's accounting system provides consolidated information on expenses. For example, the postage expenses of the major gift area, annual appeal, fall major event, and planned gift newsletter might be lumped together into one "postage" category. This makes explanation and comparison difficult. A line-item analysis and translation of the accounting information into specific program segments may be required in order to make valid comparisons.

4.5 Budgeting Special Needs

(A) ZERO-BASED BUDGETING

Zero-based budgeting is a financial technique that forces an organization to examine each and every budget item and to justify each item every year. The objective is to con-

EXHIBIT 4.20 Budget Summary Information for Comparison Review

	Actual	Budget to Date	Actual Prior Period	Remaining Year Budget	Fiscal Year-End Forecast
Income					
Expenses					
Net Income					

tinue those programs that meet the planning objectives of the charity and are financially productive. Programs that are not productive or do not meet current objectives are eliminated. The director is required to justify the existence of each program every time the budget is prepared. In addition to such justification, the director is required to rank the impact of each program and to list decisions on why the program should be continued into the next year. One major flaw of zero-based budgeting is it does not account for the historical impact of fund-raising efforts or the lifetime contributions of individual donor segments.

Fund raising is a process that builds on prior-year results. Therefore, it is difficult for zero-based budgeting to be fully implemented within the context of successful fund-raising dynamics. Certain aspects of the zero-based budgeting concept can be adapted to a fund-raising program. It is quite appropriate to examine each program every year to determine its effectiveness. Growth in program effectiveness is a sign of positive performance. Variable program performance, or declining support of a program segment, should lead to a complete examination of the reasonableness of continuing the program or program segment. A new start or a major revision in programs may be a healthy approach when enthusiasm for repeated fund-raising activities has declined.

(B) HOW TO PAY FOR THE DEVELOPMENT EFFORT

Charities have used several methods to pay for their fund-raising programs. The most common techniques are the self-supporting approach, the subsidy approach, or a combination of these approaches.

The self-supporting approach requires the fund-raising program to generate considerable unrestricted revenue. A portion of the unrestricted revenue is used to offset fund-raising expenses, and the balance is used by the charity to fulfill its mission. This approach forces the fund-raising program to concentrate on gifts of unrestricted income over those that may be used to support a restricted purpose. Support of a restricted purpose should free the charity from the costs of that purpose. To the extent that the support of a restricted purpose frees the charity's budget from expenses, the revenue originally allocated to the restricted purpose can be reallocated and used to support the fund-raising budget. Restricted-purpose support may be more easily attainable, because it provides a specific purpose to the donor's charitable gift. In the early years of starting a fund-raising program, the self-supporting approach may be difficult to use as the charity builds its donor base.

Many charities use the subsidy approach to support the fund-raising program. The entire revenue of the charity, including unrestricted gift income, is allocated to operational departments within the organization. The fund-raising program receives its allocation to pay its operating costs. The subsidy method is used mostly in the beginning of the fund-raising program. Subsidy support does not mean that the fund-raising program should not assess its progress in program growth and in donor development activities. All applicable methods used to evaluate fund-raising programs should be employed, even if the fund-raising department is being subsidized by the total organization budget.

Some charities deposit all unrestricted gift support in their board-designated unrestricted endowment fund and subsidize the fund-raising program. To the extent that the unrestricted income from development activities exceeds the subsidy, the charity grows its endowment fund principal. To the extent that the unrestricted income allocated to the endowment fund is less than the fund-raising subsidy, the organization has less of its own funds being deposited into a board-designated endowment. In using the subsidy method, the charity informs its donors that all funds are being used for direct program support without a decrease caused by fund-raising expenses. This is commonly referred to as the pass-through method of endowment growth.

Most charities use a combination approach to support fund-raising activities. Unrestricted revenue is used to offset current fund-raising expenses; restricted support is applied as the donor directs; and the organization commits to paying for the personnel, benefits, and overhead costs of fund raising while requiring the individual program segments to be self-supporting.

(C) ACCOUNTING AND FINANCIAL REPORTING ISSUES RELATED TO THE FUND-RAISING BUDGET

Budget development and accounting are two separate functions. The recent regulatory changes affecting all not-for-profit organizations aligns the results of these two functions more closely.

The Financial Accounting Standards Board (FASB), the organization that sets forth the rules for generally accepted accounting principles, has issued two standards affecting the not-for-profit sector. The new rules have a significant and far-reaching impact on how not-for-profit organizations report their financial performance and how they record fund-raising support. These rules are important to the budget process because organizations may find it reasonable to develop budget reporting and control procedures that more closely mirror the accounting requirements.

The new rules were implemented because existing accounting standards were inconsistent and caused problems in comparability between organizations. Moreover, there was no relevant guidance on how to report multiyear complex charitable estate planning arrangements or deferred charitable gifts. Charitable reporting formats differed; thus information presented was inconsistent between organizations, which led some readers to have difficulty in understanding the information.

Depending on the type of not-for-profit organization and the nature of its revenues and expenses, the changes ranged from nominal to monumental. Charities that conduct multiyear pledge campaigns will experience dramatic swings in reported revenues.

Changes in the timing of recording public support revenues and expenses will change historical financial indicators of performance, especially the fund-raising cost percentages. In addition, changes in the timing of recording public support can make a charity appear to be "too rich" or "poorly managed."

FASB rule 117 sets forth procedures for proper presentation of the financial statement format. FASB rule 116 sets forth procedures for the proper recording of contributions received.

FASB rule 116 requires the development director to know the exact terms of contributions in order to record them correctly under the new standards. It stipulates when to record a donor's gift, how to value the gift, and which gifts should not be recorded as revenue. It also stipulates three categories of contributions. Contributions include not only cash when it is received but also pledges, now called "promises to give," when they are made. All pledges must be verifiable through written documents. Multiyear pledges must be discounted for the time value of money before they are recorded as assets and as revenue.

Contributions and pledges are classified as unrestricted, temporarily restricted, or permanently restricted in the organization's financial Statement of Activities. Charities that recorded cash only when it was received from pledges must now record as revenue pledge commitments that are unrestricted or have donor-imposed restrictions. Pledges that contain restrictions, imposed by the donor as necessary to receipt of the contribution (conditional restriction), are recorded as revenue only when the pledge requirements are fulfilled. Campaigns that contain matching gifts as donor incentives for participation will be especially affected by this standard. Once the requirement has been met, the full pledge amount is recognized.

FASB rule 116 imposed requirements for the financial reporting of contributions from estates, trust, and annuities. Estates are to be recorded when management receives notification of an estate interest. The charity's recording of the estate should be based on the type and amount of support to be received and the timing of the estate distribution. Trusts and annuities are to be recorded at the net present value of the future income interest. The charity's interest in a trust must be irrevocable. The trust may be managed by the charity or managed by others for the benefit of the charity. Recording of the trust requires the charity to have complete knowledge of the terms of the future gift, the gift amount, the life interest of the trust's living beneficiaries, and any restrictions to be imposed when the trust is distributed to the charity. Annual updating of the additional net present value of the trust released should be recorded until the death of the life income beneficiaries. This new reporting requirement imposes significant new requirements on a planned gift program, especially when the assets are held and managed by a bank or trust company.

FASB rule 116 further imposes recording responsibilities and standards for the receipt of noncash gifts, contributions of time and services of volunteers, and gifts of equipment, land, and buildings. When developing a budget presentation, the organization should consider budgeting gifts and pledges by category: unrestricted, temporarily restricted, or permanently restricted. The use of these accounting categories can assist in the final comparison of the budgeted activities with the accounting presentations.

FASB rule 117 sets forth standards for developing a set of financial statements. The statements should include a balance sheet, statement of activity, statement of cash flows, and, for voluntary health and welfare organizations, a statement of functional expenses. The requirement to provide a statement of cash flows is new. This statement reports by functional categories and should include expenses broken down into categories for programs, management and general, and fund raising. According to FASB, all expenses are to be reported as an unrestricted expense, even if previously recorded as temporarily restricted or permanently restricted revenue. This is a major change, which presents problems in relating costs to particular programs. The actual end-of-period budget documents may present a more realistic representation of the support received and the expenses incurred to raise support (cash and pledges) in selected program areas.

The director should review and gain an understanding of the changes required by these new standards and begin to incorporate the changes in the cash-flow revenue and expense budget projections. Staff education and board understanding of the implications of these changes is necessary for the proper implementation of new budget and accounting procedures. A sample worksheet using the FASB format is shown in Exhibit 4.21.

(D)   FINANCIAL MODELING AND BUDGET FORECASTING

Organizations with a long fund-raising history should use financial modeling and budget forecasting for both long- and short-range periods. Financial modeling can assist the director in predicting the effect of changing the fund-raising program mix and the resulting revenues. Changing program priorities to secure endowment, unrestricted, or restricted project or capital support can have a dramatic effect on the financial well-being of an organization at any time. Failure to predict the impact can severely and negatively impact the organization and the fund-raising program.

No universally acceptable financial models have been adopted as industry standards.

EXHIBIT 4.21 FASB Budget Analysis Using Statement of Activity Reporting Format

Statement of Activities	Unrestricted	Temporarily Restricted	Permanently Restricted	Total
Revenue				
Contribution Income				
Contribution Income—Estates				
Contribution Income—Trusts				
Net Assets Released				
Total				
Expenses				
Programs				
General and Administration				
Fund Raising				
Total Expenses				
Changes in Net Assets				
Net Assets, Beginning of Year				
Net Assets, End of Year				

The best approach is to tailor a model to the specific needs and goals of a charity. To compare and contrast one organization's financial results with those of dissimilar organizations is never productive. To find like organizations with similar details is somewhat difficult. It is the impact of the financial trend over time that is important. The director should examine statements of similar organizations that show changes in financial results when program priorities are changed. It is important to note the direction and magnitude of the change. The new accounting standards that establish standard reporting formats should aid in cross-program comparisons. In modeling revenue, the director should select categories that are useful to the particular fund-raising situation. He or she should look at the history of the fund-raising results and estimate the magnitude of the changes.

The management of the total cost of fund raising is also important, and budget comparisons are very useful. The impact of increased expenses on increasing revenue is the most important measure a director can use in developing a case for fund-raising budget support. Charting the impact over time is useful in showing when increased resources have had an impact, either immediately or over a longer period. Selecting classifications such as cost per dollar raised, expenses per dollar raised per program category, and overall return on investment can help the director communicate, in financial terms, the impact of the fund-raising program. When a program has a few major gifts that skew the financial results from year to year, consider using a revenue and budget report based on five-year cumulative averages. This approach provides a leveling effect and does not overextend the financial targets in any one year. For the revenue target of an established program, use a five-year cumulative revenue average and increase it by 8 percent to 10 percent for the budget year. This method is especially useful in spotting potential problems in a mature development program when it fails to perform for several consecutive years. The first year gives a warning signal, the second year is a red flag, and poor comparison results in the third year are a sign of a significant problem. This is the time to consider changing program leadership and/or adjusting the program in a constructive manner.

(E)   CAMPAIGN BUDGET

The campaign budget, like the annual program budget, is derived from a plan for future activity. The campaign budget is normally a multiyear projection. Development of a capital campaign requires a detailed and thorough analysis of current fund-raising operations. The budget is based on planning assumptions developed over time as the campaign program process evolves.

The campaign budget should be developed as a supplement to the normal fund-raising budget. The costs and revenues should be kept separate to allow for historical and accurate comparisons. Few campaigns are conducted in isolation from normal fund-raising activities. The intensity and focus of a campaign effort normally increases all private support. The total fund-raising budget should include a presentation of information on the ongoing support activities and the campaign budget. This format gives staff and volunteers information on the total costs of all fund-raising activities. In addition to focusing on costs to conduct a campaign, the budget report should list the anticipated cash pledge activity and the long-term impact of expected estate and life income gifts.

If the director does not get adequate budget support, it is unlikely that the campaign will be successful. One of the first campaign budget decisions is the commitment of resources to conduct a feasibility study, which may include the cost of outside campaign counsel. Campaign costs may vary considerably according to the nature of the charity, the history of its fund raising, the campaign project, the campaign duration, and the nature of the planned activities. The campaign budget should be based on each particular charity's information only. Although other campaigns can serve as guidelines, their activities and associated costs are not benchmarks.

Developing a campaign budget is a staff function, which should not include intensive volunteer involvement. The campaign budget will be the sum of many parts, conducted at different times with varying intensity. It is important for a campaign to be cost efficient in its activities to raise significant sums. For example, spending $200,000 to raise $1,500,000 may be less efficient but more important than spending $100,000 to raise $1,000,000. The multiyear campaign budget should reflect the nature and scope of the planned new activities and the increasing intensity of the current fund-raising efforts.

The impact of the campaign activity may be illustrated by using a multiyear breakdown, as shown in Exhibit 4.22.

(F) ENDOWMENTS, INVESTMENT INCOME, AND SPENDING FORMULA

Endowments are funds permanently set aside by a not-for-profit organization to fulfill a designated purpose. A fund may be established by the action of the board of directors or by the wishes of a donor. Endowment funds are invested and generate income to support the charity's mission. Endowments establish quality and permanence for the charity. The income can be used to offset funding shortfalls caused by unforeseen economic events. Endowments can be board-designated funds set aside for future financial needs. Board-designated endowments are often called quasi-endowments. Because the board has made the designation, it also can undo the designation when the financial needs of a

EXHIBIT 4.22 Budget Worksheet for Multiyear Campaign Planning

	Year 1	Year 2	Year 3	Total
Expense/Budget				
Current/Ongoing Program				
Campaign Program				
Total				
Revenue/Budget				
Current Program Gifts				
Campaign Gifts				
Campaign Pledges				
Total				

new program or project require extraordinary funding. Endowment is an effective technique in permanently connecting the donor to the charity. Endowments benefit the charity because they provide a means for the donors to continually upgrade their gifts.

Endowments also protect an organization when there is a sudden or significant change in fund-raising performance. Board-designated unrestricted principal and/or income can be used to fill a gap in fund-raising revenue.

Endowments allow for the consistent funding of important programs by supplying baseline revenue support. All organizations should set aside cash reserves to protect against unexpected financial downturns. Many organizations have as a financial planning policy the immediate set-aside of unrestricted bequests and/or other significant estate or planned gift income. In larger organizations, bequest income may be somewhat predictable. Most smaller organizations would benefit from using bequest support to begin building an endowment. However, a charity should avoid using unanticipated bequest income to begin new programs that require annual operational income to sustain them.

The size of an organization's endowment is often cited as a reason not to support the charity. This is a convenient excuse, but it is not based on the reality of how a endowment helps in the financial planning of the organization. How large should an endowment become? A charity may appropriately strive for an endowment large enough that the income is equal to 25 percent, 50 percent, or 100 percent of annual fund-raising revenue. Another often used benchmark is an endowment equal to the current value of the physical plant facilities of the charity.

Endowments may be built by budgeting a planned surplus into fund-raising activities. The surplus, if realized, is transferred at the end of the budget period to a temporarily restricted endowment fund. It is temporarily restricted due to the action of the board since it can be reallocated at any time. Future endowments are built using current cash, planned gift techniques, and estate expectancies. Budget allocations to current planned gift activities reflect the commitment of the charity to acquiring future support. Once a planned gift donor is identified, it is important that the donor who will give a future gift remain connected to the charity's current programs through information and recognition of what the gift of his or her assets will accomplish in time.

It is the responsibility of the board's finance committee to set the investment objectives of the endowment funds. Most charities have adopted an investment approach that allows for the allocation of endowment assets to be invested in both domestic and international stocks and bonds. The board sets the asset allocation formula (e.g., 40 percent to 60 percent in stocks; 30 percent to 50 percent in bonds; and 10 percent to 20 percent international) and monitors the performance of the investment advisors. Once the investment formula is established, the board must determine how much of the endowment fund it will expend each year on current programs. The board should adopt a spending formula to determine the annual allocation to program support. Most spending formulas are a set percentage of the fair market value of the endowed fund. Therefore, the board may set a spending formula of 6 percent of all endowed funds. The percentage would be applied to the market value of the endowment at the end of one fiscal year, and the spending amount determined would be applied to support the budget in the following fiscal year. Because of the planning necessary to determine the spending formula amount for budget purposes, the finance director may suggest using a spending formula determination date prior to the end of the fiscal year when the final budget projections should be approved. Spending formulas allow the endowment to provide constant support over time as the principal of the endowed fund grows.

(G) COMPUTER SPREADSHEETS

Computer spreadsheets aid in the development of budget work papers, revenue and expense forecasts, and pro forma financial statements. Commercial computer programs, such as Quicken by Intuit, Excel by Microsoft, and 1-2-3 by Lotus, provide templates adaptable to the needs of the fund-raising department. When an organization's financial statements do not provide comparison statistics, or when the finance committee and board require more intensive reports, a computer-based reporting format is very helpful. With the use of a budget template, the categories can be changed to reflect organization-specific income and expense components. Computer spreadsheets also have a graphic capability to chart trends over time as well as yearly changes in revenue and expense categories. When a new event or project is started, the computer spreadsheet can be adapted to provide several planning scenarios and, once finalized, used to report budget performance to volunteers, staff, and board members. Computer spreadsheets are easy to individualize to budget requirements, and updating a program from the standard organization reports should provide more extensive and intensive information on the monthly budget's performance.

Suggested Readings

Ashton, Debra. *The Complete Guide to Planning Giving.* Cambridge, Mass.: JLA Publications, 1988.

Burns, Michael E. *Budgeting Guide for Nonprofit Administrators and Volunteers.* New Haven, Conn.: Development & Technical Assistance Center, Inc., 1995.

Costa, Nick B. "Measuring Progress and Success in Fund Raising: How to Use Comparative Statistics to Prove Your Effectiveness." Falls Church, Va.: Association for Healthcare Philanthropy, 1991.

Fink, Norman S., and Howard C. Meltzler. *The Cost and Benefits of Deferred Giving.* New York: Columbia University Press, 1982.

Greenfield, James M. *Fund-Raising Cost Effectiveness: A Self-Assessment Workbook.* New York: John Wiley & Sons, 1996.

Greenfield, James M., ed. *Financial Practices for Effective Fundraising.* San Francisco: Jossey-Bass, 1994.

Gross, Malvern J., Jr., Richard F. Larkin, Roger S. Bruttomesso, and John J. McNally, eds. *Financial and Accounting Guide for Not-for-Profit Organizations*, 5th ed. New York: John Wiley & Sons, 1995.

Kovener, Ronald R. *Accounting and Financial Reporting Issues Related to Fund Raising.* Falls Church, Va: Association for Healthcare Philanthropy and Healthcare Financial Management Association, 1993.

Rasmussen, Robert B. "The Campaign Budget." In *The Successful Capital Campaign*, edited by H. Gerald Quigg. Washington, D.C.: Council for Advancement and Support of Education, 1986.

Reynolds, Ruthie G. "Budgeting." In *Financial and Accounting Guide for Not-for-Profit Organizations*, 5th ed., edited by Malvern J. Gross Jr., Richard F. Larkin, Roger S. Bruttomesso, and John J. McNally. New York: John Wiley & Sons, 1995.

ROPES: A Model of the Fund-raising Process

KATHLEEN S. KELLY, PH.D., CFRE, APR,
FELLOW PRSA
University of Louisiana at Lafayette

Fund raising is much more than solicitation. Raising gifts involves a multistep process—one that must be systematically organized and managed. Although this concept is well understood by experienced practitioners, until recently the field lacked a theory that would explain the process to newcomers and others who are not knowledgeable about what fund raisers do (e.g., trustees, senior managers, and regulators). In addition, theory was missing that would establish standards of effective practice.

5.1 Overview of ROPES

ROPES is a new theory that meets those needs.[1] It breaks down the process of fund raising into five steps: (1) research, (2) objectives, (3) programming, (4) evaluation, and (5) stewardship. The theory is both descriptive and normative, meaning that it describes what fund raisers actually do and what they *should* do to make their work effective and efficient. Exhibit 5.1 presents the ROPES process model.

As shown in the exhibit, the fund-raising process begins with research in three consecutive areas: (1) the organization for which practitioners work; (2) the opportunity, or problem, faced by the organization; and (3) the donor publics related to both the organization and the opportunity. Failure to conduct research in all three areas dooms fund raising to sporadic results that contribute little to organizational effectiveness.

The second step in the process is setting objectives that are specific and measurable. They are of two types: (1) output objectives, which deal with the production of fund-raising *techniques*; and (2) impact objectives, which deal with the intended *effects* of programming. Regardless of type, fund-raising objectives flow from the charitable

---

[1]Kathleen S. Kelly, *Effective Fund-Raising Management* (Mahwah, N.J.: Lawrence Erlbaum Associates, 1998).

Exhibit 5.1 Fund-raising Process of ROPES

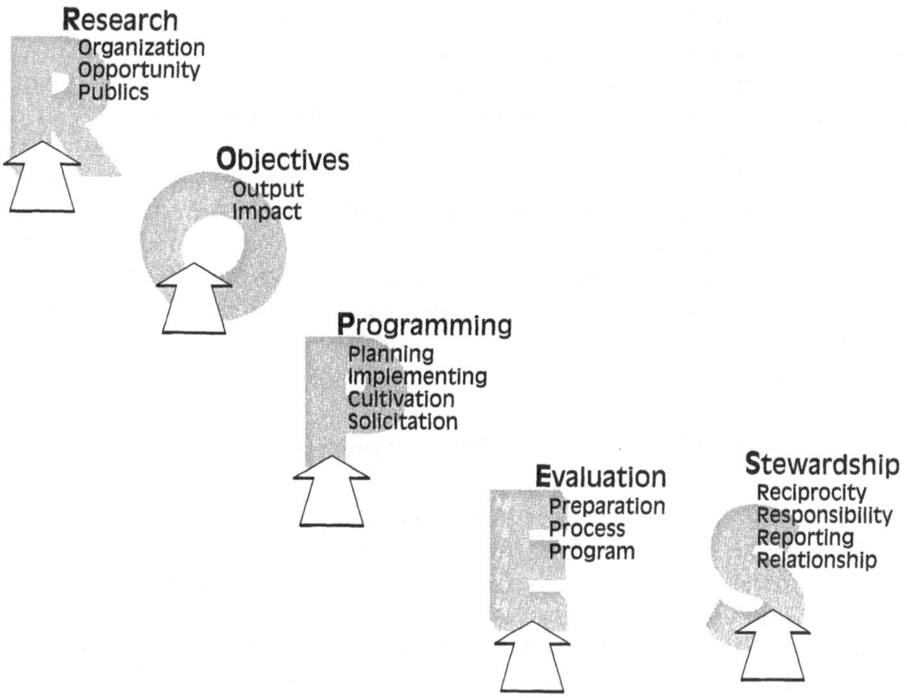

Research
Organization
Opportunity
Publics

Objectives
Output
Impact

Programming
Planning
Implementing
Cultivation
Solicitation

Evaluation
Preparation
Process
Program

Stewardship
Reciprocity
Responsibility
Reporting
Relationship

Source: Adapted from Kathleen S. Kelly, Effective Fund-Raising Management *(Mahwah, NJ: Lawrence Erlbaum Associates, 1998), p. 392.*

organization's goals; that is, their attainment directly supports organizational plans. And money is not always the main concern.

The third step, programming, consists of planning and implementing activities designed to bring about the outcomes stated in the objectives. These activities are grouped into two categories based on their desired results: (1) cultivation and (2) solicitation. Contrary to the belief of many people outside the profession, solicitation activities constitute a small portion of the fund-raising process and only part of the programming step. Efforts spent on research, cultivation, and stewardship distinguish legitimate practitioners from paid solicitors who unduly concentrate on asking for gifts.

The fourth step is evaluation, which is conducted on three progressive levels: (1) messages and techniques are tested (preparation evaluation); (2) programming is monitored and adjusted (process evaluation); and (3) results are measured and compared with the set objectives (program evaluation).

Finally, stewardship completes the process and provides an essential loop back to the beginning of fund raising. Four sequential elements are basic to stewardship: (1) reciprocity, (2) responsibility, (3) reporting, and (4) relationship nurturing.

ROPES applies to all of the traditional programs of fund raising: annual giving, major gifts, planned giving, and capital campaigns. Its application, however, focuses on the first two programs because planned giving and capital campaigns can be incorporated into the two primary programs as *strategies* for raising major gifts. Major gifts are defined as gifts of $10,000 or more and annual gifts are those of less than $10,000—typically about $25. Differences in gift size create significant differences in the number and types of donors associated with the two programs. These characteristics, in turn, affect how the steps in ROPES are carried out. Basically, the annual giving program targets a large number of donors, primarily individuals, whereas the major gifts program concentrates on a relatively small number of individuals, foundations, and corporations who are capable of giving $10,000 or more. By necessity, then, annual giving donors are treated as members of groups and receive less personal attention than donors of major gifts.

This chapter describes the five steps of ROPES, pointing out variations between the annual giving and major gifts programs.[2] It identifies theories from which the model draws and presents the wisdom of experienced practitioners to demonstrate the validity of the steps. Normative percentages of the amount of time fund raisers should spend on each step are given. The chapter concludes by reporting the results of a recent study that tested the ROPES process. The quantitative research showed that ROPES does explain what fund raisers do and that the average percentages of time practitioners spend on research, objectives, programming, evaluation, and stewardship closely resemble the theoretical norm.

5.2   Research: The First and Most Important Step

Without solid research, fund raising is little more than panhandling—hit-and-miss activities without direction and with little respect. Research provides knowledge, formulates strategy, inspires confidence, and ensures results. It is the essential ingredient that makes fund raising a management function as well as a managed function.

Methods of research range from the informal to the scientific, with qualitative methods situated in the middle. All are valuable to fund raising. Informal methods include

---

[2]For a more detailed description, see *ibid.*, pp. 391–443.

background reading, both to browse for general knowledge and to search for specific information, as well as talking, listening, and recording observations. Qualitative methods require scientific design and analysis. Of particular value to fund raisers are in-depth interviews and focus groups. Although results are not generalizable, findings do provide rich insight on the problem being studied. For example, focus groups are helpful for testing the case for support, rating prospects for major gifts, and getting reactions to a planned direct mail series. Consultants use in-depth interviews to conduct feasibility studies, which traditionally are undertaken before launching a capital campaign. Yet only quantitative research employing statistical procedures yields findings that are scientifically reliable. The three common quantitative methods are (1) surveys, (2) experiments, and (3) content analysis, with surveys used most frequently. Probability sampling and inferential statistics allow fund raisers to generalize their findings to the population studied and to make predictions.

(A) KNOWING THE ORGANIZATION

As stated earlier, research must address three consecutive areas, starting with the organization. It is crucial for practitioners to know their organization's history, finances, personnel, program services, and past fund-raising efforts. To be effective, fund raisers develop a solid working knowledge of operations and clients. They gain a clear understanding of how annual gifts serve organizational goals and learn all they can about projects requiring major gifts.

To do this, practitioners interview key managers and trustees. They also analyze budgets, audited financial statements, and IRS Form 990s. Focus groups are helpful for studying important stakeholders, such as clients of the organization and managers responsible for delivering program services. Fund raisers also are advised to do a monthly stint as a volunteer, sit in on program service sessions, and join employees outside their department for lunch. Attesting to the importance of research on the organization, practitioners Bruce Loessin and Margaret Duronio concluded from their study on characteristics of successful fund raising that "[t]he most important factor in making decisions about fund-raising programs may be insight into one's own institution."[3]

(B) UNDERSTANDING THE OPPORTUNITY

Strategic planning by the organization, which must be completed before the ROPES process begins, sets the direction of the fund-raising department and suggests the opportunities it will pursue. In this way, the purposes for which gifts are raised grow out of organizational planning and, therefore, support the organization's mission and goals. As the late consultant Thomas Broce asserted, "Without the link to institutional goals, fund-raising goals are meaningless."[4]

---

[3]Bruce A. Loessin and Margaret A. Duronio, "Characteristics of Successful Fund-Raising Programs," in *Educational Fund Raising: Principles and Practice,* edited by Michael J. Worth (Phoenix, Ariz.: Oryx Press, 1993), p. 48.
[4]Thomas E. Broce, *Fund Raising: The Guide to Raising Money from Private Sources,* 2d ed. (Norman, Okla.: University of Oklahoma Press, 1986), p. 186.

Effective practitioners find out as much as they can about their organization's planned initiatives and ask hard questions about need and cost. According to Broce, fund raisers should ask such probing questions as: Will we be duplicating the services of other organizations? How will the project be funded after gift support runs out? Broce proclaimed that it is "irresponsible" to tell fund raisers not worry about such details. He rightfully argued, "The program must be one that can be presented and defended as part of the institution's basic mission."[5]

Practitioners should study similar fund-raising efforts to learn from the triumphs and mistakes of other organizations. Most important, they need to conduct research to find out if prospective donors recognize and value the opportunities identified by the sponsoring organization. Such research is grounded in "coorientation theory," which emphasizes the importance of determining the degree of accuracy and agreement between a charitable organization's views of a fund-raising opportunity and the views of its donor publics before programming begins. If differences are found, the organization must correct misperceptions or change its intended behavior.

(C) LEARNING ABOUT DONOR PUBLICS

An inviolable principle of fund raising is that prospective donors must be matched to the organization and the opportunity—matching that can be accomplished only through research. Inquiry is guided by "the situational theory of publics" and its three predictor variables of problem recognition, involvement, and constraints, which are emulated in such applied formulas as L-A-I (linkage to the organization, ability to make a gift, and interest in the organization's mission and goals) that separate prospects from "suspects."

Fund raisers do not *make* people give. Rather, practitioners rely on research to identify those prospects who are likely to give because the gift is both possible and meaningful to them. Practitioners Victoria Steele and Stephen Elder define the *scientific* practice of fund raising as "a carefully orchestrated, purposive effort to raise substantial sums of money by identifying and cultivating potential donors and by soliciting gifts from them *when* their goals and wishes are congruent with the [organization's] goals and priorities."[6] Fund raiser Phyllis Allen elaborates: "Prospect research is the systematic acquisition and recording of data about donors and prospects that provide the basis to establish, maintain, and expand the 'exchange relationship.' "[7]

Fund raisers readily accept the need for research; however, they generally concentrate on only this last area of donor publics, and usually that research is limited to prospects for major gifts. As a rule, fund raisers never begin communication with a major donor prospect without first gathering information on the individual, foundation, or corporation. Practitioners obtain the necessary information from three sources: (1) public sources, (2) peers of the prospect, and (3) the prospect him- or herself.

---

[5]*Ibid.*, p. 31.

[6]Victoria Steele and Stephen D. Elder, *Becoming a Fundraiser: The Principles and Practice of Library Development* (Chicago: American Library Association, 1992), p. 3 (emphasis added).

[7]Phyllis A. Allen, "How to Research and Analyze Individual Donors." In *Achieving Excellence in Fund Raising: A Comprehensive Guide to Principles, Strategies, and Methods,* edited by Henry A. Rosso and associates (San Francisco: Jossey-Bass, 1991), p. 217.

The first source consists of reference materials, such as directories, and public records. The Internet has revolutionized document searches. (See Chapter 25.) Focus groups are useful for gathering information from peers. Referred to as *prospect rating* sessions, small groups of individuals are convened to assess prospects' financial capacity, interests in common with the organization and its work, linkage to the organization, readiness to give, and philanthropic nature. Regardless of these other sources, "the most valuable information is still what prospects relay in person."[8] Steele and Elder explain, "Through careful questioning, you can check on the validity of your assumptions about a person; elicit new information, uncover values, attitudes, and needs that are relevant to the potential gift; and locate the prospect's position in relation to the giving process."[9]

Large departments have at least one full-time staff person for researching just public sources. These researchers usually are trained in library science, not social science research. They rarely investigate annual giving donors.

Yet prospects for the annual giving program should not be ignored in the research step. Group analysis based on such demographics as giving history and gender accomplishes three purposes:

1. It segments previous donors for more effective and efficient communication.
2. It identifies prospects who share characteristics in common with donors.
3. It pinpoints annual giving donors who are capable of making a major gift.

Fund-raising departments must have a comprehensive computer system and staff with the necessary statistical skills to manage the annual giving program effectively.

Theory suggests that fund raisers should devote 20 percent of their time to the critical step of research. The remainder of their time should be spent as follows: 15 percent on objectives, 30 percent on programming, 15 percent on evaluation, and 20 percent on stewardship. This prescription is compatible with the few practitioner estimates found in the literature. Consultant Ernest Wood, for example, claims that when raising major gifts, fund raisers spend 25 percent of their time on research, 10 percent on stewardship, 60 percent on cultivation, and only 5 percent on solicitation.[10]

5.3 Setting Objectives

An old adage states, "If you don't know where you want to end up, then you need not fret about which direction you go!" Without objectives derived from organizational goals, "fund raising is destined to be more random than rational—an amateurish activity around which serendipitous events will occasionally occur, but by which they are rarely caused."[11] Objectives give focus and direction to program planning, provide guidance to those implementing activities and tasks, and spell out the criteria for monitoring progress and evaluating results.

---

[8]Jon Thorsen, "Spies Are (Not) Everywhere" CASE *Currents* (February 1993): 64.
[9]Steele and Elder, *Becoming a Fundraiser*, p. 67.
[10]Ernest W. Wood, "The Four R's of Major Gift Solicitation," Reid Report, 1989, pp. 1, 6.
[11]Joel P. Smith, "Rethinking the Traditional Capital Campaign," in *Handbook for Educational Fund Raising: A Guide to Successful Principles and Practices for Colleges, Universities, and Schools,* edited by Francis C. Pray (San Francisco: Jossey-Bass, 1981), p. 63.

(A) FORMULATING USEFUL OBJECTIVES

Unlike *goals,* which are general statements that express broad desired results, *objectives* are specific statements about measurable outcomes. Useful objectives consist of five parts, usually in the following order:

1. An infinitive verb
2. A single outcome stated as receiver of the verb's action
3. The magnitude of the action expressed in quantifiable terms
4. The targeted public
5. The target date or time frame for achieving the outcome

An example of a well-constructed objective for the major gifts program is as follows: To hold in-person meetings with 25 nondonors who are prospects for major gifts by December 31, 2002. An example for the annual giving program is: To increase the number of individuals who make an annual gift from 5,000 to 6,000 during the next fiscal year.

The reason for precise formulation is understandable given the key role objectives play in the fund-raising process. Yet practitioners often produce worthless objectives because they select verbs that also serve as outcomes. For example, verbs such as "to inform," "to educate," and "to persuade" describe what the staff intends to do *to* targeted publics. Rather than outcomes, publics are the receiver of the verbs' action; the only outcomes are those implied in the verbs. An example is as follows: To inform 80 percent of all previous donors about the tax benefits of charitable remainder trusts by the end of the fiscal year. Such objectives draw attention away from the results of programming and hamper meaningful evaluation. Illustrating the objective just given dictates that fund raising would be evaluated by the extent to which staff *informed* past donors (e.g., the number of messages sent), not by the percentage of donors who were aware of the tax benefits of charitable remainder trusts because of programming. The findings would be of little value for documenting the function's contribution to organizational goals.

(B) OUTPUT VS. IMPACT

The examples given in the previous section for the major gifts and annual giving programs illustrate the two types of objectives, output and impact. Output objectives deal with the production of fund-raising techniques, whereas impact objectives deal with the intended effects of programming on targeted publics. The major gifts objective (to hold in-person meetings with 25 nondonors) focuses on the technique of face-to-face conversations. A hierarchy of the techniques used by fund raisers is presented in Exhibit 5.2.

As shown in the exhibit, the major gifts program depends on interpersonal communication techniques, which are the most powerful. Annual giving, on the other hand, relies on techniques that utilize controlled media, such as direct mail, and the mass media (e.g., public service announcements on radio). These lower-level techniques are appropriate for communicating with large numbers of people; however, the probability of successful communication diminishes as fund raisers move from the top of the hierarchy to the bottom.

Output objectives are used most often for the purpose of cultivation. Whether holding meetings with major gift prospects or producing a newsletter for community resi-

Exhibit 5.2 Fund-raising Techniques by the Three Levels of Communication and Two Primary Programs

I. INTERPERSONAL COMMUNICATION

Major Gifts Program

- Face-to-Face Conversations
- Small-Group Meetings
- Speeches
- Telephone Conversations
- Personal Letters
- Personalized Proposals

II. CONTROLLED MEDIA COMMUNICATION

Annual Giving Program

- Direct Mail
- Special Events
- Publications (Newsletters, Brochures & Flyers)
- Internet (Web Sites & E-mail)
- Videos and Films
- Phonathons (Telephone Banks)
- Paid Advertisements, Billboards, Signage

III. MASS MEDIA (UNCONTROLLED) COMMUNICATION

Annual Giving Program

- Editorials and Op-Ed Pieces
- News Releases and Story Placements
- Public Service Announcements (PSAs)

NOTE:

Interpersonal:	*Direct communication between people*
Controlled Media:	*Mediated communication through channels controlled by the organization*
Mass Media:	*Mediated communication through uncontrolled channels (e.g., newspapers, television & radio)*

Source: Adapted from Kathleen S. Kelly, Effective Fund-Raising Management *(Mahwah, N.J.: Lawrence Erlbaum Associates, 1998), pp. 373–380.*

dents, fund raisers spend time and resources on activities from which they do not expect an immediate return. The investment is expected to yield future dividends as relationships with prospective donors are started and built. In such instances, output objectives address goals beyond those prompting the current cycle of fund raising. Stated another way, output objectives, strategically selected and based on research, are valuable for increasing the probability of future success; that is, they enhance the climate of giving. A well-known application of this concept is the "moves-management" strategy, whereby the major gifts program largely is directed—and evaluated—by cultivation initiatives.[12]

---

[12]David R. Dunlop, "Major Gift Programs," in *Educational Fund Raising,* Michael J. Worth (Phoenix, AZ: ACE/Oryx, 1993).

Output objectives also are used when one technique is deemed essential for the attainment of multiple impact objectives. For example, fund raisers may decide that hosting a special event such as an open house is an *activity* that is needed to accomplish all of the following: increase understanding of the organization's mission among annual giving prospects, generate major gifts for the new program service, and maintain positive attitudes among all previous donors. To avoid duplication and to streamline planning, the activity is formulated as a separate output objective: To hold a one-day open house for donors and prospects by June 31, 2002. Finally, administrative needs, or goals related to the infrastructure of fund raising, usually are addressed by output objectives. Outcomes often overlap program boundaries and range from converting to a new computer system to establishing a volunteer board.

Although valuable, output objectives are of lesser importance than impact objectives, which constitute the "meat" of the second step. Fund raising based only on output objectives lacks accountability. Impact objectives are needed to demonstrate how and how much the function contributes to achieving the organization's goals and advancing its mission. As a general rule, plans should include five impact objectives for every output objective.

Impact objectives spell out the intended effects of programming on targeted publics. Drawing from communication theory, effects are categorized by creation, change, or reinforcement of cognitions, attitudes, and behavior. Cognitions are broken down to concepts dealing with awareness, knowledge, and understanding—each a progressively higher order of thinking. The annual giving objective given earlier (to increase the number of individuals who make an annual gift) focused on changing behavior. Exhibit 5.3 presents a taxonomy of the effects that are addressed in fund-raising impact objectives.

The exhibit lists the effects of fund raising in hierarchical order, showing that the importance of the effects increases as they ascend from awareness to repeat behavior. Excluding repeat behavior, the hierarchy also portrays the increasing degree of difficulty in achieving ascending effects; that is, it is relatively easy to affect people's cognitions, but it is much more difficult to get them to adopt attitudes or behaviors. The six effects—combined with creation, change, and reinforcement—represent all possible impacts sought by fund raisers.

Exhibit 5.3 Hierarchy of Effects of Fund Raising

Repeat Behavior

Behavior

Agreement (Attitudes)

Understanding

Accuracy (Knowledge)

Awareness

Source: Adapted from Kathleen S. Kelly, Effective Fund-Raising Management *(Mahwah, N.J.: Lawrence Erlbaum Associates, 1998), pp. 369–373.*

Repeat behavior is the most important fund-raising effect because previous donors have a higher probability of making a gift than nondonors, regardless of all other factors. Consultant James Gregory Lord confirmed, "Experience shows that the best prospects for the immediate future are those who have given in the past."[13] Furthermore, repeat gifts cost significantly less to raise than new gifts. For example, gifts solicited through direct mail cost only $0.20 per $1.00 raised when they come from renewed donors, but they cost $1.00 to $1.25 per $1 raised when they come from new donors. (See chapter 6.) Third, theory predicts that changing behavior is more difficult than reinforcing behavior. Practitioners estimate that it takes five times as much work to acquire a new donor than it does to renew an existing one. As Lord warned, "It's very difficult to turn a non-giver into a giver."[14]

Based on practitioner observation, about 75 percent of an organization's annual giving donors renew their gifts the next year and almost all major gifts come from previous donors. Therefore, impact objectives dealing with repeat behavior are essential to both primary programs.

Once objectives have been formulated, they must be approved by senior managers and volunteer leaders. Approval ensures that the objectives support organizational goals and engenders the involvement of critical actors in subsequent steps of the process. Approval also provides consensus on the criteria by which the function and its practitioners will be evaluated.

5.4 Planning and Implementing Programming

In the programming step, objectives are dissected to determine what activities are needed to accomplish the stated outcomes. All objectives, except the simplest of output objectives, require multiple activities. Each activity is then broken down by the tasks involved in carrying out the activity. When the tasks are completed, the activity is completed. When all activities are done, the objective should be met. As the objectives were developed to support organizational goals, their attainment moves the organization closer to achieving its priorities. Success overall and for the function results from systematic execution.

The third step is divided into two parts: planning and implementing. The first part concentrates on producing a written fund-raising plan. A suggested format for the plan is to organize it by the annual giving and major gifts programs and then subdivide each section by the related objectives. (A third section can be added to address overlapping objectives, such as those dealing with administration.) Program sections present comprehensive budgets that incorporate both variable and fixed costs as well line items for contingency (10 percent), research (10 percent), and stewardship (3 percent). These main sections also give pertinent background information and message platforms that summarize the case for support. Subsections for each objective include the following:

- A synopsis of the research supporting and shaping the objective
- A detailed outline of the activities and tasks required to accomplish the objective (a decimal system developed by the author is helpful)[15]

[13]James G. Lord, *The Raising of Money: Thirty-Five Essentials Every Trustee Should Know* (Cleveland: Third Sector Press, 1983), p. 49.
[14]*Ibid.*, p. 85.
[15]Kelly, *Effective Fund-Raising Management*, pp. 417–418.

- Time lines and personnel assignments (e.g., Gantt charts)
- A description of how the objective will be evaluated
- Plans for stewardship
- A budget

Drafts of the plan are submitted to the managers and volunteers who approved the objectives earlier. Once the plan is approved, it becomes a blueprint for the fund-raising department's day-to-day work. An approved plan is the department's strongest deterrent to those who would make fund raising a solution to all the organization's financial problems. The plan shows that fund-raising efforts fit within a coherent system and are not subject to haphazard changes.

The second part of the programming step consists of implementing the activities and tasks outlined in the fund-raising plan. Expertise in the techniques listed in Exhibit 5.2 is necessary. Specifically, effective fund raising is dependent on practitioners who are highly skilled in oral and written communication. Those working in the major gifts program have mastered such techniques as conducting small-group meetings, giving speeches, and writing personal letters. Those working in annual giving are specialists in direct mail and special events—the techniques used most often to raise lower-level gifts—as well as in lesser-used techniques such as news releases. Increasingly, practitioners in both programs are utilizing the Internet to reach larger audiences and to personalize messages. The array of techniques, from interpersonal to mass media communication, form the backbone of activities implemented for cultivation and solicitation.

(A)   CULTIVATION

Much of programming is designed to meet objectives dealing with cultivation; for the major gifts program, it constitutes the majority. Although the mix is surprising to laypeople, experienced practitioners have long espoused the principle that cultivation takes precedence over solicitation. Consultant Fisher Howe, for example, instructed: "You cannot expect to receive donations from people until they know about your organization; you should not ask people for contributions until they are ready. Getting them ready is called cultivation."[16] Yet the emphasis on cultivation also reflects the growing belief among practitioners that fund raising is a function concerned with relationship management. Consultant Kay Sprinkle Grace summarized the new perspective: "Fund raising is about relationships more than it is about money."[17]

Empirical support for the viewpoint was provided by the Association of Fundraising Professionals' (AFP) 1999 membership survey, which showed that society members—19,000 at the time of the survey—spend the greatest percentage of their time on building relationships, followed by soliciting gifts.[18] Adding to those findings, the

---

[16]Fisher Howe, *The Board Member's Guide to Fund Raising: What Every Trustee Needs to Know About Raising Money* (San Francisco: Jossey-Bass, 1991), p. 83.

[17]Kay Sprinkel Grace, "Can We Throw Away the Tin Cup?" in *Taking Fund Raising Seriously: Advancing the Profession and Practice of Raising Money,* edited by Dwight F. Burlingame and Lamont J. Hulse (San Francisco: Jossey-Bass, 1991), p. 185.

[18]Association of Fundraising Professionals (AFP), *1999 Profile of AFP Members* (Alexandria, Va.: Author, 1999), p. 8.

research study testing ROPES, which is discussed as the end of the chapter, measured practitioners' beliefs on a set of key fund-raising issues. Using a five-point Likert-like scale on which 5 equaled strongly agree and 1 equaled strongly disagree, respondents overwhelmingly agreed that effective fund raisers spend more time building relationships than they do soliciting gifts ($M = 4.58$, $SD = .68$). The new perspective, it is important to note, is grounded in the unified theory encompassing ROPES, which defines fund raising as "the management of relationships between a charitable organization and its donor publics."[19]

Cultivation activities fall under the two categories of information and involvement. Information includes activities utilizing any of the techniques listed in Exhibit 5.2, although publications such as newsletters are the most prominent. Involvement, on the other hand, is limited to activities that employ techniques based on two-way communication, such as special events and interpersonal techniques. A combination of both types of activities provides the strongest means of cultivation; however, because of cost factors, involvement activities generally are reserved for the major gifts program. For example, prospects for major gifts are invited to dinners, asked to participate on committees, and recruited to serve on advisory boards. To the degree that it is cost efficient, similar attention (e.g., activities designed to encourage volunteering) should be given to annual giving prospects. As Lord argued, "If we want people to invest their time and resources in a program, we have to give them authentic involvement in the cause."[20]

(B)   SOLICITATION

Solicitation is the easiest part of fund raising. Howe elaborated: "It is proverbial that the success of fund raising is 90% in prospect identification, research, cultivation, and preparation, and 10% in the asking."[21] Fund raisers do not solicit gifts unless they have good reason to expect that the prospect will say yes. As explained earlier, practitioners spend much of their efforts on seeking a *goodness of fit* among their organization, the funding opportunity, and donor publics. And as Steele and Elder stated, "If the fit is right, the decision to give will follow naturally."[22]

Yet asking for gifts is a fundamental part of fund raising; that is, people do not give unless asked. Smith summarized practitioner wisdom on implementation: "The two most frequent errors are to ask too hastily and to fail to ask at all."[23]

When people outside the profession think about asking for money, they immediately conjure up images of face-to-face conversations with strangers. No wonder, then, that solicitation is viewed as uncomfortable and unpleasant. Fund raisers, however, do not solicit strangers. Furthermore, face-to-face conversations constitute only one technique employed to solicit gifts. Most annual gifts are solicited by direct mail. Major gifts from corporations and foundations usually are solicited by personal letters or personalized proposals. Solicitations of major gifts from individuals do include face-to-face conversations, but the conversations do not take place in isolation. If communication has been

---

[19]Kelly, *Effective Fund-Raising Management*, p. 8.
[20]Lord, *The Raising of Money*, p. 29.
[21]Howe, *The Board Member's Guide to Fund Raising*, p. 81.
[22]Steele and Elder, *Becoming a Fundraiser*, p. 67.
[23]Smith, "Rethinking the Traditional Capital Campaign," p. 63.

clear, the prospect signals his or her willingness to be solicited when granting an appointment for the meeting. As Michael Adams, a former fund raiser who now is president of the University of Georgia, stated, "It is often more difficult to get an appointment with a prospect than to get the money."[24]

Misunderstanding regarding the role of fund raisers contributes to flawed perceptions about solicitation. Practitioners solicit gifts on behalf of an organization; they are not asking for themselves. Therefore, rejection rarely is personal, but more likely a reflection on the organization, the opportunity, or the timing of the ask. Fund raisers have no need to apologize for requesting gifts from well-researched prospects.

Participation of the organization's chief executive officer (CEO), other senior managers, and trustees is essential to successful cultivation and solicitation. By virtue of their positions, these people speak for the organization. Their contacts, influence, and credibility have a significant impact on the amount of money raised. More important, if those who are in charge of the organization do not participate in programming, their understanding of fund raising's contribution will be distorted. Widespread misperceptions already hamper meaningful evaluation.

5.5   *Evaluating Results*

Far too often, fund raising is evaluated by the amount of dollars received in a given year. In other words, the function is considered effective when it generates the most money possible. This approach positions fund raising as a profit center more appropriate to a commercial enterprise, thereby ignoring the fundamental difference between for-profit and nonprofit organizations. Whereas businesses are successful when they earn profits for owners, nonprofits are successful when the goals they developed through strategic planning are met. As explained in a leading accounting manual, "To determine a nonprofit's success you must refer to its goals: these are the group's self-determined replacement for the bottom line of profit-making."[25] Fund raising is effective, therefore, not when it raises indiscriminate dollars, but when it helps charitable organizations achieve their goals.

The dollar approach is further flawed in three critical ways:

1. It ignores "gift utility," or the degree to which restricted gifts match organizational priorities.
2. It does not account for "delay factors" in raising major gifts.
3. It measures only impact objectives dealing with giving behavior.

(A)   FLAWS IN DOLLAR TOTALS

The concept of gift utility was introduced in the early 1980s by practitioner Joel Smith, who challenged the idea that a gift's dollar amount was more important than its pur-

---

[24]Michael F. Adams, "How to Solicit a Major Gift," in *Educational Fund Raising,* Michael J. Worth (Phoenix, AZ: ACE/Oryx, 1993), p. 136.
[25]Accountants for the Public Interest, *What a Difference Nonprofits Make: A Guide to Accounting Procedures* (Washington, D.C.: Author, 1990), p. 14.

pose.[26] Smith argued that a $1 million gift restricted for a purpose not related to the organization's goals (e.g., an unneeded chapel for a college) contributes less to the organization's well-being than a $10,000 gift made in support of the goals. He urged fund raisers to discourage the notion that the success of their programs ought to be judged by the bottom line. The fascination with large numbers, he said, "is shortsighted and superficial; it ignores the entire subject of utility."[27]

Practitioners have long acknowledged the delay factors inherent in raising major gifts; that is, gifts of $10,000 or more are made only after years of cultivation. Steele and Elder provide the following rule of thumb: "The typical major gift requires thirteen contacts over the space of two to three years."[28] In addition, major gifts often are pledged at the time of solicitation and then paid in multiyear installments, which further delays receipt. An analysis of one university's records showed that outright major gifts have delays of four to five years from solicitation to the final payment on the pledge.[29] Planned major gifts involve longer delays, with estimates ranging from 15 to 25 years.

As major gifts typically account for the majority of dollars raised, these delay factors significantly affect yearly gift totals. In other words, dollars received in a given year are a poor basis for evaluating fund-raising performance during that year. The researcher who conducted the university analysis recommended that organizations change their reporting procedures to reflect the fund-raising process and evaluate practitioners "on how well and how often they relate to the prospects."[30]

Finally, dollars received measure the outcomes of only impact objectives dealing with giving behavior. Yet, as discussed earlier, a substantial portion of fund-raising programming—for both annual giving and major gifts—is devoted to activities aimed at outcomes other than giving (i.e., cultivation activities). Furthermore, if, as practitioners claim, fund raising is a function concerned with managing relationships more so than with soliciting gifts, then the quality and quantity of relationships are more accurate measurements of performance than dollar amounts. When asked about the evaluation issue, participants in the ROPES study firmly agreed that fund raising should *not* be evaluated solely by the amount of dollars raised each year ($M = 4.13$, SD $= .92$).

(B)   MEASUREMENT BY OBJECTIVES

The ROPES process offers an approach to evaluating fund raising that is superior to counting dollar totals. Because the model's approach bases evaluation on all set objectives—those that deal with cultivation as well as those that deal with solicitation—it incorporates measurements of both dollars raised and relationships built. Because the objectives were developed to support organizational goals, resulting gifts have high utility. Because annual totals are not used to gauge performance, problems with delay factors are overcome. Most important, evaluation as prescribed by ROPES determines the effectiveness of fund raising in a manner appropriate for the nonprofit status of charita-

---

[26]Smith, "Rethinking the Traditional Capital Campaign."
[27]*Ibid.*, p. 64.
[28]Steele and Elder, *Becoming a Fundraiser*, p. 25.
[29]Wesley E. Lindahl, *Strategic Planning for Fund Raising: How to Bring in More Money Using Strategic Resource Allocation* (San Francisco: Jossey-Bass, 1992).
[30]*Ibid.*, p. 119.

ble organizations. The discussion turns now to a description of the fourth step of the ROPES process, which includes three levels of evaluation.

The first two levels of evaluation take place during the programming step. Fund raisers conduct preparation evaluation as part of planning—testing messages and techniques for their appropriateness. For example, readability tests determine whether proposed copy for publications is written in a style suitable to the educational level of targeted publics. (Most word-processing software contains such tests under Options in the grammar tool.) Focus groups provide insight on how special events should be organized.

During implementation, fund raisers conduct process evaluation to monitor progress and to make adjustments when necessary. Waiting until programming is over to evaluate results is risky. Practitioners may find that part of their planning was flawed and that changes in activities could have improved results. As the environment is constantly changing, conditions affecting fund-raising efforts also change. Established procedures for systematically assessing progress protect against failure. Using the objective for the annual giving program given earlier (to increase the number of individuals who make an annual gift from 5,000 to 6,000 during the next fiscal year), fund raisers should conduct quarterly comparisons of the number of current individual donors and the number at the same time the year before. If current numbers are not 20 percent greater than the previous year's, additional activities should be implemented (e.g., an extra phonathon).

Once programming is completed, program evaluation takes place, whereby fund raisers evaluate their efforts by comparing the results attained with the results sought, as expressed by the set objectives. Programming for output objectives usually can be evaluated by counts obtained from in-house records (e.g., call reports document the number of meetings held with prospects for major gifts). Programming for impact objectives dealing with giving behavior also is evaluated by in-house records. Evaluation of programming for other impact objectives, however, often requires surveys or other research methods.

Findings of program evaluation substantiate the contribution of fund raising to organizational success and are used to improve future efforts. A written report of the findings, backed up with numbers, should be widely circulated within the organization and among key constituencies. The report should also include measures of efficiency, such as fund-raising cost ratios for both primary programs and for the function overall. (See chapter 6.)

5.6 Stewardship: The Foundation for Future Success

As explained earlier, a fundamental fact of fund raising is that most annual gifts and almost all major gifts come from individuals, corporations, and foundations that have given to the organization in the past. Therefore, how donors are treated *after* they make their gifts largely determines future success. It also costs significantly less to raise gifts from past donors than from new donors. And it is easier. Michael Worth, vice president at George Washington University, summarized practitioner wisdom as follows: "Because the best prospects for new gifts are past donors, programs that provide careful stewardship and provide donors with timely information on the impact of their gifts can pay significant dividends in continued support."[31]

---

[31]Worth, *Educational Fund Raising*, p. 13.

Stewardship is the second most important step in the fund-raising process, after research. It consists of four elements requiring practitioners' attention:

1. *Reciprocity,* by which the organization demonstrates its gratitude
2. *Responsibility,* meaning the organization acts in a socially responsible manner to those who have supported it, including in the way it uses gifts
3. *Reporting,* a basic requirement of accountability
4. *Relationship nurturing*

Embedded in the elements are ethical standards that hold moral duty above other considerations. In other words, stewardship not only ensures continuity in fund raising, it also promotes ethical behavior by practitioners and their organizations.

(A) RECIPROCITY

The "norm of reciprocity" is a universal component of all moral codes. Studies by anthropologists have shown that it is cross-cultural and fundamental to all people: Human interaction requires stable practices of give and take. Specific to this discussion, "Gifts create an obligation for the recipient to repay the giver, and an expectation of reciprocity on the part of the giver."[32] Repaying helps maintain social balance, engenders mutual respect, and encourages further helping. In short, when donors make gifts, the organization receiving the gift must reciprocate.

At the applied level, reciprocity simply means that organizational recipients show gratitude for gifts. Gratitude is broken down by acts of appreciation and recognition appropriate to the size of the gift. The most common and expected way of demonstrating appreciation is to say "thank you." The message must be sincere and timely, usually sent within 24 hours after a gift is received.

"Recognition," according to J. Patrick Ryan, CEO and president of Staley/Robeson/Ryan/St. Lawrence, "displays your institution's style and gratitude. It shows good stewardship. It says you're thoughtful, attentive, and caring."[33] An effective and simple form of recognition is to personalize all future communications to donors, thereby recognizing their special status to the organization.

As gift size increases, acts of appreciation and recognition become more elaborate. Forms of recognition for donors of major gifts, for example, range from plaques to named gift opportunities. Formal written policies, approved by the board of trustees, are strongly recommended.

(B) RESPONSIBILITY

Charitable organizations must act in a socially responsible manner to donors as well as to other publics. The concept of social responsibility simply means that organizations act

---

[32]Barbara J. Lombardo, "Corporate Philanthropy: Gift or Business Transaction?" *Nonprofit Management & Leadership,* 5, no. 3 (1995): 297.

[33]J. Patrick Ryan, "Thanks a Million: You Need Strong Recognition Programs to Foster Healthy Donor Relations," CASE *Currents* (March 1994): 64.

as good citizens. The concept is rooted in "systems theory" in that organizations are interdependent with people and other organizations in their environment.

At its most basic level, responsibility requires charitable organizations to keep their word. Promises made when seeking support must be kept. Of particular importance to fund raising is responsible gift use, meaning gifts are used for the purposes for which donors gave them. If annual unrestricted gifts were solicited to enhance program services, they should not be used to pay for fund-raising salaries or for entertainment, for example. Restrictions placed on major gifts should not be "bent" to pay for unrelated expenses. Neither should gifts made for endowments be hoarded. When facilities are named in perpetuity for a donor, the gift should not conveniently be forgotten when the building deteriorates and new prospects appear. Good stewardship cannot be achieved when donors are misled about how their gifts are used.

More generally, charitable organizations must demonstrate through all their actions that they are worthy of support. Fund raisers counsel senior manager and trustees that promises and expectations must be fulfilled if the organization is to succeed. Betraying public trust is expensive; building goodwill with people who already are "friends" of the organization saves money.

(C)   REPORTING

Accountability demands that charitable organizations keep donors informed about developments related to the opportunity for which their support was sought and how their gifts helped. Accountability, as defined by scholars, is the degree to which organizations continually reinforce public confidence in the integrity and effectiveness of their performance. Organizations are accountable to specific publics as well as to society in general.

On a general level, accountability is closely related to the concept of social responsibility. All organizations—for-profit companies, government agencies, and nonprofits—have an obligation to serve societal needs because society grants them the opportunities to operate. Charitable organizations carry a special burden because of the privileged tax-exempt status granted to them by society through its representative government.

On the specific level, organizations are answerable to key stakeholder groups that may help or hinder the organization in fulfilling its mission. Donors are of particular importance to charitable organizations because they enable the organization to carry out its work—now and in the future. Reporting reinforces positive attitudes and increases the probability that donors will give again. Rather than receiving mere recognition publications, which list names and levels of gifts, donors should be sent annual reports with complete financial data and explicit information on how gifts helped the organization meet its goals. Reporting standards issued by accounting and fund-raising associations (e.g., the Council for Advancement and Support of Education) should be followed.

(D)   RELATIONSHIP NURTURING

Stewarding donors goes beyond reciprocity, responsibility, and reporting; relationships so critical to the organization's success must be nurtured. An important rule to remember is that relationships cannot be maintained if the organization communicates with friends only when it seeks more help. Grace said that whereas "traditional notions of stewardship refer to the gift and ensuring that it is spent wisely and in accordance with the donor's wishes," contemporary fund raisers have adopted "an expanded sense of stewardship, one that includes continued relationship building with the donor."[34] "This new view of stewardship," she explained, "lets people know on a regular basis that you care about them, respect their support, appreciate their gifts, and want their interest and involvement."

The most effective means of nurturing relationships is quite simple: Accept the importance of previous donors and keep them at the forefront of the organization's consciousness. Information and involvement activities are fundamental, and both types should flow naturally from the organization's work. For example, donors should receive copies of the organization's publications as well as news releases sent to the media. They should be among the groups represented when advisory boards are formed. Opportunities to nurture relationships are numerous and occur on a weekly basis.

Lord summarized the thrust of this discussion: "Good stewardship is well worth the extra effort it requires. It is the bedrock on which the future of an organization is built."[35]

5.7 Testing the ROPES Process Model[36]

A national survey was conducted in spring 2000 to test the ROPES model as well as to examine other concepts important to fund raising. Results of the quantitative research showed that ROPES is a valid description of the fund-raising process; that is, it depicts the "real-world" behavior of fund raisers as they go about their work. Practitioners spend time on each of the five steps, although the amount of time allotted to each step differs among organizations.

(A) POPULATION AND METHODOLOGY

Participants for the study were drawn from the membership of AFP. Because the study, in addition to testing ROPES, dealt with issues related to earning a terminal research degree, the selected population was U.S. members of AFP who hold a Ph.D. degree. Although not representative of all fund raisers, or even AFP members, this highly educated group was deemed appropriate to studying the fund-raising process because group members likely held senior positions in their organizations.

As of March 1, 2000, AFP's on-line membership directory included 225 members who listed the credential of Ph.D. after their name. Ten of the 225 were deleted from the preliminary population because their listing showed they resided outside the United States (five), held a professorial rank as their title (three), or were corporate contributions officers for well-known companies (two). The size of the qualified population, then, was 215.

A three-page questionnaire was developed by the author, which included five items that measured the percentage of time an organization's fund-raising staff spends on each of the steps of ROPES as well as demographic variables that might be related to time allotment. The latter ranged from gender of the respondent to the mission of his or her organization.

---

[34]Kay Sprinkle Grace, "Managing for Results," in *Achieving Excellence in Fund Raising,* ed. Rosso and associates, p. 158.
[35]Lord, *The Raising of Money,* p. 93.
[36]This section draws from the author's paper, "A National Study Testing the 'ROPES' Process Model of Fund Raising," presented at the Association for Research on Nonprofit Organizations and Voluntary Action (ARNOVA), twenty-ninth annual conference, New Orleans, LA, November 2000.

Students enrolled in the author's fund-raising and research methods classes administered the questionnaire by telephone. Members of the population first were sent a standardized e-mail or fax message alerting them to the study and explaining why they were selected. Follow-up telephone calls, capped at three, were made to schedule a convenient time for conducting the survey.

(B) RESULTS

Of the 215 qualified Ph.D. members, 9 reported that they were not members of the study's population (e.g., they have not practiced fund raising for a long time), 15 no longer worked at the listed organization, and 8 could not be located because of wrong telephone numbers. These problems further reduced the population to 183. Of those remaining, 74 could not be reached, 8 declined to participate, and 101 completed the questionnaire. Thus, the study's response rate was 55 percent (101 ÷ 183), which provides confidence in generalizing its findings to the entire population of U.S. practitioners who belong to AFP and hold a Ph.D.

Analysis of demographics yielded the following profile of respondents. Sixty-four percent are men and 36 percent are women. The median number of years they have worked in fund raising—meaning that half worked more years and half worked less—is 19. As hypothesized, most hold senior positions in their organizations: 44 percent are the head of fund raising, 24 percent are the CEO, 21 percent are consultants, 9 percent are staff fund raisers, and 3 percent classified themselves as "Other." On average, they spend the majority of their time, 61 percent, on fund raising, which supports their use for this study. The organizations for which they work employ a median of three full-time fund raisers and raised a median of $2.3 million in the fiscal year before the survey.[37] All major categories of organizational mission are represented, although the greatest percentage of respondents, 40 percent, work for educational institutions.

A comparison of these demographics with findings from AFP's latest membership survey showed that, as a group, respondents differ in some ways from the general membership but also share similarities.[38] For example, the gender breakdown of approximately two-thirds men and one-third women is exactly the opposite of AFP membership, which consists of 62 percent women and 39 percent men. The difference likely is due to traditional gender patterns in graduate education; that is, more men than women pursue a Ph.D. degree. Respondents to this study included proportionally more CEOs and consultants than are represented in AFP. Only 9 percent of all AFP members are CEOs and just 7 percent work as consultants, as compared to 24 percent and 21 percent, respectively, for this study. Conversely, only 9 percent of Ph.D. holders are staff fund raisers, whereas staff fund raisers constitute 28 percent of AFP's membership. These findings suggest that earning a Ph.D. pays off in higher-level positions.

Despite such differences, there are enough similarities between this study's respondents and the general membership of AFP to assume that the ROPES model applies to

[37]Readers may be interested to know that the number of fund raisers employed was significantly and positively related to the amount of money raised ($r = .37, p < .00$), which empirically supports practitioners' long-standing argument that organizations employing more fund raisers generate more dollars in private gifts.

[38]AFP, *1999 Profile of AFP Members.*

the process of raising gifts by all fund raisers and their organizations. For example, small charitable organizations, as measured by the amount of money raised, are similarly represented in this study and AFP's membership: 23 percent and 29 percent, respectively, raised less than $500,000 in the year preceding the surveys.[39] Organizational missions also are represented somewhat equally in that the majority of fund raisers in this study and AFP (62 percent and 66 percent, respectively) are employed by organizations with missions in education, human services, and health.

Turning to the major findings of the research, respondents were asked to give the percentage of time they or others on the fund-raising staff spend on each of the five steps of ROPES. They were instructed to answer so that their responses totaled 100 percent. Exhibit 5.4 presents the means of the percentages reported, the standard deviations from the means, and the normative percentages given earlier.

As the figures in the exhibit demonstrate, Ph.D. holders and the staff members with whom they work follow the ROPES process quite closely. On average, they spend 14 percent of their time on research, another 14 percent on setting objectives, 39 percent on planning and implementing programming, 11 percent on evaluation, and 21 percent on stewardship. These mean scores provide strong empirical evidence that fund raising is a systematic process that involves much more than soliciting gifts.[40] Indeed, these statistics show that fund raisers in this study spend the majority of their time, 61 percent, on activities outside the programming step, such as conducting research.

Yet a comparison of the means with the theoretical norms shows that the match between practice and theory is not perfect. Most important, Ph.D. holders and their staffs, on average, spend substantially more time on programming than recommended (39 percent vs. 30 percent) and spend less than the recommended amount of time on research (14 percent vs. 20 percent) and evaluation (11 percent vs. 15 percent).

Correlation analysis was conducted to examine the relationships between the five steps and the percentages of time spent on each. Analysis showed that time spent on the programming step has negative relationships with time spent on all other four steps—research ($r = -.34$), objectives ($r = -.43$), evaluation ($r = -.51$), and stewardship ($r = -.44$).

---

[39] Ibid.

[40] Unfortunately, the survey instrument did not break down the programming step by cultivation and solicitation. However, as reported earlier, respondents adamantly and uniformly agreed that effective fund raisers spend more time building relationships than they do soliciting gifts.

Exhibit 5.4 Percentages of Time Spent on Steps in the Fund-Raising Process of ROPES

Step	Mean	Standard Deviation	Theoretical Norm
Research	14.5%	9.2	20%
Objectives	13.8%	7.6	15%
Programming	39.3%	16.2	30%
Evaluation	11.5%	7.0	15%
Stewardship	20.9%	13.8	20%
	100.0%		100%

N = 100

The four relationships are significant at the .01 level of probability, meaning that repeated studies would find the same relationships 99 times out of 100.

The strongest relationship is between programming and evaluation, which indicates that those fund-raising staffs who spend the most time on programming also spend the least time evaluating the results of their efforts. Furthermore, as time spent on evaluation decreases, the belief that fund raising should not be evaluated solely by dollar totals increases ($r = -.24$, $p < .01$). In other words, practitioners who spend little time on the evaluation step hold the strongest attitudes about evaluating fund raising by more than just the amount of money raised each year.

These findings suggest that fund-raising effectiveness would increase if more practitioners were trained in how to set meaningful objectives and to evaluate programming results. Overall, practitioners, their organizations, and their donors would benefit from closer adherence to the prescribed norms of ROPES.

Suggested Readings

Broce, Thomas E. *Fund Raising: The Guide to Raising Money from Private Sources*, 2d ed. Norman, Okla.: University of Oklahoma Press, 1986.

Burlingame, Dwight F., and Lamont J. Hulse, eds. *Taking Fund Raising Seriously: Advancing the Profession and Practice of Raising Money*. San Francisco: Jossey-Bass, 1991.

Cutlip, Scott M. *Fund Raising in the United States: Its Role in America's Philanthropy*. New Brunswick, N.J.: Transaction Publishers, 1990. (Original work published 1965.)

Fischer, Marilyn. *Ethical Decision Making in Fund Raising*. New York: John Wiley & Sons, 2000.

Greenfield, James M. *Fund Raising: Evaluating and Managing the Fund Development Process*, 2d ed. New York: John Wiley & Sons, 1999.

Duronio, Margaret A., and Eugene R. Tempel. *Fund Raisers: Their Careers, Stories, Concerns, and Accomplishments*. San Francisco: Jossey-Bass, 1996.

Kelly, Kathleen S. *Effective Fund-Raising Management*. Mahwah, N.J.: Lawrence Erlbaum Associates, 1998.

———. *Fund Raising and Public Relations: A Critical Analysis*. Hillsdale, N.J.: Lawrence Erlbaum Associates, 1991.

———. "The Fund-Raising Behavior of U.S. Charitable Organizations: An Explanatory Study," *Journal of Public Relations Research*, 7, no. 2 (1995): 111–137.

———. Utilizing Public Relations Theory to Conceptualize and Test Models of Fund Raising. *Journalism & Mass Communication Quarterly*, 72, no. 1 (1995): 106–127.

Lord, James G. *The Raising of Money: Thirty-Five Essentials Every Trustee Should Know*. Cleveland: Third Sector Press, 1983.

Rosso, Henry A., and associates. *Achieving Excellence in Fund Raising: A Comprehensive Guide to Principles, Strategies, and Methods*. San Francisco: Jossey-Bass, 1991.

Steele, Victoria, and Stephen D. Elder. *Becoming a Fundraiser: The Principles and Practice of Library Development*. Chicago: American Library Association, 1992.

Worth, Michael J., ed. *Educational Fund Raising: Principles and Practice*. Phoenix, Ariz.: Oryx Press, 1993.

6 Fund-raising Assessment

JAMES M. GREENFIELD, ACFRE, FAHP
Hoag Memorial Hospital Presbyterian

JOHN P. DREVES, MPA
Staley/Robeson/Ryan/St. Lawrence, Inc.

6.1 Environmental Audit on Fund Raising
- (a) Type of Institution or Agency
- (b) Written Long-range and Strategic Plan
- (c) Board Leadership, Background, and Attitude
- (d) Geography
- (e) Style
- (f) Competition, Image, and Market Position
- (g) Tradition of Fund-raising Practice
- (h) Volume and Variety of Fund-raising Methods
- (i) Availability of Prospects
- (j) Existing Donors for Renewal and Upgrading
- (k) Experienced and Dedicated Volunteers
- (l) Access to Wealth
- (m) Focus on Major Gifts
- (n) Professional Staff and Fund-raising Counsel
- (o) Development Staff, Space, Budget, and Systems
- (p) Donor Recognition

6.2 Development Department and Program Audit
- (a) Comparison with Prior-Year Results
- (b) Growth in Donor Universe
- (c) Penetration of New Markets
- (d) Quality of Effort
- (e) Leadership Development
- (f) Consistent Messages and Personalization
- (g) Regular Reports and Analysis of Results
- (h) Staff Training and Development
- (i) Matching Institutional Needs
- (j) Forecasting Future Income

6.3 Development Planning (Feasibility) Study

6.4 Fund-raising Productivity Analysis
- (a) Gift Reports
- (b) Volunteer Performance
- (c) Indirect and Overhead Expenses
- (d) Cost-Effectiveness Measurement
- (e) Reasonable Cost Guidelines

Suggested Readings

The assessment of not-for-profit organizations remains underdeveloped, and evaluations have not been performed often. But times are changing. Whether because of the growth of the independent sector and the sheer magnitude of its presence, or unwanted focus as a result of public scandals and abuses, or financial pressures caused by negative economic conditions, attention to performance by not-for-profit organizations increased substantially during the 1980s and the 1990s.

Nonprofit organizations have entered the new century with more attention from the public and more internal resolve to evaluate their own performance. "Many opinions and assertions are put forth about the effectiveness and desirability of nonprofits, but evidence is scarce. Especially limited is information about whether nonprofits are better or worse at achieving certain goals than for-profit firms or government enterprises would be."[1]

Areas for assessment are broad; they include institutional mission, community benefit, governance, management, fiscal accountability, strategic planning, resource allocations, and success in fund raising.

Because fund raising is only one measurable entity of a not-for-profit organization's performance and because fund-raising results are inextricably tied to several other areas of internal operation, this chapter and the following one will explore ten separate assessment areas:

Chapter 6:

1. Environmental audit on fund raising
2. Development department and program audit
3. Development planning (feasibility) study
4. Fund-raising productivity analysis

Chapter 7:

5. Mission Statement: Review and measurements
6. Environmental audit for operations
7. Assessment criteria for management
8. Outcomes measurement for programs and services
9. Demonstrating community benefits
10. Conclusion: Public perceptions of accountability

The first four areas, beginning with an environmental audit on fund-raising readiness, relate directly to the fund-raising function. The six areas in Chapter 7 focus on the not-for-profit organization's self-evaluation of fulfillment of mission, annual operations, management, outcomes measurement, and community benefits assessments, all of which affect the success of fund-raising activities. Each of these assessment areas is framed against an audit of external environmental features to help appreciate the degree to which changing external forces limit as well as assist in the overall success of each organization. Together these 10 assessment areas demonstrate how institutional awareness and operating performance measured against defined community needs combine to affect public support so necessary to meet annual and multi-year institutional goals and objectives.

---

[1]Burton A. Weisbrod, *The Nonprofit Economy* (Cambridge, Mass.: Harvard University Press, 1988), p. 2.

6.1 Environmental Audit on Fund Raising

There is a growing conviction that not-for-profit organizations need to demonstrate efficiency in fund-raising performance. Productivity analysis will do much more than justify the cost of raising money: It will develop an appreciation of the potential of fund development programs as highly cost-effective profit centers. Each not-for-profit organization has the potential to achieve some amount of public support and to grow up to its capacity for this support. However, only a few organizations know their potential, much less their capacity, because they use fund raising only as a means to realizing a targeted amount of money.

> But a non-profit institution that becomes a prisoner of money-raising is in serious trouble and in a serious identity crisis. The purpose of a strategy for raising money is precisely to enable the nonprofit institution to carry out its mission without subordinating that mission to fund-raising. This is why nonprofit people have now changed the term they use from "fund-raising" to "fund development." Fund-raising is going around with a begging bowl, asking for money because the need is so great. Fund development is creating a constituency which supports the organization because it deserves it.[2]

An understanding of fund-raising potential and capacity begins with an assessment of the immediate environment, which has an overriding influence on fund-raising performance. Exhibit 6.1 lists the factors that address both potential and capacity to raise money, and allows a ranking of each factor on a scale of 1 to 5, in order to identify

---

[2]Peter F. Drucker, *Managing the Nonprofit Organization: Practices and Principles* (New York: Harper-Collins, 1990), p. 56.

EXHIBIT 6.1 Environmental Audit for Fund Raising

	Score				
	Low				High
1. Type of Institution or Agency	1	2	3	4	5
2. Written Long-range and Strategic Plan	1	2	3	4	5
3. Board Leadership, Background and Attitude	1	2	3	4	5
4. Geography	1	2	3	4	5
5. Style	1	2	3	4	5
6. Competition, Image, and Market Position	1	2	3	4	5
7. Tradition of Fund-Raising Practice	1	2	3	4	5
8. Volume and Variety of Fund-raising Methods	1	2	3	4	5
9. Availability of Prospects	1	2	3	4	5
10. Existing Donors for Renewal and Upgrading	1	2	3	4	5
11. Experienced and Dedicated Volunteers	1	2	3	4	5
12. Access to Wealth	1	2	3	4	5
13. Focus on Major Gifts	1	2	3	4	5
14. Professional Staff and Fund-raising Counsel	1	2	3	4	5
15. Development Staff, Space, Budget, and Systems	1	2	3	4	5
16. Donor Recognition	1	2	3	4	5

MEDIAN SCORE

strengths and weaknesses, assets and liabilities, potential and capacity. There is no "passing grade" for this test, but a median score of 3 or better reflects a positive environment for fund-raising activity. Any area scored below a 3 deserves attention. Assessment helps to increase awareness of the external factors that can affect annual and future fund-raising activities, and provides suggestions on how much impact these factors might have, the levels of reasonable expectation in generating gifts, where attention to improvements will bear fruit, and similar information. Environmental audits on fund raising should be conducted at least once every three years, or even every two years, as the pace of our world continues to accelerate. Organizations that do not anticipate change and are unable to execute decisions with speed, based on adequate assessments, will quickly fall behind.

The factors listed in the exhibit are discussed in the following paragraphs.

(A) TYPE OF INSTITUTION OR AGENCY

There are several separate classes of not-for-profit organizations whose annual contributions data has been published by the American Association of Fund Raising Counsel, for more than 35 years, in its annual report, *Giving USA*. The dominant recipient of gifts in every year has been *religion*, receiving 44 percent to 48 percent of all funds raised. At the next level of support, receiving 8 percent to 12 percent of all gifts each, are *human services*, *education*, and *health*. *The arts* and *culture* receive from 6 percent to 8 percent annually, and *public and civic benefit causes* receive 2 percent to 5 percent.[3] Based only on this data, an arts organization, for example, when setting its contributions goals, should appreciate the potential limitation to the extent of community support it may be able to achieve as compared with a college or university or the local United Way. Unrealistic expectations, resulting in a board's loss of confidence in fund raising as a viable source of revenue, can cripple any fund-raising program.

(B) WRITTEN LONG-RANGE AND STRATEGIC PLAN

The absence of a written plan for the future limits possible supporters to investigation of a single criterion: the annual operation's budget performance. More important to donors, however, is the absence of any "vision" for the organization's future or any assessment suggesting its ability to continue to provide even present-day programs and services beyond one year. This absence will inhibit their decision to make any sizable investment or commitment, whether of "time, talent, or treasure," and thus prevents any significant progress.

(C) BOARD LEADERSHIP, BACKGROUND, AND ATTITUDE

Most board members come from business and industry and may arrive with preconceived attitudes about how to manage a not-for-profit organization, derived from their for-profit training and experience. Organizations that provide their board members with

---

[3]American Association of Fund-Raising Counsel, *Giving USA* (New York: AAFRC Trust for Philanthropy, 2000), pp. 22–23.

well-prepared orientation and training activities (including their role in fund raising) will likely retain them and, with their help, grow. When board leadership is lacking, many good volunteers become frustrated and discouraged from future service.

(D) GEOGRAPHY

Demographic studies help board members and management to see how location affects response to the programs and services offered, how they should be offered and to whom, what resources will be required to deliver them, and what potential for public support (volunteers and money) is available. (See Chapter 15.) Populations shift more quickly today than ever before; they are driven by age, economics, ethnic and cultural factors, and sheer numbers, and differing local influences accompany each shift.

(E) STYLE

As the American landscape changes ever more rapidly, alertness to local community style, with its diversity of culture, tradition, and practice, will aid nonprofit organizations in determining where they "fit in" and how they may appear ("image is everything") in order to attract public support, volunteers, and contributions. Saturation with one fund-raising method (telephone calls by telemarketing professionals, or benefit-event ticket sales) can cause the public to build levels of resistance and even to reject solicitations, regardless of their legitimacy, the quality of their requests, or even their success only one year before.

(F) COMPETITION, IMAGE, AND MARKET POSITION

Each organization should assess, as accurately as possible, where its mission, purposes, goals, and objectives match the needs of the community it serves. There is always competition for volunteers, clients, employees, resources, and public dollars. Those organizations serving less popular or less well known causes will be working uphill to find people willing to share in their mission. Market research and other assessment tools greatly aid every organization to better understand public opinion and support potential.

(G) TRADITION OF FUND-RAISING PRACTICE

The methods and techniques of public solicitation, although restricted in number, are openly available to all to use equally. Some organizations use only one or two methods, limiting their capacity to develop funds by failing to use every means available. Results will vary with each method used, because causes and needs are different. Each organization's history of solicitation and breadth of methods used with success will guide it in how best to achieve consistent results and will help it to understand external realities, such as the effects of environmental factors in an ever changing, ever more competitive marketplace. Determining which fund-raising methods to use or which combinations of methods will work best for each nonprofit organization, at what level of volunteer support and at what cost (budget), requires the new evaluation techniques provided in this chapter.

(H) VOLUME AND VARIETY OF FUND-RAISING METHODS

Most not-for-profit organizations begin with one or more annual solicitation methods to produce the first donors and dollars. The same methods are used to renew these donors and to increase their numbers and dollars in the next year and the next. Several other methods can be added, once a base of donors and public support demonstrates a readiness or opportunity for acceptance. In time, an organization builds a broad base of fundraising activities that will yield more predictable levels of cash for annual purposes; special-project funds when necessary; major gifts for construction, renovation, and equipment projects (especially targeted in capital campaigns); and, eventually, endowment funds as a consequence of offering estate planning and planned giving programs. A not-for-profit organization cannot expect to begin one day and achieve success the next, using only the planned giving method, nor should it expect every technique to succeed immediately and at maximum efficiency. Development has been aptly defined as "planned promotion of understanding, participation and support,"[4] and it takes a lot of time. Each fund-raising method selected will develop to its own level of success, year after year, matched to the public's economic ability and personal conviction to support the organization. All methods in use must be integrated carefully, in a coordinated and cooperative manner. The audiences invited to participate are almost always the same people whom every other organization is soliciting at the same time. If an organization is to achieve the amount of financial and voluntary support that is adequate to meet its needs at any time, it must, at that same moment, match the capacity of its public to reply. The only limitation is the organization's own ability to ask for support with efficiency and effectiveness.

(I) AVAILABILITY OF PROSPECTS

Every fund-raising program has a geographic range or boundary within which it can effectively concentrate its search for prospects. This range is tied to the image and extent of the programs and services offered by the organization. Time and budget invested in building relationships with those who are nearby, those who are served or will be served, and those who participate in the cause or programs offered will pay higher dividends because these groups are more likely to care about the organization and its future than groups that are not so committed. People who are far away, have never been clients, and are not involved in any way are much less likely to care and to give.

(J) EXISTING DONORS FOR RENEWAL AND UPGRADING

The best prospects are those who are already supporting the organization. They must not be taken for granted, despite their commitment; they must forever be cultivated, communicated with, and rewarded. Efforts to preserve and increase donors' personal participation and their potential for even greater support in alternate ways (time, talent, and treasure are all available) will always succeed.

---

[4]Harold J. Seymour, *Designs for Fund-Raising* (New York: McGraw-Hill, 1966), p. 115.

(K) EXPERIENCED AND DEDICATED VOLUNTEERS

Although it is easy to count volunteers and to count the many areas and hours of their service, there can never be enough of them. Any expansion in community relations or philanthropic potential rests with the number of volunteers and the extent of their knowledge, experience, and commitment. The key to success in fund raising, for every not-for-profit organization, remains in the hands of its volunteers.

(L) ACCESS TO WEALTH

Attention to those few wealthy persons whose ability to participate is greater than that of others must be a priority for the board and for management. A defined program with specific objectives can be measured in terms of numbers of qualified prospects, a strategic plan for each, numbers of contacts made, and the results. People are not likely to make the biggest investment decisions of their lives in favor of any not-for-profit organization before both parties engage in an extensive effort. Wealthy individuals must be available and within reach.

(M) FOCUS ON MAJOR GIFTS

Success with annual giving programs is essential, but time and attention also must be given every year to the development of patrons and benefactors—those few best friends whose capacity for six-figure (and up) contributions is crucial for the present and the future of every not-for-profit organization. Identification and invitation, recruitment and cultivation, solicitation and recognition of significant gifts from individuals, corporations, and foundations must be annual priorities. The attention of these donors must be directed toward the "vision" of the board of directors and management and the long-range plan they intend to help complete. They must know that each major gift will help bring that vision to life in a way that allows their own aspirations to be matched and fulfilled.

(N) PROFESSIONAL STAFF AND FUND-RAISING COUNSEL

The use of competent fund-raising executives is essential to achieving success in public solicitation. Gone are the days when volunteers could provide the funds needed by staging a benefit event or nonprofit organizations could rely on the board of directors to make up the difference needed to balance the budget at the end of each year. Potential for success can be enhanced by the use of professional fund-raising counsel. Counsel adds experienced and professional methods for staff recruitment and training, board and management involvement in solicitation, adequate levels of support systems, recognition programs, and other areas to improve performance. When best used, these expert advisors define specific programs with detailed plans, prepare everyone to conduct the effort, give supervision or "coaching" along the way, evaluate results, and demonstrate personal conviction on how to proceed with an expectation of success. Most important, their guidance helps everyone concentrate on the task of raising money, which helps to prevent distractions and misdirections and promotes success.

(O)   DEVELOPMENT STAFF, SPACE, BUDGET, AND SYSTEMS

Success in fund raising is more likely to occur with an organized program led by a professional fund-raising executive who has adequate support in the form of office personnel, space, budget, and modern systems for managing all the data involved. Location is less important than competence. It costs money to raise money, and although reasonable cost levels can be targeted for each individual program, there are also costs for management functions, equipment, computers, research, support personnel, and continuing training programs, all necessary for continued success in the future.

(P)   DONOR RECOGNITION

Recognition is important to those so honored, no matter how they protest to the contrary. A program of recognition addresses how current donors are treated at *all* times, including after their gifts have been received. Recognition must be visible so that donors (and those who aspire to increased giving) can see that their support is appreciated, is valuable, and has been visibly declared to have been significant and worthwhile. Hard evidence is needed to show how donors are treated, how their names will appear on buildings, plaques, or donors' walls, and how prominently their recognition will be displayed.

6.2   *Development Department and Program Audit*

External environments can exert a pervasive influence on fund-raising success. Completing an assessment of those factors (environments) prior to a review of the fund development department and its variety of solicitation programs will be useful but is not a necessity. Assessments can and should be performed when needed or when an extensive review can help to resolve current issues or aid operating decisions.

When should a decision be made to proceed with a departmental and program audit? The need to answer any of the questions in the following list should suffice as a reason, and the need to answer two or more will verify the urgency to begin:

How can I get my staff to be more productive?
How can I more effectively use my limited budget?
What additional resources do we need?
How can we increase our prospect pool?
How should our staff and volunteers be organized?
How can we get the board more involved in fund raising?
How can we raise more money?

Before beginning, three guiding questions should be considered:

1. How will this review be used?
2. What should be measured and what criteria should be used?
3. Who should conduct the assessment?[5]

---

[5]Del Martin, "The Development Audit: Providing the Blue Print for a Better Fund-Raising Program," *AFP Journal* (Autumn 1990): 28.

In determining fund-raising performance, it may not be possible to separate the not-for-profit organization from this same scrutiny, nor may it be advisable to do so. The organization's ability to meet its mission is dependent, to a degree, on success in fund raising, and success in fund raising is dependent on a clear understanding of mission. As to when to do the assessment, there may never be an optimum time, but there is likely to be time committed if the priority is high enough or when conditions recommend it. Biannual surveys should be adequate; annual reviews could be too strenuous and may lack sufficient time for recommendations from the last assessment to progress enough to allow for any measurable change. An opportune time to do an assessment is when a change in leadership occurs and a new board chair, development committee chair, president, or executive director takes office.

Areas to be assessed can be selected from the topics listed in Exhibit 6.2. Other areas open to review include prior-year accomplishments in relation to the mission statement; present size, scope, and number of clients served in relation to the demonstrated value of programs and services (outcomes for public good); written case statement for support in relation to perceived public image and popularity; and measurements of public confidence and trust in relation to compensation levels for staff. It may be true that not-for-profit organizations vary as to how they conduct fund raising and that fund raising results are different for every organization, but there are many common criteria that justify self-analysis, objective measurements for any one organization, and comparisons with other organizations where possible.

Who does this work? Selection of the right person should follow the decision as to what is to be assessed and the objective of the assessment. A study leader from the employee pool outside the development staff may not be a suitable candidate because, generally speaking, few employees in not-for-profit organizations have enough understanding of philanthropy and resource development to be prepared to be rigorous in the right areas. Development staff are not candidates either, but they should do the work of data gathering and can help interpret the data to the study leader.

If the assessment goal is a comprehensive review of current fund-raising programs (volunteer effectiveness, funding sources and gifts received, and analysis of the programs' interaction with the rest of the organization), an experienced and knowledgeable

EXHIBIT 6.2 Areas for Department and Program Assessment

	Score				
	Low				High
1. Comparison with Prior Year Results	1	2	3	4	5
2. Growth in Donor Universe	1	2	3	4	5
3. Penetration of New Markets	1	2	3	4	5
4. Quality of Effort	1	2	3	4	5
5. Leadership Development	1	2	3	4	5
6. Consistent Messages and Personalization	1	2	3	4	5
7. Regular Reports and Analysis of Results	1	2	3	4	5
8. Staff Training and Development	1	2	3	4	5
9. Matching Institutional Needs	1	2	3	4	5
10. Forecasting Future Income	1	2	3	4	5

MEDIAN SCORE

individual from outside the organization should be retained to conduct the process. Professional fund-raising consultants have firsthand experience from program audits conducted at numerous other not-for-profit organizations in many parts of the country. Arrangements for their services should be secured by contract; voluntary or in-kind services should be avoided. A proper business relationship should be established and maintained to establish credibility of the final product among board members, management, and the public.

One of the first areas to assess is preparation and readiness of the organization to engage in fund raising. Exhibit 6.3 gives a few sample questions, excerpted from a more complete list,[6] that address the question of readiness.

The basic ingredients for development department and program assessment are documents, interviews, evaluation, and recommendations. Documents reveal results in hard-data form and bring together texts such as written policies and guidelines, gift reports, budgets, accounting reports, and audited financial statements. Private interviews with key people add information about attitudes, judgments, and other subjective details, along with their personal evaluations of program and staff performance. This data can be examined and arranged in comparative formats for analysis and comparison. The findings will include interpretation, specific recommendations and conclusions that address how the relationships among development programs are advancing the not-for-profit organization in its mission and long-range plans, and progress achieved toward realization of fund-raising potential and capacity.

No development department stands or functions alone. Each is an integrated part of the larger not-for-profit organization, and how it is attached can be instrumental to its success. Access to the board of directors, president or executive director, and board-level committees for development, finance, and nominating should be open. Good relationships with employees whose duties include planning, marketing and communications, and public relations, plus those with investment and financial management assignments, can achieve maximum coordination and cooperation in communicating the institutional priorities to be offered and explained to the community. Because development programs are conducted outside the organization, development staff can bring back information and experience-based insights about public attitudes and sensitivities, which can be valuable to others within management. Development programs will meet the expectations of the board and management more often when fully integrated into the current priorities and future goals of the organization. Without such access and integration, development programs are likely to fall short in producing the support the organization needs.

Development assessments should review the organization's annual and long-range goals in relation to the board's and management's expectations of fund-raising performance and its results. Individual appeal program performances, deadlines, and costs of time and money (budget) should be similarly reviewed. The results of each fund-raising method used should be measured against forecasts, prior-year outcomes, and estimated future results, not as a single "bottom-line" figure. (Several measurement tools are discussed in Section 6.4.) Standards of performance and reasonable-cost guidelines can be defined for every fund-raising method and used each year. Performance can then be evaluated against known criteria.

---

[6]Anne L. New, with Wilson C. Levis, *Raise More Money for Your Nonprofit Organization: A Guide to Evaluating and Improving Your Fundraising* (New York: The Foundation Center, 1991), pp. 7–8, 10–11.

EXHIBIT 6.3 Assessment of Readiness

Readiness	Yes	No
Have you listed, in writing, the possible sources of support for your organization, including:		
a. Individuals (kinds of people likely to be interested in and support what you do)?	[ ]	[ ]
b. Civic groups such as Rotary, Lions, or Soroptimists?	[ ]	[ ]
c. Religious institutions and auxiliaries?	[ ]	[ ]
d. Social clubs?	[ ]	[ ]
e. Corporations and foundations?	[ ]	[ ]
f. Federated funding sources (United Way)?	[ ]	[ ]
g. Local, county, state, and national government units?	[ ]	[ ]
Do you have evidence, such as formal endorsements, unsolicited letters, clippings, and records of oral comments, indicating what people associated with the sources think of your organization?	[ ]	[ ]
Do you communicate regularly with these groups?	[ ]	[ ]
Do you have an annual fund-raising plan that is:		
a. Written?	[ ]	[ ]
b. Board approved?	[ ]	[ ]

Fund-raising Action

	Yes	No
Last year, did the organization raise (or exceed) the amount it had budgeted for contributed income?	[ ]	[ ]
This year, have all parts of your fund-raising plan been carried out to date on schedule?	[ ]	[ ]
Have you set up a separate budget for each type of fund raising you do?	[ ]	[ ]
Does each include projected results and projected net income from this type of fund raising?	[ ]	[ ]

Source: *Excerpted by permission from New, Anne L. with Wilson C. Levis.* Raise More Money for Your Nonprofit Organization: A Guide to Evaluating and Improving Your Fundraising. © *1991 by the Foundation Center, 79 Fifth Avenue, New York, NY 10003.*

For example, suppose a decision to conduct a benefit event requires that an assistant fund-raising director and two clerical staff be assigned full time to the project for three months. A goal of $25,000 net income is established. Assessment will measure gross income against expenses, beginning with all the direct costs to conduct the event. Added to this expense are all the indirect (overhead) charges—a percentage of staff salary and benefits; a portion of the lease, heat, light, telephone, postage, and other charges incurred over three months—to arrive at the total investment of time and money required to conduct the event and to achieve the goal. Next, the event should be evaluated for its ability to achieve other, "soft" objectives—the extra development opportunities this event will make possible. These include visibility and image enhancement for the organization, community participation, volunteer and leadership training, prospect and donor cultivation, public relations gains and press coverage, recognition of donors, and more. Total value from the event must include assessments of all these areas, because $25,000 net proceeds alone may be judged to be an inadequate or inefficient gain for the cost involved, if measured only for profitability. A decision to continue or drop the event rests in part on its effectiveness to enhance the development process and its efficiency in maximizing net income. To use benefit events only as money-raising activities is to ignore their equal potential for aiding the organization and helping with several other development and institutional objectives.

Within the development program, another area worthy of assessment is departmental operations. These can be evaluated for their quality of performance, such as the effectiveness and extent of professional staff to provide leadership to the organization and the department; the training of volunteers and employees; communication of institutional priorities; efficiency in integrating planning, marketing and communications, and public relations goals; interpersonal relations with volunteers; and appropriate communications (frequency, timing, costs, effectiveness) with donors. Quantitative measurements of fund raising will always include accurate and complete gift reports and financial statements, but should add a number of other factors: complying with government regulations and filing public reports on time; completing policies and procedures and gaining their approval and acceptance; setting up efficient and accurate procedures for timely gift acknowledgments and donor records systems; and other similarly important measures. Solid departmental management is essential to the success of every fund-raising program offered. Abstract areas might be added, such as demands for nondevelopment work by development staff, stability of staff and fund-raising programs, public reputation of the department, and the like.

The operating success of the not-for-profit organization has considerable influence on the potential for success of its fund-raising activities. Assessment of an organization's support of development work can be difficult to interpret in quantitative and qualitative terms. How does one express the value of advocacy of mission and not-for-profit status; ethics in program fulfillment; public acceptance (popularity and respect) of the cause and the organization's overall performance; confidence and trust in the board of directors and top management; cultural diversity of the board of directors and the staff; board members' giving records and willingness to help to raise funds; correct use of funds raised to demonstrated outcomes of programs and services to the public; and the organization's willingness to disclose financial information?

The time period used in this assessment (fiscal year or calendar year) should, if possible, take into account the time and energy spent to identify, recruit, orient, and train volunteers. Time and money should be allotted to do prospect research, prospect cultivation, and donor relations and to measure their outcomes. The payoff from these activities will occur later in time; no direct gift income from this work will show within the current fiscal period. A similar time frame applies to corporation and foundation proposals, which are submitted in one year for a decision in the next year; actual funding may be spread over the third and fourth years. Such delays occur especially in planned giving, where it is common for charitable trusts and life insurance policies to "mature" in the form of legacies and bequests years later, following the death of the donor. Unsolicited gifts, unannounced bequests, unexpected memorial contributions, and even unwanted donations can happen at any time during the measurement period. These unpredictable results should be separated from program results that accrue from direct solicitation activities because they will easily distort the performance evaluation. Such gifts are unpredictable only to the extent that no one can forecast exactly how many, for how much money, will arrive in any one year. In reviewing these "extra" gifts, their value should be included in the total of gifts received, but in setting goals for the next year, they should be separated to avoid the impression that the receipt of unsolicited, unknown, unexpected, or unwanted gifts will continue at a dependable level.

The areas of activity common to development departments and fund-raising programs are described in the sections that follow. (They can be scored using Exhibit 6.2.) This assessment can also be used to address two overriding questions:

1. Did the department accomplish what it set out to do (that is, was it effective)?
2. Did the department accomplish this goal at an acceptable cost (that is, was it efficient, considering both monetary and nonmonetary costs)?[7]

(A) COMPARISON WITH PRIOR-YEAR RESULTS

Given the short time interval between one year and the next, a review should begin with what happened last year (and the year before, if available). Program-by-program results should be compared, on a monthly basis, with results of the most recent year. Trends, which can be spotted quickly, allow timely decisions to change direction and to make program and budgetary revisions of estimated results and the costs to achieve them.

(B) GROWTH IN DONOR UNIVERSE

The development department should always be engaged in finding new donors to replace those who leave the program. Nearly every organization wants to increase its results year after year, and, to gain the added gifts needed to meet higher goals, there must be a continuous effort to increase the numbers of donors. New donors also can be invited to participate in voluntary services, which will increase their involvement and enhance the prospect of repeat gifts from them. Acquisition of new donors is so routine to most annual giving activities that, if it is not found, in a close observation of performance (especially in test results with new audiences), its absence can be the earliest sign of change in public affection, in project appeal, in message, or in package acceptance. Percentage of response and average gift size are indicators that reflect current public attitudes and quickly illustrate donors' judgment; the turnaround time for early decisions that implement corrective (and less costly) actions must be swift. Similar scrutiny should be given to programs that renew prior donors' gifts, to monitor the number who respond and the percentage who upgrade their gifts—both indicators of growing satisfaction and of more predictable dollars. Donors who are invited to join donor clubs and become active volunteers often demonstrate increased commitment and enthusiasm for the organization.

---

[7]Dennis J. Murray, *The Guaranteed Fund-Raising System: A Systems Approach to Planning and Controlling Fund Raising,* 2d ed. (Boston: American Institute of Management, 1994), p. 353.

(C) PENETRATION OF NEW MARKETS

Test mailings, telemarketing, and membership drives are used to reach out to new constituents, including new communities and demographic groups. Testing new mail packages containing various messages about the merits and needs of the organization can show which appeal will yield the best results. Alertness to the changing community can reveal opportunities to test old groups and to approach newly arrived prospects and can help to create an awareness of when to solicit new corporations (*after* they achieve profitability) and when to submit proposals to foundations, matching a new need with their established priorities for grantmaking. Groups with declining responses can be dropped from further solicitation if appeals are likely to go unanswered and are thus unprofitable. Successful annual giving programs should be expanded to wider audiences after tests, market research, and demographic studies prove good response rates and forecast profitability. Such evidence, when matched to programs that can prove their profitability, will support requests for added budget.

(D) QUALITY OF EFFORT

Although subjective, a review of solicitation materials to determine the time and cost of their preparation, the fulfillment of their deadlines, and their delivery costs can influence success. These are hidden areas, but they offer ways of increasing net results by improving quality of performance. The texts used in letters, brochures, and proposals can be evaluated for good English usage, brevity, clarity, contemporary design, completeness, and consistency with other materials and messages sent to the same audiences. The time spent drafting the text of appropriate thank-you letters and keeping the turnaround time to less than 48 hours between receipt and response can affect public confidence and improve the potential for donor renewal. Assessment of operating areas can improve efficiency, effectiveness, and quality of the product, all leading to increased public acceptance and response.[8]

(E) LEADERSHIP DEVELOPMENT

It is most valuable to track the development of volunteers into informed and competent leaders. The support activities that sustain them during their tenure of service are equally important. Board development should be highest on this list because board candidates often evolve within the fund development area. A systematic program to identify, recruit, orient, train, evaluate, and reward volunteers at all levels should be fully in operation. The nominating committee should maintain a sizable list of candidates whose progress they can observe. There is also a continuous need for board education on current issues, to help members in the decisions they are asked to make. Finally, personal participation in giving should be part of the performance evaluation on all levels of leadership.

---

[8]Robert J. Berendt and Richard J. Taft, *How to Rate Your Development Office* (Washington, D.C.: Taft Corporation, 1983), pp. 70–73.

(F) CONSISTENT MESSAGES AND PERSONALIZATION

Several parts of the same organization are likely to be in constant communication with the general public throughout the year. Coordination and cooperation among those who communicate externally are necessary, for obvious reasons, not the least of which is the possibility that multiple and potentially conflicting messages will be sent to the same audience, with one message sender unaware of what the others are sending and when. For fund development to work well, the entire list of public communications of all kinds must be reviewed in detail: the appearance of the organization's physical plant (in videos and photographs), the materials used to describe programs and services, the consistency of style and appearance in all forms of mass communication and public relations, and other visible features. An honest sensitivity to individuals who are valuable to the organization, whether clients, employees, volunteers, or donors, results from attention to the personal relationships involved, to personalized forms of contact wherever possible, and to recognition. Nothing can beat a first-name greeting and a smile!

(G) REGULAR REPORTS AND ANALYSIS OF RESULTS

The results of fund raising are of high interest to everyone. Donors want to know their money was received safely and was spent to do good works. Volunteers want to know whether their hard work was successful. Management wants to know how much money arrived, to allow them to proceed with programs and plans. Regular fund-raising reports should cover three basic areas: sources of gifts, purposes or use of funds raised, and methods used to raise the money. (See Exhibits 6.4, 6.5, and 6.6 for examples.) Frequent reports help to demonstrate progress and success and to encourage volunteers and donors alike. These reports also help everyone to better understand the realities of fund raising—how the various methods perform and what can be expected of these methods based on results, not guesses or presumptions about what they should yield.

(H) STAFF TRAINING AND DEVELOPMENT

Employees in the development office require training for more than the items listed in their job descriptions. They must understand something about the areas of program and service that use the money raised. They need to be shown how the several fund-raising methods they help support actually perform individually and together. They must have an appreciation for the value of clients, of volunteers, and of donors; must understand why thanking donors promptly for each and every gift is important; and must be aware of the need for accuracy *always* in mail lists, gift reports, and donor records. Funds assigned to train professional and support staff at conferences and workshops are a solid investment; these staff members can improve their skills along with their understanding of the development process of which they are so vital a part. Their own performance evaluations can assess their progress in understanding the purposes of their work, the fund-raising methods used, and their role in helping to accomplish goals and objectives for the development department and the not-for-profit organization.

EXHIBIT 6.4 Gift Report on Sources of Gifts Received

Sources of Gifts	Number of Gifts	Gift Income	Average Gift Size
Trustees/Directors	15	$25,500	$1,700
Professional staff	21	3,025	144
Employees	65	3,675	57
New donors (acquisition)	285	8,030	28
Prior donors (renewal)	282	18,010	64
Corporations	17	8,500	500
Foundations	12	38,800	3,233
Associations/societies	6	2,850	475
Bequests received	3	31,500	10,500
Unsolicited gifts	42	2,950	70
Other gifts received	12	21,500	1,792
Grand Total	760	$164,340	$216

(I) MATCHING INSTITUTIONAL NEEDS

There is more to fund-raising assessment than measuring amounts of money raised against the costs of raising it. Clearly, raising the funds for the programs and services that match institutional needs with community needs are a priority. Some boards and managers believe that high goals and firm deadlines encourage volunteers and staff to work harder. In reality, results are a function of those solicited being well prepared to receive the message asking for their support, just as much as their being well asked by well-trained volunteers. Nevertheless, it is important to address these questions: Was all

EXHIBIT 6.5 Gift Report on Purposes or Uses of Gifts Received

Purposes or Uses of Gifts Received	Number of Gifts	Gift Income	Average Gift Size
Unrestricted Funds	225	$34,519	$153
Temporarily Restricted Funds			
Capital/equipment purposes	295	$26,950	$91
Programs/services purposes	138	18,500	134
Education/training purposes	14	22,500	1,607
Research/study purposes	15	26,450	1,763
Staff/employee purposes	58	3,016	52
Other restricted purposes	12	905	75
Subtotal	757	$132,840	$175
Permanently Restricted Funds			
Unrestricted endowment	2	$6,500	$3,250
Restricted endowment	1	25,000	25,000
Subtotal	3	$31,500	$10,500
Grand Total	760	$164,340	$216

EXHIBIT 6.6 Gift Report of Solicitation Activities and Results (by Program)

Solicitation Activities	Number of Gifts	Gift Income	Average Gift Size
A. Annual Giving Programs			
Direct mail (acquisition)	285	$8,030	$28
Direct mail (renewal)	282	18,010	64
Membership dues	0	0	0
Donor clubs	0	0	0
Support groups	0	0	0
Telephone gifts	0	0	0
Benefit events	2	12,850	6,425
Volunteer-led solicitations	65	3,675	57
Unsolicited gifts	42	2,950	70
Other gifts received	16	21,500	1,344
Subtotal	692	$67,015	$97
B. Major Giving Programs			
Corporations	17	$8,500	$500
Foundations	12	28,800	2,400
Individuals	36	28,525	792
Special projects	0	0	0
Capital campaigns	0	0	0
Bequests received	3	31,500	10,500
Subtotal	68	$97,325	$1,431
Grand total	760	$164,340	$216

the necessary money raised in time for the purposes needed by the organization? Were those who were asked to give ready to respond (prior marketing and public relations efforts), or were they uninformed and hesitant? Did they give the amount asked of them based on staff research and the rating and evaluation process? What other information and opinions did they express to the volunteer who called on them? Was this information reported back for evaluation and for future contact? Many details go into a solicitation, and all of them must be organized to produce happy donors, confident volunteers, and all the money needed—on time.

(J) FORECASTING FUTURE INCOME

Assessment of the prior criteria (a–i) encourages an organization to understand itself and its fund-raising programs better. It can now begin to forecast how fund-raising programs will continue to function, how they can react to changing circumstances and economic realities, and how their flexibility can be used to achieve the money when needed. Reliable analysis of external conditions measured against accurate results will increase the organization's ability to manage its public programs and services with increased confidence.

After the departmental study has been concluded, the results should be studied and interpreted in order to define recommendations for the future. Much has been learned, and, before any more time passes, this knowledge should be shared with the board and management. Outcomes from analytical work are more frequently refinements of what is already known than they are surprises. Assessments provide a means of documenting achievements and accomplishments as well as problems and shortcomings; both kinds of outcomes should be recognized for what they truly are—opportunities for attention, focus, challenge, and renewal.

Assessments of the development department provide the capability "to identify what is being done well and confer suitable rewards, to identify areas where improvement is possible and desirable, to assess the entire planning process and its critical assumptions, and to develop future plans, objectives, and standards."[9]

6.3 Development Planning (Feasibility) Study

After departmental reviews, key areas of performance within each fund development program will be much better known. But what of the future? Another year or two may pass without any change in current priorities or financial needs of the organization. During that time, existing development programs may be challenged most often only to meet and exceed their present levels of annual performance. This should be considered good fortune! There is time to refine and improve areas such as volunteer and prospect identification, recruitment, and involvement; time to complete and implement donor recognition policies; time to train volunteers and office staff and improve office systems; time to improve present capabilities, achieve greater efficiency, and realize more cost-effective results for each program. This is the time to prepare for the future. A day will come, perhaps soon, when the organization will complete its own assessments and resolve to embark on a major surge forward, to expand its programs and services, to seize an unusual challenge or opportunity, or to respond to new options that were previously unseen (mergers or takeover proposals). When this day arrives, the fund development program will be challenged to extend its performance too, perhaps with significant new monetary objectives. A multiyear, major capital campaign frequently targets an amount five times current annual performance levels and more.

How prepared will the development program be to undertake such a challenge? Is the board of directors ready to accept its role of personal leadership in the campaign? Are enough volunteers trained and experienced with major gift solicitation? Have professional staff attended conferences and workshops on major-gifts research and capital campaign preparation and direction? The challenge of a capital campaign should not come as a total surprise to the development team. Ideally, they will have been actively involved in the planning process and will be well acquainted with the projects, their cost estimates, their priority, and the timetable set for their completion. Fund development participation in the planning process allows them to begin early to conduct their own assessments of how current and past fund-raising programs, messages, and public responses can be energized to a higher capability to meet future needs.

In the for-profit business world, market research is a well-developed science that provides hard evidence on which to base large decisions. One of the best-known users of

---

[9]Murray, *Guaranteed Fund-Raising System*, p. 353.

market research is the Procter & Gamble Company, which never introduces a new product without an extensive, thoroughly tested, and exhaustive assessment of that product's predictable success in the marketplace.

Nonprofit organizations are unlikely to commit themselves to market research to this extent, but board members and management, after some market analysis, can achieve a higher degree of confidence in their product (their "vision" of the future), in the accuracy of public needs, in delivery of their programs and services, and in their sales force (fund raising). They need to accurately assess their internal strength of leadership, both volunteer and staff, plus the competence of departmental staff and proven systems.

It is now time for the final examination. What is the extent of the public's agreement with the urgency of the organization's plans? Will these plans test positive to those from whom financial support will have to come? This final exam is critical because the future of the organization is riding on the outcome. In assessing what is feasible, market research will test *everything*: the long-range plan and each of the defined projects for its priority of need, cost, and timetable for implementation. This exam will also test the financial goals, competency of leadership, campaign readiness, public concurrence with the plan, proposals to solve problems, and extent of public willingness (financial potential) to give of time, talent, and treasure to achieve the campaign goal.

The development planning study is an examination the organization must pass with high marks if it intends to go forward to fulfill its goals.

> One of the first questions to ask about a capital campaign is whether it is truly needed. This question deserves a compelling answer. Capital campaigns are not for raising significant numbers of gifts or significant numbers of large gifts, and not for achieving prestigious gifts or important objectives. A capital campaign is one means to financial security, but it should, and in most cases it must, represent the studied conclusion that all traditional funding options have been exhausted and a capital fund drive is now required to raise most or all of the money needed by a certain date.[10]

Plans must be well prepared to withstand tests of credibility, relevance, urgency, and practicality. The need for additional resources must be so convincing that those who are invited to participate will agree with the vision for the future, and its conclusions, not because of what their money will be spent on but because what their money will allow to happen is so necessary that the value of the objective compels them to act in support of it.

When a project holds such potential and value, it should not proceed without a comprehensive assessment of how it will be received. Equally important, such a critical study should not be done without experienced and professional guidance. The question is not how to do the study (a host of consulting firms are skilled in market research techniques) but who should lead the process. By every measure, objectivity is absolutely necessary, and only an experienced study director from outside the organization can perform this work with professional skill and credibility. Nearly every professional fund-raising consulting firm or seasoned fund-raising executive is experienced with a development planning study (or feasibility study) and the capital campaign that fol-

---

[10]James M. Greenfield, *Fund-Raising: Evaluating and Managing the Fund Development Process* (New York: John Wiley & Sons, 1999), p. 277.

lows. If there is adequate talent to do this work, how should the study leader be identified, interviewed, and hired for the job?

To begin, the board of directors must concur that there is a need to test their conclusions and convictions about their long-range plan on the public. The board committee on
fund development, working with the chief development officer, should conduct the
interview process and bring back to the board their recommendations for who will be
the study leader, the cost of the services, and the time required to deliver the final report.
Candidates are then invited to submit a proposal within 30 or 45 days. Board members
and development staff should be available during this period for interviews and should
fully disclose everything the study leader requires. The development committee should
invite two or three of those who submit proposals for personal interviews, to verify their
ability to secure answers to the questions the study must test. Reference checks on each
firm and its staff are mandatory before final selection. The decision will also be guided
by who the study leader will be, when the study can begin, the budget and fees required,
and the timetable to completion. There should be absolute clarity about who is hiring the
study leader and to whom the study team reports throughout the contract period. The
answer can be any of the following, and everyone on this list must agree with the decision: chairman of the board, chairman of the development committee, president or executive director, or chief development officer. The development committee should review
the written agreement for services and should understand all of its details, including
payment dates and amounts, what expenses will be included, what study team members will be assigned, and similar arrangements.

Good chemistry between the study leader and the chief development officer is
essential so that, working together, they can perform the maximum amount of work that
can be accomplished during the study period. Development staff will be active partners
throughout, to identify and contact interview prospects, help draft the case statement to
be tested, and secure appointments for the study team. The project should be managed
so that the expertise of the study team is maximized and the information necessary to
resolve how to proceed is readily available.

The conclusions and recommendations of the completed study will provide the
board of directors and management with answers on their capability to proceed with
their plans and on how much public support their future plans will inspire. Proposed
goals will be tested and verified (or adjusted), just as the plan and its details (case statement) will be verified for their acceptance. Leadership availability, public confidence,
access to volunteers and prospects, internal readiness, timing of when to start and when
to end the campaign, and a campaign plan, including details of staffing, budget, materials, and support features, will also be provided. In essence, study recommendations provide a complete road map to success from start to finish, with plenty of directions for
each bend in the road along the way. The well-prepared, well-executed study should be
a document in which the board and management can place full confidence and belief as
a forecast of what will be required for optimal success in achieving their goals. The study
will also identify the weaknesses that require attention and the process for their correction. In summary, a feasibility study can reveal:

- The response for campaign giving
- How much each audience might give
- The identity of major gift prospects
- The identity of leadership candidates
- Problem areas (case, timing, image, leadership, staff, systems, others)

- An overall campaign objective
- Specific goals for each giving audience available
- A timetable and sequence for solicitation
- Elements of the case statement and all support documentation required
- Staffing and budget required
- Public relations support plan
- Where and how campaign counsel will be needed

Martin Grenzebach, master of the feasibility study and the campaign plan it fore-tells, notes that a high-quality study and the answers it provides will spell out certain prerequisites that should be in place to enable the campaign to succeed. He summarized these prerequisites as follows:

The institution must enjoy a positive image *within its constituency and within the business, financial, and industrial community; there must be a clearly* perceived need, *well defined in the minds of those who know the institution best and which can be made to inspire a sense of commitment in the thinking of those who are asked for financial support; there must be a* presence of available funds *ample enough in depth and breadth that, when properly motivated, those who hold the key to these resources will release enough of them to the institution in such measure as to meet its goal; there must be* capa-ble leadership, *holding the complete respect of the community and willing to give the necessary time and talent to the institution and its causes; and there must be a generally* favorable economic climate *within the constituency and/or the community, such as is occasioned by a sound economic outlook and the reasonable absence of conflicting campaigns and competing enterprises.*[11]

There can easily be failures in the best of plans. Their causes are known and are added here so as not to be missed. Errors can creep into any analysis and, as Dennis Murray states in his excellent chapter on "Reviewing, Evaluating, and Rewarding the Development Effort," the potential for disaster can result.

An overly optimistic assessment, for example, can produce unattainable objectives. These, in turn, produce detailed but totally meaningless action plans. These action plans, when executed, do not produce the anticipated results. But the failure in this case was not in the action plans, much less with the individuals who tried to carry them out. The failure slipped in much earlier, in the assessment. This is why the evaluation must track back along the entire integrated model and examine each step for the causes of failure. Four common reasons for failing to meet objectives deserve special mention:

- *Lack of top leadership*
- *Insufficient cultivation of prospects*
- *Lack of realism in assessments and objectives*
- *Lack of a tradition of giving*[12]

---

[11]John Grenzebach and Associates, *Prerequisites for Provable Campaign Success Investigated by a John Grenzebach and Associates Feasibility Development Study* (corporate report). (Chicago, Ill.: John Grenzebach and Associates, 1986), 1.

[12]Murray, *Guaranteed Fund-Raising System*, pp. 360–361.

Is it not much more valuable to everyone, both inside and outside the organization, to enter and engage in this process with both eyes open? Is it not much more valuable to avoid the hard lessons of those organizations that, having decided in advance all of their campaign objectives, use the feasibility study only to alert everyone that the campaign is coming? In their eagerness to get the money they need, they may fail to achieve even their income goal, because they have not involved their potential best donors and campaign leaders in what can be accomplished with their help. They have failed to test their plan and its potential for public acceptance and have not used a proven market research technique to verify everything necessary to design their campaign for maximum success. They may achieve what they thought was possible, only to learn in the end that they could have achieved even greater goals; or, worse, they may fail to meet their goals and fulfill their plans while they incur a serious loss of confidence along with the public's resistance to provide support for years into the future.

6.4 *Fund-raising Productivity Analysis*

A fund-raising productivity analysis is not a summary of the first three assessment areas, nor is it the "big finish" wrapped up with a simple answer of what is the reasonable cost for fund raising. As in the three prior sections, performance evaluation methods are offered here to help demonstrate the productivity and "profitability" of fund development activities. This section answers questions on what to measure, shows how efficient and how effective each solicitation program is, and demonstrates the efficiency and effectiveness of volunteers in completing their assignments.

If fund-raising productivity were only a simple comparison of revenue received against cost to raise it (the "bottom line"), it would illustrate only a single money-raising ratio and would fail to show any amount of program effectiveness or efficiency. This oversimplified measurement will also fail to assess any progress toward the potential that may exist or the extent of the public's capacity for giving to the organization to satisfy its present needs and fulfill its future plans. There is much more to fund raising than raising money, and there is much more to its productivity assessment than simple bottom-line analysis.

Fund-raising departments are engaged in a variety of methods and techniques to raise the money needed by their nonprofit organizations. They have goals and objectives that go beyond how much money is raised in a single fiscal or tax year. They employ these same fund-raising methods to communicate information, to cultivate positive relationships, and to solicit a variety of positive responses in addition to money. They produce ever larger numbers of suspects, prospects, and donors, stimulating their active participation as well as their fiscal support. They inform and enthuse, build confidence and trust, offer new and old friends important roles to play and valuable work to be done, and, using gifts as but one exchange medium, bond all these supporters ever more tightly to the organization and its mission, purposes, goals, and objectives.

Time and energy are necessary to support fund raising, which must be understood to be an investment decision and a firm commitment. Each budget dollar spent and each gift received should be appreciated for its cost-benefit ratio and for its long-term return on investment, which aids in the institution's own advancement. It takes years of investing in time and energy, plus budgeting, to build a successful development program that meets planned needs for the future. One year's budget and its results can and should be measured for direct performance, but they should also be measured for their contribution toward an increase or return on the next year's and future years' results as well.

Most professional fund-raising executives employ the image of a pyramid (see Exhibit 6.7) to illustrate the design for the overall fund development program. The pyramid shows each fund-raising method available, how each relates to the others, and at what levels performance should be measured. Management tools are available to measure each fund-raising activity. Murray identified the purposes for such evaluation as follows:

Evaluation has four purposes:

- *To identify what is being done well and to confer suitable rewards*
- *To identify areas where improvement is possible and desirable*
- *To assess the entire planning process and its critical assumptions*
- *To develop future plans, objectives, and standards*[13]

---

[13]Murray, *Guaranteed Fund-Raising System,* p. 47.

EXHIBIT 6.7 Pyramid of Giving

Source: *James M. Greenfield,* Fund-Raising Cost Effectiveness: A Self-Assessment Workbook *(New York: John Wiley & Sons, 1996), p. 132. Reprinted by permission of John Wiley & Sons, Inc.*

Murray also offered these six methodologies for evaluating fund-raising programs:

- *Opinions of professional consultants*
- *Outcomes measurement*
- *Cost-revenue ratios*
- *Solicitation effectiveness*
- *Congruence between predetermined objectives and outcomes*
- *Congruence between actual performance and standards of performance based on a systems approach*[14]

Fund-raising productivity analysis is the means to examine how to measure, to explore what to measure, to explain how it should be performed, and to become educated in what the outcomes may mean. Fund raising has been defined by Seymour as "the planned promotion of understanding, participation, and support.[15] Peter Drucker has stated that "performance in the nonprofit institution must be *planned*. And this starts out with the mission . . . [f]or the mission defines what results are in this particular nonprofit institution."[16] Murray's definition adds that "fund-raising management . . . is proactive and results-oriented."[17] Each of these concepts (promotion, planning, results) can and should be measured. The results of their assessment will add a better understanding of their contribution to the overall success of a comprehensive fund development program and the nonprofit organization it serves.

Results measurement begins with adequate preparation to ensure (1) access to valid statistics and their fair comparison and (2) an easy-to-understand report format for every audience intended. Nick Costa, in his thorough study of fund-raising cost performance in healthcare institutions, defined the following criteria for compiling and comparing statistics to ensure the integrity of their results:

- *Establish clear and decisive standards for recording data for each of your reports*
- *Maintain the standards you establish*
- *Use the reports to simplify, clarify, and educate*
- *Seek a uniform standard of measurement when using external statistics*[18]

(A) GIFT REPORTS

The use of gift reports is an interesting way to display numbers and illustrate results. Preparation depends on proper record keeping and consistent handling of all the data, which is then assembled for measurement. The value of gift reports is enhanced because fund-raising performance can be measured weekly, monthly, yearly, or whenever desired. The objectives in developing such reports, beyond being able to display results,

---

[14]Murray, *Guaranteed Fund-Raising System*, pp. 354–357.

[15]Seymour, *Designs for Fund-Raising*, p. 115.

[16]Drucker, *Managing the Nonprofit Organization*, p. 109.

[17]Murray, *Guaranteed Fund-Raising System*, p. 7.

[18]Nick B. Costa, *Measuring Progress and Success in Fund Raising: How to Use Comparative Statistics to Prove Your Effectiveness* (Falls Church, Va.: Association for Healthcare Philanthropy, 1991), pp. 7–8.

are to show the level of performance at any time, to compare the results with those at the same time in the previous year or in other prior years, and to measure all areas of progress, program-by-program, toward this year's goals.

The three primary areas that should be displayed in a gift report are sources of gifts, purposes or uses of the money raised, and results of each fund-raising program, as presented earlier in Exhibits 6.4, 6.5, and 6.6. The number of donors achieved and the amount of money raised in these three summaries are important data. The volume of people participating is as significant a sign of progress and program results as the dollars they provide; money follows people. When several fund-raising programs are being used at the same time, comparative analysis helps to determine which programs to emphasize during the year and which to postpone for emphasis in the following year. Programs whose financial results are not as productive as others, in terms of numbers of participants or dollars, may still have merit because they attract a number of faithful donors each time they are offered. Achieving an overall balance of results (people and dollars at reasonable cost) year after year, among all fund-raising programs offered, is more often the desired outcome. The health and vitality of each program will be important to long-term fund development growth because each depends on the success, efficiency, and effectiveness of its own activities, acting in concert with the others as well as on its own.

Public interests and moods can change rapidly in regard to charitable causes and issues. Regular analysis of results can help to track these changing patterns of response. Each nonprofit organization needs flexibility if it is to retain donor interest and faithful giving levels each year. It must allow for a shift in emphasis or a need to concentrate more budget and volunteer time on those methods currently having a greater or lesser success; again, the measurement of fund-raising performance goes beyond just counting net proceeds. Each method and its performance should be studied in detail to gain insight in assessing the values and merits each can achieve as well as what it can contribute to the whole. The assessor might look for the following nine areas (see Exhibit 6.8); together they offer a broad measurement guide:

1. *Participants.* The number of people who reply with gifts is the first indicator as to the success of the list chosen, solicitation method, and appeal message. Counting the number of donors from each list who reply also is valuable for other reasons, such as determining accuracy of mailing list, time between solicitation and

---

EXHIBIT 6.8 Nine-Point Performance Index

1. Participants	= Number of donors responding with gifts
2. Income Received	= Gross contributions received
3. Expenses	= Fund-raising costs (direct, indirect, overhead)
4. Percent Participation	= Number of participants divided by total solicitations made
5. Average Gift Size	= Income received divided by number of participants
6. Net Income	= Expenses subtracted from income received
7. Average Cost per Gift	= Expenses divided by number of participants
8. Cost of Fund Raising	= Expenses divided by income received, × 100
9. Return	= Net income divided by expenses, × 100

Source: *James M. Greenfield,* Fund-Raising Cost Effectiveness: A Self-Assessment Workbook. © *1996 John Wiley & Sons. Reprinted with permission.*

replies, address corrections received, requests for "do not mail," correspondence without gifts and contents to be answered, and more.

2. *Income received.* Total revenue produced by each solicitation method must be accounted for and deposited correctly, which also begins the evaluation process. Gross contributions should be tracked for each solicitation activity (mailing, benefit event, grant application, etc.), as results will differ. Future decisions on solicitation methods are linked to their ability to generate income along with numbers of donor participants.

3. *Expenses.* The costs associated with each solicitation method must be understood in order to evaluate performance with accuracy. It requires some effort to document direct costs as well as to calculate indirect and overhead expenses for each solicitation method used. With these first three data elements in place, assessment of each solicitation method can provide the next six revelations.

4. *Percent participation.* The percentage of replies will vary among solicitation methods. A 1 percent rate of return on invitations to a benefit event would be disastrous, but 1 percent rate of return from broadcast mailings to nondonors is considered a success. One of the prime objectives of fund-raising activity is to stimulate numbers of participants with each effort. Monitoring the percentage who reply is a major indicator of how those solicited like what is being said to them and accept the method used to communicate with them. Monitoring percentage of participation also can provide an early signal of change in interests and moods among participants when resolicitation activities occur.

5. *Average gift size.* Fund-raising activities must assess how successful appeals are in raising money as well as in stimulating numbers of participants. Gift size illustrates donors' acceptance with the organization asking for their support and concurrence that the project identified to need money is worthwhile, and identifies them as a group who have money to give. Gift size evaluates the choices of prospect and donor lists used and amounts requested. For example, lists that stimulate a high percentage of replies but result in average gifts of $5 are not efficient. Lists and appeal methods must increase both the percentage of participation and average gift size, because their performance forecasts what these same donors may be expected to do when asked again for their support.

6. *Net income.* The amount of money available to spend on programs and services after expenses represents the net effect of each solicitation activity. This figure is important for fiscal planning. Multiyear experiences can provide reliable evidence of reasonable expectations from continued fund-raising efforts and verify the value of investing in profitable fund-raising methods. Donors also want to know how their funds were spent and the benefits (outcomes) provided the community as a consequence, both of which must be reported to them following the completion of solicitation activities.

7. *Average cost per gift.* This calculation provides a direct answer as to the efficiency for each fund-raising method as well as a planning figure for future solicitation activities. The relationship between average gift size and average cost per gift, which reflects both productivity and profitability, should also be measured.

8. *Cost of fund raising.* The percentage relationship between gross revenue and the expenditures required to achieve it represents a "bottom-line" assessment of effectiveness and efficiency. This figure may be expressed as a percentage (20 percent) or as cost per dollar raised ($0.20). Judgment on performance is likely to be based on this bottom-line figure alone. It is important to be able to explain

what this figure means so that misinterpretation does not occur. Each solicitation activity produces a different cost-benefit figure; weighing direct mail acquisition costs against corporate solicitation is an unfair and misleading comparison, whereas comparing direct mail acquisition with prior solicitation to the same mailing list is most appropriate.

9. *Return.* This is another bottom-line figure representing the relationship between net income and cost to achieve it. This analysis is similar to a return on investment comparison and can be expressed as a percentage reflecting the extent of productivity and profitability achieved by each solicitation method.

The first step is to study the immediate results of each fund-raising method used. A review of gift reports does not take much time and can be valuable to the decision making required throughout the operating year. Second, gift reports should be used to convert the results into a budget request that is tied directly to an estimate of next year's results. To convert gift results into a budget request, begin with the information prepared earlier using Exhibit 6.6 and add all the costs for each fund-raising method used in the current operating year. As a bonus, cost per dollar raised for each program is now provided. (See Exhibit 6.9.) With this data at hand, the final step is to complete a budget worksheet (see Exhibit 6.10) arranged in traditional budget categories matched to the business office and Internal Revenue Service (IRS) Form 990 report formats.

EXHIBIT 6.9 Gift Report of Solicitation Activities with Gift Income Measured against Approved Budget and Actual Expenses (by Program)

Activities	Gift Income	Approved Budget	Actual Expenses	Cost per $ Raised
A. Annual Giving Programs				
Direct mail (acquisition)	$8,030	$10,500	$9,855	$1.23
Direct mail (renewal)	18,010	3,750	3,890	0.22
Membership dues	0	0	0	0
Donor clubs	0	0	0	0
Support groups	0	0	0	0
Telephone gifts	0	0	0	0
Benefit events	2,850	1,800	1,350	0.47
Volunteer-led solicitations	3,675	500	485	0.13
Unsolicited gifts	2,950	0	0	0
Other gifts received	21,500	0	0	0
Subtotal	$57,015	$16,550	$15,580	$0.27
B. Major Giving Programs				
Corporations	$8,500	$20,215	$18,250	$2.15
Foundations	38,800	34,525	33,555	0.86
Individuals	28,525	3,210	3,250	0.11
Special projects	0	0	0	0
Capital campaigns	0	0	0	0
Bequests received	31,500	500	550	0.02
Subtotal	$107,325	$58,450	$55,605	$0.52
Grand total	$164,340	$75,000	$71,185	$0.43

EXHIBIT 6.10 Budget Worksheet for Fund Development Office

	Estimated Budget	Actual Budget	Next Year's Est. Budget
A. Salaries and Benefits			
Director of development	$	$	$
Assistant director			
Office support staff			
Part-time employees			
Temporary workers			
Fringe benefits (—%)			
Vacation/holiday pay (PTO)			
Estimated salary increases			
GROUP A TOTAL:	$	$	$
B. Office Operations			
Office supplies			
Telephone charges			
Telephone equipment			
Rental equipment			
List fees			
Postage fees			
Printing costs			
Books/periodicals			
Travel (trips)			
Travel (local)			
Entertainment			
Awards/plaques			
Dues/memberships			
Conferences			
Insurance			
Office rental/lease			
New equipment			
Equipment maintenance			
Consultant fees			
Services purchased			
Other expenses			
GROUP B TOTAL:	$	$	$
BUDGET TOTAL (A + B):	$	$	$

(B) VOLUNTEER PERFORMANCE

Fund-raising program measurement counts how and where time and money produce results. Next, the most essential ingredient for success, volunteer performance, should be assessed. Volunteers must be evaluated in ways that encourage their continued participation. Assessments must demonstrate where they have been successful and where improvements are possible. Performance evaluation linked to their success in solicitation activities can include all of the following measurements of volunteer effectiveness and efficiency:

1. Number of qualified prospects available
2. Number and percentage of prospects assigned to volunteers
3. Number and percentage of solicitation calls made and gift results (by volunteer and group total)
4. Number of upgraded gifts requested, and results
5. Number of prior donors renewed, and average gift size (by volunteer and group total)
6. Direct costs to support volunteer solicitation
7. Average cost per gift received
8. Cost to solicit any unassigned and unsolicited prospects, and results
9. Total dollars raised, average gift size, and average cost per gift (by volunteer and group total)
10. Overall program costs and results comparison (cost per dollar raised this year and in prior years)

Fund-raising activity and results vary considerably among not-for-profit organizations. Volunteer performances also vary and, among individuals, are hard to compare fairly. Years of experience in fund-raising teaches all of us that volunteers are successful in their commitments of time, energy, and talent. They also share their treasury with us, but their best performances are in seeking out other individuals whom they convert into faithful followers who will join and then succeed them. This function is much more valuable to the organization than their cost-effectiveness alone.

(C) INDIRECT AND OVERHEAD EXPENSES

A vital part of budget preparation is to include the indirect and overhead costs of fund development operations. Up to this point, assessment data has compared actual or direct costs for each of the fund-raising activities with their respective revenue results. There has been no mention of the indirect costs (most of which occur back at the development office) or other operating expenses for support activities. Typically, these costs are for gift processing, data processing, donor record keeping, donor recognition, and a portion of the expenses (salaries and benefits) for employees who do this work. These and other "soft" or "hidden" areas of the cost of fund-raising management (heat, light, rent, insurance, copy machines, computers and software, etc.) may not show up on gift reports, but they should.

Fund raising is a part of every organization's external affairs program to engage the general public. Fund development communications present the organization, its current programs and services, its future plans, and its need for "understanding, participation, and support." The fund development office shares management's goals and objectives for planning, marketing, communications, and public relations, all of which are joined together in the common cause of promoting and advocating the organization's mission. Assessing mission outcomes against indirect expenses and overhead costs is not as simple as measuring newsprint copy or client satisfaction, but there are results that fund raising certainly contributes to, in aiding these goals and objectives.

Murray defined several activities that are directly related to fund raising but are not visible in the list of budget expenses. These include time and dollars spent on identification, screening, introduction, familiarization and understanding, appreciation and commitment, involvement, rating, solicitation, prospect reaction, and organizational reaction.[19] After-gift activities of donor relations, recognition, and reward complete the list of non–income-producing but highly essential activities of any fund development program.

Indirect costs influence overall net results in such areas as the following:

- Time and money spent with volunteers to prepare them to conduct the programs they lead as well as to identify, recruit, train, and evaluate their results
- Time and money spent on prospect and donor research, on meetings and their planning, on gift processing and donor records, and on donor recognition
- Time and money spent on administrative work, such as budget preparation and accounting, gift reports, personnel supervision, and personal and professional training of staff and volunteers
- Time and money spent on office equipment and its maintenance, lighting and heat, rent and lease costs, travel and meals for staff, and entertainment of prospects and donors as well as volunteers
- Time and money spent on community relations, friend raising, overall visibility, and accessibility
- Time or money lost because of a lack of revenue, excessive demands on development staff for other management assignments, or vacations, holidays, and sick time

How are all of these realities of time and money added to the direct costs of raising money? Professional management techniques are required to establish fair and equitable means to add back these "hidden" expense areas to each fund-raising activity and to assign their fair share of cost to every solicitation method, where appropriate. Only with total indirect and overhead costs understood and included in fund-raising assessment will the organization and its leadership fully understand fund development productivity.

(D) COST-EFFECTIVENESS MEASUREMENT

Nick Costa has advocated that each organization create its own comparative reports via these four steps:

---

[19]Murray, *Guaranteed Fund-Raising System,* pp. 266–270.

1. *Defining the purpose of the report and/or the area of fund-raising under study;* . . .
2. *Determining the data necessary to make the comparisons;* . . .
3. *Obtaining the data from internal sources and, as required, external sources such as outside surveys;* . . .
4. *Ensuring that all data is compiled according to a common standard so your comparisons are fair and have integrity.*[20]

Costa also recommended that institutional plans, goals and objectives, and income forecasts be converted into TARGET™ goals that match the nonprofit organization and its environment to the purposes and direction of the fund development program, thus creating the basis for reports on activity as well as criteria for performance evaluation. These TARGET goals are as follows:

T = Targeted to specific fund-raising programs for impact
A = Achievable, given the historical experience of your program
R = Results, or numbers, oriented, and name . . .
G = Group consensus or commitment by your volunteers
E = Executive approval
T = Timetable or deadline for completion[21]

Six cost-effectiveness and productivity measurements should be applied to each fund-raising technique to demonstrate its effectiveness, efficiency, and profitability, as shown in Exhibit 6.11. These tools represent a uniform method to assess each fund-raising activity on its own results. It is commonly accepted today that direct mail acquisition performs at a different cost-benefit level than do benefit events. Equally, capital campaigns should perform with different cost-benefit standards than corporate and foundation solicitations and planned giving programs. Each has its own standard of reasonable cost for cost-benefit measurement. (See Exhibit 6.12.)

(E) REASONABLE COST GUIDELINES

Experience has shown that cost guidelines should be defined for each method of fund raising, to measure individual cost effectiveness and to demonstrate how each has a capacity for increasing its own productivity. The reasonable cost guidelines shown in Exhibit 6.12 have been developed from individual program results and experience at many not-for-profit organizations across America and should be applied to programs after *at least three years* of active operation. The guidelines are considered to reflect the current levels of reasonable performance. They can be improved on when favorable conditions, such as strong leadership, access to wealth, capable volunteers, positive economic conditions, well-managed not-for-profit programs, and quality projects recognized as having significant public benefit, all come together.

---

[20]Costa, *Measuring Progress and Success in Fund Raising*, p. 5.
[21]*Ibid.*

EXHIBIT 6.11 Cost-effectiveness and Productivity Assessments

1. Percentage of Return

   Divide number of gifts received by number
   of solicitations made.

   $$\frac{1,384}{125,000} = 01.1\%$$

2. Average Gift Size

   Divide total contributions received by number
   of gifts received.

   $$\frac{\$272,376}{1,384} = \$196.80$$

3. Average Cost Per Gift

   Divide program fund-raising costs by number
   of gifts received.

   $$\frac{\$45,927}{1,384} = \$33.18$$

4. Program Cost of Fund-Raising Percentage

   Divide program fund-raising costs by total
   contributions received, and multiply by 100.

   $$\frac{\$45,927}{\$272,376} \begin{array}{l} = 0.168 \\ \times\ 100 \\ = 16.86\% \end{array}$$

5. Overall "Bottom Line" Cost of Fund Raising

   Divide total fund-raising costs by total
   contributions received, and multiply by 100.

   $$\frac{\$325,440}{\$1,720,000} \begin{array}{l} = 0.1892 \\ \times\ 100 \\ = 18.9\% \end{array}$$

6. Net Income Return

   Divide total net income by total fund-raising
   costs, and multiply by 100.

   $$\frac{\$1,394,560}{\$325,440} \begin{array}{l} = 4.285 \\ \times\ 100 \\ = 428\% \end{array}$$

Measurement of each fund-raising program also verifies how its results can aid the performance of other programs; all contribute to one another in some fashion. Time and money required by volunteers and staff to support various annual giving programs year after year remain valid expenses, because finding new donors and renewing and upgrading prior donors must continue. Bigger gifts are possible in time, but they are not likely to arrive unless time and money first are invested in developing qualified donors and prospects through effective and efficient annual giving programs.

What should be the bottom-line cost for total fund-raising performance? Because organizations vary in how they conduct fund raising and because fund raising does not perform the same for every organization, there is no single number or percentage for all to salute and observe. The Council of Better Business Bureaus, Inc. suggested that fund-raising costs should not exceed 35 percent of related contributions.[22] The United States

---

[22]Council of Better Business Bureaus, Inc., *Standards for Charitable Solicitations* (Arlington, Va.: Council of Better Business Bureaus, 1982).

EXHIBIT 6.12 Reasonable Fund-raising Cost Guidelines

Direct mail acquisition	$1.00 to $1.25 per $1.00 raised
Direct mail renewal	$0.20 per $1.00 raised
Membership organization	$0.25 per $1.00 raised
Groups, guilds, and support group organizations	$0.25 per $1.00 raised
Donor Club program	$0.20 per $1.00 raised
Benefit events	$0.50 per $1.00 raised
Volunteer-led annual giving	$0.10 to $0.20 per $1.00 raised
Corporations and foundations	$0.20 per $1.00 raised
Individual major gift programs	$0.10 to $0.20 per $1.00 raised
Capital campaigns	$0.10 to $0.20 per $1.00 raised
Planned giving/estate planning	$0.20 to $0.30 per $1.00 raised

Source: *James M. Greenfield,* Fund-Raising Cost Effectiveness: A Self-Assessment Workbook *(New York: John Wiley & Sons, 1996), p. 281; James M. Greenfield, "Accountability, Program Performance, and Profitability." Part I: "How to Assess Fund-Raising Program Performance,"* AHP Journal *(Spring 1994): 17–25; Part II: "Comparative Analysis, Profitability, and Forecasting,"* AHP Journal *(Fall 1994): 21–30. Norman S. Fink and Howard C. Metzler,* The Costs and Benefits of Planned Giving *(New York: Columbia University Press, 1982).*

Supreme Court, in the 1980s, delivered three major decisions—*Schaumburg v. Citizens for a Better Environment,* 444 U.S. 618 (1080); *Maryland Secretary of State v. Joseph H. Munson Co.,* 467 U.S. 947 (1984); *Riley v. National Federation of the Blind of North Carolina, Inc.,* 108 S. Ct. 2667 (1988)—on this question, prohibiting any enforcement of fund raising based on an administrative percentage.[23]

Is there any answer? Yes. It is reasonable to compare the results of each fund-raising method with its own cost guidelines. The comparison is helpful for mature, well-balanced programs (those with several fund-raising methods in place for at least three years or more), but it is a bit unfair to expect such performance the very first time a method is used. It is reasonable to use an overall guideline of 35 percent ($0.65 of every dollar given goes for charitable purposes), but that performance is not to be expected for a new organization or one that has just begun fund raising. The best guideline may be stated thus: Too much emphasis on less efficient forms of fund raising (direct mail and benefit events) will push average costs upward to 50 percent. What is recommended is a balanced program with some concentration on major and planned gifts, to keep costs down while building a pyramid of future leaders and future donors of size.

The flip side to all these assessments is the use of these same measurement tools to forecast future gift revenue. Too much microanalysis of prior results can mask the results predicted as reliable future income. Fiscal planning should place high value on accurate forecasts of likely contributions revenue, especially when developed from uniform measurement tools with reasonable cost guidelines. When fund development results are added to the balance of data developed from all the other assessment areas presented in this chapter, including environment, development department operations, development planning (feasibility) study, mission, and management, the organization's path for the future can be drawn with much greater accuracy and confidence.

---

[23]Bruce R. Hopkins, *The Law of Fund Raising* (New York: John Wiley & Sons, 1994), pp. 45–46, 489.

Suggested Readings

American Association of Fund-Raising Counsel. *Giving USA.* New York: AAFRC Trust for Philanthropy, 2000.

Anthony, Robert M., and Regina Herzlinger. "Management Control in Nonprofit Organizations," unpublished study, Harvard Graduate School of Business Administration, Cambridge, Mass., 1984.

Berendt, Robert J., and J. Richard Taft. *How to Rate Your Development Office.* Washington, D.C.: Taft Corporation, 1983.

Costa, Nick B. *Measuring Progress and Success in Fund Raising: How to Use Comparative Statistics to Prove Your Effectiveness.* Falls Church, Va.: Association for Healthcare Philanthropy, 1991.

Council of Better Business Bureaus, Inc. *Standards for Charitable Solicitations.* Arlington, Va.: Council of Business Bureaus, 1982.

Drucker, Peter F. *Managing the Nonprofit Organization: Practices and Principles.* New York: HarperCollins, 1990.

Eisenberg, Pablo. "Why We Know So Little About Philanthropy." *Chronicle of Philanthropy* (17 December 1991): 37–38.

Fink, Norman S., and Howard C. Metzler. *The Costs and Benefits of Deferred Giving.* New York: Columbia University Press, 1982.

Greenfield, James M. "Accountability, Program Performance and Profitability." Part I: "How to Assess Fund-Raising Program Performance." *AHP Journal* (Spring 1994): 17–25.

———. "Comparative Analysis, Profitability, and Forecasting." *AHP Journal* (Fall 1994), 21–30.

———. *Fund-Raising: Evaluating and Managing the Fund Development Process.* New York: John Wiley & Sons, 1999.

———. *Fund Raising Cost Effectiveness: A Self-Assessment Workbook.* New York: John Wiley & Sons, 1996.

Grenzebach, John, and associates. *Prerequisites for Provable Campaign Success Investigated by a John Grenzebach and Associates Feasibility Development Study.* Corporate report. Chicago, Ill.: Author, 1986.

Hopkins, Bruce R. *The Law of Fund Raising.* 2d ed. New York: John Wiley & Sons, 1994.

———. *The Law of Tax-Exempt Organizations,* 2d ed. New York: John Wiley & Sons, 1999.

———. *A Legal Guide to Starting and Managing a Nonprofit Organization.* New York: John Wiley & Sons, 1993.

Independent Sector. *Daring Goals for a Caring Society: A Blueprint for Substantial Growth in Giving and Volunteering in America.* Washington, D.C.: Author, 1986.

Lane, Frederick S. "Enhancing the Quality of Public Reporting by Nonprofit Organizations." *The Philanthropy Monthly* (July 1991): 3–38. Reprint of Report of the Nonprofit Quality Reporting Project, Baruch College/The City University of New York.

Lindahl, Wesley A. *Strategic Planning for Fund Raising.* San Francisco: Jossey-Bass, 1992.

Lippincott, Earle, and Elling Aannestad. "Management of Voluntary Welfare Agencies." *Harvard Business Review* (November/December 1964): 87–88.

Martin, Del. "The Development Audit: Providing the Blue Print for a Better Fund-Raising Program." *AFP Journal* (Autumn 1990): 28.

Mixer, Joseph R. *Principles of Professional Fundraising.* San Francisco: Jossey-Bass, 1993.

Murray, Dennis J. *The Guaranteed Fund-Raising System: A Systems Approach to Planning and Controlling Fund Raising.* Boston: American Institute of Management, 1987.

New, Anne L., with Wilson C. Levis. *Raise More Money for Your Nonprofit Organization: A Guide to Evaluating and Improving Your Fundraising.* New York: The Foundation Center, 1991.

Schmaedick, Gerald L. *Cost-Effectiveness in the Nonprofit Sector.* Westport, Conn.: Quorum Books, 1993.

Seymour, Harold J. *Designs for Fund-Raising.* New York: McGraw-Hill, 1966; 2d ed. (paperback): Ambler, Pa.: The Fund Raising Institute, 1988.

Smith, Bucklin, and associates. *The Complete Guide to Nonprofit Management*, 2d edited by Robert H. Wilbur, Susan Kudla Finn, and Carolyn M. Freeland. New York: John Wiley & Sons, 2000.

Warwick, Mal. The Five Strategies for Fundraising Success: A Mission-Based Guide to Achieving Your Goals. San Francisco: Jossey-Bass, 1999.

Webster, George D. *The Law of Associations.* New York: Matthew Bender, 1965.

Weisbrod, Burton A. *The Nonprofit Economy.* Cambridge, Mass.: Harvard University Press, 1988.

Accountability: Delivering Community Benefits

James M. Greenfield, ACFRE, FAHP
Hoag Memorial Hospital Presbyterian

(d) Community Relations
(e) Donor Relations
(f) Measurable Outcomes
(g) Forecasting Future Gift Income
(h) Setting Performance Standards
(i) Community Benefits

7.6 Demonstrating Community Benefits
(a) Accreditation
(b) Advocacy of the Cause
(c) Disclosure (Open and Full)
(d) Effectiveness and Efficiency
(e) Enhancement of Public Confidence and Trust
(f) Enhancement of Image and Reputation
(g) Indigent Care
(h) Productivity Analysis and Proof of Profitability
(i) Quality Reporting
(j) Ethical Behavior
(k) Stewardship

7.7 Conclusion: Public Perceptions of Accountability
(a) Success as Measured by Donors
(b) Success as Measured by Volunteer Solicitors
(c) Success as Measured by Not-for-Profit Organizations
(d) Success as Measured by Fund-raising Staff

Suggested Readings

7.1 *Introduction*

The primary objective of not-for-profit accountability is to demonstrate to the community what are the quantifiable outcomes and benefits its citizens received in exchange for their personal support of not-for-profit organizations as advocates, donors, and volunteers. Among all the criteria to be examined in this chapter, the key word in all cases will be *quantifiable*. This must be true for the mission, operations, and management as well as for program and service outcomes, all of which contribute to the organization's ability to demonstrate, with measurable results, actual quantifiable benefits delivered back to the community. These documented benefits are needed by each organization to be able to retain its prized privileges as a not-for-profit, tax-exempt public benefit corporation—exemptions from federal and state income, sales and property taxes, plus qualification for the charitable contribution deduction for all gifts and contributions received.

Evaluation of all these areas is required to quantify performance but this work is not easy nor is there an acceptable set of uniform standards to be measured against. These measurements also must go beyond effectiveness and efficiency; they must be credible evaluations. Increasingly, the reasons are that general public and funding sources require reports of measured outcomes. Some organizations perform evaluations to measure for themselves how their programs and services are performing to learn if they are working or making any difference in the lives or the communities being served. Others study performance in order to improve program planning. Some debate exists around who should perform these assessments. The options include current staff, board members, outside consultants, stakeholders along with some of the above, and all of the above.[1]

(A)   NEED FOR OUTCOMES THAT MEASURE COMMUNITY BENEFITS

In general, there is evidence that the public holds its not-for-profit organizations in high esteem. This image and reputation has been built on a framework established most by older organizations achieved over time as good community citizens whose conduct was blameless. Beginning in the 1980s, organizations began to be asked pointed questions about their fund-raising performance, such as "How much money have you raised?" and "What were your fund-raising costs?" plus "How do these costs compare with those of other organizations?" As the 1990s ended, new questions were added as a result of highly publicized scandals and abuses by a few not-for-profit executives (e.g., James Bakker, William Aramony, and William Bennett) who used the money raised improperly, were found guilty, and went to jail.

The public's reaction has been to demand more accountability, especially regarding financial operations. The Taxpayer Relief Act of 1996 established two new principles to answer this demand. The first was increased access to and disclosure of information contained on Internal Revenue Service (IRS) Form 990, including its posting on the Internet. The second was "intermediate sanctions," a penalty short of withdrawal of tax-exempt status. This new law was armed with stiff monetary penalties for not-for-profit boards and executives to increase their accountability to the public. These efforts got the attention they deserved but fell short by failing to provide measurement guidelines to analyze the results achieved by programs and services provided by not-for-profit organizations.

(B)   THE "CIRCLE OF ACCOUNTABILITY"

Results are the required data that demonstrate the "circle of accountability" for every not-for-profit organization. (See Exhibit 7.1.) This circle begins with the statement of the organization's mission and vision that is based on periodic assessments of community needs and answers to the question "Why do we exist?" Next, strategic plans are prepared to define the programs and services plus the budget required to address these needs. Fund-raising goals are communicated widely inviting the public to help to achieve these needs and to answer "What's the money for?" The organization executes these priorities through rigorous application of resources to its programs and services in its annual operations. Management of these operations results in outcomes that can be measured and reported as quantifiable benefits delivered back to the community, to complete the circle.

---

[1] Allison H. Fine, Colette E. Thayer, and Anne T. Coghlan. "Program Evaluation Practice in the Non-profit Sector," *Nonprofit Management & Leadership*, 10, no. 3 (Spring 2000): 331–339.

EXHIBIT 7.1　Circle of Accountability

Outcomes
Measurement

Mission

Programs
& Services

Operations

Stewardship

Management

Fund Raising

Another challenging issue raised by the demand for more accountability is the presumption that valid comparisons can be made between like organizations based on their performance. This analysis is particularly dangerous. "If assessing mission accomplishment for a particular organization is difficult, then comparing the extent of mission accomplishment across different types of NPOs [nonprofit organizations] is impossible. How could the mission achievements of women's shelters and at-risk youth development organizations be fairly or objectively compared?"[2]

Not only are organizations not alike in how they do their work to accomplish their mission, but they also are not alike in how they practice fund raising. Further, fund raising does not perform the same for every organization. An example is the use of one year's fund-raising results in a "bottom-line" analysis for setting next year's goals. An organization that received $750,000 one year (thanks to three bequests worth a total of $150,000) at a budget cost of $125,000 or a cost-benefit ratio of 16.6 percent or $0.166 to raise $1.00 looks quite efficient. In reality, this budget was spent only to raise $600,000 in actual gifts and contributions; no expense was needed for the three bequest donors who made their estate decisions years earlier without the organization's knowledge. To assume, based on "bottom-line" results of $750,000, that the same result could be repeated and even exceeded could lead to a serious misunderstanding and misinterpretation of performance. The same solicitation programs could produce another $600,000 or perhaps $625,000 at a cost of $125,000 again, a more reasonable evaluation. No one should assume that more unknown bequests for another $150,000 will arrive on schedule. Such a result is not in the hands of the organization and its fund-raising team.

---

[2]Robert D. Herman and David O. Renz, "Nonprofit Organizational Effectiveness: Contracts Between Especially Effective and Less Effective Organizations," *Nonprofit Management & Leadership,* 9, no. 1 (Fall 1998): p. 24.

This level of scrutiny of the facts and an attempt to understand actual results in all areas of the "circle of accountability" is required to accomplish measurable outcomes to be reported to the public. Credibility is a major issue in accountability. The public is correct to demand expertise as well as accuracy by not-for-profit organizations in their analysis and reports of performance. To conduct an examination of each area of not-for-profit operations and management, begin with analysis of the mission statement.

7.2 Mission Statement: Review and Measurements

To be incorporated as a voluntary, not-for-profit public benefit corporation, an institution or agency must fulfill both state and federal legal requirements. It must have an appropriate legal form, fulfill a "charitable" purpose, receive tax-exempt status, conduct day-to-day operations within legal requirements, and complete annual public reporting requirements. Several areas of mission assessment are readily available (see Exhibit 7.2).

Not-for-profit organizations do not stand alone in their mission to provide programs and services for the public good, nor are they alone in their need to ask for and to receive a share of public support in the forms of time, talent, and treasure. The Independent Sector, in its mission to aid all not-for-profit organizations to benefit the public good, defined a program of "measurable growth" as a national objective. To this end, Independent Sector developed the following checklist, which defines what voluntary organizations can do and what benefits they can achieve from growth. The 10 recommendations that follow can serve the board of directors as a checklist for performance of both mission achievement and organization management:

1. *The Board should set fund raising goals for next year and five years that are realistic, but which stretch the Board and everyone else in the organization. . . .*
2. *The Board must commit a significant portion of the resources of the organization, including their own time, to the pursuit of the fund raising goals. For*

EXHIBIT 7.2 Assessment Criteria for the Mission

	Score				
	Low				**High**
1. Fulfills a "charitable" purpose.	1	2	3	4	5
2. Completes annual public reporting requirements.	1	2	3	4	5
3. Provides high quality of service.	1	2	3	4	5
4. Offers accessibility to service.	1	2	3	4	5
5. Increases public awareness of the cause.	1	2	3	4	5
6. Addresses five advocacy measurements.	1	2	3	4	5
7. Adequately uses audits and auditors.	1	2	3	4	5
8. Is financially accountable.	1	2	3	4	5
9. Stimulates innovative ideas.	1	2	3	4	5
10. Provides programs of value to the public.	1	2	3	4	5
11. Develops new leadership.	1	2	3	4	5
12. Is guided by written policies and procedures.	1	2	3	4	5

MEDIAN SCORE

most organizations, it will take a minimum of 20 percent of the organization's time and money to develop significant fund raising thrust. This is fully justified if, in the long run, the organization will be able to do more in the fulfillment of its program mission. . . .

3. *Similar goals and commitments should be made for increased volunteer participation. . . .*

4. *The Board should devote a portion of almost every meeting and at least one full meeting to evaluating progress toward the goals. It should resolve to make these goals central to everything the organization does. . . .*

5. *Make fund raising and the effective utilization of volunteers every bit as important and prestigious as the most important program activities of the organization. . . .*

6. *Encourage the Board and staff to participate in training efforts to improve fund raising skills and effectiveness in recruiting and involving volunteers. Where necessary, help create such training opportunities by working with experienced and successful volunteer and staff leaders from other organizations. . . .*

7. *The organization's communications to current volunteers, members, contributors and others should emphasize the message of "fiving" and the importance of all people being engaged in active citizenship and personal community service. Pay first attention to those who are already involved. They offer the greatest potential for increased participation. . . .*

8. *Help to develop a local coalition of churches, other volunteer organizations, funders, media and others to build interest and awareness of "fiving" and a spirit of contributing back to the community through support of the causes of one's choice. . . .*

9. *Honor the strong contributors and volunteers. Make it clear that the organization is aware and appreciative of how special they are. . . .*

10. *Elevate the good volunteers and fund raisers to the Board. Make it clear that their performance is what the organization respects.*[3]

Beyond these assessment areas are hard questions that need solid answers to determine the vitality of a not-for-profit organization. "Building a non-profit's capacity to carry out its mission, develop leaders, insure accountability, handle conflicts of interest, recruit new and young staff members, maintain good relations with clients and community, and plan programs that will have a serious impact—these are the key issues that need scrutiny but have largely been ignored."[4]

What standards against mission should not-for-profit organizations observe? Should they be judged only by those criteria that allow them to retain their privileges of tax exemption? Should an organization be willing to be judged on how it has served its mission, whom it has served (and how many), and its public benefit (making a measurable difference)? Has it increased its accessibility beyond those to whom it provides services? Has it increased public awareness of the cause it represents and the value of its role to

---

[3]Independent Sector, *Daring Goals for a Caring Society: A Blueprint for Substantial Growth in Giving and Volunteering in America* (Washington, D.C.: Independent Sector, 1986), pp. 11–12.
[4]Pablo Eisenberg, "Why We Know So Little About Philanthropy," *Chronicle of Philanthropy* (17 December 1991): pp. 37–38.

achieve results that are of benefit to the community? In response to these questions, five areas of mission, discussed in the following sections, are suggested.

(A)   ADVOCACY

Advocacy is an important assignment in every not-for-profit organization, even if it conducts a self-serving program to enhance its own image and reputation and to inspire public gift support. Advocacy is measured by:

- The number of legislative and regulatory changes realized
- The number and frequency of advertising pieces
- The number and frequency of mass communications (public relations), messages, and materials circulated
- Growth in the number of members and their contributions
- Market research to document altered public perceptions

(B)   FINANCIAL ACCOUNTABILITY

Too often, boards of directors and management staff give attention only to financial measurements tied to budget reviews and to completion of the fiscal year with a break-even objective or a minimum deficit. The fiscal mission of some not-for-profit organizations is to achieve an "excess of revenue over expenses" (profit) in order to secure greater financial stability and to fund current and future programs with these resources. Is that sufficient to preserve their privileged tax-exempt status?

The requirement to prepare, review, and approve the annual audit statement is often given only one brief period of scrutiny. After the auditor's analysis is reported, the audit is often set aside as an exercise of historical value rather than an instrument for continuous use in financial planning and performance evaluation.

Financial accountability is possibly the most frequently used method of assessment of not-for-profit organizations, although others may serve as standards for comparison and self-analysis. The Council of Better Business Bureaus, in its *Standards for Charitable Solicitations,* concentrates on five areas: public accountability, use of funds, solicitations and information materials, fund-raising practices, and governance.[5] The Council conducts evaluations of several not-for-profit organizations each year in its "watchdog" capacity and publishes the results of its assessment. Failure to meet these criteria can mean disqualification for corporation and foundation grants as well as a potential for diminished giving from the general public.

Other areas of assessment merit mention to not-for-profit organizations and the public. "Such matters as who benefits from philanthropy, equity in grant making, philanthropic access and accountability, ethical problems, governance, the financing of public policy and advocacy activities, innovation and risk taking in philanthropy, . . . have been, not surprisingly, overlooked or neglected."[6]

---

[5]Council of Better Business Bureaus, *Standards for Charitable Solicitations.*
[6]Eisenberg, "Why We Know So Little About Philanthropy," pp. 37–38.

(C) CHARITABLE PURPOSE

Charitable purpose, while always implied, can stand regular review. In 1985 the Supreme Court of Utah found the difference between a for-profit and a not-for-profit hospital to be "indistinguishable" in making a determination as to whether the not-for-profit hospital should pay any property taxes (*County Board of Equalization of Utah County v. Intermountain Health Care, Inc.*, 709 P.2d 265 [Sup. Ct. Utah 1985]). Tax-exemption challenges, "commerciality tests," and community benefit tests are complicated issues and already represent a serious threat to the not-for-profit status of every institution and agency. Not-for-profit organizations are, by nature and law, quite distinguishable from for-profit business corporations. Yet if they must now prove in the courts their validity for retaining their exemptions, as it appears they must, these special privileges could be lost.

Part of the American tradition in fostering voluntary action has been as a substitute for direct government support. Given greater freedoms of expression and reinforced by tax-exempt privileges, not-for-profit organizations have as their mission the implied duty to consider change, to stimulate and initiate innovative ideas, and to add programs of increased value and benefit to the public. How well have they fulfilled this duty? Boards of directors and management should evaluate their own performance in providing public leadership and innovation and should assess their ability to be an influence in meeting changing community needs in advance of legal challenges.

(D) LEADERSHIP DEVELOPMENT

Although public participation and public support are obvious ingredients for the current and future success of every not-for-profit organization, they are more vital than just part-time assistance where and when needed. The strength of each not-for-profit organization is leadership, which is vested in the composition and membership of its board of directors. Without constant attention and a commitment to developing present and future leaders, an organization will soon stagnate and wither. Board members and other volunteers are proof to the public that they can entrust their money and their confidence to the organization. The role of volunteers must be well defined, their time and expertise must be recognized and accepted, and their contributions must be rewarded. These are all easily measurable outcomes.

(E) WRITTEN POLICIES AND PROCEDURES

Much more than a book of rules, an organization's written policies and procedures are guidelines for daily operations that assist both volunteers and employees in their joint efforts to achieve the mission of the organization and to do so within well-defined and easily measurable purposes, goals, and objectives. Assessment of performance against policies and procedures is the easiest of measurements to accomplish with regularity. Along with the work required to prepare and maintain such documents, the bonus often is a consensus that knits everyone together toward the common purposes defined in the mission statement.

7.3 *Environmental Audit for Operations*

Many of the annual operating areas of not-for-profit organizations can be influenced by the external environment, which will also have an effect on fund-raising results. This section reviews 16 environmental factors that affect management operations and provides a mix of qualitative and quantitative criteria for assessment of progress in meeting the mission, purposes, goals, and objectives of the not-for-profit organization. Environmental audits paint a much different portrait for each not-for-profit organization; each has a unique mission and is no more the same in how it performs daily operations than it is in how it conducts fund raising. Operating areas do not perform in the same way for every organization. These 16 environmental criteria (arranged alphabetically, for convenience) can be scored as low to high on a scale of 1 to 5 (see Exhibit 7.3) to help identify those that may have a greater influence on the organization's potential to raise money and to fulfill its mission.

(A) AGING OF THE POPULATION

Population growth impacts nearly every area of society, and older citizens are society's fastest growing segment. Older citizens require increased support from government, business, and community programs and have high expectations for attention and service as well as for respect. Organizations whose programs and services for the elderly entitle them to financial reimbursement from government sources will find those sources of payment continually limited and shrinking, an experience already felt by the seniors themselves. Seniors are resources to not-for-profit organizations for leadership, volunteerism, and gift support, but they are likely to give first of their "time, talent and treasure" where

EXHIBIT 7.3 Environmental Audit for Operations

	Score				
	Low				High
1. Aging of the Population	1	2	3	4	5
2. Debt Financing	1	2	3	4	5
3. Coalitions, Mergers, and Acquisitions	1	2	3	4	5
4. Costs of Supplies and Services	1	2	3	4	5
5. Disclosure	1	2	3	4	5
6. Ethics and Professionalism	1	2	3	4	5
7. Financial Conditions	1	2	3	4	5
8. Globalization	1	2	3	4	5
9. Government Regulation	1	2	3	4	5
10. Leadership Development	1	2	3	4	5
11. Management Competency	1	2	3	4	5
12. Pressure for Cash	1	2	3	4	5
13. Profitability	1	2	3	4	5
14. Public Confidence	1	2	3	4	5
15. Technology	1	2	3	4	5
16. Wages and Benefits	1	2	3	4	5

MEDIAN SCORE

their relationships are strongest—the organizations they have supported throughout their lifetimes.

(B) DEBT FINANCING

Financial pressure in daily operations requires not-for-profit organizations to examine every possible source of increased revenue while maximizing the use of funds held and containing expenses. Alternative revenue sources to help achieve fiscal stability include: (1) an excess of revenue over expenses from the operating budget, (2) entrepreneurial for-profit enterprises, (3) investment earnings from endowment and other reserves, (4) cash from fund raising, and (5) debt financing. Management should exhaust its use of the first four options before considering any borrowing decisions. It is worth noting that nearly half of these are fund-raising options (3 and 4). Organizations that qualify for tax-exempt bond financing for major capital and equipment projects (a tempting solution) soon learn that debt financing increases annual operating costs and results in seriously limited financial flexibility for many years to come.

(C) COALITIONS, MERGERS, AND ACQUISITIONS

The merits of joint ventures become all the more attractive when competition, fiscal limitations, market forces, and other factors close in and cause the board and management to be concerned with the viability of the organization itself. Mergers and acquisitions are management strategies that should be considered to achieve improvements in community service as well as to ensure survival or control over market share. The public can be confused and even alarmed when too many duplicate services appear to be offered, especially when all of them are active in seeking public participation and support for what appear to be the same goals and objectives. Not-for-profit organizations should coordinate and cooperate wherever possible; joint ventures without a threat of merger or acquisition will be well received by the public, who expect the leaders of not-for-profit organizations to collaborate to resolve community problems, not compound them.

(D) COSTS OF SUPPLIES AND SERVICES

The costs of the goods and services that not-for-profit organizations have to buy for day-to-day operations are increasing each year. With good management, delivery of programs and services can sometimes be contained within available resources, but rising expenses exert pressure on operating budgets and can cause reductions in the extent of programs and services offered. Hard decisions will be forced on boards and management as they try to balance their commitment to provide public services against fiscal restraints. Any reduction by one institution or agency only seems to transfer its burden to others that already share the same restraints.

(E) DISCLOSURE

Not-for-profit organizations are public corporations. They are required to share information about programs and services offered (including their outcomes), management

PART I

MANAGING FUND DEVELOPMENT

practices, and financial affairs. Several areas of operation, including the organization's annual tax return (IRS Form 990), are required by law to be included in reports made to federal, state, county, and city governments and to the public on request. Open and full disclosure should be the policy and attitude of every organization's board and management, but many organizations are uncomfortable with this obligation—not because they are engaged in illegal or illicit practices, but because they believe their decisions, based on complex issues in areas largely unknown to the public, will not be understood or appreciated and therefore will be subject to criticism and the potential for withdrawn support. Those who cannot overcome their hesitancy about the need for disclosure may next become targets of suspicion, with a decline in public confidence and support a distinct possibility.

(F) ETHICS AND PROFESSIONALISM

Media reports of scandals and abuse harm public confidence and trust in every not-for-profit organization. Ethical behavior should be inherent in the policies and decisions of the board and management, not a tactic to escape media attention or to evade public criticism. Not-for-profit organizations are called to a higher standard of stewardship in order to merit the special privileges their tax-exempt status allows. Their actions should always meet or exceed these higher standards rather than only minimally satisfy the requirements that preserve tax status. Areas of behavior to be avoided include personal conflicts of interest by board members and employees, questionable investments, inhumane treatment of clients, improper use of funds raised (especially for personal inurement), expensive and inefficient fund-raising practices, failure to meet legal requirements, and similar offenses.

(G) FINANCIAL CONDITIONS

The overinflated U.S. economy and financial situation of the federal, state, and local governments will be the most influential driving forces in the day-to-day decisions of every sector of the country during this decade. General economic conditions remain the dominant economic force in this new century and have an ever-expanding effect on the nation and the world. Despite enormous stock market gains with frenzied rises and falls, there is the belief that until government spending at all levels can achieve a balance between public needs and public revenues, any relief measures will be short-term policy decisions. Their impact on every not-for-profit organization will affect the extent of dependence on government funding, the continuation of the privileges of income, sales, and property tax exemptions, and the preservation of the charitable contribution deduction for donors.

(H) GLOBALIZATION

Barriers between nations have all but disappeared in most parts of the world, suggesting that globalization is becoming a reality. How will this movement affect America's not-for-profit organizations and their mission? The concept of philanthropy is spreading rapidly throughout the world as the merits of voluntary association to effect solutions are accepted and replicated. Not-for-profit organizations will feel the effects of a chang-

162

ing world marketplace. Are they prepared for change as an opportunity? Change offers everyone an opportunity to reexamine their original mission statement in response to a changing world.

(I) GOVERNMENT REGULATION

Government law provides the tax-exempt privileges currently enjoyed by not-for-profit organizations and legitimizes the actions of those who support them. Changing laws and regulations can have enormous impact on not-for-profit organizations that the government now advocates and enhances with tax deductions. Some hold that not-for-profit organizations are an extension of the government's own duty to provide public programs and services. Because of this opinion, any proposals to reduce tax-exempt benefits and privileges are considered a serious threat, even when disguised as a solution to government's own larger problems. Desperate times can produce desperate ideas and can challenge even well-established principles and traditions. Not-for-profit organizations can protect themselves by organizing their supporters to respond to harmful proposals. New lobbying regulations may limit the extent of this action and may weaken the efforts of all who are threatened, with the result that charitable organizations are at risk for their fundamental privileges.

(J) LEADERSHIP DEVELOPMENT

Every not-for-profit organization should assess its leadership strengths and resolve the size, talents, cultural diversity, and other components necessary for its maximum use of volunteers. Failure to attend to leadership development will limit success and progress. No one should expect that other organizations will identify, recruit, train, retain, and otherwise develop future leaders and then make them available to competitors. Leaders are often initiated into the life of an organization through active volunteerism in the fund-raising program by personal giving, willingness to recruit gifts from others, and other voluntary roles. Volunteers often have multiple experiences with many organizations, but they must learn their role anew each time they serve, because the needs for their services are likely to be as different as the several organizations they join.

(K) MANAGEMENT COMPETENCY

Not-for-profit organizations require competent executives to lead and to supervise their operations. It is the duty of the board of directors to recruit, hire, supervise, evaluate, and dismiss senior managers. Gone are the days when individuals who were marginally successful in the business world could find a safe haven for their talents in the not-for-profit world (although that image remains prevalent). Not-for-profit management is different from other business management and requires different skills and training. Evaluation criteria can include traditional areas of planning, quality of services rendered, employment practices, and financial success. A few areas that are unique to not-for-profit management—directing volunteers, advocacy, and engaging in fund raising—can also be considered for measurement.

(L) PRESSURE FOR CASH

Every not-for-profit organization must finance its annual operations as a first priority, which places the dominant pressure on its revenue sources to meet current expenses. Managers can achieve cost-effective success in providing programs and services, but there is constant pressure for extra cash for expansion, renovation, equipment replacement, employee training, research, indigent care, and much more. It may be true that not-for-profit organizations can spend every dime they receive, but they also must be run by good financial managers who observe professional fiscal policies. The pressure for cash results more from the insistence of the public's needs for increased programs and services, for improved quality and quantity, and for the addition of new technology and modern facilities. Such pressures and hard choices affect long-range and strategic plans for programs and services as well as finances and facilities, which must remain flexible to meet the unseen and unmet needs of society. Pressure for cash also affects fund-raising operations by diverting attention away from developing lasting relationships for reliable gift income in the future, to "pocket change" of the moment.

(M) PROFITABILITY

Success in business is measured as profits. Not-for-profit organizations can achieve "profits" in their operating budget, but no person may enjoy any personal share in the excess; it can only be applied to further programs and services defined in the mission. Public understanding of both profits and deficits by not-for-profit organizations is often limited and tends to be expressed as judgments of management ability, board competency, and the like. Assessment of profitability can evaluate management and financial expertise alongside quality of programs and quantity of services provided. Management and financial success comes from following professional management practices, including attention to alternate revenue sources such as fund-raising. Any "excess of revenues over expenses" will often be used to improve programs and services provided to the public. These funds can also be applied to improve management capability, to fund depreciation, to improve physical plant and equipment, to conduct planning and market research, to train staff, and to satisfy other essential decisions that will increase the organization's ability to manage for its future with increased competence and quality.

(N) PUBLIC CONFIDENCE

The public's trust in an organization's name and reputation for commitment to its mission can and should be measured by its actions to achieve that mission. Failure in public confidence and trust will do more than damage reputation. The loss of public confidence in the quality of the public programs and services offered will cause people to hesitate to seek the organization's services, decline to serve on its board, and decide against making contributions.

(O) TECHNOLOGY

As technological advances continue at a rapid pace, society expects to see such modernization appropriately transferred to not-for-profit organizations. The pressure to add technology brings higher costs for new equipment, new and more expensive employees, maintenance, space, and other necessities. An example of the effects of technology is seen in health care, where science and technology yield better medical care but at an increased cost to the consumer where the benefits of improved quality clash with higher costs of patient care. To assess the impact of technology is to assess judgment in equipment selection, competitive pricing, group purchasing, maintenance contracts, alternative financial options, adjustments in charges after reimbursement analysis, and other business decisions.

(P) WAGES AND BENEFITS

Employees are not volunteers; they require salaries, benefits, and retirement plans that are nearly competitive with those in private businesses. Management decisions on the extent and cost of employee benefits must meet full legal requirements and aid in recruitment and retention of individuals who have the expertise necessary to provide quality programs and services. Inflation, local cost-of-living adjustments, cost of facilities, and cost of equipment and systems are factors that affect success in employee relations.

7.4 Assessment Criteria for Management

Management skill within not-for-profit organizations has grown extensively in the past two decades. No doubt there remain instances in which boards and managers practice inefficiency, laxity, indifference, and complacency, but their numbers are shrinking. Any organization at any time may fall short in one or another management area, but most are increasingly alert to the need to improve their internal management skills and are committed to do so within their means. They are also more willing to acknowledge their weaknesses, an important step toward improvement.

Business executives often make up the majority of voluntary board members of not-for-profit organizations. Trained to demonstrate success by measurement of corporate bottom-line profits, these individuals erroneously tend to use the same measurements for not-for-profit organizations. One result has been criticism of the management ability of not-for-profit executives, as in the following analysis:

All organizations use inputs to produce outputs. An organization's effectiveness is measured by the extent to which outputs accomplish its objectives, and its efficiency is measured by the relationship between inputs and outputs. In a profit-oriented organization the amount of profit provides an overall measure of both effectiveness and efficiency. In many nonprofit organizations, however, outputs cannot be measured to quantitative terms. . . . The absence of a satisfactory, single, overall measure of performance that is comparable to the profit measure is the most serious management control problem in a nonprofit organization.[7]

[7]Robert M. Anthony and Regina Herzlinger, "Management Control in Nonprofit Organizations" (unpublished study, Harvard Graduate School of Business Administration, Cambridge, Mass., 1984).

Several areas of assessment of the management function have universal standards for measurement (see Exhibit 7.4). Voluntary accreditation reviews are performed for several groups of not-for-profit organization, such as colleges and universities, hospitals, and museums. Standards of accounting used for audit preparation measure and report financial performance against criteria established by the Financial Accounting Standards Board (FASB) and the American Institute of Certified Public Accountants (AICPA). Equally known, but without any comparative standard beyond compliance, are the annual reports filed with the Internal Revenue Service and the individual states. IRS Form 990 is used by both federal and state authorities to monitor select areas of annual performance. This data is now being tabulated in a few states that publish summaries. A study led by Professor Frederick S. Lane at Baruch College/The City University of New York, found that among not-for-profit organizations that file IRS Form 990, the annual returns were "often incomplete and/or inaccurate," limiting their usefulness by not-for-profit organizations as well as by regulators, policymakers, donors, and others. The study also found that inconsistent and inaccurate IRS Form 990 filings were caused by "different applications of accounting principles" and by "board member and manager unfamiliarity with nonprofit accounting in general and the requirements of Form 990 in particular."[8]

The Baruch College project team offered three recommendations to assist not-for-profit organizations in their public reporting:

1. *Raising the consciousness of nonprofit organizations regarding the importance of quality reporting of finances and programs . . .*
2. *Education of nonprofit organizations and those who advise them on accounting, financial management, and reporting . . .*
3. *Establishing and maintaining cooperative action for nonprofit quality reporting.*[9]

---

[8]Frederick S. Lane, "Enhancing the Quality of Public Reporting by Nonprofit Organizations," *The Philanthropy Monthly* (July 1991): p. 4.
[9]*Ibid.* p. 16.

EXHIBIT 7.4 Assessment Criteria for Management

	Score				
	Low				**High**
1. Computer technology application	1	2	3	4	5
2. Successful accreditation review	1	2	3	4	5
3. Compliance with current accounting standards	1	2	3	4	5
4. Accurate IRS Form 990 submission filed by the deadline	1	2	3	4	5
5. Board checklist for liability	1	2	3	4	5
6. Governance	1	2	3	4	5
7. Accountability to the public	1	2	3	4	5
8. Financial management	1	2	3	4	5
9. Planning	1	2	3	4	5
10. Marketing and communications	1	2	3	4	5
11. Community and client relations	1	2	3	4	5
12. Human resource and employee benefits	1	2	3	4	5

MEDIAN SCORE

Public reporting is important because it helps to build public confidence in the quality of the information provided and in interpretation of the documents' contents as a valid form of management performance evaluation. In this sense, not-for-profit organizations resemble private businesses.

In this litigious age, liability has become a prominent issue to not-for-profit board members. One result is that conservatism has escalated to the extent that willingness to innovate and to take risks has been greatly diminished. To overcome such hesitation, boards and management should take the steps necessary to avoid any conduct that might be the basis for a liability suit. In this way, they can regain their confidence in fulfilling their organization's mission. The following list of directors' responsibilities will, if adhered to, eliminate or at least minimize personal liability while allowing boards and management to think more boldly. These responsibilities also represent a good checklist for board assessment purposes:

- *Make certain that all technical requirements of law have been met before the organization commences operations.*
- *Keep informed of the general activities of the organization and the general field of interest in which it functions.*
- *Ensure complete and accurate disclosure of the details of all transactions, such as the sale of securities.*
- *Avoid self-dealing in any matters relating to the organization's operations.*
- *Attend directors' meeting regularly; if meetings must be missed, be certain that the minutes reflect a valid reason for the absence.*
- *Register dissent when in disagreement with board action; be certain that it is made a matter of record in the minutes of the meeting and that the accuracy of the minutes is checked.*
- *Have a complete and competent knowledge of the duties of the office.*
- *Avoid any contract to serve personal interests or to assume any position that would bring personal interests into conflict or competition with the interests of the organization.*
- *Keep informed of the provisions of the documents creating the organization and setting forth its rules of operation, especially as they relate to the powers and duties of the directors.*
- *Exercise the utmost good faith in all deadlines with and for the organization, and be prepared to provide good faith if necessary.*
- *Obey all statutes and other forms of law that prescribe specific duties to be performed by directors.[10]*

Management standards apply to those areas of duty and responsibility that belong to voluntary members of the board of directors and hired executive officers. These men and women have a duty, directly and indirectly, to supervise seven areas of assessment, as a measurement of their own performance: governance, accountability in management, financial management, planning, marketing and communication, community and client relationships, and human resources and employee benefits. These criteria are discussed in the following sections.

---

[10]George D. Webster, *The Law of Associations* (New York: Matthew Bender, 1965), p. 2.07(2).

(A) GOVERNANCE

The ultimate responsibility for each not-for-profit organization is vested in its board of directors. Their stewardship includes the quantity and quality of programs and services provided, financial accountability for all assets and funds, and fulfillment of all laws and regulations. Boards of directors share a degree of personal and collective liability in meeting these responsibilities, and, although the not-for-profit organization may be insured to protect them insofar as it can, their personal obligation remains.

Assessment of governance can be expanded from the list for board assessment presented above, beginning with the following standards:

1. *Are the Board and staff set up to work effectively? . . .*
2. *How well defined are the needs served by the agency and its program for meeting these needs? . . .*
3. *Are adequate financial safeguards and sound controls maintained for fundraising? . . .*
4. *Is the agency's work related to that of the national organization of other planning groups in the field? . . .*
5. *Is the agency doing a good job of what it is set up to do? . . .*
6. *How many other agencies are trying to do all or parts of the same job? . . .*
7. *Does the agency function in proper relationship to government agencies?*[11]

Another method of self-evaluation is the well-established management by objectives (MBO) standard, which sets defined goals for measurable periods, such as the annual operating year, or for prepared three- or five-year strategic plans. An organization should be able to define specific goals for its public programs and services, based on its evaluation of current public needs and its ability to contribute to their fulfillment within its mission. Why else does it exist? In addition to public needs assessment, it should be able to assess specific internal goals based on current strengths and weaknesses, threats and opportunities, and should include areas of administrative competence and preparedness. For example, the goals set can be associated with the composition of the board of directors regarding size, sex, age, talents, cultural diversity, and rotation of its members. In this regard, assessment of its nominations process would include maintenance of a roster of qualified and qualifiable candidates whose development is being supervised on a regular schedule.

Does the board perform any self-evaluation and, if so, how often? What criteria are utilized? Caution may lead boards to be soft on themselves or to measure only hard data such as the volume of clients served, the fulfillment of budget objectives, and so on. The ability of the board to provide leadership and direction might be a more germane area of assessment. Criteria might include: routine educational presentations on advances in program and service areas; what similar organizations have achieved; workshops on liability issues, quality control, and long-range planning; or outside evaluations of legislative and regulatory directives that may influence current operations and future planning.

Another set of assessments might be framed as answers to the series of questions shown in Exhibit 7.5.

---

[11]Earle Lippincott and Elling Aanestad, "Management of Voluntary Welfare Agencies," *Harvard Business Review* (November/December 1964): pp. 87–88.

EXHIBIT 7.5 Assessment of Leadership

	Yes	No
Does the organization have records that enable it to document		
a. What it has achieved?	( )	( )
b. How it is continuing to carry out its mission?	( )	( )
Does the organization issue annual reports based on these records?	( )	( )
Do all board members have copies of		
a. The mission statement?	( )	( )
b. The long-range strategic plan?	( )	( )
c. The plan for the coming year?	( )	( )
d. The budget for the coming year?	( )	( )
Does the organization have a detailed, board-approved plan		
(including a plan for fund raising) for the coming year?	( )	( )
Was the most recent auditor's report an "unqualified" report?	( )	( )

Source: *Excerpted by permission from New, Anne L. with Wilson C. Levis.* Raise More Money for Your Nonprofit Organizations: A Guide to Evaluating and Improving Your Fundraising. *© 1991 by the Foundation Center, 79 Fifth Avenue, New York, NY 10003.*

(B) ACCOUNTABILITY IN MANAGEMENT

Accountability in management includes an assessment of programs and services for public benefit as well as financial details. Activities can easily be counted, but assessing their quality and the worth of their outcomes is more difficult. Performance measurement data does exist and can include, for example, comparative analysis of staff ratios to operating costs for each program, to discern cost per unit of client service. How is this data to be interpreted? Costs for a college to educate students are different from a hospital's cost to provide patient care or a museum's cost to be open daily for visitors. This data is more useful internally, to assist the board and management in cost-benefit analysis, such as the relation between staffing for service and income. The value or utility of these programs and services to the community served should also be assessed through market research methodologies.

Accountability in management also includes an assessment of the distribution of information about the not-for-profit organization, usually in the form of an annual report, newsletters, brochures, and the like, to describe its programs and services and to report its financial affairs. An attitude of open and full disclosure is important for not-for-profit organizations: Is there anything of significance that is honestly "private" about the management of a voluntary, not-for-profit, public benefit organization?

Financial information is more tangible, but its interpretation requires assistance. Not-for-profit organizations have two separate standards of accounting issued by the FASB and AICPA, depending on type of organization. The Internal Revenue Service requires all not-for-profit organizations to follow the Not-for-Profit Organizations audit guide in preparation of their annual IRS Form 990, which yields uniformity in presentation of financial information for every institution and agency—provided they know how to complete the form and do so with mathematic accuracy. Sources and amounts of revenue are separated into several categories; expenses for programs and services are separated from costs of management and administration and from fund-raising expenses—all reasonable areas for assessment and performance evaluation.

(C) FINANCIAL MANAGEMENT

Because most not-for-profit organizations have limited assets to manage, financial data should be easy to measure, including the stewardship of these resources to gain full value during their period of use. Financial management requires expertise among the board and senior managers. The scope of fiscal activities is broad and requires sophisticated supervision even in smaller organizations where some or all of the following assets may be present. Annual operating budgets report all the sources of revenue and categories of expense activity; their results are analyzed and reported in the annual audit statement. Liquid and fixed assets include property, buildings, and equipment; employee health and dental insurance, disability insurance, and pension and retirement programs that also must be supervised. Fund raising is an active source of additional revenue both for daily operations and for capital and equipment, education, research, and other purposes. Categories for active capital management include cash, management of funded depreciation and reserves in short- and long-term investments, acting as trustee for charitable trusts, and investment management of endowment funds.

(D) PLANNING

The mission statement establishes a grand design for every not-for-profit organization. Annual operations implement the mission to the extent that present ability and resources allow. Planning is a discipline for looking beyond a current operating year and its limitations and defining a future direction that seeks to fulfill the mission of the organization. This plan, or "vision," of the board and management reveals their commitment to specific and measurable goals that will achieve exciting and worthwhile activities and enterprises for the public good. Without a future plan, an organization is more apt to wander aimlessly among daily threats and new (and untried) opportunities, all likely to lead to hasty, ill-informed decisions that favor quick fix solutions. Such a plan is not likely to lead an organization in any future direction and may only allow it to survive perhaps a little while longer with minimal ability and effect; such an organization should consider closing its doors and going out of its nonbusiness.

Whether called a master plan, a long-range plan, or a strategic plan, the "vision" for the future should be written to describe its orderly assessment of the present and its informed view of the direction it has set for itself. The board and management should next develop internal and external consensus and commitment to the goals and build enthusiasm for their accomplishment. Long-range plans include the three key areas of analysis and projection in the following list. When completed, they serve as the road map to achieve that vision:

1. Sufficient details about current programs and services and their merits, plus new activities to be offered that will improve the quality and breadth of present programs and services for community benefit

2. A financial evaluation of existing resources and the extent of those required to pay for future programs and services
3. A capital and equipment needs assessment that will support the planned programs and services to be carried out within adequate facilities

(E) MARKETING AND COMMUNICATION

In prior years, the term *public relations* was adequate to cover the area of establishing and supervising public information and communications for not-for-profit organization. Different skills are required today, combining planning (both long range and strategic) with market research and strategic marketing, all carried out through multimessage advertising and multimedia communications.

Assessment of the use and outcomes of these high-tech methods is as essential as assessment of other management areas. Volumes of analytical information are available on how market research can pinpoint different attitudes within segments of the public, or identify the medium to deliver the precise messages selected to those most likely to hear and reply, or measure results within a single organization in detail. The science of market research also measures progress against long-range and strategic plans, to enable early management intervention in their likely effect on current operations. Raw and uninterpreted intelligence is essential to keep pace with a changing world that can affect current management options and decisions.

Public communications channels are jammed with messages. The quality and cost of advertising production and distribution have skyrocketed so that only larger, more affluent organizations can afford their use. Public resentment toward mail, telephone and Internet invasion of privacy limits the ability of everyone to communicate, even with a select audience. The use of multimedia outlets reinforced with repeat messages has proven to be more effective but is also the most costly method. Added to this search for a means to gain people's attention is the competition with for-profit corporations, whose larger budgets can outperform the best efforts and limited budgets of not-for-profit organizations.

Assessment of merit, value, performance, and outcomes, using modern marketing and communications techniques, adds a wealth of helpful information for planning and decision making. However, the range of management standards against which not-for-profit organizations can measure their areas of activity, as compared with the experience of others, is limited. Counting inches of newspaper space is only one indicator; others are needed. The cost of assessment itself has become a factor in budget decisions. The value of information has increased and, for those organizations whose mission is advocacy, may become more critical than analysis of routine operating programs that provide public services. Internal competition for operating dollars will increase, because funds directed to marketing and communications can be proven to influence public perceptions about quality of service (attraction) and improve market position for continued expansion (growth).

(F) COMMUNITY AND CLIENT RELATIONSHIPS

Not-for-profit organizations have always been sensitive to their local community and its residents. Renewed attention to both is necessary because of rapid shifts in demographics, evolving attitudes, and direct changes introduced into the community through economic and government influence, all reinforced through mass marketing and communications techniques. People are more likely to relocate as a consequence of factors that influence their lives; they will even incur financial loss on jobs, housing, and lifestyle in order to achieve better opportunities. Demographic changes are widespread, and each community must pay increased attention to how culturally diverse groups influence its needs for government, business, and philanthropic support to meet basic community needs. Opening or closing a major plant or business can have overnight ramifications across the spectrum of community life and can affect everyone living in the area.

Not-for-profit organizations should be active in community affairs to the extent possible, and for better reasons than preserving an inaccurate sense of corporate image. Community residents often consider programs and services provided by not-for-profit organizations to be part of its basic fabric of essential public amenities available to every resident. Board members are uniquely qualified to bridge this gap, as are senior managers, who need to join civic, service, and social groups and be visible presences in community projects. They should also be active partners in discussions on community issues, especially when their own organization's expertise can help the resolution.

(G)   HUMAN RESOURCES AND EMPLOYEE BENEFITS

Whether in hard or prosperous economic times, not-for-profit organizations must, by law, provide fair wages, comprehensive benefits, and safe working conditions for their employees. Their salaries and benefits often lag behind private business, but, to their credit, many not-for-profit employees bring to their job a sense of commitment to the cause and an honest concern for its clients. Given such favorable attitudes, the addition of a few privileges deriving from internal options (tuition remission, by a college or school; healthcare, by a hospital; tickets, by a museum or performing arts center) is valuable to employee relations. Aside from what is required, positive working conditions and benefits are needed to attract and retain competent managers, professional and technical staff, and trained employees at all levels. Their offerings will never match for-profit business packages, because shares of company stock, profit sharing, and other perks are unavailable, but not-for-profit organizations can be quite competitive.

Comparative salary and benefits surveys can also keep each institution informed of what other organizations (both for-profit and not-for-profit) provide, and an analysis of external conditions can help an organization to stay current with issues that affect employment and employee satisfaction, such as union organizing activities. Access to public transportation, parking, local housing costs, child care, and other community indicators help to make employee benefit programs competitive. Well-designed employee relations programs that offer internal values can emerge as attractive alternatives to costly benefits. Organizing car pools and offering extra privileges and prizes for participants encourages employees to be environmentally sensitive, builds camaraderie, and may help to reduce highway and parking congestion.

The broad areas of management assessment briefly examined here offer numerous criteria for assessment. Each not-for-profit organization can choose those most essential to its own success and measure progress using the scorecard in Exhibit 7.4. Continued attention to these few areas, plus all those presented in this chapter, will aid the organization in carrying out its programs of public service and will help it to become even more capable of fulfilling its mission.

7.5 Outcomes Measurement for Programs and Services

Now more than ever our public expects us to demonstrate accountability. One measure is to report on the outcomes we achieved through our programs and services. And, if we can, we also should link our measured outcomes with how we used contribution dollars so that donors who gave them and the volunteers who solicited them can know how the money they raised made a difference to others.

Outcomes are easy to measure, at first glance. How many students did you graduate? How many meals did you serve? How many patients did you treat? How many performances did you provide? At second glance, some elements of quality can be added. A consistent 75 percent of freshmen graduate after four years. Homeless meals increased to twice a day and fed 22 percent more clients per month than last year. Open-heart surgical patients showed a 97 percent survivability rate in the first year. Net operations from ticket sales allowed purchase of a replacement lighting control board. However, to demonstrate outcomes measured against the mission statement and community expectations adds a dimension beyond quantity called "quality indicators." How many graduates found employment in their major field of study? Did the homeless also receive counseling, medical care, or job training? Were heart patients faithful in completing their rehabilitation and in changing their eating, exercise, and smoking habits? How did performance reviews and marketing promotions compare against customer satisfaction studies? Calculating the quantity of outcomes achieved is one step; demonstrating accountability by improving the quality of these same outcomes is another indeed.

How are outcomes to be measured? Because not-for-profit organizations have separate missions, each must define its own outcome measurement criteria including what will be the indicators to measure, the procedures for collecting data on each indicator, and the process for review and reporting the results. United Way of America developed a comprehensive outcomes measurement system in the mid-1990s that remains in practice across the nation. Its success in using this process in so many different organizational settings is to measure funding programs according to whether they are appropriate, comprehensive, and accurate. Included is an acceptance that outcomes, indicators, and data collection methods also may be established by accrediting bodies along with national organizations and trade associations to which not-for-profit organizations belong or adhere to. It matters less which terminology and reporting formats are followed; United Way is evaluating its agencies by their commitment and dedication to the outcome measurement process.[12]

Outcome measurement also can be applied to fund-raising results and performance of the not-for-profit organization itself. Exhibit 7.6 provides nine measurement areas in a worksheet format to tabulate the data. An examination of each for fund-raising program results placed alongside measurement of the organization's program and service outcomes also will link contributions to their use in enabling programs and services to produce results.

---

[12]"Focusing on Program Outcomes: A Guide for United Ways" and "Measuring Program Outcomes: A Practical Approach" (Alexandria, Va.: United Way of America, 1996).

EXHIBIT 7.6 Demonstrating Accountability

	Score				
	Low				High
1. Participation	1	2	3	4	5
2. Involvement	1	2	3	4	5
3. Leadership development	1	2	3	4	5
4. Community relations	1	2	3	4	5
5. Donor relations	1	2	3	4	5
6. Measurable outcomes	1	2	3	4	5
7. Forecasting future income	1	2	3	4	5
8. Setting performance standards	1	2	3	4	5
9. Community benefits	1	2	3	4	5
MEDIAN SCORE					

(A) PARTICIPATION

Fund raising is a numbers game. How many new donors were acquired? How many prior donors were renewed? Growing the donor file is a strategic objective; retaining and upgrading current donors is the profit goal. More hidden results to study might include tracking major gift donors through executing a prepared cultivation strategy to achieve new contributions of size. By comparison, the organization's types of services provided could be studied to understand its clients' origins and whether any trends indicate changing community needs. It is not enough just to count the number of people served. Analysis of which programs were used, prior performance statistics compared with current data, and follow-up studies on lasting effects will help document problem sources as well as effective mediations. When contribution dollars are used to pay for these studies and for salaries and supplies of staff delivering them, the link is made with donors and their dollars who made this service possible. Communications that report these outcomes also will serve to increase public confidence and aid future gift support that will continue to provide valued services.

(B) INVOLVEMENT

Public participation is as important to fund-raising success as it is to fulfilling a not-for-profit organization's mission. Involvement by community members is essential to the life of nearly every institution or agency. Multiple layers and levels are available for people to join up, stand up, and come on board. Options for helping can begin with simple tasks, such as addressing and stuffing envelopes for a benefit event, up to and including serving as an officer on the board of directors. In between are a great variety of assignments, duties, and responsibilities. People can choose where they want to give their time and talent, energy and work within the organization in order to benefit those whom it serves. People's time has great value, and that value is increasing daily. Organizations also need more people to do more of the day-to-day work required to remain open and conduct operations. Volunteerism provides people who want to help multiple avenues to be involved in meaningful ways. It is also true that active volunteers are more generous with their personal gifts because they have witnessed firsthand the value of the services to others they helped provide.

(C) LEADERSHIP DEVELOPMENT

Every organization needs volunteer leaders just as much as it needs leadership from its professional staff. Leadership development is an action program. Each not-for-profit organization has to define how it will prepare for its future, even if that future begins the next day. Fund-raising leaders inspire other volunteers to ask their friends for money, which is a formidable assignment. Solicitation training is required along with careful strategies for cultivation and solicitation followed by the commitment to remain in personal contact with qualified prospects and important donors. Internal leaders also must be found to inspire other employees to continue to give their best in time and talent, energy and work, for which they get paid, unlike volunteers. Leaders are also managers, not only of people but also of process, products, performance, and policy. If we are not actively searching for and developing our own leadership candidates, our organization is doomed to the less productive role of struggling to survive rather than measuring and reporting its improvements in quality and quantity services delivered back to the community.

(D) COMMUNITY RELATIONS

One of the primary by-products of a comprehensive fund-raising program is its extensive engagement with the community. Public participation is a key objective, whether as volunteers or donors, friends or neighbors, advocates or clients. In exchange, employees of not-for-profit organizations are active as community activists, whether as volunteers in community organizations, as members of the chamber of commerce and school boards, as library trustees and scout leaders, and more. Community residents bring information and opinions back to their favorite not-for-profit organizations in order to assist them in understanding community needs, public perceptions of the organization, and special issues that the organization needs to know in order to perform its mission. On their side, employees who volunteer in their community bring their knowledge, skills, and experience in managing and serving people and resources to help other organizations. Both benefit their community and its people.

A high level of communications exchange is vital to both parties, in particular when not-for-profit programs and services are considered vital to community well-being. Good education and access to healthcare, for example, have risen to the level of a local community "right" that every citizen expects to be available. Little thought is given to how these public benefit organizations came to be, how they are sustained, and the vital partnership with the community that is needed for each of them to be effective. An active community in the United States, engaged with its own basic services and working in coordination and cooperation with its business, government, and not-for-profit organizations, as has been true for 200 years, can improve the quality and expand the essential services to more of its citizens through public participation.

I have since travelled over England, whence the Americans have taken some of their laws and many of their customs; and it seemed to me that the principle of association was by no means so constantly or adroitly used in that country. The English often perform great things singly, whereas the Americans form associations for the smallest undertakings. It is evident that the former people consider association as a powerful means of action, but the latter seem to regard it as the only means they have of acting. Thus, the most democratic country on the face of the earth is that in which men have, in our time, carried to the highest perfection the art of pursuing in common the object of their common desires, and have applied this new science to the greatest number of purposes.[13]

(E)   DONOR RELATIONS

After a gift has been received, a not-for-profit organization should consider the act as an investment, with expectation of a return. This transaction also requires an appropriate thank-you letter and/or gift receipt back to the donor, in appreciation. Contributions are given to help others in need, advance a cause, and solve problems. The organization has a responsibility to use the funds for charitable purposes, as the donor intended, and to report back on the results to all those who provided the help needed with their time or talent, energy or money.

If you ignore the demands of civility and stop thanking donors for their gifts, you'll also be undermining the foundation of your fundraising program: the goodwill of your donors. In fact, to involve and cultivate donors, you should probably be spending more time and money on your donor acknowledgment program, not less. Few nonprofits routinely have thank-yous in the mail (or on the phone) within seventy-two hours of the receipt of gifts—and I regard three days as a requirement, not a goal. Don't be fooled into thinking that donors don't notice. In truth, they probably notice—and remember—the absence or tardiness of a thank-you note more readily than they notice almost anything else. Long after she's forgotten what you said you were going to do with that $25 she sent you, the donor remembers that you never sent her a thank-you note! . . . thank-you letters and phone calls aren't just required by the near-universal expectation of politeness in North American cultures (even more intense in Canada than in the United States). They're a wonderful opportunity to inform, educate, and involve donors.[14]

Multiple forms of public communications are available in the form of brochures, annual reports, newspaper articles, newsletters, contents of a Web page, and more. Most discuss what the organization is doing and its internal performance and results. Few discuss what effect their work has had on the community because they do not know. Why is this? Perhaps because the organizations believe their first responsibility is to provide quality programs and services to their clients, students, patients, and more. They are focused on delivery, not on measuring how their work is improving the community. The

---

[13]Alexis de Tocqueville, *Democracy in America,* edited and abridged by Richard D. Heffner. (New York: Penguin Book USA, 1956 and 1984), pp. 198–199.
[14]Mal Warwick, *The Five Strategies for Fund Raising Success: A Mission-Based Guide to Achieving Your Goals* (San Francisco: Jossey-Bass, 2000), pp. 241–243.

time has come to evaluate their results from the community's standpoint, starting with current donors.

Donors are the best prospects an organization has to help meet its current and future needs, including its need for a willing public to participate by helping to carry out the mission. Donors are excellent advocates as well as reliable contributors. They also are investors who will continue to contribute if they see good works performed as the return on their initial gifts. How these good works are communicated is a critical obligation of the organizations they support, which can begin with finding ways to measure the outcomes.

(F)   MEASURABLE OUTCOMES

How is a not-for-profit organization useful? What is its value? The information gathered by an organization from measuring results of its work can be used in multiple ways, starting with evaluation for its own benefit. These include:

- Improving performance of its own programs and services
- Communicating measurable outcomes to staff, volunteers, donors, the public, and others
- Identifying effective program strategies to be implemented more broadly
- Developing approaches that affect identified community issues
- Defining values that funded programs deliver back to their communities
- Rewarding progress with increased volunteerism and contributions

While these measurements translate into outcomes, a natural result of applying oneself to the process, a more disciplined approach is required for consistent year-to-year analysis. The process each organization adopts for its own evaluation should be rigorous, receive the commitment of the board and senior management, and be assigned to a team of employees, perhaps even with public representatives participating. The team will be empowered to examine the work performed and initiate the data collection methods required to capture the essential information on outcomes that result. Exhibit 7.7 is one example of a series of questions a not-for-profit organization should review in building its outcomes measurement process. It is important also to note that these criteria are not directed at specific employees nor are they used in evaluation of their personal performance. More important, it looks at teamwork required and processes employed to render services. *"The potential benefits of the shift to a focus on outcomes are broad. United Ways will have evidence of their effective stewardship of donor dollars to make a difference for people and communities. Agencies will have invaluable feedback for improving the quality of their programs. Program participants will receive services that are shown to produce positive change."*[15]

(G)   FORECASTING FUTURE GIFT INCOME

The advantages of measuring fund-raising performance includes the ability to understand more completely the process of public solicitation to produce monetary support.

---

[15]"Focusing on Program Outcomes: A Guide for United Ways." Alexandria, VA: United Way of America, 1996, p. 43.

EXHIBIT 7.7 Review Team Questions Regarding an Agency's Outcome Measurement Process

1. Have the client groups to be served by the program been sufficiently identified? If identified, are they appropriate (e.g., most in need)?
2. Is the program clear as to what it aims to achieve for program participants—knowledge enhancement, skill development, attitudinal change, behavioral change, situational change? Is the program measuring the right things?
3. Are the outcomes and associated outcome indicators client or community focused?
4. Are they really outcomes, not counts of program activity or physical outputs, such as units of service?
5. Has the program identified unintended, negative outcomes it might have and made plans to track them? (Examples include encouraging teen pregnancy through an in-school child case program or escalating crime in a neighborhood that borders one engaged in a successful citizen anti-crime effort.)
6. Is the set of outcome indicators reasonably comprehensive in covering all major outcomes for the program?
7. Are the outcome indicators and data collection procedures sound/valid? Are tracking procedures in place for programs that seek to measure long-term results?
8. Are the outcome indicators and data collection procedures sufficiently sensitive to cultural differences in the client population?
9. Do data collection procedures, including any questionnaires, provide the needed data for each outcome indicator?
10. What participant or program characteristics will need to be examined to understand differences in outcome achievement? Will data be collected in a way that will allow this analysis?
11. Over what time periods will the data be collected and analyzed?

Source: Focusing on Program Outcomes: A Guide for United Way *(Alexandria, Va.: United Way of America, 1996), p. 25.*

Each individual solicitation program can and should be measured separately, as described in Chapter 6. Based on conducting multiyear performance measurements, the fund-raising staff should be able to predict with some reliability what levels of gift income can be expected. These forecasts are quite important to an organization's overall fiscal planning. The ability to make firm plans for continued delivery of services depends on a reliable level of public support; to realize this goal is to achieve a position of confidence and of gratitude.

How credible are the numbers that a forecast claims as a measure of fund-raising productivity? The answer will be found in a three-year review of results for each solicitation method. Take into account the variety of internal and external factors that affect success for any fund-raising program (see Exhibit 7.3), to define the realistic estimate of likely returns from a continued investment of budget dollars in proven fund-raising methods and techniques. This method of analysis is based on the organization's own experience and is preferred over attempts to compare results with other organizations, even of the same type in the same community. Organizations are not alike in how they conduct their fund raising, nor does fund raising perform the same for every organization—organizations do not solicit the same people at the same time using the same method for the same purpose with the same volunteers. As a result, attempts at comparative analysis based on fund-raising results of other organizations can be unfair and misleading. An organization's own results are a better guide simply because it knows what it chose to do, how it was done, and how it turned out.

(H)   SETTING PERFORMANCE STANDARDS

Once a three-year performance measurement of the entire fund-raising program is completed, these results will suggest a reasonable standard of performance that can be expected to continue, if resources and commitment remain constant. This performance standard is what the organization should use to measure its continuing fund-raising programs. If improvements continue, the criteria chosen for evaluation will focus on how progress is achieved, suggesting the merits of continued or expanded investment. If any solicitation program declines in number of donors, average gift size, or net proceeds, the cause should be investigated to learn why its performance has fallen below the standard it has proven previously for itself. The added advantage of using this standard for evaluating performance year after year is the assurance that acceptable levels of efficiency as well as effectiveness are being achieved along with the measure of profitability that will justify the budget investment required to raise the funds so necessary for annual operations.

> *What's critical is that the leadership of every nonprofit organization must think about these issues. Setting the return-on-investment ratio is one of the most important policy decisions any board of trustees can make. Unfortunately, the decision is rarely made consciously. Most boards, executive directors, and development directors make such decisions by default. They're influenced by pressures from donors, charities regulators, legislators, and their own, often untrustworthy instincts and preconceptions. They enact policies they think they ought to pursue—or still more often, no policy at all. That's no way to run a railroad—or a nonprofit organization. Measuring long-term value and acquisition cost are vital first steps toward taking the destiny of your organization into your own hands (assuming, of course, that your fundraising track record is long enough and that sufficient data are available).[16]*

(I)   COMMUNITY BENEFITS

To complete the outcomes measurement "circle of accountability" is to translate all these results of sections (a) through (h) into measurable criteria applied to what has been delivered to the community and to clients served by the organization. Again, such measurements are neither simple nor easy to accomplish and can be conducted only with the full cooperation and coordination of others inside the organization. Here are a brief set of questions each organization should use to begin to develop its answers as community benefits:

- Has your organization made a difference in the life of the community?
- Can you measure the results of your mission through your programs and services?
- Is your organization affecting change?
- Is it being a benefit to community residents?
- Has it improved their quality of life?
- Can you demonstrate both quality and quantity in terms of having made a positive difference?

---

[16]Warwick, *Five Strategies for Fund Raising Success*, p. 235.

To assist in seeing examples of what kinds of improvements can and should be reported, United Way has defined the following as a measurement report to demonstrate community benefits:

Outcomes may relate to knowledge, skills, attitudes, values, behavior, condition, or status. Examples of outcomes include greater knowledge of nutritional needs, improved reading skills, more effective responses to conflict, getting a job, or having greater financial stability.

Outcomes are benefits or changes for individuals or populations during or after participating in program activities. Outcomes are influenced by a program's outputs. They are what participants know, think, or can do; or how they behave; or what their condition is, that is different following the program.[17]

Surely your organization has a wealth of such examples of how it has helped people. Doing the homework to document more than numbers of people served and linking these results with the community's own role in the process (as volunteers and donors) will transform the work of the organization from what it claims it does into an effective partnership by demonstrating how the community has been the beneficiary of these good works.

7.6 Demonstrating Community Benefits

The final step in accountability for not-for-profit organizations is the demonstration of measurable benefits delivered to the community it serves. This goal is what the mission and vision statements broadcast as its purpose for being, its reason to exist, and its continuous quest. The contents of this chapter illustrate a variety of measurement tools, from mission and operations to management and outcomes measurement, that will aid this effort. We should no longer assume that the public will be trusting enough to let us proceed with our own sense of what is good for everyone. Today's donors want proof of returns on their investments. We must be able to translate our self-evaluations into quantifiable results that explain these community benefits. This translation is a major challenge, and, as has been illustrated in this chapter, it will not be easy to fulfill. The question remains: How does a not-for-profit organization demonstrate that the community's investment of its people as volunteers and their personal contributions result in a worthwhile return? What or where is the return that can be seen? Is that return justified adequately as a fair exchange for the three tax-exempt privileges the organization also receives—income, property, and sales tax exemption—plus the deduction from income tax its donors are able to enjoy? In combination, these are questions deserving of substantial answers of fact in the form of measurable outcomes the community can plainly see as beneficial to them, their neighbors, and the community itself.

The Commonwealth of Pennsylvania has initiated a community benefit test that healthcare organizations are required to meet as a "pure public charity." (See Exhibit 7.8.) The motive comes partly from cities and counties in Pennsylvania seeking tax revenues to support communitywide police and fire services that not-for-profit organizations also enjoy but do not pay for directly through property taxes. At issue are statewide initiatives to help relieve operating deficits for local governments. In many communities across the

---

[17]"Measuring Program Outcomes: A Practical Approach," pp. xv-2.

United States, cities and counties have already negotiated a "fee" paid voluntarily by some (but not all) of their not-for-profit organizations for such basic community services. Schools, colleges, hospitals, and museums are visible targets for these programs because of the amount of their valuable real estate holdings. However, in Pennsylvania, failing to pass the "pure public charity" test results in the requirement to pay property taxes or an assessed fee. This legislation has survived early court challenges, has seen one clarifying amendment, and may yet prevail. In the meantime, this legislation is being studied by other states, some of which have already adopted an annual requirement for public benefit measurement but have yet to decide on the penalties or enforcement proceedings.

The Pennsylvania example proves the "age of accountability" has continued into this new century and is beginning to grow teeth. If successful, every type of not-for-profit organization may be included next. In addition, these organizations also are acutely aware of the new federal requirement to disclose details on their annual operations by making their annual tax returns (Internal Revenue Service Form 990) "widely available" to any who wish to see it, including posting it on the Internet. There also is a form of "intermediate sanctions" now available to the IRS to be imposed on board members, management executives, and their organizations for errors of commission or breaches of public confidence. Both legislative measures were enacted in 1996 and are designed to provide an intermediate step before removal of tax-exempt status for major malfeasance. (See also Chapter 49 on revised accounting standards for public reporting of financial details, and Chapters 51 and 52 for more details on expanded state and federal legal requirements that reinforce these new accountability standards.)

To assist in providing guidance leading to answers for these many questions and to reinforce a not-for-profit organization's ability to demonstrate its multiple benefits to the community it serves, a discussion of 11 areas of objective measurement follows. (See Exhibit 7.9.)

EXHIBIT 7.8 Characteristics of a "Pure Public Charity"

	Score			
	Low			High
1. Advance a charitable purpose	1	2	3	4	5
2. Render gratuitously a substantial portion of its services	1	2	3	4	5
3. Benefit a substantial and indefinite class of persons who are legitimate objects of charity	1	2	3	4	5
4. Relieve government of some of its burden	1	2	3	4	5
5. Operate entirely free from private motive	1	2	3	4	5

MEDIAN SCORE

Amendment to the law, Institutions for Purely Public Charity Act, *was enacted in November, 1997, and provides three additional tests to retain tax-exempt status:*

1. Uncompensated service equal to at least 75% of net operating income but not less than 3% of total operating expenses.

2. Compensation and benefits of any director, officer or employee shall not be based primarily on financial performance of organization.

3. Institution must relieve some governmental burden, such as providing service that would otherwise be the government's responsibility.

EXHIBIT 7.9 Measurement Criteria for Demonstrating Community Benefits

	Score				
	Low				High
1. Accreditation	1	2	3	4	5
2. Advocacy of the cause	1	2	3	4	5
3. Disclosure (open and full)	1	2	3	4	5
4. Effectiveness and efficiency	1	2	3	4	5
5. Enhancement of public confidence and trust	1	2	3	4	5
6. Enhancement of image and reputation	1	2	3	4	5
7. Indigent care	1	2	3	4	5
8. Productivity analysis and proof of profitability	1	2	3	4	5
9. Quality reporting	1	2	3	4	5
10. Ethical behavior	1	2	3	4	5
11. Stewardship	1	2	3	4	5

MEDIAN SCORE

(A) ACCREDITATION

A first step a community might expect its not-for-profit organizations to pass successfully in meeting its objectives is an inspection of its programs and services by outside accrediting agencies. Some forms of accreditation are voluntary, such as the Joint Commission on Accreditation of Healthcare Organizations (JCAHO). However, federal regulations specify that Medicare and Medicaid reimbursement for patient care expenses will be denied unless the organization has passed its JCAHO inspection. Other forms of accreditation are basic requirements such as for schools, colleges, and professional schools, in order to be certified to grant academic degrees and credentials. To a similar degree, some employees in not-for-profit organizations are required to meet and maintain state licensure requirements in order to perform their professional duties as a test of competence.

There are no federal or state tests for fund-raising competency or minimum performance standards. However, not-for-profit organizations are required to be registered in all but seven states and to file annual financial reports. (See Seth Perlman's Chapter 52.) Whether the organization meets voluntary forms of accreditation or is properly registered to conduct public solicitation, failure to meet these obligations will be a first strike against it in its efforts to meet its community benefits test.

(B) ADVOCACY OF THE CAUSE

In addition to an obligation to follow its mission statement and observe the operating rules of its articles of incorporation and bylaws, not-for-profit organizations also are obligated to speak up and speak out for their purpose for being. In some instances, the only mission of the organizations is advocacy, such as those that seek to protect the environment, improve civil rights, or reduce crime and disease. In other situations, offering public access to its services fulfills an organization's obligation for advocacy of its cause. An example is a healthcare organization that advocates community residents to improve their health and prevent disease by providing programs of wellness training, regular checkups for disease screenings, prenatal care, and a variety of forms of public health education. Fund-raising programs often invite the public to give to these same services, not just to help pay for their availability but to participate in public awareness promotions.

(C)   DISCLOSURE (OPEN AND FULL)

A reliable form of accountability for a not-for-profit organization is to be public about its activities, including its fiscal operations, and to be open to reporting on its program and service outcomes. Open and full disclosure is not always comfortable. This fact is true not because an organization may wish to hide something. More often it is because the organization presumes that the public will not understand what the facts and figures mean. Granted, it is hard to correct public perceptions based on misinterpretation of fiscal reports, including audited financial statements, since not-for-profit accounting standards and guidelines are unlike those used in the for-profit business world. But it is in the organization's best interest to explain what the figures mean, beginning with briefing board members, volunteers, and donors at regular intervals on the financial condition. Any failure to disclose more than likely suggests that something is being hidden.

The IRS Form 990, the annual tax return all not-for-profit organizations must file, has become a very public document. Included are the salaries and benefits of the five highest-paid executives along with details of any financial activities with board members. Compensation is a delicate topic for both for-profit and not-for-profit executives. However, this information has been included in Form 990 for many years; only the recent awareness and "widely available" access to this data on the Internet has awakened the public to the issue. Similarly, the amount of gifts and contributions received along with the cost of fund-raising activities also is reported in the IRS Form 990. Anyone interested in comparing the two to judge the merits of giving to an organization can do so. Merely to compare funds spent on programs and services with the cost of administration and the cost of fund raising is an easy analysis on the surface, but these answers are not easy to explain. (See Chapter 50 for a full explanation of IRS Form 990 and how to interpret its information.) Such comparisons will not reveal details on the quality of programs and services rendered, information that is not provided in the IRS Form 990. Other resources must be found to evaluate these essential features of an organization's annual performance to learn its community benefits.

(D)   EFFECTIVENESS AND EFFICIENCY

Not-for-profit organizations are not banks nor are they accounting firms. No rigid and uniform regulations govern their day-to-day activities nor do regular inspectors review their operations. The simple bottom line of profits or price earnings measures does not apply here. Many participate in accreditation reviews, but in the main, organizations have the flexibility and freedom to address their mission as they choose, based on the judgment of their boards of directors and management staff alone. In most situations, reasonable men and women follow sound guidelines as adequate demonstrations of a good-faith effort to support their sound decisions.

These judgments are complicated when trying to address a cause, respond to an emergency, and attempt new programs and services to help those in need where none exist at present. As such, the more traditional measurements of cost-benefit ratio analysis may not appear positive for a while, even the first few years, until the efforts either have proven their value and grown into their expected level of competency, or they have failed and been removed from service. This ability to experiment, to attempt to meet a new or emerging public need, is where not-for-profit organizations demonstrate one of their best qualities—flexibility. The best judgment of those in charge is their only guide, along with the advice of volunteers and donors who are willing to invest personal treasure to make a best effort to succeed. Not to try often is the bigger sin of omission than playing it safe by not trying at all.

(E) ENHANCEMENT OF PUBLIC CONFIDENCE AND TRUST

The judgment of others that an organization's efforts are worthwhile enhance its attempts to measure the worth of its programs and services for benefit of its community. All not-for-profit organizations are highly dependent on public confidence and trust—not because they need this public position to seek gifts and contributions but because the public must trust that their programs and services are of high quality. When a natural disaster strikes, a person may be less concerned about who provides a blanket, a cup of coffee, or a bed for the night. But if the American Red Cross or Salvation Army is recognized as the source of these benefits, the confidence resulting from being well cared will be greater and a source of assurance when that same person is invited to help with a gift. Using this example, we can assume that the Red Cross or Salvation Army already has a high level of public confidence and trust. The next disaster reminds people of the organization's utility and will help to stimulate gift support.

(F) ENHANCEMENT OF IMAGE AND REPUTATION

Every not-for-profit organization should promote its not-for-profit status as often as possible. Not-for-profits are, after all, "public benefit corporations," so defined by statute in California. Not all citizens can easily distinguish between a not-for-profit service and a for-profit one; they seek only the service and want assurances that it will be of high quality. Whether they also have to pay for the service does not clarify the distinction between them. One reason people name an implied level of confidence in a not-for-profit enterprise is because its motives do not include making a profit from the service. The public needs to better understand this important distinction, and it is the task of not-for-profit organizations to increase public awareness and appreciation of this difference.

(G) INDIGENT CARE

It should be no surprise that many not-for-profit organizations provide their programs and services "for free." Many also may charge something or are reimbursed afterward for some or all of their operating costs. Few not-for-profits receive full payment for services from clients or even seek it from some reimbursement source. Despite payment plans of any sort, a growing number of people depend on the services provided by these charitable entities as their chief means of day-to-day life support. We read and hear that the "gap" between the poor (qualified only as "living below the poverty line") and the rest of society is growing. A prime example is the number of people who have no healthcare coverage, a figure that is approaching 50 million. These people may be unemployed, employed with no health benefits, or "illegal aliens" with no source of support. They are true indigents in need of help.

Every community in the United States has a homeless population living on the streets. Food distribution centers, homeless shelters, soup kitchens, halfway houses, and more are not welcome in many neighborhoods. This nation, the wealthiest in human history, cannot find a way to provide even minimal care for some of its own citizens or tolerate them to be near where we also live, work, and play. It is unlikely that not-for-profit organizations can hope to serve the needs of the indigent since the public's willingness to support all causes, including those that are unpopular, cannot compete with the public's desire to give to traditional, well-known causes such as religion and education, the arts, and hospitals. How comfortable will these volunteers and donors be when they learn how much indigent care their organizations provide? More established and successful organizations enjoy a greater measure of public confidence with their generous support. Their decision to provide for the indigent should be a powerful message about the validity of these community needs. If the organizations would be forthcoming and answer positively, their image and reputation will grow, and because of their respect for community needs this will yield them even greater public confidence and trust.

(H)   PRODUCTIVITY ANALYSIS AND PROOF OF PROFITABILITY

If it applies the variety of measurement tools provided in this chapter and in Chapter 6, an organization will be well prepared to document its productivity. At the same time, it can demonstrate further credibility by going public with its process for measurement, the criteria used, and its fiscal performance.

Productivity is a tool to describe how well resources have been used to meet operating needs and is not unlike the measurement of program and service outcomes except for its tendency to focus on numbers alone. Tools are available to analyze cost-benefit ratios along with efficiency, effectiveness, and profitability; however, the results must be interpreted adequately. The absence of industry-wide standards is a handicap. Again, comparing your own results with prior-year experiences will be more than adequate to demonstrate the best use of available resources. To make a "profit" as a not-for-profit organization will require repeated explanations that such a performance has the same value as a profit margin—the sign of success in the for-profit world. Attempts to disguise this fiscal performance by using terms such as "margin" or "excess of revenue over expenses" are less helpful when reporting a positive bottom line for the operating budget or the consolidated financial statement. The proof of fiscal success is disclosed in the annual audit statement and in IRS Form 990. These figures reveal the organization's ability to manage its financial resources just as successfully as it manages to deliver quality programs and services.

(I)   QUALITY REPORTING

Considerable thought and preparation should be given to how best to report all these results to the public. A variety of communications channels are available: special reports, news releases, letters from the president, newsletters, annual reports, the Web page announcements, and more. Disclosure begs for interpretation and is an excellent opportunity to educate as well as to inform the public about accomplishments and what they mean for everyone. For example, making the annual audit statement widely available is to share an independent validation of fiscal correctness by a certified public accountant. Likewise, sharing copies of the IRS Form 990 also works to build credibility because of the public's respect for federal tax returns. These forms, by themselves, can enhance the public's view that the organization is well managed and meets all of its obligations as a public charity.

The release of public reports coupled with brief explanations of what the figures mean is worthy of an organization's best communications efforts. Because the general population receives so many messages, at such a rapid pace and from every possible direction, it is advisable to repeat this information in each communication vehicle available and continue to share the details with every audience.

(J) ETHICAL BEHAVIOR

Not-for-profit organizations and their employees are called to a higher standard of performance because they are public benefit corporations and enjoy tax-exempt privileges. Most organizations have written policies and procedures to guide their day-to-day operations. Those who are subject to accreditation and certification reviews are also bound to observe these additional rules and regulations.

Fund-raising practice has its standards for professional conduct. In demonstrating its commitment to best practices, a not-for-profit organization should adopt as a policy of the board of directors the "Donor Bill of Rights." (See Exhibit 9.1.) Stewardship for funds raised requires the recipient organization to honor the wishes of each donor and to remain faithful to their trust that these funds will be used for public benefit and never for private, personal gain.

Fund-raising practice also requires active public solicitation. Far too many scandals and abuses, scams and fraudulent examples have occurred in this area. Each tests the public confidence in every new contact and every ask, no matter how correct and legitimate. Whenever there is an abuse, whatever the source or circumstances, it is usually accompanied by wide media coverage that paints every organization as suspect. Fundraising executives are trained in best practices and correct ethical conduct. Each of the professional trade associations that support fund raisers has a code of ethics. Failure to observe these guidelines results in dismissal from membership. The best-known and most comprehensive code is the "Code of Ethical Principles and Standards of Professional Practice" of the Association of Fundraising Professionals (AFP). (See Appendix 9B.) AFP also has prepared a complete enforcement process and has an active Ethics Committee reporting to its national board of directors for continuous guidance of professional conduct for its more than 22,000 members. In addition, AFP has written a "Values Statement" to serve as additional guidance to its members and their organizations in eight areas: Integrity, Fair Play, Respect, Accountability, Compassion, Loyalty, Risk, Leadership and Change, and Stewardship. (See Exhibit 9.2.)

(K) STEWARDSHIP

Last but far from least is the measurement of stewardship: of the public trust, of the commitment to the highest ethical standards, and to a faithful fulfillment of each donor's direction for the use of gift dollars for public benefit. Stewardship is the "bottom line" of accountability. Four areas can be examined as an organization measures itself against its stewardship responsibility.

1. Faithfulness to its mission, vision, and values
2. Faithfulness to its use of all its resources for public good
3. Its unwavering observance of ethical standards and professional practices
4. Its wise investment of its funds, whether they are short-term cash strategies or long-term endowment practices.

Analysis of mission, vision, and values was described earlier in this chapter. A measurement tool was provided in Exhibit 7.5 that is a starting point to evaluate performance against these carefully worded objectives.

Conducting the variety of outcomes measurement and community benefit tests described in this chapter measures stewardship as faithfulness for use of resources for public good. Being open with full disclosure and public access to the annual audit statement and IRS Form 990 will reinforce these results.

Unwavering observance of ethical standards and professional practices can be ensured by following the rules of ethical behavior, described earlier.

The fourth area of stewardship includes the careful and conservative management of *all* the funds and assets under an organization's control. These include its facilities and equipment as well as its cash and other invested resources. Professional supervision is required, usually with a volunteer committee of experts in the field who advise the board and management on each form of monetary activity. Written policies and procedures also guide internal authorization for all expenses within the budget. The budget is subjected to vigorous internal scrutiny in its development and requires full board review and approval each year. Monthly financial statements provide the board and management with current information on revenues and expenses that fulfill current operating guidelines. The placement of cash in banks or with other professional managers adds professional oversight, an audit trail, and the experience of monetary professionals. Any investments in securities of all types also are guided by written policy and subject to external performance measurement by professional evaluators.

Building an endowment with excess proceeds from annual operations, funded depreciation, or gifts restricted to endowment requires the highest form of financial integrity. Endowments represent more than a savings account strategy; they are an essential asset to the future ability of each organization to continue to meet its mission despite occasional fiscal, management, or operational changes that may be required. The "prudent-man rule" continues to serve as a proper guide for all investments by not-for-profit organizations. There is no explanation for an organization's flagrant disregard for this guide in its enthusiasm to "cash in" on a volatile market or investment "tip." The obligation to oversee all these investments is a duty of the board of directors and is one of its most important responsibilities representing the public trust.

7.7   Conclusion: Public Perceptions of Accountability

Despite all that has been written above, the public perceptions will test even further the level of accountability that not-for-profit organizations must address. One of the most challenging questions to answer is: What is a reasonable cost of fund raising? No one knows the answer because guidelines are absent. First, the accounting profession has yet to offer standards or guidelines on how to allocate costs so that there is a consistent and uniform methodology in use. Second, no empirical study by academic professionals or an accredited public opinion poll or survey has established the answer. A major national study is now in progress under the dual leadership of the Center on Philanthropy at Indiana University and the Center on Nonprofits and Philanthropy of the National Center on Charitable Statistics at The Urban Institute. Their purpose is to improve the management and reporting of fund-raising and administrative expenses (overhead expenses) for not-for-profit organizations. Most likely improved tools and guidelines that will serve to encourage consistent reporting will follow. Their report will be awaited eagerly.

The final test of success in demonstrating public accountability is one that will be conducted by the family, a constituency that hesitates not at all to point out all our warts and blemishes while remaining steadfast in their support. Their motive is to improve both quantity and quality so we cannot fault them for their sincerity or objectivity. These final arbiters—our donors and volunteers along with our not-for-profit organization's leadership and our fund-raising staff—are our best friends. The following are the criteria by which they might measure success to their own satisfaction. If we succeed in passing their final exam, surely our public can soon agree that we also merit their confidence and support.

(A) SUCCESS AS MEASURED BY DONORS

In contributing to a not-for-profit organization, donors seek to:

- Be accepted and appreciated.
- Respond positively, perform a duty.
- Respond satisfactorily; receive spiritual reward.
- Fulfill personal aspirations; be involved.
- Assuage guilt; help others in need.
- Be noticed; achieve status.
- Be invited to do more.
- Receive donor benefits and personal gains.
- Overcome fear and anxiety.
- Receive tax deductions.

(B) SUCCESS AS MEASURED BY VOLUNTEER SOLICITORS

Volunteer solicitors seek to:

- Confirm the true value of their assistance.
- Build personal confidence.
- Build a willingness to volunteer again.
- Be personally motivated to make their own best gifts.
- Achieve more results than they could provide alone.
- Enable and encourage advocacy of the cause.

- Be publicly recognized for high performance.
- Be part of a successful team effort.

(C) SUCCESS AS MEASURED BY NOT-FOR-PROFIT ORGANIZATIONS

Not-for-profits aim to:

- Help to fulfill the mission and vision.
- Tell donors they are appreciated for who they are; confirm donors' value for what they have done.
- Identify and recruit volunteers who will ask their friends for money.
- Identify and recruit leaders who are able to direct others to perform a similar assignment when asked.
- Ask current donors to increase their level of giving.
- Identify major gift prospects among individuals and organizations.
- Operate at a reasonable, cost-effective budget level.

(D) SUCCESS AS MEASURED BY FUND-RAISING STAFF

The fund-raising staff seeks to:

- Successfully manage the solicitation process.
- Successfully manage the volunteer-donor exchange.
- Successfully manage donor research data into an action plan with a cultivation and solicitation strategy.
- Successfully build confidence of volunteers and donors.
- Convert goals and objectives into programs and services that benefit others in need.
- Successfully manage the continuing donor relationship.
- Achieve personal goals and objectives.[18]

---

[18]James M. Greenfield. *Fund Raising: Evaluating and Managing the Fund Development Process.* 2d ed. (New York: John Wiley & Sons, 1999), pp. 375–376.

Suggested Readings

United Way of America, *"Focusing on Program Outcomes: A Guide for United Ways."* Alexandria, Va.: United Way of America, 1996.

United Way of America, *"Measuring Program Outcomes: A Practical Approach."* Alexandria, Va.: United Way of America, 1996.

Anthony, Robert M., and Regina Herzlinger. "Management Control in Nonprofit Organizations," unpublished study, Harvard Graduate School of Business Administration, Cambridge, Mass., 1984.

Drucker, Peter F. *Managing the Nonprofit Organization: Practices and Principles.* New York: HarperCollins, 1990.

Fetterman, D. M., S. J. Kaftarian, and A. Wandersman, eds. *Empowerment Evaluation: Knowledge and Tools for Self-Assessment and Accountability.* Thousand Oaks, Calif.: Sage, 1996.

Allison H. Fine, Colette E. Thayer, and Anne T. Coglan. "Program Evaluation Practice in the Nonprofit Sector." *Nonprofit Management & Leadership*, 10, no. 3 (Spring 2000): 331–339.

Greenfield, James M. "Beyond Cost-Benefit Analysis: Five Steps to Demonstrating Community Benefits." *AHP Journal* (Spring 2000): 34–39.

———. *Fund Raising: Evaluating and Managing the Fund Development Process*, 2d ed. New York: John Wiley & Sons, 1999.

Guba, E. D., and Y. S. Lincoln. *Fourth Generation Evaluation.* Thousand Oaks, Calif.: Sage, 1997.

Herman, Robert D., and David O. Renz. "Nonprofit Organizational Effectiveness: Contracts Between Effective and Less Effective Organizations." *Nonprofit Management & Leadership*, 9, no. 1 (Fall 1998): 24.

Hopkins, Bruce R. *A Legal Guide to Starting and Managing a Nonprofit Organization*, 2d ed. New York: John Wiley & Sons, 1993.

Lippincott, Earle, and Elling Aannestad. "Management of Voluntary Welfare Agencies." *Harvard Business Review* (November/December 1964): 87–88.

Patton, M. Q. *Utilization-Focused Evaluation*, 2d ed. Thousand Oaks, Calif.: Sage, 1997.

Smith, Bucklin, and associates. *The Complete Guide to Nonprofit Management*, edited by Robert H. Wilbur, Susan Kudla Finn, and Carolyn M. Freeland. New York: John Wiley & Sons, 1994.

Warwick, Mal. *The Five Strategies for Fundraising Success: A Mission-Based Guide to Achieving Your Goals.* San Francisco: Jossey-Bass, 2000.

8 The Balanced Scorecard: A Performance Measurement Tool for Not-for-Profit Organizations

JEAN CRAWFORD, FAHP
Jean Crawford & Company, Ltd.

8.1 Introduction

Both for-profit and not-for-profit organizations are experiencing significant and funda-mental transformation. Traditional forms of measuring success have largely been in financial terms. The information age now demands, however, that organizations develop new tools to measure their performance. Organizations as diverse as hospitals, governments, social service agencies, and foundations have adopted a new comprehen-sive tool to meet these demands—the balanced scorecard.

8.2 The Balanced Scorecard

The balanced scorecard translates an organization's mission and strategy into a compre-hensive set of performance measures that provide the framework for a strategic mea-surement and management system.[1] Although financial objectives are still emphasized, the balanced scorecard measures organizational performance across four balanced per-spectives: (1) financial performance, (2) customers' knowledge, (3) internal business processes, and (4) learning and growth.[2]

(A) HISTORY OF THE BALANCED SCORECARD

In the early 1990s, a study revealed that traditional measurements based solely on finan-cial data would become obsolete and would not accurately reflect the organization. This led to the development of the balanced scorecard. "The balanced scorecard evolved from an improved measurement system to a core management system."[3]

Robert S. Kaplan and David P. Norton advanced the key concepts in a number of *Harvard Business Review* articles, and in 1996 they published the book *The Balanced Score-card: Translating Strategy into Action.* Since then organizations have spent many hours coming to grips with mission statements, identifying who they are, what they do, and what outcomes they expect to achieve. Some more progressive organizations have developed the *vision* statement—what they wish to become. However, organizations have continued to have difficulty in linking goals, objectives, and strategies to success-fully achieve their own unique mission and vision.

The balanced scorecard provides a strategy for the translation of vision and mission into integrated measurable steps. By linking strategy to operations, it presents informa-tion in such a way that the critical success factors identified by the organization can be monitored and evaluated. Most financial measurement systems, for example, will tell you what has happened but not what is happening. The balanced scorecard combines the measurement of soft activities (service numbers) and harder reality (financial num-bers) and gives reality to both measures. It does not replace financial measures but com-plements them by presenting a balance of nonfinancial and financial information. Now the organization can measure what is happening.

---

[1]Robert S. Kaplan and David P. Norton, *The Balanced Scorecard* (Cambridge, Mass.: Harvard Busi-ness Press, 1996), p. 2.
[2]*Ibid.*
[3]*Ibid.*, p. ix.

The balanced scorecard can measure what is important to the organization's overall performance, and this can then empower the organization to make innovative decisions. The not-for-profit sector needs the balanced scorecard. In the past 20 years, the not-for-profit sector has undergone extraordinary change. The sector existed for decades in a comfortable, relatively noncompetitive environment largely funded by governments and sheltered by supportive tax laws. Donors and funders were relatively undemanding. During the 1990s, however, governments have aggressively divested themselves of day-to-day responsibility for social services. In both Canada and the United States, there has been a massive reduction in the real dollars available to support community needs. Poverty has risen, especially among single-parent families, people from first world nations, and the urban poor. The economy's demand for ever-higher minimum levels of education from its entry-level workers keeps driving unemployment higher—especially among those with a low level of postsecondary education.

Fund raising has become more competitive and demanding; more charities are requiring more dollars; and there have been a greater number of scandals in the mismanagement of funds in national not-for-profits than ever before. The resulting pressures to use better business methods are reflected in a growing chorus of demands for more accountability and transparency in not-for-profit operations. Meanwhile, the demand for innovative, educated, and effective not-for-profit leaders is forcing many not-for-profit leaders (without adequate training) into a struggle with their boards to create dynamic visions and good strategic plans and build effective teams.

Performance measurements are one area in which not-for-profit organizations are particularly weak. Just as the corporate world needed to change how it measured and reported its activities, change was becoming increasingly important for not-for-profits. Stakeholders were asking questions such as: What does the charity really do? What is the cost of their activities? What value do their activities give to individuals and their communities, and what are the outcomes of these activities?[4]

(B)   WE NEED A BALANCED SCORECARD

The most successful organizations link strategies and outcomes. They are able to move away from short-term goals toward long-term ones. Very few, however, are in this position. This level of clarity of vision demands a clear focus on the strategies needed to achieve long-term goals. "What gets measured gets done."

Customers once settled for the service that they received, but no longer. Now they demand better quality, performance, and timeliness. They insist on the best customer service and want to pay less. As a result, many organizations have moved away from a focus on internal hierarchy to an inverted pyramid customer focus. Emphasis is now on the elements that create value, while those that do not are quickly eliminated. New ways to leverage the impact of the service inputs are now the goal, and the focus on leadership development has shifted to an emphasis on the value of working closely with leaders who are strategically oriented, faster, and interactive. We are scrambling to develop intellectual capital: to transform the future into an asset and develop measurable steps to attain it.

---

[4]Stephan Murgatroyd and Don Simpson, *"Making Measurement Work, Using a Balanced Scorecard in Nonprofit Organizations,"* p. 7. A product of the AXIA Performance Centre, Calgary, Alberta.

(C) IMPORTANCE OF OUTCOMES MEASUREMENT

- *Best practice argument.* Because of greater competition for funder dollars, organizations have to demonstrate greater proof of operational success in relation to strategic goals. The same activities undertaken by different organizations may have different outcomes.
- *Consequence argument.* In social service activities, some interventions make more impact on clients than others.
- *Cost-benefit argument.* Value for money has become a more common theme for major funders. By addressing outcomes and the costs associated with producing them, funding agencies can allocate resources to those activities more likely to lead to the desired change.[5]

8.3 *Components of the Balanced Scorecard*

Each organization has its own unique mission and strategy, and will need to develop its own version of the balanced scorecard. The corporate scorecard is different from a not-for-profit scorecard, but in most cases the balanced scorecard addresses four basic components related to organizational performance:

1. *Customer perspective.* This can be translated into funder and donor satisfaction or customer/client satisfaction.
2. *Internal business perspective.* What are the internal business processes that need to be improved? Are they focused on providing value, reducing costs, eliminating waste, or improving satisfaction? Are our operations transparent?
3. *Innovation and learning perspective.* What do we have to do to innovate that can add value to our operations? What are our customers' needs, and how are they being met? What new methodologies have our employees implemented? What do our volunteers need to learn to be more effective?
4. *Financial perspective.* What is the stakeholder's perspective, whether funder, taxpayer, donor, or neighbor, and how does the stakeholder perceive our organization?

The four perspectives of the scorecard provide a balance between short- and long-term objectives; outcomes desired and the performance drivers of those outcomes; and hard objective measures and softer, more subjective measures.

8.4 *Developing the Balanced Scorecard*

The balanced scorecard is created after the organization has identified its mission and vision. Over the past few years, "the mission" has become what we do and why we exist, whereas "the vision" is what we want to become. There are four stages in developing the balanced scorecard:

---

[5]*Ibid.*, pp. 9–10.

- Stage 1: Translating the vision and mission and gaining consensus
- Stage 2: Communicating the objectives, setting goals, and linking strategies
- Stage 3: Setting targets, allocating resources, and establishing milestones
- Stage 4: Feedback and learning

(A) VISION, MISSION, AND CULTURE

Identifying who we are, what we do, and what outcomes we expect to achieve is one of the most challenging roles an organization has to accomplish. Without this step, it will take much longer to prepare the balanced scorecard program. If this step was accomplished some time ago, it may be appropriate to review the vision and mission statements to ensure that they accurately reflect the current organization. Changes in leadership both on the board and in management may have altered the integrity of the mission and vision statements. In the same respect, due to the recent upheaval in the not-for-profit sector, stakeholders may need to be approached again. The culture of the organization reflects how we carry out our work. The vision and mission tell us what we aspire to be. Not-for-profits should receive input from stakeholders and the community. What values guide us? Are we customer focused? Are we a learning organization that adapts to change and makes improvements?

(B) COMMUNICATE OBJECTIVES AND SET GOALS

In each of the four areas, the organization needs to set goals and objectives and identify leading and lagging indicators. Senior managers should communicate the strategic objectives of the organization clearly. Goals are the targets we intend to achieve, especially to achieve outcomes and improve processes. Indicators are measures we monitor in each of our strategic business units or customer target groups to tell us how we are doing in achieving our goals (e.g., percent decrease in length of services, or percent ratings of "excellent" on a client satisfaction survey).

(C) IDENTIFY CORE PROCESSES

Core processes, the central, key groups of work activities we do to achieve our purpose and attain our goals, are the heart of our business. We should ask: What are our core processes? How can we simplify them? How can we identify priorities for improvement? If we do not describe the whole process clearly and simply, then the objectives and goals have no context. Some common examples in a not-for-profit service organization include:

- Screening and intake
- Assessment
- Develop plan of service
- Implement plan of service
- Monitor quality of services and results
- Termination of service and follow-up

(D)   MEASURE AND MONITOR INDICATORS

The first step is to define specific measures for monitoring processes and outcomes. Often these are linked to quality dimensions (e.g., accessibility, appropriateness, acceptability, effectiveness, efficiency). This first step includes reporting the actual rate, as monitoring tells us how well we are meeting customer needs and carrying out our core processes.

(E)   IDENTIFY GAPS AND TAKE ACTION

Teams and individuals identify gaps between target and actual, which leads them to study the processes to achieve customer expectations. The purpose is to learn, not to control. Teams and individuals receive coaching and training to improve quality and achieve outstanding performance.

(F)   GOALS AND OBJECTIVES

Ultimately, goals and objectives are threefold. There is a continuous process of monitoring and updating. Not-for-profits should include customers and stakeholders in the process. Finally, feedback from the front line should be reported back to senior management and the board.

8.5   *What Happens in the Four Stages*

(A)   STAGE 1: TRANSLATING THE VISION AND MISSION AND GAINING CONSENSUS

Perhaps one of the most difficult steps in starting the balanced scorecard is clarifying an organization's vision. Gaining consensus in an organization is difficult, and very rarely does every stakeholder group agree. Each group needs to be asked separately, and then the common elements need to be agreed upon.

(B)   STAGE 2: COMMUNICATING THE OBJECTIVES, SETTING GOALS, AND LINKING STRATEGIES

The balanced scorecard can be used either to measure long-term goals, such as three to five years, or to develop short-term stretch goals over a 12- to 18-month period. Strategic objectives include setting goals and linking strategies.

(C)   STAGE 3: SETTING TARGETS, ALLOCATING RESOURCES, AND ESTABLISHING MILESTONES

Targets are the specific numbers or activities that the organization wishes to accomplish. For example, the agency will increase client visits from 1000 to 1500 in the year 2000.

Strategic initiatives are the specific activities that will meet the targets. Aligning all the initiatives will be crucial to achieving success. For example, to meet the target of attracting 500 new clients will mean advertising, adding new counsellors, finding additional space, etc.

Allocation of resources to meet the targets includes people to carry out the additional or new work and additional budgeting for payroll, equipment, systems, etc.

Establishing milestones to keep the program on track establish start and finish dates, weekly, monthly, or quarterly.

(D)   STAGE 4: FEEDBACK AND LEARNING

Articulating the shared feedback: As the organization moves through the various stages both clients and employees will be impacted. Regularly scheduled meetings and communications to all stakeholders in the balanced scorecard process will need an opportunity to share their knowledge.

Strategic information will become increasingly important. Major impacts such as human resource and finance availability will be crucial to the success of the program. Transparency and timing of strategic information is vital.

Facilitating new learnings: As the new initiatives are started, stakeholders in the process may need to be trained or retained in aspects of the program.

Linking outcomes to performance driver measures identifies methodologies such as surveys, and that will demonstrate the outcome. Example: Outcome is increase customer loyalty; performance measure is a customer satisfaction survey.

8.6   *Ten Steps for Implementing the Balanced Scorecard*

- *Step 1: Strategic planning retreat.* Identify strategic issues and discuss possible solutions. This process can be either top-down or bottom-up, but both have problems. If necessary, to achieve consensus regarding vision, strategies, objectives, and goals, have a second retreat.
- *Step 2: Form a strategic planning committee.* This committee will identify objectives and goals for each perspective in the balanced scorecard.
- *Step 3: Feedback and approval from entire organization.* It is necessary to have a buy-in for the corporate scorecard, because departmental and individual scorecards will be built on the corporate balanced scorecard.
- *Step 4: Revising the scorecard.* The strategic planning committee will first explain the program to everyone. Then each individual will develop his or her own balanced scorecard, which will support the larger organizational objectives and goals.
- *Step 5: Develop individual scorecards.* Break the organizational goals into smaller units and develop individual scorecards.
- *Step 6: Finalize individual and corporate scorecards.* The strategic planning committee reviews the corporate and individual balanced scorecards and suggests revisions.
- *Step 7: Formulate a five-year strategic plan.* Review individual and corporate activities to identify progress and make adjustments. Based on individual balanced scorecard evaluations, the committee will review each person's performance. The strategic planning committee then revises the corporate balanced scorecard

based on the internal and external scanning of changes in the environment. Finally, it identifies as many strategic issues as possible and considers possible solutions that the organization can employ.

- *Step 8: Review progress quarterly.* This can be done by the strategic planning or evaluation committee.
- *Step 9: Evaluate and reward individual performance.* Management will have to have a plan in place, so that employees will know what to expect.
- *Step 10: Review and revise the balanced scorecard and strategic plan.* This review should take place on an annual basis.

8.7   Major Implementation Issues

- *Coping with change.* Change in the board, management, and employees means continual education regarding the balanced scorecard.
- *Articulating the vision.* As new board members, employees, and management come on board, they will have different ideas on what the change should be, but the vision must remain constant.
- *Reducing resistance.* This represents a great deal of work initially, and many employees will not see the value and put it aside to respond to other, more pressing concerns. It will be important to communicate the value of the program over the long term.
- *Rewarding performance.* Have a system in place, for both the employees and the board. Clarify key success factors and performance indicators. Set up realistic timelines.

8.8   Using the Balanced Scorecard as a Board Tool

Although the balanced scorecard can also be used to monitor the chief executive officer (CEO), it is crucial to maintain priority for governance issues. The balanced scorecard can also help clarify the vision and its implications, prevent control failures, improve accountability for outcomes and quality, and ensure that efficient use of resources is ongoing.

(A)   BENEFITS OF THE BALANCED SCORECARD

The balanced scorecard is an asset to the maintenance of an organization. It translates the strategic plan into an integrated set of financial and nonfinancial measures. The scorecard also communicates organizational strategy, providing a holistic view of what is happening inside or outside the organization in the form of a framework that shapes work behaviors. It does so by providing meaningful measures of performance and enabling employees to determine how to measure individual performance, while empowering them by providing the data they need to make changes immediately. This in turn provides them with the feedback to guide processes and actions toward the attainment of objectives.

The balanced scorecard has become a powerful tool for linking an organization's strategic intentions with short-term stretch goals. Employees are challenged to determine what key performance indicators are most important for them in order to reach these stretch goals across all these dimensions. They take ownership and responsibility for selecting and applying the measurements that would be most helpful to them in reaching their performance goals. The best practices are searched for in their own terms, as well as looking at other organizations. By doing so, employees will learn how to improve the level of performance for each of the indicators they have chosen.

The balanced scorecard approach has been a powerful tool not only for improving performance but also for overcoming the limitation of relying purely on financial resources. Employee behavior is crucial in building customer loyalty, which makes it all the more essential to nurture their personal growth and capacity and excitement for practicing innovation. The balanced scorecard can help achieve this, and is not intended to add more pressure to the substantial burdens already facing most not-for-profits. Rather, it is a vehicle for building consensus among a diverse group of stakeholders and for broadening coalitions among the business, government, and not-for-profit sectors.

(B) DILEMMAS, DIFFICULTIES, AND PROBLEMS WITH THE BALANCED SCORECARD

Small and medium-size not-for-profits may ask, "How do we best demonstrate our efficiency and effectiveness without taking time away from the task at hand? Implementing the balanced scorecard may at the beginning create additional work for some managers and, as it is cascaded down into the organization, other employees. Outcome measurement is especially difficult to carry out with complex social problems. For example, the reasons a disabled person is unable to work may be many and complex, and one disabled person's complex situation may be very different from that of another with the same disability."

Measures are not always used correctly by those who access the data. Sometimes measures determine what actions are taken. This can be dangerous if what is being measured is the wrong thing. Different stakeholders have different perspectives on what the most significant measures are, and not-for-profits are often uneasy about government pressure for outcome measurement. The concern is that they will be pushed to defend their performance using narrow return-on-investment measures that do not reflect client or employee needs. If we do not attempt to measure and focus our efforts on those actions that produce the most returns, organizations can rightly be accused of unaccountable social spending.

8.9 Six Principles Inform the Balanced Scorecard

The scorecard is meant to be a tangible indicator of "mission-critical" activities and results within an organization. It provides a concrete set of measures arranged carefully for ease of interpretation and aimed at showing how the organization is doing in relation to its key mission and goals. It uses the best available "hard" data to examine the results stakeholders need to make good decisions. The data show actual results, wherever possible.

The balanced scorecard is available in its entirety to all stakeholders. The aim is for all stakeholders to see the same information so that decisions they are making are based on the best possible information. The data provided in the scorecard is both lag data (showing past results) and lead data (predicting future trends). It should show patterns of interrelationships between cause and effects. For example, the scorecard should show when more funds are raised because of an increase in the number of volunteers rather than from larger donations from a shrinking pool of givers. Finally, the scorecard is not used as a device to threaten anyone, though it can make clear what challenges the organization and individuals are facing.

(A)   ELEMENTS OF THE BALANCED SCORECARD

The balanced scorecard translates mission and strategy into objectives and measures and is organized into four different perspectives:

1. Customer/client satisfaction or funder and donor satisfaction
2. Financial
3. Effectiveness and efficiency of internal business processes
4. Enhanced learning and growth

The balanced scorecard is intended to provide an integrated framework that shapes the behaviors of those delivering the services, those receiving the services, and those shaping the support of governments and the private sector. In order to develop a scorecard, an organization needs to state its vision and mission very clearly and explicitly, and finally describe its strategic intentions, specifically what new achievements it hopes to accomplish in the next two to three years and how it wants to be seen as an organization in the future.

The balanced scorecard must also make clear how the organization has performed for funders and donors on some key financial measures such as fund raising, reserves, and the ratio of administrative costs to costs of service. The organization also needs to know how it has performed on improving its internal processes (measures of efficiency, cycle time, etc.); how it has invested in and secured returns in relation to learning and growth; and, most important, how it is doing in terms of customer/client satisfaction, based on the measurable outcomes.

(B)   FEEDBACK AND LEARNING

Translating the vision, communicating and linking, and business planning are vital in implementing the balanced scorecard strategy. But they are not sufficient in an unpredictable world. Together they form an important single-loop learning process—a single loop in the sense that the objective remains constant, and any departure from the planned trajectory is seen as a defect to be remedied. Most companies today operate in a turbulent environment in which

> *new threats and opportunities arise constantly, and in which companies must become capable of . . . double-loop learning—learning that produces a change in people's assumptions and theories about cause-and-effect relationships. Budget reviews and other financially based management tools cannot engage senior executives in double-loop learning, because these tools address performance from only one perspective, and do not*

involve strategic learning: gathering feedback, testing the hypotheses on which strategy was based, and making the necessary adjustments.[6]

The balanced scorecard supplies three elements essential to strategic learning. First, it articulates the company's shared vision, defining in clear and operational terms the results that the company as a team is trying to achieve. The scorecard communicates a holistic model that links individual efforts and accomplishment to business unit objectives.

Second, the balanced scorecard supplies the essential strategic feedback system. A business strategy can be viewed as a set of hypotheses about cause-and-effect relationships. A strategic feedback system should be able to test, validate, and modify the hypotheses embedded in a business unit's strategy. By establishing short-term goals within the business planning process, executives can forecast the relationship between changes in performance drivers and the associated changes in one or more specified goals.

Third, the balanced scorecard also facilitates the strategy review that is essential to strategic learning. Traditionally, companies use the monthly or quarterly meetings between corporate and business unit executives to analyze the most recent period's financial results. Discussions focus on past performance and explanations of why financial objectives were not achieved. The balanced scorecard, with its performance drivers and objectives, allows executives to use their periodic review sessions to evaluate the validity of the strategies of their organization. A company is thus able to align its management processes and focus the entire organization on implementing long-term strategies. The balanced scorecard provides a framework for managing the implementation of strategy while also allowing the strategy itself to evolve in response to changes in the company's competitive, market, and technological environments.

8.10 Important Terms Defined

- *Goals.* Goals define the long-term outcomes stated as the benefits or changes intended for the clients of the program. Example: "By the year 2010, the unemployment rate of teen mothers will be reduced by half."
- *Objectives.* Objectives define the specific shorter-term outcomes that contribute to reaching the goals of the program. Outcome objectives define the specific benefits or improvements to be expected by clients as a result of participating in a program. For an employment program, an example of outcome objective is "By the year 2005, 10 percent of unemployed single teen mothers will find full-time employment in a computer-related field." Service objectives define the specific units of service and service quality to be expected from the program. Examples of service objectives are "to train 35 teen mothers in computer skills" and "to hire instructors who have passed industry standard certification exams."
- *Outcome indicators.* Outcome indicators are the specific measures that show how well goals and objectives are being met. Example: "percent of single teen mothers that move from being unemployed to being employed full time in a computer-related field."

---

[6]Robert S. Kaplan and David P. Norton, *Using the Balanced Scorecard as a Strategic Management System* (Cambridge, Mass.: Harvard Business Press, 1996), p. 84.

- *Inputs.* The resources dedicated to or consumed by the program. Example: money, staff and staff time, volunteers and volunteer time, facilities, equipment, and supplies.
- *Activities.* What the program does with the inputs to fulfill its mission. Example: sheltering and feeding homeless families.
- *Outputs.* The direct products of program activities, usually measured in terms of the volume of work accomplished. Example: number of classes taught, counseling sessions conducted, educational materials distributed, and participants served.

Suggested Readings

Bozzo, S. L., and M. H. Hall. *A Review of Evaluation Resources for Nonprofit Organizations.* Canadian Centre for Philanthropy, 1999: Toronto, Ontario.

Kaplan, Robert S., and David P. Norton. *The Balanced Scorecard.* Cambridge, Mass.: Harvard Business School Press, 1996.

———. "Using the Balanced Scorecard as a Strategy Management System." *Harvard Business Review,* 74 no. 1 (1996): 77–85.

Love, Arnold J. "Outcome Evaluation: Putting the Balanced Scorecard to Work." Workshop, January 1999.

Murgatroyd, S., and D. Simpson. *Making Measurement Work, Using a Balanced Scorecard in Non-profit Organization.* AXIA Performance Centre, Developed in Partnership with The Peter F. Drucker Canadian Foundation and the Volunteer Centre of Calgary.

PART II Ethics and Governance

9 A Not-for-Profit Ethics Program

ALBERT ANDERSON
President, College Misericordia

9.1 Introduction

Fund-raising practitioners devoted to charitable causes should be no less professional in ethical matters than they are in maximizing contributions. Chances are that will not happen, however well disposed they are principally by instinct or codes. Nothing less than a program in principled ethical decision making integral to the organization's culture will lead to the professionalism philanthropy deserves. What follows may suggest a step in the right direction.

9.2 Not-for-Profit Ethics Today

In 1991 a blue-ribbon committee on ethics and values, sponsored by the Independent Sector (IS), issued a major report entitled *Ethics and the Nation's Voluntary and Philanthropic Community: Obedience to the Unenforceable*. A significant piece of work, it sets national ethical standards for not-for-profit organizations as well as grantmakers engaged in raising and contributing funds for various causes. It is a classic effort

204

designed to describe and exemplify the major levels at which ethical issues engage organizations, to urge them to conduct regular "audits" of their compliance with laws and best practices, and to encourage them to develop their own codes of ethics. A companion manual, *Everyday Ethics: Key Ethical Questions for Grantmakers and Grantseekers,*[1] provides a very useful format for conducting an ethics audit.

While there is no way of knowing how extensively not-for-profits have followed up on this work in the interim, the recommendations remain valid and important. Progress is most evident at national levels, where related professional associations such as the Association of Fundraising Professionals (AFP), the Association for Healthcare Philanthropy (AHP), the Council for the Advancement and Support of Education (CASE), the American Association of Fund Raising Council (AAFRC), the American Prospect Research Association (APRA), and the National Committee on Planned Giving (NCPG), among others, have done their part by developing or revising ethics codes and standards of high quality. (See Appendix 9B for selected association codes.)

Ironically, the very existence of such codes may have dampened not-for-profits' enthusiasm for developing their own codes, and so have done little to advance members' ethical proficiency. Not-for-profit professionals and volunteers may presume, for example, that these codes make it unnecessary to do further work at home. Being ethical, they may feel, is self-evident from the provisions, and all that remains is to endorse the standards and norms. Moreover, the subject of ethics in fund-raising circles is no longer the rage it was during the 1980s, prior to the emergence of most association codes. Other priorities, such as how to capitalize on "the largest generational transfer of wealth in history," seem to command greater attention.

Doubtless, the association codes have contributed to a greater awareness of ethical issues since that time. However, as a review of recent cases reported in, for example, *The Chronicle of Philanthropy, The Chronicle of Higher Education,* and elsewhere reminds us, unethical behavior is a changeless fact of life—and a major continuing threat to the public trust on which philanthropy depends.

The higher education component of the not-for-profit sector continues to struggle with issues of academic freedom, gender bias, and harassment—and, more recently, the ethical issues raised by the prospect of human cloning after the cloning of "Dolly," the sheep. Increasingly, however, institutions are facing three major areas of concern to philanthropy:

1. Issues surrounding access to and privacy of computerized information
2. Cases of potential conflict of interest arising from the changing relationships between the for-profit and not-for-profit sectors of American society
3. More noticeably, growing regulation of fund-raising activity

(A) PRIVACY ISSUES

Not strangely, reports suggest a growing number of cases of software piracy.[2] Given the widespread access to cyberspace, preventing theft of intellectual property and

---

[1]Sandra Trice Gray, ed., *Everyday Ethics: Key Ethical Questions for Grantmakers and Grantseekers* (Washington, D.C.: Independent Sector, 1993).
[2]Karla Haworth, "Publishers Press Colleges to Stop Software Piracy by their Students," *Chronicle of Higher Education* (henceforth *TCHE*), July 11, 1997.

infringement of copyright protection is increasingly more difficult; applicable laws are virtually unenforceable except as they trigger personal moral scruples. Then there are the computer hackers, some of whom create serious mischief, for example, by gaining access to extensive password files for anyone on the Web to peruse.[3] Fortunately, there is also the helpful (but scary) computer student who, in a challenge posed by an over-confident data security firm, succeeded in a few hours to break the firm's 40-bit encryption code.[4]

Fund raisers will appreciate the concern for electronic security of donor files, given the potential for embarrassment, if not litigation. Internet access makes it questionable whether development offices should continue to include personal, anecdotal information (marital problems, addictions, health condition, scandal) on donors and prospects in their files.[5] Knowledge of private affairs, exclusive of what is publicly known about a donor's assets and connections to the institution, can be very helpful but not necessarily essential to fund raisers. The risk that file information may be leaked has increased with the use of technology, and records can be subpoenaed as evidence in public probate, criminal, and civil courts. Beyond that, the ethical breaches at stake include the promise of confidentiality, the respect for individual dignity, and the responsibility to maintain constituent trust.

Evidence of the mushrooming influence of technology on not-for-profit fund raising is clear from the Winter 1995 issue of the AFP journal, *Advancing Philanthropy*, almost wholly devoted to the issue. The challenge for not-for-profit organizations, say the contributors, is to balance the emerging applications of technology with the dangers they may pose to donor impersonalization, to costly use of staff time, and so on. Still, virtually no attention is given in this discussion to the potential for unethical behavior. However, the Winter 1996–1997 issue makes a closer approach to ethics by focusing on corporate philanthropy. Milton Friedman, the economist, is the most provocative contributor, arguing that corporations that tout their "social responsibility" for philanthropy in fact undermine the free enterprise system with what amounts to socialism. Contributing to human welfare is government's job, he avers, by allocating taxes to alleviate society's ills; the job of business is to be profitable to its shareholders and employees—provided firms play by the rules—that is, avoid fraud and deceit.[6] Still, other authors in the issue laud the partnership of business and philanthropy for doing what government cannot be expected to do.

(B)   CONFLICT OF INTEREST

As to relationships with for-profits, however, current literature gives more attention to conflicts of interest. In higher education, for example, concern has been expressed that the increase in research by university faculty under contract with corporations may contribute to the publication of results favorable to the company, to the researcher who profits from the product, or to the institution that subsequently seeks the company's

---

[3]Reported by Kelly McCallum, *TCHE,* March 28, 1997.
[4]Reported in *TCHE,* February 14, 1997.
[5]Julie L. Nicklin, "Some College Fund Raisers Move to Delete Personal Information from Donor Records," *TCHE,* January 24, 1997.
[6]Milton Friedman, "The Business of Business Is Business," *Advancing Philanthropy* (Winter 1996–1997).

donation as a quid pro quo. But there is another side to this: One researcher has alleged that the university terminated him because he "blew the whistle" on a firm that threatened to sue him for publishing results unfavorable to the firm and for the jeopardy to a contribution the university sought from the firm.[7] Still another sponsored researcher was forced by the company to withdraw an unfavorable study, on the grounds of protecting patients using the product from research the firm claims is flawed.[8] One observer has suggested the formation of a national commission to examine the potential for conflicts of interest in these relationships and to offer guidelines for managing them.[9]

Meanwhile, authors have perceptively described the changing relationship of corporate America to philanthropy[10] as well as the motivation with which companies are increasingly inclined to give.[11] In addition to noting a discernible shift in corporate objectives from community responsibility to greater profitability, these studies offer evidence of corporate funding (or "investment"), beyond advertising budgets, to serve self-interests—for example, to enhance reputation and image, even to attract the campus specialists the corporations wish to recruit. Or, as another author notes, if the firm has a poor record on environmental concerns, for example, it may be moved to award grants for projects designed to correct its reputation.[12]

With mounting public concern that many charity-related organizations are abusing their tax-exempt status, Congress enacted the Taxpayer Bill of Rights Act of 1996. Exempting private foundations, it requires not-for-profits to strengthen—through full disclosure on their Internal Revenue Service (IRS) Form 990s—their accountability to the public. The law is aimed at determining whether a tax-exempt organization is engaging in excess benefit transactions, which would then subject it to significant penalty taxes. The test of such a transaction is whether people in a position to exercise substantial influence over an organization's affairs ("disqualified persons") receive economic benefits that exceed the value these people provide. For example, excessive benefits can take the form of the payment of unreasonable compensation or of improper revenue-sharing arrangements. The executive of a tax-exempt nursing home who serves as a paid director of the firm that supplies the home's food, or the director of development whose compensation, when reimbursed expenses are added to income is excessive, may turn out to be disqualified unless the organizations demonstrate otherwise. Clearly, not-for-profits will want to review with expert counsel the act's implications as they apply; however, even in compliance, the organization will want to review its general practices and policies for ethical accountability.

---

[7]Kim Strosnider, "Medical Professor Charges Brown University with Failing to Protect His Academic Freedom," *TCHE*, July 18, 1997.

[8]David L. Wheeler, "Article in Drug Study Spurs Call to Resist Corporate Influence on Research," *TCHE*, April 25, 1997.

[9]Mildred Cho, "Secrecy and Financial Conflicts in University-Industry Research Must Get Closer Scrutiny," *TCHE*, August 1, 1997.

[10]Dwight F. Burlingame and Dennis R. Young, eds., *Corporate Philanthropy at the Crossroads* (Bloomington: Indiana University Press, 1996).

[11]Jerome Himmelstein, *Looking Good and Doing Good: Corporate Philanthropy and Corporate Power* (Bloomington: Indiana University Press, 1997).

[12]Amy Magaro Rubin, "More Colleges Solicit 'Green' Gifts for Environmental Research and Education," *TCHE*, March 7, 1997.

(C) FUND-RAISING REGULATION

It follows that, in addition to technology-related issues and corporate responsibility, there is another troubling trend affecting the ethics of philanthropy: the growing role of regulators, state and federal, in monitoring and imposing sanctions on organizations for various fund-raising abuses, including fraud. A disproportionate number of scams exploiting the cause of public safety groups—police officers and firefighters—is a particular concern. Usually presented on the telephone by paid solicitors or well-meaning volunteers, the request to help the officers and families of such groups is appealing to unwary donors, not least because they may fear that declining to give will mean less public protection.[13]

At worst, in these cases donors—and public safety groups—are the victims of fraud, if solicitors misrepresent themselves, or, more often, donors may assume, unless they ask the solicitor, that their gift is tax-deductible, when it is not. While the Federal Trade Commission is beginning to crack down on these fund-raising efforts, a dozen states to date now require fund-raising telemarketers to disclose the percentages of the gift that will go to the charity and to the paid solicitor.[14] The unfortunate fact is, however, that as not-for-profits pay less attention to keeping their own houses in good ethical order, regulators will see fit to do it in the name of serving the public good.

9.3 The Ethical Task

This sampling of ethical concerns among not-for-profits may be sufficient to make the case for rededicating ourselves as practitioners in philanthropy, corporately and personally, to the task of developing organizations that are both ethically accountable and proficient.

However, the emergence of new professional codes, noted at the outset, is only part of the solution. The naked truth is that most practitioners who mean to be ethical are either ignorant of or very vague about how to be ethical; and norms that urge us, for example, to protect donor confidentiality or to avoid conflicts of interest do little to guide us in identifying or resolving the actual cases we experience. Thus, it is not enough even to develop codes for our own organizations beyond those of the associations. It requires nothing less than a *program* integral to the organization's day-to-day life—one that enables practitioners to make ethically adequate decisions and aids in developing a code that represents the organization's ongoing ethical posture, exemplified and tested on regular occasions by the actual (and hypothetical) experiences of its members.

What follows, therefore, is added encouragement to reaffirm the Independent Sector's recommendations, together with some suggestions and guidelines that essentially complement them by helping to advance practitioners' proficiency for ethical decision making.

9.4 Doing the Right Thing

As Aristotle reminded us well over two millennia ago in his classic *Nichomachean Ethics*, doing the right thing is more art than science, but nonetheless a finely developed craft essential to our well-being, and thus demands our lifelong attention. In his judgment, it

---

[13]Debra E. Blum, "Hiding Behind a Badge," *Chronicle of Philanthropy* (henceforth *TCP*), April 17, 1997.
[14]Debra E. Blum, "The Right to Raise Money?" *TCP,* July 10, 1997.

was a matter of building character around two primary and specifically moral traits or virtues: justice and beneficence.

Essentially, by applying his version of a Golden Rule, one distinguishes right from wrong and so acts responsibly by consistently "drawing the line"—the familiar metaphor we use to this day—between too much and too little, the excesses (abuses) and deficiencies of behavior we experience or intend. Ideas like moderation and balance come to mind. For example, to be beneficent one must draw and walk the line between aggrandizement and penury. Aristotle recognizes that every situation is different, so that what actually counts as beneficent is relative—and artfully discerned; however, the principle of avoiding extremes, of finding that perfect middle ground, is universally applicable. Indeed, beneficence, which puts philanthropy on a par with justice, is a distinctively moral aspect of character and human well-being.

The concept of drawing lines continues to represent one of the *two major categories of ethical issues* we as practitioners (and human beings) are asked to address. The first includes the many cases of *potential abuse or inadequate action* that pose a constant challenge to our sense of well-being. The second major category represents situations in which we are faced with *competing or conflicting interests and values*, which cannot be resolved without the aid of some more encompassing, priority-ruling principle.

Various thinkers since Aristotle have proposed what they regard as more adequate ethical decision-making principles. Though the reasoning that grounds them differs radically, two stand out over time for their ability to address most of the ethical issues we face:

1. A course of action is ethical that, experience suggests, will likely result in more benefit than harm for most people; and
2. Action is ethical that, rationally considered, accords with what would be intrinsically obligatory for all, regardless of anticipated consequences.

With variations, (1) is often termed *consequentialism* or *benefit-based ethics*, taking its lead from the classic Utilitarianism of the nineteenth-century English thinker John Stuart Mill. With similar variations, (2) may be called *formalism* or *duty-based ethics*, inspired by Immanuel Kant, the eighteenth-century German philosopher, whose guiding principle, the categorical imperative, provides a rational template or "form" for ensuring that one's intended course of action is one's moral duty. Again, consequentialism finds its final justification in empirical science and human experience; formalism implies total confidence in human reason, the discernment and personal obligation to do what seems right independently of probable outcomes. In crassly simplistic terms, their respective differences are sometimes depicted as best results vs. best intentions, and majority satisfaction vs. everyone's best interest. They are two good examples of comprehensive, though competing, *ethical frameworks*.[15]

Despite their profound differences, Mill and Kant, like Aristotle and others before them, were at one in insisting that morality be *principled*, not arbitrary or whimsical. That is, they affirmed the desirability, even necessity, to live in a moral order structured by principles, such as regard for human dignity, fairness, truth-telling, and promise-keeping; and they insisted that behavior is *ethically adequate only if justified by such principles*.

---

[15]Much of what follows is explained more fully, with actual or hypothetical cases, in my book, *Ethics for Fundraisers* (Bloomington: Indiana University Press, 1996). The book includes a wide range of bibliographic references as well as selected corporate and association codes of ethics.

9.5   *Ethically Adequate Decision Making*

This brings us to the practical use of ethical principles in philanthropy. They are embedded in the decision-making process we employ in the face of an ethical issue—that is, in
drawing lines or resolving competing values. Briefly, the process for ethically adequate
decision making entails answers to the following questions.

(A)   WHAT IS THE ETHICAL ISSUE?

Typically, we confront an apparent ethical issue with a feeling of tension or unease. Relying on the moral influences that have shaped us, we sense that something is not as it
"ought" to be—the language of morality. We are on the verge of making a moral judgment but cannot until the issue is clear—if indeed there is a moral issue. Often, by carefully examining the case, we find no reason to challenge it, at least on moral grounds. For
example, our discomfort may in fact be some reservation we have about the "right" way
of doing things—that is, a questioning of effective policy, process, or strategy is not necessarily an ethical issue. The difference is doing things right vs. doing the right thing.
Thus, the first step is to clarify the situation by establishing the facts, a step that may go
a long way toward resolving one's initial uneasiness. If the facts seem to compel a judgment that some action or behavior is morally wrong, then by implication some corrective
course of action is in order.

(B)   WHAT PRINCIPLES(S) MIGHT I EMPLOY TO SUPPORT MY MORAL JUDGMENT?

Suppose as the organization's chief fund-raising officer the board urges you to mount a
campaign targeted at your vendors, on the grounds that they owe the not-for-profit
something in return for its business. You are uneasy about it. You reason that while your
vendors do have a close and valuable relationship to the organization, and thus represent good prospects for solicitation, the approach suggests potential for abuse, say, a
quid pro quo or a subtle form of extortion—which seems (morally) wrong. But why is it
wrong? Because, you conclude, it seems to violate the very ideas of beneficence and
charitable intent—so basic as to suggest *guiding principles*—on which the organization's
mission relies. That is, the organization ought to draw some lines, to keep separate its
business transactions from its funding efforts. Vendors are under no other obligation
than to supply necessary goods and services. Ideally, you believe, philanthropy ought to
occur in a free and unconditional context: A philanthropic organization should not
coerce a vendor into becoming a donor; and a donor should expect no favor in return for
a gift, other than the satisfaction of supporting a good cause.

(C)   WHAT ACTIONS SHOULD I TAKE?

The possibilities range from many, perhaps alternative, courses of action to no action at
all (which is sometimes the best decision). You choose to explain to the board that you do

not recommend any specially targeted campaign to vendors, first, because most of them already contribute, or are solicited along with other firms as part of the organization's annual community drive; and second, because of the guiding principles involved—principles generally endorsed by reputable philanthropic-related associations. You may also suggest the timeliness and usefulness of discussing such norms at a future meeting and of considering developing a code of ethics, incorporating principles like beneficence tailored to fit and guide the organization's particular mission.

(D) WHAT ETHICAL PRINCIPLES ARE ADEQUATE FOR PHILANTHROPIC PURPOSES?

Typically, the norms (normative statements) or provisions that make up a code of ethics are based on principles such as beneficence or trustworthiness. An ethical principle may be thought of as a concept recognized for its unusually influential place in human experience with moral matters. These concepts come to mind as possible guides for identifying and justifying the practitioner's ethical stance, and thus achieve the status of principles. The principles, in turn, are reflected in the norms of the code; for example, the principle of trustworthiness would in some form express the norm "One ought always to be worthy of trust." However, there are many ethical principles distinctive of philanthropy, some more dominant or wide-ranging in their conceptual richness than others (no less important). These three philanthropic principles are:

1. *Beneficence.* A dominant principle, this acknowledges one of Aristotle's primary ethical virtues, central to philanthropy: the responsibility to share one's surplus wealth to further human well-being. Subject like planets to this principle's orbit are:
   The public good that the mission of every worthy not-for-profit cause is intended to serve
   Charitable intent, which reflects the governing motive on which philanthropic activity rests, to include both fund raising and fund giving.
2. *Respect.* Another dominant ethical principle for practitioners, this embraces the fundamental dignity and worth we accord every human being. It attracts to its sphere of influence three additional principles:
   Individual autonomy, the right of every able person, uncoerced, to make his or her own choices, secure his or her own well-being, and determine his or her own destiny
   Personal privacy, which recognizes the sanctity and confidentiality of one's personal, family, and nonpublic business or financial affairs
   Protection from harm, which urges that no action be taken that could be harmful to oneself or others
3. *Trust.* The third dominant ethical principle, trust represents the fundamental relationship among not-for-profit practitioners and the constituents and general public they serve. Philanthropy would disappear without it, as would the ground of every relationship between persons. Accordingly, this principle attracts several others:
   Truth-telling, the obligation to be honest and forthright, to convey information as fully and accurately as possible, avoiding deceptive or misleading information

Promise-keeping, which acknowledges the commitments entailed by mutual understandings, agreements, and contractual arrangements

Accountability, the responsibility one assumes for performing, or failing to perform, the legitimate assignments or expectations of others

Fairness, the capacity and willingness to deal justly, equitably, and objectively with others, avoiding preferential, arbitrary, or prejudicial actions

Fidelity of purpose, which recognizes the necessity for dedication to the mission and aims of philanthropy, the organization, and one's profession

These are the ethical principles of greatest moment to all who have a part in furthering not-for-profit philanthropy. (Not strangely, they are principles we find applicable in our personal, nonprofessional lives as well.) In the course of the challenges to know and do the right thing, we mentally scan them for proper fit and justification. Nonetheless, ethically adequate decision making, as noted above, may well require that the principles *themselves* be justified, by reference to an all-inclusive ethical framework.

(E) HOW DO I JUSTIFY THESE (PHILANTHROPIC) PRINCIPLES?

Clearly, in most cases the principles on which the norms or provisions of a code of ethics rest may be sufficient for justifying one's positions and actions. However, while no code provision is justifiable without recourse to ethical principle, so it is that no such principle can stand on its own without a deeper grounding in human experience. Hence, we ultimately rely on more comprehensive *ethical frameworks* like consequentialism and formalism.

Consider the principle of promise-keeping. Suppose as the development officer (the chief executive officer, chief financial officer, or anyone with authority over expenses), you are under pressure to raise operating funds, but you know that the prospective donor's sole interest is in general endowment. You assure him or her that the gift will support that interest; but after receiving the contribution, and feeling that the donor will never discover the difference, you instruct the financial officer to apply it to current operations. Of course, your instruction is contrary to IRS regulations, and the financial officer may remind you of that, provided she does not fear that what sounds like insubordination will cost her her job. However, ethically you have violated the principle of promise-keeping in relation to the donor. But if you can do it with impunity and to your own advantage, why not do it?

The consequentialist would say that experience shows that, generally, it is more *beneficial* than harmful to keep one's promises (though one might imagine exceptions); otherwise, relationships, understandings, and agreements we regularly assume with others lose their force, and offer little assurance they will endure. The formalist would say that it is never right under any circumstances to break one's promises, though it might seem expedient to do so; the very idea is self-defeating, and therefore absurd to think that this particular course of action, with or without impunity, could become a universal moral rule. Promise-keeping is one's *duty.*

In summary, ethically adequate decision making requires that one identify the ethical issue, make a moral judgment, support it with ethical principle that is framed in a comprehensive ethical stance, and take appropriate action. (For extensive explanation of how consequentialism and formalism apply to a variety of cases see my *Ethics for Fundraisers.*)

9.6 Developing an Organizational Code

A code of ethics represents the values and intentions an organization shares with all who have a stake in it. The committee sponsored by the Independent Sector, noted earlier, identified a number of ethical values and behaviors it felt should be evident in every not-for-profit organization. Explained more fully in the committee study (with helpful examples), the values are also reasonably self-evident and provide a valuable checklist for approaching the development of a code:

- Commitment beyond self
- Obedience to the laws
- Commitment beyond the law
- Commitment to the public good
- Respect for the value and dignity of individuals
- Tolerance, diversity, and social justice
- Accountability to the public
- Openness and honesty
- Prudent use of resources

The codes of national associations also offer thoughtful and useful insights into the character and content of ethics codes suitable for not-for-profit organizations. And some of the best models for developing one's own organizational code come from successful firms and corporations such as Levi Strauss & Co. and Johnson & Johnson. (See Appendix 9B for examples.)

Of course, except for purely public relations value, no code is worth the paper it is written on if it is not espoused by top management and embodied throughout the organization. And if executives need inspiration for taking the lead in code development central to the organization's culture, they should read the history of Johnson & Johnson. No event so tested the firm's longstanding code, or enhanced the company's priceless reputation, than the decision to remove Tylenol from the market and develop a tamper-resistant cap for the product, once it was discovered that someone had tampered with it.[16] Above all, a code of ethics is a dynamic, not a static, instrument, designed to be understood, tested regularly for adequacy, and lived.

While every corporate or organizational code of ethics will be unique, tailored to the aims and constituents it serves, most codes seem to have certain elements in common. Typically, they:

- Begin with a statement of *purpose* that implies or affirms service for the public good
- Assume explicit responsibility toward the key *constituencies* that have a stake in the purpose
- Pledge good *citizenship*, upholding the laws and rights that a democratic society provides

---

[16]See Anderson, *Ethics for Fundraisers,* for a reprint of this code and the tradition the firm's employees continue for reviewing and upholding it.

- Express a commitment to *ethical principles* that goes beyond compliance with the law, principles that might include fairness, truthful communications, respect for privacy, and for the general welfare of employees, clients, and vendors
- Often reflect a *dominant ethical concept* such as trust or integrity, which underlies their relationships with constituents
- Give significant attention to *conflict of interest*, often with examples that warn against personal gain at the expense of the goodwill earned by the organization

9.7   *Installing an Ethics Program at Home*

A good *first step* in the process of initiating the organization's ethics program might be to review the Independent Sector work. Members would also find it instructive to collect and compare available codes, both those of the various associations devoted to philanthropy, and those of reputable local and national firms.[17]

The *second step* is to decide on the elements essential to the code that will represent the organization to the public—such as those noted above, but also those that may be unique to one's mission and constituencies. In general, the code should reflect as many of the ethical principles characteristic of philanthropic work as possible. However, the code is intended to form a profile of the organization's ethical stance. Some suggested templates (my language, which need not be yours) for discussion follow.

For example, the *purpose* provision may need to reflect the *idea* that:

> *As responsible persons organized to advance and support [here, state in a sentence the organization's purpose/mission/cause], an ongoing need is to aid [the name of the organization] to accomplish its aims by rightly soliciting and thus meriting the contributions and enduring goodwill of our constituents.*

As part of this preamble, the organization may wish to add a statement reflecting its general responsibility to its *stakeholders*. Again (my language):

> *In partnership with the philanthropic community, we seek to build and strengthen professional and ethical relationships with all our constituents: donors whose gifts are entrusted to us; volunteers on whose aid we depend; staff who are accountable for their actions; and the public whose good we serve.*

Further provisions might affirm norms of citizenship, compliance with the letter and spirit of the law, and, above all, the organization's commitment to key *ethical concepts, values, or implied principles* that go beyond the law. One could also underscore the theme or foundation of *trust* we seek in philanthropy and at the same time introduce specific organizational norms—for example, acknowledging the line between privacy and public disclosure.

That is, the not-for-profit organization balances twin obligations: to disclose information, such as policies and financial data, that adds to public understanding and con-

---

[17]Chapter 5 of *Ethics for Fundraisers* provides a detailed account of what is entailed in developing a code of ethics for not-for-profit practitioners.

fidence; and to guard against unwarranted interference and intrusiveness into private or confidential matters, such as a donor's personal life or gift history.

Given the increasingly sophisticated means available to not-for-profit organizations for the gathering and analysis of donor/prospect information, it may be prudent to include a provision that assures stakeholders concerning the organization's *use and management of data*. That is, we make it clear that while we are thorough and discreet in the process of learning to know and engage our donors and prospective supporters, to earn their enduring support, we do so with sensitivity and respect for individual and corporate dignity, with particular concern for the protection of private, even anecdotal information.[18]

Conflict of interest provisions are a prominent part of codes, perhaps because many people are inclined (mistakenly) to believe that the issue is virtually synonymous with ethics, which they characterize as the conflict of values. At best, this view would cover only a fraction of the ethical issues we face. Nonetheless, conflict of interest does denote a broad class of moral tensions that the organization will want to identify and discuss at length.[19]

Moreover, these provisions will have added value in today's codes, considering the issues surrounding the rightful place and protection of the "whistle-blower." This is the most difficult dilemma for a loyal not-for-profit practitioner to face, because it suggests that doing the right thing offers the legitimate whistle-blower nothing but grief; hence, anticipating the issue may be prudent in our litigious climate. This, and the more conventional norms that address conflict of interest, will include the following ideas:

> *As persons employed or enlisted for our willingness and competence to carry out [this organization's] mission, we are committed to integrity in all our relationships, and place the long-term best interests of [the organization], its constituents, and the profession, before our own.*
> *To avoid even the appearance of conflicting or competing interests, we will take no actions that could be viewed as favoritism, unfair advantage, or monetarily significant reward for ourselves or [the organization].*
> *Concerns about any practice, action, or relationship that could embarrass [the organization], breach confidentiality, or violate conscience will be discussed with those to whom we are accountable, fairly and without fear of recrimination.*

Finally, the organization may see fit to add norms that reflect the ethical behavior it seeks to instill in its staff and volunteers, behavior worthy of both personal and professional development. Tailored to the organization's character, these norms may aid in establishing an appropriate moral culture for operations and activities. Here one might include respect and consideration of others, accurate claims for reimbursement of expenses, careful and legitimate use of the organization's property, prudent use of budgeted resources, acknowledgment of others' ideas, readiness to take constructive criticism and to improve one's performance, and the like.

As we learn, however, to become ethically proficient, it is not enough to rely on a code of ethics. A code is neither self-clarifying nor self-justifying. Its norms stand exposed, without benefit of meaningful experience and principled reasoning. Norms are

---

[18]Here, the American Prospect Research Association (APRA) code of ethics will be very helpful.
[19]For a sense of the breadth of conflicts of interest, see Anderson, *Ethics for Fundraisers*.

abstractions lacking the real-life moral tensions and conflicts that would make sense of our professed responsibilities, and even if we understand them, they lack the justification that would compel us to affirm them.

Thus, the *capstone of the ethics program* is the organization's commitment to practice ethical decision making as well as to test and refine the code's viability, on a regularly scheduled basis, in light of actual and hypothetical situations. For practitioners of philanthropy, both professionals and volunteers, helping the organization make the right decisions will be engaging and satisfying. The whole point, of course, is to do the right thing.

Suggested Readings

Anderson, Albert. *Ethics for Fundraisers.* Bloomington: Indiana University Press, 1996.

Aristotle. *The Nichomachaen Ethics,* many versions, especially Chapters 1 and 2, Book IV, and Books I, II, and III for context. For one excellent version, see J.A.K. Thomson, *The Ethics of Aristotle.* New York: Penguin, 1956.

Briscoe, Marianne, ed. *Ethics in Fundraising: Putting Values into Practice.* San Francisco: Jossey-Bass, 1994.

Burlingame, Dwight, ed. *The Responsibilities of Wealth.* Bloomington: Indiana University Press, 1992.

Currents (January 1987) (the periodical of the Council for Advancement and Support of Education). This entire issue is devoted to ethical problems that can plague not-for-profit organizations, particularly educational institutions.

Fischer, Marilyn. "Ethical Fund Raising: Deciding What's Right." *Advancing Philanthropy* (Spring 1994).

Goodpaster, Kenneth. "Ethical Frameworks for Management," case study. Boston: Harvard Business School, President and Fellows of Harvard College, 1983.

Independent Sector's Committee on Values and Ethics. *Ethics and the Nation's Voluntary and Philanthropic Community: Obedience to the Unenforceable.* Washington, D.C.: 1991. A companion manual for use by not-for-profits is Sandra Trice Gray, ed., *Everyday Ethics: Key Ethical Questions for Grantmakers and Grantseekers.* Washington, D.C.: Independent Sector, 1993.

Josephson, Michael. *Ethical Issues in the Philanthropic and Non-Profit Community.* Joseph & Edna Josephson Institute for the Advancement of Ethics: *Ethics Easier Said Than Done,* issue 18, January 8, 1992.

Kant, Immanuel. *Foundations of the Metaphysics of Morals* (1785), translated by Lewis White Beck. Indianapolis: Library of Liberal Arts, Bobbs-Merrill, 1959. This is the classic source of formalism, or duty-based ethics.

Mill, John Stuart. *Utilitarianism* (1861), many editions; for example, George Sher, ed. Indianapolis: Hackett, 1979. This is the classic source of consequentialism, or benefits-based ethics.

O'Neill, Michael. *Ethics in Nonprofit Management.* San Francisco: Institute for Nonprofit Organization Management, University of San Francisco, 1990. See also his "Fund Raising as an Ethical Act," *Advancing Philanthropy* (Fall 1993), a good summary of the ethics of Aristotle, Kant, and Mill applied to fund raising; and "A Spare Literature," *Journal of the National Society of Fund-Raising Executives* (Summer 1997).

Pastin, Mark. *The Hard Problems of Management: Gaining the Ethics Edge.* San Francisco: Jossey-Bass, 1991. See also his "Bright Lines, Big Deals," *Advancing Philanthropy* (Summer 1997), an issue devoted to the state of the public trust.

Payton, Robert L. *Philanthropy: Voluntary Action for the Public Good.* New York: American Council on Education/Macmillan, 1988.

Shannon, James P., ed. *The Corporate Contributions Handbook: Devoting Private Means to Public Needs.* San Francisco: Jossey-Bass, 1991. An excellent collection of essays by representative leaders in corporate philanthropy; for example, chapters on grant-making ethics and the ethical concerns about cause-related marketing.

Singer, Peter. "Ethics," in *The New Encyclopedia Britannica,* vol. 18 of the *Macropaedia,* 15th edition. Chicago: Encyclopaedia Britannica, 1992. An excellent review of the history of ethical thought.

White, Douglas E. *The Art of Planned Giving: Understanding Donors and the Culture of Giving.* New York: John Wiley & Sons, 1995. See also his chapter, "Why Do People Donate to Charity?" in James M. Greenfield, ed., *The Nonprofit Handbook: Fund Raising,* 2d ed. New York: John Wiley & Sons, 1997.

Appendix 9A   Elements of Ethical Decision Making in Not-for-Profit Organizations

Moral Awareness

- Rooted in upbringing, accepted behavior, personal values, self-interest, conscience.
- Unexamined sense, feeling, or opinion of what is right and wrong, good and bad, just and unjust,
  - affecting me (egoism), and
  - affecting others (altruism).
- Presupposes some concept of self-worth, of the human condition, and of individual capacity based on
  - self-realization (secular), or
  - other-worldly assistance (religious).
- Assumes a basic climate of trust; in philanthropy, relationships
  - affecting clients, constituents, and
  - affecting colleagues, organizations.

Ethically Adequate Decision Making

- *Examine* the initial tension or discomfort one has about a situation,
  - to determine the ethical issue (if there is one),
  - by establishing the facts.
- *Propose* a course of action, what ought or ought not to be done, recognizing
  - two kinds of decision-making:
    - Drawing lines (to avoid inadequate or abusive action).
    - Choosing from competing or conflicting values.
- *Justify* a course of ethical action (below).

Model of Ethical Justification

- *Judge* that a certain actual or proposed action is right or wrong based on moral awareness and examination of the facts (above).
- *Apply* the moral principle that seems to support the judgment and suggests an appropriate (principled) course of action.
- *Employ* a comprehensive ethical framework to justify one's choice of principled action.

Principled Action in Philanthropy

- Principles are forces or spheres of enduring ethical influence in the form of concepts we mentally explore for application to a morally puzzling issue. Each can be transformed into a normative statement, for example, honesty means one ought always to be forthcoming, to tell the truth.
- In philanthropy there are three dominant forces or spheres of influence supported by other principles (logically related, but no less important):

- *Beneficence*
  - The public good
  - Charitable intent
- *Respect*
  - Individual autonomy
  - Personal privacy
  - Protection from harm
- *Trust*
  - Truth-telling
  - Promise-keeping
  - Accountability
  - Fairness
  - Fidelity of purpose

Comprehensive Ethical Frameworks

- *Consequentialism (benefit-based ethics):*
  - Action is ethical that results in greater benefit than harm, for most people.
- *Formalism (duty-based ethics):*
  - Action is ethical that accords with what is intrinsically and rationally obligatory for all, independent of balancing outcomes.

Appendix 9B   Selected Ethics Codes, Principles, and Standards

The following material is taken from the appendix to Anderson, *Ethics for Fundraisers*, where it was reprinted with the permission of the organizations represented. Readers are advised to contact these organizations directly for possibly revised or updated versions of materials.

EXHIBIT 9.1 A Donor Bill of Rights

A Donor Bill of Rights

PHILANTHROPY is based on voluntary action for the common good. It is a tradition of giving and sharing that is primary to the quality of life. To assure that philanthropy merits the respect and trust of the general public, and that donors and prospective donors can have full confidence in the not-for-profit organizations and causes they are asked to support, we declare that all donors have these rights:

I. To be informed of the organization's mission, of the way the organization intends to use donated resources, and of its capacity to use donations effectively for their intended purposes

II. To be informed of the identity of those serving on the organization's governing board, and to expect the board to exercise prudent judgment in its stewardship responsibilities

III. To have access to the organization's most recent financial statements

IV. To be assured their gifts will be used for the purposes for which they were given

V. To receive appropriate acknowledgment and recognition

VI. To be assured that information about their donations is handled with respect and with confidentiality to the extent provided by law

VII. To expect that all relationships with individuals representing organizations of interest to the donor will be professional in nature

VIII. To be informed whether those seeking donations are volunteers, employees of the organization or hired solicitors.

IX. To have the opportunity for their names to be deleted from mailing lists that an organization may intend to share

X. To feel free to ask questions when making a donation and to receive prompt, truthful and forthright answers.

Developed jointly by American Association of Fund Raising Counsel, Association for Healthcare Philanthropy, Council for Advancement and Support of Education, National Society of Fund Raising Executives; endorsed by Independent Sector, National Catholic Development Conference, National Committee on Planned Giving, National Council for Resource Development, United Way of America.

AFP CODE OF ETHICAL PRINCIPLES AND STANDARDS OF PROFESSIONAL PRACTICE

Statement of Ethical Principles
Adopted November 1991

The Association of Fundraising Professionals (AFP) exists to foster the development and growth of fund-raising professionals and the profession, to promote high ethical standards in the fund-raising profession and to preserve and enhance philanthropy and volunteerism. Members of AFP are motivated by an inner drive to improve the quality of life through the causes they serve. They serve the ideal of philanthropy; are committed to the preservation and enhancement of volunteerism; and hold stewardship of these concepts as the overriding principle of their professional life. They recognize their responsibility to ensure that needed resources are vigorously and ethically sought and that the intent of the donor is honestly fulfilled. To these ends, AFP members embrace certain values that they strive to uphold in performing their responsibilities for generating philanthropic support.

AFP members aspire to:

- practice their profession with integrity, honesty, truthfulness and adherence to the absolute obligation to safeguard the public trust;
- act according to the highest standards and visions of their organization, profession and conscience;
- put philanthropic mission above personal gain;
- inspire others through their own sense of dedication and high purpose;
- improve their professional knowledge and skills in order that their performance will better serve others;
- demonstrate concern for the interests and well being of individuals affected by their actions;
- value the privacy, freedom of choice and interests of all those affected by their actions;
- foster cultural diversity and pluralistic values, and treat all people with dignity and respect;
- affirm, through personal giving, a commitment to philanthropy and its role in society;
- adhere to the spirit as well as the letter of all applicable laws and regulations;
- advocate within their organizations, adherence to all applicable laws and regulations;
- avoid even the appearance of any criminal offense or professional misconduct;
- bring credit to the fund-raising profession by their public demeanor;
- encourage colleagues to embrace and practice these ethical principles and standards of professional practice; and
- be aware of the codes of ethics promulgated by other professional organizations that serve philanthropy.

Standards of Professional Practice
Adopted and incorporated into the AFP Code of Ethical Principles November 1992

Furthermore, while striving to act according to the above values, AFP members agree to abide by the AFP Standards of Professional Practice, which are adopted and incorporated into the AFP Code of Ethical Principles. Violation of the Standards may subject the member to disciplinary sanctions, including expulsion, as provided in the AFP Ethics Enforcement Procedures.

Professional Obligations

1. Members shall not engage in activities that harm the member's organization, clients, or profession.

EXHIBIT 9.2 Values Statement of the Association of Fundraising Professionals

Our mission says what we will do. Our values describe how we will do it. As individuals and an organization, we are committed to our mission and these values. Everything we do—and the way we do it—is guided by these values.

INTEGRITY
We act ethically, with honesty and sincerity. We honor privacy and confidentiality. We remain true to our organizational values and our own personal values. Our discussions are open and we ensure that all information is available.

FAIR PLAY
We believe in parity. We ensure that the opinions and perspectives of all are heard. We deal objectively with issues. We are accessible regardless of geography, culture, finance, experience, physical challenge or other. We resolve conflict with honesty, respect and compassion.

RESPECT
All people have worth and value. We welcome and encourage diversity in all forms, be it gender, generation, ethnicity, experience, faith, sexual orientation or other.

We welcome different opinions and agree to disagree. We respect the group and honor the will of the group to move forward cohesively, focusing on the good of the organization. We have faith and confidence in ourselves, our colleagues and those we serve as volunteers, donors and members. We are professional in our treatment of each other.

ACCOUNTABILITY
We are ever vigilant about our moral and legal responsibilities to each other, the group and our own selves. As individuals and an organization, we acknowledge strengths and opportunities, weaknesses and threats. We address these issues in a responsible manner.

We strive for excellence, pursue continuous quality improvement, and seek cutting edge opportunity in all areas of service, management and governance. We stay close to our customers—whether members, donors, volunteers or collegial organizations—in order to respond to their expectations and anticipate their needs. We seek the highest level of competency in our practice through education and professional development. We take pride in our work, are accountable for our own actions, and take responsibility for contributing to solutions.

We respect teamwork. We create opportunities for personal and professional growth. We honor our commitments to each other and to the group. We serve and support each other—staff to volunteer, volunteer to volunteer, volunteer to staff, staff to staff, and to the community.

We recognize our responsibility to our members and donors for appropriate stewardship of their dues and gifts.

COMPASSION
We are caring and sensitive. We promote an atmosphere of tolerance, respect, inclusion, sensitivity and humor. We are sympathetic to the distress of others and seek to alleviate it. We support our colleagues in AFP and the people in our communities.

LOYALTY
We are faithful to the diverse colleagues who make up AFP. We acknowledge our duty to those not present. We recognize our allegiance to the many constituents who comprise our various communities.

RISK, LEADERSHIP AND CHANGE
We believe that leaders take risks. We try to be courageous as individuals and an organization. To this end, we create a safe, trusting and stable environment where the individual and group can take risks.

EXHIBIT 9.2 (*Continued*)

We recognize that risk and leadership require authenticity, honesty, creativity and change. We are responsive to change and its attendant risks, opportunities and challenges. We respect questioning and self-examination. As leaders, we strive to find the balance between following and leading the group.

STEWARDSHIP

We believe in love of humankind and voluntary action for the common good. We commit ourselves to the philanthropic process here at AFP and in our own organizations and communities. We pledge to protect and enhance philanthropy for future generations. We are philanthropists ourselves. We recognize that other individuals and organizations also work to advance philanthropy and that we are a part of a larger universe.

Created by the Board of Directors, Staff and Delegate Assembly
Adopted by the AFP Board of Directors, July 15, 1995; amended with input from the Delegate Assembly, November 5, 1995.

2. Members shall not engage in activities that conflict with their fiduciary, ethical, and legal obligations to their organizations and their clients.
3. Members shall effectively disclose all potential and actual conflicts of interest; such disclosure does not preclude or imply ethical impropriety.
4. Members shall not exploit any relationship with a donor, prospect, volunteer, or employee to the benefit of the member or the member's organization.
5. Members shall comply with all applicable local, state, provincial, federal, civil, and criminal laws.
6. Members recognize their individual boundaries of competence and are forthcoming and truthful about their professional experience and qualifications.

Solicitation and Use of Charitable Funds

7. Members shall take care to ensure that all solicitation materials are accurate and correctly reflect the organization's mission and use of solicited funds.
8. Members shall take care to ensure that donors receive informed, accurate and ethical advice about the value and tax implications of potential gifts.
9. Members shall take care to ensure that contributions are used in accordance with donors' intentions.
10. Members shall take care to ensure proper stewardship of charitable contributions, including timely reports on the use and management of funds.
11. Members shall obtain explicit consent by the donor before altering the conditions of a gift.

Presentation of Information

12. Members shall not disclose privileged or confidential information to unauthorized parties.

13. Members shall adhere to the principle that all donor and prospect information created by, or on behalf of, an organization is the property of that organization and shall not be transferred or utilized except on behalf of that organization.
14. Members shall give donors the opportunity to have their names removed from lists that are sold to, rented to, or exchanged with other organizations.
15. Members shall, when stating fund-raising results, use accurate and consistent accounting methods that conform to the appropriate guidelines adopted by the American Institute of Certified Public Accountants (AICPA)* for the type of organization involved. (* In countries outside of the United States, comparable authority should be utilized.)

Compensation

16. Members shall not accept compensation that is based on a percentage of charitable contributions; nor shall they accept finder's fees.
17. Members may accept performance-based compensation, such as bonuses, provided such bonuses are in accord with prevailing practices within the members' own organizations, and are not based on a percentage of charitable contributions.
18. Members shall not pay finder's fees, commissions, or percentage compensation based on charitable contributions and shall take care to discourage their organizations from making such payments.

Association for Healthcare Philanthropy Statement of Professional Standards and Conduct

Preamble

Association for Healthcare Philanthropy members represent to the public, by personal example and conduct, both their employer and their profession. They have, therefore, a duty to faithfully adhere to the highest standards and conduct in:

    I. Their promotion of the merits of their institutions and of excellence in health care generally, providing community leadership in cooperation with health, educational, cultural, and other organizations;

   II. Their words and actions, embodying respect for truth, honesty, fairness, free inquiry, and the opinions of others, treating all with equality and dignity;

  III. Their respect for all individuals without regard to race, color, sex, creed, ethnic or national identity, handicap or age;

  IV. Their commitment to strive to increase professional and personal skills for improved service to their donors and institutions, to encourage and actively participate in career development for themselves and others whose roles include support for resource development functions, and to share freely their knowledge and experience with others as appropriate;

   V. Their continuing effort and energy to pursue new ideas and modifications to improve conditions for, and benefits to, donors and their institutions;

    VI. Their avoidance of activities that might damage the reputation of any donor, their institution, any other resource development professional or the profession as a whole, or themselves, and to give full credit for the ideas, words, or images originated by others;

    VII. Their respect for the rights of privacy of others and the confidentiality of information gained in the pursuit of their professional duties;

    VIII. Their acceptance of a compensation method freely agreed upon and based on their institution's usual and customary compensation guidelines which have been established and approved for general institutional use while always remembering that: (a) any compensation agreement should fully reflect the standards of professional conduct; and, (b) antitrust laws in the United States prohibit limitation on compensation methods;

    IX. Their respect for the law and professional ethics as a standard of personal conduct, with full adherence to the policies and procedures of their institution;

    X. Their pledge to adhere to this statement of Professional Standards and Conduct, and to encourage others to join them in observance of its guidelines.

The National Committee on Planned Giving Model Standards of Practice for the Charitable Gift Planner

Preamble

The purpose of this statement is to encourage responsible charitable gift planning by urging the adoption of the following Standards of Practice by all who work in the charitable gift planning process, including charitable institutions and their gift planning officers, independent fund-raising consultants, attorneys, accountants, financial planners and life insurance agents, collectively referred to hereafter as "Gift Planners."

This statement recognizes that the solicitation, planning, and administration of a charitable gift is a complex process involving philanthropic, personal, financial, and tax considerations, and as such often involves professionals from various disciplines whose goals should include working together to structure a gift that achieves a fair and proper balance between the interests of the donor and the purposes of the charitable institution.

I. Primacy of Philanthropic Motivation

The principal basis for making a charitable gift should be a desire on the part of the donor to support the work of charitable institutions.

II. Explanation of Tax Implications

Congress has provided tax incentives for charitable giving, and the emphasis in this statement on philanthropic motivation in no way minimizes the necessity and appropriateness of a full and accurate explanation by the Gift Planner of those incentives and their implications.

III. Full Disclosure

It is essential to the gift planning process that the role and relationships of all parties involved, including how and by whom each is compensated, be fully disclosed to the donor. A Gift Planner shall not act or purport to act as a representative of any charity without the express knowledge and approval of the charity, and shall not, while employed by the charity, act or purport to act as a representative of the donor, without the express consent of both the charity and the donor.

IV. Compensation

Compensation paid to Gift Planners shall be reasonable and proportionate to the services provided. Payments of finders fees, commissions or other fees by a donee organization to an independent Gift Planner as a condition for the delivery of a gift are never appropriate. Such payments lead to abusive practices and may violate certain state and federal regulations. Likewise, commission-based compensation for Gift Planners who are employed by a charitable institution is never appropriate.

V. Competence and Professionalism

The Gift Planner should strive to achieve and maintain a high degree of competence in his or her chosen area, and shall advise donors only in areas in which he or she is professionally qualified. It is the hallmark of professionalism for the Gift Planners that they realize when they have reached the limits of their knowledge and expertise, and as a result, should include other professionals in the process. Such relationships should be characterized by courtesy, tact and mutual respect.

VI. Consultations with Independent Advisors

A Gift Planner acting on behalf of a charity shall in all cases strongly encourage the donor to discuss the proposed gift with competent independent legal and tax advisors of the donor's choice.

VII. Consultation with Charities

Although Gift Planners frequently and properly counsel donors concerning specific charitable gifts without the prior knowledge or approval of the donee organization, the Gift Planner, in order to ensure that the gift will accomplish the donor's objectives, should encourage the donor, early in the gift planning process, to discuss the proposed gift with the charity to whom the gift is to be made. In cases where the donor desires anonymity, the Gift Planner shall endeavor, on behalf of the undisclosed donor, to obtain the charity's input in the gift planning process.

VIII. Explanation of Gift

The Gift Planner shall make every effort, insofar as possible, to insure that the donor receives a full and accurate explanation of all aspects of the proposed gift.

IX. Full Compliance

A Gift Planner shall fully comply with and shall encourage other parties in the gift planning process to fully comply with both the letter and the spirit of all applicable federal and state laws and regulations.

X. Public Trust

Gift Planners shall, in all dealings with donors, institutions, and other professionals, act with fairness, honesty, integrity, and openness. Except for compensation received for services, the terms of which have been disclosed to the donor, they shall have no vested interest that could result in personal gain.

APRA Mission Statement

The mission of the Association of Professional Researchers for Advancement is to foster professional development and promote standards that enhance the expertise and status of development research and information service professionals worldwide.

To fulfill its mission, APRA will direct its energies to the following goals:

- To promote professional growth and advancement
- To advocate the highest standards of performance and ethical behavior
- To facilitate interaction among research, development and information professionals, and their representative organizations
- To advance the role of research in the development field
- To develop and maintain an administrative organizational plan that will support the association

APRA Statement of Ethics

As representatives of the profession, Association of Professional Researchers for Advancement (APRA) members shall be respectful of all people and organizations. They shall support and further the individual's fundamental right to privacy. APRA members are committed to the ethical collection and use of information in the pursuit of legitimate institutional goals.

Code of Ethics

In their work, prospect researchers must balance the needs of their institutions/organizations to collect and record information with the prospects' right to privacy. This balance is not always easy to maintain. However, the following ethical principles apply:

I. Fundamental Principles
A. Relevance
Prospect researchers shall seek and record only information that is relevant to the fund raising effort of the institutions that employ them.

B. Honesty

Prospect researchers shall be truthful with regard to their identity, purpose and the identity of their institution during the course of their work.

C. Confidentiality

Confidential information pertaining to donors or prospective donors shall be scrupulously protected so that the relationship of trust between donor and donee and the integrity of the prospect research professional is upheld.

D. Accuracy

Prospect researchers shall record all data accurately. Such information must be verifiable or attributable to its source.

II. Procedures

A. Collection

1. The collection and use of information shall be done lawfully.
2. Information sought and recorded may include all public records.
3. Written requests for public information shall be made on institutional stationery clearly identifying the sender.
4. Whenever possible, payments for public records shall be made through the institution.
5. When requesting information in person or by telephone, neither individual nor institutional identity shall be concealed.

B. Recording

1. Researchers shall state information in an objective and factual manner.
2. Documents pertaining to donors or prospective donors shall be irreversibly disposed of when no longer needed (e.g., by shredding).

C. Use

1. Non-public information is the property of the institution for which it was collected and shall not be given to persons other than those who are involved with the cultivation or solicitation effort or those who need that information in the performance of their duties for that institution.
2. Only public or published information may be shared with colleagues at other institutions as a professional courtesy.
3. Prospect information is the property of the institution for which it was gathered and shall not be taken to another institution.
4. Prospect information shall be stored securely to prevent access by unauthorized persons.
5. Research documents containing donor or prospective donor information that are to be used outside Research offices shall be clearly marked "confidential."
6. Special protection shall be afforded all giving records pertaining to anonymous donors.

Recommendations

1. Prospect researchers shall urge their institutions to develop written policies based upon the laws of their state defining what information shall be gathered and under what conditions it may be released and to whom.

2. Prospect researchers shall urge the development of written policies at their institutions defining who may authorize access to prospect files and under what conditions.
3. Prospect researchers shall urge their colleagues to abide by these principles of conduct.

Mission and Values

Stanford University Office of Development

Our Mission

Our collective and individual objective in the Office of Development is to support the mission of the University by maximizing, over the long term, useful gift support to Stanford, and doing so in ways that bring credit and benefit to the University, satisfaction to our donors, and fulfillment to our volunteers and staff. We underscore the importance of gift utility, acknowledging that funding priorities, which become our goals, are set by Stanford's senior academic administrators. Also, we avoid actions that would compromise the long term for the sake of short-term expediency. In addition, we recognize a dual responsibility to our donors as well as to the institution, and the pivotal role our volunteers play in making our mission possible.

Values Key to Our Mission

- Responsibility to Donors
  We consider the donor's best financial interest, including capacity to give, taxes, cash flow, and estate planning. We disclose fully the conditions and status of any proposed or outstanding fund balance or pledge. Unless given permission by the donor, we regard gifts as confidential transactions between the donor and the University. We respect the privacy of donors and prospects, including requests for anonymity, and treat with great care any potentially sensitive information.
- Integrity
  We live up to both the spirit and letter of promises to donors. As staff members, we avoid conflicts of interest between our Stanford jobs and outside activities, both paid and voluntary. We do not exploit relationships with donors or volunteers for personal benefit. We utilize University facilities and property only for official business. We travel with a sense of fiscal responsibility. When in doubt about the compatibility of an action or expenditure with these values, we have a responsibility to disclose and discuss the situation with relevant O[ffice] O[f] D[evelopment] managers.
- Teamwork
  We recognize that success in our mission is always the result of team effort— staff teamwork, teamwork between staff and volunteers, and teamwork with other parts of the University. We pursue honest and open communication with volunteers, between supervisors and staff members, among peers and with officers, faculty, and staff throughout the University.

- Quality
  Because for many of Stanford's friends, we are their primary contact with the University, we recognize our responsibility to reinforce the excellence of this University by the quality of our own work: our correspondence and communication, our personal interactions, the accuracy of our data, files, reports, and gift acknowledgments. Moreover, we believe that the pursuit of excellence is cost-efficient.
- Enthusiasm
  We understand that unless we are supportive and positive about the mission of the University and our role in fulfilling that mission, we cannot be effective in our work. We understand that our public behavior must be guided by our dedication to the University.
- Initiative
  We must initiate action and not simply respond to events and circumstances. We know that we must be willing to make our own decisions, take bold and independent action, and assume certain attendant personal (but not ethical) risks. When the best interests of the University are at stake, we are willing to undertake responsibilities beyond the normal scope of our jobs.

Henry E. Riggs
Vice President for Development

Levi Strauss & Co. Ethical Principles

Our ethical principles are the values that set the ground rules for all that we do as employees of Levi Strauss & Co. As we seek to achieve responsible commercial success, we will be challenged to balance these principles against each other, always mindful of our promise to shareholders that we will achieve responsible commercial success.

The ethical principles are:

HONESTY: We will not say things that are false. We will never deliberately mislead. We will be as candid as possible, openly and freely sharing information, as appropriate to the relationship.

PROMISE-KEEPING: We will go to great lengths to keep our commitments. We will not make promises that can't be kept and we will not make promises on behalf of the company unless we have the authority to do so.

FAIRNESS: We will create and follow a process and achieve outcomes that a reasonable person would call just, even-handed and nonarbitrary.

RESPECT FOR OTHERS: We will be open and direct in our communication and receptive to influence. We will honor and value the abilities and contributions of others, embracing the responsibility and accountability for our actions in this regard.

COMPASSION: We will maintain an awareness of the needs of others and act to meet those needs whenever possible. We will also minimize harm whenever possible. We will act in ways that are consistent with our commitment to social responsibility.

INTEGRITY: We will live up to LS&Co's ethical principles, even when confronted by personal, professional and social risks, as well as economic pressures.

Levi Strauss & Co.
Code of Ethics

Levi Strauss & Co. has a long and distinguished history of ethical conduct and community involvement. Essentially, these are a reflection of the mutually shared values of the founding families and of our employees.

Our ethical values are based on the following elements:

- A commitment to commercial success in terms broader than merely financial measures.
- A respect for our employees, suppliers, customers, consumers and stockholders.
- A commitment to conduct which is not only legal but fair and morally correct in a fundamental sense.
- Avoidance of not only real, but the appearance of conflict of interest.

From time to time the Company will publish specific guidelines, policies and procedures. However, the best test whether something is ethically correct is whether you would be prepared to present it to our senior management and board of directors as being consistent with our ethical traditions. If you have any uneasiness about an action you are about to take or which you see, you should discuss the action with your supervisor or management.

10 ▼ Professionalism, Ethics, and Certification

TED BAYLEY, ACFRE, ASSOCIATE VICE PRESIDENT
Alford Group, Inc.

10.1 Introduction

The purpose of this chapter is to bring focus on professionalism for fund raisers. Having been a "professional fund raiser" for almost 40 years, I had always seen myself as a professional. Many of my friends and colleagues felt the same way. However, a good many people practicing the art of fund raising argued that we were not professionals and that we did not receive professional recognition by those for whom we worked or by the public. In some ways they were correct. We did not have the recognition that physicians, attorneys, or accountants had in their professions. About 20 years ago, when I became especially interested in helping fund raising become a recognized profession, I applied for certification, was accepted, and passed the written test required. By becoming "certified," I felt I was helping all fund raisers who wanted to be seen as professionals. It seems in order to have the right to be recognized as a profession, those who would lead the way had to exhibit strong commitment to certification as well as ethical behavior.

A simple analogy is the good way to start. A three-leg stool is the foundation that this chapter will be built on. The three legs represent professionalism, ethics, and certification. The first leg, professionalism, is recognition based on knowledge, experience, and performance within the profession of fund raising.

The second leg, certification, supports professionalism. Certification is a statement to the public at large that an individual has been willing to be tested on his or her understanding of the common body of knowledge that the profession considers the baseline and indicates the individual's successful experience.

The third leg, perhaps the most critical, is the individual commitment to abide by a code of ethical behavior.

A growing number of fund raisers see themselves as professionals and believe that a code of ethics and the standards of professional performance are critical elements required of all fund raisers. Adding the credential Certified Fund Raising Executive after one's name is a way to claim full recognition of professionalism.

Those familiar with the history of fund raising in the United States would probably all agree with Scott M. Cutlip's conclusion that "generally speaking, organized philanthropy supported by systematic fund raising is a twentieth-century development in the United States. Philanthropy, in America's first three centuries, was carried along on a small scale, largely financed by the wealthy few in response to personal begging appeals."[1] The early thoughts about professionalism probably started with the successful capital funding programs conducted on behalf of the YMCA by Charles Sumner Ward and Lyman L. Pierce. As noted by Cutlip, "These two imaginative, resourceful fund-raising pioneers trained many of today's professional fund raisers, passionate disciples who insist one, not the other, is the father of the fund drive."[2] The success of these pioneers was shared throughout the YMCA, and by the beginning of the twentieth century, many of these "trained fund raisers" became the founders of consulting firms across America. From this group the organization of AAFRC was founded "to advance professional and ethical standards in philanthropic fund-raising consulting and to promote philanthropy in general."

In 1996 the Professional Certification Board was organized to bring together the previously existing certification programs of the Association of Fundraising Professionals (AFP) and the Association of Healthcare Philanthropy (AHP). Although these two organizations had existing certification programs and codes of ethical behavior, they agreed to combine the baseline credentialing into one program. A number of other fund-raising associations were invited to join this effort and have done so.

From the very founding of what has now become the Association of Fundraising Professionals in 1965, there has been a commitment to professionalism and a concern for ethical behavior. Likewise, the Association of Healthcare Philanthropy, founded in 1965, had very similar aspirations.

10.2 Professionalism

When one begins to study the evolving history of fund raising, it is clear that professionalism has always had a strong link to ethical codes. While our culture and economic system operates with the assumption that there are "professionals" who have special training to provide special services, few understand when professional certification

---

[1]Scott M. Cutlip, *Fund Raising in the United States: Its Role in American Philanthropy* (New Brunswick, NJ: Rutgers University Press, 1990).
[2]*Ibid.*

started. Professional certification programs have existed since the Middle Ages, when the thirteenth-century Holy Roman Emperor Frederick II developed a credentialing program for physicians. In the United States, the earliest certification programs appeared in the field of education. They were affiliated with churches to ensure schoolmasters held orthodox religious beliefs. During the eighteenth and nineteenth centuries, the labor force started evolving from craft guilds to professions. Access to university education made it possible for individuals to understand scientific research and to seek better ways to solve problems. Practitioners began to understand the concept of a common body of knowledge. It is fair to assume that in the early days of these professions, many people practicing them were not as competent as one would like. When critical services were not completed satisfactorily, legislatures began to create licensing programs to ensure that only individuals whose particular skills were competent and beneficial to the public at large were granted a license.

(A)   DEFINING PROFESSIONALISM

Multiple definitions exist for the terms "profession," "professional," and "professionalism." Dictionaries often refer to probably the oldest understanding of the concept by using theology, law, and medicine as examples.

If asked to define a professional most of us would probably start with character, education, skills, and commitment to ethical and moral values. Some might say it is the opposite of amateur. Still others would want to talk about experience, management, and recognition.

There is no end to this debate. Clearly, the public recognizes attorneys, physicians, nurses, accountants, and educators. All of these professions clearly have a common body of knowledge and academic credentials attesting to people's mastery of that knowledge. However, remember, all of these people cannot practice their profession without taking special examinations that qualify them to practice. Once in practice, a great many of these people seek higher recognition for their skills and abilities by becoming credentialed by professional societies and associations.

Therefore, we need not debate the issue about our "profession." We have traveled and are traveling the same path as physicians, teachers, accountants, and lawyers. We have a common body of knowledge for our profession that is growing every year, as it does with the older professions. We have available to us the opportunity to acquire certification credentials through practice, examination, and continuing education.

10.3   Codes of Ethics

In Chapter 9, Albert Anderson does a superb job of outlining the roots of ethical behavior from the writings of Aristotle and Englishman John Stuart Mill and German Immanuel Kant. In his assessment, two statements stand out and address most of the ethical issues we face:

1. *A course of action is ethical that, experience suggests, will likely result in more benefit than harm for most people; and*
2. *Action is ethical that, rationally considered, accords with what would be intrinsically obligatory for all, regardless of anticipated consequences.*

(A)   DEFINING ETHICS FOR THE PROFESSIONAL

In *Ethics for Fundraisers*, Anderson cautions readers to understand that it is not an easy task to "act ethically," because of the very nature of defining ethics. "It is simply the nature of ethics, unlike arithmetic, to be uncertain. Its issues, choices, and actions can provoke head-shaking, demand for thoughtfulness, consistency, and decisiveness—with no clear or certain prospect that one's decision is wholly right."[3]

To discuss or even to debate the concept of ethics can be helpful, perhaps insightful, but probably is frustrating because the professional fund raiser usually wants an answer that is correct for the situation. As Anderson said, it's not arithmetic; the answers add up differently for those involved in the situation.

(B)   UNDERSTANDING ETHICAL BEHAVIOR

Those who have served over the years on committees trying to define an "ethical code" or who conducted seminars and programs about the subject share the same frustration. It is buried in local cultures around the world and cannot be defined in absolute terms. Also, the environment of fund-raising practice is constantly changing. Scandals uncovered in one organization will create a negative image for similar nonprofit organizations and in some instances, negative feelings about all nonprofit organizations. The disclosure uncovered by the press about massive fraud some years ago by William Aramony, President of United Way of America, had a significant negative impact on local United Ways there were not at all involved.

When the press brings this type of behavior to light, the public has a right to know how their gifts were used. Most fund raisers would agree that the loss of public confidence could make future solicitation of gifts very difficult for any nonprofit institution. National scandals can and do harm all nonprofits, making it hard for those who do ethical fund raising to work.

The challenge to the fund-raising profession is to ensure that beyond the commitment to an ethics code, members receive continuing education about how to behave ethically, ensuring that not only the fund raisers but the non-for-profit organizations they work for, understand what the code means. Yet certain "fund raisers" have chosen not to participate in the professional fund-raising associations because they do not want to be bound to an ethical code. Therefore, it is critically important that professional fund raisers who do sign a commitment to the code of ethics for an association do act responsibly. This is not an easy task.

(C)   ADMINISTRATION OF ETHICAL CODES

Currently there are two codes of ethical principles accepted by the CFRE Professional Certification Board, AFP and AHP. Other organizations that have joined the CFRE Certification Program have agreed to utilize the AFP Code of Ethical Principles and Standards of Professional Practice. All members of AFP, AHP, and other associations must annually sign the AFP code and/or the AHP code.

---

[3] Albert Anderson, *Ethics for Fundraisers* (Bloomington, IN: Indiana University Press, 1996), p. xii.

The CFRE Professional Certification program has recently developed a contract with the professional association of fund raisers in Australia and New Zealand. Their code is basically the same as the AFP code, although it is longer. As the CFRE board works with other fund-raising associations around the world, similar contracts will arise. The important point is that fund raisers are of one mind about the importance of ethical behavior for all fund raisers. It should also be noted that one does not have to be a member of any of these professional associations to seek certification. Like members, non-members must sign annually the AFP code or a board acceptable code of other countries participating in the certification program.

(D) HOW CHARGES MAY BE BROUGHT TO ATTENTION

The Ethics Board of AFP has a thorough process in place to enable any individual, whether a member or not, to file a complaint with the Service Office of AFP. When such a complaint is made, it is given to AFP Ethics Committee for answer or investigation. AHP has a similar procedure.

Once a qualified complaint has been filed, the Ethics Committee conducts an investigation. After investigation, the member or certificant is notified and has an opportunity to answer the complaint. That person can have legal advice and a right to confront the person(s) who initiated the complaint.

The Ethics Board ensures confidentially throughout the process. Appeal policies are in place to ensure fairness to all parties.

(E) SANCTIONS

There are four levels of sanction in the AFP code, starting with a letter of reprimand, then a letter of censure that would provide a probationary period during which the offender could hold no office in the local or the national association. The third level is suspension. This removes membership for a period of time or under certain conditions.

The highest sanction is permanent expulsion as well as a recommendation of revocation of certification sent to the CFRE Board. All of these sanctions can be appealed through existing policies and procedures.

10.4 *Certification*

Phillip Barnhardt's introduction in the *Guide to National Professional Certification Programs* suggests:

> *Three trends act together to make professional certification important to both the organization and the individual. University degrees no longer represent, if they ever did, the ultimate measure of professional knowledge and capability. The downsizing of corporations, coupled with teaming, outsourcing, and temping, has forced professionals to take control of their own careers independent of their employer. Finally business environment requires almost constant training, development, and professional involvement beyond one's particular job title.*
>
> *Companies now use many forms of professional assessment. College degrees, references, and resumes are used to evaluate individual capabilities. What distinguishes pro-*

fessional certification is what it says about the individual. The basic requirements for many programs require extensive personal commitment. Individuals who show motivation, provide time, and the expense necessary to pursue and maintain certification have made a commitment to their profession.

Most professional certifications have a knowledge segment based on real-world requirements. Many certifications are based on a profession's common body of knowledge. Passing a certification examination based on professional requirements may be the only tool available to measure a candidate's knowledge. A certification program may be the only group defining the knowledge required for a specific job.[4]

(A) COMMON BODY OF KNOWLEDGE

The common body of knowledge usually emerges slowly for a given profession. It evolves as individuals in similar jobs learn from mentors, colleagues, and a few who are successful in their responsibilities. These individuals begin to apply what they learned as they gain basic education presented through 12 years for most students, followed by four years of college, often with a liberal arts focus. They begin to recognize the behavior of individuals, organizations, and the economic sector about how society works. Fund raisers begin to appreciate that their role in the philanthropic process is to understand the concept that a gift to a nonprofit organization is an exchange action, very much like how an individual might make a decision to drop by a local doughnut shop to enjoy a snack and a cup of coffee. In this case, an exchange of $2.50 will get the coffee and doughnut. They then realize that a donor makes a gift to the institution they represent by presenting a gift of $100 and in return gets a good feeling for helping a person in need served by their institution.

This simple process is always going on as one thinks about a "common body of knowledge." As more and more people in this same vocation get more experience, and some begin to write articles and books on their experience, others begin to teach.

Over the past 20 years or so, a good number of colleges and universities have realized that there exists a professional group of people who have special skills that help them raise the philanthropic support that the institutions need. This has led to for-credit courses in colleges and universities. In the process, individual faculty members begin to do research, which adds a very important component of the common body of knowledge.

As practitioners and educators continue in dialogue, a consensus evolves that yes, we do have a common body of knowledge that is the foundation of the certification examination.

(B) RECOGNITION OF THE PUBLIC

Because the philanthropic process works as it does means that both professionals and volunteers are intimately involved in the exchange process. These volunteers are from

---

[4]Philip Barnhardt, "Introduction," in *Guide to National Professional Certification Programs.* Human Resource Development Press, Inc. Amherst, MA, p. xvii–xxix.

that large number of individuals that we often call "the public." As volunteers become involved in the mission of the institution that invites them to provide leadership, they become the first not only in evaluating the "good" that the organization does but in helping communicate the good works to the larger community.

Every professional fund raiser who has been facilitating the exchange process with volunteers understands that without the confidence of the public, the organization will have a very difficult job in continuing to receive philanthropic gifts.

(C)   WHY PROFESSIONAL ASSOCIATIONS ESTABLISH CERTIFICATION PROGRAMS

Jerry W. Gilley's article in *Association Management* gives us some insights on why associations create certification programs. He conducted a survey of 70 national associations that had established certification programs in the past 20 years. His study found 12 issues common to these associations. The following list condenses his findings:[5]

1. *Administration.* In general, associations administer their own professional programs.
2. *Finance.* Almost all provide financial support for the program's development.
3. *Content.* Professional competencies lie at the heart of the certification program.
4. *Acceptance.* Members generally welcome certification programs.
5. *Promotion.* Eighty percent of the programs developed public relations programs to gain member support.
6. *Grandfathering.* Most avoided grandfathering (awarding the credential without having to fulfill the formal requirements for certification).
7. *Legal problems.* Most retained legal counsel, but few expected legal problems resulting from certification. Only three of the 70 reported any legal action.
8. *Examinations.* Applicants must take formal examinations in 88 percent of those in the sample.
9. *Ethics.* Nearly 75 percent have written codes of ethics and will revoke the certification for individuals whose behavior violates the code.
10. *Fees.* Candidates generally pay a processing fee for certification.
11. *Evaluation.* A paper-and-pencil multiple-choice question is the most common tool for evaluating applicants.
12. *Recertification.* Surprisingly, most did not require recertification or encourage continuing education. Some said they might require recertification in the future.

(D)   BASIC REQUIREMENTS FOR CERTIFICATION

The CFRE Professional Certification Board has established the basic requirements for certification. As stated in its *Preparing to Take the Certified Fund Raising Executive (CFRE) Examination:* "In order to be eligible to apply to the CFRE program, an individual must

---

[5]Jerry W. Gilley, *Association Management*, August 1985, p. 125–127.

have been employed as a paid fund-raising professional for a minimum of five (5) of the most recent eight (8) years (allowing for career gaps)."[6]

"The written application requires a candidate to satisfactorily document achievement in four (4) areas: 1) Professional Practice; 2) Education; 3) Professional Performance, and 4) Service." The application requires documentation of employment as a fund development officer; education includes both academic and continuing education courses; professional performance is measured in three areas: actual dollars raised, communication efforts, and management projects; and evidence of service to philanthropy by volunteer activities in fund-raising associations and community organizations.[7]

If the points needed in each category are documented, the applicant is invited to take the certification examination.

(E) TESTING METHODS FOR CERTIFICATION PROGRAMS

The handbook states:

> The competencies required of fund-raising executives who work in any area of fund raising are the basis upon which a CFRE examination is developed. Fund-raising executives who are experts in the field (subject matter experts) develop a comprehensive list of task statements, activities that competent professionals perform in the course of their job requirements. The subject matter experts then list all of the tasks and skills, which would be required to carry out each of those responsibilities satisfactorily. All of these items are assembled into a survey format, called a Role Delineation Study or Job Analysis.
>
> This survey is then sent to a random selection of currently certified individuals who are asked to complete it. The survey specifically asks respondents to rate the task and skill statements in terms of importance of the statement; the frequency in which the statement is performed; and how much harm, if any, would come (to donor, organization or individual) if a professional did not carry out that responsibility satisfactorily.
>
> The results of the survey are analyzed and the outcome is those task and skill statements which your colleagues believe are essential for a competent fund-raising professional. This becomes the core body of knowledge a professional must have to be a Certified Fund Raising Executive.[8]

(F) GUIDELINES FOR STANDARDIZED TESTING

Why should there exist such a complex study of the common body of knowledge and evaluation of the test to ensure it is reflective of core competencies? The handbook gives us a strong answer:

> Just as all CFRE candidates must adhere to Standards of Professional Practice, so must those involved in carrying out standardized examination activities. The Standards for

---

[6]CFRE Professional Certification Board, *Preparing to Take the Certified Fund Raising Executive (CFRE) Examination*, p. 1.
[7]*Ibid.*, pp. 1–2.
[8]*Ibid.*, p. 3.

Educational and Psychological Testing *published jointly by the American Psychological Association, the American Educational Research Association, and the National Council on Measurement in Education in 1985 sets those standards. Both the CFRE Professional Certification Board and PES (Professional Education Services) are committed to adhering to these guidelines.*[9]

10.5 Certification and Licensure

It is important to define and clarify some of the jargon that surrounds certification. Ann Touringy, Ph.D., CAE,[10] explains that there exist significant differences between certification and licensure. In the certification process, an institution or association seeks to recognize an individual who has met predetermined qualifications set by the organization and grants the individual the right to use the title or designation associated with that recognition.

Licensure is the process used by a governmental agency to define the minimal degree of competency needed to authorize an individual to engage in a given occupation. While most certification programs are national or international in scope and have uniform standards, licensure requirements can vary by state or other political subdivision.

(A) WHAT IS THE DIFFERENCE?

While consumer protection is inherent in licensure and certification, neither guarantees quality of service. Licensure laws define the scope of practice for a specific profession or occupation. Certification focuses on role delineation that includes a common body of knowledge inherent to the profession. Touringy notes that "certification offers an alternative path to professional status particularly for those professions for which there is no universal academic track. Continuing education coupled with experience requirements usually plays an important role in certification for these professions."[11]

When government agencies seek to establish licensure requirements, they seek the minimal standards that, they hope, will ensure that citizens using these skills receive competent service. Law requires licensure, and one cannot "practice" without a license. Certification focuses on a common body of knowledge inherent to the profession and often includes skill sets that are obtained by training beyond formal academic credentials.

While consumer protection is inherent in licensure and certification, neither can guarantee quality of service. In almost all cases, however, certification seeks to establish evidence of knowledge, skills, and practice based excellence.

(B) WHY RECERTIFICATION?

As discussed earlier, much of the credibility of certification is comes from the competence of the individual. Much of this is learned on the job. In fund raising, it is critically

---

[9]*Ibid.* p. 10.

[10] "Certification: What, Why, and How?", Unpublished paper, Ann Tourigny Ph.D., CAE President, Special Assignments, 7052 Idylwood Rd., Falls Church, VA 22043.

[11]*Ibid.*

important to be competent in skills that are continuously influenced by high technology. Therefore, the National Organization for Competency Assurance (NOCA), the governing board for certification programs, insists that certification programs largely based on competency require continuing education to ensure that practitioners are fully competent.

10.6   Closing Observations

It is impossible to lay out all of the details of what it means to be a professional fund raiser in one chapter.

Over the past three years, the new CFRE Professional Certification Board has established a complete set of policies that will ensure that the program is testing the right competencies, is fair to all who seek certification, and is expanding the number of associations that want the benefits of certification for its members. The board's work has not been completed. However, the new certification will, in all likelihood, be ready to submit its certification application to become a "certified" program under the standards of the National Commission for Certification Agencies (NCCA), most probably in 2001. Even though a number of associations are involved in the new program, there is strong interest in fund-raising certification in many parts of the world. As this interest grows, the CFRE board will have to ensure that the common body of knowledge is the same in other countries and that the code of ethics and standards of professional performance are consistent. Exams will have to be written in multiple languages and be responsive to the differences in commerce, banking, and country-specific taxation regulations. This will not be easy, but there is evidence that philanthropy exists around the world and the methods of solicitation of gifts are similar. The future is marked by change; the population of every country and culture will always be greatly helped because of the philanthropic process of exchange that aims to make things better or, at the least, to not do harm.

Good Governance: Requisites for Successful Philanthropy

GEORGE F. MAYNARD III, FAHP
Jerold Panas, Linzy & Partners, Inc.

JAMES A. RICE, PHD
The Governance Institute

This chapter is adapted from *Governing Health Care Foundations at the Dawn of the 21st Century,* an Association for Healthcare Philanthropy (AHP) publication (© 1998). It is based on the 1997 AHP

11.1 Introduction: Good Governance Is the Requisite for Philanthropy

But the guiding truth is that the human soul is built to give. We are fashioned in the image of the Giver of all life, and nothing proves this more dramatically and repeatedly than the glow of fulfillment that accompanies every act of generosity. To challenge people to give is to do them a favor—the favor of acting out of their highest selves, made in the innermost pattern of the self-giving Servant God.

—*Bennett J. Sims*[1]

Bennett J. Sims, president of the Institute for Servant Leadership and Bishop Emeritus of the Episcopal diocese of Atlanta, Georgia, in his book *Servanthood: Leadership for the Third Millennium* boldly states what is so true about giving—"that the human soul is built to give."

The governance of health systems and hospital-related foundations deserves more explicit attention if we are to maximize the contribution of philanthropy to integrated health systems in the twenty-first century. Philanthropy, as part of the soul of humankind, will always rise above a particular environment or trend, and it needs to be understood within the context of the times. A recent fax poll of selected health system–related foundation executives indicates the need for greater attention to the effectiveness of foundation governance structures and functions. (See Appendix 11A.)

This chapter, based on the 1998 AHP publication *Governing Health Care Foundations at the Dawn of the 21st Century*, is intended as a guide to help healthcare foundation executives and board leaders improve the performance of their philanthropic initiatives by improving their governance performance within the context of today's integrated health system (IHS). Exhibit 11.1 provides a summary of the importance of good governance to maximize the contributions of philanthropy within these systems. Such enhanced performance is important if philanthropy is to maximize the following four contributions that it can make.

(A) CONTRIBUTION 1: DEVELOP RISK MANAGEMENT TOOLS

The new integrated health systems are being held accountable for health risks under new payment contracts. Philanthropy can support the development and use of modern tools that an IHS needs for active risk management. To thrive, the IHS must self-fund the use of managed care pathways, clinical guidelines, utilization review, and continuous quality and process improvement. Resources are also needed to support the research, information systems, and staff education to mobilize and continuously refine these tools.

Think Tank Project led by George F. Maynard III, FAHP, and James A. Rice, PhD, President of The Governance Institute. Mr. Maynard was at that time president of the Orlando Regional Healthcare Foundation in Orlando, Florida. This text is focused on challenges specific to raising philanthropic funds in a multi-institutional setting. The editor greatly appreciates permission from the Association for Healthcare Philanthropy to include this text.

[1]Bennett J. Sims, *Servanthood: Leadership for the Third Millennium* (Boston: Cowley Publications, 1997), p. 33.

EXHIBIT 11.1 Successful Philanthropy in the Integrated Health System

Five contextual
factors that
support
successful "P"

Five Keys
to
successful "P"

2

There is
cohesive
coordination
between
parts of the IHS.

2

1
The IHS has
an excellent
reputation for
care giving.

Laser-
clear case
that speaks to
philanthropist

Informed
and
committed
leadership

The IHS has a
clear plan and
commitment to
health gain.
3

1
Mission
anchored on
community
need, not
institutional
need for
money

**Maximum
Success
of "P"**

Excellent
communication
capabilities

Trusted
steward of
resources

The IHS
visibly supports
patient-physician
needs.

5

The IHS has
full engagement
of key
stakeholders from
the community.

4

5

4

(B) CONTRIBUTION 2: ATTACK RISK FACTORS

Additional resources that depend on the positive relationships of philanthropic practice can help forge and support new healthy community partnerships and alliances that remove or reduce such varied risk factors as high-risk pregnancies, breast and skin cancers, alcohol- and social tension–related violence that increases illness and injury, and a myriad of other behavior and lifestyle-related obstacles to "health gain" or health status improvement.

(C) CONTRIBUTION 3: ENHANCE INFRASTRUCTURE FOR HEALTHCARE

Philanthropic practice also can strengthen the IHS's capabilities and technologies needed for cost-effective healthcare and the restoration of optimal patient health and well-being. Traditional investments provided by charitable contributions for equipment, capital expansion, program operations, and research/education can help the IHS meet its new contractual obligations for reasonably priced services that yield demonstrable clinical outcomes.

(D) CONTRIBUTION 4: ENHANCE IMAGE TO ATTRACT COVERED LIVES

The resources, relationships, and alliances established from philanthropic practice also can add a positive public image of innovation, trust, and a commitment to quality and excellence to encourage large groups of subscribers or enrollees to turn to the IHS as their personal choice for their healthcare and health gain.

To be successful in providing the new IHS a strategic lever for success, philanthropy must improve the performance of foundation boards. This requires a more explicit understanding about the critical factors that contribute to good governance. To really govern well, foundation boards should consider the following five criteria:

1. Dimensions of philanthropy's success in the new IHSs
2. Dimensions of good governance
3. Characteristics of good board membership
4. Obstacles to good governance
5. Important governance process factors

11.2   What Is Successful Philanthropic Practice in the New Integrated Healthcare System?

During the Association for Healthcare Philanthropy's 1997 Institute for Healthcare Philanthropy at the University of Wisconsin–Madison, a group of experienced foundation executives and consultants explored answers to two essential questions:

1. What is the value of philanthropic practice in this new era of managed care and integrated health systems?
2. What factors help maximize the contribution of philanthropy to the new integrated system?

The exchange of ideas during this AHP Think Tank session suggests that a useful orientation to philanthropy can be reflected in the cycle of influence. (See Exhibit 11.2.)

Understanding philanthropy as the "heart's desire to benefit others as one has been benefited in life and as the courage to act by giving" can help maximize the success of the new integrated health systems, but only if certain key factors are carefully balanced. These factors are set forth in Exhibit 11.1, which illustrates how the maximum success of philanthropy is a function of how well the leaders of the foundation implement five factors within a supportive context consisting of five dimensions.

The five keys for successful philanthropy are not new, but they do require rigor in their execution:

EXHIBIT 11.2 The Cycle of Influence

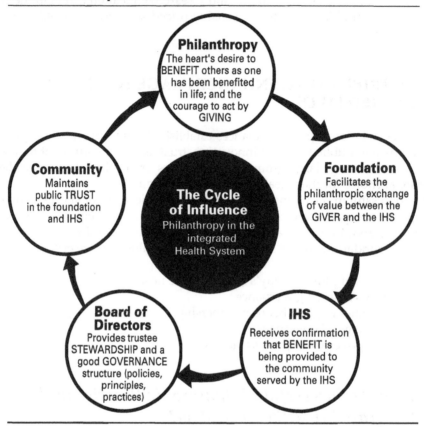

1. Mission anchored on community need, not institutional need for money
2. Laser-clear case for support that speaks to the philanthropist's reason for giving
3. Informed and committed leadership
4. Excellent communication capabilities
5. Trusted stewardship of resources given

The five contextual dimensions that can support good philanthropy are:

1. Excellent reputation of the IHS as a caregiver
2. Cohesive coordination among parts of the IHS
3. An IHS that has a clear plan and commitment to health gain
4. Full engagement of key community stakeholders
5. An IHS perceived as clearly supporting patient-physician needs

11.3 What Is Good Governance?

Good governance is a decision-making process that defines an organization's strategic direction and determines how its resources will best be used to achieve its goals.

Governance within a nonprofit institution begins with a basic understanding of stewardship. A steward is one called to exercise responsible care over possessions entrusted to him or her. Stewardship is therefore a trust and involves a sense of being accountable to someone or something higher than self. This should be the basic premise upon which all governance models are built. One who governs in an IHS is a steward. Not only do members of a nonprofit foundation board affiliated with an IHS hold a charter of public trust, but they also are charged with the responsibility of providing stewardship for the gifts made on behalf of the IHS for the community's benefit. Every action taken by the foundation's board should be measured against its benefit to the community, as well as against its contribution to achieving the foundation's mission, vision, purpose, and strategic goals.

According to Charles Ewell and Dennis Pointer, good governance and stewardship rest upon how well board members discharge certain basic responsibilities.[2]

There are three common-law fiduciary duties of every board member:

1. *The duty of care.* Acting the way that a prudent individual would in similar circumstances
2. *The duty of loyalty.* Placing the organization's interest above an individual's own
3. *The duty of obedience.* Acting in accordance with the law and the organization's own charter bylaws and policies

Modern governance, however, must move beyond these basic duties to encompass three important roles of effective board members:

1. *Role 1: policy formulation.* Policy is the primary mechanism through which boards influence their organizations. As such, they provide the most tangible evidence that boards are fulfilling their responsibilities. Policies should be formulated with great care; written, explicit, and brief; and reviewed periodically. Foundation boards need policies to guide how they intend to catalyze and nurture philanthropy.
2. *Role 2: decision making.* Decision making is considered to be the central and most important role of governance. Decisions are made on the basis of policy. Board decisions are made in two different ways: (1) a board can choose to retain authority; or (2) a board can choose to delegate decision-making authority.
3. *Role 3: oversight.* Oversight entails three functions that require information: (1) monitoring; (2) assessment; and (3) feedback. Information generated to support these functions should be selective and of high support; comparative; clear, concise, and user friendly; valid, accurate, and timely; and presented graphically where appropriate.

As the boards of prominent health system foundations seek to carry out these roles and duties, they also must be prepared to focus on five key functional responsibilities. Exhibit 11.3 provides a matrix that seeks to balance the three roles and five responsibilities. The five ultimate responsibilities for any board that cannot be delegated are:

---

[2]Charles M. Ewell and Dennis D. Pointer, *Really Governing: How Health Systems and Hospital Boards Can Make More of a Difference* (Albany, N.Y.: Delmar Publishers, 1994).

EXHIBIT 11.3 Board Work Matrix

		Core Roles		
		Policy Formulation	Decision Making	Oversight
ULTIMATE RESPONSIBILITIES	Ends			
	Executive Management Performance			
	Quality			
	Finances			
	Self			

Source: Charles M. Ewell and Dennis D. Pointer, Really Governing: How Health Systems and Hospital Boards Can Make More of a Difference (Albany, N.Y.: Delmar Publishers, 1994).

1. *Ends.* Boards are responsible for envisioning and formulating organizational ends. In doing so, boards define their organizations in both present and future tenses. The ends usually are stated in terms of a board's guiding principles, purpose, mission, vision, strategic and short-term philanthropic goals. (See Appendix 11B.)
2. *Executive management performance.* The board's attention is focused on the only employee who reports directly to the board—the chief executive officer (CEO). Fulfilling this responsibility entails items such as recruiting, selecting, and evaluating the CEO.
3. *Quality.* Boards are committed to providing quality services to the organizations and the philanthropists they serve. Relationship is the most important aspect of

quality between the organization and the philanthropist. A foundation's success is realized when these relationships are deep and lasting.

4. *Finance.* Boards are responsible for ensuring the organization's financial health (protecting, enhancing, and investing resources) and for ensuring that resources are used for legitimate purposes and in legitimate ways, as directed by philanthropists.

5. *Self.* A board must assume responsibility for its own effective and efficient performance. Periodic self-assessment of both the board and individual board members is essential for good governance, and for continuous governance improvement. (See Appendix 11E.)

In the literature, the terms "roles" and "responsibilities" of boards generally are employed interchangeably. However, there is an important difference between the "what" (responsibilities) and the "how" (roles) aspects of governance. As IHS-related foundations explore new strategies to enhance the effectiveness of their boards, these factors should be considered carefully during a formal process of governance redesign and enhancement.

Ewell and Pointer's work suggests important considerations for boards as they execute their three primary roles: policy formulation, decision making, and oversight.

Policies provide an organization with direction and are the means by which authority and specific tasks are delegated to management of the foundation. Board policy both guides and constrains management's decisions and actions. Policies also provide a framework for the board to execute its decision-making role. Decisions must be made by the board in each of its areas of ultimate responsibility and regarding recommendations forwarded to it by management. The board then engages in oversight. It monitors and evaluates decisions and actions to ensure that they conform with policy and produce the intended results.

(A) ROLE 1: POLICY FORMULATION

It is through the formulation of policy that foundation boards can lead their organizations. Policies provide the most tangible evidence that boards are fulfilling their ultimate governance responsibilities. Additionally, effective execution of the decision making and oversight roles depends on how well policies are formulated.

Yet most boards spend little time formulating policy. After studying the boards of 33 *Fortune* 500 companies, W. P. Clendenin wrote: "In general, board involvement in policy . . . tends to be superficial. Two-thirds of the executives interviewed stated that the board discussed important issues of policy only occasionally."[3] This statement is as true now as it was 30 years ago, and it is equally applicable to IHSs and the foundations that have been created to serve them.

At its core, the concept of policy is relatively simple. Policies are statements of intent that guide and constrain further governance decision making and action, and limit subsequent choices. They reflect the values and preferences of the policymaker and state his or her expectations.

---

[3]W. D. Clendenin, "Company Presidents Look at the Board of Directors," *California Management Review,* 14, no. 3 (1972): pp. 60–66.

Based on the ideas of Chait[4] and Hodgetts and Wortman,[5] there are three different levels of policy: (1) statements of board responsibility, (2) board policy, and (3) operating policy. These levels provide a basis for developing operating rules, regulations, and procedures, which then structure specific decisions and actions. Boards should formulate policy regarding strategic planning, board recruitment, evaluation of progress toward goal accomplishment, coordination of donor contacts and relationship building, and CEO performance review. With only one exception (the responsibility for itself), boards should not become involved in developing routine operating policy or rules and procedures.

Statements of board responsibility describe the nature and scope of the board's obligations for formulating organizational ends (philanthropic strategic directions) and for ensuring high levels of executive management performance, the quality of philanthropic relationships, financial health, and the board's own performance. One statement should be formulated for each of a board's five ultimate responsibilities, as identified earlier in Ewell and Pointer's schematic.

One such statement, which describes a board's responsibility for foundation finance, is provided below. It is taken from The Orlando Regional Healthcare Foundation and is a statement of policy:

> *The Orlando Regional Healthcare Foundation Board of Directors is responsible for protecting and enhancing the philanthropists' investment in Orlando Regional Healthcare Foundation as stewards of the assets contributed. To accomplish its mission the Foundation must provide a significant rate of return for every dollar spent required to generate a dollar contributed. The Board: establishes philanthropic revenue objectives in support of Orlando Regional Healthcare Foundation; ensures that financial and programmatic methods are undertaken in a manner that leads to accomplishment of such objectives; monitors and assesses financial and investment performance; ensures that necessary control systems and procedures are in place; and ensures that Foundation funds are invested prudently.*

Such statements of responsibility are critically important. They describe what a board's focus should be, define the domain of governance, and differentiate board responsibilities from those of management.

Board policies, therefore, flow directly out of, and are based on, statements of responsibility. These policies provide direction and convey the board's expectations in the areas for which it bears ultimate responsibility. Board policies provide guidance to management and volunteers as they go about accomplishing the foundation's work.

For each of its five ultimate governance responsibilities, a board could formulate an infinite number of such policies. In this regard, a board must address two critical questions:

1. How directive does it want to be? Because of its authority and status, a board can be as directive as it wishes, limited only by laws and regulations.
2. To what extent and in what ways does the board want to constrain management and volunteers as it delegates tasks and authority to them?

---

[4]R. P. Chait et al., *The Effective Board of Trustees* (New York: Macmillan, 1991).
[5]R. M. Hodgetts and M. S. Wortman, *Administrative Policy: Text and Cases in the Policy Sciences* (New York: John Wiley & Sons, 1975).

The answers to these questions establish the dividing line between board and operating policy; they also define where governance ends and the practice of management begins. Consider the extremes. If a board formulates only a few broad policies, it abdicates its ultimate responsibilities to management. If it formulates a mountain of very detailed policies that direct management regarding what to do (and how to do it), the board assumes the task of operating the institution. How does a board avoid these inappropriate and dysfunctional extremes?

Pointer and Ewell suggest that board policies be thought of as a set of progressively smaller concentric boxes. Each box represents a more narrowly drawn policy that restricts further choices. As a board formulates more policies and makes them more specific, the operational degrees of freedom for the foundation's management are narrowed.

With respect to each of its ultimate responsibilities, a board must determine how directive and restrictive it wants and needs to be. The board must define its comfort zone. Based on the work of Carver,[6] we forward the following principle:

With respect to each of its ultimate governance responsibilities, a board should continue to formulate policy that sequentially narrows the discretion of management . . . up to the point where it is comfortable with any reasonable interpretation, application, and/or implementation of that policy.

For example, in a given area of responsibility (e.g., formulating a strategic plan or defining ends) and with respect to a particular issue (e.g., defining the IHS's philanthropic potential), a board continues to formulate policies of greater and greater specificity until it reaches a point where it feels comfortable delegating all further decision making to management. The board has operationally defined its "comfort zone" by being willing to accept all reasonable applications and interpretations of the policy it has formulated. When applied, this principle defines the point where governance ends and operations begins.

There are two different ways that board policy can narrow degrees of freedom: through prescriptions and/or through prohibitions. Prescriptions are "thou shalts"; prohibitions are usually more efficient than prescriptions because boards do not have the time, energy, or expertise to specify everything management or the volunteers should do.

Board comfort zones vary depending on the preferences of the board itself. Some foundation boards are inherently directive; others are much less so. Comfort levels also vary across responsibilities.

As a foundation board formulates increasingly specific policies that narrow management's operational freedom, the number of policies that must be formulated increases rapidly. The policy pyramid becomes very wide very fast, imposing a practical limit on a board's directives and forcing it to consider how far it needs to go to fulfill its ultimate responsibilities. Every board must determine the point at which policy specificity becomes more of a burden than a benefit to the organization.

For each of its five ultimate governance responsibilities, then, a board must formulate a comprehensive set of policies, leaving no gaps. As mentioned previously, the following should be kept in mind when formulating a board's responsibility statements and governance policies:

---

[6]J. Carver, *Boards That Make a Difference: A New Design for Leadership in Nonprofit and Public Organizations* (San Francisco: Jossey-Bass, 1991).

- *Policies should be formulated with great care.* Board policies are among the organization's most important statements.
- *They should be written.* Reducing policies to writing forces a board to be precise regarding what it wants and expects from management, its committees, and itself. Without written policies, board directives are literally nothing more than hot air. An organization's most important statements must be codified.
- *They should be explicit.* A board often operates in the realm of ideas and its principal product is words. These words must be clear. A board must state what it expects in a way that is understandable.
- *They should be brief.* Wordiness confuses rather than clarifies. To have the desired impact, a policy must be easily digested. Most policies should be expressed in a page or less.
- *They should be reviewed periodically.* Like old clothing, outdated policies must be tossed out or altered. Nothing decreases the quality of a board's voice as much as policies that have been rendered irrelevant because of changed circumstances.

Policies should be grouped by responsibility area, compiled in a loose-leaf manual, and disseminated among board members and throughout the foundation(s) and associated integrated health systems, as appropriate.

(B)   ROLE 2: DECISION MAKING

Decision making is often considered to be the board's central and most important role because nearly everything a board does requires making choices. To cite some examples:

- Should philanthropic revenues be allocated to providing health promotion and/or subsidize cancer care within the affiliated health care system? If so, how much? (This decision deals with a board's responsibility for ends and finances.)
- To what extent did the CEO achieve his or her stated performance objectives last year? Should a salary increase be recommended? (This decision deals with a board's responsibility for executive performance.)
- Should an external research firm be engaged to conduct a giver satisfaction survey? (This decision deals with a board's responsibility for quality.)
- Should targets for net funds distributed be increased to 15 percent next year? (This decision deals with a board's responsibility for finances.)
- Should the size of the board be reduced? (This decision deals with a board's responsibility for itself.)

Decisions like these are clearly important, and foundation boards will need to do a better job of making them in the twenty-first century. However, such decisions must be based on good board-formulated policy. Without the framework provided by policy, decisions run a high risk of being disjointed and ineffective.

For example, consider the decision facing a board on whether to provide philanthropic support for the free community care provided by the not-for-profit healthcare system. This decision will certainly require an analysis of the IHS's strategic plans and the local market as well as an analysis of financial and operational factors. However, at its very root, the decision must be made in light of the IHS's and foundation's ends; it depends on policy. Simply put, policy provides the context for, and guide to, decision making. Good board decision making depends on good policy.

As the pressure mounts for foundation boards to become more assertive and sophisticated in their general governance roles, board decisions are made in two different ways. First, a board can choose to retain authority over issues related to their responsibilities and to make decisions regarding them. For example, boards invariably choose to retain complete decision-making authority over their own performance. Accordingly, they make decisions regarding such issues as board size, new member selection, and the number and types of standing committees.

Second, a board can choose to delegate decision-making authority to selected standing committees and/or to management. The nature and scope of this authority is specified by board policy. A board has two options here:

1. It can allow management or the committee to make decisions within certain limits (the board's comfort zone). For example, management might be permitted to make capital equipment decisions up to $10,000 without board approval. Such decisions, of course, are subject to board oversight (a topic addressed in the next section).
2. Management can be directed to forward recommendations that serve as the basis for a board decision.

Employing these approaches, a board optimizes its leverage and effort. It retains total authority in some areas, completely delegates decision making in others, and seeks recommendations from management prior to making decisions in yet others. All such decisions, however, should be policy driven.

(C)   ROLE 3: OVERSIGHT

Execution of the oversight role closes the loop with respect to the board's five ultimate governance responsibilities. Management is accountable to the board (and often to the CEO of the integrated health system) for the decisions it makes and the actions it undertakes. Proper oversight assures this managerial accountability.

Board policies, once formulated, can be ignored, misinterpreted, and subverted. Oversight protects against all of these possibilities and entails three functions: monitoring, assessment, and feedback. Each function is essential if a board is to fulfill its responsibilities. The monitoring and assessment functions guarantee that delegated tasks and authority are executed in ways that meet board expectations, as expressed in its policies. Feedback provides a board with the information it needs to modify existing policies and formulate new ones.

Oversight begins with the delineation of performance standards by the foundation's board. Like decision making, such standards must be policy driven. Board policy must either contain explicit standards within the policy itself or provide the context for developing them. In the former, for example, a board might formulate a policy stating: "The financial performance of the foundation's endowed capital will be such as to result in at least a 13 percent return on invested capital." In the latter, a policy might state: "Foundation funds must be invested prudently." To develop a standard, the board would have to define prudent. A standard should be included in, or developed from, every board policy. If a policy is important enough to be formulated, it warrants a standard. If a policy is so trivial that it does not need to be monitored and assessed, it should have not been formulated in the first place.

In order to effectively and efficiently execute its oversight role, a board must put in place a consistent method for receiving governance information. Most foundation boards do not lack information; on the contrary, they are flooded with it. Often this information is not the type they need to govern effectively. Rather, it is designed by either management or consultants to support the work of administration—not necessarily to help the board do its job. Boards have different responsibilities and execute different roles, however. They need governance information, not management information.

The process of developing governance information is relatively straightforward.[7] A board, in consultation with executive management, should specify the information it needs based on its policies. Management can then translate board information needs into specific data collection and reporting requirements.

Governance information reports should be:

- *Selective and of high leverage.* Boards do not require information about everything; they need only information regarding the most important things—their policies. Valuable information is highly selective. Too much information—particularly if it is of the wrong type—is worse than too little. High-leverage and selective information helps the board determine whether its expectations are being fulfilled and if the intended results are being achieved. The information provides the answer to a straightforward question: Are things working as intended regarding the development of relationships and resources?
- *Comparative.* By far, the most meaningful and useful information has a high degree of contrast. Data can be presented in the context of a standard, portrayed across time, and/or compared (benchmarked) to similar information from other institutions. Such comparisons allow a board to put information into context and, thereby, make more meaningful evaluations based on that information.
- *Clear, concise, and user friendly.* In order to be clear, information must be easy to assimilate and understand, and presented and organized in the simplest manner possible. Information is generally compiled and formatted by specialists in a particular area. Accordingly, to be user friendly, extra effort needs to be made to ensure that information products are not wrapped in veils of esoteric jargon and technical minutia.
- *Valid, accurate, and timely.* Board oversight can be no better than the quality and timeliness of the information it receives.
- *Presented graphically, where appropriate.* Most of us have great difficulty making sense of page upon page of numbers or words. To be useful, information must be organized and summarized. With few exceptions, the best type of organization is graphical.

Well-designed and properly reported governance information is as important to the success of a philanthropic program as its fund development and management information systems.

---

[7]Chait et al., *Effective Board of Trustees.*

(D) OTHER SUGGESTED GOVERNANCE ACTIVITIES

There are many other activities that boards and their members can do on behalf of their philanthropic organizations.[8] Among the most widely cited:

- *Serving as a sounding board for, and advisor to, the CEO.* The boardroom provides a confidential place for management to test ideas. Board members are valuable sources of advice and counsel. Quite naturally, CEOs want to tap the experience and expertise of individuals who understand the foundation but also stand somewhat outside of it.
- *Serving as institutional advocates and links to constituents.* Because of their positions in the community, board members often speak on behalf of the foundation and the related IHS. Board members can forge relationships with individuals, groups, and organizations upon which the IHS depends for support and resources.
- *Making and securing philanthropic gifts.* Making and securing philanthropic gifts are two of the most important functions foundation board members serve. (*Note:* Too many foundation board members are recruited only because they have money or know people who do. Today, an affinity to the IHS is an extremely important criteria for board member selection, especially if that affinity has led to philanthropic giving to your organization. Nevertheless, board members also should be committed to fulfilling their governance responsibilities. The best foundation board members give time, talent, and treasure to ensure that the philanthropic tradition of the nonprofit IHS is protected and enhanced.)

In addition, board members are occasionally asked, or volunteer, to provide consultation services, or to undertake specific managementlike tasks on behalf of the foundation. For example, a board member with expertise in real estate is asked to appraise property that may be donated to the IHS; an investment advisor who serves on the board is requested to assess the foundation's portfolio.

Such activities do not directly contribute to fulfilling the ultimate responsibilities of governance, and, thereby, they do not qualify as board roles. Nevertheless, they must be well defined; if not, trouble may result in any one of several ways.

First, when a board member provides services to the foundation, the critical distinction between governance and the roles of management and staff can become blurred. The result can be confusion and potential conflict. Second, practical difficulties often arise. For example, what if a board member's advice is not taken, his or her work is performed poorly, or bad outcomes result? These possibilities can place both the board member and management in extremely awkward positions. Accordingly, the authors recommend that a board member avoid performing consultation or managementlike tasks for the foundation unless expectations have been clearly defined by the board of

---

[8]See R. N. Carpenter, "Cooperative Governance, Part II: Directors' Responsibilities," *Management Quarterly,* 29, no. 3 (1988): 3–6; L. A. Gordon et al., "The Challenge of Governing for Value," *Directors and Boards,* 16, no. 3 (1992): 13–17; W. M. Hageman and R. J. Umbdenstock, "Organizing and Focusing the Board's Work: Keys to Effectiveness," *Frontiers of Health Services Management,* 6, no. 3 (1990): 29–46; A. R. Kovner, "Hospital Board Members as Policy-makers: Role, Priorities and Quantifications," *Medical Care* 12, no. 4 (1974): 971–982; and D. Starkweather, "Hospital Board Power," *Health Services Management Research,* 1, no. 2 (1999): 74–86.

directors in advance. The temptation to use board members in this way is hard to resist. They inevitably have knowledge and skills that are of value to the foundation; they are available; and, in many cases, their services are free. However, the benefits may not be worth the costs without a clear understanding of outcome.

(E)   BOARD WORK MATRIX

Utilizing the concepts presented thus far, we see that a foundation board must fill each of the 15 cells of the Ewell and Powell matrix (see Exhibit 11.3) if it is to govern effectively. In keeping with its core roles, the board must formulate policy, make decisions, and engage in oversight while fulfilling its ultimate responsibilities. A board that is missing any one row, column, or cell is impaired and cannot do all that it should be doing.

When combined, the five ultimate responsibilities and three core roles provide a paradigm of governance that can be used to focus and direct the work of the board. This paradigm helps answer two key questions: (1) What should the board be doing? and (2) How should it go about doing it?"

Every foundation affiliated with a health system or hospital has distinctive board work fingerprints. These fingerprints are determined by two things: (1) How much effort is devoted to board work vs. the many other ways in which a board can choose to spend its time; and (2) the way in which the effort devoted to board work is allocated across the 15 cells of the Ewell and Powell matrix. Boards vary significantly on both of these dimensions.

Board fingerprints also change across time. For example, a board that spent the last year refining its policies might now devote less effort to this role. Moreover, there is no typical or ideal fingerprint. A fingerprint that is effective for one board might be dysfunctional for a board facing different circumstances. It also is true that extremes portend problems. For example, it is difficult to imagine that a board could be governing effectively if it devotes no effort to executing its oversight role or if it pays no attention to its responsibility for quality.

What are the additional characteristics that should be represented on your foundation board? What are some of the practical responsibilities you will need to consider as you plan for better governance?

An effective board builds support for the purpose, mission, and vision of the foundation. Board members act as liaisons with the broad base of the community while providing continuity for purpose and policy.

(F)   BOARD OBLIGATIONS

When individuals agree to sit on a board, they become part of a group that offers camaraderie. They also get a chance to make a difference in their communities, to support a cause they care about, and to further develop their skills. But board participation also involves certain obligations that new members should consider carefully before accepting a position. For example, they should be expected to:

- Be familiar with the programs and services of the IHS
- Be familiar with the foundation's goals, objectives, and programs

- Know as much as possible about the board of directors, board member expectations, criteria for selection, financial condition, programs, and staff before accepting membership
- Attend board and committee meetings regularly
- Be familiar with the minutes of the board and standing committees, especially those to which they are assigned
- Be familiar with the foundation's publications; treat the foundation's affairs as they would their own
- Learn (and use) the skills needed to motivate charitable giving by philanthropists
- Be certain the foundation's records are audited by a reputable certified public accountant (CPA) firm and that tax returns are prepared and submitted on a timely basis to the state and federal authorities (IRS, charity review bodies, etc.)
- Know the foundation's budget, budget process, and financial situation
- Know who is authorized to sign checks and in what amount
- Avoid self-serving policies
- Ask for advice if there is something they do not understand or something that raises questions about policy or practice
- Avoid the substance or appearance of conflict of interest
- Be certain the foundation is fulfilling all aspects of its nonprofit and tax-exempt status
- Insist on a written nominating procedure
- Monitor the foundation's community and professional image
- Be certain that policies are clearly identified and that the board acts on them as a whole rather than by action of a small group of individuals
- Require that the organization has proper legal counsel
- Monitor the activities of the executive committee to ensure it does not overstep its authority

(G) BOARD COMMITTEE RELATIONSHIPS

The foundation board's performance and the contribution it makes to the IHS and the community are significantly affected by the committees the board establishes and how well they perform. Properly structured and well-functioning committees are an asset. Poorly functioning ones waste valuable time and deflect, or even subvert, a board's attention and energy.

To fully tap the potential of committees, a foundation board must resolve two questions: (1) How many and what types of committees should be created? and (2) How should tasks be subdivided between the full board and its committees? Too often, these questions are not explicitly addressed; as a consequence, foundation board effectiveness and efficiency suffer.

It is likely that the board will need to form five core committees, one for each ultimate governance responsibility:

1. A committee on ends, to assist the board in fulfilling its responsibility for formulating the vision, mission, and goals for philanthropy
2. A committee on executive management performance, to ensure that the board is fulfilling its responsibility for high-level executive management

3. A committee on service effectiveness, or quality, to assist the board in fulfilling its responsibility regarding the relationship between philanthropists and the health system foundation

4. A committee on finance to assist the board in fulfilling its responsibility for enhancing the foundation's financial health and investment strategies

5. A committee on self or governance effectiveness, which, in addition to other duties, assists the board in assuming responsibility for its own high levels of performance and the selection, orientation, education, and training of members

Ad hoc committees also will be needed from time to time. They should only be formed, however, when standing committees are not the appropriate mechanism for addressing a particular issue. An ad hoc committee should have a very specific charge, and it should be disbanded when its assigned task has been completed.

Board committees exist to enhance the effectiveness and efficiency of the full board when it meets. They do this by performing much of the work for the board, in addition to directing work done by others on their behalf. Standing committees should assist the board in formulating policymaking decisions and engaging in oversight with respect to each ultimate responsibility. Some examples of tasks that might be undertaken by board committees are:

- *Policy formulation.* Employing data provided by the governance information system to identify areas in which new board policies should be formulated; preparing drafts of board policies; and facilitating the implementation of board policy by working with executive leadership
- *Decision making.* Reviewing proposals and recommendations forwarded to the board by management; requesting analyses needed by the board to make decisions; and drafting recommendations to the full board regarding decisions that it must make
- *Oversight.* Designing the component of the governance information system that focuses on its area of responsibility; proposing standards and performance measures; analyzing products of the governance information system; facilitating discussion of those analyses by the full board; and making recommendations regarding changes in functioning of the governance information system, standards, performance measures, and reports generated for the board.

Committees cannot and should not do the work of the full board. They cannot assume the ultimate responsibility that is the board's alone. Committees can, however, help the full board fulfill its responsibilities and execute its core roles. Given the volume of work that must be done, it is difficult to imagine a board functioning without committees. It is up to the board to ensure that committees function properly.

(H) TIERED GOVERNANCE IN INTEGRATED HEALTH SYSTEMS

Up to this point, discussion of board work has been incomplete and overly simplified. To better understand its full and complex nature, we must look at tiered governance structures, or multiple layers of boards, as found in multihospital or integrated health systems.

Examples of typical merged governance arrangements are helpful; nevertheless, the authors maintain that, in most instances, the need for multiple, separately incorporated foundations is unnecessary. Often the rationale for keeping them separate has more to do with turf than need.

- *Example 1.* Two or more hospitals may be part of an integrated system that chooses to have more than one foundation lead its philanthropic efforts. In this case, there may be both a system foundation board and separate foundation boards for each hospital and/or market.
- *Example 2.* Two or more hospitals merge and form a parent holding company. There may only be a parent holding company foundation board, with no foundation board for each hospital or program.
- *Example 3.* A hospital undergoes corporate reorganization and creates one or more subsidiary organizations with only one corporate foundation. In this case, the hospital and each subsidiary may have its own philanthropic initiatives.

In each of these illustrations, there are multiple layers of governance wherein some boards have superordinate relationships, while others have subordinate relationships.

These types of governance arrangements seem to be more evident to nonprofit health care organizations. Commercial corporations usually do not have boards for each subsidiary or component. For example, General Motors does not have separate boards for each of its divisions; when American Hospital Supply and Baxter Laboratories merged, the American Hospital Supply board was eliminated.

Irrespective of the specific form of governance employed, the combination of multiple organizations into one entity prompts several questions: Should there be separate legal entities to house local philanthropy programs? Should there be separate boards for each organizational component? If yes, then how should responsibilities and roles be allocated between corporate and subordinate boards? In the new IHS and their related attempts at integrated philanthropy systems, these questions are often addressed in haphazard manner. Good governance, however, requires consensus.

The decision whether to have a single board or multiple boards within the same corporate entity eventually comes down to weighing the assets and liabilities of centralization against decentralization.[9] That is, should philanthropic governance responsibilities and roles be concentrated or dispersed?

Probably the single most important asset governance offers is the opportunity to push selected foundation board responsibilities and roles down to a level where they can be fulfilled with a greater sensitivity to the distinctive circumstances faced by the component organization and their defined constituency base of support. On the other hand, having multiple boards also can create problems.

First, coordination can be difficult. Creating multiple layers of governance increases the possibility that different components will pursue their own ends in ways that impede the performance of the whole. For example, what might be viewed by a foundation board as being best for the local hospital or health program might not be in the best interest of the system or community philanthropists. Second, having more boards inevitably results in more work. A greater number of people are involved in governance,

---

[9]R. L. Daft, *Organization Theory and Design* (St. Paul, Minn.: West Publishing Company, 1992).

and more time and energy must be devoted to it. System executives and officers, if they hold seats on local foundation boards, must attend more meetings. Proposals and recommendations must be reviewed at multiple levels.

The following factors should be considered when deciding whether to have a single board or multiple boards:

- The number of separate organizational components and their geographic proximity
- The actual need for autonomy
- Legal considerations
- Philanthropic constituency interest

First, as the number of organizational components increases, the centralization of governance becomes more difficult and, at some point, becomes impossible. As the governance span of control widens, more and more issues must flow from individual organizations up to the corporate board, which can quickly become overwhelmed.

Second, when the component organizations are geographically dispersed, the attractiveness and benefits of tiered governance increase significantly. Consider, for example, a geographically dispersed integrated system with five hospitals located in different regions versus a local system in which all of the hospitals are in the same area. A single-system foundation board is possible in the latter situation, whereas it would be virtually impossible in the former. Distance can dramatically increase the cost and difficulty of coordination and weaken the effectiveness of the philanthropic programs.

Third, the benefits of tiered governance increase as component organizations perceive a need for more autonomy. The two most important factors here are differences between the types of markets or constituencies associated with the organization, and, in the case of hospitals, whether it is feasible for foundations of separate hospitals to be combined. When an integrated system is composed of organizations that operate in markets with highly dissimilar characteristics, greater governance autonomy may be warranted. This situation is confounded by the number of organizations in the system and their degree of geographic dispersion and/or autonomy. In an integrated system, the feasibility of tiered governance depends more on the ability to maximize philanthropic revenues from local markets and constituents than on any other factor. If the constituents for separate foundations can be combined and coordinated on behalf of the constituents, centralized governance for the philanthropic initiatives is possible and desired.

Fourth, legal considerations are a factor. Some states require charities or hospital-related entities to have separate foundations in order to be eligible for tax exemption, particularly if located in more than one state.

If tiered governance is employed, decisions must be made about how responsibilities and roles will be subdivided among corporate and subordinate boards. This issue is often not explicitly addressed. The result can be confusion, conflict, and less-than-optimal levels of board performance.

A framework for subdividing responsibilities and roles among corporate and subordinate boards is needed. For each ultimate responsibility, explicit choices must be made regarding who will formulate policy, who will make decisions, and who will engage in oversight. Additionally, a determination must be made regarding how these roles will be executed. For each of the 15 cells that define board work (as found in the Ewell and Pointer matrix, Exhibit 11.4), there are three alternatives:

EXHIBIT 11.4 Completed Board Work Matrix

Core Roles

ULTIMATE RESPONSIBILITIES		Policy Formulation	Decision Making	Oversight
	Ends	CORPORATE ↑ retain share ↓ delegate *subordinate*	CORPORATE ↑ retain share ↓ delegate *subordinate*	CORPORATE ↑ retain share ↓ delegate *subordinate*
	Executive Management Performance	CORPORATE ↑ retain share ↓ delegate *subordinate*	CORPORATE ↑ retain share ↓ delegate *subordinate*	CORPORATE ↑ retain share ↓ delegate *subordinate*
	Quality	Co...	CORPORATE ↑ retain share ↓ delegate *subordinate*	CORPORATE ↑ retain share ↓ delegate *subordinate*
	Finances		CORPORATE ↑ retain share ↓ delegate *subordinate*	CORPORATE ↑ retain share ↓ delegate *subordinate*
	Self	CORPORATE ↑ retain share ↓ delegate *subordinate*	CORPORATE ↑ retain share ↓ delegate *subordinate*	CORPORATE ↑ retain share ↓ delegate *subordinate*

Source: Charles M. Ewell and Dennis D. Pointer, Really Governing: How Health Systems and Hospital Boards Can Make More of a Difference *(Albany, N.Y.: Delmar Publishers, 1994).*

1. The system foundation board can retain responsibility and authority.
2. The system foundation board can delegate responsibility and authority to the subordinate board. Here are two options: The system board can delegate a given responsibility or a specific aspect of it to the subordinate board; or it can delegate with specific constraints and limitations.
3. Responsibility and authority can be shared by the system and subordinate boards. An example is a corporate board requesting recommendations from the subordinate board prior to making a decision.

The choice of alternatives for each of the 15 separate aspects of board work and their components can be made independently of one another. For example, a foundation board dealing with its responsibility for system effectiveness might choose to: retain the right of developing policies regarding financial investment of assets; delegate decision making to local community foundations for determining philanthropic revenue needs; or share the oversight role, wherein the quality of donor relationships (level of time, talent, treasure given) are reviewed by the system foundation board.

The extent to which policy formulation, decision making, and oversight rules will be retained, delegated, or shared by the corporate and subordinate boards for each ultimate responsibility must be explicit. The authors suggest that the system foundation board (in consultation with subordinate boards) prepare a responsibility statement that:

- Describes the nature and scope of corporate and subordinate board responsibilities
- Specifies which decisions will be retained by the corporate board, which will be delegated to the subordinate boards (in addition to any limitations) and which will be shared
- Specifies which aspects of the oversight role will be delegated to the subordinate boards and which will be shared

This process, although complex and time consuming, is necessary if board work is to be effectively and efficiently coordinated within a multiunit organization having tiered governance. The alternative is chaos.

11.4 *Changing Board Member Behavior to Enhance Governance*

(A) SIX PHASES OF BEHAVIOR CHANGE

Improving a foundation board's performance usually requires individual and collective behavioral changes. Changing the behavior of an institution requires changing the behavior of those who guide and manage the institution.

There are six vital prerequisites to bringing about the behavioral change needed to try a new product, idea, or role (such as board membership).

1. *Awareness.* Before any changes can be made, organizations must make their market constituents aware of what they have to offer. Market constituents (or customers) are linked to IHS by exchange relationships that bind them to our organizations and are vital to our success. Examples of market constituents include: external (suppliers, regulators, community, givers); internal (employees, physicians, volunteers, board members); and clients (patients, family members, visitors).
2. *Knowledge.* Once market constituents are aware of what an organization has to offer or wishes to communicate, the next step is to help them gain an understanding of the service.
3. *Image.* Image is collective perception based on the knowledge gained from Step 2 above and demonstrates how the service meets the market constituent's needs (personality, expectations, etc.).
4. *Sampling.* Sampling occurs when the market constituent, as a result of having a positive image and having made an internal or external decision to fill a need, elects to try the organization's product or service.

5. *Preference.* Preference is gained when, after sampling, the market constituent prefers your product or service over other alternatives. This step is the result of product performance or operations, not marketing, which can only move market constituents to sample.

6. *Advocacy.* Advocacy is a measure of the loyalty that an organization can garner through positive marketing and performance. This step usually represents heavy users and those who will recommend your product or service to others.

(B) BOARD MEMBER AS ADVOCATE

The best board members are those who conscientiously, consistently, and creatively drive themselves to serve the foundation. For them, the foundation is a vehicle for enhancing the health system through philanthropic gifts and in turn for enhancing the system's service to the broader community. This will happen only if the foundation board attracts, develops, and retains excellent board members.

The job for foundation managers then is to "capture" people of influence—opinion leaders—who must become (1) strong advocates of the IHS's cause for better health care; and (2) effective marketing agents. In effect, we want these individuals to be salespeople for our cause. The quality of a foundation's board membership is directly related to three things: (1) how well the foundation has sold itself; (2) what image it has communicated; and (3) how well it performs. For instance, the IHS's CEO, if an advocate, carries enthusiasm for the foundation and IHS, among other area corporate executives—his or her peers.

The board member must market the IHS by endorsement on a personal and/or corporate basis. In addition, a board member who is an advocate carries the message into family circles, into social activities, and into business activities on an informal basis; this "advertising" is absolutely free. Multiply this by the number of board members you have, and the marketing potential becomes tremendous in terms of influencing and ultimately securing philanthropic revenues.

Good governance, however, does not just happen. Board members function best as individuals and collectively when the "rules of the game" are available and well defined. You must have bylaws; strong committee structures; descriptions of roles and responsibilities; and board member manuals that outline governance policies, decision making and oversight, and define your foundation's purpose, mission, vision, goals, expectations, and so forth.

Often this element of establishing the "foundation" of the foundation is overlooked in order to see the immediate results of funds raised. It is like the old oil filter television commercial adage, "You can pay me now or pay me later." The implication is that the "cost" is much less if "foundational" work is done first. Good governance requires that the board's work, organization, and management be addressed first in any program for sustained philanthropy. Good governance also requires an understanding of why people invest their time, talent, and treasure in the foundation.

(C) WHY BOARD MEMBERS AGREE TO JOIN BOARDS

Most candidates for board membership have an abundance of opportunities to serve on community boards. Many nonprofit institutions compete for their time, talent, and treasure. Many candidates who accept a board position know little about the internal workings of the foundation or the IHS when asked to serve. Many join because of the foundation's or IHS's image and not because of a preference or desire to advocate for the foundation or system. One must know where the new board member fits within the six stages of behavioral change just listed; one also must be prepared to help them evolve beyond their entry level.

The elements that attract people to "sample" our foundation as board members deal with awareness, knowledge, and image (reputation, status, quality, prestige of other board members, etc.). These are factors that lead people to say yes. Saying yes does not automatically give us an active, involved board member. Our efforts should be to secure new board members who have preference for our IHS to ensure a likelihood of success.

(D)   WHAT BOARD MEMBERS EXPECT FROM THE FOUNDATION

When board members agree to serve, they do so believing that the IHS and foundation will help them do their jobs well and make an important contribution. They also expect to use their talents and capabilities in ways that truly are interesting, instructive, and rewarding. It is at this point that we succeed or fail in turning new board members into effective advocates. Some specific elements needed and expected by board members are:

- *Accurate, up-to-date information.* Board members do not want to be surprised. They want you to keep in touch with them and keep them informed, particularly on those items affecting public trust.
- *Accountability.* Many board members come from businesses in which they must report to their directorship, shareholders, and other regulating agencies. They expect the foundation to be accountable and responsible to the community for its actions.
- *Involvement and participation.* Most board members expect to be asked to share their expertise and to participate and lead efforts to obtain philanthropic resources and build constituencies through defined policies, procedures, strategic plans, and short-term objectives.
- *An opportunity to know and be known by the IHS's staff, management, and board of directors*
- *Opportunity to help build public trust.* Board members do not become advocates if they are only caretakers. Board members who help build and strengthen their foundations greatly increase their personal investment in the organization.
- *Economical use of their time.* Meetings should be planned in advance. Minutes and the agenda should be sent out ahead of time, and the agenda followed closely during the meetings.
- *Staff members who help them understand their roles and help them to be effective board members*
- *Stewardship.* Board members who become advocates are deeply interested in the foundation's investment and care of resources, property, and assets.
- *Opportunity to ask questions, to probe, to explore available options.* Each board member will not have the same knowledge base about the foundation or IHS. Most entry-level board members will have very little knowledge about either organization. If they are to become advocates they must have access to the foundation

and IHS so that the image they bring with them is confirmed by demonstrated operational performance and the knowledge gained is confirmed as fact. Structured orientation, training, and continuing education opportunities are essential to effective leadership.

• *Recognition, appreciation, and thanks.* The exchange value for a board member comes in many forms, but as one knows, financial exchange is not one of them. Because foundations cannot give financial incentives to board members, some of the most important items given are recognition, appreciation, and thanks, which demonstrate the value of their service. While most board members say they do not need recognition and thanks, both should be made as a "gift" for a job well done.

(E) DESIRABLE BOARD MEMBER CHARACTERISTICS

Good governance within a foundation affiliated with an IHS also requires certain predominant board member characteristics:

• *Integrity and accountability.* High ethical standards and integrity should be the guiding factors that drive the accountability for boardroom decisions.
• *Informed judgment.* Board members should provide wise, thoughtful counsel on a broad range of issues, including foundation programs, finance, and community philanthropy.
• *Financial literacy.* One of the important roles of a board member is to plan and monitor financial performance.
• *Mature confidence.* Openness to opinions and the willingness to listen among board members should rank as highly as the ability to communicate persuasively.
• *High performance standards.* In today's highly competitive world, only foundations capable of performing at the highest levels are likely to prosper.

11.5   Obstacles to Good Governance

Foundation board members and volunteers provide a quality of insight and caring that cannot be replaced by theoretical expertise or legislated services. The volunteer who feels needed and valued as a board member will experience personal growth and continue to be concerned and involved in the foundation. This concern and involvement is essential to the vitality of the foundation. Unfortunately, there are many obstacles to effective governance. A review of these potential problems should precede a discussion of strategies that will not only attract, engage, and empower effective board members, but continuously enhance their effectiveness and that of the foundation.

Most problems that develop within foundation boards evolve from one of the five areas listed below. By identifying those that face your board, you are in a better position to begin to resolve them. For example, if board members seem uncertain about the dimensions of their jobs, it is time to develop updated job descriptions for each position or committee.

1. Fears about:
   • Looking inept to others
   • What others might think

- Not being up to the job
- Asking questions and appearing inexperienced
- Expressing opinions that might differ
- Other board members because of the position they hold in the community

2. Lack of skills in:
   - Working with others as a group
   - Organization, administration, and planning
   - Decision making and problem solving
   - Research and development
   - Being an effective meeting participant
   - Asking for a philanthropic gift
   - Understanding the motives of a philanthropist

3. Lack of information regarding:
   - Changes in health care delivery and finance
   - Modern portfolios of philanthropy programs
   - Lines and extent of authority
   - Their specific roles
   - Their responsibility and accountability

4. Lack of leadership:
   - Serving under an unskilled or ill-equipped board chair
   - No preparation for specific responsibilities

5. Lack of understanding due to:
   - No information on how philanthropy can maximize its contribution to modern IHSs
   - Being "rubber stamps"
   - No significant board orientation, annual training, and/or education self-assessment
   - Inability to recognize how the philanthropic board fits with the overall health system

All too often, money is not sufficiently allocated for board training, nor is time. Even experienced board members need time to build a sense of team in a new group, with new people and new challenges. Board members need structured time in which to build a sense of trust, to develop pertinent skills, and to assess needs and opportunities. Board orientation and training should be annual events, at least. Good governance in new integrated philanthropy systems demand good board members that are ready, willing, and able to continuously enhance their knowledge, skills, and attitudes. Time spent by board members in this area reflects their investment of personal time, talent, and treasure for the benefit of those served by the IHS.

Robert Greenleaf in *Trustees as Servants* states: "*A society dominated by large corporations with governing boards, both for-profit and nonprofit, is a historical development that belongs almost entirely to this century. Too much of the public concern for the quality of society is still devoted to caring directly for individuals and not enough attention goes to caring for institutions and the way they are structured*"[10]

With this in mind, many foundation governing boards focus more on raising philanthropic funds than on governing the foundation they have been chosen to serve.

---

[10]Robert K. Greenleaf, *Trustees as Servants* (Indianapolis: The Robert K. Greenleaf Center, 1974), p. 6.

Many board members make the assumption that the paid administration and staff will see to it that the foundation performs as it should. Board member selection is often made for the name value rather than the affinity and/or commitment to the health care foundation's purpose, mission, and vision. Once the strategic plan and goals are set, board members, in many cases, fail to provide adequate oversight and a necessary critical eye to ensure success. Board members who are not fully committed can accept somewhat customarily and uncritically data supplied by staff and make no effort to equip themselves to be critical in their oversight.

The volunteer board member must be one of the most loyal, dedicated advocates of the IHS. An advocate not only prefers the health system or his or her needs but will turn that preference into supportive action. Board members must know and act on their governance responsibility and have the courage to seek and receive philanthropic revenues. The ability to serve effectively becomes stronger as the volunteer member develops:

- A better understanding of, and loyalty to, the IHS
- A belief in the worthiness of the IHS to receive philanthropic gifts
- A personal commitment to give in time, talent, and treasure in support of the IHS

Governing boards do not automatically receive an advocate when someone says yes to membership. Close attention must be paid to a new board member's cultivation, just as we do our philanthropic givers.

The corporate philanthropic officer in an IHS must have an understanding regarding the care and nurturing of volunteer board members. The lack of understanding about board members helps destroy many potentially good programs and corporate philanthropic officers. Too often, the initial efforts of a new foundation concentrate too quickly on raising dollars and overlook governance issues, and the selection, orientation, training, and education of the volunteer leadership necessary for ultimate success.

In today's competitive, ever-changing environment, the leadership that supports philanthropy within the IHS must be responsive to its surroundings or face certain failure. To meet the challenges as we move into the twenty-first century, one behavior that is essential is advocacy. If foundation board members are advocates for the IHS they serve, they are more likely to think ahead, anticipate problems, and make it their business to be on the forefront of change so that they can be proactive, rather than controlled by outside pressures.

11.6   The Foundation as a Learning Organization: New Leadership Roles

Foundation board leaders, especially the chairperson and the CEO, play essential roles in the new movement to evolve from individual board member performance to group responsibility, and they share responsibility for performance enhancement. In the new "learning organization," they are often the first to hear board members' concerns. Instead of avoiding these concerns or defending the status quo, they should invite the board members' desire to improve board performance.

Old board habits may suggest avoiding discontent, questions, or challenges to customary practice, but nonresponse can exacerbate divisiveness and create win-lose traps. Instead of repressing questions or allowing polarizations to develop, effective leaders should solicit honest member assessments of meetings and bring concerns to the full group for its attention and response.

Not every complaint will meet with group consensus, but it may be easier for the complainant to take a different stance if all members listen and respond respectfully to the concern. Sometimes the initial issue or suggestion is reformulated by the group into a broader or more basic concern that all can join in addressing.

Savvy CEOs understand that board members are their best partners in creating stronger foundations. Accordingly, they invest time in assessing board performance and educating members in order to maximize their time, talent, and contributions. This is especially important when major changes are on the horizon, for example, when a foundation is considering whether to merge with another body or to undertake a capital campaign.

CEOs must be committed to improving board performance and for bringing such matters up with the full board. Working with the board chair, the executive raises performance questions before the group to see if others have similar concerns. Together, they raise aspirations about what the board could be achieving and suggest alternative approaches. On issues for which there is group interest and shared concern, leaders help the groups sharpen expectations and aspirations by initiating questions about group performance, suggesting alternative approaches to dealing with issues, and offering new possibilities for improving group effectiveness.

Holland and associates[11] have found that by opening up discussion about the board's performance, leaders show that it is appropriate to direct attention to the quality of the board's own work and to explore ways to continuously improve. Thus, they shift concerns from back channels to the forefront of everyone's attention to foster discussions of the ways in which the group can better expedite its future work. Leaders provide opportunities for others to join in problem analysis and form a constituency for mutual action in seeking solutions.

Leaders use these discussions not as occasions to find fault or point fingers but as opportunities to model respectful feedback, improve performance quality, and invite others to join in similar efforts. In doing so, leaders confirm that they and the board members are committed to doing their jobs more effectively. This encourages dedication to improving the quality of group performance, even at the expense of traditional practices or assumptions.

Effective leaders expect and allow old ways of doing business to be questioned. They welcome new ideas and alternatives, and encourage board members to do the same. They also recognize and celebrate incremental steps toward the achievement of goals for improved performance and continuous governance enhancement.

Visionary leaders apply Peter Senge's[12] advice about creating organizations that learn to work better as they move forward. Outstanding orchestras and winning sports teams exemplify groups that take time to reflect on each performance to assess how well they did and to determine what changes might improve future efforts. Reflecting on experiences, identifying areas of change, and then implementing the changes are all crucial steps to their success. Boards that follow this model by examining and reflecting on their

---

[11]Thomas P. Holland, Roger A. Ritvo, and Anthony R. Kovner, *Improving Board Effectiveness: Practical Lessons for Nonprofit Health Care Organizations* (Chicago: American Hospital Association, 1997).
[12]Peter M. Senge, *The Fifth Discipline: The Art and Practice of the Learning Organization* (New York: Doubleday, 1990).

own performance can learn useful lessons and reveal changes that can turn them into more effective leaders who establish the learning curve throughout their organization.

11.7 Good Governance: A Journey, Not a Destination

When one says yes to board membership, the work is not over—it has just begun. Board members are important because they are the essential ingredient in the relationships and revenue dimensions of success in philanthropic programs. In the words of Harold J. Seymour from his classic work *Designs for Fund Raising: Principles, Patterns, Techniques: Every cause needs people more than money, for when the people are with you and are giving your cause their attention, interest, confidence, service and advocacy, financial support should just about take care of itself; whereas, without them in the right quality and quantity in the right places and the right states of mind and spirit, you might as well go and get lost!*[13]

The board chair and CEO must be ever diligent to work with board members for continuous governance enhancement. Boards must continuously challenge their performance and continuously develop the knowledge, skills, and attitudes of its members. Good governance is a lifelong pursuit of excellence. Good board members are committed to continuously improve their understanding and advocacy of the purpose, mission, vision, and case for support of the foundation. This will not come easily nor quickly. Explicit attention must be directed to the challenge of continuous governance enhancement, as defined earlier in this publication.

A farmer does not grow crops, he creates the conditions in which crops grow. Likewise, we do not raise funds; we create the conditions in which philanthropy grows and flourishes. In working to create those conditions, we, like the farmer, understand that we cannot control most variables in the external environment. We must learn, act, and adapt to what comes before us. We shall never be able to achieve an ideal future, but we can have successful movement in an understood direction. Continuous progress on a continually changing strategic agenda, learning, adapting, and improving along the way is what Margaret Wheatley called "tinkering" in her work *A Simpler Way.*[14]

It is the hope of the authors that a basic introduction to foundation governance has been provided that may help you raise the levels of philanthropic support for IHSs emerging as we approach the twenty-first century.

Suggested Readings

Carpenter, R. N. "Cooperative Governance, Part II: Directors' Responsibilities." *Management Quarterly*, 29, no. 3 (1988): 3–6.

Carver, J. *Boards That Make a Difference: A New Design for Leadership in Nonprofit and Public Organizations.* San Francisco: Jossey-Bass, 1991.

Chait, R. P., et al. *The Effective Board of Trustees.* New York: Macmillan, 1991.

---

[13]Harold J. Seymour, *Designs for Fund Raising: Principles, Patterns, Techniques* (New York: McGraw-Hill, 1966), p. ix.

[14]Margaret J. Wheatley and Myron Kellner-Rogers, *A Simpler Way* (San Francisco: Berrett-Koehler Publishers, 1996).

Daft, R. L. *Organization Theory and Design*. St. Paul, Minn.: West Publishing Company, 1992.

Ewell, Charles M., and Dennis D. Pointer. *Really Governing: How Health Systems and Hospital Boards Can Make More of a Difference*. Albany: Delmar Publishers, 1994.

Gordon, L. A., et al. "The Challenge of Governing for Value." *Directors and Boards*, 16, no. 3 (1992): 13–17.

Greenleaf, Robert K. *Trustees as Servants*. Indianapolis: The Robert K. Greenleaf Center, 1974.

Hageman, W. M., and R. J. Umbdenstock. "Organizing and Focusing the Board's Work: Keys to Effectiveness." *Frontiers of Health Services Management*, 6, no. 3 (1990): 29–46.

Hodgetts, R. M., and M. S. Wortman. *Administrative Policy: Text and Cases in the Policy Sciences*. New York: John Wiley & Sons, 1975.

Holland, Thomas P., Roger A. Ritvo, and Anthony R. Kovner. *Improving Board Effectiveness: Practical Lessons for Nonprofit Health Care Organizations* (Chicago: American Hospital Association, 1997).

Kovner, A. R. "Hospital Board Members as Policy-makers: Roles, Priorities and Qualifications." *Medical Care*, 12, no. 4 (1974): 971–982.

Mintzberg, H. *Structuring in Fives: Designing Effective Organizations*. Englewood Cliffs, N.J.: Prentice-Hall, 1983.

Parsons, T. *Structure and Process in Modern Society*. Glencoe, Il.: Free Press, 1960.

Selznick, P. *Leadership in Administration*. New York: Harper & Row, 1957.

Senge, Peter M. *The Fifth Discipline: The Art and Practice of the Learning Organization*. New York: Doubleday, 1990.

Seymour, Harold J. *Design for Fund Raising: Principles, Patterns, Techniques*. New York: McGraw-Hill, 1966. (A second edition was reissued in 1988 in paperback by The Fund Raising Institute, Ambler, PA.)

Starkweather, D. "Hospital Board Power." *Health Services Management Research*, 1, no. 2 (1988): 74–86.

Wheatley, Margaret J., and Myron Kellner-Rogers. *A Simpler Way*. San Francisco: Berrett-Koehler Publishers, Inc., 1996.

Appendix 11A   Fax Poll on Governance Issues

FAX POLL— GOVERNANCE ISSUES FOR FOUNDATION BOARDS
"Decision Making for Better Performance of 21st Century Foundation Boards"
DEGREE OF CONCERN TO YOUR BOARD—AVERAGE RATINGS

FAX POLL—GOVERNANCE ISSUES FOR FOUNDATION BOARDS
"Decision Making for Better Performance of 21st Century Foundation Boards"

May 1997

"Degree of Concern to Your Board"	Board understanding strategic issues	Board understanding role of philanthropy	Role of board in strategic planning	Level/nature of managers' compensation	Role of board in fund raising performance target	Role of board in funds distribution priorities	Continuing education of board	Evaluation of board performance & effectiveness	Strategies to recruit new board members	Efficiency of board meetings	Written governing board responsibilities policy
Very Low — Very High											
1 Butterworth Foundation	10	10	10	1	10	10	5	5	7	3	1
2 Calgary General Hospital Foundation	5	5	10	10	8	9	5	5	9	4	6
3 Carondolet Foundation	6	7	8	2	7	7	8	4	8	8	5
4 Centura	8	7	7	6	8	8	8	7	7	6	9
5 CHS Foundations	5	3	9	4	3	6	8	1	5	7	7
6 Eastern Connecticut Health Network, Inc.	10	6	9	4	10	6	4	4	8	9	5
7 First Health of the Carolinas	9	9	6	4	5	4	7	5	7	8	4
8 Franciscan Sister	9	10	6	6	4	8	9	9	10	10	10
9 General Health System Foundation	9	10	7	5	9	7	9	8	10	8	7
10 Grossmont Hospital Foundation	9	4	4	1	4	9	5	4	5	6	8
11 HealthEast Foundation	7	8	9	2	6	7	4	1	5	8	9
12 Hillcrest Medical Center Foundation	8	7	6	8	5	4	4	4	7	8	6
13 John Muir Foundation	7	7	5	4	8	5	5	5	9	9	9
14 Little Company of Mary Hospital Found.	10	6	7	6	7	7	5	4	5	6	6
15 Memorial Healthcare System (Houston, TX)	8	6	4	3	4	3	4	3	3	8	3
16 Mercy Health Services (Farmington, MI)	10	6	6	9	9	9	9	7	9	9	6
17 Methodist Health Care System	10	10	7	5	8	8	7	6	9	10	6
18 Monmouth Health Care Foundation	6	3	8	7	7	8	6	7	6	7	6
19 Parkview Foundation	6	7	6	5	8	8	7	3	6	5	5
20 PGH Mercy Foundation	8	4	8	7	7	7	9	4	8	4	4
21 Samaritan Foundation	7	8	6	4	5	7	7	5	6	6	9
22 Seton	6	6	7	3	3		3	3	6	10	6
23 Seton Healthcare	8	9	9	9	7	6	6	4	9	10	8
24 SJHHC			4	1	6	8	9	9	10	8	10
25 Srs of Providence Hlth Sys (Holyoke, MA)	10	6	9	5	8	9	8	6	9	7	7
26 St. Mary Med Ctr Found. (Long Beach, CA)	7	8	3	3	3	9	6	8	9	7	3
27 Stamford Health Foundation	9	9	7	7	4	3	8	8	8	9	9
28 Sun Health Foundation	9	8	8	6	8	4	8	7	7	7	5
29 University of Texas Health Science Center	5	5	8	2	7	7	7	7	8	8	8
30 (name withheld)	4	3	2	2	2	4	2	1	4	4	4
AVERAGES:	7.9	6.9	7.0	4.8	6.5	6.9	6.6	5.3	7.4	7.4	6.4

Appendix 11B   Sample Foundation Strategic Plan

ORLANDO REGIONAL HEALTHCARE FOUNDATION STRATEGIC PLAN

PRINCIPLES OF GOVERNANCE AND OPERATION

At ORHF all philanthropic activity:

- Serves the Orlando Regional Healthcare System (ORHS) priorities
- Advances the Purpose, Mission and Vision of ORHF
- Follows an approved strategic plan
- Considers the mutual interest of the philanthropist and ORHS
- Creates an exchange of values between the philanthropist and ORHS
- Utilizes an integrated approach
- Adheres to the Association of Healthcare Philanthropy Standards of Ethics

Purpose
Benefiting Our Community

Our purpose at Orlando Regional Healthcare Foundation (ORHF) is to benefit our community. This primary directive holds special meaning as we strive to advance and preserve meritorious healthcare causes within the mission of ORHS by making dreams reality.

To provide benefit is to add value. All that we do must benefit our various communities. Adding value is measured in tangible and intangible terms, including economic. We strive to meaningfully satisfy the diversified needs of our various communities.

Our community within ORHS involves the patients, families and friends, caregivers, ORHS board, administrators, managers and the Foundation staff and board. Our service community includes residents and visitors in our area. Our serving community is the charitable giver to ORHS.

Our specific communities benefit as follows:

Patients	• Have access to advanced healthcare
Families & Friends	• Receive comfort and support while they themselves provide comfort and support to ORHS patients
Residents & Visitors	• Receive pre-eminent healthcare services
Caregivers	• Have access to advanced medical resources and technologies
ORHS Board, Administrators, Managers	• Have access to funding for unmet capabilities
Foundation Staff and Board	• Receive the satisfaction of making the dreams of today become the reality of tomorrow for all communities of ORHS
Charitable Givers	• Support a great cause and give back the good that has been done for them

Mission
Improving the Quality of Life and Health

Our mission will be achieved by:

- Expanding and preserving essential patient services
- Equipping caregivers with unique resources and technologies

- Helping create a healthier community for greater Orlando
- Communicating the good news stories from "inside the walls"
- Marketing the special dreams that attract significant giving
- Enabling ambassadors to participate in making dreams reality
- Cooperating with other community organizations who share the ORHS mission

Vision
Making Dreams Reality

Our vision is achieved as we constantly strive to add value to, and improve, the community's health status one life at a time through philanthropy.

Values

- **Integrity:** Taking pride in our work while holding ourselves to high personal and professional standards
- **Learning:** Embracing experience and education as important to improvement and accomplishment in both personal and team goals
- **Team:** Respecting each member as a significant contributor to the potential, strength and growth of the Foundation
- **Visible Leadership:** Every team member is a leader in, and an advocate for, philanthropy
- **Philanthropy:** Matching donor needs with ORHS opportunities
- **Service:** Building relationships that serve the needs of our community

Key Assumptions

- Our primary customer is the ORHS community
- We can only serve ORHS successfully through the charitable giving community
- The world is abundant; there are no money problems, only idea limitations
- Giving contributes to personal wellness
- Alignment with ORHS is imperative
- Giver satisfaction is essential

Outcomes

The following are *specific* outcomes sought:

- Maintain new philanthropic revenues at a minimum of $10 million per year
- Contribute a minimum of $3–5 million per year to ORHS
- Provide M.D. Anderson Cancer Center up to $20 million in philanthropic funds over the next three to five years
- Determine potential for $100 million philanthropic effort for ORHS into the 21st century
- Develop ORHF as the premier philanthropic organization in Central Florida and within the top 5% of all healthcare foundations nationally

Appendix 11C   Sample Partnership Plan/Board Commitment

ORLANDO REGIONAL HEALTHCARE FOUNDATION, INC.

Purpose   **Benefiting Our Community**
Mission   **Improving the Quality of Life and Health**
Vision   **Making Dreams Reality**

BOARD OF DIRECTORS

PARTNERSHIP SUCCESS PLAN

I,_____, recognizing the important responsibility I am undertaking in serving as a member of the Board of Directors of this Orlando Regional Healthcare Foundation (ORHF), hereby pledge to carry out in a trustworthy and diligent manner the duties and obligations in my role as a board member.

My role:

I acknowledge that my primary roles as a board member are to: 1) abide by the ORHF Principles of Governance and Operations (**attachment A**); 2) contribute to the ORHF purpose, mission and vision, and governing the fulfillment of that purpose, mission, vision; 3) carry out the functions of the office of board member and/or officer as stated in the bylaws; and 4) work to fulfill the expectations outlined in this my personal Partnership Success Plan.

My role as a board member will focus on the development of policies that govern the work of the ORHF Board of Directors and Membership. This role is separate and distinct from the role of the ORHF administration and staff, who determine the means of implementation.

I understand that philanthropic revenues are the primary focus of the Board of Directors because: 1) philanthropic revenues are essential to fulfill the C.A.R.E. matrix outlining the philanthropic revenue needs of ORHS, and 2) assuring that all philanthropic funds are properly and prudently managed is the fiduciary of the ORHF Board of Directors.
With my personal commitment, I pledge to:

- Exercise the duties and responsibilities of this office with prudence, integrity, collegiality, and stewardship
- Meet or exceed attendance requirement at meetings of the ORHF board and committees on which I serve
- Be prepared to discuss the issues and business addressed at scheduled meetings, having read the agenda and all background materials relevant to the topics at hand
- Work with, and respect, the opinions of my peers who serve this board and to leave my personal prejudices out of board discussions
- Act for the good of the community
- Represent ORHF/ORHS in a positive and supportive manner at all times and in all places
- Participate in yearly philanthropic activities. During 1998 I shall do the following: (**attachment B**)

- _____
- _____
- _____
- _____
- _____

- Observe parliamentary procedures and display courteous conduct in all board and committee meetings
- Refrain from intruding on administrative issues that are the responsibility of management, except to provide designated policy oversight for the ORHF board policy decision responsibilities
- If a conflict of interest between my position as a board member and my personal life should arise, I will declare that conflict before the board and refrain from voting on matters in which I have a conflict
- Support in a positive manner all actions taken by the board of directors even when I am in a minority position on such actions
- Ensure all necessary financial support for C.A.R.E. matrix is secured
- If I chair the board, a committee, or a task force I will:

   1. Call meetings as necessary until objectives are met
   2. Ensure the agenda and support materials are mailed to all members in advance of the meetings
   3. Conduct the meeting in an orderly, fair, open, and effective manner
   4. Make committee progress reports/minutes to the board at its scheduled meetings, using the adopted format

- Participate in:
   1. At least two of the annual ORHF Board retreats during my three-year term
   2. Annual board self-examination based upon this personal Partnership Success Plan
   3. Board orientation, development workshops, seminars, and other educational events to enhance my skills as a board member. During 1998 I shall participate in the following: (**attachment C**)

   - _____
   - _____
   - _____

In return, ORHF is responsible to me in the following ways:

   1. I will be sent quarterly policy oversight reports that allow me to meet the policy requirements of the ORHF Governance Policies.
   2. I can call on the ORHF President to discuss governance policy, program goals and objectives.
   3. Board members and staff will respond in a straightforward and thorough fashion to any questions I have that are necessary to carry out my fiscal, legal or moral responsibilities to this organization.

If, for any reason, I find myself unable to carry out the above duties as best as I can, I agree to resign my position as board director/officer.

_____   _____

Board Member's Signature   Date

PARTNERSHIP SUCCESS PLAN ADDENDUM

". . . making the most of your orientation and education for ORHF"

Summary:

The following outlines the orientation and educational programs available to help board members complete the process annually and fulfill their PARTNERSHIP SUCCESS PLAN commitments. The calendar outlines a suggested strategic opportunity for each board member to take advantage of the programs offered to meet their individual needs. A suggested calendar outlines how each person should easily be able to plan their specific orientation and educational programs within the desired time frames.

Orientation and Education Schedule

One of the concepts within the Partnership Success Plan is an ongoing orientation and educational process for Foundation Board members. A suggested process for each board member to follow consists of 6-month intervals of educational milestones within their 3-year term. Your program track could look something like the following:

- *6-month milestone.* Each board member would complete the **general orientation** program and review the corresponding information packet that would give them an overview of Orlando Regional Healthcare System, the Orlando Regional Healthcare Foundation, and the relationships that exist between the different entities.
- *12-month milestone.* The board member would have completed a general tour of Orlando Regional Healthcare System accompanied by a member of the Foundation's Development Officer Team (actually provided at the general orientation).
- *18-month milestone.* The board member would have completed an in-depth learning session within one of the key areas of Orlando Regional Healthcare System (i.e., The Chatlos Center for Trauma Care, surgical half-day session, pediatric half-day session, cancer care half-day session, telemedicine session, research and training session).
- *24-month milestone.* The board member will have completed the Orlando Regional Healthcare System's Board program called "A Day in the Life" where they spend an entire day working through areas of individual choice within Orlando Regional Healthcare System. In this program, the day is broken down by time in a selected number of places that fall into the continuum of care. This gives them a global perspective of healthcare today through the eyes of the employees who deliver it each day within ORHS.
- *30-month milestone.* The board member will have visited all nine of the campus service areas that provide patient care through Orlando Regional Healthcare System.
- *36-month milestone.* As the board member completes their first term of service, the self-governance process will be best tested as they review their commitment and fulfillment and through one-on-one interaction determine their future commitment.
- In the area of education, the Foundation Board could pursue a learning track of varying topical issues relating to its role within the system. In addition, the Organizational Development programs within ORHS would be available for personal enhancement for the board.

ORLANDO REGIONAL HEALTHCARE FOUNDATION
GENERAL ORIENTATION

This is the **required** orientation component for new board members and their mentors. The program encompasses a half-day and will include all of the following.

NOTE: You may also come to a morning program beginning at 9 A.M. that includes a planning session with staff, Directors Committee Chair and a walking tour of the downtown campus.

12:00 noon–2:45 P.M.	Luncheon
	Summary/overview of ORHS presented by John
	Hillenmeyer, ORHS President/CEO
	Site-specific educational program presented by
	Chief Development Officers
3:00 P.M.–5:00 P.M.	Tour of Campus
	Arnold Palmer Hospital for Children & Women
	Health Research Institute
	ORMC Trauma/Air Care
	Hubbard House
5:00 P.M.–6:30 P.M.	Reception/Social

THE ORIENTATION OPPORTUNITY MENU

To ensure that each board member and friend to ORHS has the opportunity to acquire the knowledge and skills that capitalize on their time, treasure, and talents, the following menu of ongoing ORHS orientation has been established. This will allow you to plan the important opportunities you will take to learn more about the issues we face as a community or for you to take advantage of personal enhancement programs provided by ORHS.

Customized Orientation Enhancement

Each of these three programs provides participants with an in-depth look at ORHS from the inside. Each program is customized to look from your perspective at how the system works to provide healthcare from a variety of observation points—some more in depth than others.

Behind the Scenes

Format: Active participation tour of ORHS service
Time: 2.5 Hours
Schedule: 2nd Tuesday of the month, 11:00 A.M.–1:30 P.M.
                    3rd Thursday of the month, 6:00 P.M.–8:30 P.M.
                    4th Tuesday of the month, 7:00 A.M.–9:30 A.M.
Contact: Sharon Williams, Mgr. Board Governance & Stewardship, 841-5111 x-8794.

This two-hour program will walk you and a guest through differentiating areas within ORHS from top to bottom. You will experience an area from a patient perspective, with a unique opportunity to hear from the medical professionals how the situation is dealt with first hand.

A Day in The Life

Format: Hands-on tour of ORHS downtown campus service areas
Time: 8 hours (optional half-day with morning or afternoon preference)
Schedule: 8:00 A.M.–4:30 P.M.
Contact: Sharon Williams, Mgr. Board Governance & Stewardship, 841-5111 x-8794.

Step inside ORHS for a day—to experience it "up close and personal." The program allows you to design a day that meets your personal schedule and interest areas across a continuum of care. You will work alongside team members as they go about their typical work activities, and you will be hosted throughout the day by one of the administrative assistants.

The ORHF Healthcare Experience

Format: Half-day in-depth tour opportunities to tour the areas supported by the Foundation
Time: Both morning and afternoon programs are available
Schedule: flexible depending on the area(s) toured
Contact: Sharon Williams, Mgr. Board Governance & Stewardship, 841-5111 x-8794.

Arnold Palmer Hospital for Children & Women, M.D. Cancer Center Orlando, The Chatlos Center for Trauma Care, Hubbard House and the Health Research Institute represent some of the key areas within ORHS you can experience from the vantage point of our "care" givers. Learn how the areas are supported through the generosity of our community and what the staff is accomplishing daily.

THE EDUCATIONAL OPPORTUNITY MENU

Programs within this series will allow board members to meet their educational expectations and learn about issues, enhance their personal portfolio of information and take classes that will benefit themselves and their career track.

Organizational Development presents Quality Leadership Process training as outlined in the attached Curriculum Guide for Behavioral Development.

Information Services provides ongoing computer training according to a monthly published schedule. Beginner, Intermediate and Advanced classes include: Intro to PCs/Windows, Microsoft Word, Windows Basics, GroupWise, Excel and Access. Classes are filled in the order in which registrations are received.

Programs can be scheduled through Sharon Williams, Mgr. Board Governance & Stewardship, 841-5111 x-8794.

LIST OF BOARD RESPONSIBILITIES

PHILANTHROPIC ACTIVITY

"WAYS YOU CAN HELP AS A BOARD MEMBER"

1. Provide prospect names, addresses, telephone numbers. Share some pertinent information about interests and giving potential of your contacts.
2. Provide prospective board members for consideration. Share some pertinent information about interests and giving potential of your contacts (see nomination form).
3. Introduce people to ORHF Chairman and/or ORHS/ORHF President. Cultivate regularly. Friend raise!
4. Speak on behalf of ORHF to an outside group.
5. Write a personal testimonial for public use or offer to be quoted as to why you are supporting ORHF.
6. Work on a special events committee.
7. Edit a case statement, grant proposal, C.A.R.E. matrix, and so forth.
8. Complete ORHS-sponsored continuing education programs relevant to ORHF membership.
9. Visit a person of affluence and/or influence within the community to explain need within C.A.R.E. matrix.
10. Host in your home, business, ORHS, or restaurant a small group of prospects so they learn more about the value of services provided by ORHS.
11. Solicit direct support from service clubs, civic groups or churches/temples requesting their sponsorship for a gift opportunity within the C.A.R.E. matrix.
12. Secure an irrevocable gift that can be documented for auditing purposes (i.e., cash, pledge, or in-kind).
13. Personalize gift solicitation and/or recognition by providing givers one of these:
    • Put a handwritten postscript or thank you on prepared acknowledgments.
    • Write a handwritten note of appreciation for gifts and mail.
    • Phone to thank some of those who have given.
14. Complete a philanthropic training workshop to learn how to better carry out your role, responsibilities, and expectations.
15. Telephone-lapsed givers to ORHF using follow-up instructions.
16. Accept a campaign leadership role, chairmanship of an organized event, or other solicitation effort.
17. Participate in local, state or national programs providing information on philanthropy and/or foundation related activities.
18. Ask for a gift from an individual with help from an ORHS/ORHF staff member.
19. Ask for a gift from an individual on your own.
20. Follow-up on a specific giver concern with service.

Appendix 11D   Sample Committee Charges

EXECUTIVE COMMITTEE: Shall have the authority of the board of directors with respect to the operation of ORHF in the normal course of its business (including the investment and reinvestment of ORHF funds) between regular meetings of the board, and it shall be responsible for the self-governance activities of ORHF and for any corrective actions regarding director effectiveness, and the performance of the President/CEO of ORHF. In addition, it shall have such authority with respect to extraordinary transactions as the board of directors may, by resolution, delegate to it. However, unless expressly delegated by the board, the Executive Committee shall not have the authority to: amend the bylaws of ORHF; elect, appoint, or remove any Director, officer or member of ORHF; amend the Articles of Incorporation; adopt a plan of merger or consolidation; authorize the sale, lease, exchange or mortgage of the property or assets of ORHF; authorize dissolution or liquidation of ORHF; adopt a plan of distribution of the assets of ORHF; or amend or repeal any resolution of the board of directors.

Structure:

- Chairman will be the Chairman of the board of directors.
- Other members will be the Vice Chairman, President, Secretary/Treasurer, the immediate past chairman of ORHF, and the President/CEO of ORHS

Composition: Members should possess and have demonstrated leadership qualities while serving as members of the board in various committee activities; understand the basic mission of ORHS and its scope of services, and be a giver to the Foundation.

Primary responsibilities:

- Keep minutes of all meetings and furnish to ORHF board before the full board meetings.
- Set the full board agendas.
- Annually conducts survey of board membership based on defined expectations prior to the election of ORHF Officers and Directors to determine level of understanding regarding responsibility as a director, assessment of personal performance and contribution to the board's effectiveness, as well as any improvements that need to be made in the governance of the Foundation.
- Call for the resignation of directors, as needed.
- Conducts search for new President/CEO based on board policy #BD-005.
- Between October and December of each year, evaluates the performance of the President/CEO based upon the following criteria: goal achievement based upon the approved strategic plan including results against priority revenue needs defined in the C.A.R.E. matrix; achievement of critical success factors; results of the Leadership Index and Team Survey; and adherence to the ORHF Principles and Values.
- Submits written President/CEO performance evaluation to the ORHS President/CEO through Chairman.

STRATEGIC PLANNING COMMITTEE: Shall recommend to ORHF the organizational purpose, mission, vision toward which the efforts of ORHF shall be directed. In conjunction with each "community" board and ORHS, the committee shall formulate and recommend to the ORHF Board a strategic plan for ORHF, a C.A.R.E. matrix outlining philanthropic priorities, and policies to ensure that resources and capacities of ORHF are directed toward helping accomplish these stated ends.

Structure:

- Vice Chairman shall serve as Chairman of the committee.
- Up to ten (10) members of which six (6) shall be ORHF Directors, and one (1) member shall be selected by each "community" board, which selection shall be approved by the Chairman of ORHF.
- Other members may be appointed at the discretion of the Chairman of ORHF because of expertise. They shall not have voting privileges and may not be directors.

Composition: Members must be able to understand the ORHS priorities and develop plans that relate to the "whole" of ORHS. Special interests should be set aside in determining the ultimate goals and priorities of ORHF.

Primary Responsibilities:

- At least every five years, the committee causes to be produced a strategic plan with measurable results.
- Before the end of the fiscal year, the strategic plan's measurable results and outcomes are reviewed, modified, and updated by the committee with input from the "community" boards.
- The committee causes to be presented to the annual meeting of ORHF the strategic plan for approval or reconfirmation; as well, the strategic plan of ORHS to ORHF Board by the ORHS President/CEO.
- Establish policies for review and recommend grant requests above $15,000 submitted by ORHS that request ORHF unrestricted funds.
- Periodically review grant request policy and procedure to ensure the relationship, communications and process between ORHS and the Foundation is positive.
- Evaluate approved and funded projects on a yearly basis and measure success.
- Prioritize the C.A.R.E. matrix submitted by each "community" board into a unified whole, and ensure its continuity with the strategic plan (BD-002).
- Cause to be created the C.A.R.E matrix for those parts not operationally covered by ORHF and approve new areas for operational support by ORHF.
- Receive quarterly reports from the "community" boards regarding success in achieving C.A.R.E matrix outcomes.
- Report C.A.R.E. matrix success at the ORHF annual meeting.
- Provide oversight that insures the major operational processes and procedures of ORHF reflect adherence to the Statements of Principle (BD-001).

PHILANTHROPY COMMITTEE: Shall recommend to ORHF measures which shall enhance deep and lasting relationships between ORHF and the philanthropist who choose to share their time, talent and/or treasure for the improvement of the community served by ORHS. The committee shall monitor and evaluate methods to maximize the satisfaction, acknowledgment, recognition and management of the ORHF givers.

Structure:

- Committee Chairman appointed by the Chairman of the Board of Directors.
- Shall consist of up to six (6) members
- Other members may be appointed at the discretion of the Chairman of ORHF because of expertise. They shall not have voting privileges and may not be directors. The Director of Giving serves in a staff capacity.

Composition: Chairman should have marketing/public relations interest/experience. Membership is comprised of directors who have an interest in, and knowledge of, relationship marketing, customer service outcomes, etc.

Primary responsibilities:

- Conduct a full scientific satisfaction survey of the giver base at least every three years. Evaluate results of the satisfaction survey and cause to be created an action plan based on the findings that are likely to increase giver satisfaction.
- Approve a process to annually monitor giver satisfaction, which could include monitoring of day-to-day feedback via telephones, mail, personal contacts, etc. based on a response rate of 5 as outstanding, 4.5 as satisfactory and 4 as minimum.
- Provide oversight of the giver satisfaction processes in place by receiving at least quarterly reports from foundation staff. Report findings to ORHF on the same frequency.
- Provide oversight for giver acknowledgment that: sets as a standard two (2) business days for written acknowledgment of all gifts; uses the correct legal language to ensure givers are in compliance with the law; and includes other appropriate acknowledgments, i.e., telephone calls, invitations to special ORHS/ORHF events, personal visits, tangible recognition, etc.
- Recommends to ORHF Board the ORHF giver recognition plan in consultation with the ORHF team and giver representatives which includes all tangible recognition within the ORHF sites, printed materials, etc. As a standard, recognition is completed within one month of the gift, unless new construction prohibits the completion.
- Address with ORHS administration any conflicts vs. recognition requests vs. institutional/structural requirements.
- Provide oversight in consultation with the "community" boards and ORHF staff regarding the effectiveness of the information systems in support of the Strategic Plan. Report status annually to ORHF.

FINANCE/INVESTMENT COMMITTEE: Shall cause to be prepared a budget showing the expected philanthropic receipts and other income for the ensuing year in relation to the expense budget approved by the Member. It shall monitor the actual performance as compared to the budget, and it shall cause to be audited on an annual basis financial statements of ORHF. It shall cause to be prepared a resolution of fiscal policy which shall include but not be limited to treatment of depreciation, debt retirement, auditing, handling of fund accounts, employee bonding requirements, purchasing authorization of officers of ORHF, authority of officers of ORHF to sell or otherwise dispose of investment property of ORHF. The Committee shall arrange for all funds of ORHF to be properly invested with one or more investment managers duly authorized to conduct business in the State of Florida, and shall require quarterly reports concerning such investments. The Committee shall adopt and monitor the performance of policies to ensure that all gifts, grants, endowments and other funds and properties donated to ORHF are in the proper fund account of ORHF so that principal and income are used in accordance with the terms of any gift or grant.

Structure:

- Chairman will be appointed by Chairman of the Board of Directors.
- Up to six (6) members including the Treasurer.
- Other staff members to the committee include Director of Gift and Estate Planning and Manager of Finance and Accounting.
- Other members may be appointed at the discretion of the Chairman of ORHF because of expertise. They shall not have voting privileges, and may not be directors.

Composition: Members should: have a working knowledge of corporate/personal investment strategies; be familiar with corporate accounting principles; a working knowledge and understanding of foundation financial documents.

Primary responsibilities:

- Cause to be audited the financial statements of the corporation on an annual basis.
- Establish the process for raising, disbursement and allocation of all philanthropic funds. Reviews the process annually to ensure the integrity of the process and proper stewardship of philanthropic gifts.
- Determine the availability of funds for distribution, and notify the ORHF Board on a semi-annual basis of such amounts for distribution to facilities and programs within ORHS.
- Receive quarterly reports on fund distribution/allocation from each "community" board.
- In the event there is need for an "emergency" distribution of unrestricted funds, the committee determines the availability from which fund pool the distribution is made.
- In the event there is an "emergency" requiring the invasion of the principle of the ORHF Board restricted endowment, the committee determines the most appropriate endowment to invade, the manner and timing, and any other related matters regarding the withdrawal. The ORHF Board has final decision-making authority regarding the withdrawal of funds.
- Recommend the investment policy(s) for all funds to ORHS, and communicate the policy(s) to the "community" boards upon approval. Review annually.
- Recommend the fund investment manager(s), and use of consultants in the management of ORHF investments, their selection process, compensation, and issues regarding conflict of interest.
- Provide ORHF quarterly reports regarding investment management performance.
- Review a financial statement at least quarterly that includes: comparison to budget from current year and last year, external benchmark financial data, and balance sheet. Present to Board on same frequency.
- Recommend a special events policy regarding expense/revenue expectations. Monitor effectiveness based upon signature event outcomes of ORHF. Review policy annually.

DIRECTORS COMMITTEE: Shall recommend to the Executive Committee for further consideration by the Member, persons to serve as members of the ORHF Board of Directors. In addition, this committee shall annually recommend to the Board persons to serve as officers of ORHF (except the President/CEO who serves in such capacity at the direction of the President/CEO of ORHS), and shall be responsible for the orientation and education of new members of ORHF.

Structure:

- Chairman will be appointed by Chairman of the board of directors.
- Shall consist of up to six (6) members and may include the immediate past chairman.

Composition: Members should possess and have demonstrated leadership qualities while serving as members of the board in various committee activities; understand the basic mission of ORHS and its scope of services; and should have served at least two years as a Director.

Primary responsibilities:

- Recommends new ORHF directors and officers annually (except the President/CEO who serves in such capacity at the direction of the President/CEO of ORHS). Approval of Officers and Directors is by the ORHF Membership at its annual meeting. Final approval is given by the ORHS Board of Directors.
- Ensures an ORHF approved process is established for recruitment, selection, orientation, training and education of ORHF directors and members.
- Serve as mentors for new directors.
- Ensures the expectations of ORHF directors are understood by all directors, and reports achievement of expectation requirements of directors to the Executive Committee quarterly.

Appendix 11E   Sample Self-Assessment Survey Form

THE GOVERNANCE INSTITUTE'S

**15-MINUTE SELF-ASSESSMENT FOR A FOUNDATION BOARD
THAT IS PART OF A SYSTEM***

© 1997, The Governance Institute

*Systems usually have either a "corporate," "parent," or "system" board which oversees the entire organization.

Section 1—MISSION AND PLANNING OVERSIGHT

A. Each board member has received a copy of our system's and foundation's mission statements.

   Our Rating: Excellent _____   Good ____   Fair ____   Poor ____

B. Our board has developed guiding principles that establish parameters for all foundation operations.

   Our Rating: Excellent _____   Good ____   Fair ____   Poor ____

C. We have reviewed and discussed our system's and foundation's mission statements within the past 12 months to ensure that they are current and consistent with each other.

   Our Rating: Excellent _____   Good ____   Fair ____   Poor ____

D. Our board helped develop the strategic plan for our foundation to determine that it is consistent with and supportive of the system's strategic plan.

   Our Rating: Excellent _____   Good ____   Fair ____   Poor ____

E. The administration, medical staff, corporate system board members, and other advisors participate in planning foundation activities.

   Our Rating: Excellent _____   Good ____   Fair ____   Poor ____

F. Our foundation board reviews proposals for major development programs and services to ensure they are consistent with the system's mission statement and strategic plan and priorities.

   Our Rating: Excellent _____   Good ____   Fair ____   Poor ____

G. The foundation board regularly reviews progress toward meeting goals in our strategic plan to assess the degree to which the foundation is meeting its mission and needs of the system.

   Our Rating: Excellent _____   Good ____   Fair ____   Poor ____

H. The foundation's board members are active and effective in representing the community's health care interest and serve as a communication link between the system, foundation, hospitals, government officials and others important to the provision of community health services.

   Our Rating: Excellent _____   Good ____   Fair ____   Poor ____

Section 2—QUALITY OVERSIGHT

A. Our foundation board is well informed about the quality of care provided by the system's and hospitals' services.

    Our Performance: Excellent _____ Good _____ Fair ____ Poor ____

B. We carefully review recommendations of the system's and hospitals' administration and medical staff regarding new programs, services, equipment, and politics needed to provide quality care.

    Our Performance: Excellent _____ Good _____ Fair ____ Poor ____

C. We seek physician participation in the work of the foundation board to assist us in our responsibilities for the development of financial resources needed to provide quality care.

    Our Performance: Excellent _____ Good _____ Fair ____ Poor ____

D. We require, receive on a regular basis, and discuss quality of donor satisfaction data reflecting our foundation's relationship with our donors.

    Our Performance: Excellent _____ Good _____ Fair ____ Poor ____

E. We regularly receive and discuss data about recognition systems and acknowledgment programs of importance to our donors.

    Our Performance: Excellent _____ Good _____ Fair ____ Poor ____

F. We periodically receive reports which review and assess the attitudes and opinions of patients served by the system and its hospitals and services to identify our strengths, weaknesses, and opportunities for improvement.

    Our Performance: Excellent _____ Good _____ Fair ____ Poor ____

G. Our board insures that foundation information systems support and enhance the building of relationships with our donors.

    Our Performance: Excellent _____ Good _____ Fair ____ Poor ____

Section 3—FINANCIAL OVERSIGHT

A. Our board reviews financial needs and development goals of the system and hospitals and considers how the foundation can help meet these needs.

    Our Performance: Excellent _____ Good _____ Fair ____ Poor ____

B. Our board reviews the foundation's goals for financial development and for specific projects and purposes.

    Our Performance: Excellent _____ Good _____ Fair ____ Poor ____

C. Our board receives and reviews periodic financial reports concerning the results of the foundation's development activities related to return on investment and expenses to revenues generated.

    Our Performance: Excellent _____ Good _____ Fair ____ Poor ____

D. Our board has a written investment policy(s) governing asset management.

   Our Performance: Excellent ____ Good ____ Fair ____ Poor ____

Section 4—MANAGEMENT OVERSIGHT

A. Our board approves development policies for the foundation that are consistent with system policies and directives.

   Our Rating: Excellent _____ Good ____ Fair ____ Poor ____

B. Our board supports and assists the system and hospital CEOs to achieve their mission.

   Our Rating: Excellent _____ Good ____ Fair ____ Poor ____

C. Our board participates in the periodic evaluation and review of the performance of the principal foundation executive.

   Our Rating: Excellent _____ Good ____ Fair ____ Poor ____

D. Our board participates in the hiring of the principal foundation executive.

   Our Rating: Excellent _____ Good ____ Fair ____ Poor ____

Section 5—BOARD EFFECTIVENESS

A. Our system or foundation board evaluates board performance and the individual performance of each board member.

   Our Rating: Excellent _____ Good ____ Fair ____ Poor ____

B. Our foundation board has governing statements of responsibility.

   Our Rating: Excellent _____ Good ____ Fair ____ Poor ____

C. Our board has a yearly calendar of standing board oversight responsibilities.

   Our Rating: Excellent _____ Good ____ Fair ____ Poor ____

D. We have a written conflict of interest policy that includes guidelines for the resolution of any existing or apparent conflicts of interest.

   Our Rating: Excellent _____ Good ____ Fair ____ Poor ____

E. All members of the foundation board understand and fulfill their responsibilities and each foundation board member has received written descriptions of the board's duties and reporting relationships.

   Our Rating: Excellent _____ Good ____ Fair ____ Poor ____

F. All members of the foundation board participate in the foundation board orientation program and continuing education.

   Our Rating: Excellent _____ Good ____ Fair ____ Poor ____

G. The frequency and duration of foundation board and committee meetings are adequate to conduct the foundation board's responsibilities, but do not discourage attendance and participation by misusing valuable board members' time.

Our Rating: Excellent _____ Good _____ Fair _____ Poor _____

H. Our chairman exercises a firm and fair hand with individual board members to ensure that all have equal opportunity to participate, time is not monopolized by a few, and agenda items are dispatched after reasonable discussion.

Our Rating: Excellent _____ Good _____ Fair _____ Poor _____

I. The board members receive the agenda and back-up materials well in advance of meetings.

Our Rating: Excellent _____ Good _____ Fair _____ Poor _____

J. Our foundation board members come to meetings well prepared to discuss agenda items.

Our Rating: Excellent _____ Good _____ Fair _____ Poor _____

K. The system board maintains an up-to-date policy manual which includes specific policies covering foundation activities and governance responsibilities.

Our Rating: Excellent _____ Good _____ Fair _____ Poor _____

Section 6—INDIVIDUAL SELF-ASSESSMENT

A. **Continuing Education.** I participate in educational opportunities outside the system hospitals and foundation to remain current on changing trends and issues affecting healthcare and our governance.

My Performance: Excellent _____ Good _____ Fair _____ Poor _____

B. **Demonstrated Interest.** I prepare for, attend, participate, and assume a fair workload at board and committee meetings.

My Performance: Excellent _____ Good _____ Fair _____ Poor _____

C. **Development Activities.** I participate actively in development programs and projects of the foundation.

My Performance: Excellent _____ Good _____ Fair _____ Poor _____

D. **Interpersonal Relations.** I deal fairly and appropriately with other foundation members, management, and professional staff.

My Performance: Excellent _____ Good _____ Fair _____ Poor _____

E. **Confidentiality.** I understand the confidential nature of foundation board deliberations and maintain privacy regarding issues and information discussed in board and committee meetings.

My Performance: Excellent _____ Good _____ Fair _____ Poor _____

F. **Donor Identification.** I participate in identifying individuals who could be interested in providing financial or other gifts to the hospitals and system.

My Performance: Excellent _____ Good _____ Fair _____ Poor _____

G. **Community Representation.** As a foundation board member, I strive to represent the healthcare needs of the community and share the system's and the hospitals' needs and concerns with external constituencies, especially prospective donors.

    My Performance: Excellent _____ Good _____ Fair _____ Poor _____

H. **Philanthropy.** I contribute financial resources to the work of the foundation that serves the system.

    My Performance: Excellent _____ Good _____ Fair _____ Poor _____

This 15-minute self-evaluation was developed by THE GOVERNANCE INSTITUTE to assist boards of foundations that are part of a System to identify the most important areas in which they can improve their performance.

For further information about the use of this or other resources for board development contact:

THE GOVERNANCE 100 · 737 Pearl Street, Suite 201 · La Jolla, CA 92037
(619) 551-0144

The Board Chair, Chief Executive Officer, and Development Officer

GAIL L. WARDEN, MHCM
Henry Ford Health System

R. GLEN SMILEY, FAHP, CFRE
Henry Ford Health System

12.1 Introduction

The chairman of the board, the chief executive officer (CEO), and the chief development officer must be the backbone of an organization's-fund raising effort. Arm in arm as lead volunteer, executive leader, and fund-raising leader, they provide the leadership, direction, accountability, credibility, and technical knowledge to successfully execute a fund-raising plan that may be quite elaborate. They have linkage to donors, prospective donors, volunteers, community leadership, the organization's staff, and a large base of knowledge essential to fund-raising success. Their enthusiastic support for an organization's fund-raising efforts and an acceptance by each of his or her role greatly increases the chance of success even before the actual fund raising begins. Agreement on the fund-raising needs and priorities is the bond that makes this trio a strong and consistent force in the successful pursuit of an organization's *mission*. The first and possibly most important task for each is in assuring an organizational plan from which the fund-raising agenda will be set, a task that will require working together closely.

12.2 *Organizational Planning*

In the absence of purpose, perfection in the execution of any task or activity will be judged as failure. This is true because any activity without purpose has no value. Unfortunately, in some organizations the fund raisers decide on the projects for which they will seek gifts without regard to the priority of the projects. They may be successful raising funds for worthy but low-priority projects and, in the process, may "waste" key prospects who should be asked to support high-priority projects. Fund raisers should not be making such decisions in isolation. If a list of priorities does not exist, the board chair, CEO, and chief fund raiser have an obligation to see that one is developed. And the list needs to be a vertical list with the most important project at the top. The fund raisers and all who speak for the organization should know its priorities and the reasons why those projects are important.

(A) VISION

An organization's board and executive leadership must determine the specific needs for which private funds are raised. Those needs and priorities should be keystones of a plan to realize the organization's current vision of what it would like to become in the next five to 10 years. Consistent with the organization's mission (which is timeless), the vision should be for a specified period of time. Ideally, an organization's history is a succession of realized visions since the organization's inception. The current vision for an organization represents the next major milestone in the provision of service.

(i) *Roles*
The board and executive leadership set the vision with input from board members, the community, constituents, and key people inside the organization. Ideally the CEO takes the lead in promoting a specific vision. Often it is his or her vision that prevails. That vision and ability to help the organization realize it may be the basis of the board's confidence in the CEO.

At Henry Ford Health System (HFHS) in Detroit, the vision was developed with the help of a futures committee that was charged with developing a stretch view of the future for health care, the HFHS market, the challenges/opportunities for HFHS in dealing with that future, and recommended strategies. The committee heard from futurists, assessed the environment of HFHS, and established the key organizational requirements for the next century. An important key to their findings was that the vision had to recognize the needs of all HFHS stakeholders. They also felt the vision should include initiatives that are unique . . . that are appealing to potential donors.

The board chair working with the CEO will shepherd the planning process, and the chair may well share the CEO's vision. The process should also include the chief development officer, who, as at HFHS, will be looking for a vision with maximum appeal to current donors and to others with no prior giving history to the organization. Since most plans and needs are developed from an internal perspective, it is important to have the fund raiser's external view of the plan and needs on behalf of those unfamiliar with the organization.

(B) STRATEGIC PLAN

Once the vision has been established, a strategic plan to realize the vision is developed. The strategic plan includes the actions necessary to make the vision a reality. Many of the necessary actions require funding beyond what currently may be available. Those opportunities that are potentially appealing to donors should become the fund-raising priorities. Other needs will require redirection of operating funds or outside commercial financing.

(C) GOAL SETTING

"Never set fund raising goals by subtraction."

The late Sheldon Garber,
former vice president for Philanthropy,
Rush-Presbyterian-St. Luke's Medical Center, Chicago

Elaborating, Garber said that setting a fund-raising goal by subtracting money **available** from money **needed;**

1. Incorrectly assumes that donors will contribute blindly to anything the organization calls a "need."
2. Does not take into account the organization's fund-raising potential.

Generally speaking, the more broadly and externally appealing the vision, the more of an organization's needs that can be included in the fund-raising goal. If the vision is viewed enthusiastically, even by those who have not supported the organization in the past, it is possible to attract new donors at high levels of giving. If the vision is viewed enthusiastically only by those with an existing allegiance to the organization, the fund-raising effort will depend almost entirely on previous donors and existing constituents and is likely to raise less money. These considerations are important to setting an achievable goal. The external appeal of the vision should be tested before setting an especially ambitious fund-raising goal.

(i) Assessment of Fund-raising Potential
Using the list of needs and priorities suitable for fund raising and results of an assessment of the organization's current fund-raising potential, specific dollar goals for fund

raising can be set for each of the years covered by the vision. The assessment may be done either internally or with the help of a consultant. A goal that is only a total of needs that might be attractive to donors may be far beyond the organization's realistic fund-raising potential. The right goal is likely to be one that goes slightly beyond the potential shown in the organization's assessment of fund-raising potential. The annual "stretch" in goal beyond known potential may lengthen over time as the organization successfully cultivates new prospects and sources of giving. (See Chapters 2 and 6.)

(ii) Use of Consultants for Assessment of Potential

Using a fund-raising consultant to assess an organization's fund-raising potential should be done realizing that the board, leadership, and staff of the organization usually know the prospects for future gifts to the organization far better than the outside consultant. Organization personnel also best understand current relationships with key prospects and how those relationships may affect future gifts.

A consultant may properly facilitate the assessment and, as an objective third party, assess the fund-raising climate for the organization and the external appeal of its vision, but the final determination of who is likely to give and at what levels should be made by the organization's board and staff rather than a consultant. Beware the consultants who offer to do an independent assessment and then to submit a report recommending the right fund-raising goal for an organization.

(iii) Evaluation

Evaluation of the fund-raising function should be easy once the fund-raising needs and priorities are identified and after dollar goals have been set by agreement of the board chair, CEO, and chief development officer for each year of time spanned by the vision.

These three individuals share a responsibility for assuring that the planning occurs, that there is a common vision for the organization's future, for determining the role fund raising will have in assuring realization of the vision, and for setting the annual fund-raising goals. After the planning is done, they must continue working together, but each has a distinct and somewhat different role to play in the ongoing fund-raising process.

12.3   The Board Chair

The prestige and influence of the board chair as the not-for-profit organization's volunteer leader helps galvanize support both internally and externally during the planning process and in raising the funds required to implement the resulting plan. As a volunteer, the chair uses knowledge gained outside the realm of the organization's sphere that is helpful to predicting the organization's future level of success in the marketplace. The chair also helps anticipate community reaction to new programs and services. Internally, this view helps reassure staff that the plan can be successful. Externally, the chair's passionate belief in the organization and its vision also heightens community interest in the organization and its mission.

(A)   MARSHALING BOARD SUPPORT

The chair's leadership in assuring enthusiastic support of the full board for the vision and the strategic plan will greatly impact the plan's eventual success. The chair is also in the best position to read board interest and commitment. Most board chairs are not viewed as "empire builders." In this way, the chair's view may be an important complement to that of the organization's chief executive who, in some organizations, may be seen as pushing the vision/strategic plan to advance a personal agenda. It is hoped that generosity and a substantial commitment of time become the manifestations of board enthusiasm for the plan, the vision and the fund-raising effort to assure realization of the vision.

(B) THE "MODEL" CHAIR

Once the fund-raising effort is under way, the "model" chair monitors its success, is available to make calls on key prospects (especially for major gifts), and addresses key groups about the organization's vision, plans, and need for support. If the fund-raising effort is a capital campaign, the chair helps the campaign leader in every way necessary to ensure success and to make certain the board is doing its part. The board should never delegate its responsibility for fund raising to a campaign committee or other organization (such as a foundation). Ultimately it is the board that is responsible for assuring the resources necessary to an organization's success.

What characteristics would be most desirable in a board chair that will help assure fund-raising success? Here are a few:

- Unwavering devotion to the organization and the importance of its mission
- Passionate belief in the vision and strategic plan
- Views the role of the chair:
  - To be nonoperational
  - To be supportive of organization leadership
  - To hold the board and management accountable to high expectations of organization success
- Perceived as a visionary and enlightened leader
- Is proud to be identified with the organization
- Leads by example through word and deed
- Is an enthusiastic ambassador for the organization in all settings
- Will spend his or her "chips" in the community for the organization
- Makes an impassioned plea for thoughtful consideration of support at a significant level at a fund-raising kick-off meeting
- Enthusiastically asks peers for their support of the organization
- Is an eager participant in fund-raising report meetings and offers encouragement to all in their future efforts to obtain needed funds
- Inspires other volunteers with his or her own commitment of support and time and enthusiasm
- Makes fund-raising calls on the most important prospects, alone or with the CEO, the chief development officer, other board members, or key organization staff
- Is willing to be pictured representing the organization in local publications
- Is willing to share knowledge helpful to fund raising with appropriate staff and the CEO

(C) COMMUNITY RECOGNITION

In words and actions, the chair signals to the community that someone important in the community who is outside the walls of an organization and who is not its paid staff thinks it is very important. Community acceptance of the organization's programs and support for its future aspirations is thus made much more probable.

(D) CHAIRS AND HISTORY

Not surprisingly, the history of many successful not-for-profit organizations is characterized by periods of especially effective board chairs. In the early 1980s when Henry Ford II was board chair at Henry Ford Hospital, a decision was made to establish a large number of outpatient clinics in the metropolitan Detroit area to make the hospital more easily accessible to a wider number of people. That visionary decision helped make the HFHS of today a possibility. The idea had Mr. Ford's enthusiastic support, and he is often given principal credit for that decision. It is one of the landmarks of his era in the Henry Ford Health System.

The history of other organizations may be characterized by a successful combination of board chair and chief executive. After its formal and amicable separation from Baylor University in 1969, Baylor College of Medicine had to recruit many new department chairs and find enough money to attract them. The combination of former Conoco chief executive L. F. McCollum as board chair and heart surgery pioneer Dr. Michael DeBakey as chief executive was perfect to secure the medical talent and requisite private support to propel the new free-standing medical school toward the upper echelon of academic medicine, where it remains today.

As with any successful enterprise, there is no substitute for effective leadership. An able and committed board chair offers a degree of external credibility, influence, and knowledge that cannot be realized from staff. Without these advantages, it is nearly impossible for an organization to reach its potential. Since the perceived strength of boards and board members is often characterized by the leadership and influence of the board chair, generally no one other than the board chair is in a position to help assure that all of these important factors are present.

12.4   *The Chief Executive Officer*

An organization's chief executive is the key to a successful fund-raising team. The CEO reports to the board, and the chief development officer usually reports to the CEO. A CEO who makes fund raising a priority thus can assure a coordinated effort involving the three key leaders. Without a committed CEO, the job is much more difficult and can lose the momentum successful fund-raising efforts require.

(A)   TIME COMMITMENT

The CEO must be willing to commit the required time. The skills required of a not-for-profit CEO today are many and the demands on the CEO's time far exceed time available. Finding time for fund raising requires making it a priority. If the CEO adopts the attitude of "I'll do it if and when I have time," it may not get done, and almost assuredly not in a timely manner. And in fund raising, very often timing is everything.

(B)   ROLE OF PHILANTHROPY IN AN ORGANIZATION—NOT A "QUICK FIX"

Recognizing the proper role for philanthropy in the ability of an organization to address its mission is another important contribution of the CEO. Philanthropy is a long-range strategy, not a "quick fix" to balance an unforeseen deficit in the operating budget or to meet spur-of-the-moment capital requirements/opportunities. In some types of organizations, such as social service organizations, philanthropy is the source of the entire operating budget. In others it provides principally capital for buildings and equipment. Some use philanthropy principally for program development and endowment of existing programs.

The smart CEO understands that successful philanthropy programs are the result of careful planning and consistent effort over time to build enduring relationships that will yield consistently high levels of support from foundations, corporations, and individuals who know the organization well and believe its work is important. The resulting support also is consistent with the ongoing role the organization has chosen for philanthropy.

(C)   THE CEO AND ORGANIZATION IDENTITY

The CEO also must communicate the vision to the board, volunteers, staff, and other stakeholders. Everyone needs to know the importance of achieving the vision and that they too can play a role as donors *and* as fund raisers. It is the CEO's "call to action" in support of the vision that will first gain the attention of those with the ability to make the vision reality. If the CEO is not enthusiastic about the vision and the importance of pursuing it, there will be little support from others for an all-out effort to achieve it.

A high level of CEO visibility in the fund-raising effort assures a higher level of constituent awareness of the importance of private support. Speeches to constituent groups, motivational speeches to fund-raising volunteer gatherings, making calls on key prospects, press conferences to announce important gifts: These are all important to keeping the need for support high in the consciousness of those who can help.

Most highly successful organizations have a leader whose name is almost synonymous with the organization. That name gives constituents and potential supporters an answer to the questions "Who is (*name of organization*)?" and "Who runs (*name of organization*)?" The image of an organization with a recognizable name and face is far more warm, personable, and desirable than that of a faceless and nameless, even if renowned, organization. A public identity for the CEO also provides public accountability that is desirable among organizations seeking public support.

Making calls on key prospects is extremely important to obtaining gifts from those prospects. Powerful and visionary decision makers want to know far more than the facts and figures of the organization. They want to size up the person running things (the CEO) and decide whether that person is someone who can successfully carry out the organization's plan and realize the vision. It is true that, in the end, people give to people. Most often the person on the receiving end of a substantial charitable gift is the organization's CEO whom the donor has judged to be "capable" of running the organization successfully. Securing large gifts usually will require a face-to-face meeting of the donor prospect and the CEO.

(D)   CEO SELF-IDENTITY

A CEO whose self-identity is that of "builder" rather than "fund raiser" has a greater chance of realizing fund-raising success. The same can be said of fund raisers who see themselves as helping to build worthwhile programs and services rather than merely raising money. The builder is committed to the project. A fund raiser might be committed only to raising money.

The builder-CEO is not only interested in bricks and mortar. The builder builds quality programs and has a clear vision of the next milestone of service for the organization. The builder also has the motivation and skill to marshal the resources needed to realize the vision.

The late Boone Powell, Sr., former CEO of Baylor University Medical Center in Dallas and one of the best-known hospital administrators in history, once bristled at being called a great fund raiser. He said to us, "I don't know anything about fundraising. I'm a builder and if it takes money to build what Baylor needs, I'll get it, but I am *not* a fund raiser. I don't know anything about fundraising."

Powell built Baylor University Hospital into one of the nation's premier healthcare facilities in the wake of a 1943 decision by Baylor University College of Medicine to desert Dallas and the hospital for a move to Houston to become the first tenant of the Texas Medical Center. Powell's skill as a builder included an ability to raise large amounts of private funds from the community to build what is today Baylor University Medical Center.

Coincidentally, the medical school's decision to move to Houston also worked out well. While Powell was building Baylor University Hospital in Dallas, Dr. Michael DeBakey was making medical history and headlines at Baylor University College of Medicine in Houston's Texas Medical Center. Today that medical center is the largest medical center in the world and employs more than 50,000 people in over 44 organizations housed there.

(E)   CORPORATE CITIZENSHIP

Community involvement by the CEO is also important to successful fund raising. Even not-for-profits must be seen as good corporate citizens working to better the entire community, not just their organizations. The relationships with other community leaders built through community involvement help assure at least a cordial reception when the organization needs community support. Others in the organization including the chief development officer should also be serving the community in a volunteer capacity.

(F) WORKING RELATIONSHIP WITH CHIEF DEVELOPMENT OFFICER

(i) Providing Information

The CEO and chief development officer (CDO) relationship has to work. Because the CDO is not involved in the operational heart of the organization, the CEO must regularly step outside the operational lines and make certain the CDO is up to date on what is happening in the organization, what is planned and why, and how these things may influence the perception of donors and potential donors in the community. Sometimes knowing enough to know what *not* to say to external constituents is most important. If donors and prospects get the impression that the CDO is not in the organization's "inner circle," they may lose interest in discussing the organization with him or her.

(ii) Timing

Since timing is often critical to obtaining certain gifts, it is essential that the CEO have an open door (to the extent that is possible) for the CDO to share important information that may require swift action. A high level of CEO confidence in the judgment of the CDO will require some orientation to the CEO's preferences and enough interaction for the CDO to develop an intuitive sense of the way in which both understand how the CEO wants to conduct the organization's business. Since fund raisers are often the interface with donors and people of influence in the community, the CEO cannot afford to have them representing the organization unprofessionally or in a way that lacks credibility. The CDO must know what is happening in the organization and how the CEO wants to have the organization represented externally.

(iii) Confidence in CDO

While the CEO should always offer opinions on how best to solicit/cultivate gifts from certain prospects, the CEO should also respect the judgment and suggested strategies of the CDO. Presumably prospects have been carefully researched and their previous links to the organization chronicled prior to formation of a recommended strategy.

(iv) Who Asks?

The CEO does not always have to be the "asker" in a solicitation call. Some CEOs would prefer to "sing the song" and let someone else ask. The CEO needs to make clear to the CDO his or her desired role in solicitation calls to ensure that the CEO's presence on the call is taken maximum advantage of.

(v) Board Contact

CEO comfort with the CDO and other fund raisers regularly dealing with board members and other community leaders is essential to successful fund raising. This comfort comes from a solid relationship between the two that results in loyalty and a willingness to share information helpful in all aspects of fund raising.

    The CEO must do many things to make the CEO/CDO relationship work well for fund raising, but the CDO must do even more.

12.5   The Chief Development Officer

Tending to the day-to-day requirements and details of the fund-raising program is the role of the chief development officer. Making certain that appropriate actions are taken in a timely fashion, managing volunteers, assuring acknowledgment and organizational memory of all gifts, making cultivation and solicitation calls with and without volunteers, gathering information on projects for which funding is needed, researching prospects to assure an intelligent solicitation for something in which the prospect may be genuinely interested, preparing written proposals to be delivered to prospects being solicited, helping existing donors and volunteers with personal needs they have relating to the organization . . . these are some of the important activities of the fund-raising office.

The CDO is the catalyst for perpetual pursuit of private support by a not-for-profit organization. Since fund raising is a staff function, the CDO has no direct authority over any part of the organization. The CDO must instead rely on cooperation from organization staff, leadership, and volunteers to help create fund-raising success. There is a premium, therefore, on working effectively with others in the organization, foremost among whom is the CEO.

Assuring a steady flow of new prospects, cultivation, gift solicitation, acknowledgment and recording of gifts, maintenance of meaningful donor relations after the gift, and then another solicitation: That is the cycle of fund raising. In prospecting, cultivation, solicitation, and donor relations, working closely with the CEO is central to success.

(A)   PROFESSIONALISM AND LOYALTY

First and foremost, the CEO expects professionalism and loyalty from everyone in the organization and especially from direct reports. These qualities may be especially important in the CDO, since, as lead fund raiser, he or she will represent the organization to some important donors, volunteers, and prospects for gifts. Unprofessional behavior by a CDO can reflect negatively on both the organization and the CEO who presumably chose (or at least supervises) the CDO.

In appearance, word, and deed the CDO and other fund-raising staff must represent the organization on a high plane. Another way of saying it is "Look sharp, speak well, and do what is right morally and professionally."

(i)   Appearance
To be assured that the organization is represented well, a CDO's clothing should never be an issue either inside or outside of the organization. Overdressing, dressing shabbily, dressing outlandishly: Each can result in unwanted distraction from the goal of raising private funds for the organization. Party attire is also inappropriate in the workplace. Clean, neat, and conservative (given the type of organization and its constituents) business attire is the route to assuring that appearance does not interfere with the job.

(ii)   Knowledge
The CDO needs to know the organization and the business of fund raising. People will expect it. What makes the organization work, its history, its people, its plans, its current status, its next milestone of service, and knowledge of how charitable gifts can be made

and the benefits to both donor and organization are all areas in which the CDO will be expected to be fully knowledgeable.

Though not often in the line management of an organization, the CDO must demonstrate insider's knowledge to an organization's constituents. How can the CDO be effective if donors and volunteers perceive that they know more about the organization than the professional staff charged with fund raising? Unfortunately this is all too common in meetings with board members to discuss their gifts or a gift from someone the board member is being asked to help solicit.

(iii) *Organization Before Self*

By always presenting a positive view of the organization and its CEO, never talking "out of school" or negatively behind someone's back, and putting the organization first, the ethical CDO never becomes more important than the organization in the eyes of a donor, prospect, or volunteer. Over time, leadership and staff regularly change in organizations, so it is essential to insulate the organization from loss of donors and friends by working to assure that their loyalty is to the organization first.

(B) ASKING THE KEY QUESTIONS

The CDO is always thinking about how to present the organization's vision and attendant needs knowledgeably and accurately to external constituents. Very often the questions asked by the fund raisers are of great importance and have not yet been addressed:

- Of what benefit will that (*need for which gift funding is being sought*) be to humankind?
- Is that (*need for which funding is being sought*) unique or new in our market/service area? Will it help distinguish us from other organizations doing similar work?
- What is the organization's vision for the next three to five or five to 10 years? Do we have a strategic plan to realize that vision?
- Will the community at large and people who have no current allegiance to our organization find this appealing? If not, should we try to fund it some other way?
- What should be the ongoing role of philanthropy in our organization? Capital for buildings/equipment? Endowment of key people/programs? Seed money for new programs? Operating budget?

The CEO can either provide these answers or direct the work necessary to obtain them. The questions will resharpen the focus of an organization and help assure a more complete plan. Certainly if public support is desired, the plan should be seen as important externally as well as internally.

The logical source of these questions most often is the CDO.

(C) COMMUNICATING WITH THE CEO

The CDO's extensive external communications will elicit a substantial amount of information. Pertinent details and significant impressions from these discussions should be shared with the CEO, who, as an important corporate citizen in the community, should know how key people view the organization and other matters important to them. Presumably the CEO has shared with the CDO his or her knowledge of key donors and prospects. That knowledge base should be updated after calls on those people by the fund raisers.

When the CEO is not acquainted with a promising prospect or major donor, see if a meeting can be arranged. Important people like knowing the CEO, the CEO likes knowing important people, and through personal contact chances of a significant gift for the organization can also be greatly improved.

(D) DOING HOMEWORK CAREFULLY

Before making a call on a board member, major donor, or key community leader, the CDO must do the homework necessary to ensure that the CEO has updated knowledge of the individual's current business and personal (if applicable and appropriate) circumstances. Do not guess and risk embarrassing of the CEO and possibly losing an important gift.

(E) PREPARING A THOROUGH PLAN

Do not expect the CEO to offer "the plan" for fund raising. The CEO will assure availability of information regarding needs and priorities. It is the CDO's job to take that information and offer a plan that includes a dollar goal for fund raising, a staffing plan, and budget. The plan will be discussed with the CEO and perhaps with the board chair and a fund-raising committee of the board, and may be altered in the process, but it is up to the CDO to offer a comprehensive plan to begin the discussions.

(F) PROMPTNESS

The CEO wants to be prompt with important people. Keep organizational response time to a minimum when prompt action is desired. The impression of a purposeful, competent, responsive, "heads-up" organization is very positive.

(G) BEING SUPPORTIVE

Not-for-profit CEOs have a difficult job. Success in fund raising or even some good news from a discussion with a prospect, board member, or donor can offer some relief from organizational stress. The CDO can be understanding of the challenges faced by the CEO and can look for ways to be supportive.

Being supportive also means being considerate of the time demands on the CEO. The CEO will appreciate the CDO who makes effective use of time in meetings.

12.6   *Summary*

The pivotal person in the board chair–CEO–CDO triumvirate is the CEO. As the CEO's comfort level with the fund-raising effort increases, so can the effectiveness of this team in leading the effort. Working together to assure a solid organizational vision, strategic plan, and fund-raising effort to help assure realization of the vision, this trio can provide the leadership on all fronts to help assure success.

Suggested Readings

Broce, Thomas E. *Fund Raising: A Guide to Raising Money from Private Sources*, 2nd edition. Norman: University of Oklahoma Press, 1986.

Carver, John. *Boards that Make a Difference: A New Design for Leadership in Nonprofit and Public Organizations*. San Francisco: Jossey-Bass, 1990.

Panas, Jerold. *Boardroom Verities*. Chicago: Precept Press, 1991.

The Board's Role in Fund Raising

FISHER HOWE, CFRE

Lavender/Howe & Associates

13.1 Introduction

Although many people are involved in fund raising—the chief executive, the staff, and volunteers—the board and its members individually are central to success.

Moreover, in fund raising the board's role is quite different from its other activities. In almost all they do, board members are deliberating, discussing, and deciding; in fund raising they are *participating*. This distinction is important because it calls upon board members to play a more active part than in most of their other responsibilities.

To be clear on the board's role in fund raising, two matters must be faced squarely. First, it is important to look at what both boards and staffs must *understand* about raising money. The elements of fund raising are often misunderstood, yet their full appreciation by board members and staff is key to success.

Understanding leads to *fund-raising action*, knowing who is responsible, what board members and staff can do in fund raising, and the role of each.

13.2 Understanding Fund Raising

It is common for board members to be reluctant, sometimes resistant, to participate in fund raising. Many associate fund raising with preying on friends or begging; others fear

---

This chapter is adapted from Fisher Howe, *Welcome to the Board: Your Guide to Effective Participation* (San Francisco: Jossey-Bass, 1995).

the embarrassment of being turned down. Some like to think their contribution to the organization is in the program, or administration, not in fund raising. Others will say they were not told that fund raising was part of being a board member.

To overcome resistance and to get engaged in fund raising, board members and staffs need to identify the differing *characteristics of nonprofit organizations;* to be aware of the *sources and kinds of income,* especially contributed income; to understand the nature of *giving and asking,* the importance of *strategic planning,* and the special nature of *capital fund raising;* and to be alert to some *special problems* in overseeing fund-raising programs.

(A)   CHARACTERISTICS OF ORGANIZATIONS

No two not-for-profit organizations are the same. The world of philanthropy is as varied as our national culture and social endeavors. Not-for-profits are of different sizes and at varying stages of growth, serving widely different purposes, and each organization handles its fund raising in its own way. Boards and staffs must be clear about where their own organization fits into the scheme of all other local charitable organizations. Exhibits 13.1 and 13.2 present a checklist of characteristics of *purpose, type, size,* and *stage of growth.*

EXHIBIT 13.1 Checklist: Characteristics of Not-for-Profit Organizations

A. Purpose
Exist *to serve the public* _____
Exist *to serve members* _____
Exist as *grantmaker* _____
Exist for *religious purposes* _____
B. Type
Health Care _____
Culture/The Arts _____
   Performances/Exhibits _____
   Education _____
Education _____
   Higher _____
   Secondary _____
   Specialized _____
Community Services _____
Advocacy _____
Research _____
C. Size
National _____
Local _____
Budget over $5 million _____
Budget $1 to 5 million _____
Budget under $1 million _____
D. Stage of Growth (see Exhibit 13.2)
Start-Up _____
Expansion _____
Consolidation _____
Maturity _____

EXHIBIT 13.2 Checklist: Organization Development of a Not-for-Profit Organization

Stages of Growth

1 Start-up	2 Expansion	3 Consolidation	4 Maturity
Characterized by: Dedicated volunteer staff	**Characterized by:** Full-time staff	**Characterized by:** Stable staff	**Characterized by:** Steady/complacent staff
	• Program • Management	• Program • Management	
Almost no *board*	Small *board*	Strong *board*	Indifferent *board*
Fund-raising Need: Survival	**Fund-raising Need:** A fund-raising program Involvement of community leaders	**Fund-raising Need:** Strategic planning Redefining mission Program choices Board leadership	**Fund-raising Need:** Maintain momentum Renewal

For example, an independent secondary school, serving the public as an educational institution, having a budget of $5 million, and in the "consolidation" phase, will have some clearly defined fund-raising needs. On the other hand, a center for abused women, serving a select public community service, with a budget of $1 million, and in the "start-up" phase of development, faces a different set of fund-raising challenges. The perspectives that emerge from these factors can help board members understand the challenges.

(B) SOURCES AND KINDS OF SUPPORT

Board members and staffs must not be confused by the various sources of income; in particular, they need to be clear on what part of income is derived from contributions. To start with, these sources of income should be distinguished:

- *Government contracts*. Fees and reimbursements
- *Earned revenues*. Sales, fees for service, admissions, and tuitions
- *Unearned income*. Investments and rentals
- *Contributions*

Although all sources are important to the financial well-being of an organization, the term "fund raising" is concerned only with contributions.

Contributions come in many forms:

Government grants
Foundation grants
Corporate grants
Grants from other nonprofit organizations (United Way, religious institutions, labor unions, service clubs)

Individual contributions—from regular givers and from mass-mail appeals
Contributions received from fund-raising events

Organizations must be sure to take advantage of all the sources and kinds of contributed income that may be available to them, rather than concentrating on just one or two. They must put their efforts where the money is.

Exhibit 13.3 is a checklist to display the amounts an organization receives from each source and kind of income, the percentage of overall income, or the percentage of contributed income each source and kind represents.

(C) GIVING AND ASKING

Some basic truths that underlie giving and, therefore, of the asking for money are often overlooked, which accounts for resistance to fund raising by board members and staff, particularly their reluctance actually to ask for a contribution. It helps to remember these reasons that people contribute support:

- People give money because *they want to;* in raising money you do not need to twist arms or beg.
- People want to give to worthy endeavors that are *making a difference;* you must believe your organization makes a change for the good and emphasize that change for the good in asking for support.
- People *give money to people*—a cliché, but nevertheless true; the personal relationship underlies most contributions, especially major gifts.
- People give to *success*, not distress; show the winning side.

(D) STRATEGIC PLANNING

Although it may be recognized that sound strategic planning is important for management—the executive and staff—and for governance—the board—it is not generally

---

EXHIBIT 13.3 Principal Sources of Support for a Not-for-Profit Organization

	$	%
Government: fees, contracts reimbursements	_____	_____%
Earned: sales, fees, admissions, tuitions	_____	_____%
Unearned: investment return	_____	_____%
Contributed (fund raising):	_____	_____%
Government grants	_____	_____%
Foundation grants	_____	_____%
Corporate grants	_____	_____%
Other not-for-profits' grants	_____	_____%
Individuals (regular, noncapital):		
Constituency	_____	_____%
Mass mail	_____	_____%
Special Events	_____	_____%

understood how critical such planning is to successful fund raising. Strategic planning calls on an organization to think through and articulate:

- Its *mission*—the purposes, programs, and priorities; and the *values*—not what it does but how it does it; and
- Its *vision*—what kind of an organization it wants to be in the coming years.

Only on the basis of such thoughtful planning can an organization arrive at two determinations on which the whole fund-raising program depends: a realistic estimate of its *funding needs* and a persuasive *case* articulating why people should support the organization with contributions.

The board must ensure that strategic planning takes place and must participate in the planning.

(E) RAISING CAPITAL FUNDS

A new dimension of board participation comes into play when an organization turns to raising capital funds for buildings, endowment, or a reserve fund established to function as endowment, or when it seeks capital donations through planned giving. Boards cannot assume, as too often they do, that capital fund raising is just more of the same.

A planned giving program, a special kind of capital fund raising, is a structured form of contributing assets that allows donors to give to an organization over time more than they are able to give outright. The recipient institution receives the donation only after an intervening period, often years, during which time the donor and a beneficiary may retain the use of the property or the lifetime right to receive its income. Such gifts, closely associated with estate planning, can be in the form of bequests, insurance, real property, or securities.

Mounting campaigns to raise capital funds, or undertaking a planned giving program, involves extensive planning, an organization, a not inconsiderable amount of expense, and the full commitment and participation of the board. Capital donations, by definition large, usually involve board members directly in the identification, evaluation, cultivation, and solicitation of donors.

(F) OVERSIGHT

In overseeing the fund-raising program, the board must understand that it has to keep a watchful eye on three troublesome areas: (1) *ethics*, (2) *costs*, and (3) *donor unhappiness*.

(i) Ethics
Ethical problems are difficult because they almost always are unclear. For instance, through innocence or unrestrained aggressiveness, an organization can easily overstep the bounds of acceptable practice in seeking funding support. One clear unethical step to guard against is any fund raising carried out on a commission basis. Rewarding a fund raiser with a percentage of the money received, although not illegal, is considered professionally unethical—a fact not understood by many board members unfamiliar with unscrupulous fund-raising agencies.

It is also considered unethical to pay finder's fees to those who are in a position to help people with their estate planning, for steering bequests or major gifts to an organization the donor may not have shown any interest in supporting. The donor's wish to make the contribution to a specific organization should be the dominant motivation.

The Association of Fundraising Professionals (AFP) has a clear Code of Ethics, which should be strictly adhered to. (See Appendix 9B.)

(ii)   Costs

The costs of fund raising should not be excessive in relation to the amount raised. Determining reasonable fund-raising costs, however, is by no means simple. Costs vary widely with the size and kind of organization and with different types of fund raising. For example, the costs of soliciting corporations, foundations, and individuals that are part of the organization's own constituency are unlikely to be worrisome. On the other hand, large national, high-profile organizations depend heavily on mass mailing techniques, which can be very expensive, generating a high ratio of dollars spent to dollars received.

In any event, board members must be cautious about using mass mailings, often called direct mail. The important distinction to make is between appeals to the organization's own mailing list—constituency mailing—and mass mailings to lists purchased, leased, or exchanged. The costs of constituency mailings tend to be modest; mass mailing are expensive.

(iii)   Donor Unhappiness

Public or donor unhappiness with an organization's fund raising is not infrequent. Excessively repetitious mail appeals, aggressive phone solicitations, and indiscriminate sales and exchanges of mailing lists can be causes of complaints.

Several leading philanthropic associations, including AFP, have developed a Donor Bill of Rights (See Exhibit 9.1, page 220.), which serves as a reasonable guide in dealing with the unhappiness factor.

13.3   Fund-raising Action

The first step in taking action in fund raising is to be clear on where responsibility lies, which is unequivocal.

The board is responsible for the entire organization, and that includes attracting the resources to carry out its program. The board does not pass to anyone else the responsibility for raising funding support: not to the staff, not to a committee, not to a foundation, not to a consultant or outside agent. The board puts the organization in place, hires the executive, and approves the budget. The buck stops with the board.

It is true that some health care and educational institutions create foundations to raise contributed funds, usually to separate donated money from government appropriations or reimbursements. Boards of other public service organizations sometimes consider setting up a separate organization to do the unwelcome work of fund raising, or they may think about hiring someone to raise money for them. In the end, however, the board of the institution stands responsible for the success or failure of the fund-raising effort, no matter who does the work.

But make no mistake: The board is helpless without strong staff support. Rarely, if ever, can a board by itself raise the money required to support a program. Therefore, fund raising must be a partnership of board and staff. In no other way can it work. Neither board nor staff can succeed without the other. Accordingly, the key is to give attention to the roles of each, defining what the staff can do and what the board can do in the fund-raising effort.

(A) WHAT STAFFS CAN DO

The staff must always keep the files, records, and mailing lists. The staff does the research so essential to successful fund raising and prepares correspondence, acknowledgments of donations, and proposals that seek the support of foundations, corporations, or government agencies.

As in any program, fund raising must be planned. Preparing thorough program plans for raising money is clearly part of the staff role. Such plans can be discussed with a board development committee, and bringing them before the board for approval can help to ensure the participation of all members. To be most helpful, a fund-raising plan should identify the various sources or fund-raising projects, and for each should include the following five components:

1. A simple statement of the basic *purpose* of the program element or project
2. What is currently being done—the current status
3. What is planned for the future—courses of action
4. Specific targets of achievement
5. Administration—who is responsible and how much it will cost

Presented in this fashion, such a guiding plan will not only give management a clear focus, it will offer the board a sound basis for oversight and for evaluating performance.

Above all, however, the staff—whether the executive, a development officer, or volunteers acting as staff—must take the initiative, constantly generating ideas that will move the fund raising forward and motivate board members' action. Without that initiative, an organization's fund raising is lifeless.

Motivating board members, especially those who have demonstrated a reluctance about fund raising, although heavily dependent on the board's own leadership, is a job that falls principally to the staff. The executive and staff can stimulate board members' participation. They can engage trustees in simple projects, not necessarily related to fund raising: one project at a time, small tasks before large ones, making each task specific and limited. If board members are asked individually to carry out a particular job, rather than appealed to collectively in a board meeting, they will respond. Board members are no different from other people: They need to be individually stimulated, instructed, encouraged, thanked profusely, and given the credit. This motivating task for the executive and staff is not easy, but successful fund raising depends on its being fulfilled.

(B) WHAT MEMBERS CAN DO

Board members' reluctance to get involved in fund raising almost always centers on the act of asking. Money is tawdry; they resist asking for it. Although raising money ultimately does depend on someone asking someone else for a grant or contribution, and some board members will have to do some asking, there is much else to do other than the asking. The key is to demonstrate to board members all the things they can do materially to assist in fund raising without actually asking for money. Here, in summary form, are the many aspects of fund raising in which board members can help—indeed, board members will be the essential ingredient of effectiveness:

- *Personal contribution.* All trustees of an organization, without exception, should make their own personal, annual contribution. Regardless of the donations they may help to secure from other sources, this personal contribution is an essential act of commitment, no matter how small it has to be. No organization can expect others to invest in it if its own leaders do not do so first. The investment starts with annual giving by board members.

- *Strategic planning.* Because institutional planning is so important to successful fund raising, a board member must participate in determining its mission and plans for the future, on which are based both the *funding needs* and the *case* articulating why people should support the organization.

- *Development plans.* Although the executive and staff will appropriately prepare the fund-raising plans, the board should regularly approve them as part of its oversight responsibility, assuring familiarity with the plans by all members.

- *Adding to the mailing list.* The mailing list is at the core of the entire fund-raising program. The names board members add to that list are more valuable than those drawn from any other source.

- *Identifying and evaluating prospects.* Board members are the peers of important prospective donors—individuals, officials of companies, and foundations. They know these donors personally and their help in evaluation is invaluable.

- *Cultivating prospects.* A board member identified with the organization can speak out in the community and help to interest prospective donors.

- *Introductions.* Often the most difficult part of a solicitation is gaining the first introduction, arranging for the first meeting, especially with corporations and foundations. Board members, because of their familiarity with corporate officials and their standing in the community, can make the all-important introductions.

- *Annual appeal letters.* When board members append personal notes to appeal letters, success can increase four- to fivefold. Appeals preceded or followed by phonathons give further opportunity for valuable board member participation.

- *Supporting letters.* Organizations seeking support from a government agency, foundation, or company must submit a formal proposal. A separate supporting letter from a trustee does much to ensure a favorable reading.

- *Special events.* Special benefit events are not only sources of money, they also help raise public awareness and give exposure to the organization; they are forms of public relations, of cultivation. Certainly board members will attend these events, but, in addition, it is particularly appropriate for board volunteers to manage them. This involvement ensures that the event will not divert staff from their program responsibilities—a common problem.

- *Acknowledgments.* Letters of thanks for a donation are the first step toward the next asking. When a board member adds an acknowledging thanks—to companies and foundations as well as to individuals—such letters are particularly effective.

- *Accompanying on an ask.* When a board member accompanies the executive, a staff member, or another board member in making a solicitation, such participation adds weight to the appeal. Moreover, it is the best way for a trustee to become familiar with the process of asking.

The checklist presented in Exhibit 13.4 can be used to evaluate annually the participation of the board as a whole and of its individual members in each of the fund-raising functions that board members can perform.

13.4 Conclusion

Not-for-profit organizations vary in their approach to fund raising according to type of organization and the kind of fund raising that fits its place in the community. However, fund raising is a process made up of key elements that apply to the manner in which almost all organizations seek contributed support. These elements are identified in this chapter in the discussions of understanding fund raising and the responsibility for fund raising. Success in raising money, in significant measure, can be gauged by the effectiveness of boards, supported by staffs, in addressing each of these key elements. The final review (see Exhibit 13.5) assembles the key elements of what it takes to achieve success in fund raising. These factors also can be examined annually and their scores, resulting from the combined tally of all board members, can serve as a report card on the board's role in fund raising.

EXHIBIT 13.4 Annual Evaluation of Board Participation in Fund Raising

	Checklist (Score 1–5 high)	
	Self	**Board**
1. Board members make personal contributions	____	____
2. Participate in strategic planning	____	____
3. Understand and endorse development plans	____	____
4. Add names to the mailing lists	____	____

5. Help identify and evaluate prospects
     Individuals, foundations, corporations,
     religious institutions, service clubs
	____	____

6. Share in cultivation of key prospects	____	____
7. Make introductions to prospects	____	____
8. Write notes on annual appeal letters	____	____
9. Participate in phonathons	____	____
10. Write supporting letters	____	____
11. Help manage fund-raising events	____	____
12. Write thank-you letters	____	____
13. Accompany others in a solicitation	____	____
14. Ask for a contribution	____	____
In addition, board members		
15. Actually do what they undertake to do	____	____
16. Do not procrastinate	____	____

EXHIBIT 13.5 Overall Factors of Board Involvement in Fund Raising

(Score 1–5 high)

1. *Board and board chair*—committed and supportive; willing to work tirelessly at raising money. _____
2. *Chief executive*—committed even if not experienced. _____
3. *Development staff person*—a self-starter; writes well; gets on with people; willing to do the tough, hard work without recognition. _____
4. *Strategic Planning*—a clear and agreed-upon mission and a vision of what the organization wants to be in the coming years. _____
5. *The case*—a compelling statement of *why someone should support*, emphasizing the difference that needs to be made. _____
6. *Procedures*—good records, mailing lists, acknowledgments. _____
7. *Research*—relentless, methodical prospect research and preparation of each ask. _____
8. *Development plan*—comprehensive strategy with realistic targets of achievement. _____
9. *Patience*—acceptance that fund raising takes time. _____
10. *Enthusiasm.* _____

Suggested Readings

Howe, F. *Fund Raising and the Nonprofit Board Member.* NCNB Governance Series Paper No. 3. Washington, D.C.: National Center for Nonprofit Boards, 1988.

———. *The Board Member's Guide to Fund Raising.* San Francisco: Jossey-Bass, 1991.

———. *Welcome to the Board; Your Guide to Effective Participation.* San Francisco: Jossey-Bass, 1995.

Lord, James Gregory. *The Raising of Money: Thirty-Five Essentials Every Trustee Should Know.* Cleveland, OH: Third Sector Press, 1983.

O'Connell, B. *The Board Member's Book.* New York: The Foundation Center, 1985.

Verdery, J. D. *Dear Chris: Advice to a Volunteer Fund Raiser.* Washington, D.C.: The Taft Group, 1986.

14 Leadership Reengineering: The Not-for-Profit Board for Tomorrow

AUGUST A. NAPOLI, JR., PRESIDENT
Catholic Diocese of Cleveland Foundation

14.1 Introduction

There is a popular maxim shared by the leaders of not-for-profit organizations: In order to be successful, not-for-profits must be run more like businesses. So often have the words been spoken that they have taken on the sacred character of Holy Writ, accepted as an act of faith. This chapter begins, then, with a statement of blasphemy: Not-for-profit organizations are not businesses and should not be run like them. It likewise begins with a thesis most not-for-profit executives would consider to be an impossible dream: It is possible to forge a healthy, productive, mutually beneficial relationship with a board of trustees.

The business analogy is examined first. Consider the most elementary rule of success in the business world: Demand and revenues go hand in hand. As consumers' needs or desires for a product or service increase, the businesses lucky or smart enough to meet those needs or desires sell more of their products or services and, hence, earn more money. It is a matter of simple economics. But in the world of not-for-profits, that basic rule is turned inside out. For not-for-profit organizations, revenues often dwindle at the very moment demand skyrockets. Certainly that is true of the Catholic Charities Corporation in Cleveland, Ohio, which is used as a model for discussion in this chapter. The corporation raises money for direct human services administered by agencies owned and operated by the Catholic Charities System of the Diocese of Cleveland. It also manages a large endowment and assists other entities of the diocese with fund raising.

Like so many other not-for-profits, Catholic Charities struggle with a never-ending dilemma. Economic hard times produce a two-edged sword: Donations (revenue) increase but do not keep pace with expanding needs (demands). This is hardly the rule of business. Yet despite this disparity, many of the organizational management concepts traditionally embraced by not-for-profits have been "borrowed" from the world of for-profits. This is understandable, given that most not-for-profit boards are composed predominantly of corporate executives and other business practitioners who, in general, are likely to view the world through the prism of profit and loss. Contributing to this bias is the fact that, more often than not, boards of not-for-profits include a majority of "lay people" rather than professional not-for-profit administrators. The reason is obvious: Laypeople, successful in the world of commerce, have greater influence and greater access to money, along with broad management experiences.

Yet even though the advantages—management expertise and access to money and power—that business leaders bring to not-for-profit boards cannot be denied, there are distinct disadvantages as well. Most troublesome is that the business leaders who lend their time and insights to not-for-profit boards frequently approach them in precisely the same way they approach their for-profit businesses.

Given the differences between the not-for-profit and for-profit worlds, it is also helpful to acknowledge some important similarities. More than at any other time in history, not-for-profits face many of the same issues encountered by for-profits:

- Greater competition for financial support
- Competitive services and programs
- An untrusting public
- Fewer "home-grown" and locally managed organizations, thus less ability to curry favor through networking

Not-for-profits are caught between the need to avail themselves of the undeniable strength that business leaders bring to their boards and the inherent weakness that comes from too much reliance on the principles and approaches of for-profit business. Fortunately, and contrary to popular belief, not-for-profits can indeed achieve the balance necessary to have a dynamic relationship with their boards. But like high-wire performers, they must possess the self-confidence, trust, and courage to step away from safety and take a risk.

14.2   Toward a More Effective Board

Perhaps the most sweeping reform to be instituted at the highest levels of Fortune 500 firms over the past few years has been the movement to ensure that their boardrooms are populated less by "celebrity" and "buddy" board members and more by board members who truly work and who truly contribute to the company's progress. Witness the dramatic step taken by the International Brotherhood of Teamsters' pension fund, which in 1996 released a list of what it called the "least valuable directors" in corporate America. Bill Patterson, the Teamsters' director of corporate affairs, called the list "an attempt to put a face on inefficient board oversight." He said the Teamsters' $46 billion pension fund would vote against the reelection of board members on the list.

Because of such aggressive and highly public efforts, the days of boards made up of "good ol' boys"—friends and supporters of the chief executive officer who return the favor by awarding him or her a spot on their own "easy-money" boards—are rapidly disappearing. Shareholders no longer get starry-eyed over big names on corporate letterheads; they insist, instead, that directors bring practical knowledge to the boardroom table. This is one movement taking place in business that not-for-profit organizations would do well to emulate. The managers of not-for-profits must treat their constituencies as shareholders and incorporate their concerns into the operation of their boards. That means creating accountability.

Any effort to reengineer the board of a not-for-profit organization, then, can succeed only if three revolutionary principles are effectively communicated to and accepted by all who participate in the process:

1. Not-for-profits are fundamentally different from for-profits and, thus, must be run differently.
2. Board members must understand the philosophy and mission of the not-for-profits they represent.
3. Board members must be fully engaged in the not-for-profits' work and must be willing to be held accountable for the not-for-profits' performance.

The term "revolutionary" does not overstate the point. The principles listed here are at odds with the ingrained character of most not-for-profits. Not-for-profit executives generally have a reactive, rather than proactive, relationship with their boards. Boards tend to set policy and issue directives, whereas the role of the not-for-profit executive tends toward implementation and execution.

Yet although the management of not-for-profits dutifully follows board directives in strategic planning, marketing, and other areas, these activities often fall short of fulfilling their promise. Such failures should not be surprising. The executive often does not "buy in" to the directives he or she is given and so serves as less than an inspirational force among staff. In addition, the plans may not, in fact, be well advised, because they are formed unilaterally by board members who are not fully engaged in the organizations they are charged to direct. Clearly, a more cooperative relationship must be forged. And the process of forging it must be carried out by the executive and board member together.

The first step is self-examination. Not-for-profit leaders must refocus their vision of their organizations and must revisit, restate, and recommit to their mission. Furthermore, management must:

- Ensure that the board participates in the implementation of all strategic plans.
- Accept and encourage the board in its role to set policy.
- Vest itself in the outcomes of all initiatives through participatory leadership on an ongoing basis.

Is it possible to meet such ambitious goals? Yes. It is made possible through reengineering. Reengineering consists of six essential steps:

1. Reacquainting current trustees with the organization as it has evolved over the years
2. Putting ongoing systems into place to replenish the board's knowledge base as the demands on, and approaches of, the organization change
3. Finding new trustees suited to the organization's ever-changing needs
4. Acquainting new trustees with the philosophy and mission of the organization, as well as with the roles they are expected to perform within it
5. Adapting existing programs, and adopting new ones, to reflect the organization as it currently exists
6. Identifying "emerging talent," potential trustees for the future who will be appropriate to anticipated future needs

14.3 Diagnosing the Problem

No two not-for-profits, of course, are made alike. Still, the Catholic Charities experience contains lessons that apply across a broad spectrum of not-for-profits. As the organization's strategic planning process commenced, both the staff and the board executive committee agreed that the organization's greatest structural need was to increase board involvement. In that regard, of course, Catholic Charities was no different from the great majority of not-for-profits. But the organization did distinguish itself by making a firm commitment to address the problem and solve it.

At the urging of the executive leadership, the board's nominating and planning committees recommended that a reengineering of the board of trustees occur. It was further recommended that this initiative be conducted in a sensitive manner but with a determined focus.

In any new initiative, the feelings of long-standing trustees, many of whom have made significant contributions to the organization's success, must never be dismissed or ignored. The input of veteran trustees during the process of reengineering, in fact, may well be vital to the endeavor's success. At the same time, however, staff leadership must maintain its resolve to see the process through, handling opposition in a respectful rather than confrontational manner. In other words, they let chips fall where they might—but softly.

Three important initial steps were undertaken:

1. A profile of the board was drawn, along with a profile of the "ideal" board member, which included the following characteristics (see Exhibits 14.1 and 14.2):
   - Ability to listen; analyze; think clearly and creatively; work well with people individually and in a group
   - Willingness to prepare for and attend board and committee meetings; ask questions; take responsibility and follow through on a given assignment; contribute personal resources generously, according to acquired, personal circumstances; open doors in the community; evaluate oneself
   - Willingness to develop certain skills, if not already acquired, such as to cultivate and solicit funds; cultivate and recruit board members and other volunteers; read and understand financial statements; and learn more about the program areas of the Catholic Charities system
   - Honesty; sensitivity to and tolerance of differing views; a friendly, responsive, and patient approach; community-building skills; personal integrity; a developed sense of values; concern for Catholic Charities development; sense of humor

   This effort also focused on the following: people who will work; well-known people who may only lend their names; people who are "on the way up" in the community but not already overcommitted; well-positioned community leaders who can contribute "time, talent, and treasure," or to put it another way, "work, wealth, and wisdom"; leaders who can and will "give and get"; active, involved, and mature young leaders; upper-level and middle-level managers of corporations.
2. Differences between the actual and the theoretical were candidly noted.
3. A survey of board members was made to determine their own views about their role in the organization and what could be done to improve it. The survey was

EXHIBIT 14.1 Current Board of Trustees Profile

Area of Expertise	Class "A"	Class "B"	Class "C"	Class "D"
Administration				
Business/Corporate				
Finance: • Accounting • Banking Trusts • Investments				
Fund Raising (both professional fund raisers and those with leverage in getting funds)				
Government Representative				
Law				
Marketing/Public Relations				
Personnel				
Physical Plant (architect, engineer, contractors)				
Strategic or Long-range Planning				
Public Relations				
Real Estate				
Representative of Clients Served by Catholic Charities				
Other				
Age Under 35				
From 35 to 50				
From 51 to 65				
Over 65				

Gender
  Women
  Men				

Race/Ethnic Background Asian				
Black				
Hispanic/Latino				
Caucasian				
Other				

EXHIBIT 14.1 *(Continued)*

Area of Expertise	Class "A"	Class "B"	Class "C"	Class "D"
Financial Position Self Employed				
Salaried				
Philanthropic Reputation				
Prospective Major Donor				
Board Committees Executive				
Nominating				
Development				
Finance				
Marketing/Public Relations				
Audit/Pension				
Other—Appeal				
Length of Past Board Service Over Ten Years				
5–10 Years				
2–5 Years				
Geographical Location *City (Cleveland, Akron, Lorain/Elyria)				
Suburbs				
Regional				
Retired				

conducted through a Trustee Visitation Project, wherein trustees were engaged in thoughtful and detailed interviews. (See Exhibits 14.3 and 14.4.)

All of these assessment profiles and surveys, of course, are activities that take place at regular intervals in most well-managed organizations. Seldom, however, are the activities connected in a coherent strategy to truly reform and reenergize—that is, reengineer—the organization. Conducting the board assessment merely sets the scene. Once the assessment is in hand, the real work begins.

14.4 Writing the Prescription

Unless he or she is fully prepared, psychologically as well as institutionally, to confront difficult problems and personalities in order to bring about systemic change, the not-for-profit executive is advised to avoid the question of reengineering altogether. Because the

EXHIBIT 14.2 Sample Trustee Profile

The following characteristics are those used *in part* to define potential trustees for the Catholic Charities Corporation. It is intended only as a guide in describing a range of characteristics that are desirable in recruiting new trustees.

Age: 35–50 years of age.

Religion: Preference given to Catholics; however, individuals from other denominations with an interest in the work of Catholic Charities and possessing the other requisite skills and talents should be given consideration.

Occupation:
- Professionals in business, industry, government, law, medicine, fund raising, marketing/public relations, finance, and human services, with at least five years experience in their chosen field.

- Persons who work in the home with not-for-profit volunteer experience and/or with a strong interest in the mission of the Catholic Charities Corporation.

Education: College education (baccalaureate degree) or some college experience as a minimum.

Geographic Location: Resident within the Diocese of Cleveland.

Gender: Aspire toward equal balance of male and female.

Race/Ethnic Background: Aspire to equal balance of race/ethnic background as reflected within the composition of the church in this diocese and in those served by the Catholic Charities system.

Catholic Charities Experience: Not required; however, individuals who have served the Catholic Charities Corporation as fund-raising or public relations volunteers within their parish, through an agency, or as members of the Catholic Charities Associate Board, should be given special consideration.

process of reengineering involves two broad efforts—identifying problems and then solving them—anything less than a full commitment is destined to open more wounds than it will close.

Strategic planning is critical to treating any organizational illness, and to ensuring its future health. True strategic planning:

- Defines leadership
- Demonstrates organizational commitment to the future
- Promotes risk and change within an organization

In short, planning allows growth to happen. Only organizations with a plan—with a vision—have a chance to flourish. And fully engaged board members are important assets

EXHIBIT 14.3 Sample Survey of Board Members

Trustee Visitation Committee Suggested Interview Topics

I. History

1. When did you become involved in Catholic Charities?
2. Why did you become involved in Catholic Charities?
3. Who recruited you to be involved in Catholic Charities?
4. What committees or other involvement have you been part of as a member of the Catholic Charities Board of Trustees?
5. Do you have any observations on the evolution of Catholic Charities over your tenure? What do you think about Catholic Charities today?

II. Opinion

6. Have you enjoyed your involvement in Catholic Charities? What have been the most enjoyable experiences?
7. Do you know enough about this organization? What's the best way to tell you more?
8. If you were a new trustee all over again, should we do anything differently to make you feel welcome? (For example, have a better board member orientation program.)
9. Do you feel you are being utilized effectively as a trustee? How can we better utilize you as a resource on our behalf?
10. Do you wish there were more social occasions so that you could get to know your fellow board members better?

III. Giving/Involvement

11. Thank you for making your gift to Catholic Charities, or, will you be making your gift to Catholic Charities?
12. As a trustee of Catholic Charities, would you be willing to visit some of our donors to talk about the organization, thank them for their support and encourage their continued support?
13. Have you thought about a gift to Catholic Charities in your estate plan, and is this something you'd be interested in hearing more information on?
14. We want to involve our trustees in a way that they find meaningful. Are you interested in serving on a subcommittee of the board or as an advocate to donors and in the community?
15. Is there anything else that you've wanted to say, about which no one ever asked you before?

IV. Other Suggested Topics

16. Information and their careers. What they do and when do they plan to retire?
17. Their history in Cleveland. Have they grown up here?
18. Their involvement in their parish and other civic organizations.
19. Their families, including spouse and children. Do children attend Catholic schools?
20. Any other information that you consider worth knowing.

EXHIBIT 14.4 Sample Instructions for Survey Interviews with Trustees

---

10 Secrets for a Terrific Talk with a Trustee

1. Read the list of questions 10 times over to get a conversational familiarity.
2. Prioritize your list of contacts. Visit your most familiar one first.
3. Save the toughest contact for last. After your conversational skills are honed, take on your toughest assignment.
4. If a trustee declines to be visited or otherwise indicates he or she no longer wishes to be involved, thank the person for past participation and note this information on the interview summary sheet. *This information will be forwarded to the nominating committee for future consideration.*
5. There is safety in numbers. If you want additional support, make arrangements for a member of the staff to visit a trustee with you.
6. If you are asked a question to which you do not know the answer, proudly admit your ignorance, promise to get the answer, and call the office.
7. Take notes on the meeting while they are fresh in your mind: key words, thoughts, ideas, follow-up actions necessary.
8. Return your notes as quickly as possible to the Catholic Charities Corporation office.
9. When you are finished, tell yourself: "Because I am a successful person, I am ready for more contacts."
10. When you wake up in the morning, look in the mirror and remind yourself, "The trailblazing work I am accomplishing will benefit Catholic Charities for years to come."

---

in providing any organization's vision. Unless this principle is accepted, the question of board reengineering is moot. The goal of board reengineering, after all, is to achieve a fully engaged board, and that can come about only if trustees are fully informed.

At Catholic Charities, results of the board survey served as a mandate for change. Central to that change was a concerted effort to educate and inform both new and continuing trustees about the role, mission, and operational complexities of the organization—not once for now, but lasting for always. For an organization to maintain its vitality, it must be dynamic, and *dynamic* means *changing*. Thus all parts of the organization—programs, structure, and leadership—must be dynamic as well.

The mission of the organization, of course, remains constant. The change occurs in the approach, the tactics, best suited to fulfill the mission in an ever-changing society. In the case of Catholic Charities, for example, the days of door-to-door fund raising, once a staple of the organization, are long since past, replaced by methods far more effective and efficient in the information age.

Board members steeped in past traditions must fully understand the need for change in order to become fully involved in it. Thus, at Catholic Charities it was determined that any efforts to increase board involvement would not be merely "window dressing." Board members would be encouraged to participate only in truly meaningful ways (see Exhibit 14.5). Six bold moves were taken to fill the prescription for change:

1. Committees were created or re-created to fit the current profile of the organization. In doing this, the not-for-profit leader must take care to adapt the committees to the organization and its programs rather than to the board members and their preferences and interests.

EXHIBIT 14.5 Catholic Charities Corporation
Statement on Trustee Leadership

By definition, we, as members of the Board of Trustees, are responsible for providing leadership to the Catholic Charities Corporation.

We, as Trustees, fully support and subscribe to the following list of Basic Responsibilities of the Board of Trustees as set forth in the Corporation's *Trustee Handbook:*

1. *Determine the mission and goals of the Catholic Charities Corporation.*
2. *Select the Chief Executive Officer.*
3. *Support the Chief Executive Officer and review his/her performance.*
4. *Ensure effective organizational planning.*
5. *Ensure that adequate resources are available.*
6. *See that resources are managed effectively.*
7. *Determine and monitor the Corporation's programs and services.*
8. *Participate in the Corporation's programs and committees as a donor, fund raiser and public advocate.*
9. *Serve as a court of appeal.*
10. *Assess the performance of the Board of Trustees.*

We, the Trustees and Honorary Trustees of the Catholic Charities Corporation, have the responsibility to demonstrate commitment to the mission, vision and programs that embody the Catholic Charities Corporation. That commitment takes many forms and is evidenced in many ways. Key among these are personal giving, peer solicitation and community advocacy.

Trustee leadership: Personal giving
Personal giving is one component of Trustee leadership. All Trustees are expected to make an annual contribution to the full measure of individual capability. Trustees should aspire to major donor status. Leadership gifts by Trustees provide a crucial foundation for other development efforts.

We, as Trustees, set a goal of 100% participation by Trustees as donors.

Trustee leadership: Peer solicitation
Peer solicitation by Trustees is a crucial component of successful fund raising. Major donors want to deal with their peers, members of the Board of Trustees.
We, as Trustees, pledge our full commitment to peer solicitation.

Trustee leadership: Community advocacy
As Trustees, we must first educate ourselves about the Catholic Charities System and convey that knowledge as ambassadors to the community.

We, as Trustees, commit to serve as advocates for Catholic Charities throughout the community.

2. An Education and Training Committee was created to develop a continuum of programs to go beyond the superficialities of a typical orientation. The importance of this committee was underscored in all presentations to the board by emphasizing its high standing in the hierarchy of board responsibilities. A series of educational workshops and site visits were designed to fully communicate

the mission and goals of the organization, and to emphasize the vital steward-ship role the trustee must play so that the organization meets its objectives.

3. The identification-and-recruitment function of the old Nominating Committee was made part of a new Committee on Trustees. Besides annually recommend-ing nominees to the board and a slate of officers, the Committee on Trustees reg-ularly assesses the board structure and composition, recommends enhancements to governance, and evaluates the contributions made by each trustee. The Com-mittee on Trustees also provides oversight of the "trustee experience," mentor-ing their colleagues to ensure that the experience is mutually satisfying.

4. The trustees wrote their own manifesto of sorts, a "Statement on Trustee Leader-ship." This is comprised of ten points that outline a trustees' job relative to the organization's mission, goals, resources, programs, and services. Moreover, the manifesto commits trustees to three core activities: Personal Giving, Peer Solici-tation, and Community Advocacy. An activities chart was created to track trustee involvement and progress in their tasks. (See Exhibits 14.5 and 14.6.)

5. We created an associate board, consisting exclusively of "rising stars," those whose background, experience, achievements, and position in the community might not yet qualify them for full board membership. This allows the organiza-tion to "grow its own" trustees for the future.

6. A newsletter, "*Re: Philanthropy*," was created to keep trustees engaged, focused on their mission, and informed about the organization's activities. The Office of the President of Catholic Charities distributed the newsletter four times a year as a component of the trustees' education continuum. The newsletter's discus-sions of major trends and ideas in philanthropic fund development and fund management gave weight to the supra-mundane aspect of trustee stewardship.

"*Re: Philanthropy*" operates on another level, one germane to the management strat-egy behind the reengineering as well. The newsletter is a component of the ongoing edu-cation continuum in which, it is hoped, the trustees are by now immersed.

14.5   *Education, Participation*

Catholic Charities, like most not-for-profits, has hundreds of volunteers. It also has 100 trustees. The two roles cannot be confused. Trustees are much more than just volunteers; trustee commitment and responsibilities run much deeper. Therefore, the education and training of new and existing trustees is a vital component of the efforts to reengineer the board of trustees. Education equals participation. Catholic Charities designed the New Trustee Orientation Program (see Exhibit 14.7) and the Trustee Continuing Education program (see Exhibit 14.8).

All new trustees take part in two half-day orientation sessions prior to their first meeting. The curriculum for the initial session includes an overview of the Catholic Char-ities mission, history, agencies and programs, operational units of the corporation, board governance, and strategic planning. The second session includes a site visit to various agencies, an explanation of management services provided, and a tour of the physical plant. Future directions for Catholic Charities also are discussed as a part of this session.

The New Trustee Orientation Program was designed to provide new trustees with the basic information necessary to become effective board participants and working

EXHIBIT 14.6 Catholic Charities Corporation
2000 Board of Trustees

Trustee	First Elected (New Code)	Class/ Term	Terms Completed	BOT Attendance				Committee Activities		
				96	97	98	99	1996	1997	
1										
2										
3										
4										
5										
6										
7										
8										
9										
10										
11										
12										
13										

KEY:

Committee Assignments:

AGS = Annual Giving Societies Subcommittee (formerly MajorGiving)
AP = Annual Appeal (now Parish Promotions Subcommittee)
CT = Committee on Trustees (formerly the NominatingCommittee)
D = Development
EM = Education & Marketing
ET = Education & Training (now Education & Marketing)
FAC = Facilities Corporation
FD = Foundation
FI = Finance
HS = Heritage Society Subcommittee (no longer exists)

MC = Marketing & Communications (now Education & Marketing)
MG = Major Giving Subcommittee (now Annual Giving Societies)
Par = Parish Promotion Subcommittee
PL = Planning (now part of Executive Committee)
PP = Past Presidents/Chairs
RT = Corporate Retirement
75 = 75th Anniversary Steering (no longer exists)
USA = Catholic Charities, USA—1996 (no longer exists)

A = Active I = Inactive

Committee Activities			Donations						Personal Involvement		Special Designation
1998		1999	1994	1995	1996	1997	1998	1999	1998	1999	

Donor Codes: Personal Involvement Codes:

AD = Annual Donor　　　　　　　ADV = Advocacy Program
SD = Special Donor　　　　　　　AGS = Annual Gift Solicitation
UW = United Way Donor　　　　　SGS = Special Gift Solicitation
PGS = Planned Gift Solicitation　　PAGS = Phonathon Annual Gift Solicitation

(TRUSTEE TRACKING CHART.DOC)

EXHIBIT 14.7 Sample New Trustee Orientation Program

Session I

Title:	The History, Mission, and Operation of the Catholic Charities Corporation
Time Allocated:	Five hours (half day)
Faculty:	Catholic Charities Corporation Senior Staff
	Catholic Charities Services Corporation president
	Board chairperson
	Board of Trustees Education and Training Committee chair and committee members
	Board Development Committee chair
	Board Marketing/Communications Committee chair
Location:	Catholic Charities Corporation Board Room
	1111 Superior Avenue
	Cleveland, Ohio 44114
Content:	• Introductions to program and of participants
	• Mission of the Catholic Charities Corporation and history of the Catholic Charities system of corporations, agencies, and programs
	• Vision for the future and strategic long-range plan for the Catholic Charities Corporation.
	• Overview of the operating units of the Catholic Charities Corporation
	Development
	Marketing and Communications
	Administration and Business Affairs
	Office of the President
	The Catholic Charities Foundation and Catholic Charities Facilities Corporation
	• Board Governance of the Catholic Charities Corporation
	Board Meetings
	Board Self Assessment
	Board Orientation and Continuing Education
	Board Responsibilities
	Committee Structure *(continued)*

members of the board committee structure. Completion of the program is *required* of all new trustees. It also is recommended that existing trustees be required to participate in two continuing education units per year, designed specifically for them.

The continuing education sessions are even more important than the new trustee orientations because they keep trustees keyed into the organization's mission and the approaches taken to fulfill it.

In addition, a Trustees Issue Briefing program has been developed to help board members stay abreast of crucial issues affecting the organization. Topics relate to philanthropy, not-for-profit management and trusteeship, and human services. The Education and Training Committee selects topics and invites presenters as the first agenda item on each of the regular board meetings each year. Presenters provide trustees with a written paper on their topic, and those not in attendance receive their copies enclosed with the minutes of the meeting. The annual collection of Issue Briefing Topic papers become part

EXHIBIT 14.7 *(Continued)*

Session II

Title: The Services and Agencies of the Catholic Charities System

Time Allocated: Five hours (half day)

Faculty: Catholic Charities Corporation president
Board chairperson or other officers
Board of Trustees Education and Training Committee chairperson and
   committee members
Various agency directors and/or program staff

Location: Various locations throughout the Diocese of Cleveland

Content: The new trustees will first gather at a predetermined central location and
then proceed together to meet and tour facilities representative of
Catholic Charities work in the three program disciplines of the system:
Hunger/Homeless, Children/Family, and Older Adults.
- Overview of the management of the typical Catholic Charities agency
(on site)
   Staffing
   Budget (allocation, fees, and reimbursement)
   Planning process and interaction with the Catholic Charities Service
     Corporation
- Overview of the services provided by the agency (on site)
   Description of services rendered
   Demographics of client base
   Projected service trends
   Quality assurance
- Overview and tour of the physical plant (on site)
   Renovation/expansion projects under construction
   New construction projects under consideration
   Facility maintenance quality control
   Relations with the local community
- Future directions for the Catholic Charities Corporation
   Short term, 3–5 years
   Long term, 5 years and beyond
- Presentation of the board manual and review of contents
- Open discussion
   Questions and answers

of the permanent body of information and are then used as appropriate in other trustee and staff orientation, education, and training forums.

If the formal meetings of a board are the essence of trusteeship, the board meetings themselves must be meaningful. Thus, a program of Trustee Roundtable Sessions has also been established. The purpose is to provide detailed briefings on the business aspects of the organization's programs.

These sessions, scheduled one hour prior to each regular meeting, act as tutorials on subjects vital for the board to understand in order to make sound, well-informed decisions. The sessions allow the regular board meetings to proceed in a businesslike manner, free of elementary questions. Appropriate staff members prepare a detailed

EXHIBIT 14.8 Sample Agenda for a Trustee Continuing Education Program

Unit I: Techniques of Personal Solicitation
(Insert date, time, and location)

The purpose of this Continuing Education Unit is to provide training to trustees on how to solicit gifts for the Catholic Charities Annual Appeal in preparation for active solicitation. This unit is scheduled during the first four months of each calendar year.

15 Minutes	• Donor Motivation: Why do People Give?
15 Minutes	• The Catholic Charities Case for Support
	15-minute break
15 Minutes	• How to Ask for the Gift: Tips on Fund Raising
1 Hour	• Solicitation: Role Play Video and Exercise
20 Minutes	• Questions and Answers
40 Minutes	• Prospect Assignment
	Adjournment

Unit II: Catholic Charities Service System
(Insert date, time, and location)

The purpose of this Continuing Education Unit is to provide training to trustees on how the planning and distribution process works within the Catholic Charities Services Corporation. This unit is scheduled during the second half of each calendar year.

15 Minutes	• History/Mission/Goals of the Catholic Charities Services Corporation
15 Minutes	• Present Structure and New Directions
15 Minutes	• Planning and Distribution of Catholic Charities Resources
	15-minute break
	• Roundtable Discussion of Services:
20 Minutes	Children and Families
20 Minutes	Emergency Assistance
20 Minutes	Older Adults and Developmental Disabilities
	Adjournment

overview of a particular topic, such as "Reading and Understanding the Catholic Charities Corporation Financial Statements," "Trustee Liability and Responsibility," and "Market-Research Results." Several roundtable sessions run concurrently, allowing each trustee to choose the one most appropriate and useful.

Augmenting these efforts is "Re: philanthropy," the newsletter from the organization president. Each issue is dedicated to a single topic so that the ideas have breathing room, but the text is kept short, to about 750 words. Surveys show that busy executives—many of whom are trustees—receive dozens of newsletters every month, and the

EXHIBIT 14.9 Trustee and Volunteer Service Opportunities			
Areas of Service	*Exec. Com.*	*Trustee*	*Volunteer*
Nominating Committee (Governance)	•	•	
Education and Training Committee	•	•	
Planning Committee	•	•	
Marketing & Communications Committee	•	•	
Associate Board	•	•	•
Annual Parish Appeal	•	•	•
Annual Giving Societies	•	•	•
Corporate Awareness Program	•	•	•
Diocesan Fund Development Program	•	•	•
Proposal Development Program	•	•	•
Visions for the Future Program	•	•	•
Foundation Board	•		
Special Review Committee	•		
Corporation Retirement Committee	•		

newsletters that get read are those that are brief, useful, and attractive. "Re: philanthropy" is a custom creation, nicely designed and printed on good paper, with an original logo; its high quality reinforces trustees' sense that Catholic Charities in Cleveland is among the most respected and successful Catholic Charities organizations in America.

In all these efforts, opportunities for meaningful participation are stressed. Board members are continually reminded of the various areas of service in which they may participate as board members, volunteers, or both. (See Exhibit 14.9.) Involvement in two or more service areas is recommended; keeping track of experience and knowledge gained by board members and volunteers from active service is key to identifying potential leaders for the future.

14.6   Conclusion

Trusteeship should never be just a name on a letterhead. That is a disservice to both the trustee and the organization he or she serves.

All of the steps in reengineering a board, then, must be taken with a focus on full participation as a goal. The steps must not be external to the life of the organization but, rather, woven into its fabric.

Unfortunately, many not-for-profits are driven solely by the personality of its leaders on the board and in the executive ranks. When those individuals leave the organization or there is an unexpected crisis, the organization faces a leadership vacuum. Successful reengineering, however, demystifies the organization and enables it to endure through all challenges, regardless of who is at its helm. Reengineering keeps the organization vital, dynamic, and continually responsive to changing needs.

PART III

Environmental and Institutional Readiness

15 Demographics: Our Changing World and How It Affects Raising Money

JUDITH E. NICHOLS, MBA, PHD, CFRE

15.1 Introduction

15.2 Overview of Our Changing Audiences
   (a) Increasing Longevity
   (b) Increasing Diversity

15.3 Understanding Generational Differences
   (a) Depression Babies
   (b) World War II Babies
   (c) Baby Boomers
   (d) Baby Busters
   (e) Baby Boomlet

15.4 A Culturally and Ethnically Diverse Population

15.5 How Can Fund Raisers Use Demographic and Psychographic Information?

Suggested Readings

To effectively raise money, you must understand how the world is changing.

—Judith E. Nichols, *Growing from Good to Great*

15.1 Introduction

Change presents both opportunities and challenges. Although it can be threatening, disruptive, and anxiety provoking, change is also transforming, revitalizing, and a source of energy. *Unfortunately, too often, change takes us unaware.* Then we play "catch-up," trying desperately to move to the new reality. David Parradine, the recently retired chief executive officer of the United Way of Columbia-Willamette, Oregon, notes that "change is not negotiable. It's inevitable." In fact, the Chinese proverb and curse "May you live in interesting times" is especially apropos given the tumultuous changes that are happening all around us. The one thing we know with certainty about the future is that it is likely to be different from the present.

The material for this chapter is drawn heavily from Judith Nichols' books, *Global Demographics: Fund Raising for a New World* (1996), *Growing from Good to Great: Positioning Your Fund Raising for BIG Gains* (1995), *Pinpointing Affluence: Increasing Your Share of Major Donor Dollars* (1994), *Targeted Fund Raising: Defining and Refining Your Development Strategy for the 1990s* (1991), and *Changing Demographics: Fund Raising in the 1990s* (1990), which are available through Bonus Books, Chicago.

Simon George, director of development at Good Shepherd Trust, Great Britain, suggests trying this test to check your response to change. Does your organization:

- Predict change and move ahead of it?
- Recognize that things have changed and manage to catch up?
- Not even notice that change has occurred?

Notes George, "No prizes for guessing which [organizations] will survive to meet tomorrow's needs!"

We live our lives based on paradigms, assumptions that help establish boundaries. They provide us with:

- Rules for success
- A filter for incoming experiences and data so that we can accept what fits and ignore the rest

Paradigms are both common and useful. However, when you develop a terminal case of certainty, you wind up with "paradigm paralysis." To thrive, not just survive, you need to understand the changing paradigms in population, values, and technology. Futurist Joel Barker notes that when the paradigm shifts, everyone goes back to zero. Your past successes no longer count, they guarantee you nothing! In fact, your successful past can block your vision of the future.

The increasing longevity and diversity of our populations will change the way we do fund raising in fundamental ways. Too many fund raisers are still working under the old rules, assuming an unlimited pool of donors to be acquired, treating all people as if they share common "generational anchors," and clinging to methodologies that today's savvy consumers are rejecting.

15.2 Overview of Our Changing Audiences

You cannot plan for the future if you are evaluating from the past and present. Unfortunately, there is a natural resistance to change. To overcome this resistance, you need to have solid, useful information to evaluate. Fund raisers deal with individuals of all ages, either directly as prospects or indirectly because they influence those who give. During the last decade of the twentieth century, dramatic changes occurred in our population. (See Exhibit 15.1.) The changing demographic paradigms that fund raisers must understand to succeed in the years ahead fall into two general areas: (1) increasing longevity and (2) increasing diversity.

(A) INCREASING LONGEVITY

In case you have not noticed, the world is turning gray. (See Exhibit 15.2.) According to demographer Peter Laslett, "Europe and the West are growing old and will never be young again." Increasing longevity, the results of gains in medicine, education, and nutrition and declining birth rates are contributing to dramatic increases of older people throughout the world.

EXHIBIT 15.1 A Population Overview

U.S. Population Through 2020

Between 1990 and the year 2020,
the under-50 population is projected to grow by only 1 percent.

- Fewer young adults:
  By 1995, there will be 20 percent fewer 18- to 24-year olds
  (nearly 5 million fewer prospects) than there were in 1988.
  But the 50+ population is projected to grow by 74 percent.
- An older population:
  In 1989, the majority of U.S. adults were over the age of 40.
  By 2002, the majority of U.S. adults will be over the age of 50.
  63 million people alive today have celebrated their 50th birthdays—34 percent of the
  entire adult population.
- The fastest growing segments are Boomers:
  50 to 54-year-olds, followed by 45 to 49-year-olds, followed by those 55 to 59.
- Increasing numbers of the elderly are female:
  60 percent of the 65+ population are women, and because women usually live longer,
  they outnumber men by *nearly three to one* past the age of 85.

Source: David B. Wolfe, Marketing to Boomers and Beyond: Strategies for Reaching America's Wealthiest Market *(New York: McGraw-Hill, 1993).*

Another major reason for the increase in numbers of older people is the aging of the
large group of those born in the years directly after World War II: the baby boomers,
twice as large in numbers as the preceding generation. Currently in their late 30s
through early 50s, as boomers move through life, they substantially increase whatever
age group they occupy. Between 1990 and 2020, the under-50 population is projected to
grow by only 1 percent, but the 50-plus population is projected to grow by 74 percent.

By 1995, there were 20 percent fewer 18- to 24-year olds (nearly 5 million fewer
young adults) than there were in 1988. By 1989, thanks to the middle aging of the 76 mil-
lion+ baby boomers born between 1946 and 1964, the majority of U.S. adults were over
the age of 40. The first 7,745 baby boomers turned 50 on January 1, 1996. By the end of
1996, 3.4 million had crossed the great divide. Each day for the next 10 years 10,000
boomers will turn 50. As a result, the 55+ market, presently 21 percent of the U.S. population, will gradually increase to 33 percent during the next 5 years. By 2002 the majority
of U.S. adults will be over the age of 50.

Medical advances have lengthened life expectancy from 45 years in 1900 to over 79
years for American women, 72 years for American men. And increasingly, because
women live an average of seven years longer than men, the elderly will be female.

EXHIBIT 15.2 Aging in the United States

Current 65+ population	28.5 million or 12 percent of population
Projected by 2020	51.4 million or 17.3 percent of population
Life expectancy	78 years for women; 71 years for men

Source: U.S. Census Bureau, 1990.

Women outnumber men by nearly three to one past the age of 85. Older women are increasingly single. There are 14 million single women older than 55 and only 4 million single men. Moreover, most women marry older men. As a result, nearly half of all elderly women are widowed, as compared with just 14 percent of elderly men. "The land of the old will be a land of women."

And looking at median life expectancy does not truly explain the aging phenomenon. For those reaching the median expectancy of 79 years (women) and 72 years (men), for every year they live past the median they can expect to live another two to three years. This makes true life expectancy for many Americans over 90!

(B)   INCREASING DIVERSITY

No longer will the best prospects in a fund-raising effort be similar to one another. We will deal with diversity across age groups, lifestyles, and ethnic/racial backgrounds. (See Exhibit 15.3.)

As life lengthens out, there will be more differences among age groups. Our "generational anchors" will not be the same. Our points of reference and childhood experiences will vary substantially. Throughout the developed world, more adults are alive who were born after World War II than before: 70 percent of adults do not remember a time "before TV." Different life experiences means that fund raisers and prospects may lack common life "triggers." Our philanthropic personalities and our attitudes toward money will not be the same. Fund raisers will need to do more "intergenerational" selling.

In addition to the differences between age groups, we will need to factor in differences in lifestyles and life stages. (See Exhibit 15.4.) A growing number of adults are moving through life at their own pace: postponing or not having children, taking sabbaticals from careers, returning to school, starting new businesses, and so on. Remarriage, second families, and caregiving change the way adults of similar ages look at their ability to be charitable.

15.3   *Understanding Generational Differences*

Rebecca Piirto, in *Beyond Mind Games: The Marketing Power of Psychographics*, describes a study by DuPont and Management Horizons that focused on shared experiences. It uses as a starting point an assumption that people are shaped by the events they experience during youth: "People of the same age tend to behave in similar ways because they went through the same formative experiences. During the formative years—between the ages of 7 and 21—core values and attitudes are shaped that will affect an individual for life."

EXHIBIT 15.3 Increasing Diversity

- Distinct Generational Differences
- Growing Ethnic/Racial Pluralism
- Differences in Life Stages and Lifestyles

EXHIBIT 15.4 Lifestyles and Life Stages

Try targeting to MOBYs (Mommy Older, Baby Younger) and DOBY's (the daddies). Once Yuppies (Young Urban Professionals), now they're PUPPIES (Poor Urban Professionals) and WOOFs (Well-Off Older Folks).

We've got Sandwichers (adults caught between caring for their children and their older parents); SKIPPIEs (School Kids with Income and Purchasing Power) as well as groups based on special interests like Global Kids (children with strong feelings about the environment plus strong influence over family purchase choices); and New Health Age Adults (consumers who consider their health and the health of the planet top priorities).

Source: Rebecca Piirto, Beyond Mind Games: The Marketing Power of Psychographics *(Ithaca, NY: American Demographics Books, 1991).*

As people mature, other influences take over, such as college, marriage, pursuing a career, and/or raising a family. Overriding all of these personal influences are the broader events—political, social, international, technological, and economic—that shape all of our lives. As a result, those of different age groups have different points of reference and different childhood experiences.

Each generation has its own personality. To understand the differences between generations, we need to ask people how they were raised as children, what public events they witnessed in adolescence, and what social mission elders gave them as they came of age.

Projecting the cycle is a new way of predicting consumer attitudes and lifestyles. Historians William Strauss and Neil Howe in their book, *Generations: The History of America's Future, 1584 to 2069,* suggest that we can read behavior along a "generational diagonal." According to the authors, there are four "generational personalities"—idealistic, reactive, civic, and adaptive—that recur in that order throughout history. To succeed in reaching the generations, your messages will have to pay attention not only to where a generation has been but also to where it is headed.

Currently we are dealing with seven generational groupings, or cohorts, spanning those born before 1901 to those born today. The term "cohort" and "generation," though often used interchangeably, are not exactly the same. A generation is usually defined by its years of birth. Cohorts are better defined by events that occur at various critical points in the group's lifetime. To make this information useful for fund raisers, a number of demographic and psychographic theories concerning cohorts have been used to combine the oldest groupings, as their numbers are extremely small, into a total of five age groups, as shown in Exhibit 15.5.

(A) DEPRESSION BABIES

Currently aged 65 and older, persons born prior to 1935 have "civic" personalities, believing it is the role of the citizen to fit into society and make it better. Civics are today's activist elderly.

Civics came of age during the depression, and many of them fought in World War II. Their shared experiences gave them two key characteristics: frugality and patriotism. They are the twentieth century's confident, rational problem solvers, those who have always known how to get big things done.

EXHIBIT 15.5 Generation Gaps in Values

Depression Babies   The Civics
(Born prior to 1935)
            "We fought for it."
      Money personality: "Save, save, save"

World War II Babies   The Silents
(Born 1935–1945)
            "We earned it."
    Money personality: "Save a little, spend a little."

Baby Boomers   The Idealists
(Born 1946–1964)
            "We've owned it."
  Money personality: "First spend, then save for it."

Baby Busters   The Reactives
(Born 1964–1977)
      "We deserve it, but probably won't get it."
        Money personality: "It's hopeless."

Boomlet   The Civics
(1978–1994)
            "We'll be taken care of."

Civics have boundless civic optimism and a sense of public entitlement. Former Boy and Girl Scouts, they volunteer and give because it is part of their inner image. They respect authority, leadership, civic-mindedness, and discipline.

- *Preferred message style.* Those in this group prefer a rational and constructive approach, with an undertone of optimism.

    "And now you want to know if there is anything good
    to say about getting older"

    We're quicker to laugh, and not as eager to blame.
       There's time left in this game.
    May we find (along with the inability to tell ourselves
       that we'll keep playing forever)
    A few compensations.

                    —Judith Viorst, *Forever Fifty and Other Negotiations*

- *Financial style.* Shaped by memories of the stock market crash and the Great Depression, those in this group have cautious spending habits. Always mindful of the lessons of their childhood, their money personalities are conservative. They tend to be cash payers and to distrust the technology of the "cashless" society.
- *Key life events.* The depression and World War II are common experiences of people in this age group.

(B) WORLD WAR II BABIES

Born between 1935 and 1945, a smaller group of "young elders" was taught to be "silent," believing in the will of the group rather than individuality. World War II babies growing up during the war learned to be "seen but not heard." Followers rather than leaders, they respond to appeals to their other-directed pluralism, their trust in expertise, their emulation of the young, and their unquenched thirst for adventure.

Consensus builders rather than leaders, Silents give freely to charity, are inclined to see both sides of every issue, and believe in fair process more than in final results. They are organization-loyal and value-oriented.

- *Preferred message style.* Those in this group prefer an approach that is sensitive and personal, *with a reliance on technical detail.*
- *Financial style.* Their parents repeated the lessons of the Great Depression to them, but Silents reached adulthood in golden economic days, benefiting from real estate appreciation, a booming stock market, portable pensions, government entitlements, and inflation. Now in early retirement, many Silents are willing to spend on themselves if not on charity. Their financial style is to "save a little, spend a little."
- *Key life events.* Members of this age group recall World War II and the dropping of the bomb on Hiroshima, the Cold War as symbolized by the Berlin Wall, the McCarthy hearings, and the popularity of Marilyn Monroe.

(C) BABY BOOMERS

Our society's adult "Idealists" (born between 1946 and 1964), the baby boomers, were told that they could do anything, that life is a voyage of self-discovery. They display a bent toward inner absorption, perfectionism, and individual self-esteem. Taught from birth that they were special, boomers believe in changing the world, not changing to fit it. In midlife, they will see virtue in austerity and a well-ordered inner life. They will also demand a new assertion of community values over individual wants. (See Exhibit 15.6.)

- *Preferred message style.* Those in this age group prefer a mediative and principled approach, with an undertone of pessimism.

"They're the only generation that ended a war and fired a president," notes Barbara Caplan, vice president at Yankelovich Clancy Shulman, marketing research firm. "To this day, they have a higher level of optimism, a sense that the world is their oyster."

"This will be a much more open and challenging and possibly skeptical set of people" states Rena Bartos, marketer, on the aging of baby boomers.
- *Financial style.* Having always lived in a world of inflation and having no memories of the depression, members of this group have a different understanding of money. This is the generation that saw money lose clout: More is worth less. Financial planning is viewed as a sign of status in its own right. However, they are coming out of the free-spending 1980s to focus on nonmaterialistic values. They tend to buy first, pay later, and like monthly payment plans and credit cards.

EXHIBIT 15.6 Boomer Aspirations

"I plan to do the 'someday' things."
—Robert Goodnow,
42-year-old who became mayor of Old Saybrook, Connecticut, in 1989.

"The nineties will be like the fifties but less conventional."
—Sally Jackson,
PR consultant, defining the aging baby boomer style as "New Fogy."

Source: Judith E. Nichols, Pinpointing Affluence: Increasing Your Share of Major Donor Dollars *(Chicago: Bonus Books, 1994), p. 10.*

- *Key life events.* Baby boomers recall the assassinations of John and Robert Kennedy, Martin Luther King Jr.; worldwide rock music, the Red Brigade, and other campus/youth-based terrorism.

(D) BABY BUSTERS

The "reactive" young adults born between 1965 and 1977 are the first generation that does not believe life will be better for them than for their parents. Following the much-heralded boom, the media convinced us that busters could do nothing right.

Many busters believe the boomers let them down. (See Exhibit 15.7.) Busters were the throwaway children of divorce and poverty, the latchkey kids. The reactives were not trusted or appreciated as youth and carry the scars into adulthood. They are the most Republican-leaning youths of the twentieth century. Busters will need convincing proof that an organization is reliable and will simplify rather than complicate their lives.

- *Preferred message style.* Members of this group prefer a blunt and kinetic approach, with an appeal to brash survivalism. "I want us to be the generation that leads, that votes, that earns, that spends, that doesn't continue to let our parents fight our wars for us," noted Nicholas W. Nyhan, graduating senior, in a

EXHIBIT 15.7 The Boomer/Buster Debate

"*My generation considers the baby-boomers too self-absorbed and frivolous.* While our parents—the "Happy Days" generation—were the pampered children of the 1950s, my generation grew up in a period of social ferment. We grew up with childhood memories of waiting in long gasoline lines. The first of us came of political age during the Iranian hostage crisis. And while the nation appeared prosperous during the Reagan years, many of us now know that our generation was left with the bill for a decade of budget deficits and an enormous savings-and-loan bailout," says Taegan Goddard, 26, in an interview in *New York Newsday.*

Source: Taegan Goddard, "4 Big Worries for Twentysomethings," New York Newsday, October 26, 1992, p. 71.

1992 commencement speech at the University of Massachusetts at Amherst, Massachusetts. They see their role in life pragmatically. They want to fix rather than change. They are highly influenced by technology and television.

- *Financial style.* Twentysomething has a different view of the the good life. Only 21 percent say the most important measure of living the good life is financial success, and a scant 4 percent believe that the criterion is owning a home. The rest are more concerned with the acquisition of intangibles: a rich family or spiritual life, a rewarding job, a chance to help others, and an opportunity for leisure and travel or for intellectual and creative enrichment.

  Many who are still being supported in adulthood by parents have substantial discretionary income that they will give to charities with which they work. Highly computer literate, they prefer the cashless society.

- *Key life events.* This age group saw the crumbling of the Berlin Wall and the opening of Eastern Europe.

(E) BABY BOOMLET

The "civic" children of boomers, born between 1978 and 1994, hold many of the values of an earlier generation. Although it may be too early to tell what events in their lives will be significant, it is likely that technology and globalism will play important roles. They are growing up in a world without boundaries and are likely to extend their philanthropy well past their own countries. (See Exhibit 15.8 for summary.)

15.4   *A Culturally and Ethnically Diverse Population*

Today, one in three people in the USA is black, Hispanic, Asian or Native American. Fueled by immigration and high birthrates, populations of ethnic and racial minorities in the United States will grow seven times faster than the white, non-Hispanic population over the next decade, according to the U.S. Census Bureau. Fourteen percent speak a language other than English at home. The 1990s became the decade of diversity. And tomorrow's adults are today's youth. Twenty-five percent of California's 4.5 million kindergarten-through-high school students, for example, are Hispanics.

Nationwide, the Hispanic and Asian populations of the United States surged during the 1990s, with the number of Hispanics growing by more than 35 percent and Asians more than 40 percent, *the Census Bureau said.* The national Hispanic population is expected to overtake the non-Hispanic black population (with 12.7 percent or 34.4 million—of the nation's population of 270 million) to become the largest minority group by the end of 2004. Four states—Arkansas, Georgia, Nevada, and North Carolina—had their Hispanic populations double. The Asian and Pacific Islander population grew in the 1990s from 3 percent of the overall population to almost 4 percent at 10.5 million. (See Exhibit 15.9.)

The Black, Hispanic, and Asian populations are expected to increase their share of births and immigration, adding 110 million more people than the non-Hispanic white population over the next sixty years:

EXHIBIT 15.8 Summary of Target Market Groups

Targeting Mature Individuals

- Avoid ageism and negative myths.
- Segment
    50–64: In transition, preretirees.
    65–74: Traditional givers, low numbers.
    75+: Asset rich, concerns about outliving their financial resources.
- Market positively
    Like direct mail, "literate."
    Communicate in length/depth.
    Use appropriate age models.
    Watch signage, type size, color usage.

Targeting Baby Boomers

- Have been held back 10 years economically.
- Not donor/customer loyal.
- Grew up being told they were special, yet overwhelmed by their numbers.
- Don't trust anyone.
- Very nostalgic for "the good days."
- Key concerns:
    Retirement
    College for their kids
    Their parents' aging
- Created networking as a way of life.
- Concentrate on recognition, instant gratification, accountability.

Targeting Baby Busters

- Second largest population grouping: 33 million individuals born 1964–1976.
- Currently, have high disposable incomes.
- Grew up in the "shadow of the boom."
    Cautious, conformist
    Anti-intellectual/pessimistic
    Often fearful, frustrated, angry
- Key concerns are "quality of life"
    The environment
    Positive self-issues
    Parenting
    Ongoing education
- Friends first, then extended family.

Boomlet Values*

Racial Harmony

73% Have friends of another race.
63% Welcome someone of another race as a next-door neighbor.
61% Want to go to school with someone from another country.

Charitable Giving

61% Would give up some of their pocket money to help feed kids.
50%+ Would go without some presents at Christmas.
37% Would give up money for summer vacations.
27% Would give up their back-to-school clothing allowance.

*Source: Karen S. Peterson, "Kids Believe in Welcome Racial Integration," USA Today, October 9, 1992, p. 1.

EXHIBIT 15.9 Percentage of USA Population by Race & Ethnicity

	2000	2010	2050
Non-Hispanic White	71.8%	68.0%	52.5%
African-American And Black	12.2%	12.6%	14.4%
Hispanic	11.4%	13.8%	22.5%
Asian and Pacific Islander	3.9%	4.8%	9.7%
Native American	0.7%	0.8%	0.9%

U.S. Census Bureau and American Demographics, June 2000

- Blacks are the largest minority except in the West. *As of June 2000, about 33 percent of the country's 35 million blacks are age 18 or younger, compared with 24 percent of America's 193 million whites.* The statistics offer more proof that America's population will become even more diverse in the 21st century. According to the Census Bureau, the black population would rise to 59.2 million in 2050, a 70 percent increase. Under this projection, the black share of the total population would increase slightly, from 13 percent to 15 percent.

  Today's black population is 27 million or 12 percent of the U.S. population. It is growing at a rate nearly three times faster than the white population. The Black population will grow 94% to 62 million in 2050. After 2005, more blacks than non-Hispanic whites will be added each year.

- Hispanic, a designation that includes people from all four races, will add more people to the U.S. population than any other group. Hispanics are increasing about 3.3 percent per year, or about three times the overall U.S. growth rate. The number of U.S.-born Latinos and Latin American immigrants to the United States doubled from 1980 to 1990 according to U.S. Census Bureau data. Latinos residing in the U.S. total 27 million people, make up nearly 10% of the population, and are expected to become the largest minority by early in the next century. By 2010, it's estimated that Hispanic-Americans will surpass African-Americans as the largest USA minority group. Noteworthy is the relative youth of this demographic segment: 35 percent are under the age of 18. In 2010, Hispanics are projected to account for 13.8 percent of the U.S. population, up from 11.4 percent today.

  The Hispanic population will be 81 million strong by 2050 (246% growth), representing a total increase of 57 million people after 1992. Within a century, Hispanics could comprise up to 30% of the U.S. population, approximately 99,000,000 people.

- Spurred by the 2.4 million Asian immigrants who arrived in the United States during the 1980s, there has been an 80 per cent increase in the number of Asian Americans. Asian Americans are the fastest-growing minority group in the United States. The number of Asian Americans (which also includes Pacific Islanders) grew from 3.8 million in 1980 to an estimated 6.9 in 1989 and onwards to 9 million in 1992. Asians will continue to be the fastest-growing group, increasing from 9 million in 1992 to 41 million in 2050 (356% growth).

By 2050, "minorities" will make up just under half the United State's population. Non-hispanic whites will decrease to 53% of the population from 72% today. By 2050, the projected population of 383 million will be: 23% Hispanic, 15% black, 10% Asian, 1% Native American. In California, New York, and Florida "minorities" are already the majority.

According to Urban Institute projections, the white population (Hispanic and non-Hispanic whites) is projected to be the slowest-growing racial group during the next 60 years, increasing only 29% by 2050 (62 million after 1992). The non-Hispanic white share of the population will decline from 75% in 1992 to 53% in 2050.

The African American population will increase by 68 percent; the Asian, Pacific Islander, and Native American populations will increase by 79 percent; and the Hispanic population will increase by 187 percent. The Population Reference Bureau has forecast that by the year 2030, the USA may well be 49 percent white American, 15 percent African American, 12 percent of Asian ancestry, and 24 percent Hispanic.

Blacks, Asians and Pacific Islanders, and Hispanic Americans need to feel their participation is genuinely welcome and valued. These ethnic communities may not perceive some organizations as welcoming. The starting place is to be sure that our boards and key volunteer committees reflect the diversity of the populations we serve and wish to attract as donors. There are four key areas that not-for-profits should examine:

1. *Formal qualifications for participation.* The qualifications for participation may be exclusive or have financial/occupational restrictions. Few members of minority groups are persons of wealth. As board members, they may not be able to make large gifts. Yet if they cannot bring "wealth," they can bring "wisdom and work."

2. *An organizational inability to assess the "talent pool" of minorities.* Traditionally, not-for-profit organizations have looked for board leadership among those from the corporate sector. Many who belong to minority groups are not making it in corporate America. The problem is not simply one of racism. There are few role models, few means by which even ambitious minority members can rise. They often choose to run their own businesses because they are intimidated by lack of access to the corporate "club."

3. *A refusal to recruit aggressively.* The majority of not-for-profit organizations have not been proactive. To involve minorities, you must make an explicit commitment to increase minority participation and make special efforts to recruit members of minority groups. To find persons of color possessing the qualifications you desire in a board volunteer, you must seek out networking opportunities at professional meetings and social and church events. For example:

- *Make direct contact with minority communities.* Demonstrate your respect for the diversity within your local Black, Hispanic, and Asian communities by participating in or cosponsoring festivals and celebrations. Festivals, fairs, and other community events draw large crowds and provide an ideal opportunity to build awareness for your organization.
- *Recruit one on one.* Regularly make use of alternative media and community-based organizations for identification of up-and-coming minority group members. Some of the national ethnically targeted magazines regularly run articles with biographical information on upwardly mobile men and women in a variety of communities. Several publications present yearly lists of individuals who are doing well in a variety of occupational areas. Most have regular features, such as a newsmakers column, that list accomplishments and promotions.

Who's Who Among Hispanic Americans is a biographical guide listing more than 5,000 prominent Hispanics. The book includes geographic, occupation, and ethnic/cultural heritage indexes. *The Asian Americans Information Directory* lists more than 5,200 resources concerned with Asian American life and culture. Listing more than 7,500 minority organizations and covering all minority groups, *Minority Organizations: A National Directory* is the largest single sourcebook on the subject. National publications such as *Minority Business Entrepreneur, Hispanic, Hispanic Business, Minorities and Women in Business,* as well as your local media, are good sources as well.

You can also seek out executive recruitment, search, and professional organizations that specialize in minority job placement. *Black Enterprise* publishes a yearly list of black-owned executive recruitment firms. The Black and Hispanic National MBA Associations provide a national network of business executives working in a broad variety of industries.

Once you have found an individual who interests your organization, write or call. Refer to the article or listing that caught your attention so that the potential candidate knows you proactively reach into his or her community. Be careful, however, not to insult the individual by making race or ethnic background the sole criterion for your interest in him or her; explain what qualities you think he or she will contribute to the board as a successful businessperson or community leader. Although a person's ability to contribute to the diversity of viewpoints is also a valid recruitment aim, it should never be the only reason.

4. *Cultural insensitivity.* Cultural differences make recruitment of minority members difficult for nonminority management. Organizations often fail to recognize:

- Stereotypes and their associated assumptions
- Actual cultural differences
- The exclusivity of the "white male club" and its associated access to important information and relationships
- The unwritten rules and double standards for success that are often unknown to women and members of minority groups
- A lack of communication about differences

Those who truly understand "the changing face of America" must demonstrate that that they value diversity. Organizations must show by their actions that they understand and appreciate that individuals are different and that such differences are not simply to be tolerated but must be encouraged, supported, and nurtured.

15.5　How Can Fund Raisers Use Demographic and Psychographic Information?

Remember, "when the paradigm shifts, everyone goes back to zero." No matter how successful you have been, you must change your methodologies or lose ground. Because audiences have diversified, you must differentiate between donors by generational triggers, life stage and lifestyle, and cultural and ethnic backgrounds.

For example, different life experiences mean that fund raisers and prospects may lack common life "triggers." Our philanthropic personalities and our attitudes toward money will not be the same. Moreover, fund raisers will need to do more "intergenerational" selling. People in their 50s and older tend to be cash payers, distrusting newer technologies. They tend to listen to society's recommendations and like to support traditional, well-established charities. Younger people are likely to look for more "personal" charities and to dislike workplace giving. They may be more participatory in style, supporting only those organizations with which they actively work. They grew up budgeting for purchases and are apt to use newer technologies. Fund raisers can use demographic and psychographic profiles to meet the challenges of matching audiences with fund raising messages.

Because people are living longer:

- *Concentrate on renewal and upgrading donors rather than acquisition of new prospects.* Research has shown that it takes five times as much work to attract a new customer (donor) as to renew and upgrade an existing one. Because of their increasing longevity, the donors you attract at age 40 can continue to give, year after year, for 30, 40, 50 or more years.
- *Concentrate on planned giving rather than current sacrificial (major) giving.* It takes about 15 years for our perceptions to catch up with reality. Right now, most adults do not understand their own increasing longevity. But soon they will, and with this understanding, their willingness to part with assets during their lifetime will decrease.

Because the majority of adults were born after World War II:

- $100 is a meaningful level of giving. Whereas prewar and World War II generations tend to believe that $25 is a meaningful gift, boomers and younger adults believe it takes $100 to make a difference. As there are more adults who were born after World War II than before, make sure your message fits the larger audience.
- There is less donor loyalty. Having grown up in a world where they were always in competition for resources and recognition, middle-age and younger adults tend to be less forgiving of poor service, mistakes made by an organization, and being taken for granted. There is no second chance with these donors and prospects. You must constantly recultivate. For the rest of this decade, savvy development officers will view the mature market as one "in transition" and will work both to engage the more traditional audience and to build for the future.

The years ahead will be challenging ones for not-for-profits. By studying the demographic and psychographic information available on our changing populations, fund raisers will be able to increase their opportunities for fund-raising success.

Suggested Readings

Dychtwald, Ken, with Joe Flower. *Agewave.* Los Angeles: Tarcher, 1988.
Jones, Landony. *Great Expectations: America and the Baby Boom Generation.* New York: Ballantine, 1980.

Joseph, James A. *Remaking America*. San Francisco: Jossey-Bass, 1995.

Murdock, Steven H. *An America Challenged*. Bolder, Colo.: Westview Press, 1995.

Piirto, Rebecca. *Beyond Mind Games: The Marketing Power of Psychographics*. Ithaca, N.Y.: American Demographics Books, 1991.

Roberts, Sam. *Who We Are: A Portrait of America*. New York: Times Books, 1993.

Russell, Cheryl. *The Master Trend: How the Baby Boom Generation Is Remaking America*. New York: Plenum Press, 1993.

Smith, Bradford, et al. *Ethnic Philanthropy*. San Francisco: University of San Francisco Press, 1994.

Strauss, William, and Neil Howe. *Generations: The History of America's Future, 1584 to 2069*. New York: William Morrow & Company, 1991.

Wolfe, David B. *Marketing to Boomers and Beyond*. New York: McGraw-Hill, 1993.

Wong, Angi Ma. *Target: The U.S. Asian Market*. Palos Verdes, Calif.: Pacific Heritage Books, 1994.

Why Do People Donate to Charity?

Douglas E. White
Kaspick & Co

16.1 Introduction

Why do people donate to charity? Simple question. Complex answer. Would that this chapter were entitled "The Tax Benefits of Establishing a Charitable Remainder Trust" or "Why People Should Consider Donating Retirement Assets to Charity at Their Death." Although mathematically much more quantifiable, the answers to these questions pale against the powerful complexity of human emotions underlying the *why* of giving away money.

Often we hear about tax benefits. Peruse the literature sent to donors; the words read something like this: "You can give away a dollar and spend only 60 cents in your 40 percent tax bracket. That's a savings of 40 cents." Thus charity is helped through government intervention, the largest matching company in the United States. No money, of course, is actually saved; the donor still parts with 60 cents. What is true and exciting, though, about the federal income tax system's deduction structure is that the charity is helped by an amount greater than the donor spends, the result of a tax code at once sympathetic to the needs of charities, yet realistic about its own inability to help them directly.

In almost every study conducted on the motives behind philanthropy, donors have ranked tax savings at or near the bottom of a priority list of reasons they give away money. Thus, listing for a donor the tax reasons for making a gift is, if not an exercise in futility, at least a process of upending priorities.

16.2 Culture of Expectation

In a counterintuitive way, the mechanical processes of fund raising have done their part to divert our attention from the question of why people donate money to charity. The telethon, for example, is a popular fund-raising device. Development office employees may from time to time throughout the year visit a site where volunteers gather to make telephone calls to their friends and others to ask for money. "This year our annual fund goal is $200,000," one caller might say. "We're hoping to build a new wing for . . ." or "We'll be using the money to hire 10 additional nurse's aides . . ." The request comes quickly: "So, for how much can I put you down?" The caller listens to the response, and, when it is positive, replies, "Thank you very much for your generosity again this year. We'll send you a card confirming your gift, and we'd appreciate your prompt attention." This is a mechanical but effective process. Often the conversation is cheery, as it should be; the caller records the results of the solicitation and is then on to the next prospect. The hubbub of the routine is striking in that those involved are often removed from asking the fundamental question: *Why* do these people give? They—both the development office staff and, often, the volunteers of the moment—come to expect, as unconsciously as a server expects a tip, the money to be raised.

Charities all over the world routinely deal with the matter of raising money. Whether at a prestigious well-endowed university or a small community-based service organization, the palms are out and people give. Some organizations raise more money than others; rarely is it ever enough, despite the successes and gains over prior years, to cover its intended uses. Those who work in charitable organizations are quickly caught up in the activity of raising money, whether the process involves sending a letter of appeal or visiting a prospect or, for complicated gifts, visiting with a prospect's advisors. Even many organizations with only modest budgets have development offices with one person, and often more, whose sole responsibility is to raise money.

The development office begins its day much like any other office: Coffee is made, computers are turned on, mail is opened, a letter is drafted, and phone calls are placed and accepted. Unique to development offices, however, the mail often brings new delights: checks from those already solicited, from those who wish to support the organization. Often the person who opens the envelopes records the gifts in a computer database and then sends a summary of the day's intake to the person responsible for the program. The thank-you letters have already been generated by computer by the time anyone pauses to think about what has happened. This system is not bad; actually, it is necessary for an efficient fund-raising office. But the joy of accepting a check is often lost to the mechanical routine.

Why do people give away their money? Who knows? And most of the time during the day's activities, who cares? Those who work in the not-for-profit community routinely raising money can easily forget what an extraordinary concept giving away money is. In a world where annual fund goals reach new highs each year, and the largest capital gift at one charity seems to better the largest at another charity only a short time ago, those who work in the philanthropic community tend to harden themselves to the extraordinary miracle of giving. Yet that it takes place many times every day should not diminish the miracle.

Consider this from the donor's perspective. Most people work so they can earn an income to pay their bills and provide a satisfying lifestyle for themselves and their families. Those with mortgages or children to educate must look at their incomes with a protectiveness that puts the idea of giving away money at or near the bottom of any list of priorities. Even those who earn or already possess more than they need—a rare concept—usually think first of saving their money for a variety of reasons: anticipated future expenses, emergencies, retirement, or just the comforting thought that they own a growing base of assets. In a society where the goals of home ownership and the growth of capital is almost a ritual of citizenship, giving away money certainly is not an easy idea to grasp. Even those who know they do not need all their money do not usually leap to the conclusion that they should give it away to charity.

Yet Americans give away more dollars and a greater percentage of their incomes than people in any other country. They also continue to increase their giving. According to the 2000 edition of *Giving USA*, an annual study conducted by the American Association of Fund-Raising Counsel (AAFRC) Trust for Philanthropy, corporations, foundations, and individuals gave $190 billion to American charities in 1999, $15 billion more than in the previous year. With statistics like that, no wonder fund raisers have come to assume so much. The culture of expectation distances them from asking why this happens. The fund-raising environment does much to dissolve the appreciation of miracles.

16.3　Humanity Inherent in Charitable Giving

The answer to why people support charity is complex. The question itself—Why do people donate to charity?—sounds simple, but it belies the difficulty of the answer, an answer so elusive it defies research. Studies and surveys have occasionally been conducted, and the results yield a list of reasons that people give to charity. On those lists, the tax advantages are almost never at or even near the top. Instead, the donor's relationship to an organization or its mission is more prominent. In addition, more important than tax incentives are the organization's needs (but be careful: too needy an organization may receive little; the donor must know that the money will be spent productively); the value of the charity to its constituency; and a sense of history and continuity, a measure for many to gauge the charity's ability to provide services in the future. A charity that effectively communicates its societal purpose will do well in its fundraising efforts.

Such studies, however, convey only the statistical side of our wonderful and deeply human profession. They cannot convey the heart and soul of why people give to charity. A statistical analysis is valid for many purposes, and much can be learned from it, but the most convincing arguments are to be found at the kitchen table or in the donor's office. Ultimately, to truly convey the idea of philanthropy, the question must be answered by the anecdotal, by what is told by a donor, for inherent in the answer is the humanity that cannot be captured through statistical analysis.

(A)   CHARLIE'S GIFT

In 1988 Charlie gave $50,000 to his favorite charity, Phillips Exeter Academy, the well-known independent college preparatory school in New Hampshire he attended from 1946 to 1949. After talking with the director of capital giving at Exeter, Charlie established a charitable remainder unitrust, a gift that would pay him and his wife an income of 6 percent of the asset's value for the rest of their lives. In 1994 he added $10,000 to the unitrust. So far he has given away $60,000 in major gifts—all to a charitable remainder trust—and he plans to make more significant gifts. This is in addition to the many annual gifts he has made to Exeter over the last several decades and those he has made to several other charities during his lifetime.

"I remember sitting at a meeting in New York in 1988," he recalled. "It was one of those prereunion meetings where the class leadership gather to discuss who can contribute to next year's fortieth reunion campaign. As we were going through the list, I wondered what they would have asked of me; that is, if I didn't happen to be in the room. Here we were, looking through a list of my classmates and talking about this person giving $100,000, and that person giving $500,000. We pegged one individual at $1 million. Imagine that—a million dollars. But the guys around the table were serious, and, as I recall, everybody who was asked for a large gift gave one. They didn't all give what they were asked, of course, and the million-dollar guy, I think he ended up giving only $500,000. We were pretty successful that year, breaking the fortieth-year reunion record. As I think about it now, years later, that was pretty bold on our part, asking so much from one person. But he gave, and he gave a lot." Charlie, as he said the words, softened his timbre in reflection. Then, as if to convince himself, he repeated the figure: "A half-million dollars."

Charlie then described how he decided to make his own gift. "That was the first time I even thought about making a gift myself, at least larger than the relatively small annual checks I'd been sending over the years." Charlie's annual support had grown to a few hundred dollars in recent years. "I went home to think about it some more, and then I called the director of capital giving at Exeter and he sent me some information about the various ways to give. Then, when he was in New York, he stopped by to discuss the idea. Before he left, I knew what I was going to do. All he did was get me to think about the options, and then he helped me realize which one would be best for me. His assistance was undoubtedly helpful, but I already knew I wanted to make a major contribution. At least for me." Charlie was the president of his class at the time and had spent several years as part of the class leadership. He was a dedicated and active volunteer, and that participation was instrumental in his decision to make the gift. "After all, I knew all about the place."

Knowing all about the place helps. How many times do charities try to convert a person into a donor without doing the requisite work to win the donor's heart, without a home for that heart's strings? Although Charlie will talk about the taxes he saved and the income he's earned, the first chapter of the story of that gift—major for him—was written 40 years earlier. The first sentence may have been written on the day Charlie, as a young boy of 12, first saw the campus of the imposing private school, where minds such as those of Daniel Webster (statesman), Gore Vidal (author), and John Heinz and Jay Rockefeller (senators), along with many others', were improved. "It was hell," he said in a way that makes hell sound not so bad. "But it was the best experience of my life.

They made me work like I never worked before. I had to be responsible. I had to grow up fast. Because I was only 12, the other kids took advantage of me, made me do things—their chores and such—and teased me a lot. But those were great learning years, nevertheless. After I left there, college was a breeze." Charlie enrolled at the age of 16 at a prestigious university, a few years later a member of the newly formed Ivy League, but he felt his college experience was not as challenging. "As a result I don't have the same feelings about my college as I do about Exeter." Charlie's feelings about the organization he supports most were born many years before the gift was made.

But the feelings had to be nourished as time passed. Although Charlie's memories of his experiences were extremely positive, his continued loyalty required more than mere memories. Exeter, like almost any educational organization, was not passive. In 1970, against the wishes of many influential alumni, the trustees made a historic decision to accept women. "I was against Exeter going coed," Charlie recalled. "With the Vietnam War in full stride and civil strife at new heights, the late 1960s and early '70s were rough on everything and everybody in the country, but it seems that places like Exeter and the colleges and universities took the brunt of the revolts. Nothing came out the same after. I'm a pretty conservative guy, and feel—I still feel—that there should be boys' schools as well as schools for girls. I'm not against coeducation per se, but I thought that part of what made Exeter great was the fact that it was single sex." Yet the relationship between Charlie and Exeter did not die or even lessen.

"Even though I was dead set against the idea, they kept me informed as to their reasons," he said. "I felt they respected me. And back then, I wasn't really as active as I am now. To them I was just another alumnus who happened to support the annual fund. They had plenty of those guys. I was nothing more than that, yet they wrote to me and answered my phone calls whenever I had a question. Look, there were plenty of alumni who were much more influential than I who were against coeducation; if they couldn't keep the place single sex, how could I have had any influence? But they always listened. I was impressed by that." In other words they cultivated Charlie. "They" were the people in the administration, including the school's principal, and every one of them had respect for the alumni. The same continues to be true today. Respect is the backbone of cultivation.

Charlie will gladly explain that he used highly appreciated stocks to fund the gift. Because the gift was a charitable remainder unitrust, from which he and his wife will receive an income for the rest of their lives, he wanted to use those stocks that also paid the least before the gift was made. "That way I got two benefits: one, I avoided the tax on the capital gain, and two, I increased my income from the assets. I was receiving about 2 or 3 percent for the stocks beforehand, and I've been receiving 6 percent ever since." Not bad—and his words do as much as those found in any brochure to describe the economic advantages of establishing a charitable remainder unitrust. It is strange how donors are better than professional brochure writers at explaining these matters in words that convey real meaning. "But don't get me wrong. Sure, we made certain that the tax and income benefits would be to the greatest advantage, but none of that would have meant a hill of beans if I didn't care about the place. I mean, I still haven't done the same thing for my college, and they can provide the same gift benefits as Exeter."

At the time, a specific aspect of the tax environment was relevant and, although it did not, could have created a problem. Charlie made his gift in 1988, when the tax law designated the appreciated portion of charitable gifts as a preference item in computing the alternative minimum tax (AMT). This provision, which was in effect from 1987 until its repeal in 1993, effectively prevented many gifts from being made to charitable organizations. That so many aborted gifts were documented, most notably at museums, so broadly affected the charitable community that political pressure eventually led to its repeal. This was a good result, because the tax code had unfairly discouraged charitable giving.

What is not widely known, however, is that despite the many complaints, the AMT did not play as large a role in the financial affairs of donors as was commonly believed. That is, many donors, despite the AMT provision, were not subject to the AMT even when making gifts of appreciated property. Charlie was clearly in a minority whose legal and financial counsel thoroughly examined the impact of a gift of appreciated property. The examination found that despite the high appreciation of approximately 90 percent of the gift, the AMT would not apply in his situation. Thus, to Charlie's credit and that of Exeter, he made his gift and was able to deduct the full fair market value of the remainder interest in his gift. "Oh, yes, I know all about the AMT," Charlie said. "Exeter pointed out that it might have an impact on my gift, but they said I should look at some of the numbers and that I needed to talk to my advisors. I looked at the numbers and talked to my advisors and they all added up to the same thing: the AMT did not affect the deduction of my gift. It was irrelevant, at least in my situation." Then he added, "But even if it did have an impact, I still would have made my gift. After all, it was our fortieth reunion."

This story is not about Exeter, of course. It is about giving. Exeter is just one of more than a half million charitable organizations in the United States that can accept tax-deductible gifts. Although the school does a good job at fulfilling its educational mission, Exeter is not unique in its ability to raise money and cultivate donors. Charlie is active in other charities, and not all of Exeter's alumni feel the same way Charlie does about the school. Many of those alumni have chosen to spend their time and donate their money for other charities. Such charities include colleges and universities, hospitals, mental health centers, community centers, churches and synagogues, museums, and many other organizations, large and small, that take part in the largest effort of private support for the public good in the world. Exeter is only the forum here, an example to display the larger issue: the reasons people donate to charity.

An examination of Charlie's story reveals a great deal about the ingredients of a successful gift.

(B) INITIAL EXPERIENCE

Charlie's first experiences with Exeter were, at least in retrospect, positive. Think of the doctor or the medical assistant who treats you without respect during your first hospital visit. Although an examination conducted for a head injury may be routine to the specialist, it is not so routine for the patient. If the doctor appears indifferent to the patient's plight, the patient will not have fond memories (assuming the injuries heal sufficiently to allow memories). Initial impressions are always important, even if they are modified by later experiences. Many impressions are not modified, of course, but are instead confirmed by later experiences. Although many prospective donors identify themselves voluntarily to a charity—as docents at art museums or ushers at religious services, for example—the charity cannot make the assumption that the person is not worthy of respect from the outset.

Think back to when you first met a friend. Then, not knowing how the relationship would evolve, you were equipped to act only with what experience and training taught you about dealing with strangers. All representatives of charities, not just those employed in the development office, must be aware that at any time they could be speaking with a person who is not only a potential future user of services but a provider of resources as well. Even the janitors at Exeter are helpful to strangers wandering the halls of the academic buildings.

(C) CULTIVATION

As the *Giving USA* statistics indicate, fund raising has become a huge business. While headlines announce the cutback of government finances to assist charitable organizations and the cost of providing services escalates, fund raising is becoming an increasingly important component of balancing a not-for-profit's budget. University presidents, only a few years ago primarily academicians, today find themselves embroiled in the fund-raising activities of their development offices. Executive directors of environmental organizations are reluctantly taught by their fund raisers that they must often consign pollution or species extinction to a secondary priority. Many small charities, historically unused to broad annual solicitations and sophisticated capital campaigns, find themselves forced to rely more heavily than ever before on the generosity of the communities they serve. As periodicals, newsletters, and books announce the need for more and better fund raising, the idea that money can be acquired simply by employing formulaic strategies distorts the idea of how raising money should be conducted. Such formulas and strategies are important, of course, but they can be effective only in the context of mission and understanding prospective donors.

In the flurry of fund-raising activity, the human relationship is often lost. Partly because society seems to give more importance to what is instant than to what is valuable, the notion that an organization must take time, often many years, to win a person's loyalty is losing ground. But without a relationship, which is to say, at least in part, cultivation, how can a charity claim the right to ask for a gift of any size? To think that fund raising will succeed merely by identifying a person who has the financial means, but without establishing a relationship is absurd. Charlie had a long relationship with Exeter before he made a major gift.

Further, the relationship between Charlie and Exeter was neither self-perpetuating nor one-sided. Charities must be realistic in assessing a person's interest. A charity can do only so much cultivating; if a person is not interested, nothing can force him or her to support the organization. Charlie expressed his interest in and shared his opinions about Exeter's future. Although they at times differed with the school's, those opinions were an important measure of his interest. No charity can expect to please all of its supporters all the time; if it tried, the mission would be lost to the ambiguity of the masses. Just look at political campaigns to see the results of efforts to please everyone.

A charity must stay true to its purposes, and donors must realize that they cannot mandate changes simply because they support the organization. Colleges and universities whose admissions policies are challenged or modified by donors lose more in integrity than they can ever gain with money. This may be hard to grasp in the moment of the financial offer, but it is true and always will be. After the dimwitted daughter is accepted, what other situation will arise in the future when an alumnus can wield his financial influence? Although providing charitable services cannot always be absolutely and fully impartial—the donor who receives an advance viewing of the Monet, preferred tickets at the opera, reduced bureaucracy at the hospital admissions desk, a private visit with the pope—how many manipulative donors does it take to tarnish an ideal? A donor who tries to steer a charity's course from his pocketbook is pathetic. Allowing the donor to do so is even worse. Thus, although an ongoing relationship is part of the reason people support charity, it must be a healthy relationship.

16.4 *Financial Ability and Donative Intent*

Of course, in order to give, no matter how strong the relationship, one must have the means to give. Although Charlie spent his life managing money, in the 1950s that profession did not have the same potential for immediate financial success as many think it does today. Although he made modest annual gifts, Charlie did not have the means in his early years to support Exeter or any other charity substantially. Charlie's story is partly one of assessing his own ability to make a major gift.

But wait. When we speak of charitable support—why people give money to charity—does that support have to be significant to count? Furthermore, how much is "significant"? We sometimes trap ourselves into thinking that the only people who matter in the halls of development are those who can make $100,000 or $1 million gifts. KQED, the public television station in San Francisco, reported in a 1996 pledge break that its average annual gift—and therefore of meaningful size to the station—was $48. Forty-eight dollars—this is about the price of a dinner for two at most restaurants in the country; in San Francisco it buys less. Not everyone in the San Francisco area, however, gives to its public television station or to any other charity. To many, a dinner is often more palatable than giving away money, even if it has less beneficial effect on society.

The $50,000 gift that Charlie made in 1988 was significant by any measure, of course, but the ability to give is relative. Think of a graph that measures the size of donations against income. Certainly, at the $48 level, not much extra income is required; at the $100,000, a much greater ability to give is required. Thus, the lower gift levels require less ability, which, ironically (not measured in the graph), may be a better measure of a person's charitable intent. That such a gift is made or not made is hardly a question of ability, but one of being connected to a charity's mission. The larger gift, because it is so much more a separation from money, is clearly meaningful both in terms of ability to give and donative intent. Clearly, an ability to give is a prerequisite to giving, but because giving can be at any level, donative intent is one ingredient that crosses all levels of giving.

16.5 *Timing*

At the time of his meeting in New York, Charlie was approaching an important milestone in his relationship with Exeter. Until that time, even though he had fond memories of his school days, he had never considered making such a substantial gift. He had made small annual gifts, used to defray operating expenses, but no capital gifts, either to the endowment or for the purchase of a building, nothing that could be considered a major gift. In addition, he was, in effect, asked to give. Charlie was at the table where his classmates were being rated on their ability and willingness to make reunion gifts. The only reason he was not asked directly was that he was present at the meeting. He knew better than to wait. Many of Charlie's classmates who were not at the meeting, those who had the means to make a gift, did make a gift when they were asked. How many people do not make a gift because they are not asked? Too many. Several points converged when Charlie made his gift: His relationship was strong; he was approaching a reunion, a moment when alumni are expected to reflect on their giving histories; and he was able. The timing was right.

Yet donors are sometimes asked to give when they are unable, or at least unprepared given their circumstances. Not all capital campaigns, when most significant gifts are made, conveniently coincide with a donor's financial trajectory. Not many donors wait to dispose of their businesses until their favorite charity is ready to count the gift in a major fund-raising effort. Exeter, perhaps realizing this—perhaps employing the customer-service theory of business to its not-for-profit persona—has not had a major capital campaign since its bicentennial celebration in 1981. Since then the school has continued to raise substantial amounts of money, but in the context of more regular events, such as reunions, which allow Exeter to acknowledge gifts when donors are most prepared to make them. Charlie's gift was connected to a reunion. His own situation did not require the sale of a business or the inheritance of a relative's fortune. Most gifts, especially major gifts, are made when donors are prepared to make them, not when charities are most prepared to accept or celebrate them.

16.6 Good Professional Advice

In making gifts, legal and other professional advice is often required, and not only for deferred gifts such as Charlie's. In fact, many current gifts are planned. Anyone who makes a gift that requires thinking about the effects on income taxes, family members, future estate distributions, business growth, or other philanthropic gifts is making a planned gift. (Deferred giving, in which the gift's benefit to the charity is deferred, is a subdivision of planned giving.) Despite the many jokes wafting through fund-raising conventions, most planned gifts are all the better when they result from competent financial and legal advice.

Charities can go only so far on this point. The credible development professional will know much about the technical intricacies surrounding the effects of making a gift, but the donor needs his or her own advisor. Charlie received his own advice and made his gift with confidence that all was well, both financially and legally. Donors who make gifts without their own professional advice make gifts at their peril; similarly, charities that accept gifts from donors who forego their own paid-for counsel are in danger of becoming subject to legal action, not only by the donor but also by disgruntled relatives. Nothing brings out long-lost heirs more quickly than the scent of money. That a charity is the recipient of that money is not a deterrent. The most well-known example is a 1994 lawsuit in Texas, the legal action brought by the disgruntled heir of a woman who had established several gifts to benefit the Lutheran Church. The sting of that assault, which eventually targeted almost 2,000 charities throughout the United States, was assuaged, if not fully remedied, by nothing less than an act of Congress. Of late charities have become popular targets.

Charities must realize—and respect—that donors' advisors play a role that often opposes a charity's efforts: The charity tries to convince a person to give away assets, and an attorney's or accountant's job is to protect those assets. The battle lines are clearly drawn. Despite much whining heard from development offices, however, this is not only natural, but proper. If an attorney did not ask the hard questions, she would not be doing her job: "I know you'll increase your income and save capital gains taxes, but do you realize that you will no longer own this asset?" "Do you realize that your children will not receive these assets?" "Do you realize you could name the charity in your will and retain control over how the assets are invested?"

Unfortunately, much of the marketing material distributed by charities not only fails to address these questions, but goes a long way to ignore the issues. A sign along a California highway declares: "Donate your old car and receive a tax deduction." The person answering a call to the toll-free number under the words on the sign reveals that the deductible amount is equal to the car's original value. This, when the car's deductible value, assuming the donor itemizes gifts on his income tax return, is the lower trade-in value. Because the IRS is interested only in the taxpayer's accountability, the potential car donor would be wise to acquire the advice of an attorney or an accountant, who would say that the information received was wrong.

Advice has, or should have, its limits. An advisor is hired to help execute a decision. The advisor is not the *decision maker*. An individual's decision to help a charity can and should be his or her own. Thus, if a person talks with a charity about a gift, the idea of making the gift rests best in the bosom of the donor; in addition to asking questions about the gift that the donor may not have considered, an advisor should also explain how best to accomplish the objective of making the gift. This is where many advisors, despite their paid obligation to protect the donor's assets, get it wrong. The way a charity can best combat this problem is to prepare the donor with the technique of making a gift and how the money will be spent, either immediately if it is an outright gift, or eventually if it is a deferred gift. The charity must connect the donor to the eventual good works of the gift. The more donors know about how the gift is to be made, the better prepared they will be when they visit—as they must—their advisors.

The capital giving director at Exeter was able to advise Charlie in the technique and potential consequences of the gift. This information, along with his relationship to the school, helped Charlie approach his advisors. They, to their credit, did not try to dissuade him from making the gift. They did, however, also to their credit, alert Charlie to the potential alternative minimum tax problem and to several other financial consequences of making the gift. They then worked with Charlie and Exeter until the gift was complete.

16.7   Tax and Income Benefits

Although tax benefits do not drive most gift decisions, and certainly no truly eleemosynary gift decisions, only the naive planner would ignore the effects of taxes on the mechanics of structuring the gift. After all, Congress provides deductions for charitable gifts; charitable deductions and the provisions in the tax code defining deferred gifts are not loopholes. The gift decision should be made for charitable reasons—to support the mission of the organization—but once that decision is made, the gift should provide the greatest tax advantage legally available to the donor. Income, capital gains, gift and estate, and generation-skipping transfer taxes should all be considered when a gift is made.

(A)　INCOME TAX DEDUCTION

An income tax deduction reduces tax on income. Although the most common deduction is the interest paid on home mortgages, the charitable income tax deduction is also popular. For donors who do not itemize, no income tax deduction is currently available for charitable gifts. This may change in the future (and for a few years in the mid-1980s, non-itemizers could deduct an amount up to a certain dollar limit), but right now those who do not complete Internal Revenue Service (IRS) Form Schedule A cannot deduct their gifts to charity. Thus, a charitable gift yields no tax benefit for a nonitemizer, no matter in what income tax bracket a donor is or how large the gift.

Large gifts—those of more than approximately $5,000, and certainly those that are larger than the standard deduction, the amount automatically deducted from income before an income tax is calculated—are often made by those who do itemize, however, and only the foolish person would fail to declare a deduction for such charitable gifts. This does not mean that small gifts are too small to deduct; the mortgage deduction allows most of those who itemize to take tax advantage of their charitable gifts. Approximately 20 percent of all taxpayers itemize, and those people may deduct their charitable gifts. Still, for those who earn more than $100,000 (adjusted upward for inflation each year), deductions are reduced by 3 percent, another misguided attempt by Congress to deny legitimate deductions.

(B)　CAPITAL GAINS TAX AVOIDANCE

A capital gain is the amount an asset's value increases. Stock purchased 10 years ago for $1,000 and sold today for $10,000 has a capital gain of $9,000. Under current law, when the asset is held for more than a year, the owner of the asset pays a reduced tax on its appreciation when the asset is sold. (Appreciated assets held for less than a year generate ordinary income tax, the highest level of tax.) Although a capital gains tax is often less than ordinary income tax, it is still a tax that many people prefer to avoid if they are able. When donors make a noncash gift that has grown in value, such as publicly traded stock, they avoid paying a capital gains tax on the transfer to charity. (By the way, although fund raisers often distinguish between income tax and capital gains tax, a capital gains tax is an income tax.) A person who donates stock valued at $10,000, which cost $1,000 many years ago, can give away that stock without incurring a tax on the growth. Thus, charity benefits by $10,000 with an asset that cost the donor only one-tenth its value. The sense of this standard may seem obvious, but from 1987 to 1993, many people were not allowed to deduct the appreciated portion of a property gift. That amount was a preference item in calculating the alternative minimum tax. Not only did charities receive fewer gifts during that time because of the AMT problem, but there was no economic argument to support the measure. (Not much was gained in new tax revenue by the government.) Some taxpayers were affected by this ruling (and many more were scared away by the prospect) and could not deduct the entire amount of the gift, even though charity received the entire amount. Fortunately, this is no longer true. Moreover, and not incidentally, charity benefits in full from the gift.

However, fund raisers must remember that the deduction does not mean the donor saves money. The donor still parts with the difference between the amount of the gift and the tax savings. Unless the tax code ever allows for a deduction of more than 100 percent, the donor will always pay to be charitable.

(C) ESTATE TAX DEDUCTION

For estates of more than a certain size, an estate tax is imposed on the right to transfer assets at death. Donors may save estate taxes when they make charitable gifts. Similar to the way donors must itemize to save income taxes when they make a lifetime gift, a donor must have a taxable estate to save estate taxes for gifts made at death. Currently, a taxable estate is one with assets whose value plus prior lifetime taxable gifts exceeds $600,000. If a donor leaves to charity $100,000 in a will, the estate will receive a corresponding deduction. The value of the deduction, as with an income tax deduction, depends on the estate tax bracket of the decedent. Estate tax rates currently range from a low of 37 percent for estates of more than $600,000 to a high of 55 percent for estates of more than $3,000,000. At the 55 percent bracket, a person saves $55,000 on a $100,000 gift to charity. However, the donor still pays $45,000 in taxes.

A gift tax is similar to an estate tax and is often a consideration in making charitable gifts. It, too, is a tax on the right to transfer assets. The difference is that a gift tax is imposed on *lifetime* transfers. Most people never pay a gift tax even though a gift may be large (exceeding the current $10,000 annual exclusion for outright gifts), because it draws from the same tax credit applied to the $600,000 amount that the estate has at death. This means that taxable gifts made during life reduce the $600,000 available at death. Gifts to charity, however, are excluded from gift tax consideration. No matter the size of a charitable gift, assuming the gift is properly made, a donor does not pay a tax on the gift.

(D) GENERATION-SKIPPING TRANSFER TAX AVOIDANCE

People who make gifts during life or at death to their grandchildren pay a transfer tax in addition to the estate tax. The generation-skipping transfer (GST) tax prevents people from avoiding an estate tax by skipping a generation when transferring assets to family members. Congress effectively taxes twice, although at the same time, transfers that skip a generation, such as gifts from a grandparent to a grandchild. The result is not positive for the grandchild.

A $10 million estate taxed at 50 percent would be reduced to $5 million when assets are transferred to children. Then, assuming no growth (this is a simplified example, in both growth and tax bracket assumptions), the children's assets, taxed at 50 percent, would provide $2.5 million for their children. To avoid the middle generation's tax, some people used to make transfers to grandchildren, either during life or at death, simply skipping the middle generation. (The children were not disinherited, however; often they had access to the asset's income, but not to the asset itself.) The goal of saving $2.5 million in taxes by giving $5 million to the grandchildren is defeated by the GST tax.

(E) TAX CONSIDERATIONS ARE IMPORTANT

Charlie's gift was not the largest that Exeter had ever received, but all of the taxes previously described, except for the GST tax (he has no grandchildren), were either reduced or eliminated when he made his gift. As described earlier, in a healthy transaction tax savings do not give birth to or dominate a gift decision, but once a person has decided to be charitable, they certainly need to be considered. Considering tax advantages thoroughly and properly, however, is not an easy process. Many large gifts for which tax savings are a consideration are the result of the detailed efforts of the charity's development staff, the donor's advisor, and, of course, the donor.

16.8 Need

Often a charity will tell its donors that it needs money for a specific purpose: a new building, more scholarships, the operating budget, a new program. Although these are all worthy objectives, there is a line between asking donors to support a financially healthy need and begging for money to enable a charity to stay in business. Charities should be careful not to cross this line. Donors are suspect when they are asked to support a cause that may fail. Large, well-endowed charities (you know them) do not run the risk of asking for money in the context of survival, but many others do have that problem. Even those whose existence is not threatened too frequently sound desperate, rather than healthy. A donor will want to invest in a charity's future only if he or she knows the charity has a future.

To Charlie, the health of the institution was not an issue. He knew Exeter intimately through a lifelong association with the school, and he knew it would thrive; he was concerned about what its future would look like, perhaps, but not whether the school would have a future. His gift, when it becomes available, will be placed in the general endowment. The income from the gift will be used in any manner Exeter wishes. In this respect, Charlie's gift was slightly different from most other large gifts. Donors who establish endowment funds typically designate the income from those funds to a specific purpose, such as financial aid or continuing research at a university, or for some other ongoing purpose at the charity.

16.9 Dark Side of Why People Donate

A discussion of donor motives cannot be complete without a realistic look at personal ego and guilt. This is where philanthropy confronts the act of charitable giving. Philanthropy is pure. It is defined as the "love of humankind." It evokes altruistic feelings. But not all charitable giving is philanthropic. Charitable gifts *may* be the result of philanthropy; many are, but some are not. They are, instead, the result of less than honorable intentions. The board member who responds to peer pressure to contribute to the capital campaign is an example of a gift made for reasons other than love of humanity. The person who makes a gift of ill-gotten gains—drug money or insider trading profits, for example—acts out of guilt more than out of philanthropic considerations.

Individuals who establish charitable foundations to address a personal concern often act out of self-interest. Funding the science center or the cancer wing may be as much a business decision for the corporation as it is a charitable gift. Peer pressure, guilt, self-interest, marketing—all are to a degree nonphilanthropic benefits, benefits to which the IRS, because it is not able, has not yet attached a value.

16.10   Conclusion

Despite the frequent lack of altruistic purity, good work is done in the area of charitable giving. Most actions are the result of many causal feelings and experiences, not all of which are known to be related to the action. Given how little we know of human motivations, we must appreciate and deal with what we do know: the results. Yet we are left with a question: How is philanthropy conceived? From what seed are charitable gifts born? If personal financial gain were the only consideration, no one would make charitable gifts. Social status and community recognition are hardly quid pro quos, and we have seen that tax considerations only make a gift less expensive, not cost-free. Therefore, that people make charitable gifts must mean that something else is at work.

An economic analysis does not often enough take into account noneconomic considerations. What Charlie did in 1988 might stupefy an economist. That he gave away a large sum of money—twice—boggles the quantitative mind. Understanding why people make charitable gifts requires a mind that is receptive to a complexity that encompasses more than income and tax savings. Beyond the numbers is a whole layer of feelings—the result of experiences and innate, intuitive predispositions about people and society—which we may never fully understand, that do much to help philanthropy. We may never know the root causes of philanthropy, but we can continue the quest to learn. Fund raisers need to know as much as they can about the technical aspects of the job, but they also need to realize that much of the motivation in donors will be found in the process of connecting their desires to a worthy cause. As a result of that primarily personal process, charitable organizations grow. Altruism lives; the unique charitable sector of our American society is proof of that.

Women as Philanthropists: A New Approach and a New Voice in Major Gifts

ANDREA KAMINSKI, B.S., M.S.
Women's Philanthropy Institute

17.1 Why Focus on Women as Philanthropists?

Dorothy Bryson is a colleague working for a women's program in a coeducational university. She recently sent a letter to the Women's Philanthropy Institute in which she admitted having misgivings about her role in the development profession until she understood that women donors call for a different approach from those she had learned from her colleagues. She wrote:

> *After 12 years in various student services positions, I switched career paths and accepted the position of Director of Development at the University of Tennessee. This was in 1990 and I was the first person assigned to the College of Human Ecology to develop a constituency fund-raising program. The college has an alumni base of mostly women, but only sporadic work had been done to cultivate these wonderful graduates. After about 18 months with only small returns, I began to think I had entered the wrong profession.*
>
> *Just as I was ready to prepare my resume and begin a job hunt, Martha Taylor was quoted in the* Chronicle of Philanthropy *with some of her seminal work on the topic of Women & Philanthropy. At that point I realized that maybe it wasn't me! Maybe the models I had been taught were just not quite right for the women I was approaching. It did take much longer to cultivate a woman to make a major gift. Women did want to be involved before making a significant gift. Public recognition was not a motivating factor for most of the women I saw; in fact it was often a negative.*

This chapter is dedicated to my mentors, Martha Taylor and Sondra Shaw-Hardy, who literally wrote the book.

Dorothy went on to learn all she could about women and philanthropy. She sponsored a women and philanthropy workshop for her university and eventually established the University of Tennessee Alliance for Women's Philanthropy. She attributes part of her college's current success in the university's capital campaign to the education of alumni and staff leaders around the issues we will cover in this chapter.

Philanthropy has been referred to as the last frontier of the women's movement, yet of course it is nothing new for women. As early as the thirteenth century, religious women of wealth founded hospitals and homes to assist the poor in cities across Europe.[1] Kathleen D. McCarthy traces the women's philanthropy movement in the United States back to the eighteenth century, when women were establishing charitable associations to aid the poor and promote social change. Women's contributions to these early organizations remained relatively invisible because common law doctrine prohibited women from controlling their inheritances, possessions, or earnings. "Once an organization became legally incorporated its officers were collectively empowered to sue and be sued, buy and sell property, and sign legally binding contracts—things that married women generally could not do as individuals," according to McCarthy.[2]

For the next 150 years, women contributed their voluntary time and financial resources from behind the scenes to benefit society through their work in the areas of moral and social reform, abolition of slavery, child labor reform, education, suffrage, and women's rights.

A few examples of pioneering women philanthropists in these areas include: Sojourner Truth (1797–1883), the abolitionist and Quaker missionary; Lucretia Mott (1793–1880), an abolitionist who later took up the cause of women's rights; Mary Lyon (1797–1849) and Sophia Smith (1796–1859), who were dedicated to providing an education for women equal to the best available for men; Mary McLeod Bethune (1875–1955), a teacher and advisor to presidents who with only $1.50 began a school to help educate young black women and developed it into a college; Jane Addams (1860–1935) and Madame C. J. Walker (1867–1919), who devoted their financial resources and much of their lives to social justice and improving the lives of the poor.[3]

Canada's heroes in philanthropy include: Adelaide Hoodless (1857–1910), who founded a number of women's service organizations; Mary Shadd Cary (1823–1893), who set up a school for slaves who escaped to Canada; and Marie Lacoste Gerin-Lajoie (1867–1945), who in 1907 founded an organization of French Canadian women dedicated to promoting civil and political rights of women.[4]

Indeed, women philanthropists created many of the institutions and organizations that continue to serve society today, long beyond the lives of their mortal founders. Yet until recently women's philanthropy took place behind the scenes, and it was expected only of women of great wealth.

---

[1] L. S. Moerschbaecher, "Don't You Worry Your Pretty Little Head," presentation by LMNOP Seminars and Publications, San Rafael, CA, 1996.

[2] Kathleen D. McCarthy, *Women and Philanthropy in the United States, 1790–1990*, Curriculum Guide #1 (Spring 1998), Center for the Study of Philanthropy, Graduate School and University Center, City University of New York.

[3] Sources include: Amy Alexander, *Fifty Black Women Who Changed America* (Secaucus, N.J.: Carol Publishing Group, 1999). Also the National Women's Hall of Fame Web page, "The Women of the Hall," www.greatwomen.org/grtwmn.htm.

[4] National Library of Canada/Bibliotheque Nationale du Canada Web page, "Celebrating Women's Achievements," www.nlc-bnc.ca/digiproj/women/ewomen.htm.

What has changed is that now more women

- Have more control over more money
- See their potential to apply their charitable dollars to shape the future of society

What are the facts related to women, wealth, and giving?

- There were almost 1.3 million female top wealth holders in 1992 with a combined net worth of almost $1.8 trillion. The average net worth for the group was $1.37 million, slightly higher than for male wealth holders, and the females carried less debt.[5]
- Women own 38 percent of U.S. businesses. As of 1999 there were 9.1 million women-owned firms, employing almost 28 million people and generating over $3.6 trillion in sales.[6]
- Baby boomer men (ages 35 to 49) give to six to 10 nonprofits annually, while boomer women give to fewer than five.[7]
- Boomer women give evenly to charities, public interest groups, and their places of worship. Boomer men focus on public interest groups and charities and secondarily on their churches.[8]
- There are more than 90 women's funds across the United States, up from the "original 11" created in the 1970s.[9]
- In charitable bequests, men left nearly 40 percent of their gifts to private foundations; women bequeathed less than 25 percent to such foundations.[10]
- At least $41 trillion will be passing from one generation to the next by 2044. Women outlive men by an average of 7 years.[11] It can be expected that women will determine what becomes of much of this money.

So we know that women do have money and women do give. But what do we know about *how* women give? What do we know about their philanthropic motivations and their giving behavior?

Women have the same core motivations for giving as do men—altruism, gratitude, the desire to have a positive influence on the world we will pass on to future generations. These core motivations are valid for women and men alike.

---

[5]*Statistics of Income Bulletin, 1997–1998.* Also the NFWBO Web page, Key Facts, www.nfwbo.org.
[6]*Key Facts,* National Foundation for Women Business Owners, Washington, DC, 1999.
[7]Special Report, "Toward 2000 and Beyond: Charitable and Social Change Giving in the New Millennium, Part 2, A Craver, Mathews, Smith & Company Donor Study," *Fund Raising Management,* June 1999, p. 27.
[8]*Ibid.*
[9]Capek, M. E., "Foundation Support for Women and Girls: 'Special Interest' Funding or Effective Philanthropy?" *Volume Two of the Monograph Series, Women and Philanthropy: Old Stereotypes, New Challenges,* St. Paul: Women's Funding Network, 1999, p. 22.
[10]*Statistics of Income Bulletin,* Internal Revenue Service, Summer 1999.
[11]Schervish, Paul and John Havens. "Report Reveals Significantly Higher Forecasts for Upcoming U.S. Wealth Transfer: Boston College Researchers Project Range of $41–136 Trillion in First New Wealth-Transfer Estimates Since 1990," press release, Chestnut Hill: Boston College Social Welfare Research Institute (SWRI), October 20, 1999.

However, we know from gender-based research in the areas of education, communication, management, and marketing that men and women respond to different "triggers." This is a result of our socialization in a society that has long had a double standard—in our economic, social, and power structures. As a result, women and men have different approaches to management, different communication and learning styles, and *they have a different culture of giving.*

17.2 What Do We Know about Women as Philanthropists?

(A) THE SIX Cs OF WOMEN'S GIVING

A number of studies have examined women's giving patterns through focus groups and personal interviews with hundreds of women nationally.[12] The culture of women's giving is written in the book *Reinventing Fundraising: Realizing the Potential of Women's Philanthropy,* by Sondra C. Shaw and Martha A. Taylor, cofounders of the Women's Philanthropy Institute. These authors summarize the recurring themes in their discussions with women philanthropists in six words beginning with the letter C:

(i) Create
Women often give to *create* something, as did the women philanthropists in history who created the charitable, educational, medical, and advocacy institutions and organizations that have shaped our society and continue to serve today.

In other cases, women create new programs in existing institutions, as did Lucille Puette Giles, who recently left $2 million in her estate to Randolph-Macon Women's College (Va.) to create a Global Studies Initiative in her name at the college, and Jean Manchester-Biddick, who created a Center for Excellence in Family Studies at the University of Wisconsin-Madison.

(ii) Change
Women give to bring about social *change.* Mary Elizabeth Garrett did this in 1881, when she gave $350,000 to Johns Hopkins University to establish a medical school on the condition that the medical school open its doors to women.[13] The women suffragists for decades devoted their time, their work, and their fortunes to the suffrage movement. An example is Carrie Chapman Catt, the suffragist who established the League of Women Voters.

Modern-day women philanthropists who have created a nonprofit designed to bring about change include Winsome McIntosh, Liz Sutherland, and Tjiska Van Wyk. They are the founders of Rachel's Network, named for author Rachel Carson, who challenged chemical companies for their irresponsible use of chemical pesticides. These women had noted that although women traditionally make up the majority of those

---

[12]S. C. Shaw and M. A. Taylor, *Reinventing Fundraising: Realizing the Potential of Women's Philanthropy* (San Francisco: Jossey-Bass, 1995); The UCLA Women and Philanthropy Focus Groups (Los Angeles: The UCLA Foundation, 1992 1999); *Perspectives on Women's Giving: Findings from the 1999 Focus Groups* (Los Angeles: The UCLA Foundation, 1999); M. A. Taylor, "Study on Women's Philanthropy for Health Care: St. Luke's Medical Center" Milwaukee. Women's Philanthropy Institute, 1995.
[13]Joan M. Fisher, "Celebrating the Heroines of Philanthropy," in A. I. Thompson, and A. R. Kaminski, *Women and Philanthropy: A National Agenda* (Madison: Center for Women and Philanthropy, University of Wisconsin-Madison, 1993).

who support environmental issues, they are underrepresented in decision-making roles within the conservation movement. Rachel's Network works with women funders to help them become more strategic in their philanthropy in support of the environment. It will also provide training and peer support to place women in leadership positions in environmental policy and procedures.

(iii)   Connect

The third C is connect: Women often seek a sense of personal *connection* with the program or project they fund. It was a very personal motivation—her twin sister's breast cancer—that motivated Yvonne Jackson to contribute $100,000 to Spelman College to advance women in science and medicine. She believed that if there were more women in these fields, there would be more work done on women's health.

To cultivate this sense of connection, women donors often seek continuing information after the gift has been made. They want to know:

- How money will be used
- How the project is progressing
- How it is helping people

This is consistent with the findings of a recent study by Deloitte and Touche on the personal financial management practices of affluent women.[14] In particular, the investigators were looking at what these women seek in a personal financial advisor. They found that women seek to build a close working connection or relationship with their financial advisors. "They want a provider who hires and retains high-quality personnel who will listen and custom-tailor products and services to meet their needs. They like having one person to meet with and look after their matters," says the report.

The women in the study also expressed a desire for ongoing guidance and information. "Their provider should offer both easy-to-understand statements and the latest technology for tracking account information," according to the report.

Women seek the same type of partnership with people at the institutions they fund. It is up to us to provide opportunities for these partnerships.

(iv)   Collaborate

Women like to *collaborate,* or work together as a group—in part this is why they often don't respond to competitive fund-raising appeals. Quite the opposite. Many women like to pool their gifts to make a project possible. At the University of Virginia, a group of law school alumnae had noted that the influence of women in the school's history was not apparent in the names and photographs on the walls, and they were concerned about the effect this would have on young women just entering the profession. The women lawyers pooled their gifts to fund a highly visible lobby in the law school's new wing. The names of the women who participated in the gift were announced on a wall of the lobby for young women entering the law school to see. In 2000 a group of eight anonymous alumnae pooled their contributions for a $2.2 million gift to Mary Baldwin College (VA), in honor of President Cynthia Haldenby Tyson, to establish a new endowment fund to support leadership development programs.

---

[14]*She Said: A Study of Affluent Women and Personal Finances* (Philadelphia: Deloitte & Touche, 1998), page 21.

The women's funds, women's giving circles, and women's philanthropy councils in higher education are examples of collaborative philanthropy. These programs usually engage in donor education and involvement, which build a sense of connection. A number of collaborative program models designed to encourage women as philanthropists are described later in this chapter.

The high value women place on collaboration and connection is consistent with what we have learned about women's management styles in business settings.[15] Women managers in general foster cooperation, consensus, and networking. That's how women do business.

(v) Committed

Women are *committed* to the causes they support—they want to give not only their money but also their time. According to *Independent Sector*, 62 percent of women and 49 percent of men volunteered in 1998, and volunteers make larger contributions—on average, two and a half times more.[16] Although many longtime community volunteers express concern that increased participation by women in the paid labor force will result in a diminished volunteer labor supply, these fears appear to be unfounded, according to a new study by John Wilson of Duke University and Marc Musick of the University of Texas at Austin.[17] To the contrary, the study reveals that rates of volunteering for nonprofits among younger women are higher than they were among women of the previous generation at the same age. Moreover, the researchers found that both women who work part time and women whose work weeks exceed 40 hours actually tend to volunteer more than those who work a conventional full-time schedule.

This goes back to the days when all that most women had to give was their time, and so they raised money with events. Now more women are capable of making major gifts and can have more impact on the organizations they support by doing so. It is up to the development profession to help them understand and realize that potential. At the same time, we must affirm their contributions of unpaid service and make them aware of opportunities for meaningful volunteer involvement. This is particularly important when working with individuals who came of age during the Great Depression and the world wars. That experience has shaped their outlook on sharing, service, and civic participation. For more information about generational differences, consult the books by Judith E. Nichols, CFRE.[18]

(vi) Celebrate

Finally, women like to *celebrate* their accomplishments and have fun with philanthropy. This too goes back to the days when all most women could give was their time, so they

---

[15]"Styles of Success: The Thinking and Management Styles of Women and Men Business Owners." Washington, DC: National Foundation for Women Business Owners, 1994.

[16]"Giving and Volunteering in the United States: Findings from a National Survey," Washington, DC: Independent Sector, 1999.

[17]John Wilson, and Marc Musick, "Women's Labor Force Participation and Volunteer Work," Nonprofit Sector Research Fund of The Aspen Institute, www.nonprofitresearch.org/newsletter1525/newsletter_show.htm?doc_id=27560, April 5, 2000.

[18]Judith E. Nichols, *Changing Demographics: Fund Raising in the 1990s* (Chicago: Bonus Books, 1990); Judith E. Nichols, *Transforming Fundraising: A Practical Guide to Evaluating and Strengthening Fundraising to Grow with Change* (San Francisco: Jossey-Bass, 1999).

raised money with events. Events are still an important way to recognize the contributions of major donors and volunteers and to have fun. Toby Ansin did this when she celebrated her fiftieth birthday by commissioning a ballet, in her name, by the Miami City Ballet, which she founded. A recent professional seminar on women and philanthropy inspired an administrator at a historically black women's college to celebrate her upcoming fiftieth birthday by contributing $5,000 to a scholarship fund and inviting her friends and relatives to give to their ability.

(B)   OVERCOMING THE BARRIERS TO WOMEN'S GIVING

But the unique culture of women's giving also has a downside. There are some unique reasons why women *do not* give that arise from their socialization with regard to money and decision making. Women are less likely to be moved by the surface motivators of competition and public recognition, and fund-raising appeals based on these factors are likely to backfire. For older women in particular, there are barriers to giving, such as the bag lady syndrome—the fear of outliving one's resources. This fear crosses all levels of wealth, education, and charitable impulse. Other barriers include a lack of a sense of ownership of the family's resources—a need for permission to give. Many women have been raised to believe it is impolite to talk about money or to draw attention to one's wealth in any way. The desire not to flaunt one's wealth may be compounded by a fear that making a sizable public donation will attract the attention of other fund raisers or unscrupulous individuals who wish to take advantage of the donor.

For many women, these barriers are internal fears that they themselves have to overcome. But the most pernicious barrier—one that came up again and again in the focus groups—is that women do not believe they are being asked to give at the same level as men. This was found even in 1999 in a study of high-achieving businesswomen, members of the prestigious Committee of 200. These are women who own businesses grossing more than $15 million a year or who manage corporate divisions with annual revenues above $100 million. More than half the women in the study donate $25,000 or more annually, yet one out of four of them said they do not think they are taken as seriously as men by the fund-raising community.[19] Fully 40 percent of the younger women in the study, those under age 45, reported that they are not taken seriously as philanthropists. Almost half of the women reported that the way they are asked to give is a barrier to giving for them. Unfortunately, the initial study did not explore the details of this finding. Surely this is an area for further research.

Interestingly, in the Deloitte & Touche study, those women who considered themselves savvy investors believed they needed more money ($25,000 median) to be taken seriously as investors than did the general population ($10,000 median).

"Being young and female, I don't always seem to be taken seriously or given appropriate respect by some of the 'old school' brokers. I would like them to make the effort to get to know me and what I can afford, without making assumptions based on my age and sex," said one respondent.[20]

---

[19]"Philanthropy Among Business Women of Achievement: A Summary of Key Findings," Washington, DC: National Foundation for Women Business Owners. November 1999.
[20]*She Said,* p. 29.

The key to overcoming these barriers to women's philanthropy is *knowledge*. Dorothy Bryson found that to be true for her donors and staff at University of Tennessee. For women, the key is knowledge of financial management (and of their own financial situation), of the needs of nonprofits, and of the power of money to make things happen in a nonprofit. For development professionals, the key is knowledge of how to approach, ask, and acknowledge women appropriately. In the focus groups women gave low scores to the fund-raising methods used by many nonprofit institutions. They said most fund-raising methods are based on competition, status, and public recognition, methods based on a male model. Women are seeking a new approach—one based on collaboration, connection, and philanthropic partnership.

17.3 Motivating Women as Major Donors and Volunteer Leaders

(A) TRANSFORMING YOUR STANDARD DEVELOPMENT PROCEDURES

In the focus groups and interviews, women shared several suggestions—truly their gifts of wisdom to the nonprofit community. They illuminated ways that development officers and nonprofits can partner with them to shape a better world for future generations. They told us what motivates them as philanthropists as well as what turns them off. Following are nine suggestions for transforming your everyday development procedures to help nonprofits reach, involve, and motivate more women as major donors and volunteer leaders:

1. First and foremost, be a philanthropist yourself. Give generously to your own institution as well as other causes about which you are passionate. Focus your giving, rather than scattering many smaller gifts, so that your contributions have impact. Women want to see that you are as committed to your institution as you hope they will be.

2. In your development work, concentrate on relationship building. This often begins with annual giving, but do not overlook your volunteers and those who attend your events. This is often how women begin building a relationship, and financial giving may come later.

As the relationship develops, shift your focus to major and planned gifts. Remember that people make major gift decisions based on their experiences and socialization with regard to money. Recent pacesetting research by Cindy Sterling, director of Gift Planning at Vassar College, indicates that women are more likely to choose straight bequests, while men are more likely to select income-producing planned giving vehicles. Sterling speculates that a simple bequest may feel "safer" to women who may fear outliving their resources than would an irrevocable, income-producing gift.[21]

3. Examine what women see when they look at your organization. Review your boards, committees, and administration as well as your publications. Are women represented? In leading roles or supporting roles? Women want to see that your nonprofit affirms and values their contributions of expertise and talent.

---

[21]Cindy Sterling, "Planned Giving: Not an Afterthought," Presentation at CASE Women in Philanthropy Conference, April 13, 2000.

4. Review your standard development procedures. Are the six Cs represented in your work? Are you letting women know about opportunities to be involved in creating new programs? Are you telling them about how your programs will do more than help—but will bring about change? Are there opportunities for donors to become involved as volunteers? Do you provide ongoing information so they feel connected? Do you provide personal recognition?

5. Analyze your current giving statistics, broken down by gender. This will help you understand the current level of support by women to your organization or institution. Choose a time period, say the past three years, and answer the following questions:

- What percentage of your donors were women?
- What percentage of your total gift dollars came from women?
- What percentage of your major gift clubs or higher giving categories are women?
- What percentage of your planned gifts, and of the total dollars given in planned gifts, came from women?
- What percentage of those on prospect tracking are women? (How many women are you actively talking to about major gifts?)

When Martha Taylor examined giving statistics at the University of Wisconsin Foundation for the campaign period of 1988 to 1992, she found that women:

- Made up 40 percent of living alumni from UW-Madison
- Gave 51 percent of the gifts during the campaign
- Gave 37 percent of the total dollars

Another large, public research institution in the Midwest ran statistics for 1996, and found that women made up:

- 40 percent of living alumni
- 43 percent of the planned giving recognition society
- 54 percent of the $50,000 giving circle
- 48 to 50 percent of the giving circles at the $100,000 to $1 million levels
- Yet only 21 percent of major donor prospects (individuals on prospect tracking)[22]

Note that in the last example women were giving in greater proportion than they are being asked. This leads to suggestion 6 below.

Note: Your results will depend, in part, on how your nonprofit credits contributions, in particular those from married couples. When looking at the raw data, it may be impossible to know which spouse had more influence on the philanthropic decision. Start by examining how your nonprofit credits joint gifts, and you may want to recommend a change in policy for the future. A recent study of women's philanthropy programming at research universities found that all of the development offices surveyed used systems, including BSR Advance, Ascend or Millennium, that are capable of crediting spouses separately when a gift is received from a married couple.[23]

---

[22]Personal communication, 1997.
[23]M. Marcello, G. Van Dien, and K. Vehrs, "Women's Philanthropy at Research Universities: 1998–1999 Study," University of Wisconsin Survey Research Center, Madison, February 21, 2000.

For college fund raising, it can be a challenge to decide how to credit a gift from a married couple when one spouse is a graduate of the institution and the other is not. Just over one-third of the development offices (38.2 percent) will contact the donor and ask how to credit the gift; half automatically credit the spouse who is a graduate; and 14.7 percent credit the signer of the check. Another 11.7 percent give split credit for the gift, and 8.8 percent credit each partner individually. Only one university automatically defaults to give credit to the male spouse—a practice that was not so unusual just 10 years ago. Contacting the donor and asking how to credit the gift may be the best approach, as it demonstrates respect for the donor(s) and strengthens the connection to the organization.

6. If you do nothing else, make at least 50 percent of your fund-raising calls on women. If women are giving in greater proportion than they are being asked, this could mean one of two things: that asking is detrimental (and we should all lose our jobs) or that the potential for women's giving is enormous. I believe the latter is true. Imagine the good work our nonprofits can accomplish if we help women realize their philanthropic potential!

7. Be sensitive to differences in communication styles. Women's colleges are so successful in part because they are sensitive to women's learning styles. Read the books by Deborah Tannen, such as *You Just Don't Understand: Men and Women in Conversation.*[24] There are also communication differences based on generational and cultural factors. While you want to approach each donor or potential donor as an individual, it helps to understand some of these differences in communication styles and keep them in mind when working with your donors.[25]

In particular, the women in the research were sensitive to sales language. Avoid jargon. People are not *targets.* They do not want to be thought of as *prospects* or *suspects.* They do not want nonprofits *going after them.* These terms and phrases are sometimes all but impossible to avoid for internal use, but they reflect a mind-set that is offensive to women donors. Instead of prospects, refer to potential donors. Watch your language—the women philanthropists who have participated in our research certainly are.

8. Partner with both partners. If you are working with a committed couple, include both spouses, or partners, in your solicitation calls and recognition. If you set up a meeting with one member of a couple, ask if the other partner—or other family members—should be present. Often older women hold back in their giving because they are afraid their adult children will not approve. And nearly as often, the adult children, when they hear about their mother's intention, are very supportive and proud. Remember that the older woman may not feel it is her place to make major decisions about the family's financial resources, which she may believe her husband earned without her participation. She may feel she needs permission to give. Build a relationship with the family, and you will build trust. And the relationship may continue even after your woman donor passes away.

9. Pay attention to stewardship. How you accept the gift, acknowledge the donor, and maintain the relationship is crucial. In research, women have expressed an overwhelming preference for personal, as opposed to public, recognition. Men might say the

[24]Tannen, D. *You Just Don't Understand: Women and Men in Conversation,* New York: Ballantine Books, 1991.

[25]Nichols, *Changing Demographics;* M. A. Abbe, "Inspiring Philanthropy by Women of Color." *Women's Philanthropy Institute News* (May 2000).

same in a similar situation; this suggests another area for further investigation. As more new groups—women, young entrepreneurs, and racial/ethnic minorities—enter major gift philanthropy, the best approach is to talk with your donors about recognition and listen to their preferences. The worst thing to do is to assume that the white male model, which has served the development profession for decades, can be universally applied.

Beyond acknowledgment and recognition, it is essential to maintain the relationship through ongoing contacts, invitations, information, and opportunities for volunteer involvement. The following comment from a note from a woman who had attended a women and philanthropy seminar illustrates how this kind of cultivation bonds the woman donor to the program: "As a woman, I want to focus on how I can further integrate philanthropy throughout my life. . . . I was delighted to accept an offer to chair a sub-group of the board. . . . I am convinced that such a group of vital women will make a difference."[26]

Note that these comments illustrate how the six Cs permeate this woman's philanthropy. She demonstrates a strong interest in *connection* with the programs she funds, *commitment* to volunteer service, a desire to *collaborate* with others, and to bring about *change* (make a difference) with her philanthropy.

(B) PROGRAMS THAT ENCOURAGE WOMEN AS PHILANTHROPISTS

The above suggestions offer ways to transform your standard operating procedures in development work. You may also wish to establish a formal program to involve and educate women as donors for your nonprofit. There are several excellent program models from which to learn. The model you choose, and the program that results, must be appropriate for your organization and its constituents. In the long run, a women's initiative will help you address the culture of women's giving. Ideally, the women will be involved in *creating* the program. It obviously is an opportunity for *connection, collaboration,* and *commitment* to volunteerism. It will help you understand your female donors, and they will appreciate the opportunity to have a voice in your institutional planning. UCLA's experience in organizing their first round of focus groups in 1992 is instructive: "When women were approached by letter to participate in focus groups for UCLA's Women and Philanthropy Program their response was unusually enthusiastic. Before the follow-up calls promised in the invitation could even begin, a full third of the invitees initiated their own response, calling UCLA to make sure they would be included. The number of groups originally planned were soon doubled. . . ."[27]

Elements of a successful women's program include:

1. *Committed staff.* The development profession has a relatively high turnover rate, and donors often stay with a nonprofit longer than development officers do. Women donors want to work with a staff member who is as dedicated to the nonprofit as they are. If you want to establish a women's council, think of it as a long-term project. It is major gift work, and it takes cultivation.

---

[26]Personal communication, 1992.
[27]UCLA Women and Philanthropy Focus Groups.

2. *Active volunteer committee.* To heighten a sense of connection and ownership, it is crucial to involve a core group of women volunteers in the formative stage of the initiative. Of course, you must not let volunteers create a program that the staff, or the organization itself, cannot uphold. Nonetheless, it is important to let the women participate in developing the mission, purpose, goals and tone of the program. In your initial investigative work, whether it takes the form of focus groups, personal interviews, or a survey, you may want to suggest a number of possible activities and ask which ones would be of interest to the women you wish to involve.

Your volunteer committee should be made up of women who are established financial donors to your institution and respected leaders in their community. This is not a place for well-meaning volunteers or well-known philanthropists who do not give to your nonprofit. Except in the rare case where a women's philanthropy council actually advances your organizational mission, you probably could not justify the expenditure of staff time unless there is an expectation that the program will advance your fund-raising efforts. Although some women will almost surely prefer to avoid the issue of money at least at first, this tendency runs counter to the purpose of a women's philanthropy program. It is critical to make the expectation clear from the outset that the program is intended to inspire women to become philanthropists for your nonprofit and secondarily for others.

3. *Commitment of institution.* While it is important to focus the program on giving to your nonprofit, it is equally important to communicate to women that the program is an opportunity for them to become involved as leaders in advancing the organization's central mission. Women philanthropists do not want to belong to a "ladies' auxiliary," nor do they want to be valued only for their money. The best way to demonstrate that the nonprofit values women's interests, and their multifaceted contributions, is to show support for your women's program from the main administration and governing body of your nonprofit. Involve your chief executive officer and/or board chair in hosting, addressing, or at the very least attending your women's philanthropy meetings and events.

4. *Donor research.* You may want to run focus groups or have the top development officer conduct a series of personal interviews of women donors. This effort will generate valuable information for you about how your women donors view your nonprofit and how you can better serve them. At the same time, your interest in their views will increase the women's sense of connection to your nonprofit.

5. *Full philanthropy education.* Donor education seminars and publications enlighten your women donors while solidifying their connection with your nonprofit. Just as women seek user-friendly opportunities to learn how to be better investors, they appreciate similar guidance in learning to become a more effective philanthropist. The discussions should begin with the concept that philanthropy involves gifts of time, talent, and treasure and that nonprofits need all three to function at full capacity.

The Women's Philanthropy Institute has developed an innovative donor curriculum that takes women through three stages of development as philanthropists: motivation, knowledge, and leadership.

(i) Motivation
The goal of the motivation stage is to get women to think of themselves as philanthropists or at least as potential philanthropists. Women may be giving very generously to a num-

ber of nonprofit institutions and organizations but still not identify with the word "philanthropist." They may believe that a philanthropist has to be white, male, and richer, smarter, or more powerful than they are. Often women are impressed when they see the facts and figures about women, wealth, and giving as well as some outstanding examples of women's philanthropy. It also may help for women to see examples of collective giving in which women of relatively modest means make a transforming collective gift.

But women philanthropists are primarily motivated by a cause. The Women's Philanthropy Institute often takes women through a process of identifying the most pressing needs of society that can be met through increased funding. Then we ask them what they would do if they had $1 million (or another "stretch" figure, depending on the audience) to give today. We impose some parameters, such as a limit of three causes or organizations, to encourage the women to think strategically. Then we tell them to use their imagination.

Some women set right to work, because they have been thinking about philanthropy for some time and they know just what they would do. (All they needed was the million dollars.) Others turn to their neighbors and get ideas. Usually at least one table of eight will pool their funds to create a foundation or a program within an existing nonprofit to address a societal need. The six Cs are always evident in the results.

In 1993 Lorene Burkhart, a successful businesswoman in Indianapolis, attended a donor education seminar for women at the Felker Leadership Conference, sponsored by the School of Consumer and Family Sciences at Purdue University.[28] At one point the speaker, Martha Taylor, asked the women in the workshop to write down what they would do if they had $1 million dollars to give philanthropically that day. Later, during the coffee break, Burkhart approached Taylor and said: "I'm going to do what I said I would do this morning. I'm going to commit $1 million to the School of Consumer and Family Sciences to create a center that will study the effects of legislation and government policy on the family. *I'm doing this because you gave me permission to follow my heart!*"

An astute businesswoman, Burkhart decided to make the gift over 10 years, with a challenge to encourage at least 25 others to give the center $10,000 each over the same period. In the first year there were 30 donors, allowing the center to begin research and programming immediately.

"By structuring it very carefully, we could provide a vehicle for other women to make major gifts, women who never expected to make a major gift. And that's what happened," Burkhart said. In addition, several men on Purdue's national fund-raising campaign committee and their wives also contributed.

Of course, it was not one seminar that inspired Lorene Burkhart to make her momentous decision. She had no doubt been thinking about her legacy for some time, but the discussion about philanthropy emboldened her.

(ii) Knowledge

By the time the women have completed the Million Dollar Exercise, they are motivated. The next stage is knowledge. At this level, women learn about the six Cs and the barriers to women's giving. They examine ways that women's giving patterns result in less impact on society, and they learn specific strategies to increase the effectiveness of their philanthropic giving. Following are a few of the strategies we teach that help women overcome barriers and increase their joy in giving:

---

[28]Cited in *Women's Philanthropy Institute News* (October 1998): 6.

- *Focus your philanthropy.* The principles taught in the book *Inspired Philanthropy: Creating a Giving Plan* by Tracy Gary and Melissa Kohner are particularly helpful for individuals who wish to define their personal philanthropic mission.
- *Work for parity in giving in your household.* This is an important point to cover, particularly with women who have not brought in a paycheck. It is an affirmation of the value of unpaid work—both in the community and in the home. It is a crucial issue of discussion with women philanthropists.
- *If you can, give out of principal to the causes you are passionate about.* There is an unchallenged taboo against invading principal, and as a result women often do not live to see the fruits of their philanthropy. We encourage women to think of their philanthropy as they would a child, their investment in the future of our world.
- *If you do not have so much money, consider the strength of numbers.* Examples follow of model programs in collective giving by women.
- *Leverage your giving.* Most women appreciate a bargain, and they appreciate learning how they can increase their philanthropic impact by challenging others to support the causes they hold dear.
- *Teach the art of philanthropy to the next generation.* The women who participated in the focus groups and other studies were very concerned about how to pass on to their children, grandchildren, and other young people the value of philanthropy. This is a required topic in your donor education program for women.

(iii) Leadership

The third developmental stage in philanthropy is leadership. Leadership in philanthropy includes such activities as:

- Being a role model by making a public gift
- Serving on a governing board or committee, in particular on a financial committee, where women are often represented
- Asking others to give major gifts

(C) MODEL WOMEN'S PHILANTHROPY INITIATIVES

Over the past decade, an increasing number of nonprofits have identified the need for special programming designed to reach and involve more women as donors. The number of such programs has mushroomed from a few women's councils at institutions of higher education in 1990 to countless programs at a variety of nonprofits today. In addition, women donors have initiated their own collective giving circles in several communities. There is no single best program for all nonprofits or all communities. The program model that is best is one that takes into consideration such factors as the demographics of the women and the community, as well as the mission and customs of the nonprofit. Following are descriptions and examples of several program models.

(i) Top-level Women's Council

The top-level women's council is a membership program that deals directly with philanthropy as well as, in some cases, other women's issues related to the nonprofit. This program model is seen most often in institutions of higher education. Examples include the highly developed programs at the University of Wisconsin Foundation, Purdue University, Oklahoma State University, Cornell University, University of Tennessee, Ohio State University, UCLA, and California State University, Long Beach. For a list of women's philanthropy programs, each with a description and the name of a contact person, contact the Women's Philanthropy Institute at 608-270-5205.

Members of top-level women's councils are major donors to the institution. There is usually a minimum contribution, which may range from less than $1,000 to $25,000. Of course, many members contribute significantly more than the minimum. These programs provide philanthropic education through regular seminars and publications. Because women are generally concerned about teaching philanthropic values to younger generations, mentoring is often an important activity of the council. Members may mentor students or younger women in philanthropy or other skills. In addition, many of these programs foster women's leadership skills through volunteer training. The women are trained to ask others—both men and women—for major gifts.

Women's councils are important vehicles for institutional change at the leadership and governance level. Outstanding women donors and volunteers are often identified and cultivated through the program. These women then are invited to serve on influential institutional boards and committees. At the University of Wisconsin Foundation, the Council on Women's Giving now holds a seat on the board of trustees, and a cofounder of the council went on to become president of the Foundation Board.

The Council on Women's Giving has also brought about an important change in development procedures at the UW Foundation. "Twelve years ago, when we started, our volunteer manual said: 'Solicit the man for the gift in his office.' There was no mention of the spouse's involvement in the gift decision," recalled Martha Taylor in April 2000. "Now the Foundation instructions are to seek gifts from both husband and wife."

Women's councils often support and advocate for women staff, faculty, and students of the institution. The President's Council of Cornell Women began as an advisory group. Although the council has taken on several diverse additional roles in the 10 years since inception, it continues to be an important advocate for women on campus. In some cases, the women's council raises money for student scholarships and faculty grants. These funds provide important support that helps women succeed as students and advance as faculty and administrators.

(ii) Focus on Connection

Some institutions prefer not to form a membership council, but they nonetheless establish a carefully researched and planned program designed to strengthen women's connection to the nonprofit. Through educational presentations on philanthropy and other topics of interest to women, the nonprofit demonstrates a concern for women's interests and input. While this approach is effective in many educational institutions and community-based nonprofits, it may vary greatly in scope and form.

In educational institutions, what works in one setting would fail in another. This focus on connection can take the form of small-group breakfasts with the president, as is the case at Michigan Technological University, or it may be a prestigious and visible annual forum with high-profile speakers, such as the annual Colloquium for Women of Indiana University. Both programs invite high-achieving alumnae to participate. The invitation list is developed from nominations made by staff and volunteer leaders. At Michigan Tech, the program is a joint effort between the advancement department and the educational opportunities department, according to Paula Nutini, director of Annual

Gifts at the Michigan Tech Fund. The president and the advancement office provide the annual budget of $10,000 to $15,000.

The Colloquium for Women of Indiana University brings approximately 100 women to campus to hear faculty and such big names as Beverly Sills, Jeanne Kirkpatrick, and Anna Quindlen. Curt Simic, president of IU Foundation, says this about the colloquium:

> *Some years ago, I attended a meeting at which Martha Taylor and Sondra Shaw spoke about the potential of women as philanthropists. Even without specific numbers from my own institution, I knew that they were correct, and we undertook a formal look at the involvement and contribution patterns of our women donors and volunteers. As a result of our research, we initiated five years ago a program called The Colloquium for Women of Indiana University. The program has involved 240 women, who are or have the potential to be major donors and volunteer leaders, in a unique and very special way of connecting and reconnecting with Indiana University. As a direct result, we have increased the number of women on our Foundation Board of Directors; all of the five women appointed were Colloquium attendees. In addition, we have received several significant gifts which we can attribute directly to the Colloquium experience, including a $1 million chair and a $500,000 endowment for the program. At their own initiative, the Colloquium women have formed "action groups," some of which are involved in fund raising. Most recently, the women have asked the Foundation to develop a large-scale fund-raising program that would benefit women at Indiana University.[29]*

In this case, the women invited to attend the colloquium were not asked to belong to a membership council. Nonetheless, they are involved closely with the institution. True to the six Cs, the women have—on their own—begun to apply their commitment to collaborative volunteer action and fund raising.

Many community-based nonprofits and affiliates have increased their programming on topics of interest to women. An example is United Way of Morris County (New Jersey), which held its second annual Women's Leadership Initiative "Rise and Shine" breakfast celebration in October 1999. Patricia Lewis, president of the Women's Philanthropy Institute, spoke at the program and provided a national perspective for the initiative.

The Women's Leadership Initiative of United Way of Morris County goes beyond presenting programs of interest to women. The initiative was established in 1998 to recognize the community involvement and support of area women and inspire them to reach their potential as philanthropic leaders. A steering committee composed of women leaders from local corporations and small businesses gave shape to the initiative and defined two broad goals: increasing the financial participation of women and expanding their personal involvement in the community.

"We see our efforts to increase women's financial participation as breaking the final glass ceiling, helping women recognize that they too have the resources to give at the same level as men have been giving for years now," said Sharon McCullen Prince, volunteer chair of the initiative.[30]

Across the continent, the women members of the Alexis de Tocqueville Society of United Way of Snohomish County (Washington) established a program called Women

---

[29]Personal communication, Feb. 2000.
[30]Personal communication, 2000.

Leading the Way in 1998 to encourage and realize the potential of women to take a significant leadership role in building healthy communities in Snohomish County through volunteer and philanthropic efforts. For more information about Women Leading the Way, contact Heather Whitehill at 425-921-3456 or e-mail events@uwsc.org.

(iii)   Women's Campaign

Some nonprofits are benefiting from campaigns initiated and to a great extent carried out by women. For example, the United Way of Greater Greensboro (North Carolina) increased its giving by at least 10 percent in 1998–1999, in part because of an effort led by philanthropist Bonnie McElveen-Hunter to motivate women to make donations of $10,000 or more.[31] Under McElveen-Hunter's direction, the United Way approached businesswomen, women who were active community leaders or volunteers, and housewives with financially successful husbands. In some cases, the women's husbands were asked to make gifts in honor of their wives. McElveen-Hunter began by making her own gift in honor of her mother. She made 43 personal visits and obtained 40 new donations from or in honor of women. Then she persuaded Merrill Lynch to place a $50,000 full-page ad in the *Wall Street Journal* featuring photographs of the women. Her own publishing company designed the piece.

A leading example of women's philanthropy took place in Columbus, Ohio. The YWCA is housed in the Griswold Building, the only downtown Columbus edifice built, owned, and operated by a group of women.[32] In 1990 the board convened a committee to weigh the relative advantages of renovating the dilapidated structure or moving to another site.

To affirm women's skills and abilities, the board selected only women for this committee, which included architects, bankers, real estate professionals, and lawyers. They eventually chose to renovate for two reasons:

1. To preserve the historical significance of the Griswold Building
2. Because the city of Columbus promised substantial funding, in order to maintain the YWCA as a downtown residence for low-income women

In all, city, county, and state agencies yielded nearly $8 million in grants and loans. It was up to the board to raise the remaining $7 million in private funds, the largest such goal in the history of Columbus.

In 1994 the board appointed a 50-member, all-female campaign cabinet. Abigail Wexner, wife of Leslie H. Wexner, chairman of The Limited, was general chair for the campaign. After viewing the dilapidated building, she called in a pledge of $1 million toward the campaign in the annual phonathon and committed to raising the remaining $6 million. Consistent with the YWCA's tradition of community involvement, the cabinet raised funds from small businesses, religious congregations, civic organizations, union and trade associations, YWCA members and friends, and the general public.

---

[31]Domenica Marchetti, "Magazine Publisher's Charity Begins—But Doesn't End—at the Office," *Chronicle of Philanthropy*, January 13, 2000, p. 22.

[32]Karen Schwarzwalder, "Focus on the Future: A Partnership of Women in the Campaign to Renovate the YWCA of Columbus, Ohio," in Julie C. Conry, ed., *Women as Fundraisers: Their Experience in and Influence on an Emerging Profession* (San Francisco: Jossey-Bass, 1998), p. 111.

Karen Schwarzwalder, CEO of the YWCA, wrote: "From its inception, this project demonstrated the abilities of the contemporary woman, and many donors made contributions simply because they wanted to be in support of a women's project."[33]

The YWCA of Rock County (Wisconsin) has also initiated a grass-roots women's campaign, called 100 Caring Women, to raise $100,000 toward a $500,000 need for a new shelter for victims of violence. The vision for the campaign is that of 100 women contributing (or raising from others) $1,000.

(iv) Women's Fund

A women's fund is a philanthropy that focuses its grantmaking and other programs on issues that principally affect women and girls and that is governed and managed predominantly by women, according to Susan Church, former executive director of the Michigan Women's Foundation, and Carol Mollner, founder and former executive director of the Women's Funding Network.[34] Although the first women's funds were created in the 1970s, most are considerably less than 20 years old. There are now more than 90 such philanthropies internationally, although mostly in the United States. The women's funds were created in response to findings that less than 5 percent of grant dollars awarded by traditional foundations and corporate giving programs were directed to programs designed specifically to serve women and girls—a figure that has not significantly changed over the past 20 years.

The women's funds are devoted to "changing the face of philanthropy," as the Women's Funding Network motto declares. They are very mindful of diversity and can be credited with bringing many new individuals into philanthropy through their educational programs, outreach to often-overlooked population groups, and highly democratic governance structures.

Research indicates that women philanthropists are very concerned about passing on their philanthropic values to the next generation. Some women's funds and women's circles are working to do just that. For example, in 1994 Susan Church and Twink Frey created a program under the Michigan Women's Foundation (MWF) called Young Women for Change.[35] The initiative allows girls age 12 to 17 to research and recommend how the foundation will allocate $20,000 annually to benefit girls in West Michigan. The program is supported by a $375,000 designated gift from Frey's family foundation. In 1998 MWF established a second program in Detroit.

Although the vast majority of the women's funds and foundations are devoted to raising money for projects that serve women and girls, one very successful group, the Washington Women's Foundation (WWF), in Seattle, does not by charter limit its grantmaking in this way. The WWF is a new model of women's foundation that, in part, has led to the evolution to the women's giving circles.

(v) Women's Giving Circle

The women's giving circle is a most exciting model for women's collective philanthropy. Its core features are equal membership shares, member involvement in grantmaking,

---

[33] *Ibid.*

[34] Susan Church, and Carol Mollner, "By Women, for Women: The Women's Funding Movement," in Abbie J. von Schlegell and Joan M. Fisher, eds, *Women as Donors, Women as Philanthropists* (San Francisco: Jossey-Bass, 1993), page 98.

[35] "Cultivating Young Philanthropists" *Women's Philanthropy Institute News* (May 1999).

funding in the community, and philanthropic education. Like many of the women's funds, women's giving circles bring new individuals into major gift philanthropy, embolden those capable of giving larger amounts, and provide opportunities for mentoring and learning. A difference is that funding is not limited to projects that serve women and girls.

Women's giving circles are often the creation of a group of individual women acting on their own desire to invest in the future health of their community. Some, however, are organized under the sponsorship, and in support of, a particular nonprofit. For example, the Seven Generations Circle of Women, in Columbus, Ohio, was founded in 1997 to celebrate the twenty-fifth anniversary of Action for Children, a local child care resource center. Each member contributes $1,000 annually to support the organization. The Women's Philanthropic Healthcare Fund supports programs of interest to the members at the Saint Alphonsus (Hospital) Foundation in Boise, Idaho.

Although every women's giving circle is unique, the common factors include the following[36]:

- Equal contributions are pooled so the group can make sizable grants. Sondra Shaw-Hardy encourages giving circles to make the contribution from members at least $1,000 annually for two to five years. This amount is significant for most donors, and the pooled fund will be capable of making a genuine impact in the community. This amount may be a stretch for many women, but it helps women of modest means to think of themselves as philanthropists. In some giving circles, a $1,000 membership may be split among two or three women, or a mother may sponsor membership for her daughter.
- Women's giving circles are generally devoted to funding in the community. While some circles are created to support a particular nonprofit, others are set up as donor-advised funds in a community foundation. In New York, members of The WellMet Group contribute $5,000 annually for three years to a donor-advised fund in The New York Community Trust. In Traverse City, Michigan, the Three Generations Circle of Women is sponsored by the Women's Resource Center. Half of each member's $1,000 annual contribution stays with the center. The other half goes into the pooled fund, which may be invested in other projects in the community.
- Perhaps the most exciting—and educational—aspect of a giving circle is that the members are actively involved in grantmaking. There is usually a grants committee that researches and recommends specific projects to the membership, which makes the final decision by vote. Shaw-Hardy advises giving circle organizers to recommend that each member serve on the grants committee with some frequency. She points out that the experience will help donors learn how to plan their own philanthropy as well as experience the joy of directing larger gifts. In its first year of grants, The WellMet Group will give out grants of up to $20,000 for two purposes: to help emerging or grass-roots groups and to help organizations that encourage people to become self-sufficient. The circle's 16

---

[36]Sondra C. Shaw-Hardy, *Creating a Women's Giving Circle* (Madison WI: Women's Philanthropy Institute, 2000), pp. 4–5.

members have formed two groups of eight to research and identify organizations that are doing such work.

- Giving circles generally provide education for women in financial issues and philanthropic leadership. The Seven Generations Circle sponsors a three-part Leadership Institute, bringing in nationally renowned experts on women's philanthropy. Their speakers in 1999 and 2000 have included Tracy Gary, Sondra Shaw-Hardy, and Jane Leighty Justis. Giving circles are most educational for women who are discovering their philanthropic potential. However, many highly experienced philanthropists enjoy the collegiality of the group as well as the meaningful opportunities to mentor younger—or newer—women donors.

- Women's giving circles are donor focused. There is almost as much attention paid to providing education and support for the members as there is to the grantmaking, according to Shaw-Hardy. Yet, she points out, there is usually little in the way of individual donor recognition. The rewards the women report are more likely to include the joys of:
  - Collaboration and cooperation
  - Financial and philanthropic education
  - The ability to direct a larger grant and have more impact
  - The friendships that result from working together to accomplish a goal.

17.4   Conclusion

All of the women's councils, circles, funds, and programs that have been described contribute to women's self-confidence as donors. Through educational programs, women develop knowledge, skills, and belief in their potential abilities. The programs are generally inclusive and nonthreatening, and they provide opportunities for women to share their experiences in a "safe" environment, where they can admit their fears about money and their ambivalence about being "public" philanthropists. They provide opportunities for women to help others by serving as role models and to learn from others who may be a step ahead in their philanthropic development. They allow women who may not be able—or may think they are not able—to give large gifts to nonetheless experience the sense of clout that comes from helping to direct a pooled fund. This experience may well inspire those who are capable to make larger gifts on their own in the future. For some women, the discussions that take place in such a program give them *permission* to make a significant decision.

Women are poised to make a major impact with their philanthropy. They are seeking connection and guidance to help them make active choices about what becomes of their wealth—how much they spend, how they invest, how much goes back to society in the form of taxes, and what they accomplish through active philanthropic choices.

Nonprofit professionals can help women become stewards of their wealth, by providing guidance from our development offices in our publications, our programs, and in every contact we have with women donors and their families. Together, we can help women become philanthropic leaders and stewards of their wealth, and the benefits will be shared by our institutions, our society as a whole, our next generation of young women and men, and by the women donors themselves.

Suggested Readings

Ballard, Kay. "Marketing to Older Women: Ideas and Opinions from the Trenches," *Journal of Gift Planning*, Indianapolis: National Committee on Planned Giving, 1st Quarter 2000, pp. 9–11, 36–37.

Cox-Chapman, Mally. "The Heart's Currency," *New Age*, January/February 2000, pp. 78–83.

Edwards, T.M. "The Power of the Purse," *Time*, May 17, 1999, p. 64.

Gary, T., and Kohner, M. *Inspired Philanthropy: Creating a Giving Plan*. Berkeley: Chardon Press, 1998.

Ginsberg, Lori D., *Women and the Work of Benevolence: Morality, Politics, and Class in the Nineteenth-Century United States*. New Haven: Yale University Press, 1990.

Hicks, Zoe M., *The Women's Estate Planning Guide*. Chicago: Contemporary Books, 1998.

Kaminski, Andrea. "The Hidden Philanthropists," *Currents*, Washington, DC: Council for Advancement and Support of Education, Feb. 1999, pp. 20–25.

Kaminski, A., and Taylor, M. "Women in Philanthropy," *AHP Journal* (Association for Healthcare Philanthropy), Spring 1998, pp. 6–12.

McCarthy, Kathleen D., *Noblesse Oblige*. Chicago: University of Chicago Press, 1982.

McCarthy, Kathleen D., ed., *Lady Bountiful Revisited: Women, Philanthropy and Power*. New Brunswick and London, Rutgers University Press, 1990.

McCarthy, K.D., *Women and Philanthropy in the United States, 1790–1990, Curriculum Guide #1, Spring 1998*. Center for the Study of Philanthropy, The Graduate School and Univ. Center, City University of New York, 33 W. 42nd St., Rm. 1525 GB, NY, NY 10036, 212/642-2130.

Nichols, J., *Changing Demographics: Fund Raising in the 1990s*. Chicago, IL: Bonus Books, Inc., 1990.

Nichols, J., *Global Demographics: Fund Raising for a New World*. Chicago, IL: Bonus Books, Inc., 1995.

Nichols, J., *Transforming Fundraising: A Practical Guide to Evaluating and Strengthening Fundraising*. San Francisco: Jossey-Bass, Publishers, Inc., 1999.

Rosenberg, Claude. *Wealthy and Wise: How You and America Can Get the Most Out of Your Giving*. Boston, New York, Toronto, London: Little, Brown and Company, 1994.

Rubin, B. and Klelman, C. "As Women Amass Wealth, Social Causes Feel Their Gain," *Chicago Tribune*, May 23, 1999, pp. 1, 11.

Shaw, S.C., and Taylor, M.A., Reinventing Fundraising: Realizing the Potential of Women's Philanthropy. San Francisco: Jossey-Bass Publishers, 1995.

Women's Philanthropy Institute News, Madison, Wis.: Women's Philanthropy Institute, 608/270-5205, www.women-philanthropy.org

Leading Learning Communities: Implications of the New Science for Not-for-Profit Organizations

SALLY J. SMITH, MAT, CFRE
Coviello & Associates

18.1 Introduction

A concern common to all not-for-profit organizations deals with building future leaders and leadership capability. How can leadership be developed? What skills, knowledge, and values help leaders to be effective? How can leaders cope with the environment of change that is ever present? Much of current management and leadership practice is founded on principles first articulated by Sir Isaac Newton. More recently, however, contemporary thinkers have identified the handicaps imposed by those seventeenth-century Newtonian perspectives. Now newer concepts are catching on, replacing those old, familiar maxims and strategies. Popularized by Fritjof Capra, Peter Senge, Margaret Wheatley, Danah Zohar, and others, twentieth-century new science ideas are proving to be relevant and effective to not-for-profits and their leaders.

18.2 Old Newtonian Views and Their Outcomes

In the seventeenth century, Sir Isaac Newton observed the world around him from which he deduced an orderly and predictable universe, one that was like the mechanical clocks of his era. His worldview with its mechanistic clock metaphor provided an extremely useful perspective for thinkers and leaders in the centuries to follow. With this Newtonian perspective, one could rely on the world being predictable. Its systems were made up of finite, knowable components. To deal with any problems within Newton's universe, all one had to do was to isolate the component that had the problem and fix it. Hierarchical, bureaucratic control made sense and was trusted. This understanding of the natural world and its systems was so compelling that it was enthusiastically applied to the workings and structure of human society as well.

Newton's perspective was a major step on the road to greater understanding of our world and how it operates. By the twentieth century, however, many of its basic tenets had been found to be seriously limited. Scientists increasingly noted that their observations of nature's systems did not conform to Newton's orderly, predictable model. Newton's laws of how the universe works no longer seem sufficient.

Furthermore, society, with its various forms of government, business enterprise, and cultural, environmental, health, and educational institutions, has become more complex. Organizations structured and run according to a 300-year-old paradigm are increasingly dysfunctional. Built to resist change and to enforce control, the resulting systems are rigid, inflexible, and bureaucratic. People are treated as parts of the system, along with materials and methods. Complexity is seen as a problem to be resolved by breaking things down into smaller fragments. Efficiency is the final goal. By focusing on the proverbial trees in life, leaders have lost the ability to see, understand, and appreciate the forest as something greater than its collected arboreal components.

So, after three centuries of structuring our societal systems on the orderly universe principles of Newton, what are the results? Everywhere we look, according to Dee Hock, founder and chairman emeritus of VISA International, we see massive institutional failure.[1] Providing specific examples of Hock's point, Peter Senge and Daniel Kim write of our educational system, which is constantly criticized for not preparing children adequately to meet the demands of the future.[2] In fact, U.S. corporations are spending millions to teach high school graduates in their workforces to read, write, and do basic math. Healthcare systems in America are also in acute crisis. We spend more money than any other industrialized nation and yet the health of our citizens is among the worst. At the same time, religious institutions are struggling for a relevant role; and our government seems caught in a vicious cycle of growing self-interest groups, distrust, and corruption.

How has this happened? Senge and Kim conclude that the knowledge-creating system, by which we *collectively* learn and through which our institutions improve and revitalize themselves, is deeply fragmented and only minimally functional. The skills

---

[1]Hock, Dee. Speech to 1995 Systems Thinking Conference, quoted by Peter Senge and Daniel Kim in article, "Building Organizational Learning Infrastructures," *The Systems Thinker*, October 1995. Cambridge, MA: Pegasus Communications, p. 6.

[2]Senge, Peter and Daniel Kim, "From Fragmentation to Integration: Building Learning Communities," *The Systems Thinker*, May 1997. Cambridge, MA: Pegasus Communications, p. 1.

advanced by Newton's model, such as analysis, planning based on a predictable model, focus on components, and building change-resistant organizational structures, actually block organizations from learning. They discourage the development of timely, collective responses to the changing environment.

18.3   New Science: Different Understandings of Our World

(A)   SCIENTIFIC CHANGES IN THE TWENTIETH CENTURY

In the last century, massive changes occurred in the disciplines of physics, biology, and chemistry as well as in theories of evolution and chaos that span several disciplines. The new perspectives emerging from these changes, which have come to be called the new science, have revolutionized our understanding of the universe and how it works.

Margaret Wheatley in her book, *Leadership and the New Science*, identifies four eras as the milestones along this road of change (See Exhibit 18.1.).[3]

With these breakthroughs in scientific understanding have come new ways of seeing our world, new ways that go beyond Newton's clockwork universe that was believed to be predictable and controllable. Gone are the comforting days of belief in either-or choices.

Replacing these beliefs are new perspectives that offer a different kind of comfort. The new science data now manifests a natural world that works well "without a net." We now realize that we live in a world that is holistic and contextual. It is also self-organizing, free, experimental, renewing, responsible, and spiritual. Life is full of uncertainty, increasingly rapid change, and untold complexity. Captivated by Newtonian ideas, we have made *control* of our world the object of our efforts. Instead, we should have been seeking *order*. For it is only by being attentive to and appreciative of the nat-

---

EXHIBIT 18.1 New Science Milestones of the Twentieth Century

In the 1920s and 1930s, systems concepts emerged, including:
- organismic biology
- gestalt psychology
- quantum physics
- ecology

In the 1940s, two classical systems theories were formulated:
- general systems theory
- cybernetics

In the 1960s and 1970s, new mathematics of complexity were postulated, which included:
- chaos theory
- fractal geometry

During the 1970s and 1980s, theories of self-organizing systems were developed.

---

[3]Fritjof Capra, notes from Myron Kellner-Rogers and Margaret Wheatley seminar entitled "Self-Organizing Systems—A Simpler Way," April 1997.

ural order and applying its lessons to our man-made systems that our society will survive and thrive. Control is illusory, but order and patterns can and do emerge over time.[4]

"A system is a perceived whole, whose elements 'hang together' because they continually affect each other over time and operate toward a common purpose."[5] As seen through the lenses of the new science, the natural world serves up wonderful examples of systems—*living* systems—at work, systems that are continuously adapting and changing, in fact, learning. The universe, Earth, weather, the oceans, rain forests, individual plants, animals, and humans are all living systems.

(B) SHIFT IN EMPHASIS

What defines a living system? According to Fritjof Capra, every living system has three components: its pattern of organization (i.e., the relationships that determine a system's essential characteristics), its structure (the physical reality or form the patterns take), and processes (the activity involved in realizing the pattern).[6] These components constitute all living systems. Now we can see that the whole is much greater than the sum of its parts; and with that reorientation comes a powerful shift in emphasis. (See Exhibit 18.2.)

With the advent of modern computers, scientists have been able for the first time graphically to plot complex systems. Their work has revealed unexpected results. What had in the past appeared to be disconnected or chaotic behavior, when plotted over time, has been shown to contain ordered patterns of great beauty. Furthermore, we have learned that minute changes can lead to large-scale consequences. Previously it was believed that we could ignore small influences; but results of work with complex living systems show that they have an exquisite sensitivity that makes long-range behavior ultimately unpredictable. Since *living* systems are constantly using feedback to reinforce or reinvent themselves, they are indeed *learning* systems.

All of these findings indicate that organizations and their leaders must shift from quantitative to qualitative analysis for greater understanding and knowledge. Just as in nature, it is critical to revitalize our knowledge-creating systems. There is a great need to build the capacity in our organizations, including for-profit *and* not-for-profit entities to

EXHIBIT 18.2 Living Systems: A Shift in Emphasis

From		To
Focusing on parts, components	→	Focusing on the whole
Focusing on objects	→	Focusing on relationships
Measuring	→	Mapping
Contents	→	Patterns
Quantity	→	Quality

[4]As you will see later, most not-for-profit organizations were founded as innovative or adaptive responses by individuals and groups to fill gaps in society's fabric, whether they were gaps in the social service support network or improved cultural or educational opportunities or other perceived needs.

[5]Peter M. Senge et al., *The Fifth Discipline Fieldbook* (New York: Doubleday, 1994), p. 90.

[6]Fritjof Capra, *The Web of Life* (New York: Anchor Books Doubleday, 1996), p. 6.

identify environmental changes at the earliest possible moment, respond collectively to them, work together efficiently, and perceive the emergent larger systemic patterns. Thus, we must transform our command and control agencies into learning communities where teams and groups strive to think strategically and are prepared to respond to even small alterations in the workplace or its surrounding milieu.

18.4   *Learning Systems and Organizations*

Thanks to the new science, it is now clear that life organizes itself from several imperatives:

- The freedom to create a self
- The need to preserve a self
- The desire to form systems and relationships
- The capacity to invent, to discover original newness, in effect, to learn
- The need for meaning, contribution and growth, at least in humans[7]

Furthermore, living systems cannot be directed. An outside force cannot determine the behavior or direction that a living system takes. However, one can "disturb" a living system, making it aware of new stimuli or changes to its surroundings, and in so doing, the system, itself, may alter its course or behavior.[8]

Living systems are found not only in nature but also in the social structures created by humankind. Nations, cities, governments, religious institutions, corporations, clubs and not-for-profit organizations are also living, and thus, learning systems. Like systems in nature, societal systems must be constantly learning in order to remain viable. As always, change is the organizing force. Structure and solutions are temporary, but self-organizing systems have the capacity to respond continuously to change. They are constantly adjusting to new circumstances. Some adjustments do not work, others work well for a time, still others not only work in the short term but also help to generate new possibilities for the longer term.

(A)   THE LEARNING COMMUNITY[9]

As with life, a learning community is attracted to pattern and order. Nonetheless, both life and learning communities use "messy" tactics like experimentation, some of which is not successful, or diverse responses to the same problem, some of which work better than others, to achieve such order. There is a lot of bumping, even bumbling around.

---

[7]Myron Kellner-Rogers and Margaret Wheatley, seminar entitled "Self-Organizing Systems—A Simpler Way," April 1997.

[8]Humberto Maturana and Francisco Varela, quoted in Margaret J. Wheatley and Myron Kellner-Rogers, *A Simpler Way* (San Francisco: Berrett-Koehler Publishers, 1996), p. 47.

[9]For the purposes of this chapter, I will use the terms "learning organization" and "learning community" interchangeably. I prefer the phrase "learning community" as it carries overtones of caring, commitment and interdependence, but the reader should assume the same implications regardless of which term is used.

Images of dancers working out their moves or of jazz ensembles improvising their riffs serve as helpful models. Nothing is preplanned and yet, with practice and developing intuition, patterns of behavior emerge. Not-for-profit organizations should see themselves as communities of practice.

By seeing employees and volunteers as valued ensemble members, leaders can reorient their approach to problem-solving by entrusting the ensemble to "improvise" solutions. Not-for-profits have capitalized on the valuable creativity of their diverse volunteers to develop innovative responses to challenges facing them. Inasmuch as the volunteers come from the very community being served, the likelihood increases that their solutions are more aligned with the community's needs. In many cases, an agency's responses, guided by past practice and established skills, will be right on target. Yet in other unexpected situations, their improvisations may yield only modest outcomes. Nevertheless, in both circumstances, the team or ensemble continues to learn and grow, as does the organization.

Most not-for-profit institutions or agencies were started by individuals to solve a problem or meet a need in their community. Their founders wove their own webs connecting various members of the community to accomplish specific tasks. With the proliferation of not-for-profits, our institutions are increasingly challenged by funders and others in the community to continue to develop creative and proactive links, now with each other to maximize their potential and minimize operational costs. These networks are filled with potential new ideas, better understandings, greater connections by which not-for-profit missions can best be realized.

Since all activity occurs in the context of a larger system like society or a community, even a field of inquiry, it is vital that an agency's learning community be able to think systemically. Such systems thinking includes both *process thinking*, as the example of the jazz ensemble that practices to build its skills and subliminal connections between its members, and *contextual thinking*, as represented by the funders' requests that not-for-profits keep the community's current needs in mind and seek creative partnerships with other groups.

(B) CHARACTERISTICS OF LEARNING ORGANIZATIONS

New science research shows that a true learning organization will have:

- Continuous learning at the systems level; knowledge generation and sharing; and critical, systemic thinking.
- A culture of learning; a spirit of flexibility and experimentation. It is a place where people are continually discovering how they create their own reality and how they can change it. Its culture supports and rewards learning and innovation; promotes inquiry, dialogue, risk-taking, experimentation; allows mistakes to be shared and viewed as learning opportunities; values the well-being of all employees; is trusting and open.
- Decentralized authority organized around tasks instead of roles or hierarchy.
- Many prescriptions for success instead of only one. Diversity and even redundancy are seen as enriching opportunities for new perspectives and new responses to the changes that constantly bombard the organization. Thus, it will value its people and see them as central to their success.

Danah Zohar, in *Rewiring the Corporate Brain,* offers a new model for structuring and leading organizations that builds on new science data, one that incorporates not only mental systems and skills but also emotional and spiritual ones as well.[10] She argues that learning organizations must strive to become "quantum" organizations, that is, truly outstanding examples of self-renewing, self-developing learning systems. She sees such quantum organizations having eight characteristics:

A quantum organization is:

1. Holistic
2. Flexible and responsive—at the edge
3. Bottom-up, self-organizing, emergent
4. Thriving on diversity
5. Operating like a jazz "jam session," always practicing, experimenting, evolving, encouraging different questions, goals, products, and roles
6. Playful
7. Deeply green (ecological)
8. Vision-centered and values-driven

Groups having these features will:

- Be dynamic and continuously learning
- Be inclusive with decentralized authority, accommodating multiple perspectives and dealing gracefully with dissent
- Have power centered around tasks

In *Built to Last: Successful Habits of Visionary Companies,* James Collins and Jerry Porras share their conclusions from studying outstandingly successful companies around the world such as 3M, Hewlett-Packard, IBM, Johnson & Johnson, Marriott, Nordstrom, Sony, Wal-Mart, and Disney.[11] In comparing them to other companies with good performance, they identified four concepts that set these industry icons apart from the others.[12]

1. These companies focus on "clock building, not time telling." That is, they are primarily concerned with capacity building and not the details prescribing how to do the work.
2. They deliberately avoid seeing either/or situations or issues, and instead they embrace and encourage seeing them as both/and situations.
3. Driving everything is the third key concept of preserving the company's core ideology, values, and home-grown management while simultaneously stimulating progress through "audacious" stretch goals, continuous quality improvement efforts, and natural evolution.
4. Everything else aligns with the first three ideas.

---

[10]Danah Zohar, *Rewiring the Corporate Brain: Using the New Science to Rethink How We Structure and Lead Organizations* (San Francisco: Berrett-Koehler Publishers, 1997), pp. 122–128.

[11]James C. Collins and Jerry I. Porras, *Built to Last: Successful Habits of Visionary Companies* (New York: HarperCollins, 1994).

[12]Jerry Porras, "Building Lasting Organizational Communities," speech to Systems Thinking Conference, September 1998.

18.5 Applying the Learning Community Concept to Not-for-Profits

(A) CHAOS THEORY

Like all of society's structures and processes, not-for-profit organizations are experiencing change—massive, continuous, and accelerating change—as a normal part of daily existence. However, few systems or structures are in place that enable effective and efficient responses to those changes. Organizational charts and long-range plans increasingly are found to be insufficient and out-of-date almost as soon as they are adopted. These sources from which not-for-profit organizations have traditionally derived their management strategies no longer guarantee progress or success for the agencies' leadership.

For example, think of local hospitals. For years they were stable and respected aspects of the community. They were financially sound and enjoyed a comfortable relationship with private citizens and government leaders, who endorsed their value to the community. As aggregations of highly trained and well-paid doctors and other medical professionals, hospitals generally made their governance and service decisions without having to be concerned about public reaction. Basic trust predominated public opinion.

But that apparently stable and dependable scenario has been drastically changed. In recent decades, the healthcare industry and most certainly hospitals have been on the edge of chaos. Dramatic shifts in government and insurance regulations coupled with reduced payments from price controls have spawned a new paradigm in healthcare. Survival strategies prevailed in the 1990s and inhibited learning opportunities. According to the *Los Angeles Times*, 70 percent of U.S. hospitals will show negative balances in the next several years.[13]

As hospitals were faced with the threat of acquisitions, mergers, and buyouts due to managed care and cost-control strategies, the result has been public confusion, irritation, and loss of trust. Healthcare is in danger of becoming more of a commodity than a community service. Clearly, a new leadership is needed.

This constancy and frequency of change and its concomitant complexity and uncertainty are often described as being "on the edge of chaos." Were organizations actually to descend into chaos, they would lose all ability to contend with their environment; so they and their leaders teeter on the edge, nervous, tense, exhausted, and insecure. The image of a tightrope walker comes to mind, as he tries to stay balanced and keep his forward momentum on a minuscule wire while always swaying back and forth to compensate for the natural forces that would otherwise cause him to fall. Feelings of inadequacy and failure are ever-present as managers strive to improve their ability to adapt easily and quickly to new near-chaotic conditions. Control, once viewed through Newtonian eyes as achievable and ideal, is now seen as illusory and counterproductive.

Instead of desiring safe, controlled circumstances, successful organizations are now working to be increasingly adaptive and comfortable with feeling almost out of control. Being on the edge of chaos is the hallmark of any natural system, and as such is the only place where progress and new learning can happen.[14]

---

[13]Julie Marquis, "Many Academic Medical Centers Struggling Financially, Panel Says," *Los Angeles Times,* May 5, 2000.
[14]Margaret Wheatley, Speech to Systems Thinking Conference, October 1996.

(B) SURVIVAL KIT FOR LIVING ON THE EDGE OF CHAOS

New science research suggests four basic shifts in thinking and orientation that leaders must make in order for an organization to survive and thrive in such near chaos. (See Exhibit 18.3). These shifts are no less vital for not-for-profits than for-profit companies, as attested to by the healthcare example cited earlier.

(i) Shift 1: To Focus on the Whole: The Need for a Strong Core Identity

Developing a strong core identity is indispensable for successful companies in shifting focus from their component parts to the whole. In the not-for-profit world, agencies have long recognized the value of having vision, mission, and values statements, for they help to distinguish each institution's uniqueness and contribution to society. They further have come to recognize how important it is that every member of the not-for-profit community, from the lowest employee to the highest, from part-time volunteers to involved trustees, understands and embraces these mutual goals. In our chaotic world, the not-for-profit's organizational identity needs to be its most stable aspect. The significance of a shared vision cannot be overemphasized.

There are many examples in the not-for-profit arena of organizations that are highly successful in creating strong core identities. It is interesting to consider how such a well-established core generates an aura or field that can pull new organization members, staff and volunteers alike, into the group. Field theory postulates that people who are introduced into this environment will be positively influenced by this field. In fact, the field itself somehow transmits the core identity to new employees, volunteers, prospective and current donors, clients, or visitors without extensive effort on the part of leaders. Now, there's both effectiveness and efficiency!

(ii) Shift 2: To Adapt Faster by Understanding Processes

According to Arie de Geus, former head of Royal Dutch/Shell's planning division, the ability to learn faster than your competitors may be the only sustainable competitive advantage.[15] While de Geus comes from the for-profit world, his statement is no less applicable to not-for-profits. The challenge, Einstein once said, is that the knowledge

---

EXHIBIT 18.3 Shifts in Thinking to Survive Near Chaos

From		To
Focusing on parts	→	Focusing on the whole
Understanding structures	→	Understanding processes
Seeing the universe as static and definite	→	Understanding the universe as a web of relationships and potentials, constantly shifting and growing
Believing that reality is predictable and absolute	→	Realizing that we can never know absolutely or predict anything

---

[15]de Geus, Ari quoted by Bob Guns, "The Faster Learning Organization (FLO)," *Learning Organizations,* Sarita Chawla and John Renesch (eds.) (Portland, OR: Productivity Press, 1995), p. 337.

base that created today's problems will not solve them.[16] Therefore, learning communities must move beyond their former thinking to new mental models that overcome past problems and achieve positive results.

The charitable institutions and agencies that will survive and thrive in the future will be those that can constantly update themselves, stay connected to the world at large, be in touch, find necessary information, and know how to interpret that data. This will require more fluid and flexible structures, such as self-directed work teams, which are established around tasks on an as-needed basis and which disband and re-form with others when the original task is completed.

Driven to continuously improve their systems, teams will routinely monitor and assess both their short-term and long-term activities and results. The focus will be more on processes and outcomes. Furthermore, input, not only from employees but also from other stakeholders of the organization, raises the potential for strategically significant adjustments being made as well as optimally positive outcomes.

(iii) Shift 3: To See Webs of Relationships and Nurture Community Members
Not-for-profit organizations will also expand their capacity for creating relationships as they recognize their limits and the value of diverse *inter*dependent connections with other groups and individuals, both internally and externally.

By discovering how to tap people's commitment and capacity to learn at *all* levels, not-for-profits will endorse their constituents—paid *and* volunteer, service providers *and* receivers—as their most valuable resources. In this environment, leaders and subordinates will be dependent on each other with far less hierarchical control.

Fortunately, not-for-profits with their volunteer boards and active involvement of private citizens have good grass-roots systems for keeping in touch with what the community needs. Without such open conduits of information, it would be all too easy for institutions to fail to identify emerging changes in local needs, service or program concerns that might be developing, or new opportunities to reach out with appropriate programs. Examples of charities collaborating with other not-for-profits, government, and corporate or private entities on behalf of the collective good manifest the value of expanding these innovative and interdependent relationships. Collaboration is in!

Underlying the notion of interdependence is another concept to be nurtured and promoted: the understanding that each person, again whether paid or unpaid, whether high in the organizational structure or not, can and usually does contribute to the best of his or her ability. Recognition and credit should be given for each contribution. It is vital to ensure that an individual's or a work group's success contributes to the success of the common enterprise and to the success of others. A not-for-profit's value to society is directly related to the quality of its commitment and effort.

As stated earlier, operating on the edge of chaos is exceedingly stressful. Therefore, it is vitally important to take care of one another. Not-for-profits have long held a special distinction in our culture as the work environment where there was a greater likelihood of some person-centered approach to its employees and other community members. New science data strongly suggests that this uniqueness is a great strength that should

---

[16]Einstein, Albert, quoted by John Thompson, "The Renaissance of Learning in Business," *Learning Organizations,* Sarita Chawla and John Renesch (eds.) (Portland, OR: Productivity Press, 1995), p. 97.

be exploited and built on. Our charitable organizations must take to heart the implications of being communities, and not merely places of work, albeit very worthy work.[17]

(iv) Shift 4: To Embrace Uncertainty

Finally, all living systems, including not-for-profit groups, need to accept the notion that nothing is certain. Putting aside the old desire for predictability and certainty can liberate organizations and their members from outdated mental models. It can also reduce the stresses incurred when members of the organization try to resist change. By embracing uncertainty and being flexible, not-for-profit organizations are in a much better position to recognize early and take advantage of opportunities for growth and change. Indeed, being seen as a change agent in the vanguard of the field can be most effective. Perceiving the need and acting on it with dispatch will be key.

18.6 How Leaders Can Help

Given the increasingly numerous changes in all our organizational environments and the unforeseen challenges they will pose, it is crucial for not-for-profit leaders to nurture and build their organizations into learning communities that will be resilient and dynamic enough to meet these future circumstances successfully.

(A) SERVANT LEADERSHIP

The concept of servant leadership as described by Robert Greenleaf provides an important first step for not-for-profit leaders.[18] Servant leadership starts within each person who hopes to become a positive and leading force in any organization. As individuals strive to achieve their own *personal* transformation, they will then be able to concentrate on the practical activities of transforming the corporate culture into a learning entity.

If individuals see themselves as servants *first,* they greatly enhance their potential for truly effective leadership. When the intention and desire to serve is firmly established in their hearts and minds first, then can they aspire to lead. This is a vastly different point of view from the one of wanting to lead first, and it takes several different perspectives. Servant leaders consciously put ego aside. So, too, do servant leaders recognize that the autocratic, decision-making role model of the past simply is not the one that will accomplish today's desired transformation. By learning to trust others and acting on that trust, leaders will also generate trustworthiness, thereby increasing their leadership potential.[19]

Benchmarks of successful servant leadership can be determined by asking the following questions: Are those in our organization, whom we serve, growing as persons? While being served, are they becoming healthier, wiser, freer, and more autonomous? Are they themselves exhibiting the traits of becoming servants to others?[20]

---

[17]James A. Autry, *Love and Profit: The Art of Caring Leadership* (New York: Avon Books, 1991), p. 19.
[18]Robert Greenleaf, *The Servant as Leader.* (Indianapolis: The Robert Greenleaf Center, 1991).
[19]Stephen Covey, *The Seven Habits of Highly Effective People* (New York: Simon and Schuster, 1989), p. 188.
[20]Greenleaf, *The Servant as Leader,* 7.

Servant leadership is a powerful tool. In the most successful learning organizations, it cascades throughout hierarchy, crossing and connecting what had formerly been lateral division "silos" and empowering employees at all levels to claim their rightful investment in the products and achievements being produced. It is critical, however, that those at the very top of the organization's pyramid embrace this concept. Only with their personal change will it succeed.

(B)   KEY LEADERSHIP ACTIVITIES

Having committed to his or her personal journey, what steps can a leader take to help the organization undertake its own collective transformation? The following four strategic leadership activities provide great leverage and value.

1. Ensure that there is a shared vision of what your organization is all about.
2. Provide *all* staff members with the tools they need to accomplish that vision.
3. Remove the barriers that might inhibit or block personnel from doing quality work.
4. Facilitate change, and celebrate milestones along the way.

(i)   *Shared Vision*
From Collins and Porras, Wheatley, and others, it is clear that not-for-profit organizations lose an enormous organizing advantage when they fail to create a clear and coherent identity. In a near-chaotic world, organizational identity needs to be the *most* stable aspect of the endeavor. Without a strong, universally understood and embraced identity and vision of itself at its core, the organization will never be able to communicate its value and message to the rest of the world. Instead, there will be multiple, perhaps conflicting, messages, all confusing, none compelling or convincing.

It is also important that vision *not* be the perspective of the leader only but that it be shared. *Shared* vision requires the involvement and contributions of many stakeholders throughout the organization. These might include: employees at all levels, trustees and other volunteers, clients or beneficiaries, donors, or other interested community members. It is the leader's role, while ensuring that a vision is created and maintained, to promote conversations at all levels of the organization and beyond that involve as many stakeholders as possible in the development of the vision statement.

(ii)   *Importance of Free-Flowing Information*
Providing *all* staff members with the proper tools so they can accomplish their jobs can mean assuring that the physical resources are available and in working order. But it also refers to the importance of a free flow of information. Information should belong to everyone. *Access* to information, of all sorts, is vital.

We have all heard arguments supporting a contrary point of view. The need for secrecy to protect unique, distinctive, or sensitive aspects of work, the importance of not burdening employees with details they do not need to do their jobs, the importance of respecting confidential information immediately come to mind. However, too often these arguments are merely diversions from the vital point, that access to most—if not all—information may be life-saving for any living system, not-for-profit organizations included.

It is, after all, information—unplanned, uncontrolled, abundant, instantaneous—that creates conditions for the emergence of fast, well-integrated, effective responses. And, in our ever-changing world, quick responses are critical. However, to respond with speed *and* effectiveness, people need access to the intelligence of the *whole* system. Without that access, decisions or actions may be taken that are ill-conceived if not totally wrong-headed. By providing such access, all members of the organization have the informational tools available whenever they are confronted with new or unexpected situations.

Not-for-profit leaders understand that meaningful relationships with customers, clients, and donors are a natural and positive opportunity for enriching the informational (and financial) input into our system. Like continuous quality improvement guru Edwards Deming, they also realize that a single person, team, or an entire organization cannot achieve quality alone. The focus must also be on connections. It is through better relationships that the agency's health is assured. Only through relationships is information created and transformed. Assuredly, relationships cultivated with donors are crucial to the success of their fund-raising efforts. Without connections, nothing happens.

As free-flowing information is vital to an organization's success, it is useful to focus on two areas:

1. Conversation as a core business practice
2. The power of dialogue

Since information is most often transmitted verbally, leaders must clearly understand and sincerely embrace the idea of conversation as a core business practice. One of a leader's primary roles should be to serve as a convener or host for good conversations about questions that matter. How much time do you and your colleagues spend discovering the right questions to ask in relation to time spent finding the right answers? How much of your training budget is devoted to supporting *informal* learning conversations and *sharing* effective practices across organizational boundaries? Leaders have the opportunity and an obligation to their institutions to create a space for these kinds of verbal exchanges. By honoring the unique contributions of each and every member, they build a strong and vibrant community of commitment.

To facilitate the desired diversity of contributions, leaders can actively maintain a forum in which all voices may be heard. This also means that members of the not-for-profit community can disagree without withdrawing from the group. Furthermore, all are free to express what they *feel* as well as what they *think*.[21] By focusing less on training programs and more on how to engage people in determining how to resolve quality issues, leaders will promote the active investment of all group members. If those in leadership could provide better resources to support their inquiry, rather than limiting that inquiry to issues imposed from outside, they would also generate many more solution-seeking processes and many more sources of feedback.

Even with the best of intentions, however, leaders often find it difficult to unlearn years of training in and reliance on discussion skills, because they have attained personal success with them. Unfortunately, those same skills are counterproductive to promoting a learning community environment. Think about it. Most discussions are conducted like

---

[21] Autry, *Love and Profit*, p. 48.

an indoor sport where the object is winning, whether it is an actual argument or merely ensuring that one's perspective dominates. The seminal work of Harvard professor Chris Argyris, a highly respected observer of learning in corporate management teams, on the problems in communications in meetings has led to greater awareness of the negative results of our usual business discussions.[22]

Dialogue approaches verbal exchange quite differently from discussion. It forges a very different environment where participants strive to discover *shared meaning* through their individual contributions.[23] Rather than opposing others, as happens most often in discussion (a word that has the same root as percussion), dialogue promotes a joint exploration of topics and ideas without preconceived outcomes.

Dialogue relies on four skills:

1. Identification of assumptions
2. Suspension of judgments
3. Listening
4. Inquiry and reflection for understanding and, indeed, new meaning[24]

This is a powerful tool for any not-for-profit group or business that is serious about becoming a learning community. It slows down verbal deliberations and helps participants be more intentional as listeners as well as contributors to the collective search for a shared foundation for understanding and, ultimately, action.

(iii) Promoting "Messiness" and Supporting Learning

While having high expectations and managing for the best, leaders should also foster creativity, surprise, and even messiness. Just as in nature, organizational learning often comes from the messy, unexpected, even playful moments when new thinking emerges. Leaders can facilitate change by encouraging the creativity that lies within each member and team in the community. Promoting a spirit of exploration, a leader can cultivate the readiness, mental flexibility, and openness to meet new challenges as they arise.

It is also crucial to remember to keep local solutions localized. Just because a good idea works for one unit or section of the organization does not mean that it will work for others. Information about what has worked well elsewhere can be very helpful, but not if imposed. As new science teaches, a plurality of solutions, even a redundancy of them, is desirable. Managers cannot "direct" colleagues into perfection; they can only engage and encourage them so that they themselves will *want* to do perfect work. Thus, fostering creativity and even injecting "disturbances" or surprises into the environment are useful tools of today's leader.

In promoting this spirit of experimentation, leaders should assume that all individuals have skills—including, perhaps, those needed for the task at hand. However, they should also establish an environment in which subordinates can ask questions or seek additional guidance and training easily and without retribution. Employees, or volunteers for that matter, should understand that they are trusted to determine their capabil-

---

[22]Chris Argyris, *Overcoming Organizational Defenses: Facilitating Organizational Learning* (New York: Prentice-Hall, 1990).

[23]David Bohm, *On Dialogue* (Ojai, CA: David Bohm Seminars, 1990).

[24]Linda Ellinor and Glenna Gerard, *Dialogue: Rediscover the Transforming Power of Conversation* (New York: John Wiley & Sons, 1998).

ity of tackling a project. Learning communities need to be based on a concern for people and a belief that they can and will learn. Such a culture will have shared beliefs that people have the capacity for change.

A note of caution, however. In the midst of promoting various, different responses and projects, the not-for-profit leader should always keep in mind his or her first responsibility—to ensure a clarity and consistency of the organization's vision, mission, and values. As Mort Meyerson, chairman & CEO of Perot Industries, says, "The essence of being a leader is to make sure the organization knows itself."[25] Thus, it is imperative for leaders to call everyone together often to promote new information sharing and to ensure that people remain clear about who they are collectively, where they have been, who they have just become, and who they still want to be.

Such meetings will include feedback and input from clients, society at large, and the marketplace as well as the group's history. Data and deductions from the organization's mistakes are also important. As stated before, organizations that are clear at their core hold themselves together because of their deep congruence. People are then free to explore new avenues of activity and to support diversity, freedom, and creativity. A wonderful sense of camaraderie will emerge, and true community, which is inclusive and which honors the gifts of all members, will result.

Thus, leaders need to make available some "slack" time for generative learning to develop. Such generative learning depends on open and extensive communication, the ability to think systemically, and interdependent coordination and cooperation. Senge has identified that different types of leaders exist at all levels of an organization.[26] In learning communities, all leaders and managers model learning behavior, facilitate learning, encourage people to contribute their ideas, ensure dissemination of knowledge and learning, make needed resources available, and share the leadership.

(iv) Facilitating Change

An important component in facilitating change is *celebration*. We all need encouragement and recognition. Not-for-profits recognize the value of acknowledging and thanking their volunteers and donors; but they may not always extend that behavior to staff members. Leaders have an especially important role to play in helping *all* members of the group to celebrate, not only the big achievements, but also the small, incremental milestones. Both are equally significant to the ongoing effort of collective transformation.

Not-for-profit leaders need to understand that if they:

- Impose structure, they create resistance.
- Ignore relationships, they create irresponsibility.
- Deny participation, they create anger and resentment.
- Impose traits and behaviors, they create lifeless performance.

---

[25]Meyerson, Mort, quoted by Margaret Wheatley, "Goodbye Command and Control," *Leader to Leader,* Summer 1997. (San Francisco: Peter F. Drucker Foundation and Jossey-Bass Inc.), p. 24.
[26]Peter Senge, "Rethinking Leadership in the Learning Organization," *The Systems Thinker* (February 1996). He refers to three types of leaders: local line leaders, who can undertake meaningful experiments to test whether new learning capabilities actually lead to improved results; executive leaders, who provide support for the line leaders, develop learning infrastructures, and lead by example; and internal networkers, who move freely about the organization identifying those who are predisposed to bring about change and aid in the diffusion of new learning.

- Allow incoherence, they create withdrawal and paralysis.
- Ignore meaning, they create selfishness.[27]

In the quest to improve the capacity of their organizations to meet future change as effectively and as quickly as possible, leaders also need to recognize that there are no right answers. Long-learned reliance on analysis of situations may yield some helpful hints; but it is also important to factor in new science learning that cause and effect will most likely not be closely related in time and space. Thus, nibbling away at a large systemic problem will *not* produce long-term improvements. It may even worsen the situation. Beware! The easiest way out of the problem will always lead you back in. Again, what new science has revealed is that we should be seeking to discover the natural, emerging order of things rather than imposing controls, which are illusory anyway.

Leaders can do a great deal of good for themselves, their organization, and their colleagues to help others *deal with change*. First, they should set the stage by providing a historical perspective for the anticipated change, establishing present conditions, and outlining expected benefits. By clearly stating the problem or reason for change, along with its antecedents and the intended outcomes, leaders can educate the volunteers and staff and build in them not only an understanding but also an endorsement of the change.

This initial phase also implies that they have taken the time to identify all the stakeholders in this process: staff members, volunteers, people affected, individuals or representatives of community groups. This list may also include donors, people who have supported the organization in the past, with perhaps even a particular investment in the area or program affected by the proposed change. Reaching out to all of these constituents is a very important leadership role of change agents. In this day and age, it is crucial to ensuring the alignment of their services with the community's perceived needs and the benefits it desires.

In the process of describing the need for change, it is also good to define specifically what processes, programs, systems, or structures of the institution will be affected or influenced by the change. Again, the more clarity leaders can help the others of their group to have about the situation, the greater likelihood that they will be able to buy in to the coming activities.

By identifying the skills and experiences people currently have and also those they will need to acquire in the future, leaders can help them begin to understand the potential to themselves and the organization. Throughout this process, it is vital to listen carefully to the questions and concerns that are raised. In addition, leaders also should be clear about what will not be changed.

Listing the pros and cons associated with the change can help others identify both inhibiting and positive forces for the change. Leaders need to ensure consensus about needed resources, strategies, and activities with a timetable. Once again, by bringing some celebration to the moment, leaders can acknowledge and thank people for their cooperation and collaboration.

Not-for-profit leaders facilitate these wrenching transformations by also keeping in mind that relationships make up the fabric of our organization. The work and friendship connections among employees, trustees, and volunteers, donors, clients, and others are critical to the group's mission and structure. So, discerning how proposed change might impact on those relationships is equally important.

---

[27]Kellner-Rogers and Wheatley seminar: "Self-Organizing Systems," April, 1997.

As leaders, they can help others to think through what probable effects may result from the impending changes. By following those speculations, the organization's members can think through various scenarios and, it is hoped, determine which ones will create the most desirable long-term result. We all know how painful big change is; but, paradoxically, what we may not grasp is that our community members may actually adjust to big changes more easily than they do to smaller ones.[28]

Regardless, sweeping change takes several years to accomplish, and in the meantime, behavior may grow worse before it grows better. Therefore, having a strong and clear intention of the direction in which we wish to head without laying out a too finely prescribed set of action plans will facilitate the learning orientation needed to successfully meet the unknown challenges ahead. A strategic alignment of the proposed change with the community's needs also ensures a much higher awareness of the not-for-profit's benefit and value to its community, something for which all agency leaders strive.

18.7 Conclusion

Given the rate and scope of the changes occurring in today's society, not-for-profits, as well as other businesses, must be able to respond effectively and efficiently. This requires that *all* members, both paid and volunteer, have the skills and understandings that heretofore may not have been developed in order to understand and use change to advantage.

What would be different if leaders truly believed that most people have a deep desire to do quality work, want to make things work better, and want to develop sustaining relationships beyond narrow self-interest? What would occur if a leader focused not on control but on emerging patterns and order? What would happen if persons in leadership held those beliefs and promoted them throughout their organizations?

By applying new science concepts in this new millennium, not-for-profit institutions will see themselves as communities of endeavor, with members who are continuously learning and leaders who serve as models for others. Employees and volunteers will find themselves encouraged to try new approaches; and managers will attempt to remove all barriers hindering others' ability to meet the new challenges confronting them.

Not-for-profit organizations will think systemically, seeing the forest as well as the trees and taking time to appreciate its intrinsic beauty and value to the world. They will be reinventing themselves in response to the changing needs of their communities. Both internally and externally, such agencies will extend and generate new networks thereby increasing their capacity to solve problems and to deliver benefits back to their communities. Included in those networks will be clients, donors, and people walking in off the street, who will be welcomed and valued for the potential learning they bring to the organization, not merely as recipients of services or as potential contributors.

Leaders will release their need for control. They will value the people who are involved and invested in their organization and will promote among them all a shared vision of where they have been, where they are headed, and how they intend to get there. They will not only promote conversation as a core business practice, they will also

---

[28]Richard Farson, *Management of the Absurd: Paradoxes in Leadership* (New York: Simon & Schuster, 1996), p. 112.

trust colleagues with access to information, lots of information, to increase their potential for quick and effective responses to emergent problems or issues.

By trusting paid and volunteer members to want to do their best, leaders will nurture a spirit of risk-taking; and if unintended consequences arise, they will step back and learn what they can from them without judgment or retaliation. Often it is the "messes" that yield rich, new possibilities.

Thus, the organization as a whole will transform itself into a true learning community, where, as a result of the change process, both individuals and the organization continuously become:

- More intelligent and competent
- More committed to achieving purpose
- More valued for their contributions
- More prepared for the next wave of change[29]

Through it all, not-for-profit learning organizations will help their members to see change as a normal part of life and to cope with the challenges and opportunities it presents.

Suggested Readings

Argyris, Chris. *Overcoming Organizational Defenses: Facilitating Organizational Learning.* New York: Prentice-Hall, 1990.

Autry, James A. *Love and Profit: The Art of Caring Leadership.* New York: Avon Books, 1991.

Belasco, James A., and R. C. Strayer. *Flight of the Buffalo: Soaring to Excellence, Learning to Let Employees Lead.* New York: Warner Books, 1993.

Bennis, Warren. *Why Leaders Can't Lead: The Unconscious Conspiracy Continues.* San Francisco: Jossey-Bass, 1989.

Block, Peter. *Stewardship: Choosing Service Over Self-interest.* San Francisco: Berrett-Koehler Publishers, 1993.

Bohm, David. *On Dialogue.* David Bohm Seminars, P.O. Box 1452, Ojai, CA 93023, 1989.

Bolman, Lee G., and Terrence E. Deal. *Leading with Soul: An Uncommon Journey of Spirit.* San Francisco: Jossey-Bass, 1995.

Capra, Fritjof. *The Tao of Physics.* Boston: Shambhala Publications, 1975.

———. *The Turning Point: Science, Society, and The Rising Culture.* New York: Simon & Schuster, 1982.

———. *The Web of Life.* New York: Anchor Books Doubleday, 1996.

Chawla, Sarita, and John Renesch, eds. *Learning Organizations: Developing Cultures for Tomorrow's Workplace.* Portland, Ore.: Productivity Press, 1995.

Collins, James C., and Jerry I. Porras. *Built to Last: Successful Habits of Visionary Companies.* New York: Harper Collins, 1994.

Covey, Stephen R. *Principle-Centered Leadership.* New York: Summit Books, 1990.

———. *The Seven Habits of Highly Effective People.* New York: Simon & Schuster, 1989.

---

[29]Kellner-Rogers and Wheatley Seminar, "Self-Organizing Systems."

DePree, Max. *Leadership Is an Art*. New York: Dell, 1989.

Ellinor, Linda, and Glenna Gerard. *Dialogue: Rediscover the Transforming Power of Conversation*. New York: John Wiley & Sons, 1998.

Farson, Richard. *Management of the Absurd: Paradoxes in Leadership*. New York: Simon & Schuster, 1996.

Ferguson, Marilyn. *The Aquarian Conspiracy: Personal and Social Transformation in Our Time*. Los Angeles: J.P. Tarcher, 1976.

Greenleaf, Robert K. *The Servant as Leader*. Indianapolis: The Robert K. Greenleaf Center, 1991.

———. *Servant Leadership: A Journey into the Nature of Legitimate Power and Greatness*. New York: Paulist Press, 1977.

Hesselbein, F., M. Goldsmith, and R. Beckhard, eds. *The Leader of the Future*. San Francisco: Jossey-Bass, 1996.

Nirenberg, John. *The Living Organization: Transforming Teams into Workplace Communities*. San Diego: Pfeiffer & Company, 1993.

Senge, Peter M. *The Fifth Discipline: The Art and Practice of the Learning Organization*. New York: Doubleday, 1990.

Senge, Peter M., et al. *The Fifth Discipline Fieldbook*. New York: Doubleday, 1994.

Senge, Peter & Daniel Kim, "From Fragmentation to Integration: Building Learning Communities," *The Systems Thinker*, May 1997. Cambridge, MA: Pegasus Communications, page 1.

Senge, Peter M., et al. *The Dance of Change*. New York: Doubleday, 1999.

Wheatley, Margaret J. *Leadership and the New Science: Learning About Organization from an Orderly Universe*. San Francisco: Berrett-Koehler Publishers, 1992.

Wheatley, Margaret J., and Myron Kellner-Rogers. *A Simpler Way*. San Francisco: Berrett-Koehler Publishers, 1996.

Meyerson, Mort, quoted by Margaret Wheatley, "Goodbye Command and Control," *Leader to Leader*, Summer 1997. San Francisco: Peter F. Drucker Foundation and Jossey-Bass Inc., page 24.

Zohar, Danah. *Rewiring the Corporate Brain: Using the New Science to Rethink How We Structure and Lead Organizations*. San Francisco: Berrett-Koehler Publishers, 1997.

Philanthropy in the New Economy: The Quantum Civics Paradigm of Leadership

RICHARD D. CHESHIRE, PH.D.
Co-founder and Director, Institute for
Voluntary Leadership

19.1   Being Part of the Leading Edge

New science and high technology are leading the new information economy. The global information revolution now sweeping the world, best epitomized by the Internet, is changing our lives faster and more profoundly than we know. Philanthropy, the love of humankind, can be a more important influence for change than perhaps it has ever been before. That is because the capacity to lead people is more important than any other, and leading them involves loving them, having compassion for them, and caring about them deeply.

Now philanthropy is inspiring a new leadership science that can work in organizations of all types, especially in nonprofit organizations. This new leadership science is *quantum civics*, an applied social science that describes the dynamic interactions of voluntary associations in the civic sector or first sector, not the third sector, of society. Nonprofit professionals who are interested in a growing role for philanthropy should consider the significance of this development for their futures.

At the heart of the new economy is the new entrepreneur who wants to make a life for him- or herself by making a real contribution to the world. This new economy entrepreneur wants to do that by doing something that has never been done before and that makes a difference for the better. This is a wonderful impulse. It is an impulse that, happily, can overcome greed even though, sadly, it cannot eliminate it.

We who are in the world of philanthropy must understand and adopt this impulse to make it our own. By doing so, we become part of the leading edge that can take the world to a radically new place of unprecedented prosperity and peace. I invite you to take an exciting leap of faith into the emerging twenty-first century world in which we will begin seeing what we have never seen before. In this world, we will learn that leading is believing, that believing is seeing, and that seeing is leading. We will have new eyes. We will experience a creative process that circuitously finds its way to patterns of change and that makes things happen at the edge of the future. (See Exhibit 19.1 for a step-by-step progression of leadership change.)

19.2   The Best of Times and the Worst of Times

In *A Tale of Two Cities* Charles Dickens wrote the memorable lines that he might have written were he alive today: "It was the best of times, it was the worst of times, it was the age of wisdom, it was the age of foolishness, it was the epoch of belief, it was the epoch of incredulity, it was the season of Light, it was the season of Darkness, it was the spring of hope, it was the winter of despair."[1]

As he saw his own times, life was lived at the edge, one might speculate between the rich and the poor, triumph and disaster, happiness and sadness, wellness and illness, knowledge and ignorance, God and the devil. Today life has become more complex and faster paced. Statistically, we have never been healthier or wealthier, smarter or swifter, bigger or better. Trillions of dollars are being created in new wealth. Trillions more are about to be transferred from one generation to the next.

Yet there are multiple crises nearly everywhere we look: in homes and families, in personal and professional relationships, in healthcare access and quality, in preschool to postgraduate education, in voluntary civic participation from voting to running for office, in drug and alcohol abuse, in spouse and child abuse, in employment and unemployment, in faith and ideology, and in seemingly unprecedented stress. (See Exhibit 19.2.)

EXHIBIT 19.1 Patterns of Change

21st-century philanthropy→new leadership science→quantum civics→dynamic interactions→voluntary associations→first sector

---

[1]Quoted by Earl Babbie in *You Can Make a Difference: The Heroic Potential Within Us All* (Anaheim Hills, Calif.: Opening Books, 1985), p. 4.

EXHIBIT 19.2 Modern Complexities

Faster Paced	Multiple Crises
Healthier and wealthier	Families
Smarter and swifter	Healthcare
Bigger and better	Education
	Civic life
	Drug abuse
	Faith
	Stress

Our philanthropy continues to grow year by year; in the latest 1999 figures, it reached $190 billion in voluntary support plus another $225 billion in volunteered services. This $400 billion in philanthropy, which I believe is a conservative estimate, was roughly equivalent to 5 percent of the $8 trillion plus economy of that year. But for years voluntary support has been stuck at about 2 percent of gross domestic product and voluntary services have been stuck at about 50 percent of American adults, judging from published figures in widely accepted surveys.

There is growing awareness, fostered especially by the new sciences of the twentieth century, that our global civic society is living at the critical edge of chaos and order, struggling for balance. The same appears to be true about our leadership, since our leading can only come from where we are living. If we are living at the edge, then we must be leading at the edge, from the same place, right? If it is true that we are leading our lives, as the saying goes, then it is only logical to realize that we are living where we are led, from where our hearts and minds as well as our bodies and our souls are beckoning us.

19.3   The New Economy Is the Leading Edge

The leading edge is an evolution of information processes, and the new economy is an information economy driven by high technology. These processes are changing and creative. They are putting increasing pressure on the fundamentals of philanthropy to produce creative change that yields effective results. Never before have we faced such challenging complexities, and never before has the challenge been more exciting.

We are creating wealth in the new economy faster than at any other time in history, yet we continue to harvest only 5 percent of our productivity for worthy causes while the need for help gives every sign of outrunning the capacity of philanthropy to deliver it. We need to double and redouble our philanthropy in the coming years in order to meet the real needs of a viable global community that is here and now. And we can.

When Claude Rosenberg published his findings about how America could get more out of philanthropy in his 1994 book *Wealthy and Wise*, he found that "no matter how you slice it, the overwhelming evidence suggests that the giving percentages of high-end earners have not been even close to what they might have been."[2] His research persuasively

---

[2]Claude Rosenberg Jr., *Wealthy and Wise: How You and America Can Get the Most Out of Your Giving* (Boston: Little, Brown & Company, 1994), p. 48.

demonstrated that at least $100 billion more could have been raised in voluntary gifts without affecting the lifestyles of all contributors. Since then the estimates have increased to at least $250 billion in charitable gifts that could have been given but were not.

It does not seem unreasonable to me to assume that a similar relationship exists between unrealized volunteerism and unrealized contributions as exists between their realities. If that is so, then unrealized volunteerism would approximate $320 billion on top of the $250 billion in unrealized contributions for a total of $570 billion in unrealized philanthropy that could have been given without sacrifice of lifestyle! Since there is good reason to believe, in my mind, that these figures are conservative, I believe that philanthropy in America could now be at the annual level of $1 trillion if only we—the givers and the getters—knew how! (See Exhibit 19.3.)

Rosenberg's answer is information, awareness, education, attitude. I believe he is right. But I believe that this is only the beginning of the answer. The rest of the answer is leadership, specifically voluntary leadership given with civic intent. Education and leadership are like thought and action. They are reciprocals. They have a complementary relationship to each other. They are like the yin and yang of Chinese philosophy, the female and male who together create the universe.

Since the new economy is an information economy, we have potentially an ideal foundation for creating new awareness of the role that philanthropy can play for increased prosperity and peace. Rosenberg estimated that, at current tax rates, "two and a half to three dollars of impetus to the economy can, *if properly directed*, occur from every dollar of tax deduction taken. A one-dollar contribution might cost the Treasury about thirty to forty cents in lost revenues, but every philanthropic dollar that flows directly into the economy obviously adds considerably more in the way of services."[3]

The new economy has brought with it an increasing sense that people are its heart and soul, its mind and body, the primary asset with which it is endowed. With that growing appreciation has come not only a heightened awareness of the importance of education but also of leadership. People need to know in order to produce, and they prefer to lead and be led knowingly and freely. It has become more and more clear that leadership is most effectively pursued on a voluntary basis. People do not care much for being pushed around, and it diminishes their dignity to do so. Voluntary leadership is most commonly found in nonprofit organizations. And the most effective nonprofit organizations are run in a businesslike way dedicated to their philanthropic missions.

19.4   Philanthropy @ the Speed of Light

In 1999 Bill Gates of Microsoft published a new book called *Business @ The Speed of Thought*.[4] It is very thoughtful and I recommend it to all who seek a better understand-

EXHIBIT 19.3 Philanthropic Potential

Realized philanthropy	Unrealized potential	Philanthropic capacity
$190B + $225B = $400B	$250B + $320B = $570B	$400B + $570B = $970B

[3]*Ibid*, p. 30.
[4]Bill Gates, *Business @ The Speed of Thought: Using a Digital Nervous System* (New York: Warner Books, 1999).

ing of the possibilities of communication at the speed of the electronic net among people who are working together.

I suggest that there are a couple of related ideas that need to be added to Gates's insight. One is the idea that leadership is always needed for success in business, and the key to that is *leading @ the speed of vision*. We can never go far where we cannot see, or envision the way ahead, and since we are leading our lives, we need to see where we are going.

The second idea is that philanthropy is necessary for the good of humankind and therefore needs to move at the same speed at which people are moving at its leading edge. Today that leads to the necessity of creating *philanthropy @ the speed of light*. The light I am referring to is both physical light, as in the form of the sun's rays, and non-physical light, as in awareness of the timeless and the eternal, how the many come from the One and return there.

Twenty-first-century philanthropy will be conducted at the speed of light because the leading edge of our emerging global civic society is already moving ahead at that speed. What does this mean? Physical light speed is electronic, moving from place to place across the universe, thanks to high-speed technology, as invisible electromagnetic waves that can reach everywhere they can be received. Nonphysical light speed is self-consciously human in the fullest sense, moving at the speed of all our senses, especially our intuitive sixth sense that connects our spirits with our hearts and minds. (See Exhibit 19.4.)

In order to see the light, we need to be the light. In order to connect at the speed of light, we need to act at the speed of light. If we do not like how we are perceived, then we need to change what we are doing. Our being intimately affects our doing. The same goes for philanthropy. If we are unhappy with philanthropy as usual, then we must create philanthropy as unusual. The status quo is always changing, I like to say. Nothing ever stays quite the same. That is why we must embrace creativity and guide it to wherever it naturally leads.

We are, of course, dependent on high technology for our electronic communication and on human technology for our personal connections. We seem to know more about how to use the high technology of communication than we do about how to use the human technology of connections. This is partly because we do not usually think of human technology, or if we do, we probably assume it's an oxymoron. Technology is hard, right, as in hardware? Yes, but it is also soft, as in software.

The human technology we should consider most carefully as we approach philanthropy in the new economy is the technology of organized leading. It will help us to know that technology is, as *Webster's Dictionary* reminds us, "a method, a process, for handling a specific technical problem" and a "system by which a society provides its members with those things needed or desired." Leadership is a technical challenge in that it is practical, industrial, and mechanical in applying the principles and rules of both

EXHIBIT 19.4 Physical vs. Nonphysical Light

Physical Light	Nonphysical Light
Electronic	Personal
Five senses	Sixth sense
Net speed	Speed of the soul
186,000 mps	Instantaneous

the arts and the sciences. It can be learned, and it requires the use of particular skills. Voluntary leadership of the most effective order is necessary for mobilizing philanthropy.

19.5   Leading @ the Speed of Vision

In voluntary leadership, the leading of volunteer-led organizations, vision is pivotal. Vision is the focus on which attention and interest are concentrated. This, of course, is true for all leadership. But in voluntary leadership vision plays an accentuated role because it supplants the lack of control that exists in administrative structures. Vision supplies a grip on time and effort that is beyond the influence of managed commands.

Voluntary leadership is quite demanding even as it is pursued quite gently. That is because leadership, in addition to being an art, is also a science, an applied social science. As such, it is a discipline with rules that govern the way it is practiced. Of course, it is more often practiced without a sense of governing principles, and sometimes very effectively so. But experience strongly suggests that this is the exception rather than the rule. Our task now is to take a good look at the rules. We need to know them so well that we use them instinctively. Therefore, we need to be sold on them, and that means we need to know why they are the rules as well as how they work.

The rules of voluntary leadership can be simplified and set up as a prototype for leading voluntary action. The prototype we are about to look at is a new architecture that takes the place of the current infrastructure of philanthropy that was built for a bygone era in which the old management ethic, trickle-down economics, and tin-cup fund raising dominated. Now the problems of a global civic society have gotten way too big for that. We need to rebuild philanthropy to make it more aware, more accessible, more authentic, more accelerated, and more accountable than ever before.

In order to do that, we need to look at the information coming to us from the new sciences of the twentieth century, particularly quantum physics, relativity theory, genetics, and complex systems. We can discover there a set of rules, or principles, from which we may extrapolate new applications that release the potential of much greater energy when the right conditions are developed.

First, let's take a look at quantum physics, the physics of atomic scale phenomena that exist everywhere in the universe, including in you and me, and which feature the dynamic interactions of fixed elemental units of energy that are the basis of living systems, like us. The first publication of quantum principles came after a famous gathering of physicists in Copenhagen in 1927 that was convened by Nobel laureate Niels Bohr and attended by Nobel laureate Albert Einstein, among others. The so-called Copenhagen Interpretation has since been challenged and revised but remains the standard origin of the revolutionary new science, though there are other quantum interpretations now in the arena.

From this gathering we get a package of ideas in the form of principles—called uncertainty, complementarity, observer-participancy, and probability—that stood the world of classical science on its head. Later, with breakthroughs coming from Geneva in 1964 and Paris in 1982, another controversial idea was developed and experimentally tested—called nonlocality—that we shall add to the original four. These five principles, now experimentally demonstrated though not yet universally accepted, are the basis of our new prototype model of leadership.

I call it the quantum civics paradigm because it is an overall concept that guides the interactions of citizens working together and investing energy in pursuit of their rights

---

EXHIBIT 19.5 Quantum Civics Paradigm of Leadership

Uncertainty→Creative Information

Complementarity→Collaborative Participation

Observer-Participancy→Visionary Cause

Probability→Concerted Strategy

Non-locality→Connecting Resources

---

and responsibilities. It is the model I suggest as a standard for nonprofit leadership. (See Exhibit 19.5.).

19.6 Uncertainty Leads to Creative Information

The quantum principle of uncertainty indicates that we cannot observe both the position of something and its momentum at the same time. We may observe them in sequence, one after the other, but when we observe one, we lose momentary touch with the other. For people in motion, this leads us to lack of certainty about exactly what may be coming next, though experience is still a good teacher. This is a different kind of world from what we thought. It is a world we can help create.

In the absence of certainty, intention can be decisive. A pattern of information can lead to impressions that elicit response. This represents opportunity. Opportunity is the essence of freedom. Freedom is at the core of humanity. We begin, therefore, with creativity. People are endowed with creative impulses. The natural information that flows to human situations is an invaluable resource. It asks: Why are we here?

This is a crucial point, because it reveals the true intentions of participants. They must ask themselves the question or face the consequences. They must realize that their answer reveals their creative impulse. And here is the opportunity as well as the danger. Is their creative impulse one that will serve a greater good—not only for those immediately involved, but also for others who are not and will have to live with a decision in which they did not participate? (See Exhibit 19.6.)

A front-page story in the *Los Angeles Times* of May 10, 2000 reported a $40 million gift of telecommunications entrepreneur Gary Winnick to help make possible an institute for peace and tolerance being built by the Simon Wiesenthal Center on a three-acre hillside in Jerusalem that is scheduled to open in 2004.[5] Rabbi Marvin Hier, Wiesenthal Center founder, initiated the $120 million project as an extension of the center's mission to promote human dignity and understanding. "Israel is the world center," he said, "the spiritual cradle for three monotheistic religions. It's the right place and this is the right time." He went on to say that "in the 20th century, the biggest issue was the external threat. There were wars. There was the Holocaust. But most historians and philosophers think that in the 21st century, the most important question will be: 'Can we live with each other?' The Winnick Institute Jerusalem (as the new museum and conference center will be known) will focus on the great internal question."

---

[5]Susan Freudenheim, "$40-Million Gift to Fund Israeli Tolerance Center," *Los Angeles Times,* May 10, 2000, p. A1.

EXHIBIT 19.6 Creative Information

Uncertainty
Opportunity
Creativity
Compassion

Winnick, the founder of Global Crossing Ltd. and a fiber optic pioneer, has served on the board of the Wiesenthal Center since 1980. His commitment to the project was a direct response to Rabbi Hier's request and is a culmination of a "vision combining education and philanthropic interests he has long pursued." He described himself as a "modern-day contemporary Jew. But more than that I'm a person who has been given more than my fair share of good fortune. And I recognize it, as opposed to saying I want more. Funny thing is," he continued, "I feel so much better about making a larger commitment than a smaller commitment because I know its going to be more lasting. It's going to have much more impact. . . . It's for the Arab, it's for the Jew, it's for the Christian. It's for anyone who lives in oppression, anyone who lives in prejudice."

The institute will include a "museum equipped with high-tech interactive programming, as well as a theater for lectures and films and a large hall intended for meetings with world leaders as well as scholars," the report said. World-renowned Los Angeles architect Frank O. Gehry has been retained to design the 130,000-square-foot facility, which will be built on land under the jurisdiction of Israel's National Land Authority and the Jerusalem Municipality and leased to the Wiesenthal Center on a long-term basis at terms favorable to a nonprofit institution.

Notice that the Winnick gift was prompted by a request that arose from a long-held commitment. It matched a man reputed to be worth $3.2 billion with a cause in which he deeply believes. And it occurred because his interest was well known and he was asked by one who was in an excellent position to ask. Winnick stepped into the uncertainty of peace and tolerance with a creative response to an opportunity to make a difference.

I believe that Winnick acted out of compassion for a cause in which he had come to be deeply involved. He was led by his heart and guided by his mind to a vision of the future in line with his desire for a better world.

19.7 Complementarity Mandates Collaborative Participation

The quantum principle of complementarity indicates to us that apparent opposites are actually like two sides of a coin, and we need to understand both as well as we can to get as nearly complete a picture as possible. The challenging point about this is that, in a complex world, 95 percent of the problems we face contain paradoxical dilemmas, that is, they appear to have no clear common ground for resolution. On the other hand, on closer examination, they do have a connection, they share a boundary, they are attached. For example, there is no south without north, no tall without short, no big without small, no dry without wet, no cold without warm, no male without female. Each helps define the other. As Richard Farson quipped in *Management of the Absurd*, "the opposite of the

---

EXHIBIT 19.7 Collaborative Participation

Complementarity
Two sides of a coin
Resolving dilemmas
Attracting opposites
Opposite of truth also true

---

truth is also true."[6] They are contrasts of the same phenomenon, such as in the examples of: direction, height, size, climate, heat, gender. So what? (See Exhibit 19.7.)

The implication of this built-in paradox is that it is both part of Mother Nature and part of human nature as well. So, we can make sense of the world in which we live because we are the self-conscious extensions of its food chain, of the universe itself, and as such can reflect upon what it is and what it means. We are the children of Mother Nature and Father God, of the finite body and the infinite spirit. We are the consummation of our physical and nonphysical worlds in the whole of the universe. What a thought!

We need to work together. We need to do that collaboratively, by mutual consent and with mutual respect. Collaborating volunteers are a major part of leadership in voluntary organizations. Acting collaboratively, and with compassion, they forge a common sense of mission and develop it into a shared vision that embodies a cause. This sense of commonality keeps them going, keeps their energy flowing, and drives them beyond whatever obstacles seem to be in the way.

No one can undertake a complex task alone and expect to complete it successfully. All of us need help, no matter how powerful or wealthy we are, and especially if we are not members of the elite or the ruling class. That help will come from people we connect with who have complementary relationships to us and our cause. Let's look at a prominent example.

Bill and Melinda Gates reportedly contributed more than $11.5 billion in 1999 to various charitable causes, most of it to their own foundation in Seattle, but also including $1 billion for minority scholarships, $750 million for world health, $200 million for their library initiative, $30 million to the United Way of King County, Washington, $1.7 million to International Planned Parenthood, $1.5 million to the American Red Cross, and many other major grants to significant organizations and institutions of special interest.

Aside from the generosity demonstrated by these grants, it is especially interesting to note their scope: from local and regional to national and international programs and purposes. Most of their philanthropic investment went to improving healthcare access and disease prevention as well as to educational opportunity and advancement. Their emphasis clearly was on helping people in need to improve their standards of living.

This would be entirely consistent with the interest of philanthropists whose wealth is produced by a hugely successful global software company that is one of the leaders of the new economy, regardless of their court battle with the federal government. The Gateses' giving is quite complementary with their getting, seen in the broadest terms. The

---

[6]Richard Farson, *Management of the Absurd: Paradoxes in Leadership* (New York: Simon & Schuster, 1996), p. 5.

future success of Microsoft, whether or how it may be subdivided, will be dependent both on the creativity of its technology people and its competitiveness with potential technology customers. Educators and healthcare professionals are very important to the company. The wellness and intelligence of people everywhere will help shape the worldwide market for computer technology in which Microsoft competes.

Complementarity plays a welcome role in philanthropy by insisting that voluntary leaders match up with wealth creators who are interested in what they are doing and by assuring that the potential for abundance is inherent in the association.

19.8   Observer-Participancy Focuses on the Vision

The quantum principle of observer-participancy indicates that all observers are always participants in a situation because they choose what they are observing and therefore limit what they will find. Vision is the key to leadership, and leadership is the key to philanthropy.

The vision must be clear and must be shared. It must include a vivid description of a desired future state that is imagined in the mind's eye of collaborating participants. The vision must be built on the foundation of the organization's mission, that is, its day-to-day guiding purpose. It must be strengthened by a set of values that support it. In short, the vision should be a compelling picture of the end result you see being accomplished as a result of the actions you take.

There is no more critical task you perform than to lead your group in the process of creating a shared vision. It is a challenging requirement worth all the time and effort you may devote to getting it right. The highest and best form a vision can take is to be a cause, something people would sacrifice to achieve. (See Exhibit 19.8.)

A cause is an intellectually justifiable, emotionally held, moral imperative that surpasses an exciting vision and a commitment to mission. In the extreme, a cause seems impossible and is something to die for, like saving a loved one from harm or realizing a lifetime ambition or fulfilling a marvelous dream or preventing a terrorizing threat from occurring. A cause is something sacred that enraptures its followers. It is extremely powerful in concentrating attention on what must be done to support it.

At the Greater Washington (D.C.) Business Philanthropy Summit on March 16, 2000, MicroStrategy chief executive officer Michael Saylor announced his vision of a free online university for which he will invest $100 million as a deposit, with more to come.[7] His concept of a "Cyber-U," as the *Washington Post* dubbed it, is to offer an "Ivy League–

EXHIBIT 19.8 Visionary Cause

Observer-participancy
Mission→responsibility
Values→heartfelt
Vision→excitement
Cause→sacrifice

---

[7]Cindy Loose, "N. Va. Billionaire Envisions Cyber-U," *Washington Post,* March 15, 2000, p. A1.

quality" education free to anyone in the world. He envisions online courses taught by "geniuses and leaders" from around the world, appealing to the best minds everywhere. "Done right," Saylor said, "this will impact the lives of millions of people forever." He is reported by a friend to have said "there is no reason someone in a jungle in Colombia couldn't get a first-rate exposure to the finest teachers in the world through the Internet." A profound thought that is destined to open access to higher learning for all.

Interestingly, Saylor could have done something more conventional. He attended the Massachusetts Institute of Technology on a scholarship without which he could not have afforded the tuition. While a college buddy pointed out that "$1 billion would fund scholarships for every student there, forever," instead it got him thinking the Internet might allow him to offer a free education to everyone, forever, to make education ubiquitous.

Saylor calls traditional contributions for such things as scholarships "20th century philanthropy," adding that "I want to do 21st century philanthropy," or, as one of his associates said: "We're a cutting-edge company. Michael wants his philanthropy to be cutting-edge."

At the time of the announcement, Saylor's 44 million shares of MicroStrategy were worth about $13 billion. Since then, a corporate report of an earnings shortfall sent the stock tumbling, and possibly slowing the schedule for getting Cyber-U up and running. In any case, what a vision Saylor has! In his mind's eye, he can see a better future for the global community and is committed to doing something important to make it happen.

19.9 *Probability Is the Foundation of Strategy*

The quantum principle of probability indicates that everything is the result of a tendency to exist; all phenomena of the universe are demonstrations of successful tendencies that have become reality. Leadership is about converting possibilities into actualities, potential energy into kinetic energy. Probability has become a well-established scientific principle underlying all of nature, including human nature.

Scientists have discovered that the tiny subatomic particle-wave energy resonance inhabiting the subliminal quantum universe is in constant motion everywhere and demonstrates certain tendencies toward increasing complexity and consciousness. In fact, chain reactions can be stimulated by natural or technological means, and enormous explosions of energy can be released, as in an erupting volcano, a political rally, a sports event, or a nuclear bomb, the firing of armament, the launch of a rocket.

When this happens, it sets in motion a quantum leap, or a sequence of such leaps, that catapults energy into higher orbits. The leap is produced when an aggregate of potentials converge to produce a supercharge powerful enough to send one or more of them into a new orbit while momentarily setting aside any other potentials. A quantum leap makes a sharp break from a current state as it jumps to another order of magnitude. This is transformational, as in everyday life when a caterpillar morphs into a butterfly or when an ordinary actor becomes an overnight star. (See Exhibit 19.9.)

Just recently, television star Oprah Winfrey launched, as part of a multipart strategy to implement her vision of a better world for everyone, what she calls the *Use Your Life Awards*, which are being given to people who are dedicating themselves to changing the world for others in need. Her first recipient was a young man named Val Joseph who

---

EXHIBIT 19.9 Concerted Strategy

Probability
Converting possibilities
Chain reactions
Quantum leaps

---

was once homeless on the streets of New York. With the help of a wonderful mentor, he was rescued, blossomed as a person, went on to Morehouse College in Atlanta, and turned down an opportunity to go to Harvard Law School in order to develop a mentoring program for inner city kids. His program appears to be destined as a role model for such programs around the nation.

Oprah's award provided $50,000 for Val's charity, a lot of money for the neighborhood scale on which he is operating. The award was funded by donors whose gifts were matched two for one by Jeff Bezos, the chief executive of Amazon.com, who is underwriting an Internet challenge fund that is intended to change lives across the country. While Amazon.com has not yet begun to turn a profit, Bezos has become a multibillionaire through his ownership of company stock that investors have traded up to a huge price earnings ratio on their vision of the company's prospects for the future.

This strategy seems to fit in beautifully for Oprah because it can be dramatized on her television shows in front of a widely sympathetic audience in the studio and wherever her syndication appears around the country. It fits in too because it reflects Oprah's own values, which are manifested in the daily format and content of her show, in the books she regularly recommends to her audience, as well as in what she refuses to show or to be part of in her professional decisions. Oprah manifests in her public persona what appears to be a deeply philanthropic ethic that sets a magnificent example for millions. To work most effectively, strategy must reflect alignment with the vision it purports to implement, must embrace internally consistent activities that are mutually reinforcing, and must link directly to funding sources that support the cost requirements.

19.10   Nonlocality Is about Connected Resources

The quantum principle of nonlocality indicates that everything can be connected with everything else at the deepest levels in which the universe functions, no matter how far removed they are in distance. Nonlocality places central importance on the connections between dynamic systems, such as people, where they have bonded relationships. This principle means, in effect, that an electrical connection must exist before an electrical current can flow. A switch must be flipped before a light turns on.

Leadership makes connections among people and succeeds, or does not do so and fails. There is no leadership of organizations without connections to dynamic resources, the wherewithal of success. Making connections makes sense when considering resources. When we want to get something done, we have got to be wired for results. This includes being plugged in, ready to go, arrangements made, preparations in place, trusted people in charge, resources in the pipeline, awaiting a turn-on to stimulate a power surge.

We think about people when we think about making connections. We think about being on the same wavelength, sharing similar thoughts and feelings. These are coded into our memories, depending on how deep are the impressions they have made. Our memories retain information inscribed in our brains at birth, which we inherit from our ancestors. Our memories also retain information from our personal experiences, which we take from our lifelong encounters.

A memory is a coherent quantum energy field held together with electromagnetic force from the high impact of memorable moments or genetic impulse. Can we imagine that we hold our thoughts and feelings in nonmaterial memory fields embedded in the circuitry of our minds? Can we imagine with Danah Zohar, whose book on *Rewiring the Corporate Brain* is built around the idea that our minds are like an organically wired neural network, that our mental circuitry can be changed and that this is what we mean when we talk about changing our minds?[8] Can we imagine our memories, therefore, as being embodied in a quantum memory chip of our minds that would be our own leader chip something like an organic version of a computer memory chip? It is this leader chip in our minds that we must concentrate on developing. (See Exhibit 19.10.)

New economy entrepreneurs are destined to become increasingly influential in the future, regardless of ups and downs in the stock market. First of all, they will because they want to change the world. Second of all, they will because the new economy is an information economy that is changing the world at the speed of light. This will not end. These entrepreneurs are developing their own momentum investments and are always looking for new opportunities. Momentum investment is the new term, often used negatively by the media, for the idea of generating capital on the prospect of future earnings, the news about which feeds on itself rather than on profits already earned. Obviously, this is not a risk-averse game. The dangers are there, but so is the adventure. And a stock market bubble can burst at any time. All investing has always had something to do with momentum in stock trading. We want to catch and contribute to momentum wherever we can in order to improve our prospects for return on investment.

Steve Jurvetson, a top Silicon Valley venture capitalist, said recently: "Certainly there are people out there who just want to make a quick buck. That sort of thinking is shortsighted, shallow, and potentially destructive. As individuals, we must strive for excellence in everything that we do. Life is too short to sacrifice personal fulfillment for near-term financial gain. Right now, the pace of life in the Internet economy is making it all too easy to lose sight of that principle."[9]

But, he went on to say: "Most entrepreneurs have a fundamental need for symbolic immortality. . . . More and more people will find fulfillment in the expression of their ideas through small organizations—and in the dramatic impact that they can have at the

---

EXHIBIT 19.10 Connecting Resources

Nonlocality
Making connections
Coded memories
Brain circuitry
Leader chips

---

[8]Danah Zohar, *Rewiring the Corporate Brain: Using the New Science to Rethink How We Structure and Lead Organizations* (San Francisco: Berrett-Koehler, 1997).
[9]Steve Jurvetson, "Built to Flip: Where Do you Come Down?" *Fast Company* (March 2000), p. 148.

product or project level. A good idea no longer needs the support of a corporate behemoth to change the world."

A new book I heartily recommend is *The Cluetrain Manifesto*,[10] which Thomas Petzinger, Jr., former featured columnist of the *Wall Street Journal*, said is "about to drive business to a full boil." It was written by four Internet denizens who are fixtures of the high-tech establishment and who renounce business-as-usual in favor of a future centered around the human voice of the Internet. They set forth 95 theses "for the people of the earth," similar to Martin Luther's 95 theses on theology and church practices, which he posted on the door of the city church in Wittenberg, Germany almost five centuries ago.

With due respect to Luther, whose subsequent role is widely known, I will quote just the first few of these theses from *Cluetrain*, whose potential role is not yet so widely known:

> *One. Markets are conversations. Two. Markets consist of human beings, not demographic sectors. Three. Conversations among human beings sound human. They are conducted in a human voice. Four. Whether delivering information, opinions, perspectives, dissenting arguments or human asides, the human voice is typically open, natural, uncontrived. Five. People recognize each other as such by the sound of this voice. Six. The Internet is enabling conversations among human beings that were simply not possible in the era of mass media.*[11]

Wow!

The primary resource we all have is other people. Our connecting resources are really people. It is people who create wealth and have the money. I saw a very interesting piece by Juan Hovey on the business page of the *Los Angeles Times* the other day that described a new group of angel investors in Pasadena who

> *don't want to hear from you. They don't want you to call them or fax them your business plan or stop them on the street or barrage them with e-mail. They want to hear about you from other people—your attorney, your accountant, your banker, maybe a business acquaintance or another angel. That is, someone whose judgment they can trust and who can vouch for you and your idea. They want you to get them, in short, by networking. Why? Angels care just as much about your connections as about your idea because your connections say important things about your idea.*[12]

19.11   *Momentum Philanthropy Is a New Economy Necessity*

For leadership to work, there must be sustaining resources. These resources increasingly will be the philanthropy of new economy entrepreneurs. To develop this potential philanthropy in the quantum leap terms I am suggesting will require a strategy of visionary leadership. The impetus of this visionary leadership must be strong enough to transform

---

[10]Rick Levine, Christopher Locke, Doc Searles, and David Weinberger, *The Cluetrain Manifesto: The End of Business as Usual* (Cambridge, Mass.: Perseus Books, 2000), p. iii.

[11]*Ibid.*

[12]Juan Hovey, "Finding Angel Investors Is About Who You Know," *Los Angeles Times*, May 3, 2000, p. C9.

the actions of individual donors into the self-amplifying momentum of participating investors.

The innovative spirit of these participating investors will convert the fundamentals and discipline of their momentum investment into *momentum philanthropy*. This philanthropy will keep pace with basic, underlying, transforming change because it will be given from the new wealth that is leading market growth, appreciated securities with substantial promise still ahead. This philanthropy will be a leading part of the twenty-first-century world because it will be invested in the most innovative charitable organizations and institutions.

New economy entrepreneurs are looking for philanthropic investments where they can make a difference with the assets they are generating. They are looking for dynamic possibilities, opportunities to be directly involved, and the prospect of significant returns they can see. They are not interested in business as usual because they know that the new Internet world is revolutionizing the way business is being done as well as the way lives are being lived.

For us, as seekers of philanthropy in the new economy, this means that we must be civic entrepreneurs. In this role, we will be innovative thinkers, high-energy collaborators, champions of a visionary cause, and demonstrators of breakthrough potential who are offering new investment opportunities that will address unmet community needs. Sheryl Schwartz, partner in charge of the new training program recently established at KPMG, the corporate management consulting leader, has a major point to make: "If we want to work for Net companies, then we have to act like a Net company. We have to embed the Internet in everything we do. It's a credibility thing."[13] The same is true if we want the entrepreneurs who lead them to invest in us. (See Exhibit 19.11.)

We have to ask ourselves, Schwartz says, if our people "can adapt the new mindsets and acquire the new skill sets that are necessary in order to win in the new world of business." As a recent ad touting new software products says: "Net net: it's e-business or out of business." That is not a threat that can be ignored for long. Every organization on the planet, without exception, is affected by the earth-shaking change now under way. Some are aware of what it means for them in the adjustments they must make, and some are not. For KPMG and other organizations struck by the change in the air, the message is about how to use the Internet-driven changes to get people to do business in creative and productive new ways. For philanthropy, this may be the most important lesson of all.

Even John Reed, former co-chief of Citigroup, the banking giant from New York, weighs in: "I am a revolutionary. Any time you give me a fork in the road, where the choice

---

EXHIBIT 19.11 Momentum Philanthropy

new entrepreneurs
dynamic possibilities
involvement opportunities
significant returns
breakthrough potential
revolutionary times

---

[13]Cited in Rekha Balu, "KPMG Faces the Internet Test," *Fast Company* (March 2000), p. 50.

is slow change or revolution, I will always take the revolution. The Internet is real. It is fundamental. And it is a young person's game."[14] We must be willing to think differently.

19.12 *The DNA of Momentum Philanthropy*

Regardless of what type of philanthropy we are pursuing, we need look no further than to biotechnology for our first clue about where the future is going. Leading scientists and investors expect the cracking of the human genetic code to have a most profound impact on life in the twenty-first century. Its potential for identifying, isolating, and eliminating the genetic origins of disease are exciting.

As our advancing technology makes this possible, we must call attention to a second genetic code it is time to examine. This is the organizational DNA, or ODNA. Organizations are first and foremost aggregates of people. Just as an individual person is a single organism, the organization as a corporate person is a superorganism. Just as a human being develops according to a DNA, therefore, so must an organizational being develop according to an ODNA. Both are dynamic living systems.

The DNA "life molecule" consists of four chemical bases—adenine, thymine, guanine, and cytosine, or A, T, G, and C for short—that in different combinations make up the gene code of every living system. I believe that the ODNA has counterparts not only to A, T, G, and C but also to its molecular life stream that can be identified and described. These are comprised of complementary sets of movers and shakers as well as starters and finishers. All four need to be present in creating the body of any living system.

The counterparts are the leading properties of the quantum civics paradigm, our philanthropic model of information, participation, vision, strategy, and resources. In essence, this is a metaphorical prototype of philanthropy in general, and momentum philanthropy in particular, when taken to its highest potential.

The first property is creative information, which corresponds with the nucleoplasm that is the life stream from which DNA chemical bases emerge. This is the essential living matter of all cells. Nucleoplasm appears to be comparable to the creative information from which all organized activity formulates, because it is the substance from which all life arises. In voluntary organizations, its equivalent is compassion.

The second property is collaborative participation, which corresponds with the adenine chemical base. It is one of the two larger chemical bases and one of the two that are less well bonded. I see it, therefore, as the starting mover or initiating base that gets things going. In voluntary organizations, its equivalent is volunteers.

The third property is visionary cause, which corresponds with the guanine chemical base. It is the other of the two larger chemical bases and one of the two that are more securely bonded. I see it, therefore, as the starting shaker or incubating base that gets things focused. In voluntary organizations, its equivalent is a cause.

The fourth property is concerted strategy, which corresponds with the thymine chemical base. It is the other of the two less well bonded bases and one of the two that are smaller. I see it, therefore, as the finishing mover or implementing base that follows up the direction. In voluntary organizations, its equivalent is trustees.

The fifth property is connecting resources, which correspond with the cytosine chemical base. It is the other of the two smaller bases and one of the two that are

---

[14]Cited in *ibid.*, p. 50.

more securely bonded. I see it, therefore, as the finishing shaker or improving base that provides support for the rest. In voluntary organizations, its equivalent is philanthropy.

These five properties, the four bases and their life stream, are the ODNA key to leading organizations into their futures.

19.13   *The New Leadership Ethic of Philanthropy*

Philanthropy, we will remember, is the desire to help humankind and is expressed in acts of voluntary service and support in many different ways. As of the most recently reported year, in 1999, contributed service time amounted to $225 billion and contributed gift support amounted to $190 billion, for an estimated total of $400 billion, the equivalent of close to 5 percent of the $8 trillion plus in gross domestic product that year. As I have mentioned, I believe those are conservative figures, especially because they fail to measure what people do for others informally and voluntarily every day just for purposes of getting along that is not tabulated in our surveys.

What philanthropy does, in essence, is to feed the civic sector of society and the economy. The civic sector is that sector which is outside the private enterprise role of business and the public enterprise role of government. It is both the sector of nonprofit philanthropic organizations and the sector of actions by citizens acting alone and together in fulfillment of their civic rights and responsibilities through voluntary associations and organizations.

For years the civic sector has been considered the nonprofit sector or third sector, and a whole industry has been built on that notion. The civic sector has always consisted of individuals acting as citizens, people acting as members of a community, upon whom all else depends. Today, in the ascendancy of the global information age, we must recognize the fact of this transition. There is no such thing any longer as a nonprofit third sector, if there ever was. There is only the civic first sector acknowledging the primacy of people in their different communities.

We need to acknowledge a new leadership ethic to define this phenomenon more effectively. This ethic creates a new foundation with a mix of old notions. It is a way of seeing opportunities by looking at the greatest good for the largest number over the longest period with the least effort, all at once and every time.

This is a daunting challenge that some may think we are incapable of meeting. If that is the reaction, we must think again. Our future depends on it. As Rabbi Hier of Jerusalem's Wiesenthal Center asked: "Can we live together?"[15] This is the question of the twenty-first century, the first century of the new creative world that is our future.

In seeking the greatest good, we are putting first a vision of service. In seeking to do so for the greatest number, we are putting first the people we will serve. In seeking to do so over the longest period, we are putting our plans for the future in plain sight. In seeking to do so with the least effort, we are conserving resources for the most important priorities we share as a global civic society.

To have the most realistic chance of meeting such a challenge, and doing so time after time, we must be practical and constantly seek to be morally pragmatic in the context of the situations we face. Following a path of moral pragmatism means pursuing

---

[15]Cited in Freudenheim, "$40-Million Gift," p. A1.

EXHIBIT 19.12 Leadership Ethic

New Leadership Ethic	Moral Pragmatism	Win-Win-Win
The greatest good for the largest number over the longest period at the lowest cost	Doing what works for people through strategic thinking, competitive excellence, and ethical values	Stakeholders all benefit

what works for people, all those who have a stake in what we are doing. It means that we must prepare to think strategically, to act competitively, and to do so using ethical values. (See Exhibit 19.12.)

Most important in giving life to a new leadership ethic and to pursuing it in morally pragmatic ways is to think in terms of seeking always about how we all—you and I and everyone else—can win from the actions taken. If you and I cut a deal that hurts others, where is the ethical value in that? Win-win is not good enough in leadership situations.

In order to make a difference that is more than fleeting, we must think again, we must act in ways that help others, we must evaluate situations from more than our own points of view. In this way we will make a mark. We will also be rid of avoidable community backlash from those who are injured by what we do.

19.14 A Twenty-First-Century Leadership Formula

Complexity science has turned up fascinating evidence of what physicists call the critical state, a state that appears to exist in all complex systems. Complex systems operate in all but the simplest situations and involve multiple interactions of various factors that are part of a given event or activity. The critical state is the condition of life at the edge of complexity in which an uncertain balance is maintained by constantly adjusting to whatever changes are going on. Can we imagine ourselves walking a tightrope in the wind? Maintaining our balance on a seesaw with two or more people on either end? That is what complex systems can be like in leadership situations and how precarious they can be if we are not paying attention.

Keeping our balance is a matter, it seems, of making just the right moves, not too much and not too little. At any moment a slight disturbance can upset our equilibrium. This is what physicists call punctuated equilibrium. It is where a slight change of something produces what is called a catastrophic effect, that is, an effect that tips the balance from order to chaos, from tranquility to avalanche.

It is like the old story of the straw that broke the camel's back. A very small thing brings down a very large body. It is like the song about little things meaning a lot, such as a slight of forgetfulness or thoughtlessness. Think of tiny termites eating away the foundation of a house. Think of a spark igniting an explosion.

Albert Einstein was a struggling Jewish schoolboy who eventually got himself a job as a clerk in the Swiss patent office where, as a complete unknown to the scientific community of 1905, he completed three groundbreaking papers that changed the world. One of them contained the first draft of a new formula in physics that became the well-known though not well understood formula of creativity, or energy-matter convertibility, we now know as $E = mc^2$.

This formula is most widely known because of its later use to build the atomic bomb, a use that horrified Einstein, who was a lifelong pacifist. It is thought to be of little use in everyday affairs because the right physical conditions for explosion are not often present. But there is another use, yet unexplored, that some far-seeing leadership practitioners are beginning to talk about. Most recently, Burt Nanus and Stephen Dobbs raise the question about the applicability of the $E = mc^2$ equation in their 1999 book about essential strategies for nonprofit organizations.[16]

Nanus and Dobbs suggest that "social energy," as they call it, "is the energy that is generated when a nonprofit organization marshals common action for the common good."[16] They like to think of the generation of social energy "as being analogous to another familiar equation for energy: $E = mc^2$ where E = social energy, m = strength of mandate and c = organizational capital that is invested in addressing the mandate."[17] They go on to say that "squaring the term for organizational capital indicates that investing organizational capital has a self-amplifying effect."[18] However, though they indicate that "this may seem a bit whimsical (and we make no claims for its mathematical accuracy)",[19] I think they are headed in the right direction.

In 1998 I proposed to a conference on community leadership at Chapman University that I thought there was a formula for civic energy that could be extrapolated from $E = mc^2$ and asked what the participants thought of the idea. The answer came back that it sounded like a bit of a stretch. During my spring semester 1999 Executive Certificate in Voluntary Leadership classes at Chapman I introduced a formula in which the quantum civics leadership paradigm was embedded: $I = am^2$. Initial response was mixed, ranging from "wow!" to "whoa!"

Subsequent investigation and discussion led to a more effective presentation of the concept, which I will summarize this way: The impetus or driving force of leadership is the equivalent of that which transforms the actions of individual people into the momentum of a unified group. We begin by taking this as our measurable definition of leadership. It can be described in a formula where I = the impetus of leadership, a = the action of individual people, and m = the momentum of a unified group. Squaring the term for momentum seemed necessary to acknowledge the relationship between the speed of light in Einstein's formula and the speed of vision in the leadership formula.

The quantum civics leadership paradigm is embedded in the formula in several steps:

1. By equating the impetus of leadership with an assessment of the creative information that energizes leadership in the paradigm
2. By multiplying assessments of collaborative participation and the concerted strategy that implements it and equating the product to the action of individual people
3. By multiplying assessments of vision and resources that implement it and equating the product to the momentum of a unified group

---

[16]Burt Nanus and Stephen M. Dobbs, *Leaders Who Make a Difference: Essential Strategies for Meeting the Nonprofit Challenge* (San Francisco: Jossey-Bass, 1999), p. 41.
[17]*Ibid.*, p. 43.
[18]*Ibid.*, p. 43.
[19]*Ibid.*, p. 43.

4. By multiplying action times the square of momentum to produce an overall assessment.

In its recent millennium edition, *Time Magazine* named Albert Einstein the person of the twentieth century. Walter Isaacson, one of its co-authors, wrote that "Einstein often invoked God [who] 'reveals himself in the harmony of all that exists.' " He went on to say that, according to Einstein, "searching for God's design was 'the source of all true art and science.' "[20]

When Hank Lamb, a graduate of the program at Chapman and director of the Pro's and Con's Project based in nearby Garden Grove, first saw the $I = am^2$ formula, he thought of the biblical reference in Exodus 3:14 where "God said to Moses, 'I AM WHO I AM' " and implored Moses to tell the people that He would lead them to 'a land flowing with milk and honey.' "

After reading Joe Jaworski's very interesting book *Synchronicity: The Inner Path of Leadership*,[21] I have had more of a tendency to be on the lookout for the "meaningful coincidence of two or more events, where something other than the probability of chance is involved," or at least seems to be. I was struck by the thought that $I = am^2$ might coincidentally symbolize the complementarity of I and Thou, you and me, us and them, the one and the many. Something to think about. God, Einstein, people, and community.

19.15   *Building Momentum Philanthropy*

Now, what do we do? Think of yourself and your organization as a beta site or proving ground where innovation is part of the way in which you regularly seek to improve your effectiveness. New economy entrepreneurs are attracted to opportunities where it appears that innovation is leading or likely to lead to creative solutions of significance. We need to exude the energy of new economy entrepreneurship in the manner with which we approach our visions of attracting the new philanthropists.

If you have not done so already, put an alpha Web site up on the Internet, that is, one that attracts attention because of its leading qualities. It will need to be well designed, and it will need to be stocked with regularly changing information of interest to first-time visitors that will keep them coming back. So you will need to be sure, before you start, that you are prepared to devote the resources necessary to keep it current and to be responsive to the inquiries you receive from visitors. The purpose of your site will be to develop two-way communication with more people who might be interested in what you are doing than you could by other, less efficient means.

Consider that Internet values coincide with philanthropic values in that the Internet is the most accessible tool ever devised for giving long-distance expression to the human voice in an authentically personal way. People of like mind can communicate electronically with each other without the filter of corporate speak. Philanthropic values involved with helping people correspond nicely with the human voice that reaches out for help. Think of the Internet as a giant network of conversationalists who are interested in con-

---

[20]Walter Isaacson, "Who Mattered and Why?" *Time Millennium Collector's Edition*, December 31, 1999, p. 24.

[21]Joseph Jaworski, *Synchronicity: The Inner Path of Leadership* (San Francisco: Berrett-Koehler Publishers, 1996), p. ix.

necting with sources of information that can assist them. You can assist at least some of them by the opportunities of interest that you offer.

Consider that philanthropic values coincide with competitive values via the service motive. If you and your organization are serving a constituency of value to a new entrepreneur, then you may have an overlapping interest that would benefit you both. You might be able to offer the entrepreneur a comparative advantage that would help the business and would carry some reward for your purposes. Servant leadership, as Robert Greenleaf so effectively formulated the concept, pertains to any leadership that puts service first, whether that leadership occurs in a for-profit or not-for-profit setting.

Consider that competitive values coincide with collaborative values in a business model, particularly in a model for leading philanthropy, such as the quantum civics paradigm. It helps to realize that competition and collaboration are only apparent contradictions. Actually, they are complementary variables, two sides of the same coin of exchange that work in different aspects of business relationships. It helps to think of competitors as potential collaborators with whom you might be able to develop a positive-sum rather than the usual zero-sum relationship.

Finally, consider that collaborative values coincide with visionary values in a leadership ethic. To collaborate effectively two or more parties obviously must share a vision. If that vision holds the promise of leading to a better place for both, which presumably it would or it would not have been consummated, then the prospect of success could be especially exciting. In building momentum philanthropy we are always looking to match collaborators with shared visions to produce something of greater value.

19.16 Initiating Dot Com Conversations

Think about how you would like the world to change in a way in which you might be able to help. We do not often think about that. When we do, we should realize that every day we have opportunities to do that by the choices we make. Think about what you know that you think others ought to know but perhaps do not. Think about who you know who might help you do that. Connect with them and start a conversation about your thoughts, and theirs.

Think about how your ideas might be different from those of others. Okay, you can connect with others who think as you do, but how about how you offer something different from what they do? This is not a frivolous exercise. Your response to the question might surprise you and might make a difference to others. Think about your difference as possibly being of interest to others, interesting enough to get them involved in what you are doing or are interested in doing.

Think about the fundamentals. They have not changed. Yes, we are discovering new insights about what they actually are. But they have always been thus, as my dad used to say. We just need to understand what in fact these fundamentals are, and what they mean, for us. The fundamentals are the basis for our discipline, and disciplined we must be about the right things. But we must keep an open mind to new insights to avoid becoming relics of the past, like dinosaurs, never to visit again.

As George Gilder, author and senior fellow at Discovery Institute, has so persuasively argued, our world is advancing from the microcosm to the telecosm, that is, from the world of the computer microchip to the world of networking bandwidth. We are coming to the perceived physical limits of microchip technology and are shifting gears toward the "speed-of-light world of the all-optical network." Gilder tells us that it is "a new industrial era in which the Internet is the defining force." He says that "bandwidth can handle far more data, far faster, and with fewer problems."[22]

Bandwidth technologies include fiber optics, wireless communication, orbital technologies, cable modem—all linked to the Internet. We must be familiar with their opportunities as well as their limits. We must be alert and open to whatever their consequences may be. Technology has always driven civilization, from fire and knife, to domesticated animals and lethal weapons, to wagons and automobiles, to robots and rockets.

The marketplace is a giant bazaar, as *The Cluetrain Manifesto* points out. It is now increasingly propelled by the electronic waves of the Internet. And that may be the new paradox: The more we communicate with each other electronically, the more personal we get. Do not forget it. It will reward you and everyone touched by your presence.

19.17 *Summary*

The circumstances of twenty-first-century philanthropy are inspiring a new leadership science. This applied social science is quantum civics. It is marked by dynamic interactions of people acting together in voluntary associations. They comprise the first sector of our society upon which private and public enterprise are dependent.

We have never been healthier or wealthier, smarter or swifter, bigger or better. At the same time we are in the midst of multiple crises in families, healthcare, education, civic life, drug abuse, faith, and stress.

Our realized philanthropy of $400 billion is less than our unrealized potential of $570 billion and less than half our conservatively estimated philanthropic capacity of $970 billion, actually over $1 trillion in current dollars.

Philanthropy is traveling @ the speed of light. We must realize that this light consists of physical light—that is, electronic, is received through the five physical senses, at net speed, traveling 186,000 miles per second—and nonphysical light—that is, personal, is received through the sixth sense of intuition, traveling at the speed of the soul, and connecting instantaneously.

Philanthropy operates through the quantum civics paradigm of leadership—from the uncertainty principle to creative information, from the complementarity principle to collaborative participation, from the observer-participancy principle to visionary cause, from the probability principle to concerted strategy, and from the nonlocality principle to connecting resources.

Following these principles leads to momentum philanthropy through the new economy entrepreneurs, pursuing dynamic possibilities that have opportunities for their personal involvement, significant return on investment, breakthrough potential, and revolutionary change.

The DNA of momentum philanthropy consists of the five leading properties of the quantum civics paradigm in a dynamic living system that is creatively interacting in evolutionary patterns with philanthropic momentum.

Momentum philanthropy works most effectively through a new leadership ethic devoted to the greatest good for the largest number over the longest period at the lowest

---

[22]George Gilder, "Grow Rich on the Coming Technology Revolution," *Gilder Technology Report* (Fall 1999), p. 5.

EXHIBIT 19.13 Leadership Formula

$$I = am^2$$
Where the impetus of leadership is I,
the action of individual people (their participation multiplied by their strategy) is a,
and the momentum of a unified group (their vision multiplied by their resources,
then squared) is m^2.

cost. It entails an outlook of moral pragmatism to achieve what works for people and consists of strategic thinking, competitive excellence, and ethical values. It seeks always to produce a win-win-win result from which all stakeholders benefit.

Momentum philanthropy relies on the $I = am^2$ formula of leadership in which the impetus of leadership transforms the actions of individual people into the momentum of a unified group through strategies that multiply participation and resources that multiply vision. (See Exhibit 19.13.)

In momentum philanthropy we—ourselves and our organizations—are thinking like Internet innovators, which means considering how Internet and philanthropic values coincide, how philanthropic and competitive values coincide, how competitive and collaborative values coincide, and how collaborative and visionary values coincide.

Finally, in momentum philanthropy, we are thinking about the fundamentals. They have not changed, but the way we see them has changed, and these changes must be the basis for a new discipline. The new discipline will, then, lead us to realizing our visions of a better future.

Suggested Readings

Babbie, Earl. *You Can Make A Difference: The Heroic Potential Within Us All*, Anaheim Hills, California: Opening Books, 1985.

Farson, Richard. *Management of the Absurd: Paradoxes in Leadership*, New York: Simon & Schuster, 1996.

Gates, Bill. *Business @ The Speed of Thought: Using a Digital Nervous System*, New York: Warner Books, 1999.

Jaworski, Joseph. *Synchronicity: The Inner Path of Leadership*, San Francisco: Berrett-Koehler, 1996.

Levine, Rick; Christopher Locke, Doc Searles, and David Weinberger. *The Cluetrain Manifesto: The End of Business as Usual*, Cambridge, Massachusetts: Perseus Books, 2000.

Nanus, Burt and Stephen M. Dodds. *Leaders Who Make A Difference: Essential Strategies for Meeting the Nonprofit Challenge*, San Francisco: Jossey-Bass, 1999.

Rosenberg, Jr., Claude. *Wealthy and Wise: How You and America Can Get the Most Out of Your Giving*, Boston: Little Brown & Company, 1994.

Zohar, Danah. *Rewiring the Corporate Brain: Using the New Science to Rethink How We Structure and Lead Organizations*, San Francisco: Berrett-Koehler, 1997.

20 Accountability for Leadership Volunteers

PATRICK S. GUZMAN, CPA, CFP
Guzman & Gray

20.1 Introduction

Shortly after I was introduced to Dr. Richard Cheshire, a professor in organizational leadership at Chapman University in Orange, California, he gave me an interesting directive. He asked me to put together a lecture on accountability, something that had never been thought of before, something new and different. Well, in one sense this seemed like an ominous assignment, but I thought at least I do not have to do any heavy-duty research since if I could find it in research, it did not meet the directive of never being thought of before, something new and different. After much thought I was able to develop a model that I have found to be quite useful. Over the last five years we have been studying, reviewing, and testing the model I have developed to analyze accountability for leaders, and now I would like to share it with you.

On one hand, accountability seems to be something everyone is calling for; on the other hand, it seems to be something no one is willing to admit. Just listen to the news and all you hear is that something was "not my fault, it was their fault," that it was "not my job, I was not responsible for that," and on and on. I guess it is part of human nature; from the beginning Adam blamed Eve for eating the forbidden fruit and Eve blamed the serpent. Over the last half of the twentieth century several presidents of the United States have not been stellar examples of accountability. Even our cartoons, such as television's *The Simpsons*, depict a lack of willingness to accept responsibility as Bart Simpson is always saying: "I didn't do it."

It seems that only a few people really understand accountability. Abraham Lincoln had a handle on it with his famous quote, "You can fool some of the people some of the time, and all of the people some of the time, but you can't fool all of the people all of the time" Harry Truman was a great example with his THE BUCK STOPS HERE sign on his desk.

Why do people exhibit a lack of accountability? Do they think they can get away with something? Gain an advantage? Think they can hide behind the veil of the inability of people to investigate? Does society place more value on not being blamed than on finding the right answer? It is probably all of these and more.

Part of the problem is that no tools have been developed to analyze accountability—that is, until now. In this chapter we will work through a tool I have developed, based on leadership theories developed by Dr. Richard Cheshire, at Chapman University in Orange, California, in conjunction with our work at the Institute for Voluntary Leadership. First let us briefly look at what is accountability and what or who is a leader.

20.2 Accountability

Webster's Dictionary defines "accountable" as "1. Subject to giving an account: answerable, 2. Capable of being accounted for: explainable." It then defines accountability as "1. The quality or state of being accountable; an obligation or willingness to accept responsibility or to account for one's actions."

From the standpoint of a nonprofit organization, this could be phrased as "leading the efficient acquisition and use of resources for the accomplishment of your vision statement."

20.3 Leadership

According to *Webster's*, a "leader" is "1. something that leads; 2. a person who has commanding authority or influence." Leadership is defined as "1. the office or position of a leader 2. capacity to lead 3. the act or an instance of leading 4. leaders."

But who are leaders? All of us are leaders to the extent we choose to be leaders. We lead our own lives. Whether we choose to lead ourselves, to follow someone else's lead, or to be our own leader, we all, in fact, in some respects, are leaders. How good we are is another question, but leadership is something that can be improved and learned through study and action.

20.4 Basic Concept of Model to Analyze Accountability

I have developed two acronyms to assist in analyzing accountability. I call it the LIFE/DEAD model, where LIFE and DEAD correspond to each other and are an acronym for the following:

The *L* represents leading participants. A leader is accountable for leading participants toward a vision, mission, or goal, even if those participants consist only of the leader him- or herself. The corresponding letter *D* represents darkness of outlook. If a leader is not leading the participants, there will certainly be a darkness of outlook, a vision that will not be realized. Vision and communication are important elements of this section.

The *I* represents integrity of vision. If a leader does not exhibit and promote integrity, the building of the vision will be weakened, most likely to the point of crumbling. The corresponding letter *E* represents ethical void. Relationships and data are important elements of this section.

The *F* represents favorable results. The leader is accountable for the results of the effort to attain the vision. If results are not favorable or at least promising, the energy to sustain the effort to attain the vision will not exist. The corresponding letter *A* represents adverse consequences. Financial and program concerns are important elements of this section.

The *E* represents evaluate. Once a vision is put in place with followers, integrity is achieved; the plan must be executed. Once results are in, the leader is accountable to evaluate the effort and determine what adjustments are necessary to sustain the energy. The corresponding letter *D* represents disastrous results. Data collection, analysis, and adjustments are important elements of this section.

I like to look at the model as a continuum as follows, where your project can be plotted for each letter of the acronym:

```
L  ------- D
I  ------- E
F  ------- A
E  ------- D
```

Each situation falls on a continuum between each acronym. The closer each situation is to each of the LIFE acronyms, the better the situation. The closer a situation is to the DEAD part of the continuum, the worse the situation. This model allows users to analyze a situation quickly, to determine the root of a problem so that users can quickly start working toward a better result.

To assist in the analysis of accountability, I have developed a series of questions for each area based on the who, what, when, where, why, and how. The answers to these questions will give good insight to where a situation subjectively lies on the continuum. The situation could relate to the organization as a whole, a cost or profit center, or the fund-raising effort, for example.

Fund raisers first need to review the organization to determine its strengths and weaknesses. No one wants to start a fund-raising campaign and then find that there are some unknown skeletons in the closet that ambush their efforts. Then fund raisers can use this model to monitor their own leadership in the fund-raising efforts.

20.5   *Leading Participants/Darkness of Outlook*

(A)   INTRODUCTION

A leader is accountable to leading participants toward a common vision. An essential ingredient is good communication. To analyze a situation regarding leading participants, look at what the leader is doing in respect to the vision and communication.

(B)   VISION

The vision must be something that gets people to act and excited about the eventual results. Fund raisers need to review their nonprofit organization vision as well as their own fund-raising vision for the organization—in effect, they must ask the questions from both angles, the organization and fund raising—to get a better grasp of the situation.

Questions
- Who are the players? Fund raisers need to know who will be involved and affected by their vision. This can be grantors, the organization, board, community, beneficiaries, volunteers. A good grasp of who the players are will allow one to cover all aspects affecting the situation.
- What is the vision; what does the leader want the players to do? Simple question, but many projects do not adequately spell this out. Everyone needs to know how his or her efforts fit in with the vision.
- When do we act? Everyone needs to be on the same page; timing can mean everything.
- Where is everyone focused, is it on the same vision? Side agendas by seemingly well-intentioned individuals can sabotage any good project.
- Why are we doing this? This goes back to being able to sell the vision. If getting people excited about the vision is a problem, the leader is not communicating this point.
- How is the vision communicated? The leader needs to be able to determine the most effective way of communicating to get the best results.

(C)   COMMUNICATION

Communication is essential in leading participants. Without communication, how will they know where to go? A fund raiser needs to analyze this not only from an organizational point of view but also from the fund-raising point of view.

Questions
- Whom are we communicating to? This gets back to knowing the players and how they fit in with the accomplishment of the vision.
- What are we communicating? Is the message being sent the message being received?
- When do we communicate? Again, timing and coordinating actions are all important.

- Where does the message go? The leader must make sure that the right players are receiving the right message at the right time.
- Why are we communicating the information? Communication for communication's sake is nothing but a waste of time.
- How is the message delivered? This can relate to both the form and the content, as both can be equally important.

(D) INTERRELATIONSHIPS WITH OTHER PARTS OF THE MODEL

A leader who lacks integrity will eventually drag even a successful cause to a halt. Without favorable results, the eventual success will depend on the ability to evaluate and make adjustments and on having the necessary resources to recover. Without evaluation, the leader will not be able to react to changes in the environment.

As a certified public accountant, a large part of my practice is auditing the financial records on not-for-profit organizations. One day when I was presenting the audited financial statements to a client, a board member asked how they could add a few zeros to the bottom line. This was the first time that I used the LIFE model under fire. I quickly analyzed the situation using the model and within a few seconds started giving them an answer. Basically the board had one vision and the members had another vision. The board was not effectively communicating the vision and was doing absolutely nothing to evaluate their programs in order to make adjustments. The board was doing all of the communicating but not listening. Once board members started communicating to their members, they were able to make adjustments to their operations that resulted in halting the membership decline and even started adding a few more zeros to the bottom line.

To illustrate how this measurement tool can be applied to each situation, Exhibit 20.1 is a diagram of a communications analysis in a leading participant example where the left edge represents a high score and the right edge a low score.

EXHIBIT 20.1 Diagram of Leading Participant Example

Leading Participants	Darkness of Outlook
Vision	L_____X_____ l
Communication	L_____X____ l

Integrity of Vision	Ethical Void
Relationships	L_____X____ l
Data	L_X_____ l

Favorable Results	Adverse Consequences
Financial	L____X_____ l
Program	L_____X___ l

Evaluate	Disastrous Results
Data Gathering	L___X_____ l
Analysis	L_____X___ l
Adjustments	L_____X l

20.6   *Integrity of Vision/Ethical Void*

(A)   INTRODUCTION

Integrity is an essential quality of leadership. A lack of integrity can be overcome only if it occurs in an area that is not that important to the overall situation, or other areas in the model are so successful as to render integrity secondary. This is not to say that integrity is not important, but the real world takes other factors into consideration before a lack of integrity will bring down a leader or a cause.

To analyze integrity, you need to see what the leader is doing in the areas of relationships and data.

(B)   RELATIONSHIPS

The leader must develop sound positive relationships with the identified players. Personalities, styles, morals, ethics, feelings, and trust are all involved in how the leader can communicate the vision. Approach these questions from the point of view of what the organization is doing to foster relationships and what your own fund-raising efforts need regarding relationships.

Questions
- Who is the most important? Developing a hierarchy of importance will assist in decision making.
- What do you do to foster a meaningful relationship to support the vision? If the leader does not care, why should anyone else?
- When are people informed? Again, timing of information to the right players is a necessity.
- Where do you stand with your relationships—Straightforward, evasive, elusive? Players need to know where a leader stands in relationship to them.
- Why—does everyone know why they are doing what they are doing and how it fits in with the overall vision? People need to feel important.
- How does the leader treat people? "Do what I say, not what I do" is a little hypocritical.

(C)   DATA

Data, or information, must have integrity. Without integrity, no one will believe in the leader and then possibly even the vision. The leader is accountable to ensure that data that supports the efforts is obtained in a manner that is verifiable and believable. Proper internal controls over financial as well as program data is essential. Organization controls may be outside of the expertise of a person in charge of fund raising, but that person should know what the organization is doing in this regard. The fund raiser should also make sure that data concerning fund-raising efforts are verifiable and believable.

Questions
- Who is collecting the data? Duties must be segregated. No one person should be able to alter records without discovery. In other words, do not have the fox guarding the chicken coop.

- What data is needed? It is a waste of time to gather information that means nothing toward the analysis of the accomplishment of the vision.
- When is it needed? Proper analysis cannot be done if the information is not received in a timely basis.
- Where does it go? The information must be communicated to the players who can use it.
- Why is it needed? Always review the meaning of what is being done.
- How do we measure and verify? Sometimes measuring the results of efforts can be very difficult. The leader needs to determine what act best lends itself to measurement and communicates accomplishment or lack of it. The measurement must also be verifiable and believable; without this, results can be questioned without rebuttal.

(D) INTERRELATIONSHIPS WITH OTHER PARTS OF THE MODEL

Integrity without leading participants with a vision may have good intentions but will leave participants wandering without any apparent goals or vision. Integrity without favorable results or evaluation will again be well intentioned but the cause will be short-lived.

I am aware of a particular not-for-profit organization that had a key word from its vision as part of the name of the organization. This organization had fallen on hard times and was reaching out to the community for assistance. One potentially large benefactor asked what the organization was doing to fulfill its vision as stated in the name. No one could come up with an answer. The organization had strayed so far from its original purpose that it had lost any relationship with the players that meant the most to the organization. As a result this organization went bankrupt.

To diagram this situation, the left edge of the diagram in Exhibit 20.2 illustrates how this organization has scored low in all four critical areas, signaling it is on its way to the DEAD model.

EXHIBIT 20.2 Diagram of Integrity Vision Example #1

Leading Participants	Darkness of Outlook
Vision	L_____X_⌋
Communication	L_____X_⌋

Integrity of Vision	Ethical Void
Relationships	L_____X_⌋
Data	L_____X____⌋

Favorable Results	Adverse Consequences
Financial	L_____X__⌋
Program	L_____X_⌋

Evaluate	Disastrous Results
Data Gathering	L_____X_⌋
Analysis	L_____X_⌋
Adjustments	L_____X⌋

In another case, a not-for-profit organization was overflowing with well-intentioned people. Networking and relationships were not a problem. The problem was control over data, both program and financial. Accusations of special interest transactions started being made to the detriment of the people involved and the organization. Initially these accusations could not be adequately defended against because the underlying data was not organized or collected in a manner that would give one confidence as to its integrity. The organization survived only because it had had phenomenal favorable results in the past, both financial and program related, and was able to successfully reconstruct the data to the satisfaction of the parties involved.

Using the diagram to illustrate this organization's situation, Exhibit 20.3 reports high scores in the leadership and favorable results areas, mixed performance in integrity of vision, and disastrous results in evaluation.

20.7 Favorable Results/Adverse Consequences

(A) INTRODUCTION

Favorable results are required to sustain the effort toward the vision. This does not mean that favorable results must be immediate, but at least they must be foreseeable. The leader is accountable for favorable results in both the financial and the program areas.

(B) FINANCIAL RESULTS

An organization's fund-raising effort needs to be able to generate funds toward continuing operations. It goes almost without saying that without favorable financial results, any cause will have adverse consequences and will cease to exist.

EXHIBIT 20.3 Diagram of Integrity of Vision Example #2

Leading Participants	Darkness of Outlook
Vision	└X_____┘
Communication	└_____X_____┘

Integrity of Vision	Ethical Void
Relationships	└__X_____┘
Data	└_____X_┘

Favorable Results	Adverse Consequences
Financial	└____X_____┘
Program	└____X_____┘

Evaluate	Disastrous Results
Data Gathering	└_____X_┘
Analysis	└_____X_┘
Adjustments	└_____X_┘

(C) PROGRAMS

An organization must be able to demonstrate success with its programs. The programs should be in some way connected to its vision, for without success with its programs, it weakens the very core of the organization and its fund-raising messages. The organization's programs would be aimed at assisting its beneficiaries while the fund-raisers' activities would be aimed at coordinating successful fund-raising efforts to help fund the programs.

Combined Questions
The same questions can apply analysis of both financial and program aspects.

- Who does the job? Well-defined job description analysis helps prevent a duplication of work.
- What do they do? Not knowing what to do will most certainly lead to adverse consequences. People need to be able to make decisions without consulting with the leader every step of the way. The vision should be structured in such a way as to aid the participants in knowing what to do.
- Why do they do it? What is the purpose of the vision?
- When do they do it? Coordination of functions is essential to not wasting resources.
- Where does it lead? People need to know how their job fits in the overall success toward the vision.
- How do they do it? Knowledge of how to perform the job is essential to successful completion.

(D) INTERRELATIONSHIPS WITH OTHER PARTS OF THE MODEL

Favorable results without participants will lead to a short-lived cause without followers. Favorable results without integrity will not be for the overall good of all of the participants. A lack of integrity eventually will undermine any initial favorable results. Favorable results without evaluation will not allow for any modifications required, assuring that the results are favorable on an ongoing basis.

As noted in the example of integrity, organizations that do not stick to their vision have a hard time creating favorable results, financially or program. If leaders do not believe in their vision, why should anyone else? The organizations and fund-raising efforts that pay attention to executing their programs with vigor inevitably succeed both financially and in their programs.

The diagram in Exhibit 20.4 points out the consistency and positive performance that careful observance of the organization's vision can have on all four areas of performance measurement.

20.8   Evaluate/Disastrous Results

(A) INTRODUCTION

Objectivity is the most important aspect to evaluation. Leaders must be honest with themselves. They should not be blaming someone else but instead should be thinking

EXHIBIT 20.4 Diagram of Favorable Results Example

Leading Participants **Darkness of Outlook**

Vision	L___X_____J
Communication	L___X_____J

Integrity of Vision **Ethical Void**

Relationships	L__X_____J
Data	L_____X_____J

Favorable Results **Adverse Consequences**

Financial	L_____X_____J
Program	L_____X_____J

Evaluate **Disastrous Results**

Data Gathering	L____X_____J
Analysis	L____X_____J
Adjustments	L____X_____J

what can be done to make it better. They should not blindly do the same old things but rather think outside the box, try something new. They should look at the situation from not only their eyes but from everyone else's viewpoint. Their attitude should be: How I am going to make this work! Anything less means failure! The leader is accountable to making sure that evaluations are fair and get the job done, rather than ending up in a finger-pointing session. They must focus on the vision, not the blame.

Other aspects of the evaluation process are data gathering, analysis, and adjustments.

Questions

Regarding data gathering, consider:

- Who is evaluated? This may involve more than one person.
- What do we measure? Be sure to evaluate what needs to be measured and how that will assist in success. For an organization, this could be number of beneficiaries served. For the fund raiser, this could be dollars raised.
- When do we measure? You want to measure the right thing at the right time, not the right thing at the wrong time.

Regarding analysis, consider:

- Where did the results fall? Was the program successful?
- Why did it happen? This requires an open mind to discover the underlying reasons for success or failure. An errant analysis can mean inappropriate decisions.

Regarding adjustments, consider:

- How do we get better? A plan of action to correct any deviations from desired results.

(B) INTERRELATIONSHIPS WITH OTHER PARTS OF THE MODEL

Evaluation without participants should lead one to a reason as to why there are no participants. Evaluation without integrity means one has errant information in which to base adjustments. Disastrous results are sure to follow. Evaluation without favorable results requires further evaluation. If at first you don't succeed, try, try again.

A few years ago I came across a case where a not-for-profit organization did not know why it was losing constituents at an alarming rate. A quick review of the situation revealed that the organization not only did not know why it was declining in numbers, but it was not even implementing any efforts to determine why. Once the organization organized itself to gather the data, communicate with former members, and analyze the reasons, it was able to make adjustments to reach out to constituents and eventually halted the declining number of participants.

The final diagram (see Exhibit 20.5) points out how a positive appearance in three out of four areas of measurement may obscure an awareness of a disastrous trend in one area, in this case the analysis and adjustments from data gathered in the evaluation area.

20.9 Conflict

What happens when the vision runs up against a formidable foe? This is where one needs not only to review the LIFE/DEAD model from one's point of view but also from the opposition's point of view. Evaluation of strengths and weaknesses of both forces and making necessary adjustments is necessary for survival. Whoever can operate closer to the LIFE side of the model will have the most success.

EXHIBIT 20.5 Diagram of Disastrous Results in Evaluation Example

Leading Participants		Darkness of Outlook
Vision	⌊_____X_____⌋	
Communication	⌊_____X_____⌋	

Integrity of Vision		Ethical Void
Relationships	⌊_____X_____⌋	
Data	⌊_X_____⌋	

Favorable Results		Adverse Consequences
Financial	⌊___X_____⌋	
Program	⌊_____X_____⌋	

Evaluate		Disastrous Results
Data Gathering	⌊___X_____⌋	
Analysis	⌊_____X_⌋	
Adjustments	⌊_____X⌋	

20.10   Summary

In this day and age when accountability is becoming ever more important in our society, we need tools to better analyze leaders, whoever they may be. With the computer age demanding a need for quicker analysis and situations changing at an ever-alarming increasing rate, the need to analyze situations quickly is paramount.

A leader is accountable and responsible for LIFE. A leader must be accountable for leading participants with a vision and good communication. Integrity in relationships and data is a necessity. Favorable results in both finances and programs are a must in the long run. Evaluation is a requirement for anyone to react to changes.

An analysis of LIFE will assist in determining how accountable a leader has been, evaluating strengths and weaknesses, and determining the interrelationships between various factors that affect a situation or organization. Inevitably if a leader is having a problem in one area, it will affect other areas. This is where I have found the model so useful. The roots of a problem may be obscure, and everyone may be looking in the wrong direction for the answer.

In the simplest form, one need only remember the acronym LIFE/DEAD to assist in a quick analysis of a situation. Application of the basic questions who, what, when, where, why, and how provide one the ability to quickly analyze situations and arrive at solutions with amazing speed.

Suggested Readings

William Hendricks, Sam Bartless, and Joe Gilliam, editors. *Coaching, Mentoring and Managing,* Franklin Lakes, New Jersey: Career Press, 1996.

Warren Bennis and Burt Nanus, *Leaders: Strategies for Taking Charge,* New York: Harperbusiness, 1997.

PART IV ▼ Annual Giving Programs

21 Overview of Annual Giving

NAN D. DOTY
Doty & Cox

BARBARA M. COX
Doty & Cox

21.1 Annual vs. Capital Campaigns

(A) ANNUAL CAMPAIGNS

Annual campaigns are designed to provide funds for basic program operations and normal growth. They address relatively short-term needs (a year or less) and focus on individual giving, corporations, foundations, and civic groups.

Annual campaigns are, by their very nature, intended to be repeatable. Each campaign becomes the foundation for an expanded effort the following year. Donors understand that their support this year will be rewarded by a request for renewed and often increased support the year after.

Virtually any and every technique of fund raising can be useful in an annual giving campaign. Phonathons, direct mail, one-on-one solicitations, and major or minor special events are some common options. Crafting an annual giving plan that makes the best use of agency, human, and fiscal resources is the key to effectiveness.

The public sector provides a large portion of the annual income for many not-for-profit organizations, but public grant seeking is not ordinarily considered a component of annual giving.

(B) CAPITAL CAMPAIGNS

Capital campaigns are undertaken to achieve a major organizational goal for which an extraordinary investment is required. For example, a local hospital wishes to establish a cancer treatment center. The YWCA demonstrates the need for a child care facility. The Girl Scout Council believes an endowment can be created to support programs that will serve low-income communities.

Instead of the thousands typically raised in annual giving campaigns, capital goals are often in the millions of dollars. Often top corporate executives are enlisted to lead the effort. Wealthy individuals agree to give and to seek special gifts from other people who are in a position to make significant commitments. Big gifts are encouraged by utilizing multiyear pledges.

Prominent people are willing to get involved and to make extraordinary contributions because capital campaigns are rare events in the life of an organization. The defined goal and limited timetable are also attractive to volunteers.

Although special events, particularly *cultivation* events, can be part of a capital campaign, these campaigns rely primarily on face-to-face solicitation. Each request is carefully planned to match the strongest asker with the right prospect. The prospect universe is limited to major donors, in contrast to annual giving campaigns, which often emphasize small gifts from large numbers of people.

With the exception of the Kresge Foundation in Michigan, few professionally staffed foundations give to capital campaigns outside their own locality.

In recent years, a trend has been the decision to precede the capital campaign with a campaign planning study (also known as a feasibility study) conducted by fund-raising consultants. (Most capital campaigns are themselves organized with the help of consultants who specialize in this area.) A campaign planning study, a particular kind of market research, is designed to test potential donor support and to identify people who are ready, willing, and able to lead such an effort.

21.2   Getting Started: Developing a Fund-raising Plan

(A) EVALUATE PAST ACTIVITIES

Where an organization is going depends, at least initially, on where it has been. A good annual giving plan is a road map for a 12-month journey that will bring the organization home to as many different donors as possible. The plan begins with an analysis of contributions over the past three to five years:

- What sources have been tapped?
- How was the income obtained?
- Is the income from a particular source growing, declining, or staying the same?
- What are the direct (i.e., printing, postage, rental fees) and indirect (staff salaries, agency overhead) costs of raising these funds?

(B)   DETERMINE WHERE SUPPORT IS NEEDED

If the agency has multiple programs, which ones cover their own costs or break even? Which ones have a deficit? Who is served by each program? Can the program generate more earned income—by increasing fees, for example—thereby reducing the need for charitable contributions?

(C)   IDENTIFY POTENTIAL FUND-RAISING MARKETS

This part of the plan has three phases. First, list the various sources of contributions and the techniques for obtaining them. (One technique may apply to a variety of sources.) Exhibit 21.1 shows a typical list.

Second, determine the answers to the following questions:

- How much money might be anticipated from each sector?
- What are the agency's strengths and weaknesses in terms of contacting each sector?
- What will it cost in time (staff and volunteer) and direct expenditures to pursue each opportunity?

Finally, set supportable priorities. Where is the potentially biggest payoff, the maximum return on the investment of time and effort? What is expected to be the least productive source?

EXHIBIT 21.1 List of Potential Contributors and Proposed Solicitation Techniques

Sources	Techniques
Individuals (major gifts)	Personal solicitation
Individuals (small gifts)	Direct mail
Individuals (bequests)	Phonathons
Foundations	Proposals
Corporations	Joint ventures
Civic groups	Raffles
	Special events (specify options)

(D) ESTABLISH A DOLLAR GOAL

A realistic goal is important, and it can be set only after some careful analysis:

- Look at the shortfall between anticipated revenue and desired program expenditures.
- Evaluate that figure in light of prior fund-raising results.
- Consider what might be accomplished if a growth goal of X percent were established.
- Ask whether this is realistic, based on an assessment of where contributions are likely to be obtained.
- Divide the total dollar goal among the different elements of the annual giving program: $X from the year-end mail appeal; $Y from the dinner dance; $Z from foundations, corporations, and civic groups.

(E) CREATE A CALENDAR AND PUT SOMEONE IN CHARGE OF EACH PROJECT

Designate a person who is assigned specific responsibility for each element, and devise project timetables that can be used to match actual events with the plan's schedule. Each plan should start with the completion date and build backward. As shown in Exhibit 21.2, the overall plan is the sum total of the particular activities.

(F) GIVE RECOGNITION

It is just about impossible to say thank you too often. Every volunteer who works on any aspect of annual giving should receive a letter of thanks or a phone call from the chief volunteer officer (usually the president or chairperson of the board).

EXHIBIT 21.2 Sample Year-End Appeal Work Plan

Completion Date	Activity	Responsibility
Daily, as gifts are received	Gifts logged; director of development notified	Staff (specify)
	Acknowledgment sent with copy to personal contact	Staff or volunteers
Weekly	Report generated for Appeal Committee	Staff or volunteers
November 22–24	Follow-up calls (Phonathon)	Appeal Committee, board members
November 15	Letters mailed	Staff or volunteers
November 1	Personal notes added	Appeal Committee, board members
October 15	Appeal printed	Staff or volunteers
October 1	Appeal drafted and approved	Staff or volunteers, Appeal Committee
September 15	List updated, expanded	All

Work efforts should also be acknowledged publicly at board meetings, at membership meetings, and—with a tangible expression of thanks—at the annual meeting. Donors *and* annual giving volunteers should be saluted in agency newsletters.

The *primary* purpose of the annual report should be donor recognition. Keep the narrative lively (and brief) and prominently list every donor within categories or "giving clubs" that signal large gifts.

These "giving clubs" should be listed on the gift information card included with the appeal. (See an example in Exhibit 21.3.) Each organization must determine appropriate target levels based on the history and potential of its donors.

Send *every* donor a copy of the annual report. Include a brief note of thanks and point out that the agency would not have accomplished all that it did "without your generosity."

If it is too expensive to send the report to every donor, print an 8½- by 14-inch *Highlights of the Annual Report* for smaller donors, or make one issue of the newsletter, wholly or in part, the Annual Report.

21.3 Fund-raising Markets

(A) INDIVIDUALS

Individual donors should receive the lion's share of attention in any annual giving plan. The numbers tell why: 80 percent of all giving comes from individuals. When planned giving and bequests are included, the total rises to nearly 90 percent.

Individuals who are close to the organization and who have the ability to make significant contributions should be solicited in person; others may be most efficiently contacted by mail. Volunteers and staff can create lists of people who, they believe, would be interested in agency programs. A special event that offers a fun experience or something of value may bring in people who have had no previous connection to the organization.

The annual giving plan should include the creation of lists that build on the agency's constituencies:

- Present donors
- Prior donors
- Volunteers (They are giving their time, but they can be educated to give money too.)
- Prior leadership (Stay in touch with past board members, not just as donors; too many organizations let them slip away without a ripple.)

EXHIBIT 21.3 Giving Clubs

The President's Circle	(Gifts of $5,000 and above)
Benefactors	(Gifts of $1,000 to $4,999)
Community Builders	(Gifts of $500 to $999)
Patrons	(Gifts of $100 to $499)
Sponsors	(All others)

- Members (They are paying for a service, but they can be reminded that they are getting a bargain.)
- Friends of board and staff members (who will receive a personal note on the appeal)

(B) INSTITUTIONS

(i) Corporations

For most organizations the corporate sector will produce scant income for basic operations. Overall, corporate giving accounts for less than 5 percent of total philanthropy.

Corporate giving has been further reduced in recent years by mergers, takeovers, and purchases by foreign companies.

Most corporate gifts are small, even from giant companies. Significant corporate gifts are almost always elicited through personal relationship with top executives. It is virtually useless to send "cold" letters to a list of companies where no personal contacts exist.

An important new trend is the policy of linking corporate philanthropy to employee volunteerism and to services received. It is vital to capture employer information from volunteers and the people participating in or assisted by agency programs.

Many large companies have, within their marketing budgets, funds that can be made available to underwrite activities that may enhance their visibility in markets they value.

(ii) Foundations

Foundation giving accounts for another 5 percent (approximately) of total giving. Well-known, professionally staffed foundations rarely give to ongoing local programs. Directors of development of major organizations spend countless hours trying to recast their proposals so that they are "innovative" and "national models."

Community foundations present the best opportunity for obtaining a significant grant for local or regional organizations. These foundations, formed by gifts from many unrelated individuals, will readily provide information about how to apply for a contribution, and they like to fund new programs or programs that provide services to new populations. Most grants are for one year (occasionally, two). Applicants must be prepared with a good answer as to how the program will be funded after the grant money has been spent.

"Family foundations" can be a resource for local groups. There are thousands of these small, unstaffed foundations. Personal contacts are essential: "Cold" requests will not even be acknowledged. *The National Data Book,* published by the Foundation Center and available in many libraries, lists family foundations by state, including information about assets and, usually, the name and address of an officer. Additional information about these small foundations appears in state foundation directories, available in most public libraries, or in the "990" (tax return) files maintained at branches of the Foundation Center. (See Section 21.8, "Resources.")

(iii) Service Clubs

The Rotary, Kiwanis, Junior League, and Women's Club—each has a host of service clubs that award financial grants among their other activities. Some like to support scholarships; others like to give equipment. Some sponsor specific program interests. With a little digging, a member can be found who will serve as guide and advocate for the request.

21.4   The Case for Giving

Effective fund raising is rooted in the organization's mission statement and the program priorities established through a long-range or strategic planning process. (See Chapter 2.) The term "case statement" comes from capital campaigns. Often presented in the form of a brochure, the case statement contains the rationale on which requests for support are based.

The case statement is a marketing or advocacy piece. It establishes that the need being addressed is important to potential donors by providing information about the people to be helped. It positions the organization as well qualified to address the targeted problems.

A case statement for annual giving may be only one or two pages long. It should answer as many of these questions as possible:

- What are the problems or opportunities?
- Who is affected?
- What is the proposed solution?
- How will the problem be solved? (What steps will be taken?)
- Who will do the work?
- What will be the result?
- What difference will it make to the people with the problem? To the community?
- Why is this organization uniquely qualified to address this problem?
- What will it cost?
- What is in it for the donor (good feelings, a healthier community, reduced crime, a more just society)?

The case material is designed to support the volunteer who will make the request in person. It should contain just enough information to give the volunteer confidence in making the presentation. The material should be attractive enough to leave with donors, to review while they are considering their contribution. An example of case material is given in Exhibit 21.4.

Donors respond best to appeals that allow them to see how their gifts help a person or a cause. (See Exhibit 21.5.) Instead of a general request for "a gift for [*name of agency*]," the development of a table of giving opportunities enlivens or personalizes the appeal and covers a range of dollar amounts.

The list of opportunities can be included in the case material or printed on the gift response card.

21.5   Responsibility for Fund Raising

(A)   ROLE OF BOARD MEMBERS

Responsibility for ensuring that an agency has the funding it needs to fulfill its commitments is one of the board members' most important functions. It is a dual responsibility: to give personally at a level commensurate with one's resources and to get funds from outside sources. It is up to the Nominating Committee to communicate this responsibil-

EXHIBIT 21.4 Sample Case Statement

Meeting the Challenge

For four decades, AGENCY has been a lifeline for people with developmental and physical disabilities—and a bridge to friendship, work, and self-reliance.

During these years, we have wept together, laughed together, and celebrated small steps and large. Families with great wealth and families with little or none have found an understanding and supportive community dedicated to helping their special person be the best he or she can be.

Today, however, AGENCY itself must seek extraordinary help. Our ability to meet the needs of families in our community is in jeopardy. At a time when state funding has been cut back, AGENCY faces pressing demands for *increased* service:

- This year, AGENCY has been asked by area school systems to serve 20 graduates who have severe multiple disabilities;
- Our pioneering work with younger and younger infants is straining our resources;
- We have eliminated nine staff positions and have told the staff there will be no salary increases, in response to this year's budget.

A special campaign is being launched by board members, other volunteers, and staff, to strengthen AGENCY's financial resources. This effort is being greatly aided by a challenge gift made by an AGENCY family. They have pledged $25,000 if the campaign's donors will match that amount, to allow AGENCY to continue to serve all the children and adults who need our varied programs.

AGENCY's involvement sometimes begins prenatally, when a family anticipating the birth of an infant with Down syndrome seeks information about the quality of life and community support that await their child.

- *Our Center for Infant and Child Development* provides integrated early intervention services through the age of five. These services enhance development and minimize developmental delay.
- *Employment Training* includes training and placement in competitive positions, employment as the member of an AGENCY work crew within a business, and placement in our sheltered workshop.
- *Senior Services* offer exercise, lectures, arts and crafts, and trips to stores, restaurants, parks, and nature centers.
- *Social Services* provide counseling, advocacy, assessment, and help in securing housing, financial, medical, and legal assistance.

From the youngest baby in our infant program to the oldest senior who comes to AGENCY to be with friends, everyone AGENCY touches, every family we support, and every employer who depends on a valued worker is a link strengthening a society that cares about the quality of life for every person. This is AGENCY's challenge and AGENCY's reward.

Reprinted by permission of Doty & Cox.

---

ity fully and positively to candidates for the board of directors. When this does not occur, board members may feel they were recruited under false pretenses. (See Chapter 13.)

The role of board members in fund raising is central to the success of the development program. Board members are unique and significant advocates for the organization; they must set the pace for other donors with their own contributions. As people giving not only money but time, they can elicit contributions that even the most experienced staff member cannot duplicate.

Board members can also be invaluable in extending an agency's outreach to other markets. They become ambassadors to the professions, to the business community, and

---

EXHIBIT 21.5 Sample List of Giving Opportunities

What Your Gift Can Provide

$500	One month of summer camp for an inner-city child.
250	Three months of hot breakfasts for a preschool child in the nursery program.
100	Four well-baby checkups
50	Three nights in a "safe house" for a battered woman
25	Four flu shots for homeless seniors

---

to personal friends who are in a position to lend their support to a good cause. They can recruit additional leadership to strengthen the agency's network and experts to help with specialized tasks.

(B) FUND DEVELOPMENT COMMITTEE

Although every board member should be involved in some aspect of annual giving, the work of the board should be organized through a Fund Development Committee. The board member who chairs this committee should present a report at every board meeting. Staff members should also be assigned to work on the Fund Development Committee and on specific fund-raising projects.

The basic tasks of the Fund Development Committee are to develop the annual giving plan, to recruit people who will take responsibility for specific items in the plan, and to encourage other members of the board to give and to help. These tasks are incorporated into the board's charge for the committee. (See Exhibit 21.6.)

(C) ROLE OF THE STAFF

Fund-raising staff work in two dimensions. First, they provide support and guidance for board members and other development volunteers, ensuring that the annual giving plan and calendar proceed on schedule. Second, they initiate and implement fund-raising activities that can be accomplished mostly at the staff level. (See Exhibit 21.7.)

EXHIBIT 21.6 Sample Charge for Fund Development Committee, from Board of Directors

---

The Fund Development Committee is responsible for raising contributions to help support the work of AGENCY.

The Committee will develop an annual plan of work and a direct-expense budget. It will recommend a dollar goal to be adopted by the board. The Committee will recruit people to implement the plan and will keep the board informed of progress toward the goal.

The Committee will give input to the Nominating Committee to ensure the recruitment of board members able and willing to secure financial and other resources for AGENCY.

EXHIBIT 21.7 Sample Job Description: Director of Development

- Design and implement an annual mail and telephone appeal.
- Identify and research major gift prospects.
- Provide training and support for AGENCY's president and other volunteers who will person-ally solicit people in a position to make gifts of $1,000, $5,000, and above.
- Organize annual Corporate Awards Breakfast.
- Seek special gifts and grants from foundations, corporations, civic groups, and other institu-tional givers.
- Develop a cultivation and solicitation program to reach out to the people who have benefited from AGENCY services.
- Produce a newsletter to be mailed twice a year to individual donors, corporations, families, and community leaders.
- Provide staff support for an ongoing bequest program to build AGENCY's endowment.
- Create and implement a donor recognition system to ensure timely expression of thanks, and activities to encourage continued support.
- Maintain donor records and provide periodic reports on income and expenses.
- Provide staff support to the Fund Development Committee.

Reproduced by permission of Doty & Cox.

(i) Prospect Research

The goal of prospect research is to enable the organization to identify people who have major gift potential. A combination of science and diplomacy is required. The key questions are: How much can they give? Who should ask? The scientific part can be accomplished at the local library, where the following kinds of resources may shed light on prospects' interests, income, and business and social circles. (See also Chapter 35.):

Who's Who (national, regional, or by specialization, e.g., "Finance and Industry")
Who Was Who
New York Times Index (information on parents, family, other relatives; obituaries and wedding announcements can be especially helpful)
New York Times Annual Index (by person)
Wall Street Journal Index (by year, by person)
Local papers (if indexed)

Many good prospects will have only a brief (or no) entry in these sources; "diplomacy" is often all one has to go on. Confidential discussions with knowledgeable board members or other volunteers who are active in community philanthropy are the next step.

The starting point is the organization's lists of present and former donors and volunteers. Auxiliaries can be excellent places to spot potential donors. A small group of people can be brought together to review the lists, to share any information that will be helpful in deciding potential levels of giving, and to provide advice on relationships with people associated with the agency who might be effective solicitors. This information should be discreetly recorded and brought to bear in the orchestration of personal solicitations.

(ii) Record Keeping

Data processing technology has made it relatively easy to maintain donor records and to tailor personal requests to a large number of people. A wide variety of off-the-shelf fund-raising management software is available, with varying degrees of flexibility and ease of utilization. Most agencies will find, however, that their needs can be well met by setting up their own system using standard database and word processing programs. The following basic information should be collected:

Full name (and nickname, if any)
Home address and telephone
Employer's name, address, and telephone
Prospect's title
Spouse's name and occupation
Children: names, ages, schools
Prospect's relationship to agency
Committee assignments (past and present)
Programs of special interest
Giving history
Other community affiliations
Religious affiliation
Education
General comments

(iii) Reports

Giving information should be captured in such a way as to make it easy to generate progress reports on individual gifts. Although information about specific contributions is confidential and should be limited to a small number of people, periodic summary reports help keep campaigns moving forward. The formats recommended for these reports are shown in Exhibit 21.8.

(D) ROLE OF CONSULTANTS

Fund-raising consultants can be engaged to handle any and all of the work involved in planning and implementing a campaign *except* face-to-face solicitations of major donors

---

EXHIBIT 21.8 Sample Report Formats

Individual gifts prospect worksheet:

Prospect	Solicitor	Amount to Request	Status	Gift/ Pledge

Corporate gifts prospect worksheet:

Company	Contact	Solicitor	Amount to Request	Status	Gift/ Pledge

Campaign summary:

Team	Goal	Total Pledged	Percentage of Goal	Requests Pending ($)	To Be Solicited ($)

and leadership recruitment. No matter how hard it may be to recruit people willing to ask, there is no better solicitor than a volunteer who is giving his or her time and money in support of a valued organization.

Sometimes it is suggested that fund raisers be paid on a contingency basis, perhaps as a percentage of funds raised. Although this approach sounds appealing because it appears not to cost anything, it is almost never in an organization's best interest. Many experienced consultants believe contingency arrangements are unethical because they can encourage fund raisers to advocate high-pressure tactics, which may raise more money in the short term but end up alienating donors from future support.

Consultants frequently are used to handle specific pieces of an annual giving program—for example, organizing a corporate dinner. Some consultants specialize in identifying foundation or government sources and preparing written proposals; others provide advice on board development or train volunteers to solicit major gifts. Some consultants will analyze an agency's giving program, put together an overall plan, and provide periodic advice to the executive director or the director of development as the various activities take effect. Consultants write brochures and annual reports. Capital campaign consultants may place a member of their staff in the agency's offices to handle the day-to-day aspects of a complicated fund drive.

Most states regulate professional fund raisers, especially those known as "professional solicitors," who actually ask for and may personally handle contributions. Copies of such regulations can ordinarily be obtained through the office of the state attorney general.

Any relationship with a fund-raising consultant should be governed by a written contract specifying exactly what is to be done and at what cost. (See Exhibit 21.9 for an example.)

21.6 Fund-raising Techniques

(A) DONOR RELATIONS

Careful cultivation and attention to the individual dreams, fears, and needs of each major gift prospect will reap huge rewards over the years. Let "the Golden Rule" be the guide: Treat all donors with the respect, honesty, and consideration that everyone appreciates.

Cultivation is the art of gradually developing personal links between the organization and its constituency. The first link might be a personal phone call of thanks from the president or chairperson when a significant gift is received. An invitation to a small gathering in the private home of a board member, "to thank our special supporters and give them an advance look at important trends in our work," will coax some donors to draw closer.

Cultivation can be made a priority for top volunteers and the executive director. If three people commit themselves to having lunch twice a month with different major donors (or donors targeted for major upgrading), at the end of the first year 72 supporters will have been flattered and their commitment heightened.

Emphasis on cultivation is important: Donors at all levels do not like being thought of only when money is involved. A twice-yearly or quarterly newsletter, simple and attractive, is an efficient way to strengthen relationships with average donors. The newsletter can be used to recognize special gifts—memorials, bequests, and grants from local corporations.

EXHIBIT 21.9 Sample Consultant Contract

This letter is to confirm and constitute the understanding between WORTHY AGENCY and SUPE-RIOR CONSULTANTS, a [name of state] partnership conducting the business of fund-raising consultation for not-for-profit organizations.

SUPERIOR CONSULTANTS will design and implement a fund-raising plan to increase contributions from individual donors.

[Person's name] will coordinate the delivery of service under this contract, with the support of SUPERIOR CONSULTANTS.

It will be SUPERIOR CONSULTANTS' responsibility to:

1. Direct the development of a contributions database containing information about past and present giving. Train volunteers in basic research techniques.
2. Identify potential contributors to the "challenge fund." Prepare and assist the president and board members in soliciting selected individuals for this purpose.
3. Develop and implement both short-term and ongoing fund-raising strategies involving board members, parents, and friends of WORTHY AGENCY.
4. Review suggestions for fund raising for WORTHY AGENCY. Help set priorities and advise on the implementation of the best ideas.
5. Outline the basic functions of a development office for WORTHY AGENCY and prepare a model job description for a Director of Development.
6. Develop a proposal for a feasibility study for an Endowment Campaign and advise on sources of underwriting for such a study.

It will be WORTHY AGENCY's responsibility to:

1. Provide SUPERIOR CONSULTANTS with information on prior and ongoing fund-raising efforts and outreach.
2. Identify key volunteers, donors, and community leaders for fund-raising leadership, and help with involving them in the annual giving program.
3. Enable the Executive Director to work closely with the consultants to ensure full and timely communication.
4. Furnish whatever secretarial and other office services the contributions program requires.
5. Pay or reimburse any out-of-pocket expenses, such as printed materials, special-event costs, and recognition items. All expenditures will be subject to prior approval.
6. Receive all monies; log and collect gifts and pledges; and provide periodic reports on income and expenses.
7. Implement public relations aspects of the campaign, if any.

All information about donors to WORTHY AGENCY is confidential and the sole property of WORTHY AGENCY and may not be used by SUPERIOR CONSULTANTS except for the benefit of WORTHY AGENCY.

WORTHY AGENCY will not be billed for telephone, postage, photocopying, clerical, and similar expenses incurred by SUPERIOR CONSULTANTS in WORTHY AGENCY's offices, or for travel within Home County.

WORTHY AGENCY has the right to cancel this contract upon 30 days' written notice. WORTHY AGENCY is responsible for all authorized expenditures committed up to the date of notification and for the final 30 days' fee owed to SUPERIOR CONSULTANTS.

The period covered by this contract is [date] through [date]. The fee for these services is [$X,000], payable monthly at the beginning of each service period. Should WORTHY AGENCY wish to continue to receive these services after [date], SUPERIOR CONSULTANTS will provide them at no increase in fee.

If this letter correctly expresses our mutual understanding, please signify approval by signing the original and the attached copy and returning the original to me at SUPERIOR CONSULTANTS.

AGREED

[Signature]	[Signature]
EXECUTIVE DIRECTOR	Partner
WORTHY AGENCY	SUPERIOR CONSULTANTS

Dated _____

Reproduced by permission of Doty & Cox.

The executive director should keep a list of actual and potential major donors on his or her desk. When there is a news article about an agency program or an issue of prime concern, a copy of the article should be sent to selected donors with a handwritten notation making a connection between the donors and the article—for example, "Thank you again for helping make this program possible. We're reaching even more kids than we had expected!"

Or a phone call can be made: "I hope you saw today's editorial about. . . . I know you're interested in this, and it's encouraging that other people are starting to pay attention too."

Any agency representative who will be speaking at a community event should call and invite donors being cultivated. Most will not come, but they will be pleased to be remembered.

Recognizing and acting on these kinds of opportunities will be no trouble if they become part of one's regular way of work. Either the director of development (if such a position exists) or the executive director should have a list of the organization's best actual and potential donors. The list should be reviewed weekly and specific actions taken.

(B) PERSONAL SOLICITATION

The goal of cultivation is to pave the way for face-to-face solicitation of major donors. Personal solicitation is almost always the best way to elicit large gifts. Because it is also a very frightening prospect for many otherwise indomitable volunteers, the guidelines in Exhibit 21.10 will be helpful.

Volunteers who accept responsibility for face-to-face solicitation need and deserve training and support. They need coaching in how to make a phone call to set up a solicitation appointment, often the toughest part of the entire transaction. They need to know as much as possible about the person they will solicit—his or her relationship with the agency; special program interests, if any; and what size gift is appropriate to request. They need an attractive brochure (the case material) and a pledge card.

EXHIBIT 21.10 Keys to Successful Solicitations

- The $XXXXX goal is attainable.
- Make your own gift first. Your personal commitment empowers you to ask for "stretch" gifts from others.
- Be familiar with your prospect's primary interest in the Agency.
- See your prospect in person.
- Work in teams.
- Express appreciation for prior contributions and indicate their importance to the organization.
- Use the case material and brochure to briefly describe Agency programs and the purpose of the request.
- Listen and respond to the prospect's questions and interests.
- Ask for a specific amount, mentioning your own commitment and that of other donors.
- Hold on to the pledge card if an immediate decision is not forthcoming.
- Send a follow-up letter.
- Report back to the appropriate person at the Agency.
  DO IT TODAY!

Reproduced by permission of Doty & Cox.

Gathering this information is the job of the director of development or the executive director. If outside expertise is desired, people known to be effective fund raisers should be asked to conduct a training session. Development directors from other organizations may be glad to help, or professional consultants might be retained for this specific purpose.

(C) FINDING NEW DONORS

Building a donor base works on the same principle as dropping a rock in a pool. Once the process begins, ripples create widening ripples and, gradually, outreach develops throughout the entire system. The key elements are described here.

- Start with the *board of directors*. Ask each trustee to provide a list of people who are to receive a personalized letter emphasizing the sender's commitment to the work of the agency and asking the prospect to lend his or her support to this good cause. Involve as many nonmembers as possible on the Fund Development Committee and ask each of them to write to their friends and colleagues. As lists are provided, note any information that might be useful in building a donor record—particularly if there is the potential for significant support.
- To stimulate *list creation*, collect donor and board lists from other organizations and have them reviewed by the Fund Development Committee. In many communities, the local hospital, library, or family service agency regularly lists donors in an annual report. "Cold" letters probably will not produce much, but volunteers can identify people they know when prodded by such a list.
- Consider creating a *prestigious award* to be given annually to three or more prominent people whose association with the organization would be valuable. Be straightforward about the fact that this is a fund-raising event. Arrange a simple reception in a private home. Ask the honorees to provide invitation lists, and construct others based on information about their networks. Charge $100 a person and make it the responsibility of every board member to obtain 10 pledges and the use of the donor's name on the listing of the Award Committee. Print the names of the Award Committee on the invitation. Each year, expand the number of people charged with obtaining pledges. An organization that used exactly this technique raised $10,000 the first year (100 gifts at $100 each). Eight years later, the event netted $75,000, and the agency has made many new friends it would never otherwise have had.
- Be willing to *start small*. Everyone else did.

(D) BEQUESTS

Bequests are usually categorized with some highly specialized giving vehicles called "planned giving," as if the rest of fund raising is the product of happy spontaneity. The subject of planned giving is often filled with daunting, technical discussions of "charitable remainder trusts" or "pooled income funds," and volunteers leave seminars convinced they have to become estate planning experts. Universities and major health and cultural institutions do secure impressive "planned gifts" by drawing on special professional expertise; however, for organizations that are just getting started in this area, the simplest and the most productive focus is on bequests.

A bequest, like any other special gift, must be solicited: Donors must be told that the agency would like to be remembered in their wills. When a bequest is received, it should be highlighted in a newsletter, with information on what the gift will make possible. Mail solicitations should include a place on the gift card for a donor to indicate: "I have provided for [*name of organization*] in my will." A special mailing concentrating solely on bequests should be considered.

Because state laws differ, an attorney should draw up simple language to include in newsletters, in the annual report, and on pledge cards. For example:

After payment of all debts, taxes, and administration expenses, I leave _____ *percent of my estate to* [name of organization].

Donors can bequeath:

- A percentage of their estate
- A specific amount of money
- A "contingent" bequest (comes to the organization only after other heirs have died)
- A "residuary" bequest: "I leave $1 million to my husband, Faithful Spouse. The rest and residue of my estate I leave to [*name of organization*]."

Bequests can also be a topic during the face-to-face discussions with major donors. It is important that the people soliciting bequests have themselves made such a commitment. This process should start with the board of directors. Even a young person or one of relatively modest means can comfortably provide in a will that a percentage of his or her estate will go to the organization and thus be in a position to ask someone else to do likewise.

When it becomes known, by whatever means, that someone has made a bequest, that person belongs high on the list for continuing cultivation.

21.7 *Special Events*

It is no accident that special events constitute the final topic in a chapter on annual giving. A special event is often the first thing that comes to mind when people meet to discuss fund raising. However, for many organizations, it is the worst possible use of staff and volunteer energy, time, and commitment.

The annual giving plan must realistically evaluate every option under consideration. A special event has initial appeal: It sounds like fun, it may be glamorous, and it minimizes the sensitive (but almost always more productive) issues of personal solicitation.

But will the event raise money? How many hours and how many dollars will it cost to produce?

There are four questions to ask in deciding whether a proposed special event makes sense:

1. What is the event's primary purpose? Is it fund raising or something else? Be wary of trying to accomplish too many things with one event. If the purpose *is* fund raising, the focus must stay on the bottom line.

2. Is there an existing event to which a fund-raising component could be added, for example, an annual luncheon honoring businesses that employ people trained or rehabilitated by the agency? It will take nothing away from the existing event to overlay it with an appeal to major corporations in the area to purchase tables or make contributions.
3. Are there volunteers who are eager to take responsibility? This is vital. The event will still need a good helping of staff support, but unless the event is "owned" by one or more volunteers, do not try it!
4. Will organizing the event foreclose the opportunity to do something more "profitable?" (Again, consider priorities.)

There are hundreds (probably thousands) of formats for special events. They all work, and they are all opportunities for disaster. Much depends on the culture of the community and the nature of the audience. In some places, gala dinner dances are popular. In other communities, auctions, bike-a-thons, golf or tennis tournaments, or concerts attract enthusiastic support.

Special events need not be ruled out, but they must fit firmly within the total development program.

21.8 Resources

There are many very helpful books and periodicals about every aspect of fund raising. The following are superior, in our opinion; at a minimum, they are good places to seek specific materials.

Chronicle of Philanthropy (biweekly magazine), 1255 23rd Street NW, Washington, DC 20037. Invaluable information about trends and developments affecting all kinds and sizes of not-for-profit organizations. Essential reading for development professionals and highly recommended for executive directors.

The Foundation Center, 79 Fifth Avenue, New York, NY (212) 620-4230. Maintains a free library, including at least the last 12 months of many publications. Has information on many aspects of fund raising, not just foundations. Microfiche copies of tax returns of all private foundations are available. Call for information about branches in other parts of the country. (This information can be obtained by phone by paying an annual membership fee.)

The Grantsmanship Center, P.O. Box 6210, Los Angeles, CA 90014. Publications catalog has many good articles and how-to pieces on fund raising, public relations, and other aspects of not-for-profit management. Provides information and advice on public funding.

National Center for Nonprofit Boards, 2000 L Street NW, Suite 411, Washington, DC 20036. Established in 1988 by the Association of Governing Boards of Universities and Colleges and Independent Sector. Publications list and Nonprofit Governance Series booklets are especially worthwhile.

Information resources are widely available on CD-ROM and online. Technology and software in this area is developing so rapidly that our best advice is to find an information superhighway guru to advise you.

Suggested Readings

Alexander O'Neill Haas & Martin. Videotape. *Would You Rather Jump Out of an Airplane Than Ask for Money?* Atlanta, GA: Alexander, GA: Alexander O'Neill Haas & Martin, 1995.

AAFRC Trust for Philanthropy. *Giving USA: The Annual Report of Philanthropy.* New York: American Association of Fund Raising Counsel, 2000.

Federation for Community Planning. *Fund-Raising Events: Strategies for Success.* Cleveland, OH: Federation for Community Planning, 1993.

Foundation Center World Wide Web site. New York: The Foundation Center: *fdncenter.org/index.html*

Gee, Ann D., ed. *Annual Giving Strategies: A Comprehensive Guide to Better Results.* Washington, DC: Council for Advancement and Support of Education, 1990.

Geever, Jane, and Patricia McNeill. *The Foundation Center's Guide to Proposal Writing.* New York: The Foundation Center, 1993.

Greenfield, James M. *Fund-Raising Fundamentals: A Guide to Annual Giving for Professionals and Volunteers.* New York: John Wiley & Sons, 1994.

Howe, Fisher. *Fund Raising and the Nonprofit Board Member.* Washington, DC: National Center for Nonprofit Boards, 1988.

Lant, Jeffrey. *How to Raise Money for Your Nonprofit Organization with an Annual Phonathon.* Cambridge, MA: Jeffrey Lant Associates, 1996.

Seymour, Harold J. *Designs for Fund-Raising.* Ambler, PA: The Taft Group, 1988.

Direct Mail

KAY PARTNEY LAUTMAN, CFRE
Lautman & Company

22.1 Introduction

Are you reading this chapter because you love direct mail? Or because you hate it? Is it because your new job has a direct mail component and you need to know how to implement or supervise it? Is your organization considering testing direct mail for the first time? Or is your present campaign declining in profitability?

The answers to these questions are important to this chapter, just as they are to any fund-raising effort. The first question—Who is the intended audience?—is the single most important question to ask, for if a message is targeted incorrectly, it will fall on unreceptive ears (or worse, be discarded in the trash).

So, who are you and why are you reading this chapter? Whoever you are, there is one thing known about you for certain. You are interested in the subject of direct mail fund raising.

In that one statement lies the key to successful direct mail: A winning campaign is one that conveys useful information to a person who is already interested in the subject matter. Or, as someone once said, "Junk mail is any mail sent to the wrong person."

If you learn that lesson well, it will stand you in better stead than anything you could learn about copy writing, production techniques, and other strategies. Nevertheless, this chapter discusses the basics of those very subjects. Moreover, it focuses on why direct mail is the most creative and rewarding area in all of fund raising.

It would be impossible, in the space allowed, to present a complete how-to chapter on any subject, let alone one so detail-oriented as direct mail. For an in-depth study of the subject, a suggested reading list is included. Instead, this chapter provides the following critical information:

- *For the novice.* For those considering a first-time foray into direct mail fund raising, a simple test is provided to help you decide whether direct mail is for you. Also included is a guide to what direct mail is, what it can and cannot do, what cost and income expectations might be, how to get started, and how to evaluate the campaign.
- *For the committed.* For those already committed to a mail program, a review process to help in evaluating how the program is going and suggestions for improving all segments of the program, from acquisition to renewals and house appeals, to monthly donor and high-amount donor programs.
- *Evaluation tools.* Includes two checklists, (1) for writing a compelling fund-raising letter and (2) for fail-safe strategy and production methods.

22.2 *What Is Direct Mail?*

Every year individual Americans donate tens of billions of dollars to not-for-profit organizations. Some write small checks for $10 or $20; others make contributions for many thousands of dollars. But the odds are that even such vastly different donors have something in common: a first gift that was made when they received a letter asking for financial support. Eighty percent of the gifts Americans give each year start out just that way—with a letter.

For organizations, even new ones that have not yet had a chance to establish their reputations, that letter represents an opportunity to begin developing a dependable source of funding. For donors, it offers a way to belong and to help those less fortunate.

For some donors, that letter may have been a personal note from someone they knew at an organization. For the vast majority of givers, however, even those who eventually become very large donors, that first letter was probably a direct mail letter like those you find in your own mailbox every day. How those letters transform total strangers into the loyal friends whose generosity supports an organization is what direct mail is all about.

First, a word about terminology. Like "telemarketing," "direct mail" is a greatly maligned term. To many it means only large-volume, preprinted, impersonal, commercial letters that arrive by the pound in the mailbox.

That *is* direct mail at one end of the scale for certain very large businesses and organizations. But the fact is that almost any mailing of more than 10 pieces (wherein each letter is virtually the same as every other) is also direct mail.

Thus, regardless of the size of the effort, such mailings classify as direct mail. Renewal mailings to members are direct mail, personalized letters to high-amount donors are direct mail, newsletters to supporters are direct mail, and invitations to join or give to an organization—regardless of the quality of paper or class of postage used—are still direct mail. Thus, virtually 98 percent of all charitable organizations in the country utilize direct mail in their fund raising and public relations programs, even though they may think of such an activity as "letter writing."

You, too, may prefer to think of it as "letter writing" and prefer to use the term "telephoning a donor" rather than "telemarketing campaign." One immediately sees the difference in response on people's faces merely as a result of using different terminology.

The following section considers direct mail in its most common form, a tool to enlist new donors and build a constituency through the use of what most people call "bought" lists.

22.3   *Direct Mail Constituency Building*

Too often, organizations have unrealistic expectations when they undertake their first constituency-building effort through direct mail. They tally the donations, figure in their costs, and declare their verdict. If their mailing does not make a profit, does not make at least a 1 percent return and/or return $1 for every $1 spent (as they have always heard a mailing should), they conclude that direct mail just is not for them.

In many cases, that decision has cost an organization all of the growth and money a properly managed campaign, even one thought to have "failed," might have given them. The organization's mistake was in looking at direct mail as a limited campaign, when it should have been looking at it as an *ongoing, long-term process of building a program.*

Properly executed, a direct mail program can provide an organization with loyal supporters and a consistent source of working capital. Equally important, it can systematically identify the people capable of making the very large gifts and bequests on which so much of the organization's future success depend.

22.4   *Is Direct Mail Constituency Building for You?*

Even though you may be ready and willing to begin a full-fledged program, there is a critical question that must be answered before committing your organization's time, effort, and money: Is my organization a good candidate for direct mail? The answer has nothing to do with the virtues of your cause. Many causes, no matter how worthwhile, simply do not tend to work well in the mail. Others may work only at a particular time in history, when current events and the public mood make the people most receptive to their mission.

To learn whether direct mail is likely to be right for your organization, it is a good idea to ask a direct mail professional or, even better, to ask questions of at least three reputable firms.

If two out of three believe your organization to be mail viable, your chances of success are strong. But if two out of three (or all three) warn you away from direct mail, you should heed their wisdom, even over pressure from a well-intended board of directors. If the professionals advise you to forget about using direct mail, you are probably wasting your time by going in search of a fourth or fifth firm that will tell you what you want to hear.

Another way to take your organization's direct mail temperature (instead of or in addition to calling on a consultant) is to complete the test in Exhibit 22.1.

If you answer "yes" to more than half of the questions, direct mail may be appropriate for your cause and a test mailing can be made at minimal risk. However, if you answered "no" to questions 9 and 10, think twice. Newcomers to direct mail must not view it as a fix for immediate financial problems, but as a calculated investment in the organization's future.

EXHIBIT 22.1 Basic Test: Is Direct Mail Appropriate for Your Cause?

1. Does your organization or cause have broad name recognition?
   (a) In the local community?   ( ) Yes   ( ) No
   (b) In the state?   ( ) Yes   ( ) No
   (c) Nationally?   ( ) Yes   ( ) No

2. Does it deal with specific issues rather than broad or abstract ideas?   ( ) Yes   ( ) No

3. Does it serve or help sympathy-engendering constituencies—for   ( ) Yes   ( ) No
   example, minorities, the ill, the elderly, children, disabled people,
   the poor or disadvantaged, or animals?

4. Are there other organizations performing the same or similar services?   ( ) Yes   ( ) No
   If so, how is your organization unique?

5. Does your organization have a demonstrable track record?   ( ) Yes   ( ) No

6. If your organization is new, does it expect to respond to a critical issue   ( ) Yes   ( ) No
   in a dynamic way?

7. Is there a threat to the organization, those it serves, or to traditional   ( ) Yes   ( ) No
   funding sources? In other words, is there an issue, a crisis, or an
   emergency to be dramatized?

8. If yours is a membership organization, are tangible membership   ( ) Yes   ( ) No
   benefits offered? If yours is a cause-oriented organization, can you
   show the donor how his or her gift will make a difference?

9. Would your organization be financially able to survive a loss of 40   ( ) Yes   ( ) No
   percent or more of its investment should the test mailing fail
   to recoup costs?

10. Do you (and your CEO and board of directors) have the patience   ( ) Yes   ( ) No
    (and the investment capital) to wait for two to four years before
    realizing so-called spendable net income?

Source: Kay Partney Lautman. From a direct mail test form in Dear Friend: Mastering the Art of Direct Mail Fund Raising. *Edited by Kay Lautman and Henry Goldstein. © 1991, Fund Raising Institute, The Taft Group, a division of Gale Research, Inc. All rights reserved. Reproduced by permission.*

(A)   YOUR FIRST DIRECT MAIL EFFORT

If you passed the test and wish to undertake a test mailing, there are the three areas on which you need to concentrate: the market, the business plan, and the creative effort.

(B)   THE MARKET AND LISTS

The only way to learn whether you can enlist a constituency is to test a sufficient number of lists (usually between 10 and 20), composed of at least 3,000 to 5,000 names each. Test criteria differ, depending on each set of circumstances.

You will not, in fact, "buy" or "purchase" mailing lists. You will either "exchange" lists (if you have one) on a one-for-one exchange basis with other organizations, or you will "rent" lists at an average cost of $85 per thousand names, for a *one time use* for a specific purpose. You should go through an experienced list broker specializing in fund raising. You will agree to a specific mail week, and the list owners from whom you are renting or with whom you are exchanging may request to approve your mail package in advance (and vice versa).

By seeing how well your appeal performs on a cross section of these first test lists, your consultant or list broker can determine whether the "universe" of direct mail donors is likely to support your organization.

If so, a plan will be developed to "roll out" your mailing to larger and larger segments of the original mailing lists, while you continue to test additional new lists of the type that worked well in the first test mailing.

(C)   THE LIST BROKER

Be sure to ask prospective list brokers whether they specialize in fund raising; ask for names of their clients and check references.

The broker should recommend lists of members/donors/readers/buyers whose giving and spending patterns indicate a potential interest in the area your organization represents. They also provide you with data cards for each list—literally, index cards that detail all relevant information, including quantity or universe, cost per thousand names, source of list, average gift or purchase, minimum order, selection, and key coding and addressing format. Of all these, the most important is the list source because you want lists that are derived primarily from direct mail, not from door-to-door canvassing, telemarketing, or special events, as such donors are not particularly responsive to direct mail.

Insist that your broker categorize the areas in which his or her recommended lists fall (i.e., environment, civil rights, religious, health, social services, travel magazines, etc.). Thus, when several lists from a particular category work, you can focus on other lists within that category.

Good brokers will give you their best advice. After all, they want their lists to work, too, so that you will return for more (brokers work on commissions paid by the list owner, not by you). Nevertheless, it is the wise mailer who questions the broker about "usage"—specifically, what other organizations have successfully used each list more than once. (A test is one thing; returning for additional quantities is quite another.)

(D) COMPETITORS

Do not leave everything to your list broker. If yours is a small, local, and/or grass-roots organization, some of your best prospect lists will not be available on the open market. If an especially good list is not available through your broker, call your colleagues and competitors and ask favors (a one-for-one name exchange for your mailing). They need good lists too.

Do not be afraid to exchange with your competitors. Their best lists will be your best lists too. By all means, suppress your major donors from the exchange, but do not worry that you will lose a member or a donor to the competition. When a person is interested in a particular subject, he or she tends to give to two, three, and as many as 10 organizations that work in that field, tackling the problem from different perspectives.

If your board is unconvinced about exchanging, here are the most important arguments to put forth.

- *Cost.* List rentals are very expensive, representing the second largest item in a direct mail budget (average $85 per thousand names and higher). List exchanges are virtually free except for a small handling fee.
- *Availability.* Many of the best lists are available only through exchange, as the owners do not rent them commercially. Thus, if you will not exchange, your best source of productive lists is not available to you.
- *The annoyance factor.* Most donors deal with minor annoyances by trashing unwanted mail, not by complaining. However, you can protect your board members and major donors from exchanges by simply flagging their names on your computer file. Donors who do complain should be sent an apology and their names flagged for no further exchange. If you do not overexchange your list, such correspondence will be minimal.

22.5 *Business Plan*

For some organizations, acquisition (prospect) mailing earns more money than it costs, but that outcome is rare indeed. The goal of most not-for-profits is to break even on the direct costs of the mailing, spending a dollar for every dollar raised. Usually, however, more money will be spent than earned,[1] but most experienced development officers are willing to subsidize manageable losses as long as the campaign is attracting quality donors. Organizations experienced in raising funds by mail understand that *a donor's worth must be measured over time.* The longer an organization remains active in using the mail, as a rule, the more cost efficient the process becomes, and the increasing net amount of money raised in the long run more than justifies a reasonable investment made to acquire a large base of donors.

Do not let anyone convince you that you should test first and make long-range projections *after* the test. If you are using a consultant, the firm knows how to run out five-

---

[1]An average size acquisition test of 75,000 to 150,000 pieces should cost between $350 and $400 per thousand names mailed including writing, art, lists, postage, printing, and mailing. It does not include a consultant.

year cost and income projections based on a best-case scenario *before* you mail. If the money you will lose during the first couple of years is an amount you cannot afford, do not even test. If you cannot afford the best outcome, you surely cannot afford the worst.

If you are doing your own projections, use reasonable estimates as to percentage of return and gift average, not what you *hope* to achieve. Returns vary widely, and average gifts vary even more. As a rule, the higher the gift average you are able to command, the lower the percentage of return (and vice versa). The reason is that more specialized causes attract fewer supporters, but those few tend to give generously. On the other hand, causes with wide appeal attract so many donors that they can afford to market giving at a lower request level.

Either way, you usually get what you ask for. Therefore, it is critical that your lowest asking amount, or entry level, be competitive in your market. For example, animal causes attract gifts of fairly low amounts, whereas environmental causes attract larger gifts. Similarly, health causes attract smaller gifts as compared with education and advocacy causes.

Most organizations are advised to set their entry level at $20 or $25, because smaller gifts are initially given without much thought and are, therefore, more difficult to renew or upgrade.

In making your own projections or in evaluating those supplied by a consultant, make sure to account for back-end costs, because no one but your organization is going to pay for them. It is not enough to estimate that getting the mail out (including the most expensive costs of lists and postage) will cost a total of, for instance, $380 per thousand names mailed. You also have to figure what it will cost to receive gifts, computerize records, acknowledge gifts, maintain the file, send newsletters and other materials, and so on. On average, this cost can be estimated at between $2 and $5 a person, depending on benefits, with an average of $2.50 per member/donor.

22.6 *Creative Strategy*

To begin, you and your organization must decide on the image you wish to project and the type of package that will best enhance that image. You must also decide whether your organization should offer membership or should simply seek charitable contributions.

(A)   MEMBERS OR DONORS?

For some organizations, a decision on whether to offer memberships or simply ask for contributions is easy. The following checklist can help you decide.

The more of the following you can check off as representing your organization, the more likely that it is a candidate for a Membership Appeal.

Checklist for Membership Organization

( ) Is well known and/or prestigious
( ) Has a facility that members can visit

( ) Holds at least one annual event in the community
( ) Has a good publication, at least quarterly
( ) Offers tangible benefits
( ) Can offer discounts on products at a gift shop, at other locations, or through the mail

Members are probably easier to renew than donors. If a person is deeply involved with your organization, it is much easier to make a compelling case for renewal (simply "It is time to renew" . . . or "Your membership has expired" . . . , etc.). For a donor, you must explain in greater detail and with greater urgency, just why he or she should write a check.

Some organizations that do not fit the museum-type category can still undertake effective membership programs, sometime called Friends Programs (i.e., Friends of the Zoo, Friends of the Hospital, Friends of the Soup Kitchen, etc.). One benefit of membership all such groups need, however, is a good publication. Otherwise, you will be unable to write effective renewal copy that says "Renew today or your subscription will expire."

22.7 Creating an Image

When you have decided whether your offer will be for membership or for a charitable contribution, you must focus on the image you want to project through a fund-raising appeal.

If your organization is well known, it would be futile to think that direct mail can change its image for better or worse. That would require a great deal of mail—an amount you are unlikely ever to undertake.

What direct mail can do, however, is enhance your image and help carry the message you want. No fund-raising letter is composed entirely of requests for money. And with the recommended four pages (two pieces of paper, front and back) to fill, there is quite a bit of leeway in telling your story as you want it told.

The type of organization helps to set the tone of the appeal from the beginning. Letters from museums, hospitals, religious organizations, and so forth should probably have a somewhat more restrained look than those from environmental organizations, animal groups, political causes or candidates, and youth organizations.

This is not to say that museums and similar institutions should have stuffy, dignified, case statement–type letters. Each should have an appropriate, attractive image. It is important that the direct mail reflect the organization, especially if members are actually able to visit its building or campus. When someone comes to call, you want them to recognize the place they have been supporting over the years.

Many factors must be considered in creating an image. First, decide who will be the spokesperson for your organization—the president or board chairman? Do you need a celebrity spokesperson? Should a beneficiary of your services sign the appeal?

The look of your package also helps to create an image. The decision as to whether to use photographs is an important one. Choice of paper stock, ink colors, typeface, whether to use photo or teaser copy—each decision has an impact on the image.

There are many choices to be made in creating an image through a direct mail package; Exhibit 22.2 is a checklist of those that matter most.

EXHIBIT 22.2 Creating an Image

The Look of the Package

Attitude	( )	Modern, on the cutting edge
	( )	Homey, struggling
	( )	Professional, inspiring confidence
	( )	Institutional
Size of package	( )	#10 business envelope size
	( )	Monarch or similar personal size
	( )	Oversize package
Paper Stock	( )	Lightweight, inexpensive looking
	( )	Heavier, more impressive
Paper Color	( )	White or off-white
	( )	Cream, gray, or other neutral
Second Ink Color	( )	Only one color (black), to save money
	( )	Introduce a second "safe" color, such as blue
	( )	Introduce a bright second color, such as red
	( )	Include a four-color insert (brochure, buckslip, etc.)
Typeface	( )	Attention-getting, bold typefaces
	( )	Elegant, conservative typefaces
	( )	Modern, unusual typefaces
Photographs	( )	No photos at all
	( )	One photo on the reply card
	( )	Photos in brochure enclosure
	( )	Loose photos, like photo cards
	( )	Photos throughout the letter

Delivery of the Message

Signer	( )	CEO or other person at the top
	( )	Celebrity signer
	( )	Service beneficiary
	( )	Expert in field
Length of Letter	( )	4 or more pages (two pieces of paper)
	( )	Two pages
	( )	One page
	( )	Note instead of letter
	( )	Will be an appeal that highlights successes
	( )	Will provide a great deal of history about the organization's founding

Teasers, Offers

( )	An envelope teaser is needed
( )	A photo on the envelope is needed
( )	An up-front premium or discount offer
( )	Not-for-profit stamp
( )	A "back-end" or thank you premium

Postage

( )	Not-for-profit meter or indicia
( )	First class stamp
( )	First class meter or indicia

(A) CONTENTS OF THE PACKAGE

Every direct mail package must have the following components: outside or carrier envelope, letter, reply envelope, and reply card (response device), which is where the recipient's name and address go.

Which of the following additional components might you utilize in your appeal? Choose carefully only those that might help create the image you need and enhance response to the appeal.

- Brochure
- Photo cards
- Newspaper reprint
- Decal/stamps/bookmark or other premium
- Endorsement letter (called a "lift letter" in the trade as it is designed to "lift" (increase) returns)
- Survey or questionnaire
- Petition
- Newsletter or report
- Name and address stickers
- Notecards
- Other

Of all the possibilities, the most commonly used additional insert (in an acquisition package especially) is a brochure. If you plan to include a brochure, have a justifiable reason. If possible, test your package with and without the brochure. Often brochures do not increase returns, but they always increase package costs.

To help you decide whether a brochure is necessary, complete the following sentence with one of the options below. The purpose of the brochure is to:

( ) Offer benefits and show photos of benefits
( ) Contain a membership subscription form
( ) Show photos of objects (as in a museum)
( ) Show photos of clients (students, animals, patients, children, etc.)
( ) Tell the story of the organization
( ) Reinforce the message of the letter
( ) Other

Note: If you chose any of the first three reasons, you may actually need a brochure. If you chose only the latter three reasons, you are probably wasting your money on a brochure. Very few people want that much information on your history, no matter how fascinating. If you really need to show photos, include them on the reply card, on the letter itself, or as a slip-in photo card that looks like a real photo. The reason is that a brochure is not only expensive, but it is diversionary from the appeal and can actually *lower* the return rate.

Discussion of the merits of using other package inserts, whether in an acquisition appeal or in a renewal or special appeal, is beyond the scope of this chapter. Enclosures such as stickers, notecards, decals, and stamps often work, but these are expensive and must be tested for cost effectiveness. Really good newspaper or magazine articles on your organization can be dynamite, as can the right endorsement letter. For some organizations, a survey or questionnaire can be extremely effective in enlisting new members/donors. Inclusion of a newsletter, normally a "benefit" of membership, can be deadly—especially to a prospect for whom this is far too much information about your cause.

22.8 Testing

The cardinal rule of testing is to test only one thing at a time. You cannot test two variables simultaneously, no matter how minor. For example, you cannot send one half of your mailing with only a letter and the other half of the mailing with the letter *and* the brochure if you are also testing envelope teaser copy vs. no teaser. If you try, you will never know whether it was the addition of the brochure that increased or depressed the average gift, rather than the envelope teaser copy.

If you want to test two new things in a mailing, you must create three mail panels or test list and test your control (original) package against each of your new items. Moreover, each panel must be of sufficient quantity to make the test numbers valid. For example, you should not test a mailing of 20,000 pieces three ways (6,660 pieces per panel), because on each panel, at a 1 percent return, you will receive only 67 gifts—an insufficient number to be statistically valid.

A statistically valid test should have a minimum of 10,000 pieces in each panel with an expected percentage of return of at least 85 percent. Even then results will not be as accurate as they would had each panel been of at least 20,000 pieces.

Rules for Testing

1. Test only one thing at a time. (This rule excludes lists, which you are always testing).
2. Mail test packages within the same week. Poor timing can play havoc with response.
3. Mail test packages at the same postal rate, unless it is postage you are testing.
4. Mail test packages to the same lists and split the lists on a *n*th (random sample) select. In other words, a test in which half of the mailing goes to a different ZIP selection or a different part of the alphabet than the other half, is *not* a valid test.
5. Test in sufficient quantities for valid results.
6. After test results are in, test the same thing once again to validate your findings.

(A) WRITING THE LETTER

After deciding on the image you wish to project, selecting a list broker and choosing lists, developing a plan and a budget, and choosing your tests, it is time to write the fund-raising letter.

The letter you are going to write, if you are just beginning a program, is an acquisition appeal (also called a prospect appeal). That is, you are going to write a letter to enlist brand-new members or donors. Because the prospective member or donor knows nothing or very little about your organization, it is necessary to provide enough information and motivation to elicit a contribution or membership dues.

The five most important aspects of an acquisition letter are as follows:

1. It must be interesting, simple in concept, and easy to read. (Do not strive for creativity; instead, be sure it makes sense to the reader.)
2. It must contain an *irresistible* offer (benefits, premium, urgent deadline, overwhelming need, or other motivation). A good cause unto itself will perish amid the competition.
3. It must emphasize the people or animals you serve, not your organization, its founders, and their tenets.
4. It must not be afraid to ask for money straightforwardly, and it should suggest a minimum gift and a reason for such a gift.
5. It must address one person (the recipient), not a group (i.e., never say, "Dear Friends" [plural] or "I hope that all of you will . . .").

Exhibit 22.3 is a checklist for writing a winning fund-raising letter. It is not only for beginners writing an acquisition package, but also for current practitioners of direct mail, whether they are writing an acquisition, renewal, or special appeal. The checklist can be used as an evaluation tool for every letter you send, but it is most valuable to use *before* you write your letter.

After you have carefully graded your letter, using the checklist, you may want to make some revisions. When you feel you have a perfect letter, you may be very protective of it. Nevertheless, you will probably have to make further changes after a supervisor, the fund-raising committee chair, and the letter signer reads it.

As a professional, welcome any appropriate changes, no matter how good you think the letter is. Changes and suggestions mean that others are taking a real interest, and not just rubber-stamping your work. On the other hand, you may need to remind your associates that a good letter was never written by a committee.

It is difficult to research, write, rewrite, and circulate a letter for approval, but this is how you create a strong acquisition letter. If it works, you do not have to write another such letter for at least a year, possibly longer. This letter will be appropriate for potential new donors for a long time to come, as few people will ever see it twice in the same year. It is not necessary to write a new letter for every mailing. If you have a winning package, why discard it until it has lived a full life of usefulness, which is at least one year and sometimes as long as five or ten years? If you want an opportunity to be creative, you can test envelopes, lift letters, enclosures, and other items to see whether you can enhance your basic acquisition package.

22.9 Renewing Gifts and Raising Money

As mentioned earlier, acquisition/prospect mailings rarely earn spendable net income. Once you have established that you can acquire members/donors in the mail, however, you are ready for the next step. In order to maximize income from your donors and keep them interested and involved, you must develop a communications strategy that includes a strong fund-raising component.

EXHIBIT 22.3 Checklist for a Winning Fund-raising Letter

(1 = poor; 4 = excellent)

	1	2	3	4

1. *Lead.* Does it create immediate interest? Hint: A better lead can often be found in the body copy a few paragraphs down. If you find one, move it up and raise your rating as well. _____

2. *Writing Style.* Is the letter easy to read, friendly, and personal? Strive for the absence of jargon and of complicated, overlong sentences. Use down-to-earth words that no one will have to look up. Does the letter try to be funny? Humor has little place in fund raising. _____

3. *Focus.* Is the focus simple and clear? Or does the letter try to tell too much? Base your rating on whether the letter focuses on a specific problem, need, or goal. _____

4. *Problem Solving.* Does the letter offer solutions and hope? Solutions should be time- or money-related. Hint: Referring to a track record in past situations adds credibility to the solution. _____

5. *Reader Recognition.* Does the letter make the reader feel important? That his or her donation would be important? Is the letter written only to one person? Does it use the word "you" several times on every page? _____

6. *Benefits.* Are the benefits that come with a membership or donation emphasized? Does the donor receive a publication, discounts, or other services? If so, are they described effusively? If the benefits are exceptional, does the mailing package devote sufficient space (perhaps even a separate piece) to describing them? _____

7. *The Request.* Have you actually, clearly, asked for a contribution? Base your rating on a strong, straightforward request for a gift, without apology. Has the best case been made for *why* the money is needed? Is the need stated several times and in several ways before the final request? _____

8. *Urgency.* Will the donor understand that he or she must move quickly—must get the gift back to you while it still can help? Is an immediate response urged? Hint: Offer a strong reason to give *now*—a crisis, budget deficit, deadline, tremendous opportunity, whatever is true. _____

9. *Suggested Gift.* Does the donor know exactly how much money you want? Have you eliminated any chance that the donor will wonder how much to send? Remember, you get what you ask for. Hint: On a donor appeal, ask for $3 more than the average gift you seek. Try using "odd" dollar figures ($17.27, for example) for credibility. On a member appeal, the *most* attractive benefit should be offered at the base category, as most entry-level memberships will come in that category. _____

10. *The P.S.* Is it as good as the lead? Would the letter be badly damaged if the P.S. were left off entirely? If it would not, rewrite the P.S. so that it cannot be left off. Remember, the P.S. and the lead are usually read, even if the body of the letter is not. _____

11. *Length.* Is the letter long enough to create interest, to state the problem, to tell the story in its most interesting form, to arouse emotion, to offer hope and the opportunity to participate in something significant, to state your credentials, to ask for the gift, and to offer attractive personal benefits? _____

12. *Format.* Does it *look* like a letter? Is it typewritten? Is there good use of white space? Are short paragraphs mixed with medium-length paragraphs? If it is a long letter, does it make good use of graphic devices like subtitles, underlines, indented copy blocks, call-outs, and bulleted lines to increase readability? Remember, if it cannot be *easily* read, it will not be read at all.

Source: Based on the checklist in Kay Partney Lautman and Henry Goldstein, Dear Friend: Mastering the Art of Direct Mail Fund Raising. *Rockville, MD: Fund Raising Institute, 1991. Based on Con Squires's CopyRater™, from his newsletter* Techniques for Success in Direct Mail Fund-Raising.

(A) FREQUENCY OF MAILINGS

It is recommended to send, at a minimum, between 6 and 10 fund-raising mailings annually to donors or members. This does not include sending a newsletter or other informational communications, nor does it include planned gift/bequest mailings or invitations to special events.

Some organizations believe that sending more than two renewals is in bad form and will not consider using more. If an organization does not mail at least six times a year to donors, it should not become involved with direct mail in the first place.

The reason for this advice is that an organization cannot renew 65 percent to 80 percent of its donors annually (which should be the goal) with only two mailings. Suppose an organization gets an extraordinary return on its first renewal mailing of 25 percent and another 25 percent on a second mailing. The result is that it has renewed 50 percent of its donors. What about the other 50 percent in whom the organization invested a great deal of money to acquire? By mailing only twice, the organization has not given donors sufficient opportunities to renew (or to make a second or even a third gift during the year).

However many mailings you decide to send, estimate that each mailing should bring in a return of between 5 percent and 25 percent and an average gift some 15 percent to 20 percent higher than the acquisition average (i.e., if someone joined at $20, a 15 percent natural upgrade would produce a gift of $23).

The general rule of thumb is that you should continue mailing to nonrenewing donors until it is no longer profitable. Some say that as long as your "lapsed" donors are producing as well as your acquisition mailings, you should continue appealing to them.

(B) BENEFIT/COST EXPECTATIONS

The gratifying aspect of renewal mailings is that they constitute true fund raising. You will always make a net profit on house mailings (current donor and volunteer mail lists); it is impossible not to. The reason is that the costs are so much less and the return so much greater. Costs are lowered by the price of the rental lists, a full $85 per thousand on a much smaller volume. Returns increase from an average of 1 percent to between 5 percent and 25 percent per mailing, and the average gift is upgraded by at least 15 percent, as stated earlier. This means that profitability soars.

After you have mailed for a full year, you will have a good idea of how your renewals perform and can better understand the type of appeals that do best. After a few years, you will also learn which seasons of the year are best for mailings for your particular cause.

(C) TYPE OF RENEWAL PACKAGE

Renewal mailings are not as expensive as initial mailing because they are not as elaborate. Once donors or members have declared their interest in your organization, it is much easier to get their attention.

Four-page letters have been advocated for acquisition because the organization has a big story to tell to those who do not know it well. In a subsequent appeal, the message can often be shortened. After all, donors read the first appeal, read your acknowledgment letter, and, it is hoped, read or scanned your newsletter or other "cultivation" mailings. So when you write for a renewal or second or third gift, your message can be shorter.

Yet it is a mistake to strive for brevity in renewals. If the story you are telling requires three or four pages, use them. A letter of less than two pages is not recommended even in a renewal or special appeal.

(D) RENEWING TRUE MEMBERSHIP GIFTS

True membership organizations will want to establish a renewal series of between five and eight drops, scheduled dates for delivery of the full mailing to the post office. In this plan, the first renewal drops three months prior to expiration, the second, two months prior to expiration, and the third on the month of expiration. If a member has not renewed by his or her anniversary date, a fourth notice is sent the month following expiration, often followed by a final telemarketing effort.

Naturally, a first notice brings in the largest number of renewals (highest percentage of return) from the most committed members. The percentage of response (not average gift) drops somewhat with each subsequent appeal, but the organization is still renewing members at a profit.

(E) APPEALS IN ADDITION TO RENEWALS

Membership organizations can successfully raise money from members in addition to membership dues. A recommended method is to establish a plan to send between four and six special appeals throughout the year to members who have renewed. No special appeal should be sent to members who are in the first stage of the renewal cycle (i.e., not to members who are receiving notices 1 through 3). Once a member has renewed, however, he or she should be given an opportunity to contribute to the needs of the organization with additional gifts.

Each special appeal should have a theme and an explanation as to why the additional gift is needed. It should be written in a very personal vein, striving to make the member feel like a true insider.

Stories about the people (or animals, etc.) served are especially good at gaining interest among members, as are emergencies and the occasional crisis. Letters to donors of high amounts ($100 or more) should be personalized and possibly sent in closed-face envelopes with first-class postage to make these donors feel special. This treatment will not necessarily increase the net amount of money you make but may bond the donor to the organization for a longer period of time.

Some organizations, in order not to send too much fund-raising mail to donors, make it a habit to eliminate donors from an appeal who have just given to the preceding appeal. The logic is that the donor has already been generous twice in one year (once in renewing and once in giving an extra gift). If you decide to do this, however, do not fail to send your final, year-end (November or December) appeal to all donors, regardless of whether they have already given during the year. In the next *calendar* year (members and donors do not figure on a fiscal year, even if you do) start fresh. That is, ask all donors for a gift the first time you send a special appeal even if they have given in the last quarter of the previous year.

22.10   *Producing the Mailing*

Strategic planning and copywriting are only two-thirds of the process. Production and analysis are the final third. Space does not allow complete production instructions here; after reading the basics outlined, see "Suggested Readings" at the end of this chapter.

(A)   POSTAL REGULATIONS

If you are beginning your first mailing effort, you need to obtain the appropriate permits to mail at the discounted not-for-profit rate—the savings are substantial. The qualifying mail requirements as of 1996 are as follows:

- Mailings must consist of at least 200 pieces or 50 pounds.
- Mailings must be presorted by ZIP codes, in packages and sacks, to the greatest extent possible.
- Mailing pieces must be identical in weight and must be mailed at the post office from which the permit was issued. In addition, the name and return address of the authorized permit holder must appear in a prominent location, usually the upper left hand corner. If the mailing piece bears any name and return address, it must be that of the authorized permit holder.

Note: The Postal Service is constantly changing regulations. Keep abreast of them. Everything you need to know about postal permits and regulations is contained in the *Postal Service Manual* issued by the U.S. Postal Service. If you cannot obtain this manual, or if you find it confusing, the following regulations should be of help.

If yours is a 501(c)(3) organization, it is a simple matter to obtain a bulk-rate mailing permit. Obtain and submit completed Form 3624 to your local postmaster with the following proofs of status:

- Articles of incorporation and bylaws (including a dissolution statement)
- Certificate of tax exemption
- Samples of existing brochures and direct mail packages
- A summary of your organization's activities for the last 12 months (a financial statement is acceptable)

Organizations classified as 501(c)(4) and 501(c)(6) may also obtain a bulk-rate mailing permit, providing they are able to show that their primary purpose is one of the following: religious, educational, scientific, philanthropic, agricultural, labor, veteran, or fraternal; or that it is a qualified political committee.

(B)   PRODUCTION SCHEDULE

To produce each mailing, allow fully 10 to 12 weeks from start to finish. In an ideal world, the ideal schedule requires 7 weeks, but most organizations usually require a longer time.

Exhibit 22.4 presents an ideal schedule, describing all you will need to do from start to finish. In reality, this schedule will be adjusted as time goes on, but it can be used as a guide for planning.

Finally, in producing your mailing, be assured that Murphy's Law will prevail if you are not extremely careful about details (and, often, even if you are). There are so many details that go into producing a mailing that someone needs to be on top of them at all times. Use the checklist in Exhibit 22.5 to save grief and money.

(C) WHEN TO MAIL

You cannot conduct a "Send a kid to camp" appeal in the winter months, but you *can* do your most successful campaigns for homeless organizations when the weather is cold. Certain types of organizations have their own best time periods, but, by and large, fall and winter mailings produce the best returns for most organizations.

EXHIBIT 22.4 Ideal Mailing Schedule

Weeks 1 and 2	Discuss list schedule with broker. Contract with mail house.	Write first-draft copy. Write second and third drafts. Discuss concept with artist.
Week 3	Broker orders lists and sends confirmations (minimum of 2½ weeks from list order to delivery). Obtain postal permits (first class for reply envelope and not-for-profit for mailing envelope.)	Present revised-draft copy and rough art to signer or whoever must approve package. (Allow a minimum of 3 days to revise or approve.) Get bids from printers.
Week 4	Send written order to mail house.	Revise copy (2 days) and return to signer for final approval (3 days). Artist prepares camera-ready mechanicals (6 days).
Week 5	Request postage check (to arrive at mail house 1 week prior to mail date). Check in lists as they arrive. Allow one week for late list arrivals; alert broker.	Camera-ready art to printer. Bluelines due at week's end.
Week 6	Send labels to mail house.	Return corrected bluelines to printer. Most printers want 7 working days to print (can be done in 4–5 days).
Week 7	Mail drops at end of the week. Most mail houses require 5 working days unless special arrangements are made.	Deliver materials to mail house on Monday or earlier if possible.
Week 8	Set up a system for receiving returns and acknowledging gifts.	
Week 9	Begin tabulating first returns.	

EXHIBIT 22.5 Production Checklist

	YES
1. Postage permits obtained or renewed?	___
2. Written list confirmations received and checked for correct quantities, print color selections, and codes?	___
3. Final copy carefully proofed by someone who did not work on the project?	___
4. All approvals (your supervisor, the letter signer, etc.) obtained in writing?	___
5. Prototype of package made at early stage to make sure everything fits? If it is to be mailed first class, make sure it is not overweight.	___
6. When reprinting old materials: Copy checked for possible changes in statistics, dates, board listings, and other variables?	___
7. Instructions to printer, computer bureau, and mail house verified in writing? (Remember, nothing you say by phone can be proven.)	___
8. If inventory is to be used: Have items been double-checked to make sure that what you need exists?	___
9. Bluelines checked for correct folds, color breaks, and size, as well as text? PMS color selections verified?	___
10. Arrival of all tapes or labels from list owner or merge house verified in advance of mail date (if this is an acquisition mailing)?	___
11. Computer selects carefully chosen and verified by computer department or outside bureau (if a "house" or current donor file mailing)?	___
12. Postage check to cover mailing requisitioned and sent in advance to mail house?	___
13. Printed samples checked before delivery to mail house? (This is indeed your last chance to catch a fatal error.)	___
14. Inserted samples checked prior to mailing? (Is it your Business Reply Envelope [BRE] in the package or someone else's? Are the pieces inserted in the correct order?)	___
15. Quantities verified by mail house immediately when delivered by printer (so as not to come up short halfway through the process)?	___
16. Drop count verification received from mail house within 24 hours after mail date? (Are 10 sacks of your mail still sitting in a broom closet at the mail house?)	___
17. Sufficient funds deposited in lock box account to pay for donations returned in BREs?	___

As you become experienced with mailings through testing of various seasons, you will learn what is best for your organization. Meanwhile, if you are just beginning an acquisition campaign, fall (September and October) is recommended. Unless your cause and Christmas are directly related, avoid December for new acquisition mailings. There is too much competition for renewal gifts at this time. Wait for a better opening in January, February, and March.

Spring (April, May, and June) is a fairly good time of year, and, for a very few mailers, summer is also fine. Most organizations, however, should avoid summer mailings.

When you begin renewing donors and establishing additional programs, you will not be able to avoid the less desirable months. It is better to ask in June than not to ask at all. It is better still to ask in January, April, June, October, *and* December.

22.11   Campaign Self-Evaluation

Use Exhibit 22.6 to evaluate a direct mail campaign. Correct answers are provided at the end of the analysis.

EXHIBIT 22.6 Campaign Self-Analysis

---

1. How long has it been since you evaluated your campaign?
   a ( ) Within the last year
   b ( ) More than 5 years
   c ( ) Never or do not know

2. Are you reaching your goals for
   Acquisitions   a ( ) Yes   b ( ) No   c ( ) Occasionally
   Renewals   a ( ) Yes   b ( ) No   c ( ) Occasionally
   Special Appeals   a ( ) Yes   b ( ) No   c ( ) Occasionally
   Other Programs   a ( ) Yes   b ( ) No   c ( ) Occasionally

3. Is your *active* member/donor file
   a ( ) Growing
   b ( ) Shrinking
   c ( ) Stable

4. Are your acquisition results (percentage of return, average gift, and benefit/cost ratio)
   a ( ) Stable
   b ( ) Improving
   c ( ) Declining somewhat
   d ( ) Declining rapidly

5. Are your house results (percentage of return, average gift, and benefit/cost ratio)
   a ( ) Stable
   b ( ) Improving
   c ( ) Declining somewhat
   d ( ) Declining rapidly

6. If your percentage of return and average gift are declining, is it because
   a ( ) You have cut back in quantity on acquisition/prospect mail
   b ( ) You have had a bout of unfavorable publicity
   c ( ) Your list broker is not resourceful
   d ( ) You have had a membership price increase
   e ( ) Your program has changed dramatically
   f ( ) You changed your acquisition package or envelope without testing first
   g ( ) You have changed consultants or employees
   h ( ) Other _____

7. If your benefit/cost ratio is declining even though your percentage of return and average gift are holding their own, is it because of
   a ( ) Normal cost inflation
   b ( ) Unchecked price increases
   c ( ) Not bidding out printing
   d ( ) Cutback in number of list exchanges resulting in more list rentals
   e ( ) Expensive premiums
   f ( ) Other _____

(continued)

8. Have you instituted most or all appropriate programs to maximize results on your house mailings?

a Lapsed donor campaign		( ) Yes	( ) No
b Monthly donor campaign		( ) Yes	( ) No
c High-amount donor campaign		( ) Yes	( ) No
d Telemarketing donor campaign		( ) Yes	( ) No
e Card and/or calendar program		( ) Yes	( ) No
f Other _____			

9. How many times a year do you send fund-raising appeals to your house file? (Do not include magazines, newsletters, etc. that are not fund-raising oriented.)
   a ( ) 8–12 times per year
   b ( ) 6–8 times per year
   c ( ) 3–6 times per year
   d ( ) Less than 3 times per year

10. Has your list broker done a thorough analysis of results in the past
    a ( ) Year
    b ( ) Two years
    c ( ) Six months

11. Do you have creative meetings with your staff/consultant every
    a ( ) Three months
    b ( ) Six months
    c ( ) Year
    d ( ) Other _____

12. Have you tested an all-new acquisition/prospect package in the past
    a ( ) Year
    b ( ) Two years
    c ( ) Three years

13. Have you tested any of the following on either acquisition or renewal mailings?

a Basic membership price or ask		( ) Yes	( ) No
b Look of package with same copy		( ) Yes	( ) No
c Envelope teaser		( ) Yes	( ) No
d Time of year for mailing		( ) Yes	( ) No
e Additional enclosures (decals, lift letters, news clips, brochures, etc.)		( ) Yes	( ) No
f Other _____		( ) Yes	( ) No

14. Acknowledgment Programs
   I. Do you acknowledge
      a ( ) All donors
      b ( ) Donors who give $50 or more
      c ( ) Donors who give $100 or more
      d ( ) Other cutoff
   II. Do you acknowledge gifts
      a ( ) Within 48 hours
      b ( ) Within 1 week
      c ( ) Within 2 weeks
      d ( ) Longer
   III. Is your acknowledgment program satisfactory to your needs?   _____Yes   _____No

(A)   ANSWERS TO EXHIBIT 22.6

The "best" answers to the questions in Exhibit 22.6 are obvious in some cases. If you are in doubt, however, you may consider the following, generally accepted as the best answers.

1. **a** (within the last year)
2. **a** (ideally for all)
   If your goal setting is realistic, your cause popular, and your campaign well managed, you should be within 15 percent or better of your overall goal. It is natural that some programs will, almost inexplicably, fall short of goal (acquisitions are the most vulnerable), but other in-house programs usually make up for the shortfall. Failure to make goal is often the result of unrealistic goal setting. Just because you need the money does not mean you can raise it.
3. **a** (growing) if campaign is less than five years old, or **c** (stable) if older or if cause has peaked.
4. **a** (stable) or **b** (improving) unless past results are poor.
5. **a** (stable) or **b** (improving). Results will vary from appeal to appeal but should balance out.
6. All of these reasons (**a–g**) can have a devastating impact on your campaigns. Items **a, b,** and **c** are factors over which you have control, as you can increase your mailings, put your list broker on notice or find another, or start testing carefully. Items **d, e,** and **f** are things you will just have to live with while trying to present a positive image to your constituents through your direct mail copy, house publications, special events, and so forth. Reason **g** is more difficult to address, as changing employees and/or consultants is traumatic and not always the best idea, especially if either is new to the job. First ask yourself whether you are devoting enough time to the new employee or new consultant. If you believe you are and suspect that the problem lies with the employee, you may wish to have your consultant evaluate him or her. (If you do not have a consultant, it may be worthwhile to engage one for the purpose if you or another person on your staff is not equipped to undertake the job.) If the problem seems to lie with the consultant, request a detailed analytical report and proposal. If the consultant is new, you will remember how much work it was to change over the first time you transferred all your data to them, so you will not want to rush into another change now unless it proves absolutely necessary.
7. **a** (Normal cost inflation). This is an unfortunate but acceptable reason that affects every mailer, and item **d** (Cutback in number of list exchanges) sometimes cannot be helped, because other organizations are in control of their own lists. However, you should bid out printing frequently and carefully evaluate the benefits of expensive premiums.
8. There is no absolute best answer. Most medium-size organizations (donor list of 25,000 and over) and virtually all large organizations can institute all of these programs. Smaller organizations often cannot make monthly donor and card or calendar programs cost effective. But even if your organization has a file of only 5,000 supporters, you can utilize telemarketing, especially for lapsed donors.

9. The correct answer may be **a** (8–12 times a year), **b** (6–8 times) or **c** (3–6 times). However, fewer than five fund-raising mailings to a file within a year is not recommended. Some mailers are afraid of offending supporters by asking more than two or three times per year and will argue that they get better returns on each mailing than those organizations that mail more frequently.

It is true that the less often you mail to your file, the larger return rates will be. However, you will make far more money by mailing more frequently because two mailings that each get a 10 percent return renew only 20 percent of your file, whereas six mailings that each get a 7 percent return renew 42 percent of your file and eight mailings renew 56 percent, and so on.

10. Your list broker should provide (**a**) a thorough annual analysis of results. However, you should study carefully the results of each mailing and share and discuss mailing results with the broker on an ongoing basis.

11. The correct answer should be **a** (every three months) at a minimum.

12. There is probably no correct answer to this question, but there are certain considerations. A new acquisition package should never be developed because the organization (or you) are bored with the current control package. Rather, a new package should be developed in an effort to "beat" the control (i.e., raise the percentage of return or average gift on acquisitions). A new test package should be tested at least twice to confirm that it worked or did not work. If it did beat the control, it should probably be carefully tested in different markets (i.e., to different types of lists) because it may not outperform the other package universally. Some control packages have an incredibly long life—20 or more years.

13. The correct answers are **a, b, c, d, e,** and **f.** At some time or another, you should test the look of the package, the envelope teaser or art, the time of the year, and additional enclosures such as decals, lift letters, news clips, brochures, and so on—whatever you believe will enhance results.

Some organizations cannot test price because their organization has a firm basic entry level. If yours is flexible, however, consider price testing. It is well known that the lower the average gift you are able to enlist, the higher your percentage of return is likely to be. Conversely, the higher the average gift, the lower the percentage of return.

After several tests (perhaps of $20 vs. $35, or $15 vs. $18) evaluate mailing results, but go a step further. Figure out which approach will be more profitable in the long run. Will you earn enough income with a lower average gift to sustain your program while bringing in more donors/members? If so, you may be able to add a larger number of people to your in-house programs, including renewals, monthly donor programs, bequests, and so forth which will earn you more money in the long run. Test carefully, however, and test nothing but price.

14. Part I. The best answer is **a** (all donors who give at least the basic level). Regardless of the size of your basic category, gifts of $25 should also be acknowledged with at least a form letter, because a gift of that size is prompted by real consideration.

Acknowledgments need not all be the same, however, and it seems obvious that a donor making a gift of $100 or $1,000 should receive a more personal letter more promptly than a donor giving $25.

Part II. The desired answer is **c** (within 2 weeks) for most donors. However, if you can acknowledge gifts within one week, or even within 48 hours, you may enhance the organization's reputation. Unusually large gifts should generally be acknowledged by telephone *and* letter with IRS gift substantiation text included. Part III. The correct answer should be yes.

22.12 *Upgrading Donors*

Proper management of a donor base means systematically identifying each donor's giving potential—then moving each one to that point as quickly as possible. Most donors can be upgraded to higher giving levels. Some can be cultivated into "multiple donors," those who give more than two or three times a year. And some can even become major donors, who can then be graduated out of the direct mail program and into a more personalized program, wherein the contacts are made through face-to-face meetings or, at least, by phone.

The larger an organization's initial base of quality smaller donors, the faster this process works to develop major givers. Because direct mail can find and acquire that initial base of donors faster than any other kind of solicitation, the entire fund-raising cycle will be as cost effective as possible.

The payoff of a well-managed direct mail campaign is more than just a healthy cash flow. Through cultivation of direct mail donors, you uncover a number who will become actively involved, who may become volunteers and even board members, and who will make major financial commitments to your organization.

Such donors are not "out there," as too many organizations believe. They are largely in your own files. But they must be nurtured through a well-managed program from the day they write their first small check.

Best of all, your donor base will enable you to institute a healthy bequest program and raise more money from other sources, including foundations and corporations. You may wonder how a large donor base can help raise money from foundations and corporations. The reason is that a broad base of support says to the world that there is a real need for your services—and there is virtually nothing more compelling to a potential major donor than that.

Acknowledgments

Special thanks to the Fund Raising Institute, a division of the Taft Group, for allowing use of materials from *Dear Friend: Mastering the Art of Direct Mail Fund Raising* by Kay Partney Lautman and Henry Goldstein.

Special thanks also to the Association of Direct Response Fund Raising Counsel (ADRFCO), Washington, D.C., Robert Tigner, executive director, for its guidance and the use of various printed materials. ADRFCO members subscribe to a comprehensive ethics code. Not-for-profits are advised to acquaint themselves with these rules before entering into contracts with direct mail fund raising consultants.

Suggested Readings

Jones, Susan K. *Creative Strategy in Direct Marketing.* Chicago: NTC Business Books, 1990.

Kuniholm, Roland. *The Complete Book of Model Fund Raising Letters.* Englewood Cliffs, N.J.: Prentice-Hall, 1995.

Lautman, Kay Partney, and Henry Goldstein. *Dear Friend: Mastering the Art of Direct Mail Fund Raising.* Rockville, Md.: Fund Raising Institute, 1991.

Trenbeth, Richard P. *The Membership Mystique.* Rockville, Md.: Fund Raising Institute, 1986.

Warwick, Mal. *Revolution in the Mailbox.* Rockville, Md.: Fund Raising Institute, 1990.

23 Benefit Event Fundamentals

SYLVIA ALLEN, MA
Allen Consulting, Inc.

23.1 Introduction

Special events fund raising is the process of using special events, including sports, arts, entertainment, festivals, fairs, street shows, local/regional/national events, and the like, to generate revenue. The need for this activity has intensified as a result of the recent economic downturn, which has reduced the availability of government funds for grants, reduced individual giving, and reduced corporate contributions. By either participating in existing events or designing your own events for the purpose of fund raising, your organization can reverse this downward trend in available funds.

Not-for-profit organizations are currently in a unique position to benefit from participating in events designed for fund raising. Special events attract consumers during their leisure time. However, these sophisticated consumers want their participation, whether as spectators or participants, to have some value. As a result, for-profit events often align themselves with a not-for-profit organization to satisfy the consumer as well as to generate positive media coverage. This creates a win-win situation for everyone because it attracts more people to the event, generates more revenue for the not-for-profit, and creates the perception that the for-profit event is "doing good" as a public service.

A recent Cone/Roper Benchmark Survey confirmed this mind-set. Findings from the Cone/Roper survey include:

- 78 percent of adults said they would be more likely to buy a product associated with a cause they care about.
- 66 percent of adults said they would be likely to switch brands, and 62 percent would likely switch retailers, to support a cause about which they care.
- 54 percent of adults said they would pay more for a product that supports a cause they care about; 30 percent would pay 5 percent more and 24 percent would pay 10 percent or more.

In addition, the Cone/Roper survey discovered that the public regarded local issues (55 percent) as more important than national (30 percent) or global issues (10 percent).

The poll also found that, after price and quality, one-third of Americans consider a company's responsible business practices the most important factor in deciding whether to buy that company's brand. Indeed, social responsibility was found to be more influential than advertising in making a buying decision. In addition, 18 percent of consumers could name companies that were deemed *least* socially responsible. Companies that have been consistently cited as polluting the environment, that have failed to recognize the need for a culturally diverse workforce, and that have flagrantly defied society's laws are determined not to be socially responsible. These statistics are important to know and will be invaluable when determining what sponsors you want to align with, whether in an existing event or in your own.

This chapter introduces special events fund raising and shows how to take advantage of this revenue-generating opportunity for your organization. This chapter includes resources to help you identify special event fund raising opportunities; an overview of special events and their component parts; ways to get involved; a discussion of whether to develop your own program or participate in an existing program; levels of participation; ways of capitalizing on your event participation; what to expect; methods of maximizing the payback; and two case histories of effective special event fund raising.

23.2 *Identifying the Opportunities*

There are two primary ways to become involved in sponsorship. The first is to align yourself with an existing event and receive either a predetermined flat amount or net proceeds from the event. The second is to create your own event, from which all the proceeds come to your organization.

The simplest way to get involved in special events fund raising is to hitchhike on existing events. To find these events at the local level, call the Chamber of Commerce, Visitors and Convention Bureau, city permit office, Kiwanis, Rotary, or other social service organizations. On the state level, contact the Department of Travel and Tourism, Department of Commerce, Department of Cultural Affairs or Community Affairs, and Department of State. Nationally, you can check on event availability by reading the national trade media and contacting national organizations. By reading *Brand Week, Promo, Advertising Age*, and other industry trade publications, you will quickly be able to identify a number of opportunities.

Another way is to start your own event. Hostelling International, based in New York City, has successfully done this with its annual Bike New York. Through what is basically a local event, Bike New York has generated national sponsorship and national media exposure via celebrity participation and endorsements. Also, rather than being a secondary beneficiary of the event, which would occur if it were hitchhiking on an existing event, it is the primary beneficiary. Bike New York approaches the management of this event as would any for-profit organization, from the standpoint of management and sponsorships. All the proceeds from the event go to Bike New York after expenses have been met. At the end of this chapter are two case histories, one from Bike New York and the other from Women in Sports & Events (WISE).

23.3 Special Events Elements and Organization

Special events come in all sizes, from the simple car wash to raise money for the local church group to the Olympics. Although event sizes vary dramatically, the basic administrative and organizational components do not. In fact, organizing an event is very similar to setting up a small business. You need a marketing plan with clearly defined goals and objectives, someone in charge (manager, director, president, etc.), a budget, and an operating plan (who is going to do what, when, and where).

The major categories of an event are management and administration, revenue generation, and on-site management. Within each of these categories are subcategories of function and responsibility.

(A) MANAGEMENT AND ADMINISTRATION

In the category of management and administration you will find the event manager, the volunteer coordinator, and those who handle marketing, finance, legal matters, and insurance. As a team they have determined the operating budget, the expenses that must be covered, and the amount of money that must be raised—first, to break even and, second, to generate a surplus. Of course, for a small event all these responsibilities might be handled by one person. For larger events, specific individuals are responsible for each of these areas.

(i) Event Manager
The person responsible for the overall management of the event is the event manager. He or she is involved in site negotiations, sponsorship sales, volunteer coordination, determination of a production time line, and pre-event site surveys as well as overseeing the activities of the people in marketing, finance, and legal. The event manager is pivotal to the success of the event. The more "hands-on" the event manager, the more successful the event.

(ii) Volunteer Coordinator
The volunteer coordinator is responsible for ensuring that there are sufficient funds to pay staff and enough volunteers to make the event function efficiently. A key resource for volunteers is the not-for-profit organization's corps of volunteers and/or members. One of the major benefits realized by an event aligned with a not-for-profit organization is the availability of that organization's extensive volunteer base. This helps events by providing more personnel and offering the volunteers an opportunity to participate in something that is not only fun but also generates funds for the organization.

(iii) Marketing

The individual handling marketing is responsible for advertising and public relations, graphic design, production of collateral material (brochures, posters, etc.), sponsorship sales, sales promotion, exhibit space sales, program book sales, and development of not-for-profit relationships. Obviously, this is your prime contact person for an existing event. If you are forming your own event, this person is vital to its financial success, because he or she is responsible for generating sponsorship dollars to support the event and for helping to ensure that enough funds beyond costs are generated to make the event a successful fund-raising effort. The following section, "Revenue Generation," discusses the many different ways you can raise money, in addition to sponsorship.

(iv) Finance

The finance person is responsible for putting into place a system that effectively controls expenditures, as well as ensuring that income exceeds expenditures. A simple numbered purchase order system, with two signatures for approval on ordering and a two-signature check payout system, is very effective. With the general availability of computer spreadsheet programs, there is no reason that the finance person cannot update the income and expenses on a weekly basis. As in any business venture, this allows the management team to track and adjust the budget to accurately reflect changes in income and/or expenses.

(v) Legal

Whenever you negotiate a relationship, with celebrities, sponsors, venues, teams, or other organizations, you need a contract. The contract should be prepared by a lawyer. This helps to ensure that all major commitments made are clearly defined and that there is no room for future misunderstandings. The contract should very clearly define areas of responsibility, limitations, confidentiality or nondisclosure, indemnification, individual rights, and recommendations for an equitable resolution if a dispute arises.

For more details on specific contract elements, there are two very good resources to consult, including *IEG Legal Guide to Sponsorship*, published by the International Events Group in Chicago, Illinois, and the two-volume *Sports Law Practice*, published by Lexus Law Publishing in Charlottesville, Virginia.

(vi) Insurance

Just as you need legal safeguards, you need to provide additional protection. Insurance can protect your event against greed, weather, accidents, violence, and human error. The types of insurance most common to special events include comprehensive, general liability, errors and omissions, accidents, cancellation, spectator/participant coverage, sponsorship, and weather. Several major insurance companies specialize in event insurance and can be contacted through your local insurance agent.

Event insurance is usually expensive. When the extensive liability of the alternative is considered, however, one quickly realizes it is an essential investment for the event.

(B) REVENUE GENERATION

How does an event make money? Most important, how does a not-for-profit benefit from special events participation? Again, as stated earlier, you can participate in an existing event or you can have your own event. Either way, you need to know how revenues are generated and how they are distributed.

One of the prime ways of generating money is to sell sponsorships. Sold in various dollar increments, sponsorships are designed to provide the sponsoring organization with an opportunity to support a worthwhile event while getting its message to its target customers or the public. The sponsor's target customers may include its own employees, consumers, others within the trade, and the media, to name just a few. Keep these realities in mind if you are selling sponsorships; understanding the reason sponsorship is being done helps you define a sponsorship program that will achieve the stated objective. (For a concise overview on sponsorship, read *Sponsorship Principles and Practices,* published by Amusement Business, Nashville, Tennessee.)

How do you determine the value of a sponsorship package, both in its pricing and in evaluating it from the buyer's point of view? There is no set formula. In fact, there are almost as many ways of arriving at sponsorship prices as there are types of events being sponsored. Because there are no set formulas and no Standard Rate and Data Services listing of rate cards, as are available for electronic and print media, sponsorship packages are unique and vary substantially.

From the event organizer's perspective, there must be enough anticipated sponsorship revenue to warrant holding the event. From the sponsor's view, measurable value must be received from the sponsorship. In both instances, one of the keys to successful sponsorship is having sufficient lead time to properly implement the sponsorship to develop its full potential. The less lead time there is, the less likely the sponsor will have time to totally integrate the sponsorship program into its marketing strategy. Conversely, when the event organizer's lead time for collecting sponsorship dollars is reduced, so too are the benefits that can be offered. Assume that the sponsor and event organizer have a minimum of six months to determine how they can work together and what the sponsorship commitment will be.

In discussing sponsorship, there are two different approaches. The first is a prepackaged approach that centers on levels of sponsorship—gold, silver, bronze, and so on—representing ascending values of sponsorship benefits. The second focuses on custom-designed packages that contain specific customer-selected elements that will help a particular sponsor achieve the desired marketing goals. Either way, prepackaged or custom-designed, the sponsorship must have perceived value or sponsors just will not participate.

What attracts sponsors? One of the prime interests is attendance: Who and how many will there be? It stands to reason that the more people potentially exposed to the sponsor's marketing message, the more value that sponsorship will be perceived to have. There is a direct correlation between attendees and revenue: the greater the attendance, the higher the investment.

Another "hot button" is media. Will there be radio and television coverage? What print media are involved? How visible will the sponsor's participation be in the various media? When preparing sponsorship packages, take into consideration the dollar level of participation and then determine what media coverage will be included at each level. Again, the greater the media exposure, the higher the sponsorship commitment.

Another point of high interest with sponsors involves the issue of whether they can generate additional sales from participation in this sponsorship. Some of the questions sponsors typically ask include: Can we sell a product on site? Can we do product sampling? What about pre-event in-store promotions? Can we offer the event attendees some incentive for coming back to purchase more product? Events that offer additional value, beyond the price of sponsorship, are those that lead to increased sales and bottom-line profitability.

Exclusivity is a topic of particular importance to beverage and tobacco companies. However, when offering exclusivity as part of a sponsorship package, understand that it should be assigned greater value, because it limits the promoter's ability to get additional sponsorship dollars from competitive products. If Coca-Cola demands exclusivity, that prohibits the event from soliciting Evian, Snapple, or Apple & Eve, because the soft drink category would be exclusively Coca-Cola's. Thus, exclusivity carries a higher price tag.

Bonus items, such as tickets for the event, priority parking, hospitality, and other "rewards" for associating with the event, are important sponsorship benefits. Again, the more that are included, the higher the price of the actual sponsorship package. The promoter is giving up potential revenue that could be generated from the general public and must be compensated for this lost revenue.

An easy way to determine the value of a sponsorship package is to take all the items listed in the benefits and price them out as if they were to be purchased separately. If the value is 10 percent or more than the actual sponsorship price quoted, it is priced fairly and equitably. You will encounter difficulties in determining pricing when considering such intangibles as goodwill, exclusivity, on-site visibility, and the like. However, these items also can be assigned a value and included in the total evaluation of the sponsorship package.

Another way to raise funds for an event is to have a variety of activities with specific fees attached to participation. For example, participants pay a fee to compete, exhibitors pay a fee for display space, parade participants pay a fee for placement, attendees pay a fee for photographs with celebrities, spectators pay an entry fee, and so on.

Yet another way is to have various collateral materials in which (or on which) people can advertise. These include a program book or some sort of commemorative piece, display boards (with sports it can be the scoreboard or leader board), event maps, event posters, and the like. These elements can also be included in the various sponsor packages as benefits for participation.

Other ways of bringing in additional monies include having a carnival as part of your event, for which the proceeds are split 75/25 (75 to the carnival, 25 to you); a raffle with a 50/50 split; games of skill; electronic games, and so on.

If you are simply hitchhiking on an existing event, much of this information is merely nice to know. However, if you are running your own event, it is vital to know, as you will be responsible for raising as much money as possible to (1) ensure event success and (2) have funds left over for your organization's operating budget.

(C) ON-SITE MANAGEMENT

Staff for on-site management is provided by the event manager and volunteer coordinator and includes both paid and unpaid personnel. The function of this group is to see that sufficient planning and preparation have taken place to ensure a smooth-running event. Because the event occurs in "real time," with no rehearsal and no opportunities to do it again, all logistical issues and problems have to be solved before they happen.

On-site management is responsible for such mundane, but necessary, items as the following, to name just a few.

- Portable sanitation facilities
- Tents
- Lighting
- Security and crowd control
- Audio systems
- Fencing
- Bleachers
- Tables and chairs
- Paper towels and toilet paper
- Traffic control
- VIP treatment
- Communications
- Food handling and distribution

To be effective, on-site workers do a pre-event site survey to determine the problem areas and how most efficiently to lay out the event. Then, 12 hours before the event, they do another survey to ensure that nothing has changed. On-site persons are usually at the event many hours before its official opening: tents, chairs, and other physical setup do not go up quickly (or easily), and there are always last-minute details that need attention before the successful start of the event. They are also the last ones on-site, long after the event is over, tending to the cleanup operation and overseeing the return of all rented equipment. Their primary objectives are to return the site to its original pre-event condition and see that all contracted and purchased goods are returned intact.

23.4 How to Get Started

The easiest way to get started is to become part of an existing event. This will give you an opportunity to observe, firsthand, what is happening and what is needed to have a successful event.

How do you determine the appropriate "fit" for your not-for-profit and a specific event? One easy way, once you have determined those events in which you are interested, is to send the Promoter/Producer Worksheet (see Exhibit 23.1) to the event organizers and ask them to complete it for you. You should also run a credit check on the event organizers to make sure they are part of a legitimate organization and not a fly-by-night group.

The worksheet provides you with a wealth of information that can help you make your decision on participation. For example, use great caution before getting involved in a first-year event. Generally, it is not recommended. Wait and see whether this is a one-shot opportunity or will become an annual event.

Be careful of an event that has had constant sponsor turnover—something is wrong. Check out previous charitable tie-ins—why are they no longer involved? Ask to interview previous sponsors and previous participants. Get their impressions of the event.

In addition, ask the producers or promoters about the audience the event attracts. Is it primarily male? Female? Family? What age groups are represented? What social strata attend the event? What ethnic groups are represented? What geographic area do they come from? What types of jobs or positions do the attendees and participants have?

Through this questionnaire you can get both the demographics and psychographics of the event. Then, look at the profile of persons who contribute to your organization.

EXHIBIT 23.1 Promoter/Producer Worksheet

1. Background Information on _____(event name)

   A. Company name:_____

      Address:_____

      City:_____ State: _____ Zip:_____

      Telephone: (___)_____ Fax: (___)_____

      Contact person: _____

      Title: _____

   B. Other locations (if any):_____

      _____

   C. Number of years in business: _____ Number of years managing event: _____

   D. Other events produced/promoted: _____

      _____

   E. Number of full-time staff: _____

   F. Names and titles of executives working in this organization, including number of years
      with organization, experience with event, and any additional background:

      1. _____

          _____

      2. _____

          _____

      3. _____

          _____

   G. Any lawsuits pending? Yes_____ No_____ If yes, what are the circumstances?
      Please explain.

      _____

      _____

   H. Ever declared bankruptcy? Yes_____ No_____ If yes, what are the circumstances?
      Please explain.

      _____

      _____

   I. Current sponsor(s):_____

      _____

      _____

   J. Number of years sponsor(s) has been involved:_____

      _____

      _____

   K. What is the event's insurance coverage (type/dollar amount)?

      _____

      _____

EXHIBIT 23.1 (*Continued*)

II. Event Background

    A. Name of event: _____

    B. Number of years in existence: _____ Initial date: _____

    C. Date of event: _____ Length of event: _____

    D. What other events occur in the area on the same date as this event? _____

        _____

    Please detail: _____

        _____

        _____

    E. Current title sponsor: _____ How long? _____

    F. Past title sponsor: _____

       Why not renewed? _____

       _____

    G. List other current sponsors, length of time with event, dollar commitment: _____

        _____

        _____

    H. Exact location of event: _____

        _____

    I. Event objectives: _____

        _____

    J. Anticipated attendance: _____

    Previous year's attendance: _____

    K. Composition percentage of attendance per category:

        General public____%   Invited guests____%   Trade____%

        Press____%   Staff____%   Spouses____%   Other____%

    L. Ticket required?_____ If yes, prepaid or payable at gate? _____

    M. Ticket prices and classifications:_____

    N. Tax exemption/taxable:_____ Are tickets marked taxed?_____

    O. Are tickets torn?_____ Deposit box for stubs?_____ Door prize arrangements?_____

       Ticket-back promotions? _____

    P. Readmission procedure: Hand stamp _____Pass _____Half ticket_____

       Scanning light_____ Other_____

III. Not-for-Profit Tie-in

    A. Is a not-for-profit group benefiting from the event? _____ If yes, name the organization and benefit amount:_____

        _____

    B. Any connection between sponsor and beneficiary? _____If yes, describe: _____

        _____

    C. Are any specific promotions related to the not-for-profit group? ____If yes, please detail:

        _____

EXHIBIT 23.1 (*Continued*)

D. If you do not have a current not-for-profit relationship, are you interested in establishing one?_____ If yes, describe the relationship you are seeking:_____
_____

IV Event Attendance/Participation Profile

A. Describe the event's target audience: _____
_____

B. Is this event unique?_____ If yes, why: _____
_____

C. What is the composition of attendees? (men, women, children, ages, etc.)
_____

D. Profile the participants: _____

V. Media Coverage and Signage

A. Is there television coverage of the event?_____ If yes, cable or network? _____
_____

Is the coverage national, regional, or local? _____

Dates and times of airings: _____

Previous year's ratings? _____

B. If televised, is event covered by Sponsor's Report or some other third-party measurement?_____

C. What other types of coverage are offered? Radio _____

Magazine _____ Newspaper_____ Other _____

D. What type of signage is available? (quantity, size, placement)_____
_____

E. Please check all of the following that would be promoting the not-for-profit organization's participation in the event:

Press kits

Schedules

Press releases

Scoreboards

Press conferences

Event posters

Pre-event publicity tours

Ribbons

Print interviews

Trophies

Radio/TV interviews

Flags

Event brochures

Billboards

EXHIBIT 23.1 (*Continued*)

    PA announcements

    Transit

    Tickets

    Uniforms

    Other:_____

    _____

VI. Merchandising and Promotion

  A. Which, and how many, of the following items will carry your logo? Hats _____

    T-shirts_____ Sweatshirts_____ Pins_____ Balloons_____ Cups/mugs_____ Bags_____

    Other _____

  B. Can the not-for-profit organization have a display booth? Size:

             Quantity: Any restrictions:

  C. Can an on-site drawing or contest be conducted?_____Are there any restrictions? Please

    detail: _____

    _____

  D. What is the total advertising budget for the event? _____

    _____

  E. How is the advertising budget allocated? _____

    TV $_____ number of spots_____

    Stations: _____

    Radio $_____number of spots_____

    Stations: _____

    Print $_____number of ads _____

    Which publications:_____

  F. Program/books? _____ If yes, how many? _____

    Ad rates: _____

    Distribution:_____

  G. Can not-for-profit be present at awards presentation? _____

  H. Can not-for-profit have access to athletes/celebrities for special appearances? _____

  I. Check all sales promotions planned:

    Contests/sweepstakes

    Couponing

    Premiums

    Sampling

    Point-of-purchase

    Incentives

    Other:_____

  J. Other merchandising/promotion/publicity opportunities:

    _____

    _____

EXHIBIT 23.1 (*Continued*)

VII. Customer Relations/Corporate Hospitality

    A. Check hospitality opportunities: _____

       Skybox/suite

       Parties with celebrities

       Exclusive tent area

       Food/beverage functions

       Priority seating/viewing

       Other (please detail)

    B. Check any of the following that are provided by the event:

       Tents

       Tables and chairs

       Audio system

       Food and beverage

       Wait staff

       Special event seating

       Travel

       Accommodations

       Welcome gifts

       Auto rental

       Other:_____

VIII. Security/On-Site Protection

    A. On-site security? _____

    B. Constant on-site communication?_____

    C. On-site lost and found? _____

    D. Traffic control? _____

    E. Medical and safety?_____

Are the two profiles similar? If your objective is to attract more of the same, go with the events that have similar profiles. Conversely, if you have identified new donor target areas into which you wish to expand, select the events that match the new profile.

Once you have successfully worked with an existing event, you can initiate your own. Look around and see where there is a need—then start small. You do not have to organize a big event to be effective in your fund raising. Give yourself enough time to plan the event (at least a year) and be realistic in your expectations and goals. If you decide to produce your own event, a good reference for step-by-step details and production checklists is David Wilkinson's *The Event Management and Marketing Institute Manual.*

In addition, New York University has a Sports, Events, and Entertainment Marketing program available through the Management Institute, with a wide selection of courses as well as an intensive two-week summer institute. This is the only program of its kind in the country. It provides practical, useful knowledge and introduces a wide range of industry leaders.

23.5 *Levels of Participation*

Hitchhiking on an existing event and starting your own event entail dramatically different levels of participation.

(A) EXISTING EVENT

Participating in an existing event, you can take as small a position as merely having a table with literature at the event and accepting whatever the event organizers decide to donate to your organization. This, of course, puts you at the mercy of the organizers and will probably not generate more than $1,000 for your not-for-profit.

A better approach is to align your organization with an existing event early in the planning process. In fact, you should attend the event you have selected and approach the organizers concerning participation in the following year. This gives you one full year of planning and involvement with the event and allows you greater input on distribution of funds. Conversely, it gives the event the cachet of your organization's legitimacy, which has strong marketing value and impact.

Your organization's strength, besides its not-for-profit status, is in its volunteer base. By providing the selected event with an existing group of volunteers, the event management is relieved of one of its most difficult tasks—volunteer recruitment—and can get on with generating sponsorships and event organization.

Once you have met with the event organizers and established a working relationship with defined areas of responsibility, establish a revenue goal for the amount to be donated to your not-for-profit group. An equitable amount would be 10 percent of gross revenues; however, if that is not possible, you might negotiate for all revenues from one specific function of the event. For example, if a program book is produced, your organization could get the net proceeds from the sale of advertising as well as all the proceeds from sale of the book to event attendees. Or net proceeds of the ticket sales could be given to your organization. Yet another approach is to have an event within the event—a band concert, a celebrity guest appearance, a raffle—where all the proceeds of that particular activity go to your not-for-profit. Be creative and remember that it is to the event's advantage to have your participation. It is an asset to the event organizers, and a token payment for it is unacceptable.

(B) OWN EVENT

Of course, if you are conducting your own event, you are in charge and have the full benefit of all proceeds coming to your organization. However, you also have all the work of planning and running the event. This means being responsible for all the special events elements and organization outlined in Section 23.3 of this chapter. (You may want to reread that section several times before starting your own event.) Unless you are experienced in event management, you would be well advised to seek outside professional help.

Bike New York is an excellent example of an event organized by a not-for-profit. Retaining total control of the event, Bike New York handles everything in-house with their own staff.

Another approach to sponsoring your own event is to hire outside people but retain management of the event. The Greater Fort Myers Beach Chamber of Commerce did just that with the American Sandsculpting Championship. Designed to bring tourists to the beach during the off-season, the event is held annually on the second weekend in November. The brainchild of the chamber executive, the event was totally handled by an outside professional with input from a chamber advisory committee. In this way the event generated funds for the not-for-profit with minimal expenditure of time on the part of chamber staff, yet the chamber retained ownership of the event.

Whether participating in an existing event or developing your own event, be sure you understand the event planning, management, and implementation process to maximize your organization's involvement and fund-raising efforts.

23.6   Enhancing Event Participation

As a beneficiary of an existing event, you have the same rights as any of the participating sponsors. These include all media coverage, signage, prominence on all collateral materials, and inclusion in all marketing efforts. Make sure your organization's logo is included on all signage, on the merchandise (T-shirts, hats, etc.), and during the event. In fact, you should enter into a sponsorship contract, just as the other sponsors have for the event, that spells out exactly what your organization and the event expect of each other. To facilitate this discussion, the checklist in Exhibit 23.2 outlines items to be discussed with the event organizers. (This process is not necessary when you own the event but is vital when you are part of an existing event.)

By using this checklist for contract negotiations, you can protect your organization from negative publicity and assure your organization of fair and equitable treatment by the event organizers.

23.7   Increasing Payback

To be effective in fund raising through special events, you must approach your participation as you would any other business venture. Here are some very simple dos and don'ts to make your participation in an existing event more cost effective:

Do:

Take an active part in the event planning and administration.
Enter into an event contract.
Follow through with your commitments to the event.
Protect your organization against any negative publicity.
Clearly delineate your expectations.
Enlist the help of your volunteer base.

Do Not:

Wait until the day of the event to get involved.

EXHIBIT 23.2 Checklist for Not-for-Profit Rights

1. Signage
   Logo placement on signage
   Approval of logo usage/placement
   Number of signs with your logo
   Signage placement at event
   Pre-event signage
2. Advertising credits
   Logo placement in advertising
   Approval of logo usage/placement
   Advertising placement
   Pre-event advertising
3. Merchandising rights
   Logo placement on merchandise
   Approval of logo usage/placement
   Revenue sharing from sales
4. Public relations rights
   Logo placement on media releases
   Approval of logo usage/placement
   Approval of your organization's involvement in event
   Right to distribute media releases through your organization's media list
5. Benefits
   Pre-event appearances
   On-site participation
   Dollars for nonprofit
   Visibility at event functions
   Public acknowledgment of participation
   Not-for-profit employee hospitality
   Donor hospitality
6. Future options
   Right of first refusal for following year
   Cancellation terms
   Increased revenue benefits
7. Indemnification/liability
   Hold harmless clause
   Insurance protection
   Errors and omission protection
   Force majeure, rain date
8. Nondisclosure
   Contract confidentiality
   Control information for public knowledge

23.8 Case Histories

(A) BIKE NEW YORK CASE HISTORY

Since its inception in 1977, Bike New York: The Great Five Boro Bike Tour has grown to be America's largest mass-bicycling event. In 1999, 29,000 cyclists participated in the ride. The tour was originally named The Five Boro Challenge, then the Citibank Five Boro Bike Tour in the years of Citibank's sponsorship. Bike New York, held annually on the first Sunday in May, is a 42-mile noncompetitive bicycle ride through New York City's five boroughs on traffic-free roads.

Starting from Battery Park in Manhattan, the tour travels through the canyons of Midtown, into Central Park and Harlem. After a loop into the Bronx, the ride continues on the FDR Drive along the East River and over the Queensboro Bridge. The tour weaves through the Queens and Brooklyn waterfront areas to Brooklyn's Greenpoint and Williamsburg neighborhoods, and then up and over the Verrazanno-Narrows Bridge spanning spectacular New York Harbor. On the Staten Island side, the tour takes riders into a festival celebration staged at Fort Wadsworth in Gateway National Recreation Area. A free Staten Island Ferry ride returns participants to Manhattan.

Hostelling International-American Youth Hostels produces Bike New York in association with the New York City Department of Transportation. The City of New York considers the event a city-celebration that brings travelers to the city, and enhances its image for both residents and visitors. When scheduling permits, the Mayor participates in the opening ceremonies at the Tour start line.

Proceeds from the event supported the development of New York City's first official Youth Hostel, opened in 1990, and today supports the programs that make the hostel a popular destination for young international visitors to the city. In addition, beginning in 1996, the event also benefits the New York City Traffic Safety Foundation. Revenue generators include rider registration fees, royalties from a merchandising agreement for Bike New York clothing, advertising in the official program, festival exhibitor fees, the festival food concession, and sponsorships.

Sponsor benefits include corporate/product identification on start and finish line banners, signage at rest stops, signage at start and finish lines, rider vests, and volunteer T-shirts; the corporate/product name and/or logo in event press releases, advertising, the registration brochure, the event program, and the Bike New York Web page on the Internet; public service announcements on WCBS-FM radio; and public address announcements at the event start and finish. Sponsor marketing opportunities include product sampling and demonstration at rest stops and the festival, sweepstakes and contests, promotions, key client participation and recognition, couponing, and a database of 72,000-plus.

Exhibit 23.3 shows a production time line for Bike New York: The Great Five Boro Bike Tour.

Participants in the Bike New York event are 68 percent male and 32 percent female, professionally employed, and look upon the event as a recreational lifestyle choice. The median age is 34.

(B)   WOMEN IN SPORTS & EVENTS (WISE) CASE HISTORY

(i)   WISE
Women in Sports & Events (WISE) was created by women, for women, to provide professional access and guidance, present and explore career-related issues, and offer a forum for problem-solving and enrichment for women in the sports industry and other major event markets.

Founded in November 1993, the WISE membership consists of individuals who range from emerging professionals to key decision makers in companies and organizations such as CBS Sports, Danskin, IMG, Lady Foot Locker, Madison Square Garden, MLB, NBA, NHL, Reebok, and Timex Corporation.

EXHIBIT 23.3 Bike New York Production Schedule

June/July
- Complete assessment of previous year's event.
- Write thank-you letters to sponsors, support service organizations, volunteers.
- Evaluation of benefits to sponsors.
- Prepare marketing analysis for sponsors.
- Review and organize photos; develop a library of prints and slides for subsequent use.
- Tabulate and evaluate press coverage.
- Prepare sponsorship presentations.

August/September/October/November
- Renew current sponsors.
- Research and contact potential new sponsors.
- Negotiate for media partners.
- Begin writing and design of printed material, including registration brochure.
- Plan public relations campaign, hire consultant.
- Hire additional staff, negotiate staffing contracts.

December/January
- First round of city agency meetings to negotiate route changes, assess relationships, apply for permits.
- Media alert to long-lead publications.
- Print participant registration brochure.
- Negotiate contract with fulfillment house.
- Order participants' vests.
- Begin Advisory Group meetings.
- Review and update databases.
- Write the Program.
- Sell advertising in Program.

February/March
- Mail and distribute participant registration brochure.
- Begin public relations campaign.
- Begin volunteer recruitment.
- Print program.
- Processing and fulfilling registration and clothing orders begins (March).
- Negotiate per-diem and short-term event management contracts.
- Prepare volunteer training material.
- Interview and place event interns.
- Staff office to handle telephone, e-mail, and in-person inquiries.
- Plan Festival, negotiate vendor and exhibitor contracts.
- Order signage, tents, prepare supplies lists.
- Make insurance arrangements, order certificates.

April
- Intense training and site planning, including volunteers.
- Operations plans and site maps completed.
- Production schedule completed.
- Supplies purchasing.
- Public relations campaign intensifies; media announcements, press kits distributed; photo shoots of events planned.
- Pre-ride of Tour route for volunteers.
- Inter-Agency planning meeting.
- Entertainment and stage arrangements for start line and Festival completed.

EXHIBIT 23.3 Bike New York Production Schedule (Continued)

- VIP agenda completed (invitations, speeches, hospitality).
- Finalize arrangements with all suppliers (vendors, sponsors).

May
- Pre-event final meetings of key volunteers.
- Final days of participant fulfillment.
- Route signage, route preparation, truck loading, final site details.
- EVENT DAY!
- Debriefings with various volunteers, staff, vendors, agencies.
- Thank-you party, thank-you letters, thank-you dinners. Wrap Tour office.

June
- Staff prepare final reports.

Bimonthly functions featuring key industry leaders are designed to inform the members on industry issues and to provide strategies for success in their own careers. Quarterly newsletters highlight member news and profiles, market trends, anecdotes, and survey reports from WISE polls.

(ii) Sponsorship

The sponsorship program is focused on the annual Woman of the Year luncheon in which five finalists are honored for their contribution in the fields of sports and events. Since WISE is a relatively new organization with minimal media exposure, the main benefit to the sponsorship package is the purchase of tables to the lunch, which has attracted the "who's who" of the industry. Additional benefits include logo inclusion on the invitation, program, letterhead, brochure, and listing in the WISE quarterly newsletter. The pre- and post-Olympic attention to women's sports has helped to spotlight the value of WISE to individuals and corporate supporters.

To add value to the package, WISE was successful in upgrading its affiliation with the *New York Times* and secured three to four ads in a national run. A top-level sponsor would have its logo included in this ad and therefore receive national exposure.

Companies were approached for sponsorship based on the following: past participation with WISE, current activities within the sports industry, and some commitment to targeting women and, even more specifically, women in sports. This "research" is compiled on a year-round basis by reading marketing publications and having a general awareness of what is happening in the business of sports.

(iii) Time Line

The lunch has been held each year in June, and it is preferable to send out sponsorship packages for the next year's event approximately one year prior to the next year. However, since it is a luncheon event, without media buys or tie-ins, six months in advance has been more than enough of a time frame in which to work.

The deadline for a sponsor to respond should be approximately two months prior to the event. This allows enough time for invitation preparation, which should include the company's logo or listing. The invitations should be in the mail to individuals and sponsors approximately six weeks in advance of the event.

A rough schedule follows:

October

- *Sponsorship package revised for upcoming event and submitted to Executive Committee for review.*

November/December

- *Adjustments to the package are made for finalization.*
- List of potential supporters and contacts is compiled.

December/January

- *Proposals are sent out.*
- Sponsorship subcommittee meets to discuss new target companies.

February/March/April

- *Proposals continue to be sent out to any new prospects.*
- Follow-up on proposals already submitted.

April

- Sponsor deadline for inclusion on invitation.

23.9 Conclusion

Of course, there can be problems. Another Hurricane Andrew can devastate your event; the onset of an overseas U.S. military action can dampen your plans; however, these are forces beyond your control. What you should worry about, instead, are the items that are under your control.

The key to the success of any special event—whether an existing one from which you will benefit or one you manage yourself—is good planning. Make sure you have hired people who know what they are doing, prepare a workable budget, put together a time line that is realistic, and be prepared to handle emergencies. Remember, the reason for doing all this is to generate more funds for your not-for-profit organization and, while you're at it, to *have a good time.*

Suggested Readings

Advertising Age, Crain Communications, Inc., 740 North Rush Street, Chicago, IL 60611; 312-649-5200.

Agent and Manager, Bedrock Communications, Inc., 650 First Avenue, 7th Floor, New York, NY 10016.

Amusement Business, BPI Communications, Inc., Box 24970, 49 Music Square West, Nashville, TN 37203.

Brand Week, A/S/M Communications, Inc., 1515 Broadway, New York, NY 10036; 212-536-5336.

Cable Marketing, Associated Cable Enterprises, Inc., 352 Park Avenue South, New York, NY 10010.

CableVision, International Thomson Communications, Inc., 600 Grant Street, Suite 600, Denver, CO 80203.

Directory of Sponsorship Marketing, IEG, 213 West Institute Place, Suite 303, Chicago, IL 60610; 312-944-1727.

Entertainment Marketing Letter, 160 Mercer Street, NY NY 10012; 212-941-1633.

Fairs, Festivals and Expositions, Amusement Business, P.O. Box 24970, Nashville, TN 37202; 615-321-4250.

IEG Sponsorship Report, 213 West Institute Place, Suite 303, Chicago, IL 60610; 312-944-1727.

Motorsports Marketing News, 1448 Hollywood Avenue, Langhorne, PA 19047.

New York Daily News, 220 East 42nd Street, New York, NY 10017; 212-210-2100.

New York Post, 210 South Street, New York, NY 10002-7807; 212-813-8000.

New York Times (Advertising Article, Section D), 229 West 43rd Street, New York, NY 10036; 212-556-1234.

Promo, 45 Old Ridgefield Road, Wilton, CT 06897; 203-222-0279.

The Sponsorship Newsletter, 89 Middletown Road, Holmdel, NJ 07733; 732-946-2711.

Sporting News, Sporting News Publishing Company, 1212 North Lindberg Boulevard, St. Louis, MO 63132; 314-997-7111.

Sports Industry News, Game Point Publishing, P.O. Box 946, Camden, ME 06843.

The Sports Marketing Newsletter, 1771 Post Road East, Suite 180, Westport, CT 06880; 203-225-1787.

Team Marketing Report, Full Court Press, 1147 West Ohio, Suite 506, Chicago, IL 60622; 312-829-7060.

Television/Radio Age, Television Editorial Corporation, 1270 Avenue of the Americas, New York, NY 10020.

USA Today, Gannett Company, 1001 Wilson Boulevard, Arlington, VA 22229; 703-276-3400.

24 ▼ Benefit Event Enhancements

Susan B. Ulin, MS
Susan Ulin Associates, Ltd.

24.1 Introduction

Although special events are appealing to many not-for-profit organizations, few realize the amount of work that is involved in planning, organizing, and managing a successful event. There are many different ways in which your organization can improve or enhance its special events. The strategies discussed here are those that occur in all phases of the event process, building on the basic mechanics of planning an event.

Events are labor-intensive and require much planning, but they are fun and an enjoyable way of involving people in your organization.

24.2 Purpose of Events

Special events are important for many different reasons. Most people hold special events to raise money for their organization; however, it is important to realize that in addition to fund raising, cultivation and public relations are also primary goals. Unlike most fundraising efforts, such as a direct mail campaign and grant writing, which target specific audiences, the event may extend beyond its target group to reach the general public.

By means of large-scale mailings and extensive follow-up, you can reach many individuals. Newspaper and magazine coverage, advertisements, and media coverage such as radio, television, and the Internet all serve to inform the public. Although the content may be directly related to the event itself, it can also highlight the mission of your agency. Increased visibility leads to increased public awareness.

In addition, events provide an opportunity to reach people who will not support an organization in any other way. Participation can result from a social or business obligation, a desire to meet people, or an interest in the event activity. This is, in summary, a unique opportunity for your organization to reach out to prospective donors who may not be familiar with your not-for-profit agency.

Events also provide the impetus for post-event cultivation of donors through followup activities such as distributing newsletters and membership mailings. A special event should not be viewed as an end in itself, but rather as a component of the entire development effort, and should be part of the annual budget.

24.3 Assessing Your Organization

Before launching a special event, it is important to examine your organization and determine whether this is an appropriate time to undertake such an initiative. A thorough evaluation of the organization is needed to make an informed decision regarding your ability to implement an event. While planning an event, it is imperative that one keep in mind all the other fund-raising activities that may be taking place during the months prior to the actual event. In addition, evaluation should include an examination of your organization's staff, volunteer support, budget, board involvement, and resources.

(A) STAFF AND VOLUNTEERS

Commitment across all levels of the organization is necessary to implement a special event. It is important for the board of directors, as well as staff and volunteers, to support the planned event.

The involvement of the board is especially important. Board members must have a clear understanding of their responsibilities in regard to the event and a willingness to carry them out. Board members may be expected to reach out to friends and other prospective event participants, secure corporate sponsorship, and help to identify leadership for the event. In addition, the board must be willing to participate in the event. If the board is not willing or capable of completing these critical functions, it is unlikely that the event will be successful.

Even with the support of the board, staff and volunteers must also be committed to the event. All of the details of the event will require much of their time and energy. Because they will be responsible for the planning and the management of the event from start to finish, their support is critical. These duties, which are discussed later in this chapter, include such varied functions as deciding what kind of event complements the personality of the organization; the selection of an appropriate site; research, updating, and collection of prospective donor/participant lists from within the organization and outside resources; and day-to-day management of the event. Good management must focus on the proper dissemination of information, financial accountability, and coordination of all event components.

It is crucial that information concerning the progress of your event is communicated appropriately to the organization's regular leadership as well as to the event leadership. Careful financial recording of receipts and expenses is essential for fulfillment of legal requirements. It is also the basis for proper tracking of responses, evaluation of participant response, and knowing which sources are yielding the responses.

Accurate records must be kept for proper follow-up of potential participants. You want to avoid wasted effort and, even worse, angering your list by continuing to solicit those who have already made a commitment.

Acknowledgments and, if appropriate, receipts for tax records must be sent to all event participants. Letters and printed information must be drafted. Schedules and projected budgets must be respected, and bills must be paid. In addition, all of these various components must be coordinated together to present an efficient and successful event.

Clearly, special events are extremely time-consuming for all involved. Even a small event can drain the energy of board, staff, and volunteers. Therefore, before your organization decides to hold an event, you must be certain that all key players are committed.

(B) FINANCIAL RESOURCES

Aside from evaluating the commitment of board members, staff, and volunteers, you must assess whether your organization has the financial resources necessary to successfully implement an event.

The preliminary costs of events can vary dramatically. Therefore, an evaluation of your annual budget as well as of the resources of your constituency must be done to decide whether your organization is ready to undertake a particular special event. The organization must select an event that can be managed successfully.

There are many direct costs associated with an event. They are often obvious and may include such items as location fees and the costs of entertainment, decorations, and catering. However, it is important to remember that there are other costs that must not be overlooked in planning an event.

Overhead costs, such as hours of staff time and increased usage of telephone, fax, and photocopying, should be factored into the cost of an event. Other costs that must be considered include printing and mailing. These expenses and their payment schedules must be carefully reviewed before you decide to hold an event. When planning your expense budget, also keep in mind that there are some costs that cannot be anticipated. A line item should be placed in the budget to allow for emergencies.

Once you have examined all costs associated with an event, a thorough evaluation of your organization's financial resources is necessary to determine whether an event is feasible for your organization at this time. Setting unrealistic goals is a common problem for many organizations planning an event. It is important to be truthful in your evaluation of the money you expect to raise, the costs, and the participation you can expect. You can avoid this pitfall by undertaking a careful analysis of your organization and its resources and by researching what similar organizations have achieved.

The best events require considerable time, planning and commitment, and the necessary financial resources. Without all of these components, it is difficult to execute a special event effectively.

24.4   Determining the Type of Event

Once you have decided that you have the necessary resources to implement a special event, you must determine the type of event that is consistent with the needs, goals, and character of your organization. The variety of events is endless; you are limited only by your imagination and your energy. Use your creative spirit when brainstorming event ideas. The event you may sponsor must compete with those of many other organizations, so yours must be planned to attract an audience in order to succeed. For example, people like locations that are not generally available, such as private homes and galleries. People also like events that are innovative and provide a new twist on an old theme.

Your event can be a breakfast, luncheon, dinner, or cocktail reception. It can take place on one or several days. The following is a list of a few traditional events:

Anniversary events	Corporate tribute dinners	Auctions—silent or live
Sporting events	Festivals	Privately hosted parties
Donor recognition	"A-thons"	Theatrical events
Gallery openings	Bake sales	Awards presentations
Fashion shows	Book sales	Pot-lucks
Cultivation events	Fairs	Campaign kick-offs/conclusions

To find an event that will work for your organization, it is important to determine what makes your institution unique. Factors to consider in deciding on an appropriate event include the mission of the organization, its geographic location, and the size and nature of your support. For example, a small community-based organization's event will be very different from an event for a major urban institution.

Consider the following questions:

- *What is the purpose of the organization?* The purpose of your organization will help determine the type of event to hold. For example, a music school may want to hold a concert featuring its students, or a neighborhood association may want to hold a block party.
- *Where is the organization located?* Certain events are better suited to particular geographic locations. For instance, an ice carnival is more appropriate for a location that always has heavy winters.
- *Whom does the organization serve?* The planned event should not be offensive to or conflict with the values of your constituency. For example, an organization that serves disabled people should not hold an event in a location that is not accessible to people with disabilities.

- *Who are the organization's current donors?* An analysis of current donors can help in determining the appropriate event. Review demographics such as age, income, and past participation in your organization. More than likely you will find a diverse population, but you will have determined the amount of support you can expect for a given event.
- *What are the interests of the organization's constituency?* An assessment of the interests and hobbies of your organization's donors is also important. If many of your donors are active golfers, it is likely that a golf tournament will appeal to them.
- *Whom are you trying to attract?* Special events may be used to attract people who are not currently involved with the organization. For example, if you would like to involve younger donors for the first time, you may want to plan an event that will appeal to them. When the Children's Hope Foundation wanted to introduce the foundation to a younger generation, it transformed a parking garage into a combination nightclub/flea market that featured disco music and items such as an armchair with Elvis Presley's face on it.
- *What are the financial resources of the potential participants?* You must consider the financial circumstances of your target audience. For instance, although the Children's Hope Foundation wanted to attract a younger audience, it also recognized that their group of young adults did not have a significant amount of disposable income and charged only $35 per ticket.

An evaluation of your organization's mission, constituency, and donors will help you determine the type of event that best suits the needs of the organization. Events that fit the culture of the organization have the greatest chance for success.

24.5   *Planning the Event*

Once you have decided on the type of event, the planning process begins. The success of any event is contingent on careful planning. One person should be appointed as the event manager. In choosing an event manager, it is important to select someone with appropriate skills. This individual will be responsible for overseeing all aspects of the event process.

An event manager should be well organized, detail oriented, and able to handle multiple tasks at once. He or she must ensure that all relevant parties are fulfilling their responsibilities. The manager will work with the board, the executive director, event leadership, outside vendors, staff, and volunteers. A good event manager coordinates all the various components of the event and helps it to run smoothly.

(A)   SETTING THE DATE AND SELECTING THE SITE

One of the first steps in planning any event is setting a date and selecting the site. Even the simplest events require much planning; therefore, it is not uncommon for organizations to begin making arrangements for an event six or more months in advance. Arrangements for a community-based fair will naturally demand more time and organization than a simple bake sale.

In scheduling a date, be mindful of holidays and other major competing events in your community. You should also be wary of approaching your donors too frequently within a given time period. Your event should not be scheduled too close to major fundraising efforts such as your annual campaign. It is also essential to have a signed contract for the site which has been selected.

Do not overlook the demands made on the organization's staff, board, volunteers, and event leadership. Are they available for the designated period? Do you risk burnout of your human resources by having too many activities back to back?

(B) BUDGET

You must also develop a projected budget of expenses and revenues. A careful evaluation of projected expenses and revenues allows you to determine the size and scope of the event. For example, if you need to raise $25,000, a traditional bake sale would not be the best choice of event to achieve your goal.

Tracking expenses can ensure that you do not exceed your event budget. It is important to base the projected budget on realistic costs and not exceed the stated amounts. Some expenses may be offset by securing in-kind donations, sponsorship, or underwriting.

Projecting potential revenue is as important as projecting expenses. When projecting revenue, the break-even point must be considered. You must determine how many individual sales are necessary to meet expenses. After evaluating your potential audience, it may be appropriate to institute tiered pricing.

Tiered pricing is often used to boost the amount of revenue received in comparison to projected expenses. For example, it is common practice to charge multiple ticket prices for tribute dinners that attract corporate attendees. Tables for 10 may be priced at $5,000, $10,000, $15,000, and an underwriting benefactor level at $25,000. Ticket prices may range from $500 to $2,500. Participants receive varying benefits, depending on the price paid. Those who participate at the highest levels by reserving a table of 10 seats might receive preferential treatment for seating, special listing in the program, and a special reception. By offering multiple levels of participation, the organization is able to increase its net profit.

It is important to continually track where you are in terms of securing revenue. This will allow you to determine whether your event is proceeding as planned. If it is falling behind projections, you can address the problem by taking corrective action. Event leadership, board members, staff, and volunteers should be informed and strategies devised to enhance their efforts.

The budget is an evolving process. Both revenues and expenses should be reviewed and evaluated periodically to ensure that you do not overspend and to keep you on track in regard to revenues. Reviewing revenues and expenses can help you to catch problems quickly before they become disasters. See Exhibit 24.1 for an example of a budget.

(C) TIME LINE

The next step is to create a time line for the event. The time line includes all activities leading up to the event as well as post-event activities. It should be a detailed list, encompassing everything that must occur to execute the event. See Exhibit 24.2 for a sample time line for a gala with a seven-month lead.

EXHIBIT 24.1 Sample Event Budget

Project Expense Report

(as of April 1, 2xxx)

XYZ Charitable Organization
2xxx Gala Benefit
600 attending

Hotel	$110,000
Graphic Design and Printing	15,000
Save the Date	
Reply Card/Envelopes	
Program	
Letter Service	
Preparation and Mailing	2,500
Table Cards	500
Centerpieces/Decor	9,000
Music	4,000
Photography	1,500
Miscellaneous	
Messengers, Clerical Overtime	1,000
Postage	3,000
Photocopying	500
Public Relations	2,000
Awards/Gifts	600
Staff Time	60,000
TOTAL EXPENSES	**$209,100**

(D) LEADERSHIP

One of the most important aspects of planning an event is securing leadership. The nature of leadership will depend on the event. Ideally, the leader is familiar with the organization, has many contacts, and is willing to commit him- or herself to the success of the event.

Leaders with social prominence in the community and corporate chief executives are the ideal people to seek as honorees or chairs, because they have a large number of contacts and can use their networks to bring participants to the event.

Among the many different responsibilities associated with leadership of an event are the following:

- *Development of a guest list.* Ideally, chairs and honorees should provide lists of their own social and professional contacts; otherwise, the organization must prepare such lists for the chair to personalize. Board members should also be solicited for lists.
- *Lending name to materials.* Chairs and honorees should be willing to let the organization use their names publicly in association with the event. The chair should be asked to sign letters on his or her letterhead for both his or her own list and

EXHIBIT 24.2 Sample Event Time Line

Gala Benefit Time Line (7-month lead)

Date and site selection and securing of event leadership to precede the following:

Month 1   Preparation of drafts for initial mailings
            Development and organization of mailing lists (collection, targeting for
                corporations and other table reservations, updating)
            Selection of designer/printer
            Production of initial mailing pieces

Month 2   Organization of committees
              • Steering Committee
              • Special committees (corporate, juniors, etc.)
            First mailings (Save the Date)
            Select music, entertainment, decor
            Preparation of advance table mailings
            Personalization of lists provided to corporate chair and other appropriate
                leadership

Month 3   Mailing to committee members
            Development of lists for general invitation
            Follow-up of initial mailings
            Preparation of invitation and tickets
            Financial reporting begins—reports designated by source
            Preparation of simple acknowledgments

Month 4   Continued follow-up of initial mailings
            Printing of invitation
            Invitation listing
            Plan other printed material for event
            Plan remaining details of evening (menu, video, photography, etc.)
            Continue financial reporting (tables, tickets, contributions)
            Follow-up of corporate mailing begins and continues throughout

Month 5   Addressing invitations
            Mailing invitations
            Design printed program
            Financial reporting continues
            Continue follow-up (table, tickets, contributions)

Month 6   Finalize all details of event
            Finalize printed program for the event
            Plan program for the evening and prepare necessary materials
            Continue follow-up (table, tickets, contributions)
            Weekly financial reports begin

Month of Event
            Continue follow-up (table, tickets, contributions)
            Complete preparation of all components for the event (e.g., seating
                assignments, seating lists, table cards, place cards, distribution of tickets,
                printed program, draft remarks, press coverage, event checklist, schedule for
                the evening)
            Weekly financial reports and daily updates
            Thank-you notes with tax information
            Collection of unpaid pledges
            Prepare minute-by-minute schedule for the evening event

Post Event Thank-yous to leadership, volunteers, and staff
            Final report
            Evaluation meeting
            Complete collection of pledges

larger lists developed by the organization. The chair should also be willing to be listed prominently on promotional materials, press releases, the printed invitation, and the program of the evening.

- *Financial support.* A chair should be responsible for bringing in a certain amount of revenue for the event. His or her level of support serves as encouragement to others to participate. If the chosen chair does not make a financial commitment to the event, it is less likely that he or she will be able to persuade others to do so.
- *Recruiting committee members.* An important task of the leadership is to recruit vice chairs and/or committee members. These people may also take leadership roles by bringing in financial support for the event. A good chair targets individuals who will make strong committee members and potential chairs at future events.
- *Time commitment.* In recruiting a chair, consider whether the person is capable of providing the support necessary for the success of the event. Do not select a chair who is already overcommitted, particularly someone who is currently serving or has recently served in a leadership role for another event. In some cases it may be possible for leadership duties to be shared among a few committed individuals (a group of co-chairs).

Commitment and enthusiasm are vital to the success of any event. A good deal of thought should be put into choosing the right leadership.

(E) COMMITTEES

The formation of committees can increase the number of people working actively on an event. Their effective use can significantly improve chances for success and can reach more people. The wider the targeted audience, the greater the possibility of achieving or surpassing the goal of the event.

By developing well-organized committee structures, your organization can utilize the skills and interests of its volunteers to enhance the event. In addition to raising funds, some of the tasks associated with implementing the event may be handled by members of the committee (e.g., decor, food, entertainment).

Given the importance of their roles, all committee members should be thanked, honored, and recognized whenever possible. Without their hard work and dedication, your organization's staff would have to assume complete responsibility for the event. The contributions of committee members should be recognized at meetings and mentioned in the invitation and other relevant event materials.

(F) SPONSORSHIPS

Another way of ensuring the success of an event is to utilize corporate sponsorship. Sponsorship, which has become more popular in recent years, allows either the entire cost of an event or a portion of the cost to be covered by a sponsoring corporation.

There are many different ways to locate corporations that may have an interest in sponsoring an event:

- *Organizational relationships.* There may be people involved with your organization who have connections with a potential corporate sponsor. Look first to the board, donors, and volunteers to determine whether such relationships exist. These contacts make it easier to sell the idea of sponsorship.
- *Ties to the organization's mission.* Look for corporations that may have a direct relationship with the mission of the organization. For example, a publishing company would be a likely sponsor for a literacy organization.
- *Ties to constituency.* Corporations also want to reach their potential clients—the segment of the population that patronizes their business. If your organization is a dance company planning a benefit performance, corporations that produce or sell dance accessories may be likely sponsors. Try to involve those corporations that have an interest in reaching your organization's constituents.

Even when there is no existing link between a company and your organization, it is still possible to secure sponsorship. Corporations often have other reasons for supporting an event:

- *Visibility.* High-profile events can attract many types of corporations. Their ability to reach a large number of participants is a major selling point. For example, in return for sponsorship, the company logo and product may be featured at the event.
- *Connection to the community.* Corporations are often looking for an event that can connect them to a particular community. By sponsoring an event, a corporation can be recognized as a community partner. For example, a business with many local employees may support the event of an organization if it benefits that community.
- *Benefit to employees.* Corporations may sponsor events that provide direct benefits to their employees. Corporations may sponsor a sporting event or tribute dinner and provide its employees with tickets.

The greater the amount of event expenses covered by sponsorship, the greater the net revenues. In addition to financial support, corporate sponsorship may also be a means of bringing greater visibility to your organization. The sponsor may want to promote its goodwill effort by assisting in public relations efforts. Association with a major corporation can also lend greater credibility to your organization and its event. For more information on sponsorship, see Chapter 32.

(G) LISTS

Developing a good invitation list is a key component of any successful event. The board of directors and leadership can provide lists of their personal and professional contacts. Committee members should also be asked for lists of their friends and colleagues. The organization's donor files, particularly of participants in past events and donors above a given level, are good sources for an in-house list. You can also trade with, or purchase lists from, other organizations.

If these sources do not yield enough names, general lists must be developed. To expand your list, evaluate the relationships of leadership, board members, and honorees. For example, corporations in related fields to those of the event leadership are good candidates.

Other possible list candidates include those who serve on other boards with your directors or leadership. Vendors of your chair and honorees should be included (e.g., accountants, advertising agencies, and law firms).

Once your lists are complete, they should be categorized in order of likelihood of participation. Those who are most likely to participate may receive advance mailings and be asked to join the committee at a designated level, such as associate chairs. Ranking the list can also be helpful in determining where staff and volunteers should focus their follow-up efforts.

The development of good lists is the foundation of implementing a successful event. A specific list that targets those connected with your organization, board, or leadership can significantly increase the likelihood of participation.

(H) PRINTED MATERIALS

Anything that is created to announce an event should convey its excitement and enthusiasm. The style of the materials should be consistent with the type of event and the type of organization. Well-thought-out promotional materials may result in increased interest and participation. A tightly drafted program is another opportunity to present information to the guests and to give credit to participants. All printed materials should be graphically consistent.

(I) PROGRAM OF THE EVENING

The actual program should be considered as soon as the leadership is in place. The program provides an opportunity for the organization to "present itself"—its mission and goals—to the assembled audience. How well you plan this presentation will, in large part, determine the success of the event from the guests' viewpoint. Programs should be short—less than 30 minutes. An event is not the time for speeches. If you are making an audiovisual presentation, consider carefully the type and timing. Videos can be very costly and must be short and extremely well done if they are to be effective. If you are considering the use of a video, it is wise to consider a format that can easily be adapted for future fund-raising activities.

Once the program has been planned, it is important to contact all the participants, "script" the program, and prepare a minute-by-minute schedule to implement it at the event. People appreciate a tightly organized event with activities occurring on time.

(J) PUBLIC RELATIONS

Public relations is an important element of successful event planning. This is the way your organization communicates not only information about the event but also its mission and information on its programs to the public.

To be effective, public relations tools must be used creatively. The strategy you employ depends on the type of event, participant characteristics, and the culture of the organization. Opportunities for promoting your organization and event are numerous and require imagination and resourcefulness.

Various media have specific audiences. Focus on those that target your potential audience. Although general radio announcements may be effective in drawing people to a city-wide walk-a-thon, this may not be the appropriate medium to bring participants to a church bake sale. To reach this population it may be more helpful to place ads in the local community paper and church newsletter or to post flyers throughout the neighborhood.

A strong public relations initiative can attract attention to your organization and help to bring in more participants, members, and donors. Planning in advance and thoroughly examining the options for public relations can enhance the positive impact of an event.

24.6   Event Management

Organizing and effectively producing all aspects of an event is the definition of event management. To produce any event, managers must coordinate many different elements. Competent management, based either within or outside the organization, can make the difference between a mediocre and a superb event.

(A)   FOLLOWING THE TIME LINE

A time line can assist in keeping all those involved with the event on track. The time line should be referred to frequently in order to check on and evaluate the progress of event planning. If you are behind schedule, the event manager must identify and take corrective action to put the event back on schedule.

(B)   FINANCIAL OVERSIGHT

The event manager should continually assess how the event is proceeding financially. This oversight can determine whether your organization is on track in regard to expenses and revenues.

Following an established budget can make a big difference in net profit at the end of the event. If you do not control expenses, they can easily exceed initial projections, which diminishes the amount of revenue available to the organization. The event manager plays an important role in this process. Through careful monitoring, decisions can be made to keep expenses within budget.

Evaluating projected revenue against actual revenue is an equally important aspect of financial oversight. The event manager should periodically review financial records to determine whether actual revenues are consistent with projections. A careful review allows the organization to take corrective action when necessary. For example, if you are behind in terms of revenues, you will want to increase the amount of follow-up work in order to increase the participation rate and/or level.

(C)   RECOGNIZING PARTICIPANTS

Event participants should always be recognized in some manner. Recognition may vary according to the type of support. Sponsors may have their logos used in all promotional materials and at the event, and leadership, board, and committee members can be listed in invitations, the printed program, and mentioned at the event. Recognition of participants conveys the message that they are a vital part of the organization, which can often encourage future participation.

It is also important to acknowledge those who make a contribution to the event. All those who make financial gifts should receive a personal letter from the organization thanking them for their participation and including the appropriate tax deduction information. (See Exhibit 24.3.) Well in advance of thank-you letters, it is a good idea to send simple acknowledgments of reservations as they are made. All letters should be sent in a timely fashion; do not wait until after the event.

Keep in mind that tax laws require not-for-profits to give donors a receipt for any gifts above $250. In addition, acknowledgment letters and other printed materials should indicate what portion of each ticket is tax deductible. For example, a ticket to a benefit dinner may cost $500. However, if the value derived from the dinner is worth $125, the tax-deductible amount is only $375 per ticket.

(D)   RECORD KEEPING

Managing an event requires one to keep impeccable records. Meticulous record keeping can help the event manager implement the event and plan future events.

Records are useful for tracking the process from start to finish. During the initial phase of event planning, records should be kept of contact information, contributions

---

EXHIBIT 24.3 Sample Acknowledgment Letter

November 3, 2xxx

Ms. Jane Smith
President and CEO
JS Corporation
100 Elm Street
Somewhere, USA 00000

Dear Ms. Smith:

The XYZ Charitable Organization gratefully acknowledges your gift to the annual benefit dinner, which is scheduled for December 12, 2xxx, at the Hotel Erehwon.

In fulfillment of current tax regulations, we confirm that the tax-deductible portion of your gift of $5,000 for one Sponsor Table is $3,900.

Thank you again for your support of the XYZ Charitable Organization.

Sincerely,

John Brown
Executive Director

---

received, correspondence, contracts, and so on. This information should be readily available. For example, the board may want to know the status of contributions above a particular level. The development office may request the addresses of participants for a direct mail campaign. A donor may lose the original tax receipt and need another copy for his or her accountant.

Records are also essential in evaluating an event. It is important to know what worked successfully and which areas need to be improved. For example, it would be useful to know that this year you raised only 60 percent of your projected revenues one month before the event, although you successfully reached your goal. On the surface it did not appear that there was a problem with ticket sales. However, accurate record keeping allows event managers to identify and address problems. In the future perhaps you can encourage committee members to become active earlier in order to prevent anxiety just before the event.

There should be a defined process for record keeping. This allows for consistency. A database can easily store all the information you need regarding your participants and can be helpful in tracking the financial progress of the event. There are specific special events databases, such as Jask, but ordinary database programs, such as Filemaker Pro, are sufficient for the needs of most events.

(E) ACCOUNTABILITY

Because events usually involve a variety of outside professionals (caterers, musicians, florists, etc.), it is important to ensure that they are accountable for their work. Contracts provide the best means of holding vendors responsible. Secure contracts or written agreements that detail the services they will provide, their fees, payment schedules, and any other specific promises they have made. This will alleviate problems that might result from miscommunication. Carefully review all contracts and make changes before signing. Contracts should be signed by the person with proper authority within the organization. Signatories might include the director of development, the executive director, or the event manager.

(F) TROUBLESHOOTING

In planning any event, there are many possible pitfalls that must be avoided. The event manager should be aware of all the various aspects of the event. Sometimes, despite planning, the worst happens. The event manager must identify the problems that can be solved and those that cannot. In some situations it may be proper and cost effective to cancel an event. In this instance the board and chairpersons should be notified about the problem.

Oversight of the planning and implementation process can allow the manager to respond effectively to problems and seize new opportunities.

24.7 *The Event*

Although most of the work involved in implementing an event occurs well in advance, there are still many activities that must be accomplished during the week prior to the event. If the planning process has been well managed, the event should run smoothly.

All of the diverse components merge on the day of the special event. Therefore, it is important to develop a checklist of what needs to be accomplished during this period. The function of a checklist is much the same as that of a time line. However, a checklist is usually much more specific and detailed.

With so many tasks to complete, it is easy to forget even the most obvious ones. Develop a checklist well in advance of the event and continue to update it so that it is both complete and accurate. Some items to keep in mind are included in Exhibit 24.4. This list is not exhaustive. You will have to determine what else should be included for your particular event.

Many volunteers may be involved the day of the event. To make their role easier, prepare a checklist including the responsibilities of each volunteer and staff member. This decreases the possibility of confusion and miscommunication on the day of the event.

If possible, meet with the staff and volunteers prior to the event to "walk through" the occasion and their roles. This is a good time to answer any questions and to reorganize responsibilities if there is a problem.

The event is the culmination of everyone's hard work. If attention is paid to the details throughout the process, the event should be fun and entertaining for all. Remember, too, that your event is a public relations and cultivation opportunity. Have literature about your organization on hand for those interested, and treat everyone as a prospective donor.

EXHIBIT 24.4 Sample Pre-Event Checklist

One Week Before Event
- Develop seating charts.
- Follow-up with guests.
- Prepare media information kit.
- Prepare printed program.
- Prepare place cards.
- Prepare table cards.
- Prepare presentation items.

Day Before Event
- Reconfirm all arrangements.
- Confirm with staff, volunteers, speakers, etc.
- Prepare complete guest list.
- Prepare table seating assignments.
- Give caterers final attendance guarantees.

Day of Event
- Take along phone numbers of relevant parties (vendors, staff, volunteers).
- Check facility.
- Put up any needed directional signs.
- Place items for registration table or other display (including alphabetical guest list, seating charts, table cards).
- Have information on organization available.
- Carry paper/pen/business cards on person.

24.8 Post-Event Activities

Once the excitement of the event is over, people tend to overlook the importance of post-event activities. They are, however, as essential as planning the event. Post-event activities bring closure to the event and assist you in planning future events.

(A) THANK-YOUS

It is important to thank all those who have participated in the event, no matter what their roles. When people are recognized for their contributions, they are more likely to participate in the future.

(B) COLLECTION OF PLEDGES

There will be many instances in which a financial pledge has not been prepaid. This often occurs in dealing with corporations that may have a lengthy check approval process. Your staff must keep track of outstanding pledges and follow up with telephone calls or written reminders.

(C) EVENT ASSESSMENT

Following the event, meet with key players, such as event leadership, board, management, staff, and volunteers. During this meeting, they should be asked to point out what made the event successful as well as any shortcomings or obstacles. The meeting should be held as soon after the event as possible while memories are fresh. The information should be recorded, shared with key players, and used in planning future events.

(D) CULTIVATION

It is important to view an event as part of an organization's overall fund-raising strategy. An event can provide the foundation on which to build a relationship with prospective donors and prospective leadership for future events. Information gathered through the event process will help you determine how individuals might fit into your fund-raising efforts. Those who seemed particularly interested in your organization should be noted and targeted for additional cultivation.

(E) RECORD KEEPING

After the event, compile all records and place them in one location so they can be retrieved when necessary. It is also beneficial to create an event book that holds crucial information about the event. Useful items include guest lists, budget, actual revenues and expenses, a copy of the program and other printed materials, letter formats, and anything else that might be of value in planning a future event.

(F) PLANNING NEXT YEAR'S EVENT

The energy developed in a first-time event will quickly dissipate if the event is not repeated the next year. Much as with any other fund-raising project, it takes time and repetition before one can judge the effectiveness of an event, financially as well as in terms of organizational goals.

Budgeted events, like direct mail and an annual fund campaign, are part of the annual fund-raising process. It takes time to "grow" an event. Initially, one needs to develop an event constituency that is, in large measure, different from the annual fund donor base. Appropriate leadership, cultivation of new prospects, and recognition of large donors are essential to a growing event.

In considering a new event, plan to repeat it for a minimum of three years so that you can adequately judge whether it meets your organizational as well as your budgetary needs. Once it is established, an event should be able to meet a predictable annual fiscal goal. In addition, it should serve as a significant marketing tool.

It is a mistake to expend all the energy required to produce a successful event without allowing for its healthy growth. It is much easier and often more profitable to manage the same event in its second and third year.

It is necessary to evaluate your event carefully to determine which aspects should be continued next year and which need to be changed. Although people enjoy consistency (e.g., as to location and time of year) they will enjoy the addition of a new element to keep this repeat event fresh and to maintain a level of enthusiasm. One might, for example, add an auction or entertainment or celebrities, change the format of the program, or have a totally different theme each year. The possibilities are endless.

It is important to develop long-range goals for your event and to see each year as part of a continuum.

24.9 Using a Professional Consultant

If your organization does not have adequate staff or time to implement a special event itself, consider hiring a consultant to organize the event. Consultants have a great deal of experience and can help you determine whether your organization is ready for an event, plan the type of event that is best for you, and assist with as few or as many of the details as necessary.

Consultants can also help to reduce the cost of your event. Their contacts with vendors may allow them to negotiate better prices or services than are possible for one-time users. Their experience with various vendors also means that they often know which are the best and most reliable, thus enabling your organization to avoid unprofessional or unreliable vendors.

The more aspects of an event you want a consultant to handle, the more it will cost. You must consider whether the cost is realistic for your organization and the event you have selected.

If you hire a consultant, be sure to do your research. Examine past clients and types of events the consultant has managed. Obtain a contract that spells out the services that are provided and the cost of these services. Laws regarding fund-raising consultants vary from state to state. It is important to examine such laws before entering into any contract.

Hiring an outside consultant does not mean that you do not have any responsibilities in planning for the event. Throughout the planning process, you must remain in contact with the consultant to ensure that everything is going according to plan. Hiring a consultant enhances your ability to attend to the cultivation of your constituency and relinquish many of the clerical duties which are inherent to the special event.

24.10 Conclusion

Special events, although time-consuming and labor-intensive, can be a very positive experience for your organization. If well planned and executed, they can bring greater recognition, increase the donor base, and provide more funding. With the exercise of a little care and attention, you can emerge from the event process unscathed with your sense of humor intact. The goodwill generated and a sense of accomplishment are the intangible goals of any event. The cooperative spirit, sense of community, and renewed energy an event can provide to an organization are benefits that are lasting and not easily replaced.

Fund Raising on the Net

MICHAEL JOHNSTON, PRESIDENT
Hewitt and Johnston Consultants

25.1 Introduction

During the early 1970's, running water was installed in the houses of Ibieca, a small village in northeast Spain. With pipes running directly to their homes, Ibiecans no longer had to fetch water from the village fountain. Families gradually purchased washing machines and women stopped gathering to scrub laundry by hand at the village washbasin.

Arduous tasks were rendered technologically superfluous, but village social life unexpectedly changed. The public fountain and washbasin, once scenes of vigorous social interaction, became nearly deserted. Men began losing their sense of familiarity with the children and the donkeys that had once helped them to haul water. Women stopped congregating at the washbasin to intermix their scrubbing with politically empowering gossip about village life.

In hindsight, the installation of running water helped break down the Ibiecans' strong bonds—with one another, with their animals, and with the land—that had knit them together as a community.[1]

---

[1] Richard E. Sclove, *Democracy and Technology* (New York: The Guilford Press, 1995), p. 3.

Is this a parable for nonprofit fund raising at the start of the twenty-first century? Like Ibiecans, we seem to acquiesce to seemingly innocuous technological changes. We adopt more advanced databases, more powerful computers and their networks, e-mail, and Internet solutions—sometimes willy-nilly.

Have we thought clearly about the implications of these technologies for our sector and on the donors we serve, and do we need to?

If we think that Internet technology can have a profound impact on our sector and fund raising, then the pace of technological change should make us pay even more attention. It took over 20 years for radio to reach 50 million households in North America—50 million being a benchmark indicating some form of mass communication maturity. It took just 12 years for television to reach the same saturation level and only four years for the World Wide Web to do it.

If technological advances are reaching more people faster, then we need to study, discuss, and review these new fund-raising technologies, strategies, and tactics more thoroughly in order to decide how to best use them in fund raising. This chapter will remind us that there are as many fund-raising opportunities on-line as there are in the "real world," but more important than the opportunities are some of the fundamental changes in on-line fund raising over the last three years. Those changes have changed the questions we should be asking about on-line fund raising.

Two years ago we asked: Should we get online? What are other groups up to with the Internet? Will it be profitable to our organization to use it for fund-raising purposes?

These questions emphasized a medium in its infancy. Before anyone wanted to act, we wanted to know what everyone else was doing and would it work. The evidence in this chapter shows that the answer is yes to all three questions.

Now the medium is reaching its first level of maturity and the information in this chapter will emphasize that maturity. On-line fund raising over the last few years has been passive. Nonprofit organizations have been content to build giving forms, hope donors find their way to the form, and then count the unsolicited gifts that trickle in.

The new trends in online fund raising emphasize a proactive approach that includes:

- E-mail fund raising
- Use of application service providers
- Rigorousness in planning, testing, and tracking results
- More sophisticated on-line marketing plans

Nonprofit organizations are now soliciting gifts on-line instead of simply waiting for an electronic manna from heaven.

Almost every nonprofit organization has to get on-line. There are just too many people on the Internet now and in the future to ignore. It is a new medium that nonprofit organizations are already using to reach a wider audience to help them accomplish their mission and mandate, including new ways to raise money. Every nonprofit organization should make the small investment to have it as a part of their media mix.

25.2 Now It Is Not Just the Web

The Internet is not just the World Wide Web anymore. The meteoric rise of wireless technologies (e.g., Palm Pilots, Web-enabled cellular phones, etc.) give nonprofit organizations the opportunity to reach donors on the street.

Imagine running an emergency relief organization and being able to send out an emergency appeal to every donor who has a Web-enabled cellular phone. They would receive a message from your organization asking them to press a series of buttons to make an immediate gift—while they are standing at a hot dog stand!

If giving is, in part, impulsive, I cannot think of a better way to get individuals to give than to reach them at the same time a disaster is striking.

Every nonprofit organization needs to investigate the possibilities of using wireless technology to capture gifts.

This chapter will outline Internet fund raising in the following way:

- Fund-raising behavior on-line (part of Greenpeace Canada study)
- Membership fund raising
- E-mail solicitations
- Telethons
- Major gifts
- Pledges
- On-line auctions
- Lotteries
- Managing the .com relationship
- Application Service Providers (ASPs)
- Online marketing

It is important to note that many of the following examples are from organizations that have been doing their own fund raising in-house. The new trend is for nonprofit organizations to acquire on-line fund-raising abilities out of house. After the listing and explanation of what some organizations have been doing themselves, there follows a section that explains the rise of Application Service Providers (organizations that give nonprofits the software and abilities) to raise money on-line.

Now, just what are nonprofit organizations around the world doing on the Internet to raise money?

25.3   Donor Behavior On-line

What kinds of gifts do on-line supporters make? Do they like to make large gifts? Small gifts? Merchandise purchases?

Greenpeace Canada received 74 gifts or purchases on-line over a set period. They decided to look at those on-line transactions over that time and uncover who was doing what online. Of those 74 on-line transactions, 35 of them were one-time donations, 21 were individuals joining the monthly donor plan, and 18 individuals purchased merchandise (either a T-shirt or ball cap).

The 35 donors who made one-time donations gave a total of $1,705. That works out to an average donation of $48.71 per donor—more than one-and-a-half times the average donation from a direct mail donor, and two times more than a door-to-door donor.

The 21 donors who joined the monthly donor club gave a total of $297 per month, which extended over 12 months, is $3,564. The average gift was $14 a month deducted automatically from their credit card.

The 18 donors who purchased a T-shirt or ball cap gave a total of $270 dollars. The average purchase amount was $15.

How does all of this compare to "real-world" donors? Most of these on-line donors were first-time donors to Greenpeace Canada, and it is instructive to notice that first-time donors through direct mail give an average of $29 while they give $24 at the door. So, on-line donors seem to be more generous—giving an average of $20 to $25 more per gift. Those on-line donors who already give to Greenpeace gave on-line gifts $8 to $9 higher per donor.

The most telling difference is in the number of on-line donors who decided to make a commitment to the monthly giving club in comparison to the "real-world" donors through the mail and door to door. Approximately 10 percent of all Greenpeace donors are members of the monthly giving club. But this pales in comparison to the 28 percent of on-line donors who chose a monthly giving club over a one-time donation or a merchandise purchase.

What can any nonprofit learn from this? The on-line environment is automated. It is an electronic and computer-driven medium that seems to align itself with the most things like automatic deductions from a credit card. That is why almost three times as many on-line donors for Greenpeace Canada chose the automated, monthly giving club over any other kind of on-line generosity in comparison to "real-world" donors.

25.4   On-line Fund-raising Methods

(A)   MEMBERSHIP FUND RAISING

Is it possible for nonprofit organizations to find on-line members? The evidence from the World Wildlife Fund (WWF) USA is a cautious but tantalizing yes.

The World Wildlife Fund USA has created an on-line membership opportunity for visitors. In the bottom right-hand corner of the home page, the text "join" takes visitors to a membership form that presents the visitor with the following offer:

> *Your membership donation of $15 or more entitles you to 12 months of benefits including WWF's bimonthly newsletter FOCUS with reports from the field and an annual WWF Members Travel Issue.*
>
> *When you join, you will also receive by mail the WWF members' only Panda T-shirt pictured at right, one size (XL) fits all.*
>
> *To join, either fill out the credit card form below or select from the other join options at right.*

The on-line visitor can make an immediate on-line membership donation or call the 1-800 number.

WWF has a slowly growing membership response on-line. For its first year of electronic solicitation (March 1996 to April 1997), 312 individuals took out a membership through an on-line credit card transaction. That is an average of 26 people per month. From April 1997 until April 1998, 836 on-line memberships were taken out (with an average donation of $35). That is an average of 70 memberships per month. Over one year was a 270 percent growth in membership donations!

In what other medium are not-for-profit organizations experiencing a 270 percent increase in membership donations with little or no extra effort? Probably none. Obviously not-for-profit organizations should start to invest in on-line membership/donor cultivation and solicitation.

(B) E-MAIL FUND RAISING

A relatively simple and inexpensive tool like e-mail can be an effective means for a not-for profit to raise money and raise its presence. Unlike existing media, with e-mail many of the rules are yet to be established, let alone tested. Yet the opportunities for not-for-profits are increasingly clear.

E-mail offers fresh channels of communication with key audiences: prospects, supporters, partners, beneficiaries, or sponsors. More important, it can allow organizations to interact and respond with their supporters in the way that they choose and to track the interactions in sufficient detail to treat these supporters as individuals. The cost of entry for e-mail is relatively low, and, in a sense, the Internet offers a level playing field in terms of audience reach for both big corporate brands and small not-for-profits. Therefore, creativity and ingenuity can go a long way to maximizing a modest budget.

Much of what is known from work in other direct response media can be used to good effect with e-mail marketing. It is, however, very important to test different approaches and evaluate results because we still do not know enough what works the best in the on-line environment. As with other marketing work, remember to coordinate with existing campaigns in other areas in terms of form and timing. See the section on fund raising later in this chapter.

(C) LARGE GIFTS ON-LINE

Many not-for-profit managers are skeptical that not-for-profit organizations can receive large gifts via the Internet. The experience of the American Red Cross since November of 1996 shows otherwise.

From November of 1996 until April of 1998, the American Red Cross received 22 on-line credit card donations for a total of $49,400. That is an astounding $2,245.45 per donation! The on-line credit card gifts went from a low of $1,000 to as high as $12,000. These were not pledges. These were not donations that needed to be confirmed by the donor. They were simply electronic transactions where the prospective donor entered information on-line, sent it to the American Red Cross and then the organization processed the gift. It is important to realize that on-line consumers generally do not make transactions of this size; it may be easier for citizens to make large transactions on-line if they involve helping a charity instead of buying consumer goods. (See Exhibit 25.1.)

At a minimum, these findings dictate that not-for-profit organizations test the efficacy of large gifts on their own Web sites. Most Web site gift arrays do not provide on-line donors with a chance to choose a $1,000 gift option, but the findings from the American Red Cross show that a small but important segment of on-line donors like to make a "millennial contribution." Every not-for-profit organization should make sure it offers on-line donors a chance to choose significant gift amounts (of $1,000 or more) either through a pledge or in credit card donations. With thirteen $1,000 gifts, the American Red Cross has shown this amount seems to be a comfortable and attractive larger gift amount. As a minimum effort, every not-for-profit organization should provide an on-line giving opportunity set at $1,000.

On-line donors need to be coddled and cultivated like all other kinds of donors. The American Red Cross has made sure that their on-line donors get a personal approach. Richard Renn, director of Development Operations at the American Red Cross National

EXHIBIT 25.1 Red Cross Transactions

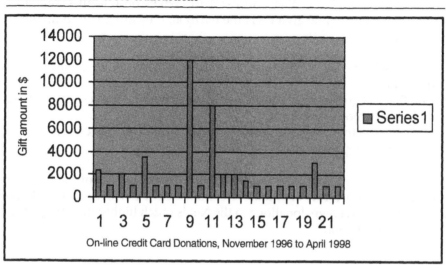

On-line Credit Card Donations, November 1996 to April 1998

Offices, states that "all Internet donor information is sent to the local chapters across the country for a more personalized follow-up after we at national send the initial acknowledgment. (The initial acknowledgment is the same for all Internet donors.) Although some chapters may cultivate their donors differently, I expect that most or all high-end donors receive a special acknowledgment, along with phone calls and other cultivation techniques."[2]

Two on-line gifts to the American Red Cross, one for $8,000 and another for $12,000, qualify as major gifts, according to Kathleen Kelly, in *Effective Fund-Raising Management*.[3] In the case of the American Red Cross, there is an immediate problem (a disaster and people to help) that needs to be solved with a major gift, but with many other not-for-profit organizations, donors may want their on-line major gifts to help for years to come. A gift in the range of $10,000 is often seen as the minimum for an endowment,[4] thus, many not-for-profit organizations should start to offer on-line giving information about major gift opportunities and what a major gift and the resulting endowment could do for a donor's chosen cause.

(D) TELETHONS

A number of not-for-profit organizations are raising money on the Net when they run telethons. The Foundation for Research into Children's Diseases ran its annual telethon in December 1999. Victor Drury, the executive director, recounts the fact that they

---

[2]Michael Johnston, *The Fund Raiser's Guide to the Internet* (New York: John Wiley and Sons, Inc., 1998), p. 4.
[3]Kathleen Kelly, *Effective Fund-Raising Management* (Mahwah, N.J.: Lawrence Erlbaum Associates, 1997), p. 476.
[4]*Ibid.*, p. 482.

received over 100,000 individual gifts and of those gifts, over 1,000 were made on-line.[5] The TV telethon highlighted a Web address (URL) where on-line gifts could be made.

To improve their on-line giving via the telethon, they are going to do the following three things next year:

1. Have celebrities use a computer on-air to highlight how to make an on-line donation.
2. Run the URL (or "web site address") at the bottom of the screen and make the giving URL more prominent.
3. Offer prospective on-line donors the ability to click their mouse and begin to talk to a live representative (via voice).

The integration of all media is evident in this example. The Internet is offering this organization the opportunity to link the telephone with TV with the Internet. It is important to note that the average donation via the Net is much higher than the gifts made via telephone for the telethon.

(E) PLEDGING

Although many individuals are now giving on-line, it is still important to give people the opportunity to pledge on-line. An example of on-line pledging comes from WPLN, a Nashville public radio station. There are three important characteristics of on-line pledgers, as revealed by WPLN supporters, that all not-for-profit organizations should take notice:

1. On-line pledgers use credit cards in 25 to 30 percent of their pledges—the same as real-life pledgers.
2. On-line pledgers, in the case of WPLN, and most likely true of other nonprofits, pledged an average of $75 per person—much higher than the average real-life pledge.
3. The on-line pledger fulfilled at the 60 percent rate, which is approximately the same as telephone pledge fulfillment rates. The pledge fulfillment rate for on-line donors at the American Civil Liberties Union Web site was also much like its telephone pledges.

Every not-for-profit organization that already conducts pledge drives in their fund-raising campaigns (especially with pledge campaigns through the telephone, TV, and radio) should think of adding the on-line pledge campaign to complement their other pledge fund raising. However, WPLN staff offer some sober perspective: "We have found that on-line pledging has significant results for us only when it is being reinforced in other ways: on the air, in print, etc. It seems to be helpful as an additional tool and an additional opportunity for those interested in using this method, but does not seem to yield results significant enough to warrant using it in replacement of other methods."

---

[5]Interview with Mike Johnston, AFP Montreal Chapter, April 14, 2000.

(F) MERCHANDISE SALES

The Rainforest Action Network (RAN) (www.ran.org/ran/) has discovered its Web site is a good place to sell merchandise. (See Exhibit 25.2.)

Mark Westlund, media director at RAN, states that, "The site has been a great place to get rid of extra stock. If we had to get rid of stock in the real world, it could have entailed sending out a mailing with a more expensive color reproduction of the T-shirts or phoning supporters—both cost money. Instead, we used the relatively free method of showing our beautiful T-shirts online."

RAN quickly ran through its overstock of approximately 800 T-shirts through on-line sales. It also has had success selling calendars on its Web site—making approximately 700 sales during the holiday season.

Many not-for-profit organizations have begun to offer their expertise to the private sector to raise additional revenue. Without a doubt, this kind of product should be advertised on-line. The business community is already offering, and finding, professional services on-line; the charitable sector should be there as well.

The Family Service Association of Metropolitan Toronto offers its counseling services to the commercial sector through its Employee Assistance Program. That kind of service could, and should, be offered on-line because commercial companies are already scouring the net for human resource assistance.

(G) AUCTIONS

The not-for-profit community has made auctions a part of its fund-raising repertoire. Many special events have included an auction as part of the event's agenda. Now the Internet provides an opportunity for not-for-profit organizations to raise money through

---

EXHIBIT 25.2 Merchandise Sales: Rainforest Action Network

1997 Rainforest Calendar: Celebrate biodiversity year-round!

We're back with another beautiful, full-color rainforest calendar, just in time for the holidays! It's got photographs of rainforest canopies and landscapes, each one a framable work of art-and lots of animals, from the malachite butterfly to the jaguar.

You'll see breathtaking scenes of nature's power-from the awesome splendor of La Hacha falls in Venezuela, to the terrible beauty of Costa Rica's erupting Mt. Arenal volcano.

Enjoy rainforest beauty month by month- and buy extra copies to share with friends! They're a bargain at $10.99 each. And the proceeds go to benefit Rainforest Action Network. Last year's calendars sold out early. Be sure to get yours today!

Order yours here! (Netscape required)

| Top of Page | Search | Join | Email RAN | Homepage |

on-line auctions. However, along with opportunity comes risk. This is a new medium and less accumulated experience exists among not-for-profits on exactly how to be successful with on-line auctions. Therefore, the author turned to an experienced on-line auctioneer, Brian Erman, the self-described "owner, Webmaster, and janitor" at www.keybuy.com. He has been running on-line auctions for over three years, and he has failed to sell only one or two items among tens of thousands of sales. His seasoned advice has 10 points.

1. The first thing any not-for-profit organization needs to do is decide what items it is going to sell and then visit an index site like www.bidfind.com to see what auction site might be most appropriate for its auction items.
2. Once a not-for-profit has found an auction site that looks suitable, it needs to contact the owner/managers of the auction site.
3. The not-for-profit needs to find out if the auction site will reduce its sales commission for the not-for-profit. Commission fees range from 2.5 percent with www.keybuy.com to 5 percent for www.ebuy.com. www.keybuy.com offers a 50 percent reduction in commission fees, and that is what every not-for-profit should fight for as a minimum reduction.
4. A number of auction sites also charge a listing fee. Every not-for-profit organization should ask that the listing fee to be waived for its items. Often a listing fee is a minimum fee (e.g., 10 cents) that helps to reduce the number of items that are posted with outrageously high beginning bids. On-line auction sites that charge listing fees are trying to have only serious on-line sellers post items.
5. Every not-for-profit organization should be prepared to provide the following for each auction item:
   a. A short, one-paragraph description of the item. The description should include the brand/make or specifications of the item (especially for computer goods). This is important. For example, if a not-for-profit organization is selling a computer, then the make of each component is vital in getting the item sold. Some organizations provide a link to a manufacturer's Web site from the description of the item, but often this drives people out of the auction item Web page, and many will not come back to buy.
   b. A picture should almost always be included. It boosts sales and final price.
   c. It is often effective to include a hypertext link from a description of the auction item to the not-for-profit's home page to find out more about the organization.
   d. It is also effective when the not-for-profit includes a hypertext link to a list of other auction items the organization has for sale.
   e. A one-sentence explanation of the mission and mandate of the not-for-profit organization, included in the description of the auction item, is also important.
   f. To receive a reduction in commission or listing fee, most on-line auction houses need a letter, on the not-for-profit's letterhead, asking for the fee reduction. In addition, a brief explanation of the organization's work is helpful.
   g. Many on-line auction houses will shy away from more controversial advocacy not-for-profits because showing favor to a group representing one side or another may upset some of their repeat customers.

    h. Studies by www.keybuy.com have shown that on-line bidders spend an average of $80. However, the value of the item will dictate the final bid—if a $1,200 antique is offered, the final bid will be higher than for a $12 computer part.

6. Not-for-profit organizations need to think carefully about a starting price for their on-line auction items. According to Erman, starting every item at $1 is a successful strategy for on-line auctioneering. A psychology major in college, Erman has been carefully tracking on-line buyers' motivations. He has found that on-line buyers are afraid to make the first bid. They are wary of bidding too high for an item with an initial high bid amount because other on-line bidders will ridicule their bid. Others will say, "That bid is too high, is this person a sucker or what!" By starting at $1, individuals are not afraid to begin bidding, and in Erman's experience, once people make that first bid they are hooked.

7. Furthermore, people are even more hooked into the bidding process on-line when they get an e-mail notice telling them they have been outbid. That means every not-for-profit organization should make sure that the on-line auction house they are going to use, or their own system, include such an e-mail notification system that tells bidders if they have got the highest bid or not.

8. Not-for-profit organizations should think carefully about how long they would like to offer items. According to Erman, a seven-day bid period is usually the most effective. His service offers a three-day, five-day, seven-day, and 14-day auction period to choose from.

9. Not-for-profit organizations must understand standard activity during that bid period. Usually almost all of the activity is on the first and the last days of the seven-day bid period. If a not-for-profit is thinking about bumping up the bidding, it may want to state that the bidding might be cut off at any time during the seven-day period if a high enough bid is received. This termination threat may be enough to get bidders to be active before the last day of bidding and help drive up the selling price.

10. Not-for-profits that are going to use an on-line auction house must make sure the site has been around for at least one year.

(H) ON-LINE LOTTERIES

Sue Schneider, editor of *RGT OnLine* and *Interactive Gaming News* (www.rtgonline.com), is a veteran observer of the on-line gambling scene and spent 12 years as a staff member of a youth services not-for-profit organization.

    She believes "It's just a matter of time until governments in North America, Australia and other jurisdictions allow nonprofit organizations to raise money through on-line gambling." Why? Because a number of charitable on-line gambling operations are setting up companies on offshore locations, such as the Caribbean, Gibraltar, Finland, and Lichtenstein (Internet casinos are bound by the laws of their host country) and are beginning to raise a large percentage of their profits from North American and Australian players yet give a percentage of profits to charitable organizations that exist outside of the countries of the largest percentage of players.

New technologies are becoming more important to gambling. In Canada, bingo halls are being linked by satellite through the Satellite Bingo Network—www.satellite-bingo.com. A central studio broadcasts the game to whoever pays to hook up to it. This is a purely commercial venture, but not-for-profit organizations could offer the same kind of gambling service. It is also important to note that indigenous groups in North America are moving to on-line gambling services.

It is up to not-for-profit organizations to keep up in charitable gaming on-line. The International Red Cross has been running an on-line lottery, Plus Lotto, since April 1997. Dwight Mihalicz, director of the Revenue Generation Department of the International Federation of Red Cross and Red Crescent Societies in Geneva, states that the site "is a qualified success." It is the qualifications to success that can prove very helpful to other not-for-profit organizations that are contemplating an online lottery. The International Red Cross first decided to enter into a partnership with a commercial organization, the International Lottery in Liechtenstein Foundation (InterLotto). Together, they operate the PLUS Lotto, authorized by the Liechtenstein government.

25.5   Regulation of Internet Fund Raising

The Internet presents vast opportunities while at the same time introducing a major challenge, that challenge of finding a way to regulate the practice of on-line solicitation. While there is no clear consensus on how or who should regulate this activity, most agree that the existing state regulations regarding charitable solicitations are no longer applicable in this on-line era.

The current laws were primarily put in place to protect the common citizen from fraud, and this has become even more necessary with the advent of on-line fund raising. Posting a Web site is an easy and inexpensive way for an organization to reach a large number of people, but with this convenience there is also a greater risk of unethical solicitation.

While the intention for regulation is the same for conventional solicitation as it is with the Internet, such that the public must be protected from fraud, the method used must be different, as the media themselves are different. According to Dan Burk, Assistant Professor of Law, Seton Hall University, "Much of the difference stems from the Internet's telepresence features, which render the network technologically indifferent to physical location. So insensitive is the network to geography that it is frequently impossible to determine the physical location of a resource or user."[6] In essence, the power of the medium transcends local, national, and international borders, making jurisdiction an impossible concept to establish. For example, if a charity based in California posts a Web site that is viewed in Connecticut, the question is who has the authority to regulate its activity and can Connecticut require this charity to register with it?

The present laws require not-for-profit organizations to register in every state they solicit for a donation. However, with the pervasive nature of the Internet, an organization's Web site may appear in outside states without its knowledge. Even if the organi-

---

[6]Dan L. Burk, "Jurisdiction in a World Without Borders," in *Virginia Journal of Law and Technology*, Volume 3 (Spring 1997).

zation knew its site was being viewed in every state, the idea of registering in each is one that many do not entertain due to the cost and time it would take.[7]

From a government perspective, the task of maintaining registration for these organizations is arduous. Most state regulators do not have the capacity to keep track of all the organizations that pass through their jurisdiction. According to Geoffrey Peters, Managing Director, Creative Direct Marketing International, Ltd., "if only 10% of charities maintain a website that 'passively' asks for donations, the typical state will see an increase from 1,500 to 62,000 in the number of charities which must register. The resources which could otherwise be devoted to detection and prosecution of charitable fraud would thus be devoted to registration compliance."[8] With these facts in mind, the question is not should something be done but what can be done and when?

Most states and not-for-profit organizations for that matter are taking a wait-and-see approach and applying the standard solicitation regulations to the Internet until "someone tells them otherwise." In many cases that "someone" has become the courts. Organizations and state governments are now bringing cases to court as a way to determine who has jurisdiction over Internet activities and whether applying the existing laws to on-line practices violates basic constitutional rights.

A case involving Pinellas County, Florida, is an example of the type of suit under debate. The constitutional validity of the Pinellas Charitable Solicitations Ordinance was brought before a District Court in 1997. The ordinance requires all those who solicit funds in Pinellas, including not-for-profits as well as professional fund-raising consultants, to register with the county, provide all requested information, and pay an annual fee. The plaintiffs, who did not reside in Florida, claimed the ordinance was unconstitutional because it inhibited interstate commerce and imposed an undue burden on those within the not-for-profit sector. The court ruled in favor of the county in November of 1998, stating that the provisions within the ordinance were in fact constitutional.[9]

In contrast to the Pinellas case, *GTE v. Bellsouth Corp.* questioned whether the court was even the proper institution to exercise personal jurisdiction over Internet matters. GTE argued that because of the overwhelming presence of Bellsouth and other similar organizations on the Internet, residents of Washington, D.C. were being diverted away from GTE's Web site and therefore the defendants were in violation of antitrust legislation. On January 11, 2000, the U.S. Court of Appeals for the District of Columbia decided that merely having an accessible Web site was not sufficient evidence for the courts to exercise jurisdiction.[10] What this verdict means for on-line fund raising is that simply

---

[7]A study conducted by Eric Mercer found that an estimated 268 to 750 organizations are actually registered nationwide. For further details see: Online Compendium of Federal & State Regulations for U.S. Nonprofit Organizations, www.muridae.com/nporegulation.

[8]Taken from a memo distributed at the National Federation of Nonprofits Annual Conference entitled "Critical Issues Facing Nonprofits in the 21st Century: How Will Fundraising on the Internet Be Regulated?"

[9]*American Charities for Reasonable Fundraising Regulation v. Pinellas County, Florida.* Case No. 97-2058-CIV-T-17B (1998) (U.S. District Court, Florida, Middle District). Similar cases include: *American Target Advertising v. Giani*, Civil Case No. 2:97-CV-610B (1998) (U.S. District Court, Utah); *American Charities for Reasonable Fundraising Regulation v. Shiffrin*, Civil Action No. 3:98-CV-01050 (JBA) (U.S. District Court, Connecticut).

[10]See: *GTE New Media Services Incorporates v. Bellsouth Corporation, et al.*, Case No. 99-7097.

having a Web site is not regarded as a violation and states cannot require charities to register if their only contact with residents is an accessible Web site. However, once a site includes a solicitation, the organization will more than likely be required to register.

In addition to the judicial involvement, some states have begun to take matters into their own hands by bringing forward legislation that incorporates on-line business. In 1998 California passed a law that includes regulating the use of electronic mail for the purpose of solicitation.[11] This bill consists of three components:

1. Donors must give not-for-profit organizations permission to solicit them.
2. A prior relationship must exist.
3. If a prior relationship does not exist, the e-mail must be labeled as unsolicited.

Like California, other states have begun to pass comparable legislation involving unsolicited commercial e-mail.[12]

In a clearer approach to the issue of Internet jurisdiction, the Minnesota Attorney General's office issued a memorandum in September of 1998 regarding their position. According to the statement: "Persons outside of Minnesota who transmit information via the Internet knowing that information will be disseminated in Minnesota are subject to jurisdiction in Minnesota courts for violations of state criminal and civil laws."[13] In this instance the Attorney General's office refers to the practice of on-line gambling as an example, but the jurisdictional statement applies to "any illegal activity." This may have implications for not-for-profit organizations with Web sites that may be seen in Minnesota but are not registered in the state. Likewise, Pennsylvania has taken the position that if a charity's Web site is seen in that state, the charity is in violation of state regulation unless it is registered with Pennsylvania.

These are just a few examples of the regulation environment not-for-profit organizations encounter when developing their on-line fund-raising strategies. Obviously, the wait-and-see approach to dealing with the Internet can no longer be applied. Governments and not-for-profit organizations alike need to take a proactive approach and begin working on a dialogue concerning how to turn this regulation challenge into an opportunity that will benefit the regulators as well as the regulated. The regulation of the Internet must be simple enough to keep up with the changing nature of the technology, be unified enough in the different states to ensure compliance, and maintain basic standards to provide the necessary protection for donors. Only then will Internet activities benefit all those who participate.

25.6 .Com Relationships

Many not-for-profit organizations will be entering into relationships with .com companies to give them the on-line fund-raising abilities they need but could not afford to cre-

---

[11]Bill number AB1629 was filed with the California Secretary of State on September 12, 1998.
[12]See Connecticut Bill number HB5028, *An Act Concerning Unsolicited Commercial E-mail.* Massachusetts has also passed legislation (H4483) concerning the privacy of consumer information that has effected the use of e-mail for solicitation.
[13]See: The Statement of Minnesota Attorney General on Internet Jurisdiction at www.ag.state.mn. us/home/consumer/consumernews/OnlineScams/memo.html.

ate and run in-house. It is vital for every not-for-profit organization to understand how to structure a relationship with a .com company that protects the integrity of the organization and the donors it serves on-line.

(A) SOME GUIDELINES FOR WORKING WITH .COMS

The following questions can help not-for-profit organizations manage their relationships with a .com company for on-line fund raising.

- *Is there a contract*, and does it guarantee that the affinity .com will not use the not-for-profit's name without permission—in every instance?
- *Are there hidden requirements for consumers (donors/members) who come use a .com service because of participation in the .com's affinity service?* Can the not-for-profit ensure that those hidden requirements are made explicit?
- *Are all common questions clearly outlined on the Web site?* Donors need to have a clear explanation of what a .com is offering to them and to the participating not-for-profit organization.
- *Will proceeds from the affinity relationship be delivered in a timely and transparent manner?* Any not-for-profit organization deserves to get the proceeds of the .com relationship within 30 to 60 working days (or sooner). If that is not the case, then that should be stated on the .com site.
- *What kinds of not-for-profits are allowed to participate with a particular .com?* Every not-for-profit organization needs to know what other organizations are a part of the same service.
- *Does the .com believe in an open-book policy?* Every not-for-profit organization should be able to review its proceeds and results through the .com 24 hours a day, via a Web interface that is presented in a clear, understandable manner.
- *Are prices inflated in product affinity relationships?* Every not-for-profit organization wants to be in a .com product relationship that gives the consumer a fair price, the .com a profit, and money back to the not-for-profit. The price of the product should not be inflated beyond principles of profit and fairness. Nothing could be worse for a not-for-profit than to be seen as a price gouger!
- *Is the transaction/information secure?* Every not-for-profit organization needs to know that .com has security systems in place that protect the not-for-profit, the .com, and the donor.
- *Does the not-for-profit get access to supporter information in a timely and transparent manner?* Does it have access to the on-line donor information 24 hours a day? Is it Web-interfaced? Can it be easily downloaded into any database? Is it a real-time database of on-line donors?
- *Does the .com have a list of happy clients?* There are so many new .coms that it is hard to know if the service is effective. Ask for not-for-profit client references. If there are none, or very few, then drive a very hard bargain.
- *Is the .com well capitalized?* Will it be a .com that appears one day and is gone the next? Is it committed to improving its applications? Does it have a system in place of taking not-for-profit experiences and comments and working them into the applications?

25.7   *Why Internet Outsourcing?*

The world of not-for-profit organizations on the Internet has matured rapidly recently. Gone are the days when organizations could be satisfied with an "on-line brochure" Web site that sat waiting for on-line visitors to come calling. Today's most successful not-for-profit Web sites are interactive, fully functional, and backed up by carefully constructed and well-resourced marketing and outreach campaigns to attract increasing numbers of visitors.

The price for these "next-generation" Web sites can be prohibitive for many organizations—both in dollars for all of the programming time and in human resources to maintain and refresh the on-line content. Fortunately, a new kind of on-line service company has emerged to assist not-for-profits to expand and enhance their on-line presence.

For a fraction of the cost of a custom, in-house solution, these outsourced services can provide fully developed, state-of-the-art functions that plug seamlessly into or compliment an organization's existing Web presence.

(A)   APPLICATION SERVICE PROVIDERS (ASPs)

Application service providers (ASPs) are commercial companies offering add-in services to an organization's Web site. These services have arisen in response to the rising aspirations and expectations (and associated costs) for not-for-profit websites. Typically, an ASP offers to host one or more special-function Web pages that will integrate seamlessly into a not-for-profit's Web site. Web site visitors may be entirely unaware that they are temporarily "leaving" the not-for-profit's Web site in order to make a donation or send an e-postcard, for instance. ASPs offer quick, cost-effective ways for an organization to add sophisticated features to its Web site without all of the extensive cost and delay to develop the programming code and commit human resources internally.

Typical ASP services include secure donation forms, shopping carts, event registration, and community-building features like bulletin board and chat rooms designed to plug in to an organization's existing Web site. Usually there will be a setup fee, which will include some customization work to make the ASP pages look and feel like the rest of the organization's Web site.

There are many new ASPs, and more are appearing each day. Deciding which service to use and negotiating the terms can be a daunting task.

(B)   OTHER OUTSOURCING SOLUTIONS

ASPs are "add-in" services, intended to integrate in with an organization's Web site. But there are other avenues to pursue in looking for on-line services to augment an on-line presence. Affinity opportunities abound for those organizations that are willing to lend their good names to an on-line auction or shopping venue. Affinity portals allow membership-based organizations to turn their membership numbers into revenue streams.

As in the real world, affinity opportunities typically require more consideration for a not-for-profit's public image and credibility, since an organization's good name is being associated with an outside company—often a for-profit company. Special care should be taken to scrutinize the terms of the affinity contract to ensure that the not-for-profit's name is not going to be misrepresented or used in ways that are contrary to its mission and mandate.

To help nonprofit organizations make sense of all of these .com options, there is an on-line resource—The Matrix—at www.hjc.on.ca/matrix. It is a compendium of ASPs for every not-for-profit to review, analyze, and use.

These application service providers are giving not-for-profit organizations wonderful abilities and opportunities for on-line fund raising. If managed properly, an organization should benefit from:

- Better capture, storage, and use of data
- Improvements in fund-raising service
- Improved fund-raising consistency
- Improved fund-raising flexibility
- Getting ahead of competition
- Savings on nonlabor and labor costs
- Greater efficiencies

However, if the .com relationship is not properly managed, a not-for-profit organization may experience:

- Disintermediation—.coms cutting not-for-profits out of their traditional stewardship role in philanthropy
- A growing distance between the donor and the not-for-profit organization
- Estrangement of volunteers and staff
- Loss of human touch in philanthropy
- Falling behind the competition
- Overallocation of financial and human resources
- Bad publicity

25.8 On-line Marketing

Many not-for-profit organizations have built on-line fund-raising forms and are beginning to accept on-line donations. However, many have forgotten to create on-line marketing *plans* that drive prospective donors to their giving forms. What follows is an on-line marketing template for any organization to adopt.

Any on-line marketing strategies should do three vital things:

1. *Protect your brand.* The banner strategies outlined below are designed on banner strategies proven to strengthen brand awareness. In addition, nonbanner strategies will ensure that you understand who is linked to you and whether any hypertext links affect the public's perception of your organization.
2. *Increase traffic to the giving sections of your Web site.* Thereby they will increase the number of dollars raised on-line.
3. *Plan, test, and track results.* Staff needs to understand how to create on-line marketing plans that can be executed every few months. Once staff understands where likeminded people exist on-line, future on-line fund-raising marketing plans can be conducted more quickly and more cheaply.

There are four main areas for on-line marketing:

1. *E-advocacy.* Not-for-profit organizations should test the efficacy of paid and volunteer e-advocates. E-advocates use a script and sit in front of connected computers, advocating for a particular raise directly, in chat rooms & newsgroups.
2. *E-wire service: reaching opinion leaders on-line.* Information gatekeepers, like Eric Ward—a premier on-line consultant in announcing Web sites through the use of his URL wire service. The use of e-wire services will help announce the new on-line campaigns.
3. *Banners—paid and pro bono.* A wide variety of high-volume sites, such as juno.com and doubleclick.com, can put up banners to drive fund-raising traffic to an organization.
4. *Niche broker advertising.* A new phenonmenon in U.S. on-line marketing services consists of service companies that handle the on-line environments of hundreds of Web sites that have a particular theme or content approach, such as campuspipeline.com and mybytes.com. These sites broker Web sites that can focus on just university or college environments. There are many other niche and broad broker advertisers.

25.9   *An Internet Fund-raising Test Guide*

The Internet and fund raising are a very new partnership. In other areas of direct response fund raising, a long list of studies, books, practitioner results, and publications provide a liturgy for direct response fund raising (especially direct mail). In deciding what to test on-line, it is very important to set a goal. Whatever the on-line test is, it should be designed to do one of the following:

- Simply acquire that first on-line gift
- Increase the on-line response rate
- Increase the on-line average gift

If the test is not expected to do one of these three things, it really is not worth testing, particularly since testing will almost always, in the short run, add to the human resource and programming costs of on-line fund raising. Of course, if the winning on-line fund-raising strategy is less expensive overall, it is worth it. It is also important to remember that many on-line fund-raising endeavors are loss leaders at the present, so organizations should use testing to find ways to reduce the return on investment in on-line fund raising (especially in prospecting for on-line donors).

Some general guidelines and rules for on-line fund-raising testing follow. (Many of these may seem familiar. That is because the basic rules for testing on-line do not differ significantly from the basic rules for direct mail testing. The more things change, the more they stay the same.

- In general, test only one thing at a time—unless you have experience with testing or a file large enough to support multiple test Web pages. This is doubly important on-line because the ease of on-line publishing can lead to testitis, too many tests at once. Succumbing to the urge may actually invalidate all the results.

- Launch test Web areas or elements within the same day—or even hours. Conditions in the world change rapidly, and things move even more rapidly on-line. The news that a devastating earthquake in Mexico City has just occurred may be read on-line almost immediately by millions—and they might click immediately to a fund-raising area. Even a one-hour difference could ruin a test. Launch test areas and elements simultaneously.
- House test areas and elements on servers that have the same capabilities. If one test page takes longer to download because it sits on a less capable computer, that could ruin a test. Studies from Sun Microsystems indicate that for every 10 seconds it takes for a Web page to download, 10 percent of visitors are lost. Imagine how this could destroy an on-line test.
- If an e-mail solicitation is sent out, send it to the same lists (or segments of the e-house file) and split the lists on an nth (random sample) selection. In other words, a test in which half the mailing goes to addresses at aol.com and the other half goes to random ISP providers is not a valid test. Splitting the file A–M and N–Z is not random either.
- Conduct e-mail solicitation tests in sufficient quantities for valid results.
- After test results are in, test the same thing once again to validate the findings.

Because the Internet is a new fund-raising medium, not-for-profit organizations need to understand the basics of direct response fund raising on-line. Following on the idea that direct mail fund raising has much to teach us on-line, try to test the following:

- *Personalization.* Not-for-profit organizations are beginning to build personalization into their fund-raising Web sites. Visit an example at www.alumni .utoronto.ca. The University of Toronto allows an alumna to personalize her own alumni Web page. Does this cookie-driven personalization improve the relationship with a supporter and improve fund raising? Conduct a test. Offer half of the on-line supporters the chance to personalize their experience with the organization's Web site. Do not give the other half the same personalized experience and instead give them a more static experience. Now let them interact with the Web site and, after a set period of time, send each group an e-mail solicitation and see which group gives more money to your organization.
- *Premiums.* Upfront premiums in direct mail can improve lapsed renewal rates, acquisition response rates, and relationships with past supporters. On the Web site, test the efficacy of on-line premiums directly related to computers, such as screensavers, software, hardware, mousepads, and a mouse.
- *Calendar.* Mal Warwick, a seasoned direct response fund raiser, often mentions that the annual cycle is an ecological human constant that should not be ignored in any fund-raising endeavor—no matter the technology. This needs to be tested in the on-line environment. An e-mail solicitation cycle should be created that follows the traditional times of the year solicitation is sent (whether is a special appeal, annual renewal, or reminder); this cycle should be tested against a cycle that is more personalized—allowing each on-line donor to choose when he or she receives an on-line solicitation. After a year, the results should be analyzed carefully.
- *The little things.* Excellent direct response fund raisers often outline how the small things (like type face and teaser copy) should be tested in direct mail fund raising. The same should be done on-line. Try to test factors like:

- Does a flashing GIVE icon on the home page draw more traffic to the giving area and improve on-line giving results?
- What kind of storytelling improves results on-line—something interactive, like a quick survey, or something multimedia, like audio or video? Test different storytelling leading to the on-line reply form.
- What graphics, colors, font sizes, and font types improve on-line fund-raising results?
- Can an e-mail follow-up after an on-line gift is made improve the future giving pattern for an on-line donor?

25.10   Conclusion

This is a time of incredible pressure for not-for-profit organizations. They are being asked to do more in an increasingly competitive environment. And the Internet is a part of that incredible pressure. Not-for-profit fund raisers are being asked to master a new medium as quickly as possible. Luckily for every fund raiser, there have been some important trends in the last two years that can make on-line fund raising more successful:

- E-mail fund raising
- The use of application service providers
- Rigor in planning, testing, and tracking results
- More sophisticated on-line marketing plans

New technologies (especially the Internet) are reaching important saturation levels of use in a very short time. Not-for-profit organizations are scrambling to use these new technologies, often with the help of governments and business, without fully understanding the impact they will have on their organizations—and on the communities they serve.

At the beginning of this chapter, I made reference to the town of Ibieca and its adoption of running water. This story could be the parable for the not-for-profit fund raising.

The not-for-profit fund-raising community at the start of the twenty-first century needs to create a tradition of asking hard questions about the efficacy of new fund-raising technologies on the sector. These new technologies (especially e-mail fund raising, online marketing, and the rise of ASPs) hold incredible potential, but adopting them without proper planning, testing, and rigorous analysis means using new technologies without understanding their impact on each not-for-profit and on the communities we serve.

New Media and Direct-Response Fund Raising

JASON POTTS, BA

26.1 Introduction

The term "new media" is a cover-all term that describes different data storage and transfer devices—the World Wide Web, e-mail, computer diskettes, DVDs, interactive television, touch-screen kiosks, and CD-ROMs. New media is playing an increasing part in direct-response fund-raising initiatives around the world. It is also making an increasing claim to be added to fund raisers' armory of responsive media in its own right. Whether it is a diskette in a mail pack, a CD-ROM linking a specific target audience to a Web site, or a secure credit card donation facility promoted through a Web address on a direct-response television (DRTV) advertisement, new media are rapidly becoming credible responsive media (inquiries and donations) for fund raisers worldwide.

This chapter has been adapted from Michael Johnston, ed., *Direct-Response Fund-Raising* (New York: John Wiley & Sons, 2000).

The increasing availability of Web-ready devices, big investment from leading commercial brands, and the transformation of certain types of business through e-commerce are just some of the factors contributing to massive worldwide on-line audience growth. Unlike existing direct-response media, many of the rules are yet to be established, let alone tested. Yet the opportunities for fund raisers are increasingly clear. This chapter looks at these opportunities and how some organizations around the world are beginning to take advantage of them. It is divided into five key areas:

1. New media—setting the scene for fund raisers
2. Applying the tried and tested techniques of direct response to new media
3. Integrating new media components into existing initiatives
4. The impact of new media technologies on recruitment and supporter communications
5. A look at how new media technologies could develop over the next few years, with the possible impacts on not-for-profits

The fast-changing nature of new media means that anything printed on this subject has the danger of being out of date before the ink has had time to dry on the page. With this in mind, this chapter looks at general trends rather than specifics, with some indicative not-for-profit examples.

(A) WHAT ARE NEW MEDIA?

First, let's take a step back. "New media" is a cover-all term, which at its most basic level describes different data storage and transfer devices, as specified. The various devices are grouped together because they are comparatively new (most of the terms would have been unfamiliar to many a year or so ago) and because they all use the same basic language: digital. Because digital information can be transferred effortlessly through existing communications networks (satellite, cable, or the telephone) and can be viewed easily on differing output devices (TV, personal computer, a hybrid, mobile phone, or wristwatch), the convergence of new media is potentially the biggest advance in communications technology since movable type.

When one talks about new media and direct-response fund raising today, one is talking mainly about the Web and e-mail. But that's not the new media of the future. The rapid convergence of this technology with existing networks—TV, telephone, and global intranets—means that the global information infrastructure, much vaunted in the writings of U.S. Vice President Al Gore, is becoming an increasing reality. What is called the Internet today will be a far more widely accessed global information channel in the not-too-distant future.

For fund raisers, digital media offer new channels of communication with key audiences: prospects, supporters, partners, beneficiaries, or sponsors. These communication channels allow audience(s) to interact and respond as they choose and allows tracking in enough detail to treat them as individuals.

Clearly, the new media's ability to individualize fund raising should be of interest to fund-raising practitioners worldwide, particularly as the cost of entry to some of these technologies is often not great. (For example, I've included the costs and capabilities for a screensaver for a not-for-profit organization at the end of this chapter.) Also, the Web offers a level playing field in terms of audience reach to both big corporate brands and small nonprofits. In many cases creativity and ingenuity can go a long way toward maximizing a modest budget. (See Exhibit 26.1 and visit Greenpeace UK's Web site at www.greenpeace.org.uk. The area of the site focusing on genetically modified food includes interactive games and competitions that are engaging, exciting, and not expensive.)

(B) SETTING THE SCENE

Tracking the growth of new media worldwide is far from an exact science, and a great deal of hyperbole has preceded actual fact. Audience figures vary from survey to survey, but the general consensus is one of massive growth in a very short space of time, growth that at the moment is showing no signs of slowing down. Quite the opposite, in fact.

EXHIBIT 26.1 Greenpeace Web Site/Interactive Games

Source: Used with permission from Greenpeace UK.

Figures for usage and user demographics are changing as quickly as new media grow, diversify, and converge. According to Anne Leer of Financial Times Management in *Masters of the Wired World:*[1]

- In five years the number of computers connected to the Internet has grown from 1.3 million to 37 million
- Traffic on the Web doubles every 100 days
- Content grows at a rate of 1.5 million pages per day and its size doubles every eight months

The ability to visit the Web on a TV set will undoubtedly add to this remarkable growth. TV penetration worldwide is far greater than PC penetration, and the cost of using an existing TV compared to investing in a Web-ready PC allows lower-income households access. Interactive TV is just beginning to deliver statistically meaningful audiences, as a percentage of the overall population, in the more developed economies. According to www.datamonitor.com, there will be an estimated 67 million interactive households across the United States and Europe by the year 2003, up from 10.3 million in 1998.

The Internet first developed within a particular demographic slice: young educated males, in a particular geographic location, the United States and Canada. Large worldwide growth, the increasing ease of access (there are around 3,000 Internet service providers in Europe alone), support infrastructures (24-hour help lines), and the commercialization of the Web for e-business (.coms continue to capitalize on the stock markets at incredible levels, although those without sound business models are finding that the investment money is increasingly drying up) have meant that all existing profiles are rapidly flattening. Trends for the millennium indicate:

- The rest of the world is catching up to the United States and Canada as the major user base.
- Women are set to overtake men as the most represented gender.
- People over 50 are the fastest-growing audience (according to www.nua.com), and they are using new media. Dan Goldhar, the general manager of Fifty Plus Net (www.fifty-plus.net), a nonprofit organization that provides Internet community services to individuals over 50, presents some intriguing information about over-50 Net users.
- WebTV is the number-one access point for his 5,000 plus visitors. Over 50 percent of visitors get access that way, and the number is growing for over-50 users.
- There are two distant groups of seniors on-line. The first have low-end computers, often old machines given to them by kids or grandkids. The second group has jumped right over the computer and gotten on-line with WebTV.

A broad look at the on-line audience shows that the main users of the Web, e-mail, and digital TV are no longer college students and academics but instead businesses and individuals who fit more with existing not-for-profit supporter databases. The audience also consists of new younger people that not-for-profits traditionally have had difficulty reaching through more conventional communications channels.

---

[1] Anne Leer, Masters of the Wired World (New York: Prentice Hall Publishing, 1999).

26.2 New Media and the Techniques of Direct Response

Now that the scene has been set, let us begin by looking at how tried and tested techniques of direct response can be used to get results through new media. Simply putting a mail pack on-line or digitizing a TV ad and waiting for the donations to come flooding in has proved a frustrating experience for many nonprofit organizations.

By studying the lessons learned from years of direct mail and direct-response TV in the sector, by doing as much testing as possible, and by sticking to their off-line brand values, Amnesty International UK (www.amnesty.org.uk) was able to make a success of its fund-raising site.

(A) CASE STUDY—AMNESTY INTERNATIONAL UK

The objective for the site was to learn as much as possible about fund raising on-line and at the same time recruit supporters at a profit. When entering the support area of the site from the home page, the visitor was given one of three randomly generated appeals. These test both creative and technological sophistication. Creatively:

- Appeal 1 (see Exhibit 26.2) tells a good news story of an individual released from prison because of the letters received by Amnesty supporters worldwide.

EXHIBIT 26.2 Amnesty International Letters

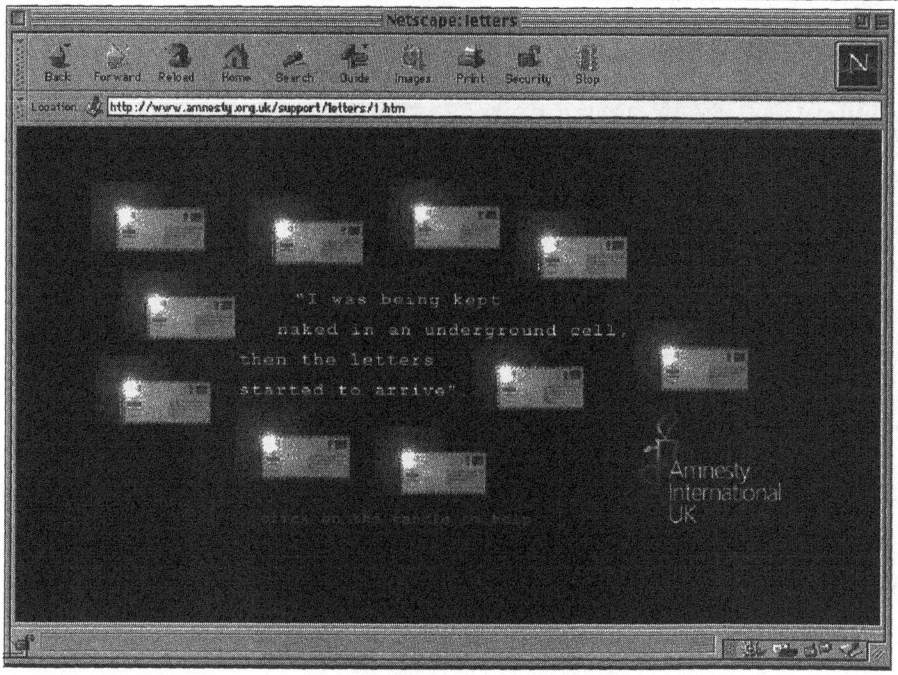

Source: Used with permission from Amnesty International UK.

- Appeal 2 (see Exhibit 26.3) invites the visitor to click on a series of yes/no boxes to answer questions (it might be compared to a questionnaire mailing) such as: Have you ever read a book? or Would you defend your family?
- Appeal 3 (see Exhibit 26.4) is very hard hitting and uses animation and sound to bring to life the story of Maria, imprisoned and brutally tortured by an oppressive regime

As in all good fund raising, these were real stories about real people. And the way to give was made very simple; on two of the screens the phrase "click the candle (the Amnesty logo) to help" was prominent.

The appeals also tested Web technology. At one end of the scale the appeals were simple HTML pages; at the other end, they were complicated JavaScript animation with accompanying sound files. So as not to disappoint prospective donors, the site sensed what type of browser each visitor had and served up only that appeal that the browser could view. (I will explain more about this later.)

With such a new medium, it was necessary to test as much as possible to lay the groundwork for what works and what does not for future on-line activities. And so,

---

EXHIBIT 26.3 Amnesty International Question Box

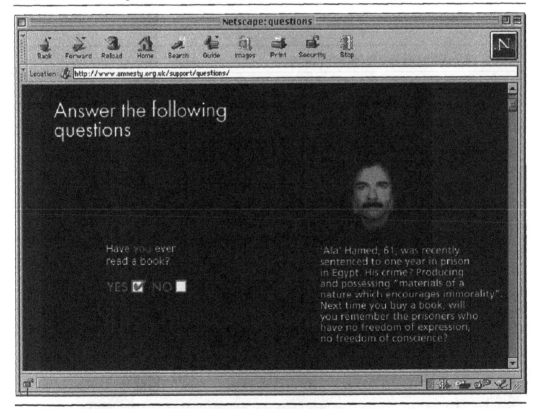

Source: Used with permission from Amnesty International UK.

EXHIBIT 26.4 Amnesty International Maria Story

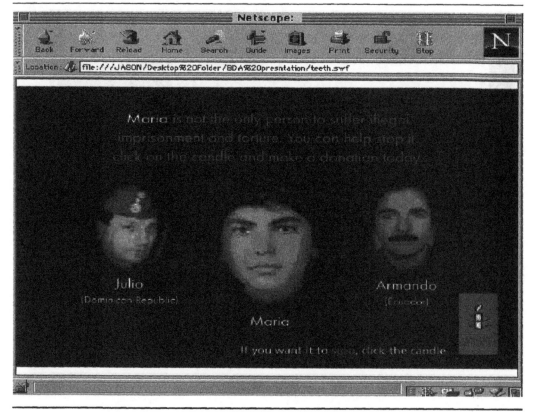

Source: Used with permission from Amnesty International UK.

membership was tested against one-time donations, and two different reply forms were created and were served up randomly from each appeal. (See Exhibits 26.5a and 26.5b.) This area of the site also featured a questionnaire to capture more qualitative data about site visitors.

After six months the site produced a return on investment of 1 to 1.8. This favorable quick return on investment is set against a backdrop of the vast majority of organizations in the United Kingdom, which are unable to make such recruitment through other forms of advertising cost effective. In addition, the costs of recruiting a new supporter through cold mail can cost anywhere between £3 to £10. A total number of 846 new members recruited shows that the medium has become a viable alternative to conventional channels. The total number of donations (regular, ad hoc, or with membership subscription) was 101. In addition, over 600 questionnaires were returned.

Perhaps not surprisingly, membership worked better than one-time donations. Amnesty is, after all, a membership organization. Appeal 2, the interactive one, and the multimedia appeal (3) outperformed the more static appeal (1).

EXHIBIT 26.5A Amnesty International UK Membership Form

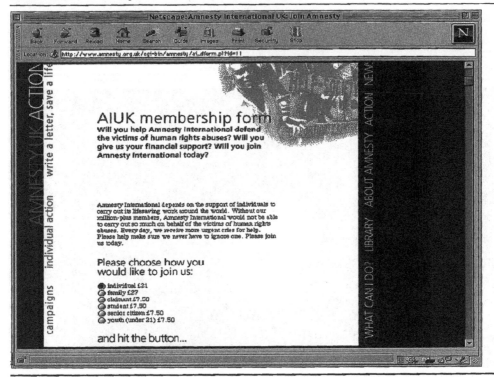

Source: Used with permission from Amnesty International UK.

26.3   Adding New Media to the Mix

Integrating new media into a fund raising campaign can open up new audiences and facilitate responses that might otherwise have gotten away. What follows are several examples of not-for-profits that are already adding new media elements to their fund-raising campaigns.

(A)   CASE STUDY—PRESS ADVERTISING

The aim of the Greenpeace U.K.—True Food Campaign was to publicize Greenpeace's call to ban genetically modified foods and promote organically grown alternatives. The campaign saw Greenpeace UK adding a Web site (see Exhibit 26.6) and e-mail communications program to a national press campaign (see Exhibit 26.7). Time was very much of the essence to make the most of the surrounding news media coverage about genetically modified foods. The direct-response media chosen needed to be enabled rapidly. The day after the issue became front-page news in most U.K. broadsheets, the press advertisements appeared and the Web site was launched.

EXHIBIT 26.5B Amnesty International UK Donation Form

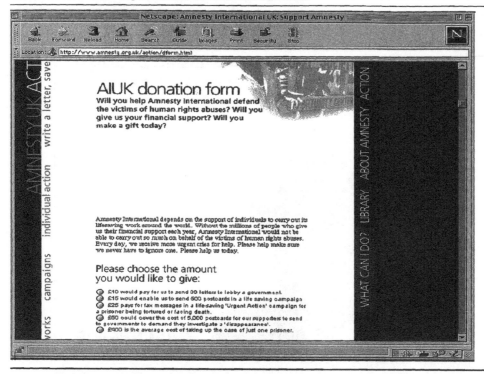

Source: Used with permission from Amnesty International UK.

The press advertisements allowed respondents to request more information through the mail or directed those with Internet access to a Web site that was regularly updated with new campaign developments. The site was created specifically for this activity and taken off-line afterward. Once on-line, visitors were able to make a donation or request more information about the issues via post or e-mail. Not surprisingly, most opted for e-mail.

The press activity stimulated traffic on the Web site while offering site visitors an e-mail communication option stimulated response. From a standing start, as the site had no existing traffic, 600 new names with e-mail addresses were generated.

The direct mail pack sent to 100,000 Greenpeace members generated £75,000, and the entire activity including phone, Web, and press inserts generated 8,000 requests for more information. With such a fast-moving campaign, Greenpeace learned that the more flexible response mechanisms of e-mail and telemarketing were far more effective than traditional supporter communications channels.

(B) CASE STUDY—DRTV

Comic Relief's Red Nose Day 1999 was called the "record breaker," in the fund-raising sense. The eight-hour live telethon on national TV offered great exposure to a large audi-

EXHIBIT 26.6 Greenpeace UK True Food Campaign Web Site

Tony has swallowed the false promises of US chemical companies like Monsanto. He believes:

"...If GM foods were properly tested and approved it could mean products being healthier, tastier and cheaper."

There is already a food production technology involving groundbreaking science which is experiencing unprecedented levels of demand and could deliver all these benefits and more – without the risks. It's called organic farming. It works with nature not against it.

Greenpeace is campaigning to ban genetically engineered foods and transform food production to make organic available to everyone.

for more info   to make a donation

Source: Used with permission from Greenpeace UK.

ence. The Web site address, www.rednoseday.org.uk and www.rednoseday.beeb.com, was repeated at regular intervals during the TV show. (See Exhibit 26.8.) To attract a global audience, the show was Webcast live. The site opened up a new fund-raising route for Comic Relief, and approximately 2 percent of all donations were made via the Web on the night of the appeal. Almost 14,000 donations came in from all over the world; 13,508 donations were in British sterling; 83 in U.S. dollars; 11 in Australian dollars; nine in Canadian dollars; 134 in euros; and 107 in Irish punts.

Overall, 5 million "click-throughs," or page impressions, were served with nearly 700,000 visits over a seven-week period. The sites generated nearly 9,000 extra e-mail addresses.

One of the biggest challenges for not-for-profits using new media will be their e-mail solicitations. This little-understood area needs further experimentation.

26.4 New Media as a Stand-alone Direct-Response Tool

Fund raisers around the world such as Amnesty International are also finding that digital media can be used as a relatively low-cost recruitment and retention medium in its

EXHIBIT 26.7 Greenpeace Press Campaign "Leave It Out Tony!"

Genetically engineered foods are, well, look, you know, kind of terrific, aren't they?

Leave it out Tony!

To find out more about the genetic food fiasco and what the alternatives are, call free on 0800 269 065 or visit www.greenpeace.org.uk/truefood

GREENPEACE

Source: Used with permission from Greenpeace UK.

own right. Recruitment is all about attracting as many people as possible to a Web site and converting them into donors or members, or at least collecting e-mail addresses for future communications.

Several organizations have found that once visitors have been attracted to a site, allowing them to join e-mail mailing lists or enter member-only areas are good ways of strengthening their commitment to a cause.

EXHIBIT 26.8 Comic Relief/Red Nose Day

Source: Used with permission from Comic Relief.

(A) SEARCH ENGINES/ON-LINE PUBLIC RELATIONS

With 70 percent of Web visitors beginning on-line sessions by visiting a search engine, the art of positioning a site prominently on these listings is worth investment. Few other direct-response media provide such low-cost access to such a vast global audience. Key words and phrases to describe an organization and its work need to be chosen carefully. Finding an individual or company to do the registration and meta-tags (ways of submitting key words to search engines to ensure a high ranking) also should be done very carefully. Organizations serious about their on-line presence should not allow well-meaning amateurs to do these jobs.

Check the organization's positioning on search engine listings, as it will change. Listings can be checked by visiting www.rankthis.com. Interestingly, the word "environment" on Yahoo! does not list Greenpeace in the top 200. It is also important to note that time lines vary with each search engine. However, allow approximately six weeks for an organization's listing on a search engine to appear.

Many larger organizations suffer from too many site listings, either from regional or country offices or from well-meaning supporters putting up a site in the belief they are doing the organization in question a good turn. For example, searching for the Red Cross on Lycos, a typical search engine, produces over 88,000 listings, the first of which mentions Elizabeth Dole leaving the Red Cross. No disrespect to Mrs. Dole, but this is perhaps not the best way to introduce a potential supporter to a global organization. This problem is certainly not unusual. Clearly it is every bit as important to protect a brand image on-line as in off-line direct response materials. Providing prospects with the easiest path possible to finding and joining an organization on-line is crucial.

Other low-cost promotional opportunities exist through on-line public relations, organizing reciprocal links with high-traffic sites, getting links on listings and What's Hot sites, and also informing likely news groups. Links can generate enormous traffic. Greenpeace International currently has over 28,500 sites linked to www.greenpeace.org, and, not surprisingly, it is one of the most visited sites in the not-for-profit sector.

To find out who is linked to a site, visit www.altavista.com and type link: followed by the Web address (i.e., link: www.greenpeace.org). This will return a list of all sites linked to a site. Viewers may well be surprised.

(B) BANNER ADVERTISING

Banner advertising can be described most simply as a link on a third-party site that is designed to grab visitors' attention and take them to another site. As with all direct-response media, the key is to place a banner advertisement on a site that has a large percentage of the target market as regular visitors (at the right price). Click-through rates from banners are usually reckoned to be between 0.2 to 5 percent. The percentage of people who will then request more information or donate is no more than 5 to 10 percent.

From these statistics, it is plain to see that banner advertising, like most marketing, is very much a numbers game. The good news for not-for-profits looking to get people to their Web site is that the cost of banner advertising is not prohibitive. For most high-traffic sites a cost of £25 to £30 per 1,000 views is not uncommon. Testing is very economical because many high-traffic sites will allow potential users to pay for several thousand views to get an idea of how the banners are performing and what revenue or inquiries are being generated. Based on results, it is possible to revise the banner, concentrate further views on the most successful areas of the site, change the ask, or look for another host site with a different audience profile.

For forward-thinking fund raisers, opportunities exist to negotiate good banner deals with high-traffic sites or by putting banners on existing corporate sponsors' sites. Many blue-chip companies have many site visitors and probably a global intranet. Having a banner on the intranet, which can link to the Web, of a large global corporate presents enormous opportunity for interoffice competitive fund-raising challenges. It is also a low-cost way to keep donors informed of how much they have raised and how this money has been put to good use.

26.5 *Making Effective Banners*

Studies conducted by Milward Brown Interactive in 1999 found the following five facts about banners that are directly applicable to any nonprofit organization:

1. Multimedia banners are more likely to be noticed by visitors than standard, static GIF banners.
2. Multimedia banners increased customers' positive perception of a branded product over static GIF banners.
3. Click-through rates increased from 50 to 400 percent with multimedia banners.
4. Multimedia banners had a positive impact on those consumers who were ready to buy right away (as well as those who were not ready to buy at that moment but could be influenced positively for a possible future purchase).
5. Brand recall was improved with multimedia banners over static banners.

The multimedia banners were built using FLASH and JAVA script animation software tools. Nonprofit organizations should pay only $150 to $200 for an animated banner. Yehoshua Bendah, a programmer and Internet consultant for Hewitt and Johnston Consultants, offers the following advice for creating effective banners:

- Make it interesting enough so that there is some *mystery* in it, so people will be attracted to read them, and click.
- If possible, use at least three shifts (panels), if it can remain small enough in size—for all intents and purposes you can build a few teasers one on top of one another leading to the demand for an action.
- Organizations should tantalize the reader into clicking on the banner to "find something out" or make a difference.
- As commercial banner advertising becomes increasingly ineffective, not-for-profits are advised to clearly identify their charitable brand as well as provide a compelling call to action.

(A) A BANNER CASE STUDY

Besides targeting banners by host site visitor profile, most search engines will also allow banners triggered by the search for key words. For example, animal charities might want a banner to appear when someone searches for the words "cat" or "dog."

Recently the National Abortion Rights Action League (NARAL) tested banner ads with juno.com. (Juno provides Internet services for over 7 million Americans.) When a prospective supporter clicked on the NARAL banner, a survey popped up. NARAL was out to build an on-line database of activists. Another organization might have had a click take someone to a donation page. In their case, NARAL got the following results:

- It was able to select 130,000 Juno members who fit a favorable demographic for NARAL.
- Those 130,000 members saw a NARAL banner that asked them to get involved in abortion rights.
- When they clicked on the banner, up popped a survey.
- Twenty-five thousand of these individuals actually filled out the survey that popped up after the banner was clicked.
- Of these, 15,000 gave home and e-mail addresses.
- These 15,000 were e-mailed and asked to take an action (e.g., send an e-mail).
- Of these 15,000, 3,000 took an action on-line or made a donation.

In a very short time, NARAL built a database of 15,000 prospective supporters. This banner case study should remind every not-for-profit organization that banner ads can help it think big: imagine finding 15,000 new supporters in a week—or even one day. The new media have accelerated a not-for-profit's time line to build a database of like-minded people.

(B) WHAT TO DO AFTER GETTING THE E-MAIL ADDRESSES

Moveon.org is a political reform organization that began as a grass-roots movement to force U.S. federal politicians to leave the Clinton sex scandal behind and get on to an agenda focused on issues. Their site, at www.moveon.org, collected 500,000 on-line signatures and received 25,000 on-line pledges, all of it to get Congress and the Senate to move on from impeachment.

Moveon.org decided not to approach these pledgers to actually give a gift. After about a six-month delay, the organization sent out 16,000 e-mails. Recipients of the e-mail could visit a site that showed the politicians who backed Clinton's impeachment process, and they could make an immediate on-line gift. The organization made $250,000 in just five days on-line. The average gift was $10, and 92 percent of gifts were under $50. While this example shows that organizations can wait to e-mail prospective supporters, Yahoo! has found that almost 50 percent of e-mail addresses change in one year, so do not wait too long.

The Environmental Defense Fund collected 125,000 e-mail addresses for its action-focused e-mail newsletter. It got 50,000 e-mail addresses from a juno.com promotion (similar to NARAL), then sent an e-mail newsletter every three weeks to on-line newsletter subscribers. Of the 125,000 people asked for money, 0.3 percent responded to e-mail by going to the on-line giving form, and 75 percent of those individuals gave on-line.[2]

(i) NSPCC Virtual Collecting Tin

As part of the Full Stop initiative, a campaign launched in 1999 to end child abuse forever, the NSPCC (National Society for the Prevention of Cruelty to Children) developed an on-line icon, the Virtual Collecting Tin (VCT). This allowed corporate sponsors to visit a Web address (www.nspcc.org.uk/vct/hosts) (see Exhibit 26.9) and pick up a banner to put on their site. The campaign was to continue over the course of 1999 and 2000, so it was important to make the process of putting the banner on a host site as simple and automated as possible.

Prospective hosts were approached through the NSPCC's existing corporate supporters, and an on-line public relations campaign was mounted to approach various selected high-traffic sites.

True to conventional direct-response logic, various aspects of the campaign were tested. Three different types of banners (see Exhibits 26.10, 26.11, 26.12) were produced with different creative approaches. Three different appeals were created to present to the visitors once they had clicked through to the NSPCC site. The data from these tests were

---

[2]All of the above banner and e-mail results come from Nick Allen's presentation at the DMA Conference in Toronto, November 1999.

EXHIBIT 26.9 NSPCC Virtual Collecting Tin

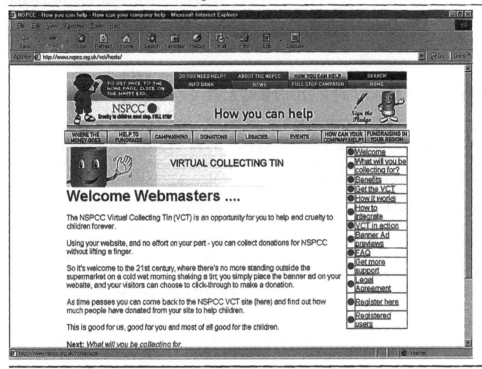

Source: Used with permission from NSPCC.

automatically logged and fed into a database that had an on-line password-protected viewing area.

The NSPCC site was populated with the image of the Virtual Collecting Tin. (See Exhibit 26.13). Various categories of visitor were identified and given appropriate content based on what the site knew about them. For example, those who had already made a donation were not given an appeal again when they clicked on the VCT but were taken straight through to the donation option page. Because of some nervousness in Europe about on-line secure credit card transactions, visitors were given the option of secure credit card or print, post, or fax donations.

The early results show that from the big-traffic sites, many people can be directed to the NSPCC's site and encouraged to get involved with the campaign. So far, the VCT has over 70 host sites, 10,725 people have clicked through to the NSPCC donation area, 125 on-line donations have been made, 244 print and mail donation forms have been requested, and 477 requests for more information have been logged.

26.6   Other Media

(A)   ON-LINE EMERGENCY APPEALS

The urgent nature of the Web as a communications medium is giving fund raisers around the world involved with disaster relief organizations a new channel through

EXHIBIT 26.10 NSPCC VCT "Don't Close Your Eyes to Child Abuse"

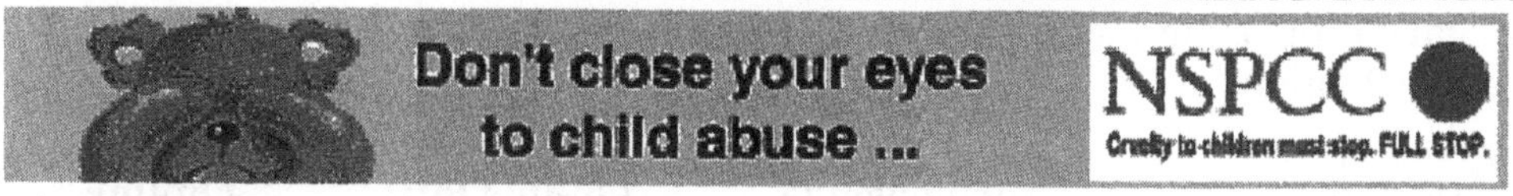

Source: Used with permission from NSPCC.

EXHIBIT 26.11 NSPCC VCT "Cruelty to Children Must Stop. Full Stop."

Source: Used with permission from NSPCC.

EXHIBIT 26.12 NSPCC VCT "It's 'Virtually' Here . . ."

Source: Used with permission from NSPCC.

EXHIBIT 26.13 NSPCC VCT "Click Here to Make a Donation"

CLICK HERE TO
MAKE A DONATION.

Source: Used with permission from NSPCC.

which to instantly communicate their needs to potential and existing supporters. The crisis in Kosovo set the on-line cash registers ringing on both sides of the Atlantic. In the United States on-line fund raising makes up a significant percentage of monies raised in emergency situations.

Organization	Total revenue	On-line total	On-line %
Oxfam America	$ 300,000	$ 43,000	14 %
Save the Children	$ 125,000	$ 40,000	32 %
American Red Cross	$6,100,000	$545,000	8.9 %

The American Red Cross, perhaps the most successful on-line fund-raising organization in the world, is reported to have raised over $9 million in Web donations in 1999. Along with larger and larger gift totals for emergency appeals, organizations are building larger e-mail databases. The American Red Cross built a database of over 15,000 individuals during the Kosovo crisis. The fund-raising potential of this e-mail database is exciting.

In the United Kingdom, the Charities Aid Foundation received over £30,000 in less than a month in on-line donations through its CharityCard Web site (www.charity-card.org) in support of Kosovan refugees. This took the total donated through the site since its launch just one year earlier to £170,000.

(B) CD-ROMS

CD-ROMs are a good way to target a specific audience and provide them with lots of high-quality, multimedia information. They also can be used to link audiences to an organization's Web site. The problem is that CD-ROMs often are prohibitively expensive to produce without a guaranteed return on investment. However, low-cost alternatives exist to producing a CD-ROM. One is putting material on other CDs that are already being distributed to likely target audiences. Amnesty International, Greenpeace, and Great Ormond Street Children's Hospital were all able to put information on a CD-ROM that goes to every final-year college and university student in the United Kingdom. The main function of the disk is to enable students to search through a large database of prospective employers. Among this career-matching facility are other offers and promotions.

The three charities put on some simple information and several pieces of video to appeal to this audience and make them aware of the work they do. The students were then able to link to the organizations' Web sites to find out more, join, or volunteer. This was inexpensive and in this case very well targeted. Linked to competitions or interactive content, this kind of activity can stimulate interest from younger age groups that are not traditionally known for their philanthropic nature.

(C) COLD E-MAIL

Cold e-mail, or "spamming," has created mixed results for not-for-profits. Organizations that have attempted large-scale mailings have run into severe problems. A European-based land mine charity had so many complaints after sending out an unsolicited e-mail that its service provider pulled the plug on its account. Oxfam in the United Kingdom began and then aborted e-mail recruitment tests due to adverse initial reactions.

A good example of what *not* to do comes from the Children's Hunger Fund, which bought 1 million e-mail names for $700 and sent 1 million e-mail messages out as part of a Kosovo appeal. It raised a measly $1,600 but received a pile of negative reactions, including warnings from two U.S. State attorneys general. An antispammer activist contacted the fund's Internet service provider to pressure it to not allow that kind of mass e-mail solicitation to be sent out again.

Organizations using more targeting are having more success. For example, the University of Maryland generated $100,000. The audience it mailed belonged to news groups that discussed the particular medical issues the university was asking readers to support. The equivalent of on-line member-get-member schemes have also proved popular. Tearfund (a U.K.-based development agency) invited supporters visiting the site to send e-mail postcards to their friends directing them to the site to pick up a message and find out more.

With 18 percent response levels currently being generated from unpersonalized e-mail in the commercial sector, according to Forrester, a marketing research company, not-for-profits should not give up but should wait for the right moment and the right targeted audience to come along.

26.7 Retention Methods

In addition to the straightforward recruitment of new supporters, new media also offer fund raisers the opportunity to build relationships with donors or supporters.

Ken Burnett, a fund-raising guru in the United Kingdom, emphasizes something called relationship fund raising.[3] Relationship fund raising preaches a donor-based focus to the business of fund raising. This donor focus holds true as much for this direct-response medium as any other. Indeed, the automated segmentation and data storage capacity of the backend technologies underpinning a database-driven site allow fund raisers to get closer than ever before to genuine two-way dialogues built on supporter choice.

The nature of digital communication allows the storage of a great deal of information that can be pulled into predesigned templates easily. Digital tools also allow site visitors to choose the information they require and customize and personalize their information. The next time they return to the site, digital tools (software and hardware) will remember their preferences and exhibit a personalized approach for them. (See Exhibit 26.14 a–g.)

Exhibit 26.14 shows how database technology differs from static HTML Web site production.

Effectively, all site visitors could have their own individual home page based on only the content in which they are interested. Knowing what it is that interests an individual about a cause is clearly very valuable knowledge for a fund raiser in terms of targeting future correspondence of all kinds and maximizing the impact of any ask.

---

[3]His books, *Friends for Life: Relationship Fundraising in Practice* (1996) and *Relationship Fundraising: A Donor-Based Approach to the Business of Raising Money* (1989) (London, UK: Whitelion Press).

EXHIBIT 26.14A–G Database-Driven Web Sites: The Theory

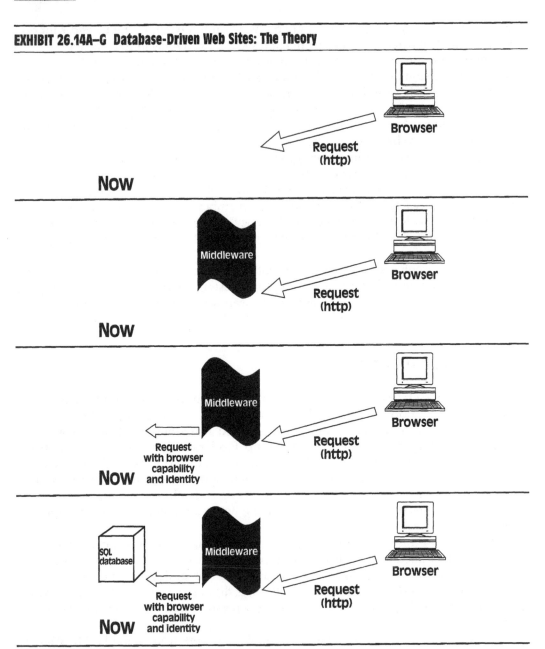

Source: Used with permission from Burnett & Associates.

Add to this push technology, where an e-mail can be generated automatically whenever a particular area of the site in which a supporter has shown an interest is updated, and it is easy to see how inexpensive relationships can be managed effectively and successfully.

The site of a U.K.-based development charity, Tearfund (see Exhibits 26.15 and 26.16) employs just such a database-driven system. It uses a product called Microsoft Site-

EXHIBIT 26.14A–G Continued

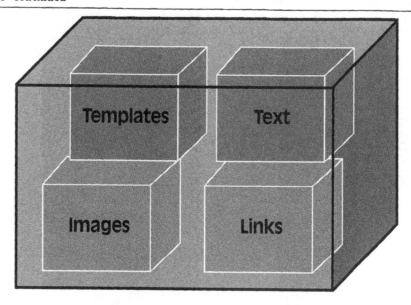

Now

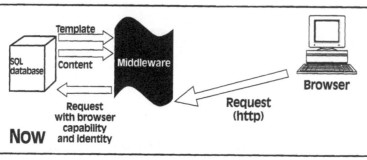

Now

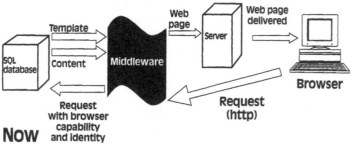

Now

EXHIBIT 26.15 Tearfund "Your Profile"

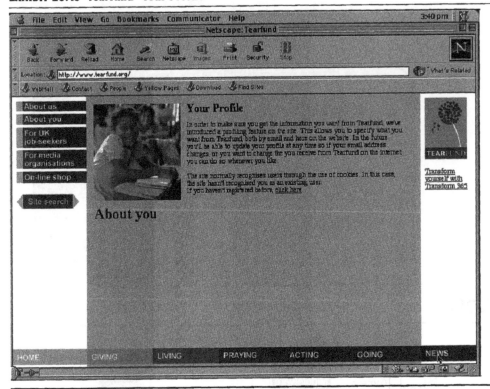

Source: Used with permission from Tearfund.

Server to enable some of the backend data tracking and e-mail list servers. On arriving at the home page, visitors are presented with a series of buttons that allow them to make choices about the content they wish to see. Tearfund works in many places all over the world, and visitors are allowed to select countries that interest them most. The site does this automatically by tracking viewers' behavior over time and then relegating areas of less interest to lower levels of navigation.

During the Kosovo crisis, the site raised over £14,000 in under two weeks by e-mailing 3,000 warm supporters, names that the site had collected over time. In keeping with other on-line giving trends, the fund received several healthy donations of £1,000 as part of that total. Tearfund was able to put up an appeal within a day and send out e-mails asking supporters to visit the site and make a donation.

Greenpeace Sweden employs a different model with its 3,000 on-line supporters. In the same way that regular giving schemes bring the supporter closer to the organization, Greenpeace Sweden uses its site and e-mail to give supporters access to all kinds of information and to regularly update them about news items affecting the organization's campaigns. It uses the immediacy of the medium to inform supporters that Greenpeace might be appearing on the news that evening and can present its side of the issue and offer background information.

EXHIBIT 26.16 Tearfund "Thanks for Registering"

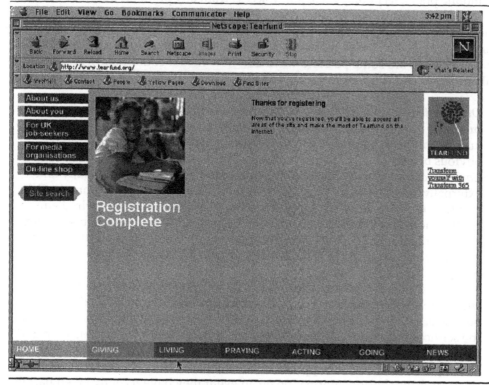

Source: Used with permission from Tearfund.

26.8   Conclusion: New Media and Direct Response Tomorrow

Some of the key ways that not-for-profits around the world are beginning to use new media as a direct-response medium have been outlined. Of course, there are many other ways: lotteries, auctions, treasure hunts, and on-line petitions, to name but a few.

Several factors are stimulating the environment of opportunity. Politicians and chief executives across the globe are investing time and, more important, money in making the digital future a reality. Major investments include equipping educational institutions and public facilities (i.e., libraries) as well as the home user market and local government initiatives to empower those groups that are traditionally information poor. Technological advances are creating further openings:

- Moore's Law dictates that computing power will double while its cost will halve over a 12- to 18-month period for the foreseeable future, most likely spelling an end to the user's wait many experience on the World Wide Web.
- Interactive TV in many homes will unlock a larger audience, with a demographic profile more representative of society as a whole.

559

- Low-level communication satellites and WAP (wireless application protocol) mobile phone technology will allow access from any point on the globe.

Increasingly it is not the technology, the audience, or the resources that are holding organizations back but the *imagination*. So, where could fund raisers go with a little imagination? Here are some possible ways that new media could help with both individual initiatives and supporter lifetime values:

- *Digital interactive TV.* The massive proliferation of channels will allow not-for-profits to provide programming, or "documercials." The ability of viewers to jump from this programming to a Web site to make an instant donation has obvious benefits.
- *Communications.* The ability to share digital information, both internally and externally. A new media office will draw information in digitally from the field and turn it into material for supporters and the general public by wired editors. Furthermore, it will be checked at a senior level and posted to a Web site within a matter of hours or perhaps minutes or sent as an e-mail report to those supporters who have given to that scheme or particular fund-raising initiative in the past.
- *Revolutionizing volunteering.* The new media will empower retired supporters, such as teachers or engineers, to communicate with an organization's partners or beneficiaries either locally or globally, to offer help and advice, improving both the services the organization offers and the bond between the organization and that supporter.
- *Creating on-line advocates.* Supporters will be able to communicate with each other, perhaps sharing information on an event they have recently taken part in, such as a bike ride or marathon. It is often at this grass-roots level that the best fund-raising case studies are found.
- *Education.* Curriculum-based on-line educational materials to familiarize a younger audience with a cause can be combined with school fund-raising initiatives or volunteering.
- *Twinning.* Facilitating fund-raising initiatives in one area for beneficiaries in another and using the technology to put donors directly in touch with the people or project they are supporting.
- *E-mail communications programs.* These include strategies for allowing donors access to as much or as little information about an organization as required, coupled with the use of push technologies to maximize the use of automated information distribution. This would allow an organization to concentrate on one-to-one communications for key relationship-building customer services issues.
- *The daily me.* This allows increasingly busy supporters to download key updates (top-line topical information) from a site to their desktops or handheld devices, where the information can read at their own convenience. Syndicating information through other content providers would give reach beyond existing on-line supporters.
- *Subscription services.* For those organizations that complete research or develop technology or information (publications) that has a commercial value, on-line subscription services provide an easy, low-cost distribution channel.

- *Portals.* A portal is a definitive site on a particular subject area. For example, an environmental organization might develop a single portal that would contain various content, services, and e-commerce around one environmental issue.
- *Selling third-party advertising.* This is a common aim for current high-traffic sites, but if the Internet makes the transition to a televisional broadcast medium, those on-line broadcasters with large or well-targeted audiences will be able to sell conventional TV commercials between their programming.
- *Supporter relationship management.* Using the flexibility and cost effectiveness of information products and delivery, combined with the ability to trade people at an individual level, to provide exceptional customer service.

This list should provide food for thought for future planning. Clearly future-gazing has no guarantees, but many of these suggestions seem logical developments of increased digital communications channels.

In conclusion, new media applications are today beginning to produce results for fund raisers worldwide. The way the new media are growing and are set to develop should offer further encouragement. But competition for audience is fierce, and consumer expectations from both a content and a customer service perspective are high. Failure to investigate these new fund-raising channels and to explore the low-cost supporter communications opportunities the new media provide would be a big mistake for not-for-profits.

APPENDIX 26A: *Low Cost of Staying Top of Mind through a Screensaver*

A screensaver can be a very effective, low-cost piece of new media for a not-for-profit organization. A wide range of such organizations have created screensavers that can be downloaded from a Web site and/or can be sent on a diskette to a supporter.

A screensaver can use graphics, animation, and sound to communicate a mission and mandate through new media. For fund raisers, giving messages in screensavers would be ideal.

What follows are some standard points in creating a screensaver. Creating one with the listed functionality should cost approximately $2,500. Imagine spending $2,500 and having thousands of supporters putting your screensaver on their computers. Every time their computers are inactive, the message will be scrolling across their screens. Now, that's top of mind!

A new media nonprofit screensaver should include:

- PC and Mac versions of screensaver up to approximately 4 MB
- Compatibility: Windows 3.1, 95, 98, NT
- The not-for-profit should send the supplier with raw images in digital format (pict, PCX, PhotoShop, GID, JPG, whatever) at highest possible resolution.
- Not-for-profit corporate logos or images for the icon and control panel should be included as well as copyright notice and/or disclaimers.
- The supplier should reproduce as closely as possible the look and feel of the not-for-profit organization's brand.

- The supplier should work with the not-for-profit to provide additional creative/ conceptual value to the screensaver. It should not be a static new media product. It needs to make supporters sit up and notice what is on their screen. It should be pleasing to look at. Ideally, it should be passed on from supporter to family and friends.
- The supplier needs to include bug testing.
- The supplier needs to provide an installation copy for Web site, plus trouble-shooting copy.
- The supplier should work with the not-for-profit to link a direct-response function with the screensaver. For example, supporters might get the opportunity to download the screensaver only if they fill out an on-line survey.

27 Telemarketing

WILLIAM FREYD
Founder, IDC

DIANE M. CARLSON
Chairman, IDC

27.1 Introduction

Every day, the multiplicity of human need seems to increase. Our mail becomes more laden with fund appeals, and the technology associated with the solicitation process becomes more sophisticated. A key aspect of the competition for the charitable dollar involves the increasing necessity to get "personal."

(A) NEED TO PERSONALIZE

Most fund raisers would agree that *personalization* provides the competitive edge. The more personal the approach, the higher the response rate and the larger the gift. Clearly, the face-to-face appeal is the best solicitation approach. However, for large groups of donors or prospects about whom little is known—people whose names appear on a rented list, for instance—face-to-face solicitation is out of the question. In this case direct mail may be the most viable, cost-effective option. But what other choices are available? Consider small to medium previous donors or persons with a known affinity for your cause or organization. How do we reach this "mass" market in the most effective and most personal way possible? More and more often, the answer to that question is "By phone."

(B) WHAT ARE THE OPTIONS?

In recent years, the telephone has proved to be one of the most profitable tools for fund raising. However, the methods by which the phone is used in the overall appeal process are almost as varied as the institutions and causes using it. For new and senior fund raisers alike, the range of options can be mind-boggling. What, exactly, are the alternatives, and under what circumstances might we select one over another?

27.2 *Phonathons*

By definition, phonathons are fund-raising efforts in which volunteers solicit gifts or pledges by telephone. They are relatively inexpensive and uncomplicated, and they permit personal contact with a large number of people over a short period of time. Based on direct-response techniques, they are used most frequently to make advance calls on special gift club prospects, to wrap up annual appeal efforts, or to conclude a capital or other special campaign.

Phonathons also offer a way to generate goodwill about an institution from coast to coast. They have proved to be a successful form of fund raising, capable of outdoing traditional mass solicitation techniques, such as direct mail, by as much as 100 to one. There is no question that the phonathon is an especially effective solicitation method when the caller knows the prospect or shares a common association with the prospect. Volunteer callers like phoning people they know, so as to reduce the potential of rejection.

Generally staffed by volunteer callers, phonathons lend themselves particularly well to the educational setting where an in-house base of callers can be found. Alumni and parents already know about the school or college and are often pleased to receive a call, enabling them to ask specific questions and renew warm feelings of association with the institution. When student volunteers are engaged in the effort, the phonathon offers a wonderful opportunity to groom a cadre of enthusiastic and giving-conscious alumni. Any other type of not-for-profit organization can also give the volunteer caller an opportunity to serve. Social service agencies have used this technique quite effectively for the purposes of community outreach and fund raising.

(A) PLANNING FOR SUCCESS

Although phonathons are still among the least advanced methods of personalizing the appeal process, success does depend in some measure on careful planning, monitoring, and follow-up. Four key ingredients for a successful phonathon include the following:

1. *Planning and preparation.* This means researching phone numbers, preparing prospect cards and report forms, and designing and printing the follow-up mailing pieces. A pre-call postcard is often used to tell prospects that a representative will be calling.
2. *Location.* Calls should be made in a place, preferably free of charge, with ample office space and an adequate number of phones. The type of phone service available helps in making decisions about the wisdom and cost effectiveness of long-distance calling. In some instances, it may be advisable to arrange phonathons on a regional basis.
3. *Solicitors.* A dependable group of capable and enthusiastic callers constitute the phonathon solicitors. These people may be volunteers or, in some instances, paid participants. Expect them to work four to eight hours total. The training program for these callers should be brief (20–30 minutes) so that their time can be spent on the phone.
4. *Follow-up.* A prompt follow-up mailing confirming each pledge should be sent within a day of the phone call.

Volumes have been written on the how-tos of phonathons, and samples of prospect cards, mailing packages, report forms, scripts, and so forth, abound. Any and all of this material is worth examining by those planning a phonathon. (See "Suggested Readings" at the end of this chapter for sources of further information.) But what are the factors that might suggest the wisdom of a phonathon in the first place?

(B) WHEN TO USE A PHONATHON

If the following four circumstances apply, a phonathon is probably worth consideration:

1. You are interested in reaching a constituency who already has some knowledge about the organization and/or its cause and has a sense of loyalty to it.
2. You are raising funds for a purpose with which prospects are already familiar, or one that can be explained in a brief introductory statement on the phone.
3. You have a willing group of volunteers.
4. You do not wish to commit yourself to more than a few weeks of weekday evening calls; or the number of people you really want to reach by phone is small enough to be contacted within that amount of time.

In conducting a phonathon, a major investment of time and energy is demanded of staff members in planning, recruiting volunteers, and administering the program. Working full days on other annual giving programs and running a phonathon at night over an extended period of time is practically impossible.

(C)   WHAT TO EXPECT IN RESULTS

Although results of a phonathon vary by type of prospect (previous donor, lapsed donor, nondonor), participation rates are higher than those of direct mail. Assuming that the prospects are part of the "organizational family," pledge rates generally range from 25 percent to 35 percent for nondonors and from 60 percent to 90 percent for donors.

Average gifts are usually small one-time pledges, and typically range from $20 to $50 for nondonors and $35 to $100 for donors.

(D)   ESTIMATING COSTS

In most cases, staff costs are not factored into a phonathon cost analysis mainly because staff expenses are generally costed out to the overall solicitation program (i.e., annual giving). These are regarded as "indirect costs."

Direct costs, such as pre-call mail, phone charges, food for callers, and so on are tracked. Where possible, phone charges are kept to a minimum because most calls are local.

In summary, the successful phonathon strengthens relationships with members of an organization's "family"; enables them to reach a great many people in a short amount of time; is financially productive and its out-of-pocket costs relatively low; and, most important, it is *personal*.

27.3   *Telemarketing*

Phonathons, in actuality, are a form of telemarketing. However, as technology has become more sophisticated, so has its terminology. Today "telemarketing" generally implies a serious focus on the marketing aspects of the task. It means combining professional marketing and communication techniques in a variety of ways to sell products or services or even to raise funds. It is a sophisticated communications tool, which can be used by professionals representing all kinds of not-for-profit organizations to gain support. Whereas phonathons are useful for smaller organizations that want to call a relatively small number of people, telemarketing involves calling on a larger scale, employing paid callers rather than volunteers.

Telemarketing is, however, often described as a "sales tool," and with good reason. In the case of direct mail, there is generally no way of knowing whether the customer is interested in the product in the first place, and customer feedback is limited to returning a reply card (and a check). Mail that arrives at a person's home and sits passively on the desk does nothing to press a response, elicit concerns or objections, or communicate personally in any way with the recipient. A phone call, on the other hand, as sales companies across the country attest, commands attention. It is far more difficult to ignore. A phone call is more personal and enables the caller to make the pitch, answer questions, and counter objections—in short, to make the "sale."

(A)   KEY STEPS IN THE PROCESS

The five key steps in conducting a telemarketing campaign are as follows:

1. Establish the objective.
2. Conduct a market test.
3. Select and train personnel.
4. Decide on the quota for each caller (usually the number of calls to be made within a particular time period).
5. Determine a means of evaluating the success of the program.

Telemarketing is more expensive than direct mail and usually more expensive than a phonathon. However, the rate of return can be rewarding, and this activity can be used successfully in concert with other fund-raising techniques.

The risks of "negative telemarketing" can be reduced by calling only those people who have a *prior relationship* with the organization, such as former patients, alumni, consumers of services, and the like. Most telemarketing that uses "cold calling" is negative telemarketing. This happens when prospects who have no relationship to the organization are called from phone directories or rented lists. Organizations that are concerned about image should beware of cold calling programs that use high-pressure, commission-based callers.

Telemarketing can be used to test a market group much faster than direct mail. It can raise money, find new subscribers, sell tickets, and build a personal bridge between the organization and the prospect or donor. Most important, it permits *two-way dialogue* about the organization's needs even if the prospect does not donate, buy a ticket, or respond otherwise.

(B)   WHO SHOULD USE IT?

Today a wide variety of institutions and agencies use telemarketing techniques with enormous success. Educational institutions use telemarketing to raise money for everything from annual campaigns to capital campaigns to creating endowment funds; hospitals use it to solicit funds for wellness programs and new services and to promote special events; arts and cultural organizations use it to raise money, find new subscribers, and sell tickets. Significantly, telemarketing is used much more effectively than phonathons to find new donors for not-for-profits of all kinds.

(C)   DONOR ACQUISITION

Most organizations are using telemarketing for large donor acquisition campaigns. Because of the magnitude of the task, it is generally impossible to use volunteer callers. Thus, a paid staff must be recruited. Because this staff may have little familiarity with the cause, training is vital and adherence to a script may be a necessity. The nature of the job requires cheerfulness and enthusiasm. It is also repetitive. Most workers cannot be expected to be effective for more than four hours a day. When using hired workers, not related in any way to the cause, some organizations have found that a taped message or a pre-call video (video message sent ahead of the call) is a great way to carry the burden of the case for support. The caller, upon reaching the prospect, asks whether he or she is willing to listen to a short, recorded message from the president or other respected representative of the cause. When the tape ends, the caller returns to the line to conclude the "ask."

(D)   DONOR RENEWAL

Calls to the "converted" (previous donors) should be more personalized than calls aimed at donor acquisition. This group has already made a commitment to the mission and goals of the organization. Donor renewal should focus on *thanking* the donors for their previous support as well as *upgrading* giving in relation to the most recent gifts.

Donor renewal rates in a telemarketing campaign are usually 70 to 90 percent, depending on the quality of the solicitation. Giving the opportunity for installment payment (known as a multipayment plan) either in one fiscal year or over several years can greatly increase the average gift.

(E)   DECIDING FACTORS

How do you decide whether to conduct a telemarketing campaign? Eight factors that can influence that decision include:

1. You want to build a large donor base.
2. You need to reach a great many people.
3. You are aware of a large number of LYBUNTs (people who gave Last Year But Not This Year) and SYBUNTs (people who gave Some Years But Not This Year).
4. You need to find many new subscribers or donors, and there is a reasonably natural constituency within which they may be found.
5. Your primary objective is donor *acquisition*; an intense long-term cultivation effort is not the priority.
6. Prospects require some education and cultivation prior to the "ask."
7. Your current donors need upgrading.
8. Your case is complex and requires explanation.

27.4   *Phone/Mail® Campaign*

The most personalized solicitation approach short of a face-to-face visit is a PHONE/MAIL® campaign. With the use of this methodology (see Exhibit 27.1), *personalized pre-call mailings* are sent in advance of phoning.

(A)   GOALS IN USING PHONE/MAIL® METHODOLOGY

The PHONE/MAIL® calling is used to reach certain solicitation goals, contingent on the following four circumstances:

1. The "family" of the organization (alumni, parents, former patients, lapsed donors, etc.) require a very personalized approach.
2. The case for support is well planned and requires two-way dialogue to maximize the solicitation potential.

EXHIBIT 27.1 PHONE/MAIL® Flow Chart

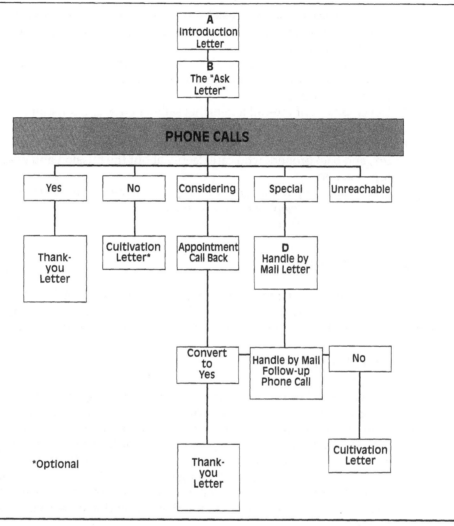

PHONE/MAIL® is a registered trademark of IDC.

3. You want to communicate with your "family" even if they do not become donors (public relations/cultivation).

4. There are too many prospects to solicit effectively in a phonathon.

(B) KEY INGREDIENTS FOR SUCCESS

The more personalized the approach in fund raising, the more successful are the results. Use the following checklist to achieve both:

____ 1. Segmentation of database into "interest groups" (i.e., parents, alumni, former patients, subscribers, etc.)

_____ **2.** Segmentation of the database into solicitation groups (i.e., previous donors, lapsed donors, nondonors)

_____ **3.** Further segmentation for "ask" amounts, such as by using previous gift history for previous donors and using acquisition statistics to set ask amounts for nondonors

_____ **4.** Selection of credible letter signers who have an appropriate, identifiable relationship with the organization (board chairman, former patient, campaign chairman, etc.)

_____ **5.** Development of pre-call letters that set forth the case for support, focusing on the value of meeting the need in very human terms

_____ **6.** Recruitment of a paid calling cadre of individuals appropriate as to age, sex, and background, who care deeply about the mission and goals of the organization

_____ **7.** Quick follow-up to pledges, sending out payment materials within 48 hours after the telephone calls are made

_____ **8.** Reminder notices to collect pledges

27.5 *Calling Cadre*

Although the preparation of pre-call mailings is important to maximize solicitation results, the deciding factor in all telemarketing is the quality of the paid calling cadre. The recruitment, training, and retention of callers require planning and regular monitoring.

(A) RECRUITMENT

A recruitment plan should be prepared prior to actual recruiting. Decisions must first be made concerning the *caller profile*, the characteristics of the callers you need to recruit. The profile addresses questions of age, background, and familiarity with your organization. Two weeks should be allowed for recruitment, prior to the start of calling. Where possible, recruit from the organization's family before "going to the street." If you need to advertise for callers, use newspapers that target your profile as their audience.

Callers should be interviewed by telephone, inasmuch as their jobs will be on the phone. Personal, face-to-face interviews should then be conducted with those who pass the phone interview.

Callers should be compensated with an hourly wage rather than by commission. Callers paid on commission (often used by telemarketers) are naturally more aggressive, because their self-interest is at stake. It is best that there be no correlation between callers' "take home pay" and their calling results. High-pressure tactics can be one of the negative aspects of callers paid on commission, and although this may work in some sales approaches, it cannot make donors feel good and is a questionable practice in not-for-profit fund raising.

(B) TRAINING

Once callers are recruited according to the established profile, the next important step is caller training. The training program must be organized in two segments: (1) education about the organization and the case for support and (2) instruction on the housekeeping details of the job.

An agenda for caller training should include the following 10 steps:

1. Mission and goals of the organization.
2. Case for support—why the organization needs money and how it will be used.
3. Review of any pre-call materials sent in advance of calling to familiarize callers with information the prospect has already received.
4. Training on the script—use role play.
5. Review of the type of people who will be contacted (alumni, former patients, subscribers, etc.).
6. Key objections the caller may encounter and answers to those objections.
7. Discussion of any public relations problems the organization may have had.
8. Information about the fund-raising goals and how caller performance will be measured.
9. Particulars about the job—hours, employment policies, and so on. Follow the laws in your state for part-time employees.
10. Payment of callers. If there are incentives, how they will be used.

When possible, someone who has credibility in regard to the case for support (a physician, a faculty member, a patient, etc.) should participate in caller training. Obviously, an enthusiastic, committed presentation of the case will enable callers to better relate to the need and to communicate it over the phone.

Scripts for callers are best when they are *not read* to prospects but are communicated in the callers' own words. The best calling occurs when callers are *listening to prospects* rather than to themselves.

Role-playing is a useful training tool to prepare callers for phone work. It can be a great asset in teaching callers to focus on the prospect and to listen.

(C) RETENTION

The workplace environment probably has more to do with caller retention than anything else. Even if callers are experiencing some measure of rejection from prospects, they are more likely to stay with the job if the workplace is pleasant, well managed, and reflects an interest in the well-being of both callers and prospects.

Because members of the calling cadre are key to bringing closure to the solicitation, caller performance must be regularly evaluated. The "rules of the game" must be communicated clearly and fairly during the interview phase, so that callers know the standards for keeping the job. Even the most effective callers must be dismissed if they do not perform within the standards set (i.e., those applying to absenteeism) so that fairness prevails.

Caller retention is less important in short calling programs, such as a phonathon. It is, however, critical to the success of long-term programs so that a learning curve can be established. There is no better way to maximize fund-raising results than retaining a well-trained cadre of callers.

27.6 Budget/Costs

Among the key concerns in both direct mail and telephone solicitation is the cost per dollar raised, or "How much is going to the charity?" Donors, as well as fund raisers, should be concerned about this issue.

Generally speaking, the lower the budget for phone programs, the higher the cost per dollar raised. Although pre-call mailings, low supervisor/caller ratios, and extensive caller training cost money, these investments also yield better results. The return on investment (ROI) will be better with higher-quality calling.

(A) ACQUISITION COSTS

The standard for fund-raising costs for acquisition (acquiring the first gift from a non-donor) has generally been that $1 in costs raises $1. This ratio for acquisition is impacted upward or downward as follows:

- The greater the affiliation of the prospect with the organization (former patient, classmate, etc.), the better the results (participation rates and average gifts).
- The more personalized the solicitation approach, the better the results.
- Computerized segmentation for better ZIP codes, better demographic profiles, and closer organization affiliation increases results. There are demographic screening services available for purchase for those who do not have computer capability to use census information and other data.

(B) RENEWAL COSTS

Cost-per-dollar standards for renewal of donors vary greatly according to type of organization, loyalty of the donor base, and other factors. Generally speaking, $0.10 to $0.20 is the usual ratio. Donor loyalty, amount of time lapsed since last gift, and the quality of the case for support impact costs negatively or positively. High-end donor recognition renewals ($1,000 club) will experience less than $0.10 cost per dollar raised.

(C) MIXING NONDONORS AND DONORS

When a telemarketing campaign includes both donors for renewal and nondonors for acquisition, the overall cost per dollar raised should be evaluated. Although many development programs do not track cost per dollar raised by constituency, this is critical to program evaluation in both direct mail and telemarketing. The higher the cost per dollar raised for a constituency, the less effective the solicitation program. It is important to be certain that the return on investment is good for both the organization and the donor.

27.7 *Legislative Environment*

Because of abuses in telemarketing specifically, and in fund raising generally, most states have enacted regulatory legislation regarding telemarketing. Both not-for-profits and vendors conducting solicitation on behalf of not-for-profits are required to register with the office of the attorney general in all but five states. Some states also require not-for-profits to post a bond in order to conduct telemarketing activities to residents of the state. It is probably just a matter of time before there will be similar federal legislation.

Although it goes without saying that not-for-profit fund-raising activities must be above reproach, it is imperative that both charities and vendors employ self-regulation to avoid both donor embarrassment and injury to the organization's image.

For not-for-profits to continue to enjoy their favorable tax-deductible status at both the federal and state levels, ethical conduct in fund raising is more important than ever. Donors, too, benefit in tax savings from deductible charitable giving. Charities have a stewardship responsibility to donors in this regard. Chapters 51 and 52, on federal and state regulation, respectively, present more in-depth information on these concerns.

27.8 Selecting an Outside Vendor

Once a not-for-profit organization decides to consider the use of telemarketing as a solicitation tool, the question arises about in-house operation vs. outsourcing. Quality control is usually better with an in-house program, because the mission and goals of the organization become part of the phone program "culture." Although most organizations, in theory, favor an in-house program, some may decide to outsource this work owing to a lack of space, staff size, scope of the overall fund-raising program, or for other reasons.

If an organization chooses to engage an off-site vendor, the following five considerations are important to the selection of a quality vendor:

1. The program should be custom-designed by the vendor to fit with the mission and goals of the organization.
2. The vendor should be as invisible as possible to the prospects being called so that the charitable organization is presented with a positive image.
3. The callers should be paid a flat hourly rate, not on commission. Incentives for a job well done can be used but should not be a major part of the overall compensation for callers. Commission often leads to high pressure on the phone.
4. Funds collected from the pledges should be sent by the donor directly to the charity rather than to the telemarketing vendor. Most reported abuses have included a violation of this policy.
5. Prospects who prefer not to be called in the future must be tracked and removed from future calling lists so that their wishes are respected. This provision requires database maintenance capability some vendors and charities do not have.

27.9 Conclusion

It appears that telemarketing is here to stay as a strong tool for charitable fund raising. By the year 2006, it is estimated that one in three jobs will be in telemarketing and/or related activities. Both the not-for-profit and for-profit sectors will use various forms of telemarketing to solicit charitable gifts and to sell their wares. It is predicted that continued public acceptance of telemarketing techniques will result in more ethical measures and standards enforced by federal and state regulators. There is now an important opportunity for the independent sector to participate in shaping legislation and public policy in this area of charitable solicitation.

Suggested Readings

Carlson, Diane M. "Mail and Phone Solicitation Offer a Winning Combination." *Association for Healthcare Philanthropy News* (February 1995): 5.

Dunn, Stephen. "Telemarketing in the 90's: Rising Above the Plateau." *Fund Raising Management* (April 1995): 25–27.

Goerlich, Ellen, and Mark Kinney. "University Builds Successful Phonathon." *Fund Raising Management* (March 1996): 29–33.

Hazen, Harold P. "Oh, No! Not Another Telemarketing Call!" *Fund Raising Management* (March 1996): 35–37.

Liebeskind, Ken. "Calls Flow for Victims in Oklahoma City." *Direct Mail News* (May 1995): 2.

———. "L.A. Mission Raises $1 Million by Phone." *Direct Mail News* (November 1995): 18.

Logan, Timothy D. "Managing the Telemarketing Process: Forecasting Fund-Raising Income." *Fund Raising Management* (April 1995): 30–33.

28 Volunteer-led Solicitations

WALTER P. PIDGEON JR., PhD, CAE, CFRE
Wild Life Conservation Fund of America

28.1 Volunteering: The Magic Ingredient of Successful Campaigns

In his book *Philanthropy*, Robert L. Payton notes, "Sociologists may tell us that we are becoming more isolated and atomized as individuals, but this is still a country of irrepressible joiners"[1] and Richard Lyman has said that "not-for-profits are perhaps the

---

[1]Robert L. Payton, *Philanthropy: Voluntary Action for the Public Good* (New York: Macmillan, 1988), p. 3.

biggest unknown success story in American history."[2] This success is due, in large part, to the proper use of talented individuals who become active volunteers in not-for-profits. As Peter F. Drucker notes, "Volunteers are the largest single group in the American workforce."[3] Drucker feels that not-for-profit organizations have created distinct values as well as an active and effective citizenship through the process of volunteerism. Volunteers can, therefore, be a ready resource for fund development activities in not-for-profits.

Volunteer-led annual campaigns have been the basis for most of the successful fundraising solicitation efforts of not-for-profit organizations. These successes traditionally have not been isolated undertakings within an institution but, rather, part of a strategic process that encourages a cooperative effort between the institution's staff and volunteers in order to fulfill its mission through the procurement of funds. Exhibit 28.1 provides an example of a volunteer-led solicitation annual campaign schedule.

The method of solicitation and the use of volunteers often depend on a number of factors, including the not-for-profit's culture, the staff and volunteer talent, the available resources, and the unique requirements of the institution. The vision of an institution can play a key role in what happens in the ongoing day-to-day activities. If the vision is not clear or exciting, volunteers will not be attracted to the organization. A vision provides guidance and motivation, and it should include the following seven elements:

1. A mission statement
2. Basic core values and philosophic values
3. Goals
4. Basic strategies
5. Performance criteria
6. Important policies and procedures
7. Ethical standards[4]

The organization's vision should drive the strategic planning process; it should not be simply a projection of the current operations into the future.[5] The strategic plan, however, needs to be broken down into annual sets of priorities that address the projected steps to achieve the vision and are flexible enough to cope with the unexpected. Exhibit 28.2 shows an organizational chart for a volunteer-led annual giving campaign committee.[6]

(A) VOLUNTEERS AND THE EVOLUTION OF NOT-FOR-PROFITS

Not-for-profit institutions experience a number of evolutions as they mature and/or reinvent themselves. Start-up organizations are often completely volunteer-led. Funding

---

[2]Michael O'Neill, *The Third America: The Emergence of the Nonprofit Sector in the United States* (San Francisco: Jossey-Bass, 1989), p. 1.

[3]Peter F. Drucker, *The New Realities* (New York: Harper & Row, 1989), p. 187.

[4]John M. Bryson, *Strategic Planning for Public and Nonprofit Organizations* (San Francisco: Jossey-Bass, 1989), p. 186.

[5]Paul B. Firstenberg, *Managing for Profit in the Nonprofit World* (New York: The Foundation Center, 1986), p. 118.

[6]James M. Greenfield, *Fund-Raising Fundamentals: A Guide to Annual Giving for Professionals and Volunteers* (New York: John Wiley & Sons, 1994), p. 286.

EXHIBIT 28.1 Volunteer-led Solicitation Annual Campaign Schedule

The following campaign schedule is designed for use in both a start-up campaign and an existing annual campaign.

Days	Item
−180	Define the culture of the not-for-profit or bring it up to date based on past campaign evaluations, internal audits, and volunteer surveys.
−150	Determine the volunteer and professional structure for the campaign. Develop individual guides for each position.
−120	Hold a strategy meeting with key leaders of the not-for-profit to review prospects for the next chair of the annual campaign.
−100	Meet with the prospects and recruit the new chair.
−90	The first campaign meeting is held. The new chair leads the meeting.
−60	The volunteer recruiting process is completed by selecting the remaining individuals needed.
−45	Hold the volunteer selection meeting to match volunteers to donor prospects.
−24	Hold a strategy meeting for all volunteers to build team spirit and to ensure that all is ready. Introduce the campaign control process.
−0	Hold a kick-off meeting.
+1–5	Hold report meeting number 1.
+15	Hold report meeting number 2.
+30	Hold report meeting number 3, which is the mop-up meeting.
+45	Complete the evaluation report.
+60	Hold the volunteer recognition rally.
+75	Close the annual campaign by holding a meeting of key volunteers and professionals to review the evaluation report and set plans for next year.

for new institutions, for the most part, traditionally comes from the core group of people who are dedicated to the mission of the institution. This is the first major test, or cycle, for a not-for-profit: Survival is the prime motivation.

If the entity survives this period, it tends to move into the next cycle. In this cycle, the volunteer leadership discovers that they cannot perform the quantity or quality of work required for the institution to grow and prosper and that they are unable to underwrite the full cost of the budget. The organization now needs full-time professional assistance. The careful selection and proper assignment of the first professional is crucially important. The new professional is asked to perform a number of programmatic duties; it is crucial that fund raising is a major duty as well, but this can happen only if two important assumptions are made:

1. That outside funding is necessary
2. That a staff professional must be part of the process of procuring that funding

The solicitation process that results from this experience often provides the basis for the organization's funding culture far into the future. It will act as a guide to future leaders in establishing the relationship between the process of raising funds and the functions of both the professional(s) and the volunteers.

EXHIBIT 28.2 Organizational Chart for a Volunteer-led Annual Campaign Committee

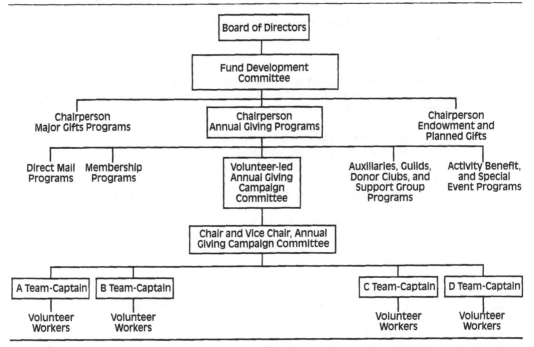

Source: James M. Greenfield, *Fund-Raising Fundamentals (New York: John Wiley & Sons, 1994), p. 286. Reprinted by permission of John Wiley & Sons, Inc.*

One of three general methods of cultivating and soliciting funds emerge:

1. A totally volunteer-driven model that tends to use the professional(s) to provide backup resources but does not consider the full-time employee(s) an equal partner in the process.
2. A model in which the first professional hired is given the total responsibility of raising funds. In this case volunteers avoid the solicitation process altogether and spend their time totally on various programmatic functions.
3. A model that is a blend of the first two. It places a shared responsibility on the professional in performing a leadership role within the solicitation process and clearly defines leadership roles for the volunteers as well.

As not-for-profit organizations continue to mature, they become more complicated and their functions more diverse. In many cases, their solicitation process is based on a culture established early in the life of the institution through a number of unrelated circumstances, including leadership decisions that have become dated or were not valid in the first place.

The best approach to have in place is the third model, which encourages a partnership between professionals and volunteers. This is the model that is illustrated in this chapter, and it is the model that should be used in most not-for-profit institutions. (Of course, there are always exceptions.) In some cases part of a campaign, or even an entire campaign, may be better served by the first or second model. For the most part, however, the partnership of professionals and volunteers is the "magic" of highly successful campaigns. Chapter 21, "Overview of Annual Giving," provides details on this process.

(B) DEFINING THE CULTURE

Understanding the culture of the not-for-profit is essential to being successful in any fund development endeavor. Not-for-profits are constantly challenged on how to effectively manage funding programs.[7] The vision and the methods used by organizations to procure funds provides an interesting road map to what is saleable; how it can be sold, to whom it is best to sell it, and, most important, who can make the sale.

It is also essential in determining whether an organization has been or would be receptive to a volunteer-led solicitation campaign. At first glance many organizations give the impression that they are receptive to volunteer-led campaigns. Yet it is worth a closer look to ensure that the volunteer commitment is really in place. To test the volunteer role in a not-for-profit institution, one needs to review the past annual campaign records to determine the performance of volunteers within the fund development function. Check to determine, for example, whether there is documentation that volunteers were assigned to solicit individual donors and if solicitors were assigned the same prospects over a period of time. Check the ratio of volunteers to the number of donors. Inquire about the methods used to solicit donors, that is, one-on-one solicitation, direct mail, or telephone. Review the current volunteer recognition plan and gather any other information available on past annual campaigns. The information gathered or the lack of information will help in measuring volunteer involvement in the past. Exhibit 28.3 provides a guide to obtaining data from a not-for-profit's campaign records.

Conducting a small survey of key volunteer leaders, including past annual campaign workers and current/past board members, can reveal the roles they have played in raising funds. It is important to compare these responses, describing perceived involvement, to the actual records on volunteer solicitation within the organization. Exhibit 28.4 illustrates a sample annual campaign volunteer survey.

The research can provide a clearer view of the volunteer involvement in the annual campaign and a reasonably measured base from which to work. The following six items are examples of what some basic measurements can reveal:

1. The number of donor prospects assigned to each volunteer reveals the level of volunteer involvement beyond the organizational level.
2. The percentage of donations that were obtained through volunteer involvement shows the level of commitment to volunteer-led solicitations.
3. The extent of detailed records on past campaigns can reveal a number of things. For instance, a lack of information (particularly volunteer recognition data) reveals low-level volunteer involvement and a more professional-driven campaign.
4. The ratio of volunteers assigned to prospective donors reveals the level of refinement in the annual campaign. A one-to-five ratio is ideal—one volunteer to five prospective donors. This is the realistic number of individuals a volunteer can cultivate and solicit funds from in a given year.

[7]Kirsten A. Gronsjerg, *Understanding Nonprofit Funding* (San Francisco: Jossey-Bass, 1993), p. 6.

EXHIBIT 28.3 Questionnaire for Obtaining Data From Not-for-Profit Campaign Records

1. Has the not-for-profit conducted fund-raising campaigns previously? Yes/No.
2. If the answer to question 1 is yes, what types of fund raising campaigns has the not-for-profit conducted?

Type of Campaign	Last Year Conducted	How Much Raised	Did It Make Goal?
Annual			
Capital			
Planned Giving			
Other			

3. What divisions of funding did the last annual campaign use?

Area	Division	% of Participation	Funds Collected	Goal Met
Internal	Board			
	Volunteers			
	Members			
	Alumni/Past Clients, etc.			
	Employees			
External	Individuals			
	Businesses			
	Foundations			
	Vendors			
	Other Organizations			
	Government			
	Other			

4. What is the ratio of volunteers to number of donor prospects?
   Number of volunteers ____ divided by number of donor prospects ____ = ____.
   (Ideal answer is 5.)
5. What have been the methods of soliciting funds?

Types	Number of Donor Prospects	Percentage of Campaign
One-on-one		
Telephone		
Mail		
Other		
Total		

(The one-on-one comparison reveals the level of direct volunteer involvement.)

6. Is there a donor recognition plan in place? ____ Yes/No ____. If so, what is it based on?

5. The methods used to solicit funds from prospective donors also provide evidence of the level of volunteer involvement. If the one-to-one cultivation and solicitation percentage was high, the campaign tended to be a more volunteer-driven effort. If direct mail and/or telephone methods were predominantly used, then the campaign was relying on indirect contacts, which tend to be less volunteer-led and traditionally produce a significantly lower value.
6. Finally, if a volunteer recognition program is in place, inquire about the qualifications for receiving recognition. Is the program value-driven? Is it based on the percentage of donations procured from prospects assigned, the total income pro-

EXHIBIT 28.4 Sample Annual Campaign Volunteer Survey

This survey is designed to assist (*name of organization*) to better serve its members and the community. As a volunteer of this organization, you have dedicated your time and energy to ensure that its work continues. Your advice and consultation will be greatly appreciated. We will also make sure that you are provided with a copy of the findings.

1. How many years have you been a volunteer for this organization? ____ Years

2. Why have you volunteered for this organization?

_____

3. What volunteer positions have you held with the organization?

	Position	**Number of Years**
(a)	_____	____
(b)	_____	____
(c)	_____	____
(d)	_____	____

4. What involvement have you had with the fund-raising function of the organization?

   (a) Do you donate funds to the organization? ____ If so, for how many years? ____

   (b) Have you been a volunteer within the fund-raising function? ____ If so, for how many years? ____

   (c) How many donor prospects did you solicit last year? ____ Is this higher or lower than the year before? ____

   (d) Do you think that the campaign was successful last year? ____ The year before? ____

   (e) How many individuals volunteered for last year's campaign? ____ (estimate)

   (f) Do you think the campaign needs more volunteers? ____ Yes/No ____

   (g) Will you be volunteering for next year's campaign? ____ Yes/No ____

5. What do you think are the major concerns facing this not-for-profit organization?

   Present: _____

   _____

   Future: _____

   _____

6. Comments:

   _____

   _____

   _____

   _____

Name: _____

Title: _____

Employer: _____

Business Address: _____   Home Address: _____

_____   _____

Business Telephone: _____   Home Telephone: _____

Business Fax: _____   Home Fax: _____

E-mail: _____   E-mail: _____

duced, the percentage increase over last year, the average gift procured as compared with those procured by other volunteers in the same category, or the level of personal volunteer contributions made to the annual campaign?

Data can be obtained through these measurements, which reveal the percentage of funds raised by volunteers as compared with the percentage raised by the professionals who work for the not-for-profit. The true volunteer-led campaign produces a higher level of donations, because volunteers tend to ask people and/or entities with whom they are familiar or have influence.

The volunteer survey is as important as internal research. The survey can reveal the thoughts and desires of past and present leaders of the organization and can allow a comparison with data found in the records of the organization. The survey can reveal the personal aspirations of the opinion makers who have the power to define the role of the volunteer in the annual campaign. What they think and how they react can play a significant role in how future annual campaigns will be conducted. Therefore, the survey often has a dual purpose:

1. To gather comparative data,
2. To act as a way of measuring key leader response to volunteer-led solicitation campaigns

Exhibit 28.5 lists six measurements of volunteer commitment from a personal standpoint.

Defining the organizational culture through internal research and a leadership survey can be more than revealing. It can provide a measurable base from which to work and can reveal the level of internal commitment to a volunteer-led campaign.

(C) START AT THE TOP

There is an old saying: "For the best results, start at the top." This is applicable in all aspects of fund raising, from procuring donations to increasing the involvement of volunteers. The data obtained from research can reveal the level of volunteer involvement in the annual campaign. If additional volunteer involvement is desired, it is important to

---

EXHIBIT 28.5 Measurement of Volunteer Commitment from a Personal Standpoint

It is often quite revealing to compare past annual campaign results to the perceptions of individual responses. One of the most revealing bits of information is the measurement of the volunteer's true commitment from a personal standpoint. This can be identified through gathering data based on the following standards:

- The level of personal donations to the not-for-profit that the volunteer provides each year;
- The extent of the role the volunteer played in the annual campaign;
- The success the volunteer has had in the cultivation and solicitation of others in past campaigns;
- The volunteer's opinion of the effectiveness of past annual campaigns;
- The volunteer's opinion on the sufficiency of volunteer involvement; and
- The volunteer's intention of participating in future annual campaigns.

secure the endorsement of the volunteer and/or professional leadership of the institution. Increased volunteer involvement in the annual campaign cannot be achieved without this support. The best way to obtain support is to demonstrate two advantages of volunteer-led solicitation:

1. From the volunteer leader's standpoint, emphasis can be placed on current operational factors as well as how increased volunteer support can put the institution in a better position to obtain funds for current needs and long-term goals.
2. If the professional leadership requires persuasion, then the motivation can focus on the advantages of strengthening long-term volunteer support to ensure that the necessary funds can be obtained through a greater volunteer/professional partnership to meet the present and the future financial demands of the institution.

(D) ANNUAL CAMPAIGN: THE BASIS FOR ALL OTHER FUND-RAISING EFFORTS

Setting the standard for significant volunteer involvement at the annual campaign level can assist greatly in the natural progression of volunteer involvement in other types of campaigns, ranging from major gifts to planned giving. It is important to establish the annual campaign as a volunteer-led effort. This is true of new organizations as well as established ones. Traditionally, the entire fund development effort for an institution is built on the annual campaign. Chapter 21, "Overview of Annual Giving," provides greater detail on the annual giving process. The key elements in a successful volunteer-driven annual campaign schedule include:

- Understand and define the culture of the not-for-profit and adapt the campaign to fit its traditions.
- Understand the traditional role of volunteers in the not-for-profit and measure its effectiveness in raising funds.
- Ensure that the leadership, both volunteer and professional, understands and approves of a volunteer-driven campaign.
- Develop a sound volunteer-driven annual campaign before embarking on other campaigns.
- Secure the best-qualified annual campaign chair even if an external search is necessary.
- Develop a schedule of highly charged meetings and rallies that lends excitement and fun to the process.
- Develop a volunteer recruitment plan that encourages retention of successful solicitors and maintains an open environment to encourage new volunteers to join the process.
- Create and maintain a close team effort between volunteers and the not-for-profit's professionals.
- Understand the important role of recognition in the attraction and retention of volunteers.
- Maintain a quality-evaluation component for the annual campaign that reviews volunteer performance based on individual success.

28.2 Volunteer Campaign Structure

No matter what the size of the institution, the structure of a volunteer-led annual campaign is based on the principle that volunteers can successfully cultivate an average of five prospects in a campaign cycle. This formula is due to a number of factors, including the limited time of volunteers, the desire to have a speedy campaign solicitation period and, most important, the desire to conduct a quality cultivation and solicitation plan. Therefore, it is essential to translate your needs into an integrated program of action steps.[8]

(A) DEVELOPING A SYSTEMATIC APPROACH TO DETERMINE THE APPROPRIATE ROLES FOR VOLUNTEERS AND PROFESSIONALS

The roles of volunteers and professionals vary among not-for-profit organizations. This is why it is important to have all functions clearly defined. The professional(s) is a full time employee of the institution and, therefore, is responsible for the day-to-day administrative and logistical needs of the annual campaign. These are the detailed items that can make or break a campaign, including material preparation, prospects research, meeting planning, and recording/reporting funds procured. The volunteer, on the other hand, should be utilized as much as possible to cultivate and solicit prospects for funds. Although this separation of roles sounds rather simple, in practice it often becomes blurred. People tend to see such functions differently, and what may seem logical to one person may seem quite different to another. It is the growth and sustaining of effective teams of both volunteers and professionals that makes an annual campaign successful. Effective leadership is the dynamic.[9] Chapter 2, "Strategic Planning for Fund Raising," can provide additional information on this process.

It is important to determine, through a strategic process, the tasks that are best performed by volunteers within an institution's annual campaign. Once the general areas or tasks are defined, a written plan should be developed that outlines the roles of both volunteers and professionals. This is a general overview statement. It should be short and to the point and agreed upon by both the volunteer and professional leadership. This must be a genuine agreement that is not forced on either side; otherwise, it will not work. The process, if properly presented, can help to cement a closer bond between volunteers and professionals. It can be an exciting moment in the process when everyone realizes that one of the by-products of the annual campaign plan is a new level of teamwork between volunteers and professionals—which can lead to successes far beyond the annual campaign. Exhibit 28.6 outlines an example of a volunteer-professional plan for the annual campaign.

The next step is to define both the traditional and unique needs of the campaign. This plan may include categories of prospects such as alumni, corporations, vendors; functional

---

[8]Patrick J. Below, George L. Morrisey, and Betty L. Acomb, *The Executive Guide to Strategic Planning* (San Francisco: Jossey-Bass, 1987), p. 75.
[9]Tracy D. Connors, *The Nonprofit Management Handbook: Operating Policies and Procedures* (New York: John Wiley & Sons, 1993), p. 117.

EXHIBIT 28.6 A Volunteer-Professional Plan for the Annual Campaign

The relationship between the volunteer and the professional varies among not-for-profit organization. A volunteer-professional plan for the annual campaign can ensure that an understanding is reached that clearly defines the roles that everyone will play in the campaign.

The professional support plan

The professional staff of the not-for-profit will provide the day-to-day support for the annual campaign. This will include the meeting planning functions, materials development, record keeping, and other appropriate support areas.

Direct professional assistance will be provided by:

- The chief executive officer
- The development director
- Two support staff

The professional staff will ensure that volunteers are recruited through a joint partnership between the professional staff and the volunteer leadership.

The volunteer support plan

The volunteers of the not-for-profit will provide part-time assistance to ensure that the not-for-profit conducts a successful annual campaign. This will include the recruitment of sufficient numbers of volunteers to ensure success.

The volunteer leadership will be provided by:

- The board chair
- Board members
- The annual campaign chair
- Volunteers

The volunteer members of the not-for-profit understand that the annual campaign cannot be successful without the direct involvement of volunteers to conduct the direct solicitation of donor prospects. It is the goal of the volunteer leadership to recruit one volunteer for every five donor prospects.

Volunteer Leader	Professional Leader
Date	Date

(Greater detail would be needed for an actual agreement. The key is to have an understanding of who performs what duties.)

---

positions such as marketing and communications; and, most important, the top leadership needs for the campaign. Each of the functions in the plan will have one or more volunteers and/or professionals assigned to it. Before such assignments are made, however, a general guide must be developed that details the overall projected duties of each position, the projected schedule, the proposed outcomes, and the evaluation process, as shown in Exhibit 28.7. This is not a job description but, rather, a guide or road map to what is needed to be accomplished in the particular function. The ultimate agreement on what will be accomplished within that function should be mutually agreed on by the individual who accepts the position and the volunteer and/or professional who is responsible for the overall success of that function. The ultimate agreement remains flexible, in order to take advantage of the unique skills of the individual who accepts the position and to ensure that he or she has an opportunity to play a vital part in creating the agreement. Such attention to individual preferences and aspirations can attract and retain quality volunteers.

(B) HOW TO ATTRACT AND RETAIN VOLUNTEERS

According to an Independent Sector report, *Giving & Volunteering in the United States,* more than 89.2 million adults volunteered in 1993 for thousands of worthy causes. Why do people volunteer their time to these institutions? There are perhaps 89.2 million unique answers to that question. In general, however, there are three major reasons:

1. To satisfy psychological needs, including security, socialization, self-esteem, and self-actualization

---

EXHIBIT 28.7 Volunteer Position Guide

Each volunteer needs a written guide to assist in understanding the role that the not-for-profit is asking him or her to perform. The length and detail will depend on the position. The following is a suggested outline:

Name: _____   Date accepted position: _____

Title: _____   Reports to: _____

Position begins: _____   Position ends: _____

Estimated number of volunteer hours needed per week: _____
Assigned Responsibilities

_____

_____

Vice chair and team captains need to be recruited:

_____

_____

Meeting dates scheduled:

_____

_____

_____

_____

_____

Support to be provided and who will provide it:

_____

_____

Other information:

_____

_____

2. To fulfill a conscious desire to help others or serve the community or other altruistic intentions
3. To attain benefits received through the process

Although the level of volunteering in 1993 (89.2 million) was impressive, it represented a 5 percent decline from the 94.2 million adults who volunteered in 1991. The decline of volunteering could have significant implications for a volunteer-driven annual campaign. Annual campaigns often require hundreds of volunteers to make the effort a success. It is important in today's environment to be sensitive to this reality and to structure the campaign accordingly. Volunteers have individual reasons for providing their valuable time to a particular project. It is this personal reason that motivates people to participate and to make a vital contribution to the success of a not-for-profit. *The National College Graduate Survey on Volunteering*, conducted in 1991, discovered that individuals are indeed self-motivated to volunteer and, in fact, gain leadership traits in the process. Not-for-profits will have to find new ways to attract volunteers and retain quality volunteers. This effort should include strategies that allow volunteers to assume smaller but more frequent "bytes" of a needed activity.[10] As Peter Drucker points out, "people decisions" are the ultimate—perhaps the only—control of a not-for-profit organization.[11] These decisions largely determine whether the organization's objectives are real, whether its mission has value, and whether it is meaningful to people. The attraction and motivation of volunteers to enthusiastically assist an institution in conducting a successful annual campaign is of prime concern.

Armed with the completed guides for the functions needed, analyze the types of individuals who would be the ideal candidates for positions in meeting the needs of the organization. For example, if the corporate division wishes to raise funds through approaching the area's businesses, the logical candidate for that function would be a business executive, who could easily approach fellow business leaders.

If an institution does not have a volunteer who fits that profile, where would it find such a person, and, more important, how would its leadership convince that person to chair the corporation division? Volunteers can be found in every profession and every station of life. They are either self-motivated to volunteer or waiting for someone to ask them. A 1991 Gallup survey revealed that people of all ages are three times as likely to volunteer if someone asks them, particularly if it is someone they know.[12] There are logical methods to identify volunteers. In the search for a corporate division chair, for example:

1. Within the institution's data system there may be records of business executives or their families who have received your services directly or indirectly.
2. The present volunteer base may have contacts with business executives.
3. Your institution's mission may have a direct or indirect relationship with one or more businesses due to the nature of their product or other factors.
4. Certain businesses may be striving to increase their visibility in your area of expertise or client base.

[10]Glenn Tecker and Marybeth Fidler, *Successful Association Leadership* (Washington, D.C.: American Society of Association Executives Foundation, 1993), p. 52.
[11]Peter F. Drucker, *Managing the Non-Profit Organization* (New York: HarperCollins, 1990), p. 145.
[12]Tracy D. Connors, *The Volunteer Management Handbook* (New York: John Wiley & Sons, 1995), p. 64.

It can still be difficult to measure volunteer potential. The best way to approach this challenge is through a systematic approach of matching the needed functions with the top volunteer candidates available in your area. The process is quite similar to prospect research. Chapter 35, "Prospect Development—An Art," may provide additional information.

(C) FINDING THE CHAIR

A quality chair to lead the annual campaign is the most important volunteer position to fill. The five key attributes to seek in the volunteer to assume this position are:

1. Perceived willingness to volunteer
2. Leadership qualities to attract and motivate volunteers
3. A no-nonsense attitude—a person who is too busy to lead a prolonged campaign
4. Visibility within the constituency to be solicited
5. An ability to give personally and attract others to give to the campaign

The annual campaign chair should have ready access to the top volunteer and professional leadership of the not-for-profit organization, including the board of directors. The annual campaign is a core objective for the organization, and everyone—at all levels—should be involved with its success. The board of directors, in particular, has an obligation, as part of its fiduciary role, to make sure that the campaign is conducted successfully each year.[13] If the board of directors is less than enthusiastic about taking an active role in the annual campaign, it will have a direct effect on the success of the effort.

Most not-for-profit leaders understand the need to have board members heavily involved in the annual campaign. Active board members become the first givers to the campaign, and at a significant level to encourage others to do the same. They also become the core solicitors for the campaign, taking the lead donor prospects to ensure that the campaign gets off to a great start. If board members are not committed to the annual campaign, measures must be taken to encourage their commitment. In today's economic environment, not-for-profits cannot afford to retain volunteers at the board level who do not believe in fund raising and volunteer-led solicitation.

Under ideal circumstances, the annual campaign chair is a seasoned volunteer of the not-for-profit and is on the board of the organization. However, as a rule of thumb, it is unwise to attempt to persuade a board member who does not wish to or is not capable of raising funds, to take the chair of the annual campaign. If the board does not have the talent needed to successfully conduct the annual campaign, use this opportunity to attract a new person to the position. This is a key judgment call, made jointly by the volunteer and professional leaders of the not-for-profit.

If an external person is required, a search must be conducted among the available volunteer and professional talent. Bring the key leadership of the organization together for a strategy meeting. The annual campaign chair's position should be designed to attract the type of candidate desired. The design can have a major effect on motivating an individual to accept the position and, more importantly, on achieving maximum success.[14]

---

[13]Cyril O. Houle, *Governing Boards* (San Francisco: Jossey-Bass, 1989), p. 93.
[14]Edward E. Lawler, *Motivation in Work Organizations* (San Francisco: Jossey-Bass, 1994), p. 196.

The six-step agenda should be brief and to the point:

1. To update or develop a guide (job description) on the position
2. To list the attributes sought for the position
3. To create a list of the top five individuals who could fill that position
4. To discover the best way to approach each candidate
5. To list the best team, of no more than three, to approach each prospect
6. To draft a schedule, including sufficient time to gather the appropriate materials to take to the appointments, to verify the discovered linkages between each candidate and the organization, and to make appointments and visit with candidates

The process should be coordinated through one person to ensure that the recruiting plan is on schedule. The actual visit to a prospective chair should be well orchestrated. Each member of the team should have a key part in the presentation.

The presentation to a candidate should include the following four steps:

1. An introduction to the mission of the not-for-profit. This step should be included even if the organization is well known to the candidate. The candidate may not be aware of the overall role of the institution in the community or its area of expertise.
2. An affirmation linking the candidate to the organization, using the information found during the research phase.
3. A review of the position, including the support and resources to be provided.
4. Answering questions presented by the prospective chair.

Note: If the candidate asks for time to think about the opportunity, do not be discouraged. This is often a good sign. If the institution has selected the right prospect, and the candidate does not want to volunteer for the not-for-profit, he or she will tell you so immediately. Individuals who are busy may wish to determine whether the opportunity can fit into a schedule. A follow-up call by the key person on the team within 48 hours can assist in closing the deal.

(D)   FIRST CAMPAIGN MEETING

When a chair has been secured, it is important to bring together the top leadership of the not-for-profit to begin to lay out the campaign strategy and to create an effective organizational system. Exhibit 28.8 outlines a sample agenda for the first campaign meeting. This should be an exciting event, perhaps held in the new chair's boardroom. The chair of the board, the professional/chief executive officer (CEO), and appropriate volunteers and staff should attend. This will be the key control group for the campaign. The chair of the board should lead the meeting and explain the role of the campaign's volunteer leaders. Although the functions and titles of key volunteer positions will vary, it is important that current volunteer campaign leaders are present and that a link to the last campaign is maintained by having the chair or vice chair of that campaign attend. The professional/CEO should review the role of this office and the roles of other staff members in the campaign. If the organization employs a development officer, that person should be present and should be introduced by the CEO. The CEO should review the role of the development officer as the chief professional advisor/coordinator to the annual campaign chair.

A complete review of past campaigns and the campaign process should be conducted, including:

- The proposed goal and how it related to past performance
- The number of qualified prospects
- The anticipated volunteer needs and the recruitment process
- The structure of the campaign
- The timetable
- The reporting process

The plan should be presented in a proposal format, suggesting that it is still flexible enough to be refined. Such a format provides an opportunity for fresh input from all who have attended, including the annual campaign chair. Moreover, it offers a way of making everyone present buy into the plan and encourages a sense of ownership in the campaign.[15] Some of the most imaginative ideas can come out of this experience, particularly from the campaign chair.

One of the key parts of the meeting is the review and selection of the next level of volunteers to recruit. Campaign structures vary, depending on the size of the organization, but the traditional needs of an annual campaign dictate the inclusion of certain elements. Most campaigns have two major areas to cover:

1. *Internal prospects* (those individuals who are directly involved with the organization)
   Board members
   Volunteers
   Current members
   Alumni/past clients/past members

EXHIBIT 28.8 Sample Agenda for the First Campaign Meeting

Opening:	Setting the stage for the campaign	Chair of the board
Introduction:	Volunteer leaders and their roles	Chair of the board
	Introduce the president/CEO	
Campaign Support:	Review of staff roles and functions	President/CEO
	Introduce the development officer and other key staff	
Past Campaign:	A brief review	Past campaign chair
		Development officer
This Year's Plan:	A complete review	New campaign chair
		Development officer
Volunteers:	Review and select the next level of volunteers	New campaign chair
Plan Approval:	The plan and schedule are approved	New campaign chair
Other Business:		New campaign chair
Closing:		

---

[15]Richard Lynch, *Lead* (San Francisco: Jossey-Bass, 1993), pp. 79–94.

Staff/employees
Prior donors

2. *External prospects* (those who have indirect or little involvement with the organization)

Individuals
Businesses
Foundations
Vendors
Other organizations
Government (as it pertains to annual contracts—projects)
Prior donors

Larger organizations may have to create a structure that includes two vice chairs, with division chairs for each of the key funding sources. Smaller organizations can consolidate the campaign to fit the size of the prospect list and the volunteer potential. The objective is to set a standard by which no more than five volunteers report to one supervising volunteer. Completing the key leaders' strategy meeting with the structure in place and a time line to recruit the next level of volunteers positions the campaign well on the way to success.

(E) VOLUNTEER RECRUITING PROCESS

The process of recruiting volunteers who will make up the various teams is similar to the process used to recruit top-level volunteers. The recruiting process is a joint effort of the appropriate volunteer(s) and professional staff personnel. Volunteers should recruit the individuals who will make up their teams. The professional staff person should assist, providing the support needed to attract volunteer team members, including, if appropriate, being present at the time of recruitment. The most obvious difference in this process is the number of people involved. The annual campaign chair and the area chairs who will report to the chair and represent the working areas of the campaign, may each have suggestions on who may fit well in various parts of the campaign structure that they will lead. Most of the volunteers who will work on the campaign at the next level will be known individuals within the organization. There will be exceptions (external prospects, for example), but for the most part the pool of volunteers needed for the rest of the campaign will be known. The challenge, therefore, is to match the volunteers to the appropriate divisions and to the appropriate prospects for cultivation and solicitation.

To accomplish this task, it is suggested that one or more training sessions take place. The number of sessions depends on the size and scope of the organization; smaller organizations might accomplish this task in one meeting. The volunteer selection meeting is a must for all organizations, no matter their size. This is a gathering of all the volunteers recruited to date and the volunteer/professional leadership of the organization. The session's objective is to shift part of the responsibility for the campaign to additional volunteers who may, if needed, become empowered and self-directed to recruit other volunteers themselves. This process can create a successful team approach to the annual campaign plan.[16]

---

[16]Richard S. Wellins, William C. Byham, and Jeanne M. Wilson, *Empowered Teams* (San Francisco: Jossey-Bass, 1991), p. 31.

(F) VOLUNTEER SELECTION MEETING

Detailed preparation for the volunteer selection meeting is a must. Exhibit 28.9 outlines a simple agenda to use for the volunteer selection meeting. For a new campaign, create a list of current members, alumni or prior clients, and other interested parties, and make available enough copies for all who attend. If the annual campaign has been an ongoing effort, develop an additional list including the volunteers who participated in the annual campaign for at least the last three years. Another listing should include past donors and prospects and their giving history. This data can provide a good historical base. Past volunteers who have successfully cultivated and solicited funds should be recruited to visit with the same prospects this year. A large percentage of volunteers will return each year if they have had a positive experience in the previous year's campaign. This is the key to building a successful volunteer team for the annual campaign. However, if you identify past volunteers who have not reached the expected goal, it is best to replace them and to submit their donor prospects to the general pool. Past campaign volunteers are valuable assets to an annual campaign. They possess a sense of history about the organization's campaign and act as a stabilization factor or base for the campaign to build upon.

Once returning campaign volunteers are assigned to the same donor prospects they solicited last year, the focus centers on the remaining donor prospects and the remaining pool of potential volunteers. Matching the right volunteer to the right prospect is the true key to success, yet it is often difficult. The meeting will at least begin the match. Start by considering the areas and divisions of the campaign: for example, Mary Johnson is best suited for the external campaign and the vendors division, because she is well known in the business services field; Jim Smith should be placed in the internal campaign, alumni division, because he is a past alumni president and is quite respected by his peers. Other prospective volunteers who do not immediately fit a profile for a particular campaign may be selected by individuals who know them. The remaining volunteers, who should be low in number, can be asked to volunteer for the campaign for general purposes. When they are recruited, they should be encouraged to request an area to serve.

EXHIBIT 28.9 Sample Agenda for a Volunteer Selection Meeting

Opening:	Setting the stage for the meeting	New Campaign Chair
Materials:	Review materials for the campaign	Development Officer
Past Volunteers:	Review of past volunteers and suggested matches with donor prospects based on documented results	Past Campaign Chair
Other Donor Prospects:	Match with the pool of volunteers remaining	New Campaign Chair
Review of Needs:	Volunteer needs for donor prospects not assigned	New Campaign Chair
Schedule:	Set time lines for notifying volunteers of assignments and for recruiting additional volunteers, if needed	New Campaign Chair
Other Business:		New Campaign Chair
Closing:		

The three control points of the meeting should include:

1. All donor prospects are assigned an area (e.g., Internal or External Campaign) and placed in a division (e.g., Alumni or Foundations). Exhibit 28.10 illustrates how assignments may develop, based on an organizational chart. (See Exhibit 28.11.) The volunteer chairs of the area and/or the divisions take responsibility for soliciting all prospects given;
2. All volunteers are assigned an area and/or a division. The chairs of the areas and/or divisions take responsibility to formally recruit all volunteers assigned; and
3. Documentation includes the name of persons responsible for each donor prospect and for each volunteer. (Note Exhibit 28.11.)

One of the best parts of this process, particularly for new campaigns, is the introduction of new volunteer prospects. Do not overlook this opportunity. The meeting attendees consist of the leading volunteers of the not-for-profit, who will have in mind individuals who may not be on the lists provided. Take a few minutes to brainstorm. Spending time to discover new volunteer potentials, based on the prospects to be covered, can add new life to the volunteer pool. New prospects should be carefully screened. Keep in mind that the heart of the annual campaign is its volunteers. Careful selection of each new volunteer can ensure that a new or seasoned campaign will improve. The characteristics of a good annual campaign volunteer include:

- An ability to give at the level at which he or she will be asking. Successful campaigns rely on volunteers to give a measurable percentage of the goal.
- An eagerness for asking donor prospects to give to a worthy cause.
- A desire for recognition and an eagerness to give recognition to others.
- A willingness to donate the time and energy needed.
- An ability to bring in at least one new prospect.
- An ability to recruit the additional volunteers needed for the area of the campaign assigned.

The key objective of the volunteer selection meeting is to ensure that all donor prospects are assigned to recruited or proposed volunteers. Following up on the recruit-

---

EXHIBIT 28.10 Suggested Format for a Volunteer Organization Chart

Area 2:   The Internal Campaign
Division 4: Alumni

(The teams can be based on a number of factors, i.e., class year, levels of giving, location, etc.)

Action Steps for Each Team	Team A	Team B	Team C	Team D
1. Match all returning volunteers to donor prospects from last year.				
2. Match new volunteers to donor prospects not taken.				
3. List potential volunteers needed for donor prospects still not assigned.				

EXHIBIT 28.11 Sample Volunteer Solicitation and Donor Prospect Documentation

Great Mountain Boys Club
D Team—Section 3
Tom Smith, Chair

Volunteer Assigned	Donor Prospect	Giving History	Rating/Goal	Comments
Susan Wallace	1. James Smith	$50	$75	
	2. Mary Johnson	$35	$35	
	3. Henry Brown	$75	$100	CEO of XYZ
	4. Susan Simon	$50	$75	
	5. Jack Jones	$50	$60	
Subtotal	5	$260	$345	
Jane Weber	1. Jane Adams	$50	$70	
	2. Robert Jones	$75	$100	
	3. Henry Green	$50	$75	Boy in program
	4. Jean Hayes	$45	$60	
	5. Peter Dill	$50	$65	
Subtotal	5	$270	$370	
Pat Smith	1. Jill Jackson	$80	$125	
	2. Tim Sacks	$50	$60	
	3. Jerry Kats	$75	$85	
	4. Joan Waters	$75	$125	
	5. Robert Smith	$50	$75	
Subtotal	5	$330	$460	
Nancy Wallace	1. Jack Kimble	$75	$100	
	2. Lisa Lemon	$55	$70	
	3. Gerald Rink	$50	$75	
	4. Melinda Clemens	$75	$100	
	5. Jim James	$50	$60	
Subtotal	5	$305	$405	
Richard Deacon	1. Henry Homes	$50	$60	
	2. Mary Martin	$60	$75	
	3. Jan Jacobs	$55	$80	
	4. Blake Rubin	$60	$75	
	5. Kevin Burns	$75	$100	
Subtotal	5	$300	$390	
Total	25	$1,465	$1,970	

ment of the remaining volunteers is a necessary part of the final phase of the recruiting process. In this process, be sure that a single volunteer is assigned to recruit no more than five other volunteers. It is important that each new volunteer is recruited in the same personalized manner as the top volunteers. Taking time to ask each person individually can produce a higher number of acceptances and a higher giving ratio for the campaign as well. This is one of the chief ways to attain and retain good people.[17] Even with the ideal ratio of one to five and a successful volunteer selection meeting, volunteer recruit-

---

[17]Paul J. Ilsley, *Enhancing the Volunteer Experience* (San Francisco: Jossey-Bass, 1990), p. 94.

ment will not be fully accomplished. Immediate and constant follow-up by volunteer and professional leaders is needed to ensure that all positions are filled. This is even more important if your campaign has a multilayer structure. If a volunteer is not recruited at a mid-high level in the campaign structure, several other volunteer positions may also be unfilled. Exhibit 28.12 illustrates the progression that could take place. The recruiting process will succeed to the degree that the volunteering experience is perceived as providing a sense of meaning and/or fulfillment.[18] One of the key means of ensuring success is to utilize volunteers who have not been assigned, or have been placed in a pool for general purposes as a back-up or an alternative group to fulfill tasks that do not attract volunteers, to bolster areas in which performance is low, or to replace volunteers who had to drop out of the campaign.

(G) FORMATION OF THE TEAM

When volunteers have been recruited, it is time to mold the volunteer group into an exciting and productive team. The steps to accomplish this task can, and in most cases should, be conducted at a strategy meeting that includes all volunteer workers. The meeting should be designed to encourage a one-on-one dialogue between the volunteers and their volunteer chairs. This is not a kick-off meeting but, rather, a meeting to establish needs and to generate enthusiasm. Exhibit 28.13 details a suggested three-part agenda for this

---

EXHIBIT 28.12 Structure of Campaign Unable to Recruit Enough Key Volunteers

The recruitment of the proper number of volunteers, based on the standard of one volunteer for five donor prospects, can have a profound effect on campaign results. It is the best way to ensure that the most donor prospects are solicited in a timely fashion. It is important, however, to make sure that key positions are filled and that enough volunteers are recruited. The structure below illustrates the results of not recruiting enough volunteers. A total of 650 donor prospects could not be covered, resulting in a loss of revenue of $50,000. It is important to have a volunteer recruitment plan that anticipates volunteer needs and has a general pool of volunteers ready to fill in wherever necessary.

Campaign Chair			
Board	Alumni	Members	External
5 V	200 V	175 V	20 V
25 DP	1500 DP	1000 DP	125 DP
0 DPS	500 DPS	125 DPS	25 DPS
$200 AG	$50 AG	$100 AG	$500 AG
$00 L	$25,000 L	$12,500 L	$12,500 L

V = Volunteers
DP = Donor prospects
DPS = Donor prospects not seen
AG = Average gift
L = Possible loss

---

[18]Jeffrey L. Brudney, *Fostering Volunteer Programs in the Public Sector* (San Francisco: Jossey-Bass, 1990), 159.

meeting, which acts as a dress rehearsal for the kick-off and the active solicitation phase of the campaign. If there are problems, there is still time to refine the plan.

(H) CONTROL FACTOR

Control of the campaign is imperative. The campaign now has its volunteers in place. Most, or all, of the prospects have been assigned. As preparations are being made for the kick-off meeting, the process must include the steps needed to ensure full control of the campaign. There must be documentation as to who will solicit whom, when each volunteer receives the prospect cards (or other documents that are used), when the solicitation takes place, the total donation cash/pledge, when the pledge is turned in, credit given to the donor and to the volunteer solicitor, recognitions ordered for both giver and volunteer solicitor, and refusals, moves, and so forth. All prospect cards should be returned and processed. This is the only way to determine that the campaign was fully conducted and the only way to calculate the true value of each volunteer solicitor. Exhibit 28.14 is a sample control sheet for an annual campaign. The control factor for a volunteer-driven campaign must be a collaborative method. Such a method allows both volunteer and professional participants to work together to ensure that the plan is successful.[19]

(I) KICK-OFF

The importance of the kick-off meeting should not be underestimated. Although the annual campaign schedule has included a number of meetings to date, they are not the same as the formal kick-off meeting of a campaign. This event announces the formal

---

EXHIBIT 28.13 Agenda for a Volunteer Strategy Meeting

1. Introduction:
   - A quick review of the campaign; and
   - A review of the schedule.
2. Group breaks up according to areas/divisions:
   - Review of the campaign structure at the area/division level;
   - Review of individual positions for full understanding of each volunteer's role;
   - Review of prospects to ensure that each person has selected the best prospects to see;
   - Ensure clear understanding of the schedule and reporting process;
   - Complete review of the materials and their use;
   - Ample time for questions and answers; and
   - Request each volunteer to be ready to provide/pledge his or her donation at the kick-off meeting.
3. The entire group is reassembled:
   - Reports given by each area/division;
   - Campaign chair reviews the schedule and the importance of the kick-off;
   - The not-for-profit's lead volunteer (chair of the board) provides inspiration; and
   - Recognition is given to top volunteers who have already pledged.

---

[19]Alvin Zander, *Effective Social Action by Community Groups* (San Francisco: Jossey-Bass, 1990), pp. 218–219.

EXHIBIT 28.14 Sample Annual Campaign Control Sheet

Great Mountain Boys Club
D Team—Section 3 Report #2
Tom Smith, Chair
Date: 10-15-97

Volunteer	Prospective Donor	Date Pledge Cards Issued	Solicitation Scheduled	Donation: Cash (C) or Pledge (P) Amount	Refusal (R) Not Seen (NS) Not Home (NH)	Recognition Ordered Date
G. Wallace	1. J. Smith	9-19	10-05	P—$ 75		10-07
	2. M. Johnson	9-19	9-25		R	
	3. H. Brown	9-19	10-01	C—$100		10-05
	4. S. Simon	9-19	9-21		NS	
	5. J. Jones	9-19	10-10	P—$ 60		10-12
Total	5			$235	2	3

This report would be extended to include each campaign worker's assignments within each team and then a total would be tabulated for a summary report by all teams.

solicitation phase of the campaign. It is highly desirable to have a grand kick-off for the entire campaign, but additional kick-off events for area/division levels, or for geographical reasons, should not be ruled out. It is highly desirable to include a social component in the program. Sharing a meal is always a good bet. Breakfast meetings may work best, because they tend to be less expensive and convey, by being held in the morning, a sense of importance. The timing of this event, however, should fit the lifestyle of most of your volunteers. If a number of volunteers commute and have to leave for work at 6:30 A.M., an evening event may be best.

The event itself should project an atmosphere of success. The proper use of decorations and, perhaps, a theme can signal that this not just another meeting. The agenda should be simple, move quickly, and end on time with an inspirational message. Volunteers who attend should feel that they are part of something grand and that funding the organization is important. Exhibit 28.15 outlines a suggested agenda for a kick-off meeting. The kick-off meeting is a major volunteer recognition device; the beginning phase of the volunteer recognition program. This is the time to motivate and to inspire. A properly executed kick-off meeting can result in a smoother and more highly productive campaign.

(J) REPORTING PROCESS

A clearly defined reporting process is a must. The easier and quicker the process is, the better it is. A local or area not-for-profit might hold a one-day solicitation and reporting process by conducting a breakfast kick-off meeting, then holding the first report meeting at a social gathering in late afternoon of the same day. This type of quick turnaround has proven to net high returns. A one-day focused solicitation plan is not for every not-for-profit, but it can be effective for a number of grassroots organizations. Most volunteer solicitors will spend the same amount of time visiting with their prospects. The key is to have volunteers do it in a condensed period of time. The length of the campaign will dic-

---

EXHIBIT 28.15 Suggested Agenda for a Kick-off Meeting

1. Opening
   - The campaign chair acts as the master of ceremonies;
   - The lead volunteer for the not-for-profit provides opening remarks; and
   - The lead professional of the not-for-profit provides remarks as well.
2. The Social Event/Meal
3. Submeetings of Areas/Divisions (may be accomplished at assigned tables)
   - Prospect cards and materials are handed out;
   - The schedule and the reporting process are reviewed; and
   - Volunteer gifts/pledges are solicited.
4. Oral Reports by Area/Division Chairs (Each chair includes the following information in his or her report.)
   - Number of volunteers present and other volunteers who will participate;
   - Number of prospects to be covered;
   - The total gifts/pledges collected from volunteers to date including personal donations; and
   - The proposed plan to ensure that all prospects will be covered (if needed).
5. Special Address (by a speaker who has been a recipient of the services of the not-for-profit).
6. A Tally of the Gifts/Pledges Given and a Special Thank-You to Volunteer Donators.
7. Inspirational Message (audiovisual, etc.).
8. Closing
   - Concluding remarks and review of the reporting process.

---

tate the best time to hold report meetings. A report meeting should not be a series of dragged-out events that everyone dreads. It must be designed to recognize success and to encourage and educate others on how to complete their visits successfully. Three report meetings should be enough. All prospect cards should be returned by the third meeting and should then be evaluated as to the following results:

- The total number of solicitations made and the number of successes
- The number of refusals and why they occurred
- The total number of prospects who could not be seen

The prospects who were unable to be seen should be reviewed to determine whether they are still viable prospects. The prospects who were unable to be reached or were not contacted should be designated as prospective prospects for the last phase of the solicitation campaign.

(K) MOP-UP

No matter how successful the annual campaign has been, there will remain prospects who were not seen. The last part of the solicitation process is the true measure of the quality and perseverance of the volunteer team. This can be the hardest part of the campaign if the campaign plan did not anticipate the mop-up phase. The volunteers have worked to ensure that all the other prospects were seen. The campaign is running down, and it is losing steam. The mop-up phase is generally less than 10 percent of the total campaign. This an ideal time to call on your reserve pool of volunteers and a few other dedicated volunteers to assist. Hold a cleanup rally. Bring as many volunteers together as possible to review the remaining prospect cards. Have each person select the donor prospects they wish to solicit. Suggest one week to contact the prospects, and hold a report meeting at the end of the week. If prospects still have not been seen, find out why. If most prospects have been seen, suggest that a letter be sent to them and that a volunteer follow up by telephone. Allow two weeks for the process to be completed, then formally close the campaign. It is important to note that striving to achieve the projected funding goal is important but it is not the entire objective. The annual campaign provides an opportunity for donors to fulfill an important role in the community by offering a way for them to support a program or cause they feel is important. Therefore, the cultivation-solicitation process must be a delicate system of events that engages both the giver and the receiver to complete the philanthropic cycle.

28.3 Evaluation

(A) OVERALL EVALUATION

The annual campaign should have an overall review to determine its success. This should include the process itself, its results, and its impact on the organization. The professional staff of the not-for-profit will want to know whether the support they provided was appropriate and how it might be improved for next year. Volunteer leaders will want to know whether the structure of the campaign was appropriate and whether the support given to the volunteer solicitors by staff was adequate. An evaluation report should be submitted by the annual campaign chair to the board of directors of the not-for-profit no more than 60 days after the end of the campaign.[20]

(B) VOLUNTEERS' STANDPOINT

Volunteers are an important resource in the evaluation of an annual campaign. They can provide insight on the areas that can use refinement and the areas that may open new opportunities for the campaign next year. An individual evaluation program can assist in the overall volunteer evaluation of the annual campaign. This process should be led by the campaign chair and supported by the not-for-profit professional staff. Exhibit 28.16 outlines a suggested evaluation sheet for volunteers.

28.4 Volunteer Recognition

(A) VOLUNTEERS WANT TO BE RECOGNIZED

When the campaign is completed, all solicitations are in, and the evaluation report is submitted, is the campaign over? The answer is no, not unless you have made provisions for the recognition of the volunteers who made it possible. Volunteers want to be recog-

---

[20]James C. Fisher and Kathleen M. Cole, *Leadership and Management of Volunteer Programs* (San Francisco: Jossey-Bass, 1993), pp. 138–143.

EXHIBIT 28.16 Sample Volunteer Evaluation Sheet

Great Mountain Boys Club
Annual Campaign Evaluation

Name: *Tom Smith*   Campaign Position: *Chair Section 3, D Team*   Date: *10-15-97*

This is a self-evaluation of your experience during the annual campaign. It is designed to assist the Great Mountain Boys Club to better prepare and execute future campaigns. The volunteers and professional staff deeply appreciate your assistance during this year's campaign. Your personal effort helped to make our campaign a success. This is an opportunity to provide written feedback on your volunteer experience.

1. How many donor prospects did you originally commit to solicit? *5*
2. How many donor prospects did you solicit? *4*
3. What was your goal? *$1,980*
4. What did you actually collect? *$2000*
5. How would you rate the campaign support? (on a scale of 1 to 10, with 10 being the highest) *8.* Please explain your answer:

   For the most part I found the support really great, but do think that the information on each donor prospect could be more detailed.
6. What is your opinion of the materials used?

   Excellent _ Good *X* Fair _ Poor _

   Please explain your answer:

   The materials were as good as they could be in light of the Boys Club's budget for the campaign.
7. What is your reaction to the meetings you attended?

   Excellent _ Good *X* Fair _ Poor _

   Please explain your answer:

   The meetings were designed to meet the need to promote and to report progress. I do think we should begin and end on time more often.
8. Do you have any advice on how the Boys Club could improve the annual campaign?
   I suggest that additional time be spent on gathering more detailed profiles on higher-level donor prospects and then matching them with volunteer solicitors to achieve a greater return.

nized for what they have accomplished. As *The Nonprofit Management Handbook* reveals, recognition can come in a number of forms. Although thank-you letters from key leaders to all volunteers are appropriate, they should not constitute the only form of recognition.[21] Volunteer recognition can also occur in the not-for-profit's publications, news releases can be sent to area newspapers, letters can be sent to the volunteers' employers thanking them for their employees' contribution to the community, and so on. A written recognition plan should be in place to honor annual campaign volunteers. Chapter 47, "Donor Recognition and Relations," provides additional details on the subject.

---

[21]Tracy Daniel Connors, *Nonprofit Management Handbook: Operating Policies and Procedures* (New York: John Wiley & Sons, 1993), p. 117.

(B) VOLUNTEER RECOGNITION RALLY

No matter how many written thank-you recognitions a volunteer receives, a volunteer recognition rally should be conducted. This is a formal event, staged to thank volunteers for a job well done. Spouses and significant others should be encouraged to attend. The event should be of such quality that sponsorships are sought to cover the expenses of the affair. This is the time to present individual awards to each volunteer, as well as other types of awards. These awards should include recognition of achievement based on the various goals met. Recognition awards for volunteers to the annual campaign should be both meaningful and consistent from year to year. Traditional awards such as plaques and certificates are still used, but an increasing number of campaigns are turning to awards that recipients will more likely display or use in their homes or offices. Limited art prints, tabletop awards, and personal items such as key rings provide ongoing reminders to volunteers of the positive experiences they had in the campaign. This final rally completes the recognition of volunteers who have made a significant contribution of time, money, and energy to the success of the annual campaign.

The volunteer recognition rally is also the informal beginning of the next year's annual campaign. It puts closure to the present campaign and psychologically prepares volunteers to be asked to serve for the following year. Ideally, the new campaign chair for the following year's annual campaign should be introduced at this time.

28.5 Closing the Annual Campaign

The key volunteers and professionals should get together to review the evaluation report and to set plans for the next year. Last year's chair as well as the new annual campaign chair should attend. All reports and workbooks documenting the annual campaign should be turned in and placed for safekeeping in the not-for-profit's office. The new annual campaign chair should be given a proposed schedule for the following year. This meeting can pay real dividends when the time comes to begin the campaign process again. The key elements in a volunteer-led annual campaign schedule were cited earlier.

28.6 Conclusion

Volunteer-led solicitations provide the essence of what not-for-profits are designed to perform. Not-for-profits are volunteer-led organizations that are supported by a full-time professional staff. Annual campaigns are not successful unless volunteers assist. Not-for-profits are successful only when volunteers and professionals work together as a team, performing the tasks they are assigned. The annual campaign is a prime example of how this combined team can work to make a difference. In today's environment, where the loss of government funding and overdependence on foundation grants have had a negative effect on a number of not-for-profits, the reliable annual campaign can help build a steady base of income. The average not-for-profit needs to build beyond the three- to five-year window that grant funds tend to provide.[22] The tried and true volunteer-driven annual fund campaign should be reinstituted or revitalized as the base fund-

---

[22]Holly Hall, "Planning Ahead for Survival," *Chronicle of Philanthropy,* January 11, 1996, p. 22.

raising component for not-for-profits. Joseph R. Mixer has noted, "For more than two hundred years, fund-raising has been practiced in the United States to support charitable organizations and their causes. Yet, systematic, organization solicitations of funds came into being only during the last eighty years."[23] It is the systematic use of volunteers to build the annual campaigns of not-for-profits that will assist in the preservation of the philanthropic tradition for the next two hundred years.

Suggested Readings

Below, Patrick J., George L. Morrisey, and Betty L. Acomb. *The Executive Guide to Strategic Planning.* San Francisco: Jossey-Bass, 1987.

Brudney, Jeffrey L. *Fostering Volunteer Programs in the Public Sector.* San Francisco: Jossey-Bass, 1990.

Bryson, John M. *Strategic Planning for Public and Nonprofit Organizations.* San Francisco: Jossey-Bass, 1989.

Connors, Tracy D. *The Nonprofit Management Handbook: Operating Policies and Procedures.* New York: John Wiley & Sons, 1993.

————. *The Volunteer Management Handbook.* New York: John Wiley & Sons, 1995.

Drucker, Peter F. *The New Realities.* New York: Harper & Row, 1989.

————. *Managing the Non-Profit Organization.* New York: HarperCollins, 1990.

Firstenberg, Paul B. *Managing for Profit in the Nonprofit World.* New York: The Foundation Center, 1986.

Fisher, James C., and Kathleen M. Cole. *Leadership and Management of Volunteer Programs.* San Francisco: Jossey-Bass, 1993.

Greenfield, James M. *Fund-Raising Fundamentals.* New York: John Wiley & Sons, 1994.

Gronsjerg, Kirsten A. *Understanding Nonprofit Funding.* San Francisco: Jossey-Bass, 1993.

Hall, Holly. "Planning Ahead for Survival." *Chronicle of Philanthropy,* January 11, 1996, p. 22.

Hodgkinson, Virginia A., and Murray S. Weitzman. *Giving and Volunteering in the United States.* Washington, D.C.: Independent Sector, 1994.

Houle, Cyril O. *Governing Boards.* San Francisco: Jossey-Bass, 1989.

Ilsley, Paul J. *Enhancing the Volunteer Experience.* San Francisco: Jossey-Bass, 1990.

Lawler, Edward E. *Motivation in Work Organizations.* San Francisco: Jossey-Bass, 1994.

Lynch, Richard. *Lead.* San Francisco: Jossey-Bass, 1993.

Mixer, Joseph R. *Principles of Professional Fundraising.* San Francisco: Jossey-Bass, 1993.

O'Neill, Michael. *The Third America.* San Francisco: Jossey-Bass, 1989.

Payton, Robert L. *Philanthropy.* New York: Macmillan, 1988.

Pidgeon, Walter P. *Volunteering: The Leader's Competitive Edge.* The National College Graduate Survey on Volunteering. Cincinnati: Union Institute, 1991.

Stratton, Jeff, ed. *Nonprofit Volunteer Management.* Gaithersburg, Md.: Aspen Publications, 1994.

Tecker, Glenn, and Marybeth Fidler. *Successful Association Leadership.* Washington, D.C.: American Society of Association Executives Foundation, 1993.

Wellins, Richard S., William C. Byham, and Jeanne M. Wilson. *Empowered Teams.* San Francisco: Jossey-Bass, 1991.

Zander, Alvin. *Effective Social Action by Community Groups.* San Francisco: Jossey-Bass, 1990.

---

[23]Joseph R. Mixer, *Principles of Professional Fundraising* (San Francisco: Jossey-Bass, 1993,) p. 241.

PART V

Major Giving Programs

Overview of Major Giving

M. JANE WILLIAMS, MBA, MED

Schultz & Williams, Inc.

29.1 What Are Major Gifts?

All not-for-profits, from large, national causes to the smallest, local organization, have the potential to raise significant gifts from those who really care about their services. However, to raise major gifts, not-for-profits must focus on the process and draw potential large donors close enough to their organizations so that major gifts become a real possibility.

This chapter addresses how to build major prospect potential. It discusses how best to approach major prospects, including individuals, corporations, and foundations, both on an ongoing basis and during a capital campaign. This overview deals with broad issues that have an impact on attracting major support and that help put the elements of major gift fund raising in perspective.

What is a major gift? The dollar amount of a major gift varies according to the type of organization and its fund-raising history. One definition of a major gift is a gift to a project or program that may not be recurrent each year. Major gifts are often made to specific projects and are marketed as gifts that can make a real difference to an organization by making projects, programs, and facilities happen. Major gifts can be categorized by size. To make the work necessary to raise the gift worthwhile, major gifts should be of a size that will truly make a difference. A "major" donor may be a giver of an amount far above the average gift for an annual funding effort or, more often, a donor to a special project. The simplest way to define a major gift is that it is of a size that requires personal interaction (cultivation and then a face-to-face solicitation). Major gifts usually come from individuals, corporations, and foundations that have already been annual donors and that have had significant involvement with the organization.

Most fund-raising programs begin by building an annual support program through the use of mailings, events, and/or phone contacts. Annual campaigns provide excellent opportunities to cultivate donor interest, but they can be expensive to operate if there are no especially large gifts made to the annual program or for specific projects. Major gift fund raising is the most cost-effective type of development activity in that the gift return is far larger than the cost of cultivating the donor.

Major gifts are valuable because they can make a significant difference to an organization. They can serve as seed money to get projects started or can actually fund entire programs. Major gifts also help to raise the gift sights of all donors.

In many capital campaigns, a few major donors lead the way. The top-level donors in some campaigns provide as much as 70 percent of the goal. Major donors can make projects happen. Their involvement also puts a stamp of approval on a project, which encourages other donors to support it.

The motivations to make a major gift vary. The eight reasons (in order of frequency) that many individuals make major gifts are as follows.

1. The prospect is sincerely committed to the organization's programs and goals.
2. The prospect, a family member, or a close friend is directly involved with the organization.
3. The prospect respects the solicitor and will give because it is the solicitor who asks.
4. The prospect owes the solicitor a favor.
5. The prospect wants the name of his or her family permanently identified with the cause.
6. The prospect could use the tax advantages a gift will provide.
7. The prospect has a real sense of responsibility to the organization.
8. The prospect feels his or her family or friends can benefit from the facilities funded by the gift.

29.2 Structure of Major Gift Programs

(A) ORGANIZATION

To raise major gifts, a not-for-profit must focus on a select number of prospects and create opportunities for those prospects to make meaningful gifts. To be successful, a major gift program must be well organized. Identified major prospects must be targeted for a number of cultivation steps. Major gift programs should be aimed at those prospects who have the greatest ability to give and the strongest interest in the organization. Focusing on the most likely prospects is key. It is often best, especially with limited staff resources, to confine major prospect activity to the number of prospects that can be managed—even if that number is only 10 or fewer. It is better to have organized interaction with a few prospects than to be overwhelmed because there are "too many" prospects. The seven steps in interacting with major prospects are as follows.

1. Identification
   Prospect's history of giving to your organization and others
   Staff contacts
   Board contacts
   Other connections
2. Evaluation
   Target amount (rating)
   Specific project or interest
   Unrestricted or restricted gift potential or both
3. Assignment
   Cultivator/solicitor
   Staff support
4. Cultivation
   Event attendance
   Mailings
   Individual contacts
5. Readiness Decision
   Solicitation team
   Reassessment after contact
   Revisit and next steps to decision
6. Stewardship
   Acknowledgment and results reports
   Invitations/donor relations
7. Resolicitation

(B) TRACKING SYSTEM

To be well organized in approaching major prospects, especially in a larger organization with many people involved in the process, it is helpful to create a computer tracking system. A tracking system is different from complete biographical data on prospects. It should include only the briefest gift and background data. The purpose of a tracking system is to know just where the organization is with each prospect at any given time. The most important elements to include in a tracking system include:

- Prospect name
- Region (general address information)
- Project focus
- Gift rating
- Cultivators' names
- Solicitor's name
- Name of the staff person assigned to the prospect
- Names of other people who have connections with the prospect
- Date of last interaction with the prospect
- Brief review of recent interaction
- Next steps
- Date of next action

A tracking system is a management tool that should be updated regularly so that the current status of interaction with each prospect can be accessed quickly. Keeping biographical data at a minimum means updates can be streamlined. Users also need the ability to sort prospects by the elements listed so that progress with prospects can be reported regularly to volunteers and staff.

29.3 *Individual Donor*

(A) IMPORTANCE

Individuals, through outright gifts and bequests, are providing nearly 90 percent of all philanthropic dollars given to not-for-profits every year. Total gifts from individuals have grown each year for more than 40 years. Gifts from individuals, including annual support and major and planned gifts, are *the* growth area in philanthropy.

The decline in government funding of not-for-profits is causing many organizations to step up their funding activities with individuals. Each not-for-profit organization can have its own group of individual supporters that not only give financially but also become active participants in the organization's activities.

(B) INVOLVEMENT

Major donors are usually involved in some way with a not-for-profit before they make significant gifts. Individuals, corporations, and foundations invest in causes that are linked to their interests. Interest in causes can be created by careful, targeted interactions orchestrated by the not-for-profit and including its staff and volunteers. *Involvement* and a sense that a major gift can make a real impact on an organization are the key motivators for making sizable gifts.

(C) CONTINUUM OF GIVING

One way to begin supporters' involvement with an organization is to draw in prospects as annual donors. To maximize support from individuals, the goal of all development programs should be to attract regular annual support each year at the highest possible level and then, from those annual donors with significant gift potential, to seek major gifts for specific projects. Some individuals may also be prospects for planned gifts. Planned giving techniques may allow some prospects to make a larger gift than they could make using outright assets. Moreover, for some who are already major donors, a planned gift might allow a truly significant gift through estate planning.

The continuum of giving for individuals is:

annual → major → planned

The constituencies for major and planned gifts are not necessarily different. Prospects may make large outright gifts and then further expand their gift sights by using planned gift options.

(D) HOW DO YOU SPOT A MAJOR PROSPECT?

Most not-for-profit organizations have connections with major prospects that have evolved over time. To be an individual with real potential, a prospect must have assets to draw on to make a significant gift. The following list of factors are good indicators that an individual has gift capability.

- Over 55
- Married
- Religious
- Approaching retirement
- Philanthropic
- History of involvement with not-for-profits
- Personal or family interest in the organization
- Holds mixed assets (a combination of stocks, bonds, real estate, venture holdings, etc.)
- Has a family foundation
- Owns a business
- Has inherited wealth
- Single with few heirs

The most important of these characteristics is holding mixed assets. Most major gifts are made from assets; therefore, a prospect must be able to sell or reorganize assets in order to make a gift.

Changes in lifestyle and in the type of assets owned are also excellent indicators of major gift potential. The following situations should be considered when identifying prospects:

- A death in the family that leads to inherited wealth
- Retirement—especially with a "golden parachute"
- Marriage into wealth
- Sale of a business or property
- Success in a venture capital or real estate deal
- No dependents or heirs
- Financial windfall
- Company takeover

(E) CULTIVATION

Cultivation is necessary for every major gift. Cultivation is a continuous process of interacting with a prospect through mass communications and personal contacts. The prospect should be aware that an organization is building contacts, but these initiatives should be informative and natural, not forced and contrived.

Cultivation is 80 to 90 percent of the process of securing a major gift. It is a process of educating potential donors about an organization's purposes and needs. If cultivation is done effectively and the prospect has the ability to give, support will follow. The real challenge is to maximize the size of the gift.

One way to think of the cultivation process is as a series of "moves," or initiatives that attract a prospect's interest. This concept, first defined by G. T. (Buck) Smith, a veteran development officer and college president, is based on the theory that the best way to cultivate the interest of prospects over a period of time is to engage them in a series of regular but unexpected contacts. These "moves" planned by the development staff to advance a person's relationship with the organization can include anything from a personal visit to a letter, a newsletter, or participation in the organization—an almost endless list of possibilities. To stimulate interest on the part of individuals to make significant gifts, they must frequently be made to feel that the organization is part of their lives. The extent of a prospect's involvement must be real, not artificial. In other words, those moves or initiatives must seem natural to the prospective donor rather than contrived. Therefore, the system of moves is not the same for every prospect; in almost every case, each must be designed specially.

The objective of this stream of initiatives is to move the donor along a continuum of involvement with the organization. This continuum starts with awareness, moves on to interest and involvement and, finally, to commitment, which, it is hoped, will lead to a gift. The development staff of an organization should be the orchestrators of this series of initiatives with major prospects.

(F) THE ASK

Asking is the final stage of seeking a major gift, but many people (particularly nervous volunteers) think fund raising is nothing but asking. The secret to success in major gift fund raising is the ability to identify capable prospects and link them effectively to an organization before asking.

To make major prospect solicitations work, the participants must be prepared and comfortable with the process. Team solicitations often work well when a volunteer is linked with an administrative leader of an organization.

Guidelines for a successful ask follow; keep these points in mind when starting a solicitation.

- Relax.
- You are not begging or asking for charity.
- You are talking to someone you know and who knows about your organization.
- You are most likely talking to someone who is already philanthropic, encouraging him or her to make a new commitment.
- You are giving the prospect an opportunity to do something important.
- Your role is to help people see how they can make an important project happen.
- Enjoy the process.
- Be ready to handle any objections or questions the prospect might have—or to get the answers.
- No matter what the outcome, you have taken an important step in strengthening the relationship between the prospect and the organization.

For many not-for-profits, volunteers still play an important role in major prospect solicitations. Some helpful hints from volunteers who have been successful askers follow.

- Preparation is 90 percent of the process.
- Know as much as you can about the prospect.
- Put yourself in the prospect's shoes; figure out what will capture his or her interest.
- Know the case well enough to internalize it; make the case your own statement.
- Tell why the project is important to you and to the prospect. Stress the specifics you feel strongly about.
- Tailor the request to the prospect.
- Determine what is special to the prospect.
- Know what you are going to do before the meeting.
- Recognize the prospect's mental attitude.
- Concentrate on reading the prospect.
- Present the case; tell it like a story. Put the case in your own words.
- Make the request specific.
- Mention your own commitment; speak of it with enthusiasm and passion.
- Once you make the ask, stop talking and listen.
- After the ask, confirm the agreement, clarify the terms and the pledge period.
- Keep in mind that you are giving the prospect an opportunity to do something rewarding for him- or herself.
- Be confident; nothing is impossible.
- Be ready for a "no" and for objections.
- Convince the prospect the investment is worthwhile.
- Show the prospect you have a personal interest in him or her.
- Recognize the competition; go out and beat it.
- Ask for an investment.
- Set aside the time to be effective as a solicitor.
- Most people do not give because they have not been asked.
- Talk about the benefits of giving.
- People give because they want to.
- Most people respond positively.
- Bring the cause to life.
- Make your case; then listen!

29.4 Role of Volunteers

Volunteers are *key* to increasing the size of major gifts through their interaction with prospects. They can also be very helpful in identifying prospects with major gift potential and in figuring out the best way to draw prospects into an organization. The board, especially if it is a governing board, should take the lead in major gift activity. Some organizations, either without a governing board or with board members who are appointed by other sources, are finding it necessary to create leadership groups for fund raising.

Enlisting a volunteer group just for major gift fund raising or a capital campaign usually requires that some board members be part of the group and that it be carefully staffed. Moreover, for such a group, a finite list of responsibilities should be drawn up, with a time frame.

The eight duties of a major gifts/development committee member are as follows:

1. To understand and appreciate the activities of the organization.
2. To learn about the organization's overall financial picture and about the projects within the organization for which private funding is being sought.
3. To act as spokesperson with the organization's constituencies—individuals, foundations, and the corporate and business community.
4. To help interpret and react to the fund-raising climate in the area.
5. To spearhead an organization's development/major gift activities by:
   • Supporting the organization financially
   • Actively cultivating the interest of potential supporters and soliciting prospects
   • Taking the case for private support of the organization to its constituencies
6. To be directly involved with (*number*) prospects on a regular basis and/or to host cultivation events.
7. To serve as an advisor to the chief executive officer (CEO) or president and the development staff on all issues related to fund raising.
8. As requested, to provide additional counsel related to specific issues having an impact on the organization's fund-raising activities.

(A)   THE BOARD

The expected role of the board in development should be made clear as board members are recruited. This role might include the following:

- *Giving.* Annual support plus gifts to special projects according to the means of the member; also consideration of making a planned gift.
- *Prospect interaction.* Helping to identify, cultivate, and solicit major prospects.
- *Representing* the organization within the community.
- *Setting policies* that relate to gift acceptance and gift management.
- *Approving the necessary* budget for development activities with guidance from administrative leadership.

Some board members will say they cannot be involved in fund raising because they are not "good solicitors." But 80 to 90 percent of the effort in raising major gifts occurs before the "ask." Board members must be convinced that their most crucial role is helping to identify and cultivate prospects. Each board member should have some capability to bring prospects into the organization.

Involvement by the board and other volunteers is key to increasing the impact of a major gift program. Making board members and volunteers comfortable with the fund-raising process can encourage their participation. If volunteers work with staff to prepare prospects for a solicitation, they may actually *want* to be part of a solicitation team when the time comes to ask. Limit the number of prospects being assigned to a board member at any one time to five or so. The task must seem doable.

To be effective in interacting with major prospects, volunteers and board members need certain materials: a case statement that explains current funding needs, a statement of named gift opportunities, and a pledge card. Volunteers are much more comfortable approaching prospects if they have supporting materials to legitimize their mission.

The best way to motivate board members to become involved with major gift activity is to show how the process works and illustrate success with a prospect. Set up a team with the CEO and an effective board member and position them to close a gift with a likely prospect. Once a carefully planned major gift cultivation and solicitation process works with one prospect, volunteers will be less hesitant to help with others.

To be effective, major gift fund raising must be an organizational priority. That means the development staff, administrative leadership, the board, and other volunteers must work together to draw prospects into the cause and to show how important major private funding is. Seven suggestions for involving the board follow.

1. Manage the board well. Set reachable goals for members' involvement in development.
2. Tell board members what is expected of them when they are enlisted.
3. Inform board members in detail about the organization.
4. Encourage board members to be active in the selection, recruitment, and training of new board members.
5. Have realistic expectations about board giving. Be careful about setting a minimum annual gift requirement—it may actually limit giving.
6. Nurture board members; make them feel they play an important role.
7. Enlist and train an effective major gifts/development committee to position development as key to the organization's future.

29.5 *Role of Staff*

(A) DEVELOPMENT STAFF

Development officers are the orchestrators of the major gift process. To be successful, they should know the organization and its needs extremely well and have the competence and ability to interact directly with prospects. Those responsible for major gifts must engage in behind-the-scenes strategizing as well as have direct contact with prospects. Often a development staff person makes the first call on a major prospect to further define his or her gift potential and then becomes the link between the prospect and the organization. That staff person identifies the individual within the organization who should help to cultivate the prospect and then oversees the steps in that interaction. The staff person also has to decide when is the appropriate time to ask and push for the solicitation to occur. A development staff person who is responsible for major gifts needs the following traits.

- Self-starting
- Confident
- Has a can-do attitude
- Competent
- Energetic
- Risk-taking
- Honest
- Committed to the cause
- Willing to travel
- Enthusiastic
- Interesting
- Courteous and sensitive

- Professional
- Always prepared
- Patient
- Persistent
- A good listener

Development staff members involved with major prospects need direct access to board members and the organization's management so that appropriate contacts with prospects can be organized. Development staff should be seen as partners with the board and managers in major prospect activity.

Development staff also have to research prospects to justify their inclusion as targets for intensified activity. They then track all initiatives with prospects to be sure the interaction is continuous and leading to a solicitation.

(B) ADMINISTRATIVE LEADERSHIP

The paid managers of a not-for-profit organization must understand the process of developing major prospects and must play a role in the effort. First, the CEO or president must hire effective development staff and give them the contacts and resources to do their jobs. The head of a not-for-profit is the titular head of the development program. He or she should also be a chief cultivator and solicitor of major prospects. Key donors want to see the involvement of the president so that they know the leadership is aware of their interest and is shepherding their involvement with the organization.

The CEO and other managers must also be the definers of funding priorities so that the development staff know what options to present to major prospects. In addition, they must provide an adequate budget to carry out development activities.

Ideally, development, especially major prospect activity, is seen as an institutional priority, so that key leaders are willing to be drawn into the process of developing major prospect potential. The leaders of a not-for-profit are the best people to sell its programs to prospective supporters. They must convey, in a compelling way, a vision of the future of the organization.

29.6 *Corporate and Foundation Giving Trends*

Gifts from corporations and foundations are an important part of the private funding environment for most not-for-profits. In many regions, support from leading foundations and corporations is a barometer for the success of funding efforts. Foundations often lead donors to new initiatives, and corporate support can broadly publicize an organization's objectives.

In recent years, corporate giving nationally has leveled off, whereas foundation giving has grown. The following is a list of a few key trends in the evolution of giving by these institutional sources.

- Many corporations are changing what they do to support not-for-profits. Outright gifts are being supplemented by support from marketing and sponsorship budgets.

- Many large corporate giving programs are under review and face significant change.
- Corporations are seeking to bring the giving process in line with business goals. "Corporate social investment" requires a quid pro quo in return for gifts.
- Corporate giving is increasingly directed to specific projects in regions tied to company operations.
- Unrestricted corporate giving, except from small businesses, has nearly disappeared.
- Large national foundations are seeking to have an impact on broad issues by starting initiatives and then inviting participation by selected not-for-profits.
- Some foundations are declining to support not-for-profits that have annual operating deficits.
- Downsizing and consolidation make it difficult to justify corporate philanthropy to shareholders.
- Corporations and foundations are increasingly being asked to support programs that were previously supported by tax dollars, such as public libraries and public school projects.
- Newly emerging entrepreneurs may be prospects in the long run but often do not have time to think about philanthropy as their businesses grow.

Suggested Readings

AAFRC Trust for Philanthropy. *Giving USA: The Annual Report of Philanthropy*. New York: American Association of Fund-Raising Counsel, annual editions.

Arthur Anderson & Co. *Tax Economics of Charitable Giving*. Chicago: Arthur Anderson & Co., annual editions.

Ashton, Debra. *The Complete Guide to Planned Giving*. Cambridge, Mass.: JLA Publications, 1988.

Barrett, Richard D., and Molly E. Ware. *Planned Giving Essentials*. Gaithersburg, Md.: Aspen Publishers, 1997.

Bowen, William G. *Inside the Boardroom: Governance by Directors and Trustees*. New York: John Wiley & Sons, 1994.

Burnett, Ken. *Relationship Fundraising: A Donor-Based Approach to the Business of Raising Money*. London: White Lion Press, 1992.

Conrad, Daniel Lynn. *How to Solicit Big Gifts*. Detroit: Public Management Institute, 1978.

Kihlstedt, Andrea, and Catherine R. Schwartz. *Capital Campaigns, Strategies That Work*. Gaithersburg, Md.: Aspen Publishers, 1997.

Nichols, Judith. *Pinpointing Affluence*. Chicago: Precept Press, 1994.

O'Connell, Brian. *The Board Member's Book*. New York: The Foundation Center, 1985.

Panas, Jerold. *Born to Raise*. Chicago: Pluribus Press, 1988.

———. *Mega Gifts: Who Gives Them, Who Gets Them*. Chicago: Pluribus Press, 1984.

Prince, Russ Alan, and Karen Maru File. *The Seven Faces of Philanthropy: A New Approach to Cultivating Major Donors*. San Francisco: Jossey-Bass, 1994.

Schneiter, Paul H. *The Art of Asking*. New York: Walker & Co., 1978.

Seymour, Harold J. *Designs for Fund-Raising*. New York: McGraw-Hill, 1966.

White, Douglas E. *The Art of Planned Giving*. New York: John Wiley & Sons, 1995.

The Corporate Support Marketplace

Lester A. Picker, EdD
Picker & Associates

30.1 Introduction

Corporate charitable giving is as old as our nation. It is based on the belief that corporations have a stake in helping the communities in which they operate. Since the earliest times in our nation's history, American business has been concerned with the quality of the workforce and the social conditions that have an impact on the business climate. In this context, one could view corporate charitable giving as self-serving.

In the quasi-capitalist system within which American business operates, corporations must be concerned with the bottom line; after all, no one in the community benefits if a legitimate business fails. The fallout from business closures goes far beyond the loss of income by the company's workers. A ripple effect is felt by suppliers, and the tax revenue to support critical social programs and community infrastructures like roads and schools is lost. Given the need to earn a profit, corporate charitable giving must be placed in its proper context. Despite its flaws, this quasi-capitalist system works and is lent credence by the recent events in Eastern Europe.

There are, however, other reasons for corporate giving programs. Many of these programs begin with self-serving interests and, over the years, evolve into a culture of caring. In these cases, giving is often divorced from the marketing interests of the business and exists to do good for its own sake. This caring attitude extends to the executive corps within the company, so that personal giving and volunteerism become norms of the business culture.

30.2   The Marketplace Today

(A)   OVERVIEW

The not-for-profit field is an enormous enterprise in the United States. Annually, more than $621.4 *billion* flows through the books of the more than 1 million not-for-profits recognized by the Internal Revenue Service. Collectively, these not-for-profits control assets worth more than $1 trillion and employ between 6.9% of the total workforce.

Corporate support of charities is also big business in the United States, but it is by no means the major source of charitable dollars. In 1999, corporations gave approximately $11.02 billion of the estimated total charitable giving of $190.1 billion—a mere 5.7 percent of all charitable gifts, according to the American Association of Fund-Raising Counsel.

Private foundations, another source of not-for-profit revenues, play a larger role in charitable giving. In 1999, the nation's more than 58,000 private foundations contributed approximately $19.81 billion, or 10.4 percent of total charitable contributions. However, because of a variety of factors, the giving by foundations has a far greater impact on the not-for-profit community than does corporate giving.

Private individuals donate the overwhelming preponderance of charitable dollars. In 1999, individual Americans gave approximately 83.7 percent of charitable dollars, a total of more than $159.32 billion in total giving and bequests. Of interest to all not-for-profit leaders is the fact that a sizable number of private givers are corporate executives or executive retirees, a group that tends to give larger gifts than the population at large. This fact should be calculated into a not-for-profit's strategic plan for resource development. Specifically, the implications of giving by this market segment demonstrate that, once a relationship with rising starts in the corporate world is cemented, the not-for-profit benefits not only from corporate support, but from private dollars as well.

(B)   PROGRAMS SUPPORTED

The range of programs supported by corporate giving is as broad as philanthropy itself. Corporate gifts are applied to scholarships, endowments, capital campaigns, seed money for new program initiatives, operating support, and deficit reduction.

Although funding for some categories is undoubtedly easier to secure than for others, development officers can recount for willing listeners war stories of how traditional taboos against certain categories, deficit reduction in particular, have been overcome.

As one would expect, corporations are cautious about the programs they choose to support. Negative publicity can adversely affect the bottom line, especially in today's volatile stock market. It is not uncommon for a company to lose 10 percent of its value overnight because of negative press coverage. Therefore, it is considerably more difficult for controversial programs to receive corporate support than more traditional, conservative causes. Examples abound. Corporations regularly withdraw advertising support for television shows that may offend viewers, or choose not to advertise in publications that are considered offensive to sizable market segments. Often these withdrawals draw as much attention and negative publicity as the controversial programming. This type of controversy is most evident in the highly charged, emotional, and polarized area of reproductive rights.

Many companies choose to support issues that directly affect their client markets: A sneaker company may support youth programs or a pharmaceutical company may support population planning or other health-related programs.

(C) ATTITUDES

The relationship between not-for-profits and their for-profit counterparts is, and has always been, a tenuous one. Many factors are responsible for this shaky relationship, not the least of which is the widely different profiles of the individuals who have historically led the two types of institutions.

Executives of not-for-profits have traditionally been raised through the social caring network; in other words, they tend to be experts in their public service field, not necessarily in business management. They are typically caring individuals who place people's needs first, often at great cost to themselves. They frequently lack understanding of business needs and have a mistrust of businesspeople who are motivated by profit. This description represents a somewhat generalized stereotype. In recent years, the "third sector" has improved its management training and development.

Businesspeople, on the other hand, often have difficulty understanding the not-for-profit environment. They almost universally recognize the good works that not-for-profit organizations do, but they often do not speak the same language as not-for-profit staff. Further, they are often in conflict between the desire to attend to the bottom line of the charity and the intense human needs that not-for-profits address on a daily basis.

This mutual lack of understanding has several serious consequences. First, not-for-profit executives are often reluctant to approach corporations for funding. When they do, they can be ill at ease and not terribly successful in terms of securing needed funds. Another consequence is that through lack of understanding of the business environment, not-for-profits are not particularly effective in designing strategies in which both parties benefit.

30.3 *Seeking Corporate Support*

(A) THE CASE *FOR* CORPORATE SUPPORT

The case for corporate support is a compelling one for many not-for-profit organizations. Even during the best of times, there never seems to be enough money to support the ever-increasing costs of operations. In today's turbulent economic climate, it is extremely hard to predict program fees, investment income, interest rates, and other financial vehicles on which not-for-profits depend for revenues. As a result, most not-for-profit organizations will at some time seek corporate support for their good works.

The following paragraphs discuss management issues that are addressed by a not-for-profit organization in achieving corporate support.

(i) Revenue for Current Operations

Corporate funding is one of several sources that not-for-profits can approach to fund current operations. Admittedly, corporate funding is not the most likely source to cover this type of revenue need. Most corporate chiefs believe that not-for-profits should develop detailed strategic plans and accompanying budgets that will allow them to live within their means, much as the company's stockholders require. Therefore, raising corporate funds to support current operations is a difficult, but not impossible, sell.

The scenarios most likely to result in funding for current operations occur when a not-for-profit has a longtime board member who has an influential position in a company. A not-for-profit that supports an area of critical interest to a company will have a greater chance for success, as when a science education program seeks support from a high-technology company. In most cases, though, support for current operations should be viewed as difficult to obtain and a temporary measure.

(ii) Predictable Cash Flow

Receiving a grant from a corporate source helps a not-for-profit to plan better for the immediate future. Because most companies rarely commit to a funding initiative more than two or three years in advance, overoptimistic revenue assumptions based on this approach are dangerous. However, most not-for-profits estimate budgets based on a mix of revenue sources, so a small percentage of anticipated corporate funding is healthy and frequently indicates a broad resource base.

(iii) Seed Money for New Programs

The likelihood of corporate support is increased when the request is for seed money for new programs. This is especially true when the program addresses social issues that have direct appeal to the business community, such as improved science education, reform of public schools, university research, or healthcare initiatives designed to lower overall healthcare costs for the community.

Corporations tend to fund short-term projects, and most require some evidence that the program either will be self-supporting or will attract new dollars after the seed period is over. No company leaders will agree to seed funding if they believe they will inherit a public relations nightmare when they stop the cash infusion and no one is able to pick it up.

(iv) Broadening the Resource Base

People like to support winners. Nowhere is this truer than in the not-for-profit fundraising environment. How do corporate funders perceive winners? First and foremost, by their ability to attract donations from a diverse group of funding sources, including board members, private individuals, foundations, corporations, fees for services, and government agencies. This broadened base also enables the not-for-profit to weather economic storms by diversifying its revenue sources. In this case, corporate support can play a strong role by improving a not-for-profit's ability to attract or leverage other revenue sources.

(v) Credibility and Stature

Receiving funds from corporate sources lends an air of credibility to a not-for-profit organization. It is a vote of confidence from the business community. Rightly or wrongly, other donors view such support as an indication that the not-for-profit has a track record and programs worthy of support.

As a result of intense competition for limited corporate dollars, not-for-profits that are regularly funded by corporations gain additional stature and respect.

(vi) Entry to Other Funding

Another major benefit derived from corporate funding is the leverage it provides to other funding. When a company with an established, reputable giving program decides to fund a not-for-profit organization, it often accompanies the gift with additional resources, including volunteers and loans of executives.

Often corporations help open doors to other corporations, believing that they have already made a significant investment and wishing to do whatever they can to ensure that the investment is successful.

(vii) Noncash Contributions

A further benefit of corporate support is the multitude of noncash resources that tend to flow, once trust and credibility are established. Such noncash resources include volunteers, donations of depreciated assets and excess inventory, board members, executives-on-loan, and other creative contributions. If the supported program(s) are successful, the leader of the not-for-profit can augment its management resources with counsel from its for-profit counterparts. This has proven to be an invaluable asset to many not-for-profit organizations.

(B) THE CASE *AGAINST* CORPORATE SUPPORT

(i) The Odds Are Not Good

For every corporate donation to a charitable institution, there are often more than 100 requests. In today's competitive philanthropic environment, it is common for corporations with $1 million giving programs to receive more than 1,000 requests for help per year. The odds of a particular not-for-profit's obtaining corporate funding are slim, even after absorbing the high costs of staff time spent researching the company and soliciting the corporate decision makers.

There are many actions a not-for-profit can take to improve dramatically the odds of obtaining corporate support and funding. But even under the best of circumstances, sustained corporate funding is far from a sure thing.

(ii) It Is a Tough Sell

Many naive or beginning not-for-profit executives think that garnering corporate support is not very difficult. Some take a shotgun approach to funding, broadcasting hundreds of letters or proposals in the hope that one will find a receptive audience. That premature optimism is quickly extinguished.

Successful corporate solicitation processes involve planning time, staff-consuming and painstaking research, cultivation of potential donors, writing and rewriting proposals, and meticulous follow-up. Often, even after extensive cultivation, the gift can dissolve under the pressures of declining corporate profits or be received in an amount far lower than anticipated.

(iii) Integrity

For many not-for-profits, the "circus" of corporate solicitation is more a can't-make-any-misstep tightrope walk than a center ring attraction. Consider a large environmental organization, for example. Should it accept gifts from corporations that have documented pollution histories? Should the American Cancer Society accept an offer of a large gift from a tobacco company? In these cases, the answers seem obvious. But every day not-for-profits face decisions involving corporate gifts and support that take them deep into ethical gray areas.

Integrity is the ethical foundation and "currency" of most not-for-profit organizations. Many, therefore, consciously choose not to solicit corporations for fear of comprising this major asset.

(iv) It Is Not the Real Thing

For many not-for-profits, the search for the envisioned cornucopia of corporate support is undertaken to avoid dealing with major underlying problems, such as financial instability. There is simply no substitute for detailed strategic planning by the board and staff of a not-for-profit, including financial planning. Most major corporate giving and support is contingent on a sound financial plan before any significant commitment is made.

30.4 Corporate Support for Not-for-Profit Organizations

(A) THE CASE *FOR* SUPPORTING NOT-FOR-PROFIT ORGANIZATIONS

All too often, not-for-profit organizations imagine the corporate "pocket" as stuffed with cash, failing to realize the underlying dynamic rationale and process. Corporations give away ("target" might be more accurate) their pretax profits for a variety of reasons, some of them more fully thought out than others. It is critical for the eventual success of a corporate solicitation program that not-for-profit managers understand the rationale for corporate support *from the corporate perspective*. Some of the major reasons that corporations choose to invest in not-for-profit causes are described in the following paragraphs.

(i) Support of Business-related Community Infrastructure

American business cannot gain a competitive edge in the long term if community infrastructures are not strong. Significant media attention has been devoted to documenting problems with public education, housing, drug abuse, and illiteracy. In one major United States automobile assembly plant, management has had to revert to instructions in sign language and graphics, to overcome the severe illiteracy problems it is facing.

By investing in public schools, affordable housing, and literacy programs, for example, the business community is ensuring its own survival.

(ii)   Social Investment

Closely related to the issue of infrastructure is the issue of social investment. In the enlightened times in which we now find ourselves, corporations realize they have a responsibility to address and help to solve social problems. Many social issues overlap (and, at times, undermine) those that support the infrastructure of American business. Teenage pregnancy, for example, although not necessarily a direct problem for American business, imposes enormous drains on the tax base, removes needed workers from the labor pool, and perpetuates a cycle of poverty, all of which have significant implications for business.

Although no one would argue that the goal of any business is to earn a profit, many citizens advocate that part of a company's mission includes investing "social capital." Enlightened corporate executives understand the role that their company should play in the community and are prepared to exercise their responsibility in the area of social investment.

(iii)   Doing Good While Doing Well

Doing social good while doing well in business is a value of long standing among corporations that have a strong history of charitable giving. These corporations produce and support a significant number of corporate senior leaders who are highly motivated to do good works for and within the community, whether local, national, or international.

(iv)   Marketing

Most corporations integrate their charitable support into the overall marketing strategy designed to increase market share. Some social activists attack this approach, but most philanthropy professionals understand, accept, and support it as entirely ethical within the context of a quasi-capitalist economic system.

There are countless examples of charitable giving and support provided in ways that boost marketing efforts. They include, for example, the following:

- Producers of products for youth supporting drug reduction programs
- Computer makers donating inventories to schools
- Manufacturers of house construction goods donating items for use by community development groups

(v)   Influencing Public Policy

There is no doubt that strategically placed social investment can be part of an overall plan to affect public policy as it applies to the industry in question. Some companies develop plans that weave corporate giving, public relations, government relations, and community affairs into one fabric designed to achieve their public policy objectives. It is important for not-for-profits to recognize when this motivation for giving is operating and to decide whether it is in their best interests to participate. In some cases, there is no conflict; in others, there may be actual or perceived conflicts.

(B)   THE CASE *AGAINST* CORPORATE SUPPORT OF NOT-FOR-PROFIT ORGANIZATIONS

(i)   Profits

Most large-company executives and directors understand the need for social investment, but the same cannot be said for small to medium-size businesses, especially in today's strongly entrepreneurial business climate. Many of these businesses were started by individuals who had little or no prior business experience, are family owned and family grown, or were created small and then experienced explosive revenue growth within a few brief years.

These companies may not have a tradition or culture of giving. The individual who started the business is usually so closely focused on business goals that a giving program is the last thing on his or her mind. Finally, such people may be so completely caught up with their hard-won business success, and their history of fighting to stretch every dollar in their company's formative years, that they view handing out pretax profits as anathema.

Although this outlook could be a real problem for not-for-profit resource development, it also presents an exciting opportunity to bring these corporations into the philanthropic community. Then, as the company grows, a culture of giving and caring may take root and translate into strong programs of community investment.

(ii) Time

In many companies, corporate giving is viewed as a waste of staff time, and, in business, time translates into money. If anything characterizes business today as opposed to decades ago, it is executives' never-ending search for more time to accomplish business goals.

As a result of this outlook, many businesses choose not to involve themselves in philanthropic activities or may delegate those responsibilities to lower management. Again, this situation is not all bad: A not-for-profit can hitch itself to a rising corporate star and harvest the fruits of its efforts as the executive climbs the corporate ladder.

(iii) Philosophical Orientation

Although their viewpoint is less common today, some corporate chief executive officers see philanthropy as a private, individual activity, not properly within the province of business. These people believe that they help the community best when they conduct a profitable business in such a way that jobs are created and taxes are paid, which in turn creates a better standard of living and supports services for those who cannot afford them.

(iv) Unfamiliarity

It is a fact that many corporations do not participate in philanthropic activities simply because they have no history of doing so and are unfamiliar with how to get started. With the public service needs of not-for-profit organizations at an all-time high, it is hard to accept this explanation; however, it is the most frequently cited reason among those small to mid-size corporate chiefs who are not involved in philanthropy. This sad state of affairs signals that not-for-profits must do a far better job of educating and involving these businesses in charitable activities, through committee work, board memberships, and, eventually, donations of cash and assets.

(C) TYPES OF CORPORATE SUPPORT

The types of corporate support available are even more varied than the reasons corporations choose to involve themselves in corporate philanthropy. Many not-for-profit leaders, not fully appreciating the wide scope of help available from corporations, mistakenly ask only for cash assistance. Very often that is entirely the wrong approach and will result in outright rejection or, if funded, minimal gifts.

The following paragraphs present the broad categories of gifts and brief discussions of when a not-for-profit agency might choose to request each type of assistance.

(i) Cash

Direct gifts of cash are obviously always welcome by not-for-profit organizations. Cash gifts are the most sought after and the most difficult to obtain. Cash gifts from corporate sources are most often requested to seed the start of new programs or for capital campaigns, but they are also requested for benefit events, such as sponsorship of a table at the annual dinner. Generally, corporations are not receptive to requests for cash grants for operating support or deficit reduction.

(ii) In-Kind Services

Corporations often contribute in-kind services to help not-for-profit organizations. In-kind services usually involve the donation of employee time and experience, which would otherwise contribute to overhead costs for the not-for-profit. For example, a corporation may donate the services of its in-house accounting staff for tax preparation. Or a corporation may donate the use of its four-color press to produce a capital campaign brochure, saving the not-for-profit many thousands of dollars in printing costs.

(iii) Executive Loan

Throughout the country, large corporations have established executive loan programs in partnership with the not-for-profit community. Competition is keen for the few available slots. These programs are effective for three basic reasons. First, they provide not-for-profits with needed skills in such specialized areas as management, financing, and marketing. Second, they give corporate executives a more realistic understanding of the needs facing the not-for-profit community, often followed by a deeper commitment to a cause, with all its resource development implications. Finally, the loan experience enables not-for-profit leaders to gain more understanding of operations, issues, and policies within the corporate sector. Usually such loan programs are the province of large corporations, which can better afford a temporary loss of some middle managers.

(iv) Employee Matching

Increasing numbers of corporations are establishing employee matching programs. In these programs, employee gifts to not-for-profit agencies are matched by the corporation, thereby leveraging every dollar given. This has an immediate and long-lasting effect on employee morale and retention, while benefiting social causes.

(v) Gifts of Inventory or Depreciated Assets

Corporations' gifts of inventory or depreciated assets are a boon to not-for-profit organizations. Almost every manufacturing company in North America gives such gifts; most gain tax incentives or warehouse savings for doing so. In many locations throughout the country, specialized clearinghouses have been established to solicit, collect, and redistribute such gifts.

(vi) Cause-Related Marketing

The term "cause-related marketing" (CRM) was coined by American Express in the early 1980s. In its most basic form, CRM is a way for a company to increase its market share by trading on the name and good works of a charity. For example, a company might offer a cents-off coupon for which, when redeemed, it will donate a specified amount of money to a not-for-profit cause.

In the original American Express promotion, 10 cents was donated to the Statue of Liberty restoration fund each time its card was used. Results were impressive: American Express cardholders increased their card usage by more than 30 percent. More than $1.7 million was generated for the statue's restoration fund.

CRM is an excellent vehicle for generating revenues for a not-for-profit organization. It also enables the not-for-profit to market its services to a wider audience, because it enlists the efforts of the for-profit company to promote its products. On the downside, any not-for-profit must be very careful about lending its name to a for-profit marketing effort. Surveys, focus groups, or other appropriate data gathering should be conducted by the not-for-profit to ensure that client groups are comfortable with the proposed marketing relationship. The not-for-profit should also ensure that the company is not embroiled in controversial causes that have a bearing on the same audiences served by the not-for-profit organization. Prior to seeking a CRM agreement, a not-for-profit must develop guidelines and policies that will enable it to make solid judgments regarding which CRM agreements to pursue.

Prudence is required on both sides of a CRM agreement, but the negatives are often overstated by those who have little experience in the corporate world. Most corporate executives do understand the implications of a CRM agreement entered into for spurious reasons—that ultimately this type of arrangement will backfire, with potentially disastrous consequences for the for-profit company.

The trend continues toward more CRM relationships between the corporate and not-for-profit sectors, extending even to smaller businesses and not-for-profits. The reason is, primarily, that following massive federal cutbacks, not-for-profits are being expected to play an increasing role in resolving social issues. This expanded role provides corporations with the potential to reach significant new market segments through creative, mutually beneficial partnering with not-for-profit organizations.

30.5 Researching Potential Corporate Sources

As in any fund-raising approach, potential corporate donors should be carefully researched, screened, and cultivated prior to requesting funds. No matter how compelling the need, gifts are invariably larger and extend over longer periods of support when a relationship has been carefully nurtured with corporate donors.

The odds of a not-for-profit organization receiving corporate support increases dramatically if the corporation being solicited is local or has a local operating division. The reasons for this are both obvious and subtle. Corporations understand that they must invest in the community's social infrastructure in order to promote a quality of life that will be attractive to new employees and will retain existing ones. They also recognize that by investing in educational facilities, for example, they are ensuring a viable work force for their future business needs.

How does one begin the process of researching corporate sources close to home? Fortunately, many sources of information and methods are available to help not-for-profits do the background research needed for corporate solicitation. However, as in any type of donor research, the entire process should be organized (so that priorities can be set), comparisons should be made between likely donors, and successful approaches with one category of companies should be tested with others in that category.

Exhibit 30.1 gives an example of a generic research organizer. Using a simplified systems approach to corporate research, a separate organizer sheet can be filled out for each corporate source. A corresponding file folder can be created with that company's name. All corporate sources should be identically color-coded (foundations, private individuals, federal, state, and local sources each receive other color designations). Into the file folder would go news clippings relevant to that company or its industry, the annual report, marketing brochures, notes on meetings with executives, research on alumni working for the company, profiles of important executives, and other pertinent facts. Strong corporate potentials might have a separate, dedicated notebook. If the records are computerized (entered into a database file), reminders should be entered to request annual report updates.

(A) LOCAL CORPORATE SUPPORT

Too often, not-for-profit executives think in terms of national corporations and their large, highly visible gifts to not-for-profit organizations. What are not readily apparent are the countless hours of cultivation that typically precede such gifts. In most cases, *years* of relationship building and several incrementally larger gifts have preceded a large donation. Relationship building today does not come cheap nor happen overnight. For example, there are (usually) travel and staff costs that must be incurred before gifts are received.

The best means of securing corporate support is by carefully researching local support possibilities, then approaching, developing, and nurturing those relationships. Most not-for-profits, in pursuit of the one large corporate gift, lose sight of the broad-base resource building they can accomplish by developing relationships with many smaller companies.

EXHIBIT 30.1 Sample Funding Prospect Form

Keys _____

Name of Corporation _____

Name of Contact _____

Telephone No.   (   )

Address _____

Deadline(s)

Assets _____ High _____ Average _____

Priorities _____

Notes

Reproduced with permission from Picker & Associates.

One of the most effective means of accessing local corporations is to obtain a list of members of the local, county, and state chambers of commerce. These lists can provide the names of corporate officers and the addresses, telephone numbers, and SIC codes of members.

SIC codes provide an excellent means of determining the operating areas of a company. The eight-digit code classifies corporations into one of several increasingly finer categories. For example, the first four digits of a hypothetical company, 2542, reveal that the company is a manufacturer (25) of office fixtures (42). (The last four digits provide even more detail but are usually not needed by most not-for-profits and can provide misleading data for mail campaigns.) Not-for-profits should be sure that they enter the SIC codes into their databases, to allow for retrieval by industry affiliation when soliciting specialized program support. Lists of SIC code designations are available from the U.S. Department of Labor, mailing list vendors, and libraries.

Another way to secure local corporate support is by identifying rising corporate stars. This can be done through a thorough reading of the business sections of local newspapers and regional business magazines. Concurrently, a not-for-profit should ask to be on the mailing list for corporate press releases, corporate newsletters, and annual reports of key companies in its service area.

The development function, as applied to corporate resource building, may involve many different levels and activities. Once a promising individual is identified, a not-for-profit can ask that person to share his or her expertise and get involved—for example, serving on a committee researching some aspect of the not-for-profit's work, including quality control, service delivery, client needs identification, and others. Or a potential board member, volunteer leader, or advocate can be asked to serve on a committee developing a "white paper" on a significant social issue that involves the public service interests of the not-for-profit organization. Businesspeople often willingly take such assignments; they are specific in nature and have a finite time commitment. Still, the not-for-profit must make expectations clear. *It is critical that the first assignments end in success.*

Once a businessperson is involved, and assuming an initial good experience, the not-for-profit can ask the executive to serve on the board or, alternately, on an advisory group. In either case, the organization should make certain that the individual receives challenging assignments. Many not-for-profits, especially smaller ones, mistakenly believe that it is best to simply name an important corporate executive to a committee without requiring him or her to work hard on an assignment. Nothing could be further from the truth. Challenging assignments help the corporate executive see that the not-for-profit is serious about its mission and about meeting the needs of its clientele.

A good way to gain access to a corporate leader is through the not-for-profit's board members and leading volunteers. If a professional or personal relationship already exists between a board member and a corporate leader, it will make the process of education and confidence building that much easier. The fund-raising maxim "People give money to people" is particularly appropriate for corporate solicitations.

(B) NATIONAL CORPORATIONS

Aside from local corporate support, including national corporations that have local operating locations or subsidiaries, there is a possibility of support from national corporations outside the not-for-profit's immediate locale. Corporate giants such as International Business Machines (IBM), American Telephone and Telegraph (AT&T), and Xerox have national giving programs that distribute huge sums of money.

In general, national corporate giving programs are well staffed and have carefully focused programs. The programs are frequently run by a corporate foundation or administered directly by the community affairs office.

There are many sources of information concerning national corporate giving programs. (Recommended research sources are listed in Section 30.10.) The first thing any not-for-profit should do is request a copy of the guidelines and an annual report from the corporate giving program. This is most easily accomplished with a personal letter.

With the guidelines in hand, the not-for-profit should carefully determine whether its organization and/or programs qualify. The number-one reason that grant applications are rejected is that the requesting agency does not fit the published guidelines of the corporate program.

(C) FOREIGN CORPORATIONS

There are millions of foreign corporations operating throughout the world, but those to which an American not-for-profit has access are limited by two major factors:

1. Does the corporation have a significant operating presence in the United States?
2. Does the not-for-profit have an operating presence in the corporation's homeland?

The major barrier to accessing foreign corporations is the culture gap that may exist, especially in the area of corporate involvement in social issues. A prime example is the influx of Japanese industry to the United States. For many years, it was very difficult for American not-for-profits to access these corporations in terms of funding or volunteers. This was primarily traceable to an absence of corporate social programs in Japanese industrial culture. Only in recent years have Japanese companies doing business in the United States begun full-blown social investment programs.

Several reference works detail foreign corporations that operate in the United States. Most of the standard rules of approach apply to a not-for-profit's search for foreign corporate support. One of the more interesting developments in foreign corporate support for American not-for-profits has been in the area of corporate response time in the solicitation process. For example, Honda Corporation of America has published guidelines that pledge unusually quick turnaround time in evaluating and responding to query letters and telephone calls from program officers. It appears that corporate philanthropy is transferring to its customers some of the attention emphasized in product sales and service.

30.6 *Planning and Cultivation*

With the proper research materials, a strategic plan can be developed to guide the not-for-profit organization in cultivating corporate sources and fostering enduring relationships. There is a distinct difference between cultivation and solicitation. Cultivation refers to the long-term relationship-building process. This may entail several layers of involvement, during which time the corporate officers complete committee work and learn about the not-for-profit and the needs of its clients. Cultivation may also include the not-for-profit's performance of services for the corporation, ranging from breast cancer screenings at the corporate site to a string quartet in the corporate cafetet in. Solicitation generally refers to the actual process of asking for support for specific projects or programs.

Perhaps nowhere else in not-for-profit management is relationship so important to meeting long-term objectives. In the corporate world, those in authority prefer to deal with people they trust. This applies not only to agreements and deal making, but also to the many occasions when business colleagues serve together on not-for-profit boards or committees. Therefore, it is critical that a not-for-profit have on its board several businesspersons with the ability (and credibility) to network with the larger business community.

Contrary to the perception of some who may be new to development, solicitation ideally begins with cultivation and an institutional commitment to keep potential donors informed about the organization. Even organizational failures can be used to advantage with potential corporate donors. If a not-for-profit honors a corporate executive by asking for help in resolving an institutional problem, more often than not he or she will end up being a diehard supporter.

(A)   THE APPROACH

(i)   *Personal Meeting*

In the actual solicitation process, creativity and persistence are prerequisites for success. In the solicitation approach itself, relationships are all-important. Corporate giving officers are continually barraged by well-meaning not-for-profits seeking funding. Most requests for funding arrive through the mail and are rejected out of hand—in most cases, rightfully so. Cutting through barriers to obtain a face-to-face meeting with the corporative executives responsible for making the funding decisions should be a primary goal of any corporate solicitation process.

The personal meeting may concern or even frighten those new to the fund-seeking arena. Some people go to great lengths to avoid personal interviews, despite the fact that this is the single most effective way to secure funds for an agency. Some experts estimate that the chances of funding increase by 70 percent if the proposal is preceded by personal contacts. This is understandable on several grounds. First, corporate officers get to learn about the agency and its programs, staff, and board; that knowledge increases the comfort factor when close decisions on funding are made. Given the choice of funding a known vs. an unknown entity, the known almost always prevails. Second, the not-for-profit representatives learn what the latest priorities are; what lessons concerning other funded projects have recently been learned by the corporate officers, which may impact the proposal being discussed; and what key issues, phrases, and concepts are mentioned frequently by the corporate officials and should be included in the proposal. Based on this data, all fund- and support-seeking efforts should be focused on obtaining a face-to-face meeting with carefully targeted corporate funding sources.

Many development officers use a form similar to that shown in Exhibit 30.2 to organize the calling process. It should be noted that busy executives are often best reached *prior* to 9:00 A.M. and *after* 5:00 P.M. Calling at these times frequently has the added advantage of bypassing secretarial interference. Once the meeting is set, not-for-profit representatives should:

EXHIBIT 30.2 Sample Form for Prospect Follow-up Calls

Week of _____
Day _____
Date _____

Proposal _____

	Name	Corp/Agency/Fund	Tel #	Follow-Up Call	Appointment	Decision By
7:00						
7:30						
8:00						
8:30						
9:00						
9:30						
10:00						
10:30						
11:00						
11:30						
12:00						
12:30						
1:00						
1:30						
2:00						
2:30						
3:00						
3:30						
4:00						
4:30						
5:00						

Reproduced with permission from Picker & Associates.

1. Obtain all useful and appropriate information about the corporation before initiating any contact.
2. Dress according to accepted professional or business standards for the meeting.
3. Shake hands firmly.
4. Act assured and behave assertively. (No one feels comfortable handing over limited financial resources to a hesitant asker.)
5. Be honest. (No amount of money is worth compromising one's integrity; if there are questions that cannot be answered during the meeting, the not-for-profit's representatives should promise to get back to the corporate executives by a definite date—and then do so.)
6. Ask questions. (What will be expected of the agency if funded? Is continued funding a possibility, assuming all present program objectives have been met? What materials need to be forwarded following this meeting? How will payments be made?)
7. Actively listen and not act defensively. (If questions by the not-for-profit representative are well designed, the funding official will provide answers that can be incorporated into the formal proposal and will markedly increase chances of being funded.)
8. Not mention a price tag. (Funding officials receive requests totaling many times what they can give; psychologically, funders look for ways to reject proposals quickly, and cost is the most frequently cited reason—yet, when a project excites corporate officials, financial resources are almost never an obstacle.)
9. Treat rejection graciously and look at it as an opportunity. (Perhaps the present request did not meet the funder's current objectives; however, such meetings help not-for-profits understand the funding agency's priorities, establish rapport, and provide personal entry to their personnel.)
10. Keep detailed notes.
11. Always follow up the meeting with a letter, thanking the funder for the opportunity to share the agency's aspirations and recounting any items agreed on.
12. Add the funding source representative to the agency's informational system mailing list.

(ii) Telephone Contact

At the beginning of the solicitation process, a not-for-profit executive may need to resort to the telephone, especially with the high costs associated with travel. In the process of telephone solicitation, the following points should be kept in mind.

1. Thoughts and questions should be organized and written down before the telephone is picked up. All relevant facts and figures should be at the fingertips of the not-for-profit representative. Previous contacts with the funding source, collected in a file folder on the individual or company, should be thoroughly reviewed.
2. The highest-ranking corporate contact person should be requested. Secondary sources should be avoided, unless absolutely necessary (e.g., the higher-ranking person is no longer with the company).
3. The not-for-profit representative should speak clearly and authoritatively. He or she should state the agency's name and get directly to the point. If the contact person has only a few minutes available, the not-for-profit representative should arrange to call back.

4. If the funder asks a question that the not-for-profit representative cannot answer, he or she should agree to get back to the corporate officer with the information and should be sure to follow through. Often the opportunity to get back to the person with follow-up information actually increases a not-for-profit's chances of being funded.
5. Rapport should be established by asking questions and advice of the funder.
6. The not-for-profit representative should convey enthusiasm and a positive attitude for the agency and the program.
7. Active listening skills are imperative. The not-for-profit representative should not monopolize the conversation. Often the representative will be able to suggest program or funding alternatives to a reluctant funder.
8. A secretary should never make the solicitation calls for the not-for-profit representative; it degrades the funder.
9. Every attempt should be made to arrange for a person-to-person meeting to explain the project. As noted previously, a personal meeting increases chances for funding 70 percent, according to some estimates.
10. Good telephone etiquette is a prerequisite to telephone contact with funding sources.
11. Careful records of all pertinent details of conversations with funding sources should be logged.
12. If a follow-up meeting has been scheduled or the not-for-profit representative agrees to send additional information, a one-page follow-up letter should be mailed (or faxed) within 24 hours. The main points of the conversation should be recounted, and the letter should end by stating that the not-for-profit representative is looking forward to a meeting regarding the agency's request.
13. Not-for-profit representatives should try to avoid getting pigeonholed regarding a price tag for the proposal. Beleaguered funding officers look for ways to reject proposals quickly, and the "too-costly" label is the easiest to apply. Yet if they like the concepts, they will often fund part of the project and help the agency to leverage that contribution to secure gifts from other sources. A good approach is for the not-for-profit representative to tell the funding agency representative that his or her input is being sought and evaluated before finalizing the program and request. Following such a meeting, the agency can ask what the funder feels the realistic request range might be.

(B) PARTNERSHIPS

Prior to requesting large sums of money, not-for-profits have been successful in developing partnership arrangements with receptive corporations. As an example, health-related not-for-profits can offer corporate site screenings for high blood pressure, breast cancer, or diabetes. Smoking cessation, stress reduction, and exercise classes are also popular with the corporate community. A key factor improving the chances for success is the perceived benefit to the corporation in terms of public perception or employee relations.

In the same vein, there are many case histories of corporations offering in-kind help to not-for-profits, including accounting, marketing, public relations, and printing. These partnerships are vitally important; they attach a human involvement element to the partnership. These human partnerships are the best leverage a not-for-profit has to eventually obtain a commitment of financial support.

(C) SUBMITTING A FORMAL PROPOSAL

Finally, after the cultivation and solicitation processes begin to bear fruit, the not-for-profit may be asked to submit a formal proposal to the corporate giving committee. There is a strong tendency on the part of not-for-profit organizations to throw at the corporate source every document the agency has ever produced, lengthy descriptions of the agency's history, rambling lists of programs, and program descriptions that are impossibly detailed. After all, according to this train of thought, this is the agency's chance to showcase itself to the corporation.

In reality, a formal proposal to a corporate source is the briefest of all formal proposals. A not-for-profit agency should make every possible attempt to keep the proposal to fewer than five single-spaced or 10 double-spaced pages, excluding cover letter and any appendices. Most giving committee executives simply do not have the time or inclination to thoroughly read lengthy proposals. Instead, they rely on the program officer's analysis and recommendations.

Corporate solicitation proposals are really supplemental follow-ups to the relationship building that has preceded the submission by months or years. By then the corporate source (a "critical mass" of corporate advocates) knows the essentials about the not-for-profit and simply wants to know about the problem, the proposed solution, the methods of assessing success or failure, other funding sources, and the corporation's role.

In corporate solicitations, conciseness is the rule of the game. Be brief, make every word count, and use high-impact, simple graphics to make important points that would otherwise be buried in the narrative.

If supporting materials must be included, be highly selective about which are truly needed. Move cumbersome supporting materials, such as letters of support, to the appendixes. This shows readers that you care about their time and effort and allows them to consult appendixes only if and as needed.

Be sure to give the proposal to two or more naive readers for comment. A naive reader is someone who knows little or nothing about the problem being addressed, which is certain to be the case for many of the corporate decision makers. Ask businesspeople on the board or committees also to review and comment on the proposal before it is submitted.

A cover letter should *always* accompany a proposal, whether the funding contact expects the submission or not. The cover letter is critical; it must secure the reader's interest immediately. The cover letter should:

- Summarize the request concisely.
- Grab the reader's interest quickly. (Do not be afraid to use modifiers to make your concepts sparkle; however, avoid using words like *unique*.)
- Link the not-for-profit's request to the company's expressed interests. (Determine those interests through careful research, reading its published guidelines, telephone and personal contacts, and discussions with others familiar with those funding sources, especially agency board members.)
- Not ramble on any of the issues addressed in the proposal.
- Be confined to one page and *never* exceed two.

- *Always* be addressed to a person, not to "Dear Friend" or "Dear Corporate Director." (Reference sources should be consulted to obtain the names of contacts, *and* accuracy should be confirmed by telephone. (See Exhibit 30.3.)
- Reference previous telephone or personal contact with the addressee.
- Be cleanly typed on agency letterhead, grammatically correct, and free of typos. If the agency letterhead does not include a telephone number, it must be included in the cover letter.

30.7 Follow-up

Too many not-for-profit agencies tend to suffer from the take-the-money-and-run syndrome. Whether because of embarrassment, ignorance, or both, many agencies receive

---

EXHIBIT 30.3 Sample Letter Seeking Corporate Support

Mr. Jack Jones
Vice President
AB Corporation
100 Main Street
Hometown, MD 20001

Dear Mr. Jones,

Thank you again for taking the time to meet with us concerning The Wellness Community of Baltimore's upcoming Wellness Olympic Weekend.

In follow-up to our meeting, we are submitting the enclosed request for support from AB Corporation. Specifically, we are requesting that AB serve as the lead sponsor of the event for the next two years, which we estimate will involve costs not to exceed $25,000 each year.

As we discussed, sponsorship represents an extraordinary opportunity for a company to gain statewide visibility and advance its marketing goals. Our last exclusive sponsor, Maryland Big Bucks Bank, exceeded its recognition goals by some 30 percent owing to the joint promotion, a fact which its president, John Jacobs, attributed to its success in opening branches statewide. Bank employee involvement in the event was highlighted on all three television networks and helped the bank network into new communities. If it were not for a major corporate charitable initiative in homelessness and public housing, the bank would certainly retain its sponsorship. Mr. Jacobs was kind enough to encourage any serious contenders for corporate sponsorship to contact him directly at (301) 555-3333.

The enclosed proposal provides the data you requested in terms of the number of scheduled public messages, media we use, types of promotional materials, and market segments.

We look forward to your response and to the possibility of working with you on the Wellness Olympic Weekend to help people with cancer and their families.

Sincerely,

Suzanne Bryce
Executive Director

Sydney Darnell
Chair of the Board

---

their corporate check, spend it on the intended purpose, and then avoid approaching that company again—until it is time to request new funding.

Once an agency secures funding for a project or capital campaign, it should redouble its efforts to maintain a positive relationship with the funder. Agencies show respect for their funders by providing ongoing communication. It should always be remembered that the ultimate goal is not to fund a single need but to develop a consistent donor and supporter. The following are some suggestions for keeping an agency's funding base informed and involved.

- *Thank-you letters.* First and foremost, all funding must be acknowledged with a personal thank-you letter that accepts the support and briefly reiterates the need and intended use. This letter should be signed by both the board chairperson and the executive director. It should again state clearly and concisely what the funds will be used for; in many cases, the acknowledgment letter will be the first communication to a chief executive on the specifics of the gift.
- *Press clippings.* Copies of local press clippings publicizing any aspect of the project and giving credit to funders should be forwarded to the funding agencies. Such clippings should be accompanied by a brief letter explaining the general content of the news article and how the gift made some of the newsworthy items possible. A handwritten personal note in the margins of such clippings is usually well received by corporate decision makers.
- *Committee work and progress reports.* The funder should be kept informed of work accomplished by the project. Agencies should be careful never to let their first communication with the funder be a request for continuance of funding! Funders should be asked for advice and/or to be on a working committee.
- *Personal visits.* Representatives of the funder should be invited to kick-off ceremonies and project openings. Notices of all important milestones should be mailed to funders, with follow-up calls inviting them to lunch when the board chairperson or executive director is in the funder's neighborhood.
- *Telephone calls.* Agency heads should be available to receive and to initiate telephone calls from and to the funding source and should be responsive to questions that show continued interest in the project.
- *Newsletters.* Funding agencies should be placed on the mailing lists for general organizational newsletters.
- *Donor recognition.* It is always a good idea to plan donor recognition events. One way to handle this is to use opportunities inherent in program milestones and newsworthy success stories. Linking a corporate donor to well-publicized successes in social programs is highly prized by corporate marketing departments.
- *Donor clubs.* Another excellent way to encourage relationships and future funding success is in the establishment of donor clubs. Corporate donors appreciate the opportunity to be viewed as community leaders and to rub elbows with others of influence in the community. In fact, donor clubs are an excellent means of getting small to medium-size companies to stretch their gifts. The extra financial pain is often worth the gains in access to larger corporate decision makers.
- *Requests for continuing funds.* The request for continuing support is as important as the initial fund solicitation. Funded agencies should never simply send a letter asking for additional money. Instead, they should state the progress and accomplishments of the project and outline opportunities for continuance and

expansion. In particular, funded agencies should detail for funders how their contributions made success possible. Funded agencies should ask funders for input on requests for continuing funds. If a funded agency has done its job properly, the road to continued funding will have already been paved.

30.8 Handling Rejection

To a successful not-for-profit executive or development officer, there is no such thing as rejection; there are only situations in which a company temporarily cannot fund a specific proposal. Development officers and top executives of not-for-profits can spin many a yarn about initial project rejections that were subsequently turned into major gifts. The secret is wrapped in how one handles the initial rejection.

First, the not-for-profit chief executive should acknowledge the rejection and thank his or her corporate counterpart for taking time to hear the request and making an effort to evaluate it. Next, by personal call or meeting, preferably the latter, the not-for-profit representative should debrief the funding source as follows:

- What caused the proposal to fail?
- Was the proposal written clearly enough for the giving committee?
- In what ways could the proposal have been improved?
- Would the company entertain a modified request?
- What actions could the not-for-profit take to bolster chances for success in the next go-around?
- Given the nature of the program for which funding was requested, does the corporate contact know of any other corporations that would be more receptive to such a program? If so, would he or she agree to help in the initial contact?

In 90 percent of cases of corporate rejection of a funding request, corporate giving officers report never hearing from the agency again until the next round of requests. This is a strategic error. Instead, an initial rejection should be viewed as the starting point for relationship and confidence building, which will result in larger corporate support in the future. If debriefing and other follow-up procedures are employed with a corporate funding source, the chances of future proposals being funded increase dramatically.

The fact is that no matter how well written a proposal may be, no matter how well connected to the corporation a not-for-profit's board may be, some proposals will fail because a finite amount of funding is available. That means that a company may like a program but be unable to fund it. Here lies an opportunity for a savvy not-for-profit.

Are there ways that noncash involvement can substitute for program components? In the area of philanthropy, an old maxim says that involvement leads to commitment and commitment leads to a host of resources. Would the company agree to lend an officer to help with program committee work? Are there depreciated assets that can support the program, such as used furniture or excess product inventory?

Corporate officers must be kept abreast of the progress a not-for-profit is making toward its stated goals. This includes placing receptive officers on mailing lists for newsletters and publicity releases, inviting them to key social functions, placing them on blue-ribbon panels, assigning them committee work, requesting that they serve on boards—in essence, keeping them informed and involved. Only through such means can rejections be turned into gifts, and gifts into consistent donors.

30.9 Leveraging Gifts

Corporate gifts can be used to secure other gifts. Corporate executives generally understand the concept of leveraging, whereby every dollar earns many times its value in results. Most people, given the choice between two worthwhile causes, would rather give to the one that will match their gifts with gifts from other sources, thereby magnifying their own gift. Corporations are no exception.

Leveraging works on both sides of the giving equation. First, during the solicitation phase, leveraging helps to secure corporate support. A company prefers to give knowing that it is not the only one that believes in the approach the not-for-profit is taking. Call it security, confidence, aversion to risk taking, or whatever other words critics and supporters use; most corporate givers are swayed by the argument that others, too, support the program.

After a corporate gift is secured, it can be used to secure other corporate gifts. In many cases, the corporate donor will work with the solicitation committee or its representative to cull the list of other potential corporate givers. This cooperation is based on the premise that every dollar the donor gives will attract other dollars, thereby diversifying the resource pool. There are many consequences. For example, in cases in which a particular industry is hard hit by economic trends, another industry group of companies may take up the slack. Diversity in funding sources also has the effect of making sure that the project is not undercapitalized, a situation to which any corporate donor is sensitive. Finally, a diverse resource pool offers the potential of many more people, with a wide range of experience and skills, for the not-for-profit to draw from, thereby increasing the likelihood of program success.

30.10 Sources of Information

The following are excellent sources of information for researching corporate sources. However, the keys to successful corporate solicitation are to keep abreast of developments in the field of corporate giving, maintain regular contact with likely corporate prospects, and develop a strategy that ties marketing efforts to fund raising. This usually means that a not-for-profit must dedicate a staff position to these activities or, in a smaller not-for-profit, highly focus the corporate solicitation effort so that associated activities can be part of a staff position.

> *Local chambers of commerce.* Find the listing in the local phone directory. Keep in mind that local chambers (town or city) are separate entities from statewide chambers of commerce. Each may have a role to play in research. It may also be a good idea to join the local chamber as an associate member.
> *The Foundation Center,* 79 Fifth Avenue, New York, NY 10003. A not-for-profit organization headquartered in New York City, with major branches throughout the United States and holdings in every state. Its main mission is to disseminate accurate and timely information concerning private foundations to the not-for-

profit community. It maintains a detailed database on more than 30,000 private foundations in the United States, including corporate foundations.

The Foundation Center issues annual publications that update earlier databases and bulletins that report on trends in private and corporate foundations. It also hosts training and informational seminars on foundation-related issues. Its entire database is available for on-line computer retrievals. Retrieving the materials from an on-line source, such as DIALOG Information Services (3460 Hillview Avenue, Palo Alto, CA 94304; 1-800-3-DIALOG), has distinct advantages. A researcher can save the search parameters and simply request that the file be updated regularly, automatically.

The Foundation Center also offers an Associates Program. For an annual fee, this program offers telephone help to researchers, database searches, and printouts.

The Taft Group, c/o Gale Research, Inc., PO Box 33477, Detroit, MI 48232. 1-(800)-877-GALE. A for-profit publishing company focusing on the largest private foundation and corporate giving programs. The materials (books, newsletters, and special-topic publications) are generally well researched and comprehensive, although the coverage is not as broad as that of the Foundation Center's materials. Data is updated annually.

Publicly held corporations. An excellent source of information for potential approaches by not-for-profit organizations. Request a copy of these corporations' annual 10-K reports or quarterly 8-K update reports, which every publicly traded corporation must file with the Securities and Exchange Commission (SEC). The forms are also available from the SEC regional offices, from major libraries, and on-line through DIALOG. The 10-K forms give a great deal of information about the company, its executive compensation, board members, and other details that may help with your cultivation efforts.

A not-for-profit organization should request to be placed on the public affairs mailing list of all potential corporate sources in its geographic area, including the national headquarters of firms with a local presence.

Who's Who in Business and Industry, Marquis Who's Who, Inc., 200 East Ohio Street, Chicago, IL 60611. This is one of several specialty publications by Marquis. It can be used to cross-match information on likely corporate prospects with their officers and directors. Also available on-line from DIALOG.

31 Corporate Fund Raising

Dwight F. Burlingame, PhD

Associate Executive Director

Indiana University Center on Philanthropy

31.1 Introduction

In 1994 Dennis Young and I cochaired a conference on corporate philanthropy, which was sponsored by the Indiana University Center on Philanthropy and the Mandel Center for Nonprofit Organizations at Case Western Reserve University. The purpose of this meeting of selected corporate grantmakers, fund raisers, and academics was to explore a mutually attractive research agenda on corporate philanthropy for the last part of the twentieth century and the beginnings of the twenty-first century. That discussion led to the publication of *Corporate Philanthropy at the Crossroads* by Indiana University Press in 1996, along with many other publications and discussions in the field about whether corporate philanthropy still existed. Indeed, I think "corporate philanthropy" is no longer an appropriate term to characterize the giving that is provided to not-for-profits, mainly because philanthropy implies action for the public good, and corporate giving is more characterized by action for self-interest—albeit enlightened self-interest. The use of the phrase "do well by doing good" is not empty in its meaning within the corporate community.

31.2 Corporate Giving

Therefore, for purposes of this chapter I am using the term "corporate giving" to represent those funds or services provided by corporate entities (businesses) to not-for-profits that provide for some common or public good, usually in the enlightened self-interest of the company. Although many argue corporate giving is as old as corporations themselves, it is a relatively recent phenomenon. Emerson Andrews points out that the seeds of corporate giving were planted when the railroad companies supported the development of YMCAs in the late nineteenth century.[1] Even with this example, it is noteworthy that the YMCA development was to benefit the railroads by providing safe housing for their workers. In other words, enlightened self-interest was at work much as it is today in most corporate giving.

(A) HISTORY

Corporate giving in the United States began in 1936 with what Hayden Smith refers to as the modern era.[2] It was in 1936 that we have the first recorded figures of amounts reported by corporations on their income tax returns for charitable contributions. This deduction was enacted into law with the 1935 amendments to the Internal Revenue Code. Corporate giving has risen from about $30 million in 1936 to about $9 billion at the end of the 1990s.

According to *Giving USA*, most of this growth has been concentrated in the last 25 years.[3] This growth can be explained mostly by the remarkable growth in size and number of businesses in the United States as well as by the removal of certain historical legal obstacles. The legal improvements began with the adoption of the Texas Amendment in 1917, which allowed corporations in Texas to make charitable gifts. This process continued with the 1935 Internal Revenue Service (IRS) tax amendment mentioned above and ended with the historical case in New Jersey of *A.P. Smith Mfg. Co. v. Barlow,* where the court refused to overturn the decision of corporate management in regard to contributions made to charities.

(B) PERCENT OF PROFITS

On the economic side, corporate profits have risen at a much faster rate than corporate giving. For example, from 1986 to 1996 the Conference Board noted that corporate profits (before taxes) rose from $218 billion to $850 billion.[4] In that same time period, corporate giving (as a percentage of profits) went from 2.3 to 1.3 percent. By the end of the century, corporate giving had declined even further to an estimated 1 percent. Why have we seen this erosion in the percent of giving by corporations? Certainly many factors have been at work, but some on the major reasons include changing philosophy, chief

---

[1]Emerson F. Andrews, *Corporation Giving* (New York: Russell Sage), 1952, pp. 23–26.
[2]Hayden W. Smith, "If Not Corporate Philanthropy, Then What?" *New York Law School Law Review,* 31, nos. 3 & 4, 1997.
[3]*Giving USA* 1999 (New York: AAFRC Trust for Philanthropy), 1999.
[4]Audris Tillman, *Corporate Contributions in 1997* (New York: The Conference Board), 1999.

executive officer's role, change of corporate culture, increased global competitiveness, and change in corporate giving.

31.3   Changing Philosophy

The "business of business is business" is an expression that has been around in some form since Adam Smith (although it gained its more recent meaning from the arguments of neoconservative economist Milton Friedman, who has argued that corporations have no money to give away since it really belongs to the shareholders). The way to appeal to corporations is through their own self-interests. After all, the main function of business is to create jobs and make a profit. Ever since 1935 the debate has been on how much of the company's profits or expenses should be considered for charitable purposes. Although there still are those who argue for the moral obligation of corporations to continue their social responsibility by making contributions, the let's-focus-on-our-core-business approach has gained acceptance in recent years. In fact, in the last 50 years we have seen a full circle change—starting from a way to serve a company's business bottom line, to a more socially responsible position (less commercial), and now back again to a mostly business-driven approach.

31.4   Chief Executive Officer's Role

Much of corporate giving has been determined by the interest of the chief executive officer (CEO). The importance of the CEO in leading the company in giving is as important today as it was yesterday. The interest, however, has waned in recent years—partly because of business concerns, such as shareholder profit pressures, merger and buyout fears, and the mobility of corporations and their executives. Charles Heying in 1997 argued that destabilization of communities results when corporate ownership is disconnected from place. This delocalization causes a decline in the elite leadership in a community, which in turn negatively impacts the philanthropic giving of companies.[5] Some have argued that business school training vs. a liberal arts education has created executives who do not have an appreciation of the larger societal context of business, and are trained only to think of the bottom-line contribution. As Curt Weeden has noted, "Visionaries are hard to find when it comes to corporate social responsibility."[6]

31.5   Change of Corporate Culture

The recognition of a company's giving program by a chamber of commerce or a similar group has greatly declined in the last 15 years. Two and 5 percent clubs hardly exist. The corporate culture no longer rewards such activity. Thus, little time and importance are granted to the corporate contributions function within the company. The current environment calls for a strategic investment that will support the company's primary goal of

---

[5]Charles H. Heying, "Civic Elites and Corporate Delocalization: An Alternative Explanation for Declining Civic Engagement," *American Behavioral Scientist*, 40, 5, 657–668.
[6]Curt Weeden, *Corporate Social Investing* (San Francisco: Berrett-Koehler Publishers, 1998), p. 7.

producing more profit. This is commonly referred to as "corporate social investing" or "obtaining business value" from contributions. A company's success under this scenario is measured not by percentage of net income that is given to charity but rather by using tools and techniques that answer such questions as:

- Will the activity increase company revenues?
- Will the activity reduce overall costs?
- Will customers know more about company products?
- Will the image of the company be improved?
- Will the activity improve employee morale?
- Will the activity lead to greater success by the company?
- Will shareholders consider the activity important?

Notable efforts to increase corporate giving have been made recently. In particular, the Prince of Wales Business Leaders Forum has promoted the improvement of the practice of good corporate citizenship and sustainable development internationally by raising awareness of the value of corporate citizenship in business practice and by encouraging partnership action between business and communities. The London Benchmarking Group's template for reporting community involvement has been another major effort on benchmarking social investing. Finally, toward the end of 1999 we saw new efforts being made to increase corporate giving in the United States by a new nonprofit called the Committee to Encourage Corporate Philanthropy. About two dozen CEOs of the country's largest companies, including Xerox, America Online, and Chase Manhattan, started the group, along with businessman/actor Paul Newman. The group's function is to prod companies to give more by helping them expand or establish corporate giving programs through the identification and sharing of effective practices. The success of this venture is yet to be seen.

31.6 *Increased Global Competitiveness*

The argument is advanced that, because of increased global competition, functions perceived as inessential need to be cut. The giving budget is one area that is often seen as an easy target for reduction. The argument is also used when companies are consolidated. Craig Smith and others have estimated that the number of full-time staff devoted to the corporate giving function has been reduced by over 75 percent during the 1990s.[7]

31.7 *Change in Corporate Giving*

The way companies give to not-for-profits changed significantly in the 1990s. The importance of volunteer labor provided by companies, cause-related marketing, cause branding, sponsorships, and support for research are all aspects of involvement not recorded by the corporate giving figures reported in *Giving USA*. The Boston-based strategic market-

---

[7]See Burlingame, D. F. and Smith, C. "Corporate Giving's Future," unpublished manuscript, August, 1999.

ing firm Cone Inc. refers to cause branding as "a business strategy that integrates a social cause or issue into a brand's personality and organizational identity . . . and can truly differentiate a brand."[8] The combined total of these forms of monetary support for not-for-profits may be close to the amount of annual giving recorded by traditional means.

31.8   *Implications for Fund Raising*

In an earlier work, Dennis Young and I developed four models of corporate giving.[9] The utilization of those models suggests implications for how a not-for-profit should approach a company for support. The four paradigms, derived from alternative ways of thinking about how companies approach their giving and volunteering, are:

1. Corporate productivity or neoclassical model
2. Altruistic or ethical model
3. Political model (external and internal versions)
4. Stakeholder model

A summary of each along with its implications for fund raising follows.

(A)   CORPORATE PRODUCTIVITY MODEL

This model is based on the premise that corporate giving will help the company increase profits and return more value to the shareholder. Corporate giving activities must demonstrate how their contributions enhance the bottom line of the company. This may be done directly, by giving away product to try to influence people's taste, or it may be long term and indirect—for example, by improving company morale and ultimately worker productivity. The notion of "enlightened self-interest" mentioned earlier is very consistent with the neoclassical model as long as the focus remains on the long-term profitability of the corporation. It further suggests that the term "corporate philanthropy" is an oxymoron, since it implies that the action is at least in part for the public or common good. Types of giving that are consistent with this model are:

- Projects that help improve public images of the company
- Projects that help market corporate products, such as cause-related marketing and sponsorships
- Projects that increase employee morale and productivity
- Projects that lower corporate costs, such as grants for research by nonprofits that lower internal research costs

The challenge for the fund raiser is to find the match between the company's desire for improved productivity and the mission of the nonprofit. In addition, fund raisers

---

[8]*Corporate Philanthropy Report* (July 1999), p. 4.
[9]Dwight F. Burlingame and Dennis R. Young, *Corporate Philanthropy at the Crossroads* (Bloomington: Indiana University Press), 1996.

will want to assist corporate giving officers with arguments and evidence on how the project contributions can add to the bottom line of the company making the gift.

(B) POLITICAL MODEL

The political model is of two different forms—external and internal. The external form is based on the premise that corporations use giving to build relationships that protect corporate power and limit governmental influence over companies. Under this paradigm, the corporate giving program serves as a liaison to important allies within the community at large. Types of giving that are consistent with this model are projects that build closer relationships between corporations and not-for-profits, efforts that substitute for government initiative or minimize the need for government intervention, and programs that portray the corporation as a good public citizen, for example environmental or arts projects.

The implication for fund raisers is to cultivate long-term relationships with corporate leaders and giving officers and to give corporations credit for community benefits that result from their funding. In addition, bringing forth projects that have important public sector benefits for funding by the corporation is a useful strategy for the nonprofit.

The internal political model is based on the premise that the corporate giving officer is a player in a larger corporate game in which departments attempt to build allies and prove their worth to their fellow workers. In this plan, corporate giving programs must build alliances with departments such as human resources, marketing, research, and public relations and demonstrate that such alliances are useful. Giving that is consistent with this model includes sponsorships and cause-related marketing, employee volunteerism, social service and educational programs for employees, and research support that is in the interest of the short- and long-term objectives of the company.

The implication for fund raisers is to take a look at the total company and work with various corporate departments, not just the corporate giving unit. The relevance and design of projects that address internal corporate needs and also meet the needs of the not-for-profit become central to this model. Finally, the collection of documents that describe how initiatives increased departmental effectiveness will be crucial.

(C) ETHICAL/ALTRUISTIC MODEL

Behind this model is the premise that corporate leaders understand the necessity of the company being a good corporate citizen and the company's perceived obligation to play the socially responsible part of supporting societal needs.

It also assumes that corporations have some discretionary resources. The giving program must identify community priorities and be able to alert corporate leaders to those needs where the company can be a partner in seeking solutions. Types of giving consistent with this paradigm are:

- Projects that address major community needs
- Projects that appeal to the preferences of corporate leaders both as individuals and as citizens
- Projects involving corporate employees in community efforts to solve local problems

Implications for fund raisers are to make the case for community benefit and to involve corporate leaders or their employees in the projects.

(D) STAKEHOLDER MODEL

The stakeholder model of corporate giving holds the premise that the corporation is a complex entity that responds to the pressures of a variety of key stakeholder groups including stockholders, employees, customers, suppliers, community groups, and governmental regulators. Under this perception, managing the corporation is seen as an exercise in managing the stakeholders. To be effective, corporate giving programs must help or represent the various stakeholders. Types of giving consistent with this model include:

- Employee benefit or volunteerism projects
- Community education or environmental projects
- Projects that help consumers of corporate products

Fund raisers will want to identify key stakeholder groups and develop projects that appeal to their interest. The ability to demonstrate how projects improve corporate relations with specific stakeholder groups will be key. An overall strategy on the part of the not-for-profit will be to position itself as a community stakeholder championed by the corporate giving program.

These models not only provide a theoretical framework for understanding corporate giving and thus a basis for doing empirical research and debating the various approaches; they also provide different implications for research and the practice of corporate giving. These models actually try to get at how the corporation works. Thus, we can gain an understanding through corporate giving of what the company is all about. Each model attempts to bring a unique dimension to the understanding of corporate giving. Recognizing that all or some of the models may be operating within any one particular corporation at any particular time is an important caveat. Within the current global corporate environment, the political activity is more complex and the networks of corporate stakeholders more diverse. Changes in these environments domestically and internationally have made for even more pressure to show a stronger bottom line. Thus, corporate giving must be understood from all of the four perspectives that the models offer.

31.9 Cause-related Marketing and Sponsorship

Recent trends in corporate giving are built on the idea that fund raisers need to build a corporate giving model, based on a collaboration with business, that not only recognizes that the company needs to see economic gain based on a nonprofit partnership but also demonstrates the potential for social change. Two important trends of corporate dollars going to not-to-profits include cause-related marketing and sponsorship. It is important to note the distinction between the two. Cause-related marketing is characterized by the company providing a contribution to a not-for-profit with the amount of the contribution depending on how much of a product or service was purchased by consumers during a specified period of time. In good practice the company and the not-for-profit form a partnership with each other to market a product or service for mutual gain. In essence, it is enlightened self-interest on the part of the company, since it raises funds for a cause while enhancing consumer loyalty and purchase of its products or services. Continuing cause-related marketing activities over the long term by eliminating the short-term promotional aspect has become known as "cause branding." That is, a strategic plan to integrate social issues into the identity of a particular brand or company, not only by increasing consumer loyalty but by also influencing employee morale and loyalty. In addition, other stakeholders of the company are considered in developing cause-related partnerships with not-for-profits.

Sponsorship, in contrast, is not directly tied to consumers' purchase behavior. However, there are certainly investments in causes or events that support corporate objectives.

Cause-related marketing began with the American Express Company's effort to help fund the 1981 San Francisco Arts Festival. The company went national with its 1983 campaign to assist in the Statue of Liberty restoration. Its success in increasing card usage and in new cardholders was impressive. At the same time, the Liberty restoration fund received $1.7 million from American Express.[10]

(A) ADVANTAGES

Corporations engage in cause-related marketing, sponsorships, and branding because there is direct payoff to the business. Influencing consumer behavior, reflecting the company as a responsible citizen in the community, and building employee morale are all good business decisions. Studies by Roper Starch Worldwide and Cone Inc. have found that American employees and consumers support cause-related marketing. Companies have found that such programs increase sales and customer loyalty, improve employee morale, and enhance the image of the company. In a 1999 study, Cone and Roper found that from 1993 to 1998 acceptability of cause programs as good business practice had increased by 8 percentage points, to a 74 percent acceptance rate. Eight out of 10 Americans have a more positive image of companies that support causes they care about. Further, nearly two-thirds of American consumers would likely switch brands or retailers to one associated with a good cause. Finally, employees working at companies with cause programs feel a stronger sense of loyalty to their company than those who do not have such a program.[11] These are important findings for fund raisers to be aware of as they discuss cause or sponsorship programs with businesses.

Some of the advantages for nonprofits of cause-related marketing, sponsorships, and branding are:

- It produces needed revenue.
- It attracts volunteers who otherwise might not be involved to the not-for-profit.
- It increases public awareness of the not-for-profit's mission.
- It increases the public's participation in the not-for-profit.

---

[10]W. L. Wall, "Companies Change the Ways They Make Charitable Donations," *Wall Street Journal*, June 21, 1984, p. 1.

[11]1999 Cone/Roper Cause Trends Report, *The Evolution of Cause Branding* (Boston: Cone Inc.), 1999.

(B) DISADVANTAGES

Potential problems for the not-for-profit related to cause-related marketing, sponsorships, and branding include:

- Negative reactions on the part of some donors and potential donors to the not-for-profit may develop because negative perceptions of the company exist.
- The marketing strategy may detract from the case for support of the not-for-profit.
- The commercial aspects of the arrangement may decrease the public's trust level in the not-for-profit.
- Too much reliance may develop on an uneven income stream.
- As individuals make donations through the purchase of cause-related marketed products, they may think they do not need to make regular gift donations. Corporations may also see such activity as their only method of support for the not-for-profit. Further, individuals who think that the not-for-profit no longer needs their support may reduce their gifts, and corporations that used to support a not-for-profit may take their giving elsewhere if they think that the organization and the issue it supports have been "co-opted" by its corporate partner.

Marketing relationships with not-for-profits can also be problematic for the corporation. The time it takes to maintain the relationship may not be worth it. Some consumers may worry whether their dollars are really going to the not-for-profit; more complicated accounting procedures must be followed; and not-for-profits may not be aware of what the company wants from the relationship.

These concerns can educate the fund raiser on what to be aware of in building a marketing relationship with a company. Keeping an eye on the issues and developing procedures to prevent management error will go a long way to building successful ventures with businesses that can benefit both the not-for-profit and the corporation. One of the best ways to avoid ethical problems is to eschew anything that could be perceived as inappropriate. Sponsorship guidelines should be developed and approved by the not-for-profit's board of directors. Many organizations will place the responsibility for sponsorship and cause-related marketing with the development office. If this is not the case, effective coordination and communication with the development officer, the sponsorship or cause officer, and the chief executive must be in place. Management needs to take an active role in shaping a business partnership and in monitoring its progress.

31.10 Conclusion

Corporate giving has been full circle in its purposes: from being at the center of business purposes, to more publicly concerned giving, back to being predominantly business-driven. Cash contributions have declined as a percentage of all company giving, and gifts of company products and volunteer time have increased. In addition, more companies seek to add value to their giving by gaining favorable publicity and improved economic bottom lines.

The charitable giving function is now linked to other business functions. This trend has spawned the growth of cause-related marketing, branding, and sponsorship. The implication for not-for-profit fund raisers is clear. They must match their goals with those of the corporate sponsors. Where there are fits, benefits for the not-for-profit will be realized from the for-profits. Using the various models of corporate giving can facilitate the development of a realistic approach to businesses for greater involvement in working with not-for-profits in meeting societal needs.

Suggested Readings

Burlingame, Dwight F., and Dennis R. Young. *Corporate Philanthropy at the Crossroads.* Bloomington: Indiana University Press, 1996.

Hemphill, Thomas A. "Cause-Related Marketing, Fundraising and Environmental Nonprofit Organizations." *Nonprofit Management & Leadership,* 6, no. 4 (Summer 1996).

Muirhead, Sophia. *Corporate Contributions: The Views—From 50 Years.* New York: The Conference Board, 1999.

Weeden, Curt. *Corporate Social Investing.* San Francisco: Berrett-Koehler Publishers, 1998.

32 ▼ Cause-related Marketing and Sponsorship

SYLVIA ALLEN, MA
Allen Consulting, Inc.

32.1 Introduction

With money becoming tighter and tighter, grants becoming fewer and fewer, and direct mail fund raising becoming less and less effective, not-for-profit organizations are having to turn to sponsorship to maintain their programs. Although both sponsorship and fund raising consist of generating revenue for the not-for-profit organization, the approaches are different. The primary difference lies in the definition of sponsorship, as follows: Sponsorship is an *investment*, in cash or in kind, in return for *access* to an *exploitable* business opportunity through a special event, sport, or other public association. The highlighted words offer a clue to the difference. Basically, fund raising is a gift; sponsorship is an investment which implies a payback. So, if not-for-profit organizations are getting involved in sponsorship, they must realize that the investor (the sponsor) expects a payback. These organizations also must hone up on their sales skills since the competition for corporate dollars is fierce. With hundreds of thousands of media (radio, television, cable, billboards, direct mail, etc.) and just as many events/sports/ entertainment opportunities, the not-for-profit organization must have the same level of professionalism in its presentation of materials as its competitors. This chapter will provide you with the professional strategies and techniques that will allow you to be competitive.

Keep in mind that terrific value to a sponsor is available through cause-related marketing (CRM).

32.2 Evaluating Cause-related Marketing: A Strategic Approach

Cause-related marketing is a growing trend as corporations are discovering that what is good for the community is also good for business. *Cause-related marketing* ties a company's charitable contributions to the sale of products and services, to increase consumer awareness and company image.

Organized to increase the bottom line, cause-related business sponsorship has gone from approximately 1,000 companies spending $450 million in 1984, to over 15,000 companies spending $8.8 billion in 1999. Cause marketing will continue to increase as more and more companies seek nontraditional methods of supporting products. Is cause marketing suited for every corporation? Maybe. The key is to understand what a program is trying to achieve and to maintain a positive relationship with, and understanding of, the charity.

Every company and not-for-profit organization will develop its own format for choosing and evaluating a cause marketing program, but see Exhibit 32.1 for some introductory guidelines.

Cause marketing is here to stay. As with all marketing, the corporations successful with it will be the ones that take the time to understand it, evaluate it, and improve upon it. Unfortunately, like so many other marketing strategies, "cause marketing" has become a buzzword that many not-for-profit organizations and corporations toss around but have no idea how to incorporate into their plans. A successful cause marketing program must create a "win-win" situation for both the corporation and the not-for-profit organization.

The standard for a successful cause marketing program was set with the joint restoration committee for the Statue of Liberty. During a three-month period in 1983, American Express donated $0.1 cent for each transaction on its American Express Card. This program resulted in a $1.7 million donation to the restoration of the Statue of Liberty and increased the use of the card by over 20 percent. This is a classic example of a true "win-win" program.

Today, not-for-profit organizations often view cause marketing as a simple donation to a charity without understanding that the corporation must benefit. Corporations have also tried to shy away from their responsibility by soliciting programs that use a charity's name but do not deliver solid financial rewards to the not-for-profit organization. Cause-related marketing is a tested winner and has earned exceptional marketing results for corporations, but as with any strategy, it needs to be done with the right resources and the proper thought process.

EXHIBIT 32.1 Guidelines for Choosing and Evaluating a Cause-Related Marketing Program

- **Good company citizenship is good business.** It has been proven time and again that those companies exhibiting conscience are consistently the most successful. The recent Cone/Roper Benchmark Survey found that 75 percent of all questions expressed the importance of buying from companies that make charitable contributions.
- **Check references.** Corporations and charities should check each other out with the same due diligence as hiring a new employee. Corporations need to analyze how a charity spends its money, and they should talk with other corporations who have worked with the charity to determine its credibility. Charities need to take the time to study a corporation to determine its reputation in the community.
- **Target audience.** A successful cause marketing campaign must match the cause to the desired target audience of a corporation. An alcohol company would typically not look toward a children's charity; obviously, a tobacco company would not either.
- **Lead time.** One of the most important elements of a successful cause-related program marketing effort is lead time. Packaged goods manufacturers were some of the first to use cause marketing, and have reaped the most benefits, in part because they have more time to work on a campaign than other corporations.
- **Timing.** The timing of the program itself is important. Companies often try cause-related marketing when sales are low. This type of approach almost always fails. The best programs should not be run in the best months or worst months for a company. Somewhere between is the best.
- **Involve employees.** The best cause marketing programs are team efforts that involve all levels of employees. When the CEO of a corporation stands shoulder-to-shoulder with employees in a program, it makes for a winner.
- **State your goals.** Do not merely announce a cause-related tie-in. Say what it is for. The promotional message should state the amount of money trying to be raised, and what it will be used for. This will help people identify with and develop empathy for the cause.
- **Dominate a cause.** Corporations will see the most benefit if they can be the pre-eminent benefactor. If you are splitting your efforts among several charitable organizations, you tend to lose exposure.

32.3 Enhancing Event Participation as a Not-for-Profit Organization

This section applies to not-for-profit beneficiaries receiving net funds or a designated amount from the organizers, not having ownership of the event.

A beneficiary of an existing event has the same rights as any of the participating sponsors. This includes all media coverage, signage, prominence on all collateral material, and inclusion in all marketing efforts. Make sure the organization's logo is included in all signage, on the merchandise (T-shirts, hats, etc.), and during the event. In fact, enter into a sponsorship contract, just as the other sponsors have for the event, that spells out exactly what the organization and the event expect of each other. See Exhibit 32.2 for an outline of those items to be discussed with the event organizers. (This process is not necessary when the not-for-profit owns the event but is vital when it is part of an existing event.)

By using this checklist for contract negotiations, fund raisers can protect their organizations from negative public relations and ensure the organization of fair and equitable treatment by the event organizers.

EXHIBIT 32.2 Rights of Not-for-Profit Organizations

---

1. Signage
   —Logo placement on signage
   —Approval of logo usage/placement
   —Number of signs with your logo
   —Signage placement at event
   —Pre-event signage
2. Advertising credits
   —Logo placement in advertising
   —Approval of logo usage/placement
   —Advertising placement
   —Pre-event advertising
3. Merchandising rights
   —Logo placement on merchandise
   —Approval of logo usage/placement
   —Revenue sharing from sales
4. Public relations rights
   —Logo placement on media releases
   —Approval of logo usage/placement
   —Approval of your organizations' involvement in event
   —Right to distribute media releases through your organization's media list
5. Benefits
   —Pre-event appearances
   —On-site participation
   —Revenue for the not-for-profit
   —Visibility at event functions
   —Public acknowledgment of participation
   —Not-for-profit employee hospitality
   —Donor hospitality
6. Future options
   —Right of first refusal for following year
   —Cancellation terms
   —Increased revenue benefits
7. Indemnification/liability
   —Hold harmless clause
   —Insurance protection
   —Errors and omission protection
   —Force majeure, rain date
8. Nondisclosure
   —Contract confidentiality
   —Control information for public knowledge

32.4 *Winning Sponsorships with Effective Proposals*

Like inventors rushing to find venture capital, not-for-profit organizations have gone after sponsorships with great interest—and the private sector is responding. Almost $19 billion in sponsorships was distributed in 2000 by corporations.

But the quest has exacted a price. With so many not-for-profit organizations pursuing sponsorships as a means of coping with government cutbacks, corporations have become very selective with their gifts. Nowadays, a standard form denying a request is very common at most large companies.

The heightened competition puts more pressure than ever before on not-for-profit organizations to do their homework to make their proposals stand out.

How to do this? The first step is to fully evaluate the event or program that needs sponsorship. Analyze the value of the product and its marketability to a potential sponsor. This is where many not-for-profit organizations make a mistake: They greatly over-estimate the value of their product. There is no quicker way to court rejection than to simply look at the bottom-line cost of the sponsorship and declare that to be the project's value. An example: If a not-for-profit organization is holding a celebrity golf tournament, determines that its "hard" costs are $40,000, and decides to package a title sponsorship for that amount, it is probably overpricing the package. That same event may not hold similar value to a sponsor. That is where the evaluation process comes in. A few considerations can determine whether a product has value to a sponsor:

- Is television involved in the event? If so, can a potential sponsor tap into the coverage with a commercial or somehow attract coverage of the company name? If there is coverage, it is easy to evaluate the dollar value to a sponsor by calculating the advertising rates.
- Who will be attending the event? Is it a demographic group desirable to the corporation? A group of high-level physicians might be of tremendous interest to a pharmaceutical company, even if the event is a relatively small one. An event with mass appeal, such as a walk in New York City that may draw hundreds of thousands of people, will have interest to corporate sponsors, particularly if they can tie in their products. Listerine pursued that marketing strategy at the Taste of Chicago event, and it paid off. Local sales of Listerine increased.
- Was the event a success last year? Why or why not? Document programs and sponsor exposure. It is a lot easier to sell a track record to potential sponsors than mere promises.

After taking an inventory of the product value, fundraisers may decide to enhance the program to make it more viable for a sponsor. A consulting firm working on a program for the Leukemia Society of America did just that. The firm was developing a sponsorship program based on the society's Team in Training event, a program that trains people to run a marathon while raising money to fight leukemia. After evaluating the plan, the consultants determined it would be difficult selling the idea to a national sponsor without a media partner. Before sending out corporate sponsor proposals, they contacted *Runner's World* magazine and secured it as the national media sponsor for the program. The participation of *Runner's World* made the proposal package much more attractive to corporate sponsors and added considerable value to the product.

Proposals take on all sizes and forms of quality. Some are sophisticated four-color brochures, while others are simply one-page letters. There is no set rule on how long or short a proposal should be, but it should be tailored to the size and scope of the project and the corporations being approached. And it should be simple and easy to read as well as having a strong benefits orientation.

32.5 *Sponsorship Fund-raising Tips*

To be effective at raising funds through special events, fund raisers must approach participation as they would any other business venture. Here are some very simple rules that will make your participation in an existing event more cost-effective:

DO:

- *Take an active part in the event planning and administration.*
- *Enter into an event contract.*
- *Follow through with commitments to the event.*
- *Protect the organization against any negative publicity.*
- *Clearly delineate expectations.*
- *Enlist the help of the volunteer base.*

DO NOT:

- *Wait until the day of the event to get involved.*
- *Trust agreements or planning details to memory or vague conversations.*
- *Make extraordinary demands.*
- *Expect to reap all the benefits without any effort.*

Working in partnership with event management will create a positive relationship that will lead to increased funds for the not-for-profit organization.

Selling sponsorships is just like selling anything else; fund raisers who follow the principles of good salesmanship will have greater success than their competitors. Each year we see an increase in the number of lifestyle activities that can be sponsored. Dollar amounts invested in sponsorships continue to grow and more and more companies are recognizing the value of lifestyle marketing in helping achieve their marketing objectives. All of this means there is more competition for corporate dollars.

How can one not-for-profit differentiate itself from the competition? Here are 10 suggestions that will help increase sponsorship sales and improve renewals of existing sponsorships:

1. *Produce quality materials.* How many times have you received a proposal with typos, misspelled names, page numbers out of sequence, poor-quality photos? If fund raisers are trying to convince a prospective buyer of their professionalism, they must demonstrate it through their materials. Double-check the spelling of the individual's name as well as his/her title, company name, and other pertinent information as it relates to each proposal. If a presentation is to be customized, make sure the company is referred to properly and make sure the change is made universally throughout the presentation. Do not merely rely on the spell-checker in the computer—read through the presentation before it goes out to the potential sponsor, to ensure there are no errors.

2. *Understand the sponsor's corporate culture.* Learn something about each company being solicited for sponsorship. If it is a publicly traded company, request a copy of the most recent annual report. Do a data search at the library, checking industry periodicals for the last year, to get a sense of the company's media exposure and activities. Read trade newsletters for a clear picture of what the company is interested in and what its sponsorship expectations are. Understanding the customer is one of the first rules of successful consultative selling.

3. *Understand the property.* As simplistic as this sounds, fund raisers must know their product. Know and understand all the opportunities that can be afforded a sponsor—hospitality, signage, tickets, product sampling, and so on. Be prepared to provide potential sponsors with photos, videos, and other visual elements that will further enhance the sponsorship proposal and entire participation.

4. *Have good follow-through.* Be consistent in the approach, deliver what has been promised, and be sensitive to the individual sponsor's needs.

5. *Demonstrate good selling skills.* One of the first skills is good listening. Potential sponsors will quickly explain what their marketing objectives are and how a not-for-profit's program will or will not fit into their marketing program. If as a fund raiser you agree it is not a good fit, move on to the next one. Do not waste time arguing or attempting to fit a square peg into a round hole. Conversely, you may need to reposition a proposal to better comply with the potential sponsor's needs before giving up completely.

6. *Maintain a sense of humor.* Selling sponsorships is serious! However, people often can get through a difficult negotiation process if they maintain their sense of humor. Keep in mind that difficult and/or tense negotiations can be eased with tasteful humor.

7. *Be specific in contract benefits.* When preparing the sponsorship contract, be specific in listing benefits and rights. For example, rather than say "Sponsor has the right to hang four banners in highly visible locations," state "Sponsor has the right to hang four banners (size) at the following locations: _____." If all benefits and rights are clearly delineated, there is no room for misunderstanding.

8. *Delineate responsibilities.* Within this same contract, define who is responsible for what. For example, in the previous instance, who will hang the banners and who will be responsible for taking them down, storing them? Again, spell out these responsibilities precisely so they are easily understood.

9. *Deal with problems before they get out of hand.* No situation is perfect, and no matter how clearly the contract is written, there are bound to be minor misunderstandings. Address them quickly, get clarification on matters where either side is confused, and get concurrence on the resolution of the problem(s). If handled quickly, problems can be eliminated and not allowed to compound and escalate.

10. *Be honest.* Tell the truth about attendance, media exposure, and former sponsor relationships. Lies will not build a long-term, trusting relationship. Honesty has long-term paybacks.

These 10 tips will help fund raisers improve sponsorship sales ratio as well as enhance renewals. And, remember, sponsorship sales are fun . . . enjoy yourself!

32.6 *Understand What Sponsors Want*

When reading a newspaper or magazine article about a sport or special event, see if there is any mention of the participating sponsor's name. If so, the sponsor has just scored a publicity coup that cannot be measured in dollars. The public relations impact is so much stronger than the same amount of coverage in advertising space that there is no comparison. More and more companies are realizing that sponsorship, carefully planned and skillfully executed, can be a win-win situation—a boon for both the sponsor and the event. Poorly thought out, sponsorship can be a costly mistake.

Each year more sports and special events take place, creating a greater number of sponsorship opportunities for a diversity of products and services. However, not all of these opportunities are for all sponsors. To get the most from sponsorship, make sure that both sponsor and event organizers' needs and expectations are being met.

Here are some questions sponsors ask when deciding whether an event is right for them:

1. *Who is attracted to the event, in terms of both spectators and participants?* Are these the people I am trying to reach through my marketing efforts, or will my message be misdirected?
2. *Who are the other sponsors?* Am I in good company? Do I have too much company? One of the appeals of event sponsorship is that it helps corporations avoid the "ad clutter" of television. If there are too many sponsors, one name could be lost.
3. *What are the sponsorship benefits?* Am I included in the press kits? Do I participate in all the media events? What on-site recognition/acknowledgment—signage, introductions, opportunities for product demonstration—will I have? What is my visibility to those who are attending? To those who are watching on TV?
4. *What is the goal of my sponsorship, and do the answers to the previous questions indicate that I will reach it?* The goal is not always a direct sell of a product or service. Firms may use special event involvement to provide sales incentives; to enhance dealer and employee loyalty by inviting them to events; to provide an opportunity for product demonstration; for goodwill, giving current customers the opportunity to rub shoulders with top brass; and/or to build a company's image.
5. *Will I get my money's worth?* What is the history of the event? How have other sponsors fared? If this is a first-time event, what bonus breaks are being offered as an inducement to participate? What is its potential longevity? Do I have right-of-first-refusal for upcoming years?

Results—particularly those geared to image enhancement—may be difficult to quantify. Some companies do ask their sales forces to track sales before and after, and indicate those figures show a positive response. Others hire a tracking service that measures exposure time and offers advice on such topics as how to increase logo visibility.

In the final analysis, each sponsor must answer the question Is it worth it? based on its own investment, goals, and results. Sponsors want to reach their market at their lifestyle level, making sure the audience is receptive and qualified to receiving their message. They want to be assured of maximum coverage. And they want to know that their involvement is long-term, to ensure maximum benefit.

In general, companies get involved in sponsorship for 15 reasons:

1. Generate more sales
2. Introduce new products
3. Entertain prime customers
4. Entertain potential new customers
5. Entertain/reward employees
6. Introduce product changes: "new" Pepsi, etc.
7. Introduce product extensions: how many ways can you use baking soda?
8. Reach new markets to expand market share
9. Reinforce trade relationships
10. Block the competition
11. Increase media exposure
12. Meet customers (sales, market research, database building)
13. Offer an opportunity for product trial through sampling
14. Demonstrate category leadership (to distributors)
15. Forge new links with opinion leaders

32.7   Sponsorship Is No Longer Linear

Before sponsorship became sophisticated, it was simple. In the late 1970s the corporate chief executive said, "I want to sponsor football." And a couple of banners and several tickets on the 50-yard line later, the company was a sponsor. If it had a good time, it participated again. No one questioned the benefits, such as media exposure, the sales gains, the return on investment, the marketing partners, the long-term strategy, and on and on. Sponsors handed the check to the sport or event organizers, tickets were handed to them . . . it was done.

Today's sponsorships are multidimensional, with multiple partners and multiple components. Sponsors have certain expectations of rights and benefits as well as a much greater sophistication about how sponsorships work and how they can maximize their investment. Today's economic climate requires sponsors to have greater accountability and the investments are expected to have a return, whether it is greater exposure, more sales, increased visibility, enhanced image, better trade relations, improved public perception . . . and the list could go on and on. Just think about the many marketing objectives that can be achieved through sponsorship, and you will begin to understand the complexities of becoming involved.

Added to this is the fact that each year more and more sports, events, and organizations are seeking sponsorships. Competition for sponsor dollars is also coming from the not-for-profit sector where museums, dance troupes, theater companies, charities, and other agencies are having to become more creative in their fund-raising efforts and are therefore turning to sponsorship.

Last, sponsors want to extend their investment as far as they can before and after the event. This is done through integrated marketing activities, seeking additional sponsors for cross promotions, tying sponsors into the media activities to get greater visibility and exposure, and having the opportunity to measure the results.

To be successful in sponsorship sales, fund raisers have to be creative, bringing together multiple partners that create a synergy for success, and recognizing that the competition is heavy. How well one stands out from that competition, with forward-thinking, creative ideas and clever strategies, will determine sponsorship sales success.

32.8   Twenty Cross-promotion Ideas

Sponsorship is no longer a matter of hanging a banner, getting a bunch of seats on the 50-yard line, and meeting the star players. Sports and special events are now part of the marketing mix and are expected to deliver. For that reason, fund raisers will be asked to incorporate various types of promotions as part of the total sponsorship package. Here are 20 basic ideas that can be used singly or combined in any number of ways that will help a not-for-profit achieve marketing success:

1. *Bouncebacks.* Using something at the event to bring the customer back to the store. For example, bring your ticket stub to XYZ store and redeem for your product. Or, at some time during the event, give the customer a coupon that is a special offering and is redeemable after the event. It literally "bounces the customer back" to the retail store and allows the product sponsor to measure

the sales effectiveness of sponsorship as well as the retail store's ability to do the same.

2. *Buy one, get one free (BOGO)*. Taken alone, this is a product sale enticement. If combined with one of the other elements of sales promotion, it can not only increase product sales but also tie in with event sponsorship. For example, as part of the BOGO promotion, you receive a sweepstakes entry form for a free trip, free tickets, etc. (whatever you wish).

3. *Contests/sweepstakes*. These can be unlimited! There can be registration at the point of purchase, at the event, even through the mail. One word of caution: Do not undertake a contest without consulting a lawyer, since each state has very specific rules about entry requirements, probability-of-winning clauses, and the like.

4. *Coupons*. These can be either pre-event or at the event. If they are distributed through a retail facility, they can be used to promote an organization's sponsorship before an event and, it is hoped, to drive additional traffic to the event. In fact, the coupon could be distributed through the retail partner and used for event admission discounts. Or coupons can be distributed at the event to drive sales after the event.

5. *Database development*. As more and more companies get involved in marketing directly to their customers, take advantage of generating a list of customer names. Have a booth at the event where people can participate in a survey, enter a contest, or just register to win with hourly drawings at the event.

6. *Discounted sales*. Taken alone, this is a way to drive traffic into a store. Combined with a coupon or bounceback, this is a way to reward an event attendee with an additional "bonus" for attending that event. Then combine it with a "register-to-win" promotion and one not only measures the results of attendance at the sponsored event but also generate names for the database.

7. *FSIs (free-standing inserts)*. These can combine coupons, register to win, sweepstakes, and contests. They are the four-color, advertising-only inserts so prevalent in the Sunday paper. For a recent Super Bowl, a number of Super Bowl sponsors participated in a 36-page FSI that was distributed nationally one week before the big game.

8. *Hang tags* (literally, tags that hang off the product). These can be used with soft goods and food products, particularly bottled beverages. Again, design the tag like a coupon to drive traffic to the event—or an entry form to win tickets to the event—whatever is desired.

9. *Holusion*. This a hologram, a Polaroid trademark. Recent Super Bowl tickets have taken advantage of this promotion concept. It can be used for program books, tickets, or large on-site displays. Again, if combined with any of the other sales promotion ideas presented here, it can drive traffic, sales, or generate names for target marketing.

10. *The Internet*. The entire cyberspace concept is wide open for sales promotion ideas. Special offers or discounts, pre-event, can be designed as well as additional sponsor/event information that will entice customers to the event as well as encourage them to purchase the product.

11. *Media coupons*. Similar to FSIs, these coupons are included in coupon mailings, newspaper and magazine ads, and other print coupon distribution. Again, use

them like coupons or bouncebacks to enhance pre- and post-event sales and participation.

12. *On-air promotions.* Using radio, television, and cable, fund raisers can make the same offers as they would with coupons, only using the electronic media. Same activity and results as in item 11.

13. *On-pack promotions.* These are special offers on the product package. They can either be cut out or easily peeled off and are similar to coupons and bouncebacks to generate pre- and post-event coverage as well as database development.

14. *On-site sampling.* Use sponsorship either to sample a new product or to introduce consumers to a new product application through sampling. This can be actually tasting a product or giving a demonstration. Combine this with bouncebacks and/or a register-to-win promotion for additional sales as well as development of a potential customer database.

15. *Phone cards.* Prepaid phone cards can be distributed at the event—with the sponsor's name clearly in evidence—and used to drive customers back to the sponsor's place of business to get their pin code activated. Or the cards can be distributed before the event with the requirement that the consumer attend the event to get a specific pin code activated.

16. *Point-of-purchase tie-ins.* These can consist of instant coupons at the checkout counter, on-shelf promotions, and end-cap displays with "take ones." Again, combine this with some of the other sales promotion ideas to enhance results.

17. *Point-of-purchase promotions.* These can include product sampling with coupons, point-of-sale promotions, and contests. And point-of-purchase can be at the retail partner's location before the event or at the event itself.

18. *Product promotions.* These can include on-pack coupons or entry forms, register receipt with UPC codes, or any other form of promotion that is specifically tied to proof of purchase. As with contests, check with a lawyer on the exact wording and application to ensure that the promotions do not violate the law.

19. *Product sales.* Very simply, sell the product at the event! This is a viable sponsorship benefit and allows fund raisers to add one of the other promotion ideas presented here—coupons, bouncebacks, register to win, contests—to measure impact and effectiveness.

20. *Shelf talkers/take-ones.* These are point-of-purchase promotions, usually right where the product is located on the retail shelves, with additional incentive for purchase. Similar to coupons and bouncebacks with similar applications.

The basics have been presented; now let your imagination run wild! Any number of combinations will help fund raisers successfully drive product sales, measure effectiveness of a sponsorship investment, and even increase event attendance. Good luck!

32.9   How to Write a Sponsorship Letter That Gets Response . . . Cover Letters that Work

The cover letter sent with a sponsorship proposal often can make the difference between getting the sponsorship package read or receiving a nice thanks-but-no-thanks letter. What makes the difference between a "good" sponsorship letter and a "bad" one? The same things that make the difference between a "good" sales letter and a "bad" one.

When preparing an event's sponsorship package, fund raisers took great care to outline the various sponsorship elements and the benefits they provide. The media, hospitality, sales promotion, signage, and on-site offerings were carefully packaged to provide a fair and equitable package, whether title sponsorship or one of the supporting sponsorship packages. The potential market was researched to identify which sponsors would be most qualified to participate: which ones had audience and marketing needs that were parallel to those of the sponsorship offering. In short, fund raisers did their homework.

Then they quickly wrote a generic cover letter that allowed them to customize each package by name and company and mailed them off. This mailing was then followed by a series of telephone calls to the people who received the sponsorship packages to determine their interest. Fund raisers who did not have a good cover letter and had not prequalified the potential sponsors before the mailing probably experienced a low interest/response to their mailing. Next time, apply the following principles of good sales letter writing to see a difference in the response.

(A) RULE #1: GET THE SPELLING RIGHT

Make sure to have the proper spelling of the person's name, title, and company as well as a correct address. Call to confirm this information before mailing, if necessary.

(B) RULE #2: LOSE THE "I" AND "ME" WORDS

Eliminate as many references to "I" or "me" as possible. Here is an example of a terrible paragraph:

> *I would like to have an opportunity to sit down and show you why my event is so important. I've worked on this for over 5 years and I need to have at least 10 sponsors who will give me $100,000 so I can have a successful event.*

Six times in one paragraph . . . not good!

(C) RULE #3: KEEP IT BENEFITS ORIENTED

Make sure the letter is benefits oriented. And the benefits orientation must be custom tailored. Do not make the following mistake:

> *Title Sponsorship of $100,000 for XYZ Event offers your organization exclusive rights to distribute the product of your choice.*

Instead, take time to know a potential sponsor. The above paragraph would be written differently for each sponsor with specific elements itemized. For example, assume that XYZ Event is looking for a carbonated beverage sponsor. And, further, assume the targeted carbonated beverage sponsors are Coca-Cola, RC Cola, and Cadbury Schweppes Ginger Ale. Each of these companies has a different marketing strategy and need. The above paragraph would be written as follows for each of these potential sponsors:

- *Coca-Cola:*

    As title sponsor of the XYZ Event, Coca-Cola would continue its dominance of the XYZ market as well as enjoy exclusive pouring rights at the XYZ Event. With event attendance estimated at (number of attendees) and the audience primarily consisting of young men and women ages 18 to 35, you have an ideal opportunity to get exposure for (specific name of product).

- *RC Cola:*

    As title sponsor of XYZ Event, RC Cola would be presented with the opportunity to have exclusive beverage rights at an event that attracts your competition's primary market. Between in-store promotions, product sales, signage, and sampling opportunities, XYZ Event offers RC Cola an opportunity to dramatically impact sales.

- *Cadbury Schweppes Ginger Ale:*

    XYZ Event offers Cadbury Schweppes Ginger Ale an opportunity to market to its target audience . . . young men and women ages 18 to 35 . . . plus have the bonus opportunity of trade promotions. Title sponsorship would give Cadbury Schweppes exclusive pouring rights for Ginger Ale, as well as signage, trade hospitality, and new-product sampling.

As you can see, specific benefits *as they relate to the specific company* are provided in the cover letter.

(D)   RULE #4: BE SPECIFIC

Never make a general statement that cannot be substantiated by solid facts. For example:

The response to the event has been terrific and the support by other sponsors is overwhelming. All the media are excited about participating in XYZ Event.

This is fluff. Rather, this same paragraph could be written as follows:

The initial mailing to 100 sponsors has provided us with at least 20 major companies that are interested in some level of participation in XYZ Event. These sponsors include such well-known names as _____, _____, and _____. In addition, _____ newspaper, _____ radio station, and _____ TV will be providing extensive coverage of XYZ Event. All of this has a positive impact by generating more interest in a greater attendance at XYZ Event. Through your sponsorship of this event, you too will benefit from this exposure and attendance.

(E)   RULE #5: TAKE RESPONSIBILITY FOR THE FOLLOW-UP

Fund raisers must always state when they will follow up; never make it the sponsor's responsibility to call. For example:

Thanks for your interest and I look forward to hearing from you.

Rather, word the final paragraph this way:

Thanks for taking time to read this proposal and see how XYZ Event offers (name of company) a viable lifestyle marketing opportunity. I will call you the week of (date) to discuss the feasibility of our meeting to discuss this further.

Put as much effort into the cover letter as on the whole proposal. Research sponsors; find out what their marketing strategies are and what products are logical choices for event sponsorship. Understand their marketing needs and tailor the letter to satisfy their needs. Eliminate "I/me/my" from the focus . . . begin to think in terms of "you" and have a strong benefits orientation. And do not think this letter can be written quickly. It might take three or four hours to craft a good letter that will create interest in an event, inspire the reader to go through the proposal, and generate a desire to discuss it further. That time will be well invested if one is successful in generating sponsorship dollars for an event.

To help with letter writing, where appropriate, incorporate the following powerful (and effective) phrases:

- "Measurable response"
- "Qualified media coverage"
- "Diverse, integrated marketing opportunities"
- "Targeted marketing messages"
- "Database marketing opportunities"
- "Generous hospitality components"
- "Enhance existing marketing efforts"
- "Increase product exposure"
- "Improve market share"
- "Reinforce market position"
- "Develop qualified sales leads"
- "Solidify client relationships"
- "Increase sales!"

Remember, the letter is a reinforcement of the powerful sponsorship value associated with the not-for-profit activity.

32.10 Guaranteed Sponsors for Any Event

Sometimes it is hard to know where to start when soliciting sponsorships. Here is a list of the top-20 potential sponsors that can be approached for almost any event:

1. Local electronics retailer
2. Local beer bottler
3. Local soda bottler
4. Local banks
5. Local restaurant association
6. Local retailers association
7. Car dealers

8. Automobile aftermarket
9. Long distance carriers
10. Mobile telephone companies
11. Network marketing companies (Amway, Nu Skin, Mary Kaye, etc.)
12. Craftspeople
13. Antique dealers
14. Fresh produce dealers (mini-farmer's markets)
15. Local radio
16. Local cable
17. Local newspapers
18. T-shirt vendors
19. Food vendors
20. .com companies

32.11 *What Television and Radio Look for in a Sponsorship or Partnership*

Often fund raisers should start their search for sponsors with a television partner. This is an important first step because of the guaranteed publicity muscle of the media. The added value of media exposure is a key marketing tool in attracting top corporate sponsors. Audience size and demographics are important, but they are not the sole criteria a television station will use in deciding if it will sponsor an event. Here are some of the guidelines used by the media in evaluating an event sponsorship package:

- It must be consistent with who we are and who we want to be.
- Is it consistent with our branding?
- Does it meet the needs of the community?
- It must increase awareness of our station, programming, and talent.
- It must help differentiate us from our competition.
- Does the event have revenue-generating opportunities?
- What is the track record of the event organizers?
- Does it provide a database opportunity?
- How far away is the event? (We like to plan one year in advance.)
- Judgments are based on our resources, people, and inventory.

It is imperative to reach an agreement at the onset with event organizers on the responsibilities of each partner and determine exactly what each partner will bring to the table. Just as imperative is establishing a time line for the completion of tasks. Missed deadlines are often the first sign that a partner is falling behind or unable to handle a task.

It is also very important for the organizer and partners to create a post-event report to properly analyze the value of the sponsorship, share database information, and maintain a good relationship with key contacts. Event sponsors look for high recognition of their sponsorship. It is great to be identified on press releases, signage, flyers, entry forms, and posters, but it loses its value if we are lost in a "sea of logos."

Everyone wants event organizers who understand their individual business. Such people become valuable partners. It is important to have the partner understand the value of a station's on-air commitment of time. On-air time is money.

32.12   Developing the Post-Event Report

The event is over. The last tent is gone, the grounds are cleaned up, the last food vendor has left, sponsors were happy . . . it is done! Or so one might think. However, fund raisers still have work to do.

Always provide sponsors with a post-event report. Fund raisers will have maintained a good, close working relationship with sponsors during the pre-event and at the event process. The fund raisers were meticulous about writing a contract that properly outlined all the various rights and benefits associated with the sponsorship. The not-for-profit organization worked closely with the sponsor's representatives, on site, to ensure that all contractual obligations (and more!) were met. Now the fund raiser needs to report back to the sponsor.

Remember the old presentation saying: "Tell them what you are going to tell them; tell them; then tell them what you have told them"? The latter part of that statement refers to the post-event evaluation report. During the event, fund raisers should take lots of pictures, particularly pictures of crowds, signs, banners, tents . . . anything that demonstrated that people were there and that the sponsors' logos and other branded materials had high visibility and exposure. Keep samples of all printed materials: tickets, site maps, program books, press releases, newspaper and magazine clippings (with sponsor's names), posters, flyers, branded merchandise (T-shirts, hats, coolies, etc.), samples of in-store promotions, samples of coupons or bouncebacks, samples of entry forms. Make sure to have enough of these materials for all sponsors for the post-event report.

Next, summarize all the component parts of the not-for-profit event. This includes total attendance (and profile of attendees, when possible: kids, parents, teens, etc.), summary of media exposure (radio and TV will provide the not-for-profit with a notarized log of the times and dates when commercials/promotions ran; newspapers and magazines will send tear sheets), how many posters and flyers were distributed and in what geographic areas, how many banners were hung and where, the number of audio announcements made (sample script too) and how many times each sponsor's name was mentioned, number of contest/promotion entries (database development, etc.), number of coupons or bouncebacks distributed: in short, anything that had a sponsor's name on it or gave sponsor exposure.

Now, put it into a list and attach a value to the component parts. The media will be easy since the summary report will have a value attached to it. The tougher part is attaching a value to some of the components, such as banner exposure, ticket stud exposure, and audio announcements. However, here are three simple estimates to use in providing sponsors with a post-event evaluation of their investment. The elements that must be included are dollar value and number of exposures:

1. For banners and signage at the event, contact the Traffic Audio Bureau for Media Measurement, 212-972-8075, and get them to help evaluate the value. To use a "straw man" figure, use $50/1,000 people who see the sign. Therefore, if an event attracts 10,000 people, the value of the signage exposure is $500/sign. For banners and signage that are put up *before* the event, contact the local Department of Transportation (DOT) to get traffic counts (cars/pedestrians) and then use the same media measurement used for the event exposure.

2. For the media (radio/TV/print), break out each sponsor's exposure (were they all mentioned in all the spots, or was the campaign divided, with each sponsor given a selected number of exposures?) and use the media's evaluation. Then get the media to tell how many people those messages reached (circulation for newspapers and magazines, listeners for radio, viewers for TV) and include those exposure numbers.

3. For branded merchandise, tickets, and hospitality, break out figures the same way: number of exposures and dollar value.

When preparing a post-event report, use a three-column report (going left to right) with the following three headings:

- Column 1 (sponsor components): banners, tickets, media, etc.
- Column 2 (number of impressions): listeners, attendance, viewers, etc.
- Column 3 (dollar value): tickets, value of media, banner expense, etc.

Then just total the columns. This post-event report should be delivered within 30 days after the completion of the event. It is hoped that fund raisers underpromise and overdeliver, showing a minimum return on investment of 3 to 1. Any questions? Give us a call at *The Sponsorship Newsletter* and we will walk you through it. This is my own newsletter, a promotional flyer relating to my consulting practice.

What is the bonus value of the post-event report? Besides letting the sponsor understand the full value of the sponsorship, it is a terrific sales tool for renewal or extension of the sponsorship. See Exhibit 32.3 for an example of a post-event report.

32.13 Sins of Sponsorship

Selling sponsorships takes knowledge and time. One of the biggest sponsor complaints is "The person selling the sponsorship doesn't understand *my* business." This does not have to be an issue *if* one does one's homework.

If the company is publicly traded, get a recent copy of the annual report. No, it does not tell how much money it spends on sponsorship; however, it does tell if it was a good year, a bad year, what divisions made money and what ones did not, what its growth plans are, areas where it will be adding/expanding/cutting back, and the like. Then do a data search: *Brandweek, Advertising Age, Promo, The Sponsorship Newsletter* ... any media that have carried stories on potential sponsors so you know what they are doing.

Fund raisers also need to know who the "players" are in the company. Doing a review of the previous year's media coverage provides the names and contact people, which helps fund raisers decide who is best suited to receive sponsorship solicitation. By researching and reviewing a company's activities over the last year, they are prepared to discuss, intelligently, how sponsorship of an event/sport/activity fits into the company's overall marketing strategy. Preparation will impress the potential sponsor and facilitate the selling process.

32.14 Conclusion

To conclude, keep in mind the following seven strategies for sponsorship success:

1. Start the selling process early—a minimum of six months in advance, preferably one year.

2. Have enthusiasm and passion for your project.

EXHIBIT 32.3 Sample Post-event Report

Event title: _____

Date/times of event: _____

Location: _____

Attendance: _____

Sponsor Components	Number of Impressions	Dollar Value
Banners (size/location/#) _____	_____	_____
Signage (size/location/#) _____	_____	_____
Posters (size/location/#) _____	_____	_____
Tickets (quantity) _____	_____	_____
Media		
Radio (# of spots) _____	_____	_____
TV (# of spots) _____	_____	_____
Newspapers (# of ads) _____	_____	_____
Public relations _____	_____	_____
Radio (coverage) _____	_____	_____
TV (coverage) _____	_____	_____
Newspapers (coverage) _____	_____	_____

Other (list contests, promotions, audio billboards, etc. . . . everything that was in your inventory that was committed to the sponsor plus the value of each component).

TOTAL: _____   _____   _____

3. Be honest—underpromise and overdeliver.
4. Be flexible—willingness to modify and change the sponsorship benefits gives you a better chance at success.
5. Have your materials organized and easy to read.
6. Follow-up and follow-through when promised. Keep your word!
7. Communicate regularly with sponsors; keep them involved and they will return.

The Grant-seeking Process

SUSAN L. GOLDEN, PHD, CFRE

The Golden Group

33.1 Introduction

This chapter focuses on the realities of the grant-seeking process and the most effective methods of preparing a grant proposal. However, the art of grantsmanship is permeated with myths, the most dangerous of which are frequently encountered among people new to fund raising:

1. If you want to raise money quickly, you should seek a grant.
2. When you want to get a grant, the first thing to do is to write a proposal.
3. It is the quality of the proposal that will determine whether a grant is awarded.

Consider the flaws in each of these myths:

1. If you want to raise money, seeking a grant is *not* the best or quickest way. Grants make up less than 10 percent of all private philanthropy. The fastest and easiest way to raise money is for fund raisers to *ask someone they know* who has money and is interested in their organization.[1]

---

[1]Leonard Wright Bucklin, "Basic Planned Giving Workshop," September 18, 1981, Cleveland, Ohio.

2. Preparing a proposal is *not* the first or most important thing to do. A more helpful statement is: "When you want to get a grant, the thing to do is to *begin a dialogue with a grantmaker.*"

As discussed later, preparing a proposal is worth your while only in certain conditions, and submitting a proposal is only one step in the process of building a relationship between grant seeker and grantmaker. Although a proposal is a necessary part of effective grant seeking, it is seldom sufficient to generate a grant.

3. In real life, the quality of a proposal is less important than the quality of your *relationship and dialogue* with the grantmaker. Even well-crafted proposals are turned down; conversely, a poorly crafted proposal sometimes results in a grant. It is wise to keep the importance of the proposal in proper perspective.[2]

A proposal, however, is an essential element of the relationship between the grant seeker and grantmaker, so it is to your advantage to know how to prepare one effectively. The following sections identify the conditions under which it is worthwhile to prepare a proposal, and the conditions under which it is not, and explain how to obtain maximum benefit for an organization by preparing a proposal.

33.2 *The Grant-seeking Process: Seven Scenarios*

The following seven scenarios represent the range of preliminary exchanges between grant seeker and grantmaker. For each of these scenarios, the best course of action in preparing a proposal is suggested.

(A) WHEN IS IT WORTHWHILE TO PREPARE A PROPOSAL?

There are three sets of circumstances in which it is worthwhile to prepare a proposal:

1. When there is reason to believe that submitting a proposal will result in either the immediate or eventual awarding of a grant.
2. When the grant seeker is looking for a way to expedite the planning of a project.
3. To open a dialogue with a grantmaker, and the awarding of a grant is really secondary.

The first set of favorable circumstances—when obtaining a grant is the highest priority—may be reflected in any of three scenarios, depending on how promising the situation is for an award.

Scenario 1: The Optimal. The optimal scenario for you as a grant seeker is to be told by a grantmaker that funds have already been earmarked for your organization, and that if you prepare and submit a proposal documenting the agreement reached verbally, an award will be forthcoming. Although this is not an everyday occurrence in the world of fund raising, it does happen (more often with govern-

---

[2]For a comprehensive treatment of the grant-seeking process, see Susan L. Golden, *Secrets of Successful Grantsmanship: A Guerilla Guide to Fundraising* (San Francisco: Jossey-Bass, 1997).

ment funding sources than private sources). When it does happen, rejoice—then get to work on the writing.

Scenario 2: High Level of Promise. If a grantmaker initiates a conversation in which he or she clearly invites you to submit a request, chances of being awarded a grant are high and you can approach the task of preparing a proposal with optimism.

Scenario 3: Good Level of Promise. The odds of being awarded a grant may also be favorable if you initiate the contact and the grantmaker responds with enthusiasm, inviting you explicitly or implicitly to submit a proposal.

The second set of favorable circumstances, when obtaining a grant is a secondary concern, are reflected in two different scenarios.

Scenario 4: Expediting the Planning Process. The fourth scenario prevails when your highest priority is to expedite your internal planning process. An imminent proposal submission deadline may be one of the best tools in your motivational arsenal, helping you to marshal your resources and get people moving quickly. As Boswell's Johnson pointed out, "Depend upon it, sir, when a man knows he is to be hanged in a fortnight, it concentrates his mind wonderfully." Although grant opportunities are not as threatening as a noose, if you miss deadlines you are "dead," at least in terms of securing a grant during the next funding period.

Scenario 5: Opening a Dialogue. You may find yourself in a situation in which you realize that you need to build a relationship with a grantmaker, but it proves impossible to make the initial contact directly—by phone, preliminary letter, or personal visit. You may think, and it may indeed be the reality, that the only avenue open to you is to submit a proposal.

As discussed later, the odds of your receiving a grant in response to a "cold" proposal are slim. But if you view the proposal as an opening gambit in the dialogue you hope to establish—and on this basis, you can afford the time, energy, and resources required to prepare the proposal—it may be worth your while to proceed.

(B) WHEN IS IT NOT WORTHWHILE TO PREPARE A PROPOSAL?

It is generally *not* worthwhile to prepare a proposal in one of the two following situations:

Scenario 6: Unenthusiastic Response. Suppose you initiated a contact with a grantmaker and told her about your idea, either in a conversation or in writing, but her response was lacking in enthusiasm and interest. In this case, it is probably a waste of time to prepare a proposal, because the chances of your being awarded a grant are very slim.

Scenario 7: No Prior Contact. Assume, for instance, that your sole purpose is to secure a grant from this particular funder at this particular time, but you have not spoken nor had any personal correspondence with the grantmaker. In that event, it is probably not worthwhile to submit a proposal.

Although there seems to be no consensus on how slim the odds are, various scholars estimate the number of proposals that result in grants at somewhere between *one in five* and *one in 20.* Whatever the exact odds, it is obvious that grant seeking is a highly competitive arena and that the vast majority of proposals that result in grant awards are submitted by people who have had direct contact with the grantmaker.

33.3   *Preparing a Grant Proposal*

Assume that you find yourself in a position in which it makes sense for you to submit a proposal. If you have never prepared a successful proposal, you may well be uncertain about how best to proceed. Yet before you embark on the preparation of a proposal, you will have already completed the first step. That is, you will have emerged from the creative struggle of figuring out how to solve a problem or meet a need. You will have generated an idea. This is by far the most challenging and exciting part of the entire process.

The rest of this chapter outlines the steps you should take to obtain the greatest benefit from the process and maximize chances of success. It describes in detail the kinds of tasks that must be completed by you and the officer in charge of the process, and those that can or should be completed by other staff members.

(A)   SCULPTING THE PROJECT

You have probably conceived your project on a fairly abstract level and discussed it in a conceptual fashion with the grantmaker and, perhaps, with others. Now you need to concentrate on making all aspects of the project as concrete as possible. You might find it helpful to think of this process as mental "sculpting." You have the basic materials and a general idea of what you want the finished product to be. From now on, you will be shaping your project and adding detail to prepare it for exhibition before a select, sophisticated, and demanding audience.

On a mundane level, of course, your purpose is to describe in a way that sells your project the *activities* it includes. But this is a creative process, so use your ingenuity. If you are a verbal thinker, develop a list of phrases to describe your project. If you are a visual thinker, envision a series of scenes. If you are familiar with the technique of storyboarding, you could use it to illustrate how you believe events will unfold as the project becomes a reality.

Very few grant seekers go to their offices, sit down at their desks, and sculpt their projects. The process requires less creativity than generating ideas, but your subconscious can still play a role. You can mull over a project while performing routine activities. Your project will take shape organically, evolving as you live with the idea for some time, until, one day, you recognize the project's shape and direction.

Given the evolutionary nature of project development, it does not require full-time, focused attention. As the sculpting process continues, you will be able to carry on other activities to advance the preparation of your proposal.

(B)   CRITERIA FOR ELIGIBILITY

As ideas evolve, a number of tasks must be performed. The first of these is to determine whether your organization meets the criteria for eligibility established by the grantmaker. Some requirements, such as tax-exempt status, are almost universal. Only about 5 percent of all grantmaking organizations award grants to individuals. The other 95 percent require that recipients be qualified by the Internal Revenue Service (IRS) as charitable tax-exempt organizations, according to Section 501(c)(3) of the Internal Revenue Code.[3]

Other requirements are peculiar to specific funders. Some, for example, require that an organization be in operation for three years before it can be eligible for consideration.

33.4 Planning the Work: Six Steps

Once it has been determined that your organization is, in fact, eligible for a grant, review your funder's proposal guidelines and map out a plan for preparing all the sections, which eventually will be assembled into the document you submit. Word processing and spreadsheet software will make it easier for you to do the work in the sequence that makes the most sense, and then to cut and paste to achieve the order in which the information must be presented.

What information do grantmakers request? In what order do they want it presented, and how much detail do they want to see? The guidelines published by the Cleveland Foundation, the oldest and second largest community foundation in the United States, are fairly typical. (See Exhibit 33.1.)

It is recommended that you prepare the sections in the following order (which is quite different from the order in which you will present the information in the assembled document).

- *Task 1.* The agency's background (Section 1)
- *Task 2.* Project implementation plan (Section 3)
- *Task 3.* Financial information (Section 6)
- *Task 4.* Project evaluation (Section 5)
- *Task 5.* Project continuation (Section 4)
- *Task 6.* The project you propose (Section 2)

Over a period of several days, weeks, or even months, you will be cogitating about your project, the work that must precede Task 6. In the meantime, you can begin working on the other sections of this document. If you follow the order described here, each task will lead organically to the next, and the final document, once assembled, will be cogent and compelling.

(A) TASK 1: THE AGENCY'S BACKGROUND

While assembling the information listed in Section 1 of Exhibit 33.1 (describing the organization's mission, programs, staff, and the like), you can also collect the key documents that grantmakers often require as appendixes or enclosures:

- Letters from the IRS designating the organization as tax-exempt
- List of members and officers of the board of trustees, including their business affiliations and positions
- The organization's current annual report

---

[3]C. Edward Murphy, ed., *Guide to U.S. Foundations, Their Trustees, Officers and Donors,* vol. 1 (New York: The Foundation Center, 1995), p. vii; and L. Victoria Hall, ed., *Foundation Grants to Individuals,* 9th ed. (New York: The Foundation Center, 1995), p. vii.

EXHIBIT 33.1 Cleveland Foundation Application Guidelines

Section 1: Your agency's background
- Mission
- Founding date
- Major programs
- Links with similar organizations
- Number and capacity of staff

Section 2: The project you propose
- The specific community need or policy issue you will address, or
- The contribution your project will make to the community
- Your project's goals and objectives
- The activities you propose to tackle the problem
- Why your organization wants to do the work
- Why your plan is cost effective
- Expected immediate and long-term results
- Other providers of this service in the area
- Distinctive features of your project
- Expected contribution to knowledge in the field
- Relationship to your agency's overall program
- Professional support or other evidence of the project's value

Section 3: Your project implementation plan
- Your time line: steps to be taken, by whom, and when
- How many people, and whom, will be served
- Names of cooperating organizations
- Project staff and/or consultants
- Any advisory groups

Section 4: Project continuation
- If the project is ongoing, your plans to continue after the funding period
- Future funding sources
- Other current funding sources

Section 5: Project evaluation
- Your criteria for effectiveness
- Methods and schedule for measuring results
- Methods and schedule for short- and long-term evaluation of results
- Who will assess the results

Section 6: Financial information
- A line-item income and expense budget for the project
- A budget narrative explaining each line item for which you are requesting support
- The amount your organization will contribute to the project
- A list of other foundations or sources to which you have submitted this proposal (indicate whether funds have been committed, declined, or are pending)
- Your organization's current annual operating budget. (Note any deficits and describe your plans to correct them.)

Source: The Cleveland Foundation, "Guidelines for Grantseekers" (February 1996).

- A current audit or financial statement
- Job descriptions for project personnel

If this is the first proposal your organization has submitted, or the first submitted in a long time, you can help the organization by setting up a grant-seeking file. Place in this file copies of all the documents you assemble so that they will be readily available to you and your colleagues in the future.

If, on the other hand, your organization has submitted successful proposals in the past, and it is only your personal involvement that is new, you may be able to take a shortcut. Save time by updating information in the grant-seeking file that is no longer current and simply appropriate the other information.

At this stage, you must also start to work with people outside the organization on at least two issues, which will be fleshed out later.

1. Future funding for the project
2. If your project is collaborative, the nature of the partnership and how it will work

(i)　Future Funding Partners

You may have already given some thought to the long-term financial viability of the project, but many grant seekers do not think about this until the grantmaker insists on it. The earlier you address the question of how the project will be supported after the grant period, the more attractive your project will be to prospective investors—and the more likely you will be to secure both the start-up and continuing support you require. If future funders are closely involved in the planning of a project, they are more likely to continue their involvement.

Therefore, if you have not already done so, now is the time to begin building good relationships with prospective permanent funders, sponsors, and customers. Inform these people about the plans you are developing and build their interests into your planning process. Although this will require an investment of time and energy, their results will be worthwhile.

(ii)　Collaborating Organizations

Your project may involve partner organizations that will be collaborating on your grant-seeking venture and providing services as part of your project. If so, you have probably established contact with your prospective partners and inquired in general terms about the possibility of working together. Now it is time to confirm your plans for collaboration. Meet with at least one representative of each of the organizations with whom you wish to collaborate, in order to determine:

- The role the collaborative partner is interested in undertaking
- The level of commitment with which the prospective partner is comfortable

Developing collaborative relationships is usually a wise investment of time and energy, inasmuch as many grantmakers currently prefer to support collaborative efforts rather than single-organization projects. These funders maintain that collaboration is generally more efficient and more cost effective than single-organization efforts, because costly duplication of effort is avoided.

Although involving collaborative partners may make your project more attractive to funders, a collaborative project is far more complex in its planning and organizing requirements. In fact, in dealing with multiple sources of information and multiple administrative approvals, the process may seem not just arithmetically, but geometrically, more complex. It is important to accept this reality.

Another reality of today's grant-seeking environment is that funders' expectations are rising in respect to the level of advance planning and commitment to collaboration. As recently as a few years ago, some funders accepted letters of support—committing little more than hearty best wishes—as documentation of involvement. Today, however, most grantmakers require contracts, or at least firm, formal commitments, contingent upon the receipt of funds. When organizational resources are being committed, of course, appropriate authorization is required. This almost always involves a good deal of negotiation, which naturally takes time.

Therefore, if a project involves one or more collaborating organizations, you cannot afford to defer discussions on how the arrangement will work. "Fudging" the details in the grant proposal is no longer an option.

(B) TASK 2: PROJECT IMPLEMENTATION PLAN

The evolutionary process of sculpting your project generally produces a list of activities or a series of scenarios. With this information in hand, you can move on to the next task: the project implementation plan.

One way to approach this task is to create a time line matrix. In the process of constructing this grid, you will develop the information on the project time line requested in Section 3 of Exhibit 33.1. You will also develop much of the budget information requested in Section 6. In short, you will answer all of the subquestions posed in this mega-question: *Who will do what, for whom, with what, at what cost, by when—and how will we know it is done and how effective it was?*

To answer the mega-question, you must identify:

- All tasks involved in the project
- Who will be responsible for completing each task
- The resources that will be employed in completing each task
- The costs that will be incurred in employing these resources
- How long it will take to complete each task
- The milestones that will indicate the completion of each task
- Evaluation and outcome metrics, as well as benchmark data to measure change

(i) Developing a Time Line Matrix: An Example
In developing a marketing project for a performing arts organization, one of the activities was to "conduct an advertising campaign."

A time line matrix was constructed in order to spell out exactly how this will be accomplished. The questions that had to be addressed are listed in Exhibit 33.2.

To answer such questions and develop a sound plan, you will have to make some decisions based on incomplete information. If the organization is located in a major metropolitan area, for example, it may not be practical to obtain advertising rates for all TV and radio stations. Therefore, you and your colleagues will have to come to at least a tentative agreement about the scope of the advertising campaign. As soon as you begin this detailed planning, you must make choices and, as a consequence, limit the potential of your project.

Many issues will arise as you address questions, such as those listed in the exhibit, and gather the information you need in order to arrive at answers that make sense.

EXHIBIT 33.2 Sample Marketing Time Line Matrix

- What media are to be used in the advertising campaign?
- How are funds to be distributed among direct mail, print, radio, television, billboards, and bus cards?
- Which mailing list(s) are to be used for direct mail?
- How is mail to be sent (bulk rate or first class)?
- Who will prepare the mailing?
- What percentage of the ads in print and electronic media are to be public service ads (free of charge to the not-for-profit)?
- Which radio and TV stations will attract the audience the not-for-profit organization wants to target?
- How long will each advertisement be?
- At what time of day will the ads be aired?
- Who will compose the ad copy?
- Who will design the graphics?
- Who will reproduce the graphics?
- What items are to be printed, and how many copies of each will be needed?
- What size audience can each radio and TV station promise?
- Who will perform in the ads?
- Will royalties have to be paid for music used in the ads? If so, how much and to whom?
- How long a commitment will the organization have to make to the advertising media?
- How will the impact of the advertising be measured?
- How will the organization know that this evaluation was impartial and accurate?
- How will the organization analyze the cost-benefit ratio for future planning proposed?

When you have finished constructing the time line matrix, you will have completed much of the planning for your project.

(ii) Allocating Resources to Proposal Preparation

Developing a matrix will be easier if you adopt two strategic approaches to preparing the proposal:

1. Budget sufficient time and resources for the planning and research involved. Before you commit to preparing a proposal, consider how much time you have available and the kind of help available to you. Factor in this information in deciding whether you can realistically meet the deadline under discussion.
2. Involve colleagues in planning and proposal preparation. If you do so, the project will be better planned, and its implementation will go more smoothly.

Participating colleagues represent disciplines or functions that will be involved in implementing the project. For instance, if you are planning an educational project, you may involve teachers; if you are planning a research effort, you may involve researchers.

Service colleagues represent functions that support the mission-oriented work of the organization. The fiscal management and advancement function, for example, includes fund development, marketing, public relations, and planning. If you need to know the value of 10 percent of a staff member's time or the cost of health insurance, you would ask a person who works in your organization's fiscal management function. If you need to know how much it will cost to produce a brochure, you would ask someone who works in public relations to help you develop the estimate.

When you involve colleagues in the planning and proposal preparation process, it helps to lighten the burden. Beyond that, when you involve those who will be responsible for implementing and supporting the project, they will develop ownership of the venture. People who have been involved in planning a project are motivated to implement it with greater enthusiasm than those who are merely presented with a fait accompli.

Most assistance in preparing a time line matrix may be provided by staff members, but you may have to seek help outside the organization as well. Do not hesitate to ask professionals or vendors to develop bids. Remember, everyone who is in business is concerned about developing new business.

The ethical approach to securing bids or estimates is to make it clear that you do not currently have funding in hand for the work you are discussing. To encourage a prompt response from a vendor, point out that the estimate or bid process is part of your fundraising effort, and that once you do have the funds in hand, you will consider that vendor in purchasing the product or service on which he or she is bidding.

An ancillary benefit of preparing proposals is that you often gain more valuable information than you set out to acquire. In most instances, for example, you follow sound business practice and secure at least two or three bids for each major product or service involved in the project. In the process, you also learn which vendors are easiest to work with and which professionals best fit the culture and style of your organization.

The difference between seeking a preliminary bid and signing a contract to work together is analogous to the relationship between dating and marriage. If a vendor fails to return phone calls promptly when you are making initial inquiries, his performance will probably not improve if you select him to help implement your project.

The time line matrix can provide the information needed to prepare two key sections of the proposal: the time line (for Section 3 of Exhibit 33.1) and the budget (for Section 6).

(iii) Project Time Line

The project time line identifies each activity within the project, the person who will be responsible for completing it, and the period of time it will require. The time scale selected for your presentation depends on the nature of the project. Whether events are outlined week by week or quarter by quarter, what counts is to demonstrate that you know what needs to be done, have a clear understanding of the order in which tasks must be accomplished, and understand the time and resources required.

A proposal has a more professional appearance if this information is presented in graphic as well as narrative form. You can accomplish this fairly easily by using project management software to generate a Gantt or PERT (Project Evaluation and Review Technique) chart.

Most grant seekers significantly underestimate the time required to complete the activities involved in their projects. Therefore, it may be wise to double the original estimates. In your project implementation plan, try to accommodate the operation of Murphy's Law. Most grantmakers have extensive experience with a broad range of projects. If you underestimate the time required to accomplish your goals, you will be seen as naive, a poor planner, or both, which can discourage funders from getting involved with your plan.

(C) TASK 3: FINANCIAL INFORMATION

Most grantmakers agree that they look at the budget first and scrutinize it more rigorously than any other part of a proposal. If the grantmaker specifies a format for your budget information, be sure to follow it. If there is no format specified, a template that seems to accommodate most situations is that provided by The Cleveland Foundation.[4] A number of the Foundation's forms are included as samples in the Exhibits of this chapter.

Before you begin to build a budget, be sure to think through all the basic components and parameters of your project:

- Its duration
- The duration of the period for which you are seeking grant support
- The level of resource commitment from your organization
- The number and identity of collaborating organizations and the levels of their resource commitments
- The number and identity of external funders to whom you are applying
- The preferences of specific external funders and any restrictions they will place on the use of funds

As you plan a budget, you can make it more attractive to funders by applying the following guidelines:

Nine "Golden" Rules of Budget Building

1. *Keep it simple.* Whenever possible, divide the support you request from multiple sources on a percentage basis. If an expense item costs $1,000 and you have four funders who are equally capable of supporting it and equally likely to do so, the simplest thing to do is to request $250 from each of the four.

2. *Give yourself full credit.* Document as high a level of organizational support as you honestly can. Many people fail through mere oversight to credit their organizations for support in the form of standard business operating costs. Every time someone inserts a new toner cartridge, runs a letter through a postage meter, or staples two pieces of paper together, there are costs involved. Give your organization full credit for providing this support. The higher the degree of organizational support you can demonstrate, the more committed your organization will appear, and the more attractive your project will be to external funders.

Organizational support can be provided in cash, in-kind services, or both.

Commitment is most clearly demonstrated by an allocation of cash for direct expenses. Such expenses may include compensation for an individual hired specifically to work on the project or the purchase of a piece of equipment specifically for use in the project.

In-kind services are normally services, staff time, supplies, or equipment provided by the organization without reimbursement. For example, office space may be donated by the organization to support the project, or the fiscal officer may undertake oversight of the project budget along with her other responsibilities. Indirect expenses are overhead or administrative costs that are necessary if the project is to function but do not directly provide a service to clients. Frequently, indirect costs are provided as an in-kind donation by the sponsoring agency.

To determine whether organizational resources should be considered cash or in-kind services, ask yourself whether you expect a check to be cut specifically for a given expen-

---

[4]Format used with permission of Susan L. Eagan, Ph.D., associate director, The Cleveland Foundation. Sample budgets are adapted from the Capacity-Building Project of the Cleveland Rape Crisis Center; used with permission of Mary Brigid, executive director.

diture. If so, that expense probably involves a cash commitment. If you do not expect a check to be cut to cover an expense, such as 5 percent of the rent or 10 percent of an existing staff person's time, then the commitment is probably in-kind.

3. *Detail the commitments of partners.* If the project involves one or more collaborating organizations, then identify them in your budget and detail their commitment of resources. This will demonstrate their level of involvement and their enthusiasm for the project.

4. *Be specific.* Wherever possible, give the budget specificity by spelling out the number of units and the unit cost before multiplying to arrive at a forecast expense. For instance, if the project involves mailing a newsletter, determine how many copies of the newsletter must be printed and the unit cost. Add the postage cost per copy. Then multiply this figure by the number of copies to estimate the total mailing costs.

5. *If you cannot be specific, create a reasonable fiction.* When it is impossible to forecast precisely what something will cost, create a reasonable, fact-based fiction. For instance, many funders expect you to be able to forecast exact costs for copying, which is extremely difficult to do. However, if you review your organization's expenditures for copying over a recent period, you can probably extrapolate from that level of activity to the project you are planning. Thus, you can arrive at a number that is fictional but reasonable.

6. *Change is constant.* No costs will remain static over the life of a project, especially if it is expected to last more than a year. You should allow for inflation and for annual increases in staff compensation.

Make sure that your year-to-year budget projections reflect any changes in the activities involved in your project. Costs will increase as you introduce new activities or expand existing activities to serve more people. Start-up costs should disappear after the first year. For example, once software has been developed, costs for maintenance should be included, but the original cost of development is eliminated.

7. *Nothing lasts forever.* Although all funders recognize that external support is usually required to get a project "up and running," no funder wants to support a project that can never become self-supporting. Over time, your budget should reflect a diminishing reliance on external funding—and an increasing reliance on your own donor base, together with any revenues the project may be able to generate for itself.

8. *Be consistent.* If you are applying to more than one grantmaker for support, bear in mind that funders are likely to compare notes. They tend to develop their grantmaking strategies in relation to what their counterparts at other foundations or agencies are doing. To maintain your credibility, keep your budget numbers consistent in all the proposals you submit.

9. *Be respectful.* We all like to think that our organizations are distinctive, even unique, and we are not pleased when others make unwarranted assumptions about us. Grantmakers feel much the same way, so try to respect the preferences and limitations of individual funders.

For instance, in asking for support for computers, some funders prefer that their money be used to purchase hardware and some prefer that it buy software. If you are aware of such preferences, they should be reflected in the way you build your budget.

(i) Building a Budget: An Example

To see how these guidelines are used in practice, consider how one grant seeker built a budget and the thinking that went into its presentation. Various sections of the budget are developed in much the same way as the proposal narrative: The work is done in one sequence, and the presentation in another.

Project expenses. Accounting convention requires that revenues be listed before expenses. In putting together a proposal budget, however, you must calculate expenses first, so you can decide how much grant support to request.

With this in mind, use the project expenses form (see Exhibit 33.3) to begin building your budget. This sample has been filled in for a one-year period. If your project will last more than one year, make copies of this form and do each year separately. When all years have been completed, total them on another form, which can serve as a summary.

As we review each section of this form, we will suggest guidelines for developing both the *line items* and the *narrative* which must accompany the budget.

Personnel. In estimating the percentage of a person's time that will be allocated to a project, it is usually easier to think about how much time the individual will spend on a weekly basis, then multiply by 52. If a person will be spending a major portion of his or her time on the project, base your calculations on a total of 2,080 paid work-hours in the year.

Consult your fiscal office to obtain information on fringe benefits. Be sure to ask what costs are covered, because these vary considerably from one organization to another and even from one position to another.

Nonpersonnel expenses. The area of contract services, especially for consultants, can present problems in a review by a program officer. Because foundations generally base their own payments to consultants on the "government rate," the program officers who scrutinize your proposal may not be well informed about current market rates.

You are advised to contact a national organization in the consultant's field of expertise and request a written statement that documents the generally accepted market rates in the field. If you cannot obtain a written statement, at least discuss the matter with an objective third party and take notes on what market rates are perceived to be.

To estimate a consulting fee, you will need an hourly or daily rate and the consultant's estimate of the amount of time the job will require, or the consultant's estimated total fee.

Your project may or may not involve other contract services. If it does, retain the information on which you based your estimate (i.e., hourly rate and number of hours).

Office space. You may have given minimal thought to some line items, such as the cost of insurance or utilities. Wherever costs are unknown to you, work with your business office personnel to do the research and estimate the numbers.

Equipment/supplies. It is very difficult to forecast many of these line items. The best method is to prorate your organization's annual expenditures, based on the relationship of your project to the rest of the organization's activities.

Travel/related expenses. Because so many scandals and abuses have involved the inappropriate use of grant, government, or not-for-profit funds, this section will be very closely scrutinized. To make sure your budget holds up, take extra care in estimating any travel expenses for which you are seeking support.

One of the problems you may encounter is that hotel and airline rates change frequently and, sometimes, dramatically. Another complexity is that when you begin to prepare a budget, you may not know where your professional meetings and conferences

EXHIBIT 33.3 Sample Form—Project Expenses

Personnel Expenses	Percent on Project	Organizational Contribution	Other Funding Sources	Cleveland Foundation Request	Total
Staff Costs					
Position Title					
Executive Director	60%	$_____	$13,500	$16,500	$30,000
Administrative Assistant	40%	$_____	$4,500	$5,500	$10,000
_____	___%	$_____	$_____	$_____	$_____
_____	___%	$_____	$_____	$_____	$_____
Staff Costs Subtotal		$_____	$18,000	$22,000	$40,000
Fringe Benefits		$_____	$4,500	$5,500	$10,000
(explain in narrative)					
Fringe Benefits Subtotal		$_____	$4,500	$5,500	$10,000
Total Personnel Expenses		$_____	$22,500	$27,500	$50,000
Nonpersonnel Expenses					
Contract Services					
Consultants		$_____	$15,750	$19,250	$35,000
Legal services		$_____	$1,080	$1,320	$2,400
Temporary services		$_____	$_____	$_____	$_____
Audit services		$_____	$_____	$_____	$_____
Other (explain in narrative)		$_____	$_____	$_____	$_____
Contract Services Subtotal		$_____	$16,830	$20,570	$37,400
Office Space					
Rent		$14,400	$_____	$_____	$14,400
Utilities		$960	$_____	$_____	$960
Furnishings		$_____	$_____	$_____	$_____
Maintenance		$_____	$_____	$_____	$_____
Insurance		$1,200	$_____	$_____	$1,200
Other (explain in narrative)		$_____	$_____	$_____	$_____
Office Space Subtotal		$16,560	$_____	$_____	$16,560
Equipment/Supplies					
Office supplies		$_____	$128	$155	$283
Printing		$_____	$653	$797	$1,450
Postage and delivery		$_____	$225	$275	$500
Copier rental/supplies		$_____	$338	$412	$750
Telephone/fax (local/long distance)		$_____	$1,899	$2,321	$4,220
Repairs/maintenance		$_____	$0	$0	$0
Computer supplies/maintenance		$_____	$0	$14,850	$14,850
Other (explain in narrative)		$_____	$23,372	$0	$23,372
Equipment/Supplies Subtotal		$_____	$26,615	$18,810	$45,425

EXHIBIT 33.3 (*Continued*)

	Percent on Project	Organizational Contribution	Other Funding Sources	Cleveland Foundation Request	Total
Travel/Related Expenses					
Air travel		$_____	$_____	$_____	$_____
Out-of-town expenses		$_____	$_____	$_____	$_____
In-town expenses (parking/mileage)		$_____	$_____	$_____	$_____
Meetings/seminars/conference fees		$_____	$_____	$_____	$_____
Other (explain in narrative)		$_____	$_____	$_____	$_____
Travel/Related Expenses Subtotal		$_____	$_____	$_____	$_____
Other					
Indirect cost (explain in narrative)		$_____	$_____	$_____	$_____
Volunteer Recognition Banquet		$_____	$3,000	$_____	$3,000
		$_____	$_____	$_____	$_____
Other Subtotal		$_____	$3,000	$_____	$3,000
		$_____			
Total Non-Personnel Expenses		$_____	$29,615	$18,810	$48,425
TOTAL PROJECT EXPENSES		$16,560	$68,945	$66,880	$152,385

Requesting Organization: Cleveland Rape Crisis Center
Prepared by: Mary Brigid
Phone Number: (216) 555-3914

will be held two or three years from now. Many large organizations book hotel space as far in advance as possible, but smaller organizations may not select a site for a meeting two or three years ahead of time. If this is the case, you need to:

- Review actual travel costs for the last few years.
- Select a few representative meeting sites.
- Contact a travel agent to determine the current travel and hotel costs for these sites.
- Hope that the organization does not select a site that is much more distant or a hotel that is much more expensive.

Revenues. When you have finished estimating your project expenses, move on to the next section of the budget, project revenues. An example is shown in Exhibit 33.4.

As you can see, this form requires you to distinguish between those funds that are committed and those that are anticipated. Under "Committed" list only those grants for which you have a written, legally binding commitment.

Organizational income may be challenging to forecast. You will usually be close if you review your organization's budget history and base your calculations on the trends of the past several years.

EXHIBIT 33.4 Sample Form—Project Budget Request

THE CLEVELAND FOUNDATION
PROJECT BUDGET REQUEST

(Please copy form for multiple year projects)

Requesting Organization: Cleveland Rape Crisis Center
Project Title: _____ Capacity Building Project ____
Project Duration: From ____1/1/98____ To 2/31/98
Total amount requested from The Cleveland Foundation: $66,680

SUMMARY OF PROJECT REVENUES

Grants and other support

GOVERNMENT	Committed	Anticipated	Total
City	$_____	$_____	$_____
County	$_____	$_____	$_____
State	$_____	$_____	$_____
Federal	$_____	$_____	$_____
Government Subtotal	$_____	$_____	$_____
Foundations and Corporations (list separately)			
__The Cleveland Foundation___	$_____	$66,880	$66,880
__The George Gund Foundation___	$_____	$45,505	$45,505
__The Bruening Foundation___	$_____	$23,441	$23,441
_____	$_____	$_____	$_____
Foundations and Corporations Subtotal	$_____	$135,826	$135,826
Organizational Income			
Membership fees/dues	$_____	$_____	$_____
Contract services	$_____	$_____	$_____
Fundraising events	$_____	$_____	$_____
Other	$_____	$_____	$_____
Organizational Income Subtotal	$_____	$_____	$_____
Other (specify)			
—	$_____	$_____	$_____
—	$_____	$_____	$_____
Other Subtotal	$_____	$_____	$_____
TOTAL PROJECT REVENUES	$_____	$_____	$_____
In-Kind (list below: do not include in total)			
Office Space/Utilities	$15,360	$_____	$15,360
Insurance	$1,200	$_____	$1,200
—	$16,560	$_____	$16,560

For obvious reasons, most grantmakers are more interested in the funds you are requesting from them than the funds you are seeking elsewhere. Prior to any meeting or conversation with a grantmaker regarding the budget, review your backup material. When you discuss the funds you are seeking from this grantmaker, be prepared to discuss in detail the reasoning behind each line item.

With all of this detail completed, you are now in a position to prepare a budget summary. An example is presented in Exhibit 33.5.

The numbers in the summary should be taken directly from the detail and should be consistent throughout your budget sheets.

If you use spreadsheet software to develop your budget, the numbers will be subject to rounding. Be sure to review all sums manually so you can correct the effects of rounding. You can be sure that the grantmaker will check your math manually. Any errors, even those produced by automatic rounding, can damage your credibility.

Budget narrative. In the format provided by The Cleveland Foundation, the grantmaker suggests the level of detail grant seekers should include in the budget narrative. A few of these suggestions follow.

For staff involvement, an example of a staff position for which support is sought is:

> *Project director.* This position is accountable for planning, organizing, and directing the implementation and operations of the project. Specific responsibilities include directing staff, orientation, training, and evaluation in accordance with department standards. The project director also directly supervises three case managers.

An example of a nonpersonnel item for which support is sought is:

> *Postage.* The total requested postage budget is $2,500. This includes mailing routine correspondence as well as the community health assessment questionnaire. The questionnaire is an integral component of our activities in year one, as outlined on page 22 of our proposal. The total number of questionnaires to be mailed is 7,500, at a cost of $2,175. The $325 balance is for the mailing of routine correspondence.[5]

(D) TASK 4: PROJECT EVALUATION

At this point, you have to flesh out the plan for evaluating your project, which you included in your time line. This will become Section 5 (see Exhibit 33.1) of your completed proposal.

As the format suggests, you must define the criteria for a successful project. You must explain when and how you plan to measure your results, both short-term and long-term, and who will be responsible for the evaluation process.

Whenever possible, use standard instruments to measure progress. If no one within your organization understands project evaluation, consult an expert from an area university for advice.

---

[5]Used with permission of Susan L. Eagen, Ph.D., associate director, The Cleveland Foundation.

EXHIBIT 33.5 Sample Form—Budget Summary

THE CLEVELAND FOUNDATION
BUDGET SUMMARY

Requesting Organization: Cleveland Rape Crisis Center
Project Title: Capacity Building Project

SUMMARY OF PROJECT REVENUES

Revenue (committed and anticipated)

Government	$_____	
Foundations and Corporations		
__The Cleveland Foundation_____		$66,880
__The George Gund Foundation_____		$45,505
__The Bruening Foundation_____		$23,440
_____	$_____	
Foundations and Corporations Subtotal		$135,825
Organizational Income	$_____	
Other	$_____	
Total Project Revenue		$135,825
In-Kind (not included in total)		$16,560

SUMMARY OF PROJECT EXPENSES

Expenses

Personnel Expenses	
Staff Costs	$40,000
Fringes	$10,000
Personnel Expenses Subtotal	$50,000
Non-Personnel Expenses	
Contract Services	$37,400
Office Space	$15,360
Equipment/Supplies	$45,425
Travel/Related Expenses	$0
Other	$4,200
Non-Personnel Expenses Subtotal	$102,385
Total Project Expenses	$152,385

(E) TASK 5: PROJECT CONTINUATION

At the outset of this process, you were encouraged to pursue discussions with future funders, beneficiaries of your services, and other key constituencies in order to incorporate their interests into your planning and proposal preparation process. In developing budget projections, you were encouraged to show progressively less dependence on external sources of funding over time.

To complete this task (Section 4 of the finished proposal—see Exhibit 33.1), provide as much detail as you can on how you plan to continue the project after termination of the grant. Refer to the projected budget revenues and explain how each source of committed funds and anticipated funds will contribute to the ongoing support of the project. This may include increased support from your own donor base, as well as any revenues generated by the project.

(F) TASK 6: DESCRIPTION OF PROJECT

Strange as it may seem, this is truly the best point at which to develop your statement of need (Section 2 of the completed proposal—see Exhibit 33.1), describing in detail the problem the organization is hoping to solve or the issue it is planning to address by implementing the project. Here you will also explain the project's goals and objectives and provide other information you may have skipped over in your "first pass." Show how your project goals relate to the organization's overall mission, purpose, and long-range plan.

Why formulate goals and objectives *after* the time line and budget? The reason is that only now have you thought through what it is you are really going to do. You will not be indulging in vague rhetoric, as so many grant seekers do, but making definite statements that can be fully supported by all the detailed information you developed in the course of completing the preceding tasks.

At this point, of course, the goals and objectives should clearly reflect the activities you are going to conduct, including the evaluation of the project.

33.5 Final Steps: The Executive Summary, Cover Letter, and Letters of Support

Once the proposal narrative and budget are complete, move on to the part of the package that will get most attention: the executive summary.

This is one of the most challenging tasks a writer can be assigned. You are asked to summarize, in a few hundred words, in a coherent and persuasive fashion, the most important points you have made in the six sections of the proposal and to convince the reader that your project deserves her full attention and close consideration.

Faced with this challenge, many grant seekers resort to vague generalizations. Others struggle to include as many facts as possible. Instead, try to select those "significant few" facts that best support the major points you want to get across. The task is comparable to writing a highly effective five-minute speech or a 500-word editorial.

Most grantmakers do specify a length limit for this section, and that limit should be strictly observed. Some grant seekers are tempted to reduce the point size of the type in order to cram in more copy. Do not succumb to this temptation. If a grantmaker has to squint, your presentation will put her in a bad mood. She will be more critical of your document, if she reads it at all.

In your cover letter, you will have even less room for facts, or even persuasion. You can use a paragraph to describe the nature of the project, its cost, and the amount of the grant you are seeking (which should be mentioned as early as possible). In another paragraph, emphasize why you chose to approach this particular grantmaker and mention the benefits to your constituents that will be most important to the grantmaker.

The cover letter should be signed by the officials specified by the grantmaker, usually the chief executive officer and board officer. (They may be willing to include their own sentiments about the importance of your project.) If someone else in your organization has had direct contact with the grantmaker, try to develop a way to refer to this person so that the grantmaker can identify your organization with someone with whom she has had contact.

If you wish to impress the grantmaker with the fact that others in the community are supportive of the project, or if the project is collaborative and you have to document intent to participate by your partners, you have one more set of tasks to perform before you have completed your materials for submission, and these are the tasks involved in preparing appropriate letters of support or participation.

Although these letters will be signed by people who head other organizations, for several reasons it would be naive to count on the people who sign the letters to draft them within your time constraints. First of all, these are usually very busy people, and your project is a higher priority for you than it is for them, which means that the preparation of these letters is more urgent for you than for them. Second, you probably know your project in much greater detail than they do, which means that it is easier for you to draft a letter that is relevant to your project than it is for them.

To ensure that you receive the letters you need in a timely fashion, and that you enhance your relationship with colleagues with whom you will be working on the project, follow these four steps:

1. Call the person whom you are asking to sign a letter and explain that you would appreciate having a letter of support (or participation) for a project for which you are seeking funding.
2. Offer to provide a draft of the letter, to make it as easy as possible for him to comply with your request.
3. Once he indicates that he is willing to sign a letter, make arrangements to send him the draft, making sure to inquire about word processing software if you are sending the draft on a computer disk, or his electronic mail address if you are e-mailing the draft, or his actual street address if you are sending the draft by courier or overnight mail service.
4. In the same conversation, make sure to provide similar details for your receipt so that the person can return the finished letter to you in a timely fashion.

Draft the letter as you would like it to read. As for how to do this, the same principles apply to letters of support as to proposals in general: keep them specific and keep them short.

Exhibits 33.6 through 33.9 are examples of letters of participation, submitted as part of an application for Y-Haven, a transitional housing project developed by the YMCA of Cleveland to provide residential and training services to mentally ill, homeless men.[6]

As you may notice, the four letters appear as if they had been prepared by four different individuals. In fact, they were all drafted by the grant seeker on the same morning, on the same computer. But to convey the impression that they were actually prepared in

---

[6]These letters are reprinted with permission of Kenneth W. McLaughlin, president and CEO, YMCA of Greater Cleveland.

EXHIBIT 33.6 Sample Letter of Participation

May 9, 1991

Mr. Clifford Smith, President
YMCA of Greater Cleveland
2200 Prospect Avenue
Cleveland, Ohio 44115

Dear Cliff:

The West Side Ecumenical Ministry is looking forward to collaborating with the West Side YMCA on your transitional housing project, Y-Haven.

This letter will confirm the agreement I made on May 6, 1991 with Elving Otero, Vice President of the Y.

We will be pleased to develop a Cooperative Connections group which will meet at the West Side YMCA, and we will pair a small group of Y-Haven participants with a small group of suburban people who are economically independent for self-help and mutual resourcefulness.

Cooperative Connections is an innovative program which has been operating successfully in several sites on the Near West Side since we began it in 1988, and the results have been most gratifying. We are seeing people becoming employed, finishing their education, and getting their family relationships improved. All of this is being accomplished in a highly cost-effective way.

The fee for the first year's staffing of the Y-Haven Cooperative Connections group leader will be $4,680, with 5 percent increases per year for subsequent years.

We look forward to working with you and hope you are successful in obtaining HUD funding.

Yours sincerely,

Robert T. Begin

Rev. Robert T. Begin
Executive Director

WEST SIDE ECUMENICAL MINISTRY · 4315 BRIDGE AVENUE · CLEVELAND, OHIO 44113 · 651-2037

EXHIBIT 33.7 Sample Letter of Participation

M&M

MENTAL HEALTH SERVICES FOR HOMELESS PERSONS INC

MONEY & MAILBOXES

1761 E. 24th Street, Suite 200, Cleveland Ohio 44114 • (212)574-9393
Fax No : 574-9551

May 6, 1991

Mr. Cliff Smith, President
YMCA of Greater Cleveland
2200 Prospect
Cleveland, OH 44115

Dear Mr. Smith:

This letter will confirm the agreement we reached when I met on May 2, 1991 with Elving Otero, Vice President for Development of the YMCA.

Money & Mailboxes is an intensive case management agency serving persons who are homeless and mentally ill. We are certified by the State of Ohio as a provider of mental health services. Since our founding in 1988, our agency has served 472 clients. Our staff includes 12 case managers and five psychiatrists.

We are enthusiastic about the possibility of collaborating with the YMCA on their proposed Y-Haven Transitional Housing Project.

We would be able to serve approximately 15 participants in the Y-Haven project who meet our criteria for participation in our program if this housing would be their choice. We would provide the following services: reaching entitlement benefits; reaching psychiatric support through psychiatrists; providing employment assistance support; providing supportive developmental relationships; offering outreach to engage potential clients in the community; providing representative payee service; and, when the time is appropriate, finding affordable housing. Employment assistance services will be provided through appropriate referrals to the Bureau of Vocational Rehabilitation, and services will include counseling, identification of training needs and placement.

Our case management services will be provided at no fee to the YMCA, and are currently valued and reimbursed at $46.00 per hour by Medicaid.

These services will be monitored by standard staff practice which carefully logs and tracks all client contacts and referrals.

We wish you luck in securing funding from HUD and look forward to working with you.

Yours sincerely,

Cathy Steinecker

Cathy Steinecker
Director

Providing a countrywide system of case management services to the severely mentally disabled homeless population. A contract agency at County Community Mental Health Board and supported by the National Institute of Mental Health and Ohio Department of Mega.

EXHIBIT 33.8 Sample Letter of Participation

COUNTY OF
CUYAHOGA

Department of Human Services

Commissioners
Mary O. Boyle
Virgil E. Brown
Timothy F. Hagan

Gladys V. Hall
Director

May 3, 1991

Mr. Clifford Smith, President
YMCA Cleveland
2200 Prospect Avenue
Cleveland, Ohio 44115

Dear Mr. Smith:

I have been made aware that YMCA Cleveland has applied to the United States Department of Housing and Urban Development for transitional housing funds.

As an Associate Director at the Cuyahoga County Department of Human Services responsible for the FairWork Department, I know well the needs of the population you propose to serve.

This is to convey the responsibilities of Cuyahoga County Department of Human Services Job Opportunities & Basic Skills Training (JOBS) as they relate to your clients. If these transitional housing participants are public assistance recipients, they qualify for JOBS Program services. These services include remedial education, vocational training, job search assistance, transportation and expense allowance and, in the cases of ADC recipients, child care services.

Since your program proposes to provide counseling services to these participants, I believe that the JOBS program intensive Social Service unit could be a particularly effective service for clients. I look forward to working with you on this project.

Sincerely,

CUYAHOGA COUNTY DEPARTMENT OF HUMAN
SERVICES

Maureen O. Weigand

Maureen O. Weigand,
Administrator, FairWork Program

MW/cg

220 St. Clair Avenue, Cleveland, Ohio 44113   216/987-7000

EXHIBIT 33.9 Sample Letter of Participation

Saint Vincent
Charity
Hospital
& Health Center

2351 East 22nd St.
Cleveland, Ohio 44115
(216) 861-6200

May 7, 1991

Mr. Cliff Smith, President
YMCA
2200 Prospect Avenue
Cleveland, Ohio 44115

Dear Mr. Smith:

I am pleased to learn that the YMCA is embarking on a transitional housing program at the West Side YMCA! The shortage of transitional housing for homeless people has long been a concern of ours, and we applaud your efforts in this direction.

This letter will serve to document the agreement we reached about our working together on this project. We will be pleased to serve up to 10 people suffering from chemical dependency and needing detoxification service each year, depending on their Medicaid coverage and availability of appropriate funding.

As you may be aware, Rosary Hall is the oldest chemical dependency treatment program in Ohio, having opened in 1956. Our long and distinguished practice of successful rehabilitation will serve your clients well.

We wish you well in your efforts to obtain HUD funding for this important project.

Yours sincerely,

Mary C. Reed

Mary C. Reed
Administrative Director
Psychiatry and Chemical Dependency Services

 A Sisters of Charity of Saint Augustine Hospital

four different offices, the grant seeker varied the dates on the letters, used different salutations and closings, used different type fonts, chose different styles for the inside address on each, and in her quest to achieve a high level of verisimilitude, even included a mistake in the zip code of the inside address on one of the letters. The point of going to such lengths is to make the preparation of the letter as easy as possible for the person who will be signing it. Ideally, as soon as that person receives your draft, his or her secretary merely prints out the draft on their letterhead, has it signed, and sends it back to you.

Once you receive all the letters (which you drafted) from your collaborating partners or supporting organizations, add them to the proposal packet and ship it off to the grantmaker.

If the grantmaker you are soliciting is a government agency, your proposal positively must arrive by the deadline specified. Bureaucrats are not known for being flexible.[7]

If you get caught in a last-minute crunch, as many grant seekers do, if it is allowed, take an additional step just in case the weather prevents your carrier from delivering on time. Different carriers have their air "hubs" in different parts of the country, so if you send duplicate packages by two different carriers, at least one is almost certain to arrive on time—this is very cheap insurance. Be sure to check with your grantmaker to see if this is acceptable.

Finally, be sure to mail copies of the completed proposal package promptly to your collaborating partners, to reinforce your partnership, and to your board president or chair.

33.6   Conclusion: The Benefits of Preparing a Proposal

The aim of this chapter is to demystify the process of planning and preparing a grant proposal, to enable the grant seeker and his or her organization to obtain the maximum benefits. Keeping this process in its proper perspective—as an element that is necessary but not sufficient to win a grant award—the grant seeker should be able to judge when it is worthwhile to commit to the hard work required to prepare a high-quality proposal.

As a grant seeker, you should be prepared to approach this complex task in an efficient and effective manner. If you follow the steps described in this chapter, you can accomplish much of the planning required to shape the project you are seeking to fund. In the process, you will be developing and refining many skills that can help you to become a more effective manager: allocating time and resources, collaborating with colleagues and with others outside your organization, conducting research, planning, and budgeting. More important, you will greatly increase your chances of winning an award—and advancing the work of your organization.

---

[7]Another myth that must be dispelled is that applications for government funds are fundamentally different from requests to private foundations. Many people believe that preparing an application to a government agency requires special expertise and arcane knowledge. It is true that there are often more technical requirements for government applications than for private foundation proposals. However, nothing that any government agency requires is beyond the grasp of a well-educated layperson. Remember, if it is public money that is being awarded, it is *your* money, in a sense. As a taxpayer, you have as much right to go after it as any other taxpayer. You can demand that the instructions be explained so that you understand them.

Suggested Readings

Belcher, Jane C., and Julia M. Jacobsen. *From Idea to Funded Project: Grant Proposals That Work.* Phoenix, Ariz.: Oryx Press, 1992.

Carlson, Mim. *Winning Grants Step by Step: Support Centers of America's Complete Workbook for Planning, Developing, and Writing Successful Proposals.* San Francisco: Jossey-Bass, 1995.

Geever, Jane C., and Patricia McNeill. *The Foundation Center's Guide to Proposal Writing.* New York: The Foundation Center, 1993.

Gooch, Judith Mirick. *Writing Winning Proposals.* Washington, D.C.: Council for Advancement and Support of Education, 1987.

Hall, Mary S. *Getting Funded: A Complete Guide to Proposal Writing,* 3d ed. Portland, Oreg.: Continuing Education Publications, 1988.

Kiritz, Norton J. *Program Planning & Proposal Writing,* expanded version. Los Angeles: The Grantsmanship Center, 1980.

Lefferts, Robert. *Getting a Grant in the 1990s: How to Write Successful Grant Proposals.* New York: Simon & Schuster, 1990.

Meador, Roy. *Guidelines for Preparing Proposals,* 2d ed. Chelsea, Mich.: Lewis Publishers, 1991.

Miner, Lynn E., and Jerry Griffith. *Proposal Planning and Writing.* Phoenix, Ariz.: Oryx Press, 1993.

34 Grants from the Government

CHERYL NEW

Polaris, Inc.

34.1 Federal Programs

Virtually every department, agency, and division of the United States Government has grant funds to offer. The government consists of three branches: legislative, executive and judicial. Almost all grant-funding departments, agencies, and divisions come under the executive branch. These departments include that of Education; of Health and Human Services; of Agriculture; of Labor; and others. In addition to these very familiar entities, there are 57 independent establishments and government corporations, including the African Development Foundation, the National Foundation on the Arts and Humanities, the Small Business Administration, the Environmental Protection Agency, and the National Science Foundation. Each of these independent establishments has grant funding to offer.

Some of the departments encompass a few giant agencies or institutes that are so large that they act somewhat independently of the department under which they are organized. The Public Health Services, located within the U.S. Department of Health and Human Services, is one such entity. Within the Public Health Services is the National Institutes of Health, one of eight health agencies. The National Institutes of Health alone has 25 institutes and centers covering over 300 acres of land and a budget of more than $15 billion, much of which is devoted to grant-funding efforts.

Within each department there are institutes, divisions, offices, and/or agencies, each of which has grant funding to let. An example of an office is the Office of Elementary and Secondary Education, which is housed under the U.S. Department of Education. Another example is the Office of Justice Programs within the Department of Justice. This office funds many grant programs designed to test programs to alleviate youth violence, drug abuse, and crime. A third example is National Endowment for the Arts, administered within the independent establishment, the National Foundation of the Arts and Humanities. One office within the National Endowment for the Arts is Office of Folk Traditional/Literature/Theater/Musical Theater/Planning & Stabilization. Is this confusing? Of course it is. But our federal government is a very large organization made up of many smaller and more manageable subdivisions.

To repeat one important point: *Virtually every department, agency, and division of the United States Government has grant funds to offer.* As an indication of how many possible granting opportunities there are, the following four exhibits provide organizational charts. Exhibit 34.1 presents the federal government. Three of the more commonly recognized departments or independent establishments include the U.S. Department of Health and Human Services (Exhibit 34.2); the U.S. Department of Education (Exhibit 34.3); and the National Science Foundation (Exhibit 34.4). For a very good guide to all the departments and divisions of the federal government, see *The United States Government Manual,* published annually by the Office of the Federal Register, National Archives and Records Administration and for sale by the U.S. Government Printing Office.[1]

34.2 Relationship of Grant Funding and Problems to Solve

Grant funding results when problems are recognized as significant by enough people to encourage legislation of funds for projects that might provide solutions. To predict what grant funding will be available, read the newspaper or newsmagazines, watch the news on television, listen to the radio, or subscribe to a news "listserve" or clipping service through an Internet provider. It is almost as simple as that. If school violence is in the news, there will be grant funds targeted to finding solutions to that problem. If there is a new disease affecting enough people, there will be grant funds targeted to finding a cure. If there is a recognized need for support for artists who create stone sculptures, then there will be grant funding for that—the problem is that without support, cultural achievement in stone sculpture may not be encouraged and preserved. If there are not enough doctors to serve a growing elderly population, there will be grant funding to train medical students with gerontological specialties and then locate the graduating doctors in areas where there are high numbers of elderly people.

The connection between the grant seeker and the grant funder is a mutual desire to solve the same problem. The grant seeker proposes a project that, in the opinion of the

---

[1]U.S. Government Printing Office, Superintendent of Documents, Mail Stop SSPO, Washington, DC 20402-9328, ISBN 0-16-050117-2, www.gpo.gov

EXHIBIT 34.1 Organizational Chart for the Federal Government

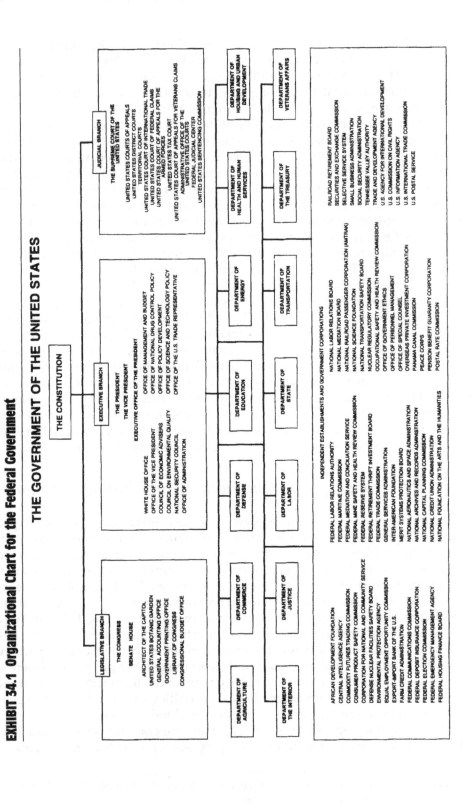

THE GOVERNMENT OF THE UNITED STATES

EXHIBIT 34.2 Organizational Chart for the Department of Health and Human Services

DEPARTMENT OF HEALTH AND HUMAN SERVICES

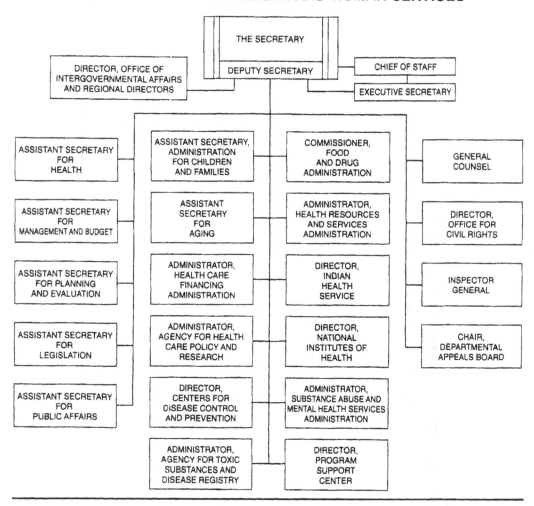

grant funder, has a very good chance of providing at least a partial solution. The method of communicating the pertinent information about the project is the grant proposal. The grant seeker writes a grant proposal to the grant funder describing his or her project. Usually the proposal is in response to a request for proposal (RFP), which is discussed later in this chapter.

34.3 Types of Federal Grant Funds

There are a number of types of federal grant programs. While all are directly related to solving a problem, the approach is very different from type to type.

EXHIBIT 34.3 Organizational Chart for the United States Department of Education

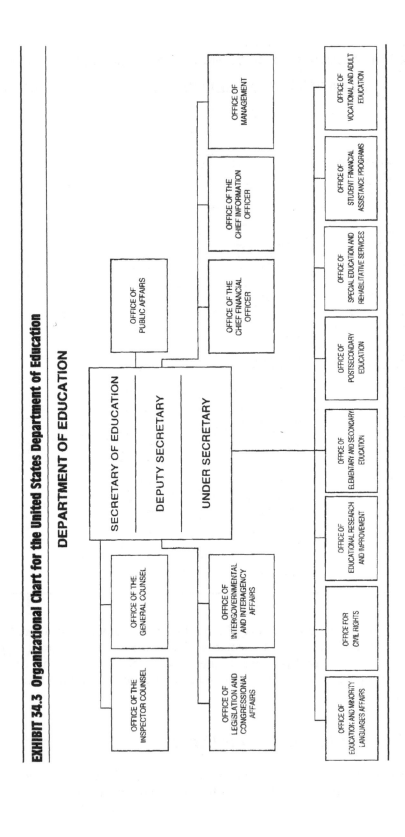

DEPARTMENT OF EDUCATION

NATIONAL SCIENCE FOUNDATION

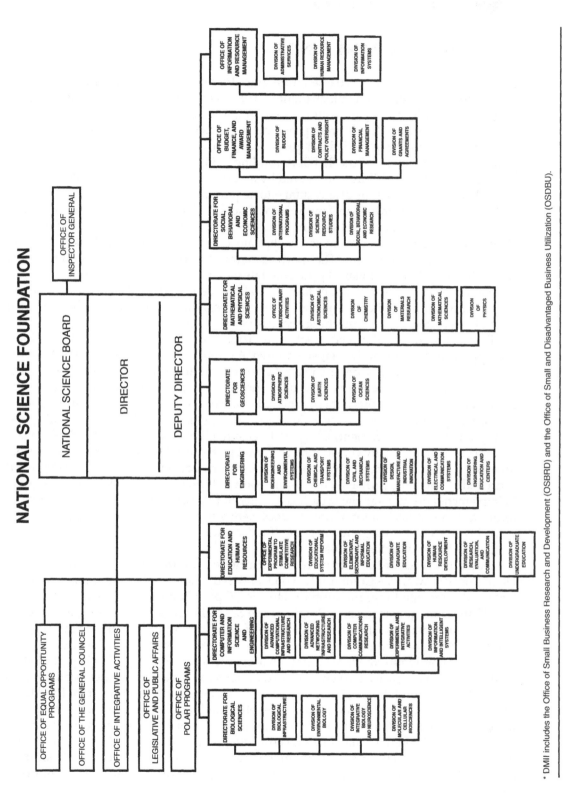

* DMII includes the Office of Small Business Research and Development (OSBRD) and the Office of Small and Disadvantaged Business Utilization (OSDBU).

(A) FORMULA GRANT FUNDS

A formula grant is one that is passed from grant funder to grantee by formula. Formula grants are sometimes called "block grants." This means that if the grantee fits a certain category or profile, money is awarded according to an established formula. The federal government frequently funds grant programs to states through a formula. One example of this type of funding is the federal government's involvement in public education for disadvantaged children—Title I, ESEA funding. This funding is dependent on how many disadvantaged children are served by a particular state public education department. The requisite level of disadvantage to acquire funding is determined by the federal government according to family income levels. Those children of families with incomes below a certain level qualify. The state gets a specific dollar figure for every child its public education system serves that meets the income standard set by the funder—the federal government. The more economically disadvantaged children a state serves, the more federal dollars it gets. The state then passes on the federal dollars by formula to the local school districts or local education agencies (LEAs). The more economically disadvantaged children a school district serves, the more federal dollars (passed through the state government) the school district receives.

Formula funds are allocated to solve problems—in this case to help equalize education opportunities for disadvantaged children. A grant "proposal" is written by both the state receiving the funds from the federal government and the school district receiving funds from the state government. The difference in this type of proposal and others to be discussed is significant. Since these funds are not competitive, the proposal consists of answers to questions posed by the federal government (and if the funding is a state pass-through, the state government) designed to ensure eligibility for funding. Experienced grant seekers do not really consider these "grant proposals," because there is no competition and little, if any, creativity involved. The governments have already decided what is needed to solve the problem and simply want to know that the grant seeker is going to implement and manage the project according to their guidance. Yes, there are a lot of forms, and yes, it takes a lot of time to document a formula grant. Not to minimize the work involved, formula grants are not "fund-raising" grants in the true sense of the word. One either qualifies or does not qualify.

Other examples of formula grant funds include: Community Services Block Grant Discretionary Awards—Community Food and Nutrition; Water Pollution Control—State and Interstate Program Support; Housing Opportunities for Persons with AIDS; HOME Investment Partnerships Program; and Special Programs for the Aging, Title III.

Every organization should keep abreast of all formula funds available through the federal or state government to ensure that it is aware of every dollar for which it qualifies. There is no requirement for a state to accept federal funding—this is part of state autonomy. In many cases, the state has no requirement that a local agency participate in a given formula fund. In fact, if a state does not participate in a formula grant fund from the federal government, then the state is not obligated to follow the related federal regulations. If a state opts not to receive federal funds for public education, for example, then it is not obligated to follow federal education regulations and reforms. The "hold" the federal government or state government has on the recipient is through the funding, which always comes with stipulations and regulations. There are no unmixed blessings.

(B) DIRECT PAYMENTS FOR SPECIFIED USE

Some federal "grant" programs are really contracts for services and not "granted" funds in the purest sense of the definition. Direct payments are provided directly to individuals, private companies, and other private organizations to support a specific service or activity that the federal government wants to provide to benefit the citizenry. Proposals are written for these "grants," and the funding source has been established to solve a particular problem, as with other types of grants to be discussed. However, again, there is little room for creativity. In this type of grant program, the federal government decides what is to be done and how. The government then seeks individuals or organizations that will do exactly what it wants them to do on a contractual basis. Once an organization has won the contract, then it is usually renewed for a number of years unless the organization fails to fulfill the contractual agreement.

This type of program is competitive but within very strict parameters. A proposing individual or organization is not offering one solution to a problem in competition with another. The proposing organizations or individuals are only competing on their respective capabilities to perform the tasks identified by the federal government. Some examples of this type of program are Museum Leadership Initiatives, the Wildlife Habitat Incentive Program, Tax Counseling for the Elderly, and the Federal Work-Study Program.

Some of these direct payment programs are based on former successful competitive grant projects that have become institutionalized.

(C) FEDERAL CONTRACTS

All federal departments, agencies, divisions, and offices contract for services they themselves require. They all have needs for office cleaning, catering, training, technical support, and other services used by any business. Because these departments, agencies, divisions, and offices are public entities, every contractual arrangement is considered on a competitive basis. Unlike most private businesses, which can contract with whichever service providers they choose, the federal government has an elaborate method of offering contractual opportunities and then evaluating the proposals they receive.

Some confuse this contracting process with a grant process and even call these contract opportunities "grants," but that is a misnomer. In fact, the federal entity is simply putting a service or product needed up for bid. The government entity letting the bid determines the parameters of the job to be done, and organizations or individuals then submit a proposal to compete for the job. A contract is awarded to the organization or individual that best meets the parameters for the job in the opinion of the agency that let the bid. The bid process was instituted to afford more companies the opportunity to do business with the federal government in a relatively objective format. Most entities that contract with the federal government in this way are for-profit businesses. To find out about contractual opportunities, see *Commerce Business Daily*.[2]

---

[2]*Commerce Business Daily*, 11300 Rockville Pike, Suite 1100, Rockville, MD 20852-3030, 800-824-1195, or 301-287-2700; Fax 301/816-8945, www.cbd.com.

(D) SCHOLARSHIPS, FELLOWSHIPS, AND GRANTS-IN-AID

The federal government offers many programs designed for the individual. These are lumped by federal agencies under the umbrella title of project grant; however, they are for one specific purpose—for furthering one's education in one way or another. An organization would not apply for any of these programs as a part of its fund-raising effort. But because the average person first thinks of these—scholarships, fellowships, or grants-in-aid—when he or she hears the word "grant," this form of grant program is included in our list of types of government grants.

As discussed in Chapter 33, some organizations seek grant funding to support their own scholarship or fellowship programs. The federal government does not seek donations for such funding—rather it offers its own programs, as do some corporations and foundations. Since these programs are for an individual and for a specific educational purpose, they are not the focus of our discussion.

(E) COMPETITIVE PROJECT GRANTS

When an experienced grant seeker speaks of federal grants, most likely he or she is talking about competitive project grants. These grants are for research, experimental programs, demonstration programs, planning projects, surveys and studies, training, technical assistance, construction, and unsolicited contractual arrangements. The various departments, divisions, and offices of the government seek good projects that solve problems they have identified. The projects may be in the form of research, experiment or demonstration, planning, and study. The nature of the problem usually guides the type of project that "fits."

Research projects run the gamut from highly complex test-tube type activities to paper-and-pencil studies. Organizations of higher education, profit and nonprofit laboratories, medical clinics, hospitals, and other such entities have been involved in grant-funded research for years. In the last few years federal funders have expanded into prekindergarten to grade 12 public and private education and smaller, more focused projects and grantees.

Experimental and demonstration projects are projects that are designed to test a solution to a problem for modeling or replicating. If the experiment or demonstration project succeeds or can be modified to succeed, then other similar organizations can apply the lessons learned.

Surveys and studies are other forms of research. Many times a project lends itself to contributing significantly to the body of knowledge about a given subject. The federal government funds projects to do just that—to provide data to expand information to contribute ultimately to a solution to a problem.

Training and technical assistance grants work two ways. Some grant programs fund training or projects oriented toward technical assistance. There are also grant programs that fund the federal government's training and technical assistance involvement with an organization. In other words, these latter projects fund government representatives to come to an organization and provide training or technical assistance to its personnel.

Construction projects are funded, but not often. One current program, CFDA #11.550, Public Telecommunications Facilities—Planning and Construction, assists "in the planning, acquisition, installation and modernization of public telecommunications facilities, through planning grants and matching construction grants." Contrary to popular opinion, there is not a lot of "brick-and-mortar" funding available, and it is not available for ordinary uses.

Unsolicited contractual projects are projects that an entity "suggests" to a federal funding department, division, or office that manages a related grant program without being "invited" to propose it. Unsolicited proposals are discussed in more depth later in this chapter.

(F) DEVELOPING A FUNDABLE GRANT PROJECT

What kinds of projects are fundable through the federal government? First of all, it is important to talk a little bit about grant projects in general. Many people have the mistaken idea that all you have to do is have a good idea, describe it to the potential funder in a letter, and then you are awarded a grant. Another fallacy is that if you have a need that is dire enough, all you have to do is write to a government agency and acquire grant funds.

First of all, to acquire funding one has to write a detailed proposal that responds to a program solicitation by the department, division, or office offering the grant. Second, by the time one usually finds out about a grant program solicited by the federal government, it is so close to the deadline that one has very much difficulty responding if one has not already thought through the problem and developed a project solution.

A common mistake novice (and some experienced) grant seekers make is to try to develop their project while writing the proposal at the same time. The single most common reason a project fails to acquire grant funding is that it is not really a project—it is just a vague or half-developed, though perhaps good, idea.

Federal as well as most other grantmakers are not really "into" charity, although their activities are listed as "charitable" or "philanthropic." As we have already said, grantmakers are interested in solving problems. They are focused on one or more issues, such as stopping drug abuse or illiteracy, and are looking for a targeted *investment*. They want to fund a project that will potentially offer a solution to the problem they are interested in. They are interested in the grant seeker testing a solution that might be applied in other communities to solve the problem in which they are interested. Grantmakers want to envision a complete project when they read a proposal. They want a proposal that specifically addresses the issues they have identified. They want grant seekers to persuade them that the project is the best investment they can make. Do not approach a grantmaker by tugging heartstrings; rather, do so by making a professional, businesslike case for a project. In this way grantmaking is very different from some kinds of fund raising.

Funders will not take a chance on investing in a project that is not fully developed, and for good reason. They have no assurance that the people who propose the project can actually make it succeed. Most people who submit proposals without first having worked out their projects have not truly thought about all the details and do not actually know if their project has a good chance of success. Such still-in-the-egg projects have very little chance of competing with those projects that are well hatched and presented in clear, concise detail. So what can you, as a conscientious grant seeker, do to solve this problem?

Following is a very abbreviated discussion of a comprehensive process for succeeding in the federal competitive grants arena. There is not space here in this chapter to go into the process in any depth; however, *Grantseeker's Toolkit: Project Management and Eval-*

uation and *Grant Winner's Toolkit: Project Management and Evaluation* discuss the process in a step-by-step, in-depth manner.[3]

(i)   Constantly and Consistently Study and Plan

Your organization was established to fill some need. You serve or service a particular population. Whether you realize it or not, your service or product likely exists to solve a particular problem for your target population. If you are an educator, you serve the student and the community. You exist because lack of education presents problems. If you are a hospital, you serve the patient. You exist because people are unhealthy. If you are a United Way, you serve your member agencies. You exist because smaller not-for-profits need assistance, organization, training, support, and funding—because they have problems if they do not have these things. If you produce widgets, you serve widget seekers. You exist because widget seekers need widgets.

Leaders of every viable organization want their organizations to grow and thrive. For the organization to succeed, constant and consistent study and planning should be done. Study and planning should be focused on how your service or product is meeting the needs of—solving problems for—the target service population. Determine if your services or products are meeting the needs—solving the problems—effectively. Determine if your services or products can be improved to meet the needs better. You might even identify additional problems for the target population that you could solve if you added to or modified your current operation. Whatever the outcome, a process of study and planning should be an integral part of your organization.

(ii)   Specify Problems You Want to Solve (or Solve Better) for the Target Population

If your planning is effective, you will naturally identify your target population's problems or needs. You will then decide which ones are met effectively by your current service or product. You will also determine which needs are not met effectively, which ones have not been considered but should be, and which ones are outside your area of interest or expertise. It is critical to look at your organization's purpose from the point of view of problem solving for your target population. If your only reason for being is to perpetuate your own organization, you are destined to fail. When an organization fails to meet the needs of those it serves, it withers and dies.

(iii)   Choose and Further Specify the Problems You Wish to Solve (or Solve Better)

The next step is to look at the problems you wish to solve (or solve better). You should be sure you have stated the actual problem rather than a symptom of it. For example, suppose you serve senior citizens. One of the problems you identified is that "the elderly people we serve are entering nursing homes at very young ages." That sounds like a problem, but it is really a symptom in disguise. The fact that the elderly people you serve are entering nursing homes at a young age is most probably reflective of their physical and/or mental conditions. What is the cause of the premature weakening of physical and mental conditions? When you come up with potential *causes*, then you have stated the real problem rather than the symptom. You can solve real problems, you can only bandage symptoms.

---

[3]See *Grantseeker's Toolkit: A Comprehensive Guide to Finding Funding* (New York: John Wiley & Sons, 1998), and *Grant Winner's Toolkit: Project Management and Evaluation* (New York: John Wiley & Sons, 2000).

(iv)   Design a Project Likely to Solve the Identified Problem

Now comes the fun part. Design a project that has a good chance of solving the real problem you have identified. Always stay focused on the problems of your service population. In focusing on and solving their problems through appropriate project development and planning, you will solve your own.

When designing a project, rough out the what, who, for how many, for how much, when, where, and with what result. The *what* is what you intend to do. *Who* is who will do it. *For how many*—how many people do you intend to serve? *How much* will it cost? *When* should you begin and end various activities? *Where* will the project be implemented? Finally, and most important, *what result*—outcome—do you expect and desire? If you answer these questions in detail, project measurability will be virtually built-in.

You might need to do some research to adapt some projects that have already been successful. You might have to modify one of your current projects. You might even have to create something totally new. All of these activities are part of good project design.

(v)   Build a File of Well-designed, Well-developed Projects

To be prepared to respond to federal or any other grant solicitation, have well-designed projects available and ready to go. When an opportunity arises, you are ready to write that proposal. Only if you have a well-designed and well-developed project do you have anything to write about. If you do not, what in the world are you going to put in your proposal?

(vi)   Actively Look for a Matching Funder

If you are constantly planning and developing, you will be able to respond to grant solicitations when they arise. We recommend, however, that you take these good projects and actively seek a matching funder. If you have good projects designed, you are ready to become proactive in your grant seeking.

34.4   How to Find a Federal Grant Funder

The grant funder has received funding from Congress to test projects designed to solve a particular problem. How does the grant funder know about these potential solution-providing projects? It advertises for them. How? For programs within the United States, primarily through a volume called the *Catalog for Federal Domestic Assistance* (CFDA), fondly known as *The Catalog* to those in the grant-seeking business.

The Catalog has in it a description of every—yes *every*—federal domestic grant program. It is published once a year with an update or supplement in the summer. Grant programs are organized by Department or Independent Agency. It can be purchased as a hard-copy publication, a CD-ROM, and on 3.5-inch diskettes, and is available for free on the Internet, at www.cfda.gov, presented in an easy-to-use, searchable format.

The hard-copy publication is three-hole punched and costs $87 a year, which includes the full catalog published each June and a supplement published each December. The CD-ROM comes with an additional database, the U.S. Census Bureau's Federal Assistance Award Data System (FAADS), which tells who received funding and how much. The CD-ROM is issued semiannually. A single copy costs $50, or you can purchase an annual subscription for $85. You will get the June publication and the December supplement. *The Catalog* is also available on 3.5-inch diskettes semiannually. The cost is the same as for the CD-ROM, $85. Search software is not included.

All versions can be purchased from the United States General Service Administration by mail at Superintendent of Documents, PO Box 371954, Pittsburgh, PA, 15250-7954; by phone at 202-512-1800; or by fax at 202-512-2250. The General Service Administration takes Visa, MasterCard, and Discover/Novus credit cards.

Each department or independent agency has a set of identification numbers, called CFDA numbers. CFDA numbers look like this: 84.132 or 93.111 or 15.046. The first two numbers refer to the agency by which the funding is administered. The numbers after the period refer to the specific grant program. The catalog is cross-referenced by the functional area, by agency, by subagency, alphabetically by program title, by applicant eligibility, by beneficiary, by program deadline, and by type of assistance.

Within each department, grant programs are organized roughly according to the problem each is designed to solve. Of course, many problems affect several departments, and each department has its own way of approaching the problem. Thus, looking under just one department, division, agency, or office may cause you to miss many good opportunities.

34.5   Searching the Catalog for Federal Domestic Assistance for Grant Programs

The CFDA is cross-referenced in many ways. Explanation of a few organizational patterns follows.

(A)   CATALOG FOR FEDERAL DOMESTIC ASSISTANCE ORGANIZED BY FUNCTIONAL AREA

One look at all the categories of operation listed in *The Catalog* will indicate just how many possibilities for grant funding exist. Exhibit 34.5 lists the functional areas within which the CFDA is organized and by which you can search for a matching funding program. *The number in parentheses is the number of subcategories under the primary listing.* To search for a matching funding program for your project by functional area, you would find the area most closely related to your project and look there.

(B)   CATALOG FOR FEDERAL DOMESTIC ASSISTANCE ORGANIZED BY AGENCY

Remember that every single agency has grant funding. Exhibit 34.6 shows the CDFA organized by agency. The numbers in parentheses following the agency name indicate how many program areas from that agency are listed in *The Catalog*. Each program area may have a number of grant-funding programs.

(C)   CATALOG FOR FEDERAL DOMESTIC ASSISTANCE ORGANIZED BY TYPE OF ASSISTANCE

Investigating programs by type of assistance provided can be very helpful to grant seekers. The CFDA organizes its programs by these types of assistance:

EXHIBIT 34.5 CFDA Organized by Functional Area

1. Agriculture
   - Resource Conservation and Development (26)
   - Production and Operations (6)
   - Marketing (18)
   - Research and Development (27)
   - Technical Assistance, Information, and Services (36)
   - Forestry (15)
   - Stabilization and Conservation Service (12)
2. Business and Commerce
   - Maritime (15)
   - Statistics (20)
   - Special Services (26)
   - Minority Business Enterprises (21)
   - Small Business (36)
   - Economic Development (53)
   - Economic Injury and Natural Disaster (28)
   - Commercial Fisheries (24)
   - International (16)
3. Community Development
   - Planning and Research (41)
   - Construction, Renewal, and Operations (39)
   - Historical Preservation (24)
   - Rural Community Development (36)
   - Recreation (32)
   - Site Acquisition (8)
   - Indian Action Services (34)
   - Federal Surplus Property (15)
   - Technical Assistance and Services (52)
   - Land Acquisition (14)
   - Fire Protection (10)
4. Consumer Protection
   - Regulation, Inspection, Enforcement (15)
   - Complaint Investigation (14)
   - Information and Education Services (7)
5. Cultural Affairs
   - Promotion of the Arts (16)
   - Promotion of the Humanities (11)
6. Disaster Prevention and Relief
   - Emergency Preparedness, Civil Relief (28)
   - Flood Prevention and Control (22)
   - Emergency Health Services (9)
   - Disaster Relief (34)
7. Education
   - Dental Education and Training (10)
   - Educational Equipment and Resources (31)
   - Educational Facilities (18)
   - Elementary and Secondary (64)
   - General Research and Evaluation (49)
   - Handicapped Education (35)
   - Health Education and Training (46)
   - Higher Education - General (131)
   - Indian Education (37)
   - Libraries and Technical Information Services (41)
   - Medical Education and Training (36)
   - Nuclear Education and Training (4)
   - Nursing Education (17)
   - Resource Development and Support - Elementary, Secondary Education (43)
   - Resource Development and Support - General and Special Interest Organizations (48)
   - Resource Development and Support - Higher Education (49)
   - Resource Development and Support - Land and Equipment (5)
   - Resource Development and Support - School Aid (9)
   - Resource Development and Support - Sciences (26)
   - Resource Development and Support - Student Financial Aid (24)
   - Resource Development and Support - Vocational Education and Handicapped Education (35)
   - Teacher Training (45)
   - Vocational Development (32)
8. Employment, Labor, and Training
   - Planning, Research, and Demonstration (13)
   - Program Development (18)
   - Job Training, Employment (61)
   - Federal Employment (11)
   - Bonding and Certification (4)
   - Equal Employment Opportunity (17)
   - Assistance and Services for the Unemployed (23)
   - Assistance to State and Local Governments (14)
   - Statistical (4)
   - Labor Management Services (12)
   - Facilities, Planning, Construction, and Equipment (8)
9. Energy
   - Conservation (18)
   - Research and Development (17)
   - Education and Training (12)
   - Facilities and Equipment (6)
   - Specialized Technical Services (10)
   - General Information Services (4)
10. Environmental Quality
    - Water Pollution Control (40)
    - Air Pollution Control (20)
    - Solid Waste Management (24)
    - Pesticides Control (15)
    - Radiation Control (9)
    - Research, Education, Training (43)
11. Food and Nutrition
    - Food and Nutrition for Children (15)
    - Food Inspection (12)
    - Food and Nutrition for Individual and Families (4)
    - Research (7)

(continued)

EXHIBIT 34.5 *(Continued)*

12. Health
    - Alcoholism, Drug Abuse, and Mental Health - General (20)
    - Alcoholism, Drug Abuse, and Mental Health - Law Enforcement (6)
    - Alcoholism, Drug Abuse, and Mental Health - Planning (9)
    - Alcoholism, Drug Abuse, and Mental Health - Research (13)
    - Communicable Diseases (30)
    - Education and Training (77)
    - Facility Loans and Insurance (6)
    - Facility Planning and Construction (21)
    - General Health and Medical (37)
    - Health Research - General (39)
    - Health Services Planning and Technical Assistance (64)
    - Indian Health (23)
    - Libraries, Information and Education Services (29)
    - Maternity, Infants, Children (28)
    - Mental Health (15)
    - Occupational Safety and Health (20)
    - Physical Fitness (3)
    - Prevention and Control (70)
    - Program Development (65)
    - Specialized Health Research and Training (82)
    - Veterans Health (17)

13. Housing
    - Property and Mortgage Insurance (8)
    - Homebuying, Homeownership (45)
    - Home Improvement (37)
    - Cooperatives, Rental (23)
    - Rural Housing (17)
    - Multifamily (26)
    - Experimental and Development Projects (15)
    - Indian Housing (18)
    - Construction Rehabilitation (41)
    - Planning (17)
    - Land Acquisition (11)
    - Site Preparation for Housing (10)

14. Income Security and Social Services
    - Disabled and Handicapped Services (31)
    - Disabled Veterans (12)
    - Emergency and Crisis Assistance (19)
    - Families and Child Welfare Services (45)
    - Indian Services (14)
    - Information and Referral Services (46)
    - Legal and Advocacy Services (29)
    - Nutrition (25)
    - Old Age Assistance (21)
    - Prevention (21)
    - Public Assistance (14)
    - Refugees, Alien Services (9)
    - Research, Demonstration (13)
    - Social Security and Insurance (17)
    - Specialized Family and Child Welfare Services (31)
    - Specialized Services (28)
    - Training Assistance (13)
    - Veterans Services (23)
    - Youth Services (15)

15. Information and Statistics
    - Census Data (7)
    - General (69)
    - Libraries, Clearinghouses, Archives (14)
    - Library of Congress (6)

16. Law, Justice, and Legal Services
    - Law Enforcement - Planning and Operations (45)
    - Law Enforcement - Research, Education, Training (46)
    - Law Enforcement - Narcotics and Dangerous Drugs (20)
    - Law Enforcement - Crime Analysis and Data (24)
    - Legal Services - General Services (26)
    - Legal Services - Employment Rights (8)
    - Legal Services - Labor Management (7)
    - Legal Services - Housing Rights (7)
    - Legal Services - Claims Against Foreign Government (2)

17. Natural Resources
    - Mineral Research (11)
    - Water Conservation and Research (25)
    - Community Water Supply Services (18)
    - Community Sewage Treatment Assistance (10)
    - Wildlife Research and Preservation (33)
    - Land Conservation (16)
    - Recreation (19)

18. Regional Development
    - Economic Development (6)
    - Planning and Technical Assistance (3)
    - Land Acquisition and Rehabilitation and Facilities Construction (3)
    - Transportation (3)
    - Energy (1)
    Housing
    - Education (3)
    - Health and Nutrition (2)
    - Resources and Development (3)

19. Science and Technology
    - Research - General (17)
    - Research - Specialized (56)
    - Information and Technical (20)

20. Transportation (5)
    - Urban Mass Transit (15)
    - Highways, Public Roads, and Bridges (19)
    - Rail Transportation (9)
    - Air Transportation (6)
    - Water Navigation (10)

EXHIBIT 34.6 CFDA Organized by Agency

Department of Agriculture (137)

Department of Commerce (90)

Department of Defense (40)

Department of Housing and Urban Development (104)

Department of the Interior (98)

Department of Justice (89)

Department of Labor (44)

Department of State (5)

Department of Transportation (52)

Department of Treasury (8)

Appalachian Regional Commission (6)

Office of Personnel Management (7)

Civil Rights Commission (1)

Equal Employment Opportunity Commission (7)

Federal Communications Commission (1)

Federal Maritime Commission (1)

Federal Mediation Conciliation Service (2)

Federal Trade Commission (1)

General Services Administration (6)

Government Printing Office (2)

Library of Congress (7)

National Aeronautics and Space Administration (2)

National Credit Union Administration (2)

National Foundation of Arts and the Humanities (21)

National Labor Relations Board (1)

National Science Foundation (8)

Social Security Administration (7)

President's Committee on Employment of People with Disabilities (1)

Railroad Retirement Board (1)

Securities Exchange Commission (1)

Small Business Administration (15)

International Trade Commission (1)

Tennessee Valley Authority (1)

Department of Veterans' Affairs (41)

Environmental Protection Agency (49)

National Gallery of Art (1)

Overseas Private Investment Corporation (2)

Nuclear Regulatory Commission (2)

Commodity Futures Trading Commission (1)

Department of Energy (27)

US Information Agency (19)

Federal Emergency Management Agency (30)

Department of Education (151)

Scholarship and Fellowship Foundations (8)

Pension Benefit Guaranty Corporation (1)

Architecture and Transportation Barriers Compliance Board (1)

National Archives and Records Administration (2)

United States Institute of Peace (2)

National Council on Disability (1)

Department of Health and Human Services (307)

Corporation for National & Community Service (10)

Formula grants
Project grants
Direct payments for specified use
Direct payments with unrestricted use
Direct loans
Guaranteed/insured loans
Insurance
Sale, exchange, or donation of property and goods

Use of property, facilities, and equipment
Provision of specialized services
Advisory services and counseling
Dissemination of technical information
Training
Investigation of complaints
Federal employment

(D) OTHER CATALOG FOR FEDERAL DOMESTIC ASSISTANCE ORGANIZATIONAL PATTERNS

The CFDA is cross-referenced in a number of other ways, including:

By sub-agency
Alphabetically by program title
By applicant eligibility
By beneficiary
By program deadline

By type of assistance
By programs requiring executive order 12372
Review
Numerically (more than 1,500 listings)

34.6 *What to Look for to Ensure a Match*

Armed with your well-developed project, search the CFDA in the manner that makes the most sense to you. When you find a program that sounds like it might fit your project, closely consider the following parts of the project entry. Each grant program description in the CFDA follows a specific format.

- *Applicant eligibility.* Is your organization eligible for the program, or if not, is one of your partners eligible? Are the beneficiaries those who you intend to serve?
- *Program objectives.* How closely do they match your project objectives?
- Under *assistance considerations.* Are there any requirements with which you cannot live?
- Under *financial information.* Does the average amount awarded fit with the figures you have drafted in your project design? Keep in mind that no one goes to a $100,000 funder for $500, nor does anyone go to a $500 funder for $100,000.
- Under *assistance considerations.* Can you live with the time frames allowed for program funding? Keep in mind that no grant is forever. You will have to plan what to do when funding runs out when you plan your project. This is called "continuation," and you will have to explain to the potential funder just how you intend to continue the program. After all, no funder wants to fund a project that disappears as soon as the funding dries up. The subject of continuation is covered extensively in both the *Grantseeker's Toolkit* and *Grant Winner's Toolkit*.

If, after you have read the program description and have carefully considered the points just cited, you think there is a match between your project and the grant program, then the next step is to acquire the request for proposal (RFP).

34.7 *Acquiring the Request for Proposal*

As mentioned, federal granting agencies publish strict guidelines for submitting a proposal that include information about the content of the proposal, special areas of interest, and publishing requirements. Guidelines are not optional. Grant seekers must follow the directions to the absolute letter if an award is expected. This is an ironclad rule. Over 60 percent of the total proposals received by a funder are rejected because the proposal was "unresponsive." *Unresponsive* means that the proposal did not match the funder's priorities in some way or did not follow directions. This is a sad statement about the quality of proposals submitted.

First go to the Department Web site under which your targeted program is administered. You will find an area devoted to funding and grants on every such site. See if there is a direct link to your program from the department Web site. Due to the Paperwork Reduction Act of 1995, many programs are not offering printed hard copies of their RFP any longer. Instead the RFP is posted on the Web site in either word processing or Adobe PDF format, so that you can download and print it yourself.

If the method of acquiring the RFP is not obvious from the Web site, call the program coordinator listed and ask for one. If there is no RFP, see if you can download or otherwise acquire last year's RFP. Most programs are similar from year to year, though they may have a slightly different priority; they were designed for a specific purpose that does not change. If you have last year's RFP, you can begin your development and writing with a long-range plan to revise after the new RFP has been published.

If there is no current RFP, how will you know when the RFP will be available? The Web site may tell you. If not, call the program coordinator and ask. Usually you will get a good general answer, such as "We intend to publish that sometime this fall" or "Normally, we publish early in November." Then what? You can look for the actual publishing notice in the *Federal Register*.

The *Federal Register* is a document published daily by the National Archives and Records Administration (NARA). It contains agency regulations, rules and notices, executive orders, presidential proclamations, and other information about the daily activity of the federal government. Among the things published in the *Federal Register* are notices of publishing of grants information and Requests for Proposals. Sometimes the entire RFP will appear in the *Federal Register*. The specific pertinent information, special considerations, and deadlines are always published. Information about grants is organized by CFDA number.

Each issue of the *Federal Register* is organized into four categories:

1. Executive orders and proclamations
2. Rules and regulations
3. Proposed rules
4. Notices, including grant applications

You can subscribe to the *Federal Register* in hard copy or microfiche by calling 202-512-1800. Fax inquiries to 202-512-2250. Mail orders go to the Superintendent of Documents, PO Box 371954, Pittsburgh, PA 15250-7954. Free access to the information in the *Federal Register* can be accessed at www.nara.gov/fedreg. You can e-mail questions on the *Federal Register* at info@fedreg.nara.gov.

34.8 What to Do after You Find a Matching Program and the RFP

Again, space does not allow for elaboration, but once you receive the RFP for the matching project, which you have already developed, then you need to analyze the request thoroughly. We strongly advise you to make three outlines or lists.

1. *Content required in the RFP.* This will include such things as: a description of the problem you are addressing; measurable goals and objectives; brief biographical data on the key personnel; a time line for project setup and implementation; continuation plan; and evaluation plan.
2. *Publishing requirements.* This will include such things as: a page limit on the narrative portion of the proposal; type size and page size and format; numbers of copies to make; address to deliver the proposal; and what forms to include where.
3. *Key points or items of critical importance* from the funder's viewpoint. Sometimes figuring this out takes some reading between the lines. It is very important to your success that your project has the impact desired by the funder.

Once you have this information, determine how much space you have to write about each item required. This is a good practice for any writing assignment, but especially good for diminishing fear about writing a proposal. Once you divide up the task, you may find that you only have two pages to write the description of your problem. That is not much. For a problem as significant as the one you are addressing, that should be easy to do. As you work your way through the planning for the proposal, you will find it easier and easier to see what to do *if* you have already developed a good project and are sure of a match. If you just have the RFP and have not considered a project until now, you have a very difficult task ahead of you.

Next comes writing the proposal. Here are a few tips to help you:

- Follow directions! Follow directions! Follow directions!
- No jargon. Remember, the reader may not be privy to your lingo
- If the average person on the street cannot read your proposal and immediately understand what you intend to do, it needs to be rewritten.
- Remember the reader—make it very easy for him or her.
- Regarding the reader, assume ignorance but not stupidity.
- Use the same language that the funder uses—if the funder discusses goals and activities rather than goals and objectives, use the former terms.
- Use the funder's topics as headings.
- Use headings, bullets, charts, and white space liberally.
- Remember that the funder's agenda is what is important, not yours.
- Never ever lie to the funder.
- Never ever cheat—whether with regard to the font size or margins or within your project budget.
- Never ever leave anything out.
- If you have a question, call and ask the program coordinator—do not guess.
- Do not hide anything—it will come back to haunt you.
- Be sure your organization can handle the grant if it wins; if not, do not write the proposal.
- If there is no way to continue the project after the grant funding runs out, do not submit the proposal.
- If you are awarded a grant, it is a *legal contract* between you and the funder to do what you said you would do in the grant proposal.

34.9   State and Local Governments

State and local government grants work much like federal grants. Follow the same guidelines listed for acquiring federal grants. To refresh your memory, they are as follows:

1. Constantly and consistently study and plan
2. Specify problems you want to solve (or solve better) for the target population
3. Choose and further specify the problems you wish to solve (or solve better)
4. Design a project likely to solve the identified problem
5. Build a file of well-designed, well-developed projects
6. Actively look for a matching funder
7. Research the funder and choose the best match
8. Obtain the proposal guidelines
9. Write the proposal according to the directions
10. Wait anxiously, but confidently, for a reply

34.10   Kinds of State and Local Government Grants

(A)   FORMULA

States have formula grants just like the federal government. Many state grants are pass-throughs from the federal government. In other words, the original grant is from the federal government, which stipulates for whom the grant is intended and what the formula will be. Then the states distribute the grant money according to that formula.

For example, the federal government might fund a program to help homeless people. The state government applies to the federal government to acquire funding through the federal homeless program. The federal government stipulates that the state gets $1,000 per homeless person it can validate. The state validates a certain number of homeless people within its boundaries. Once the state acquires the funding, it then publishes notice that local communities can apply for the funding based on the number of homeless people they serve. The local government then must validate its numbers of homeless and apply to the state government for $1,000 for each validated homeless person served. Thus the formula is passed down from federal to state to local entities.

(B)   COMPETITIVE PROJECT GRANTS

States are organized differently from each other but have some of the same basic departments as the federal government. There is always a department of education, a department of health and human services (sometimes called the department of social services), a state health department, an arts council, and so on. State departments may or may not have grant funding to offer. While most do, it depends on the state and the decisions of the individual departments.

As does the federal government, various departments and divisions of state governments publish competitive project grant programs. These programs are sometimes federal programs that have been awarded to the particular state department with the stipulation that the state must award grants based on a competitive process. Again, the state is not required to participate in these federal programs but must follow the guidelines if it does. State government departments may also decide to fund competitive project grants on their own.

State and local level project grants differ from federal project grants in that the state grants are not as interested in establishing a model program. As state and local project grant programs are developed with an awareness of community needs and differences, projects that are very specific to a particular state problem or area in the state can be very viable grant projects for a state or local funder. By contrast, the federal government is more interested in funding projects that can be modified and replicated in other parts of the nation.

State and local project grant programs also tend to be much more political than federal programs in the sense that favorite or well-known organizations may tend to get the majority of funding. It is critical to acquisition of state and local project grant funding that the applicant maintains good networking practices to keep abreast of the grant programs and in touch with those that control them. A personal touch is critical to acquiring state and local funding.

(C)   HOW TO FIND OUT ABOUT STATE AND LOCAL GRANT FUNDING

Most grant programs are publicized on the related department's Web site. If you are interested in state and local funding, you should regularly visit the Web sites of the departments related to your project focus.

You also should subscribe to state and local journals and association newsletters in your field. Grant funding is one of the primary topics of interest in those publications.

In addition, it is very important that you network with people in your field to hear about grant opportunities. Forming an association of like-minded grant seekers is sometimes a good idea, just to acquire information and hone skills.

34.11   Summary

Government grant funding is a rigorous but highly rewarding endeavor. Most government grants are for multiple-year projects. Most government grant programs fund projects in larger dollar amounts than the average overall grant. But nothing comes for free. There is usually more paperwork to do and there are more hoops to jump through with government grant programs. This is largely because governments must answer to the public, and we, the public, are a demanding group. Organizations that acquire a government grant and perform that grant to a high degree of quality have a very much increased chance of acquiring more grant funding from that government agency as well as others. As with most types of grant funding, the first one is the hardest to get.

35 Prospect Development—An Art

Bobbie J. Strand
Bentz Whaley Flessner

35.1   Introduction

The essence of major gift fund raising is building strong relationships with those who are able and willing to support the cause. *Able* is the key word for prospect identification and research. *Willing* is a condition that skilled development officers and volunteers may be able to influence. This chapter deals with basic resources, standard processes, and a strategic approach to finding the answer to the basic, critical questions concerning major donor prospects.

The days of in-depth digging for every detail of an individual's history are over. The pace of most fund-raising programs has quickened too much to allow the creation of lengthy prospect reports. Strategic prospect development should be focused on finding the information required to support a personal contact by the organization's chief executive officer, a development officer, or a volunteer. Basically, one is able to have a profitable prospect visit based on reasonable amounts of data relating to the following:

- Assets—Real estate, investments, company ownership, income, and bonuses
- Personal Information—Career track, family, business development
- Connections—Links to the organization or to other leading players
- Access—Individuals who can open the door; level of interest and involvement

35.2   Understanding the Art

As competition for the philanthropic dollar increases, the organization that is prepared to find and develop prospective donors and present an effective case for support to them will be the most successful. Think in terms of a computer company, Compaq for instance. Theoretically, almost everyone is a potential customer for Compaq. Realistically, however, Compaq manufactures different models of computers because it realizes different people want different things in a computer. An impressive number of computer users want laptops. They may, in fact, be drawn to Sony's Vaio, or IBM's ThinkPad. Compaq, therefore, does research to determine who is most likely to purchase a laptop. Then it approaches these "prospects" through various means to convince the *entire group* that Compaq laptops are great performers. And they endeavor to convince *each one* that there is a Compaq laptop that is the best computer for them. Compaq targets its approach to the most likely customers.

Prospect research can help not-for-profits do the same thing. Theoretically, everyone should be interested in supporting the common good and, therefore, a particular cause. Realistically, however, there are some prospects who are more likely to support it than others are. One of the first tasks of research is to refine a target market as a first step in the identification of the best prospects. Then it is the task of the researcher or development officer to gather information about the prospect that will enable the development team to customize cultivation and solicitation strategies for each identified prospect. For some prospects, direct mail will be the most effective and efficient means. For major prospects, however, direct contact is required. The more carefully the solicitor can use solid information to customize the approach to the prospect, the better the chances for success.

A research plan should be based on the number of development officers and volunteers who are available to carry out individual prospect strategies. The support of one-on-one prospect strategies is the top priority of prospect research. (See Exhibit 35.1.)

EXHIBIT 35.1 Group Prospect Strategy

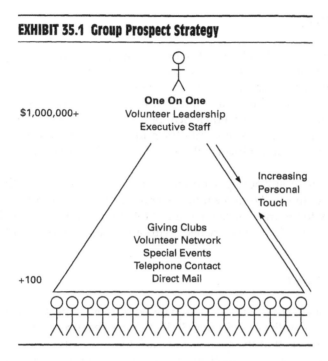

$1,000,000+   **One On One**
Volunteer Leadership
Executive Staff

Increasing
Personal
Touch

Giving Clubs
Volunteer Network
Special Events
Telephone Contact
+100   Direct Mail

Methods such as electronic screening and other uses of technology can also help researchers to support group strategies effectively.

35.3 Planning for Success

Just as invisible roots nourish a plant from deep within the earth, so the work of development officers who manage the identification, research, and development of prospects nurture the fund-raising process. These specialists may have no direct contact with prospects, yet they play a major role in the solicitation. In some cases, insiders and front-line fund raisers may be one and the same. In more complex organizations, however, it is more likely that development officers follow distinct lines of specialty.

Make no mistake about it, however; those working to research and develop prospective donors must understand fund raising and the specific nuances that grace the art of fund raising within an organization. Excellent technical skills are also vitally important. The prospector is an important member of the fund-raising team.

35.4 Investing in Fund Raising

It is better to be cost effective than cost efficient in setting up supporting systems for fund raising. Spending less can mean getting so much less that the support provided is inadequate to meet the fund-raising goals. On the other hand, it is wise to allocate resources that will produce effective end results. The following paragraphs offer some guidelines.

(A) STAFFING

A director of prospect development who is highly skilled and experienced should receive remuneration commensurate with other development officers on staff with similar levels of skill and experience within their specialties.

An organization may be too small to utilize a professional prospector, and instead may provide training to a talented clerical person or administrative assistant. Such an individual can support a development officer in the prospecting process. In such cases, however, the development officer will need to provide leadership for prospect development.

Having adequate support personnel is important because of the labor-intensive nature of research. In small organizations everyone tends to fill a number of roles, which is especially easy for an insider. Keep in mind the illustration mentioned earlier: A plant will grow stronger if it is well nourished. Without healthy roots, it will die.

(B) EQUIPMENT

A good staff is ineffective without adequate equipment. Specific needs for computer-related research are outlined in Section 35.11, "Using Technology Wisely." A principle to remember, however, is that the smaller the staff, the more urgent the need for excellent, state-of-the-art equipment. A small to medium-size organization will need to allocate $5,000 to $15,000 for research equipment, which may have broader use in the organization.

(C) RESOURCES

This is the golden age of information availability. The "public domain" (all information not specifically protected by privacy laws) is overflowing with abundant data. The challenge, therefore, is to choose wisely.

Annual budgets for prospecting resources will run from $5,000 to $100,000 or more, depending on the size of the organization. A logical proportion is approximately 15 to 25 percent for printed resources and the rest for on-line database research.

An organization's choices depend on whether it has a metropolitan, state, national, or international constituency. Location is important as well. An urban or rural location and the specific area of the country in which it is located help to determine the kind of resources an organization needs. To get started in on-line research, review the equipment and resources discussed in Section 35.11.

(D) TRAINING

Constantly changing technology and streamlined methodologies require continuing education. Research and prospecting professionals with out-of-date skills will not be able to take full advantage of the latest resources available today. Professional training, professional conferences, annual refresher courses, and networking can be critical investments. The Association for Professional Researchers for Advancement (APRA) provides these services and can be reached at 708-655-0177.

35.5 Organizing the Program

(A) PLANNING AHEAD

In beginning to organize the program, develop a broad-based, bare-bones prospecting plan to cover a period of at least three years. Whether you are in a campaign or not, your plan must be driven by the fund-raising agenda. The fund-raising programs and activities that are in place will provide guidance in developing an adequate number of prospects at appropriate times. (See Exhibit 35.2.)

(B) DEVELOPING PRODUCTS

The basic concept of "research" is ambiguous enough to defy specific expectations for production. Setting goals for the completion of carefully designed reports can be helpful. Researchers work with fund raisers to design and produce reports that meet a variety of needs. These include such pieces as the following:

- *Ranking or segmentation report.* This report is a list of newly identified prospects with initial designations of giving capability. The report may be the result of a computer selection of probable prospects or of electronic screening.
- *Prospect memo.* This report provides basic information (usually address, telephone, giving, and biographic information stored on your computer) about prospects who will have "discovery calls" or who are expected to attend events, or who have other contacts with development officers that do not require the in-depth data a solicitation call would require.
- *Prospect report.* Financial and biographical information is included in this report. It contains adequate data to allow the development officer to generate plans needed for effective strategy development. This is always a "growing" and "changing" document.

EXHIBIT 35.2 Prospecting

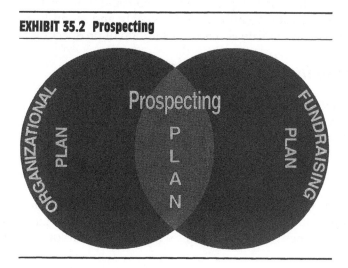

- *Management report.* This standard cultivation/solicitation status report, which is produced from the tracking system, shows the status of the work with the prospect, assignment information, and the next steps that are planned.
- *Prospect strategy plan.* Development officers may develop an outline designating specific goals in regard to the prospect and the plans that will be used to move toward those goals.

(C)   SECURING RESOURCES

Prospect research is a labor-intensive process. Excellent working tools are required to obtain the needed information from a myriad of inside and outside resources. Plan for the best possible access to the following:

Development files
Other organization files
On-line research capabilities
Printed resources
Human resources

(D)   PROVIDING TRAINING

The best of plans and resources do not produce good results without skilled staff. Researchers and the users of research should be knowledgeable concerning resources, methodologies, and program requirements. Training is available from several sources, such as fund-raising trade associations (the Association for Healthcare Philanthropy; the Council for Advancement and Support of Education; the Association of Fundraising Professionals, etc.) and the Association of Professional Researchers for Advancement.

(E)   PLANNING FOR ACTION

While annual and three-year prospecting forecasts are needed, a long-range plan will work only a step at a time. It is important to develop 90-day action plans for research that can be expanded in greater detail within the weekly and monthly agendas. This quarterly plan focuses on immediate issues for resolution of prospecting needs.

35.6   *Developing the Prospect Pool*

There often are wonderful surprises for not-for-profits when prospective donors appear unexpectedly. Most prospects for major gifts, however, will be among an organization's constituents, those with whom it already has some relationship.

(A)   PROSPECT SCREENING

Focusing research time on the constituents most likely to be major donor prospects begins with segmentation of the database. The size of the organization determines whether the development office can do this with in-house staff or needs to contract with an outside vendor.

1. Rank and segment constituents.
   - Survey in-house files.
   Organize known prospects by giving capacity.
   Identify known prospects who are ready for strategy development.
   - Use the computer to sort the database.
   The office may need help in developing a custom program to segment the database, or it may be able to develop custom programs in-house for database screening.
   If a program is developed in-house for computer ranking, it can be based on as many of the following factors as the system provides:
   Significant ZIP codes
   Business or profession
   Family names and ties
   Demonstrated interests
   Previous giving
   - If it is impossible to develop adequate programs in-house, or if the database contains more than 10,000 names, an outside vendor may be used to enhance files and rank constituents. Among the advantages of electronic database screening are the following:
   Outside data is added to the file.
   Wealth-related facts may be appended.
   Wealth ratings and other codes may be added to all records.
   Information is organized and ready to use.
2. Add the human touch to the screening of prospects. Field research by development officers will add invaluable information to the research provided in-house; likewise, the involvement of volunteers will enrich the top prospect list.
   - Volunteers add many values, including the following, to the making of a top prospect list.
   Leverage with peers
   The peer connection (Create a powerful linkage.)
   The authoritative voice (Confirm the work of the organization.)
   Influence
   Opening doors (Can often get through to those that cannot otherwise be reached.)
   A credible voice (Will be believed.)
   Understanding the "landscape" (Know how colleagues feel about supporting.)
   Enthusiasm
   Maintaining perspective (Help the organization to see itself as prospective donors may see it.)
   Concentrating energies (Help the organization to focus.)
   Presence
   Attracting others (Bring status to the organization.)
   Enhance expectations (Keep fund raisers realistic.)
   - The development staff and other staff can provide valuable assistance in prospect review.
   They can assist in reviewing the segmented lists derived from the custom computer programming described earlier.

They can also verify selected prospects who relate to each staff member's program responsibility:

Major gifts

Special projects

Annual operating gifts

Planned gifts

Other

Staff should participate in regular screening of major prospects.

Encourage staff to review, individually, selected lists of prospects and give their opinions concerning an estimate of an appropriate asking amount and information concerning the following:

Special interest areas for the prospect

The prospect's relationship with the institution

Individuals who can serve as contact persons

In prospect management committees, staff members are key players.

Prospect management meetings may be held every other week.

Meetings generally last one and a half to two hours.

The collective meetings over a period of time should follow a rule of thirds:

One-third of the time is to be spent in the review and rating of new prospects.

One-third of the time is required for strategy development.

One-third of the time is required for assigning prospects and reporting results.

• Volunteers can give valuable assistance in prospect screening.

Some volunteers respond only to one-on-one meetings. In these individual meetings, supply volunteers with two lists:

A long list to be reviewed rapidly and marked simply "yes" or "no" or with a simple alpha rating code, indicating whether constituents are major donor prospects.

A short list of approximately 25 to 50 prospects about whom you will ask for more detailed information.

Group meetings of volunteers provide a different ambiance.

Small groups of five, seven, or 11 seem to work best.

Limit the meeting time to about one and a half hours.

Do not serve meals during meetings. Refreshments before or after (preferably after) a session may be served.

Use materials similar to those supplied in one-on-one meetings.

• Screening techniques can vary to fit the setting.

Conversational exchanges can be very helpful in giving new information for strategy development. For more details, however, greater structure is needed.

The hard copy screening format shown in Exhibit 35.3 works well for detail.

The shaded areas should be filled in before the meeting. Volunteers can react, correcting or verifying this information as appropriate.

(B) RESEARCHING PROSPECTS

Fund raisers seem to know instinctively that they need certain information about prospects in order to develop the kinds of relationships through which significant support for their institutions will come. Critical information includes:

EXHIBIT 35.3 Sample Prospect Evaluation Worksheet

Name/City, State/Affiliation	Rating	Interest	Contact Persons	Comments

- An estimate of financial capability
- An evaluation of the prospect's current relationship with the organization
- A knowledge of possible contact persons and the prospect's "network" of relationships
- Some understanding of the prospect's demonstrated interests

The entire development staff and key volunteers must work together to secure information and to use it effectively in cultivation and solicitation strategies.

Decisions on cultivation and solicitation strategies must be based on a number of factors. An arbitrary figure, a potential "capability gift," can be established after a prospect's financial worth is fairly well determined, but the successful request must combine capability with many other factors. The process of research is as much an art as a science, and the right amount for a particular request must evolve with review and cultivation.

35.7 Establishing the "Capability Gift"

Corporate executives have generous salaries. Owners of privately owned companies often pay themselves lower salaries and remunerate themselves generously in other ways. Most major gifts are given from assets rather than from income. Nevertheless, finding out a prospect's salary often provides clues to other assets, stock benefits, and special financial arrangements.

(A) SALARY

Salaries for executive officers and directors of publicly-held corporations can be found through EDGAR *www.sec.gov/cgi-bin/srch-edgar.* The Web site provides full-text access to proxy statements, annual reports, 10Qs, and other documents filed with the Securities and Exchange Commission by public companies. Salaries for individuals reporting over-the-counter stocks can be found from 10K reports. Historic proxies and 10Ks back to 1986 can be found in DIALOG. Check for appropriate files on Web site: *www.dialog.com.* For lower-level executives and other individuals, knowledge of the institution that employs them will enable you to use the known salary of another individual in the company to establish an estimate of a prospect's salary. Consult with financiers—bank officers, brokers, insurance agents, attorneys, directors of United Way campaigns or other philanthropic organizations—to compile a list of estimated salaries. Government salaries are public knowledge. Last, there is the "Warren Buffet phenomenon." Although named as the world's richest person in 1996, Buffet has never reported an annual salary of more than $100,000, so salary data alone may be an incomplete picture of wealth. Among the many sources of general information about salaries are the following:

The American Almanac of Jobs and Salaries 2000 (800-238-0690)
American Salaries and Wages Survey (800-414-4253)
Available Pay Survey Reports: An Annotated Bibliography (708-672-4200)
Financial Services Industry Salary Survey (212-964-3640)
JobStar Profession-Specific Salary Surveys www.jobsmart.org/tools/salary/sal-prof.htm
The Law Department Compensation Benchmarking Survey (610-359-9900)
Medical Economics (201-358-7300)

(B)   STOCK

Stock for officers and directors of publicly-held companies is found on proxy statements or through SEC (Securities and Exchange Commission) statements. Financial advisors can assist here. Watch for stock holdings in the reading of wills. Check the DIALOG Web site for the correct files. Yearly dividend of stocks is reported in the *Wall Street Journal* immediately following the company name. To arrive at a total amount, multiply the dividend by the number of shares owned. On-line, check Dow Jones Interactive *www.askdj.dowjones.com;* Big Charts *www.BigCharts.com;* PCQuote *www.pcquote.com;* and Lexis-Nexis Development Universe under company information *www.lexis-nexis.com.* Privately-held stock information can be found in sources relating to private companies.

(C)   BONUSES

Bonuses may be on the proxy, or can be estimated by comparing to a person just ahead of the specific prospect on the executive ladder or consulting with a committee of financial experts. See EDGAR for current proxies and check DIALOG File 544.

(D)   RETIREMENT BENEFITS

Retirement benefits may be found on proxy statements, and executive recruitment packets also may be helpful. See EDGAR and DIALOG, File 544, for current proxies. Older proxy statements can be ordered from Disclosure Global Access (1-800-236-6997) or *www.primark.com/pfid.*

(E)   PROPERTY VALUE

A prospect's property value can be determined by the tax assessment available at any tax assessor's office. The property value is broken down into land, building(s), pool, improvements; and a total assessment. Ascertain the year the assessment was made and the percentage of the current fair market value used for the assessment. Electronic resources for property values include Lexis-Nexis *www.lexis-nexis.com*, Experian ($7.95 per property report) *www.experian.com*, CDB INFOTEK *www.cdb.com*, and Acxiom/ Dataquick *www.dataquick.com*. Another excellent source for property values and other asset data is the Association of Professional Researchers for Advancement Web site *www.APRAHOME.org*. Look at "Prospecting Resources" links and visit the University of Virginia or Northwestern University sites.

(F) INHERITED WEALTH

Inherited wealth may be determined by reading wills of the family connected to the prospect. Once the will is in probate, it is a public document and available at the probate court. It is wise to check "glory books" about the family and feature articles in magazines and newspapers. The APRA home page referred to earlier includes genealogy links such as the following:

> *Forbes www.forbes.com* (800-888-9896)
> *The Rich Register www.richregister.com* (512-477-8871)
> *Social Register* and *The Social Register Association* (212-685-2634)
> *Town and Country Magazine-Personal Name Index*
>   *www.tc.umn/nlhome/g248/bergq003/wa/tcindex.html* (651-905-9536)
> *Worth Magazine www.worth.com/home/html* (800-777-1851)

35.8 Creating a "Philanthropic Profile"

If individuals are already involved in charitable giving, an organization's need for private support will be somewhat easier for them to understand. Ask these questions about prospects:

- Does the prospect give charitable gifts?
- How often does he or she give?
- What is the amount of the average gift?
- Does the prospect give to an institution similar to ours?
- Are there "trends" or "pet charities" in his or her giving?
- Has the prospect recently made a major gift that might deplete immediate resources?
- Important: Has the prospect ever given your institution any kind of gift—time, materials, small cash gifts for particular activities, or financial gifts?

35.9 Determining Cultivation Status

The timing factor is crucial in developing a top prospect list. Addressing the following questions can help.

- What is the current relationship of the prospect with the institution?
- Is the relationship with the prospect close enough for major gifts to have been discussed?
- Has the prospect ever expressed a desire to make a major gift or to memorialize or honor a particular person?
- Is there a person within the institution close to the prospect or a volunteer who would be willing to introduce the chief executive officer or another staff person?
- What are the *current* interests of the prospect? Do they match the purposes of the organization or its general mission?
- Are there any major problems with the prospect, members of the family, or close friends?
- Is there a donor, similar to the prospect, willing to urge the prospect to join him or her in giving?

35.10 Developing a Strategic Approach

It is the middle of the prospect pyramid that makes the difference. (See Exhibit 35.4.) Therefore, a strategic plan for prospect development enables researchers to view prospects by category or "pool," rather than one by one. There is a tendency to "jump" from segmentation to exhaustive research without qualifying steps to identify the top level within each prospect group. These top prospects within each group are those on whom research and staff should focus. They are clearly the prospects who *may* have the potential to move upward in the prospect pyramid.

EXHIBIT 35.4 The Making of a Top Prospect List

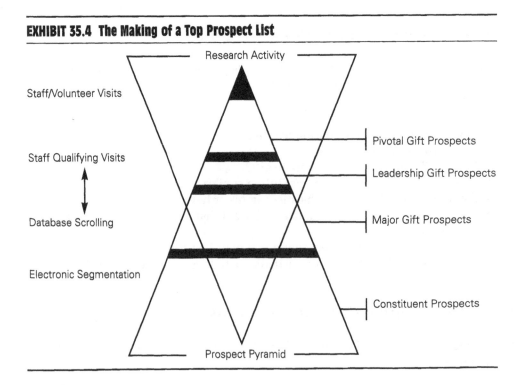

The middle of the prospect pyramid is the most challenging for research. There are too many prospects within this group for personal calls by development officers to qualify giving potential and readiness. Strategic use of electronic databases is extremely valuable to focus time and attention on the best prospects within the middle range.

Prospecting resources must be focused on the best potential at each level, but especially in the middle—the major gifts portion—of the pyramid. Technology is a critical factor in a strategic approach.

35.11   *Using Technology Wisely*

All kinds of research, including prospect research, has been revolutionized by technology. First, researchers enjoyed automated libraries and growing databases. Now they have a world of information at their fingertips. Technology does not solve all prospecting problems, and, in fact, creates different kinds of challenges.

All technology can do is give fund raisers and researchers more time to think about strategy and action. Technology cannot do their thinking. It will not correct faulty judgment in evaluating data nor make them wiser in planning a prospect strategy. And, most important, it will never raise a dime. Nevertheless, when used appropriately, CD-ROM, on-line databases, the Internet, and the World Wide Web are a researcher's dream come true.

> *The possession of facts is knowledge; the use of them is wisdom; the choice of them education. Knowledge is not power but riches, and like them, has its value in spending.*
>
> —*Thomas Jefferson*

(A)   CD-ROM—COMPACT AND SEARCHABLE

Although not technically "on-line" through use of a modem, Compact Disk Read-Only Memory (CD-ROM) technology is of great benefit to those needing access to large amounts of data. One CD-ROM disk can save the equivalent of a ton and a half of paper, from which 250,000 pages of information could be produced. This paper would cost $4,000 to mail, as compared with the $0.70 it costs to mail a CD-ROM. One CD-ROM disk can replace 1,500 floppy disks and contains data, graphics, and sound. To transmit the data on a CD-ROM over a phone by way of a modem, it would take several days at the standard 54.4 baud.

Needless to say, there is a place for CD-ROM in any researcher's toolbox. The interactive potential available with CD-ROM makes it an impressive learning tool. CD-ROM provides a very effective way to store and search bibliographies, specialized dictionaries, histories, scientific and other database collections. It provides the same detail and quality of data found in printed issues with the ease of searching on-line.

CD-ROM readers are available in most libraries and can be purchased for a reasonable price. Drives for Macintosh attach with a cable to the SCSI port in the back. For IBM PC compatibles, the user must insert an interface card and MS-DOS CD-ROM extensions (software drivers).

A CD-ROM disk is only as current as the issue available and does not benefit from the same level of updating as on-line databases. Use CD-ROM for static and historical data and complement this information with more easily updated on-line databases. The *CD-ROM Directory*, published by Pemberton Press, Inc. (800-248-8466), provides complete details on many titles and companies. *CD-ROM Finder*, from Learned Information, Inc. (Medford, NJ), lists information resources available on CD-ROM.

(B) ON-LINE DATABASES—POWERFUL TOOLS IN PROSPECT RESEARCH

On-line searching is simply the accessing of other computers' information by telephone with the help of a modem. On-line databases can greatly assist in strategic management of the prospect research process. Selecting appropriate resources, securing the best in on-line research training, and developing search methodologies tailored to an organization's specific needs are critical to a development officer's success.

Careful search techniques can help to control the amount of time and money used in on-line searching. The ability to interact between files and conduct simultaneous multiple-prospect searches makes this resource the top choice in prospect development.

(C) GETTING STARTED

Don't skimp in the setup process. You will need a computer with an equivalent to a Pentium 100 processor and a modem powerful enough to complete the transfer of data quickly, because it is the on-line time for which you pay. A 28,000 baud ranges in price from $300 to $500 and is the level recommended for this use.

DIALOG is a collection of databases conducive to creative search strategies because of its cost-effective techniques such as "pre-searching" the databases for matches through its exclusive DialIndex file (File #411). There are a wide range of other services and products, including DataStar. DIALOG's collection contains over nine terabytes of information. This equates to more than six billion pages of text contained in more than 900 databases. It includes *The Foundation Directory, Grants Index*, and the *Biography Master Index*. The communications software, DIALOGLINK, is free to anyone in the program (888-809-6193; 919-462-8600) *www.dialog.com*. Some of the following databases can be accessed through DIALOG or they can be accessed directly.

ABI/Inform www.bellhowell.com includes abstracts and indexes on over 1,450 business journals and publications. *InfoUSA www.infousa.com* accesses a nationwide database of 104 million businesses and households. *Lexis-Nexis www.lexis-nexis.com* contains two databases: *Nexis*, featuring newswire, newspaper, financial, patent and government information, magazine and journal articles, property holdings (assets), and extensive company information and accounting; *Lexis*, featuring legal data. *Bio-Base Master Cumulation www.galegroup.com* indexes more than 700 biographical directories and is a valuable resource for information on older prospects. A packet of materials from DIALOG will provide the current "blue sheets" that list all currently available files, and will enable the researcher to choose other database services.

Whether through DIALOG or directly, you will find that *The Foundation Directory www.fdncenter.org* and *Standard & Poors www.standard&poors.com* are a joy to search on-line. In addition to these resources, you may wish to add additional databases, depending on the particular characteristics of your constituency.

- *CARL UnCover www.uncweb.carl.org* permits complex searching for more than 18,000 multi-disciplinary journals.
- *Database Technologies www.dbtonline.com* provides online searching of public records in Florida, New York, Texas, and some national.
- *Disclosure-Global Access—Primark www.primark.com/pfid* presents full copies of company reports, corporate resumes, and updates on each day's insider transactions and trading patterns.
- *Dow Jones Interactive www.askdjdowjones.com* contains major financial resources such as *The Wall Street Journal, New York Times, Barron's, Financial World,* and others. Includes publications previously available through *DataTimes.*
- *Dun & Bradstreet Million Dollar Data Base* (Internet) *www.dnb.com* combines three D&B directories: D&B Million Dollar Directory; D&B Reference Book of Corporate Managements; and D&B Business Rankings.
- *GrantScape: Electronic Fundraising Database www.aspenpub.com* provides lists of funders for grant seekers and fund raisers.

The information that can be found on-line is varied and extensive. For example, a particular researcher sought basic information on a prospect to help a development officer planning a cultivation trip. A search of 51 files available from one vendor, and containing literally thousands of information sources, uncovered references to more than a dozen printed biographies on the individual as well as a match to his name in 43 of the 51 files. This initial step cost $13.12. Further examination of minimal information on selected matches cost $18.28 but uncovered the following additional data:

Existence of a personal foundation
Existence of dozens of stock transactions, date of the transactions, and company names
The year of birth
A middle name
Membership on four corporate boards
Names of other members of those companies
Occupation and career track
A wide variety of interests

Printing additional information from several of the matches uncovered the following vital prospect information for less than $18:

Financial information on personal foundation
Current stock holdings in four companies in which the individual was a director
Purchase or sale price and date for most recent stock transactions
Birth place and year
Business and home address
Employment history
Education
Business affiliations

The total cost of this search was approximately $50. It would have been less if the last step had been eliminated and copies of the desired articles obtained from print sources that are available in many development offices or in most libraries. By combining traditional prospect research methods with on-line searching, the researcher quickly uncovered vital prospect information and produced a report that was more comprehensive than standard reports based on traditional research methods alone.

(D) THE METHOD CONTROLS THE METER

Development officers are often loath to invest in the setup costs for on-line database research because beginning efforts so often run up enormous on-line charges. To save time and money, be sure that the search is well planned before logging on. Develop standard strategies for various types of research. Use the information already at hand to select the best databases for various types of individuals—for example, those who have inherited wealth, those who are corporate officers, and those who own private businesses. Corporate and foundation search strategies can be developed as well.

A macro or type-ahead buffer will also save time. You can develop a worksheet to help you move through the following eight steps before you log on and during the on-line search.

1. Evaluate any prospect information you already have.
2. Choose appropriate databases.
3. Search for a printed biography for individuals.
4. Use *DialIndex* to search for information in DIALOG about your prospect.
5. Log off and analyze the results.
6. Examine minimal information in select files.
7. Log off and analyze the data.
8. Log on and print text from files with the best information.

Develop appropriate steps for corporate and foundation on-line searching. These searches are more standardized than those on individuals or private businesses. The following is a basic guide:

- Search *The Foundation Directory* for corporate and foundation prospects that are funding projects similar to yours.
- Search *Grants Index* for corporations and foundations that have made recent grants for similar projects.
- Also search *Grants Index* for grants to institutions similar to yours.
- Search *The Foundation Giving Watch* or *Corporate Giving Watch* (on *NewsNet*) for new giving objectives of corporations and foundations.

(E) TWEAK THE SYSTEM TO MEET YOUR NEEDS

Try a variety of search techniques to accomplish your goals and track potential prospects. By entering a list of corporations, foundations, or individuals in a type-ahead buffer, you can set up a virtual electronic clipping process to track news about them. Select appropriate news databases and activate the search as often as you like—weekly, monthly, or quarterly.

Develop your own electronic segmentation process for small lists. Set up a scrolling process to cut lists of 100 or 200 prospects into small groups, isolating those you have been able to confirm as having the financial assets to make major gifts. Enter the names in a preset macro and screen through the *Biography Master Index www.galegroup.com*. Then search selected biographical and financial databases through *DialIndex* to locate information.

Using this preliminary search, you can find the prospects who appear to be the most prominent and are included in files that indicate wealth. You can now follow up with in-depth research on this select group. The average on-line time to complete this list-cutting search for 100 names is two hours at an average cost of $0.25 to $0.40 ($2 to $2.50 with printed biography) per name. The entire process should take less than half a day.

(F)   THE INTERNET: HOW HELPFUL IS IT?

From a prospect research point of view, a few year's ago the Internet resembled the old two-lane highway bordered with billboards pitching various products and services. Those billboards were not the place to find a list of the city's four-star restaurants, but the choice among hamburgers was plentiful. Although the situation has improved, there still is a resemblance to that crowded highway.

LISTSERVs on the Internet are still crowded with messages from users who are as likely to be newcomers as experienced researchers, as likely to be limited in skill as accomplished, and as likely to be impulsive as thoughtful. Too few Internet users take the time to learn the principles relating to it through the old-fashioned art of reading. And although many excellent resources are available on the Internet, they are not accompanied by the level of accuracy, quality, and customer service the information industry has taught us to expect.

Advantages of Internet prospect research include cost savings and accessibility to information. One possible disadvantage is losing sight of the quality of the information while watching what appear to be dollar savings. It is possible to lose substantially if the investment in additional hours is out of line with the overall cost. The most expensive research resource an institution buys is staff time.

LISTSERVS do provide informative discussion forums for users. The number of available Internet discussion groups grows every day. Some that are worth exploring include the following:

- PRSPCT-L serves as a forum to discuss tools, techniques and issues, for prospect development. To subscribe, send a message to *PRSPCT-Lsubscribe@ONElist.com*.
- ANNUAL FUND focuses on all aspects of the annual fund. Send a message reading SUBSCRIBE ANNUAL_FUND<insert your name> to *Listserv@Charity-Channel.com*.
- CHRONICLE-REQUEST gives a summary of the current issue to subscribers. Send message: SUBSCRIBE CHARITYTALK<insert your name> to *chronicle-request@nonprofit.com*.
- FUNDLIST serves as a discussion group for fund-raising professionals. Send message: SUB FUNDLIST<insert your name> to *listproc@listproc.hcf.jhn.edu*.
- GIFT-PL is dedicated to planned giving topics. Send message: subscribe gift pl<insert your name> to *listserv@indycms.iupui.edu*.

- GRANTS focuses on grants and foundations. To subscribe, send message: SUB-SCRIBE GRANTS<insert your name> to *Listserve@CharityChannel.com*.
- PROFNET is a list serve for public relations. Send message: SUBSCRIBE PROFNET<insert your name> to *listserv@ccve.sunysb.edu*.
- ROOTS-L provides a discussion of genealogical issues and tools. To subscribe, send a message to *ROOTS-L-request@rootweb.com*.

Donor prospect research information available on Internet sites is much improved and growing every day. These Internet sites open a new world to the fund raiser and prospect researcher. Visit the APRA Home Page: *www.APRAhome.org* to find the best sites. Among top resources are the following:

- AJR Newslink links to 8,000 newspapers, magazines, broadcasts, and news services worldwide. *www.newslink.org*
- American City Business Journals provides access to 41 regional business papers. *www.amcity.com*
- Corporate Information contains information on privately held companies, as well as international firms. *www.corporateinformation.com*
- EDGAR provides a three-page instruction manual on finding and transferring files. It includes documents companies file, including the 10K and 10Q with proxy statements. Proxies are coded as form DEF 14A. *www.sec.gov/cgi-bin/srch-edgar*
- Forbes: World's Richest People profiles over 400 people. *www.forbes.com/tool/toolbox/billnew/index.asp*
- The Foundation Center Home Page contains a directory to the Center's libraries and cooperating collections. *www.fdncenter.org*
- NET *Source@USC* is a comprehensive index of web sites for prospect research maintained by the University of Southern California. *www.usc.edu/source*
- Newspapers can be found at *www.mediainfo.com*

(G) USE RELIABLE GUIDES

Spend some time learning the sign language of the superhighway and choose a reliable vehicle such as CompuServe or America Online. The World Wide Web is a global hypertext system that allows computers to communicate information on a common platform.

Two good ways to increase understanding of the Web, the Internet, and the benefits of prospect research are to invest in good references about the use of the Internet and to log on to the Web sites that are in place and can serve as custom guides to lead you to the best resources available to support fund raising. The following guides are recommended: Web sites that offer help in the use of technology include the following:

www.//myhelpdesk./lycos.com addresses a variety of issues regarding using the Internet and CD

ROM products; *www.internet.com* offers a variety of aids such as *Virtual Dr.* and *Internet*

Seminars. One of the best guides to Internet sites designed for research is *The Internet Prospector www.internet-prospector.org/index.html*. If you are searching for company information, *Net Partners www.netpart.com* will be of great assistance.

Other excellent "guides" include the collections contained on the home pages of a variety of institutions that offer access to their bookmarks. Bookmarks deal with company profiles, foundations, local, state, and federal government, grants, legal documents, lists, newspapers, people, reference volumes, other Web pages, securities, and search mechanisms. Some of the most helpful include: *Manuscripts Department, Southern Historical Collection, University of North Carolina www.lib.unc.edu/mss; Martha Murphy's Virtual Valpo www.valpo.edu/home/staff/mmurphy;* and *University Library: Special Collections IUPUI www-lib.iupui.edu/special.* A number of other sites mentioned throughout the chapter serve as virtual guides to a wide variety of research data.

35.12 *Worksheet for Estimated Giving Capacity*

When initial research and the input of staff and volunteers provide an adequate basis, researchers may estimate a giving capacity rating. This should not be confused with the final asking amount, which will depend on the prospect's relationship to the organization and his or her readiness to give as well as capacity. Consider all specific data and clues concerning the following:

- Age and current marital status, home address, telephone
- Business/career history
- Business affiliations
- Social and business peers
- Relationship to your organization
- Salary, fees, and bonuses
- Investment portfolio
  Known information
  Logical expectations
- Property holdings
- Other income
  Trusts
  Practices
  Consultants
  Various family interests
- Inherited wealth
- Origins of prospect
- Awards
- Major interests and hobbies
- Family history and indications of family wealth
- Lifestyle wealth indices
- Known encumbrances
  Mortgages
  Inventory
  Alimony
  Special responsibilities
    Children in college
    Elderly relatives
    Disabled dependents

35.13 *Prospect Tracking*

As the number of major donor prospects identified and researched grows, prospect tracking becomes increasingly important. Because multiple contacts are usually required to close major gifts, tracking the assignment of contacts with prospects is crucial to the success of a fund-raising program.

A prospect-tracking system includes critical data elements and is used to produce information needed for staff review of major prospect assignments. Among factors that must be traced for effective prospect management are the following:

- Staff and volunteer assignment
- Date of the last contact with the prospect
- Step or status in the cultivation and solicitation process, which may indicate:
  Research needed
  Information ready for evaluation
  Solicitor assignment made, under cultivation
  Solicitation made
  Gift made
  Request declined
- Solicitation readiness
- Capability rating indicating *financial* capability
- Area of interest, related to the organization's needs
- Strategy summary describing the overall approach
- A plan of action, including:
  Next step with a date for action
  Description of planned activity (letter, telephone call, personal visit, etc.)
  Person responsible for the action
  Date by which action is to be accomplished
- An action summary:
  Date the action occurred
  Summary of the contact

The prospect researcher and the individual who meets with the potential donor are a powerful and effective team for the good of the not-for-profit organization and its cause.

36 ▼ Major Gifts from Individuals

GEORGE A. BRAKELEY JR., CFRE
Brakeley, John Price Jones Inc.

36.1   *Why Major Gifts?*

(A)   MAJOR GIFTS IN THE TWENTY-FIRST CENTURY

The pace and dimensions of philanthropy have changed dramatically in the past few years. This fact has become particularly and immediately evident with Harvard University's recent announcement on the success of its $2.1 billion capital campaign, which raised $2.5 billion in five years, with revenues still coming in. This is described as the "biggest campaign in the history of American colleges" and is a prime example of recent changes in terms of dollars and leadership participation in the giving process. The campaign is of particular significance inasmuch as 86 gifts were "greater than $5 million" and "relenting demands compel the University to maintain the current rate of fund raising, about $430 million annually."

There are, or were, recently 20 other university capital campaigns in the billion-dollar class; among those that successfully finished their campaigns in the latter part of the 1990s are Yale, Cornell, Pennsylvania, Michigan, Stanford, and New York University. These campaigns were and are over seven-year periods, although Columbia is doing comparatively very well over a period of 10 years.

Based on recent conversations with Thomas J. Reardon, vice president of Alumni Affairs and Development, Harvard; John B. Ford, vice president for Development, Stanford; and John J. Piva Jr., vice president for Alumni Affairs and Development at Duke, and his assistant, Ellen Medearis, director of Major and Leadership Gifts, and from related research, six facts can be determined:

1. The amount of discretionary income *and* capital available to American philanthropy, compared to its past and present history, is almost unbelievable. This is most evident in the dramatically increased fund-raising objectives, up from a few hundred million 10 or 15 years ago, to the billions today. To some extent this is due to the increased costs of doing business in the not-for-profit field; it is due more to the availability of discretionary income and, to a growing extent, of discretionary capital. Inevitably the process of capital fund raising itself has become more sophisticated, although in general it still depends on the information described in the rest of the chapter.

2. The changes that have occurred recently reflect changes in the world itself: social, political, economic, scientific, and certainly financial. Capital fund raising, particularly at the university levels, is adjusting accordingly, as are the lower levels of fund raising for the great variety of organizations and institutions which compete, often effectively, with the "big boys."

3. Fund-raising leadership has been broadened and refined to focus on some 400 or 500 alumni and a few other prospects for lifelong giving, for overall dollar totals never before seen by their institutions. Some 50 or 60 board-level solicitors focus on specific long-term, even lifetime, commitments. This group might be called "the Committee on University Resources." Of particular interest at this level is that usually all prospect-related information is shared. There must be focus and clarity of purpose at all levels for this ongoing process. Presidential involvement is absolutely essential. An undergirding philosophy relates to lifetime giving, starting at least at the $1 million level and often at $5 million.

4. New prospect sources must be under development constantly. Research shows that people who start businesses own 40 percent of the national wealth; 3 percent is held by corporate executives, and just 10 percent is inherited. The word "new" relates mostly to the process of taking lower-level donors into the big time. Most of these prospects are alumni, but some parents are rated equally. In the words of one expert, "you've got to look past the alumni for the sleepers." This requires a high level of confidential prospect research and sensitivity to related factors such as spouses, children, and grandchildren.

5. "The principal gifts approach" is designed to take key donors to new levels both in annual and capital giving. The process itself is particularly important for priming prospects for the next campaign and/or a continuing level of annual capital giving. So much new wealth has developed and old wealth increased that Tom Reardon says, "It is easier now to get them back and into the pattern of big giving." He also says that the "principal gift" idea started with Stanford, but John Ford gives credit to Duke and John Piva for this concept. Ford says that there is nothing really new here, just much more concentration on big gifts. "We have isolated the potential for 300 to 400 prospects, realizing that this is between campaigns, but our emphasis is on building on success, up to the $20 million level. Often we locate at the $200,000 level for starters. This is our biggest year, we are picking up seven- to nine-figure contributions with a nine-year payoff; most of the money is project and/or program related."

6. Campaign costs seem to be hard to identify. Estimates are probably accurate excluding costs of major staff participation, starting with the president, which are typically ignored, as are office space, maintenance, and secretarial costs. The costs of this type of campaign are really minimal, basically the ongoing maintenance costs of a typical development operation. Typically included are salaries for the director of "principal gifts" and a couple of other executives as principal participants with the volunteer leadership and institutional leadership. Due mostly to the very large gifts from old and new wealth, costs as a percentage of funds raised is minimal, probably not more than 1.5 percent.

(B)   THE PARAMETERS OF MAJOR GIFTS

In defining the parameters of a major gift, it should be noted first that, proportionately, size is incidental to function. This level of giving in a capital campaign usually provides at least 80 percent of total funds received; in an annual campaign, probably a third. (In both instances, however, the percentage can vary greatly, particularly for secondary schools.)

The six functions of major gifts in capital fund raising are to:

- Jump-start the campaign or program; if a capital campaign, to provide the 35 percent or so of goals traditionally needed for public announcement
- Show leadership commitment and capacity
- Particularly, provide pace-setters at the top of the major gift level
- Raise giving sights and, therefore, influence later giving at all levels
- Provide insurance for eventual success
- Provide a vehicle for appropriate publicity and to tell the institutional story

Major gifts have the same role to play in a campaign for $500,000 as for $5 million or for $1 billion. Major gifts can take various forms; in a capital campaign, the process emphasizes capital needs mostly from individuals, usually pledged over three or five years.

(After all, 90 percent of philanthropy comes from individuals.) Deferred and other planned gifts, essential to the process in almost every capital campaign, can include real estate, actuarially valued bequests, trusts and insurance, works of art, personal foundation and related general foundation grants, and, on occasion, various combinations of these.

In most capital campaigns, the top 10 or so commitments provide between 45 and 50 percent of the overall *capital* campaign objective, or the *capital* portion of so-called comprehensive campaigns, which also include annual giving over the years of the campaign. The next 100 or so commitments provide 25 to 35 percent, so there are major gifts often accounting for 70 to 85 percent of the money sought on account.

Although there may be a few exceptions, instances when the need is so apparent that anything is better than nothing, most fund raisers are not likely to take on a capital campaign client without a "fighting chance of success." This requirement is often based on preliminary assessment of a client's or, occasionally, a potential client's situation and is inevitably influenced by the findings of a confidential, in-depth market study, often called a feasibility study. This involves a rather sophisticated process of confidential interviewing with a carefully selected cross section of the key prospects on whose generosity major gifts, and therefore campaign success, will depend.

In most major accounts in which I have been involved, I have always personally interviewed most of the top 10 to 15 major pace-setting prospects to gain a fair idea as to each respondent's financial potential and possible leadership involvement; for instance, as campaign and major gifts chairs the amount each might give and under what circumstances.

36.2   *Money Is "Out There"*

An absolutely basic requirement for success in major gift fund raising is the reasonable availability of the funds needed, largely from individuals (i.e., trustees, alumni, grateful patients, subscribers, parishioners, and good neighbors). In 1984 Brakeley, John Price Jones published the *Philanthropic Index,* which received some note in the press, based on the fact that personal philanthropy essentially comes out of discretionary income[1] (which should be expanded to include discretionary "capital," a relatively astronomical figure, which is much more difficult to estimate than income). The index was intended to measure the relationship of total annual national philanthropy to the total of estimated annual national discretionary income. In addition to continuing research for its *Philanthropic Digest,* Brakely, John Price Jones consulted experts from appropriate discussions with the Departments of Commerce, Treasury and IRS, and the Conference Board of New York[2]; they estimated discretionary personal income to be about $755 billion. The American Association of Fund-Raising Counsel (AAFRC) that year estimated philanthropy at $68.78 billion, about 9 percent of the $755 billion.

Discretionary personal income in 1995 was estimated at $3.5 to $4 billion; philanthropy in that year was about $144 billion. In 1999, philanthropy was at $190 billion, which estimates discretionary income at $7 to $8 billion. However, regardless of whether

---

[1]Author's definition: "That personal annual income available for discretionary expenditures including philanthropy, *after* taxes, fixed expenses, transfer payments, and costs of maintaining the donor's *normal* life style."

[2]Apparently none of these has since kept estimate records on discretionary income.

these financial estimates are accurate, the fact is that there is clearly enough money "out there" to go a long way toward meeting most reasonable, current, third-sector needs, with a few exceptions such as the massive capital costs of replacing the aged buildings on so many campuses *and* proposed reduced federal commitments to the third sector.

A major part of the problem is epitomized at the level of major gifts and the obvious "uninvited billions" (and therefore uncommitted donors), because fund raisers often do not know who they are; if fund raisers know who they are, they do not know enough about these potential donors or how to get to them, nor, perhaps, how to do it (a major question beyond the scope of this chapter). The potential appears to be adequate to cover many, if not most, urgent and demonstrable major capital projects or programs for almost any significant institution, organization, or cause in the country—assuming, of course, a reasonable measure of continuing support from the federal and state governments and continued tax deductibility for contributions.

There are those who theorize that a minimum of $8 trillion will pass from the present senior generations to the baby boomers and thence to children and grandchildren. However, it is likely that much of this money will remain in the families of those who already have it—money begets money—the top 3 or 4 percent, the so-called well-to-do and the truly wealthy. As in the past, there will be a filtering process as succeeding generations spread out these assets. The senior generation is living longer, presumably benefiting from Social Security and Medicare, spending more, and is less concerned about its children, who usually have many more opportunities to save and accumulate than had their parents. The good life will prevail, but certainly there will be many billions available in addition to the current amounts.

36.3 Basic Documents

Typically, a "case" statement, emphasizing unique, urgent, and demonstrable needs and their costs is made available for major leadership "education," to ensure that all will tell the same story, to instruct that leadership before it solicits its peer-level prospects, and to use in such early, pace-setting solicitations.

This document in condensed form is used in oral and/or written presentations, personalized in terms of each prospect's known or anticipated interests, priced at least one step up from the best peer-level estimates (or knowledge, if available) of his or her financial capacity. (A real major gift prospect is not likely to be offended by being asked for "too much" if the amount is not unreasonable.)

A table of gift opportunities available to be named for donor(s), audiovisuals, photographs, charts, architectural drawings, and site maps can play a role in the cultivation/solicitation process, but should be used with care and fitted to each prospect's apparent receptiveness; their use *can* be perceived as a hard sell. Success in most large major gift solicitations depends mostly on the personal element, the relationship between solicitor(s) and prospect.

36.4 Prospect Resources, Rating, and Assignments

There is no substitute for prospect research, an essential and continuing process, often supplemented by information obtained through the confidential interview procedure in the market study. Then, in the rating and assignment process, a small committee including the top chairs, key cultivators, and, later, solicitors adds personal knowledge to that obtained through the normal research process. In considering individual prospects, it is important to be aware of their families, which can be very important, if not vital.

There was an incident during a recent university capital campaign when the leadership was advised to go for a major lead gift because the key prospect had three daughters and a number of grandchildren, and there were good indications in counsel's mind that the daughters would want to protect the family fortune in the interest of their offspring. However, the board chair and university president were eager to ask for a major capital commitment, which they did without bringing the daughters into the cultivation discussion, and it almost died there when the daughters learned of the proposal. When things calmed down, there was an opportunity to revisit the prospect about a lead gift for the campaign. It was agreed to and turned out to be a sizable gift, but it could have been more if the leaders had heeded the research information and counsel's advice in the beginning.

Occasionally, a carefully selected "cultivator/solicitor" will be enlisted for one very special prospect. This person must have previously made a pace-setting gift, as proportionate as possible to the amount that will be asked of the special prospect, and must be politely "trained" for the assignment.

The "sequential fund-raising" process works best, but do not ignore the possibility that a somewhat lower-level gift may be considered a pace-setting gift, encouraging others of greater wealth to give proportionally more than they had planned. For example, an unexpectedly large gift from a major second-level bank may encourage larger and senior banks to do more than they had expected, in accordance with the pecking order.

At truly large-gift levels, whatever the proportion may be according to the objectives and needs of a particular cause, proper research and initial evaluation and, later, peer-level rating and assignment of each prospect for cultivation and solicitation (about five for each solicitor) are essential. Typically, the fund raiser starts with 25 to 30 prospects for 10 or more probable gifts; when the soliciting team gets to the actual solicitation the number of prospects will be narrowed to the 10 or 12.

The solicitors should be confident, know who will say what, when, and how much to ask for, and know that they have better than a fighting chance of success. Assigning peer-level solicitation is essential. An exception is often made to involve institutional chief executive officers (CEOs) and key staff; although only occasionally are they financially and socially at a peer level with the key prospects, they can be particularly effective in cultivation. For instance, university, college, and school alumni have fond memories of their professors and their schools; the appropriate academics can be effective resources in cultivation and, often, in solicitation.

The team approach works better than that of the single solicitor, usually by a factor of three to one. In either approach, some rehearsal prior to the confrontation is essential. The institutional CEO or equivalent (or sometimes the senior development officer) can serve as a resource and develop the opportunity for the solicitors, who have already given proportionally generously, to do the asking. If one person weakens in the ask, the team should be capable of taking over. Information on related major pace-setting gifts can be used effectively to raise sights and provide examples of methods of giving. Donor recognition can be essential and should be mentioned. Some prospects, however, may want confidentiality, if not total anonymity, and this must be guaranteed.

Examples of prime gift opportunities offered at their cost can be used to raise sights and develop interest—in effect, indicating to the prospect the level of giving that the solicitor (or team) expects him or her to consider. This may be easier than asking for a specific amount, and it is often wise to present descriptive material on these gift opportunities pointed toward the prospect's known and anticipated interests, or to suggest other related interests—all in a price range higher than that expected from the prospect.

36.5   Take Time for Prospect Cultivation

In any capital campaign, taking time for cultivation prior to solicitation is essential. Consider the case of a senior trustee-level "big-gift" prospect, George Woodruff (now deceased), who became a friend over a period of seven years, through two capital campaigns in Atlanta, *not* as a prospect, but something much more.

> *In the first campaign, I met George at monthly leadership meetings and usually called on him if he missed an occasion. In both campaigns, I called on him almost every month during my consulting visits at his Trust Company of Georgia office. He was in his early 90s, with an attention span of about 15 minutes. During these visits I reviewed progress and plans for the first (Emory) and then the second campaign (Georgia Tech), in both of which he was vitally interested as a major donor and as an alumnus and honorary campaign chairman of the latter. He had been key to a $105 million personal foundation gift to Emory in preparation for which we had several one-on-one conversations, as urged by the campaign chairman. (This was the largest known personal gift in the history of philanthropy, $105 million in Coca-Cola stock from the Emily and Ernest Woodruff Fund, Inc., and one of a number of vehicles for Robert Woodruff's [George's brother] generosity over many years.)*
>
> *In the second conversation with George, I had said that if, as reported, the trustees were thinking of giving the entire corpus of the fund's endowment to Emory, it would be the largest personal dollar gift in the history of philanthropy and would raise gift sights, especially in higher education, to new levels. It would have a national impact. He asked one question: "Would it be larger than the Rockefeller gift to [the University of] Chicago?" To which I replied, "George, it would." The fund's trustees, led by George (who had cleared this with his brother), voted the gift the next week. A key player was the donor's principal legal consultant (also a trustee of the fund), joined by the president of the donor's bank (and campaign chairman), Emory's president (a minister and the donor's spiritual consultant), and the donor's physician. So, with George and the senior fund-raising consultant, we had quite a team.*
>
> *Midway through the succeeding Georgia Tech campaign, I told the monthly leadership meeting that it was time to call on our same friend who had already verbally indicated a probable $12 million bequest; we had increased the campaign goal by 50 percent to $150 million. George was getting older, and I thought his health was failing. His principal stock holdings (Coca-Cola) were up, and I thought he should be asked for $20 million to put his name on the main building of the Tech college from which he had graduated. The institute's president volunteered, and others said they would team up and do it. The chairman called me aside and said, "You really know him better than any of us; would you do it?" I pointed out that I couldn't and wouldn't solicit, but I would talk to him about the gift, which I did on my next monthly visit. I never asked him for money, but simply said that I thought there was an opportunity in which he might be interested and described it briefly in, at most, three minutes. He asked me what it would*

cost, and I said $20 million. He pulled some papers over, glanced at them briefly, and said, "Fine, I'd like to do that. Whom should I write to about it?" To the president, I told him, and he did so. He died a year and a half later, and his bequest was $40 million.

Cornell's Dave Dunlop, who is quoted later, and others have organized many such long-range cultivations. This sounds like a contradiction with what has been said about peer-level solicitation, which, perhaps, is that long-developed personal friendships can be equally or even more effective when there is an overriding prospect involvement in and affection for the cause, organization, or institution. Obviously, experienced staff attention and direction are often key to successful major gift cultivations and solicitations, especially for larger commitments. There is a vital role for the professional development officer (and sometimes the consultant) in the process. Sometimes it is easier for a consultant than a development officer to reinforce the ask; in general, a consultant is better able than paid staff to talk to institutional administrative and volunteer leadership directly and, occasionally, to a prospect, on a professional level.

36.6   Capital Gifts for Capital Needs

A limitation in major gift giving is that many prospects tend to give out of income because of tax deductibility, whereas truly major gifts should—and many do—come out of capital assets, usually in the form of pledges over three to five years (with payments annually deductible). This should be stressed with the truly wealthy. Capital campaigns are essentially for capital purposes, and efforts in the cultivation period should be encouraged to interest the prospect in giving out of capital. Smaller causes and objectives do not often have the desired effect on monied prospects, but as campaigns and large-gift programs move into the tens and hundreds of millions, they have almost an obligation to consider capital commitments.

In many large campaigns and some small ones, the "mini-campaign" or prospect-focused approach should be considered. This effort should have its own budget as well as "case" and goal, assigned staff to support volunteer solicitors, travel and entertainment funds, and print materials. Just as in any major gift effort, there should be a written plan with input from the volunteer solicitor(s), which lets everyone know how important they are to this process and how important the process is itself.

As indicated earlier, most key pace-setting major gift solicitations occur before the campaign is announced publicly, usually before major campaign printed materials, especially the so-called major pamphlets, are available. Instead, more effective use of the personalized presentation for each particular prospect is useful, starting with a brief statement of the case, then an appeal to his or her specific, known interests, sometimes sent in advance of the solicitation as part of the cultivation process. This encourages prospect interest and questions; it can be left with the prospect if not sent before, as a written reminder of what had been said.

36.7   Enlisting Major Gift Solicitors

A major problem today in most capital and comprehensive campaigns is the lack of soliciting leadership availability. The problem of enlisting solicitors for major gifts work—usually by the campaign chair and/or the chair for major gifts—is eased by promising that each will be assigned only a few prospects (up to five), carefully selected, often with good reasons as to why each prospect has been considered for a particular solicitor.

Many who have used this process have found that, if reasonably successful with his or her assignment, the involved solicitor will be willing to take on a few more prospects. Important, of course, is the peer-level, personal attention paid to each major gift solicitor by the major gift chair, institutional leadership, *and* top-level professional staff. The professional staff member assigned to each volunteer solicitor at this level plays a vital role in the process leading up to the solicitation. *Key solicitors must be cultivated at least as much as major gift prospects.* As mentioned earlier, every solicitor should have made his or her own adequate commitment before soliciting and be prepared to say so, stating the amount, to prime the pump at the time of the ask.

It is never wise to use paid staff as solicitors in capital campaigns, even though this can happen on occasion, particularly in the absence of volunteer participants and in annual campaigns where relationships (with college alumni, grateful patients, etc.) and giving patterns have been established. Stick with qualified volunteer solicitors if at all possible.

However, an exception to the use of paid staff as solicitors is the involvement of CEOs in the cultivation and solicitation process, usually in a resource capacity, leaving it to a volunteer to handle the actual solicitation. University presidents, key academics and administrators, researchers and other specialists, physicians within a hospital, opera and orchestra stars—those associated with areas of personal interest to prospects—may also be effectively involved in prospect cultivation and participate in team-level solicitations. In preparation for such solicitations, rehearsing is necessary and desirable if not essential. It is important that everyone knows who is going to say what so as to avoid overlap, to emphasize and preserve focus, and to make sure that all available influences are brought to bear on the prospect target.

At times, consultants may be involved in what might be called "a solicitation without an ask." In fulfilling what they consider to be their obligation as consultants, they will advise volunteer leadership, sometimes even a university president or CEO, as to what they felt these individuals should give under a given set of circumstances to fulfill their responsibilities in the sequential fund-raising process. A campaign may falter for lack of adequate leadership giving, particularly at the campaign chair level. The real problem may be that campaign leaders have not given what they should. Consider the experiences of one fund-raising consultant:

> *I recall a chairman of a national medical center campaign (including a well-known medical school) who had given $1 million in company stock early on and thought he had done his share, but we soon found the campaign's advance major gift fund raising faltering. One evening after a full dinner and refreshments at his New York club, when we retired to his corporate apartment for a nightcap, he asked me what the problem was, and I had to say "You haven't given enough." He asked what I was talking about, and I said, "Your peers on the board and other major prospects expected you to commit, say, $5 million, and they are apparently holding back until you do." He then tried to physically throw me out of the company apartment. From experience, I had expected a strong reaction, but, as his consultant, it was my job to answer his question, which I had done. I walked out of his apartment under my own power, and within a week, when he returned home, he com-*

mitted to a total of $5 million, and a major building was named after him. I feel it's my monument.

In another instance, at a major university, the campaign chairman committed $500,000 when he took the job, but notably thereafter, many of his fellow trustees, as they were approached, appeared to be stalling. The university president asked me what the problem was, and I told him and asked him to talk to the chairman; he called me a few days later, said he just couldn't do it, and would I please take it on. So, on my next consulting visit, I asked the chairman for some time, and when I told him what was on my mind, he asked me what he should do about it. I said, "Give $1 million." He said he would. The president of the institution, when I told him of our meeting, called the chairman and congratulated him. The chairman was furious with me; he said that he had considered our talk a confidential matter, just between the two of us. Later I gently pointed out to him that the whole purpose was to get the word around so that his fellow trustees and others would know he had done his fair share and met their expectations, and they were now doing their shares. He ended up happy.

A consultant may be asked by campaign leaders and, occasionally, corporate CEOs or their spokesmen what they and/or their corporations should give and under what circumstances. It is the consultant's professional responsibility to respond as appropriately as possible. Those in the consulting profession must be equipped and prepared to play the role of professional advisor and confidant, often on the level of legal counsel, tax advisor, or financial consultant—and sometimes a personal friend.

36.8   Donor Motivations in Major Gifts[3]

Human behavior is a complex and much-studied phenomenon. Numerous theories, often at variance with one another, have been evolved to explain why people behave as they do and what their actions really "mean." Certainly no review of philanthropy and fund raising would be complete without an exploration of the principal, identifiable reasons as to why people give money, especially at the major gift level. What actually motivated American individuals and organizations to give nearly $144 billion in 1995 to the nation's not-for-profit organizations and philanthropic causes?

Here the topic is approached from a subjective, pragmatic standpoint, based on years of professional experience. Note that the factors identified, which clearly motivate giving, sometimes correspond to various popular psychological, social, and economic explanations for certain aspects of human behavior; that altruism is one of many possible motives, but usually the chief one; and that, in most individual cases, careful analysis will reveal a number interrelated factors at work. Key factors include:

- Individuals, corporations, and foundations have the money to give.
- The right person or persons ask them, at the right time, in the right circumstances, for the right amount (or within the "right" range of giving).
- People have a sincere desire to help other people.

---

[3]Adapted from George A. Brakeley Jr., *Tested Ways to Successful Fund Raising* (New York: AMACOM, 1980), pp. 25–31.

- People wish to belong to or be identified with a group or organization they admire.
- For many people, recognition of how vital their gifts can be satisfies a need for a sense of personal power.
- People have received benefits—often personal enjoyment, as from a symphony orchestra—from the services of the organization and wish, in turn, to support it.
- People give because they "get something" out of giving.
- People receive income and estate tax benefits from giving.
- People may need to give; that is, altruism may not be an option but a love-or-perish necessity for many people.

A cynic might consider the seventh reason people give to be the most influential, and it may well be. Certainly, a corporation normally expects some kind of quid pro quo return on its philanthropic "investments," often in the form of enhanced image, or, at a university, for example, a better welcome for its corporate recruiting program and generally simple recognition for services rendered. Special interest groups naturally tend to consider how a gift to a cause will advance their own efforts. Government officials may ask themselves how well a specific grant will fulfill the requirements of the law mandating it. Individuals, among a host of other possible reasons, often want either the recognition or satisfaction (or both) that results from support of a worthy cause.

The obvious point is that most positive human behavior is motivated to some degree by enlightened self-interest, and the human need to "get something out of giving" should be steadily borne in mind by the fund-raising professional. The following paragraphs describe some of the chief factors that motivate philanthropy and how they apply to fund raising.

(A) ACCEPTANCE

People generally want to belong to worthwhile groups or causes. By giving to a particular philanthropic cause, they often gain acceptance from those already involved. An economic factor may also be important. A need for acceptance is often observed in the sequential fund-raising process. For example, in a large multimillion-dollar campaign, a group of 125 individuals might provide 85 percent of the campaign goal. Clearly, this "inner" group would include individuals of wealth, power, and influence in the community. In addition to a desire to support the cause per se, some individuals may be motivated to give because they wish to associate themselves more closely with the other members of this group.

(B) ALTRUISM

Altruism and humanitarianism are strong motivating forces. The desire to help an organization performing work beneficial to others, a wish to improve humankind, and a sense of responsibility to the next generation are, fortunately, widespread. The most direct application of this observation in fund raising is probably to take special pains, in preparing a presentation case statement, to present the institution or cause and the reason it merits support as clearly and persuasively as possible. This is an obvious requirement, but one that frequently is not fully met.

(C) APPRECIATION

Appreciation is applicable to giving in two senses: First, it can mean the gratitude and respect that accrue to a donor from the recipient organization, the community at large, and his or her friends and acquaintances; and, second, it can mean the donor's regard for the institution, cause, or organization, signified by his or her gift. An important way of relating appreciation, in the first sense, to fund raising is to provide opportunities for acknowledgment of a gift. These include publication of the donor's name in an honor roll, personal thanks by the president of the institution and the campaign chairman, recognition at a special event, presentation of a suitable honor or award, and providing for the donor's name (or the name of some other person he or she wishes to honor) to be permanently memorialized by the institution in relation to a building, an endowed academic or orchestra chair, or a scholarship fund.

(D) APPROVAL

Related to appreciation, approval in the sense employed here connotes a stronger emotion, often related to self-aggrandizement. The donor making the largest gift may be demonstrating that he or she has "arrived"; the son outgiving his father may have a particular need to assert his strength in this way (which is not directly connected with his other reasons for giving); the individual who "names" an institution or building may be seeking to consolidate the family's social position. These examples may best be viewed as the "other side" of the picture in terms of donor motivation, for few people give solely for such reasons. The applicability of these observations to major gift fund raising is to underscore the need to acquire as much knowledge as possible about each major gift prospect and his or her interests.

(E) BEING ASKED

Being asked is one of the most important motivating forces in fund raising—people simply like to be asked. They must, of course, be asked in the right way, at the right time, by the right person(s), and for the right amount. Many individuals and organizations do not give to their full capacity, because they are asked for less than they are capable of giving or not approached or cultivated effectively.

(F) BELIEF IN THE CAUSE

A primary factor in motivating giving is a donor's belief in the cause or intimate knowledge of the cause. A clear exposition of the case for the institution or cause is obviously essential. Often, but not always, the perceived degree of importance or urgency of the cause to some degree determines people's predisposition to "believe" in it. Cancer research or a children's hospital is likely to have more appeal in this sense than a library or a theater company. Once again, the importance of knowing enough about key gift prospects to intelligently match them to specific approaches and opportunities is paramount. It is usually, though not invariably, unproductive to seek significant support from an individual or organization known to have a strong interest in higher education, for instance, for a social welfare agency. And, of course, it is axiomatic that an institution or a cause that is unable to generate a reasonable degree of conviction among prospects is unlikely to be able to raise significant amounts of money.

(G) COMMUNITY SUPPORT

Frequently, the corporate or community leader who heads a philanthropic cause and makes a pace-setting gift is motivated by a desire for recognition and support from the community. The wish may be particularly strong among business leaders, and their interest in assuming leadership roles in fund-raising programs for the community's eleemosynary institutions should always be taken into account.

(H) COMPETITION

Competition can be a major motivating factor for both leadership and, particularly, giving. The need-to-win component of many individuals' personalities and its importance to their business success can be used productively in fund raising. Similarly, the competitive spirit, productively channeled, can be a significant element in the success of a capital campaign or other development effort.

(I) GRATITUDE

Gratitude is a powerful, unselfish motive for giving that often plays a major role in an institution's fund-raising programs. The student who received a scholarship, the patient whose life was saved by a critical operation, the opera lover grateful for a lifetime of enriching performances are representative of individuals whose gratitude can be an important factor in giving, or increasing the size of a gift, to a philanthropic organization.

(J) GROUP SUPPORT

Group support is a motivation based on the universal human need to belong to groups that share common interests and values. In most common applications, this belonging can be achieved in donor recognition. For example, an alumna who receives the annual honor roll of donors usually looks first for her own name, then for those of classmates who have given, particularly those she would want to see her name on the list.

(K) GUILT FEELINGS

There are people who give from a sense of guilt or in order to right a wrong for which in some way they feel responsible. Some donors are motivated to give by a feeling of guilt about not doing more for humankind; an alumnus who committed a costly prank or serious infraction might seek to atone for it by giving generously to the institution. (For instance, a wealthy alumnus of a well-known private school was kicked out but made it to Princeton; his major lifetime gift in education was to the school.) The actual applicability to fund raising of this donor motivation is obviously somewhat limited, but it should be borne in mind in approaching individuals who are known to be concerned about what they can do to improve the lot of humankind or to right social injustices.

(L)   IMMORTALITY

The desire for "immortality" or permanent remembrance of a loved one can be a strong motivating factor for giving large amounts. Individuals known to have such wishes should be offered appropriate opportunities in the form of personal proposals to permanently name an institution, a building, a program, or an endowed chair or scholarship.

(M)   "LEAVE ME ALONE"

There are individuals, including many who are extremely wealthy, who wish to be left alone. Sometimes such people are motivated by an opportunity to make one large gift, pledged over many years, on the theory—or sometimes with the specific stipulation—that the institution will henceforth "keep off their backs," giving them immunity from further solicitation.

(N)   PLAYING GOD

Sometimes a prospective donor will seek to prove his or her power by "playing God" and refusing to give. This motivation can often be turned around by means of a special presentation designed to take into account the prospect's desire for power (or for retaining control) and offering an opportunity to fund something he or she is known to favor and that only his or her money can make possible.

(O)   POWER AND INFLUENCE

It is well known that many successful individuals thrive on the daily challenge of "running" organizations and people and getting the job done, which can best be accomplished by giving generously. Such individuals should be identified also for the valuable roles they can play in campaign leadership.

(P)   PREVENTIVE GIVING

Preventive giving is a motivation with particular application to health organizations. The basic asking rationale is something like "Help find a cure for cancer now (so if you get cancer, we will be able to cure you)." Of course, application has to be made sensitively and appropriately. Circumstances often heighten the peculiar urgency of this motivation. For example, in the middle of a major capital program, a hospital's president (CEO) died of cancer. His death had a dramatic effect on giving by some large donors.

(Q)   RETURN ON INVESTMENT (AND TAX BENEFITS)

Donors are naturally most strongly motivated to give to those institutions that look as if they are "going somewhere" or, in business terms, are likely to yield a good return on investment. The return, of course, can take many forms, and virtually every worthwhile eleemosynary institution should be able to demonstrate the value and benefit of continuing, expanding, or strengthening its programs. Philanthropic giving can also result in substantial tax benefits, which can significantly affect giving decisions. Fund raisers should, of course, take pains to point out the ways in which an "investment" in a given institution is likely to pay off and the specific tax benefits that can accrue to the donor. (The latter subject is often treated in special campaign publications concerned with the ways of making gifts and their tax implications.)

(R)   SALVATION

Whether driven by guilt feelings or seeking insurance for the time when they "go to their reward," there are individuals who have a hope that they may be put in better standing with the Almighty because of their benefactions. Religious institutions are, of course, the most obvious potential beneficiaries of this motivation, but when related to altruism, it can also have valid applicability to a variety of organizations and causes.

(S)   SYMPATHY

Sympathy is used here to describe a strong emotional wish to help others in need or distress—a sense of caring, in other words, allied to powers of empathy. The individual who worked his way through college may more readily sympathize with the needs of scholarship students today; the parent with healthy children can hardly help being touched by the poster of the crippled child.

(T)   FOR FUN

Fun—in the nonfrivolous sense—is a major and positive motivation. It might better be called the "joy of giving," which has been experienced by millions of people and embraces many of the foregoing motivations. The opportunity to see one's money doing good, the sense of camaraderie that can come from working with one's peers in a worthy cause, and the satisfaction of knowing one has acted positively for good can be intensely rewarding sensations. These may reflect not only the biblical relief that it is more blessed to give than to receive, but the deep-seated psychological and emotional need present in most individuals to express their "love for humankind" through active benevolence.

(U)   ONE LAST THOUGHT

Many, if not a majority, of known—and a multitude of unknown—major gift prospects do not participate in the philanthropic process, for any one or a variety of reasons:

- They have no tradition or experience in the philanthropic process.
- Their money is relatively new and their present interests are too personalized to see beyond them.
- They have exaggerated fears of the costs of retirement, old age, catastrophic illness, and potential tax increases.
- They want to leave the maximum possible to their children and grandchildren.
- They have not been identified and/or have never been properly asked.
- Their wealth is deliberately hidden, understated, and/or undervalued.

There are unquestionably "uninvited billions" in discretionary income and capital waiting "out there" for our invitation to dance.

To summarize, effective application of donor motivations in fund raising depends on using common sense and acquiring a true understanding of people and their individual interests, ambitions, and psychological needs. More than anything else, this underscores the importance of thorough, accurate prospect research. For the philanthropic volunteer, campaign chairman, development officer, professional consultant, and others involved in fund raising on a part-time or full-time basis, one of the great rewards of their work, indeed, is that the motives of those who make it possible—the donors—are in almost every case fundamentally, and often fervently, directed toward the betterment of humankind and the many causes civilization continues to reckon among its most important endeavors.

Another approach is to identify as many prospects as possible at high levels of executive compensation in business, "golden parachutes," often tied into retirement funding; those in the entertainment and athletic worlds and overseas and other unreported individual holdings; and the large number of lower-level multimillionaires resulting from, for instance, long-term Coca-Cola or IBM holdings and the like. How to locate and motivate these individuals is perhaps the greatest challenge facing all major gift volunteer leaders, development staff, and consultants.

36.9 Gift Management

A major gift program requires administrative support. Each of these details is important on its own, and, together, they constitute the level of attention major donors deserve following their gift decision. Besides, no single gift is the only gift nor is it the last gift. A quick summary of the most essential items follows:

- Report contributions and pertinent details promptly to involved leadership, staff, and the appropriate financial office; note special action to be taken, such as selling gifts of stock, real estate, art, and so on.
- Thank donors immediately and completely; do not be afraid of overdoing it.
- Put the money to work as soon as possible and report to the donor(s).
- Check donors' desires on publicizing their contributions and the details of such publicity, especially if a project, building, or program is to be named for a donor or someone designated by the donor(s). Discuss how to handle confidentiality, even total anonymity if desired; this can be a condition of giving (sometimes also a factor to avoid family complications).
- Offer to make available tax advice. (Most large donors have their own advisors, but ask anyway *if* you have the competency.)

- Make sure both sides (donor and donee) understand conditions and implications.
- Plan to involve top donors in significant, honorary donor categories, perhaps trusteeships, honorary degrees in time; schedule donors for invitations to appropriate functions with platform or front-row seats; introduce donors for a working relationship, to the degree desired, with the professionals involved who will use their money; keep in touch with donors.
- In addition to naming facilities, programs, chairs, and so forth, recognize generosity directly by offering choice seats to athletic events, orchestra seats, and platform seats at ceremonies, so long as these do not exceed the IRS quid-pro-quo test for "give backs."
- Remember: The best prospect is a previous donor.

36.10   Thoughts for Solicitors and Lead Staff

(This section is a synthesis of the author's experiences over 55 years in the art of big, major-gift fund raising. It and the succeeding section represent a "copy package," which can be adjusted for use as such by development/campaign staff in appropriate situations, and in whole or part with volunteer leadership. These sections duplicate, for emphasis, much of the preceding discussion.)

Most successful major gift solicitors enjoy the process, have an unusual degree of dedication, and are absolutely convinced that their campaigns or programs will succeed. ("I've never failed, and I don't plan to start now.")

Remember, people give to people, and solicitors should know all there is to know about their prospects. Competent, extensive prospect research is vital and continuous: family, health, finances, directorates, investments, interests, hobbies, clubs, tax advisors, legal counsel, friends—everything is important, particularly in preparation for market study interviews, usually the first step in a capital campaign.

Get the prospect involved in the cause, organization, or institution; arrange on-site visits to meet the key people involved; make the prospect feel wanted, not just for his or her money.

The institution's CEO, as noted earlier, is a great resource and can often be a member of the task force in the "mini-campaign," recognizing that team solicitation works better than solo solicitation. Typically, the CEO or person of equivalent rank presents the case, the volunteers support it, report on their own and related gifts, and, if the time is right, present the "ask."

The cultivators and/or the solicitors should listen carefully to the prospect, draw out his or her special and (it is hoped) mutual interests and hobbies, and consider the spouse (especially if he or she is present), and be prepared to involve other members of the family. In this informal process, when the interests of the prospect are identified, determine how the prospect can be matched with a faculty member, physician, or other person in the organization.

Above all, take time. These things do not happen overnight; for a really big commitment, it may take several years for cultivation and 15 minutes for the ask.

In the process, the ways in which the prospect might want to give should be explored, particularly if there is interest in donor recognition; consider a "syndicate" gift, combining his or her companies with a family matching gift, plus a bequest, and so forth.

Obviously, a prospect has to have the money if we are dealing with large gifts. We must think big. If the atmosphere is right, when the lead solicitor has included a price or range of project costs in the ask, he might say, "I feel there's an obligation to give if you have this kind of money. I wouldn't call on you if we thought you didn't have it."

If the prospect has the kind of money you are talking about for "big" gifts, he or she probably has a sense of responsibility in regard to giving, and this is worth discussion. (A very successful, well-known campaign chairman once said facetiously, "Cultivate to the point where you think he's saying 'When are they going to ask me for money!' ") For large commitments, we must talk of giving *from* capital *to* capital purposes (the "needs") to keep the prospect away from an income-giving mentality.

David R. Dunlop, director of Capital Projects at Cornell University, speaks from many successful experiences:

> *What we're looking for is the gift that can be made only once in a lifetime because it represents such a substantial proportion of [a donor's] resources, perhaps a thousand times the size of an annual gift. These are what we call "ultimate" gifts. What we're talking about is the magnitude of and motivation for the gift.*
>
> *People give these truly major gifts because they want to express a deeply felt commitment, not just because someone happens to ask them for money. And they give when they want to, because it's the right time in their own lives and not necessarily because it's the right time for Cornell.*
>
> *So what we're trying to do is to position our institution in these people's lives so that when the time comes for them to make the ultimate philanthropic commitment, they'll feel that ours is the right cause. Ultimate-gift fund raising depends on our ability to build and develop long-term relationships with a few special givers.*
>
> *Ultimate-gift fund raising is costly, not simply in financial resources, but in the time and talent of volunteers, staff, and faculty it involves. It requires a great deal of personal attention, often over a period of many years.*
>
> *In this type of fund raising, the actual closing of the gift accounts for maybe 5 percent of the work. The other 95 percent comes earlier in building the attitudes that make people want to make these gifts. It's been said that the heart of the business here is changing people's views of the institutions from "they" and "them," to "we" and "us," and when this happens, you'll get not only financial commitments, but personal, moral, and spiritual support as well.*
>
> *The sequence is awareness, knowledge, interest, involvement, sense of commitment, and expressions of commitment.*
>
> *Major gift fund raising comes down to the business of enhancing the prospect's relationships with the institution. Ideally we'll encourage a series of experiences that will lead prospects to the point of feeling and expressing that commitment. For longer-range cultivation and the ultimate gift, the task force approach is often used, although the actual solicitation may be accomplished by a team, sometimes even a single solicitor. To start with, identify the prospect's natural partners at the institution, and this may be a development officer, the president, the campaign or other chairman, other academicians. Someone has to be in charge to be chairman of the task force, if you will, and someone has to be in charge of the staff work, track the prospect's progress, and make sure that there are the appropriate and timely contacts with the prospect.*

36.11 Package of Recommended Policies and Procedures

Recommended policies and procedures, two intertwined categories, apply to most major campaigns and are designed to set standards and directions for trustee-level, pace-setting, and other major gift solicitations. In this time sequence fund raisers are first concerned almost exclusively with precampaign capital fund raising without the paraphernalia, pressure, and costs of anything approaching the well-publicized, larger campaigns of the day, seeking financial commitments from known sources of support and exploring the often-unknown, uninvited billions "out there," which probably amount to well over $3 trillion, and infinitely more if discretionary capital, which should and, in time, will be included if the true total of the potential, can be brought into the equation.

This quiet nonpublic, highly productive, precampaign phase is *not* a "campaign" as we know the now traditional, major educational, cultural, and medical center campaigns—those of the United Way, American Cancer Society, and such. It is, in effect, a very selective, major gifts program with a limited, selective audience of those already involved and others of their persuasion.

The fundamentals of a major gifts program include the following:

- The institutional case should—if not must—be *unique, tested,* and *urgent,* in reasonable degree, and *demonstrable*—or proven—by performance and/or accepted potential.
- The case, when appropriate, must be presented in person; backed by a brief, written case statement, with a listing of "needs," their estimated costs, and the resulting financial objective as key elements of a formal presentation; stressing selected, major common denominators and, within the needs, the anticipated specific interests of the prospect, if these can be determined by earlier knowledge and/or research.

  Specifically, a case need not cover all things for all people. Rather, with variations to suit specific segments of the major gifts audience, there will be some common denominators, but the verbal and written presentations should play to the prospect's known and/or anticipated interests as best as these can be determined, both as to substance and in reference to his or her potential financial capacity. Several options at different cost levels can be useful in exploratory meetings to test a prospect's level of financial interest and ability.
- Leadership, all things being equal, is the key to fund-raising success, the sine qua non of the process; it means the ability to lead; to make and/or influence a personally connected, proportionately generous financial commitment, involve others at the peer level in the process, take the lead, often with the concerned organization's leader (usually the CEO), in key prospect cultivation and solicitation at the peer level, all based on knowledge of, affection for (it is to be hoped), and involvement with the organization, its purposes, and functions.
- The dollar objective or goal should be based on the total estimated costs of the legitimate needs, usually pretested as to acceptability by key prospects in confidential market study–type interviews.
- Solicitation, particularly with individuals, is a process (not a "quick hit") with a period of cultivation that may extend over months, even years, before solicita-

tion, for maximum impact and financial results. This process should not be rushed unless the prospect is believed to have a compelling health or financial problem.

Procedurally, the key steps building up to a successful solicitation are prospect identification, research, rating, assignment, solicitor identification and education, prospect cultivation and solicitation, and reporting results.

- *Sequential fund raising* is the key: First, board members; second, other pace-setters, on a "top-down, inside-out" pattern, soliciting the biggest and best gifts first, and working down the list using the big gifts as leverage. As discussed earlier, 45 to 50 percent of the money on capital account must be expected from the top 10 or so commitments, with the next 100 or so providing 30 to 35 percent; the rest will arrive almost by osmosis. However, campaign organization for lower-level prospects often can be essential for public relations purposes: The big fellows do not like to walk in a parade alone, and these smaller donors can become the large donors of the future, even if their considerable numbers account for only 15 to 20 percent of the final total of capital funds currently being raised.

  These initial major "pace-setting" gifts should total at least a third of the entire amount needed before going public, if that is, in fact, desired or necessary. Often, early commitments, especially if pledged over three to five years, can be renewed or payments continued with later resolicitation. Donors may request confidential treatment of their commitments, even complete anonymity.

- Planned gifts (including legal bequest commitments) can assume a proportion of up to 50 percent of the total in capital fund-raising efforts at this level; these commitments should be actuarially valued for campaign credit purposes.

- Tax-deductible commitments may be made in a variety of forms, including, as mentioned earlier, bequests credited at their actuarial value and other forms of planned gifts, often as a part of a total commitment, which can involve personal giving, personal and/or corporate foundations, corporations directly, family members, and others who might desire to pay tribute to a person they admire. Commitments in the form of appreciated securities, art, and real estate, are, of course, encouraged.

- Pledges may be paid over three to five years. Typically, five years is about as long as any not-for-profit can project its cash flow as well as its capital needs. The value of pledge segments stretching over longer periods is obviously subject to changes in the economy.

- Leadership-level prospect identification is essential in coordination with internal research on the "who's who" pattern of biographies, along with authoritatively estimated assets and incomes, health status, personal interests, clubs, hobbies, memberships, legal and tax consultants, family relations (today many personal commitments are made in the names of both husband and wife, and joint decisions are often involved), children, grandchildren, and education and medical affiliations.

- Following basic research, prospect rating or evaluation results in suggestions as to a range of asking rather than a specific amount, even for a specific need, program, or project believed to be of interest to the prospect, often involving donor recognition or opportunities for such. Then assignments are made for cultivation and, when the timing is right, for solicitation. Cultivation time is essential, particularly when planned giving is involved. Asking in a *range* of, possibly, $200 to $250 million for a specific item of need, *if* it is sufficient to cover the cost, can be easier than asking for a specific amount.

Experience indicates that the team approach—perhaps by two of the "right" people, who have made their own proportionately generous commitments, working in coordination—can be three or more times as effective as one-on-one solicitation.

- Donor recognition can be tied to specific gift opportunities, making the costs thereof palatable and can, more than any other factor except for the personal touch in the solicitation, influence the dimensions of the commitment.

36.12 Conclusion

As noted earlier, success in major gift fund raising usually ensures success in capital campaigns and programs and most annual campaigns. It is also the most involving, challenging, and rewarding, as well as profitable, aspect of fund raising for leadership, support staff, and even consultants.

Because of its proportionate dimension relative to any financial objective, and therefore its importance, and the personal element of the solicitation, major gift fund raising encourages friendships, both personal and institutional. Moreover, it allows the "professionals" to do business with the winners in life—and it can be fun!

Suggested Readings

American Association of Fund Raising Counsel, *Giving USA* (annual report). New York: AAFRC Trust for Philanthropy, 1996.

Brakeley, George A., Jr. *Tested Ways to Successful Fund Raising.* New York: AMACOM, 1980.

Broce, Thomas E. *Fund Raising: A Guide to Raising Money from Private Sources.* 2d ed. Norman: University of Oklahoma Press, 1986.

Cutlip, Scott M. *Fund-Raising in the United States: Its Role in American Philanthropy.* New Brunswick, N.J.: Rutgers University Press, 1990.

Gurin, Maurice G. *Confessions of a Fund Raiser: Lessons of an Instructive Career.* Washington, D.C.: The Taft Group, 1985.

———. *What Volunteers Should Know for Successful Fund Raising.* New York: Stein & Day, 1981.

Marts, Armaud C. *Philanthropy's Role in Civilization: Its Contributions to Human Freedom.* New Brunswick, N.J.: Transaction, 1991.

O'Connell, Brian. *America's Voluntary Spirit.* New York: The Foundation Center, 1981.

———. *Philanthropy in Action.* New York: The Foundation Center, 1988.

Panas, Jerold. *Mega Gifts: Who Gives Them, Who Gets Them.* Chicago: Pluribus Press, 1984.

Payton, Robert L. *Philanthropy: Voluntary Action for the Public Good.* New York: Macmillan, 1988.

Rosso, Henry A., and associates. *Achieving Excellence in Fund Raising.* San Francisco: Jossey-Bass, 1991.

Seymour, Harold J. *Designs for Fund-Raising: Principles, Patterns, Techniques.* New York: McGraw-Hill, 1966. (Paperback edition: Ambler, Pa.: The Fund-Raising Institute, 1988.)

Warner, Irving R. *The Art of Fund Raising.* New York: Harper & Row, 1975.

Capital Fund Appeals

CHARLES E. LAWSON, CFRE
Brakeley, John Price Jones Inc.

37.1 Definitions

(A) ANNUAL VS. CAPITAL FUND DRIVES

There are two main differences between annual and capital campaigns:

1. The impetus that drives them forward
2. The level of gifts required for success

In an annual campaign, time is the driving impetus and the time line is finite. There is one year in which to reach the goal. If, by the end of that year, the organization has reached the goal, victory! Otherwise, something less than that.

Capital campaigns offer distinct benefits, as follows:

- Accomplishing projects beyond the reach of the annual budget
- Developing volunteer spirit
- Putting the organization in the limelight with donors
- Building up the organization's image as a "winner"—especially if a study has been done to target strengths and weaknesses in the organization's case, leadership, and potential sources of support
- Cultivating new donors for ongoing annual support
- Enhancing (rather than conflicting with) the annual fund—even during the course of the capital campaign—though there is a need to coordinate the two tasks

In both capital and annual campaigns, the gift level goals are proportionate to the overall goal. But annual goals do not have the magnitude of capital campaigns; therefore, the gifts given are generally much more modest. Annual gifts can be typified as coming from cash (the donor's wallet or checkbook); capital gifts tend to come from assets and are usually paid over several years.

(B) THE BIG GIFT: A RELATIVE TERM

Amounts in the top tiers for giving in a capital campaign are much larger than in annual drives. Even within the capital fund arena, "the big gift" is a relative term. For a campaign goal of $100 million, for example, the lead gift sought might be $10 million. (The lead gift should be at least 10 percent of the overall goal.) In a campaign to raise $3.5 million, the top gift might be $350,000.

The sample gift-range tables shown in Exhibits 37.1 through 37.4 illustrate four separate capital campaigns, four separate goals, and four separate "big gifts" at the top.

(C) TOP DOWN/INSIDE OUT

The basis of successful capital campaigning is what has come to be known as "sequential solicitation," also known as the "top down/inside out" approach.

Think of a pyramid, at the pinnacle of which sits a group of people (perhaps sipping tea) whom we will call "Leadership." (See Exhibit 37.5.) Leadership people are the highest echelon of prospects—the people from whom the largest gifts are possible and should be expected, the people whose generosity will set the pattern for others. These are individuals who have a close relationship with your organization (board members and other constituencies closely related to the organization). These are the people you approach first and, figuratively speaking, have tea with.

The second tier can be envisioned as a group of people who are near the top of the pyramid, about three-fourths of the way up. These are prospects who are able to give major gifts—somewhat smaller than those given at the leadership level, but nevertheless significant in amount and impact. *These are the people you approach second*, and, because of their giving potential, you should meet with them in personal, face-to-face appointments.

The final echelon can be pictured surrounding the pyramid, perhaps wearing climbing gear but not necessarily interested in scaling the walls. They represent a variety of

EXHIBIT 37.1 Gift-Range Table: A State University

Goal: $100,000,000

Number of Gifts	Gift Range	Total in Range	Cumulative Number of Gifts	Cumulative Total
1	$10,000,000	$10,000,000	1	$10,000,000
2	5,000,000	10,000,000	3	20,000,000
2	2,500,000	5,000,000	5	25,000,000
4	1,000,000	4,000,000	9	29,000,000
*10 (endowed chairs)	1,000,000	10,000,000	19	39,000,000
.				
.				
.				
18	500,000	9,000,000	37	48,000,000
40	250,000	10,000,000	77	58,000,000
100	100,000	10,000,000	177	68,000,000
.				
.				
.				
200	50,000	10,000,000	377	78,000,000
360	25,000	9,000,000	737	87,000,000
600	10,000	6,000,000	1,337	93,000,000
1,000	5,000	5,000,000	2,337	98,000,000
1,500+	1,000–2,500	2,000,000	3,837+	100,000,000

*Endowed chairs: $600,000 private gift to be supplemented by $400,000 from state, through Eminent Scholars Act.

EXHIBIT 37.2 Gift-Range Table: A National Women's Organization

Goal: $17,000,000

Gift Range	Number of Gifts	Total	Cumulative Total
$2,000,000+	1	$2,000,000	$2,000,000
1,000,000 to 1,900,000	2	2,000,000	4,000,000
500,000 to 900,000	4	2,500,000	6,500,000
250,000 to 500,000	5	2,000,000	8,500,000
.			
.			
.			
100,000 to 250,000	20	2,500,000	11,000,000
50,000 to 100,000	30	1,500,000	12,500,000
25,000 to 50,000	40	1,500,000	14,000,000
.			
.			
.			
Under $25,000	Many	3,000,000	17,000,000

EXHIBIT 37.3 Gift-Range Table: A Specialty Hospital in New York City

Goal: $8,500,000

Number of Gifts	Gift Range	Total	Number	Cumulative Gifts	Total Received	Dollars Received
Leadership						
1	$1,000,000 or more	$1,000,000	1	$1,000,000	2	$3,137,654
3	500,000 to 999,999	1,500,000	4	2,500,000		
6	250,000 to 499,999	1,500,000	11	4,000,000	3	850,000
12	100,000 to 249,999	1,200,000	23	5,200,000	25	2,862,252
Major						
18	50,000 to 99,999	900,000	41	6,100,000	17	901,250
35	25,000 to 49,999	875,000	76	6,975,000	34	891,561
Special						
40	15,000 to 24,999		116	7,575,000	27	454,098
45	10,000 to 14,999	450,000	161	8,025,000	31	338,422
55	5,000 to 9,999	275,000	216	8,300,000	33	190,551
General						
100+/–	4,999 and less	200,000	316+/–	8,500,000	398	216,733
						$9,842,520

potential donor categories, only some of whom warrant personal cultivation. Collectively, *these are the people you approach last* (generally by telephone and/or direct mail). They are very important: A broad sense of support helps an organization demonstrate its impact on the larger community.

The pyramid amounts to a basic depiction of sequential fund raising. Top prospects closest to the institution are solicited first, progressing gradually (and sometimes slowly) to those who are farthest removed and have the lowest giving potential. The pathway is top down/inside out.

A special note is needed regarding those board members who cannot make gifts at the leadership level. In the quiet phase prior to public announcement of the goal, 100 percent participation by board members is needed at levels that are a "stretch." Sometimes outside leadership must be recruited to ensure access to big gifts and productive connections, but the board's participation is always a telling factor—and savvy donors

EXHIBIT 37.4 Gift-Range Table: A Small Catholic College in Pennsylvania

Goal: $3,500,000

Number of Gifts	Gift Range	Total	Cumulative Number of Gifts	Cumulative Total
1	$500,000	$500,000	1	$ 500,000
2	$250,000 to 500,000	500,000	3	1,000,000
5	100,000 to 250,000	500,000	8	1,500,000
8	50,000 to 100,000	400,000	16	1,900,000
12	25,000 to 50,000	300,000	28	1,200,000
25	10,000 to 25,000	250,000	53	2,450,000
50	5,000 to 10,000	250,000	103	2,700,000
100	2,500 to 5,000	250,000	203	2,950,000
200	1,000 to 2,500	250,000	403	3,150,000
Many	Under 1,000	350,000	403+	3,500,000

will ask about it. (See Exhibit 37.6.) Exhibit 37.7 transfers the pyramid categories to the format of the gift-range tables exhibited earlier.

Preparing a gift-range table helps to point out some of the general principles at work in sequential solicitation. These include the following:

- The lead gift should account for a minimum of 10 to 20 percent of the goal. Today's formula for successful campaigning is approximately 40/40/20. (At least

EXHIBIT 37.5 The Top Down/Inside Out Model

LEADERSHIP GIFTS

MAJOR GIFTS

SPECIAL GIFTS

MANY GIFTS

EXHIBIT 37.6 Board Members' Participation

> Ask for money, you'll get advice.
> Ask for advice, you'll get money.

Establish an advisory board to involve top-level prospects in helping your organization:
1. Develop its case for support.
2. Enlist fund-raising volunteers.
3. Enhance its communication with the "movers and shakers" of the community.

---

40 percent of the goal should be sought from not more than 10 gifts; the next 40 percent, from 100 gifts; and the remaining 20 percent, from hundreds or possibly thousands of gifts.) Some campaigns can succeed only with a much greater percentage (55 or 60 percent) coming from the top 10 gifts.

- Almost 90 percent of the money given in this country comes from individuals, not corporations or foundations. Efforts should be focused on individuals in most capital campaigns.
- Today it takes from 18 to 36 months to cultivate a big gift (almost triple the time it used to take). Sometimes the cultivation/solicitation period can cover five or more years.
- The influence of the solicitor is a major factor in determining the level of a prospect's gift. The "case" is important, but, in the final analysis, people give to people. Donors often rise to the solicitor's level—or sink to it.
- Large gifts today are increasingly provided through deferred giving instruments. Solicitation strategies should be geared to this approach, and staff and volunteers must be prepared to handle these opportunities.

(D) WHY SEQUENTIAL SOLICITATION WORKS

Why is strict sequencing of solicitations, in order of gift potential, recommended for capital campaigning? Perhaps the reason is best illustrated by the following true tale:

EXHIBIT 37.7 Sample Gift-Range Table

	Number of Gifts Needed	Average Gift	Total	Cumulative Total
	Goal: $17,000,000			
Leadership	1	$2,000,000	$2,000,000	$ 2,000,000
	2	1,000,000	2,000,000	4,000,000
	4	625,000	2,500,000	6,500,000
	5	400,000	2,000,000	8,500,000
Major	20	125,000	2,500,000	11,000,000
	30	50,000	1,500,000	12,500,000
	40	35,000	1,500,000	14,000,000
Special	Many	25,000	3,000,000	17,000,000

Mr. and Mrs. Charles Woodruff were solicited by one of our clients for a pace-setting fit of between $5 and $10 million. When the solicitors arrived, the philanthropically enlightened Woodruffs informed the solicitors that they had already made up their minds to pledge $100 million. At that moment, some fund raisers became instant heroes and the campaign was a guaranteed success.

This story shows the truth of an old fund-raising maxim: Start with a prospect who could, conceivably, be persuaded to give the entire amount. Failing that, look to raise the total amount from two donors; failing that, from three; and so on.

The rationale for sequential solicitation is simple: It is the only way that works. Capital goals are sufficiently large to require extraordinary levels of giving, of which only a disproportionately few donors are capable. That is why half (at least) of any capital campaign goal is raised through just a handful of leadership gifts, and why even the second half depends on substantial gifts. Only the last million or so are left to donors at the lower levels.

Deviating from sequential solicitation means that potentially big donors will tend to come in at lower levels, jeopardizing the entire goal. Many an organization has skipped merrily past the upper levels of the gift-range table, only to find themselves wishing for more gifts, more time, and more money to cover expenses.

Sequential solicitation does not work by accident, however. One key to success or failure is research capability (i.e., the ability to learn everything you can about each prospect). Research requires tremendous care, but it really pays off. (See Chapter 35.) Consider, for example, another true tale:

At Columbia-Presbyterian Medical Center (CPMC), a gift from a prominent and wealthy family was considered implausible because they were known for their generosity to New York Hospital-Cornell Medical Center, not CPMC. After mounting an intensive research effort, it was discovered that 17 of the grandchildren had been born at CPMC; one daughter had graduated from the College of Physicians and Surgeons; another had graduated from Columbia's School of Nursing. Among the relatives, there was a fragmented but nonetheless comprehensive history of involvement with CPMC. That history helped to generate a series of gifts from family members that reached, in the aggregate, more than $1 million.

(E) SPECIAL CHALLENGES OF TOP DOWN/INSIDE OUT

Sequential solicitation places tremendous emphasis on personal, face-to-face visits by volunteer solicitors. Professional staff often accompany solicitors but are not the center of focus. Put yourself in the shoes of Mr. and Mrs. Prospect, capable of giving $500,000 to your organization. Would you not be more convinced by a *peer's* belief in the cause than by that of a "hired hand" whose career may well hinge on the level of your pledge?

For most Mr. and Mrs. Prospects, the answer is yes, which means the selection of volunteer leadership is critical. Use extreme care in identifying and enlisting volunteers for the campaign—people who not only feel strongly about the worth of the organization but also are willing to give of their time, talent, and treasure. They should be people who are well connected, who can either use their peer relationships to help the cause or open doors to the people who will.

Without a team of such volunteer leaders, even the most worthy organizations would be hard-pressed to achieve success in a capital campaign effort. Thus, it behooves professional staff to learn about the special dos and don'ts of managing volunteers—for example, the need to define, as precisely as possible, the job expected of each volunteer (even providing a written job description whenever possible). It is hard to "fire" a volunteer but easy to clarify whether an individual volunteer feels suited to tackle a broadly prescribed set of objectives. Within the context of a capital campaign, several other dos and don'ts come into play in managing volunteers:

- Always remember, the volunteer gets the headlines.
- Bear in mind that the volunteer is always right in public—and always right, period.
- When confronted with a well-meaning suggestion from an overenthusiastic volunteer, tread gently. Work around bad ideas without direct confrontation.
- The campaign will benefit if professional staff can manage to put some fun into fund raising—and keep it there. Volunteers will continue to work in their spare time so long as they get some sense of satisfaction from it.

(F) SPECIAL ADVANTAGES OF TOP DOWN/INSIDE OUT

Perhaps the overall advantage of using the top down/inside out approach is that it makes clear the precise *sequence* of work, thereby expediting the completion of first things first. Take, for instance, three of the more pressing aspects of a major capital campaign: prospect research, the formation of strategies for cultivation and solicitation, and the actual asks:

1. *Prospect research* can be sequenced, restricting the "deep digging" to prospects you are approaching first, second, third, next. In even the most "mega" of capital campaigns, pace-setting gifts are targeted for just a handful of prospects. If you research (in detail) those people *first,* then you can set aside your second-tier research for later, third-tier for later still, and so on. Your campaign priorities—and staff energies—will stay focused.
2. *Formation of strategies* can be similarly sequenced. Once the overall timetable is in place (including plans for bottom-tier prospects and for campaign wrap-up), priorities will become clear. Using completed research (a sample profile appears later in Exhibit 37.8), a meeting with appropriate solicitors should produce at least one workable solicitation strategy—preferably two or even three.
3. *The actual asks.* Like strategies, "asks" often require a Plan B behind Plan A, and a Plan C in case Plan B fails. It is a good idea to work with solicitors to develop a *range* for each ask—an "ideal" gift for each prospect and an "acceptable" minimum that will not derail momentum. At times it is actually preferable to defer accepting a gift if it is more appropriate to a lower tier of the giving pyramid.

There is always a question of how to track various campaign activities, in their various stages, throughout the several-year course of the campaign. The answer given here is based on the fundamental fact that most capital campaigns (even the most ambitious) live or die on the gifts of a few. The actual number of high-level prospects may be as small as 50 or as large as 500, but it is never as extensive as one might imagine.

Numbers like these can be managed manually, especially when sequential solicitation is adhered to strictly. If sophisticated computer programs are beyond an institution's financial reach, it is possible to manage the top end of a multimillion-dollar effort out of file boxes.

37.2 *Methodology*

(A) IDENTIFYING LEADERSHIP GIFT PROSPECTS

More and more organizations are discovering that it is easier to get one $10,000 gift than to get 10 gifts of $1,000. Girl Scout councils, Red Cross chapters, local social service agencies, and other not-for-profits of every size and shape are starting to see the rewards of seeking "leadership" gifts even for annual funds.

To reap these rewards requires identifying leadership prospects, which can result only from taking at least three steps. These can be thought of as three separate phases, which, added together, can lead an organization to new heights in fund raising:

1. Change your mind-set.
2. Look for prospective donors.
3. Know what to do next.

(B) CHANGING YOUR MIND-SET

It is fair to say that most small not-for-profits are still oriented toward asking for 100 gifts of $100 rather than asking for one $10,000 gift. The reason is, in part, that most organizations (both volunteers and boards) tend to be skeptical that a donor would *want* to give such a significant amount.

The first step in changing this mind-set occurs within individuals. Each person involved with the appeal must be utterly convinced that the organization is worthy of significant, substantial, magnanimous gifts. The question is: How? The following checklist is directed at changing individuals' mind-sets *toward* positive convictions regarding a capital campaign. Your organization's "case" needs eloquent articulation. What is its work really all about? Who cares? Specifically, how much must be raised, for what, and why? What benefits will all this bring to the people of the larger community?

_____ Are you convinced personally that your organization deserves to ask for leadership gifts above and beyond those sought through annual giving?

_____ Can you articulate that conviction to someone else?

_____ Can you translate your commitment into a capital gift of your own?

_____ Are you willing to become involved in evaluating donor potential within your organization's family?

_____ Have you identified a sufficient number of major gift prospects from within your organization's constituencies? Is your leadership willing to

_____ take on the extra work (or hire extra short-term staff) to keep everything moving during the campaign?

_____ Does your organization have, or have access to, the resources (on-line research services, books, and personnel) needed to obtain background information on your prospects?

_____ Are your volunteers willing to make personal visits to your prospects?

_____ Do your volunteers have sufficient clout and/or access to open the doors you will need opened? If not, are they willing to approach such leadership for ad hoc involvement?

_____ Is everyone involved (staff, volunteers, and various institutional departments) clear about each other's role during the campaign process?

_____ Does everyone understand who is to do what—and when?

_____ If so, then you are ready for a capital campaign!

The answers to these questions are the reasons a donor will or will not choose to invest in your campaign. They constitute the basis for subsequent printed materials, brochures, and proposals—everything that is said about the program. In fund raising, there is no such thing as organizational needs.

Once convinced, each person involved with the appeal should make his or her own gift decision and be able to articulate the underlying reasons. A solicitor's gift is more convincing than anything else that solicitor can say or do; it proves that the solicitor considers this appeal an investment, not just a nice idea.

With the mind-set of the "inside family" thus shifted and demonstrated, the organization is fundamentally prepared to navigate the remaining potholes along the road to riches.

(C) LOOKING FOR PROSPECTIVE MAJOR DONORS

The "insiders" who have already committed themselves to leadership in the appeal are now your best solicitors. They are also your organization's best avenue to people who might have an interest in the organization. Members of the "inside family" should be asked to suggest potential volunteers. Widen the circle of prospects through them, looking for people who possess two characteristics: sympathy to your cause and the capability of giving "a big gift." Names of potential donors can be found in:

- Demographic analysis of your membership and annual donor/prospect lists
- Membership lists of other organizations
- Publications related to the cause or to fund raising
- Records from earlier campaigns
- Real estate records
- Foundation personnel and grants lists
- Volunteer rosters
- Reference books
- Securities exchange membership lists
- Personal inquiry among people who support the cause
- Media coverage of other recent fund raisers

(D)   KNOWING WHAT TO DO NEXT

Through your inside family and careful use of published source material, data on each prospect should begin to add up to information. Only the barest essentials are needed to determine a priority level for each prospect—whether that prospect will be solicited in the first tier, or the second, or the next, and so on.

Detailed research can then be sequenced. Do in-depth research first on those people who will be solicited first (those with the highest potential for giving to the organization). Research next those people who will be solicited next, and so on, in alignment with the solicitations to be made.

Your goal is to provide each solicitor with as much information as possible about the prospect, before the solicitation is made. A sample "prospect profile" is shown in Exhibit 37.8.

EXHIBIT 37.8 Leadership Gift Prospect Profile

Prospect
99 Rumstick Point
Kennebunkport, Maine
Telephone: 207-555-1890

Giving History:	Over the past 50 years, Prospect has given more than $800,000 to the University. Of that total, nearly $300,000 has been given in the past 5 years. Prospect's gifts have generally been made for unrestricted purposes, thereby allowing the University to use them as it deemed best. Prospect's gifts, with the exception of a pledge to the last capital campaign, have been unsolicited.
Attitude Toward the University:	Prospect has been an exceptionally active and involved member of the board since 1949. Prospect's contributions were sufficient to serve as the basis for being the 1979 recipient of the Distinguished Service Award. The fact that only on one occasion was Prospect solicited for a gift to the University is further testimony to the extent and nature of involvement. Prospect has often spontaneously stepped forward and been responsive to the institution's needs.
Interests:	Prospect began as a lawyer and formed own partnership in 1940. Has served on the boards of the Legal Aid Society, the Civil Liberties Union, and the Legal Defense Fund. At the University, Prospect has always been interested in the visiting lecturers. In recognition of this interest, the board suggested an amphitheater as a commemorative giving option in the last campaign, and Prospect accepted the proposal with some modifications.
Finances:	We do not know the extent of Prospect's family resources. It is our best estimate that it runs to several tens of millions of dollars—possibly more. Prospect is related to the former ambassador to Sweden—a family that makes its fortune in the shipping industry.
Strategy:	Prospect is rated at the top of our prospect pool with a gift potential of $5 million. Prospect is a natural leader, and we must emphasize the need for leadership in this campaign.

(E)   PERSUADING PEOPLE TO GIVE

In addition to knowing *about* each prospect, solicitors must know *how to visit* in a way that will be productive for solicitor and prospect alike. There is a direct correlation between the "sales training" your organization can provide and the solicitors' level of success.

Convincing anyone of anything generally depends primarily on listening well. This is especially true in fund raising; people do not typically give money away unless they are highly motivated to do so. Listening is the key to opening the door to insight as to what will motivate a particular donor prospect.

Your organization's solicitors must look and listen for what makes a prospect tick—philanthropically, at least. If your team of volunteer leaders can determine what might motivate a prospect to give, a proposal can be created to address specifically those interests and concerns. A comprehensive list of donors' motivations for giving follows.

Reasons People Give

Altruism
Ambition
Concern
Corporate responsibility
Corporate self-interest
Desire to belong/impress
Family custom
Fear
Generosity
Interest
Love
Loyalty
Pressure
Protection
Quid pro quo
Recognition
Religious principle
Respect
Respectability
Self-satisfaction
Sympathy
Tax advantages

The goal is to find the intersection between the donor's desires and those of your organization. Linking the case to the prospect in this way is not possible, however, if everyone is too busy talking to hear what the prospect thinks. In this chapter, three interactive case studies are provided (along with outcomes) to give some hands-on practice.

(F)   HOW TO CONDUCT SUCCESSFUL SOLICITATIONS

The foundation of a successful solicitation is listening well. Establish that fact; impress it on the mind of each solicitor. Without careful listening, all efforts to persuade will fail and all energy spent on soliciting gifts will be for naught.

The major elements of big-gift solicitation include:

- Taking the lead
- Arranging the appointment
- Conducting a successful solicitation
- Fine-tuning
- Performing in concert

The musical motif indicated in the list is not unintentional. Once solicitors have found notes that will ring true to a particular prospect, the next thing they need is a song all their own—something to which the prospect will listen and will *want* to listen. A true, well-timed theme makes the prospect want to sing along. Exhibit 37.9 is a sample conversation, to help you learn the basic tune.

37.3   *Notes for the Volunteer Solicitor*

(A)   TAKING THE LEAD

Soliciting big gifts is not a science; it is an art. As a volunteer solicitor, you will find yourself feeling graceful and accomplished in your solicitations if you:

- Believe in the institution
- Understand something of the prospects' background, interests, and capabilities
- Bring your own personality to the solicitation
- Are unafraid to ask
- Know how to listen and adapt
- Prove, by your own example of generosity, that the campaign is worthy of support

(B)   ARRANGING THE APPOINTMENT

Whether you write your prospect in advance, see the prospect at a meeting or event, or telephone directly, the following pointers are worth bearing in mind:

- Tell the prospect that it is your privilege to visit several people personally on behalf of the campaign.
- Emphasize that although you do not intend to apply pressure, you would appreciate a chance to discuss, in person, why the campaign is important.
- Suggest a specific time.
- *Do not* simply mail a sample Letter of Intent; sending one, or leaving one behind after your visit, is far less effective than filling it out with the prospect.

(C)   CONDUCTING A SUCCESSFUL SOLICITATION

A good way to start your conversation is by talking about why you are personally involved in the campaign. Set an example by telling just how much you have given—

EXHIBIT 37.9   How a Solicitation Actually Sounds

Solicitor (Anna):	John, we'd like you to consider a gift of $500,000 to endow that Herman Melville Lecture Series in Maritime Literature we discussed last March.
Prospect (John):	Heavens, Anna! I couldn't *possibly* consider a gift like that! Whatever makes you think I *can?*
Solicitor:	I'm not saying that you necessarily *can,* John. All we're asking is that you *consider* making a gift at that level . . . and with your sailing interests, the lecture series is something we thought would interest you.
Prospect:	Well . . . uh . . . I think it's a very good idea, Anna. I mean, you know where I stand on the whole maritime literature thing. I mean, wasn't it my idea in the first place? But $500,000! That's a great deal of *money!*
Solicitor:	Well, John, we are aiming high, but, as you said, you're the one who came up with the idea in the first place, and we felt you would want to make it your own. And you know a gift like this can be paid over a number of years. Remember, there are a lot of giving avenues—such as planned gift options—that are not dependent on your current income. After all, my own gift of $500,000 consists of $250,000 in cash and securities, and I've set up a life income trust arrangement for the balance.
Prospect:	I . . . I suppose Harriet and I could *think* about it. Why don't you let me have the pledge card and I'll mail it when we've made up our minds.
Solicitor:	Oh no, John. If I do that, I'll be breaking one of the cardinal rules of fund raising. Tell you what, though. You and Harriet talk about this, and then let's get together again before you put anything on paper. Why don't we agree to meet in a week?

WHATEVER YOU DO, *DON'T* LEAVE THE PLEDGE CARD BEHIND!
THERE IS NOTHING WRONG WITH TWO VISITS (OR MORE)
TO FINALIZE SUCH A LARGE COMMITMENT.

---

either personally or through your company—as evidence of your commitment. You should also be prepared to talk about what others have given or pledged. This approach invites investment in the campaign by example instead of by advice and will significantly influence the prospect's decision. Keep these pointers in mind:

- To avoid misunderstandings, listen carefully and then restate what you think you have heard. If there is any uncertainty about the donor's position, offer to return with a written proposal for the donor to consider and sign.
- It is often better to turn down a gift or postpone acceptance if a commitment is made that is considerably below expectation. If you accept, other leadership prospects could also fall by the wayside.
- If a donor is not responsive to the amount requested for a gift, be sure to suggest the possibilities of a planned gift.
- Even if you are turned down, know that you have left the prospect with a greater understanding of the institution and that you have opened the opportunity for a future solicitation.

(D) FINE-TUNING

Do not be concerned about closing a gift on the first visit. The first visit is just that—a first visit. A thoughtful gift is usually made on the second or third visit, after careful consideration of your earlier presentations. One way to make an appointment for a follow-up visit is to say: "I can appreciate that you will want to think this over before making a commitment. How about if I come back at this same time next week?" Coming back also gives you an opportunity to determine the right response to questions that remain unanswered. In essence, when you are fine-tuning:

- *Do not leave a pledge card behind.* Too often, leaving an unsigned letter or pledge card results in a much lower gift than anticipated or eventual loss of the prospect completely. All that should be left is the campaign brochure or other campaign materials, such as gift opportunity lists or planned giving brochures. Encourage the prospect to discuss the matter with family, business associates, and financial advisors.
- *Do make the follow-up visit.* On your subsequent visit, review how important the proposed gift is, and discuss the details of the gift. Try to secure the pledge verbally, and then use a Letter of Intent to record the pledge and the details of how it will be handled. Review it with the donor, and tell him or her that a confirming letter will be sent from your organization.

In soliciting a major gift, even a second visit may not close the commitment, but it should narrow the field in terms of program interest and the general nature of the gift. Remember not to rush the gift. Closing a leadership gift can take a year or longer. Go back as many times as necessary to obtain the gift.

(E) PERFORMING IN CONCERT

Remember that you are working in concert with others on this campaign. Development staff can help with techniques, strategies, and approaches to your prospects; institutional administrators can accompany you on your first call to visit the prospect or on follow-up visits if a situation warrants. Assistance is also available in the area of planned giving: You need only notify the campaign office to suggest that a planned giving expert is needed.

In summary, remember that successful solicitation, like playing good music, requires concentration and rehearsals that concentrate on:

- *Tempo.* Timing is of the essence in big-gift solicitations. Allow sufficient time for at least two face-to-face, in-person appointments. When the time is right, ask for the gift in a specific dollar amount.
- *Learning your part.* It is important that you are completely facile as to the spirit of the campaign and the importance of philanthropic investments from donors like you. Learn as much as you can about each prospect you are assigned, and try to find the link between the campaign goals and the prospect's interests. Be prepared to ask for an appropriate dollar amount, but, most important of all: *Do ask!*

(F)   YOUR ORGANIZATION'S GOAL: TRULY BIG GIFTS

When steps are completed—and completed correctly—amazing things can happen. Some examples of astoundingly big gifts follow, accompanied by brief, but true, stories to help make them memorable.

- *Gifts that are created out of necessity.* At Bayfront Medical Center, St. Petersburg, Florida, my firm counseled a $7 million campaign. We had no identifiable potential for top-level giving. What we did was establish the lead gift and its terms during the campaign planning study. The result was a $1 million lead gift, which, in turn, leveraged a matching gift of $1 million and several other large gifts from $250,000 to $500,000. Without that first gift, however, the campaign would never have gotten off the ground. And it had to be created from absolute ground-zero *scratch.*
- *Gifts that are cultivated.* A vivid example of this occurred at Milton Academy, where an anonymous donor had once made a large gift through a 10-year trust of stock in a major corporation. When we were studying the feasibility of a capital campaign, none of the leadership wanted that donor to be contacted. After all, they said, the gift had been anonymous, and they wanted that anonymity protected. The headmaster, however, took it upon himself simply to visit the anonymous donor. He told the donor what the school was doing, what it hoped to do, and generally kept in touch. These visits resulted in the conversion of the trust to an outright gift of $1.5 million plus a bequest of an additional $3 million in Dow Jones stocks.
- *Gifts that are revived.* A disillusioned donor had once headed a particular board but was removed. The new leadership was fearful of cultivating him for a major gift; our recommendation was to keep him informed and involved. After two years, he responded at least 15 times his prior annual giving level with a five-figure gift.
- *Gifts that are enlarged.* This is a classic about a campaign led by George A. Brakeley Jr. Apparently, the campaign chairman (and principal prospect) decided to take it upon himself to announce his gift unexpectedly at a board meeting. "I've decided on my contribution," he said. "It will be $4 million." To which George Brakeley replied, "That's not enough." Reportedly the donor "blew out his fuse panel and left the premises." But the next day he phoned George to say, "You're right. I've raised it to $6 million."
- *Gifts that are found almost by accident.* During Columbia-Presbyterian Medical Center's campaign for $133 million, the Dental School had been included in the program. We decided to apply the same principles of grateful patient solicitation to the Dental School as we did to the Medical School/Hospital. A Dental School professor cultivated a housekeeper (among others) who became a trustee of her employer's newly established foundation upon the employer's death. The result was receipt of the *first* fully endowed chair in dentistry.
- *Gifts that are "sleepers."* All successful campaigns attract "sleepers"—that is, large gifts that emerge from prospects not identified when the campaign is launched. My favorite is a $250,000 gift to Loyola Academy, in suburban Chicago, given by a former student who had been dismissed prior to graduation. Who could have predicted this fellow would become such a generous donor!

- *The stretch gift.* A "stretch gift" by one individual donor often determines success, but such gifts require creativity. In one case, we identified a $1 million prospect during the study. The organization needed a minimum of $2.5 million from him over five years. He declined. We knew, however, that he took great pride in managing monies for profit, so we asked him to pledge based on his managing an initial investment and personally guaranteeing the return on investment to meet his pledge total. The result? A gift of $5 million over 10 years!

- *Gifts that are loans.* Some imagination is needed for this type of gift. Consider, for example, a specialty hospital in New York City that asked a professionally administered foundation for $250,000 and was turned down. Our answer for the client was to suggest a five-year, interest-free loan rather than a one-time, direct gift. It was granted!

- *The impossible gift.* The primary potential donor to a medical university in the East was overcommitted personally and had other philanthropic priorities. During the study, we told him he must commit to a pace-setting $5 million gift from whatever resources available or the campaign would not be successful. As a board member of a large foundation, he was able to effect an exception to the existing policies and delivered a $5 million foundation gift rather than a personal gift.

- *The syndicated gift.* There are many examples of grouping a "united contribution" to overcome the lack of a single pace-setting gift. In this approach, a recipient organization accepts a group's dollar commitment to fill a need in the campaign gift chart. The most recent example I have experienced is a combined gift to a medical institution by a famous and affluent family. The family had been shown, by virtue of good research, the extent to which the institution had contributed to their health and well-being over the years. The result was a very significant family (i.e., syndicated) gift. Other syndicated gifts might be given by:
Total board
Total medical staff
Total employees
Total response-to-a-challenge gift
Total gift from employees of a corporation (e.g., the gift of $350,000 that Bear-Sterns gave to the Salvation Army of Greater New York, which resulted from one employee's soliciting other partners to come up with the total)

- *Turndowns that turn up after all.* At one of our nation's largest national charities, Shell Oil was persuaded to double its $100,000 gift and Xerox Corporation agreed to triple its initial $10,000 contribution. Our approach here is a three-part equation:
First no = Ignore.
Second no = Start to take them seriously.
Third no = Wait six months and then go back.

- *Gifts that should be rejected.* Another company solicited by the same large national charity did not want to give a penny. After three meetings, it agreed to a $20,000 grant for a specific program that would cost at least $50,000. We advised our client against accepting the grant because it would end up costing the client money. We often advise clients to turn down gifts that are too expensive to accept. Beware of real estate gifts, for instance; the horror stories are almost endless.

The worst mistakes any capital campaign can make are headlined in the following text.

- Changing needs in the midst of the campaign.
- Not asking for a gift.
- Asking for too small a gift.
- Poor campaign leadership.
- Expecting the board to do more than it is capable of doing.
- Using the wrong case.
- Conducting a campaign without a study.
- Having inexperienced development staff and/or professional counsel.
- Using the wrong public relations message.
- Not telling the story of the organization's achievements and potential for the community.
- Overlooking the organization's heritage, previous donors, and past leadership.
- Setting too low a goal.
- Not knowing the membership or the potential for leadership and key gifts.
- Wrong timing from one of two standpoints: either running into a competitive campaign or not allowing enough time to conduct the campaign.
- Having a board that is not involved.
- Concentrating only on corporations and foundations and not developing affluent individuals as prospects.
- Presenting needs in terms of the organization rather than in light of needs and benefits to the community.

The following case studies illustrate the art of soliciting big gifts.

CASE STUDY 1

Prospect: Civic-minded publishing firm in a community in which more than $3 million had never been raised through a capital campaign. Corporate giving limited largely to banks, utilities, and the prospect. Most corporate gifts to major campaigns ranged from $5,000 to $50,000.

Institution: One of two community hospitals among many proprietary hospitals serving the community. Serves the poor. Bad reputation among the upper and middle classes. Formerly owned by the city. Weak board of directors—that is, no clout and no money. Fund-raising experience limited to an auxiliary-sponsored annual event. No donors of record on file; no development staff; no history of capital or annual campaigns. Little physician loyalty to the hospital.

Circumstances: The hospital undertook a mega-million-dollar capital campaign for construction, on advice of counsel. A minimum of three $1 million gifts was projected as necessary for success, as with a new level of allegiance and extraordinary giving by the medical staff.

Preliminary research disclosed that the publishing company had been editorially harsh in its treatment of the hospital and that its top management was generally dissatisfied with physician participation in community projects and charities. One hospital board member held a management position at the publishing company—number four or five on the management roster.

Strategy Developed for Approaching Prospect

1. Ask for a $1 million gift from the publishing company, to be used to challenge a minimum of $1 million from the hospital medical staff and ultimately to help fund construction that would eliminate many of the hospital's weaknesses, which the publishing company was criticizing.
2. Persuade the publishing company that, by example, it could raise the entire standard of corporate giving in the community and, therefore, ultimately lessen the overall philanthropic burden, as well as directly provide more charitable dollars for the as yet unmet needs of the community.
3. Because the hospital board member on the publishing company's staff would not solicit the gift, and no other board member was a peer of the top management, it was decided to use an objective third party to approach the prospect.

Questions

1. Was the strategy sound?
2. What modifications in strategy would you have made, if any?
3. Did the strategy work?

Outcome   The publishing company responded with the $1 million challenge gift to our medical staff (the largest corporate gift in the community's history). The physicians surpassed their $1 million goal and then challenged the company to match an additional $250,000 in physician gifts, which the company did. The balance of the corporate community significantly increased its level of giving.

CASE STUDY 2

Institution:
A Suburban 700-bed community teaching hospital with a $25 million capital campaign. Target: A $4 million lead gift.

Prospective donor: A well-known philanthropist whose wife had been well cared for by the hospital. The husband enjoys recognition and likes to make pacesetting gifts.

The Solicitation Plan   Given the husband's preference for reserving areas in the family's name with his gifts, the plan called for offering the prospective donor the opportunity to name one of the hospital's seven-story buildings, which was to undergo renovation. The hospital assigned a gift value of $4 million to the building, roughly half the refurbishing costs.

The two co-chairs and another volunteer, who was an acquaintance and business associate of the prospect, made the call. They brought with them a proposal outlining the new programs and services the building would house and the remodeling plans. They also brought a framed photograph of the building's facade.

The Negotiations   The solicitors reported that it was clear from the outset that the husband and wife intended to make a significant gift and were intrigued by the hospital's offer of extending them the honor of dedicating the building.

The solicitors then made the gift request, asking for $800,000 a year for five years ($4 million). They suggested the couple take a few weeks to consider their request. One of the co-chairs then called and arranged a second appointment. The husband indicated that he alone would be seeing the volunteers.

At the second meeting, the hospital was represented by the one co-chair who set up the appointment and the volunteer who was the husband's acquaintance.

The solicitors reported that the husband wasted little time in getting down to business. (The husband and the two volunteers were all in the investment banking/stock brokerage business.) The husband said he was very much interested in funding the renovations and naming the building and offered to make a *total* pledge of $750,000. After exchanging counteroffers, the husband's final offer was a pledge of $2 million.

Question   Did the solicitors accept or reject the husband's final offer to name the building for $2 million?

Outcome   The volunteers accepted the husband's offer to pledge $2 million to dedicate the building (Note: The $2 million pledge did end up being the campaign's largest gift.)

Do you think this was the right decision?

Would you have handled the negotiations differently? How?

What do you see as the possible consequences of reserving the building for the $2 million gift?

CASE STUDY 3

Institution: A local community service organization serving women and their families is conducting its first capital campaign in more than 25 years. The board of directors is all female, with no connections to the major corporations and prominent citizens residing in its wealthy suburban neighborhood.

The goal is $3 million to renovate the activities center to accommodate a day-care facility and a new playground. The board has approved the campaign plan, realizing they may be faced with a fiscal crisis if the building is not renovated. Yet, the board has not accepted responsibility for the success of the campaign. This is evidenced by their token gifts (far below their giving capability) and refusal to ask people for money: "It's not ladylike." A past president is essentially *the* board's campaign volunteer.

Prospect: The founder and chairman of a local family-owned manufacturer of beauty products (geared to males) with sales of $50 to $100 million. The company employs only 300 people (most area corporations employ thousands and have revenues in the billions of dollars).

The prospect is a regular $1,000 annual donor to the organization. Gifts come in response to year-end mailings. His secretary serves as his spokesperson on all communications. He has never granted a meeting to an annual fund volunteer, the current executive director, or the president. To everyone's surprise, three years ago he attended a retirement party for an executive director, who has since moved three states away.

The prospect has given two $10,000 gifts. The first was to the last capital campaign conducted 25 years ago. The second gift came unsolicited five years ago. The prospect has a small family foundation that gives away $75,000 a year in gifts averaging $1,000. Unsolicited applications are not accepted.

His reputation with more "popular" local charities is: "He's a waste of time, and probably won't give, even if you do get to him." No volunteers know him well enough to evaluate his giving potential. Based on past giving history, his company's size, home address, and the absence of a peer-to-peer solicitation opportunity, the campaign director rates him conservatively at $100,000.

Circumstances: The campaign has reached $2 million. A lead gift of $750,000 from a trust fund was given during counsel's planning study two years ago. The board has given a total of $250,000, and the corporate committee has reached its goal of $1 million from corporations. This leaves $1 million to come from individuals.

The top and bottom of the gift-range chart have been filled, with no gifts in between (in the $75,000 to $150,000 range). It is these 10 gifts that will ensure the campaign's success. Unfortunately, the prospect list is getting shorter; those who have already been solicited have given considerably less than their capability. The volunteer committees enlisted especially for the campaign are showing the typical signs of getting tired of the effort.

The campaign chairperson will not solicit the prospect. The past president says she will give it a try, but does not think he will respond. She had met the prospect briefly at the executive director's retirement party.

Need: $100,000 gift to kick off the public phase of the campaign, and new volunteers who have peer-to-peer relationships with individual prospects in the $75,000 to $150,000 range.

The Strategy Set in Action   It is time for the campaign to go public, and a reception is planned (at the headquarters building of the largest corporate donor). The retired executive director agrees to personally invite the prospect and to attend the event. She is willing to cultivate—but not solicit—the prospect, provided the past president is with her. The past president gladly agrees. The prospect's secretary notifies the campaign office that the prospect will attend the kick-off reception.

To acquaint the prospect with the campaign, a plan is activated to cultivate him *before* he attends the reception. The past president immediately tries to schedule a meeting with the prospect. He refuses, asking that information be sent to him instead. A very general case description (not a proposal) with the subtle message "This is why we want to meet with you" is sent. No request for a contribution is made.

The plan for the reception is to get the prospect to agree to tour the facility. (The facility sells itself.) Part of the strategy is to have everyone pay special attention to the prospect. The prospect attends the reception. Upon hearing the campaign chairman announce the most generous donors to date, he whispers to the retired executive director that he would like to do something big. She suggests that he tour the facility before making a decision so as to get a better understanding of the proposed plans. He agrees and asks that someone contact his secretary to set up a date.

The past president calls the secretary and gets the usual cordial runaround. After two months and still no meeting, the past president says to the campaign director, "This guy is a waste of time. Let's forget about him." By now it is December, and he has been pulled from the year-end mailing for the annual fund.

Questions

1. Should the campaign director "forget about him?" If yes, why?
2. If no, what should the next steps be?

Outcome   The campaign director refused to give up; there were not enough prospects to ensure the campaign's success. In his own strange way, the prospect was showing discreet signs of interest. He had given to a capital campaign before, and the best solicitation tool available had yet to be used—the tour of the facility. A new 13-step plan was implemented:

1. The prospect is sent a list of named gift opportunities in the $75,000 to $150,000 range, to give him an idea of the kinds of projects available and to have him think in that range.
2. The campaign director writes a letter informing him of the new donors who had joined the effort since the kick-off. A picture of the prospect talking to the executive director is put on the front page of the campaign's newsletter. The caption reads: "Mr. X, a longtime friend of Mrs. Y, joins in the kick-off celebration."
3. Additional research is done. It is learned that the company's receptionist has resided at the organization's women's residence and that the company employs many single women and working mothers. The day-care center would be a great benefit to the prospect's employees.
4. During the last week in December, the prospect sends a foundation check for $25,000.
5. Now that he is a donor, plans are made to see whether he can be further cultivated to be a volunteer for the campaign.
6. As part of the official opening of the day-care center, the prospect is invited to visit the facility. He declines. Two days later the secretary delivers two checks for $50,000 each (one personal and one corporate). He is now the largest single individual donor to the capital campaign.
7. The past president contacts the prospect and gets him to agree to visit the facility.
8. Needing money to build a playground to complement the day-care center (government regulations), the "tour guides" decide ahead of time to emphasize the playground vs. the day-care center, which is already finished.
9. The prospect asks how much the playground will cost. Caught by surprise, the past president tells him the exact budgeted amount of $35,000. The guides also ask whether he would like to participate in any of the named gift opportunities available for his gifts totaling $125,000. He replies that he is not really interested in having his name on a wall, but that he is flattered. Instead, if the organization would notify his employees of his generosity, he would appreciate it.
10. The next day a $35,000 check is delivered.
11. Keeping in mind that a donor is a friend who can become a volunteer, the campaign director finds the ideal solicitation situation for this new major donor: an

82-year-old Forbes 400 businessman, another unreachable prospect. He would not grant a meeting, and he asked for a written proposal. A proposal requesting $100,000 was sent several months ago, and there has been no word since.

12. The past president asks the donor if he would be willing to help with "just this one" prospect. The donor volunteers to call the prospect and to ask him to match his gift. He has since done this, and the organization is waiting for a response.

13. The infusion of this lead gift and a new volunteer has ignited the campaign's momentum and the volunteers' eagerness to see the campaign to its successful completion.

(G) KEEPING TRACK OF THE WHOLE THING

There are many ways to manage a capital campaign. A "must" is the weekly staff meeting (or, in cases where the staff is only one person, the weekly staff report). Each of these should be identical in format, so that week-to-week progress can be readily assessed and shared with campaign leadership. Areas to track in most capital campaigns include:

- What was accomplished the preceding week, and by whom
- What must be undertaken during the coming week, and who is responsible for what
- Status of active solicitations and prospect cultivation activities
- Problems to be resolved, and by whom
- Emerging problems to be addressed, and strategies for doing so
- Checklist for reviewing status of leadership, budget, timetables, solicitations, prospect assignments, public relations, and research (the number of prospects, old and new; the number on whom primary research has been completed; the number on whom secondary research has been completed)
- Status of campaign gifts and pledges (in such categories as trustee gifts, staff gifts, leadership gifts, major gifts, etc.)

Whatever methods of management (and more detailed record keeping) you devise, be careful not to overdesign. What your campaign leadership needs is quick access to some very basic information: how a given area is progressing and where each prospect stands in the process. It should be possible to gain immediate, firsthand knowledge that Prospect A has moved from research to cultivation, or from cultivation to solicitation, or, finally—and more important—to *donor*.

The advent of the computer now allows us to establish a "moves management program" that tracks all activity and projected activity related to each individual prospect.

These programs are available from various software firms, although many organizations develop their own programs. The level of sophistication to be employed is dependent on your organization's needs. However, each prospect-tracking sheet should include three basic components: solicitor, last contact, next action to be taken. The nature of the next "move" should be included, along with accompanying dates and notes regarding the status of the fund-raising relationship between your organization and the prospect. (See Exhibit 37.10.) This leads to what is perhaps the most important task of any capital campaign: donor recognition.

EXHIBIT 37.10 Sample Moves Management Chart

							Tracking		Report				
Name	Grd. Yr.	State	City	Solicitor	Giving Status	Last Contact	Next Action	Nature of Next Move	Notes/ Comments	Area of Interest	DSC*	Rating Code	Status
Ayre, John	N/A	PA	Scranton	FLH				Close—Must contact University	N/A	MM			
Bent, Joe	1974	NJ	Princeton	GE	AF/Cap		1/96	Visit by GC/RD, ask $25,000	Awaiting decision	Scholarship	26-6	C	SC
Caro, Ann	1969	DE	Wilmington	MFM	AF/Cap	11-8-95		$25,000 ask made	Attended president's breakfast with Geo. Smith		21-3	C	RS
Day, Dennis	1969	PA	Philadelphia	WT	AAF/Cap		1/26/96	Ask			24-30		RS
Dean, Fred	1969	PA	Philadelphia	VL	AF/Cap				No gift, fully extended		8-5		RS
Fox, Jim	1935	VA	Richmond	FLH		11-6-95			Could help with sister Mary Perkins	Endowment		B	NC
Gates, Paul		DE	Wilmington	LIK				Son applied to university	Top VP with Prudential			B	NC
Hall, Kim	1954	VA	Williamsburg	MFM			1/11/96	Visit in VA	Has rich relative, Bill Perkins			A	SC
Hanks, Joe	1979	NJ	Marlton	PW				Asked appropriate number $			12-3		MM
Jake, Tim	1969	PA	Philadelphia	RS	AF/Cap	6-28-95					12-15	A	NC
Jonas, Peter	1964	PA	Philadelphia	VL	AF/Cap	12-2-95	1/27/96	Sending letter ? intent	Ask $100,000	Cancer research	7-20	B	SC
Kyle, Art	1979	PA	Philadelphia	IH						Music	24-6	D	NC
Loomis, Rob	1984	PA	Philadelphia	JK	AF/Cap	11-3-93		Close	Talked about gift insurance	Endowment	8-7	C	RS

Key:
- VC Verbal Commitment
- SC Has been solicited, waiting for commitment
- RS Ready to be solicited
- MM Proceeding through moves management
- NC Needs significant level of cultivation
- OS Ongoing stewardship
- *DSC Demographic screening code

(H) DONOR RECOGNITION: PREAMBLE, NOT POSTMORTEM

A statistic was once proposed: "A prospect, once converted into a donor, generally gives for the next seven years." Assume, for the sake of argument, that this is true—that a prospect, once converted to a donor, gives for the next seven years. Conversely, does it not mean that if you lose a donor, you lose seven years' worth of gifts?

That viewpoint suggests that donor recognition should be thought of not as the end of the fund-raising process, but as the *beginning:* Donor recognition should be treated as the preamble, not the postmortem. Done well, and done often, it should be the *beginning* of the next ask.

Then reality creeps in. The reality is that fund-raising professionals are often preoccupied with:

Plans for the upcoming meeting
Follow-up for those plans
Prospect research for the next solicitation
Any number of other tasks related to the wealth and welfare of the organization

Donor recognition is the *least* of their worries, which is why it tends to wind up at the end rather than the beginning. As *proof* that it is generally relegated to the end, consider an example that comes from a country day school, where everyone was impeccably polite. No one ever forgot to write a thank-you note; the notes went out as soon as a gift came in. However, that was the last time the donor heard from the solicitor until the end of the campaign. In most cases, the solicitor went right into the next solicitation, rarely, if ever, stopping to look back.

There are terrible ramifications of treating donors this way. One predictable outcome was that donors began asking about what happened to the campaign? Was it over? Had it failed? (They had not read their printed newsletters, which proves that you cannot rely on printed materials alone.)

Donor recognition, done right, means staying in touch with the donors *after* the gift is given. It means keeping them posted, visiting them for the sake of listening and conversation. Does that sound like cultivation? *It is.* Donor recognition is nothing less than the foundation of the next ask.

Perhaps an excerpt will buttress that important point. It comes from a letter written by a donor who was treated *right* (meaning that this person received a hand-written note whenever a major gift came in, was telephoned occasionally for advice, was invited to special events, and was generally made to feel a part of the in crowd). Here is what this particular person wrote at the conclusion of the campaign:

It was great having the personal touch with someone working closely with the current school activity. It made me—and I'm sure other alumnae—feel that they had some input into current and future developments—not just monetary input.

That comment is proof of the depth of opportunity that becomes available *after* the gift is given. Fund raisers should shift from thinking of donor recognition as the end and think of it instead as the preamble to subsequent solicitations—the foundation and beginning of the next ask. Exhibit 37.11 recommends four methods of giving donor recognition.

EXHIBIT 37.11 Four Ways Donor Recognition Can be Done

1. *Donors can be recognized through a systematic and speedy acknowledgment system.* Recently, some major corporate donors have had to call a medical center (unnamed) to ask whether their pledge payments had been received, how much they still owed, and whether the money is being used for the purpose designated. To make matters worse, this has often generated lengthy games of telephone tag to hospital officials, with no call-backs.
2. *Next (these are not necessarily in priority order), donor recognition can be done by giving visibility to donors* (that is, if they want it). Gift club categories, photo/press releases, a brochure on the life and times of a really high-level donor, or a gala event, with all the attendant photography of dedicated volunteers, are all possible options.
3. *Incentives, such as umbrellas, coffee mugs, and other forms of "bribes,"* might be awarded. One can easily go overboard, especially with respect to good taste, but there is a certain place for geegaws like bumper stickers, hats, pens, and so on.
4. *A higher form of incentives deserves its own category—named gift opportunities—which can also be used in annual appeals.* Commemorative gifts include *any* opportunities for donors to put their names on something—a building, a piece of a building, an academic chair, a scholarship, or an ongoing program. In annual giving, the options are more limited, but suppose Mr. Smith is giving $25,000 a year for three years, for immediate expenditure each year on scholarships. What is wrong with calling the recipients the Smith Scholars for those three years?

Consistent policies are needed in any
program of donor recognition.

(I)   CAMPAIGN WRAP-UP

Concluding a campaign can be compared to a fine cognac: Both should leave a pleasant taste, create a warm glow, and generate good feelings for the future.

Victory celebrations depend, of course, on bringing in the bottom levels of the giving pyramid. This is sometimes done through mailings; increasingly, it is done using phone/mail approaches in which a constituency first receives a written explanation of the campaign (with advance notice that a call will be forthcoming).

One last responsibility comes with the end of a campaign: documentation. Properly documented, the capital appeal can provide a valuable informational and public relations database. One company prides itself on its "campaign case books" in which the following kinds of information are preserved:

Summary of the campaign
Chronology
The planning study
The case statement(s)
Campaign design
Campaign policies
Executive committee
Gifts by category
Progress reports
Proposals

Sample letters
Prospect research
Printed materials

(J) STRATEGIC PLANNING AND CAPITAL FUND APPEALS

Goethe once said, "Whatever you can do or dream you can do, begin it. Boldness has genius, power, and magic in it."

Yet boldness, in and of itself, is like a melody unchained. Loose, it is not sufficient—not, at least, in today's fiercely competitive philanthropic marketplace, and certainly not in the arena of capital campaigns. For success, boldness must first be harnessed, defined, and tied to realities such as time frames and budget lines.

In an ideal world, every not-for-profit board would have a strategic planning committee that envisions, defines, and dreams. Once the strategic long-range plan is complete, its periodic review and updating would continue. But this is not an ideal world. Many institutions simply arrive at a crisis—a critical crossroad—when capital needs, too long deferred, are either addressed or are not. Out of crisis, a plan (of sorts) evolves—a backward sequence, but even this scenario can provide a good start on a strategic plan, so long as it is considered the beginning of the process and not its culmination.

What, specifically, is strategic planning? Simply put, it is the process through which dreams become reality. Every institution has its own unique purpose, its own set of aspirations, its own niche. However, not every institution has set them down, much less linked them to specific objectives and target dates or budget estimates. Strategic planning can help, through the following steps:

1. Define the institution's dreams (its mission, its values, its "raison d'être").
2. Determine the factors most critical to achieving the dreams set down in step 1.
3. Identify conditions that could adversely affect the institution's attainment of the dreams set down in step 1.
4. Set objectives (with action steps, deadlines, and budgets) that are required to achieve the dreams in step 1).
5. Track performance to ensure that the objectives stated in step 4 are being met.

Taking these steps helps an institution ascertain whether its development program is progressing on target, on time, and on budget. Problems do inevitably occur, and almost every campaign stalls at some point (or at least experiences a slowdown).

Should *your* campaign stall, for any reason, do not be disheartened. All that is called for is *more* creative methods of fund raising. For example:

- In bad economic times, continue the development process unabated. Raising six- and seven-figure gifts is not severely affected by economic downturns.
- If the problem is solicitor burnout, use a variety of approaches. You might form the *workers* into an especially prestigious body—named, perhaps, the "strategy group." In this way, members of the flagging committee are replaced, but not overtly. You might try harder to underscore the *fun* in fund raising—holding

meetings in "fun" places or encouraging campaign leadership to employ "fun" gimmicks. One such meeting was made unforgettable when it was started unforgivably late. But then entered the chief executive officer, leading a full-fledged high school band playing a victory march.

- At times, attendance at meetings becomes an issue. Something as simple as changing to a business location can be effective; so can faxing the agenda on the day of the meeting. A very businesslike tone can completely reverse a low-attendance problem.

An overall strategic plan is not affected by such slowdowns. In fact, slowdowns are a good reason for having a plan in the first place. Only if you know where you are headed can you see whether you are getting there. Can you imagine setting out from shore without a chart by which to navigate a ship? A capital campaign plan is no different; nor is it very different from the institution's overall strategic plan. It is just more specific. Exhibit 37.12 compares the principles that drive these two critical elements of a capital campaign.

Many campaign plans begin with a decision to conduct a professional planning study. The purpose of the study is to assess various key constituencies as to their views on the institution's case, leadership, and sources of support.

Negative as well as positive factors are considered in the study. Weaknesses help to alert the institution to obstacles that will have to be overcome. Typically, these are misconceptions about the institution or a discovery that board development is needed to heighten fund-raising clout.

The study looks for leaders, not workers. The idea is that if you have the right generals, the other ranks will fall into place. Without the right generals at the right levels, workers cannot achieve the goal.

It also seeks to establish a realistic fund-raising goal, based on the projected needs of the institution. Each study is, therefore, a tailor-made response to an institution's particular circumstances. However, certain common elements are generally included—a timetable for the campaign, a recommended organizational chart, and, in some cases, a set of pledge and cash-flow projections. Samples of each are given in Exhibits 37.13, 37.14, and 37.15, respectively.

The need for your organization to get organized—and stay organized—throughout any capital fund appeal should be clear. One step to ensure success is to conduct the study (just as a doctor consults an X ray before performing surgery). Another step is to

---

EXHIBIT 37.12 Strategic Planning Principles as Related to Capital Campaigns

Strategic Plan	Campaign Plan
Mission	Mission
Future vision	Future vision
Needed to accomplish	Needs
Strengths/weaknesses	Rationale
Issues, goals, objectives	Campaign goal
Timetable	Timetable
Budget	Budget

EXHIBIT 37.13 Campaign Timetable

Summary of campaign activity (by quarter)

	Year 1				Year 2				Year 3				Year 4			
	2nd	3rd	4th	1st	2nd	3rd	4th	1st	2nd	3rd	4th	1st	2nd	3rd	4th	

LEADERSHIP ENLISTMENT:
Enlist chairperson of the Nucleus Fund
Enlist Nucleus Fund Committee
Enlist chairperson of the campaign
Enlist honorary chairpersons
Enlist Regional Screening chairpersons/committees
Enlist Leadership Gifts Division chairperson
Enlist chairperson for Individual Gifts
Enlist chairperson for Corporate Gifts
Enlist key leaders for selected colleges
Enlist Major Gifts Division chairperson
Enlist Regional Major Gifts chairpersons
Enlist Regional Major Gifts committees
Enlist Special Gifts chairperson

PROSPECT SCREENING
Rate and assign the Board of Directors
Rate and assign Campaign Executive Committee
Research targets of opportunity
Rate and assign targets of opportunity
Screen leadership prospects
Screen regional prospects
Screen prospects in other states
Research prospects at $1,000,000 and above
Research prospects at $1,000,000 to $100,000
Research prospects at $1,000,000 to $10,000

REGIONAL ACTIVITY
Determine regional campaign goal(s)
Assign staff to regional offices
Schedule regional training for solicitors
Schedule regional cultivation

SPECIAL EVENTS AND PUBLICATIONS
Complete the case statement
Write campaign documents and audiovisual presentation
Produce campaign documents and audiovisual presentation
Schedule campaign kick-off announcement

EXHIBIT 37.14 Campaign Organizational Chart

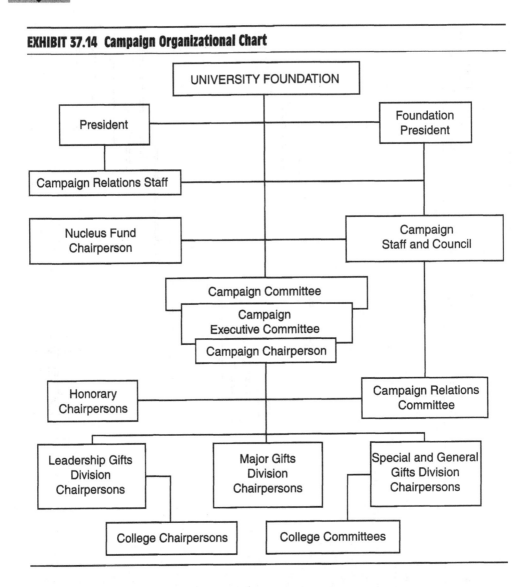

retain an experienced professional to manage the effort. Campaign management will be necessary, in some form, to succeed in the following functions (at the very least):

Keep meetings and solicitations on track.
Tend to the details of prospect research.
Develop strategies appropriate for each major solicitation.
Help prevent the campaign from stalling out or losing momentum.
Handle gift receipts, acknowledgments, and giving records.
Orchestrate donor recognition (including publicity).

When such duties are added to the workload of existing staff, critical details can (and do) tend to slip through the cracks. A preferable alternative is to bring a person aboard

EXHIBIT 37.15 Cash Flow/Pledge Flow Projections For a Capital Campaign

Campaign Quarter Ending	Projected Cash	Actual Cash	Projected Cumulative Cash	Actual Cumulative Cash	Projected Cumulative Pledges	Actual Cumulative Pledges	Projected Cumulative Expenses	Actual Cumulative Expenses	Projected Net Income	Actual Net Income
12/31/84		$80,000		$80,000		$166,131	$100,000	$55,822	$(100,000)	$24,278
03/31/85		$78,767		158,767		264,931	190,000	119,979	(190,000)	38,788
06/30/85	50,000	149,312	50,000	308,079		1,124,931	295,000	203,014	(245,000)	105,065
09/30/85	75,000	115,843	125,000	423,922	2,500,000	3,005,628	385,000	264,396	(260,000)	159,526
12/31/85	385,000	677,561	510,000	1,101,483	3,687,000	3,624,878	495,000	324,432	15,000	777,051
03/31/86	100,000	133,086	610,000	1,234,569	4,875,000	5,609,148	595,000	419,038	15,000	815,531
06/30/86	525,000	249,308	1,135,000	1,483,877	6,062,500	6,639,376	675,000	505,119	460,000	978,758
09/30/86	500,000	716,380	1,635,000	2,200,257	7,250,000	7,509,372	762,000	589,699	873,000	1,610,558
12/31/86	900,000	1,222,034	2,535,000	3,422,291	8,437,500	12,418,494	875,000	650,911	1,660,000	2,771,380
03/31/87	450,000	191,688	2,985,000	3,613,979	9,625,000	13,599,747	975,000	719,105	2,010,000	2,894,874
06/30/87	750,000	1,057,337[1]	3,735,000	4,671,316	10,812,500	14,068,066*	1,075,000	N/A	2,660,000	N/A
09/30/87	850,000		4,585,000		12,000,000		1,182,200		3,402,800	

[1] Includes $916,000 payment through the buy-back of donated closely held stock anticipated in this quarter.

*Includes three gifts totaling $400,000 that will be confirmed in writing by the end of the quarter.

who not only qualifies to direct the campaign but who might be considered for future openings in the development operation. Another alternative is to retain the services of a professional consultant to manage the effort for a specified period of time. There are three basic reasons that you might select a consultant:

1. *Objectivity.* Starting as early as the study, counsel tends to be told things by donors and prospective donors that people inside the institution have not been told. This same objectivity ensures that "the case" of the institution is conveyed in a way that will communicate to outsiders.
2. *Instant expertise.* The experience of counsel is based on a variety of campaigns. Breadth, as well as depth, helps keep the campaign on course while avoiding pitfalls along the way.
3. *Cost effectiveness.* Counsel can provide campaign staff for a precise amount of time and in the precise area of expertise required, which avoids the costs of hiring, training, and carrying benefits and eliminates the need to suffer through an expensive learning curve.

The purpose of counsel is to be both active and reactive: *active* in offering new ideas and suggesting new initiatives, and *reactive* in observing, listening, analyzing, and responding to the circumstances of the moment. Ideally, client and counsel function as a partnership, not as a hierarchy. The "horizontal" approach to counsel maximizes the sense of teamwork that is so critical to success, with counsel used primarily for purposes of planning and strategy. The benefits of hiring campaign counsel include the following:

Feasibility	Training
Planning	Expertise
Discipline	Sounding board
Ideas	Influence
Strategies and tactics	Publications
Resources	Research
Tracking systems	Guidance
Models	Enlistment of leadership
Solutions	Identification of new prospects
Access	

For more on the benefits and use of campaign counsel, refer to Chapter 46 "Fundraising Consultants."

Suggested Readings

Brakeley, George A., Jr. *Tested Ways to Successful Fund-Raising.* New York: AMACOM, 1980.

Council for the Advancement of Secondary Education. CASE Conference Presentation, Toronto, Canada (December 1980).

Gurin, Maurice G. *What Volunteers Should Know for Successful Fund-Raising.* New York: Stein and Day, 1981.

Hutler, Albert A. *Guide to Successful Fund-Raising.* New York: Business Reports, Inc., 1977.

Kerness, Elton J. *Fund-Raising.* Carteret, N.J.: Cottage Press, 1985.

National Association of Hospital Development. *Effective Utilization of Fund-Raising Counsel.* Panel Presentation Report, NAHD Convention, Chicago, 1980.

Raybin, Arthur. *How to Hire the Right Fund-Raising Consultant.* Washington, D.C.: The Taft Group, 1985.

Seymour, Harold J. *Designs for Fund-Raising.* Ambler, Pa.: Fund-Raising Institute, 1988.

Soroker, Gerald S. *Fund-Raising for Philanthropy.* Pittsburgh: Jewish Publication and Education Foundation, 1974.

Warner, Irving R. *The Art of Fund-Raising.* New York: Bantam Books, 1988.

Planned Giving: Gift Vehicles

LYNDA S. MOERSCHBAECHER, JD, MBA
ERIK D. DRYBURGH, JD, CPA
Silk, Adler & Colvin

Parts of this chapter are excerpted from *Plain English Planned Giving: Starting at Square One, Plain English Planned Giving: Working Effectively With Your Donors*, copyright © 1996 by Lynda S. Moerschbaecher, and *Marketing Magic for Major/Planned Gifts*, book and audiotapes. These books are part of the *Plain English Planned Giving* series of books and tapes, and the excerpts are reprinted with permission.

(c) Intangibles

(d) Mortgaged Property

(e) Unrelated Business Income

(f) Self-Dealing

(g) Environmental Liability

Suggested Readings

Recommended Periodicals and Newsletters

38.1 Determining the Planned Giving Program

An assessment of the current development effort is the first step in determining an organization's planned giving program. The assessment can be viewed as having three parts:

1. The organization of the development effort must be viewed in its entirety and the role and sophistication of each part of the development office must be understood.
2. The gift history and the state of the donor records must be analyzed to determine the availability of immediate markets for planned giving.
3. The internal and external capabilities of the organization must be understood.

(A) ORGANIZATION OF THE CURRENT DEVELOPMENT FUNCTION

(i) Sources of Revenue Production

The development effort consists of various programs that are revenue sources for the organization. Although they may be called different names by different institutions, generally only a handful of programs are regularly used to generate fund-raising revenue. Before a planned giving program is established, an annual giving program, to which donors are encouraged to give on a regular and recurring basis, is in place. There may also be a major gift program for the purpose of generating larger gifts, which donors would not make on a recurring basis. Typically an organization also has two types of special events: (1) those that produce revenue and (2) those that are held for the purpose of thanking or recognizing donors. The organization may also engage in special appeals by phone or by mail, which may or may not be part of the annual giving program. Finally, the organization may seek support from corporations and foundations (and, perhaps, the government).

These programs do not imply any particular organizational chart. One person may be performing all functions in a one-person development shop, or a very large organization may have 100 people staffing a development office. No matter the size or structure, these are basic, generic, revenue-raising programs of a development office. Planned giving must fit into this development effort and coordinate with the other parts of the development office. From the point of view of adding another program and making it work, the most important factors are what it is designed to achieve and how it will fit with what is already in place.

To understand this coordination, one must focus specifically on two parts of the development office—annual giving and major gifts. The annual giving program is designed to attract continual, recurring, and, ideally, increasing support that is to be used for everyday operating budgetary needs. Directly opposed in philosophy is the major gift program, which is designed to reach donors for a special-effort gift beyond the amount they can ordinarily give every year. There is an inherent possibility of tension between these two development roles. Major gifts might be viewed as "nonrecurring"; even though they may occasionally recur, they will not recur every year. If they did, the gifts would be classified as annual gifts.

If major gifts are defined as nonrecurring larger transfers that a donor undertakes once or only a few times in his or her giving life, then, in large part, planned giving must fall within this definition because planned gifts are undertaken as a special effort on the donor's part. However, major gifts and planned gifts differ in an important way. Major gifts are generally in liquid form—cash, marketable securities, and the like. Planned gifts may be viewed as a subset of these major gifts: "Planned" means that the gifts require structuring in a legal or accounting sense. Planned gifts must also be distinguished from deferred gifts. A planned gift may very well be an outright contribution of, for instance, closely held stock or real estate. It is a major gift from the donor's point of view, no matter the form or amount of gift structuring. Thus, definitionally, all planned gifts are major gifts, but not all major gifts are planned gifts. Planned giving is thus a subset of major giving.

In turn, some planned gifts are made without current receipt by the charity. These are *deferred* gifts, such as pooled income funds, charitable remainder trusts, and bequests. Some are irrevocable, others are revocable. Deferred gifts are, despite their name, made *currently* by the donor; it is the organization that views them as deferred. It would be more correct to call them deferred receipts. They are major commitments by donors and are, therefore, major gifts that are planned and structured. As such, deferred gifts are a subset of planned gifts, which are a subset of major gifts. Again, this definition does not necessarily imply organizational structure of the development office for management purposes.

(ii) Use of the Revenue Produced by Various Programs
The various fund-raising revenue sources produce spendable funds. How they may be spent falls within three categories: (1) operational use, (2) endowment, and (3) capital spending. It is really quite simple on the expenditure side. However, what is less known is that revenue from any of these sources may be used in any one of the three expenditure categories. Experience may indicate that funds raised in an annual giving program are used for operational expenses. However, those funds may be restricted to endowment if the donor so designates. Often it is assumed that major gifts feed into capital or endowment use, whereas bequests and other planned gifts generally feed into endowment; however, that is not necessarily true. Planned gifts may very well be used for any one of the three possible uses of fund-raising revenue.

It may be helpful to define endowment here. Endowment has meaning both in the law and in accounting. There are different types of endowment. If a donor places a restriction on a gift so that the income (or some percentage of the value of the assets of the endowment fund, where that type of endowment spending rule is adopted in lieu of true income) is to be spent but the principal is to be held and invested, that is true endowment, donor-restricted and respected in the law. That restriction may not be changed, other than in states that have adopted the Uniform Management of Institutional Funds Act, which permits a donor to release a written restriction by a later writing or by petition to a court on a cy-pres action (to change the purpose to another very similar). A board or other body may change the restriction where such discretion was expressly given to that body in writing by the donor.

Many organizations employ a different type of endowment in addition to true endowment. An endowment fund may be created by board resolution and then be held as if it were endowment. This type of endowment is called quasi-endowment or funds functioning as endowment. Where the board has designated funds as endowment, it may later undo the restriction. Some endowment funds are specified to be held for a definite term, after which they are to be spent. These are often called temporary endowments or term endowments.

"Endowment" is a word that is often used too loosely, and that may create problems. For example, if an organization promoted and publicized a gift-giving opportunity as one that "endows" a specific project or program, but it misused the term "endow," it would find that donors could compel it to hold the funds as endowment. A contract or understanding and reliance by the donor may have been inadvertently created. Thus, proper use of the term is essential.

Endowment also has significance for accounting. It must be separately held from operational funds and, in fact, the true endowment must be accounted for separately from the quasi-endowment.

Capital projects may have some of the same problems as caused by the use of the term "endowment." If a donor has been led to believe that his or her gift is to be used for a capital project, a contract or detrimental reliance may have occurred, and the donor may be able to compel such usage.

The end uses of funds are important to understand, especially once an organization begins an even more complex program such as planned giving.

(B) ANALYSIS OF GIFT HISTORY AND STATE OF DONOR RECORDS

The second part of the assessment is to review the past support of the organization to determine the strength of the major gift and annual giving efforts. This step is important in understanding whether the organization needs additional help in creating commitment equivalent to that required for planned gifts. Not every organization is ready to support a planned gift effort.

The donor base should be analyzed by gift level, by gift consistency (on a per-donor basis), and by the increase in giving by individual donors. This analysis can best be done with good, organized, computerized records. The process is similar to that of planning for a capital campaign. The goal is to ferret out early planned giving successes while also undertaking the planning and preparation for wider marketing.

As identified in this study, the donors who have already given to the institution should become the first to be cultivated for planned gifts. If the organization finds few or no donors who have already committed support to the organization on a consistent and increasing basis, perhaps other work is necessary before attempting a planned giving program.

(C)   INTERNAL AND EXTERNAL CAPABILITY

The third step in the assessment of the readiness of the current program involves a testing of the capability of the organization, internally and externally, to undertake a planned giving program. Internal readiness requires the ability of the development office and the finance and administration office to handle the program. Both offices must have staff time available. The development office must have a budget for planned giving, office space for the staff person, support staff assigned to the staff person, and a written understanding with the board in the form of resolutions, guidelines, or other formats, indicating the board's willingness to give the new program time (and support) to succeed. Large capital transfers do not come to an institution without considerable cultivation. Boards and executive directors too often demand immediate dollar goals. In the early stages, goals should be set in terms of identifiable steps toward successful cultivation of prospective donors. Perhaps an initial number of prospects to be seen during the first year can be set. In any event, the board and executive director must understand the different nature of this program and guarantee their willingness to become actively involved.

The finance and administration office must be willing to learn the administration and record keeping required by the new gift vehicles. It may also need to learn specific rules of investment of property transferred outright or in trust, and how to undertake the sale and reinvestment of certain types of assets. Whether gifts such as pooled income funds, charitable gift annuities, charitable remainder and lead trusts are administered inhouse or not, much new information must be processed regularly. Specific, written procedures must be developed so that gift acknowledgment, income checks, annual reports, and the like do not slip between the cracks.

How the organization conveys to the public its new program effort will set the tone for the program. External relations must be handled both by development and public relations. Planned giving requires the formation of new relationships with the outside world. The financial world can be a strong ally to the program. Relationships must be developed by the planned giving officer with trustees, investment advisors, certified public accountants, attorneys, chartered life underwriters, and certified financial planners. The public relations department must support the development office in its attempt to reach the right persons in the right way.

38.2   *Understanding the Proposed Planned Giving Program*

(A)   A PROGRAM IS MORE THAN THE SUM OF ITS VEHICLES

A planned giving program is more than the sum of the various gift vehicles to be used. It includes the gift vehicles and the gift structuring to meet an individual donor's financial situation. The program, however, is the overall effort to bring prospective donors to the institution, to utilize life income gifts to their fullest advantage, and to organize, manage, and implement staff and volunteer efforts to bring gifts of a sophisticated nature to fruition. Is it something new? Not really. A Community Chest brochure dated 1948, entitled "Looking Ahead," recited the need for long-range support and suggested ways to provide it: a bequest, a trust paying income to the donor, a trust paying income to the Community Chest, and a revocable trust. Thus, it appears that current vehicles are hardly new. Only the rules are new (and ever changing).

If not new, is the program different from other fund-raising programs? In some respects, it is not. Planned giving is fund raising and, therefore, involves general fund-raising principles. Many things are different, however. Planned giving is a highly technical, highly personalized, and highly structured area of development. It is different from other fund-raising programs because it is multifaceted. It requires significant planning and organizing in-house, it necessitates education or retraining of staff assigned to it, and it involves gift planning for prospective donors. New types of record keeping, reports to donors and governmental agencies, and choices of degree of institutional involvement are required. For example, the board must decide whether it will undertake the fiduciary responsibilities of handling the pooled income fund or being the trustee of charitable trusts, or whether it has sufficient in-house expertise to invest the funds entrusted to it.

The vehicles used are tax-oriented and require substantial time and effort to understand. A simple understanding of the gift vehicles does not mean one is capable of engaging in creative planning techniques with these vehicles. A depth of knowledge in financial and estate planning in general provides the framework for fully utilizing the charitable gift vehicles. Even with such knowledge, continual updating on events of significance is crucial. Thus, in addition to the organization, planning, and administration necessary for the development office, the planned giving officer and his or her outside advisors have continual educational needs.

"Planned giving," as the term is used here, can be defined from either of two perspectives—that of the donor or that of the organization. From the donor's point of view, it is the thinking, the planning, the garnering of the best benefits for self, spouse, family, and others (generally in that order). From the perspective of the organization, it is the consistent *effort* at developing gifts that are "structured," are not recurring annually, and are designed to meet a donor's needs and objectives, which effort includes the planning, marketing, and delivery of appropriate gift structures and vehicles.

If planned giving from the organization's point of view is a consistent effort at achieving planned gifts, that effort will require certain other things, such as a budget, a staff, time, and a plan. It will have to be evaluated. Others, such as the board and the community professionals, can be asked to help. Central to the success of the effort is the choice of the planned giving officer. Each of these items is of concern to management.

(i) Budget

The amount an organization will have to budget will depend on the scope of the program to be undertaken, but the scope of the program may be limited at the outset by budgetary constraints. Thus, budget and scope of program must be dealt with simultaneously. There are many things to consider when setting the budget, and different organizations require different budget items to be picked up by departments. For example, some offices may be required to put into their budgets an item for rent and office overhead; other institutions may not charge this item to departmental budgets. Thus, the budget model offered here (see Exhibit 38.1) is a general checklist of items to consider in light of specific practices.

A planned giving program is a person-to-person, close-contact effort, and it will require some expenses other programs do not. The marketing and cultivation are indeed different.

EXHIBIT 38.1 Budget Items to Consider

Staff salaries
Employee benefits
Rent
Phone
Office overhead (indirect costs)
Office equipment:

typewriter	calculators
computer plus software	dictaphone
printer	transcriber
modem	fax machine

Fixtures and furnishings
Office supplies: paper, letterhead, labels, other
List rental
Expenses for mailings: graphics, typesetting, printing, label or mailing house
Postage
Brochures and newsletters in bulk (custom or purchased)
Consulting/Legal/Accounting
Continuing professional education and association membership for employees
Reimbursement for volunteers
Entertainment and meals
Travel and lodging
Library: books, newsletters, journals
Seminars: speakers, refreshments, room rental, audiovisual equipment, photocopies, postage, follow-up mailings, etc.
New program development
Marketing research/consultants
Advertisements

(ii) Time Commitment

Starting a planned giving program is not dissimilar to starting a new business. An entrepreneur can provide insights about the start-up phase of the business that are definitely applicable to beginning a planned giving program. It will require a commitment of time by the staff and by the entity as a whole. The board and management must be prepared to fund the effort without expectation of immediate receipts. Even when gifts are closed, they are often in deferred form and the funds will not be available for many years. Thus, the organization starting a program must be secure enough financially to see the planned giving program through its start-up phase.

It is often said that it will take three to five years for a planned giving program to be up and running with a good flow of closed gifts. This is true not only because it is a start-up endeavor, but also because of the nature of what donors are being asked to do. A planned gift is often in the form of a bequest or a trust. To undertake such a gift, the donor must do his or her estate or financial planning. That process alone may take several months, and even years, for some people. For some donors, the thought of doing estate planning is something to put off because of the indication of finality and mortality. For these reasons, donors in this area of fund raising cannot be pushed; the time constraints of a capital campaign or annual giving do not apply.

The board and management must come to terms with this problem. Often they are eager to have a planned giving program, but, after a few months, they want to know where the money is and whether the funds they have already invested in the program have been wasted. This shortsighted attitude must be avoided if planned giving is to succeed. Management should satisfy itself that planned giving is feasible for the organization at the time it is proposed, and that the organizational efforts are proceeding at a normal pace. Projections and expectations can be a part of the plans, but the truth is that, at the beginning, dollar goals are nigh impossible to set. Later, after some experience with the particular donor base, goals may be established.

It may be wise to set out, in writing, the time commitment on the part of management and the development officer. This written understanding, although not at all binding, may serve to keep things on track. It should cover the commitment in terms of the dollars and years the board or chief executive officer (CEO) is willing to agree to. It should also cover the intended effort and time frame planned by the staff and should arrange for written evaluations to be submitted periodically, analyzing whether the program is on schedule.

(iii)   Staff Attention

No matter how many people are engaged in the planned giving effort, certain tasks must be accomplished. For example, a clerical support staff is necessary because of the volume of written materials, the amount of donor contact, and the preparation for donor and professional seminars. Legal help will no doubt be required at some point. Gift administration must be done correctly. Someone must make the actual contacts with the prospects. Finally, substantial marketing must be done to ensure continual donor acquisition. All these tasks either have to be done by or supervised by the person in charge of planned giving. If a part-time person is in charge, he or she will be very busy.

Several different models of staffing have been tried, ranging from those with a CEO who does everything to an office with several planned gift officers. In between, there may be a one-person development office or a part-time or even a full-time person assigned to planned giving. If the staffing model assigns the staff person to multiple programs in the development office for which he or she is responsible, that person is often called away from the planned gift duties for more immediate chores. As a result, the planned gift effort never gets proper attention. However, it has been shown again and again that planned giving simply will not succeed without dedicated attention. With that kind of attention, even if given part-time, a planned giving program can succeed nicely.

(iv)   Scope of the Program

An important decision at the beginning of the program is how much to undertake all at once. This concern is interwoven with concerns of staffing and budget. A planned gift program may be as simple as a bequest program or as complex as sophisticated estate planning with closely held stock, involving several generations of the donor's family. Once again, between the extremes, there are many levels to choose from.

The decision regarding how extensive a program to undertake must entail an honest examination of the numerous tasks involved in each gift vehicle selected. For example, if a pooled income fund is to be established, documents have to be prepared, an explanation for Securities and Exchange Commission (SEC) purposes must be written, a trustee must be selected, marketing materials must be chosen or created, the donor base must be studied for suitable prospects, marketing must be implemented, responses must be made to inquiries, proposals must be written, calculations must be performed, perhaps one or more visits must be made, assets must be transferred, files must be created, computer databases must be updated, administration must be set up for the gift, and so on. Even these requirements are set forth in cursory fashion; the actual job is much more detailed. When multiplied by the number of vehicles chosen, the number of tasks may become overwhelming for the time available by staff. Thus, some thought must be given to the size of the program. Too many gift vehicles undertaken at once may result in no success with any of them.

It should be made clear that selecting the scope of the program means choosing those gift vehicles the staff will consistently pursue and market. That does not prevent the organization from accepting a different type of gift offered "over the transom." Over time, of course, the organization can adopt other gift vehicles.

(v)   Chronology of the Creation of the Program

It is wise to write out a plan of action for the first year of the program, knowing that it probably will change during that year. It serves both as a guide and as a tool for evaluation of what has been achieved. Because, under the assessment described thus far, every program will have a different starting point, each chronology will be different. The scope of the program and the budget will also vary. Nevertheless, certain things have to be done in order to succeed at planned giving. Included in Exhibit 38.2 is a chronology for an organization just starting its program with a new staff person. This is only a hypothetical example; each organization must create its own chronology, based on its needs.

(vi)   Evaluating the Progress

When the chronology of action is set out month by month, the sequential steps serve as the best tool for evaluating the progress of the establishment of the program. At the beginning of the month, the planned giving officer has a set number of goals to accomplish. At the end of each month, he or she should report on whether each has been accomplished, and, if not, what obstacle may have prevented the accomplishment. If the same problem keeps cropping up month after month, it will become evident and can be dealt with by management. After six months, a formal report should outline whether the program is on track. After 12 months, a new 12-month plan should be prepared.

(B)   ROLE OF THE BOARD IN PLANNED GIVING

Commitment is critical to the success of the program, but few people adequately address what that commitment really means. It means *owning* the concept, actually taking part and making it one's own. The board must undertake this type of commitment. No major program will take place or succeed without the board's understanding and support. That is a known and accepted fact for all types of programs undertaken by a corporate body.

Although most staff people understand that commitment is necessary, many misunderstand the feelings and motivations of the board members. The idea of getting board members involved is often overdone by organizations undertaking a planned giving program. Rather than getting a board member motivated and engaged, they bludgeon the board members either by overemphasizing the necessity of involvement in the program or by insisting on contributions to the program. *Neither of these tactics will result in board involvement or commitment.* Just as philanthropy has to be voluntary, so does com-

EXHIBIT 38.2 Chronology of the Creation of a Planned Giving Program

Month	Internal Work	External Work

Month 1	Budget
	Contract (understanding of
	    employment), if not done earlier
	Current fund-raising effort analysis
	Matrix
	Volunteers
	Study of organization
	Meet key people
		Meet with consultants, interview,
		    select
		Review computer systems—data
		Meet key people

Month 2	Board treaty Plan committees Confidentiality Ethics Committee action plan	Visit prospective members
Month 3	Marketing plan Begin planned giving Case Traditional guidelines	Meet with selected marketing advisers Survey of trustees; interview
Month 4	Define scope of program Board treaty approval Begin marketing brochure, funding opportunities Products	Meet with marketing committee Meet with volunteer committee Meet with board members Meet with technical advisors
Month 5	Marketing plan Internal training lunch Case Products Seminars to attend Volunteer book Begin legal work	Meet with marketing committee Assessment of finance and administration (F&A) unit Meet with lawyers; select
Month 6	Core group prospects; assign Brochures, newsletters Staff meetings Legal work	Meet with financial community F&A procedures Meet with public relations (PR) personnel Meet with volunteer committee
Month 7	Core group strategy Bequest plan Newsletter Proposals Legal work Plan donor seminars; board seminar	Meet with marketing community F&A procedures
Month 81	Bequest plan Proposals Donor seminar Board seminar Legal documents Marketing brochure	Meet with volunteer committee Meet with lawyer

EXHIBIT 38.2 (*Continued*)

Month	Internal Work	External Work
Month 9	Gift credit; recognition Idea mailing Target seminars Core group follow-up	Computer systems—financial Meet with marketing committee Board thanks (personal) to volunteers
Month 10	Staff meeting Follow-up on idea mailing Targeted seminars Follow-up	PR—media access Meet with volunteer committee
Month 11	Replace committee members Recognition mailing Idea mailing Gift procedures	Meet with technical committee at institution Meet with board chairperson, others
Month 12	Follow-up on responses Elderly program Recognition event	Chat cultivation Visit financial advisors Volunteer committee's 12-month review

mitment. Overbearing tactics have resulted in a negative attitude: "Planned giving is just not right for us at this time."

The board has to be willing to participate in several policy decisions, among them a policy regarding the confidentiality of donor information, a decision to accept the fiduciary role that planned giving requires (not trusteeship), a policy concerning ethics in planned giving, policies and procedures for the acceptance of real estate in light of environmental liability, and others as they come up in the administration of the program. Generally, to make wise decisions regarding the liability of the institution and the board members' own liability, a committee of the board should study and analyze the issues and make recommendations to the full board. Issues such as liability for hazardous waste cannot be addressed in a crisis. They must be thought through when the board is not faced with a problem that may cost thousands or, in some cases, millions of dollars. Thus, the planned giving officer will need the attention of some or all of the board to present these issues.

Board members can also play a vital role in opening doors and making contact with prospects for the planned giving officer. They should be asked to play a role with which they feel comfortable to function; not many are comfortable with solicitations. Allowing a board member in a role in which he or she is comfortable will achieve better results and will prevent "burnout" of the board member.

(C) PLANNED GIFT COMMITTEES

For quite some time, the use of a planned giving committee has been in vogue. Most often, however, it does not seem to work well and the committee members do not quite seem to know what their function is. The problem lies in part with the selection or mix of the committee members. The wrong mix of people can result because the creator of the committee did not clearly focus on what the committee was supposed to accomplish.

Because the committee is often not focused, the planned giving officer may begin to "make work" for the committee. Soon thereafter, the committee falls apart and members start to drop out of meetings.

One must ask whether there is a role at all for a "planned giving" committee. If so, perhaps the role or job description of the committee should be written out and discussed with each prospective committee member. In fact, committees may play several different roles, such as the board policy committee, referred to earlier, to explore issues the board must address. There may be a need for a technical or professional advisory committee and, perhaps, a marketing committee. Each, then, would be focused solely on its task and not burdened with other tasks the members may not be interested in or qualified for.

The most common problem occurs when a committee of attorneys and other professionals who have never before been involved with the organization is asked to address some serious planned giving issues, such as those the board policy committee should be addressing. Concerns that involve a board member's legal exposure should not be handed off to a committee of new people who have no experience with the organization; neither should issues that affect the entity's image or legal liability. These issues and recommendations should rest with a committee that is "close to the heart" of the organization.

Thus, forming a planned giving committee of professionals who may understand a donor's perspective in financial planning may not serve the institution effectively and may produce decisions that are not in accord with long-established policies and procedures for the organization. In addition, the bulk of the work in planned giving is marketing—both the research and the outreach to appropriate markets (not the technical side). Would a group of financial professionals really understand the long-term marketing needs of a fund-raising program? Committees can be made to be very effective, but their focus and purpose for existence must be clearly understood by all before they are created.

(D) USE OF CONSULTANTS

At the beginning of a program, the organization may need the help of a consultant. How to choose a consultant is always a question, because many people offer their services as "planned giving consultants." It is necessary to separate them into categories according to the expertise they offer. These categories are as follows:

- *Donor visits and solicitations.* This type of consultant participates in a program almost as an additional staff member, helping with specifically identified donor visits for the purpose of cultivation or solicitation. This person can be a beneficial extension of the current ability to carry on a planned giving program. Quite often, this consultant works with smaller organizations in which either an executive director or a development director performs all the functions and there is no planned giving staff member.
- *Evaluations of donor records and feasibility of program.* This type of consultant often works on a project basis, as opposed to an ongoing consulting relationship. This service may be combined with other forms of consulting done on an ongoing basis. The purpose of using this consultant is to get a reading on whether the organization's donor history would support the beginnings of a planned giving program.

- *All duties—substitute for staff.* Some smaller organizations wishing to undertake planned giving cannot afford to hire a full-time staff person. A consultant may work for such an organization one or two days per week, on an independent contractor basis, and generally act as a planned giving staff person. Many of these consultants work for several organizations at the same time.
- *Technical support—tax and legal.* Some consultants who are not attorneys or CPAs are nevertheless quite competent in the areas of providing technical support for a program. Such support might include writing or reviewing brochures and newsletters and becoming involved with the organization in its gift structuring for prospects.
- *Marketing support.* Marketing consultants are not used often enough in planned giving programs. They can perform marketing studies and help to identify target markets. With their help, markets can be expanded beyond those the organization is aware of. They can also work toward designing more effective methods of communications to reach those markets.
- *Internal structure, management, and funds administration.* This type of consultant reviews the internal management structure for its strengths, weaknesses, needs for coordination, and readiness to undertake a planned giving program. At the initial stages of planned giving or in reviving a planned giving program, this consultant is absolutely necessary. Early coordination among the various offices, particularly those involving fund administration, is crucial to laying a good foundation for planned giving.
- *Board strengthening.* Consultants who work with not-for-profit boards are known to planned giving consultants and to development offices and not-for-profit organization executives as well. If there are extreme problems with the strength of the board, or with filling vacancies, this type of consultant can be very helpful.

The organization should carefully assess its own strengths and weaknesses and choose a consultant whose strengths are in the areas of the organization's weaknesses. In this way, the combination will form the best team. The purchaser may find that the consultants themselves have never considered their own strengths and weaknesses, or their areas of specialty. Very few consultants can be expert in all the areas enumerated in the preceding list. It is critical to ferret out the level of expertise of a particular consultant and to get recommendations.

The organization should address the question of fees early in its conversations with consultants. Some staff at not-for-profit organizations offer low-cost consultant services; they do not involve the overhead of a person or company in the consulting business full time. On the other hand, those in the business full time may have broader experience with different types of organizations and can carry the best and most successful ideas from one organization to the next.

In judging the qualifications of a consultant, an organization should consider these points:

- General reputation
- Referral by other organizations
- Reputation among industry groups such as NSFRE (National Society of Fund Raising Executives), AHP (Association for Healthcare Philanthropy), CASE

(Council for Advancement and Support of Education), NCPG (National Committee on Planned Giving), and the Committee on Gift Annuities (which covers *all* planned giving vehicles now, even though its specialty is still gift annuities)
- Length of time in field and breadth of contact with different types of nonprofits
- Former or current fund-raising staff:
  - Possible problem with ability to transfer skills.
  - Possible problem where planned giving staff member of an ongoing program becomes a consultant and has never created a planned giving program. A successful program at another organization does not necessarily make one a good consultant, particularly if the planned giving staff person came into an ongoing program.
  - Possible advantage of current, hands-on experience.

The consultant should also be asked to explain his or her policy regarding contracts. Some consultants require a noncancelable contract for a set period of time; others perform services on an at-will basis. (See Chapter 46, "Fund-Raising Consultants," for more information.)

(E) SELECTING AN ATTORNEY

The process of planned giving will no doubt require the help of an attorney from time to time. It would be wise to choose this person ahead of time. Attorneys with experience in planned giving, especially from the organization's point of view, are hard sometimes to find. Consider these types of attorneys when selecting:

- *Fund-raising attorney.* Certain attorneys specializing in working with fund raisers and have knowledge of both fund-raising techniques and legal questions that arise during the fund-raising process, as well as funds administration, exempt organization matters, and related questions. It is especially helpful if this attorney has had staff experience either as in-house legal counsel or directly in fund raising.
- *Exempt organization lawyer.* This lawyer often has knowledge both in exempt organization legal and tax status matters, and in charitable giving. This specialist can be very helpful with a planned giving program, but will be almost as difficult to find as a fund-raising attorney.
- *Tax lawyer or estate planner.* Many tax lawyers and estate planners have some degree of knowledge of charitable vehicles. However, even if they have a great deal of knowledge of charitable vehicles, they may not necessarily understand the donor/donee relationship or *the needs of the not-for-profit itself.* These people may be advocates or representatives of an individual client; nevertheless, they may be very knowledgeable in gift structures. The only caution for a not-for-profit organization is that the structures they propose may be for the benefit of the individual client-donor as opposed to the best structure for the organization-donee.
- *Business lawyer.* Business lawyers generally do not have a great knowledge of charitable giving, but if this is the only type of lawyer available, it may be worth-

while to undertake training him or her. A good business lawyer will try to work out creative solutions and help his or her client *make* things happen. That quality is invaluable in a charitable giving attorney as well.

- *Large general law firm.* Large law firms almost always have expertise in the various traditional areas of law. A large law firm may or may not have a charitable giving specialist; the number of law firms with an in-house charitable giving specialist is small but growing. If the firm does not have a specialist in this field, what happens when charitable giving questions arise? Sometimes these are assigned to someone the partners feel either has time to learn it or is already working in an area that is closely aligned with the question asked. The not-for-profit should follow the assignment closely, because there have been many reports of organizations being charged for the education of the attorney.

  One advantage of a law firm is that it offers many attorneys with expertise in different areas, so that when an unusual question comes up, perhaps regarding securities, contracts, patents, real estate, or the like, there will be someone in the law firm who can respond to that question—usually for an extra consulting fee. The advantages and disadvantages of the general large law firm should be carefully weighed.

- *Purchase of a name.* Quite often, not-for-profit boards are impressed with "big-name" law firms and, for specific projects, they want to attach a "big name," regardless of whether that firm has any expertise in the subject matter in question. This is almost always disastrous and very costly to the organization. The law firm may not have expertise in charitable giving and may spend a lot of chargeable time and money researching the project. A very legal-sounding opinion letter will be issued, but the organization may have been much better off using a lawyer in any of the other categories listed here.

In considering what role an attorney might play in regard to a planned giving program, these are the key points:

- *Help in certain areas.* A lawyer can help because he or she has knowledge, either personally or conjointly with others in the firm, as to questions regarding special areas—real estate, corporate law, securities contracts, estates and trusts, exempt organization problems, unrelated business income, state laws regarding solicitation, endowments, and probate.
- *Need for independent judgment.* It is only natural that when a fund raiser works with a donor, he or she will want to receive the gift. It is essential to have outside counsel review gift structures for their objectivity. Is this gift appropriate for the donee and for the donor? Simply said, the gift needs a second check.
- *Overcoming the reluctant advisor.* The attorney selected should have, or should be able to develop, the ability to work with reluctant advisors, to persuade them to understand the charitable intent of the donor and the structure proposed. An attorney can be utilized as an "expert" who is offered to other advisors because of awareness that planned giving is an area of technical specialty.
- *Respect and credibility.* In many situations, an attorney becomes a buffer or a shield, using the respect and credibility of the legal profession to advance the organization's position or to obtain things the organization needs.

(F) CHOOSING A TRUSTEE

Because many gifts will be in the form of a trust, the organization must decide whether to act as trustee or to interview corporate trustees and recommend one or more to donors. The risk of the added liability of the organization and of individual board members when acting as trustee, plus the expertise required to handle trust matters correctly in-house, should be addressed at the board level. If the decision is to recommend corporate trustees, the planned giving officer must meet with the trustees available and assess their qualifications. A survey should be made of the trustees the organization may do business with. The following questions should be asked of all prospective trustees:

- Does the trustee desire to handle charitable funds?
- How long has the trustee been in the business and what kinds of charitable trusts is it managing?
- How much money is under management?
- How much charitable money is under management?
- How much of that is in charitable trusts?
- Who does the charitable trust accounting and tax work?
- Is there legal expertise on charitable matters in the general counsel's office?
- How many trust officers are there with knowledge of charitable trusts?
- Does the trustee provide other charitable services?
- What are the fees?
- What has been the investment performance?
- What minimum levels have been established for trusts (i.e., what is the lowest fee and how does that relate to the size of the trust?)?

Once a trustee is selected, its performance should be monitored regularly.

(G) CHOICE OF PERSON TO HIRE AS PLANNED GIVING OFFICER

A not-for-profit organization is created to carry out a specific function related to the needs of society or culture. Quite often the executive director has risen through the ranks of the substantive program, rather than having been trained primarily as a manager, whether of a business, a governmental unit, or a not-for-profit organization. The development office, on the other hand, generally attracts persons from the outside world, and they often have or develop an entrepreneurial attitude. The development office is a "profit center" within an organization not based on profits. Others in the institution quite often do not understand this mentality, which leads to conflicting cultures within the organizational structure. Development officers who come from the outside sometimes have little patience or understanding of the not-for-profit bureaucratic process that prevents them from moving quickly to motivate donors or accept certain gifts (e.g., real estate). Whether such a person is from the outside or not, the development office imposes a bottom-line mentality on the not-for-profit organization. Values dear to most not-for-profits—equity, fairness, avoidance of conflict—are often obstacles to entrepreneurial ventures. Thus, fund raisers, and particularly planned giving officers, must exist in two worlds simultaneously: the money/business world of donors and the "non-money" world of not-for-profits. The tension arising from this conflict causes more of the daily problems than may at first be apparent.

A planned giving staff (in fact, all of the major gifts unit) deals with high dollar amounts and wealthy donors, from the crowded confines of a little office with indoor-outdoor carpeting and metal furniture down at the end of a narrow hall. Colleagues in other areas of the not-for-profit often cannot understand the dichotomy or the stress this may produce. The faculty of a school, the hospital personnel, the staff of an environmental organization, or a group of social workers may have no sympathy for the problems of the wealthy and may, in fact, disdain the very wealth that is the source of the gift. Meanwhile, the major gifts or planned gifts officer must maintain a balance between this attitude and the realities of dealing with a donor of wealth. Too often, the non–fund-raising staff feels it is the social responsibility of the wealthy to fund the not-for-profit organization. Therefore, when the planned gifts officer wants special consideration in the gift structuring or gift acceptance process, cooperation is not always easy to come by.

In light of the potential for conflict and tension, who is inclined to accept a position as a planned giving officer? Realism about the job and its requirements will help the person seeking such a position to adjust and will perhaps lead to job satisfaction and less job turnover. In addition, understanding the potential conflicts ahead of time will permit planning to avoid them, thereby creating an atmosphere conducive to a successful planned giving program.

From the organization's point of view, the choice of a planned giving officer is, needless to say, an important element in the success of the program. Organizations often ask: Which candidate is preferable, a marketing-oriented or a technically-oriented person? Perhaps that question is irrelevant, and other qualities should be sought. Generally, the person should understand philanthropy—the role it has played historically in building this country, the role it currently plays, and its future trends. Specifically, he or she must thoroughly understand and be committed to the program the organization delivers. Commitment is always asked of board members, whereas staff persons, who are the backbone of the operation, are often treated as "hired guns." This may be a factor in the high turnover rate of development office employees.

There are certain personal characteristics and abilities to look for in a planned giving officer. Look for someone who

1. Is good-humored, pleasant, and determined
2. Does not let constant disruption, negativity, rejection, and shoestring budgets bother him or her
3. While making $45,000 to $65,000 per year, will try to understand what it means to part with a half-million dollars
4. Will try to understand the psychology of the wealthy without ever exhibiting jealousy or insensitivity to their special needs, and will never call a donor "Mrs. Gotrocks"
5. Is willing to learn large amounts of confusing information that will change just as soon as it is learned
6. Has a "presence" that will be accepted by donors of wealth and professional advisors

The job of a planned giving officer requires a willingness to learn. One must always be seeking a little more knowledge. Although many planned giving officers come from jobs and professions outside the world of fund raising, it is important to remember that planned giving is just another form of fund raising. Perhaps it would be better to teach the field of planned giving to a person with good fund-raising skills rather than to teach fund-raising skills to a person from the outside. Sometimes those who come in from the outside world just do not see the necessity of developing good fund-raising skills and of learning basic fund-raising principles. These are as important in planned giving as in any other function of the development office. Ultimately, the organization must determine which type of person will serve its needs best and will coordinate well with other staff members.

38.3   *Marketing the Program*

(A)   TAKING MARKETING CONCEPTS FROM THE BUSINESS WORLD

Statistics show that there are 15 million businesses in this country, and about 97 percent of those are classified as small businesses. Only one in five start-up businesses survives after four to five years. Is its product or service not good? It is more likely that marketing and management have been inadequate. Planned giving is exactly like a small business. How many organizations have folded their planned giving programs, saying, "We tried it. It didn't work." What does that indicate? Probably the exact same thing as for a failed business—marketing and management have been inadequate.

If principles of marketing are to be applied to fund raising, then certain prickly concepts that have been viewed in the past as not applicable to philanthropy must be understood and assimilated into the field. For example, fund raisers must get accustomed to words and concepts such as *consumer, producer, product, consumer behavior,* and *product support,* as well as many other ideas currently deemed foreign to fund raising. In *Marketing Magic,*[1] the process of marketing in a fund-raising office is thoroughly explored, including those terms that are often unwelcome—*sales* and *closes.* Fund raisers need not become overcommercial in marketing to make it effective in the world of philanthropy, but should apply the best of the commercial thoughts on marketing in a manner consistent with the standards of the fund-raising profession.

(B)   ERAS IN MARKETING

Not-for-profits have, for the most part, been behind the times in studying and applying marketing concepts. The program delivery side of not-for-profits, however, has become much more aware of marketing in recent years. Fund raising must now catch up.

Early in the twentieth century, the prevalent marketing construct was that of "product orientation." In other words, the marketer's focus was on the product, not necessar-

---

[1]Moerschbaecher, Lynda. *Marketing Magic for Major/Planned Gifts.* (Chicago: Precept Press, 1996).

ily the audience he or she was addressing. Imaginative ways were dreamed up to make the product stand out from similar products. However, after World War II, there was a definite shift in the construct to focus on the audience side, addressing the consumer's wants and needs. This is called "consumer orientation," which became the prevalent view of marketers in the second half of the 20th century. This method of marketing challenges the marketer to learn all that he or she can about the potential end user of the product and to address the communication of the product features and benefits to those discovered needs and wants, luring the buyer into a sale.

Later in this period, the techniques became more refined, because everyone was addressing the wants and needs of the same customers. Ries and Trout have called this phase the "battle for the mind."[2] How to cut through the inundation of information to get the message across more effectively is the game in an era when the amount of information available to the consumer has skyrocketed.

To be effective in the fund-raising profession, individuals must learn to offer information that effectively competes with all the other information available to their prospects and to get a chunk of their attention long enough to "sell" their concept to prospective donors. This can be done only through the adoption of a formal marketing plan and by following up with well-planned implementation.

(C) THE MARKETING PLAN

Just as the organization itself needs a long-term planning process to understand its goals and directions, the planned giving program needs a well-considered, written plan for approaching the marketplace for planned gifts. The program needs to know how to get from point A to point B. Many, or most, planned giving programs are started without an understanding of where the organization hopes to go in what time frame. Thus, a marketing plan can be the road map for a successful planned giving program.

Many books have been written on how to create a marketing plan for the commercial market.[3] Each organization must ultimately determine its own best marketing plan. Nevertheless, as a starting point, these six steps in creating a marketing plan should be considered:

1. Understanding who the organization is in relation to the marketplace. This involves demographic and psychographic studies of the potential donor base, to determine what groups of people might realistically give to the planned giving program. Not every organization is willing to pay the cost of such a study, but those who have taken the extra step have found the study to be invaluable both for delivery of services and for fund raising.
2. Segmenting the marketplace into target markets based on identities of wants and needs of the potential donors in each of the market segments.
3. Designing planned gift strategies that may be appealing to each target market and that meet the perceived wants and needs of that target market.

---

[2]Al Ries and Jack Trout, *Positioning: Battling of the Minds* (New York: Warner Books, 1981).
[3]Lynda S. Moerschbaecher, *Marketing Magic for Major/Planned Gifts* (Chicago: Precept Press, 1996) focuses solely on major and planned gift markets.

4. Checking similarly situated organizations to see what the competition is doing and what outreach programs they are planning that may overlap or conflict.

5. Developing effective outreach efforts based on the market studies done in accordance with the preceding steps. These will no doubt include donor and professional seminars, bequest mailings, newsletters, advertisements (perhaps), and other means of reaching people who may be willing to commit to the planned giving program.

6. Creating effective private communications, once an individual prospect is identified.

(D) MARKETING CONCEPTS

For purposes of learning and communicating the marketing concepts necessary to success, basic terms must be used consistently:

Market. The market is that space or gap that separates consumers and producers; the consumer-producer relationship necessarily exists, but at a distance. The producer must survey the territory to determine who needs the product. The gap between the producer and consumer still exists.

Market relationship between producer and consumer. A *foundation* exists for an exchange but is not a substitute for it; the market is real, but it is not yet realized. While the market relationship may be in existence, it is still a *potential* exchange. A prospect is identified, but not yet a consumer.

Marketing. Marketing is the force or catalyst *that closes the gap*, the process of realization or actualization. Thus, it is the totality of the activity that makes the producer and consumer connect. Marketing is, therefore, the closing of the *gap* between the consumer and the producer.

Selling is the closing of the *deal* between the producer and a specific consumer, once found.

(E) IMPLEMENTATION

Implementation of a marketing plan includes two aspects: (1) developing the general prospect pool and then (2) identifying individual prospects from specifically defined target markets. Once this has been accomplished, the advancement officer (AO) is in familiar territory in cultivating the prospect. The difference, however, is that much more information about the prospect is already at hand, carefully studied both generally, through the marketing plan's target markets and products designed for that target market's precise wants and needs, and through individual research demographically and psychographically. By the time the marketing-oriented AO first contacts a prospect, the AO knows exactly what to do and say to lead the prospect to making a decision, on his or her own, to make a gift. Effective marketing and implementation of marketing concepts in major/planned gifts makes an ask or solicitation unnecessary. The prospect is led to "buy" on his or her own; there is no need to sell. Marketers in the commercial world have done this effectively for decades. Advancement officers can do it with equal ease.

(F) SALES AND CLOSES

The term "close" is bandied about as if everyone knows what it means. In the world of sales, writers, trainers, and others use the word "close," inventing their own meaning or twist on the word with amazing creativity.

A close is not an event, as you may have thought, but a process or an evolution; it is a series of little decisions along the way that permit a buyer to be comfortable with what he or she is about to do. There is a magic moment when the effective marketer sees that enough little decisions have been made for the buyer to be comfortable with the ultimate decision. At some point in this process the marketer has become a seller.

So, too, is the close a process for the donor. In fact, the buyer or donor himself or herself will recognize that he or she has just made a series of decisions that add up to a purchase. Once the ultimate decision is made, what does this person feel? The fund raiser must make the donor feel relaxed and good about it. Decision making, especially about a large, irrevocable gift, can be quite a jolting experience for the prospect.

(G) OUTREACH AND COMMUNICATIONS

Once a marketing plan has been established and marketing concepts have been learned, these must be implemented with the same diligence. The typical outreach and donor acquisition functions of planned giving include sponsoring seminars for donors and prospects on the subject of estate planning; presenting for the professionals in the community a seminar directly on the subject of the technical aspects of planned giving; and mailing brochures, bequest intention letters, and periodic newsletters. It is important to reach the same market in as many ways as possible and to keep the message straightforward and simple. The gift structuring phase can become complex quickly enough; in the early stages, motivation may be thwarted if the material is too complex. Outreach should not, however, be your first step; well-studied and well-planned marketing will propel a program to much earlier success.

38.4 Planned Giving Vehicles

No planned giving program can succeed without a good, basic understanding of the gift vehicles. The following paragraphs are designed to give only a quick overview of some of the technical rules.

(A) CHARITABLE REMAINDER ANNUITY TRUST

(i) Definition
Internal Revenue Code Section (IRC §) 664(d)(1) requires that a charitable remainder annuity trust (CRAT) contain the following five features. (See Exhibit 38.3.)

1. Payments to income beneficiaries of a fixed dollar amount or percentage of initial net fair market value (FMV), but at least 5 percent of initial net FMV and no more than 50%.

EXHIBIT 38.3 Charitable Remainder Annuity Trust

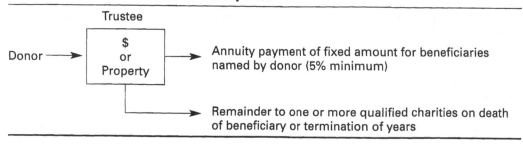

Trustee

Donor → [$ or Property] → Annuity payment of fixed amount for beneficiaries named by donor (5% minimum)

→ Remainder to one or more qualified charities on death of beneficiary or termination of years

2. One or more income beneficiaries, one of whom is not an IRC § 170(c) charity (otherwise it is a wholly charitable trust).
3. Annuity payments made for life or lives of income beneficiaries, or a term of years (not to exceed 20).
4. Ten percent minimum actuarial value remainder interest; remainder passes to IRC § 170(c) charitable organization(s).
5. Functions as a CRAT from its "creation." Creation is the earliest time no person is treated as "owner" of the trust under subchapter J of the Internal Revenue Code and property is transferred to the trust.
6. Probability test in Rev. Rul. 77-374. If the likelihood of charity receiving a remainder interest is less than a 5% probability, no charitable deduction is allowed and therefore the trust is not qualified.

(ii) Specific Features

Any person or persons may be the grantor of a CRAT. The definition of "person" under IRC § 7701(a)(1) includes an individual, a trust, an estate, a partnership, an association, or a corporation.

Any person who does not make the CRAT a grantor trust may serve as trustee. (See Revenue Ruling (Rev. Rul.) 77-285, 1977-2 Cumulative Bulletin (C.B.) 213.) An independent trustee is needed, however, if the trust holds "hard-to-value" property (i.e., closely held stock, real estate) (see the 1969 Tax Reform Act Legislative History H.R. 91-413, 91st Cong., 1st Sess. 60 (1969)), or if the trust gives the trustee a "sprinkle power" (power to allocate the annuity amount among beneficiaries) (IRC § 674(c)). An independent trustee is a trustee or trustees, none of whom is the grantor, and no more than half of whom are "related or subordinate parties" within IRC § 672(c).

Permissible income beneficiaries include individuals, trusts, estates, partnerships, associations, and corporations. At least one income beneficiary must not be an IRC § 170(c) charity. In general, individual income beneficiaries must be living at the time the CRAT is created. If the income beneficiaries are a named class of individuals (e.g., "To my children living at my death"), all members of the class must be alive at the time the CRAT is created, unless the CRAT is for a term of years (Treasury Regulation (Treas. Reg.) § 1.664-2(a)(3)). The grantor may retain the power to revoke by will the interest of any beneficiary other than an IRC § 170(c) organization (Treas. Reg. § 1.664-2(a)(4)).

The remainder interest in a CRAT must be irrevocably contributed "to" or "for the use of" a charity. Alternative remaindermen must be named, in case the named beneficiary is not in existence or not qualified when the trust terminates. Remaindermen may be revocable if the remainder interest is irrevocably dedicated to qualified charities (Rev. Rul. 76-8, 1976-1 C.B. 179).

Unlike a charitable remainder unitrust, a charitable remainder annuity trust is permitted no additional contributions after the initial transfer. However, all contributions made to a testamentary CRAT by reason of the decedent's death are deemed to be part of the initial contribution.

No payments other than the annuity amount may be made to anyone except the charity, unless full and adequate consideration is given (e.g., trustee fees). The statute and the Treasury Regulations place no restrictions on trust investments, except that the trust provisions may not prevent the trustee from realizing both income and capital gains on an annual basis (Treas. Reg. § 1.664-1(a)(3)).

The trust document should define what is income and what is principal, both as to receipts and as to charges or expenses. The trust document should also include accurate, yet flexible, wording regarding use of the funds by the charity, to avoid a restricted gift that no longer meets the needs of the organization.

(B) CHARITABLE REMAINDER UNITRUST

(i) Definition

IRC § 664(d)(2) requires that a charitable remainder unitrust (CRUT) contain the following five features. (See Exhibit 38.4.)

1. Payments to income beneficiaries of a fixed percentage (minimum 5 percent, maximum 50%) of the annual net FMV or the CRUT (the "unitrust payment" is not the same as "income"; the trust payments are based on the value of the trust assets, rather than income generated by those assets, and will thus fluctuate over the life of the trust).
2. One or more income beneficiaries, one of whom is not an IRC § 170(c) charity (otherwise it is a wholly charitable trust).
3. Unitrust payments made for life or lives of income beneficiaries, or a term of years (not to exceed 20).
4. Ten percent minimum actuarial value remainder interest; remainder passes to IRC § 170(c) charitable organization(s).
5. Functions as a CRUT from its creation. Creation is the earliest time no person is treated as "owner" under subchapter J and property is transferred to the trust.

EXHIBIT 38.4 Charitable Remainder Unitrust

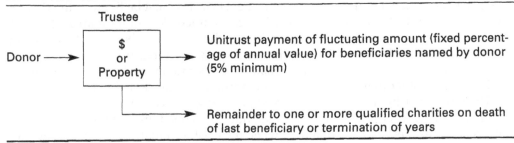

(ii) Specific Features

Any person or persons may be the grantor of a CRUT. The definition of "person" under IRC § 7701(a)(1) includes an individual, a trust, an estate, a partnership, an association, or a corporation.

Any person who does not make the CRUT a grantor trust may serve as trustee. (See Rev. Rul. 77-285, 1977-2 C.B. 213.) An independent trustee is needed, however, if the CRUT holds "hard-to-value" property (i.e., closely held stock, real estate) (see the 1969 Tax Reform Act Legislative History, H.R. 91-413, 91st Cong., 1st Sess. 60 (1969)), or if the trust gives the trustee a "sprinkle power" (power to allocate the unitrust amount among beneficiaries) (IRC § 674(c)). An independent trustee is a trustee or trustees, none of whom is the grantor, and no more than half of whom are "related or subordinate parties" within IRC § 672(c).

Permissible income beneficiaries include individuals, trusts, estates, partnerships, associations, and corporations. At least one income beneficiary must not be an IRC § 170(c) charity. In general, individual income beneficiaries must be living at the time the CRUT is created. If the income beneficiaries are a named class of individuals (e.g., "To my children living at my death"), all members of the class must be alive at the time the CRUT is created, unless the CRUT is for a term of years (Treas. Reg. § 1.664-3(a)(3)). The grantor may retain the power to revoke by will the interest of any beneficiary other than an IRC § 170(c) organization (Treas. Reg. § 1.664-3(a)(4)).

The remainder interest in a CRUT must be irrevocably contributed "to" or "for the use of" a charity. Alternative remaindermen must be named, in case the named beneficiary is not in existence or not qualified when the trust terminates. Remaindermen may be revocable if the remainder interest is irrevocably transferred to qualified charities (Rev. Rul. 76-8, 1976-1 C.B. 179).

Unlike a CRAT, a CRUT is permitted additional contributions *if* the trust instrument provides for them *and* provides for (1) valuation of property at the time of contribution and (2) determination of a prorated unitrust payment. Otherwise, the trust instrument must prohibit additional contributions.

No payments other than the unitrust amount may be made to anyone except a charity, unless full and adequate consideration is given (e.g., trustee fees). The statute and Treasury Regulations place no restrictions on trust investments, except that the trust provisions may not prevent the trustee from realizing both income and capital gains on an annual basis (Treas. Reg. § 1.664-1(a)(3)).

The trust document should define what is income and what is principal, both as to receipts and as to charges or expenses. The trust document should also include accurate, yet flexible, wording regarding use of the funds by the charity, to avoid a restricted gift that no longer meets the needs of the organization.

(C) NET INCOME UNITRUST

There is a variation of the CRUT, which has several names, the most common of which are NICRUT and NIMCRUT. NICRUT means net income unitrust without a deficiency make-up provision ("net income charitable remainder unitrust"). NIMCRUT means net income unitrust with a deficiency make-up ("net income make-up charitable remainder unitrust"). The key difference from the standard CRUT is that the unitrust payment is one of the following:

1. The *lesser* of trust income, as determined under state law, or the amount calculated using the fixed percentage of trust FMV. Thus, although the fixed percentage in the trust document may not be less than 5 percent, the trust payments will be less if the trust has insufficient earnings. This version is called the "net income" or "net income without deficiency makeup" CRUT

OR

2. All of item 1, *plus* trust income in excess of the amount calculated using the fixed percentage of trust FMV to the extent that trust income (and thus unitrust payments) in prior years (on an aggregate basis) was less than the amount determined by using the fixed percentage (on an aggregate basis). This is called a "net income unitrust with deficiency makeup," or "IOU" CRUT.

The NICRUT pays out only the amount described in the first paragraph above, or the net income of the trust whenever it is less than the stated fixed percentage. The NIMCRUT pays out an amount decribed in both the first and second paragraphs above, the net income if less. If the lesser amount is paid, the difference between what amount would have been paid out under the fixed percentage and the actual net income that was actually paid is a "deficiency" that may be made up in later years if there is income earned by the trust in excess of the stated percent. In years of excess income, the trustee pays back the accumulated deficiency (or as much as possible with the excess income on hand that year).

Property that is non–income-producing or low–income-producing and cannot meet a mandatory unitrust or annuity trust payment—such as real estate or closely held stock—is often transferred to a net income unitrust. A net income unitrust is appropriate because it allows the trust to pay the income beneficiary only the actual income earned by the trust asset. Absent such a net income provision, the trust would be required to return a portion of the contributed property to the income beneficiary in order to meet the mandatory unitrust payment. If a makeup provision is included (item 2 in the preceding list), the deficiency amount can be paid to the income beneficiary once the trust generates income in excess of the fixed percentage.

It is important to review the trust document and state law to determine exactly what constitutes "trust income." For example, the laws of many states provide that "trust income" does not reflect any gain on principal (i.e., capital gains). It may be possible to revise this general definition by careful drafting of the trust document.

(D)   COMBINATION OF METHODS UNITRUST

Newer regulations provide for a combination of the methods of payout. This trust form is called in the industry a "flip unitrust" or "FlipCRUT." It is a charitable remainder unitrust (CRUT) that starts as a net income unitrust (NIMCRUT or NICRUT) and, upon a triggering event, becomes a standard (mandatory payment of the stated percentage) unitrust. The arrangement is desirable when the trust is initially funded with property that produces low or no income, but where the beneficiary needs or wants a more steady income later.

The FlipCRUT rules in the regulations (found under "combination of methods" in Reg. § 1.664-3(a)(1)(c)-(f)) were finalized on Dec. 10, 1998 and provide as follows:

The governing instrument may provide

- The trust will pay net income (with or without deficiency makeup) for an initial period, and then
- Pay the fixed percentage for the remaining years

But only if the governing instrument also provides that

- The change is triggered (1) on a specific date or (2) by a single event whose occurrence is not discretionary with, or within the control of, the trustees or any other persons
- The change occurs beginning with the tax year following the year in which the trigger occurs
- And following the conversion, the trust will pay to the recipient *only* the fixed percentage amount and not any amount under the "income exception" method (which includes net income and any deficiency makeup)

If the triggering event is the sale of unmarketable assets or, with respect to any individual, marriage, death, divorce, or the birth of any child, the triggering event is not deemed to be "discretionary with, or within the control of, the trustees or any other persons."

(E) IRS PROTOTYPE DOCUMENTS

The IRS has published prototype, or sample, CRAT and CRUT trust instruments. The chart in Exhibit 38.5 describes these documents and sets out the Revenue Procedures in which they may be found. In reviewing these samples, it should be remembered that they are forms and most likely do not take into account the needs and wants of a donor. Nor do they address nontax issues, such as the trustee's ability to hire agents, the grantor's ability to remove a trustee, and so on.[4] New forms are being created by the IRS, but are not yet released.

(F) POOLED INCOME FUND

(i) Specific Features

To date, individuals and corporations have been permitted to contribute to a pooled income fund (PIF). There is no guidance yet regarding trusts, partnerships, or other entities as donors. (See Exhibit 38.6.)

Tax-exempt securities may not be contributed to, or purchased by, a PIF. In addition, non–income-producing property will reduce the PIF's total return, thereby reducing income to all donor/beneficiary units. Generally it is not advisable to accept such property unless the PIF can sell it quickly. Moreover, the PIF document must either prohibit the PIF from holding depreciable or depletable property (e.g., real estate) or require that a depreciation or depletion reserve be maintained in accordance with generally accepted accounting principles (GAAP) (unless state law already so provides) (Rev. Rul. 90-103, 1990-51 I.R.B. 14).

---

[4]For a careful analysis of these samples, see Lynda Moerschbaecher, Jerry J. McCoy, and Terry Simmons, "*Charitable Gift Planning*," *Charitable Gift Planning News*, 8, no. 8 (August 1990).

EXHIBIT 38.5 IRS Prototype Charitable Remainder Trust Instruments

	Intervivos	Testamentary	Revenue Procedure
Unitrusts	One life		89-20
	Two lives consecutive		90-30, § 4
	Two lives consecutive		90-30, § 5
	Two lives consecutive and concurrent		
		One life	90-30, § 6
		Two lives consecutive	90-30, § 7
		Two lives consecutive and concurrent	90-30, § 8
Net income unitrusts (with deficiency makeup)	One life		90-31, § 4
	Two lives consecutive		90-31, § 5
	Two lives consecutive and concurrent		90-31, § 6
		One life	90-31, § 7
		Two lives consecutive	90-31, § 8
		Two lives consecutive and concurrent	90-31, § 9
Annuity trusts	One life		89-21
	Two lives consecutive		90-32, § 4
	Two lives consecutive and concurrent		90-32, § 5
		One life	90-32, § 6
		Two lives consecutive	90-32, § 7
		Two lives consecutive and concurrent	90-32, § 8

No donor or beneficiary (other than the charitable remaindermen) may be trustee. However, if the charity is trustee, its officers, directors, or other officials may generally be donors or beneficiaries.

The income interest(s) retained by the donor and/or created for others must be for life. Thus, only individuals, not corporations, partnerships, trusts, or other entities, may

EXHIBIT 38.6 Pooled Income Fund

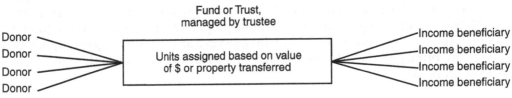

Remainderman—On death of beneficiary, value of units severed, given outright to charity.

be income beneficiaries. Income beneficiaries must be living at the time of transfer. Income payments may be made to multiple-income beneficiaries concurrently, consecutively, or concurrently and consecutively. The donor may retain the power to revoke an income beneficiary's interest by will.

Payments to income beneficiaries are of a share of net income after expenses of the fund. Net income is allocated based on the number of PIF units assigned to the value of the donor's transfer. PIF units are valued on periodic determination dates.

A PIF may have only one remainderman, which must be a public charity described in IRC § 509(a)(1). A parent entity can assign a remainder interest to its subordinate organizations, and national, regional, and other "umbrella" organizations can maintain a PIF for the benefit of their member groups. However, horizontal (or "brother-sister") organizations cannot share a PIF. The remainderman must "maintain" the PIF (i.e., be trustee or have the power to replace the trustee).

The property of the various donors is commingled and invested by the PIF. The assets of the PIF may be *jointly* invested with the trustee's other funds or endowments *if* the fund assets and income of the PIF are separately accounted for. At the death of an income beneficiary, the value of the donor's units is severed and made available to the charitable remainderman. In determining the amount severed, income is prorated to the date of death, or, where the trust provides for the last income payment to be on the last regular payment date prior to the date of death, the remainder is valued as of the last regular payment date.

The Philanthropy Protection Act of 1995 (P.L. 104-62) (PPA) amended the federal securities laws to require that PIF donors be provided with written disclosure of the material operation of the fund.

(ii)   IRS Prototype Documents

The IRS has published a prototype, or sample, PIF trust document and gift agreements (Rev. Proc. 88-53, 1988-2 C.B. 712). These forms do *not* include the disclosure statement required by the PPA.

(G)   CHARITABLE LEAD TRUST

(i)   Definition

Very little discussion of the charitable lead trust (CLT) appears in the Internal Revenue code. (See Exhibit 38.7.) There are two types of CLTs: grantor and nongrantor. The

EXHIBIT 38.7 Charitable Lead Trust

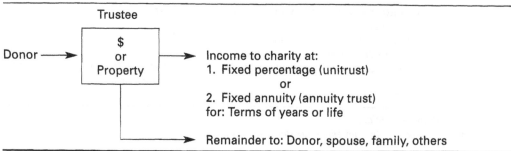

grantor lead trust comes within the definition of a grantor trust in IRC §§ 671–679; the nongrantor version does not. See Exhibit 38.8 for an outline of the differences.

The income payments to the charity can be in the form of an annuity or unitrust interest. With a charitable lead annuity trust, the charity has an irrevocable right to receive an annuity for a term of years or for the life of the donor or other individuals. With a charitable lead unitrust, the charity has an irrevocable right to receive a fixed percentage of net FMV of assets, determined annually (no net income exception as with charitable remainder unitrusts), for a term of years or for the life of the donor or other individuals.

(ii) Specific Features

Any person or persons may be the grantor of a CLT. The definition of "person" under IRC § 7701(a)(1) includes an individual, a trust, an estate, a partnership, an association, or a corporation. The property contributed to the CLT must be capable of generating income, because the payout to the charity is mandatory.

Anyone may be trustee of a CLT. However, the trust powers given to the trustee should not make the grantor the "owner" of trust assets where the grantor acts as the trustee (see IRC §§ 671–679), if a nongrantor lead trust is intended.

Any IRC § 501(c)(3) organization may be named as the income beneficiary. Private individuals may also be income beneficiaries, but only from segregated portions of the trust assets (Treas. Reg. § 1.170A-6(c)(2)(ii)(D)).

(H)   LIFE INSURANCE POLICY

A donor may make a "gift" of an insurance policy by merely changing the beneficiary designation. However, because the beneficiary designation is revocable, it is an incomplete gift and no income tax deduction is allowed. An income tax deduction for the value

EXHIBIT 38.8 Qualified Charitable Lead Trusts

	Annuity	Unitrust
Grantor	Grantor pays income tax on trust income.	Same.
	Grantor takes income tax deduction for present value of trust income.	Same.*
	Charity gets annuity for years or life.	Charity gets unitrust amount for years or life.
	Grantor (or grantor's estate) gets remainder.	Same.
Nongrantor	Grantor parts with all ownership and control.	Same.
	Grantor gets no income tax deduction,† pays no tax on income.	Same.
	Charity gets annuity for years or life.	Charity gets unitrust amount for years or life.
	Others get remainder.	Same.

*Income and gift tax deduction.
†No income tax deduction, but gift/estate tax deductions available.

of the policy will be allowed if the ownership of the policy is changed to the charity. A policy's value for this purpose is generally its replacement value if the policy is paid up, and its interpolated terminal reserve value if it is not. Local law must be checked, however. In Private Letter Ruling 9110016, the IRS concluded that, under New York law (since changed), a charity did not have an insurable interest in its donor. Because the charity's rights to the policy proceeds were thus voidable, the donor's deductions were denied.[5]

(I) CHARITABLE GIFT ANNUITIES

Charitable gift annuities are gift vehicles accomplished by means of a contract, not a trust. A donor to a charitable gift annuity transfers money or property to the charity in exchange for a fixed annuity payable over one or two lives. Each contract covers only one gift; future contributions require a new contract. (See Exhibit 38.9.)

A portion, determined by actuarial tables, of the amount transferred by the donor to the charity is deemed to be the value of the annuity and therefore for the benefit of the individual. The balance of the amount transferred is a deductible gift to the charity.

The annuity payment is an unsecured, general obligation of the issuing charity. The American Council of Gift Annuities publishes uniform annuity rates for single- and joint-plus-survivor gift annuity contracts. The Charitable Gift Annuity Antitrust Act of 1995 (P.L. 102-63) amended the federal antitrust laws to provide that it is not unlawful for two or more charities to offer the same annuity rates (e.g., the rates published by the American Council on Gift Annuities).

Some state insurance commissions regulate the issuance of gift annuities. The charity may have to maintain reserves to protect the annuitant's interest. State law should be checked to determine whether the charity must be certified or licensed to issue gift annuities and to ascertain audit and yearly filing requirements.

If certain restrictions are satisfied, the income earned by the contributed property is not unrelated business income to the charity. These five conditions are as follows:

1. One or two life contracts only.
2. The annuity portion must be worth less than 90 percent of the whole transfer.
3. The annuity must be the sole consideration issued for the property transferred.
4. There may be no guarantee of a minimum or maximum number of payments (i.e., no term-of-years annuity allowed).

EXHIBIT 38.9 Charitable Gift Annuities

```
                            $ or Property
                    ──────────────────────────────▶
        Donor       ◀──────────────────────────────        Charity
                            Annual Annuity
```

---

[5]Jonathan Tidd, "The Insurable Interest Rule and Charitable Gifts of Life Insurance," *Tax Management Estates, Gifts and Trusts Journal* (September–October 1991): 165.

5. There may be no adjustment of the annuity payment by reference to income received from the transferred property or any other property (Treas. Reg. § 1.514(c)-1(e)(1)).

In a deferred gift annuity, the first payment, as stated in the contract, is deferred at least one year. During the deferral period, the annuity rate is compounded. The American Council on Gift Annuities suggests uniform compounding rates. The effect of the deferral period is to reduce the value of the annuity and increase the charitable deduction.

(J) LIFE ESTATE—REMAINDERS IN RESIDENCE OR FARM

A remainder interest is a future interest, given now and vested in ownership, where possession arises at a preset date or at the end of the life tenant's life. (See Exhibit 38.10.) An income tax deduction is available at the date of gift for the value of a remainder interest given to charity only with respect to remainder interests in (1) a residence—any property used by the donor as a *personal* residence even though not the *principal* residence, including vacation homes, condos, and co-op apartments; and (2) a farm—any land, including improvements, used by the taxpayer or his or her tenant for the production of crops, fruit, or agricultural products, or for the sustenance of livestock.

Making a life estate-remainder gift creates joint ownership where the life tenant has possession. Certain issues must be addressed, such as which party is responsible for mortgage payments, taxes, insurance, and repairs. The laws of some states spell out some of the duties of a life tenant and the remainderman. Two major issues that should be covered in a contract are: (1) if there is a fire, flood, earthquake, or other casualty, whether the improvements will be rebuilt, and, if not, how the insurance proceeds will be split; and (2) whether the life tenant may lease the property, and whether the remaindermen may review the lease and/or tenant.

38.5 *Avoiding Pitfalls*

(A) STEP TRANSACTION OR COLLAPSIBLE GIFT RULE

Often a donor will contribute an asset to a trust (or charity) after having negotiated a sale of the asset. If the donor has fully negotiated the sale and there is a legal obligation on the part of the donee (trust or charity) to sell the asset to the buyer, the capital gain will

---

EXHIBIT 38.10 Gift of Remainder Interest

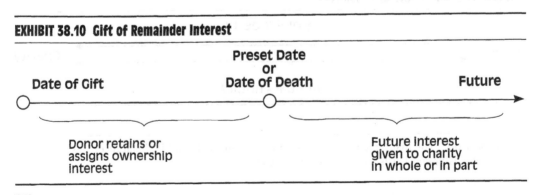

be taxed to the donor. (See *Magnolia Development Corp. v. Commissioner*, T.C. Memo 1960–177.) To avoid this result, the trust (or charity) must have free rein to negotiate the sale, change the terms of the deal, and walk away from the deal entirely. (See *Martin v. Commissioner*, 251 F. Supp. 381 (1966).)

(B)   TANGIBLE PERSONAL PROPERTY

A charitable contribution of a future interest in tangible personal property is deductible for income tax purposes only when all intervening interests to the possession or enjoyment of the property have expired or are held by persons other than the taxpayer. Thus, a transfer of art to an organization, where a donor retains a life interest, results in no income tax deduction until the donor relinquishes the intervening life interest (IRC § 170(a)(3)). The IRS has ruled that when tangible property is placed into a charitable remainder trust in which the donor retains a life income interest, and the trustee sells the asset and reinvests in stocks or other assets paying a life income to the donor, a deduction may be claimed once the art work or other tangible property is sold by the trustee.

Further, any gift of tangible personal property that is not used by the donee in a related use (related to the reason the organization exists—e.g., art to museum) generates a deduction based only on the donor's tax basis in the property (IRC § 170(e)(1)(B)). If the property is gifted for a related use, the deduction is based on the property's fair market value.

(C)   INTANGIBLES

Intangible assets such as partnership interests, trademarks, patents, and copyrights are often proposed as possible gifts. Valuation of these assets is always difficult and can be especially troublesome if the intangible is transferred to a CRT or PIF (as the income payable is based on the asset value).

As to partnership interests, the Internal Revenue Service employs either the aggregate theory or the entity theory (or both). The aggregate theory states that each partner owns an undivided interest in each and every asset of the partnership; the entity theory holds that the partnership interest itself is the item of property. If the aggregate theory is employed with respect to a gift of a partnership interest, the donor will be deemed to have made a gift of each asset and liability held by the partnership. Thus, even though the partner may hold his or her partnership interest free-and-clear; the partner may be deemed to have given encumbered property if the partnership incurred debt (see Private Letter Ruling 7943062).

(D)   MORTGAGED PROPERTY

Transferring mortgaged property into a CRT raises four issues:

1. The transfer constitutes a bargain sale (i.e., part gift, part sale), because the donor is deemed to have received "sale proceeds" in the amount of the debt relieved (Treas. Reg. § 1.1011-2(a)(3)).
2. The CRT may own debt-financed property generating unrelated business income (see Subsection e, "Unrelated Business Income").

3. The transfer may constitute an act of self-dealing (see Subsection f, "Self-Dealing").
4. If the donor remains personally liable on the debt after the transfer and the CRT makes a payment on the debt, the IRS has taken the position that the trust becomes a grantor trust and is therefore disqualified as CRT (Private Letter Ruling 9015049).

(E) UNRELATED BUSINESS INCOME

The unrelated business income (UBI) tax was enacted in the early 1950s to counteract complaints by businesses that exempt organizations were unfairly competing in business ventures because they paid no tax. (See IRC § 511 et seq.) The tax arises in two ways: (1) operationally (running a business) and (2) via "debt-financed property."

In its operational form, the tax is imposed on gross income from: a trade or business, regularly carried on, and unrelated to the exempt purpose of the charity (IRC § 512). Deductions directly connected with the activity offset the gross income, and a specific deduction of $1,000 is permitted. Certain income is "passive" and thus exempt: dividends, interest, payments on securities loans, annuities, royalties, and rent from *certain types* of leases. Gains on the sale of property are generally excluded, except for gains on the sale of property held for sale to customers in the ordinary course of business.

The income (or a portion of the income) produced by "debt-financed property" may also be unrelated business income (IRC § 514). Debt-financed property is property held for the purpose of producing income on which there is "acquisition indebtedness" at any time during the taxable year. Acquisition indebtedness is defined as the unpaid amount of:

1. Debt incurred in acquiring or improving the property.
2. Debt incurred *before* the acquisition or improvement of the property, if the debt would not have been incurred other than for the acquisition or improvement.
3. Debt incurred *after* the acquisition or improvement, if the debt would not have been incurred other than for the acquisition or improvement *and* was "reasonably foreseeable when the property was acquired or improved."

If property is acquired subject to mortgage or certain liens, the debt or lien is considered acquisition indebtedness. However, if the property is received by bequest, the debt will not be acquisition indebtedness for 10 years. If the property is received by gift, the debt will not be acquisition indebtedness for 10 years, *if* the mortgage was placed more than five years before the gift and the donor held the property more than five years before the gift (IRC § 514(c)(2)).

The Tax Court has held that if a CRT holds an interest in a partnership that has invested in encumbered property, the CRT must include its share of the partnership's income when determining UBI (*Newhall Unitrust v. Commissioner*, 104 T.C. No. 10 (1995)).

(F) SELF-DEALING

A tax is imposed on acts of self-dealing between a "disqualified person" and a "private foundation," by IRC § 4941. This section is made directly applicable to CRTs, CLTs, and

PIFs (IRC § 4947(a)(2)). The first tier is 5 percent on the self-dealer and 2½ percent on the "foundation manager" (in this case, the trustee). If not corrected, a 200 percent tax is imposed on the self-dealer and 50 percent on the foundation manager. (The maximum for the manager is $10,000 per act.)

Self-dealing includes direct or indirect:

- Sale, exchange, or leasing of property between a private foundation (trust) and a disqualified person
- Lending of money or extension of credit between a private foundation and a disqualified person
- Furnishing of goods, services, or facilities between a private foundation and a disqualified person
- Payment of compensation or reimbursement of expenses by a private foundation to a disqualified person
- Transfer to or use by a disqualified person of income or assets of the private foundation
- Agreement by the private foundation to make payment to a government official (other than for employment after termination of government services)

Five special rules apply:

1. Real estate transferred subject to a mortgage assumed by the foundation or placed on the property within 10 years prior to transfer is considered a sale or exchange.
2. Loans to the foundation without interest are not self-dealing *if* used exclusively for charitable purposes.
3. Furnishing of goods, services, and so on, *to* a foundation is not self-dealing if without charge and exclusively for charitable purposes, and *from* the foundation if made on no more favorable a basis than to the general public.
4. Payment of compensation for personal services which are reasonable and necessary to achieving the exempt purpose is not self-dealing if the compensation is not excessive.
5. A liquidation, merger, redemption, or recapitalization involving a corporate disqualified person and the foundation is not self-dealing if all securities of the same class as the foundation holds are offered the same terms, and the foundation will receive fair market value for its stock.

Five categories of disqualified persons include:

1. A substantial contributor
2. A foundation manager
3. Someone who owns 20 percent or more of a corporation's voting power, a partnership's profit interest, or a trust's beneficial interest, where that entity is a substantial contributor
4. A member of the family of a person described in items 1, 2, or 3
5. A corporation, partnership, or trust in which persons described in items 1, 2, 3, or 4 own 35 percent or more (IRC § 4946(a))

(G) ENVIRONMENTAL LIABILITY

Environmental liability and hazardous waste have become major issues in gifts of real estate. Of particular concern is the extent to which a trustee's personal assets are exposed because the trustee holds legal title to property. Every charitable organization should adopt (at board level) a policy regarding the acceptance and review of gifts of real estate, both outright and in trust, addressing the level of environmental reviews that are required and who should pay the cost of such review.

Suggested Readings

Abbin, Byrle M., Diane Cronwell, Marvin J. Dickman, Richard A. Helfand, Ross W. Nager, Joseph P. Toce, Jr., and Mark L. Vorsatz. *Tax Economics of Charitable Giving*, 12th ed. Chicago: Arthur Andersen & Co., 1995.

Ashton, Debra. *The Complete Guide to Planned Giving*, 2d ed. Cambridge, Mass.: JLA Publications, 1990.

Charitable Giving Tax Service. Chicago: R&R Newkirk, 1977.

Donaldson, and Osteen. *The Harvard Manual on Tax Aspects of Charitable Giving*, 7th ed. Boston: Harvard University Press, 1992.

Hamlin, Petkun, and Bednarz. *Charitable Income Trusts*. Washington, D.C.: Bureau of National Affairs, Portfolio, 1986.

Moerschbaecher, Lynda. *Marketing Magic for Major/Planned Gifts*. Chicago: Precept Press, 1996.

———. *Plain English Planned Giving: After the Gift Is Closed* (book and audiotapes). San Francisco: Author, 1991.

———. *Plain English Planned Giving: Starting at Square One* (book and audiotapes). San Francisco: Author, 1991.

———. *Plain English Planned Giving: The Well-Planned Gift* (book). San Francisco: Author, 2000.

———. *Build Your Endowment Right From the Start*, Chicago: Precept Press, Spring 2001.

Moerschbaecher, Lynda, Jerry J. McCoy, and Terry Simmons. "Charitable Gift Planning." *Charitable Gift Planning News*, 8, no. 8 (August 1990).

Petkun, Hamlin, and Downing. *Charitable Remainder Trusts and Pooled Income Funds*. Washington, D.C.: Bureau of National Affairs, Portfolio, 1986.

Ries, Al, and Jack Trout. *Positioning: Battling for the Minds*. New York: Warner Books, 1981.

R-Plan Manual. Los Angeles: Stanford University, Office of Planned Giving. Updated periodically.

Sharpe, Robert F. *Before You Give Another Dime*. Nashville, Tenn.: Thomas Nelson, 1979.

———. *The Planned Giving Idea Book*. Nashville, Tenn.: Thomas Nelson, 1980.

Stern, Schumacher, John L., and Patrick D. Martin. *Charitable Giving and Solicitation*. New York: Prentice-Hall/Maxwell MacMillan, 1990.

Teitell. *Charitable Lead Trusts*. Old Greenwich, Conn.: Taxwise Giving, 1991.

———. *Deferred Giving*. Old Greenwich, Conn.: Taxwise Giving, 1991.

Teuller, Alden B. *The Planned Giving Deskbook*. Rockville, Md.: The Taft Group, 1991.

Tidd, Jonathan. "The Insurable Interest Rule and Charitable Gifts of Life Insurance." *Tax Management Estates, Gifts and Trusts Journal* (September–October 1991).

Recommended Periodicals and Newsletters

Brownell, Catherine, ed. *Chronicle of Non Profit Enterprise.* Bainbridge Island, WA.
Hopkins, Bruce R. *The Nonprofit Counsel.* New York: John Wiley & Sons.
Meuhrcke, Jill, ed. *Nonprofit World.* Madison, WI: Society for Nonprofit Organizations.
Moerschbaecher, L., McCoy, and Simmons. *Charitable Gift Planning News* (monthly). (214-978-3325) Dallas.
Schoenhals, Roger. *Planned Giving Today.* Seattle, WA.
Stern, Larry, ed. *Non-Profit Times.* Skillman, NJ.
Teitell. *Taxwise Giving.* Old Greenwich, CT.
Teuller, Alden B. *The Planned Gifts Counselor.* Washington, DC: The Taft Group.

39 Marketing: Printed Materials and Publications for Donors and Prospects

RONALD R. JORDAN, JD
New Mexico State University

KATELYN L. QUYNN, JD
Massachusetts General Hospital

39.1 Introduction

Professionals new to planned giving often attempt to compare planned giving to something they already know. Planned giving is not only development and interpersonal skills, public relations, and organizational and office procedures but is similar to a business start-up with the planned giving officer in the role of entrepreneur. The most successful businesses are clear about the products they offer, understand the consumers

824

they are trying to reach, and use marketing strategies to attract constituents. Often the most overlooked and crucial part of a planned giving program is marketing. Planned giving officers may focus on technical proficiency and the building of systems, such as prospect tracking and control, but can neglect the very area that brings prospects to a planned giving program. No amount of technical expertise will generate gifts to the organization unless individuals with donative intent learn about the program. Marketing is a comprehensive, integrated campaign designed to educate an organization's constituents about the organization and its needs for funding. Marketing creates a heightened level of visibility and awareness and projects a positive image of the nonprofit and its planned giving program. Marketing means not only educating prospects about planned giving vehicles but also articulating the needs of the organization. This chapter describes the printed materials needed to market and promote a planned giving program to donors and prospects.

39.2 Marketing Fundamentals

To be successful in attracting business to a planned giving program, it is necessary to understand basic marketing fundamentals. Continuity, repetition, and perseverance are key qualities. Planned giving materials must appear continually over a long period to educate donors and prospects. Each marketing piece, whether a newsletter, advertisement, or other publication, should be produced in a consistent style and placed in approximately the same location in a publication each time it appears. Remember that planned gifts do not usually close immediately, and it is the cumulative impact of marketing to a philanthropic donor over time, along with follow-up, that results in a donor's making a planned gift.

39.3 Case Statement

A case statement educates constituents about the needs of a program or project of the not-for-profit organization. A case statement is a statement that makes a case for support; it can be an extensive document or booklet or as simple as a series of one-page integrated sheets. A case statement can focus exclusively on a particular department or program, or on the major needs of the organization. Properly drafted case statements raise awareness about the organization's needs and, like a menu, offer a variety of funding options along with their corresponding costs. This often-neglected piece is one of the most important marketing tools a development program can offer. Some organizations believe that a case statement is needed only when the organization is involved in a development campaign, but a case statement is essential for every development program, every time money is needed. It communicates the organization's message to its donors and prospects and helps to match interests with needs.

Many organizations spend too much time and money on the production of case statements. An organization may hire free-lance writers, graphic artists, design experts, and high-priced printers to create the statement. This product may be attractive, but all too often fails to connect with its intended audience. The organization should consider, if possible, drafting and producing the case statement in-house. One individual can be charged with the responsibility of drafting it, and others can participate in its creation.

(A) STEPS TO CREATE AN EFFECTIVE CASE STATEMENT

The following five steps may be followed to draft an effective case statement.

1. Design a model that illustrates the components of a case statement. These should include a title for the project, its price, and a description outlining the needs of the organization, department, program, or project.
2. Meet with the necessary dean, physician, department head, program chair, or administrator to explain the purpose of the case statement and to gather information to identify the various components.
3. Determine how the development office will handle the information it receives from the various colleges, departments, or programs assisting in the preparation of the case statement.
4. Create realistic deadlines and timetables for production.
5. Use a desktop publishing program to create a standard format, layout, and design. Arrange for final approval by the appropriate person.

(B) HOW TO USE A CASE STATEMENT

A case statement enables development professionals to show donors and prospects why the organization needs money and how specifically funds will be used, and helps donors to feel connected with the organization and its overall development effort. A case statement can help encourage a donor who has not completely committed to making a gift and can offer suggestions regarding particular areas that can benefit from the donor's planned gift.

39.4 *Guide to Charitable Gift Planning*

A guide to charitable gift planning, or a "Ways to Give" brochure, outlines the many ways that a donor can make a gift to a nonprofit through a wide variety of assets. It is probably the most important brochure in planned giving, because it goes into detail about planned giving options. The brochure may be simple or deluxe, but to be effective, it must outline the different ways to give, show various giving levels and gift minimums, and provide information on taxes, financial planning, and estate planning. A typical table of contents includes the following seven items.

1. *Description of the organization.* Emphasize the prominent and unique features of the organization and the characteristics that separate this nonprofit from other nonprofits. Various design elements, such as bullets, can be used to highlight such features.
2. *About the development office.* Describe the services and programs the development office offers to prospects and donors. This section should be designed to open the door to inquiries and encourage communication between the organization and its constituents.
3. *Menu of assets.* Communicate to the donor the broadest range of asset options that can be used to make gifts. These options include cash, stock, retirement plans, real estate, and tangible personal property.

4. *Planned giving options.* Include a complete discussion of each of the planned giving vehicles offered by the nonprofit. This section should not be overtechnical or authoritative but should pique a donor's interest. Include charitable gift annuities, deferred gift annuities, the pooled income fund, charitable remainder trusts, life insurance, and bequests. Use charts to illustrate financial benefits.
5. *Endowed funding levels.* Provide a summary of the organization's funding levels for establishing chairs, endowed funds, professorships, institutes, and scholarships. The inclusion of minimum giving levels helps to raise donors' sights for making a larger gift.
6. *Leadership and recognition societies.* Leadership and recognition societies help donors to feel that they are part of a larger group, and some donors are motivated to increase their giving to reach certain levels in such societies. Include the name of a planned giving society and list its benefits to members, including special mailings, annual meetings or events, and other membership benefits.
7. *Staff.* Decide whether to include individual staff members' names, titles, and telephone numbers to facilitate contact between staff and donors. When individual employees leave, however, this information becomes out of date.

Once the brochure is printed, send it to donors who request information about making a gift to the organization and take a copy along on a personal visit. Make sure that other development officers are provided with a number of brochures to use when meeting with donors to talk about making gifts. Print many additional copies so that there will always be an available supply.

39.5 Response Form

No planned giving communication or publication is complete without a reply device. A reply device, or response form, enables prospects to communicate with the planned giving office simply and easily. A perforated card, a card inserted into the spine of a booklet, or a tear-off device can be an appropriate response form. The card should always include the planned giving office's address and telephone number and spaces for the prospect's name, address, telephone number, and age. The card should also provide an opportunity to learn about a donor's capacity for giving by including a space for the donor to indicate the anticipated asset to be used to make the gift, and the approximate size of the gift.

39.6 Newsletters

A planned giving or development newsletter that includes planned giving information is a powerful tool in marketing a planned giving program. Consider including planned giving articles, ads, and testimonials in a development newsletter that is distributed organization-wide to donors and prospects. Create a newsletter specific to planned giving and devote the entire issue to planned giving options or to a specific gift vehicle, such as real estate or charitable remainder trusts. Segment planned giving prospects into approximate age brackets and write a newsletter about deferred gift annuities. Then send it to donors or prospects in the age range of 30 to 50 years who would be most interested in learning about deferred gift annuities. Similarly, consider producing a newsletter that features pooled income fund gifts or charitable gift annuities and send it to donors and prospects in appropriate age groups. Through such approaches, donors who would benefit most from a particular message are targeted.

Also consider segmenting prospects by geographic sections to match with asset options. For example, a newsletter that focuses on real estate may be sent to prospects in rural areas, where individuals may have more extensive real estate holdings. A newsletter that features stock options can be directed to prospects in metropolitan areas. Remember to send the newsletter to outside advisors to enhance professional outreach.

39.7   Columns in Not-for-Profit Publications

A planned giving column placed in the not-for-profit's newspaper, magazine, or newsletter affords another opportunity to communicate with planned giving donors and prospects. Emphasizing one or two planned giving vehicles or concepts per issue creates an opportunity to develop a library of informative, in-depth articles over time. These articles can be reprinted and sent as supplementary information to donors. They can also serve as the basis of a longer feature article in a newsletter as well as training materials for staff. The planned giving officer should include a picture of himself as author and planned giving specialist so that donors become more familiar with the planned giving officer and feel more comfortable approaching him or her at donor functions. Include a response box with each column to facilitate requests for information.

39.8   Planned Giving Advertisements

Use planned giving advertisements that can be placed in organization newsletters, newspapers, or magazines to attract new business to the planned giving program. Consider drafting straightforward, uncomplicated informational ads with bullets to highlight various gift benefits, as seen in Exhibit 39.1. Use one ad per gift vehicle or concept, and do not hesitate to repeat publication of the ad. Ads can be drafted and prepared by the planned giving office at little or no cost.

39.9   Buckslips

A buckslip is a valuable form of communication. An inexpensive document that is included with a mailing, it is usually smaller than a full page, often the size of a dollar bill, hence the name buckslip. Like a reply device, a buckslip enables a prospect to ask for more information. Buckslips should be enclosed with mailings such as an annual fund appeal or year-end tax letter. Use a buckslip as a way to encourage donors to request information about various life income gifts or establishing a named fund and tax, financial, and estate planning information. (See Exhibit 39.2.)

A bank, trust company, or utility company may allow not-for-profit organizations to include information about their activities in its mailing. This approach may work best when the not-for-profit is the biggest or best-known organization in the area. It also

EXHIBIT 39.1 Gifts through an Estate

Gifts through Your Estate Benefit
The Academy for Learning

Gifts through your estate provide important benefits to you and The Academy for Learning. Gifts may be made by will or trust, through which you may direct either a specific dollar amount ($25,000) or a percentage (25%). In addition, you may designate your gift to support a particular program or department of interest to you. Through your gift you can:

- Preserve current assets.
- Reduce or eliminate federal estate taxes.
- Make an enduring contribution to The Academy for Learning.
- Become a member of the <PLANNED GIVING SOCIETY>.

The Office of Planned Giving will be pleased to discuss ways to make a gift through your estate to benefit The Academy for Learning. Contact <NAME>, <TITLE>, <ADDRESS>, <CITY, STATE, ZIP>; <TELEPHONE>.

---

works well with small not-for-profits in rural areas. The use of buckslips may not be an option in major cities where there are dozens of not-for-profits, but an inquiry is worth the effort. At one not-for-profit, the planned giving officer spoke with banks in her city about including buckslips with bank statements to customers. The buckslips featured information about life income gifts and the ways in which these gifts can benefit donors as well as the charity. On the reverse side of the card was a response form. Several banks included buckslips in their bank statements, and over a three-month period the charity was able to place more than 65,000 buckslips in the hands of bank customers. Within a week several inquiries were received. This project has now run for several years and is a key component of the marketing program.

EXHIBIT 39.2 Buckslip: Life Income Gifts

The Academy for Learning
Life Income Gifts

Your life income gifts to The Academy for Learning pay dividends. There are several options to choose from depending on your age, your needs, and the way you fund your gift. A life income gift provides the following benefits:

- A stream of income for the lifetime of the donor and/or the donor's spouse
- A charitable income tax deduction
- An opportunity to establish an endowed fund in your name or in the name of a loved one
- Possible avoidance of capital gains taxes on gifts of appreciated property
- Membership in The Academy for Learning leadership club
- A reduction in federal estate taxes

The Office of Development will send you a personalized financial analysis that shows how a life income gift can benefit both you and The Academy for Learning. Please complete the form on the back of this card.

39.10   *Testimonial Advertisements*

A testimonial ad is a good way to illustrate the benefits of a planned gift. It features a donor or donors talking about the gift they made to the organization. These testimonials serve to educate other prospects about gift options, help prospects to feel part of a larger group of donors, and spark a prospect's feeling of similarity to the donor who has already made a gift. Testimonials are nontechnical and easy to read. They show "real life" donors and tend to evoke an emotional response. Be sure to include a picture of the donor(s) in the ad.

39.11   *Letters*

(A)   ANNIVERSARY LETTER

Consider sending donors who have made life income gifts a letter on the anniversary of their last gift. Send calculations that show the benefit of making a new gift this year.

(B)   DONORS WHO HAVE MADE SECURITY GIFTS

Send donors who have made a gift of securities in the last year a letter telling them about the benefits of making a gift to the not-for-profit's pooled income fund. Donors will likely be attracted to the avoidance of capital gains taxes enjoyed by making the gift.

(C)   RETIRED EMPLOYEES

If it is possible to obtain their names, send a letter targeted to retired staff of the not-for-profit. Many worked at the organization for many years and feel quite loyal. Those without children may see the charity as an heir substitute.

(D)   EXISTING PLANNED GIVING DONORS

In November, send all planned giving donors a letter telling them about any tax changes in the upcoming new year or new benefits they may receive by making a planned gift.

- *Planned giving information on annual fund appeal.* Be sure to include a check-off box for more information on the annual fund reply device. In this way, donors who are already interested in the not-for-profit may take the opportunity to learn more about planned giving.
- *Gift in honor or memory.* If the not-for-profit is a hospital, place envelopes around the hospital that provide patients with the opportunity to make a gift in honor or memory of a loved one.
- *Planned giving information in annual or donor report.* Include planned giving information in the not-for-profit's annual or donor report. A back page is an ideal location to include low-key language each year.

- *Planned giving information in tax receipt.* The not-for-profit might like to include planned giving information in tax receipts mailed to donors who have made a gift to the charity. This offers another opportunity to educate donors who already support the charity about planned giving opportunities.
- *Institutional survey.* Charities that send a survey to alumni, patients, subscribers, or members may wish to include language asking the individual to indicate whether he or she would like to receive information about making a planned gift. This language would be particularly appropriate for a survey from an alumni relations area or a hospital asking about patient services.
- *Estate administration booklet.* Donors and prospects will appreciate an informative booklet that describes the duties of an executor or personal representative. Included in the booklet may be information about making a bequest to charity.
- *Web sites.* Most charities are creating Web pages that include information about making a gift to the not-for-profit. Information can range from simple annual fund gifts to how to make a planned gift. Older donors are increasingly using computers for information and correspondence; many initially become attracted to this form of communication as a way to stay in touch with grandchildren. Web sites need to be frequently updated or they become obsolete.

39.12   Pieces in Local Newspapers

If appropriate, test market, in a local community newspaper or trade paper, a planned giving column or ad about life income gift options or gifts of real estate. Use the newspaper to expand the donor population to include those not closely affiliated with the not-for-profit but who might like to make a gift to it. Target appeals to the constituency reading the ad; for example, place planned giving ads for charitable gift annuities in appropriate sections of the newspapers that are read by an older population. Remember to emphasize that these planned giving options are gift vehicles, not traditional investment options, and should be made by individuals with donative intent.

39.13   Desktop Publishing

Desktop publishing has opened the world of printed communications. Offices can now produce printed materials that are as good as, or better than, those they can buy. Instead of using generically produced materials, an organization can generate products that reflect its own personality. To do the job well, quality computer hardware, software, and an experienced operator are needed. There are a number of appropriate hardware and software packages from which to choose. Shop for the best package to accommodate marketing needs and objectives. The largest expense will be incurred in the first year; after that, a budget can be established to purchase updates and enhancements. A first-year budget of $4,000 to $5,000 may be adequate to establish the program, and $500 to $1,000 each year thereafter should support a continued effort.

Desktop publishing software packages are complex, and it is too much to assume that a skilled word processor can excel at desktop publishing. An operator should be sent to a training course, commonly offered at colleges and universities, in the specific software selected. The operator should be part of the planned giving team and should care about the final product. A positive relationship between the writer and the operator is helpful, because production of the promotional materials requires teamwork, feedback, and attention to detail. The results can be well worth the investment in time and money.

39.14 Conclusion

One of the most important components of any planned giving program is marketing. Planned giving is the department in a development office that is most likely to market. To stimulate business, the planned giving officer plays the role of entrepreneur on behalf of the program. Without a strong marketing effort, most prospects will not know about the giving opportunities offered by the organization. The use of marketing vehicles to help prospects identify themselves to the organization will, over time, result in a greater number of planned gifts for the organization.

40 ▼ A Natural Alliance: Financial Planners and Fund Raisers

DANIEL TURSE JR., CFRE
Wayne State University School of Medicine

40.1 Introduction: A Question of Semantics

(A) FINANCIAL PLANNERS

Financial planners may be accountants, attorneys, bankers, brokers, insurance agents, or other professional financial advisors of clients. While the focus of this chapter is on the certified financial planner because of the public esteem that profession has earned over the past decade or so, much of what is written here could be applied to other planners as well. Financial planners (people who, for a fee or commission, undertake to arrange a client's assets to ensure that the client does not outlive them, can—whether alive or dead—help his or her family and others, preserve his or her own wealth, expand that wealth, and save taxes[1]) and professional fund raisers have enough in common to warrant their forming a natural alliance. The results of such a union will benefit not only the financial planner's clients but also the larger society through the institutions of the professional fund raiser.

(B) FINANCIAL PLANNING

Financial planning may be viewed in three ways.[2] The first, that of the International Association of Financial Planning, defines it as "... providing to a person, for compensation, a plan recommending strategies and actions designed to help achieve the financial goals of that person on the basis of an evaluation of the personal financial capabilities of that person."

The second, that of the Institute of Certified Financial Planners, sees financial planning as "... the organization of an individual's financial and personal data for the purposes of developing a strategic plan to constructively manage income, assets, and liabilities to meet near- and long-term goals. ..." Periodic review and monitoring are necessary to ensure that the plan continues to meet the client's needs.

The third, that of the Certified Financial Planner Board of Standards, views financial planning as "the process of determining whether and how an individual can meet life goals through the proper management of financial resources. ... Perhaps the most distinctive skill [needed by financial planners] is that of helping clients to articulate their life goals so that together [planner and client] can begin to determine, first of all, whether those goals are achievable through financial resources, and then how."

All three definitions of financial planning indicate that the planner will become intimately aware of the client's financial resources, goals, and needs. All three definitions imply that the planner is one who must have the trust and confidence of the client. All three definitions indicate that the planner is one able to suggest a charitable gift to someone with donative intent as an integral part of financial planning.

Charitable gifts may be a natural part of some financial plans. Such gifts may increase cash flows for their donors through the avoidance of capital gains taxes or the use of itemized deductions to reduce income taxes, or they may assure that their donors do not run short of money. These gifts may also leave more of an estate for the donors' heirs by reducing estate taxes.

Indeed, the variety of giving techniques opens a wide panorama for reducing taxes legally, and without controversy. As professional fund raisers, we need to be certain that the donor truly has charitable intent and complies with any applicable laws. Our natural allies in this activity should be the certified financial planners themselves.

Both professions have a code of ethics. As fund raisers, many of us[3] subscribe to the Statements of Ethical Principals, the Standards of Professional Practice, and A Donor Bill of Rights as articulated by the Association of Fundraising Professionals (AFP). Others,

---

[1]Freely adapted from the definition of "estate plan" in Robert A. Esperti, Renno L. Peterson, and Jon B. Gandelot's *Legacy: Plan, Protect & Preserve Your Estate: Practical Answers from America's Foremost Estate Planning Attorneys*, Special Edition (Denver: Esperti Peterson Institute, 1996), p. 2.

[2]Sid Mittra, with Jeffrey H. Rattiner, *Practicing Financial Planning: A Complete Guide for Professionals* (Rochester Hills, Mich.: Mittra & Associates), pp. 1–3.

[3]However, Margaret A. Duronio and Eugene R. Temple, in *Fund Raisers: Their Careers, Stories, Concerns and Accomplishments* (San Francisco: Jossey-Bass, 1997), pp. xx–xxi, estimate that less than 50 percent of all fund raisers are accessible via the membership lists of the major professional organizations.

belonging to the National Committee on Planned Giving (NCPG), adhere to the Model Standards of Practice for the Charitable Gift Planner. Whether AFP, NCPG, or both, professional fund raisers are constrained to keep the best interests of the donor in mind at all times and to avoid even the appearance of impropriety.[4] Further, we are obliged to comply with all applicable laws, thus protecting the interests of not only the donor but also the larger society and our own charitable institutions.

Certified financial planners also have their standard, the Code of Ethics and Professional Responsibility. It comprises seven principles, ranging from integrity to objectivity, through competence, fairness, and confidentiality, to professionalism and diligence. Here, too, the intention appears to be protecting the client and the larger society. (See Appendix 40A for the complete code, which is presented in full because most fund raisers are, presumably, unfamiliar with it.)

Because both professional fund raisers and certified financial planners are obliged to place the welfare of their clientele before their own and to protect the interests of the larger society, their codes of ethics make them natural allies. Because of the trust and confidence both professions inspire in that same clientele, both could easily work as allies toward a common goal: adding value to their relationship with the client and to the larger society. Because both professionals will inevitably learn not only the financial but also the social, emotional, and spiritual aspects of their clients' lives,[5] another bond exists between the financial planner and the professional fund raiser.

40.2   A Natural Alliance: An Application

(A)   PROFESSIONAL ADVISORS

It is axiomatic in the fund-raising profession that all major gift and planned giving officers should strive to develop relationships with the professional advisors (accountants, attorneys, bankers, financial planners, insurance agents, trust officers, etc.) of prospects and donors. From where else would mutually beneficial cross-referrals come? Beyond the axioms lies the Leave a Legacy program of the NCPG. The program has certainly made fund raisers and professional advisors aware of each other—and raised the level of consciousness about the importance of and need for bequests in the philanthropic community. It also seems to be the proximate cause of increasing bequests in certain communities selected for observation. Nevertheless, as good as Leave A Legacy is, it is still too early to tell if it will remain in public favor or be replaced with something else.

---

[4]Because the codes of the AFP and the NCPG and A Donor Bill of Rights span several pages of text, I will content myself with just the briefest of synopses and not repeat them here. Anyone who is not a member of the AFP and/or NCPG may secure copies by contacting the AFP at 800-666-FUND (3863) or the NCPG at 317-269-6274.

[5]As professional fund raisers, we are accustomed to searching out information about what motivates donors, what sustains their interest, what must we offer to accommodate their wishes, what really drives *this* donor, or what will change *this* prospect into a committed donor. This kind of information may come, in part, from prospect research, but, more often than not, it will come from skills in building relationships and gradually winning the donor's confidence. What we probably do not realize is that financial planners may just as easily build relationships with their clients, win their confidence, and make telling observations.

Programs all too often have halo effects and then subside into the ordinary. Perhaps something else catches the public's fancy. Perhaps mutual awareness becomes mutual taking for granted. Perhaps we shut our eyes and close our ears to the advertising din about the importance of any program. Perhaps we believe someone else will pick up the challenge. Perhaps we just become indifferent. Perhaps we are so diversified as a society that it is unreasonable to expect one program to work for all indefinitely.[6] Perhaps other factors, which can be identified only by an astute sociologist, are at work.

Ultimately, programs must reduce to people. Without programs, there is no continuity in society. Without people, there are no programs. People supply the imagination, the insight, the wisdom, the talent, and the resiliency needed for any program to flourish. Good programs will help people. But only good people will make programs succeed, which explains another fund-raising axiom: People give to people. That is, we want the right person asking for an acceptable amount at the proper time for the correct purpose of the appropriate donor. If we lack correspondences in one or more places in the preceding verbal equation, our program will suffer. If we lack such correspondences too often, our program will fail.

Again, a natural ally for any fund raiser is the financial planner. In many cases, no one else exists to take on the role of the "right" person. However, not all financial planners are adequately informed about the benefits of charitable giving. Some may even be reluctant to mention it to clients unless the client first introduces the subject.[7] We know of only one who offers a financial incentive to his clients if they include a charitable gift in their financial plans. If the client does so, the planner will remit 25 percent of his fee to a 501(c)3 charity of the donor's choice. The planner, of course, will have to claim the tax deduction, but his is the only such offer we know of among financial planners. (We do know of one attorney who makes an offer of a 10 percent reduction in his fee if the client will make a gift to charity.)

(B) *THE SEVEN FACES OF PHILANTHROPY*

One way for professional fund raisers to forge an alliance with financial planners is to make use of the intriguing book by Russ Alan Prince and Karen Maru File, *The Seven*

---

[6]Kathleen S. Kelly, Ph.D., has an intriguing article, "From Motivation to Mutual Understanding: Shifting the Domain of Donor Research," in *Critical Issues in Fund Raising*, Dwight F. Burlingame, Ph.D., ed. (New York: John Wiley & Sons, 1997), pp. 139–162. Her discussion of the magic bullet theory (also know as the hypodermic needle theory) is particularly relevant here. She cites numerous studies that have discredited any idea that communication would have a powerful effect on public attitudes and behavior. Further, scholars have even demolished the concept of a *general public*. Instead, current thinkers believe that only those who are already predisposed to the message conveyed will pay attention to it. For example, nonsmokers will absorb information about reasons for not smoking. Smokers will not. If indeed these findings are valid, then we as fund raisers must be chary about embracing any program in a mechanical way. Instead, we must constantly test, refine, or reject, keeping only what works for our unique situation at our point in time, realizing that what succeeds or fails today may fail or succeed tomorrow.

[7]I find it interesting that, having gone through eight classes in financial planning, each a semester long, only during part of one evening's class did anyone other than me ever bring up the subject of charitable giving. That person was a guest lecturer who worked for a commercial firm that created charitable plans for its clients.

Faces of Philanthropy: A New Approach to Cultivating Major Donors.[8] These two researchers have devised a system for understanding the concerns, motivations, interests, and needs that affluent donors (those having $1 million or more in a discretionary investment account and having made a gift of $50,000 or more within the past two years to a single nonprofit). At its heart, this remarkable work by two sociologists segments donors based on the similarities of their views about philanthropy.[9] Each affluent donor is fit into a category based "on the needs, motivations, and benefits the individual says are most important to him or her,"[10] each of the seven categories representing a distinct way of viewing philanthropy.[11] (An elaboration of the categories may be found in Appendix 40B.)

We have applied the *Seven Faces* criteria to two sets of clients who consented to our so doing, if we would present them incognito. A summary of their personal and financial data is included in Exhibits 40.1 and 40.2.

40.3   General Observations

For Luis and Betty Abinoja (see Exhibit 40.1), certain possibilities immediately present themselves. They have $1.2 million in securities, with a basis of $230,000. They have real estate worth $290,000, with a basis of $56,000. They have $1 million worth of life insurance, with a basis of $250,000. They have a home and personal property worth $1.5 million, with a basis of $500,000. Their goals are to live comfortably and donate generously.

For Roger Morris (see Exhibit 40.2), we immediately notice his heavy position in cash ($100,000) and securities ($5 million, with a basis of $3 million). He has life insurance of $1 million, with a basis of $40,000 and a qualified retirement plan of $1.2 million. His personal property has a basis and fair market value of $2 million. While Roger has been quite successful financially, his divorce cost him not only his first wife but also his children. Hence, everything he and his second wife leave will go to charity.

We offer the following suggestions for these prospective donors to discuss with their financial advisors. They are only suggestions. All of them are made with underlying

---

[8]Russ Alan Prince and Karen Maru File, *The Seven Faces of Philanthropy: A New Approach to Cultivating Major Donors* (San Francisco: Jossey-Bass, 1994).

[9]*Ibid.*, p. 1.

[10]*Ibid.*, p. 13.

[11]*Ibid.*, pp. 14–16. Many people would take umbrage at placing someone in a restrictive category. However, that is not the purpose behind our borrowing from the schema of Prince and File. Rather, I have asked my associates to use the patterns as norms so we could explore the theoretical construct to see if it would help present or clarify ideas about major gifts to their clientele, and so that we would have a common vocabulary to discuss the subjects of our study. In all cases, since none of the subjects was known to me and since anything tending to identify them has been concealed, I have had to rely on the judgment of the financial planner as to what was the appropriate category for the subject. (I did leave open the possibility of asking subjects to classify themselves, but this was not always practical. Moreover, a subject's answer may have changed from one point in time to another, depending on a variety of factors. Hence, I cannot comment to the timelessness of my colleagues' judgment.) In no case do I feel qualified to remark on the validity of the methodology used by Prince and File. However, their study is certainly one of the most riveting to come along in years, not only for its content but also its cross-disciplinary nature.

Exhibit 40.1 Prospect Grid for Client 1*

Name	Luis Abinoja (H)	Betty Abinoja (W)
U.S. Citizen	Yes	Yes
Marital Status		
Married	Yes	Yes
***Seven Faces* Category**	Investor	
Date of Birth		
Husband	April 1, 1933	
Wife	June 30, 1936	
Occupations		
Husband	CEO and President (retired), Michigan Bell	
Wife	Homemaker	
Children (2)		
Name	Skip Abinoja	
Age	37	
Occupation	Director of Sales	
Special Needs	Has expensive hobbies, like buying vintage cars	
Name	Marjorie Abinoja	
Age	31	
Occupation	Teacher	
Special Needs	Divorced; 1 son, age 6	
Assets		
Cash	$ 50,000	
Securities		
Basis	$ 230,000	
Fair Market Value	$1,200,000	
Real Estate		
Basis	$ 56,000	
Fair Market Value	$ 290,000	
Mortgage	0	
Life Insurance		
Basis	$ 250,000	
Face Value	$1,000,000	
Qualified Retirement Plan	$3,950,254	
Personal Property		
Kind	Home/Personal Property	
Basis	$ 500,000	
Fair Market Value	$1,500,000	
Other Information		
Condensed Cash Flow Statement		
Income	$ 150,000	
Expenditures	$ 200,000	
Taxes	$ 58,000	
Marginal Rate	39%	
Goals/Visions		
Personal	Live comfortably	
Charitable	Donate generously	

Exhibit 40.1 Prospect Grid for Client 1 (*Continued*)

Other Needed Information:
Louis and Betty Abinoja are a happy retired couple. Their children are well placed and don't need help. The Abinojas are charitable people and have been making charitable contributions all along. However, they are willing to donate a lot more if someone can demonstrate that there are major tax advantages for so doing.

Source: Sid Mittra, PhD, CFP, of Mittra Kirkman & Associates, Rochester Hills, Michigan, and professor emeritus of finance at Oakland University, Rochester, graciously supplied the numbers in this chart.

---

assumptions that may or may not fit the realities of these prospects' lives. Moreover, as fund raisers, we can only suggest. If we cross the thin line between suggesting for further discussion with the prospects' personal advisors and recommending, we may be charged with practicing accounting, financial planning, or law. (These are perfectly honorable, acceptable professions for the duly licensed who also carry the appropriate liability insurance; if we have neither license nor insurance, we have to be careful.) We may even be viewed by a disgruntled heir as exercising undue influence on a donor should a gift actually result. Consequently, we protect ourselves and our philanthropic institutions by refraining from activity that may even be perceived as outside our professional purview, or as manipulative, because we have a certain legal and vocational status not accorded to other professions. If we did not protect both, we might lose our reputations and our legal protections as charities.

40.4 General Suggestions: Client 1

We note that the Abinojas are spending $50,000 more each year than they are receiving. Since they have $1.5 million in liquid assets (cash or items quickly turned to cash without suffering an immediate loss for converting) and over $7.9 million in total assets, the $50,000 excess may be part of a spend-down strategy to contract the size of their estate in order to reduce income and estate taxes later. Perhaps the Abinojas are using this excess money as part of their charitable giving. Certainly, the purpose of the excess spending must be established in order to determine the Abinojas' total needs and to make planning more definite for this family.

(A) CHARITABLE REMAINDER UNITRUST VS. CHARITABLE REMAINDER ANNUITY TRUST

If the Abinojas really need that income to maintain their lifestyle, a look at some techniques for charitable giving would help. For example, the Abinojas could take their highly appreciated securities with a fair market value of $1.2 million and convert them into a charitable remainder unitrust (CRUT) or a charitable remainder annuity trust (CRAT), two of the more common vehicles for charitable giving today. The CRUT (at a 5 percent interest rate) would pay $60,000 the first year (and more or less in succeeding years, depending on whether the market went up or down). The CRUT would also yield a charitable deduction of $414,464, which could be written off over the current year and

Exhibit 40.2 Prospect Grid for Client 2

Name	Roger Morris	Philippa Morris
U.S. Citizen	Yes	Yes
Marital Status		
Married	Divorced. Remarried to a much younger woman.	Yes
***Seven Faces* Category**	Communitarian	
Date of Birth		
Husband	July 2, 1932	
Wife	August 10, 1957	
Occupations		
Husband	University Professor/Entrepreneur	
Wife	Homemaker	
Children		
Name	All grown up (3), married and settled No children from second marriage	
Assets		
Cash	$ 100,000	
Securities	$5,000,000	
Basis	$3,000,000	
Fair Market Value	$5,000,000	
Life Insurance		
Basis	$ 40,000	
Face Value	$1,000,000	
Qualified Retirement Plan	$1,200,000	
Personal Property		
Kind	Home	
Basis	$2,000,000	
Fair Market Value	$2,000,000	
Other Information		
Condensed Cash Flow Statement		
Income	$ 300,000	
Expenditures	$ 150,000	
Taxes	$ 70,000	
Marginal Rate	39%	
Goals/Visions		
Personal		
Charitable	After both spouses die, everything will go to charity.	

Other Needed Information:
The Morris family is very successful. Roger's divorce was bitter, and his children also divorced him. That's why nothing will pass on to ex-wife and children. Everything will eventually go to charity.

Source: Sid Mittra, PhD, CFP, of Mittra Kirkman & Associates, Rochester Hills, Michigan, and professor emeritus of finance at Oakland University, Rochester, graciously supplied the numbers in this chart.

the next five years if necessary as an itemized deduction.[12] If the CRUT had to cover only one life instead of two, the charitable deduction would increase because of the greater probability of a shorter time for payouts. (As an aside, we note that if charity is a prime consideration, the Abinojas could donate their payout from the CRUT to charity, thereby increasing the amount of their annual charitable deduction while further enhancing their flow of cash.) At a federal tax rate of 39 percent, the Abinojas could avoid more than $161,000 in taxes ($414,464 × 39 percent).

The CRAT (also at a 5 percent interest rate) would pay $60,000 each year to the Abinojas regardless of which way the market went. The CRAT would yield a charitable deduction of $545,016, which could also be written off over the current year and the next five years.

If the CRAT were limited to payments for one life, the charitable deductions would also increase. The Abinojas could avoid more than $212,000 in taxes at their current federal tax rate ($545,016 × 39 percent).

To resolve the dilemma about whether to accept either kind of a charitable giving vehicle, Mr. and Mrs. Abinoja would have to explain why they are overspending each year. They would also have to determine if the return on their securities exceeded the proposed return of 5 percent for each planned giving vehicle. Moreover, they should look at the fact that the proposed $60,000 would more than replace the $50,000 loss currently being experienced this year. (The $60,000 continues indefinitely with the CRAT; it may go up or down as previously explained in the CRUT.) Further consideration would also have to be given to the fact that they would be getting a substantial charitable deduction currently unavailable to them, they would reduce the considerable exposure (everything over $1.3 million) of their estate to income and estate taxes, and they would continue to be able to make charitable gifts.

(B) PLANNING STRATEGIES

Whatever their choice, the Abinojas must decide if they want any of their estate to pass to their children or grandson, and how much. They must also accept the fact that, like it or not, at the death of the last to survive, much of their estate will be consumed in taxes. They should consider at least three other planning strategies for their estate.

First, they should look at the life insurance policy. If Mr. Abinoja is the owner, placing the policy in an irrevocable life insurance trust (ILIT) is worth considering. If Mr. Abinoja were to die while owning the policy, the proceeds would be exposed to estate tax. If an ILIT were used instead, the proceeds could escape such taxation and be used for the benefit of Mrs. Abinoja, the children, or the grandson by contributing payments for their health, education, maintenance, or support.

Second, the Abinojas must look at the qualified retirement plan. Their financial planner must help them decide if they can expect to spend down most of this amount by the time the second member of the couple dies. If such expenditures are not realistic because of tax impediments involved at withdrawing so much money, then the Abinojas would want to consider leaving the remainder of the plan to charity.[13]

---

[12]All numbers having to do with charitable giving were derived using PGCalc software.

[13]Current discussion is under way in Congress to permit charitable deductions to be made tax free from a retirement plan. As of this writing, such deductions are not permitted. The owner of the plan must pay taxes on all withdrawals, whether they go for charity or not. Of course, if a charitable gift is made today, the itemized deduction (if taken) will efface some of the tax.

Exhibit 40.3 Deduction Calculations: 5% Charitable Unitrust

WAYNE STATE UNIVERSITY	Prepared for:
	Luis and Betty Abinoja
	August 26, 1999

Deduction Calculations
Summary of Benefits

5% Charitable Unitrust

ASSUMPTIONS:

Beneficiary Ages	66
	63
Principal Donated	$1,200,000.00
Cost Basis of Property	$230,000.00
Payout Rate	5%
Payment Schedule	Quarterly
	3 months to 1st payment

BENEFITS:

Charitable Deduction	$418,464.00
First Year's Income	$60,000.00
(future income will vary with trust value)	
	IRS Discount Rate is 7.2%

These calculations are estimates of gift benefits; your actual benefits may vary.

Third, the Abinojas should look at their home. If they remain in it, this wealth would currently be shielded from Medicare should one of them be confined to a nursing home. If the Abinojas are fortunate enough to have long-term care insurance, then the home may be something they want to remove from their estate. The removal could be effected over time by making a gift of the home via a retained life estate. That is, the Abinojas could cede their home to a charity of their choice while retaining the right to live in it until their death. Should the Abinojas accept this idea, they could acquire another charitable deduction of more than $278,000, eligible to be written off this year and the next five years. At a federal tax rate of 39 percent, the Abinojas could avoid more than $108,000 of taxes ($278,000 × 39 percent). Indeed, with all the charitable deductions available to them, the Abinojas and their financial planner should consider "laddering" their charitable gifts so that one set of charitable deductions will expire just as a new set begins while shielding the maximum amount of the family income from taxes. Exhibits 40.3 through 40.5 present the calculations necessary to determine the amount of client's charitable donation. The aforementioned conditions have been taken into consideration for these deduction calculations.

40.5   General Suggestions: Client 2

The Morrises are heavy in appreciated securities ($5 million), life insurance ($1 million), a qualified retirement plan ($1.2 million), and personal property ($2 million). Further,

Exhibit 40.3 Deduction Calculations: 5% Charitable Unitrust (*Continued*)

WAYNE STATE UNIVERSITY

Prepared for:
Luis and Betty Abinoja
August 26, 1999

Deduction Calculations
Charitable Deductions for $1,200,000 Gift

Income Rate	Charitable Unitrust 5%
Two Lives: 66, 63	$418,464
One Life 66	$581,508
One Life 63	$532,464

IRS Discount Rate is 7.2%

Deduction Calculations
Actuarial Calculations

5% Charitable Unitrust

ASSUMPTIONS:

[1]	Beneficiary Ages	66
		63
	Date of Gift	8/19/1999
[2]	Principal Donated	$1,200,000.00
	Cost Basis of Property	$230,000.00
[3]	Payout Rate	5%
[4]	Payment Schedule	Quarterly
		3 months to 1st payment
[5]	Discount Rate under IRC Section 7520(a) for 8/1999	7.2%

CALCULATIONS:

[6]	Adjustment factor for schedule on [4], rate on [5] (Table F in IRS Publication 1458 (1999))	0.957658
[7]	Adjusted unitrust payout rate ([3] × [6]) (Reg. 1.664-4(e)(3))	4.7883%
[8]	Remainder factor for values on [1] and [7] (Table U(2) in IRS Publication 1458 (1999))	0.34872
[9]	**CHARITABLE DEDUCTION** ([2] × [8])	**$418,464.00**

These calculations are estimates of gift benefits; your actual benefits may vary.

Exhibit 40.4 Deduction Calculations: 5% Charitable Annuity Trust

WAYNE STATE UNIVERSITY	Prepared for: Luis and Betty Abinoja August 26, 1999

Deduction Calculations
Summary of Benefits

5% Charitable Annuity Trust

ASSUMPTIONS:

Beneficiary Ages	66
	63
Principal Donated	$1,200,000.00
Cost Basis of Property	$230,000.00
Payout Rate	5%
Payment Schedule	Quarterly
	At end

BENEFITS:

Charitable Deduction	$545,016.00
Annual Income	$60,000.00
	IRS Discount Rate is 7.2%

Deduction Calculations
Charitable Deductions for $1,200,000 Gift

Income Rate	Charitable Annuity Trust 5%
Two Lives: 66, 63	$545,016
One Life 66	$666,708
One Life 63	$631,452
	IRS Discount Rate is 7.2%

These calculations are estimates of gift benefits; your actual benefits may vary.

their income ($300,000) exceeds their expenditures ($150,000) by $150,000. The Morrises appear to be living conservatively and accumulating wealth. They already have liquid assets of $5.1 million and total assets of $9.3 million.

Given the magnitude of their estate and the fact that they have no children by their marriage and wish to leave nothing to the children of Roger's first marriage, they must do some serious financial planning, part of which may involve charitable giving both now and through their estates. Since the disinheritance of children, for any reason, may not sit well with a judge or jury, the Morrises must decide how they want their wealth handled now, after the death of the first of them, and after the death of the second. While

Exhibit 40.4 Deduction Calculations: 5% Charitable Annuity Trust (*Continued*)

WAYNE STATE UNIVERSITY

Prepared for:
Luis and Betty Abinoja
August 26, 1999

Deduction Calculations
Actuarial Calculations

5% Charitable Annuity Trust

ASSUMPTIONS:

[1]	Beneficiary Ages	66
		63
	Date of Gift	8/19/1999
[2]	Principal Donated	$1,200,000.00
	Cost Basis of Property	$230,000.00
[3]	Payout Rate	5%
[4]	Payment Schedule	Quarterly
		At end
[5]	Discount Rate under IRC Section 7520(a) for 8/1999	7.2%

CALCULATIONS:

[6]	Value of $1 for measuring lives/term on [1], rate on [5] (Table R(2) in IRS Publication 1457 (1999))	10.6335
	[a] Adjustment factor for schedule on [4], rate on [5] (Table K in IRS Publication 1457 (1999))	1.0266
	[b] Adjusted value of $1 ([6] × [6a]) (Reg. 20.2031-7(d)(2)(iv))	10.9164
[7]	Remainder factor (1.0 − ([6b] × [3]))	0.45418
[8]	Annual Payment ([2] × [3])	$60,000.00
[9]	Value of Life Interest ([6b] × [8])	$654,984.00
[10]	**CHARITABLE DEDUCTION** ([2] − [9])	**$545,016.00**
[11]	Probability of Corpus Exhaustion (Passes 5% Probability Test of Rev. Rul. 77-374)	0.00%

These calculations are estimates of gift benefits; your actual benefits may vary.

all the estate may pass tax free to the surviving spouse and while leaving the final estate (after the death of the second spouse) to charity should avoid any estate tax, the magnitude of this estate warrants thoughtful planning by a professional financial planner to reduce the likelihood of other problems, such as lawsuits.

To avoid lawsuits by disgruntled heirs, the Morrises should look seriously at giving away as many of their assets as possible while they are still alive. While alive, it is far easier for them to refute charges of succumbing to undue influence, dementia, or whatever

Exhibit 40.5 Deduction Calculations: Retained Life Estate

WAYNE STATE UNIVERSITY	Prepared for: Luis and Betty Abinoja August 26, 1999

Deduction Calculations
Summary of Benefits

Retained Life Estate

ASSUMPTIONS:

Life Tenant Ages	66
	63
Value of Property	$1,500,000.00
Cost Basis of Property	$500,000.00
Value of Depreciable Portion	$1,000,000.00
Estimated Useful Life of Property	45 years
Salvage Value of Property	$250,000.00

BENEFITS:

Charitable Deduction	$278,032.50

IRS Discount Rate is 7.2%

Deduction Calculations
Charitable Deductions for $1,500,000 Gift

	Retained Life Estate
Two Lives: 66, 63	$278,033
One Life 66	$491,685
One Life 63	$430,980

Column 1: Asset is 50% net depreciable with useful life of 45 years.

IRS Discount Rate is 7.2%

These calculations are estimates of gift benefits; your actual benefits may vary.

else frustrated heirs may raise. While alive, the Morrises may also see the benefit of their philanthropic efforts and receive not only satisfaction but also personal thanks. After their death, only cold memorials will remain as reminders that Roger and Philippa Morris once lived and cared about others. For both of these reasons (the avoidance of future legal wrangling and the value of seeing one's investment in charity), the Morrises should consider giving away as many of their assets as they can now without compromising their lifestyle.

Exhibit 40.5 Deduction Calculations: Retained Life Estate (*Continued*)

WAYNE STATE UNIVERSITY

Prepared for:
Luis and Betty Abinoja
August 26, 1999

Deduction Calculations
Actuarial Calculations

Retained Life Estate

ASSUMPTIONS:

[1]	Life Tenant Ages	66
		63
	Date of Gift	8/19/1999
[2]	Value of Property	$1,500,000.00
	Cost Basis of Property	$500,000.00
[3]	Value of Depreciable Portion	$1,000,000.00
[4]	Estimated Useful Life of Property	45 years
[5]	Salvage Value of Property	$250,000.00
[6]	Discount Rate under IRC Section 7520(a) for 8/1999	7.2%

CALCULATIONS:

[7]	Undepreciable Factor for [1] and [6] (Reg. 1.170A-12(e)(2))	0.23439
[8]	Remainder Value of Net Undepreciable Portion ([7] × ([2] − ([3] − [5])))	$175,792.50
[9]	Depreciable Factor for [1], [4] & [6] (Reg. 1.170A-12(e)(2))	0.13632
[10]	Remainder Value of Net Depreciable Portion ([9] × ([3] − [5]))	$102,240.00
[11]	**CHARITABLE DEDUCTION** ([8] + [10])	**$278,032.50**

These calculations are estimates of gift benefits; your actual benefits may vary.

(A) CHARITABLE REMAINDER UNITRUST VS. CHARITABLE REMAINDER ANNUITY TRUST

Although the Morrises can establish a CRUT or a CRAT, the couple does not appear to need more income. (They are already $150,000 ahead of their expenditures.) A CRUT funded with $5 million of appreciated stock would yield a charitable deduction of more than $950,000 and $250,000 of income the first year, not something the Morrises need but something that will get wealth out of their estate and make charity the beneficiary. A CRAT may also be worth considering (charitable deduction of more than $1.8 million and a guaranteed annual income of $250,000) in order to remove assets from the Morrises' estate for the future benefit of charity.

(B) PLANNING STRATEGIES

Whatever their choice, the Morrises should decide if they want to leave something for his children and ex-wife in order to avoid shocking the judge or the jury, in exchange for not contesting Roger and Philippa's current financial plans. One way to do this would be to create an ILIT for the health, education, maintenance, and support of Roger's former family, with the residual (if any) going to a charity (possibly of their choice) after the death of the last survivor.

The Morrises must also look at their qualified retirement plan. They too must work with their financial planner to determine how much of this they can be expected to use during their joint lives. In order to avoid taxes on the plan, they should consider naming a charity as a contingent beneficiary since they have so many other assets on which to live and accumulation does not seem to be a problem for them.

They should also consider a gift of a retained life estate in order to remove their expensive ($2 million) home from their estate. By making such a gift, they could receive a charitable deduction of $148,070, which they could spread over the current year and the next five years if needed. Furthermore, they could avoid more than $57,000 in taxes ($148,000 × 39 percent).

Whether a CRUT, CRAT, ILIT, or retained life estate, given the Morrises' ability to accumulate and their relatively low propensity to consume, they may want to consider something else, like a family foundation or a charitable endowment that they begin funding immediately and add to at least annually. Family foundations do cost more to administer and do not create the same charitable deductions that gifts to a regular charity would, but they do give their founders the opportunity to "get into the role" of being philanthropists by being courted by eligible charities seeking gifts. They also give the founders the right to take a reasonable salary for their services and to pass on their charitable interests to family or other heirs. Charitable endowments may often be donor advised. Here, the benefactor may not only see the results of his or her generosity and receive appropriate itemized deductions but also participate in the choice of recipients of such benevolence.

Exhibits 40.6 through 40.8 present the calculations necessary to determine the amount of Client 2's charitable donation. The aforementioned conditions have been taken into consideration for these deduction calculations.

40.6   Summary of Observations and Suggestions

	Luis and Betty Abinoja	Roger and Philippa Morris
Liquid Assets	$1.5 million	$5.1 million
Total Assets	$7.9 million	$9.3 million
Excess (Loss) of Revenues over Expenditures	($50,000)	$ 150,000
Charitable Vehicles for Consideration		
CRUT @ 5% (Year I)	$ 60,000	$ 250,000
Charitable Deduction	$414,464	$ 957,650

	Luis and Betty Abinoja	Roger and Philippa Morris
CRAT @ 5% (All Years)	$ 60,000	$ 250,000
Charitable Deduction	$545,016	$1,813,450
Retained Life Estate		
Charitable Deduction	$278,032	$ 370,175
Other Considerations		
ILIT	Yes	Yes
Qualified Retirement Plan	Yes	Yes
Need for More Financial Planning	Yes	Yes
Prospect for a Planned Gift	Yes	Yes
Tangible and Intangible Benefits from Planned Gifts	Yes	Yes

40.7 Afterthoughts

(A) FINANCIAL PLANNERS AND FUND RAISERS: A NATURAL ALLIANCE BASED ON TRUST

Financial planners and fund raisers may form a natural alliance. They both have codes of ethics with sanctions attached. They both must earn the confidence of their respective clients or constituents, and often grow to know these people better than any other outsider ever will. They both are obliged to place the welfare of their clientele before their own and to protect the interests of the larger society. Should planners and fund raisers choose to collaborate, they are in a unique position to benefit society, their clientele, and each other.

Any such alliance must be based on trust. Planners need to know that their clients will not be pursued for a gift. Fund raisers need to know that they are not part of a scheme to use the system with no charitable intent on the part of the donor. Both planner and fund raiser need to help each other make the advantages of charitable giving known to prospects.

(B) ALLIANCE IS NOT A TALISMAN OR A "CURE-ALL"

Nevertheless, planners and fund raisers must be aware that their alliance is probably not going to be the talisman that cures all their ills. The program they forge will appeal to some but not all. Taking an Investor and a Communitarian from the *Seven Faces*, we were delighted to see how readily these prospects could benefit from planned gifts. To expect other prospects from other categories—or even more prospects from these same categories—to benefit from such an analysis is farther than we are prepared to go. Indeed, even persuading a prospect to let a fund raiser review confidential financial information is not easy, and getting that same prospect to sit down with that same fund raiser, *plus* the

Exhibit 40.6 Deduction Calculations: 5% Charitable Unitrust

WAYNE STATE UNIVERSITY	Prepared for: Roger and Philippa Morris August 26, 1999

Deduction Calculations
Summary of Benefits

5% Charitable Unitrust

ASSUMPTIONS:

Beneficiary Ages	67
	42
Principal Donated	$5,000,000.00
Cost Basis of Property	$3,000,000.00
Payout Rate	5%
Payment Schedule	Quarterly
	3 months to 1st payment

BENEFITS:

Charitable Deduction	$957,650.00
First Year's Income	$250,000.00
(future income will vary with trust value)	
	IRS Discount Rate is 7.2%

Deduction Calculations
Charitable Deductions for $5,000,000 Gift

Income Rate	Charitable Unitrust 5%
Two Lives: 67, 42	$957,650
One Life 67	$2,493,000
One Life 42	$1,048,300
	IRS Discount Rate is 7.2%

These calculations are estimates of gift benefits; your actual benefits may vary.

financial planner, may be equally challenging. Such an alliance may be a case in which we call to many but are chosen by few—and we must not feel frustrated if that happens.

(C) THERE IS NO PREFERRED TECHNIQUE IN PLANNED GIVING

Finally, planners and fund raisers must not tout one technique in planned giving over another. A variety of mechanisms for making a gift is available. Knowledge of some or

Exhibit 40.6 Deduction Calculations: 5% Charitable Unitrust (*Continued*)

WAYNE STATE UNIVERSITY

Prepared for:
Roger and Philippa Morris
August 26, 1999

Deduction Calculations
Actuarial Calculations

5% Charitable Unitrust

ASSUMPTIONS:

[1]	Beneficiary Ages	67
		42
	Date of Gift	8/19/1999
[2]	Principal Donated	$5,000,000.00
	Cost Basis of Property	$3,000,000.00
[3]	Payout Rate	5%
[4]	Payment Schedule	Quarterly
		3 months to 1st payment
[5]	Discount Rate under IRC Section 7520(a) for 8/1999	7.2%

CALCULATIONS:

[6]	Adjustment factor for schedule on [4], rate on [5] (Table F in IRS Publication 1458 (1999))	0.957658
[7]	Adjusted unitrust payout rate ([3] × [6]) (Reg. 1.664-4(e)(3))	4.7883%
[8]	Remainder factor for values on [1] and [7] (Table U(2) in IRS Publication 1458 (1999)	0.19153
[9]	**CHARITABLE DEDUCTION** ([2] × [8])	**$957,650.00**

These calculations are estimates of gift benefits; your actual benefits may vary.

all of them, while important, is not sufficient. The prospect's interest must be paramount at all times. If the gift is not good for the donor, it will not be good for the charitable institution (or the planner or the fund raiser) in the long run. While we chose to examine the results of the more common CRUT and the CRAT, as well as the useful retained life estate, these are not all the options we have available. Even if they were, the ages of the prospects, the amounts invested, the basis of those investments, the payout rates assumed, the discount rates mandated by the Internal Revenue Service, the tax rates in force—all would prevent facile generalizations.[14]

---

[14]For an interesting article about the relationships between just the payout rate and the IRS discount rate, see Bill Laskin's "The General Theory of Discount Rate Relativity," *Planned Giving Today* (May 1995): 3–4. I am indebted to Joshua DeLong of PGCalc for calling this article to my attention.

Exhibit 40.7 Deduction Calculations: 5% Charitable Annuity Trust

WAYNE STATE UNIVERSITY	Prepared for: Roger and Philippa Morris August 26, 1999

Deduction Calculations
Summary of Benefits

5% Charitable Annuity Trust

ASSUMPTIONS:

Beneficiary Ages	67
	42
Principal Donated	$5,000,000.00
Cost Basis of Property	$3,000,000.00
Payout Rate	5%
Payment Schedule	Quarterly
	At end

BENEFITS:

Charitable Deduction	$1,813,450.00
Annual Income	$250,000.00
	IRS Discount Rate is 7.2%

Deduction Calculations
Charitable Deductions for $5,000,000 Gift

Income Rate	Charitable Annuity Trust 5%
Two Lives: 67, 42	$1,813,450
One Life 67	$2,829,400
One Life 42	$1,881,000
	IRS Discount Rate is 7.2%

These calculations are estimates of gift benefits; your actual benefits may vary.

(D)   IMPORTANCE OF RELATIONSHIPS

We recommend going back to one of the basics of all serious fund raising. Relationships are extremely important in this business. We must build them with donors if we expect continuity in giving. We must foster them with prospects if we want to convert them into donors. We must create them with professional advisors if we expect their help. Quite naturally, one category of professional advisor with whom we might form a natural

Exhibit 40.7 Deduction Calculations: 5% Charitable Annuity Trust (*Continued*)

WAYNE STATE UNIVERSITY	Prepared for: Roger and Philippa Morris August 26, 1999

Deduction Calculations
Actuarial Calculations

5% Charitable Annuity Trust

ASSUMPTIONS:

[1]	Beneficiary Ages	67
		42
	Date of Gift	8/26/1999
[2]	Principal Donated	$5,000,000.00
	Cost Basis of Property	$3,000,000.00
[3]	Payout Rate	5%
[4]	Payment Schedule	Quarterly
		At end
[5]	Discount Rate under IRC Section 7520(a) for 8/1999	7.2%

CALCULATIONS:

[6]	Value of $1 for measuring lives/term on [1], rate on [5] (Table R(2) in IRS Publication 1457 (1999))	12.4159
	[a] Adjustment factor for schedule on [4], rate on [5] (Table K in IRS Publication 1457 (1999))	1.0266
	[b] Adjusted value of $1 ([6] × [6a]) (Reg. 20.2031-7(d)(2)(iv))	12.7462
[7]	Remainder factor (1.0 − ([6b] × [3]))	0.36269
[8]	Annual Payment ([2] × [3])	$250,000.00
[9]	Value of Life Interest ([6b] × [8])	$3,186,550.00
[10]	**CHARITABLE DEDUCTION** ([2] − [9])	**$1,813,450.00**
[11]	Probability of Corpus Exhaustion (Passes 5% Probability Test of Rev. Rul. 77-374)	0.00%

These calculations are estimates of gift benefits; your actual benefits may vary.

alliance is the financial planner, while we simultaneously build all our other relationships.

Hence, the end of this chapter is also its beginning. The past, to a degree, does contain the present. Time-tested axioms about fund raising should not be cavalierly dismissed, especially if they involve the importance of relationships, individuals, belief in the institutional mission of the charity, the importance of philanthropy, giving techniques, and ethics.

Exhibit 40.8 Deduction Calculations: Retained Life Estate

WAYNE STATE UNIVERSITY	Prepared for: Roger and Philippa Morris August 26, 1999

Deduction Calculations
Summary of Benefits

Retained Life Estate

ASSUMPTIONS:

Life Tenant Ages	67
	42
Value of Property	$2,000,000.00
Cost Basis of Property	$2,000,000.00
Value of Depreciable Portion	$1,333,333.00
Estimated Useful Life of Property	45 years
Salvage Value of Property	$333,333.00

BENEFITS:

Charitable Deduction	$148,070.00

IRS Discount Rate is 7.2%

Deduction Calculations
Charitable Deductions for $2,000,000 Gift

	Retained Life Estate
Two Lives: 67, 42	$148,070
One Life 67	$684,240
One Life 42	$185,980

Column 1: Asset is 50% net depreciable with useful life of 45 years.

IRS Discount Rate is 7.2%

These calculations are estimates of gift benefits; your actual benefits may vary.

40.8 Epilogue: On the Crafting and Sustaining of an Alliance

Prospects and donors may go from the planner to the fund raiser or vice versa. Neither professional would be totally comfortable sending the prospects or donors to the other without a clear sign from the client. The planner would much rather have the potential donor specify the charity. The fund raiser would prefer to have the potential donor choose a planner. What is important is that the planner and the fund raiser trust each other and proceed with the best interests of the prospect in mind.

Exhibit 40.8 Deduction Calculations: Retained Life Estate (*Continued*)

WAYNE STATE UNIVERSITY

Prepared for:
Roger and Philippa Morris
August 26, 1999

Deduction Calculations
Actuarial Calculations

Retained Life Estate

ASSUMPTIONS:

[1]	Life Tenant Ages	67
		42
	Date of Gift	8/26/1999
[2]	Value of Property	$2,000,000.00
	Cost Basis of Property	$2,000,000.00
[3]	Value of Depreciable Portion	$1,333,333.00
[4]	Estimated Useful Life of Property	45 years
[5]	Salvage Value of Property	$333,333.00
[6]	Discount Rate under IRC Section 7520(a) for 8/1999	7.2%

CALCULATIONS:

[7]	Undepreciable Factor for [1] and [6] (Reg. 1.170A-12(e)(2))	0.10605
[8]	Remainder Value of Net Undepreciable Portion ([7] × ([2] − ([3] − [5])))	$106,050.00
[9]	Depreciable Factor for [1], [4] & [6] (Reg. 1.170A-12(e)(2))	0.04202
[10]	Remainder Value of Net Depreciable Portion ([9] × ([3] − [5]))	$42,020.00
[11]	**CHARITABLE DEDUCTION** ([8] + [10])	**$148,070.00**

These calculations are estimates of gift benefits; your actual benefits may vary

In this particular instance, we have known Professor Mittra for two years. Both of us know some of the other's clientele. While each of us has our professional venues, we attend each other's presentations. Each tries to help the other succeed. We adhere to our respective professional codes of ethics, neither of us trying to milk or manipulate the client or each other. Were he to send us a prospect, we are confident there would be no lack of charitable intent in that prospect. We do not try to usurp Professor Mittra's role as planner. Anything less would prevent or dissolve our alliance.

For an alliance to exist, it is the planner who interacts with the client to elicit objectives, gather relevant data for addressing and resolving the client's problems, process and analyze financial data, recommend actions to the client, implement a financial plan, and monitor and review the plan.[15] This is the current sequence of steps in the financial planning process. For the alliance to exist, it is the fund raiser who tries to match a donor's needs and wants with an institution's. This match is open to negotiation on both sides and is less subject to a protocol than financial planning.

For the two cases reviewed (the Abinojas and the Morrises), Professor Mittra supplied the financial data. I vented my fund-raising reflexes and my knowledge of some financial planning techniques. I will respect the relationship both couples have with Professor Mittra and not try to persuade his clients to make gifts to my charity. Professor Mittra will review my suggestions with his clients, who will then make their own decisions about whether or not to give, when to give, how much to give, and to whom to give. That decision is totally in keeping for an ethical financial planner and an ethical fund raiser.

Sources and Suggested Readings

Duronio, Margaret A., and Eugene R. Temple. In *Fund Raisers: Their Careers, Stories, Concerns and Accomplishments*. San Francisco: Jossey-Bass, 1997.

Esperti, Robert A., Renno L. Peterson, and Jon Gadelot. *Legacy: Plan, Protect & Preserve Your Estate: Practical Answers from America's Foremost Estate Planning Attorneys*, Special Edition. Denver: Esperti Peterson Institute, 1996.

Kelly, Kathleen S. "From Motivation to Mutual Understanding: Shifting the Domain of Donor Research." Dwight F. Burlingame, ed., *Critical Issues in Fund Raising*. New York: John Wiley & Sons, 1997.

Laskin, Bill. "The General Theory of Discount Rate Relativity." *Planned Giving Today* (May 1995).

Mittra, Sid, with Jeffrey H. Rattiner. *Practicing Financial Planning: A Complete Guide for Professionals*. Rochester Hills, Mich.: Mittra & Associates, 1998.

Prince, Russ Alan, and Karen Maru File. *The Seven Faces of Philanthropy: A New Approach to Cultivating Major Donors*. San Francisco: Jossey-Bass, 1994.

*Appendix 40A   Code of Ethics and Professional Responsibility**
Preamble and Applicability

The *Code of Ethics and Professional Responsibility* (Code) has been adopted by the Certified Financial Planner Board of Standards, Inc. (CFP Board) to provide principles and rules to all persons whom it has recognized and certified to use the CFP certification mark and the marks CFP and Certified Financial Planner (collectively "the marks"). The CFP Board determines who is recognized and certified to use the marks. Implicit in the acceptance of this authorization is an obligation not only to comply with the mandates and requirements of all applicable laws and regulations but also to take responsibility to act in an ethical and professionally responsible manner in all professional services and activities.

For purposes of this Code, a person recognized and certified by the CFP Board to use the marks is called a CFP designee or Certified Financial Planner designee. This Code applies to CFP designees actively involved in the practice of personal financial planning, in other areas of financial services, in industry, in related professions, in government, in education, or in any other professional activity in which the marks are used in the performance of their professional

---

[15]Sid Mittra, with Jeffrey Rattiner, *Practicing Financial Planning: A Complete Guide for Professionals* (Rochester Hills, Mich.: Mittra & Associates, 1998), pp 1-9–1-12.

Reproduced from Licensee Standards, Denver: Certified Financial Planner Board of Standards, 1999.

responsibilities. This Code also applies to candidates for the CFP designation who are registered as such with the CFP Board. For purposes of this Code, the term CFP designee shall be deemed to include candidates.

Composition and Scope

The Code consists of two parts: **Part I—Principles** and **Part II—Rules.** The Principles are statements expressing in general terms the ethical and professional ideals expected of CFP designees and which they should strive to display in their professional activities. As such, the Principles are aspirational in character but are intended to provide a source of guidance for a CFP designee. The comments following each Principle further explain the meaning of the Principle. The Rules provide practical guidelines derived from the tenets embodied in the Principles. As such, the Rules set forth the standards of ethical and professionally responsible conduct expected to be followed in particular situations. This Code does not undertake to define standards of professional conduct of CFP designees for purposes of civil liability.

Due to the nature of a CFP designee's particular field of endeavor, certain Rules may not be applicable to that CFP designee's activities. For example, a CFP designee who is engaged solely in the sale of securities as a registered representative is not subject to the written disclosure requirements of Rule 402 (applicable to CFP designees engaged in personal financial planning) although he or she may have disclosure responsibilities under Rule 401. A CFP designee is obligated to determine what responsibilities the CFP designee has in each professional relationship including, for example, duties that arise in particular circumstances from a position of trust or confidence that a CFP designee may have. The CFP designee is obligated to meet those responsibilities.

The Code is structured so that the presentation of the Rules parallels the presentation of the Principles. For example, the Rules which relate to Principle 1—Integrity, are numbered in the 100 to 199 series while those Rules relating to Principle 2—Objectivity, are numbered in the 200 to 299 series.

Compliance

The CFP Board of Governors requires adherence to this Code by all those it recognizes and certifies to use the marks. Compliance with the Code, individually and by the profession as a whole, depends on each CFP designee's knowledge of and voluntary compliance with the Principles and applicable Rules, on the influence of fellow professionals and public opinion, and on disciplinary proceedings, when necessary, involving CFP designees who fail to comply with the applicable provisions of the Code.

Terminology In This Code

"CFP designee" denotes current licensees, candidates for certification, and individuals that have any entitlement, direct or indirect, to the federally registered service marks CFP® and Certified Financial Planner®.

"Client" denotes a person, persons, or entity who engages a practitioner and for whom professional services are rendered. For purposes of this definition, a practitioner is engaged when an individual, based upon the relevant facts and circumstances, reasonably relies upon information or service provided by that practitioner. Where the services of the practitioner are provided to an entity (corporation, trust, partnership, estate, etc.), the client is the entity acting through its legally authorized representative.

"Commission" denotes the compensation received by an agent or broker when the same is calculated as a percentage on the amount of his or her sales or purchase transactions.

"Conflict(s) of interest(s)" denotes circumstances, relationships, or other facts about the CFP designee's own financial, business, property, and/or personal interests which will or reasonably may impair the CFP designee's rendering of disinterested advice, recommendations or services.

"Fee-only" denotes a method of compensation in which compensation is received solely from a client with neither the personal financial planning practitioner nor any related party receiving compensation which is contingent upon the purchase or sale of any financial product. A "related party" for this purpose shall mean an individual or entity from whom any direct or indirect economic benefit is derived by the personal financial planning practitioner as a result of implementing a recommendation made by the personal financial planning practitioner.

"Personal financial planning" or **"financial planning"** denotes the process of determining whether and how an individual can meet life goals through the proper management of financial resources.

"Personal financial planning process" or **"financial planning process"** denotes the process which typically includes, but is not limited to, the six elements of establishing and defining the client-planner relationship, gathering client data including goals, analyzing and evaluating the client's financial status, developing and presenting financial planning recommendations and/or alternatives, implementing the financial planning recommendations, and monitoring the financial planning recommendations.

"Personal financial planning practitioner" or **"financial planning practitioner"** denotes a person who is capable and qualified to offer objective, integrated, and comprehensive financial advice to or for the benefit of clients to help them achieve their financial objectives and who engages in financial planning using the financial planning process in working with clients.

"Personal financial planning professional" or **"financial planning professional"** denotes a person who is capable and qualified to offer objective, integrated, and comprehensive financial advice to or for the benefit of individuals to help them achieve their financial objectives. A financial planning professional must have the ability to provide financial planning services to clients, using the financial planning process covering the basic financial planning subjects.

"Personal financial planning subject areas" or **"financial planning subject areas"** denotes the basic subject fields covered in the financial planning process which typically include, but are not limited to, financial statement preparation and analysis (including cash flow analysis/planning and budgeting), investment planning (including portfolio design, i.e., asset allocation, and portfolio management), income tax planning, education planning, risk management, retirement planning, and estate planning.

Part I—Principles

Introduction

These Principles of the Code express the profession's recognition of its responsibilities to the public, to clients, to colleagues, and to employers. They apply to all CFP designees and provide guidance to them in the performance of their professional services.

Principle 1—Integrity

A CFP designee shall offer and provide professional services with integrity.

As discussed in Composition and Scope, CFP designees may be placed by clients in positions of trust and confidence. The ultimate source of such public trust is the CFP designee's personal integrity. In deciding what is right and just, a CFP designee should rely on his or her integrity as the appropriate touchstone. Integrity demands honesty and candor which must not be subordinated to personal gain and advantage. Within the characteristic of integrity, allowance can be made for innocent error and legitimate difference of opinion; but integrity cannot co-exist with deceit or subordination of one's principles. Intregrity requires a CFP designee to observe not only the letter but also the spirit of this Code.

Principle 2—Objectivity

A CFP designee shall be objective in providing professional services to clients.

Objectivity requires intellectual honesty and impartiality. It is an essential quality for any professional. Regardless of the particular service rendered or the capacity in which a CFP designee functions, a CFP designee should protect the integrity of his or her work, maintain objectivity, and avoid subordination of his or her judgment that would be in violation of this Code.

Principle 3—Competence

A CFP designee shall provide services to clients competently and maintain the neccessary knowledge and skill to continue to do so in those areas in which the designee is engaged.

One is competent only when he or she has attained and maintained an adequate level of knowledge and skill, and applies that knowledge effectively in providing services to clients. Competence also includes the wisdom to recognize the limitations of that knowledge and when consultation or client referral is appropriate. A CFP designee, by virtue of having earned the CFP designation, is deemed to be qualified to practice financial planning. However, in addition to assimilating the common body of knowledge required and acquiring the necessary experience for designation, a CFP designee shall make a continuing commitment to learning and professional improvement.

Principle 4—Fairness

A CFP designee shall perform professional services in a manner that is fair and reasonable to clients, principals, partners, and employers and shall disclose conflict(s) of interest(s) in providing such services.

Fairness requires impartiality, intellectual honesty, and disclosure of conflict(s) of interest(s). It involves a subordination of one's own feelings, prejudices, and desires so as to achieve a proper balance of conflicting interests. Fairness is treating others in the same fashion that you would want to be treated and is an essential trait of any professional.

Principle 5—Confidentiality

A CFP designee shall not disclose any confidential client information without the specific consent of the client unless in response to proper legal process, to defend against charges of wrongdoing by the CFP designee or in connection with a civil dispute between the CFP designee and client.

A client, by seeking the services of a CFP designee, may be interested in creating a relationship of personal trust and confidence with the CFP designee. This type of relationship can only be built upon the understanding that information supplied to the CFP designee or other information will be confidential. In order to provide the contemplated services effectively and to protect the client's privacy, the CFP designee shall safeguard the confidentiality of such information.

Principle 6—Professionalism

A CFP designee's conduct in all matters shall reflect credit upon the profession.

Because of the importance of the professional services rendered by CFP designees, there are attendant responsibilities to behave with dignity and courtesy to all those who use those services, fellow professionals, and those in related professions. A CFP designee also has an obligation to cooperate with fellow CFP designees to enhance and maintain the profession's public image and to work jointly with other CFP designees to improve the quality of services. It is only through the combined efforts of all CFP designees in cooperation with other professionals, that this vision can be realized.

Principle 7—Diligence

A CFP designee shall act diligently in providing professional services.

Diligence is the provision of services in a reasonably prompt and thorough manner. Diligence also includes proper planning for and supervision of the rendering of professional services.

Part II—Rules

Introduction

As stated in **Part I—Principles**, the Principles apply to all CFP designees. However, due to the nature of a CFP designee's particular field of endeavor, certain Rules may not be applicable to that CFP designee's activities. The universe of activities by CFP designees is indeed diverse and a particular CFP designee may be performing all, some or none of the typical services provided by financial planning professionals. As a result, in considering the Rules in Part II, a CFP designee must first recognize what specific services he or she is rendering and then determine whether or not a specific Rule is applicable to those services. To assist the CFP designee in making these determinations, this Code includes a series of definitions of terminology used throughout the Code. Based upon these definitions, a CFP designee should be able to determine which services he or she provides and, therefore, which Rules are applicable to those services.

Rules that Relate to the Principle of Integrity

Rule 101

A CFP designee shall not solicit clients through false or misleading communications or advertisements:

(a) **Misleading Advertising:** A CFP designee shall not make a false or misleading communication about the size, scope or areas of competence of the CFP designee's practice or of any organization with which the CFP designee is associated; and

(b) **Promotional Activities:** In promotional activities, a CFP designee shall not make materially false or misleading communications to the public or create unjustified expectations regarding matters relating to financial planning or the professional activities and competence of the CFP designee. The term "promotional activities" includes, but is not limited to, speeches, interviews, books and/or printed publications, seminars, radio and television shows, and video cassettes; and

(c) **Representation of Authority:** A CFP designee shall not give the impression that a CFP designee is representing the views of the CFP Board or any other group unless the CFP designee has been authorized to do so. Personal opinions shall be clearly identified as such.

Rule 102

In the course of professional activities, a CFP designee shall not engage in conduct involving dishonesty, fraud, deceit, or misrepresentation, or knowingly make a false or misleading statement to a client, employer, employee, professional colleague, governmental or other regulatory body or official, or any other person or entity.

Rule 103

A CFP designee has the following responsibilities regarding funds and/or other property of clients:

(a) In exercising custody of or discretionary authority over client funds or other property, a CFP designee shall act only in accordance with the authority set forth in the governing legal instrument (e.g., special power of attorney, trust, letters testamentary, etc.); and

(b) A CFP designee shall identify and keep complete records of all funds or other property of a client in the custody of or under the discretionary authority of the CFP designee; and

(c) Upon receiving funds or other property of a client, a CFP designee shall promptly or as otherwise permitted by law or provided by agreement with the client, deliver to the client or third party any funds or other property which the client or third party is entitled to receive and, upon request by the client, render a full accounting regarding such funds or other property; and

(d) A CFP designee shall not commingle client funds or other property with a CFP designee's personal funds and/or other property or the funds and/or other property of a CFP designee's firm. Commingling one or more clients' funds or other property together is permitted, subject to compliance with applicable legal requirements and provided accurate records are maintained for each client's funds or other property; and

(e) A CFP designee who takes custody of all or any part of a client's assets for investment purposes, shall do so with the care required of a fiduciary.

Rules that Relate to the Principle of Objectivity

Rule 201

A CFP designee shall exercise reasonable and prudent professional judgment in providing professional services.

Rule 202

A financial planning practitioner shall act in the interest of the client.

Rules that Relate to the Principle of Competence

Rule 301

A CFP designee shall keep informed of developments in the field of financial planning and participate in continuing education throughout the CFP designee's professional career in order to improve professional competence in all areas in which the CFP designee is engaged. As a distinct part of this requirement, a CFP designee shall satisfy all minimum continuing education requirements established for CFP designees by the CFP Board.

Rule 302

A CFP designee shall offer advice only in those areas in which the CFP designee has competence. In areas where the CFP designee is not professionally competent, the CFP designee shall seek the counsel of qualified individuals and/or refer clients to such parties.

Rules that Relate to the Principle of Fairness

Rule 401

In rendering professional services, a CFP designee shall disclose to the client:

(a) Material information relevant to the professional relationship, including but not limited to conflict(s) of interest(s), changes in the CFP designee's business affiliation, address, telephone number, credentials, qualifications, licenses, compensation structure and any agency relationships, and the scope of the CFP designee's authority in that capacity.

(b) The information required by all laws applicable to the relationship in a manner complying with such laws.

Rule 402

A financial planning practitioner shall make timely written disclosure of all material information relative to the professional relationship. In all circumstances such disclosure shall include conflict(s) of interest(s) and sources of compensation. Written disclosures that include the following information are considered to be in compliance with this Rule:

(a) A statement of the basic philosophy of the CFP designee (or firm) in working with clients. The disclosure shall include the philosophy, theory, and/or principles of financial planning which will be utilized by the CFP designee; and

(b) Resumes of principals and employees of a firm who are expected to provide financial planning services to the client and a description of those services. Such disclosures shall include educational background, professional/employment history, professional designations and licenses held, and areas of competence and specialization; and

(c) A statement of compensation, which in reasonable detail discloses the source(s) and any contingencies or other aspects material to the fee and/or commission arrangement. Any estimates made shall be clearly identified as such and shall be based on reasonable assumptions. Referral fees, if any, shall be fully disclosed; and

(d) A statement indicating whether the CFP designee's compensation arrangements involve fee-only, commission-only, or fee and commission. A CFP designee shall not hold out as a fee-only financial planning practitioner if the CFP designee receives commissions or other forms of economic benefit from related parties; and

(e) A statement describing material agency or employment relationships a CFP designee (or firm) has with third parties and the fees or commissions resulting from such relationships; and

(f) A statement identifying conflict(s) of interest(s).

Rule 403

A CFP designee providing financial planning shall disclose in writing, prior to establishing a client relationship, relationships which reasonably may compromise the CFP designee's objectivity or independence.

Rule 404

Should conflict(s) of interest(s) develop after a professional relationship has been commenced, but before the services contemplated by that relationship have been completed, a CFP designee shall promptly disclose the conflict(s) of interest(s) to the client or other necessary persons.

Rule 405

In addition to the disclosure by financial planning practitioners regarding sources of compensation required under Rule 402, such disclosure shall be made annually thereafter for ongoing clients. The annual disclosure requirement may be satisfied by offering to provide clients with the current copy of SEC form ADV, Part II or the disclosure called for by Rule 402.

Rule 406

A CFP designee's compensation shall be fair and reasonable.

Rule 407

Prior to establishing a client relationship, and consistent with the confidentiality requirements of Rule 501, a CFP designee may provide references which may include recommendations from present and/or former clients.

Rule 408

When acting as an agent for a principal, a CFP designee shall assure that the scope of his or her authority is clearly defined and properly documented.

Rule 409

Whether a CFP designee is employed by a financial planning firm, an investment institution, or serves as an agent for such an organization, or is self-employed, all CFP designees shall adhere to the same standards of disclosure and service.

Rule 410

A CFP designee who is an employee shall perform professional services with dedication to the lawful objectives of the employer and in accordance with this Code.

Rule 411

A CFP designee shall:

(a) Advise the CFP designee's employer of outside affiliations which reasonably may compromise service to an employer; and

(b) Provide timely notice to the employer and clients, unless precluded by contractual obligation, in the event of change of employment or CFP Board licensing status.

Rule 412

A CFP designee doing business as a partner or principal of a financial services firm owes to the CFP designee's partners or co-owners a responsibility to act in good faith. This includes, but is not limited to, disclosure of relevant and material financial information while in business together.

Rule 413

A CFP designee shall join a financial planning firm as a partner or principal only on the basis of mutual disclosure of relevant and material information regarding credentials, competence, experience, licensing and/or legal status, and financial stability of the parties involved.

Rule 414

A CFP designee who is a partner or co-owner of a financial services firm who elects to withdraw from the firm shall do so in compliance with any applicable agreement, and shall deal with his or her business interest in a fair and equitable manner.

Rule 415

A CFP designee shall inform his or her employer, partners, or co-owners of compensation or other benefit arrangements in connection with his or her services to clients which are in addition to compensation from the employer, partners, or co-owners for such services.

Rule 416

If a CFP designee enters into a business transaction with a client, the transaction shall be on terms which are fair and reasonable to the client and the CFP designee shall disclose the risks of the transaction, conflict(s) of interest(s) of the CFP designee, and other relevant information, if any, necessary to make the transaction fair to the client.

Rules that Relate to the Principle of Confidentiality

Rule 501

A CFP designee shall not reveal—or use for his or her own benefit—without the client's consent, any personally identifiable information relating to the client relationship or the affairs of the client, except and to the extent disclosure or use is reasonably necessary:

(a) To establish an advisory or brokerage account, to effect a transaction for the client, or as otherwise impliedly authorized in order to carry out the client engagement; or

(b) To comply with legal requirements or legal process; or

(c) To defend the CFP designee against charges of wrongdoing; or

(d) In connection with a civil dispute between the CFP designee and the client.

For purposes of this rule, the proscribed use of client information is improper whether or not it actually causes harm to the client.

Rule 502

A CFP designee shall maintain the same standards of confidentiality to employers as to clients.

Rule 503

A CFP designee doing business as a partner or principal of a financial services firm owes to the CFP designee's partners or co-owners a responsibility to act in good faith. This includes, but is not limited to, adherence to reasonable expectations of confidentiality both while in business together and thereafter.

Rules that Relate to the Principle of Professionalism

Rule 601

A CFP designee shall use the marks in compliance with the rules and regulations of the CFP Board, as established and amended from time to time.

Rule 602

A CFP designee shall show respect for other financial planning professionals, and related occupational groups, by engaging in fair and honorable competitive practices. Collegiality among CFP designees shall not, however, impede enforcement of this Code.

Rule 603

A CFP designee who has knowledge, which is not required to be kept confidential under this Code, that another CFP designee has committed a violation of this Code which raises substantial questions as to the designee's honesty, trustworthiness or fitness as a CFP designee in other respects, shall promptly inform the CFP Board. This rule does not require disclosure of information or reporting based on knowledge gained as a consultant or expert witness in anticipation of or related to litigation or other dispute resolution mechanisms. For purposes of this rule, knowledge means no substantial doubt.

Rule 604

A CFP designee who has knowledge, which is not required under this Code to be kept confidential, and which raises a substantial question of unprofessional, fraudulent, or illegal conduct by a CFP designee or other financial professional, shall promptly inform the appropriate regulatory and/or professional disciplinary body. This rule does not require disclosure or reporting of information gained as a consultant or expert witness in anticipation of or related to litigation or other dispute resolution mechanisms. For purposes of this Rule, knowledge means no substantial doubt.

Rule 605

A CFP designee who has reason to suspect illegal conduct within the CFP designee's organization shall make timely disclosure of the available evidence to the CFP designee's immediate supervisor and/or partners or co-owners. If the CFP designee is convinced that illegal conduct exists within the CFP designee's organization, and that appropriate measures are not taken to remedy the situation, the CFP designee shall, where appropriate, alert the appropriate regulatory authorities including the CFP Board in a timely manner.

Rule 606

In all professional activities a CFP designee shall perform services in accordance with:

(a) Applicable laws, rules, and regulations of governmental agencies and other applicable authorities; and

(b) Applicable rules, regulations, and other established policies of the CFP Board.

Rule 607

A CFP designee shall not engage in any conduct which reflects adversely on his or her integrity or fitness as a CFP designee, upon the marks, or upon the profession.

Rule 608

The Investment Advisors Act of 1940 requires registration of investment advisors with the U.S. Securities and Exchange Commission and similar state statutes may require registration with state securities agencies. CFP designees shall disclose to clients their firm's status as registered investment advisors. Under present standards of acceptable business conduct, it is proper to use registered investment advisor if the CFP designee is registered individually. If the CFP designee is registered through his or her firm, then the CFP designee is not a registered investment advisor but a person associated with an investment advisor. The firm is the registered investment advisor. Moreover, RIA or R.I.A. following a CFP designee's name in advertising, letterhead stationery, and business cards may be misleading and is not permitted either by this Code or by SEC regulations.

Rule 609

A CFP designee shall not practice any other profession or offer to provide such services unless the CFP designee is qualified to practice in those fields and is licensed as required by state law.

Rule 610

A CFP designee shall return the client's original records in a timely manner after their return has been requested by a client.

Rule 611

A CFP designee shall not bring or threaten to bring a disciplinary proceeding under this Code, or report or threaten to report information to the CFP Board pursuant to Rules 603 and/or 604, or make or threaten to make use of this Code for no substantial purpose other than to harass, maliciously injure, embarrass and/or unfairly burden another CFP designee.

Rule 612

A CFP designee shall comply with all applicable post-certification requirements established by the CFP Board including, but not limited to, payment of the annual CFP designee fee as well as signing and returning the Licensee's Statement annually in connection with the license renewal process.

Rules that Relate to the Principle of Diligence

Rule 701

A CFP designee shall provide services diligently.

Rule 702

A financial planning practitioner shall enter into an engagement only after securing sufficient information to satisfy the CFP designee that:

(a) The relationship is warranted by the individual's needs and objectives; and

(b) The CFP designee has the ability to either provide requisite competent services or to involve other professionals who can provide such services.

Rule 703

A financial planning practitioner shall make and/or implement only recommendations which are suitable for the client.

Rule 704

Consistent with the nature and scope of the engagement, a CFP designee shall make a reasonable investigation regarding the financial products recommended to clients. Such an investigation may be made by the CFP designee or by others provided the CFP designee acts reasonably in relying upon such investigation.

Rule 705

A CFP designee shall properly supervise subordinates with regard to their delivery of financial planning services, and shall not accept or condone conduct in violation of this Code.

Appendix 40B Categories from The Seven Faces of Philanthropy

Communitarians comprise approximately 26 percent of the affluent donors studied. For them, giving is a sensible thing to do. Typically, they are local business owners, serve on boards and committees of local not-for-profits, and help their communities prosper by supporting local charities.

Devout donors make up approximately 21 percent of the affluent universe. For this group, doing good is God's will. Often, they are members of a local church, part of a larger regional or national group. More than 96 percent of their giving goes to religious institutions.

Investors, 15 percent of the giving universe, see giving as good business. They benefit the not-for-profit and themselves via tax and estate consequences. They donate to a wide range of charities to achieve their tax and estate goals and are likely to support umbrella not-for-profits (e.g., community foundations).

Socialites, 11 percent of the universe surveyed, view giving as fun. Social functions for the benefit of not-for-profits are an appealing way to ameliorate things. They are members of local networks and interact with their peers for support and for leverage in fund-raising activities. They seek opportunities to create special events for not-for-profits, rather than participating in their operations or in activities directed at constituents. They tend to support the arts and education as well as religion.

Repayers, 10 percent, give in order to do something good in return for the good they received. Usually, these people are former constituents of a not-for-profit; then they become donors. They concentrate their giving on medical and educational institutions.

Altruists, 9 percent, give because it feels right. They are the selfless donors, giving generously out of empathy. They wish to remain anonymous and give out of a sense of moral imperative. They make their gifts without advice from advisors and are usually uninterested in active roles with the not-for-profits they support. Social causes tend to be the focus of their financial generosity.

Dynasts, 8 percent, give because it is a family tradition. Typically, they inherit their wealth. Giving is something the family has "always" done, and the next generation feels the expectation to continue. However, younger dynasts will seek out different charities from their parents.

Select Audiences
and Environments

Raising Funds for a Religious Community

BARRY T. O'HARE, MANAGING DIRECTOR
Brakeley, John Price Jones Inc.

ARTHUR H. ROACH, DD, VICE PRESIDENT
Brakeley, John Price Jones Inc.

41.1 Introduction

Have you ever felt homeless? Have you ever felt the need to have a place of your own? A place of warmth and security? A place to feel comfortable and to invite family and friends?

As individuals who are responsible for raising funds for our respective organizations, we ourselves are truly homeless, for we are constantly searching for our own place in the world of fund raising—our own identity, or specialness, our uniqueness. But our home is not really a physical place; rather, it is found in our own self-esteem as fund raisers. It is found in our attitudes, our appearance, our poise, our way of doing things.

As fund raisers, we essentially influence the lives of other people in an exciting, unpredictable, and always challenging field of human endeavor. Yet, as good as we may think we are, we should always be humble. Humility is truth—knowing who we are and acting like it.

After Harry Truman became president, his aides and supposed friends kept telling him "Harry, you're great! You'll do great things for this country." Sam Rayburn, a long-time associate, warned Harry about the glowing comments he would constantly receive from people. Sam said, "Harry, let's face it. You and I both know that you're not so great."

Consider these three situations:

1. Some people do not know what is happening—ignorance.
2. Some people observe what is happening—passivity.
3. Still others make things happen—active involvement.

Which of the three describes you—ignorance, passivity, or active involvement? As fund raisers, we hope that dynamism, reflected in the third category, will continue to characterize us and our approach to the fund-raising profession.

The four basics of case, leadership, prospects, and workers are often cited; however, there is also a fifth component—the "persistent presence" of the consultant who becomes the glue, the catalytic agent that makes the other four work. The person responsible for raising funds will be less criticized for being aggressive, creative, and innovative than for being reticent, unimaginative, and passive.

In raising funds for a religious community, one way to make things happen is to broaden the nature and the scope of your strategy. Regardless of the nature and scope of a particular campaign, consider educating or reeducating the leadership and donor prospects about the concept of stewardship, the right use and management of all of God's gifts of time, talent, and treasure for people. Not only can the measurable results of raising sizable dollars be incorporated in this approach, but also the intangible ones of understanding the need to donate time and talent to the cause. Health, well-being, and personal possessions are all attributed to God's mercy—generous gifts that, in justice, are to be returned just as generously to God, most appropriately through support of the church and its ministry.

Among the particular points that can be highlighted in a stewardship approach are the following three:

1. If God had not bestowed gifts of time and personal abilities, then no money would be received.
2. The stewardship of giving is based not only on the needs of the church, diocese, or religious community, but also on the need of the giver to give.
3. The true value of money lies not in its possession but rather in its proper use.

The underlying reason for a person to be generous to a religious community can be traced to the theology of stewardship. A person gives a portion of what he or she has because he or she has received blessings from God. The receipt of these blessings requires an expression of gratitude in kind. Making a gift to a cause can be one such expression of gratitude.

Fund raising can be defined as the art of the possible practiced by believable people. The problem in fund raising lies not in raising money but in identifying the most attractive ways for people to decide to answer a request for a gift. The key is to determine the proper opportunity. If people are given the proper opportunities to make gifts, it is likely that they will do so to the best of their abilities.

41.2   Definition of Terms

The term "religious order" evokes images of "vows of silence," of men and women living in absolute poverty, garbed in exotic habits. The complex tapestry of Roman Catholic religious orders, however, represents a diversity of lifestyles and ministries. Today the benefits of professional fund raising may be required to sustain these communities and support the missions of their institutions.

The most recognizable unit of Roman Catholicism, as in most denominations, is the *parish church*. Under the jurisdiction of a bishop (or archbishop), the parish church has a body of contributing parishioners under the leadership of a priest, their pastor. At ordination, a priest takes two vows: obedience to his bishop and personal celibacy (i.e., to remain unmarried).

Very early in the history of Christianity, religious orders were founded. These groups of men and women came together for a specific calling or vocation, such as contemplative prayer and manual labor, education, or healthcare. To maintain good order, they live under a *rule* of life, which usually includes "poverty, chastity, and obedience." The members of the community, *monks, friars, nuns,* or *sisters,* are obedient to their religious superior, who may have a title such as *abbot, prior, prioress,* or *mother superior.* As a religious community grows, both in numbers of members and geographic locations of its ministries, it frequently leaves the jurisdiction of the local bishop and becomes responsible to the pope.

Because women's religious communities, and many of the men's religious communities, do not have parish churches with parishioners providing their financial support, they must earn their income to provide food and shelter as well as to maintain their ministry and outreach. Historically, they have adopted simple lifestyles in community, which keeps personal expenses to an absolute minimum and allows resources to be directed toward ministry. Starting in the late 1960s, the extraordinary decline in the numbers of men and women entering religious communities has increased the need for fund raising to provide for elderly members and to offer professional-level salaries to laypeople who must be hired to continue the community's work. In any fund-raising efforts to benefit a religious community, initial considerations include the following:

- Fund raising for a religious community can be multitiered. For example: If asked to make a proposal to the Benedictine monks of Saint Anselm's Abbey, Washington, D.C., a fund raiser must discern whether money is to be raised for the monks and the monastery, for their ministry, Saint Anselm's Abbey School, or for all of these. The case, the target audience, and the solicitation will vary according to the beneficiary.

- An institution operated by a religious community may already have its own development staff. When interfacing with that institution, the community's own development officer or consultant needs a precise organizational chart and position descriptions to define chains of command, as well as a clear idea of goals and expectations.
- Organizations of laypeople (sometimes called *oblates*) share in the spiritual life of the community and provide financial support at a level similar to offerings made to a parish church. If funds are being raised for an institution operated by the religious community, the oblates generally support the activity as a ministry and mission of the religious brothers or sisters.
- Small communities may have only one treasury for both the religious community and its institution. This can result in a lack of clarity concerning the beneficiary of the proposed fund-raising activity.

Because many religious communities have a distinguished history of earning income and benefiting from bequests of family and other benefactors, they may experience a difficult transition to organized professional fund raising. The need to promote their good works may be problematic, especially if promotional materials tend toward self-glorification. Moreover, the need to solicit gifts personally, one on one, requires a personality type rarely encountered in a religious community. Psychological profiles of entire communities, including the religious superior, have been conducted, and the profound majority are clearly introverted.

CASE STUDY

The Saint Joseph Province of Dominicans engages a development officer or consultant. This geographically based unit (Northeast United States) operates a college, spiritual retreat centers, and a seminary and staffs numerous other ministries such as hospital chaplaincies, parishes, and counseling centers. A fund raiser's first questions include the following:

- Will this be a generic fund-raising activity to help the Dominicans operate all these institutions as well as provide for the needs of the friars, or will it focus on a specific ministry?
- Who, then, will hire the consultant—the province or the institution?
- May, for instance, the college alumni be solicited for support of the Dominican Province?
- May the groups of oblates be solicited to support the college?

It is important to obtain answers to questions like these before any further discussion and information gathering as answers identify upfront. A fund raiser must recognize the organizational intricacies of Roman Catholic religious communities and translate them as clearly as possible to the public as projects worthy of gift support.

Fund raising for a religious community includes certain extra challenges:

- Recognizing and respecting that the religious have consciously rejected many of the hard business attitudes most people take for granted

- Acknowledging that print materials and solicitation techniques should be modest, to reflect the community's values
- Accepting that the entire process of undertaking a fund-raising campaign may generate hostility in some members of the community
- Adapting to the collegial but painfully slow decision-making process of a community

There are also extra rewards:

- Working with people who are accustomed to making great sacrifices of time and resources, such as those needed to undertake a fund-raising campaign
- Collaborating with men and women deeply committed to their ministry and, therefore, willing to set aside personal hesitancy when they understand what is needed from them

41.3 *Feasibility Study*

If a religious community operates a major institution, it may have experience with both the concept and the process of a fund-raising campaign. For example, Georgetown University is operated by the Jesuits and Providence Hospital (also in Washington, D.C.) is operated by the Daughters of Charity. Both of these institutions have development staffs, and their capital campaigns show few differences from any other university or hospital campaign.

Fund raising for a religious community itself, however, is usually "uncharted territory," and a feasibility study is truly necessary. A religious community, unlike a parish church, may have no base of regular donors who, more or less, understand their obligation to provide financial support on a regular and frequent basis.

Formerly, a religious community's earned income was generated from school tuitions, hospital fees, or production of communion wafers and liturgical vestments. The families of women religious, in particular, often made generous contributions at the time of entry into the community and could be counted on to include the religious in their wills. Friends of the community, appreciative of their services as teachers, nurses, missionaries, or spiritual directors contributed generously, without what we now term "sophisticated fund raising." Combined with the extraordinarily low per-person costs to feed, clothe, and house religious men and women, their earned and contributed income made organized, integrated fund raising unnecessary for many communities.

Unfortunately, these practices have resulted in a blank donor base—no cultivated relationships, no histories of giving for analysis and projection. Some communities may have begun a basic annual appeal in the form of a "Christmas letter" or a spiritual letter on the patronal feast of the congregation, but rarely has there been an aggressive building up of a donor base. Record keeping may employ the most rudimentary methods, such as the use of three-by-five-inch index cards.

A feasibility study, then, is critical in determining the possibility of soliciting major gifts to the religious community. The following questions must be answered:

- *Are those people assumed to be friends adequately informed of the community's current activities?* Because many women religious, in particular, staffed elementary schools, it can be extremely difficult to locate and cultivate adults who benefited from their ministry. Fond memories of a teacher may or may not translate into generous financial support.

- *Will the extent of the community's needs come as a shock to prospective donors?* There is an increased awareness of the critical need for financial support of religious communities; however, many people assume that "the pope" will take care of the elderly religious.
- *Will a fund-raising campaign be perceived as providing momentum to the community's mission and outreach, or will it be seen as providing oxygen to a dying body?* The vast majority of religious comprise an aging and elderly population. Either a case should be made for ongoing ministry, or a more difficult one for a "debt of gratitude" to provide for these people.

Unique and vitally important to a fund-raising campaign for religious communities will be potential donors' attitudes on how the religious express their "rule of life" in a post–Vatican II church. Many communities have abandoned both religious garb, *the habit,* and living in community. Negative feelings may arise from the sentiment people feel for these signs of sacrifice as well as a more pragmatic view—that money is now being spent unnecessarily to provide regular wardrobes and multiple apartments as residences.

As in other fund-raising campaigns, a feasibility study should identify members of the religious community who enjoy a broad range of personal appeal and whose visibility can enhance both the credibility of the campaign and the solicitation activities. At the same time, the names of laity who might serve in leadership roles should be tested, not only from credibility and appeal but also for appropriateness in serving in a church-related activity. For instance, if it is learned that an individual does not enjoy a good relationship with the local bishop, it is not advisable to invite her to hold a public position in the campaign.

The components of a feasibility study for any fund-raising campaign remain (case, achievability of goal, breakdown of needs, identification of leaders and potential donors) but in a study for a religious community, one must cut through the sentiment to see whether volunteer leadership and strong financial support really exist.

41.4 *Role of the Professional Fund Raiser*

Professional fund raising may be increasingly necessary to the efforts of religious communities, because they usually have no history of major fund raising and, therefore, lack objectivity in assessing the likelihood of fund-raising success. In particular, a fund raiser can serve as an effective catalyst in identifying potential leaders and donors and developing strategies to engage their interest in the financial needs of the religious community.

The following are examples of professional services that can be rendered:

- Assisting the religious community in defining its fund-raising objectives and strategies (capital and operating), and coordinating them with the accomplishment of its mission as a religious community.
- Introducing an outside viewpoint to the solution of internal administrative problems and decision making by objectively evaluating the ability of the religious, their staff, and volunteers to conduct a successful development program.

- Helping to identify major prospects—individuals, foundations, and corporations—and recommending strategies for approaching these prospects; providing
  information and insights on prospects or "suspected prospects."
- Responding and reacting to challenges presented by members and volunteers;
  reinforcing leadership's understanding of its responsibilities by working to raise
  prospects' sights, by helping to keep a focus on priorities, and by stressing the
  fundamentals of fund raising.
- Providing assistance (a "persistent presence") in setting time schedules, adhering to deadlines, maintaining the proper fund-raising pace, and guiding the
  community in the techniques of sequential fund raising.
- Contributing creative and innovative ideas based specifically on the community's needs; participating in brainstorming sessions with the community's
  senior religious leader, development personnel of its institutions, and selected
  members of the administrative council and advisory board.
- Working with the community in identifying those arguments for support that
  will be most effective with various audiences; providing insights on the economic and fund-raising climate based on general and current information.
- To the extent that they are necessary, making available other services, such as
  donor financial planning (bequests and planned giving), foundation and government grantsmanship, public relations and writing services, executive recruitment, direct mail, computer applications, and prospect research. Providing such
  service may require additional staff or consultants.

41.5   Case

A *case* is the rationale for financial support; it presents the collective reasons that are mar-
shaled to encourage potential donors to become involved and to make generous gifts to
a particular endeavor. At the core of any fund-raising project should be a strong belief in
the case, or reason, for the appeal.

The case for a Catholic religious community should be steeped in the language of
sacred scriptures and show an easy familiarity with Catholic vocabulary and syntax.
Although the ideas might be current, they will lose their effect if the target audience per-
ceives an absence of authenticity in expressing them. If the fund raiser lacks facility in
this kind of writing, expect—and welcome—extensive editing by the client.

Men should be very careful when writing for women religious. A careful study of
materials from other communities, for tone, diction, turns of phrase, and favorite concepts or subtexts, is recommended. This amalgam of feminism, Rogerian psychology,
and traditional and modern Catholic thought creates a style that can be learned and that
can accurately represent the women religious for whom the document is being written.

A case for support of a religious community should position the organization in the
following contexts: the entire Roman Catholic Church, the worldwide expression of the
community's unique spirituality, the vigorous history of American Roman Catholicism,
and the civic and ecclesiastical jurisdictions in which it serves.

Even if ministries are staffed primarily by laypeople, the importance of maintaining
its outreach and link to the community should be stressed. A case might be made that
continuing to minister holds out hope for attracting new members to the community.
The good effects of the ministry to date and the commitment to those currently being

served should not be overlooked. Depending on the target audience, the "debt of grati-tude" incentive may be employed. Men and women religious traditionally worked for astonishingly low remuneration, had no retirement fund or Social Security benefits, and, based on the assumption of a constant supply of young new members, expected to be cared for in old age by their communities.

Today, however, many communities have little money in reserve. Professional laypeople must be paid to staff their ministries. An increasingly elderly community, with longer life spans than those in years past, must turn to professional healthcare facilities. Those whose lives were made easier by these religious should now repay their kindness in their time of need.

Note that contemporary religious life downplays the difference between those in vows living under a rule and those whose vocation is the married or single state. Empha-sis is placed on the complementarity of religious and lay, through a sharing or partner-ship in mission. Lay "partners" historically have provided seed money for new ministries, interceded with bureaucracies and vendors, and contributed goods as well as professional skills and services. All of these elements remain necessary in today's part-nerships.

The case should identify, therefore, an existing bond between the potential donor and the religious community. Whether as student, patient, new mother, or unemployed parent, the potential donors' troubled lives were made better by this community, and, responding either in justice or mercy, they now have an opportunity to give something back in return.

41.6 Leadership

Leadership is the key ingredient in capital campaigns and major gift fund raising. It is the number-one issue in all fund-raising initiatives. *The quality of volunteer leadership will determine the attainability of a campaign goal.*

To identify the capability of candidates to serve as effective volunteer leaders in a capital campaign, the religious community should establish several objective criteria for evaluating these candidates. Exhibit 41.1 is a sample "Volunteer Leader Assessment" form, which entails a maximum of 24 points to be earned by a candidate. Each member of a leadership enlistment committee should be given this form with a list of potential leaders. Members may add other names to the list, which can then be included on a mas-ter for future reference.

Because religious leaders are immensely respected by most Catholics, they will add a great deal of weight in presenting a fund-raising campaign to potential donors. Of course, the current community superior holds a leadership position, but former senior religious leaders should also be considered. They may be held in great affection, or they may represent a happier, more secure era in religious life.

A courtesy visit to the bishop of any diocese in which major gift fund raising will take place is extremely important. It is not necessary to obtain a bishop's permission, and most religious will bristle at the thought of even appearing to ask permission. However, it would be a serious impediment to solicitation activities if the bishop resented appeals for major gifts being made to his own potential donors. At the very least, the bishop should approvingly acknowledge development activity. Ideally, if there is a campaign, he will be offered and will accept an honorary leadership position.

EXHIBIT 41.1 Volunteer Leadership Assessment Form

Please indicate the extent to which this candidate can fulfill the criteria listed below.

          Strong = 3   Moderate = 2   Limited = 1

Criteria	Degree
1. Make a strong commitment to the mission of the religious community and the objectives of the capital fund campaign	_____
2. Make a proportional and sacrificial gift	_____
3. Accept advice and direction from fund-raising counsel	_____
4. Approach five or more prospects for gifts of $100,000 or more	_____
5. Enlist at least one equally committed top volunteer leader who can make and also solicit significant gifts	_____
6. Commit time to attend key campaign meetings and events	_____
7. Draw favorable attention and financial support to the campaign in particular and to the religious community as a whole	_____
8. Act as a positive spokesperson for both the campaign and the religious community	_____
TOTAL	_____

Candidate: _____   Date: _____

Assessor: _____

Best Person(s) to Approach Candidate: _____

This information is confidential.

In testing names for volunteer lay leaders, be prepared for commentary on the person's suitability for a leadership role in a Roman Catholic fund-raising campaign. The fund raiser's opinions aside, there may be a problem if the person is divorced, is a former priest or religious, or publicly holds views considered to be at odds with church teachings on controversial subjects. On the other hand, if the community's ministry has benefited members of other denominations or if they are simply held in high regard by the general population, then peoples other than Roman Catholics can make an excellent addition to campaign leadership. Beyond these considerations, the qualities and expectations of a campaign leader are the same and are equally important as those for any fund-raising campaign.

(A) LEADERSHIP ENLISTMENT COMMITTEE

The objective of a leadership enlistment committee is to enlist the most influential group of top campaign leaders available to the religious community. The committee is generally composed of three to five people, plus ad hoc members, as required, to provide assistance in enlisting a specific prospective leader.

The following tasks of the committee are supported by the development office staff, if there is one, and the top leadership of the community:

- Approve a written position description for each of the top leadership positions.
- Identify those prospective leaders—clergy, lay, and religious—who will be most capable of leading a successful campaign on behalf of the community, whether it seems likely that they will undertake the assignment or not.
- Assemble and review background information on each leadership prospect and prioritize the candidates.
- Develop a strategy for enlisting each prospect, that is:
  — How to approach the prospect
  — Who are the best people to make the approach
  — Why the particular prospect should accept the position
- Select an enlistment team, always two people or more, to accompany the community's senior religious leader to meet with the prospective leader.
- Pursue the top leadership prospects by priority.
- Approach each prospective leader with the same care and thoughtfulness that would be practiced in soliciting a top gift—because the right leader(s) will be responsible for obtaining at least a sum equal to four or five of the top gifts made to the campaign.

(B)   ROLE OF THE COMMUNITY'S SENIOR RELIGIOUS LEADER

The senior religious leader, like the chief executive officer of any not-for-profit organization, can assist the fund-raising program in a variety of ways, including:

- Hold weekly meetings with the development director to review current progress, plans for the next week, and specific tasks to be undertaken by the community's senior religious leader.
- Act as principal spokesperson and advocate for the community's development activities.
- Provide the fund raiser with information and supportive data related to the community.
- In a campaign, participate in both key leadership enlistment meetings and key solicitation meetings, as well as special events related to the campaign.
- Attend meetings of the campaign executive committee and other campaign committees as needed.
- Convey policy decisions and provide periodic reports on campaign progress to the community's administrative council.

(C)   CAMPAIGN CHAIR

An effective campaign chair for a religious community is a civic-minded leader of the highest standing in the community and in the church, who by his or her presence or involvement in the campaign would draw attention to and foster a high level of acceptance of the needs, objectives, and plans of the community. Such a leader is characterized by:

- A deep commitment to the spiritual life of the community as well as the objectives, programs, and plans supported by a campaign

- An inclination and ability to make a generous charitable investment in the program, both as evidence of personal commitment and as an example of leadership
- A willingness and ability to approach major sources of financial support on behalf of the community
- A willingness and ability to enlist and supervise a top-level leadership team to assist the religious community in planning, policy decisions, organization, setting a timetable, and fund-raising activities
- An ability to lead a large organization of both lay and religious volunteers and to inspire others to discharge their responsibilities with enthusiasm and dispatch
- A willingness to accept advice from the development staff person or fund-raising counsel, if retained, and to prepare and adhere to the campaign plan and timetable

41.7 *Prospective Donors*

If a religious community is considering a capital campaign, and a feasibility study shows that it is not ready to begin one, the most likely reason is insufficient prospects. The painstaking process of developing and cultivating a donor base cannot be rushed, and the fund raiser should be prepared at the outset to establish a full-service, properly equipped development office with annual fund, publications, and special event activities in place. Then, leaving no stone unturned, a list of prospects should be compiled.

Every Roman Catholic diocese has a newspaper that, through the use of press releases and paid advertising, is an excellent resource. If the community formerly staffed a parish school, it might hold a reunion, announced in the diocesan newspaper and parish bulletin, with several teachers in attendance, and use the opportunity to gather names of former students. A special commemorative publication might be produced, advertised in the appropriate diocese, and offered free to anyone who requests it. Parents of former students are likely to be as grateful as the students themselves for the education that the community provided, and, if lists are still available, it is likely that the parents' addresses are still accurate.

In an ideal situation, new prospects receive a full year of newsletters and correspondence before an appeal letter is sent. The second year should include four appeals Advent/Christmas, Lent/Easter, the Feast of the Assumption (August 15), and the patronal feast of the community. The third year will find new names being added to the list, more appeals being sent to those who respond, and the elimination of names of those who do not respond. All this activity prepares a community to analyze giving histories and to identify potential major donors when a campaign is launched.

Note: The establishment of a shrine is a pious expression that many communities may not want to pursue. This is unfortunate, because many laypeople appreciate the opportunity to have their prayers offered at a site dedicated to a favorite saint, and the accompanying contributions can have a major impact on the community's income as well as build up the donor base for future solicitation.

The families and friends of the religious are the strongest prospective donors. However, it can be extremely difficult to obtain their names and addresses or permission to contact them for contributions. Many religious are frankly embarrassed at the prospect of the community's "hitting up" their loved ones for donations. Fund raisers may expect a great degree of ill will if they ignore the desires of religious for them to stay away from their families and friends.

It is possible, however, to experience success in obtaining cooperation and permission from religious brothers and sisters. First, show them the proposed materials for a specific appeal. The materials should not be too aggressive, nor should members of the community be demeaned with descriptive passages more appropriate to a "Save the Children" appeal. A simple, straightforward narrative, with specific examples of how a gift to the community will sustain its ministry and support those now retired after years of service, has won approval many times. Another method is to recruit a credible layperson to speak to the community and educate the religious to the fact that many people actually look forward to opportunities to contribute to organizations they believe in. Bombarded with solicitations, people find it refreshing to be asked by an organization they really want to help.

If a campaign soliciting major gifts is launched, the process of identifying potential donors will be familiar to experienced fund raisers. For a religious community, however, the full extent of corporate memory must be pressed into service. What former student or patient has the potential to make a major gift? Has he or she been known to express fond memories of that association with the community? Is there a particular brother or sister to whom this person "can't say no"? Will that brother or sister accompany the superior on a solicitation visit?

If the project behind the fund-raising campaign includes a new chapel or if the community has an existing chapel, a full range of named gift opportunities should be offered and can be deeply appreciated by laypeople who are seeking to honor their loved ones. Thorough research may result in a list of "memorial gifts" that completely match the breakdown of the pro forma gift range table.

Liturgical and architectural components of both new and existing chapels are especially good choices, because named gifts do not reflect at-cost expense. In assigning dollar amounts, be guided by the item's visibility and relative position of honor. For example, the purchase price of a parish church's baptismal font may be only slightly more than the cost of a chair, but a significantly higher sum may be assigned the font because the families of every infant brought for baptism will assemble there.

It is important to brainstorm rigorously the possibilities for named gifts, so that nothing is overlooked. Reconciliation rooms, garden areas adjoining the chapel, vestments, communion vessels, chairs or pews, each Station of the Cross. Keep in mind, furthermore, that a truly major gift that would permit naming the whole chapel does not preclude additional named gifts of the aforementioned components.

Anyone who is capable of making a major gift to your campaign is probably on everyone's solicitation list. The case and the needs of the other organizations may be just as compelling as your own. However, the availability of opportunities to make a named gift to a religious community can make the difference in attracting major gifts to your campaign.

41.8 Planning for a Capital Campaign

In many instances, a religious community is raising money for an institution that it sponsors. It is important to position the "campaign parent"; that is, it must be determined whether donors will be asked to contribute to the religious community or to the institution owned and administered by the community.

(A) LAYING THE FOUNDATION

Before introducing a plan of action, it is important to understand those elements that must be in place before embarking on a major fund-raising effort. Campaign success will depend on the community's ability to accomplish the following:

- Develop a case that emphasizes the community's faithfulness to its vocation, demonstrates excellence of service, and creates a focused, coherent image of the community.
- Recruit volunteer fund-raising leadership with both demonstrated commitment to the mission of the religious community and influence at the top levels of the philanthropic community in the areas being served.
- Conduct rigorous prospect research to identify and to develop strategies for cultivation and solicitation of high-level gift prospects.
- Ensure the involvement and total commitment of the religious community's leaders, the institution's board of directors, and the administration to achieve campaign objectives.
- Develop a communications program to inform both the philanthropic public and the institutional family of the full range of its services and their quality.

(B) THE NEED TO BEGIN IMMEDIATELY

To delay preparation will delay the start of fund raising and will dissipate the sense of momentum and level of expectation inevitably created by the feasibility study. The number of campaigns that are likely being conducted or planned by other local organizations and the involvement of the same "centers of influence and affluence" in these campaigns create competition for volunteer leadership and make funds more difficult to obtain in the future. Before a campaign can begin, research must be done to prepare profiles of prospective donors. Moreover, prospective donors will need significant cultivation and education before being asked to make major financial commitments.

41.9 *Campaign Organization*

As mentioned previously, effective volunteer leadership is critical to the success of any fund-raising program. Special ad hoc committees may be added to facilitate completion of specific tasks or in response to special opportunities. The following paragraphs discuss the roles and functions of each of the major volunteer committees as well as the roles and functions of staff in a campaign.

(A) ADMINISTRATIVE COUNCIL

The Administrative Council, a group of religious elected by the community, holds ultimate plenary and fiduciary responsibility for the campaign. Full endorsement of the campaign by the councillors, individually and collectively, is vital and indispensable. Although they are unable in most cases to make a monetary contribution, the councillors will be needed to enlist and encourage others with whom they have an affiliation or association.

(B) OFFICE OF THE CHAIR

The institution or religious community may wish to create an "Office of the Chair" for the campaign. Under such an arrangement, usually three to five people serve as the chair. At any given time, one would be *primus inter pares* (first among equals), for the purposes of presiding at meetings or functions and making executive decisions.

Arrangements can be adapted at any time to suit the business and personal demands of the people involved. Experience has shown that the "Office of the Chair" concept is extremely appealing, as it enables busy and successful people to feel more at ease in undertaking this critical position and secure in the knowledge that a few close colleagues will be at hand to share the tasks of leadership.

Such a construct avoids overworking one leader during a multiyear campaign effort. In addition, it enables a blending of distinctive leadership traits that may not be found in one person, however talented. The office's primary responsibilities include the following:

- Enlisting committee chairs and other campaign volunteers for key roles
- Spearheading the solicitations of pacesetting gifts
- Making a personal financial commitment of substantial dimensions
- Being a relentless advocate for the religious community and/or the institution administered by the religious community

(C) CAMPAIGN EXECUTIVE COMMITTEE

The Campaign Executive Committee provides general guidance for the organization and implementation of the campaign, focusing particularly on the definition of the case, the need for physical expansion, new services and/or an endowment fund, and the enlistment of key leadership. This committee initially consists mostly of "insiders"—the members of the Office of the Chair; the religious leader, such as the community superior; the director of development; the campaign director—and one or two "outsiders" who are already favorably inclined toward the institution and its special project. Further into the preparation period, additional outside leadership may be recruited for cultivation purposes. This committee will report on the campaign's progress to the Administrative Council of the institution sponsored by the religious community.

The Campaign Executive Committee must consist of leaders of the highest caliber that the religious community can assemble. There must be no doubt in anyone's mind that the campaign is credible, is urgent, and has the leadership committed to make it a success.

(D) SENIOR RELIGIOUS LEADERS

Working with campaign leadership, the community's senior religious leader whose title may be abbot, prior, prioress, or mother superior plays a vital role in the campaign. During the preparation period, he or she will devote a considerable amount of time in laying the groundwork for a successful campaign, especially by helping to define and articulate the case for the community. He or she will then be actively involved in cultivating prospects for pacesetting gifts and participating in actual solicitations.

(E)   DEVELOPMENT OFFICE

Essential to a capital campaign is the staff's knowledge of the donor base, past and present involvement of prominent individuals and families, and special situations that may lend themselves to cultivation events and named gift opportunities. The director of development should identify the opportunities for which the talents of the Development Office should be made available for the capital campaign.

(F)   PROSPECT RATING AND EVALUATION COMMITTEE

The Prospect Rating and Evaluation Committee has a crucial role to play. Supported by the Development Office, its members must correctly assess the proper level at which each prospect will be solicited. The members of this committee, working in confidentiality, must be extremely familiar with the philanthropic community in and around the geographic areas of service in order to do their work efficiently and effectively. They review the current prospect base, assess information compiled by the Development Office from both "hard" and "soft" sources, and determine the best matches of prospects with solicitors and the appropriate "ask" levels. The results of their work are then channeled to the respective committees and volunteers who have primary responsibility for prospect cultivation and solicitation.

(G)   COORDINATING COMMITTEE FOR CAPITAL CAMPAIGNS

In some instances, a religious community will be planning to conduct a major capital campaign for its own needs while one or more of the institutions owned by the community are also making plans for their own campaigns and will likely be approaching the same prospects for leadership and major gifts. It is essential that appropriate steps be taken in order to maximize the fund-raising success of both efforts. Therefore, the establishment of a Coordinating Committee for Capital Campaigns is recommended. The following paragraphs outline the nature and scope of a hypothetical committee, representing a religious community and a college.

(i)   Purpose
Recognizing that both the community and the college are planning capital campaigns that will approach overlapping constituencies at the upper levels of giving, a Coordinating Committee for Capital Campaigns has been formed. Its purposes are the following:

- To avoid possible confusion among donor prospects.
- To facilitate maximum giving to both campaigns.
- To expand the donor base associated with the religious community for both its campaign and the college's campaign.
- To coordinate the planning and implementation of both campaigns to the extent that such activities minimize possible conflict in approaches to the larger prospective donors.

(ii)   Membership
The Coordinating Committee for Capital Campaigns is composed of the following members:

Chair of the Steering Committee of the campaign for the community
Chair of the board of trustees of the college
Religious superior of the community
President of the college and, as volunteer campaign leadership enlistment
    evolves,
Chair of the campaign for the community
Chair of the campaign for the college

The directors of development for the religious community and the college will serve as ad hoc members at the pleasure of their respective organizations.

(iii) Scope of Activity

The committee will meet on an as-needed basis and may be convened by the senior representative of either organization. In practical terms, probably no more than three or four meetings a year will be required. Written minutes of all committee meetings will be distributed to committee members within 48 hours of each meeting. Responsibility for recording the minutes will rotate between the ad hoc representatives from both organizations.

(iv) Responsibilities

The committee will have the following three responsibilities:

1. Distribution of written descriptions of both campaigns, including goals, funding projects and their estimated costs, donor recognition opportunities, and the timetables for conducting solicitation activity.
2. Assignment of individual and foundation donor prospects targeted for potential gifts of $100,000 or more and corporation prospects of $50,000 or more. These assignments can be made to either one campaign or the other, or to joint solicitation by both organizations.
3. Approval of any plan to share the prospect pool of both organizations for capital campaign or annual giving purposes.

(v) Campaign Plans

Both organizations will submit written campaign descriptions for review and approval of the committee. Subsequent changes in either organization's campaign plan will be immediately distributed to the committee in order to enhance complementary communications by either organization.

(vi) Prospect Clearance

Each organization will submit to the committee an initial list of individual and foundation prospects of $100,000 or more and corporation prospects of $50,000 or more. In those cases where names appear on both lists, the committee will determine to which organization the prospect should be assigned, or it will assign the prospect on a joint basis.

Criteria for assignment will be the following:

- State of readiness for solicitation
- Relationship of the prospect to the organization
- Interests of the prospect
- Potential for a successful solicitation

- Availability of willing and effective solicitors
- Priority of the project to be funded
- Likelihood that an additional gift for the other organization can be obtained at a later date

As gifts are received or declined, each organization will immediately inform the other and the prospect will automatically be reassigned.

In the case of a joint solicitation, the content of the proposal and the amount to be sought or earmarked for each organization will be negotiated on a case-by-case basis, unless the committee should decide on a formula for distribution of gifts obtained through joint solicitation. It may be necessary to channel joint gifts through a third party.

(vii)   Volunteer Leadership Enlistment

It will be the responsibility of both organizations to develop independently a cadre of volunteer campaign leaders. However, as individuals accept positions of leadership, each organization will inform the other. It is probably unavoidable that some leaders will serve in both campaigns.

41.10   Communications Program

(A)   GOAL

The goal of the communications program is to increase the visibility and appreciation of the community's achievements and activities and to foster the involvement of potential key volunteer leaders and prospective donors in its fund-raising activities.

(B)   UNDERLYING PRINCIPLES

A proactive public relations philosophy necessitates early integration of publicity into the total campaign plan. The philosophy is based on five principles:

Principle 1: Creating a general ambiance to support the proposed campaign will require public relations initiatives that will impact general media exposure.

Principle 2: Communications support for a capital campaign should be sequential in nature, and targeted in approach, to reach existing and potential donor prospects.

Principle 3: Public relations activity alone does not raise money, but it does contribute to both leadership and potential donor confidence. Therefore, it should be appreciated for its supplementary value in achieving the ultimate campaign objective.

Principle 4: Highly visible expressions of gratitude for past support are critical to sustaining and increasing new support.

Principle 5: Every campaign undergoes a period during which ultimate success is openly questioned; therefore, creating the necessary aura of success early in the campaign is largely an act of faith, which must be demonstrated by a small cadre of leaders and donors and, subsequently, broadcast widely.

(C) OBJECTIVES

Know your audience! Disseminate information that will interest them, address any concerns, and generate interest in the campaign goal. Here are some suggestions:

- Establish a broad-based appreciation of the community's past contributions, current activities, and future objectives. In short, the members have made contributions, do so now, and, with financial support, will continue to do so effectively in the future.
- Record and promote the past, current, and future contributions of the community.
- Underscore the importance of the upcoming campaign.
- Publicize appropriately those volunteers who have chosen to lead and support the effort.
- Document the services of various ministries as well as other institutions in which the community is involved, and distribute this information.
- Promote donor recognition opportunities to stimulate further interest in generous giving.
- If possible, demonstrate the cost effectiveness of the community's stewardship and activities.
- Generally promote the value of the community to society as a whole.

(D) SPECIFIC RECOMMENDATIONS

The sequence of implementing specific recommendations will depend on the availability of media and volunteers. However, be as directive as possible, rather than reactive to the circumstances in which the public relations program is occurring. Seventeen ideas follow:

1. Complete and approve the campaign case statement and print it after top leadership has been enlisted.
2. Obtain letters of endorsement from church and community leaders as well as current and past organizations that have benefited from the community's efforts.
3. Place feature stories on achievements and activities in the local press and publications of organizations with which the community has been associated; also obtain reprints for distribution throughout the campaign.
4. Develop a campaign solicitor's kit that contains the following:
   - Statement of the case (major brochure)
   - Solicitor's guide, including deferred gift opportunities
   - Suggested pledge plans
   - Opportunities for memorial gifts/named gift opportunities
   - Reprints of published news releases
   - Endorsements
   - List of needs
   - Newsletter reprints
5. Expand the community's mailing list to coincide with the overall campaign prospect list.

6. Identify opportunities to make presentations in individual churches within which the community has had religious or social impact.

7. Conduct individual and group cultivation meetings at which the community's representative is given an opportunity to extol past achievements, to describe current activities and future plans, and to develop a speakers' bureau of lay leaders and members of the local community.

8. Enlist honorary campaign chairpersons.

9. Obtain "testimonials" by people on whom the community's activities have had a positive impact.

10. Aggressively pursue the talk-show circuit within the geographic areas of primary prospects for leadership and major gifts.

11. Begin a dialogue with selected members of the foundation community—not for solicitation, but for discussing the community's vocational objectives.

12. Send regular press releases to area churches, community-related organizations, and the local media (i.e., all locales in which the community retains a presence) on all events and achievements related to the community, whether they be individual achievements or those of the community as a whole.

13. Conduct special cultivation events and provide press releases to highlight campaign progress; for example, leadership enlistment top gift achievement(s), campaign kick-off, campaign progress, specific donor support, public announcement of the campaign upon achieving 50 percent of goal, etc. The objective here is to instill a belief that the campaign will be a success.

    Note: A release should be distributed to announce any gift of $25,000 or more.

14. Distribute regular progress reports to the volunteers involved in the campaign.

15. In all publications, releases, and the like, take advantage of opportunities to support the activities of organizations with which the community is associated.

16. Create a small public relations advisory committee of three to five media professionals to provide assistance with the following:
    - Specific projects
    - Strategy
    - Opening media doors

17. Develop an eight- to 10-minute video in support of campaign objectives, especially for prospect cultivation and solicitation.

(E)   TOPICS FOR NEWSLETTERS

Friends of a community look forward to receiving their newsletter. Whether separated by time or distance, these friends welcome an inside look at men and women whose lives are characterized by separation from the rest of the world or, in the vernacular, "cloister." Some content suggestions include:

- A regular "salute" to individual members of the community who have contributed many years of service to its varied ministries. The purpose is to highlight the great heritage of the community.
- A regular description of one member's activity "on a particular day." This approach is distinct from a general description of the congregation's activities.

- A feature story on a specific need addressed by the campaign.
- A "Did You Know?" column in each issue to describe a past or current activity of the community or the activity of an individual member.

It might also be helpful to use a newsletter to generate responses from readers by soliciting information about past experiences that they value as a result of their contact with the community. The newsletter can be used in this way to obtain endorsements from those who are benefiting from the various ministries.

In short, the best thing a newsletter can do is to emphasize the community's past contributions, current activities, and present challenges. An underlying theme should be the projected longevity of the community, its future viability, and a sense of "debt" to its members for all they have done and are doing on behalf of laypersons and society.

41.11 Conclusion

Raising funds for a religious community requires an understanding of the importance of the stewardship of time, talent, and treasure. Although the basic ingredients—case, leadership, prospects, and workers—are applicable to raising funds for any cause, it is important to develop a special mind-set in tailoring these fundamentals to a religious community. The traditions of religious communities may be ancient, but these institutions are facing a period of major transition. Both tradition and change must be considered.

Leadership is often the most critical factor in the formula for success. Consequently leadership recruitment methods should be tailored first to the religious themselves and then to the particular fund-raising program being designed.

The unique features of this type of fund raising illustrate the importance of listening to the concerns of each constituency. As stated in the beginning of this chapter, a dynamic approach, rooted in an appreciation of the backgrounds and viewpoints of the religious, can mean success in raising funds for a religious community.

42 Fund Development in The Salvation Army

Robert E. Gregg, MA, CFRE
The Salvation Army

42.1 Introduction

Fund development in The Salvation Army (hereinafter referred to as the Army) is similar to an English estate garden—there is much variety in the species and the variation of those species. At every twist and turn, the path unveils new arrangement patterns, colors, and landscape design.

We express particular gratitude to Dona Romine, Adrienne Finley, Bob Hemmings, Frank Mayo, and Rod Houtz for their significant contributions to this chapter.

A 135-year-old international organization, the Army's fund development is as varied as the number of countries in which it serves (103 at present). Actually, its complexity goes far beyond that. For example, in the United States alone, there are four Territories—four separate corporations (technically)—representing the four geographic areas of the country:

- The Eastern Territory, with headquarters in Nyack, New York
- The Southern Territory, with headquarters in Atlanta, Georgia
- The Central Territory, with headquarters in Des Plaines, Illinois
- The Western Territory, with headquarters in Long Beach, California

To complicate things even further, within the Western Territory (where the author works) there are 10 major administrative units called divisions, each with dozens of programmatic units. Sometimes the fund development process takes place on the divisional level with highly successful professional teams. In other situations, the local staff (usually the local Salvation Army officer trained as a pastor/administrator) will be the principal fund raiser, often with little previous experience and most often with no specific training in fund development. Thus, fund development in the Army is as varied as the over 400 programs operating in the West and the level of expertise of the professionals supporting them. Because so many needs are the same from community to community (alcoholism, unwed mothers, child care, homelessness, etc.), the Army offers many standard programs in the various locations. However, most locations develop programs that speak to the unique needs of that specific community.

42.2 Program Overview

Fund development in the Army differs significantly from university, arts organization, and hospital and health-based charities. Usually there is little direct connection between the donor/prospect and the services offered by the Army. Typical programs for the Army in the Western Territory include:

- *Christmas family relief.* Throughout the West, the Army provides food, clothing, toys, and even Christmas trees to brighten Christmas for over 1 million families.
- *Disaster relief services.*
- *Thanksgiving dinners.* The Southern California Division sponsors a Thanksgiving Eve dinner for families who call "skid row" home. The families are bused to the Los Angeles Convention Center for a complete dinner in a setting that includes tablecloths, flowers, and live entertainment.
- *Day-care centers.* The Herberger Childcare Center in Phoenix is the only licensed day-care center in the state of Arizona to care for children of alcohol- and drug-addicted parents (300 children per year) as they undergo treatment in Salvation Army programs.
- *Inner-city youth centers.* Another example from Phoenix: The South Mountain Youth Center has an innovative after-school Pregnancy Prevention Volleyball Program, designed to deter young women from becoming pregnant. (Research shows that most conception occurs between 3:00 and 7:00 P.M.) Only three of the 800 girls who participated in the program have gotten pregnant.

- *Homes and education programs for unwed mothers.* Over 100 years old, the Booth Memorial Center in Los Angeles houses 44 girls between the ages of 13 and 18. Once the girls have their babies, they can choose to stay in the program while completing high school. The support provided by the staff includes counseling, parenting classes, and employment training.
- *Transitional housing programs for homeless families.* The Lambuth Center in Denver, Colorado, provides housing for up to 84 individuals in 21 family living units. The program provides quality case assessment and management and classes in life skills, employment readiness (vocational training and placement), nutrition and cooking, child care, education services for school-aged children, health-related services, follow-up services (once out of the program), and more.
- *Shelter for AIDS families.* The Bethesda House in Los Angeles cares for 16 families in which at least one of the parents is infected with HIV or AIDS and the family is homeless. The Army staff support the family by helping to stabilize their health issues, find jobs, save money, refer the children to appropriate education opportunities, and assist the family in realistic planning for the future.
- *Alcohol and drug rehabilitation centers.* The Army has long been known for its leading-edge work therapy programs for men and women who suffer from alcoholism and drug abuse. There are over 30 such centers in the West that served over 7,354 men and women in 1998.
- *Summer camping programs* for inner-city youth and families.
- *Silvercrest Senior Residences* provide quality, safe, low-cost housing for senior citizens.
- *Missing persons bureau.* The Army in the West helped find 851 missing family members and friends in 1998.

These programs are a mere representation of the more than 400 programs that the Army operates across the West. In fund development for the Army, there are no grateful patients, few grateful families and close friends with the financial means to make a major gift, and still fewer grateful alumni with significant financial means. Currently, the predominant source for qualified major gift (current and deferred) prospects is those whom the Army served in World Wars I and II, but they are declining in number every day. Even with these donors, however, the connection is not as strong as when a prospect or his or her family is the beneficiary of particularly good medical care or education.

Rarely does an alumnus of a program go on to become successful in ways that allow him or her to help the organization financially. Thus, the Army in the West is reviewing the possibility of developing a comprehensive social service alumni program to assist with various areas of fund development. Our contention is that no one can "tell the story" of how a program affects the lives of people like the people whose lives have been changed for the good.

42.3 The Army's Role in the Growth of the Fund Development Profession

The Army's role in the growth of fund development in general as a profession is monumental. The late Ralph Chamberlain, a longtime Salvation Army professional, was a founding member of the Association of Fundraising Professionals (AFP). George Johnstone, formerly the development director for the Army's Southern California Division, was a founding member of the Los Angeles chapter of the AFP. The Army was a principal founding agency of the Community Chest, which led to the modern United Way. The Southern California Division (based in Los Angeles) innovated the first use of mass direct mail by a philanthropic organization to do donor prospecting, sending out one million pieces in the mid-1950s.

The Army also was significantly involved in the growth of planned giving as a profession and in the development of its practice. Frank Mayo, the first Planned giving Director for the Army in the West, also was the prime force in establishing the Planned Giving Round Table in Los Angeles, the first in the country, and was part of the committee that developed the National Committee on Planned Giving (NCPG). The Army also was an early player in development of the Committee on Gift Annuities (CGA), which sets the standard rates for charitable gift annuities. In recent years the Army was a principal participant in defending a lawsuit against charitable annuities, supplying expertise and significant funds to the effort.

42.4   Basic Fund Development Practices

Important as its role is in developing the profession, the Army's success in fund development today comes from leading by following the basics.

Those basics include the standard prerequisites for any successful fund development:

- A demonstrable need for the programs offered
- Programs with provable quality
- Good community visibility
- Board strength and advocacy

We'll look at each in turn.

Once these issues are in place, a more comprehensive fund development program can begin and the organization can start to accomplish its mission. We will discuss how the Army in the West addresses each of these issues in turn. As part of that discussion, we will trace the process—from acquisition to the upgrading of annual gifts, to the realization of a series of major gifts, and culminating in a large estate gift—through a case study the story of a donor family, the Larsons. The story is true, but the name is fictitious.

(A)   DEMONSTRABLE NEED FOR THE PROGRAM

The vast majority of Salvation Army programs represent a need that the local business and social service leaders currently identify as critical to improving the life of the community. For instance, no unit or program can begin the capital campaign process (to be discussed in detail later) without first engaging in a community needs assessment. The results of a needs assessment will include recommendations regarding:

- Services the community deems needed
- Services that fit within the mission of the Army

- Services currently provided by the Army that may need to be expanded or strengthened
- Needed services that would fit within the mission of, and be provided by, the Army
- Current programs and services of the Army that should be curtailed or restructured
- An assessment of the current resources of the Army—financial, personnel, property, and equipment—in relationship to a projected profile of services to be provided now and in the future

Once the study uncovers the needs of the community that the leaders believe exist, and decision makers can demonstrate that they fit within the mission of the Army, then, and only then, can any effective fund development program begin.

(B) PROGRAM QUALITY

The Army has a strong reputation for the quality of its programs based on their success in human terms of those it serves. To help ensure the consistency and continuity of this quality, the Army has in place at the territorial (corporate) level a process of internal review that ensures all social service delivery programs meet or exceed local, state, and/or national standards.

(C) COMMUNITY VISIBILITY

Most Americans recognize the name of The Salvation Army. The Army has raised more money than any other organization in the United States. A report in the November 5, 1998, issue of the *Chronicle of Philanthropy* shows that "The Salvation Army took in ($1.2 billion) more than twice what the No. 2 charity raised."[1] Thus, if money really does speak, then the Army is, as someone put it, "America's favorite charity." This success in fund development is due partly to the Army's 135-year history and the quality of the specific services it provided servicemen and their families in the two world wars.

Conversely, informal research and experience shows that most of its donors do not understand the breadth and scope of the work the Army does in all communities across the United States in general, nor in their community specifically.

CASE STUDY

The Larsons report a fairly vague awareness of, yet positive feeling about, the Army's services in their community. When the first direct-mail solicitation came (a Christmas appeal), they responded with a $25 check. They continued at that annual gift level for three years. Since then, the records report 47 separate gifts over 18 years.

One of the most visible and recognizable Army symbols is at once a fund development tool and a public relations icon—the Christmas kettle. The kettle began service in

---

[1]Debra Blum, Paul Demko, Holly Hall, Domenica Marchetti, "A Banner Year for Big Charities," *Chronicle of Philanthropy,* November 5, 1998, p. 1.

San Francisco at Christmastime in 1891 in response to the need to provide free dinners for the area's poor persons—a fund development tool. In 1901 kettle contributions provided funds for the first mammoth sit-down dinner in Madison Square Garden in New York City. Hundreds of thousands of this trademark Christmas collection device now do service in nearly every American community. Further, it is a principal collector in lands as diverse as Korea, Chile, and many European countries. In addition to actually raising funds (over $15 million raised and direct service provided to over 1 million families in the West in 1998), its presence helps to raise awareness of the Army and its work, and sets the stage for other fund development efforts, such as the Christmas mail appeal. Although there is no formal research to prove the suspicion, logic suggests that donors who pass a kettle while shopping might be more aware of, and thus receptive to, an appeal letter in their mailbox.

Whatever its history and initial purpose, the Christmas kettle is a concept that goes a long way to bring community-wide recognition about the Army itself and the services it provides to each individual community across the entire country. Only recently has the Army embarked on a national campaign ("Need Knows No Season") to supplement the existing awareness of the kettle itself.

Another facet that makes the Army "America's favorite charity" is the presence of its social service delivery system in nearly every community across the country. In communities in which there is no full-time staff, volunteers manage a program called Service Extension. Service Extension, as its name suggests, extends the service of the Army into the bergs and hamlets of every community in every state. Volunteers raise money and are further supported locally by the divisional direct-mail campaign and major gift staff. These volunteers then respond to those in their community who have needs, supplying money, food, shelter, and referrals for other services to families and individuals. The Army provides management support to the local volunteers.

Still, with the visibility as significant as it is, the Army often suffers from a lack of appropriate recognition for the depth and breadth its work. For instance, it is not at all unusual for other highly recognized organizations to be far more visible during the media phase of a natural disaster, while the Army plods along in the background serving coffee, doughnuts, and hot food; cleaning out flood-ravaged homes; supplying clothes for cold, scared children and adults; and providing counseling for grief-stricken families long after the camera lights dim and the other organizations have folded up their tents and moved on. However, this may be one secret of its position as number one in fund raising in the United States. After all, those for whom the Army provides quality, long-term disaster relief services so quietly and so consistently are those who become the major gift and planned giving prospects, not the media moguls.

The support of volunteer leadership is a key to success for most philanthropic organizations. Therefore, the Army approaches its volunteer leadership in a unique manner.

(D) BOARD STRENGTH AND ADVOCACY

This is a fascinating and challenging conundrum for the Army. Given its structure, the volunteer boards that support the Army in each community are advisory in nature only; none have any legal responsibility or voting power. This presents a challenge to Army officers; in order to have a strong, effective, supportive, and giving board, the Board Members must have meaningful work to do. The good news is that the advisory board members have neither fiduciary exposure nor liability. As with all human endeavors, the most successful boards are those where the local officers are comfortable with themselves and can attract and encourage creative and energetic members. It does happen in many locations.

One such model board is the advisory board in Monterey, California, which has a long history of strong, effective, and creative support. It began in the mid-1960s when a newly appointed Captain couple, Captains Alfred and Sherryl Van Cleef (now Colonels and Divisional Commanders in Los Angeles) were charged with the responsibility to reopen the work in the community. This creative, resourceful young officer couple began by becoming acquainted with every key individual between the post office and their rented motel room, a route they walked every day in full Salvation Army uniform. They identified, and then networked with, all of the movers and shakers in town, from service club members to the prominent social elite, from high-ranking government officials to the major business owners and community leaders.

Currently, that board significant participation in & support for most of the fund development processes, including:

- The direct-mail program (letter design, mail piece production, planning and implementation, live signatures on all renewal letters, etc.)
- 100 percent giving by members
- Major gifts
- Planned giving
- Corporate support
- Volunteer recruitment and management for many phases of social service and fund development work, and more

CASE STUDY

Mrs. Larson attended a major donor appreciation luncheon, where she was introduced to board members and fellow major donors. This interaction with board members and other major donors was a significant part of the cultivation process that led to other major gifts by the Larsons.

One secret to a successful board is to seek only top people (this board is considered the most prestigious board in the entire community), match the need of each member for participation to the opportunities of the organization, and then let them do their job. The result will be a creative, supportive group of high-level volunteers who cannot do enough for the Army in their community, as in this example. The buildings this board purchased and the programs they support are visionary in the truest sense of the word.

With the prevalence of information about the idiosyncrasies of the varying generations, Army leadership must pay close attention to attracting and developing individuals in the manner most attractive to them. Not only will donors of different generations respond differently to our cultivation and solicitation efforts, but so will those we need as advisory board members to our recruitment and management efforts. Fund development professionals in the Army is keenly aware of this issue and regularly counsels program leadership and administration about the need to cultivate support (volunteer and financial) from an ethnic, gender, profession, and age mix that truly represents the community.

The entire process (from identification through selection, recruitment, orientation, involvement, management, and exiting) must be creative and responsive to the individual's personal drives and generational differences. No longer will board members suffer a monthly "routine" just to have the honor to be on the board of a major national charity (if they ever really did). Volunteers today require a creative approach to meetings (maybe some electronic meetings and/or information dissemination?), meaningful work (as defined by the volunteer), and solid input (not just listening to reports) for a period of time they find meaningful (probably not for a lifetime in many instances). If charity X will not provide it, charity Y will. The new mantra for volunteers seems to be that hard work must be aligned to the interests and experience of the individual volunteer in concert with other volunteers they respect, not just the reputation of the organization.

Part of the success of the Army in the past—what brought it to be number one in fund development in the United States—is its ability to tap the needs of the world war generations as donors and volunteer leadership. Its success in the future will depend partly on its ability to do the same for the baby boomers and future generations. The future looks bright.

42.5 Basic Fund Development in Practice at the Army

Direct mail has long been the backbone of many philanthropic organizations, the Army included. It is the proverbial "rose" of the garden.

(A) DIRECT MAIL/ANNUAL GIVING

The Army's direct-mail program provides the basis for most of its fund development efforts. It:

- Attracts donors for annual giving, a major part of the ongoing support for local programs
- Attempts to upgrade donor gifts, again for annual giving
- Encourages volunteer involvement
- Provides significant prospect leads for major gifts (current and deferred)

We will look at each of these areas in turn.

(B) DONOR ACQUISITION AND UPGRADING

Until recently, the Army in the West depended heavily on one principal vendor to design and manage the bulk of its direct-mail program, including holding a "mirror" copy of the actual donor data. This began to change with the transition from the Alpha Micro System to a personal computer (PC) environment, requiring the selection of a new donor management system (which we will discuss in more detail later). Among other things, this change process required a strong learning curve regarding the actual design and management of the direct-mail program. While each division managed the change differently, some stand out for their success. I will relate a compilation of those that are the most successful, a sort of "best practices" survey.

(i) Purpose

The basic purpose of the change in direct-mail process is to provide objective counsel and recommendations to Army officer and program staff. Further, the change helps to ensure quality services at the most competitive prices, services that offer a variety of direct-mail packages to meet individual corps/program needs. The bottom-line goal is to increase campaign results by segmenting donors and targeting markets with direct-mail packages appropriate to their interest as demonstrated through a giving pattern.

(ii) Procedure

Prior to the change, the system had the vendor visiting each program to evaluate the prior campaigns and design the new ones. Currently the Donor Relations (direct-mail) department (a Divisional Headquarters [DHQ] function) screens each vendor who submits catalogs, samples, price lists, and campaign projections for review. The Donor Relations staff then presents all approved vendors' materials to each corps officer (local program director). The presentation includes a review of the test results and analysis of the previous campaigns, along with specific recommendations for future campaigns. The Donor Relations director accepts, processes, and manages the actual orders to ensure accuracy of the entire process, including billing. The Donor Relations director (instead of the vendor) now provides information relative to direct response marketing, including emerging trends in society, the economy, and the industry; new products; new services; common mistakes or misconceptions; and other relative information that allows the officer to make decisions on direct marketing fund raising.

Under the new system, the vendor does not (in most instances) have direct contact with the corps officer. If the officer has a question or complaint, the Donor Relations department acts as intermediary with the vendor. He or she has full responsibility for appeal code generation and file selections, transmission of files, and quality of information and format.

(iii) Results

Over the four years of its implementation, the new system and the introduction of competition shows more than a 24 percent increase in net income.

There was some reluctance to embrace this new procedure. While some were ready to try new vendors, they were unsure about the expertise of divisional staff to provide these services. There was a general fear that they would lose the control and choice they had had for years. Originally there was some question about the ability of the Donor Relations staff to be effective in this new venture, which could be expected for such a major change initiative. However, after a relatively brief period of time and positive outcomes, these concerns have been put to rest. Now, most officers welcome the proven professional recommendations and support from the DHQ staff, realizing that now they receive objective information and answers based solely on what is best for their program, not for a salesman's commission or another organization's bottom line.

The installation of the new donor management system facilitated all the above. There was no way for the Army to generate those results, create unity, and provide instant information and credibility when the donor information and campaign recommendations were not "in-house."

The new system (and the process it supports) provides an opportunity for officers, whether it be in the corps or at DHQ, to have a realistic view of how their direct-mail campaigns are performing. On behalf of those officers who so desire, the Donor Relations department can "shop" all or individual components of each and every campaign. The successes and failures of each of those trials can be shared so that mistakes become opportunities for learning and professional growth, and the benefits are spread throughout the division.

(iv) Upgrading

One of the key elements of a successful direct-mail program is upgrading the gifts of the current donors. Asking the donors to renew their previous gift at a higher amount goes beyond merely increasing the amount of the gift. It helps management to understand—and begins to pay back—the cost of acquisition.

More important in the long term, the donor upgrading program is a key initial element in the overall cultivation process that begins to identify those donors with the means and interest to become prospects for both current and deferred major gifts. We will discuss major gifts later in this chapter, but we should mention here that some novice fund development staff (or nonprofessional decision makers) express concern that continuing with regular mail appeals will clog the pipeline for major gifts. Others believe that when people become major donors, they will stop their annual gifts. However, experience suggests strongly that most major gift donors give from multiple sources of funds, including regular income, current assets, and their estates. Most often, a major gift does not inhibit continuing annual-type gifts, or vice versa.

CASE STUDY

The Larsons' first upgrade was in year three when they responded to an "association membership" appeal with a gift of $100. During the next five years, they responded to various appeals with eight $100 gifts and two $200 gifts. Twelve years after their first gift ($25), they upgraded to a request for $500. Even though they have now given over $1.4 million, they continue to respond to mail appeals: newsletters, summer camp emergencies, and Christmas.

(v) Lifetime Value

One key factor in evaluating the success of a direct-mail program is determining the lifetime value of a "typical" donor on the organization's file. The process is somewhat complicated, but the end result shows what the organization can expect average donors to contribute over their giving life, thus helping to support the planning for, and justify the cost of, an effective donor acquisition program.

Standard direct-marketing wisdom suggests that an organization should be willing to spend a third of the lifetime value of a customer/donor to acquire a new one. However, a creative donor cultivation process will impact significantly the actual lifetime value. With active donors falling off our files at an average of 30 to 33 percent per year, the evaluation tools provided in Exhibits 42.1 and 42.2 allows us to back into the size and cost of a standard donor acquisition program.

The next "path" we will explore in the garden is major gifts, the newest emphasis for not only the Army, but for many philanthropic organizations.

The initial thrust of the major-gift program is to identify those donors on our file as regular donors to the annual campaign, or who are in some other way involved with the Army, and who have the capacity to make much larger gifts. The basic process we use is as follows but will vary according to several factors.

EXHIBIT 42.1 Lifetime Value of the Average Direct Mail Donor

Process	Sample	Your Data
Donor contribution		
Average number of gifts per year	1.5	
× Average number of years active	3.5	
= Total number of gifts	5.25	
× Average (Mean) Gift	$20	
= Gross Contribution	**$105**	
Cost to acquire a donor	$22.50	
Cost of prospecting campaign ($45,000) Divided by number of new donors (100,000 mailed w/ 2% return)		
– Marketing costs (35 letters at .50 per letter)	$17.50	
Fulfillment costs = 10% of marketing cost	$1.75	
Total of costs	**$41.75**	
Gross contribution – Total costs = Lifetime value of a donor	**$63.25***	

With proper cultivation, this amount can be much higher.

(vi) Major Gifts

Major gifts (primarily we will refer here to current major gifts, rather than deferred or "planned" gifts) are principally an exercise in relationship building for the benefit of both principal parties, the donor/prospect and those whom the organization serves.

(vii) Sources of Prospects

The program the Army in the West uses began in 1995 and is a version of the one pioneered in the Army's Southern Territory a few years earlier. The principal thrust is with those donors currently on our donor file, those who have demonstrated interest by making multiple, and often increased, gifts over an extended period of time.

A principal source of information for the financial capability segment was, and remains, those donors on the direct-mail file who fit a set of criteria. Originally (and in some cases still), we set the criteria for selection of major gift prospects manually from a printed copy of the donor file itself. One method to select prospects from the donor file includes establishing a priority system. For instance:

- Size of giving over the last 12 months
- Frequency of giving (two gifts are better than one)
- Total lifetime giving
- Length of time on the donor file
- Title—often a Ms., Miss, or Mrs. tend to be more responsive candidates for cultivation (i.e., children, other family, etc.)
- ZIP code

EXHIBIT 42.2 Direct Mail/Renewal and Attrition Rate Evaluation

	1994	1995	1996	1997	1998
% of Donors who became lapsed					

Prospect Class	1994	1995	1996	1997	1998	1999	Avg. Renewal Rate
1994 # Donors Net revenue							
1995 # Donors Net revenue							
1996 # Donors Net revenue							
1997 # Donors Net revenue							
1998 # Donors Net revenue							
1999 # Donors Net revenue							
Total							

Recently the Army in the West used an electronic screening service to identify those donors on our files with significant real estate and stock holdings. This information, when added to the priority system above, makes for a reasonably qualified prospect financially. The above-mentioned criteria are flexible and designed to fit the specific situation and the individual professional involved.

(viii)   Other Sources for Names of Individuals for Cultivation

The effective major gift officer will review other sources for major gift prospects, which include:

- Advisory board and auxiliary members can be a resource for names to add to the priority list, once they are informed as to its purpose and convinced of a professional approach.
- Advisory board and auxiliary members themselves can be excellent candidates for the major-gift process.
- Active and former Service Extension volunteers make for excellent "suspects."
- Former advisory board members from as long ago as 25 or more years could still have the knowledge of, and the commitment to, the Army and the assets to make significant gifts.

- Donors to capital campaigns—recent and even those some years back—especially when the names are on similar lists from other campaigns, advisory boards, and auxiliaries.
- Local business journal/gazette; business and social section of the local newspaper.
- Donors to campaigns of other organizations with similar missions.

(ix) Prospect Review

Where possible, the major gift officer will involve the advisory board development committee in a modified version of the standard prospect review process. This committee will help establish both the priority and cultivation strategy for the names they suggest and that the major gift officer finds from the donor file, prior campaigns, and public sources. This committee should include the development director, divisional commander (or chief executive officer) and/or other officer (or program director) staff, planned giving director, development committee from the advisory board, and so on. (Here is another part of the process where former board and auxiliary members may be helpful too, either as part of this committee or as separate counsel.) The purpose of the prospect review process is to provide any information the committee members have about those on the priority list. These can include prior contacts, interests, caveats, and concerns; *any information* they know about the prospects with which the major gift officer is about to begin to build a relationship. Once the prospect review process is complete, *no one should visit the prospects on that list without first checking with the major gift officer for information, insights, and, in fact, approval.* Any chance or donor-initiated contact and additional gifts must be forwarded and made part of this donor's file. Also, the individuals on this committee may be the best people to handle the actual cultivation and/or solicitation with the professional support and planning of the major gifts officer. Finally, such involvement can and should be part of the cultivation process for their personal or corporate major gift.

The next and probably most critical piece in finding qualified major-gift prospects is attempting to determine their interest in the organization.

(C) PERSONAL CONTACT

The most important thing for major gift professionals is to *get out and see the people!* The major gift officer can and should do this even before completing the above process, because much learning is done in the field. The tendency for some is to "massage" lists and build databases and meet with committees rather than to visit donors. Although the "nonhuman" route is much easier, it will not raise much money! Therefore, we monitor the initial work of the major gift officer to help ensure that he or she does not put an inappropriate emphasis on the process to this point.

The standard process to secure personal visits that most major gift officers find effective includes a personal letter of introduction from the divisional commander. (Exhibits 42.3 and 42.4 are samples of these letters.) This letter comments on the donor's giving history, giving focus (if any), length of time on the file, and so forth. The letter will introduce the major gift officer and indicate that the donor can expect a phone call within a specified time frame. The goal is a personal visit by the major gift officer in the donor's home or place of business, an attempt to begin the relationship development process. The goal of the first visit is to begin to determine the possible level of interest on the part

EXHIBIT 42.3 Sample Personal Letter of Thanks for Contribution from Divisional Commander

(DATE)

Dear _____ :

On behalf of The Salvation Army, I would like to thank you for your exceedingly generous contributions over the past XXX years. It is only through such kindness that we are able to continue operating our programs for those in need in the Phoenix area.

In appreciation, I would like to invite you to tour our facilities at the Herberger Center, on East Van Buren Street. You can see our various programs, have lunch with us, and learn how we use your donations. Among other things, we are proud of our new, licensed Day Care facility in our Drug and Alcohol Recovery Center. We also have our Family Crisis Shelter, Senior Residences, and Family Assistance Program.

You may contact Dr. Jim Fitzpatrick, at 555-4107, to arrange a visit. It is informal, and everyone who comes finds it interesting. I have also asked Dr. Fitzpatrick to follow up on my behalf.

Let me emphasize that this letter is not seeking a donation. We just want to show our gratitude for your support.

I and others on the staff look forward to meeting you.

May God Bless You,

Olin O. Hogan, Lt. Colonel
DIVISIONAL COMMANDER

---

of the donor for increased investment (financial support) for Army programs, and what those programs might be. Some questions the major gift officer might use include:

1. *What got you started giving to The Salvation Army in the first place?* The major gift officer can ask this question straight out. Often the donor/prospect will not recall specifically, but will respond when offered some possibilities, such as "others have mentioned":
   - Service during World War I or II or the Korean conflict for them or someone in their family
   - Prison ministry
   - Influence of parents and/or family tradition
   - Volunteer service
   - Personal or family help at Christmas or in a natural disaster

   See pages 889–890 for additional services that may be of interest to donors.

   Major gift officers must know in detail the services the Army offers in their area. Even if they cannot unearth the specific reason for a donor's first gift, they will be telling donors of the services the Army offers and that "others" find important.

2. *What program that the Army operates excites you most?* The process for this question is similar to the one above. Both questions begin to paint the picture of where donor interest might lie and what shape the cultivation plan might begin to take.

EXHIBIT 42.4   Request for Camp Contributions Sample Letter

(DATE)

Dear (Name(s) of Donor(s)):

When I think back to those long, hot summer days as a child, I have many memories of fun and carefree times. Unfortunately, there are many children today that cannot live carefree and life is just not much fun for them.

The Salvation Army Camping Program is designed for children to have a week of no pressure placed upon them. That's right! **They can just be kids!** They can swim, play organized games, make crafts, and be exposed to positive role models!

For many years, The Salvation Army has bused children many miles to get them to camps. It has been decided that to: **1)** Best serve the children; and **2)** Be good stewards of the contributions we receive—that we develop a local camp. The new campground is located just southwest of Colfax, less than an hour from Sacramento. There are few structures on the site and we have erected temporary tents to house and feed the children.

However, we need to construct permanent cabins and other facilities. At present, if the weather is inclement we have no place for the children, except in their tent cabins. We need an activity/dining hall facility. **This is why I am writing to you.** You have shown through your past support that you believe in the work of The Salvation Army. Now we are in dire need of your financial support to accomplish our present task. We are looking for major supporters of our camp program. That is, we are looking for major gifts of $5,000, $10,000 or greater!

Allow me to briefly outline some of the advantages of such a major gift:
- Your entire gift is tax deductible.
- There are recognition opportunities for major supporters:
    1. Have your name placed on our Camp Donor Recognition Wall.
    2. Name a building after a loved one or yourself—THE "_____" ACTIVITY CENTER.
    3. For a very major gift, you can name our camp. How about "CAMP _____"?
- Have the personal satisfaction of knowing that you have been part of changing the lives of children.

There are many different ways that you can contribute to our new camp including:
- A gift of cash
- Appreciated securities (There are tax advantages in this type of gift)
- Gift of real estate
- Life income gifts or estate gifts

I would like to invite you to consider a major contribution to help develop our new camp. The camp development team or myself would be glad to sit down and talk with you about our camp and your possible contribution. You may wish to visit the camp this summer. However, let me warn you, if you do visit the camp this summer you will lose your heart to all those kids.

Please feel free to call or write to me with any questions.

Sincerely,

Lawrence Boettcher
Financial Development Director

3. *What competition might there be for available assets?* The questions here will focus on the donor's family: What kind of relationships do they have? How successful do they perceive their children are? It is surprising how many parents do not feel a need to—or even an obligation to—"leave it to the kids or grandkids."

   Another area to explore here is what other philanthropic interests the donors have and how the Army fits into their priorities. The *Nonprofit Times* reports that in excess of 59 percent of all donors give to three or more charitable institutions.[2] However, being a major donor to another organization is not necessarily a negative omen for the possibility of a major gift to the Army. In fact, a donor who makes major gifts to any organization usually understands the underlying philosophy of philanthropy and stewardship and, in many cases, may be an even stronger prospect for the major gift officer's cause.

4. *What concerns do you have for current use of your assets?* Financial security is a major concern for most of us. The major gift officer must carefully couch questions in this area. (Probably they will arise/surface in later meetings.) These questions will center on retirement income and concerns, as well as assets versus income. Often, this is where the discussion about planned giving comes in. It is important that the major gift officer *know the material.* He or she can begin to discuss how it is possible to take non–income-producing assets and turn them into income, even income guaranteed for life.

The major gift officer should also try to learn birthdays and anniversary dates as well as other family-related issues, career focus, interests, hobbies, education, and so on.

During a personal visit, a quick survey of the donor's home or office usually will give clues as to their interests and even a focus for the major gift officer's questions. If the major gifts officer wants information, he or she must ask questions and then listen! Most of the time, people really enjoy talking about themselves, their accomplishments, and their family.

CASE STUDY

You know you're on the right track when the donor calls you! About five years ago, Mrs. Larson called to inquire about the matching gifts program mentioned in our newsletter. During that conversation, the development director found out that her husband was self-employed and that she would have to find some organization to match their gifts.

A personal visit discussing in more detail the work of the Army resulted in Mr. Larson's comment that he would like to make a "significant" gift (Mr. Larson also is a major benefactor to his educational institution). Thinking that, to many donors, a significant upgrade from $25 would be $1,000, the development director asked him to define "significant." Imagine her response to $100,000! He expressed his desire to involve his wife in the process to learn more about the Army's work and that, if she were pleased, it might result in an even more significant gift.

---

[2] M. Sinclair, "Donors Give to More Groups: Wealth Is Being Spread Thinner," *Nonprofit Times*, May 1999, p. 1.

The planned familiarization process covered the next several months and included visits to all of the Army's major programs in the area. Part of that process included the development director's effort to involve the family in making the decisions about such a potentially major gift. Mr. Larson's response was "The children are all successful in their own right and have been provided for. Even the grandchildren have been taken care of."

Following one visit with the divisional commander, Mrs. Larson was given a proposal for the purchase of a camp that the division needed in order to carry out its mission to inner-city children and families. She took the proposal home as the basis of her own campaign with Mr. Larson. She was successful, the Larsons made a major gift, and the Army bought the camp.

(D) SPECIAL EVENTS

Special events can be very effective in support of a well-rounded fund development program. However, they are not always what they seem; they are not the panacea some fund-raising staff believe, and not always an effective tool to raise "Big" money.

Experience shows that few special events make any real money (especially when a realistic estimate of the cost for staff time is factored in). In *Achieving Excellence in Fund-Raising*, author Henry Rosso lists 13 methods to solicit gifts. Special events is number 10 on that list, leaving only three methods less effective.[3] However, they do provide a good opportunity for "friend-building" or donor/prospect cultivation. Just as cultures differ from geographic location to location and fund development practices will differ from organization to organization, so too will the tenor of special events differ by location and organization.

The Salvation Army's "garden" of special events in the Western Territory includes:

- A brass band concert attended by over 500 donors, featuring a professional musician, Phil Smith principle trumpet player for the New York Philharmonic, who is also a Salvationist (attends The Salvation Army as his church)
- A formal annual dinner honoring such luminaries as Angela Lansbury and Billy Graham
- A top-flight fashion show (*the* social event of its kind in the community) attended by several hundred, and honoring women leaders in the community
- A fashion show in another city, featuring top community leaders and media personalities wearing clothes that came from the local Salvation Army Adult Rehabilitation Center Thrift Store
- A "soup line" intended to remind the community of the Army's service during the Great Depression, but featuring gourmet soups provided by local restaurants

Most often the most striking results, again, are an increased awareness for the community at large of the myriad services the Army provides to the most needy, and the part those who are better off can play to the level of their financial ability and personal interest. (See Exhibit 42.5 for a special events evaluation checklist.)

---

[3]Henry A. Rosso, *Achieving Excellence in Fund-Raising* (San Francisco: Jossey-Bass, 1991), pp. 59–61.

EXHIBIT 42.5 Special Event Income Evaluation

(Please complete one sheet for each separate major event)

Event name:_____

Internal focus: ☐ education   ☐ acknowledgment   ☐ recognition
                        ☐ fund-raising (amount $_____)   ☐ other_____

External focus: ☐ donors   ☐ volunteers   ☐ community   ☐ other_____

	1996	1997	1998
1. Percent participation			
Response/Invitations sent			
2. Gross income			
Income/_____ # of attendees			
3. Net income			
Cost */– Income			
4. Average cost per attendee			
Fund-raising cost/# of attendees			

*Net income must *include an estimate of the cost of staff time to indicate the true cost of the event.*
Source: Adapted from James Greenfield, *Fund-Raising Cost Effectiveness (New York: John Wiley & Sons, 1996), p. 104.*

A major gift campaign is often inextricably intertwined with a capital campaign. In fact, many modern capital campaigns are essentially major gift campaigns and are continuing rather than episodic. However, capital campaigns do have some unique qualities and benefits to the philanthropic organization.

(E) BENEFITS AND PROCESS OF A CAPITAL CAMPAIGN

This is not intended to be an exhaustive treatise on capital campaigns; rather, these are some examples of internal Salvation Army procedures and responsibilities. A far more complete resource is the book *Conducting a Successful Capital Campaign*, written by Kent Dove.[4]

---

[4]Kent A. Dove, *Conducting a Successful Campaign* (San Francisco: Jossey-Bass, 1988).

A capital campaign can be a superb opportunity for a crash course in the Army's inner workings. It is a great opportunity to fully educate each advisory board about every aspect of the Army and the campaign process. How many board members could explain to a friend or business associate the impact of your programs or conduct a tour of any of your facilities? Too often, people join boards because it is the social or nice thing to do. Too often, an organization will tell prospective board members, "You won't have to do anything . . . raise money or even come to many meetings." And that's exactly what they do—nothing.

In its early (and even precampaign) stages, a capital campaign is more like the dating game. Common questions include: Are you willing to learn all about me? Can I have your time and attention? Can I meet your closest friends? What does commitment really mean to you in this context?

A capital campaign is an excellent opportunity to evaluate the true quality, strength, and support of an advisory board. Sometimes a board does not have the required influence or will not use it. Some board members believe that their role is only to promote the idea of a campaign but do not feel the responsibility to give or ask others to give. Some will even resign. Then a required phase of the campaign is the recruitment of new board members who will understand their true and proper role in the fund development efforts—who can and will carry off a campaign. That's good! The organization will be much stronger both during and after the campaign.

The first step is for the officer to articulate to the board why a campaign is necessary. The officer must provide the requisite leadership and effectively communicate a clear vision. At this point, the campaign makes clear the fundamental role of the board: to bring their resources to the table. They must get the campaign positioned in front of the financial decision makers.

One important officer responsibility is to support fund raising, especially in a capital campaign. The officer must represent the organization's constituency, telling the story and making the case for support in compelling terms. When the board opens the doors, the officer must follow through.

Often the really major prospects will want to meet and get to know the person in the organization who is on a similar social or business level. The development staff is seldom an adequate substitute; their job is to do the research and pave the way.

Most often, an organization will retain the services of a consultant or consulting firm to provide professional assistance for a capital campaign, from the needs assessment through the feasibility study to the campaign itself. The success of the campaign is more likely when supported by the insight, sensitivities, and judgment of an experienced professional. Further, a capital campaign is time-intensive for local staff, even with campaign counsel. Not having counsel tends to stretch out the time frame beyond the limits of public interest, to say nothing about other important fund development work that the local staff cannot get to.

(F)   IMPORTANT ISSUES SURROUNDING CAMPAIGN COUNSEL

(i)   Selection

The officer (or divisional commander), fund development staff, and top advisory board leadership should interview at least three (preferably five) firms. They should ensure that the person who will be the actual campaign director is part of the process. They should not select a firm and then have them select a director without their full involvement and approval.

(ii) Contract

The officer must ensure that the contract fairly represents the interests of the Army and the local leadership. The Army is the customer and should have prevailing input into the wording of the contract. The fee should be for the estimated time, not a proportion of the goal or funds raised. The phrase "customary and usual expenses" (or one similar to it) should include the requirement that Salvation Army or voluntary leadership must approve such expenses prior to their occurring. DHQ and THQ (Territorial Headquarters) development staff frequently assist in the review of the contract.

(iii) Relationship

Most of the time, working with professional campaign counsel is a positive experience. When done properly, the local staff (administrative, fund development, and volunteer) stand to learn a tremendous amount from the experience. Again, the Army is the customer, and the campaign must be of significant benefit to the local situation. The really bright, quality officer and staff will:

- Stay involved with the process.
- Learn about the process and their part in it.
- Determine how to take advantage of the increased community awareness for the benefit of other facets of the local program.
- Take the opportunity to build significant relationships that will assist in ensuring the Army's service to the community for years to come.

When it all works (and it usually does), a capital campaign enhances the program, the physical plant, and the reputation of the board and the officer, to say nothing about the significant increase in the effectiveness of the Army's program to serve the people of the community. An empowered board and other volunteers become passionately involved with a whole new esprit de corps.

(G) PREPARATION FOR A CAPITAL CAMPAIGN

In his book *Conducting a Successful Capital Campaign,* Kent Dove comments, "There is clearly an evangelical aspect to fundraising that motivates most professionals and volunteers. Never lose sight of that."[5] Thus, a successful capital campaign for the Army will be bathed in prayer and professional preparation and management. It will carry the full support and commitment of all local leadership—officer, staff, and volunteer. The three basic phases are a needs assessment study, a feasibility study, and the capital campaign itself.

We cannot stress strongly enough the need for advisory board involvement and support in the entire preparation, planning, recruitment and solicitation process. Existing development staff cannot successfully man a campaign alone, or even with the help of outside professionals. For success, the following must be in place:

---

[5]*Ibid.*, p. 2.

- The information about needs for additional and/or improved social service delivery in the community developed in a needs assessment study
- Determination of the level of support (leadership and financial) available (or that can be developed) in the community that result from a feasibility study
- Support and time commitments from all key groups, including:
  — Advisory board
  — Corps officer, program directors, and divisional administration
  — Major donors and prospects
  — Volunteer leaders
  — Campaign counsel
- A realistic assessment of the current state of the services the local command offers, clear vision of where the leadership wants to take the local unit, and a strategic plan to guide the road in between
- Important and legitimate goals, plans, and budgets validated by the community
- A program needs and feasibility study to establish the case for support
- A comprehensive, compelling case for support that is well defined and clearly articulated
- Existing major donor support
- Leadership, leadership, leadership!

Increasingly, major donor prospects will ask some tough questions about the project and how the plans were made. They will respond most positively to a well-thought-out and clearly articulated plan spanning the distance between the current reality and the envisioned future. Further, many really *major* prospects will seek more significant involvement and participation in actually planning the facility and the program that will be the result of their generosity.

The role as chief operating officer is a principal one of the officer. They need to become comfortable with that; often, these major prospects have superb credentials and/or will provide other professional help in addition to their cash gift. They are also candidates for leadership in the campaign and beyond. Barry McLeish, in *The Donor Bond,* makes it clear when he says, "A key donor strategy is to have the CEO visit the organization's key prospects and donors and let them tell him or her what their vision is for the organization. It is through involvement that one moves from outside an organization and cause to inside it. People give to people."[6]

Planned giving is usually the ultimate gift in an effective fund development program. Most often it comes from assets that are part of a donor's estate, and is part of a sequence of gifts that start small and progress up the so-called donor pyramid. (See Exhibit 42.6.)

(H)   PLANNED GIVING

Teamwork among the various fund development disciplines is evolving as a strong organizational value within the Army. Most of its professionals realize not only how crit-

---

[6]Barry McLeish, *The Donor Bond* (Rockville, Md.: Fund-Raising Institute, 1991), pp. 46–47.

EXHIBIT 42.6 The Donor Pyramid

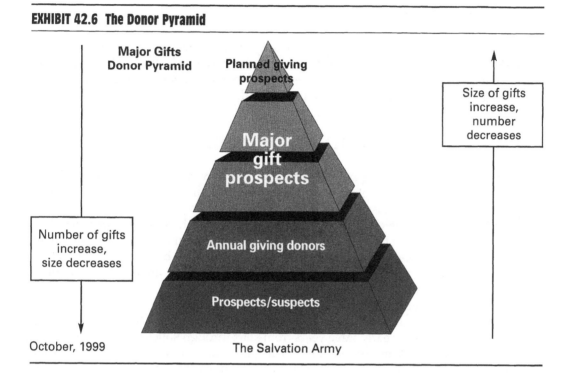

Major Gifts Donor Pyramid

Planned giving prospects

Major gift prospects

Annual giving donors

Prospects/suspects

Size of gifts increase, number decreases

Number of gifts increase, size decreases

October, 1999   The Salvation Army

ical the work of their professional counterparts is to their success but also how important their work is to the success of those working in the other disciplines.

Until recently, most planned giving work was in response to "Request for Information" coupons that donors and prospects mailed in as a result of a strong, creative marketing program and public seminars. However, with the advent of the upgraded donor management system, the planned giving staff are "mining" the donor file for candidates of planned giving agreements. Further, the planned giving officers receive an increasing number of leads from visits by the major gift staff when they determine, along with the donor, that the best gift to meet their needs and desires is a planned gift.

CASE STUDY

The Larsons had a terrific feeling about their gift that made the purchase of the camp possible. It was a beautiful site that the developer thought was a good deal financially and aesthetically. The Army staff was able to find a foundation to match the Larson's gift.

The Larsons were so happy with the entire process, including their recognition at the dedication ceremony, that they agreed to begin discussions about a gift from their estate. The work by the planned giving director resulted in a planned gift of $6.5 million, earmarked for development and expansion of the camp. The Larsons later made a separate gift of $50,000 toward the camp capital campaign, with the strong possibility of a matching gift from a foundation.

42.6 Other Issues

Several other issues have helped shape the reality of fund development within the Army in the Western Territory. The first is the fact that Salvation Army officers change appointment (which usually means location) every three years on average, and that is a challenge to a/the professional fund-development staff.

(A) DEALING WITH A CHANGE OF LEADERSHIP

Most major gift fund development efforts (both current and deferred) depend on a strong, quality relationship between the donor/prospect and the organization's leadership. An article in a recent issue of the *Chronicle of Philanthropy*, "Managing Turnover at the Top," talks about the challenge of a changeover in a philanthropic organization's leadership. In that article the author says, "Charity board members and officials say the damage that can be done by frequent changes in leadership can be severe."[7] The problem is of enough significance that some major national foundations are becoming involved in studying the problem and possible solutions.

In the Army, the administration appoints its officer leadership to their positions. The average stay in one position is under three years. Experience shows that the average significant major gift takes nearly three years from start through solicitation and closing. In most cases, Salvation Army officers are not in place long enough for the process and donor/prospect to receive the maximum benefit of their leadership and involvement. The good news is that such a system brings a fresh perspective to local issues on a regular basis. Thus, knowing the probability of the officer's moving, the key is to do as the title of the article suggests: Manage that turnover in a creative, successful way. Army fund development professionals either instinctively transfer those relationships, or learn how to do it, successfully, from one officer to the next, because it is a fact of organizational life.

CASE STUDY

> In the case of the Larsons, one divisional commander began the relationship for the gift of $1 million for the new camp; a second closed the deal; a third hosted them to the opening of the camp and began the relationship for additional major gifts toward furnishing it. The fourth divisional commander is working with them and their advisors (in concert with the planned giving staff) on an estate gift to complete the major construction. All along the way, the development director kept a strong and appropriate relationship with the donors that allowed a smooth transition in each case.

The United Way in each community is a mostly independent local organization allowed to grow and meet the needs of the community as the local leadership sees fit. Its relationship with local Army units ranges from strong, collaborative work by two major players on the local social service scene to a bare recognition of each other. The Salvation Army was a founding member of United Way's precursor (the Community Chest).

---

[7] D. Marchetti, "Managing Turnover at the Top," *Chronicle of Philanthropy* (June 5, 1999), p. 33.

However, the United Way has gone through (and in some cases is going through) a natural organizational development and change process, just like the Army.

This is not an uncommon phenomenon in the life of any "family." Sometimes the parents and child grow together as partners and friends, and sometimes they part as nearly adversaries, depending on how each matures and views the other as friend or competitor.

These two giants now stand as partners for effective community service in some instances where those in decision-making positions value collaboration and relationship building. In others they coexist in an uncomfortable, even sometimes strained relationship with parallel roles and missions.

(B)   SELECTION OF A DONOR MANAGEMENT SYSTEM

The selection of a donor management system is a process in which every charitable group will have to engage at some time (or times) during its lifetime. This process will occur as a result of growth in the database or a change in organizational structure. Most information technology professionals espouse the need to review all major systems every five to seven years due to the rapid change and improvement in technology. The Army is no exception.

The most recent process for the Army began in late 1994, when administration made the decision to move from an Alpha Micro to a PC-based system. Simply this required a new donor management system that would operate in the PC environment. In February 1995, the secretary for Business Administration for The Salvation Army Western Territory made a bellwether decision for the Army. He allowed a process to research the field and make a recommendation for a single system for all divisions in the entire Western Territory to use. This process would forever change the face of direct-mail fund development specifically, and donor management in general, for the Army in the West.

The stated goal of the process was to make a recommendation that represented the needs and desires of everyone who has to use and receive benefit from the system, not just some high-level administrators; there was no "top-down" decision here. The resulting task force was a cross-functional team in the classical, textbook sense of the concept. It included, by design, users from all disciplines including direct mail (annual funds), major gifts and planned giving, volunteers, special events, and information technology. Thus, those charged with managing the installation and operation of the system once in place were intimately involved in its selection, ensuring their buy-in for the implementation stages. An outline of the process to research and recommend a donor management system to Army leadership follows.

(C)   RESEARCHING AND RECOMMENDING A DONOR MANAGEMENT SYSTEM: THE PROCESS

The BA asked each divisional commander to initiate a local donor database committee. Each committee was to include representation from all groups who would use, have input to, and derive benefit from the database. This committee was to identify the criteria they felt they needed and wanted in a donor management system. The divisional commanders then appointed one member of the divisional committee as their representative to the territory-wide task force.

The task force met to determine the vendors from whom to invite participation, set up an initial testing and on-site visit process, and establish an extensive set of criteria representing the stated needs and desires of every division.

A small working group of the task force met to review the 16 requests for proposals (RFPs) received (out of 54 invited). They eliminated six that did not meet basic minimum standards, and approved the remaining 10 for review by the full task force.

The group sent the divisional committees the 10 successful RFPs "blind"; that is, they removed all reference to specific vendor and trade name and assigned numbers. The divisional committees assigned a weight to each "feature," which represented their feeling about the importance of each criterion.

The task force met to review the results of the committees' work, which pointed clearly to four finalists. They allowed a full day for each finalist vendor to make a formal presentation and demonstration.

In an attempt to even the playing field, the task force sent each vendor a standard Army PC system. It contained our standard Windows and Microsoft system plus approximately 100,000 donor records, 650,000 gifts, and 50,000 prospect names. The vendor was to convert the data, install its program, and bring the entire system for use during its presentation.

Each divisional committee performed a series of on-site visits with two to three clients of each vendor finalist. The purpose was to get beyond sales hype and high-level information technology presentation skills to find out how those using the product on a day-to-day basis felt about it, the real customer support provided, and the company supporting it.

During the week of the vendors' presentations, the task force required each to perform several "standard" tests the task force had designed and forwarded in advance. However, it also included a series of "surprise" tests of which none of the vendors had previous knowledge. In the discussions that followed each presentation, numbers in a "FIT" column (multiplied by the assigned weight for importance) finalized the objective portion of the review. They also factored in a subjective element. How would this organization support us *after* signing a contract?

The task force presented the final recommendation to the BA barely five months after the process began. The Territorial Finance Council (the primary decision-making body in the territory) approved it.

There are many other issues the task force reviewed and resolved beyond the technical aspects, including:

- Compatibility of the corporate culture of the vendor
- System competency
- System and program "friendliness" and speed
- Information management and control
- Perception of customer service expected

It was the overwhelming opinion of the task force that customer support was a key issue in choosing a major software package. The staff of the successful vendor repeatedly demonstrated that they and their organizational corporate culture was far stronger, more positive, more capable, more professional, and more desirous of supporting the Army as a client than all other systems reviewed.

We cannot stress too strongly the value of the open selection process that involves input from all those who will use and receive benefit from the new donor management system. The benefits to the staff and the organization far exceed the actual selection itself, and go to building the commitment on the part of those who will use the system on a daily basis. No one knows better what an organization needs in such a system than those who use it, and no one can evaluate better the merits of candidate systems.

(D) PROFESSIONAL GROWTH AND DEVELOPMENT

"Change"—the mantra of the postmodern organization—drives the need for professional development staff to keep up with new "species" (fund development programs and techniques) and "growing" (donor cultivation). Change pervades all areas of contemporary life. There is more information than ever before on how different people (generations, races, genders, etc.) respond to philanthropy, and that base of information grows and changes constantly. Professional growth and development (keeping up with the growth of relevant information) is one key to an organization's realizing increased success in fund development. In *Born to Raise*, Jerold Panas quotes Boone Powell, Sr., a 75-year-old who built Baylor University Medical Center in Dallas, as saying "You've got to grow or go."[8] That applies to any professional—certainly those of us in the field of fund development.

The more educated and better trained an organization's staff members are, the better that organization's chances are for financial success. A less obvious benefit, but one that has a similar result, is that by making professional growth and development an organizational value, the chances are better of retaining top-quality staff. (Relationships are at the core of effective major gift fund development; therefore, keeping quality staff provides a strong benefit to any organization.)

Salvation Army administration has long valued and promoted professional growth in its officers and professional and support staff, supporting the AFP's CFRE (Certified Fund Raising Executive) and ACFRE (Advanced Certified Fund Raising Executive) certification and paying a major portion of any advanced education that its staff pursues. Recently we developed a specific program to encourage advanced education and provide certificates and degrees for its fund development staff.

Often philanthropic organizations (and the Army is no exception) find that they must (or choose to) hire staff with little or no direct experience for midlevel or even senior fund development positions, for reasons such as:

- A limited budget
- Difficulty finding suitable candidates who match up to unique organizational values and/or culture
- The feeling that such personnel should work for less compensation as a sign of true personal buy-in to the mission

All these factors limit the pool of qualified candidates.

On occasion, when organizations cannot find a qualified suitable candidate for a senior position, organizational decision makers find it reasonable to identify and pro-

---

[8]Jerold Panas, *Born to Raise* (Chicago: Ruribus Press, 1988), p. 12.

mote a junior member who has strong natural competencies in general administration, leadership, critical thinking decision making, and team building. Sometimes an organization will hire from another organization, or promote from within, a junior-level fund development professional to join an experienced staff in the normal course of doing business. Whatever the driving force(s), the result is a staff member with a need for professional training and development. Finally, even for experienced fund development professionals, lifelong learning is a key to personal and professional growth.

Although there are increasing opportunities for formal education in fund development, they are not prevalent in many geographic locations in the United States. What happens usually is a learn-as-you-go, on-the-job-training situation. Unless the new staff member is tenacious in ferreting out educational opportunities, the learning can be experiential at best. This "education" can be skewed to the specific agency, or at least the "industry" (e.g., social service, hospital, education, the arts). Further, the exposure most often is not broadly based in relation to the various fund development disciplines (major gifts, both current and deferred; special events; public relations; annual fund; grants; etc.).

Thus, we developed the following plan in an attempt to make available a comprehensive yet highly individualized training and development program for the less experienced fund development professional. The six-step process is as follows:

1. *Evaluation.* The staff member candidate completes an evaluation to determine if he or she has the innate personal skills and drive that are required for success in fund development. In addition, the candidate's peers and leadership will complete the same form and submit it to a neutral party. This person will develop a mean (average) score for all the attributes and compare it to the candidate's evaluation. The object here is to ensure that the candidate has the core professional competencies that form the basis for success in fund development.

2. *Personal/professional goal.* The candidate will determine his or her own current professional goal. Next, the candidate will determine the amount of time and energy he or she is willing to put into an educational effort. From those two points, the candidate can begin to build an individualized instruction plan.

3. *Resource guide.* The resource guide is a repository of nearly 100 initial resources (including several college/university programs) available on multiple topics and in various media, such as:
   - Books
   - Audiotapes
   - Videotapes
   - Seminars
   - Conferences
   - Periodicals
   - Manuals
   - Accredited college/university courses, including those that offer certificate and degree programs via regular campus schedules, limited on-campus schedules (often referred to as "distance learning") and offerings via the Internet. See Exhibit 42.7 for a sample page from the Resource Guide.

4. *Course design.* The course will be divided into two one-year segments, each with established required material and courses, supplemented by selected elective areas of study. By no means is this program relegated solely to the specific study of fund development topics. The most effective professionals increasingly

EXHIBIT 42.7 Professional Training and Development Sample Resource Page

Territorial Financial Development Director Fund Development 101	Media	Source
Designs for Fund-Raising	Books	Harold J. Seymour—Out of print—On loan from Bob Gregg
Fund-Raising—Evaluating and Managing the Fund-Development Process		James M. Greenfield—John Wiley & Sons, Inc.
Fund-Raising Fundamentals		James M. Greenfield—John Wiley & Sons, Inc.
Rosso on Fund-Raising—Lessons From a Master's Lifetime Experience		Henry A. Rosso—Jossey-Bass Publishers
Achieving Excellence in Fund-Raising		Henry A. Rosso & Associates—Jossey-Bass Publishers
Friends for Life—Relationship Fund-Raising in Practice		Ken Burnett—The White Lion Press
Excellence in Advancement		William M. Tromble—Aspen Publishers
The Hands-on Guide to Fund-Raising Strategy and Evaluation	Manual	Mal Marwick—ASPEN PUBLICATIONS—Aspen Publishers—Gaithersburg, Maryland
The Chronicle of Philanthropy	Periodicals	
Nonprofit Times		973.734.1700
Development 101	Video Tape(s)	CSA Institute (See Bob Gregg for course information)
Principles and Techniques of Fund-Raising	Seminars	The Fund-Raising School (has a five-course certificate program)
Annual Funding/Direct Mail/Events		CSA Institute (See Bob Gregg for course information)
Small Ministry Integrated Funding		CSA Institute (See Bob Gregg for course information)
The Strategic Fund-Raising Workshop		The Grantsmanship Center (presented in several locations)
AFP National Conference	Conference(s)	
CSA (Christian Stewardship Association) National Conference		
—See section of Certificate Programs for local offerings—	College Courses	
Introduction to Advancement Services	Internet	http://interlearn.case.org/courses.htm

develop interdisciplinary knowledge and skills such as leadership, management, psychology, sociology, history, and economics.

5. *Professional support.* The candidate will select an approved mentor to support and facilitate the learning. The candidate and mentor will meet no less than bimonthly. The purpose will be to discuss the material covered in the intervening period to help ensure its internalization and its application to real-life fund-development situations. The candidate will prepare a five- to 10-page paper for the mentor to review, which will become a part of the student's records. The mentor will evaluate the paper and the interview, and with the candidate, make any midcourse corrections they agree will be beneficial to the candidate's professional growth.

6. *Outcomes.* At the end of each of the periods, the sponsoring organization will prepare a certificate of completion. This will recognize significant effort and accomplishment in the candidate's personal and professional development and his or her commitment to that process. Successful completion should be regarded as the basis for promotion and/or an increase in compensation.

An exception to the two-year program outlined here is when the candidate chooses to pursue a degree or certificate from a college or university.

(E)   EVALUATION OF THE FUND DEVELOPMENT DEPARTMENT

Finally, we will investigate the role of a comprehensive assessment process designed to foster renewal of the fund development program. There is a lot of talk in organizations today about strategic planning and visioning. Both approaches lead to the same process, asking (and, it is hoped, answering) where we are, where we want to go, and how we should get there. Again, the Army is no different. Assuring that its divisional fund development staff are keeping up with fund development tends to be a high priority for Army administration. However, the process we developed is a little more comprehensive than many we have seen. It has many features that we feel surpass the "standard" audit by an external firm.

One of the main features of this program is the use of a team (featuring the benefits of some internal and some external members) rather than a single individual. Some of the advantages to the team approach include:

- A thorough knowledge of The Salvation Army, its organizational values, and unique characteristics on the part of those providing the service.
- A broad base of current, relevant professional experience.
- In addition to the review of specific data, team interviews of a development staff, most of the divisional officer staff, and good cross-section of advisory board members to get at their thoughts, ideas, concerns, and dreams. It also briefly reviews the quality of the programs the fund development staff must support.
- The ability to process the assessment in a much shorter time frame.
- Always having two team members on an interview, who can hear more, cover more ground, and ensure a more unbiased result than with a single interviewer.

While the process uses principally Salvation Army professionals, one member of the assessment team always is a fund development professional who is not an Army staff member. This feature lends added external credibility and professional integrity to the process while keeping the cost to the division at a minimum. Further, it allows a far more candid final report than might otherwise be politically possible with only internal staff.

The other unique feature is the thorough nature of the process:

- A comprehensive assessment and detailed report with recommended changes
- Workshops for discovery and development of departmental:
  — Values (Appropriate values, when universally followed, lay the foundation for building and operating a first-class, winning organization for the long term.)
  — Mission (A clear mission allows an organization to determine on what specific functions they should concentrate.)
  — Vision (A shared vision provides the focus to keep followers and leaders alike on track. It can fill the followers' and leaders' need for some constancy in the current sea of constant change, another important element of a motivating vision.)
- A strategic plan (For long-term success, every organization must have a well-thought-out, creative strategic plan that reflects the results of the assessment and the vision development process, and is built on solid values and mission.)
- An ongoing evaluation component to help ensure that each phase of the plan is being followed over the long term and altered as circumstances dictate.

The results from the divisions that have accessed the process to date are exciting. In every instance, the divisional commander has made the decision to implement in excess of 95 percent of the recommendations, including substantive department reorganization and upgrading. The implementation is as voluntary as the initial assessment itself, it is not an administrative mandate.

In each process completed, the staff members display increased commitment to the mission of the Army and their professional work. Further, they demonstrate an increased understanding about how important it is for their department to: operate under specific shared values; discover their clear mission; develop an exciting, challenging shared vision; and learn how that process benefits their ability to support the overall mission of the Army. Each also shows increased teamwork and desire for professional growth.

42.7 Summary

Defining fund development in The Salvation Army is a challenging process because the Army is a complex organization, recognized for its service in nearly every community in America. Even when we narrow the attempt down to the western states, the effort still must recognize 10 widely dispersed and unique geographic units. Each of those has significant differences between and within them.

The professional level of the fund-development staff varies, as does the understanding of its role and support by administration. Further complicating the issue is the differing levels of financial stability and therefore the ability to provide adequate technical and clerical support. Finally, while all programs deliver quality community services and always strive for improvement, some are better than others at any given time, giving rise to the challenge of donor/volunteer involvement.

Even with all this organizational diversity and the resulting fund development challenges, the staff representing all of the fund development disciplines shows remarkable unity in its commitment to the Army's mission. Supporting this is a desire to grow professionally in order to effectively support those less fortunate men, women, boys, and girls in our communities that the Army serves.

With the focus on organizational mission and vision in the world today, it is no surprise that these factors provide a glimpse into the success the Army realizes in fund development. Commissioner Doris Noland, reflecting on the recent process to select the next general (the international leader of The Salvation Army) from among those leaders currently representing nearly every major culture in the world, made the following comment: *"We are a united Army, with differing methods and strategies but with one mission."* When we consider the almost unfathomable diversity of challenges underlying the myriad fund-development issues facing The Salvation Army, it is clear that its success lies in its determined focus to hold absolutely firm to the mission.

> *. . . to preach the gospel of Jesus Christ and to meet human needs in His name without discrimination.*

The Salvation Army both seeks and recognizes God's leading in its work; thus its success.

Suggested Readings

There are myriad books about the work of The Salvation Army, its leaders, and its work in most countries around the world. Some of these include wonderful, heart-wrenching biographies of men and women imprisoned or even killed for their determined (sometimes colorful) faith, from China to Russia to Czechoslovakia and many other places. There are stories of those famous for pushing a social agenda (radical at the time) or equally well known for their medical and surgical exploits. We will mention only three here, but they are classics.

Chesham, Sallie. *Born to Battle: The Salvation Army in America.* New York: The Salvation Army, 1965.
Collier, Richard. *The General Next to God: The Story of William Booth and The Salvation Army.* Glasgow: Fontana, 1977.
McKinley, Edward H. *Marching to Glory: The History of The Salvation Army in the United States.* Atlanta: The Salvation Army, 1980.

For a new, external view, a recent publication might prove informative:

Winston, D. *Red-Hot and Righteous: The Urban Religion of The Salvation Army.* Boston: Harvard University Press, 1999.

Books of particular value on the fund development process and professional:

Birnbaum, W. *If Your Strategy Is So Terrific, How Come It Doesn't Work?* New York: Amacom, 1990.

Bryson, J. *Strategic Planning for Public and Nonprofit Organizations.* San Francisco: Jossey-Bass, 1995.

Burnett, K. *Friends for Life.* London: White Lion Press, 1996.

————. *Relationship Fund-Raising.* London: White Lion Press, 1992.

Dove, Kent E. *Conducting a Successful Capital Campaign.* San Francisco: Jossey-Bass, 1988.

Drucker, P. *The Five Most Important Questions You Will Ever Ask About Your Nonprofit Organization.* San Francisco: Jossey-Bass, 1993.

Greenfield, J. *Fund-Raising—Evaluating and Managing the Fund-Development Process,* 2d ed. New York: John Wiley & Sons, 1999.

————. *Fund-Raising Cost Effectiveness.* New York: John Wiley & Sons, 1996.

————. *Fund-Raising Fundamentals.* New York: John Wiley & Sons, 1994.

Kotler, P., and A. Andreasen. *Strategic Marketing for Nonprofit Organizations.* Englewood Cliffs, N.J.: Prentice Hall, 1991.

Lord, J. G. *The Raising of Money.* Cleveland: Third Sector Press, 1996.

McLeish, Barry. *The Donor Bond.* Rockville, Md.: Fund-Raising Institute, 1991.

Mixer, J. *Principles of Professional Fundraising.* San Francisco: Jossey-Bass, 1993.

Nichols, J. E. *Changing Demographics: Fund-Raising in the 1990s.* Chicago: Bonus Books, 1990.

————. *Growing From Good to Great.* Chicago: Precept Press, 1995.

————. *Pinpointing Affluence: Increasing Your Share of Major Donor Dollars.* Chicago: Precept Press, 1990.

Panas, Jerold. *Boardroom Verities.* San Francisco: Jossey-Bass, 1991.

————. *Finders Keepers: Lessons I've Learned about Dynamic Fundraising.* Chicago: Bonus Books, 1999.

————. *Mega Gifts.* Chicago: Precept Press, 1984.

Rosso, H. A. *Achieving Excellence in Fund-Raising.* San Francisco: Jossey-Bass, 1991.

Seymour, H. J. *Designs for Fundraising.* Rockville, Md.: Fund-Raising Institute, 1966; reprinted 1988.

Stewart, T. *Intellectual Capital: The New Wealth of Organizations.* New York: Doubleday/Currency, 1997.

43 ▼ Grass-roots Fund Raising

JOHN HICKS, PRESIDENT & CHIEF EXECUTIVE OFFICER
J. C. Geever, Inc.

43.1 Introduction

(A) DEFINING GRASS-ROOTS FUND RAISING

Grass-roots fund raising is a key part of the longest-standing tradition of philanthropy in America. Long before the first organized fund development campaigns, Alexis de Tocqueville wrote in his book, *Democracy in America*, about "associations" through which ordinary citizens addressed needs of importance to their communities that were not met through state or federal programs.

De Tocqueville's model is applicable even today. However, the arena of grass-roots fund raising is no longer confined to community-level activities undertaken by ordinary citizens. Political campaigns that are waged on a national scale are often referred to as "grass roots." So are long-extant advocacy groups such a Greenpeace and the National Rifle Association, which have multimillion-dollar budgets, extensive networks and memberships, and an array of lobbyists and volunteers testifying in Congress or networking with significant foundation, corporate, and individual wealth in support of their agencies. So too is the local community organization fighting to save a park and the block association fighting to preserve the safety of local children.

Today's grass-roots not-for-profits are now pressured to become professional organizations in order to compete for contributions and to survive in a competitive market. The resources once available only to established not-for-profits—computers, databases, research materials and capabilities, professional-quality materials, consultants, and other professional services—are now available to grass-roots agencies for very little cost. As a result, such organizations can become professionalized, high-tech, and far-reaching virtually overnight.

(B) FUNDAMENTAL ELEMENTS OF GRASS-ROOTS FUND RAISING

Defining the "typical" grass-roots organization, especially in fund-raising terms, is probably no longer possible. There are, however, fundamental elements of grass-roots fund raising that are as applicable to a broad-based advocacy agency as to a local community group.

Grass-roots fund-raising:

- Is time and issue driven, focusing on issues of immediate concern to the community and seeking to gain maximum, immediate return based largely on the emotional response of like-minded others;
- Begins with and maintains strong ties to the community;
- Is volunteer driven as opposed to staff driven, although an organization may use professional assistance in implementing fund-raising activities; and
- Is as concerned with the amount of money being raised as the number of new adherents being drawn to the organization's cause.

(C) THREE TYPES OF GRASS-ROOTS ORGANIZATIONS

Three models of grass-roots organizations are prevalent today, each with different funding needs and fund-raising foci.

(i) *Response-Driven Organization*
Response-driven organizations are those created by an individual or group of volunteers in response to an immediate need. Fund raising for such groups is focused on low-cost,

moderate net income activities designed to raise as much money as possible from as many sources as possible to address that need as quickly as possible. As a result, both a constituency and a base of financial support are built at the same time.

(ii) Accelerated Start-up

Accelerated start-up organizations are conceptualized by their founders as long-term agencies providing continuing service to the community. These organizations begin service only after a business plan, budget, and board have been put in place and, often, the organization is duly incorporated. Although fund raising for these organizations sometimes begins with the low-cost net income activities outlined above, many organizations choose to focus immediately on seed money in the form of large grants from foundations, corporations, or governmental agencies.

(iii) Affiliate

Affiliate organizations are formed as—or become—local subsidiaries of large state or national organizations, which may themselves have begun as grass-roots organizations. Each chapter and affiliate is chartered and incorporated on its own and is usually responsible for its own operating budget. Affiliates often pay a portion of their revenues back to the national office, which provides technical support and assistance in the form of consulting, workshops, and seed funding for organization or program start-up expenses. Fund raising for such grass-roots affiliates is often left to the devices of local leadership and volunteers, and many opt for low- to moderate-level activities designed to gain members and adherents through low-dollar/low-risk gifts. Such activities include benefit concerts, charity luncheons or dinners, tag sales, raffles, and nonevent fund raisers, such as an annual letter appeal.

43.2   Overview of Different Approaches to Grass-roots Fund Raising

(A)   FUND RAISING FOR THE RESPONSE-DRIVEN ORGANIZATION

Grass-roots fund raising for a response-driven organization can be best described as low overhead, high-intensity outreach. It seeks maximum return through many small to moderate contributions.

The first months of a response-driven organization's life are quite telling, because they give all donors an opportunity to participate at many different levels—as contributors, leaders, and helpers. At this stage of the game, a grass-roots organization attracts more donations of $10 or $20 rather than $100 or $1,000. In most cases these small gifts will meet the organization's immediate needs, which in all likelihood are less expensive than longer-term needs. Easy participation by donors should be just the beginning of a long cultivation process. These donors can form the core of a longer-term, sustained annual fund effort. (See Chapter 21, "Overview of Annual Giving.")

Fund-raising activities for response-driven organizations are typically designed and undertaken by volunteers with little or no experience in fund raising and seldom with professional guidance. These activities include events with wide appeal to community citizens, such as pot-luck dinners, raffles, and holiday appeals through local newspapers and businesses. Such fund raisers are time-limited events, usually planned and executed solely by volunteers, and return a moderate net after expenses are deducted from dollars raised.

Unfortunately, such fund raising can be very time-consuming and can place demands on volunteers who are already trying to devote time to the activities and missions of the organization. Many groups address this problem by seeking grant money from local, state, or federal resources, focusing time and effort on writing a proposal to gain, in a single check, an equivalent to the net proceeds of a fund-raising event that might consume many hours of volunteer time and attention.

However, grants are highly competitive and can take a long time to acquire. Perhaps the most likely way for the response-driven organization to meet with success is to strike a balance between seeking grants and broad-appeal fund-raising activities.

(B) FUND RAISING FOR THE ACCELERATED START-UP

Accelerated start-up organizations often decide to focus completely or in part on securing large start-up grants from individual, foundation, government, or corporate resources, while at the same time providing for some community-level fund raising as a vehicle for local ownership and audience building. The Point CDC, a community development corporation located in the Hunts Point section of the South Bronx in New York City, decided to develop a mission and board and to incorporate prior to raising its first dollar. When it began to seek funding, the Point made a conscious decision to reach out to New York's foundation community for large seed grants while accepting in-kind gifts of building materials from area companies. Says Paul Lipson, associate director of programs, in an interview with the author, "We felt a strong responsibility to this community, which had seen so many great ideas fail because there wasn't the money there to fund them, to give them a win. And to do this, we needed to go to funders with a winning scenario that included them, but didn't solely depend on them. Our fund raising from Day One was designed to get the Point CDC up and running and build a great win-win for Hunts Point and for our donors."

Lipson and his colleagues, Mildred Ruiz, Steven Sapp, and Maria Torres, are all trained not-for-profit professionals who began as volunteers and have since moved into positions of paid staff. However, all are accountable to an independent board that they themselves created prior to hammering the first nail. "We think it is important to have trained professionals here to oversee the project," says Lipson, "because it builds accountability for the agency to the community. Anyone from the neighborhood has access to someone in a position of accountability and authority (one of us). Also, for the future of the Point CDC, we will have someone who can focus on continued grant writing and other fund-raising activities for the agency and the community."

(C) FUND RAISING FOR THE AFFILIATE

The affiliate grass-roots agency begins under the aegis of a parent or national office that provides or helps raise seed money. This funding is combined with local community-level fund-raising activities designed to build a constituency who will become the nucleus of a larger group of supporters. Over time, the affiliate with financial, consulting, and logistical support and training from the parent organization builds its own fund-raising program. Affiliates resemble both responsive organizations and accelerated start-ups in their dependence on larger seed grants and their conscious decision to have at least one professional staff person to oversee the day-to-day fund raising of the agency.

A highly successful grass-roots affiliate organization is Young Audiences. This organization was founded in 1952 by a group of prominent citizens who wanted to ensure that chamber music was available to schoolchildren in the Baltimore area. Friends of the original founders replicated the organization, with its blessing, in other cities. Today Young Audiences is the nation's leading source of art-in-education services. The organization has a central office in New York City, complete with a national board, a paid executive director, and a staff that works directly with 32 chapters nationwide.

B. J. Adler, education director of Young Audiences, points with pride to Young Audiences' chapters, saying in an interview with the author "Each provides us with a means to keep touch with how much importance communities—no matter how large or small—across America place on music and arts in the schools." Adler notes that the network of chapters raises more than $13 million annually from parents, educators, and concerned private citizens, as well as corporations, foundations, and government resources. "Our chapters have a combined strength of over 2,000 volunteers nationwide. Individually, each chapter may involve 50 to 200 volunteers and donors who are coordinated by a paid director. Together, with assistance and training from consultants from our national office, they work together to raise enough funds for their member dues and to underwrite workshops, residencies, and programs that reach thousands of kids. We want to place this kind of emphasis on volunteerism and community-level advocacy and fund raising to ensure that others will get involved and will help take ownership for our future."

All of these grass-roots not-for-profits find common ground in fund raising, in that their first priority is survival. This means that an organization first seeks to build a critical mass of donors who, through their collective support, are able to underwrite immediate needs and services. As a result, most grass-roots not-for-profits eschew "textbook" methods of fund development that call for planning and systematic growth of resources and instead focus on raising money as quickly as possible through any means available. Volunteer-led grassroots organizations often say that "there isn't enough time, resources, or knowledge about fund raising in our group to fund raise by the book. We can only do what we can with what we have."

Ironically, organizations that shy away from organized development activities because they perceive them as too much work often engage in low-income fund raising that is actually more time-consuming. They might consider this: Is an organization better off sending out volunteers to spend three hours selling 15 raffle tickets at $1 each, or asking them to spend the same amount of time soliciting three individuals in hopes of gaining one $25 contribution (for which no event expense will have to be deducted)?

Many grass-roots organizations fail in fund raising because they never take time to plan for what may lie *beyond* survival. This lack of foresight can get in the way of raising the sizable contributions necessary to sustain the organization, because donors of large gifts—foundations, corporations, governments, or individuals—are as interested in an organization's future as they are in its present.

43.3 Essential Elements for Long-term Fund Raising

Along with planning for what it must do beyond the survival stage, the savvy grass-roots organization will begin to accumulate some essential elements to begin and carry forth organized fund development. For many, the time and logistics of incorporation, building a board, and creating a mission statement and an operating budget seem too daunting to undertake. In some organizations, there is a fear that such things will change the character of the organization, moving it away from a position as a cause-related group dedicated solely to community good to a focus on self-perpetuation.

However, by putting into place essential elements for long-term fund raising, a grass-roots organization can:

- Attract sustained support
- Spend less effort on time-consuming, low-return fund-raising activities
- Develop greater cohesion and better focus
- Begin to plan for the long term, building for tomorrow on today's accomplishments

(A) INCORPORATION AS A 501(C)(3)

Incorporation under the Internal Revenue Code (IRC) § 501(c)(3) is critical for a not-for-profit organization and for its donors for the following reasons:

- The organization will become exempt from federal and state income taxes and may be exempt from state and local taxes, including property taxes if it has a facility.
- IRC § 501(c)(3) status allows foundation, corporate, and individual donors to declare contributions to the organization as tax deductible.
- Incorporation places the organization in the public trust. Responsibility is now formally vested in a volunteer board of directors who will collectively be bound to make critical decisions for the organization in the best interest of the community it serves.
- The organization itself will be legally liable, thus protecting board members.

To become incorporated, an organization must file an application for incorporation as a tax-exempt public charity with the state government and, once this has been approved, apply for similar status with the federal government. To ensure these two steps are done properly, seek the assistance of an experience, qualified lawyer who understands the process.[1]

If it is possible to pay for the lawyer's services, do so. Many organizations use pro bono services of legal counsel, but the process is complex and can be drawn out over time. Pro bono work is usually given lower priority than work from paying clients.

---

[1]See Bruce Hopkins, *A Legal Guide to Starting and Managing a Nonprofit Organization* (New York: John Wiley & Sons, 1993).

Agencies using pro bono legal help may wait for more than a year for confirmation of incorporation, whereas those who pay for such counsel are likely to receive a response within six to eight months after filing.

If the not-for-profit is approved, it will receive from both state and federal governments a letter declaring that the organization is exempt from taxes under § 501(c)(3). Most foundation and many corporate donors require a copy of this letter before issuing a grant check to the organization. Keep the original in a safe place and provide only copies.

A recourse for grass-roots organizations that are not yet incorporated under IRC § 501(c)(3) is to use another not-for-profit organization to receive grant income on its behalf from foundations and corporations. Many community foundations serve grass-roots organizations in this capacity, as do umbrella organizations for affiliates and established stand-alone agencies whose clients will benefit from a start-up's services.

Obviously, the benefit of using a receiving organization for grants is to enable the grass-roots agency to access grant income more immediately and, therefore, facilitate the process of building a foundation and corporate income stream and funding history. On the other hand, in receiving a grant on behalf of another organization, a recipient organization assumes responsibility to the funder to administer the grant and often retains a percentage of the grant income (10 percent is typical for most) to cover time and direct expenses related to record keeping and handling reports. As a result, the grass-roots organization does not receive 100 percent of the funds but incurs added accountability—both to the donor and to the recipient organization.

Using a recipient organization to receive grant income should be done only as a temporary measure. In fact, many foundations and corporations will not make a grant to an organization under these circumstances unless it has applied for tax-exempt status and will be able to show within a reasonable period of time (usually a maximum of one year after application for the grant) that this status has been granted. Therefore, the best route is for a grass-roots organization to incorporate as a IRC § 501(c)(3) as early in its lifetime as possible.

(B) WORKING BOARD OF DIRECTORS

A working board of directors is a critical element for long-term fund raising because the board:

- Creates and oversees the mission, vision, and values of the organization
- Provides oversight to the organization's senior professional staff, ensuring that the organization is well managed and that the public trust is well served
- Represents the community that holds the organization in trust and, as an impartial body, can objectively and effectively deal with critical issues that may arise

The *working* board of directors (note the emphasis on the term "working") consistently uses its powers of governance to ensure that fund raising occurs under those guidelines, values, and ethics it has chosen to adopt. The working board will provide ongoing oversight to all staff and volunteer fund-raising efforts. Its responsibility brings integrity, quality, and consistency to the agency's fund raising and, as a result, ensures that the organization keeps the public trust.

The board can set appropriate boundaries and guidelines for the organization in its fund raising. Not-for-profit organizations that are cash poor often accept large grants that may carry restrictions, forcing them to accept program responsibilities beyond their day-to-day activities. A mission statement, which is discussed in greater detail in the next subsection, can help the board to clarify whether such a gift would be acceptable. Additionally, corporate support for a grass-roots organization can create awkward situations because of the political and public perceptions that can accompany the acceptance of a contribution from a particular company. The organization's board can set policy on the acceptability of corporate contributions.

The governing board will also keep faith with donors by providing sufficient oversight of programs and day-to-day operations. Such a board will ensure that a donor's contribution is being well managed and well spent, giving the organization the necessary accountability that sometimes marks the difference between the established not-for-profit that will get the gift and the shakier agency that will not.

Members of the working board will lead, or at the very least be willing workers for, the fund raising. A working board can also be called upon to network with others, encouraging them to give, and to help raise money. The more an organization involves active members of a working board who provide oversight for the programs and mission of the agency, the more they become credible "evangelists" for the cause. The more these evangelists oversee fund raising and come in contact with volunteers, the more they take ownership in leading and completing fund-raising tasks. (See also Chapter 13, "The Board's Role in Fund Raising".)

(C) MISSION STATEMENT—COMMUNICATING VISION AND VALUES

Grass-roots organizations are created in response to an immediate problem and spring from the concerns of volunteers and donors alike. Although its purpose at the beginning may be very clear and well defined, as the organization looks ahead the picture may become less well defined. The voices of volunteers, staff, and donors alike must be melded into a single, cohesive statement of mission, vision, and values that is proprietary to the organization. The mission statement should, ideally, be created by the working board of directors.

A mission statement:

- Communicates an exciting vision of the solutions the organization will provide and the value of those solutions to community and society
- Underscores core values in regard to how program services and fund raising will be undertaken.

Exhibit 43.1 is a sample mission statement of a grass-roots organization.

A trap into which some grass-roots organizations fall when creating a mission statement is defining themselves in terms that are much too broad. For example, an organization whose mission is to feed homeless people daily at a soup kitchen may mistakenly define its mission in broader societal terms—"To combat hunger in our society." Although the volunteers may independently feel very passionate about the problem of world hunger, the agency does not have the resources to combat hunger on a global

---

EXHIBIT 43.1 Sample Mission Statement

The Point Community Development Corporation is an emergent neighborhood organization that is dedicated to the cultural and economic revitalization of the Hunts Point section of the Bronx. Conceived as an alternative approach to the twin problems of declining investment and unrealized community aspirations, The Point seeks to unearth the hidden strengths of an area traditionally defined solely in terms of its poverty, crime rate, poor schools, and sub-standard housing.

The Point CDC will help restore a sense of shared purpose and community pride by tapping the street-corner skills of teen entrepreneurs, the home-grown enterprise of aspiring business people, and the rich oral traditions of Latinos and African-Americans.

---

scale. (Imagine the acerbic wit of a potential donor: "It seems that the combined resources of the industrialized world have not been able to accomplish this goal—why do you think you can do it?"). Rather, the organization might better focus its efforts on identifying a tangible way to combat the problem of the growing number of hungry, homeless people in its community.

A mission statement provides consistency to the message being communicated to donors by staff and volunteers. It provides a clear description of the product in which donors are asked to invest. Put it in writing so that it can be left with a donor or mailed in advance of a solicitation.

(D) CASE STATEMENT FOR LONG-TERM SUPPORT

Whereas a mission statement reflects an organization's core values and "timeless" goals, a case statement focuses on a current or emerging need that must be met, establishes why the organization can best meet that need, and expresses how it plans to do so. The case reflects both an understanding of the climate in which the organization exists and an ability to create a realistic plan to address needs, using resources at hand or easily obtainable with the help of the donor.

Creating a case for ongoing support of a grass-roots organization is challenging. Grass-roots organizations, by their very nature, are built on the work and support of "ordinary people." The ideal of organizational permanence often raises the issue of whether to professionalize the not-for-profit's work through the addition of paid staff. Planning for such staffing or resources in future years shows the donor that the organization takes its own permanence very seriously. If the organization is not comfortable with such a change in structure, it must be prepared to articulate convincingly to a prospective donor how it plans to maintain and grow services solely through the use of volunteer labor.

An organization can craft a case statement by addressing the following questions.

- What is the purpose of the organization?
- When was the organization founded?
- What is the structure of the organization? Is it composed of volunteers only, or does it have professional staff?
- What are the key needs that must be met in the community served by the organization?

- What does the organization plan to do to meet these needs?
- How will it accomplish these tasks? Who will carry them out?
- Why is this organization best qualified to undertake these services?
- How do you define success for the program? What criteria will you use to evaluate success?
- How will success enable the organization to continue or to grow?
- What is the funding need for the program? How will the organization meet ongoing funding needs once these dollars have been raised?
- What is expected of donors? How can the donors give?

Beyond this, a case statement for ongoing support for grass-roots organizations must:

- Successfully communicate a compelling reason for the organization's continuance, based on real, documented needs
- State the organization's ability to address the need for services
- Document results to date and the tangible benefits it has delivered to the community (e.g., "Last year, we served more than 3,000 meals to indigent families and individuals in our community and referred 176 visitors to local not-for-profits providing social services, benefits counseling, drug and alcohol rehabilitation, and mental health counseling. Within a six-block radius of our center, the number of incidents of violence and drug-related crimes declined 23 percent during the last quarter of last year.")
- Communicate to the donor an exciting vision of the expected growth of the organization over the next few years.

(E) OPERATING BUDGET

An operating budget is a statement that shows both current and projected future expenses. The budget may reflect a period of months or even years, although it becomes more difficult to accurately project expenses and income beyond a year or two.

The focus of an operating budget should be the essential services or program of the organization. Carefully assess the immediate needs of the community and consider the tangible services the organization will be able to offer. Projected services should be based on the organization's capacity—through staff or volunteers—to support those services and its ability to raise enough money to pay for the additional expense of providing those services.

Budgets can be based on historical data that establishes prior patterns of spending and income. Building on these numbers, an organization can begin to construct a reasonable expectation of future expenses and income. (See Exhibit 43.2.)

Why create a budget? Workers may have a vision of your organization being around for the next two years feeding the homeless or ministering to the elderly. The mission statement may communicate this vision of relative permanence. But what is it going to cost? Who is going to do the work? Not only does it make good business sense for workers to ask these questions of themselves, but they can be guaranteed that donors—especially those who may want to make large gifts—will want to know the answers.

A budget is a way of speaking about the future of an organization in financial terms, much as a mission statement or case statement describes vision using relevant language.

EXHIBIT 43.2 Sample Three-Year Budget for a Small Grass-roots Advocacy Organization

	Year 1	Year 2	Year 3	Notes
Expenses				
Staff				
Administrative Director	$15,000	$20,000	$21,000	Year 1: Part Time; Years 2 and 3, Full Time
Secretary	$5,000	$7,500	$16,000	$10 per hour in Years 1 and 2; becomes full time (salaried) in Year 3
Benefits	$0	$0	$7,400	20% per year for full-time employees includes medical, dental insurance
Consultants	$0	$0	$5,000	Consultants to assist with agency assessment
Student Interns	$1,125	$1,125	$1,275	Work-study students (college) to assist with clerical and administrative duties and to assist volunteers; $7.50 per hour years 1 and 2; $8.50 per hour Year 2
Subtotal: Personnel	**$21,125**	**$28,625**	**$50,675**	
Other Than Personnel				
Rent	$0	$12,000	$12,000	
Utilities	$0	$6,000	$6,000	
Copier	$0	$3,600	$1,500	Lease at $300 per month
Computers	$0	$3,600	$1,000	month
Printers	$0	$3,600	$500	month
Telephone	$750	$1,300	$750	Year 1: reimbursement for phone expense for off-site use; Year 2 purchase and installation of phone system; Year 3 phone expense
Postage	$1,000	$1,500	$1,700	
Workshop and Prof. Fees	$0	$0	$1,000	
Direct Costs: Raffle	$1,000	$1,500	$1,500	Includes printing; assumes prize is donated
Direct Costs: Breakfast	$1,200	$1,200	$1,200	Includes food, printing, and other expenses
Direct Costs: Spring Sale	$1,000	$3,200	$3,500	Includes printing, other expenses
Direct Costs: Year-End Appeal	$500	$750	$1,000	Includes printing, postage
Travel: Staff	$0	$0	$750	
Travel: Interns	$0	$0	$750	Beginning in Year 2, offer stipends
Educational Sessions	$0	$1,500	$4,500	Year 1: will hold if can find underwriting in full; Year 2: budget 1 @ $1,500; Year 3 budget 3 @ $1,500 per session

EXHIBIT 43.2 (Continued)

	Year 1	Year 2	Year 3	Notes
Subtotal: OTPS	$5,450	$39,750	$37,650	
Total Expense	$26,575	$68,375	$88,325	
Income				
Breakfast	$3,000	$5,000	$7,500	
Raffle	$7,500	$10,000	$10,000	
Spring Sale	$6,000	$7,500	$10,000	$5,000 in sale income; $1,000 in vendor fees
Year-End Appeal	$5,000	$7,500	$10,000	
Other Contributions	$6,000	$7,500	$10,000	Includes gifts from board members
Foundations/Corporations	$0	$20,000	$25,000	
Government Grants	$0	$10,000	$25,000	
	$27,500	$67,500	$90,000	
Income (Net of Expense)	$925	($875)	$1,675	

Consider the example of the organization whose mission is to feed homeless people daily at a soup kitchen. Assuming that the organization does decide to expand its services to feed a growing number of hungry, homeless people, its budget should account for an increase in the number of meals served from 100 per day today to perhaps 300 per day two years from now.

A budget can also provide a tangible example to a prospective donor of how his or her grant may be used. Moreover, it can provide a prospective donor with an option when asked for pledged income by showing a short-term vision with costs to implement programs to fulfill that vision. An operating budget can make the critical difference between getting a $1,000 contribution to help out this year and convincing a donor to make a $10,000 investment to help the organization assemble staff and resources that will develop into sustained operations.

Therefore, the budget is an essential tool for an organization moving into a long-term fund development program. It can show how much the organization's income will have to be increased during the next two years, which will dictate, in turn, the types of fund raising needed to fulfill this vision.

43.4 Building a Constituency to Create a Base for Ongoing Support

Grass-roots organizations spend a great deal of energy in reaching out to build a broad base of supporters. Because these organizations are people driven, each depends on the support of a constituency made up of volunteers and donors who believe its cause or who may be personally interested in or affected by the issues it addresses.

Constituency building creates a core of supporters from which an organization can draw leadership, volunteers, and contributors. The goal of constituency building is to develop a broad base of supporters that will form a core of ongoing funding, leading to a program of long-term support.

Building a constituency takes time, energy, and a targeted, focused effort. An excellent analogy to constituency building is the "pebble in the pond" image, where a connection flows from insiders—those closest to the organization—to outsiders, who can be accessed through insiders or by cold outreach through mailings, events, or phone calls. (See Exhibit 43.3.)

Clearly, most organizations have a group of insiders—founders, board members, and volunteers who perform services. Some organizations also have members who sup-

---

EXHIBIT 43.3 The "Pebble in the Pond" Model of Constituency Building

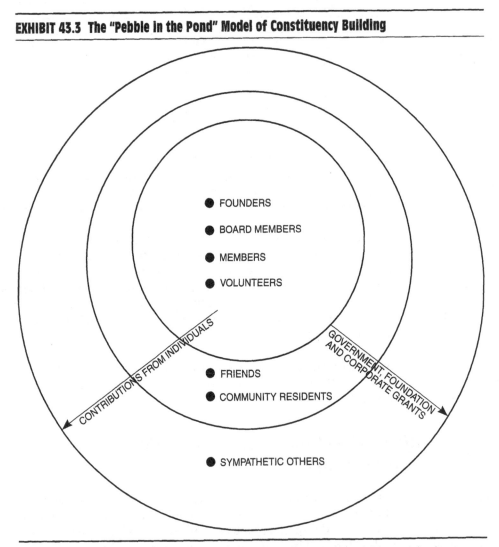

It is assumed that individual contributors will populate all three tiers of this model, whereas foundations, corporations, and government grants will come after the "insiders" have given and shown support. This model helps an organization to plan for growth once it has established a firm core of supporters.

port their missions and activities through contributions and service. All of these constituencies are made up of individuals who, at some level, are directly touched by the mission and service of the organization. How a grass-roots organization builds these "layers" of constituents depends on its resources and the methods it chooses to employ.

(A) METHODS FOR BUILDING A CONSTITUENCY

(i) Government Grant Seeking

The first grant a grass-roots organization receives is often one from a federal, state, or local government agency, such as a state or local Department of Youth Services or the federal Environmental Protection Agency. These resources periodically make grant monies available to groups that are addressing specific issues or working with particular constituencies that are of interest and importance to the government.

Opportunities for such grants are periodically announced by the offering agency, often through a request for proposal (RFP) mailed to select not-for-profits or announced in trade publications and, sometimes, in the press. An RFP provides information about the grant, such as the minimum and maximum amounts of requests that will be considered, the deadline for submission of a proposal, and how the proposal should be structured. Recently many grant opportunities have been listed on the Internet and can be found through an Internet search engine such as Yahoo! or Alta Vista. (Try searching on "grants.")

(ii) Foundation and Corporate Grant Seeking

Another area useful in funding and constituency building includes foundation and corporate grants. These grants differ from their government counterparts in that they are seldom announced in advance and can be much more competitive. Unless a grass-roots organization has secured its IRC § 501(c)(3) status or has identified an umbrella organization to accept and administer the grant, this funding is often the last to be attracted by the start-up agency. (See Section 43.6 of this chapter, "Grant Seeking for Grass-roots Organizations."[2])

(iii) Membership Clubs

Most grass-roots organizations at some time develop membership clubs. When a person becomes a member of an organization, it implies that he or she personally shares in its mission. Therefore, conferring membership on a donor draws that person into the organization's broader "family" and can create the beginning of a relationship that, if cultivated, may result in continued and increased financial support. However, because such donors can be considered "family," they demand communication (a newsletter, journal, or other media) and other benefits that reaffirm the relationship and allow them to boast of it to others (perhaps via the ubiquitous T-shirt and coffee mug).

(iv) Direct Mail and Telephone Solicitations

Direct mail and telephone solicitations are low-level, low-risk fund-raising activities and at best result in moderate net financial gains. They involve contacting individuals who

---

[2]See also Jane C. Geever and Patricia A. McNeill, *The Foundation Center Guide to Proposal Writing* (New York: The Foundation Center, 1993).

are potential contributors by telephone, through a letter and brochure sent by mail, or via e-mail messages. (You actually can search the directories of large Internet access carriers, such as America Online or CompuServe, and pull a list of prospective donors to the cause by searching on certain keywords.) Cold calling and direct mail can benefit a grass-roots organization by publicizing its name, but neither method lends itself to personal communication or interaction with a prospective contributor.

Mail and phone solicitations can be performed entirely by volunteers or be handled by a professional firm. A key difference is cost and logistical support, which are both greater when a professional firm is engaged. Of course, if an organization elects to use professionals, the utmost care should be exercised in choosing them. (See also Chapter 46, "Fund-raising Consultants.")

(v) Events

Someone once said that events "put F-U-N in fund raising." There is some truth to this, because events invite participation by promising something personal and tangible in return: a dinner at an elegant restaurant, cocktails in a stately home, a pancake breakfast on a Saturday morning for the family, a chance to drive a Mercedes that one could not otherwise afford. Used as part of an organized fund-raising plan, events provide wonderful opportunities for an organization to bond with the community, to thank contributors, volunteers, and members (the family), and to attract others to join its cause. However, events are time-consuming for staff and volunteers, and, as a result, many organizations use events for fund raising to the exclusion of other activities. Several popular types of events are outlined in Exhibit 43.4.

(B) ACQUIRING CONSTITUENTS THROUGH INSIDERS

To acquire constituents through insiders, seek first to obtain the names of potential supporters among current, active volunteers and donors. Volunteers, individually or in groups, may want to host "cultivation" events at a public place or in their homes and invite relatives, close friends, and associates to hear about the organization, its mission, and its work. Another method used by grass-roots agencies is the letter-writing campaigns whereby volunteers write to their contacts and forward information about the organization. Of the two types of activities, the cultivation event is certainly the more effective, because the face-to-face interaction between volunteers and prospective constituents provides an opportunity for all to learn. (see also Chapter 28, "Volunteer-led Solicitations.")

(C) ACQUIRING CONSTITUENTS THROUGH OUTSIDE SOURCES

Many grass-roots organizations choose to acquire prospect lists from outside resources. It may be possible to segment these lists by ZIP codes, and there may be an option of purchasing a select subset of names at a prorated price per name. Possible resources include the following:

- *Mailing lists*, which can be purchased directly from magazines or mail-order suppliers catering to a specific economic class or to people who have an interest in a

EXHIBIT 43.4 Comparisons of Fund-raising Events

Type of Event	Success Rate	Comments
Sales and Raffles	Moderate to high	• Low risk for volunteers, because they offer tangible goods to participants (for instance, a great deal on an antique lamp or a chance to go on a free vacation to Bermuda). • Depends on high number of participants for success. • Only as successful as volunteers make them through ticket sales or by personally inviting attendees. • Depends somewhat on public relations for success. • Activities are not conducive to donor education about the agency's cause; purchase of a raffle ticket does not obligate the purchaser to take information about organization. Sales see constant turnover in attendees; there is no good opportunity to educate attendees via a presentation.
Private Entertainment Events (parties and receptions)	High	• Invitation list can be select (i.e., one can invite only people who can write a fairly large check). • Event can be made exclusive; attendance can be seen as a privilege. • Success depends on host(s) follow-through on invitations to get invitees to attend. • Provide a high level of interaction between prospective contributors and volunteers of the organization. • Activity is conducive to donor education about the agency's cause (see preceding remark). • Cost to organization can be kept to a minimum (particularly if the host offers to pay for the event).
Public Entertainment Events (dinners, receptions, dances)	Low to moderate	• Involve outlay of funds by the organization (entertainment, food, drinks, printed programs). • Depends on large number of attendees to generate high net return. • Large number of attendees precludes high level of interaction between prospective contributors and volunteers. • Open to the general public; cannot place emphasis on only a select group of attendees. • Better than raffles or sales, because such events can be programmed to include a set presentation about the organization and its mission and to ask for continued support beyond event ticket purchase.

particular issue such as that addressed by the organization. Unfortunately, these lists are often quite expensive and too inclusive. The result could very well be that the organization has paid for many names that are unusable because they fall outside its community. Furthermore, mailing lists do not constitute effective prospect research, because there is no way of knowing whether the individuals whose names appear would be interested in the organization. To refine this data requires either repeated mailings or telephone calls—both expensive and time-consuming activities.

- *Membership lists* of other not-for-profits whose missions mirror that of the organization, or of local clubs that cater to wealthy individuals or leaders in the business community. Usually such lists are privately held and are obtainable only through a volunteer connection. These lists are better than mailing lists because, in most cases, they are free and because membership in a similar organization implies potential interest.

- *Public domain resources,* which list wealthy individuals, local corporations, and foundations, are usually obtainable at a public or college library and are indexed alphabetically, geographically, or by industry connection. Some key publications include Marquis's *Who's Who, Standard & Poor's* (which comes with a supplemental index of executives and directors), the *Social Register,* the *Directory of Corporate Affiliations* (which comes with supplemental indices based on geographic interests, executives, and directors), *Wealth Holders in America,* and the *Foundation Directory.* Many of these resources are now available on searchable CD-ROM, which can cut down enormously on the investment of volunteer or staff time in doing research. A downside to keeping up with these resources is that they can be expensive unless you are able to access them at a collegiate or public library.

A common pitfall encountered by organizations in building a constituency is to place too much emphasis on outside resources in hope of finding a single, wealthy individual who will send a check that takes care of all of their needs. First of all, this type of philanthropy rarely happens. Second, ignoring those closest to the organization amounts to missing a wonderful opportunity to embrace those who are most ready and willing to support it.

43.5   Assessing the Organization's Potential for Longer-term Support

Most grass-roots organizations are able to raise start-up funding solely by articulating a time-sensitive need, such as saving a landmark or providing disaster relief to residents of a neighboring town. Some organizations make a conscious decision to expand or to continue their work. In such cases, the organization must look for ongoing support to sustain itself and its mission.

In thinking about building longer-term support for the grass-roots organization, one must objectively assess how much money can be raised from its current donors. Can the organization attract new donors, and does it have the resources—volunteer, staff, and logistical—to conduct the kinds of fund raising that will bring success? This requires strategic thinking about volunteers—their networks and ability to raise funds—donors, the staff, and any further capacities to provide logistical support.

(A)   EVALUATING THE CURRENT BASE OF DONORS

The evaluation of the organization's current base of donors should be both quantitative and qualitative. To conduct such an evaluation to gain maximum results, the grass-roots organization must try to obtain as much information about each donor as possible.

Unfortunately, without staff to maintain detailed records, most organizations know little more than the names of their donors and how much they gave. If a donor bought a ticket to an event or raffle, an address and phone number may be available.

A possible solution to the lack of staffing for record-keeping purposes is to ask a volunteer who is computer literate to keep this information on a personal computer. Simple data is easy to maintain through a standard database program such as Microsoft Access or Claris FileMaker Pro. This basic information (see Exhibit 43.5 for a list of basic donor data) can enable evaluation of the following:

- *The organization's donors as a group.* The organization will be able to group donors by ZIP code or address to determine where most of its donors live. Contribution information will show the high, low, and average contribution (if more than one gift has been made) for each donor, and for all donors. It will be easy to ascertain how many donors are personally known to any given volunteer connected with the organization.
- *The potential of each donor.* The art of increasing a donor's support is based on the ability to match the contributor to the right type of fund-raising activity. Basic data can create a profile for each donor that will enable the fund raiser to think

---

EXHIBIT 43.5   Basic Donor Data

The following are the types of information a grass-roots organization may want to keep about its donors:
- Name.
- Code (e.g., Foundation, Corporation, Friend, Member, Volunteer).
- Address.
- ZIP code.
- Phone numbers (work and home).
- E-mail address (The Internet provides an inexpensive, enjoyable, and easy way to maintain contact with donors. Ask the donor to provide this information voluntarily; otherwise, you may be able to locate it via the Internet Directory, which can be accessed through any on-line service using a standard search engine such as Yahoo! or Alta Vista.)
- Volunteer contact (Who, among the organization's volunteers, personally knows the individual? By coding each donor with a name of primary contact, a fund raiser can develop a list of names of donors each volunteer has secured and generate, as needed, a "worklist" for future involvement in solicitations.)
- Date of membership.
- A record of each gift made to the organization: date of gift, amount, activity used to solicit the contribution.
- Next activity: future solicitations to send to the prospect. If coded with a date for the activity, this item can be searched to generate monthly "tickler" lists.
- *Note:* I keep a general note field with information related to the donor including, but not limited to, data about his or her involvement with the organization. This information is invaluable in developing strategy for future asks.

---

strategically about how to (1) ensure the donor's ongoing support and (2) increase that support over time. Based on the information in the database, the fund raiser can probably ascertain much of the following about a given donor: who the donor is, his or her response to various events and solicitations, how the organization attracted his or her support, and the name of the donor's volunteer contact. With the help of the volunteer contact, the organization can use this information to discuss the future potential of this donor and how best to approach the donor to ask for that support.

- *The effectiveness of events and solicitations.* A well-maintained database of donor information can also enable the organization to evaluate the effectiveness of its fund raising: which events are being well attended, which solicitations are receiving most—and fewest—responses. Compare this information with the cost of these activities to see where the return on investment is greatest. (See also Chapter 6, "Fund-raising Assessment.")

(B) EVALUATING RESOURCES

To successfully undertake sustained fund raising, grass-roots organizations must turn to volunteers who will engage their contacts to ask for their ongoing support. These volunteers will require logistical support, which can be provided by other volunteers, or paid part- or full-time staff, or can be outsourced to professionals—either paid or pro bono.

Today's grass-roots organizations can take advantage of new technologies, especially the home computer, to develop quality print materials, maintain a database of donors and potential donors, and conduct prospect research. The rule of thumb is to buy the fastest, biggest computer affordable. As of this writing, this would involve a central processing unit with Pentium III processor (or, for Macintosh aficionados, a Power PC) with the highest megahertz rating available in the organization's price range, at least 20 GB of memory (to store and run the increasingly large desktop publishing, word processing, and database programs), a 24x CD ROM drive, a 17-inch monitor (easier on the eyes and absolutely essential if the organization is going to produce its own print materials), a laser printer (Hewlett Packard makes the most reliable, followed closely by Lexmark), and at least a 56.6K BPS modem with a subscription to an on-line service for e-mail and Internet access.

How can an organization use all of the resources at its disposal to develop ongoing and increasing support? Are these resources appropriate or will they have to be upgraded or new ones obtained?

(i) Volunteers

Obtaining the continuing support of a donor depends on educating that donor, increasing his or her enthusiasm about the organization's cause, and, when the time is right, helping the donor to make the best gift possible. This process relies on personal interaction through a volunteer who is an advocate and a donor as well.

Volunteers who have been involved in fund raising at the level of selling raffle tickets or, perhaps, making a few door-to-door solicitation calls may be asked to contact donors known to them to ask for more substantial commitments. Although most are willing to undertake this type of activity, some may shy away because of fear of rejection or of being asked themselves for a gift that they may not want, or cannot afford, to give. (See Chapter 28, "Volunteer-led Solicitations.")

Grass-roots organizations that move into the arena of sustained campaigns must evaluate the willingness of their volunteers to become more deeply involved in the fund-raising process. Moreover, in seeking to attract larger contributions from wealthy individuals, foundations, and corporations, the organization must evaluate their volunteers. Do they have linkages to these circles of donors? If not, can the organization attract volunteers at this level through its current network?

(ii)   Logistical Resources

Many grass-roots organizations do not have an office or paid support staff who can maintain records or create letters, brochures, and grant proposals. Years ago, this lack of logistical support kept many fledgling organizations out of the mainstream of fund raising. Today the home computer makes it affordable and easy for any organization to produce brochures and personalized direct mail pieces and, through the Internet, to conduct prospect research and network with other volunteers and organizations that are doing similar work. With the advent of the "virtual office" it is no longer considered a stigma to provide support off-site, as more and more donors from the private sector work from their homes or from the road. (See Chapter 48, "Technology Applications.")

Key questions for grass-roots organizations that have few or no paid staff include the following: Do you have volunteers with computer and secretarial skills that can be used creatively and strategically? Will these volunteers have time to be responsive to immediate demands from donors or potential donors for information? Do these volunteers have—or can they build—professional-level fund-raising skills, including keeping files and a database, prospect research, and proposal writing?

(iii)   Print Materials

Does the organization have up-to-date materials that describe its mission, values, services, history, and need for ongoing support? How good are these materials? If there is difficulty in answering the second question, consider having a volunteer with skills in publishing, publicity, or marketing to review the promotional materials. The organization may want to seek the services of an experienced professional fund raiser or fund-raising counsel to review its documents and suggest how they might be strengthened.

(iv)   Staff and Outside Professional Resources

Response-driven grass-roots organizations typically do not have paid staff, especially during the start-up phase. As mentioned earlier, they depend on the efforts of ordinary people who volunteer their time, energies, and dollars and raise money primarily through community-level activities. Accelerated start-up agencies or affiliates may have one or more part-time or full-time professionals who oversee day-to-day operations and coordinate the activities of volunteers. Although these individuals may be experienced in managerial or not-for-profit issues, they may not have direct experience in managing a sustained fund-raising program. In either case, an organization may choose to seek professional assistance with marketing, public relations, and fund raising. Chosen wisely, professionals can provide the organization with guidance, education, structure, and products, which will pay off through an increased number and size of contributions. (See Chapter 46, "Fund-raising Consultants.")

The organization can either seek pro bono help or choose to retain the services of a professional or a firm. Both have strengths and pitfalls. Pro bono assistance is inexpensive, but such help may not be consistent, as volunteers must give first priority to company matters or paying clients. Paid professionals can guarantee attention and sign off on deliverables, but the organization must pay for quality. Before entering into a relationship with a professional, paid or pro bono, speak with those given as references and evaluate the expected return on investment. Is it reasonable to expect a beautifully designed full-color brochure to result in an increase of $5,000, to pay for itself, and $5,000 beyond that to cover increased expenses for the organization?

43.6   *Grant Seeking for Grass-roots Organizations*

Much of the literature about grass-roots fund raising published to date does not include, or go into great detail about, grant seeking. This is not surprising, because the grant-seeking process is time- and resource-consuming and does not always yield the immediate funding that most grass-roots organizations need in order to survive. (See Chapter 33, "The Grant-seeking Process.") In addition, consider these possible reasons:

- *Grass-roots organizations and grants are antithetical to each other.* The traditional definition of a grass-roots organization is a not-for-profit built around ordinary people, tackling problems on their own without professional support. Grants, however, imply that the recipient agency has professional resources in place to manage the expenditure of the contribution such that it fulfills the intent of the donor.
- *Grass-roots organizations typically do not have programs or services in place that would be of interest (or comfort) to a grantmaker.* This reason is fairly valid, particularly in the case of a start-up agency with no staff, history of success, or long-range vision. Such organizations typically are not ready to proceed with incorporation and must often depend on the financial and in-kind support of volunteers. Accelerated start-ups and affiliates, however, usually have completed incorporation and developed a budget, which gives a grantmaker the ability and, often, the incentive to provide seed funding.
- *Grass-roots organizations typically do not have access to the expertise necessary to develop a winning grant proposal.* The grant-writing and grant-seeking process is quite daunting, and most start-up grass-roots organizations shy away from it unless they have pulled together a cohesive vision that can be well articulated and identified staff or volunteers who have the time and ability to research prospective donors and spend time crafting a grant proposal.

Yet there have been recent developments that make it easier for grass-roots organizations to enter the arena of grants:

- *An increase in the number of foundations.* Over the past 10 years, a significant number of small, private family foundations were quietly created. These foundations are based on wealth created through the investment boom and were founded primarily as tax shelters for income or appreciated assets. Although this development might suggest increased availability of resources for grass-roots organizations, the best approach to such resources continues to be through personal contacts by volunteers allied with the organization.

- *An increase in entrepreneurial philanthropy.* In recent years, several foundations and corporations have created entrepreneurial grants for emerging not-for-profits that are addressing new and emerging needs. These grants usually focus on technical assistance to lead the organization toward establishing an ongoing program and sustained fund-raising activities. In the corporate giving arena, greater emphasis is being placed on providing products, technical assistance by executives, and gifts-in-kind (products and supplies—a real boon to grass-roots agencies that provide food, medicine, or other real goods to their clients) instead of cash. Corporations are also moving toward involving not-for-profits in *philanthropic marketing activities* that provide increased visibility to both the agency and the corporate donor. (See Chapter 3, "Marketing Strategies in Development.") This type of activity often raises debates within an organization concerning the prosperity of accepting such support.
- *The increasing numbers of home computers.* The personal computer allows the creation of professional documents through standard word processing programs. There is an emerging market of software and shareware (unfortunately not all of it good) created by experienced professionals to assist with creating proposals and other documents required by funders. The Internet is evolving as a marketplace for ideas; foundation, corporate, and government grant resources; and education by supportive professional and volunteer groups. *A caveat:* The quality of the Internet as a resource and marketplace is dependent on the quality of user input.
- *The increased availability of education in the grant-seeking process.* There is an increasing commitment by grantmakers and professional not-for-profit associations, such as the Association of Fundraising Professionals and the Foundation Center, to teach prospective grantees about the grant-seeking process. In addition, a number of colleges and universities are providing courses of study related to not-for-profit management and fund-raising methods, either as degree tracks or through continuing education programs. These resources are showing a growing commitment to grass-roots organizations in their educational programming.

43.7 Special Challenges in Fund Raising for Grass-roots Organizations

It is important to recognize that there are some elements in fund raising that present special challenges for the grass-roots organization: vision; the clash between fund raising and organizational culture; competition; visibility; leadership, governance, and the heightened expectations of donors; and resources. A few of these elements have been touched upon earlier in this chapter; each is examined more closely in the following subsections.

(A) VISION

In not-for-profit fund raising, *vision* can be defined to include the following: the need to be met; what will be done to meet the need; how long it is likely to take; how much it will cost; and what impact the solution will have on the immediate community and on society. Vision is one of the most powerful tools used in fund raising. As part of the mission statement, it helps staff and volunteers to be consistent among themselves in articulating to a donor how his or her contribution can make a difference and the role the donor can play in helping to achieve a set of defined needs and objectives.

Establishing or defining vision in a grass-roots organization is a challenging but important task. Because many grass-roots agencies spring up overnight in response to an immediate need that cannot (or will not) be met through conventional means, they are seen by their creators and outsiders alike as transitory. The problem or need, such as saving a local park or raising enough funds to pay for special medical treatment required for a neighbor in need, may be very time- or task-defined so as to warrant no vision of life expectancy for the organization after the goal is reached.

However, many organizations that began by meeting a very immediate and closely limited need have continued their work and expanded their reach as the need grew and never went away. In other words, these organizations have allowed their vision to evolve. The Gay Men's Health Crisis (GMHC), for example, began as a grass-roots response to a new and deadly disease, AIDS, that was being contracted by an increasing number of individuals in New York City's homosexual community. Ten years later GMHC had grown to become one of the leading advocacy and direct service agencies addressing the AIDS crisis in the United States.

(B) CLASH BETWEEN FUND RAISING AND ORGANIZATIONAL CULTURE

Not infrequently, conflicts arise between fund-raising strategies and an organization's culture. The notion of strategic planning or using professionals is sometimes seen by volunteers as being at odds with their image of a true grass-roots operation.

For example, an organization may decide not to spend time on marketing, because it fears that its image will be perceived as too "slick," or that it will lose focus on the essential work to be done in its community. In making this decision, however, the organization may be neglecting a critical activity related to developing and expanding its base of contributions. Therefore, the organization's culture impacts on its fund raising. Conversely, another not-for-profit may decide to devote a good amount of time to developing a marketing plan because of the potential for generating income. Some volunteers may consider this increased focus on fund raising to have a negative impact on the organization's focus on service.

Another example is that of the organization that moves to solicit a major gift from an individual, foundation, or corporate donor. This calls into account several issues:

- *The intent of the donor.* What restrictions will be placed on the contribution, and how can they be integrated with the intent and focus of the organization accepting the gift?
- *The intent of the organization accepting the gift.* What assurances will the organization provide the donor about how the funding will be used, and what tangible benefit or information will be derived from activities resulting from the gift?

There is an element of risk here both for the organization and the donor. Although the donor may intend his or her dollars to be used in a manner that is within the context of the agency's organization and mission, the donor him- or herself, or the manner in which the gift is made, may be at odds with the organization's mission and values. If, by accepting the gift and committing to fulfilling the intent of the donor, the organization has in any way compromised its values or ethics, then a host of issues are raised for the organization concerning both its culture and its donors.

This is a very difficult or delicate balance that any not-for-profit must address when planning, organizing, and implementing a fund-raising campaign. As grass-roots organizations move from fund-raising activities to longer-term fund development activities (such as seeking grants from foundation, corporate, and government resources), they must be careful to have developed a set of values and guidelines for soliciting and accepting contributions.

(C) COMPETITION

North Carolina, which ranks tenth in population among the states, is home to more than 14,000 not-for-profits. According to a recent study commissioned by a prominent group of New York City foundations and corporations, there are well over 19,500 not-for-profit organizations within the five boroughs of New York City alone. If an organization has identified a problem or a need, rest assured that there are dozens or even hundreds of other groups, many of them well-established, that are working to meet those or similar problems.

The challenge raised by competition is how an organization will differentiate itself from others who are doing similar work. A person may see a need to organize an environmental advocacy group in a city that has three other such groups. Fair enough, but does the person know that the group will fill a need that is currently not being met by the other groups or that its needs cannot be met through another such group? In addition, are there opportunities for collaboration with other such groups on a particular project, or at least some chance to coordinate the organization's direct services with others? This offers a wonderful opportunity to position an organization as one that is committed to partnering with others rather than standing alone and competing.

Viewed in a healthy, objective way, competition forces not-for-profits to *define* themselves either as a viable partner to other organizations doing similar work or as a viable alternative to such organizations. Organizations facing competition can define themselves according to a number of factors, which include the following:

Originality—in relation to what need is being addressed and how
Geography—in relation to what immediate community is being served
Service population—in relation to whom is being served.

(D) VISIBILITY

Surrounded by so many other not-for-profit groups, it is often very difficult for a grass-roots organization to get its story to the public or to potential donors. Often the "public" is very difficult to determine for an organization: Is it only the immediate neighborhood, or might the organization have citywide, countywide, or statewide appeal? These questions should be answered before developing a strategy to gain visibility.

Gaining visibility requires a good deal of logistical support. Most grass-roots organizations, unlike professionally staffed, established not-for-profits, must depend almost exclusively on volunteer time and resources. Sometimes the best volunteers to carry out these tasks are either too busy with daytime professions or, in the case of those organizations that are able to attract volunteers from media-related industries, unable to use their professional contacts on behalf of their own causes. This means that the ability to develop and sustain a public image through flyers, brochures, newspaper and magazine articles, television, and radio can be very limited.

Another challenge for grass-roots organizations is that once visibility has been achieved, will the organization be able to live up to expectations about what problems can or cannot be solved? To meet this challenge, two potential problems should be addressed by the grass-roots organization that has gained visibility:

1. *Lack of consistency in the message.* An organization may find itself in an embarrassing position created by volunteers who are communicating a message that is not in line with the vision, beliefs, and values of the mainstream of people involved with its cause. Work to ensure that all staff and volunteers have a clear understanding of the mission statement that has been developed by the board of directors.

2. *Not communicating results—good and bad.* Sharing successes is fun—sharing failures is not. However, because they depend on the immediate goodwill and involvement of the general public, grass-roots organizations have a heightened need to do both. Successes can show that they are winning battles and that it is worthwhile for the community and donors to continue their support. Reporting on failures or shortfalls demonstrates that the organization holds itself accountable to the public; such reports should include the lessons learned and how the organization plans to apply them to future projects and services.

(E)   LEADERSHIP, GOVERNANCE, AND THE HEIGHTENED EXPECTATIONS OF DONORS

In the aftermath of recent scandals involving very well known public organizations, donors have understandably become more skeptical about where their dollars go and how they are used. This is probably as true of the $10 donor as of the $10,000 donor. As a result, not-for-profits are facing an increasingly skeptical public that demands accountability for every contribution dollar.

In this environment, grass-roots organizations with limited or no track records are asked to provide the donor with detailed information. They must expect that everyone who is asked to contribute will want to know more about them—who they are, their mission, values, program, and method of service delivery.

Therefore, it is critical for a grass-roots organization to have a central working board, consisting of volunteers who will take responsibility for crafting its message and seeing that volunteers share it with consistency, and that the organization lives up to the values, mission, and programs it professes.

A common pitfall faced by grass-roots organizations that are created by or around a single dynamic leader is the "founder-director syndrome." This develops when a single founder for an agency either continues to sit on its board and dominate proceedings and decision making, or assumes the position of executive director and creates a board that will rubber-stamp his or her decisions. Although this individual may be involved in developing programs that will benefit the community and fund raising that will benefit the organization, and doing both as ethically and honestly as possible, this may create the impression that the organization does not stand independently on its own. As a result, founder-directors sometimes stand firmly in the path to healthy fund development for the organization by negating the involvement and input of two key constituencies: volunteers and donors.

(F) RESOURCES

Fund raising is a time- and labor-intensive process (one might adapt Thomas Edison's adage thus: "Fund raising is 90 percent perspiration and 10 percent inspiration") that requires organization and logistical support. Volunteer-led and supported grass-roots organizations face increased challenges in dealing with issues related to fund raising because they do not rely on experienced staff to provide guidance or to produce work. For such organizations, the logistics of mounting a sustained fund-raising outreach are daunting. The challenge is how to design fund raising to make the wisest and most appropriate use of human resources.

43.8   *What Lies Ahead for Grass-roots Organizations: 2000 and Beyond*

Grass-roots organizations will most likely continue to be created by concerned, ordinary citizens taking on problems that no other entity seems to be able or willing to handle. The dynamics of a fast-changing world will, of course, have an impact on how these organizations are formed, how they raise funds, and, most important, whether they survive.

As we enter the twenty-first century, the arena of grass-roots organizations will likely change. The following are two possible scenarios with implications for grass-roots organizations:

1. *An increase in the number of not-for-profits.* The Great Society programs of the 1960s provided two levels of public service organizations. On one level there developed key government-administered large-scale entitlement programs, such as Medicare, which provided relief to millions. However, millions of dollars in federal grants were also made available to another level of public service organizations: private citizens groups that created grass-roots community-based organizations in impoverished rural and urban areas. By the 1970s, these programs became a part of the largest creation of not-for-profit in our nation's history.

Today there is a growing debate over the future of federally funded and operated government programs. A federal budget deficit that skyrocketed during the past two decades has already resulted in a sustained trend of cuts in funding for several grant programs that support public service organizations. Current trends seem to augur that more and more federal public services and entitlement programs will be turned over to state and local governments. One approach being used by the federal government has been to provide block grants to states to underwrite their own entitlement programs. In addition, local municipalities may well consider increasing property taxes or other revenue-generating activities (including the establishment of user fees to be paid by not-for-profit organizations) to raise funds to underwrite community services formerly provided through federal programs.

Some local municipalities have begun to experiment with outsourcing services to not-for-profit agencies. In communities without appropriate agencies or a sufficient number of not-for-profits to undertake their programs, new organizations could be created overnight, causing a boom in the development of community-serving organizations.

> *Implication:* Grass-roots organizations may find themselves with more opportunities as local governments look beyond established not-for-profits for those with new ideas, a large base of unpaid volunteers, and less expensive overhead.

2. *A decrease in the number of not-for-profits.* Radical curtailment of federal spending within the next few years would likely hit hardest those community-based organizations that are heavily government funded. Those that have no private-sector base may be forced to curtail programs severely, go out of business, or merge with organizations that have stronger private-sector support. Foundation and corporate donors in particular may view such attrition positively—fewer organizations competing for the same philanthropic dollars. Moreover, by favoring certain mergers or circumstances for mergers, these donors may be able to broker relationships to their own advantage, or to their perceived advantage for communities where they have interests.

> *Implication:* Grass-roots organizations that want to move into the arena of fund development may face stiff competition from "sanctioned" organizations or collaborations that are already on the rolls of foundation and corporate donors. This will force start-ups to become more entrepreneurial in seeking ongoing, major support of individuals.

It is highly probable, in either case, that many of today's grass-roots organizations will emerge stronger and more competitive by combining time-honored fund-raising techniques, strategies, and tools with new technologies and resources. Staffed and led by a younger generation that is more entrepreneurial and savvy as to communication and technology, the community-based "associations" celebrated nearly two centuries ago by de Tocqueville will very likely be at the cutting edge of not-for-profit development in the twenty-first century.

Suggested Readings

Brakeley, George A., Jr. *Tested Ways to Successful Fund Raising.* New York: AMACOM, 1980.

Connors, Tracy Daniel. *The Nonprofit Organization Handbook.* New York: John Wiley & Sons, 1996.

Flanagan, Joan. *The Grassroots Fundraising Book.* Washington, D.C.: The Youth Project, 1977.

Geever, Jane C., and Patricia A. McNeill. *The Foundation Center's Guide to Proposal Writing.* New York: The Foundation Center, 1993.

Greenfield, James M. *Fund Raising Fundamentals: A Guide to Annual Giving for Professionals and Volunteers.* New York: John Wiley & Sons, 1994.

Hopkins, Bruce. *A Legal Guide to Starting and Managing a Nonprofit Organization,* 2d ed. New York: John Wiley & Sons, 1993.

Seltzer, Michael. *Securing Your Organization's Future: A Complete Guide to Fundraising Strategies.* New York: The Foundation Center, 1987.

International Fund Raising

THOMAS HARRIS
The Virtual Consulting Firm

44.1 Perspective

Given that the overwhelming market for this volume is within the United States, the American point of view has been chosen to address the issues of international fund raising, including all matters concerning fund raising outside of this country.

This perspective is much more complex than it may seem at first blush. Americans tend to have a much more organized and systematic approach to fund raising than other cultures and confuse this with "professionalism," sometimes to the resentment of others, such as the British. Also, Americans traveling abroad, professionally and personally, often cannot understand why others do not address the issues of "private" philanthropy and fund raising in the same ways as they do.

This chapter does not attempt to be exhaustive in its treatment of other countries and cultures: a recent volume[1] clearly demonstrates that it requires on average at least 25 pages to cover the highlights of fund raising within a single country. This chapter does not repeat this information but, instead, tries to take the facility for analysis one step further.

44.2 *Determinants of Fund-raising Cultures*

Research and practice has allowed thus far four paradigms or frames of reference for analyzing the kinds of fund-raising practice: sociological, religious, legal, and fiscal. A sociological scholar would argue successfully that there are large gray areas among these; however, for our purposes we will consider these areas as distinct.

(A) SOCIOLOGICAL FACTORS

The sociological structure of a society will be the strongest single determinant on fund raising. More precisely, societies that function on a tribal basis will have a radically different behavior pattern than those that are postindustrial.

As an example, the Fijian society is, sociologically, quite simple: Among "indigenous" Fijians,[2] all material wealth is shared without inhibition among the members of the extended and ill-defined family, which westerners having married into the system have found to their enormous regret. The remaining 49 percent of Fijian society is of southern Indian extraction, having "immigrated" 150 years ago during British rule. They do not intermarry; their family units are very strong and accomplishments of individuals jealously guarded. The manner in which the indigenous Fijians meet common needs is radically different from that of the Indians: The indigenous Fijians simply take what is necessary. The Indian Fijians have explicit hierarchical command and determination systems: The best students are afforded higher education opportunities (usually offshore, in Australia), for example. External fund-raising "systems" such as a United Way would probably have success only among the expatriate community and then only for expatriate needs.

Another example would be in the countries of West Africa, where the tribal system works in a much larger context. There are ruling tribes in each of these countries, and the rights of the tribes out of power are usually respected so long as the ruling tribes' positions are first recognized. This provides one explanation why Western democratic values do not take root easily: "Majority" does not usually make "right." Aid/assistance programs coming in from the outside can be doomed if they do not take this kind of tribalism into account—hiring the government minister's cousin's cousin as country director, for example. Fund raising, if done at all, usually goes into the ruling tribe's coffers with distribution according to "right," totally divorced from need.

---

[1]Thomas Harris, ed., *International Fund Raising for Not-for-Profits* (New York: John Wiley & Sons, 1999).
[2]"Indigenous" is only relative; these individuals arrived centuries ago from neighboring islands.

On the other side of the spectrum one might expect to find the United States, an open and fluid society, with individuals ascending in economic and social positions while others are descending.

Given the geographic size of the United States and its social mobility and diversity, it has served as a laboratory for fund-raising practices. Certain practices work within the New York Jewish community (but not in Los Angeles), among the Old Bostonians (but not the Catholics), and other practices that work throughout the United States (e.g., United Way).

(B) RELIGIOUS FACTORS

Each religion (excepting Buddhism) tackles the issue of a higher being differently and arrives at differing codes of acceptable behavior in this life. Not surprisingly, the manner in which the common needs are addressed and financed differs radically from religion to religion; each religion has its own formula, but a formula it has.[3]

In the Western world, the roots are undeniably Judeo-Christian, but this can be misleading. The Jewish manner of addressing common needs—as expressed at the time of Jesus—was tribal, totally appropriate to the cohesion of Jewish society and the ever-present external threats. Even then, there was strong disagreement among the Jews; the Essenes, the dry ascetic sect from which Jesus came, differed greatly with the cosmopolitan Jews of Jerusalem, with whom Jesus quarreled and was ultimately condemned. With the Diaspora, the Jewish clans addressed their needs among themselves, case by case. Today's Jewish state is manifestly socialist, and private initiatives are neither discouraged nor overtly supported by the tax and legal codes.

Christian community needs likewise cannot be addressed as a whole. True, in the first instance, the needs were naturally answered from among the immediate clan members. The spread of Christianity, and especially the Greek influences on the early church, meant that much of the early ethic changed. The Orthodox churches remain the common societal element, even being the single largest landowner in many countries. The church is the center of life. One strong indication of the level of evolution from subjective philanthropy, which is embedded locally and rooted religiously, to objective philanthropy, which has a nonsectarian world vision, seems to be the role of church/religious ownership of land: In those countries/cultures where the church or dominant religious organization is the principal or sole owner of land, philanthropy takes on a religious obligation and is directed through the church/religious organization. In the Christian Orthodox religion, Greece comes immediately to mind, with the Orthodox church running to make up for a lost century. In the Roman Catholic church, two extremes are Malta, where the church has an overpowering presence, and England, where it has a much more subdued role.

It is interesting to note that Martin Luther's famous track tacked onto the church's door was at heart an anti–fund-raising diatribe, arguing against the indulgences (the sale of pardons) by Rome. One can argue that this marked the beginning of the development of a civil society—where common needs began to be separated from the role of the church, where state began to be separated from church.

---

[3]The first volume to address this systematically is Warren F. Ilchman et al., *Philanthropy in the World's Traditions* (Bloomington: Indiana University Press, 1998).

While we can continue our *tour du monde,* let it be said that each and every society, at each stage of development, has provided for common needs and the needs of the needy. One of the beauties of the Hindu system of castes is that each person has a predefined role that, if one sticks to it, means that he or she will be taken care of. (For the Western-educated mind, the role of the Untouchables is unacceptable, of course.) The Jains of India have insisted for millennia that 10 percent of wealth generated be plowed back into the community. Muslims are obliged to take and care for anyone seeking assistance (being a fellow Muslim helps), but this principle applies to being taken into Christian monasteries also.

Buddhists were cited as exceptions at the beginning of this section, for Buddhists do not have belief in a creative being as a requisite. This does not mean that Buddhists are atheists, however. Buddhism holds that the basis of all life is suffering, and, until that is completely accepted, there can be no happiness. Buddhist charity takes this into account by first relieving suffering.

(C) LEGAL FACTORS

There are basically two legal systems today: the civil code and the common law.[4]

Common law is the system that builds up a series of cases which act as a legal back-drop for judging what is permitted and what is not. Most usually, it is underwritten by a founding document, a constitution, which outlines the overriding principles. In fact, of the common law countries—notably the United States, Canada, Australia, and India—only the "mother" of common law countries, the United Kingdom, does not have a written constitution. It is true that most common law countries flow out of the British experience. And, as befits the common law—an evolution of historical antecedents building on each other—that which is not proscribed is permitted.

Civil law derives in the first instance from church law and then from the Napoleonic Code. There is a series of basic laws that form a tightly argued logic, and each case coming before a tribunal is largely unique unto itself. Most important, that which is not permitted in the civil code is not allowed. Thus, the right to associate freely to answer a common need, commented on so famously by Alexis de Toqueville,[5] is assumed and natural to an American and a right only since 1901 in France.

The spontaneous nature of the third sector in common law countries is not missed on leaders in developing countries, especially those emerging from the collapse of the Soviet Bloc, Southeast Asia, and Africa. This is a contributing reason why many such leaders prefer the civil code system.

In fact, as the civil society/third sector has developed—in terms of educational institutes, nongovernmental organizations, churches, and sects—controlling legislation is increasingly necessary within the common law countries and enabling legislation in the civil law code countries, thus effectively blurring the distinction. Having said that, there is still a world of difference in the creativity of the U.S. third sector ("why not?!") and, for example, of the French ("ce n'est pas possible").

---

[4]For a full treatment, see Lester M. Salamon, *The International Guide to Nonprofit Law* (New York: John Wiley & Sons, 1997).
[5]Alexis de Tocqueville, *Democracy in America* (New York: Vintage Classics, 1990). First published in France in the mid-1800s.

To this author's knowledge, no free trade pact—Mercosul, NAFTA, ASEAN, or European Union—provides for transnational giving or philanthropic activities. There are, however, enabling bilateral treaties, such as between the United States and Canada and the United States and Mexico, which provide for reciprocity. A common misconception is that the reciprocity among the 15 European Union members which applies to private individuals and corporate activities must also apply to not-for-profit activities; in fact, the founding act of the European Union, the Treaty of Rome, explicitly excludes not-for-profit activities from reciprocity (§2, ¶58); the complexities of amending this provision, which also requires unanimity, excludes any realistic hope that it will occur—unless the issue is addressed "through the back door."

(D) FISCAL FACTORS

Non-Americans like to cite the tax advantages of the U.S. fiscal system as the major reason why Americans seem to give more; even if Americans do give more, experienced practitioners know that tax benefits are only one of many factors in decision making and, at best, are a determinant of the *size* of the support, not whether to support in the first place.

The example of Western Europe may serve as an example across the globe.

The Mediterranean countries have to be seen as a whole; that is, the Mediterranean basin within the limits of the Pyrenees, Alps, around to the Atlas Mountains form a diverse but cohesive cultural whole.[6] The mentality of these peoples tends to be open, vivacious, very much integrated into the Mediterranean climate. We can divide these peoples into ethnic groups: the Italians, the Spaniards, the French, the Greeks, and so on. Mediterraneans tend to be very clannish, valuing first family ties, then cultural ties.

The second major Western European grouping are the Europeans of the North—starting roughly with the Huguenot line in northern France into Germany through the Black Forest northward. These people tend to be serious, industrious, and productive. And again, subdivisions are possible among the Calvinists of various stripes; the Anthroposophics, the Lutherans, the Dutch Reformed, and even the Catholics are painted with Calvinist influences. While family plays a strong and central role, of course, the needs of the community are much more transparent than in the Mediterranean.

The third major Western European grouping is the British Isles, including Ireland. Due to their insular geography and consistently strong colonial history and the failure of all invasions for a thousand years, the British mentality is much more global than any of its neighbors. And the religious heritage in the British Isles (Ireland excluded) is much more Church of Rome without the indulgences, with the temporal power invested in the Crown. The British tend to believe much more in the power of the individual. While the infamous class system can be cited as a brake, the fact that lordships and knighthoods have always been for sale has provided a stimulus for some social mobility, at first in recognition of service to the Crown through military prowess, then through mercantile accomplishments, and, in the twentieth century, through social contributions as well. The founding act of British charity was approved by Elizabeth I in 1601—400 years

---

[6]This historiographical approach was developed most convincingly by Fernand Braudel in his two-volume work, *The Mediterranean and the Mediterranean World in the Age of Philip II* (London: William Collins & Sons, 1966), written while he was a prisoner of war during World War II.

ago—which defines charitable movements and excludes anything smacking of political pressure or partisanship. Given Britain's subsequent colonial adventures, it is not surprising to see the general concepts sprouting elsewhere.

Given that the world was largely ruled from half a dozen European capitals only 100 years ago, it is not difficult to trace some of today's practices and attitudes to the respective colonial powers.

(E) CONCLUSION

It is impossible to come to a final conclusion which states that if certain conditions are met, then the philanthropic climate will be the most favorable. Having said that, the transposition of American fund-raising techniques will be most easily accomplished in those societies that are socially very mobile, common law based, with a broad base of property ownership, and a diversity of religious beliefs.

44.3 Kinds of Organizations

As might be expected, there is no single definition of "charitable" or "not-for-profit/ nonprofit" that is universally agreed on. We shall follow the major categories as outlined in *Giving USA*.

(A) RELIGIOUS ORGANIZATIONS

In the United States, giving to religious causes accounts for two-thirds of all giving. Only in the United States does this constitute a "charitable" cause, although financial support for religion occurs in all cultures. That is, giving to religion per se does not evoke the tax rebate in the British system, does not enter on the tax returns of individuals in France, and is not accounted for in Japan. In Germany, there is very considerable giving to religion: Each taxpayer may designate which (major and recognized) religion he or she identifies with, and a set (10%) proportion of his or her taxes are diverted to that religion.

(B) HEALTH ORGANIZATIONS

Certainly health-related organizations are indisputably "charitable" and recognized as such in most legal systems, yet financial support for such is minimal. The United Kingdom has been a leader in developing private sector support, following the freezing of government assistance to the National Health Service under Mrs. Thatcher while prime minister. Private sector support has been increasing also in the Netherlands, and in Singapore it is actively encouraged, especially for treatment for specific maladies/diseases. For the most part, general healthcare is considered a responsibility of government at various levels, a raison d'être for government in the first place; Singapore's explicit policy is more typical than atypical in this respect. In developing countries, primary healthcare is a constant concern, and private support for treatment of the better off ("enlightened self interest") is not unusual.

(C)   EDUCATION ORGANIZATIONS

As with healthcare, in most countries basic education is considered the legitimate province of government. In developed countries this lasts from kindergarten through university and professional schools; in developing countries, from primary through grade school and further, with accommodations depending very much on the government's financial resources. In developing countries, elite education at all levels depends very much on user fees. Having said that, more and more universities, first in the United Kingdom and now throughout the continent, are open to the possibilities of attracting private sector support from alumni and business. In the United Kingdom, this was very much a function of the policies of the Thatcher Governments; on the Continent, much more a function of opportunism. Business schools have led the way as they have traditionally been much closer to the business (i.e., wealth-generating) community and more entrepreneurial in nature, in theory at least. Neighboring nonbusiness schools have taken notice and followed suit. In Central and South America too, universities have taken initiatives in fund raising in an organized fashion. Of course, in all cases the sums raised are tiny compared to the multibillion-dollar campaigns of U.S. universities.

(D)   ARTS AND CULTURE ORGANIZATIONS

In most countries, arts and cultural activities—museums, performing arts, visual arts—have traditionally been the domain of wealthy individuals. "Mæcenas," or patron of the arts, translates easily into many languages and, even today, can be a verb for demonstrating financial support for the arts. Private individuals continue to amass fabulous collections of the arts and for the performing arts. The leading concert hall in Tokyo was built thanks to the generosity of one beverage company. In most Western societies since 1945, the government has taken the role of individual groups of patrons to preserve cultural heritages—and to make them available to the general public. But as the antipathetic relationship between the wealth-generating sector (private individuals and companies) and government has decreased, so has the possibility for organized fund raising for the major causes increased. Most major performing arts organizations in Europe have some sort of fund raising/sponsorship today—ranging from "Friends of . . ." organizations to corporate sponsorships. North Americans are often critical of the cost-benefit ratios; what is important to note is that in the last 15 years, the divide between "public" arts and "private" support has been breached. It also should be noted that it is highly unlikely that the major cultural organizations will ever be "privatized" if only because their assets are considered to be a common heritage. Throughout Central and South America, cultural activities remain much more the province of individuals and tightly knit groups of wealthy individuals, often supported by affiliated companies.

(E)   ENVIRONMENT AND WILDLIFE ORGANIZATIONS

Again, there is a division between developing and developed countries. While the physical environment and wildlife is a universal concern, environmental alert and action organizations (e.g., Greenpeace and the World Wildlife Fund (WWF), respectively) are seen by the developing world as an obvious luxury; economic survival must take priority. In some countries, however, the wildlife funds, such as India's Worldwide Fund for Nature, thrive but their indigenous structures are minuscule in relation to the size of the country and the problems. These two leading environmental organizations—chosen by random—are Canadian and Dutch in origin, the former now headquartered in the Netherlands and the latter in Switzerland. This indicates the very nature of their activities: Greenpeace's crusades go down very well with the iconoclastic Dutch (but not with the conformist Swiss), where it has widespread support, while the WWF's much more "Establishment" approach is comfortable in the Swiss environment. Innumerable environmental groups exist throughout Western Europe and now in the former Soviet Union, all dependent more or less on direct support from the private sector. Some live on large "partnership" arrangements with corporations, some entirely on contributions from a wide audience of individuals. Japan has become cognizant of environmental issues and has come into the sights of the major environmental organizations. Australia and New Zealand have been closer to the U.S. model. Despite the recognized environment problems in Central and South America—from wheezing Mexico City to the devastation of the Amazon rain forest—the question of balancing environmental concerns with economic viability remains.

(F) INTERNATIONAL AFFAIRS ORGANIZATIONS

The international press often derides the financial support of the U.S. government to international affairs, focusing on tardiness in payment of United Nations dues, paltry contributions to aid programs, and the like. Such figures take into account only U.S. government support, of course, and thus overlook the support that U.S. foundations and nongovernmental organizations give, let alone the contributions of U.S. companies operating abroad. Most other cultures prefer to work almost entirely through their governments; that is, there is little private assistance for development or international programs. Organizations such as Médecins du Monde and Oxfam are exceptions, and, although their total budgets are large indeed and largely (but not entirely) privately funded, they are minuscule next to public/government assistance programs of developed countries—from Germany to Spain to Japan.

(G) PUBLIC/SOCIETY BENEFIT/HUMAN SERVICES
ORGANIZATIONS

For practicality of analysis, we have combined two categories—public/society benefit and human services. Indisputably these are the kinds of activities universally accepted and recognized as "charitable." As such, they are the platform from which other kinds of not-for-profit organizations spring, both functionally and historically. While in the United States these two categories account for about 15 percent of total giving (excluding the unquantifiable proportion of religious giving that is channeled to legitimate social welfare causes), they can account for close to 100 percent of charitable giving in societies such as South America and some parts of Europe. In fact, this broad category plus education would fit rather nicely into the classical and current definition of charity in the United Kingdom, among other countries.

44.4 Sources of Funds

(A) INDIVIDUALS

In general, private individuals account for the vast majority of funds donated, *although there are no hard data to support this assertion internationally.* A guesstimate is that the proportions are about the same as in the United States—individuals account for ±92 percent of total funds raised including bequests.

The motivations of individual giving are universal: the ego/social considerations, the identification with shared values, and the quest for immortality—usually progressing along this scale with the prospective donor's age.

(B) FOUNDATIONS

Foundations are very culturally specific. Many more foundations in Europe, for example, run their own programs than in the United States. Some of the largest foundations in the world are in Europe—the Wellcome pharmaceutical company was entirely owned by a foundation until its recent sale; much of the Rowntree chocolate fortune found its way into a number of grant-making trusts; in Germany, many of the leading companies are partially, and some wholly, owned by operating and grant-making foundations.

"Foundation" in Napoleonic Code countries means a legal entity with a certain endowment that runs its own programs and/or dispenses money; until very recently, any French not-for-profit organization could call itself a *fondation,* but only the Fondation de France counted as a real foundation. The threshold for the amount of founding endowment has been set intentionally very high so that there is assurance that the foundation will survive in perpetuity or to discourage the creation of foundations.

In the Netherlands, foundations known as *stichtingen* are quite easy to establish and to dissolve, and these may be operating and/or disbursing. As in Switzerland, foundations may be created to protect family assets: More than one American fund raiser has been sent astray thinking that a Swiss foundation is similar to an American one.

The movement toward a single European market has met, among many other things, the privatization of mutual savings banks which opens the question of what to do with the proceeds from privatization. In both the Netherlands and Italy, where mutual savings banks have a long and rich history, the proceeds have been put into new grant-making foundations. Those in Italy are especially flush at the moment.

There are sizable bank foundations in Spain, established so that a controlling portion of the stock in the banks would always be in friendly hands, thus warding off unwanted suitors.

Portugal has a number of wealthy foundations, mostly operating in nature. Greece also has a few. But the closer to the Mediterranean one gets, the less transparent such matters become.

Canada, Europe, and Japan have foundation centers. None has as complete or as transparent data as the American Foundation Center; each is a necessary stop in working in those respective cultures.

(C) CORPORATIONS

Corporations outside of the United States follow the same rules as those within the United States: There are those that are "good corporate citizens" with professionally directed giving programs and transparent guidelines; there are those that will give only to the projects that interest the current chief executive's spouse; and everything between. With all the risk that goes with any generality, it can be said that non-U.S. companies tend to give more in their own (enlightened) self-interest. Research case by case is necessary. No international directories of corporate giving have reliable data.

44.5 *Methods of Fund Raising*

The same means of fund raising are used outside of the United States as within, some with more sophistication in certain places, others in rather primitive forms. The individual means will be considered according to the personalization of approach.

(A) DIRECT MAIL

In one form or another, direct mail is used throughout the world. That is, the form letter can be found in each and every society, as can the highly personalized appeal letter from someone close. Mass-produced direct mail is quite another thing as this runs into a number of cultural specifics. First, there has to be a database of names, somewhere, within the organization or externally. Second, there are legal considerations: in some countries (e.g., Germany) it is not legal to use lists from one source (e.g., magazine subscriptions) for another (e.g., a not-for-profit organization). Third, it may be that it is not appropriate to be "seen" spending money on mailings, and thus organizations resort to cheap-appearing (but relatively expensive) mailings. Fourth, it may be socially unacceptable to personalize if the person "signing" the letter does not know the recipient. Fifth and most fundamentally (often overlooked), direct mail is dependent on a reliable postal system, which cannot always be assumed (e.g., Argentina).

There appears to be no country as saturated in direct mail as the United States. It is still possible for a well-constructed direct mail package to be profitable in the test phase on a cold list in those countries where this is legally permitted and practical (e.g., France and the United Kingdom). Even in those countries where the postal system is unreliable, the initial test costs can be sufficiently low to warrant the attempt.

(B) TELEMARKETING

Telemarketing is subject to many of the same caveats as direct mail—reliability of the telephone system, access to names, and the like. As telemarketing is much more invasive than direct mail, which can be ignored, it is much more culturally sensitive: In many "Latin" countries—from Spain to South America—one would be very bold indeed to initiate cold calls to a cold list by a stranger. Telemarketing has been successful in parts of "AngloSaxon" Europe (the Netherlands, Germany, Switzerland) and has been very successful in tests in reinforcing direct mail, especially with lapsed donors.

Experience shows that the single largest barrier to telemarketing is finding the individuals willing to make the telephone calls, even among alumni to their fellow alumni.

(C) GIVING CLUBS/ANNUAL GIVING

Developing fidelity among donors is a universal concern as the costs of acquiring new donors are so much more than the costs of retaining current donors. Developing annual (or quarterly or monthly) giving is somewhat culturally sensitive.

In many countries, it is possible to have a "direct debit" system: that is, donors may instruct their bank to debit their account each month/quarter/year a certain amount in favor of a third party; with the increase in electronic banking, this method has found increasing favor by individuals and their usual suppliers (electricity, gas, rent, even taxes). Many not-for-profit organizations throughout Europe find this a safe and reliable system. Once a donor has signed up, the revenues become predictable, and it takes an effort by the donor to stop the payment stream. The downside risk is that the recipient organizations often take such monthly or quarterly payments for granted and fail to acknowledge the donors.

A variation of this method is the bank debit form, the "giro" system, which is included in mailings and which donors send to their bank to order a one-time payment to a third party. This is particularly used in the Netherlands and Germany.

Giving clubs for larger donors are becoming much more fashionable, especially with those organizations that have special events, such as museums, the performing arts, and universities.

(D) SPECIAL EVENTS

Special events as a fund-raising tool are employed worldwide and, indeed, are the first types of fund raisers to come to mind in many cases. As many of the cultural meccas are also in the market to increase income, they can be hired: For example in the Paris area, the Château de Versailles is second only to the Louvre as a venue for special events. And, as in the United States, special events can take the form of a highly priced glitzy dinner to a bake sale to a piñata at New Year.

Special events are subject to same rules about income/expenses the world over and to the same caveats about "burning prospects," although in some circumstances they are the only acceptable form of fund raising.

(E) SPECIAL/MAJOR GIFTS

Special gifts are one-time or occasional gifts to an organization. These too are worldwide, although the frequency differs from culture to culture and the manner in which they are attracted is very culturally specific.

Americans are doubtless the world leaders in their boldness in asking for major gifts; Australians are probably close runners-up, and the British, subject to cultural class restraints, are not far behind. There then is a major gap before the next grouping can be found. On one hand, among the "Latins" (including the French here), the emphasis on "appearance" precludes asking another person for a personal major gift. On the other hand, the Calvinists have difficulty admitting that they might know something about someone else's financial situation. Finally (in the Western world), the Greeks are afraid that asking for a gift will necessarily invite "retribution"—that individual coming back to ask for a similar gift of similar size.

44.6 Major Gift Campaigns

The mega–billion-dollar campaign is very much American. The leading performing arts organization in the United Kingdom had much difficulty in raising the $300 million needed for restorations and extensions. A campaign for $25 million for an endowment for a major concert hall in Europe is considered enormous. A campaign for $10 million for a major Dutch university or one for $5 million in France takes every bit as much effort as a multi–billion-dollar campaign in the United States. A campaign by the leading and largest international business school in Europe (with an operating branch in Singapore) follows U.S. practices and produces an astounding $100 million. Campaigns in the order of U.S. $15 million are still noteworthy in Australia.

The trend is definitely moving toward more and larger campaigns. A few ingredients have to be in place before campaigns can grow. First, individuals have to be in the habit of giving, because in these types of campaigns private individual giving accounts for the overwhelming majority of the money. This fact requires many organizations to shift attention from "corporate sponsorship" to private individuals. Second, there has to be indigenous professional talent available to make campaigns work, and this requires professional development in parallel with fund raising itself. And third, there has to be a climate of trust and confidence.

44.7 Legacies and Planned Giving

Perhaps nothing separates U.S. fund-raising practices from that of other nations as much as legacies/deferred gifts and planned giving. Part of the explanation lies in legal logic, part in differences in mentality.

The concept that one plans one's financial support to not-for-profit organizations/ charities is not embedded in non-American minds. In many other cultures, one provides for one's immediate family, and society, history has shown, will take care of itself.

The legal logic is quite a bit more complicated but can be summarized simply by saying that in most countries, one has little discretionary power over recipients of one's estate: After the taxman has been paid, the estate is divided among surviving spouse and children, depending on the country. For example, in Scotland wives have not until recently been able to inherit real property. In France the split is 50 percent to the surviving spouse and the rest equally among all the legitimate and illegitimate children; the surviving spouse's estate is subsequently, on his or her demise, divided equally among the legitimate and illegitimate children. Depending on the number of natural inheritors, various percentages of the total estate may be designated to other individuals or to charity; more than this requires special prior approval from senior administration officials and unanimity among the natural inheritors.

"Planned giving" envelopes today's gift message with serious attention to comprehensive estate planning, based on a "win-win" approach with the taxman. Most non-U.S. taxmen are not kindly disposed to such an approach.

Having said that, the Australians have had a tradition of planned giving, from which the British have learned practical lessons. And the New Labour Government in the United Kingdom has taken matters to heart with a serious proposal for overhaul of tax and inheritance provisions. In the Netherlands, the Prins Bernhard Fonds, the national culture foundation, has been quietly working over the past decade to secure deferred gifts, with over $50 million to show for its efforts. Another Dutch organization is looking to see how it might approach potential donors with an equivalent to the charitable remainder trust. ("Trust" is a common law concept, totally absent from civil law codes.) In France, more than one organization is now working to attract deferred gifts; it is too early to tell if this might catch on. In Germany, another organization is working to attract transfer of shares in initial public offerings from the company founders, individuals who are reaching a "mature" age.

The major requirement for a fundamental change in this market is the recognition by governments that the third sector, in all its manifestations, represents a tax-efficient corollary to public sector programs; for that to happen, politicians especially will have had to have private sector experience.

Suggested Readings

Burnett, Ken. *Relationship Fundraising.* London: White Lion Press, 1995. A clear description, with many instructive anecdotes of fund raising in the United Kingdom, applicable anywhere.

Harris, Thomas. *International Fund Raising for Not-for-Profits: A Country-by-Country Profile.* New York: John Wiley & Sons, 1999. The first attempt at a global coverage of "how it is done there and why."

Ilchman, Warren F., et al. *Philanthropy in the World's Traditions.* Bloomington: Indiana University Press, 1998. A clear, irrefutable presentation that "it wasn't invented here."

Salamon, Lester M. *The International Guide to Nonprofit Law.* New York: John Wiley & Sons, 1997. A guide for layman and lawyer alike to the intricacies of not-for-profit law around the world.

Salamon, Lester M., Helmut K. Anheier, and associates. *The Third Sector Revisited: A Summary.* Baltimore: The Johns Hopkins University Institute for Policy Studies Center for Civil Society Studies, 1998.

Seymour, Harold J. *Designs for Fund-Raising.* New York: McGraw-Hill, 1966. The ageless classic on how fund raising is done, anywhere.

Useful Addresses

Fundraising Institute Australia
Suite 410
282 Victoria Avenue
Chatswood, NSW 2067
Australia

European Foundation Centre
51, rue de la Concorde
1050 Brussels
Belgium
Phone: +32 2 512 8938
Fax: +32 2 512 3265

Canadian Centre for Philanthropy
425 University Avenue
Suite 700
Toronto, Ont. M5G IT6
Canada
Phone: +1 416 597 2294
Fax: +1 416 597 2294

Association of Fundraising Professionals, Toronto Chapter
260 King Street East
Suite 510
Toronto, Ont. M5A 1K3
Canada
Phone: +1 416 941 9212
Fax: +1 416 941 9013

Union pour la Générosité
60, rue de la Boëtie
75008 Paris
France

Mæcenata: Institüt für Dritter Sektor-Forschung
Albrechtstraße 22
10117 Berlin-Mitte
Germany

Indian Centre for Philanthropy
Sector C, Pocket 8/8704
Vasant Kunj
New Delhi 110 070
India
Phone: +91 11 689 7659
Fax: +91 11 689 9368
E-mail: icp@del12.vsnl.net.in

Fundraising Institute of Ireland
9 Upper Fitzwilliam Street
Dublin 2
Ireland

Japan Foundation Center
YKB Shinjuku-gyoen Building, 5th Floor
1-3-8 Shinjuku, Shinjuku-ku
Tokyo 160
Japan
Phone: +81 3 3350 1857
Fax: +81 3 3350 1858

Asociación Mexicana de Profesionales en Obtención de Fondos y Desarrollo/AFP
Tecamachaclo 146
Lomas de Chapultepec
11650 México, DF
Mexico

Centraal Bureau voor Fondsenwerving/CBF
Anthony Fokkerweg 1
1059 CM Amsterdam
The Netherlands
Phone: +31 20 417 0003
Fax: +31 20 614 0791

National Council of Social Services
11 Penang Lane
Singapore 238485
Singapore
Phone: +65 336 1544
Fax: +65 336 7732

South African National NGO Coalition/SANGOCO
PO Box 31471
Braamfontein 2017
Republic of South Africa
Phone: +11 403 7746
Fax: +11 403 8703
E-mail: Kerry@sagoco.org.za

Centro de Fundaciones
C/Ramón de la Cruz, 36 2
28001 Madrid
Spain
Phone: +34 91 578 22 55

Schweizerische Gesellschaft der Fundraising Fachleute/SGFF
Römerstraße West 17
3296 Arch
Switzerland

Institute of Charity Fundraising Managers/ICFM
208-210 Market Towers
1 Nine Elms Lane
London SW8 5NQ
United Kingdom
Phone: +44 20 7627 3436
Fax: +44 20 7627 3508

Fund Raising in Japan: Tips from Experience

Dwain N. Fullerton, MA
Stanford University

David A. Woodruff, MBA
Massachusetts Institute of Technology

45.1 Introduction

In the late 1980s and early 1990s, the Asian economy, led by Japan, grew to be one of the strongest in the world. Optimism and pride permeated the atmosphere, and the technical prowess of major corporations was legendary and real. For fund raisers and development staffs, the territory was one of seemingly boundless opportunity. Universities, colleges, private schools, and other not-for-profit enterprises dedicated significant resources to build closer ties with Asia in hope of securing philanthropic and other types of involvement with their institutions.

Leading American research universities were among those organizations active in raising funds from Asia. For Stanford University and the Massachusetts Institute of Technology (MIT), much of the early successful fund raising occurred in Japan, where there were long-term historical connections. The experience gained in working with

Japan, although not totally transferable to strategies in other Asian cultures, informed the overall fund-raising efforts at these institutions as expansion occurred into other economies. The lessons learned in this development work should be useful to any organizations that wish to do fund raising on the Pacific Rim or other international locations. However, many of the techniques employed in Asia by Stanford and MIT were simply the result of good professional practices combined with old-fashioned luck. It was not, and is not, necessary to learn a whole new fund-raising language.

What follows are two cases of actual fund raising in Japan. The first involves the solicitation of a high-technology company to fund a "bricks-and-mortar" project at Stanford: a computer science building. The second documents the establishment of an endowed professorship in Japanese language and culture at MIT. These solicitations were intended to be philanthropic, without a quid pro quo beyond what the university and its departments were doing either as part of the academic enterprise or as part of normal stewardship to all donors of large gifts. Both cases are presented in great detail to capture and re-create the thought processes going on within the two universities. Following each case are the observations made and "take-home" lessons from each endeavor. Finally, a set of general recommendations is provided for those in charge of developing Asian or international fund-raising strategies.

45.2   Case 1: Solicitation of a Japanese High-Technology Company for Building Support at Stanford University

This is a composite history. The names are fictitious. All of the events took place, but not all occurred in one solicitation or with one company.

(A)   CASE HISTORY

Ken Harwell, the new dean of the engineering school, was elated but had a problem. He was elated because the trustees had approved a new computer science building as one of the components in the university's current capital campaign. This was a coup—the building was desperately needed. The computer science (CS) faculty were broken into small groups scattered all over campus. The new structure would reunite a technically outstanding group and put them next to colleagues in electrical engineering. The problem was cost: $40 million had to be raised. Many of the usually dependable computer companies were not doing well financially or were disinclined to make large gifts for bricks and mortar. Others preferred to offer gifts of equipment. These were welcome but of little use without a place to put them. It was beginning to look as if the campaign might be over before there was a chance to start construction.

(B)   FUND-RAISING POSSIBILITIES

Harwell knew it would be up to him to do most of the fund raising. What resources were there? The university's central fund-raising staff was helpful and competent, but they had many demands on their time for other university priorities. The engineering school's fund-raising group was small but could focus exclusively on engineering priorities. The faculty had a history of comfortable interactions with industry, including international corporations, so perhaps there were useful contacts from that source.

The majority of gifts to the school came from corporations, and a valuable part of the budgets of many departments came from industrial affiliates programs. The departments organized annual conferences and seminars and charged corporate members a fee to attend. There was also a tradition of allowing employees of member companies, for an additional fee, to spend time working with faculty and students in several of the research laboratories. The aim was to give the visitors valuable advanced training that they could then use in their own labs when they returned. Although U.S. companies provided philanthropic support, almost all visitors came from foreign companies.

With the possibility of additional help from U.S. industry fading, the fund-raising staff began to expand the list of prospects. What about Europe? Japan? The broader Pacific Rim? The foreign industrial affiliate members? There was no history of campaign giving from those sectors, or much of any philanthropy at all. Still, the school had admitted foreign students for many years, so perhaps they might be an entree into their companies. Other engineering schools were raising money in Asia, and the Japanese economy was strong.

These positives were balanced by one serious negative: the sensitivity of American companies to what they viewed as Japan's commandeering U.S. basic research without paying for it. The academics argued that the research was freely published and open to anyone who wanted to read the journals, but feelings ran high. How would American companies react to Japanese names on major portions of the building?

Another cautionary note was fund-raising cost. The largest companies were in Japan. But travel in Japan was far more expensive than in the United States, and school budgets had not been set with much foreign travel in mind. If the effort were unsuccessful, it would be hard to justify having taken the risk, especially when expense reports for a week's stay in a midrange hotel in Tokyo were exorbitant.

(C) ALUMNUS CONTACT IS FOUND

Thus, it was with mixed feelings that Dean Harwell absorbed the contents of a memo from one of the fund-raising staff in the business school. A business school alumnus, Ed Dettering, headed Hatoyama Electronics USA, a U.S. subsidiary of a major Japanese corporation. He had arranged for the business school dean to make a presentation to the company president in Japan. The dean asked for an endowed professorship but was turned down. The president's position was that the company's products relied heavily on advanced engineering technology, and future gifts would be to that field. The memo went on to say that Dettering would be glad to open the door for engineering.

Harwell surveyed the lagging gift totals for the building, checked his travel budget, and called Tim Munson, the engineering director of development, and told him to prepare a background on Hatoyama and get an appointment with Dettering. The chase was on.

Because the faculty in the school were highly independent, it was hard to know where all the ties were, who did consulting, sponsored visitors, and so on. Nevertheless, the records showed that Hatoyama had been a member of the CS industrial affiliates program for 10 years and had sent various visitors. There should be a cadre of Japanese staff who knew the school—a good sign.

Munson spent the next several weeks unsuccessfully trying to merge the dean's and Dettering's calendars. In the meantime, three senior executives from the Hatoyama Laboratories called on the president of the university. They described the company's dedication to fundamental research and the importance of ties with universities, which they hoped to strengthen, and inquired about ways to accomplish this.

Where had this come from? Baffled, the engineering staff queried the CS department. The answer was simple. One of the CS administrators, Dorothy Underwood, had been befriending the Japanese visitors for almost the entire time the affiliates program was in existence. It was superb staff work, reflecting well on the school and the department. The company had assigned a corporate executive, Kazuo Sekimoto, to be the liaison from their side, and Sekimoto and Underwood had become friends. In fact, during one of Underwood's visits to Japan, Sekimoto had invited her and her husband for dinner at Sekimoto's home, an exceptional honor in Japan. When the campaign had been announced, Sekimoto asked how they could help. Underwood said a building was needed, and the visit was the outcome.

Within a few days, the university president forwarded a generally worded proposal to the Hatoyama president, asking for their participation in the campaign. The text avoided mention of a specific building. Because the university did not want to incur heavy architectural costs for a structure that might not be funded, most of the buildings were in concept only. This led to occasional awkwardness when potential donors wanted more detail, and it was a challenge for the fund raisers to generate and maintain enthusiasm about something so amorphous.

Because Hatoyama Electronics' interest was clearly in technology, the president's cover letter suggested a visit from the engineering dean. Within a week, Harwell had blocked time for a trip to Japan, which would coincide with an October international conference in Tokyo, and wrote for an appointment. Luckily, a number of senior university administrators, including the president, were also attending and would be available for fund-raising calls as needed.

Many of the major Japanese corporations were sending representatives to the conference, including Hatoyama Electronics. Sekimoto offered to host the university group for a tour of the company's headquarters building and a meeting with the company's senior executives. The invitation was accepted with delight and anticipation that a major gift had been approved.

(D) INITIAL PROPOSAL

Sekimoto met the group at the hotel and took them by car to the headquarters in downtown Tokyo. After a tour through the public exhibits of advanced technological products, the Americans were ushered into a conference room where they had a cordial, brief, inconclusive meeting cut short by a tight schedule. It was disappointing.

Two days later, Sekimoto asked to talk with Harwell and one of the university corporate staff at their hotel in downtown Tokyo after work. His message was a surprise. Despite some clouds on the horizon, the economy was still strong—a positive sign. Although the proposal could be turned down for a variety of reasons, the retired chairman of the company was favorably inclined because of long-standing ties to the university. Just after World War II, Sekimoto related, a Professor Englehart from the engineering school was the first American academic to visit the company. Englehart had died some years earlier, but his gesture had not been forgotten.

As the conversation progressed, Sekimoto offered to serve as a "clearinghouse" and advisor. He asked to be kept up to date on fund-raising progress in Japan and informed about research projects that might be of interest. He noted that this was important with all donors, but especially so in Japan, and mentioned a new program in the management of technology that the school was considering. Sekimoto politely added that he was sure the dean knew that one of Hatoyama's senior executives was on a telecommunications committee with the chairman of the electrical engineering department. (The dean did not know.)

(E) IMPORTANCE OF COMMUNICATION

Asked for pointers in approaching Japanese corporations, Sekimoto was forthright and offered these five suggestions:

1. When making a fund-raising call, state the purpose of the call fairly soon. If the response is at all positive, ask how to take the proposal to the senior management level. A large gift is always decided at the board level, and needs support from above and below.
2. Encourage top university officials to visit Japan often. This is important, and demonstrates courtesy, respect, and mutual interest.
3. Stick to one target, in this case the building. Do not shift or broaden the scope by mentioning industrial affiliate programs or other buildings, gifts for which might release funds for computer sciences. (The university had earmarked unrestricted seed money to various buildings; a gift to one building could release money for another. But it may also have been an oblique suggestion to Harwell, who was so articulate and attuned to the audience that if he sensed resistance to one project he would switch to another without missing a beat.)
4. Keep the budget cycle in mind. The fiscal year generally runs from May 1 to April 30. It would be important to return fairly soon to make calls, possibly in February.
5. Be patient. The corporations had an internal process which they likened to preparing the roots for bonsai trees—the root work had to be done before the tree was ready, and this took time.

Sekimoto also volunteered to help with other companies, cautioning that in an economy as large as Japan's, he might not have useful contacts everywhere. The parting was exceedingly amiable, and the Americans returned to the United States more optimistic than they should have been.

From this point on, Munson took charge of the details and often wrote senior executives under his own signature. This was not the best procedure, and occasionally the answer to Munson's question would go directly to Dean Harwell. Status was important, and a person of lesser rank did not customarily address directly one of higher rank. Nevertheless, Harwell's schedule was so hectic that trying to work through him would have slowed the process unduly.

Fax was the way to communicate. Telephone connections were spectacular, but working through receptionists was rarely successful. And, unless the person being called was unusually fluent in English, information was often misunderstood. The time zone change was another factor. But a fax sent at the end of the day arrived in Japan in the morning and usually got an answer within a few hours.

In follow-up communications, Sekimoto suggested the names of the right executives in the company's research laboratory. Five months later, the dean scheduled a second trip. Munson wrote for an appointment, offering several possible days and times.

The answer came back that the president and vice president of the labs were available at 10 A.M. on March 24. Munson confirmed and set the research staff to preparing backgrounds. Maps of the train system were either unavailable from local sources or, when available, useless for the suburbs. Munson faxed the Hatoyama labs and asked for help. They sent magnificent instructions in clear English. What was learned later was that although there are bilingual signs in Tokyo, beyond the city limits there are none. An English map was useless in trying to get help from fellow passengers when one was changing trains in the suburbs. Two maps were a must—one in kanji and one in English.

On fund-raising trips, Dean Harwell and Munson usually planned to spend five working days in Japan, departing on Saturday, arriving in Japan Sunday afternoon (crossing the international date line), and beginning fund-raising appointments Monday morning. The last call would be no later than noon on Friday, leaving time to get to Narita airport and catch a late flight, which would put them back in the United States on Friday.

Scheduling appointments was a problem because they had to be requested in parallel in order to fill the week. This led to more juggling than was ideal, and embarrassments when a scheduled appointment had to be moved for a more important opportunity. Nevertheless, on average, Dean Harwell could make three to four fundraising calls a day, leaving evenings open for alumni events or meetings that could not be arranged during working hours.

Luckily, as the Hatoyama trip was being scheduled, word came that a major Japanese corporation had agreed to support the campaign and gave permission to use the information in other corporate solicitations. How significant an impact this had on other companies was hard to measure. It was undoubtedly positive, and did become a real morale booster for the Stanford fund raisers. It was almost always mentioned in later solicitations.

(F) FIRST MEETING

Three university staff members went on the first call: Dean Harwell, Munson, and the university director of corporate relations. The plan was to leave early and take the train from Tokyo to the suburbs where the laboratories were located. This looked reasonable because fares were inexpensive, trains were reliable and clean, the morning commuter crush was on the incoming trains, and taxis on city streets were slow and costly.

Everything went well until the group realized that for the last several stations there were no signs in English. Anguished attempts to communicate were total failures. None of the Japanese in the car spoke English, and the best American pronunciation of the Japanese destination drew polite blanks; it soon became clear they had probably passed the station where they had to change trains. The three leapt off at the next stop, convinced that whatever face they might have had in Japan was about to be lost. Harwell counted the stations they had passed and did a little subtracting. They went back two stops, made a guess about which was the local and which the express, changed trains, got it right, and arrived at the laboratory gate in a dead run, only four minutes late.

This was their first fund-raising meeting in Japan, and it was intimidating. The three were ushered into a paneled conference room with a broad view of the countryside. The table was long and rectangular, seating about 12 on a side. The three Americans were shown to the side of the table facing the door, as was the custom. After a few minutes, 10 Hatoyama executives and staff entered and sat down on the opposite side. The president, Tomio Nakao, was in the center, with the vice president to his right.

Everyone exchanged business cards. Fortunately, enough Japanese had visited the engineering school that the Americans knew to have business cards with English on one side and katakana on the other, and that it was important to bring gifts for everyone. What had escaped calculation was just how many gifts were needed. Munson badly underestimated, and would spend the evening on e-mail arranging to get more supplies from campus for the rest of the week's meetings.

The Hatoyama staff went first, presenting their research and significant findings. They followed with a description of the several focus areas in the laboratory. The quality of the research and engineering was exceptional, some of the best in the world. Several of the presenters had studied in the United States or the United Kingdom, and spoken English was not a problem. The discussions were lively.

Following Hatoyama's presentations, Dean Harwell outlined the directions and strengths of the CS department and the general need for a new building to house the department. The Hatoyama staff listened intently and asked for details about the configuration of the building. This became a delicate part of the meeting. Because plans were in such a preliminary stage, it was important to be as accurate as possible but avoid the impression that the building was just one item on a long university wish list. The dean was masterful in presenting the situation as it stood, eloquently describing the unknowns as positive opportunities for creative solutions, and asking permission to send further particulars as they developed, followed by a formal proposal for a $1 million gift.

Nakao then took the group on a tour of the laboratory display area and ended the day with dinner at an elegant local restaurant. Seating was arranged according to rank, with Nakao and Dean Harwell at the head of the table. The evening was a memorable display of good fellowship and toasts to the future, and concluded with pledges of further contact and mutually beneficial interactions on research and technology. It seemed to be a good start.

(G)   FOLLOW-UP AND OBSTACLES ENCOUNTERED

As soon as the group was back in the United States, Munson wrote a proposal with as many specifics about the building as were available. It contained a regrettable amount of boilerplate, faculty awards, department rankings, student quality, and so on. But it did have the most recent information in the evolving design and content of the CS building. The dean signed it and sent it to Nakao, who acknowledged receiving it.

Sekimoto's advice on frequent trips to Japan was hard to follow, in part for budget reasons and in part because of demands on the dean's schedule during the campaign. Scheduling the next visit took almost eight months. When the group arrived at the lab, this time with no mishaps on the train, Nakao received the dean warmly. The Hatoyama staff reported on new research they were undertaking. The dean presented some novel explorations in semiconductor physics and discussed the current state of planning for the CS building.

At the conclusion, Nakao reported that he had foreshadowed the proposal with senior management, and it was being reviewed for inclusion in the annual budget. However, the U.S. ambassador had just visited to discuss investments in technology, followed by a group of faculty from Japanese universities pleading for research funding. Their argument was that large companies should support the local schools as well as they did the overseas universities. The implication was that there were many supplicants for a limited amount of money. In addition, Nakao expressed concern that if the company supported a building in an American university they would be even more vulnerable to the criticism that they were stealing technology and therefore American jobs.

Dean Harwell was quick to point out that because many companies, both Japanese and American, would be involved in the building, it would be a neutral consortium with information available to all on an equal basis. Conversations with some leading U.S. businessmen had even encouraged such philanthropy from Japanese companies, as long as it did not convey an exclusive advantage. The U.S. businessmen reasoned that because the information was published openly, the Japanese might as well help pay for some of higher education's capital costs, just as American corporations did.

Nakao nodded but went on to report that business had slowed, and there was resistance at some senior levels. After that dose of cold water, he assured the dean that the proposal still had the moral support of the research group, but it was tough sledding and perhaps the amount requested would have to change or the arguments in favor strengthened.

Nakao made clear that he could not recommend any action, but it might be helpful to send a letter of inquiry to the corporate president. A day later, a fax arrived at the hotel suggesting that the letter be sent to the vice president for research at the corporate headquarters but that the letter not mention Nakao.

As soon as the group got back to campus, Munson drafted two letters—one to Nakao and one to the vice president for research. Both made essentially the same arguments, stressing research and the fruitful collaborations in basic engineering research that the visitors, students, and faculty enjoyed, and noting that the new building would make it easier to accept visiting scientists from all companies. The letter went on to report that one of the senior CS faculty members would be in Japan next summer and could describe the department's current research in more detail if that would be helpful.

A month later, Harwell got an unexpected call from Howard Dillon, a senior executive in a nearby company. Dillon grew up in Japan, worked there for part of his career, spoke Japanese fluently, and had become acquainted with Nakao. Nakao had called him and asked for help in negotiating with the engineering school. Hatoyama's financial performance was only fair, their gifts were customarily in the $20,000 to $100,000 range, and a $1 million gift would be hard to approve. They had given a like amount to another university, but that school had been willing to formalize a visitor's policy, essentially agreeing to do what they were informally doing already.

Nakao suggested that something similar would be helpful, perhaps an agreement to accept one visitor per year, or a guarantee of a fixed charge for visitors, or some sort of priority in case of a waiting list. Because faculty had absolute discretion about accepting visitors, the school administration could not guarantee a fixed number. Furthermore, graduate students always had first call on laboratory facilities. When there was space available, a faculty member could accept visitors from industry. There was an added incentive to do this. In addition to the fee paid by visitors, they were highly skilled and often contributed as much as they gained. Occasionally faculty commented that significant advances had come about because of techniques learned from foreign visitors.

Dillon suggested that one possibility might be to offer a modest discount for visitors from corporations that had contributed to the building. With that incentive, Nakao would probably prepare a two-page memo to the board, spelling out the purpose of the gift. This memo would mention long-range research advantage, the company's role in the techno-logical community, how added space in a new building would make it easier for Hatoyama visitors to be accepted, the value of information science in the twenty-first cen-tury, and how the gift's visibility could help with international relations. Also, better com-munications with faculty would boost recruiting both in the United States and Japan.

Dillon thought the memo would go to a key contact within the company hierarchy, then to an executive vice president who would take the matter up for 30 minutes in the board executive committee, which would then either approve or reject the proposal.

The dean went back to the calculator. Compared to the pledge for the building, the reduction in fees was insignificant. The gift for the building was urgent, but the engi-neering school had no experience in dealing with the arrangement Nakao proposed. There was an absolute prohibition against mixing any sort of quid pro quo with philan-thropy. (Happily, the charges for visitors were classified as fees and not gifts, eliminating that problem.) Furthermore, changes in the schedule of charges for visitors would have to be approved by the faculty in the CS department, and whatever was done for Hatoyama would have to apply to all corporations that contributed to the building. It was a thorny issue. The dean presented the situation to the faculty and left the issue open for discussion.

The debate went on for nearly a month. Finally the CS department decided in favor of offering a modest discount for corporate donors to the building, with three options the companies could choose from. The options varied by amount of pledge, length of time to pay the pledge, and the length of time and number of visitors to which the dis-count would apply. The same fees were applied to all, so there was no preferential treat-ment. The dean conveyed this to Dillon, who relayed it to Nakao in Tokyo.

Several months later, the dean and Munson traveled back to Tokyo for a visit with Nakao. At the research center he was tied up but appointed Mitsuo Kataoka, the assis-tant lab director, to be his representative. After the research presentations from both sides, Kataoka took Dean Harwell and Munson to lunch.

Kataoka was guardedly optimistic about the proposal. It would probably have to be slightly less than the $1 million originally requested, and the pledge payments spread over eight years instead of the customary five. The difficulty was that in the intervening months, Hatoyama's profitability had continued its decline. When asked about Hatoyama's situation as compared with two other Japanese companies in the same busi-ness, Kataoka replied that their competitors' situations were less serious because they were more diversified. Nevertheless, despite the bad economy, the conditions for *ringi* (the internal process of arriving at a decision) were good.

Kataoka advised sending a letter to Nakao spelling out the three alternatives, espe-cially the option that reduced the number of years the visitor discount was offered if the pledge payments extended beyond five years. This would be a key, he said, because if the economy improved, Hatoyama could accelerate the pledge payments and gain more years for the visitors discount. Kataoka asked for a fax copy of the letter (the custom was to fax the letter and send the original by overnight international air mail) and for four copies of the faculty directory, which contained brief biographies of the faculty, their research interests, e-mail addresses, and phone and fax numbers.

At the close of the meeting, Kataoka mentioned that the senior vice president for research might want to visit campus and meet with some of the faculty, and wondered if that would be acceptable. The dean immediately agreed and assigned Munson to make arrangements.

(H)   OUTCOME: A FIVE-YEAR PLEDGE

A month later, Dr. Hasegawa, a senior manager of technology planning, wrote asking for the courtesy of arranging for a visit from the senior vice president for research, Dr. Sadakaza Muroga. Hasegawa included a biography and alerted Munson to Muroga's long career and interest in basic research. Hasegawa closed the letter by noting that Muroga had just been promoted to senior executive vice president, one of only five under the corporate president.

Armed with this background, Munson focused on faculty with solid research programs. Two weeks later, Muroga visited campus and met with Dean Harwell, the associate dean for academic affairs, the chair of the electrical engineering department, and three senior faculty members in electrical engineering and computer science. Because Muroga spoke the language of advanced research fluently, the conversations in the laboratories shimmered as members of the group challenged each others' views about recent discoveries and promising new directions in technology. It was an impressive exchange.

Two weeks after Muroga's visit, Nakao wrote the dean with the information that the company had agreed to participate in funding the CS building with a five-year pledge, thus obtaining a slightly more favorable visitor discount. The foundation for the decision had been laid over a 10-year period, with scientific exchanges between corporate visitors and faculty. The philanthropic discussions had taken more than 18 months.

Funding for the CS building was completed four months later. On the ground floor is a classroom bearing the Hatoyama name, joining other Japanese and American corporations and individuals who gave for a cooperative venture benefiting engineers and scientists and their societies on both sides of the Pacific Rim.

45.3   Case 2: The Kochi–MIT Joint Program in Communications

In the world of fund raising, it is common practice to imagine how events of the past may be glorified in order to shape the future. Such thinking is generally an effective strategy for creating a dialogue between a potential donor and a viable organization whose pasts intersect and whose futures contain shared goals. The establishment of the *Kochi–MIT Joint International Program in Communication* in 1995 is an example of how drawing on history has resulted in one of the more innovative and forward-looking educational and research programs at MIT. The names of the individuals in this case are fictitious, but the events actually took place.

(A)   CASE HISTORY

It was approximately 150 years ago that Manjiro Nakahama, a fisherman and native of Kochi, a coastal prefecture (state) in Japan, was rescued at sea by Captain John Whitfield of the *John Howland*, a New Bedford whaling ship. Forbidden to return to Japan because of his contact with foreigners, Manjiro remained on board with the crew until the ship returned to its home port in Massachusetts. While in the New Bedford area, Manjiro learned English and studied the science and technology of the mid-nineteenth century.

He became known locally as John Manjiro, and he stayed in Massachusetts for six years before returning to Japan, where he then served in an important capacity as interpreter of the English language and American culture in the 1850s when Japan was opening its doors to the West. Manjiro's life and accomplishments are celebrated today in Japan and in the United States and have formed the basis for a sister-city relationship between New Bedford/Fairhaven and Tosashimizu in Kochi.

A century and a half later, in 1992, a conversation between Koichi Kinoshita, executive director of the John Manjiro–Whitfield Commemorative Center for International Exchange in Japan, and Professor Hiro Hashimura of MIT, newly hired by the School of Humanities and Social Science, took place on the MIT campus. Hashimura, an expert in the teaching of Japanese language and a scholar of linguistics, had recently come to MIT to head the Japanese Foreign Language program. In this capacity, Hashimura's mission became clear: to build a world-class program that would alleviate the excess demand by MIT students for courses in Japanese. At this point in time, approximately 70 students were being turned away each year because of a lack of instructors and classes. A key element of the MIT strategy was to raise an endowed chair for the head of the program. While few can recall the intended purpose of the 1992 meeting, what emerged was a discussion about MIT's challenge. According to Hashimura, Kinoshita listened carefully and characterized the turning away of students as tragic; more importantly, Kinoshita indicated that he could help. Undaunted by the $2 million price tag for an endowed chair at MIT, Kinoshita expressed optimism that Kochi Prefecture could be a potential source of funding for MIT and that MIT's involvement with Kochi could also assist in commemorating the life and times of Manjiro. Kinoshita offered to arrange a meeting between Hashimura and his close friend, Governor Akio Kawasaki of Kochi Prefecture. Kawasaki was highly regarded in Japan both as an expert politician and a media mogul. If Kinoshita's assessment of Kawasaki's influence was accurate, he could be a linchpin for moving forward.

(B) FUND-RAISING POSSIBILITIES

With the fund-raising objective of an endowed chair in mind, Hashimura, Dean Paul Maslow of the School of Humanities and Social Science, the senior administration, and the development staff faced several challenging questions:

- Would the prefecture of Kochi, essentially a foreign government with no record of philanthropy, make a suitable donor for an endowed chair at MIT? Could its citizenry be convinced of the merits of doing business with MIT with taxpayer money? How real was this opportunity?
- Could a package be structured to both honor the memory and achievements of Manjiro and provide substantial support to MIT's Japanese language and culture program? How would the donor's expectations be managed so as to maximize mutual benefit without onerous or distracting *quid pro quo*?

It was shortly thereafter that a series of trips to Japan began by Hashimura and the dean, which were spread over a course of about two years, the two setting out to answer the above questions. Kinoshita immediately delivered on his promise to introduce the MIT team to the governor; this meeting was critical in verifying the sincerity of the donor's interest and intent. The governor was very supportive of the objectives to celebrate Manjiro's life history and to work with MIT, but also brought a new element to the table. Kochi Prefecture was in the process of establishing a new technical university and wanted a way to receive advice and guidance, if not involvement, on its plans and strategy. Kawasaki thought that formal ties with MIT would serve as an endorsement of the new university and provide a framework for future faculty exchange. One idea that surfaced in the discussion was for MIT to serve as a sister institution with the new university. Clearly, implementation of this concept required involvement of faculty beyond the School of Humanities and Social Science; as such, the provost and president became active and critical participants in the discussion and negotiations.

It was at this juncture that some deliberate thinking on the part of the MIT team had to be done. To what length should MIT go to pursue this opportunity? Should the Commonwealth of Massachusetts also be involved in building a state-to-prefecture relationship? MIT had no heritage of formal ties with other universities that were managed on an institutional level and for such a purpose. Schools were free to operate their own kinds of faculty-driven and faculty-"owned" collaborative arrangements, but generally, these were constructed in the domain of joint research. Therefore, after some internal discussions, the conclusion was to house a potential tie with the new university in the School of Humanities and Social Science and not MIT more broadly. The faculty in this school would then be able to engage other faculty as needed and leverage their experience to address the particular challenges of the new university in Kochi. A defined time period or life of the collaboration would also be set—an arrangement that would free both parties from further obligations to each other at the conclusion or permit the two sides to extend the agreement in time.

(C)   INITIAL MEETING

Making this case to the Kochi team and the governor took place in two settings. The first was in Tokyo with Provost Samuel Lindt. The discussion actually occurred between Lindt and a member of the Japanese Diet, the Honorable Satoshi Fujimura, who represented the citizens of Kochi in the Upper House. He was very much a proponent of the new university and of MIT's involvement with Kochi. He also viewed the Manjiro story as significant in shaping early Japan–U.S. relations, and analogous to contemporary challenges. The meeting was conducted with Hashimura performing the translation. (In retrospect, this was not a wise use of Hashimura's abilities. Although he was, and is, an expert in translation, the MIT team ran the risk of losing him as a key strategy formulator. From that point on, professional translators were hired.) The provost emphasized MIT's desire to craft an agreement to establish an endowed chair based on the John Manjiro connection to Massachusetts. In closing, Lindt invited Fujimura to visit MIT and deliver a presentation on his area of expertise: Japanese political reform. Fujimura accepted the invitation and traveled to MIT four months later to deliver a speech; this was no doubt an honor for the Diet member.

In early 1994 James Berritt, president of MIT, traveled to Japan. The trip occurred just as the decline of the Japanese economy was accelerating. As budgets for prefectural expenditures began to be scrutinized more closely, serious doubt emerged over the possible outcome of these negotiations. In an attempt to keep the discussions on track, Berritt met with Kawasaki in his Tokyo office. The meeting was one of substance, in which the merits of the collaboration were discussed. Kawasaki outlined his plans for a new university and expressed hope that MIT could be involved. Berritt was personally familiar with the individuals being considered for leadership of the new institution; this pleased Kawasaki greatly. On a personal level, the meeting between the two leaders was enormously successful. Kawasaki was well read about Berritt's West Virginia heritage and likened Kochi to that American state. Kawasaki even began to sing the John Denver lyrics "Almost Heaven—West Virginia." This friendly exchange was critical to making the deal happen.

(D) FOLLOW-UP AND RESULTS

Upon his return to MIT, Berritt instructed the development staff to prepare a written proposal. The document was submitted in draft form to Kawasaki and called for the establishment of a joint exchange program in communication. The proposal featured an endowed chair in Japanese Language at MIT and cultural exchange with the Commonwealth of Massachusetts to honor John Manjiro. Collaboration between MIT and Kochi was proposed at the school level. The potential collaborators were Kochi Prefecture, the Commonwealth of Massachusetts, and MIT.

Although the governor was pleased to receive the first draft, he expressed concerns whether the terms of the agreement would be acceptable to the people of Kochi or the prefectural assembly. He offered to send a representative to MIT for further discussion. These meetings occurred in the spring of 1994, around the time that Mr. Fujimura gave his lecture at MIT. Fujimura played a key role in facilitating the discussions, but a larger delegation was sent to MIT in early autumn. It was shortly thereafter that Berritt, based on the conversations at MIT, submitted a revised proposal to the governor. The amount of the proposal was enlarged to $2.3 million, which included the endowed chair and an expendable research fund for the chair holder on the application of advanced technology to the teaching of Japanese language and culture. The Commonwealth removed itself as a participant and the agreement focused on a partnership between Kochi and MIT.

The agreement was crafted in the spirit of the John Manjiro experience and allowed for MIT students to study Japanese language using today's advanced teaching materials and methodologies. Citizens of Kochi would learn English and assist in the development of Japanese language instructional materials for use at MIT. MIT agreed to host up to five visiting scholars per year at Kochi's expense. The term of exchange was designated from June 1, 1995, to March 31, 2001, in honor of the six-year period Manjiro lived in Massachusetts. A sister-institutional relationship between the MIT School of Humanities and Social Science and the new university in Kochi was established for the same period.

Ultimately, the agreement received assembly approval in March 1995 and was signed by videoconference on May 15, 1995, almost three years later. Professor Hashimura was named the first holder of the Kochi Prefecture–John Manjiro Professorship in Japanese Language and Culture. Hashimura's appointment came as no surprise following his extensive work in pulling the agreement together; however, his appointment was never promised or implied in advance. Because of his love of language, teaching, and technology, Hashimura was considered the John Manjiro of the twentieth (and twenty-first) centuries.

(E)   OBSERVATIONS MADE AND LESSONS LEARNED

- *Stay focused on the mission and the goal in sight.* Hashimura's dedication to the goal of securing funding of a Japanese language and culture program fueled these discussions and reduced the chance for distraction or complicated quid pro quo. The discussions were always kept in a philanthropic spirit.
- *Do not jump to conclusions about a donor's ability or inability to enter into an agreement.* In this case, Kochi Prefecture represented an unusual potential donor. Conventional wisdom might have ruled out this opportunity too early.
- *Execute effective senior-level contact.* The meetings between the MIT leaders and the Kochi executives were critical. Participants were well scripted on both sides, which facilitated communication and expediency. Once the personal contact was made at the senior levels, the proposal took on an air of seriousness that had not existed prior to the meetings.
- *Take care to not be self-serving.* The fact that Professor Hashimura did not promise or market his own involvement in the agreement was important. It enabled the discussion to be maintained at the highest level. The fact that he was appointed to the chair was a logical outcome.
- *Be flexible.* The expansion of the agreement to accommodate both MIT and Kochi interests produced a win/win situation. The relationship between the new university and MIT has resulted in further exchange of merit and is the basis for ongoing discussions regarding future research.
- *Do not give up.* Although the process seems long, the trips feel endless, and the outcome appears bleak, never formally end the discussions. A "no" would have killed this opportunity at the very beginning. The easy thing would have been to walk away.

45.4   *General Recommendations*

The following recommendations are offered for those wanting to sharpen their fundraising work in Japan or elsewhere. Although not necessarily exhaustive, the list is the product of over 25 years of experience by the authors.

- *Make an inventory of your antecedents.* An absolutely essential element in Pacific Rim fund raising is an inventory of antecedents. For Stanford and MIT, these were more varied than anyone could have imagined (a faculty member who sent holiday cards to every Japanese student he had taught; a chance visit to Japan by a professor shortly after World War II; a Japanese fisherman rescued by Americans in the 1850s), but their impacts were profound. Usually the details of these contacts were never documented, at least in any place where they might be available to even the most industrious fund raiser. Nevertheless, anyone planning to do fund raising in Asia would be well advised to inventory their institution's roster of antecedents before spending the money and time serious solicitations will require.
- *Work with established contacts.* If there are no established contacts, move on to more fertile ground. Because fund raisers usually have a fairly short time to get results, it is virtually impossible to arrange a successful solicitation if too much

groundwork has to be done. An average of 10 years of prior history is typical, but as these cases demonstrate, some antecedents go back 50 years or more.

- *Understand how the corporations compete and cooperate with one another.* Companies exist within families called *keiretsu*, and there are many corporate directories that depict the historical and practical relationships. It is poor form to expect a smaller company to give more than a larger one, even though the smaller company may have the capacity and more extensive relationships with the university.
- *Bring gifts of appropriate size to the participants.* This custom was hard to get right, and the gifts were hard to select. They could not be too cheap or too expensive, and had to be small and light enough to carry through a day of meetings. For every trip, there had to be new ones, and a record kept to avoid repeats. It was also important to make sure that the gifts were made in the United States. In one case, a Japanese executive turned a university paperweight upside down and noted with approval that it was made in New Jersey and not overseas.
- *Sort out priorities, identify the basis for asking for a gift, and how the gift, if given, will relate to the donor.* By asking these tough questions before the potential donor does, everything will be speeded up. Before the first call, review your institution's academic priorities and try to match the purpose of the gift you are asking for as closely as possible to the interests of the potential donor, especially if it is a corporation. Remember that every Asian country has many pressing local needs, and there must be an acceptable reason before a gift can be made to a recipient in the United States, the wealthiest country in the world. This may sound elementary, but in practice the pressure to meet academic needs can overwhelm fund-raising common sense. There is no point in requesting computers for the undergraduate library when the company might give a professorship in electrical engineering.
- *Be prepared to make a large, continuing investment of time and effort from the beginning through the stewardship phase.* Travel in pairs—one to make the presentation and one to handle memos for the record, acknowledgment letters, gifts, and follow-up. Foreign travel is glamorous to those who do not do much of it. Being in a strange environment, jet lagged, with appointments during the day and memos to write at night, is exhausting. Furthermore, the Asian work ethic is strong, and it does not reflect well on a fund-raising team if it appears that sightseeing is a big item on the agenda.
- *Make clear what you want early in the process.* There is some conflicting advice on this subject, but being straightforward is generally the best strategy, even though it may not be what someone from within the culture might do. There is a degree of latitude afforded to a foreigner which makes such approaches acceptable and efficient given the difficulties of clear communication and geographical distance.
- *Understand the internal decision processes, whether it is at a corporation, foundation, or individual family.* Be patient. Know about status, how messages are conveyed to the decision makers, and what various answers may mean. Consider translating a technical proposal into the language of the potential donor. Unless you are very lucky, it will be a bad translation, but shows respect and understanding. Relatively few foreigners will be able quickly to scan a proposal in English. As one person said, if the proposal is in both kanji and kana (Japanese characters) and English, then the reader can switch and use the dictionary whenever there's a stumbling block.

- *Identify an advocate inside the organization.* This is a person who, within the limits of his or her own responsibilities and obligations, can show you the road you need to follow, pitfalls, amounts to ask for, the decision points that must be passed, who will make the decisions, and what particular facts the proposal should include. This is important in any solicitation, but particularly in Asia, where protocols and channels of communication may be opaque.

- *Develop trust with your donor.* In the process of any solicitation, trust is one of the fund raiser's most valuable assets. Never betray it. This is especially true in dealing with foreign organizations and their staff. For instance, the participation of the inside advocate also involves trust and places on the university staff the obligation of the utmost discretion. The advocate may provide useful information that would be embarrassing if widely shared, or ask a favor, such as arranging for a corporate scientist to meet with a faculty member, which is important to honor. Although such a scientist-to-scientist visit would normally be routine, a quick response and attention to detail may be critically important in an Asian solicitation.

- *Do not let your advocate "lose face."* This is a loss of credibility and trust, and even routine transactions can cause difficulty. For instance, international corporations frequently make pledge payments by means of a wire transfer. The money arrives without adequate identification as to its destination and languishes in a pending fund. Time passes and university accounting sends a dunning letter. This embarrasses the corporate staff in charge of the payment, and embarrasses the university, which obviously does not know what is happening in its accounts. Here quick letters of apology can save the day and restore trust.

- *Communicate, communicate, communicate.* Avoid misunderstandings at all costs, both internal and external. In most countries, when money changes hands, there is a quid pro quo of some kind, tangible or intangible. Very few people, Americans or foreigners, really understand philanthropy and its processes and consequences as they are defined in the United States. Do not assume anything. The person who nods when you talk about giving an endowed fellowship may not have the foggiest idea of how these work and will immediately assume it guarantees admission for relatives or promising employees. If the gift is given with these misunderstandings, it is almost impossible to set things right.

- *Be flexible.* Be willing to take a few risks in search of flexibility to adapt to a donor's internal needs, as long as they are consistent with the institution's policy. Do not distort the legitimate philanthropic process, which can be applied to other donors, and fail to meet ethical and legal standards.

- *Remember that, with all the differences, in many ways foreign fund raising parallels fund raising in the United States.* However, be prepared to help a willing donor understand the rules. For instance, it may be better from a corporate financial standpoint to make a gift from a U.S. subsidiary than from the parent company in Japan. Similarly, a foreign foundation may not understand how an endowed professorship works, and request periodic expenditure reports appropriate for research projects but impossible for senior faculty.

- *Maintain the contacts made in the past.* University senior executives change periodically, often more rapidly than their counterparts in Asian corporations. Development staffs need to urge presidents, deans, and department heads to nourish the contacts originated by their predecessors. Continuity and travels to the home country are important.

- *Showcase success stories and learn from failure.* Failures have their value too, and there were more of these than one likes to admit. It was easy when the potential donor said no. The problems occurred with apparently successful solicitations that encountered difficulties in midstream. Most had characteristics in common that should have raised a warning flag. These difficulties should not be an iron-clad reason for not going forward, but rather a warning to manage expectations and limit the commitment of the recipient institution until the gift is complete.

  Here are some common aspects of solicitations that did not turn out as expected:

  —*The donor or donor institution had relatively few antecedents with the recipient institution.* When this occurs, the donor's familiarity with the recipient institution is slight, which greatly magnifies the chances of misunderstanding. The motivation for giving is likely to have little real philanthropic intent, and is therefore easily deflected by anything from adverse publicity to a change in interests. Because of distance, it is hard to find out what is going on and make timely corrections.

  —*The person advocating the gift is a senior corporate executive but not a major stockholder and not so senior that decisions cannot be reversed.* Corporate gifts of this kind seem welcome at first. They tend to be straightforward. There is good communication with the executive, who understands the recipient institution. However, the senior management group within the company may acquiesce in approving the gift but not fully support or understand it. If there is a change in status (the executive's division may have a period of unprofitability, for instance) or a shift in the economy, the company will stop payments.

  —*The gift is contingent—given with an implicit understanding that the recipient institution has some kind of special performance obligation, however slight.* Many legitimate gifts have a purpose that requires the recipient institution to do something, such as establish and name an endowed scholarship, fellowship, or professorship. Usually these are directly in line with the organization's mission and relieve the operating budget. But some meritorious projects may require a commitment of institutional money as well as gift money. The awkward situation occurs when the donor requires the institution to do something, such as appoint a professor to an endowed chair, before the payments will be forthcoming.

  —*The pledge payment period is sufficiently long to be vulnerable to unexpected changes.* If the gift is offered with an unusually long pledge payment schedule, the risk is increased. The payments may become burdensome, the donor's circumstances may change, or, occasionally, the recipient institution's priorities may evolve. It is far better to direct the donor toward a smaller, completed gift than to wind up with a large, unfulfilled pledge.

  —*The gift is offered in honor of a prominent person or cause, and successful completion depends on gifts from many donors.* Horror stories abound about the universally revered professor for whom the reverence does not reach as far as the alumnus's pocketbook. Be wary of projects involving too many donors or institutions. Be especially wary if the project is in honor of a cause or person, however noble. Projects like these are difficult in the United States and impossible to manage overseas. If interest and enthusiasm begin to wane, governments reorganize, or the economy declines, the gift will not be completed.

- *Have fun.* International fund raising is both grueling and exhausting, but in the end, it brings enormous satisfaction to the development staff, the donor, and the institution. None of the work will be successful if fun is not part of the experience.

Suggested Readings

Directory of Corporate Affiliations, Who Owns Whom. National Register Publishing, 1999.
Far Eastern Economic Review by Economic Review.
Industrial Groupings in Japan—The Anatomy of the "Keiretsu." Dodwell Marketing Consultants, 1996.
Japan Company Datafile. Toyo Keizai Inc., 1992.
Japan Company Handbook. Toyo Keizai Inc. Summer 1999.

PART VII Support Ingredients

46 Fund-raising Consultants

HENRY GOLDSTEIN, CFRE
The Oram Group, Inc.

46.1 When to Use a Consultant

Among the most important decisions a not-for-profit makes is whether to work with a fund-raising consultant. A firm or an individual might be initially employed for the following reasons:

- The nature of the fund-raising project is beyond the organization's experience. *Example:* A human services agency wants to expand into its own building and will have to raise $3 million in a capital campaign. No one on the board or staff has ever been involved in this type of campaign.
- The staff is technically inexperienced or cannot undertake additional work. *Example:* One member of the development staff has conducted a capital campaign previously but feels her effort should be devoted to annual giving and government grants, which produce the bulk of the organization's annual income. She does not think it wise to be diverted from this top priority.
- The feasibility and prospects of fund-raising success are uncertain or undetermined; an objective analysis is desired. *Example:* The board is not convinced a capital campaign can produce $3 million. Having never been involved in a capital campaign, the development committee strongly feels an objective study of community attitudes, the case for philanthropic support, likely campaign leadership, and potential major gifts should be undertaken to ascertain the prospects for success.

- A specific fund-raising task is to be accomplished. *Example:* Having determined to run a capital campaign in-house, the development director has decided to use a consultant to prepare the case statement, train the solicitors, and provide strategic advice.

46.2 The Fund-raising Assignment

The decision to retain a consultant should rest on a clear understanding of the fund-raising assignment, why a consultant is sought, who in the not-for-profit board or staff structure wants (or does not want) a consultant, and realistic expectations. Whether a not-for-profit is large or small, and irrespective of the size of the development office, a consultant supplements but does not replace (except temporarily) its resources. The board and staff members involved must agree that this option is worthwhile and workable. The selection process often provides clarity.

Fund-raising consultants offer an array of services:

Alumni giving	List brokerage
Annual giving	List management
Board development	Planned giving programs
Capital campaign counsel	Printed materials
Capital campaign management	Proposal writing
Case development	Public relations
Computer systems, hardware and software	Recruitment of fund-raising executives
Corporate campaigns	Research
Direct mail	Special events
Endowment campaign counsel	Strategic planning
Endowment campaign management	Telemarketing
Foundation grants	Training for board and staff
Feasibility studies and surveys	Video production
Government funding	

Like other professionals, some are generalists; others concentrate on specific areas. An agency should select only those services that are required.

A consultant may see an assignment differently from the client. For example, suppose a not-for-profit wants to raise endowment funds but is a new organization with a very small donor base. The consultant may advise that endowment funds are generated internally and recommends developing a board-based annual giving program directed primarily to individuals and family foundations.

46.3 Initiating a Search

In most not-for-profits, hiring a consultant is a committee affair. Four to six people, staff and board, should be sufficient to encompass a variety of opinions and concerns. A typical group includes the chief executive, a board officer or two, the development director, and perhaps a major donor or someone else with a specific interest in fund raising.

Successful fund raising depends on involvement. Choosing a consultant is educational for volunteers and staff, especially when a campaign, or employment of an outsider, is a new experience.

(A) WHAT THE CONSULTANT NEEDS TO KNOW ABOUT POTENTIAL CLIENTS

To acquaint the consultant with the organization, the staff should prepare an information packet. The first enclosure, a short paper of no more than a few pages, should describe the fund-raising program. Most consultants will depend on it to gauge the organization's potential and their interest in accepting employment. Some organizations that are familiar with the governmental grant and contract process issue formal requests for proposals (RFPs). However, consultants are often reluctant to respond to an RFP from an unknown organization unless it is preceded, or followed up, by personal contact. General information—a brochure or fund-raising materials—a board list (including the members' business affiliations), a recent audit, and other financial information should be added to complete the packet delivered to a prospective consultant.

(B) FINDING CONSULTANTS

In conducting a search for the right consultant, the initial objective should be to identify three to five consultants, who will be invited to personal interviews with the hiring committee. Individual consultants, small firms, and industry leaders might all be considered. A mixed group is a good idea, so that committee members can observe their differences in style, perspective, and experience.

The best source for finding a consultant is word of mouth. The board and staff, other not-for-profits in the same field, and sources in the geographic area and among professional colleagues should all be asked for names and a critique of services. The assignment and the services sought should be specifically detailed.

Second, the American Association of Fund-Raising Counsel (AAFRC), the Association of Fundraising Professionals (AFP), and the Association of Healthcare Philanthropy (AHP) will provide lists of firms that offer services in various locales. The AAFRC is a trade association of consulting firms; the AFP and AHP enroll individual fund raisers. All set ethical fund-raising standards to which their members agree to adhere. Contact information for these organizations follows.

American Association of Fund-Raising Counsel
10293 Meridian St., Suite 175
Indianapolis, IN 46290
317-816-1313 Fax: 317-816-1633
1-800-462-2392
www.aafrc.org
Michael Ward, Executive Director

Association for Healthcare Philanthropy
313 Park Avenue, Suite 400
Falls Church, VA 22046
703-532-6243 Fax: 703-532-7170
Dr. William C. McGinly, President
www.go.ahp.org

Association of Fundraising Professionals
1101 King Street
Alexandria, VA 22314
703-684-0410 Fax: 703-684-0540
Ms. Paulette Maehara
www.nsfre.org

Not all major firms belong to AAFRC. Those reputable firms who choose not to belong accept the same ethical standards as those who do. Others offer services so specialized they do not qualify for membership. Many small firms and part-time consultants do not belong to AAFRC.

Not all individual professionals belong to AFP, but experienced people with a track record accept and abide by AFP's ethical standards.

The third step is to scan the trade press. Consultants advertise and often write for the trades. The principal media are *Nonprofit Times, The Chronicle of Philanthropy, Foundation News, AFP Journal, Giving USA,* and *Fundraising Management.*

Consultants advertise in the yellow pages as well. However, letting "your fingers do the walking" is chancy. The publishers' occupational classifications include under "Fund Raising" a mix of businesses whose relationship to fund-raising consulting is distant at best.

(C) CONTACTING POTENTIAL CONSULTANTS

A starting list of 10, or even 15, consultants is a good field. The rest of this chapter assumes that the hiring committee has provided its list and asked you to "take it from there." You can write to each name on the list, enclosing the information packet. On the other hand, unless you are experienced, you are learning nothing about the consultants and, of course, you have to wait for their responses.

Most development people agree that the feedback provided by an introductory telephone call is very useful for both parties. Your gut reaction may well be "These people sound as if we may be able to work together," or it may be "This is not a fit." The consultant may have exactly the same reaction to you.

The first few telephone calls can sharpen your presentation to others on the list. Keep a record of your first impressions. When you send a cover letter and an information packet, include a deadline for responses.

The following dos are especially recommended:

Do

- *Ask to speak to the top person.* Even in large firms, you will find that the chief executive officer is happy to talk to a prospective client. If you cannot reach him or her, ask for the next person in rank. The firm's decision to take you on as a client is made at the top, not the bottom.
- *Be as specific as possible.* You will be asked how much money you hope to raise, how large your organization is (in staff and budget), how long you have been in

business, and so on. Even though these details are covered in the information packet, the exchange is important in classifying your circumstances.

- *Ask whether the consultant's experience fits your needs.* A quick rundown of the consultant's experience, size of operation, other clients served, one or two local references, the range of fees, who might be assigned to your account, and length of time in business, is basic.
- *Ask for a brief written response, a list of the consultant's current and recent clients, and information about the firm.* Many consultants are employed full time by not-for-profits but their arrangements permit outside consulting. Be sure that the consultant (unless an independent) has such permission and that the scope of your assignment will fit the consultant's availability and competence.

Do Not

- *Expect a consultant to submit a formal proposal on the basis of a phone call or a letter.* The preparation of a proposal is time-consuming and, without fairly detailed information, meaningless. Most consultants will not do it.
- *Expect a consultant to set a fee over the telephone.* It is reasonable to discuss fees, and it is helpful to both parties if this discussion takes place up front. Consultants will respond to a preliminary question about fees, usually by providing a range of fees for the services offered. This should suffice for immediate comparative purposes.
- *Expect a consultant to respond well to an unrealistic deadline.* A request for detailed information, even if well short of a formal proposal, still takes time to prepare properly. The more you expect, the longer the time. For instance, a routine request for a brochure and a client list can be attended to immediately. For a more complete response, which considers the uniqueness of a given situation, allow at least two weeks, longer if convenient.

46.4 Selecting a Consultant

Having developed a list of possibilities, it is now time to make the initial cuts. You, your chief executive, and the chair of the selection committee should shorten the list to no more than five consultants who will be invited to personal interviews.

Some organizations like to meet consultants informally before inviting three finalists to meet with the full committee; others prefer different courses. The interaction between the parties is the most important aspect of the relationship to come. Therefore, the interview is critical.

Consultants normally do not charge a fee for an initial consultation, or even two. In most instances, the consultant's expenses incidental to the selection process are absorbed. A person based in your city incurs little expense in visiting your premises.

However, long distances pose a problem. Consultants have differing policies on speculative travel. Some will travel at no apparent expense to the potential client: Expenses are recouped later, as an overhead factor in the fees charged all clients. Others ask for reimbursement. Still others judge how much they want the client and act accordingly. As an example, a southern college in a small city called three national firms and sent information. Each firm was invited to travel many hundreds of miles at its own expense to a destination that has spotty airline service. For each, the round trip represented the better part of two billable days' time. Each consultant was to be allotted 30 minutes to appear before the trustees' development committee. Given this situation, two firms agreed to appear; the other declined.

(A) HOW TO CONDUCT AN INTERVIEW

Allow at least 60 minutes for each interview. A 15- or 20-minute break between interviews gives everyone a chance to relax and permits a bit of feedback. It is also a courtesy to the consultants not to have them stacked up like air traffic over O'Hare.

Ideally, the full selection committee will participate. However, not every person can attend every meeting. If consultants are coming a distance and repeat visits are therefore impractical, an extra effort should be made to ensure that everyone attends.

The atmosphere should be purposeful but relaxed enough to permit lively exchange among the participants. The easy way to begin is to invite the consultant to describe his or her background, the firm's experience, and why it should be selected for the assignment. The consultant should also be encouraged to ask questions of the committee.

Next, zero in on the specifics related to the assignment, and close by asking the consultant if he or she is interested in offering a written proposal.

(B) EIGHT CRITICAL QUESTIONS TO ASK A CONSULTANT

Here are eight specific questions to be sure to ask:

1. How long have you been in business?
2. Who in the firm will work on our account, and who will supervise?
3. How are you specifically qualified to handle this assignment?
4. What is your fee?
5. What is your estimate of reimbursable expenses?
6. How long will it take to complete this work?
7. Who are your current and recent clients, especially those for whom you accomplished a similar task?
8. Why do you want to work for us?

(C) HOW TO READ A PROPOSAL

Although the formats vary, a proposal addresses nine elements. If all are included, and if at the end an acceptance clause, a place for an authorizing signature and a request for a retainer are included, the executed document is considered a binding agreement.

If no authorizing action is required on your part, the proposal is nonbinding. It is ultimately attached to a shorter, binding letter of agreement (sometimes called a letter of engagement). The nonbinding proposal is useful when one party or the other has not yet made a decision. Consultants may also submit nonbinding proposals when they feel they do not yet know enough about a potential client's requirements to commit themselves.

An agreement is effective when it is signed by both parties and the retainer is paid (usually the first month's fee or 25 percent to 33 percent of a project fee).

Elements of a Proposal or Letter of Engagement

1. *Presenting information.* The consultant's understanding of the work to be done.
2. *Basic agreement.* The work to be performed by the consultant to complete the assignment addressed in the proposal.
3. *Objectives of the assignment.* A description of each element to be considered. A feasibility study, for example, usually focuses on case, constituency, leadership, staffing, cost, and duration of a campaign.
4. *Methodology.* The techniques the consultant will use to complete the assignment. These may include a specified number of interviews among defined constituents, focus groups, analysis of records, plans and materials; or the completion of a specific task: a mailing, a special event, installation of a customized computer software program; a telemarketing test, and so on.
5. *Work product.* The deliverable: It may be a written report, a test analysis, or money in the bank.
6. *Timetable.* An estimate of the time required to complete the assignment, usually presented week by week, month by month, or quarterly.
7. *Personnel.* The consultant's staff to be assigned to your account. You may ask for bios to be included on the people to be assigned; the consultant may include a clause prohibiting you from offering employment to any of his or her staff members for a specified period of time.
8. *Fees and expenses.* In the fund-raising field, it is considered unethical for consultants to work on speculation or commission, or on a percentage of fees raised. Expect a fixed fee. Reimbursable out-of-pocket expenses include telephone, fax, travel, lodging, and other than routine administrative expense, for example, reproduction of a lengthy report or extensive research. Expenses should be agreed upon in advance.
9. *References.* It is extremely important to insist on references and equally important to check them carefully. Current and former clients are the most helpful. References should be obtained by telephone; no one will say anything negative on paper. On the other hand, do not expect only accolades. Otherwise top-notch consultants occasionally do poorly, and not very good ones sometimes get lucky. Time after time, the principal reasons for client dissatisfaction are, first, the personality or, second, the competence of the staff assigned to the account.

In checking references, obtain the answers to these six key questions, and be sure to talk with someone who has direct, firsthand knowledge:

1. What services did the consultant perform?
2. Were you satisfied?
3. Who was assigned to your account?
4. Did you have regular access to a senior member of the consultant's staff?
5. Would you employ this consultant again?
6. What was the fee?

Staff and volunteers often see things differently. Include a few board members or other volunteers in checking references.

46.5   Fees, Expenses, Registration

Fees are a multiple of time and personnel and cover the consultant's salary costs, overhead, and profit margin. They are quoted on an hourly, daily, monthly, annual, or project basis.

There is nothing illegal about working on contingency, commission, or percentage. The professional associations discourage it, but the National Council of Better Business Bureaus holds that contingency fund raising might work to a not-for-profit's economic advantage. The debate has been going on for some time and is unlikely to be satisfactorily resolved anytime soon.

To new, small, impecunious not-for-profits, a contingency arrangement may look good. If you are tempted, check carefully with others who have tried it; the results have generally been poor.

(A)   WHAT IS A "FAIR" FEE?

Fund-raising consultants operate in a free market. Theoretically, they can charge whatever they wish—in fact, they are bound by competitive forces. The best way to determine whether a fee is "fair" is to ask others what they paid for the services they received, and to compare the fees various consultants propose. A low fee is not always the best choice, and a high fee does not ensure superior service.

(B)   EXPENSES

Unless an organization otherwise agrees, a consultant's out-of-pocket expenses are not included in the fee. It is possible for both parties to estimate out-of-pocket expenses in advance and to "cap" the agreement.

(C)   REGISTRATION

A thicket of state, and sometimes local, ordinances govern the relationship between consultants and clients. Whether an agreement must be registered with a government agency depends mainly on the jurisdiction and the services to be performed. Religious groups are generally exempt from all registration requirements.

46.6   Selection Process

Though it may not always be apparent, the selection process is a two-way street. Consultants turn down clients for a variety of reasons, and at any point in the selection process—up until a proposal or letter of engagement is signed by both parties, either side can walk away.

Among the reasons a consultant will turn down a potential client are the following:

- The client's mission, purpose, or methods of operation—though perfectly valid and legitimate—for one reason or another do not comport with the consultant's view of the world, his or her business plan, or strategy.
- The client does not fit the consultant's areas of specialization.
- The client is too small (or sometimes too big) for the consultant.
- The client's location is inconvenient for the consultant, an important consideration if extensive travel is required.
- The client and the consultant do not agree on a fee.
- The client makes demands or requests that the consultant believes are imprudent, impractical, or contrary to good professional practice. An example is a situation in which a client with a complex problem resists or refuses the recommendation for a planning or feasibility study, often because a board member objects.
- The chemistry is not right. No matter how careful or detailed the selection process, and no matter how good the references, a consultant-client relationship is basically an exchange of personalities, lifestyles, and professional (and often personal) confidences. The personal interview sometimes—but not always—reveals personal incompatibilities.

Experienced consultants know that client organizations possess distinct personalities and cultures. What they discern during the preliminaries is more often than not an indication of the relationship to follow.

46.7 A Happy Relationship

More than anything else, a productive relationship between a consultant and a client derives from mutual respect, shared vision, open communication, and hard work all around.

If the client-consultant relationship is working well, you will perhaps wonder why you need a written agreement. If it is not working well, a piece of paper will not save it.

47 ▼ Donor Recognition and Relations

Jerry A. Linzy, MA, AAHP
Jerold Panas, Linzy & Partners

47.1 Introduction

Thoughtful acts that are neither necessary nor expected add immeasurably to the quality of a person's life. Giving may be its own reward, but a thoughtfully conceived, donor-focused recognition program is indispensable in any not-for-profit's development program. Donor recognition builds relationships, encourages involvement, and positions the organization for future and larger gifts from donors. It is at the heart of donor relations and the cultivation process.

Donor recognition takes many forms. It can be a named building or scholarship to honor a donor. It can be a name on a plaque on a wall or a letter from the president of the organization or a personal note from an individual who benefits from the donor's philanthropy. These are important ways to recognize a donor's charitable gift, but the most important acknowledgment is that which is personal and appropriate. Recognition is determined to be appropriate through a combination of personal relationships, research, and involvement with the organization.

It is true that many donors do not want their gifts to be recognized, but it is often a challenge to distinguish between those who do want and those who *really* do not. Jerold Panas says: "I believe it is much wiser to err on the side of giving recognition. Done with a quiet flair, a certain style. But recognition."[1]

47.2 Development of Gift Recognition Policies and Procedures

The recognition of charitable gifts as an element of donor relations is vital to an organization's ability to attract continuing support. It is of such importance that policies and

---

[1]Jerold Panas, *Mega Gifts* (Chicago: Precept Press, 1984), p. 54.

procedures should be developed by staff and approved by management and trustees after thorough review. Understanding and knowledge of the program is essential for the development team. These policies and procedures should include the following:

- *Gift acknowledgments.* Describe the kinds of letters to be sent, who signs, and whether the letter should be handwritten or computer generated.
- *Memorial giving program.* Describe the kinds of acknowledgments and memorial cards and incorporate a message of sympathy from the institution. If applicable, describe the use of plaques or whatever is appropriate for a "memorial" area of the organization.
- *Donor recognition.* Describe policies for named gifts, gifts of buildings or floors, levels of giving, and gift opportunities for equipment or special programs.
- *Recognition wall design.* Describe wall displays and/or donor recognition areas within the facility. Incorporate photographs indicating levels of giving and recognition.
- *Giving clubs.* Describe the various kinds of giving clubs—accumulative, annual, or planned gift programs. Incorporate gift amounts, benefits, and the case for each giving club.
- *What constitutes a gift.* Describe what the organization deems to be a recognition gift: gifts of cash, gifts-in-kind, life insurance, other nonrevocable planned gifts, bequests, and pledges.

Remember, in developing policies and procedures, the donor recognition program has a twofold purpose. First, it is to thank a donor for a gift. Second, it is to encourage the donor to upgrade giving to higher levels. The program should be designed to accomplish this goal.

47.3 *Donor Recognition and Donor Relations*

One need only look at the names on buildings that adorn a college or hospital campus to have a sense of how important donor recognition is. Jerry Panas writes, "History has recorded few truly anonymous gifts. Most benefactors, who pretend to be anonymous, hide after conferring a gift, like Virgil's Galatea. She fled, but only after first making very certain that she had been seen by everyone."[2]

Donor recognition takes many forms. (See Exhibit 47.1 for a sample from a nonprofit.) In the organization's donor relations program, recognition is more focused on the needs of the donor and the cultivation process than the response after the gift is made, though it is all part of the continuum in seeking a donor's ultimate gift. The key in this process is to devote a significant amount of time and attention to donors and prospective donors.

James L. Bowers, former president of the Scripps Memorial Hospital Foundation, talks about the process following a successful $100 million campaign in an article in the *Chronicle of Philanthropy.* "We've been able to devote a lot of time to our donors. If we've been successful here, I think one thing has helped us: the fact that we really pay attention to our donors. And I don't mean sending a thank-you note."

---

[2]*Ibid.*, p. 53.

EXHIBIT 47.1 Sample Recognition Program and Policy

RATIONALE

The importance of voluntary contributions to Women's College Hospital has become increasingly apparent throughout the past decade, and Women's College Hospital Foundation stands as a vehicle through which the community participates in the strength and excellence of its hospital.

It is a policy of Women's College Hospital Foundation, in conjunction with Women's College Hospital Board, that plaques will not be placed throughout the hospital and that, for the following reasons, a donor recognition program is established to replace the former practice of attaching plaques to all donated capital items:

1. Equipment becomes obsolete and is discarded, and rooms that are set aside for one purpose sooner or later end up being used for something else. Plaques are often thrown out, sold while attached to old equipment, or removed and set aside during renovations and, consequently, lost. The length of time a plaque serves as a special indication of honor is limited. If the equipment or designated area becomes old and run down, it no longer associates the donor's name with something that would evoke the feelings of pride and dignity as originally intended.
2. Often contributions that are very worthy of recognition are not noticed if a plaquing system is used; for example, when plaques are affixed to expensive operating rooms or diagnostic equipment, patients rarely have an opportunity to see them and therefore, to appreciate the donor's generosity.
3. Plaques tend to compete with each other for space and visibility and to lack consistency of format.
4. Plaquing research gifts is difficult, and research donors tend to receive less recognition.

As a result of its nonplaquing policy, Women's College Hospital Foundation has created a display, in a highly visible location, of all the old plaques that could be collected and salvaged from the rest of the facility.

WHO IS HONORED?

The donor recognition policy is in place to honor all individuals, corporations, service clubs, community organizations, and philanthropic foundations that make monetary and/or gift-in-kind donations to Women's College Hospital. Donations made in memory recognize, with honor, the name of a loved one who has died.

WHAT CONSTITUTES A DONATION?

The donor recognition policy of Women's College Hospital Foundation deems the following as recognizable gifts to the institution:

1. **Gifts of cash.**
2. **Gifts-in-kind.** Fair market value.
3. **Life insurance.** The donor of a life insurance gift is recognized for the amount of the policy payments as they accumulate until the policy is paid (where the policy has been placed in the name of the institution). Once the insurance policy is paid in full, the donor is recognized for the entire value of the life insurance.
4. **Other nonrevocable planned gifts.** A planned gift, usually considered to be a gift from capital rather than from income, is recognized for the value of the gift on the day that it is legally transferred to Women's College Hospital or Women's College Hospital Foundation, providing the terms of the Planned Gift contract identify it as a nonrevocable gift.
5. **Bequests.** A bequest is recognized when it is received, not at the time it is described in the will of a prospective donor. Donors who wish to receive recognition for bequest-type contributions are encouraged to establish a nonrevocable trust or some other form of nonrevocable planned gift.

EXHIBIT 47.1 (Continued)

6. **Pledges.** A pledge is recognized for its annual payment amount only. The total amount pledged is recognized in the year that the final payment is received.

All recognition is cumulative over the lifetime of a donor in the categories described in the following section.

RECOGNITION CATEGORIES

1. **Friend** ($10 to $999)
   All donors receive a personalized thank-you letter with an income tax receipt and are placed on the hospital's mailing list to receive publications and other public relations materials. Their names are listed, by category, in the annual report of the Foundation.

2. **Companion** ($1,000 to $9,999)
   Donors in this category have their names displayed in a large leather-bound volume situated in the hospital's lobby.
   They are invited to attend an annual meeting event.
   For donors in this category, the notation in the Book of Honor will be limited to (a) the name of the donor, (b) "In Honor" wording as follows, or (c) "In Memory" wording as follows:
   In Honor/Memory of   from family and friends, or
   In Honor/Memory of   from friends & wife,   , and children,   .

3. **Benefactors** ($10,000 to $24,999)
   These donors' names will be displayed on the wall in the donor recognition garden. Their names will also be listed in the Book of Honor, according to category, and, at the discretion of the Foundation, a favorite quotation or verse of up to two lines is permitted in addition to:
   • The name of the donor
   • Whether or not the gift is from an estate or in memory
   • The names of other family members who might also be donors if the gift is in memory from several sources
   • The purpose for which the gift was made, if applicable
   In respect to wording on the donor recognition display, the following choices have been approved:
   In Honor/In Memory of _____
   From the estate of _____
   Donors name (donor's choice)
   Donors may choose whether they wish to appear as, for example, Mr. John Donor, John Donor, J.B. Donor, or Jake Donor.
   All donors of $10,000+ are invited to attend an annual President's Circle dinner to receive recognition for their outstanding support.

4. **Associate** ($25,000 to $49,999)
5. **Builder** ($50,000 to $99,999)
6. **Partner** ($100,000 to $499,999)
7. **Patrons** ($500,000 to $1,000,000)
8. **Founder** (over $1,000,000)
   Donors of more than $1 million may be offered the opportunity of having an area of the facility named in their honor at the discretion of the Foundation Board and with approval by the hospital board.
   The Donor Recognition medium is constructed in such a way that donor's names are removed from one category and placed in a different category as their contributions accumulate.

The article continues: "Mr. Bowers keeps in close touch with prospects. He sends them postcards from his business and vacation travels. He gives them flowers to mark special occasions like birthdays and anniversaries. He makes phone calls to congratulate them on big events that have nothing to do with the hospital. Looking for ways to underscore friendships with donors rather than financial ties, he also sends them newspaper clippings and other small mementos related to their hobbies and other interests, as well as invitations to social events not connected with Scripps that he thinks they might enjoy."[3]

Clearly, recognition of the donor or prospect as a person is as vital as the donor recognition that follows. Recognition of the donor, regardless of the method, should be tailored to the individual, corporation, or foundation.

According to Dr. Bowers, the essential steps in his donor solicitation process include:

- Casting a wide net to find as many people as possible who might be willing to make a large gift.
- Conducting extensive background research to determine a prospect's financial ability to make a large contribution, as well as his or her attitude toward the organization.
- Winnowing the list of prospects so that fund raisers can devote sufficient attention to each likely donor.
- Drawing up a timetable for making initial contacts with prospects.
- Determining the best strategies, based on the background research, to get leading potential donors more involved in the organization and committed to it.
- Delivering regular reports to colleagues to get advice and make certain that goals for meeting with prospects are being met.
- Updating the list of top prospects and maintaining records of contacts with them.
- Continuing contacts with the top prospects.
- Making the request for a major gift.

This process also provides information to the Donor Recognition Program, enabling the development staff to match a recognition program with the donor's personal interests and personality. It is important to understand that the development process is an integrated system. Each element of the fund-raising program supports other elements, culminating in gifts and building a relationship that will continue for the life of the donor and, done properly, continuing with future generations of the donor's family.

47.4 Use of Donor Preference Surveys

The hope underlying a donor recognition program is that the satisfaction it offers donors is more attractive than that provided by other programs. The best source for determining those factors that will enhance attractiveness are the donors themselves.

A good way to assess donors' preferences for recognition is to use a donor preference survey. (See Exhibit 47.2.) Many of the design issues—such as whether to use metal

---

[3]Holly Hunter, "These Fund Raisers Think Big," *Chronicle of Philanthropy*, March 24, 1992, pp. 18–21.

or glass, photos or engravings, systems that are highly integrated into the overall architectural design or that are more recognizable because they differ from the interior design of a building—are matters of taste and judgment and are best assessed using quantitative research methods such as focus groups. Written surveys can accurately gauge a donor's response to donor club benefits, such as services or premiums provided by the organization.

Jerold Panas, Linzy & Partners, Inc. has conducted a number of donor preference surveys and has found that such surveys have two effects. First, by comparing the responses of trustees and other leaders to the larger donor groups, it can be established that often there are very different expectations for recognition outside the leadership group, and it is these expectations that should drive planning. After all, recognition is used to nurture donative relationships already established with trustees. This new understanding can be very valuable in eliminating constraints and planning for effective donor recognition.

The second and more practical effect of surveying donors in regard to recognition is that planners can be more effective by focusing limited resources on the recognition programs that are meaningful to donors. For instance, in one study the firm found that fewer than 10 percent of the members of a hospital foundation's donor club rated as "helpful and appreciated" the pocket calendar—a "sacred" donor benefit that had been expensive to provide. The resources it had required have now been redirected to providing health-related information in a regular series, a benefit much more attractive to donors.

In another instance, donors were segmented by donor club categories for the survey and asked if they would find permanent recognition in the lobby of the institution attractive. The more generous donors responded positively, and the less generous donors

---

EXHIBIT 47.2 Sample Donor Preference Survey

Founders Society membership is a most helpful and appreciated way to support (Institution). We would like your opinion of the benefits we offer in recognition of membership gifts. Founder Society members may decline these benefits. Please rate the attractiveness of each benefit, regardless of your Founders Society membership level (x or check).

Membership Benefit	The Benefit⇒	is great	is nice	doesn't excite me	should be dropped
Founders Society Donor Reception		3	2	1	0
Founders Society donor listing in our annual report		3	2	1	0
Associate Member pocket calendar		3	2	1	0
Challenging Members name plate in hospital's lobby		3	2	1	0
Challenging Members emergency medical information card		3	2	1	0
Sustaining Members personalized notecards		3	2	1	0
Benefactors Distinguished Service Award dinner		3	2	1	0

Source: Holly Hunter, "These Fund Raisers Think Big," Chronicle of Philanthropy, *March 24, 1992, pp. 18–21. Reprinted with permission.*

were even more positive. This finding led to the creation of a cumulative donor recognition system that recognized donors of smaller gifts who were consistent in their support. These donors were thereby able to enjoy a level of recognition usually reserved for people who give single, large gifts. The end result was a substantial growth in gifts, which encouraged donors to move from one category to the next.

47.5 Role of Donor Recognition in Building a Donor Base

Experience demonstrates that donors give to organizations they believe in. The more passionate a donor feels, the more likely the organization is to receive a gift. The more the organization knows about the donor's wishes and desires, the more likely it is to advance the donor from level to level.

When an organization finds and renews a donor, it gets more than a gift. It gets an advocate. Building the donor base is not merely for the purpose of creating more annual giving; it also has to do with marketing services, advocacy, capital campaigns, bequests, planned giving, and a great deal more.

A well-developed donor base is far more important than the net dollars it delivers in a given year. It is an extraordinarily stable, predictable source of income that goes on as long as the institution does a good job of prospecting and renewal. A donor recognition program is the cornerstone of this program.

A donor recognition program can be the means for developing a continuing relationship with the donor through greater awareness, knowledge, caring, involvement, and commitment.

The following are suggestions for building relationships with donors through recognition:

- *Give greater emphasis to the continuing relationship with the donor.* In all materials, there should be an indication of the number of years a donor has given continuously to the organization. This information should also be recorded in the annual report or any other publication that lists donors. Go even a step further. Display the number of years of continuous giving on the receipt, or whatever else is given to the donors. Include in the listing, for instance:

  Jerry A. Linzy—7

  [This indicates that Mr. Linzy has been a donor without interruption for seven years.]

  A curious phenomenon occurs when continuous giving is recognized consistently. If a donor gives continuously for three years, and the gift is properly recognized and appreciated, the donor will not break the chain of continuous giving. Begin to recognize continuous giving in the second year.
- *Recognize donors of $100 and more with a phone call.* Institute a program for recognizing donors of $100 and more with a personal call, in addition to sending a receipt and/or a letter of acknowledgment and appreciation.

  Such calls probably should come from the chief development officer. In some institutions, in which trustees meet monthly, a list of donors who have given since the last board meeting is distributed to board members so they can make the calls.

In many situations, it is appropriate for a secretary to call: "Ms. Generous, I'm just typing your receipt letter now, and I wanted to make absolutely certain that we have the name spelled exactly right. And I wanted you to know, too, how much all of us at our institution appreciate your gift. Our records say that this is your third year of giving, and that's great." The reaction to this sort of contact will be very positive.

- *Use the Rule of Seven.* Jerry Panas credits Mary G. Roebling, chair of the New Jersey Trust Company in Newark, for developing the concept of the "Rule of Seven."[4] It is as simple as it is powerful: Find a way to thank a donor seven times before asking for another gift; it works.

- *Write a personal note.* One cannot write enough personal notes. The busier the world becomes—the better the technology to mass-produce personal letters and the more voice mail and e-mail invade relationships—the more donors appreciate the personal touch of a handwritten note. All forms of communication are vital, and needed, but a handwritten note of thanks, praise, or even transmittal, can pay dividends.

- *Encourage participation in the life of the organization.* Make sure donors are invited to attend appropriate organizational functions, both public and private.

  An institution in Oregon has developed a small suite for use in the cultivation and recognition program. An invitation to a private meeting or meal in the suite is a coveted activity for many. This is an effective program.

- *Make sure that gift acknowledgment and recognition are timely.* It is important that gifts be acknowledged as quickly as possible—within 24 to 48 hours is recommended. Any recognition beyond the initial letter should also be timely. If there is a long period of time between the acceptance of a gift and the act of recognition, make sure the donor is kept informed with notes, phone calls, or a personal visit.

- *Leaders play an important role.* Both management and volunteer leadership must understand how important their respective roles are in recognizing individual contributions. Recognition can be in the form of a thank-you note, a smile, the presentation of an award, a pat on the back, or public praise. The involvement of leadership in recognizing the gifts and involvement of others is essential.

- *Confirm anonymity.* If a donor requests anonymity, make sure the request is confirmed. The donor may decide later that recognition is appropriate, or, in a capital campaign, the donor may decide that recognition of the gift will lead to gifts from others. Maintaining a relationship with the donor will make this process easier.

- *Always include the spouse.* Always assume that the donor's spouse is involved in the decision to make a gift; recognition of a gift should always include the spouse.

- *Accuracy is paramount.* Whatever the form of recognition, check for accuracy, then check again. Mistakes in spelling, facts, and so forth, are financially costly to correct and are embarrassing to the donor.

---

[4]Panas, *Mega Gifts,* p. 56.

47.6   Donor Recognition Club

Donor recognition clubs constitute a critical factor in the donor recognition process. Donor clubs can help you upgrade donors to higher levels of annual giving. Recognition can be given for annual giving and for cumulative contributions. Remember that donor clubs should be promoted assertively to encourage giving upfront as well as recognition after the gift.

Exhibit 47.3 offers examples of the elements of donor recognition clubs.

47.7   Donor Recognition and the Future

It is safe to say that change is unrelenting in America. Information, technology, health-care reform, tuition costs in higher education, aid to the poor—all are undergoing constant transformation. Moreover, problems are growing faster than they can be answered. The demand for philanthropy has never been greater, and it will continue to grow apace. All not-for-profits are competing for dollars and donors.

EXHIBIT 47.3 Sample List of Donor Club Annual Giving Benefits and Privileges

Gift Amount	Club Name	Benefits and Privileges
$100	Circle of Champions	Quarterly newsletter Annual report Invitations to benefit events
$500	Ambassadors	All of the above *plus:* Name listed in annual report donor roster
$1,000	Friends	All of the above *plus:* Name added to main Donor Wall VIP identification card with 10 percent discount in gift shop Invitation to annual meeting
$2,500	Sponsors	All of the above *plus:* Name added to Sponsors' plaque at main entrance Invitation to annual recognition luncheon Subscription to *President's Letter*
$5,000	Patrons and Life Members	All of the above *plus:* Name added to Life Member plaque at main entrance Two tickets to annual black-tie ball Personal gift

Multiple gifts within the same year will be counted together in order to qualify the donor at the highest level of donor privileges achieved through cumulative giving. The donor will be honored throughout the year following this cumulative total.

Source: James M. Greenfield, Fund Raising Fundamentals *(New York: John Wiley & Sons, Inc., 1994), p. 194. Reprinted by permission of John Wiley & Sons, Inc.*

The cost of donor acquisition continues to increase dramatically; to renew a donor is much less expensive. It makes good dollars and "sense" to sustain current donors through recognition and cultivation. Moreover, effective donor recognition and cultivation can position an organization to receive a donor's ultimate gift along with many other gifts from the first to the last. Fund raising today is increasingly focused on large gifts. There is every reason to believe this focus will continue to be emphasized. Knowing that most donors do not make a major gift to an organization as a first gift, the recognition process provides the direction and impetus to higher levels of giving.

For the process to be successful, the organization in its entirety must be involved. The chief development officer must lead its management, staff, and trustees through a process of education to ensure understanding of the recognition program and its consequence to the organization's future.

Building relationships, board involvement, and leadership are required. Accord and acclaim, thoughtfulness, and a continuing appreciation that donors are individuals, not numbers, form the foundation of donor recognition. As long as an organization is as donor-focused as it is mission-focused, success will follow.

48 ▼ Technology Applications

TOM GAFFNY
Vice President and Senior Creative Director
Epsilon

48.1 Introduction

In the next year alone, the American public will be inundated with more than 60 billion (yes, billion) letters and catalogs from not-for-profit organizations. The typical donor to an organization will personally receive more than 900 of these letters and solicitations. These numbers are witness to the fact that the critical mission of raising money through the mail is getting tougher. The sheer volume of direct mail increased more than 70 percent during this decade.

The simple truth of the matter is that direct mail fund raising is more competitive, and in many ways, more difficult, today than at any other time in history. However, thanks to a massive wave of innovations in technology, fund raisers are now entering an age of extraordinary new opportunity, one that dwarfs their potential for success of 10, or even five, years ago.

This chapter examines these extraordinary changes in technology and shows how leveraging these innovations can dramatically increase an organization's fund-raising success, even in today's highly competitive marketplace.

48.2 Importance of One-to-One Communication

Mind-boggling statistics about mail volume aside, direct mail fund raising is not a mass marketing discipline but rather a one-to-one form of communication. The ultimate key to any fund-raising program rests not in mailing more, but in the ability to target the right person, with the right message, at the right time. Or, put another way, the key is to have one-to-one conversations with the people who most care about you, with the specific message they most want to hear, at the time they most want to hear it.

This may sound almost impossible, but the great news is that reaching the right person with the right message at the absolutely right time has never been more possible. Furthermore, such contact has never been more profitable for the charity that can master it.

Exhibit 48.1 illustrates the massive changes in technology that make this right person/right time paradigm a practical reality today. As this exhibit demonstrates, direct marketing has undergone a technological revolution in six key disciplines these last five years.

What do these changes mean? Consider a real-life example that shows what these technological innovations mean to today's fund raiser. Suppose, for instance, that you were the chief fund-raising officer for a disaster relief organization in California. Suddenly, a massive earthquake strikes Los Angeles, severely stretching your organization's resources to the limit. You desperately need to send out a fund-raising appeal right away. What happens next?

The following sections of this chapter describe how your task of reaching the right people, with the right message, at the right time would have unfolded in the old days (as recently as the early 1990's) and how it can be accomplished today.

48.3 Getting an Emergency Appeal in the Mail— "The Old Days"

(A) REACHING THE RIGHT PEOPLE

The first priority for any fund raiser is to determine who should get your mailing and then to extract those names in order to generate a mailing.

First, you would sit down at a personal computer right on your desk and begin to select, one by one, the specific segments you felt would react best to your appeal. For instance, you would ask your personal computer to give you the names of all major donors of the last 12 months, or all donors to earthquake appeals of the last 24 months, or another such grouping.

EXHIBIT 48.1 Key Disciplines in Direct Marketing

1. **Data Processing:** An organization's ability to collect, consolidate, and update data about its donors
2. **Data Access:** The ability to access the data in a file quickly in order to make informed judgments about the past and the best decisions about the future
3. **Analytic Tools:** The ability to break down large chunks of data and transform it into relevant pieces of actionable marketing information
4. **Segmentation:** The ability to go beyond mass marketing and instead target "groups," and even individual names, in a file for separate and distinct treatment.
5. **Design:** The ability to create a mailing piece that is sent to donors and prospects
6. **Forms and Imaging:** The ability to transform a design into a final product that can be mailed to donors and prospects—on time, on budget, and on target.

Second, after you had carefully selected each segment one by one, you would then very quickly be able to rank these audiences according to which you felt would respond best, determine counts for each segment, and finally determine exactly how many names you would like to communicate with them.

This process sounds easy, but, unfortunately, just seven to ten years ago this kind of carefully targeted, at-your-fingertips selection process was not possible. As little as seven years ago instant access to the data and information on your mainframe computer was impossible. Crafting select language and then running reports to determine audience selection used to take a minimum of a day, often as many as three days. Furthermore, after you had spent all that time crunching data and determining total available names by each segment, you might realize that there were now fewer names than you needed to mail—or more names than you could afford to contact. This meant that you had to refine the select language, run the reports—in other words, go back to the drawing board—all of which took a few more days.

The plain truth is, as recently as the early stages of last decade, it was almost impossible for most organizations to quickly select and extract a finely targeted audience from their mainframe computer. Because of this problem, one of two things usually happened to fund raisers faced with an emergency marketing challenge like that described earlier.

1. Some organizations ended up spending an entire week on the process of defining a target audience and extracting a file for their mailings. This procedure guaranteed that the appeal would be delivered much later than the optimal timing.
2. Other organizations chose to "mail to everybody" in the hope that they would reach the audiences that really counted. These organizations ended up wasting valuable dollars on audiences that were not prime prospects for their appeal and missed the opportunity to mail a specially targeted request to the top prospects in their files.

(B) CRAFTING THE RIGHT MESSAGE

What should your mailing look like? What should it say? Assume you were fortunate enough, in the "old days," to have the world's greatest copywriter and designer in Los Angeles, eager to sink their teeth into this project. By the time the designer drew layouts by hand, revised the headlines and color to make sure everything was just right, and rushed the finished layouts off to a typesetter, a minimum of a day (more likely more time) has expired. Typesetting the finished mechanicals would take another day, minimum. As for getting forms that can be personalized, the industry standard is about three weeks, but for the sake of this example, suppose you were able to get forms within a week.

In short, even assuming that the creative ideas and copy were developed instantly, it would be 10 days minimum before you had materials to send to your donors—and you still would not have imaged the letters or taken them to the post office.

(C) GETTING THE MESSAGE TO DONORS AT THE RIGHT TIME

Suppose (still in the old days) that about 10 days after the earthquake, you had turned the world upside down, pulling a mailing file, creating a mailing, and getting all the materials in place. But you were still not finished. Depending on how complicated the personalized message to donors was, it would have taken three to six days to program your letter and image it on the forms. (That in itself would have been miraculous—the industry standard five years ago was about two weeks.) Mail services (inserting letters into envelopes, adding postage, and dropping them into the mail) would have added another three to five days.

In total, if everything happened like clockwork, and the rest of the world agreed to stand still while you rushed your mailing through the system, it would have taken only two and a half to three weeks to get your emergency appeal into the mail stream. An excellent result back then—but nothing compared to what you can do now.

48.4 Getting an Emergency Appeal in the Mail—Today

(A) REACHING THE RIGHT PEOPLE

With today's changes in technology, it has never been easier to process, analyze, and access data. Whereas seven years ago managers could only dream about sitting down in front of a PC and running simple English-language queries to target segments in their files, *now you can*.

How exactly does this system work? What are the advantages? The experience of a disaster relief organization can illustrate. When, recently, natural disaster struck, it needed to contact its donors immediately.

The moment word of this disaster reached the office, a staff member was able to sit down in front of a PC and begin the process of identifying potential donor audiences by entering simple English-language commands. Within minutes, he was given immediate reports from the mainframe that told exactly how many names were included in each of the 30 audience segments that had been defined for this mailing.

Within a few hours, after reviewing a myriad of different audience selection options, the organization was able to determine exactly who should get the appeal, how many names in total were involved, and which specific segments should get which mailing packages (three different kinds of appeals were chosen for this emergency campaign).

The result was that the organization was able to reach the people it wanted to reach, with the specific message and format that was most cost effective for each individual name. All this was accomplished without wasting a nickel contacting people in the donor file who were not good prospects for this appeal and while ordering the exact amounts of materials needed. (Remember, in the "old days," it was common for organizations to order too few forms or to waste money by ordering too many.)

(B) CREATING THE RIGHT MESSAGE

Recall, in the example of the "old days" when a fund raiser was fortunate enough to have the world's greatest copywriter and designer at the disaster site to develop the creative mailings? The same players can be there again today, but the way they would go about their work would be totally different and much faster.

For instance, nowadays the designer would never go through the painstaking and time-consuming task of drawing layouts by hand, revising them, and then shipping them off to headquarters for approval. Today's designers and copywriters create their output electronically on a Mac or a PC.

By utilizing today's electronic design technology, designers can create, revise, and revise again a detailed and complete layout within a matter of hours, sometimes even minutes. Moreover, these new designs are infinitely more complete than the hand-drawn layouts of the early to mid 1990's. Each shows the exact artwork, PMS colors, type sizes, fonts—everything.

Once a design is created, a designer can modem it from one PC to another, instantly. If any revisions are needed, they can be communicated and made over the computer in a matter of minutes, not hours.

The creation of the mechanical artwork for a printer has changed as well. Nowadays it takes only a few hours to transform an approved layout into a film negative, ready to be printed. The whole process seems to be—and actually is—light-years ahead of the "old" system. The result is that an organization can develop an idea, write copy, design layouts, revise layouts, and produce film for the printing of a form in less than two days.

(C)   GETTING THE MESSAGE TO DONORS AT THE RIGHT TIME

Suppose you are two-thirds of the way to getting an emergency appeal out the door and into the donors' hands. You have analyzed audience segments and selected exactly whom you want to receive your mailing. You have crafted a mailing package (or, more likely, two or three different packages in order to tailor the approach to different audiences), and shipped it off to the printer. Now the final hurdle: getting your great ideas into the mailbox as soon as possible.

Once again, current technology comes to the rescue. With today's high-speed imagers, it is now possible to fully image more than 375,000 letters on one printer in one day—considerably more than you could generate a few years ago on the industry-standard impact printer.

Faster output, however, is only one aspect of how technology has changed the letter production process. It is now possible to run plain white rolls of paper through a laser printer and print everything (photos, logos, large headlines, hand-printed fonts—everything) on both sides. This new technology gives the ability to generate millions of high-speed, high-quality, super-personalized letters on a blank sheet of paper, in the process providing unprecedented flexibility in how you can communicate to donors, and more quickly than anyone could have dreamed just a few years ago.

Clearly, the difference between seven to ten years ago and today is extraordinary. Exhibit 48.2, contrasts these two mailings (the emergency appeal of "before" vs. the emergency appeal of today) in a simple format. As this exhibit illustrates, today's technology has dramatically lessened the time it takes to contact donors, but the benefits go far beyond saving time. As described earlier, today's technology allows you to target an audience more specifically, craft a more individualized message, and package it more effectively.

48.5   Summary—The "Old Days" vs. Today

By any measurement criteria—the speed to process information, the ability to analyze and extract data, or the available options to communicate in unique and effective ways—today's fund raiser has opportunities that could scarcely be dreamed of a while back.

Clearly, technology has changed the face of direct mail fund raising in the twenty-first century. Of course, not every fund raiser is responsible for a domestic disaster relief

EXHIBIT 48.2 Advancements in Technology—The "Old Days" vs. Today

	5 Years Ago	Time Needed	Today	Time Needed
Data Processing	Large independent mainframes.	Days to process large files	Multi-parallel processing	Hours to process large files
Data Access	Off a mainframe.	24 hours or more	Off a PC	Instantly
Analytic Tools	Complicated queries, set of "standard reports."	24 hours or more	English-language queries, learn anything, any time	Instantly
Segmentation	Clusters showing recency, frequency, amount.	N/A	A segment of one	N/A
Package Design	Drawn by hand, very loose; all edits and changes must be completely re-done.	½ day to 2 days (assuming changes)	Designed by computer, shows everything; edits take minutes.	½ day (assuming changes)
Forms and Imaging	From drawings to mechanicals to forms to imaging. Everything Courier font, one side, one size fits all.	2–3 weeks	Can now image photos, fonts, graphics on blank sheet of paper. Unlimited fonts, duplex and vertical imaging.	2–3 days

organization. Here, then, are three real-world case studies, illustrating how today's new technology helped a not-for-profit meet a tough marketing challenge.

CASE STUDY: THE NATIONAL MULTIPLE SCLEROSIS SOCIETY

Background

The National Multiple Sclerosis Society is an organization dedicated to helping those with multiple sclerosis, a disease of the central nervous system that affects more than 300,000 Americans nationwide. Through its 88 chapters, the Society provides leadership in the quest to find the cause and cure of multiple sclerosis, as well as hands-on support at the local level in the form of equipment assistance, counseling, family assistance programs, and more.

The MS Society has achieved its greatest fund-raising success by mailing appeals that come from the local chapter rather than from the national office in New York. This "positioning" works as follows: When a donor lives, for instance, in the state of Indiana, he or she receives an appeal that appears to come directly from the local chapter in Indiana. The appeal includes the Indiana address, the copy talks about the needs of people in Indiana, the request for money asks the donor to support the work of the Indiana Chapter, and the return envelope is even addressed to an Indiana post office box.

The decision to make each appeal appear to come from the "local" chapter, although a subtle point, has been a major factor in the Society's fund-raising success.

Marketing Problem

Imagine a particular marketing problem for the National Multiple Sclerosis Society. The local MS chapter in Indiana has spent a great deal of time and money identifying, and then acquiring, a local donor. The Indiana Chapter has also spent a lot of money and years nurturing and cultivating that donor in Indiana by continually mailing appeals and information that discuss the efforts of the local chapter, the needs of the local MS clients, and so on.

Then one day the donor retires or changes jobs or just decides to move to Florida. The special chapter-donor bond that has been so powerful, indeed, the centerpiece of the Society-donor relationship, is now broken. What can the National Multiple Sclerosis Society do to cement that bond quickly again and protect its "asset" before it is too late?

Technology Solution

In this case, the Society faced three major objectives:

1. To quickly reconnect with the donor in a friendly, service-oriented way
2. To somehow recreate the pivotal chapter-donor link, this time between the local Florida Chapter and the donor.
3. To establish, beyond any doubt, the key relevance of the Florida Chapter in the donor's new life.

As discussed earlier, the key to all fund raising is to reach the right person, with the right message, at the right time. Thanks to up-to-date NCOA (National Change of Address) data, which can be overlaid against the donor file, savvy marketers like the MS Society can quickly determine which donors have changed their addresses and may demand immediate special treatment. (*Note:* This marketing problem is not unusual— about 6 percent of all Americans move every year.)

But what to send these new movers? After analyzing the problem, the MS Society decided the best way to reconnect with these people was to mail them a simple "welcome" postcard coming from the local chapter. The postcard contained the following points:

- Welcome to our neighborhood.
- We wanted to be among the first to say "hi."
- We're here to offer help if you need it.
- Here's our phone number if you need help now.
- Here's our address.
- Please give us a call anytime.

In the "old days," a highly personalized postcard like this, featuring the local chapter's address, other information, and the signature of the local chapter's executive director, could not have been imaged by a laser. Because the MS Society has 88 chapters, it would have had to go through the costly exercise of ordering 88 separate lots of postcards, in tiny quantities, at enormous expense. Then, after paying the high cost of printing these cards, the Society would still have had to image the new mover's name and address so the card could be delivered.

Thanks to today's new high-speed printers, the Society now has an ongoing program in which these postcards are fully imaged from each chapter in one 88-chapter run. Each of these postcards is ultrapersonalized so it can be imaged to appear to come from any chapter, even including the handwritten signature of the chapter's executive director. (See Exhibit 48.3.)

The result is that through this program, the Society has been enormously successful in maintaining the loyalty and support of donors who move from one state to another.

CASE STUDY: PARALYZED VETERANS OF AMERICA

Background

The Paralyzed Veterans of America (PVA) is a national not-for-profit, the only organization dedicated solely to helping veterans with paraplegia. Its multifaceted objectives include helping all veterans to obtain the benefits they are due; promoting medical research on spinal cord dysfunction and other related problems, through the Spinal Cord Research Foundation and the Spinal Cord Injury Education and Training Foundation (both established by PVA); advocating on behalf of paralyzed veterans in Washington, D.C., regarding health care and other issues that affect Americans with disabilities; educating society on barrier-free access; providing wheelchair sports and recreation opportunities for paralyzed veterans; and more.

Fully 70 percent of the veterans helped by PVA served in the Vietnam War. The organization's donor base is primarily older (65 plus), a majority of which are women.

Marketing Problem

Because it is an organization dedicated to helping America's vets, PVA has achieved some of its best fund-raising results over the years by focusing its appeals on major patriotic events in the calendar year: Veterans Day and Memorial Day.

Given the significance of the day to veterans and older Americans who have enormously patriotic feelings about our country, the annual Memorial Day mailing had long been one of the tried-and-true fund-raising appeals. During this appeal, PVA historically mailed a two-page letter to its supporters, asking them to return an enclosed "Card of Thanks" to a vet being cared for in a local Veterans Administration (VA) hospital.

In recent years, PVA was finding it increasingly difficult to raise as much money as it had in the past around the Memorial Day holiday. Results of the last three Memorial Day mailings had either stayed level or declined slightly. In analyzing these results, the PVA team came to the following strategic conclusions:

- The tried-and-true idea of inviting donors to send a card to a vet at a local VA hospital was still a strong approach, relatively unique to PVA. The offer should continue, but the method of communicating that offer had to change.
- The older donors in the organization's file had seen the same kind of personalized letters from PVA for years. PVA needed a bold new approach to catch the attention of this audience and motivate donors to renew their support.
- Recent Gallup polls and PVA's own experiences clearly showed that Americans increasingly want to donate their hard-earned dollars to charities that help people "close to home." To excite these donors again, and show the work of PVA rel-

EXHIBIT 48.3 The Multiple Sclerosis Postcard Package

 NATIONAL MULTIPLE SCLEROSIS SOCIETY
Maryland Chapter

Dear Mr. Sample:
  We just got word that you've moved to
our area, and we want to say WELCOME ...
and ask if there's any way we can help
you!
  Please remember that help is just a
phone call, or a short drive away:
    Our Address:
    Maryland Chapter
    1055 Taylor Avenue, Suite 201
    Towson, MD 21286

Mr. John D. Sample
Epsilon
90 Cambridge Street
Burlington, MA 01803

We'll be keeping in touch!

        Dari DiVenti
        Executive Director

Thanks to new innovations in technology, the MS Society was able to quickly determine which donors had recently moved, and then immediately rush this postcard welcoming a donor to his or her new chapter. Today's technology gives the capability to generate 88 different versions of this card, for each of the 88 chapters, at one time, saving considerable time and expense. Note the personalization throughout the text, including the use of multiple fonts, from typeset copy to Courier to the handwritten signature.

Source: Reproduced with permission from the National Multiple Sclerosis Society.

evant as ever, it was important to communicate this donor need in a dramatic new way.

The strategy was very straightforward, but the means to achieve it were not so easy. PVA knew that many of the donors receiving the Memorial Day appeal would have received five, ten, or even more Memorial Day appeals from PVA in the past. Getting their attention, through an arresting and credible message, was a major hurdle.

Technology Solution

In preparing a marketing approach for this mailing, the planners began by putting themselves in the shoes of the target audience. Suppose for a moment you were 70 or 80 years old. You receive frequent letters from charities but all too often you feel as though you are simply being "asked to give money" instead of being "talked to by a friend." What kind of communication from PVA, or from anyone else, for that matter, would get your attention?

PVA decided to use technology to reposition the entire feel and theme of its appeal. Instead of sending donors a traditional typewritten two-page letter asking for money for all the vets in America who need help, it was instead decided to mail these donors a colorful and highly personalized greeting card. The card looked "store bought" and contained a short and very personal handwritten note about the needs of vets in the donor's home state.

This was clearly a simple concept, but until a few years back, the ability of a fundraising organization to mass-produce, for more than 500,000 donors, a personalized greeting card (duplex imaged in a believable handwritten font) was just not possible. But then new technological advancements in high-speed laser imaging came along.

Exhibit 48.4 shows the simplicity and power of this special appeal. As evident, when donors pulled this package out of the mailbox, they held in their hands a square-shaped envelope with a credible and very personal-looking handprinted address showing through the window. Technology had given PVA the tools to project a certain friendliness and intimacy to the donor even before he or she opened this envelope, as if one person had taken time to write a note to a friend.

The address block was printed on the back of the greeting card with a little note above it, inviting the reader to look inside the envelope (see Exhibit 48.5). The front of the card had a patriotic motif, with the PVA name and identity emblazoned across it, but it was the inside of the card that showed the enormous power of today's technology.

Exhibit 48.6 gives the text of this message in its entirety. Note the informal tone, beginning with the salutation and opening line and proceeding throughout the five simple paragraphs.

Clearly, this letter not only looked different, it was meant to sound different—informal, direct, like a one-to-one conversation between two friends, with substantive and meaningful personalization sprinkled through the text.

The reply slip was simple and direct, with a short handwritten note added to the front for emphasis and an extra handwritten plea added to the reply backer. It should be noted that this special feature (copy on both the front and back sides—duplex printed) was not technologically feasible for mass mailings a few years ago. Indeed, without this ability to duplex print, this format simply would not have been possible.

Topping off the package was a card, which the donor was invited to send to a vet in a local VA hospital.

That was it: a modest five-paragraph handwritten note rather than a long, emotional

EXHIBIT 48.4 Sample Envelope from the PVA Greeting Card

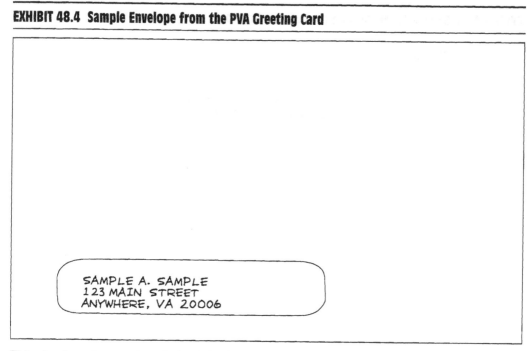

```
SAMPLE A. SAMPLE
123 MAIN STREET
ANYWHERE, VA 20006
```

This simple outer envelope helped the Paralyzed Veterans of America generate 50 percent more revenue than realized through their five previous Memorial Day appeals to donors. Note the relatively square shape of the envelope, similar to that used for a greeting card, and the text showing through the window that looks actually handwritten, real, credible—all through the magic of technology.

Source: Reproduced with permission from the Paralyzed Veterans of America.

two-page typewritten letter; a warm and very polite request for help rather than a hard-hitting plea for support; and a simple, nontraditional greeting card format rather than a traditional direct mail letter.

The result of this new approach made possible by advancements in technology was that this greeting card mailing generated more than 50 percent more revenue than previous Memorial Day appeals. (Remember, results to those appeals had been declining the past few years.) This is a perfect illustration of how advancements in technology can be used to break through the mailbox clutter, rekindle intimacy, spark a one-to-one conversation, and generate breakthrough results.

CASE HISTORY: ARTHRITIS FOUNDATION

Background

The Arthritis Foundation is the source of help and hope for nearly 40 million Americans who have arthritis. The Foundation supports research to cure and prevent arthritis and seeks to improve the quality of life for those affected by arthritis.

Formed in 1948, the Arthritis Foundation is the only national, voluntary health organization that works for all people affected by any of the more than 100 forms of arthritis

EXHIBIT 48.5 Sample Envelope from the PVA Greeting Card

This card was prepared exclusively for
Paralyzed Veterans of America

PLEASE SEE MY NOTE INSIDE.
IT'S VERY IMPORTANT.

SAMPLE A. SAMPLE
123 MAIN STREET
ANYWHERE, VA 20006

The handwritten address block showing through the outer window envelope was actually imaged on the back of the greeting card—the only space available. Thanks to new advancements in technology, today's imagers can print on both sides of a sheet at once, so PVA was able to send along a highly personalized note inside the greeting card (See also Exhibit 48.6.)

Source: Reproduced with permission from the Paralyzed Veterans of America.

or related diseases. Volunteers and staff in 65 chapters nationwide help to support research, professional and community education programs, services for people with arthritis, government advocacy, and fund-raising activities.

Marketing Problem
Like many national charities that have served the public interest for a long time, the Arthritis Foundation over the years built a number of separate "customer constituencies," which constituted its total base of support. Thanks to superior offerings and adept marketing over the years, the Foundation was able to build the following unique databases:

- Donors
- Subscriber/Members
- Prospects (inquiries, cause participants, etc.)

EXHIBIT 48.6 PVA Personalized Greeting Card

DEAR FRIEND,

    I HOPE YOU ARE ENJOYING A NICE SPRING! PLEASE KNOW THAT ALL OF US AT PVA ARE THINKING OF YOU.

    I KNOW THIS REQUEST IS OUT OF THE BLUE. BUT, SINCE YOU HAVE BEEN SUCH A SPECIAL FRIEND OF PVA, I'M WONDERING IF YOU WILL DO SOMETHING VERY SPECIAL FOR A PARALYZED VET. YOU SEE, THIS COMING MEMORIAL DAY, WHILE YOU AND I CELEBRATE OUR FREEDOM, MANY VETS IN VIRGINIA WILL SPEND THEIR DAY IN A HOSPITAL BED IN A VA MEDICAL CENTER.

    MEMORIAL DAY IS A REALLY TOUGH TIME FOR THESE PARALYZED VETS. MANY FEEL FORGOTTEN, UNAPPRECIATED, LEFT OUT. THEY REALLY NEED A FRIEND LIKE YOU TO CARE!

    WILL YOU REACH OUT TO THESE VETS TODAY, IN TWO IMPORTANT WAYS? FIRST, PLEASE SIGN THE ENCLOSED CARD AND MAIL IT TO ME RIGHT AWAY. I'LL MAKE SURE ONE OF OUR SERVICE OFFICERS PERSONALLY DELIVERS YOUR CARD TO A VET. AND SECOND? PLEASE HELP THESE VETS BY SENDING A GIFT OF $6 OR EVEN $9 TODAY. THESE BRAVE VETS URGENTLY NEED YOUR SUPPORT. YOUR GIFT NOW WILL MAKE AN INCREDIBLE DIFFERENCE.

    PLEASE GET BACK TO ME TODAY. AND THANKS FOR CARING!

              GORDON H. MANSFIELD

Here's the entire text of the letter that generated 50 percent more than the previous Memorial Day appeals. From the salutation to the thank you at the end, these words were carefully crafted to nurture a feeling of intimacy and friendship between PVA and the donor. Previous appeals with 10 times more words, and infinitely more detail, were no match for this "high-tech/high-touch" approach.

Source: Reproduced with permission from the Paralyzed Veterans of America.

    These separate "files" grew as distinct and autonomous entities, for a wide variety of reasons:

- *Positioning/services.* The Foundation made the strategic decision early on to create dedicated staff and marketing arms to build and service these databases. As the databases grew in size to become considerable databases unto themselves, they increasingly began to function as separate "silos."
- *Size.* The sheer size of each database was a major technological barrier to consolidating them into one single file. The process of updating each separate database 10 years ago was already considerable. Consolidating these already large files into one massive database would have created new marketing hurdles in terms of the timeliness of the data, the cost of processing, and the ability to access information quickly. (*Note:* To give an idea of the extent to which the new mas-

sively parallel computers have rewritten the rules regarding the speed and cost of maintaining and accessing data, consider this example. The author is familiar with the management of a massive file that took seven full days to update when it resided on a large, independent mainframe. Since its conversion to multiparallel processing, that same update now takes *four hours*.)

- *Cost.* The upfront costs of consolidating the Foundation's databases were high, especially when weighed against the benefits that would result from doing so with the limited technology that existed at the time.

As discussed, there were a number of reasons why the Arthritis Foundation chose for years not to consolidate its databases. However, there were also considerable reasons why they *wanted* to. At the most basic "service" level, the Arthritis Foundation was deeply troubled by the fact that the left hand of the organization did not always know what the right hand was doing, which had a major impact on the people listed in the databases. For example, it was not uncommon (it was indeed inevitable) that a longtime member/subscriber to the organization's magazine would receive an acquisition mailing asking him or her to become a donor. This could cause serious confusion, because the donor already viewed him- or herself as "part of the Arthritis Foundation family."

This common problem became an increasing concern on two levels:

1. How many supporters was the Arthritis Foundation upsetting and, possibly, losing? Although the Foundation could not determine an exact amount, there was a strong feeling that this lack of harmony in the marketing program was costing millions of dollars of support over the long term.
2. What were the costs in lost opportunities to the Foundation? The organization's marketing staff had proven to be among the best and savviest in the fundraising arena. Each team knew that the ability to "cross sell" among the databases (to invite a donor to also be a subscriber, and vice versa) represented an extraordinarily powerful revenue opportunity that could be valued in millions of dollars over the long term.

The alluring possibilities promised by the new technology—the ability to better serve constituents, to cross-sell fund-raising "products," and to completely leverage the enormous power of the database—led the Arthritis Foundation to make a dramatic commitment to change, one that every charity in America can learn from.

Technology Solution

The separate databases were consolidated through an elaborate process of duplicate identification and elimination, record prioritization and historical field joins.

The benefits of consolidating this data go well beyond the convenience of having everything neatly packaged under one roof at one time. The marketing and revenue implications have been enormous. At the most basic level, the Arthritis Foundation has been able to set new standards in how the organization serves and nurtures its constituents. As noted earlier, in the "old days," that is, prior to the consolidation of the databases, it was common (indeed, inevitable) that the left hand did not always know what the right hand was doing.

Today, however, the Foundation no longer has one plan for cultivating its donors and a different plan for talking to members. Instead, the Foundation has created a single marketing plan, synergistic in nature, so that it markets to the outside world with an integrated approach. Whereas years ago it was not uncommon for a name in the database to receive, in one week, two or even three different pieces of correspondence, featuring three totally different messages; the database is now carefully nurtured so that people can expect to receive appeals and information in a timely, service-oriented manner. In essence, the many "hands" of the Foundation are working in harmony, all to the benefit of those named in its donorbase.

However, effectiveness is more than a question of timing or "when" a constituent hears from the Foundation. The real power rests in the "who" (the extraordinary ways the Foundation can segment and target) and the "what" (the new ways in which the Foundation can talk to the names on its file).

For example, its completely consolidated database allows the Arthritis Foundation to segment and target its constituencies in ways that most other organizations are just dreaming about. A typical mailing from the Foundation may consist of as many as 45 to 50 unique defined segments, ranging from names of those who are merely donors, to those who are donors/members, to those who are members only, to those who are major donors. Each of these specific segments receives a unique message that reflects the nature of the individual's present relationship to the Foundation.

But this is just the beginning. The speed and "friendliness" of the new consolidated database has spurred the Foundation to collect new kinds of data, which can in turn be leveraged for marketing purposes. In the last 48 months, the direct mail program has given the member/donor the opportunity to inform the Foundation about what type of arthritis he or she has. For each kind of arthritis (more than 100 types) there are different symptoms, different issues, and different needs. Using this data, with permission from constituents supplying it, the Arthritis Foundation is now able to send completely different and tailored mailing packages to the names on the file, which speak to the very personal needs of the individual. This kind of personalized communication has been made possible by the consolidated database.

Consider the following example, which shows the incredible power of this synergistic approach. As mentioned previously, one of the major objectives of the consolidated database has been to help the Foundation "cross sell," to give donors a chance to also become members, and vice versa.

Since the introduction of the consolidated database, the Foundation has energetically pursued such cross selling to enormous effect. It has found that by talking to its constituents in one single marketing voice, it has been able to increase the value of each name considerably, indeed, far beyond what might be predictable.

For instance, suppose the Foundation determines that a donor to the organization is worth X dollars, and a member is worth Y dollars. Then it stands to reason that if you could convince either one to become both, you would double revenue to the Foundation (X + Y). However, the effect of synergy has been far greater. According to the Foundation's latest analysis, a donor who chooses to "cross over" and become both a donor and a member is not worth just X + Y but instead is worth a full 47 percent more than that.

It is results of this type that have helped the Arthritis Foundation achieve yearly double-digit growth in the past several years. In the process, the stage has been set for even more explosive growth in the years ahead.

49 Accounting for Contributions

RICHARD F. LARKIN, MBA, CPA
Lang Group, Chartered

49.1 Introduction

Contributions are the principal resource most not-for-profit organizations depend on. An organization can receive contributions with a wide range of restrictions attached. First these contributions must be *recorded* in the right fund; then they must be *reported* in such a way that the financial statement reader is fully aware of their receipt and any restrictions on them. In addition, there has been, and continues to be, considerable controversy surrounding the timing of the recording of different types of gifts as income.

Some contributions are made in the form of pledges that will be paid off over a period of time or at some future date; the main accounting questions are whether such pledges should be recorded as assets prior to their collection, and when they should be recognized as income. An organization can also receive a variety of non-cash contributions ranging from marketable securities, buildings, and equipment to contributed ser-

Based on a chapter from *Financial and Accounting Guide for Not-for-Profit Organizations*, 6th ed., Malvern J. Gross Jr., Richard F. Larkin, and John H. McCarthy (New York: John Wiley & Sons, 2000).

vices of volunteers and the use of fixed assets. All of these types of contributions present accounting and reporting problems for the organization.

In 1993 the controversy about proper accounting for contributions was settled by the issuance of Financial Accounting Standards Board (FASB) Statement of Financial Accounting Standards (SFAS) No. 116, *Accounting for Contributions Received and Contributions Made.* The details of the requirements of this statement are discussed throughout this chapter. In brief, it says that all contributions, whether unrestricted or restricted, and in whatever form: cash, gifts-in-kind, securities, pledges, or other forms, are revenue in full immediately upon receipt of the gift or an unconditional pledge. (Restricted contributions are not deferred until the restriction is met, as is now the practice by many organizations.) The revenue is reported in the class of net assets (see Section 49.4) appropriate to any donor-imposed restriction on the gift (unrestricted, if there is no donor-imposed restriction). It also contains guidance on accounting for donated services of volunteers, and an exception to the normal rule when dealing with museum collection objects.

Contributions are also discussed extensively in the new AICPA (American Institute of Certified Public Accountants) audit guide for not-for-profit organizations, issued in mid-1996.

49.2 *Expendable Current Support*

(A) UNRESTRICTED CONTRIBUTIONS

This section of the chapter discusses simple unrestricted cash gifts. Unrestricted gifts in other forms, such as pledges, gifts of securities, and gifts of equipment and supplies, are discussed in later sections. The general principles discussed here apply to all unrestricted gifts, in whatever form received.

(i) *Accounting for Unrestricted Contributions*
All unrestricted contributions should be reported in the unrestricted class of net assets in a Statement of Income and Expenses, or, if a combined Statement of Income, Expenses, and Changes in Net Assets is used, such unrestricted contributions should be shown before arriving at the "Excess of income over expenses" caption. It is *not acceptable* to report unrestricted contributions in a separate Statement of Changes in Net Assets or to report such gifts in a restricted class of net assets.

(ii) *Bargain Purchases*
Organizations are sometimes permitted to purchase goods or services at a reduced price that is granted by the seller in recognition of the organization's charitable or educational status. In such cases, the seller has effectively made a gift to the buyer. This gift should be recorded as such if the amount is significant. For example, if a charity buys a widget for $50 that normally sells for $80, the purchase should be recorded at $80, with the $30 difference being reported as a contribution.

It is important to record only true gifts in this way. If a lower price is really a normal discount available to any buyer who requests it, then there is no contribution. Such discounts include quantity discounts, normal trade discounts, promotional discounts, special offers, or lower rates (say, for professional services) to reflect the seller's desire to utilize underused staff, or sale prices to move slow-moving items from the shelves.

(B) CURRENT RESTRICTED CONTRIBUTIONS

Current restricted contributions are contributions that can be used to meet the current expenses of the organization, although restricted to use for some specific purpose, or during or after some specified time. An example of the former is a gift "for cancer research" (a "purpose restriction"), and of the latter, a gift "for your 20XX activities" (a "time restriction"). In practice, the distinction between restricted gifts and unrestricted gifts is not always clear. In many cases, the language used by the donor leaves doubt as to whether there really is a restriction on the gift.

Current restricted contributions cause reporting problems, in part because the accounting profession took a long time to resolve the appropriate accounting and reporting treatment for these types of gifts. The resolution arrived at is controversial, because many believe it is not the most desirable method of accounting for such gifts.

The principal accounting problem relates to the question of what constitutes "income" or "support" to the organization. Is a gift that can be used only for a specific project or after a specified time "income" to the organization at the time the gift is received, or does this restricted gift represent an amount that should be looked on as being held in a form of escrow until it is expended for the restricted purpose (cancer research in the previous example), or the specified time has arrived (20XX in the example)? If it is looked on as something other than income, what is it—deferred income or part of a restricted net asset balance?

If a current restricted gift is considered income or support in the period received—whether expended or not—the accounting is fairly straightforward. It would be essentially the same as for unrestricted gifts, described earlier, except that the gift is reported in the temporarily restricted class rather than in the unrestricted class of net assets. But if the other view is taken, the accounting can become quite complex.

(i) Accounting for Current Restricted Contributions: Report as Income in Full in the Year Received

The approach required by SFAS No. 116 is to report a current restricted gift as income or support in full in the year received, in the temporarily restricted class of net assets. In this approach, gifts are recognized as income as received and expenditures are recognized as incurred. The unexpended income is reflected as part of temporarily restricted net assets.

Observe, however, that in this approach a current restricted gift received on the last day of the reporting period will also be reflected as income, and this will increase the excess of support over expenses reported for the entire period. Many boards are reluctant to report such an excess in the belief this may discourage contributions or suggest that the board has not used all of its available resources. Those who are concerned about reporting an excess of income over expenses are therefore particularly concerned with the implications of this approach: A large unexpected current restricted gift may be received at the last minute, resulting in a large excess of income over expenses.

Others, in rejecting this argument, point out that the organization is merely reporting what has happened and to report the gift otherwise is to obscure its receipt. They point out that in reality all gifts, whether restricted or unrestricted, are really at least somewhat restricted and only the degree of restriction varies; even "unrestricted" gifts must be spent realizing the stated goals of the organization, and therefore such gifts are effectively restricted to this purpose even though a particular use has not been specified by the contributor.

There are valid arguments on both sides. This approach is the one recommended in the AICPA Audit Guide for Voluntary Health and Welfare Organizations and therefore has been very widely followed. It will now become the method used by all not-for-profit organizations.

(ii) Grants for Specific Projects

Many organizations receive grants from third parties to accomplish specific projects or activities. These grants differ from other current restricted gifts principally in the degree of accountability the recipient organization has in reporting back to the granting organization on the use of such monies. In some instances, the organization receives a grant to conduct a specific research project, the results of which are turned over to the grantor. The arrangement is similar to a private contractor's performance on a commercial for-profit basis. In that case, the "grant" is essentially a purchase of services. It would be accounted for in accordance with normal commercial accounting principles, which call for the revenue to be recognized as the work under the contract is performed. In other instances, the organization receives a grant for a specific project, and although the grantee must specifically account for the expenditure of the grant in detail and may have to return any unexpended amounts, the grant is to further the programs of the grantee rather than for the benefit of the grantor. This kind of grant is really a gift, not a purchase.

The line between ordinary current restricted gifts and true "grants" for specific projects is not important for accounting purposes, because the method of reporting revenue is now the same for both. What can get fuzzy is the distinction between grants and purchase of services contracts. Most donors of current restricted gifts are explicit as to how their gifts are to be used, and often the organization initiates a report back to the donors on the use of their gifts. However, restricted gifts and grants usually do not have the degree of specificity that is attached to purchase contracts.

Prepayment vs. Cost Reimbursement. Grants and contracts can be structured in either of two forms: In one, the payor remits the amount up front and the payee then spends that money. In the other, the payee must spend its own money from other sources and is reimbursed by the payor.

In the case of a purchase contract, amounts remitted to the organization in advance of their expenditure should be treated as deferred income until such time as expenditures are made that can be charged against the contract. At that time, income should be recognized to the extent earned. Where expenditures have been made but the grantor has not yet made payment, a receivable should be set up to reflect the grantor's obligation.

In the case of a true grant (gift), advance payments must be recognized as revenue immediately upon receipt, as is the case with all contributions under SFAS No. 116. Reimbursement grants are recognized as revenue reimbursements become due, that is, as money is spent that the grantor will reimburse. This is the same method as that used under cost-reimbursement purchase contracts.

Some organizations have recorded the entire amount of the grant as a receivable at the time awarded, offset by deferred grant income on the liability side of the balance sheet. This is no longer appropriate under SFAS No. 116. If the entire grant amount qualifies as an unconditional pledge (see Section 49.4(b)), then that amount must be recorded as revenue, not deferred revenue.

(C) INVESTMENT SECURITIES

Often an organization receives contributions that are in the form of investment securities: stocks and bonds. These contributions should be recorded in the same manner as cash gifts. The only problem usually encountered is difficulty in determining a reasonable basis for valuation in the case of closely held stock with no objective market value.

The value recorded should be the fair market value at the date received. Marketable stocks and bonds present no serious valuation problem. They should be recorded at their market value on the date of receipt or, if sold shortly thereafter, at the amount of proceeds actually received.

For securities without a published market value, the services of an appraiser may be required to determine the fair value of the gift.

49.3 Gifts in-Kind

(A) FIXED ASSETS (LAND, BUILDINGS, AND EQUIPMENT) AND SUPPLIES

Contributions of fixed assets can be accounted for in one of two ways. SFAS No. 116 permits such gifts to be reported as either unrestricted or temporarily restricted income at the time received. If the gift is initially reported as temporarily restricted, the restriction is deemed to expire ratably over the useful life of the asset: that is, in proportion to depreciation for depreciable assets. The expiration is reported as a reclassification from the temporarily restricted to the unrestricted class of net assets. Nondepreciable assets such as land would remain in the temporarily restricted class indefinitely—until disposed of. (Recognizing the gift as income in proportion to depreciation recognized on the asset is not in conformity with generally accepted accounting principles.)

Supplies and equipment should be recorded at the amount the organization would normally have to pay for similar items. A value for used office equipment and the like can usually be obtained from a dealer in such items. The valuation of donated real estate is more difficult, and it is usually necessary to get an outside appraisal to determine the value.

(B) MUSEUM COLLECTIONS

SFAS No. 116 makes an exception for recording a value for donated (and purchased) museum collection objects, if certain criteria are met and certain disclosures are made. Owners of such objects do not have to record them, although they may if they wish.

(C) CONTRIBUTED SERVICES OF VOLUNTEERS

Many organizations depend almost entirely on volunteers to carry out their programs and, sometimes, supporting functions. Should such organizations place a value on these contributed services and record them as "contributions" in their financial statements?

(i) Criteria for Recording

The answer is yes, under certain circumstances. These circumstances exist only when *either* of the following conditions is satisfied:

1. The services create or enhance nonfinancial assets; or
2. The services:
   a. Require specialized skills,
   b. Are provided by persons possessing those skills, and
   c. Would typically have to be purchased if not provided by donation.

If neither criterion is met, SFAS No. 116 precludes recording a value for the services, although disclosure in a footnote is encouraged. These criteria differ considerably from criteria in the earlier audit guides/statement of position.

Creating or Enhancing Fixed Assets.   The first criterion is fairly straightforward. It covers volunteers constructing or making major improvements to buildings or equipment. It also covers things like building sets or making costumes for a theater or opera company, and writing computer programs, inasmuch as the resulting assets could be capitalized on the balance sheet. The criterion says "nonfinancial" assets so as *not* to cover volunteer fund raisers who, it could be argued, are "creating" assets by soliciting gifts.

Specialized Skills.   The second criterion has three parts, all of which must be met for recording to be appropriate. The first part deals with the nature of the services themselves. The intent is deliberately to limit the types of services that must be recorded, thus reducing the burden of tracking and valuing large numbers of volunteers doing purely routine work, the aggregate financial value of which would usually be fairly small. SFAS No. 116 gives very little guidance about how to identify, in practice, those skills that would be considered "specialized," as opposed to nonspecialized. It includes a list of skills that are considered specialized, which merely recites the obvious professions such as doctors, lawyers, teachers, carpenters. What is lacking is an operational definition of *specialized* that can be applied to all types of services.

The second part of the criterion usually causes no problems in practice, as persons performing the types of services contemplated should normally possess the necessary skills (if not, why are they performing the services?)

Would Otherwise Purchase.   The third part of the criterion is the most difficult of all to consider, as it calls for a pure judgment by management. Would the organization or would it not purchase the services? This is similar to a criterion in SOP No. 78–10, which reads as follows:

> The services performed are significant and form an integral part of the efforts of the organization as it is presently constituted; the services would be performed by salaried personnel if donated services were not available . . . ; and the organization would continue the activity.

Probably the most important requirement is that the services being performed are an essential part of the organization's program. The key test is whether the organization would hire someone to perform these services if volunteers were not available.

This is a difficult criterion to meet. Many organizations have volunteers involved in peripheral areas that, while important to the organization, are not of such significance that paid staff would be hired in the absence of volunteers. But this is the acid test: If the volunteers suddenly quit, would the organization hire replacements?

(ii) Basis on Which to Value Services

An additional criterion that is not explicitly stated in SFAS No. 116 in connection with donated services is that there must be an objective basis on which to value these services. It is usually not difficult to determine a reasonable value for volunteer services where the volunteers are performing professional or clerical services. By definition, the services to be recorded are only those for which the organization would, in fact, hire paid staff if volunteers were not available. This suggests that the organization should be able to establish a reasonable estimate of what costs would be involved if employees had to be hired.

In establishing such rates, it is not necessary to establish individual rates for each volunteer. Instead, the volunteers can be grouped into general categories and a rate established for each category.

Some organizations are successful in getting local businesses to donate one of their executives on a full- or part-time basis for an extended period of time. In many instances, the amount paid by the local business to the loaned executive is far greater than the organization would have to pay for hired staff performing the same function. The rate to be used in establishing a value should be the lower rate. This also helps to get around the awkwardness of trying to discern actual compensation.

(iii) Accounting Treatment

The dollar value assigned to contributed services should be reflected as income in the section of the financial statements where other unrestricted contributions are shown. In most instances, it is appropriate to disclose the amount of such services as a separate line.

On the expense side, the value of contributed services should be allocated to program and supporting service categories, based on the nature of the work performed. The amounts allocated to each category are not normally disclosed separately. If volunteers were used for constructing fixed assets, the amounts would be capitalized rather than charged to an expense category. Unless some of the amounts are capitalized, the recording of contributed services will not affect the excess of income over expenses, because the income and expense exactly offset each other.

(D) USE OF FACILITIES

Occasionally a not-for-profit organization is given use of a building or other facilities either at no cost or at a substantially reduced cost. A value should be reflected for such a facility in the financial statements, both as income and as expense. The value to be used should be the fair market value of facilities that the organization would otherwise rent if the contributed facilities were not available. This means that if very expensive facilities are donated, the valuation to be used should be the lower value of the facilities the organization would otherwise have rented. Implicit in this rule is the ability to determine an objective basis for valuing such facilities. If an organization is given the use of facilities that are unique in design and have no alternative purpose, it may be impossible to determine what they would have to pay to rent comparable facilities. This often occurs with museums that occupy elaborate government-owned buildings.

Where a donor indicates that the organization can unconditionally use such rent-free facilities for more than a one-year period, the organization should reflect the arrangement as a pledge and record the present value of the contribution in the same way other pledges are recorded.

(E) SERVICES PROVIDED BY OTHER ORGANIZATIONS

Some not-for-profit organizations are the beneficiaries of services provided at no cost by other organizations, often organizations with which the reporting organization is affiliated in some way. An example is a corporate foundation that occupies office space belonging to the company, uses office equipment belonging to the company, and has its functions performed by personnel on the company payroll, for which no charge is made by the company to the foundation. In separate financial statements of the foundation, the value of the "free" services should be reported as both a contribution and an expense. The expense would be reported in the categories appropriate to the nature and purpose of the services provided.

49.4 Support Not Currently Expendable

(A) ENDOWMENT GIFTS

Donor-restricted endowment fund contributions should be reported as revenue upon receipt in a restricted class of net assets: temporary in the case of a term endowment gift, otherwise permanent.

Gifts of term endowment are later reclassified in the unrestricted class when the term of the endowment expires. (If upon expiration of the endowment restriction, the gift is still restricted—likely for some operating purpose—it would not be reclassified until money is spent for that purpose. If upon expiration of the term endowment restriction, the gift becomes permanently restricted, it should be recorded in that class initially.)

(B) PLEDGES (PROMISES TO GIVE)

A pledge[1] is a promise to contribute a specified amount to an organization. A pledge may or may not be legally enforceable. The point is often moot, because few organizations would think of trying to legally enforce a pledge. The unfavorable publicity that would result would only hurt future fund raising. The only relevant criteria are: Will the pledge be collected and are pledges material in amount?

If these criteria are satisfied, then there are two accounting questions: Should a pledge be recorded as an asset at the time the pledge is received? If the answer is yes, the next question is: When should the pledge be recognized as income?

---

[1]SFAS No. 116 uses the term "promise to give" to refer to what is more commonly called a pledge.

(i) Recording as an Asset

For many organizations, a significant portion of income is received by pledge. The timing of the collection of pledges is only partially under the control of the organization. Yet over the years most organizations find they can predict with reasonable accuracy the collectible portion of pledges, even when a sizable percentage will not be collected. Accounting literature requires that unconditional pledges the organization expects to collect be recorded as assets and an allowance established for the portion that is estimated to be uncollectible.

Historically, there has been considerable difference of opinion on this subject, with the AICPA Audit Guides and the Statement of Position taking different positions. The college audit guide said that recording of pledges was optional, and most colleges did not record them until collected. The other three guides required recording pledges, although their criteria and method of recording differed slightly. Now SFAS No. 116 requires *all* organizations to record unconditional pledges.

(ii) Conditions vs. Restrictions

The requirement in SFAS No. 116 is to record *unconditional* pledges as assets. *Unconditional* means "without conditions." What is meant by *conditions*? The Financial Accounting Standards Board defines a condition as "a future and uncertain event" that must occur for a pledge to become binding on the pledgor. There are two elements of this definition: future and uncertain. *Future* means it has not happened yet; this is fairly clear. *Uncertain* is, however, more subject to interpretation. How uncertain? This will be a matter of judgment in many cases.

If a donor pledges to give to a charity "if the sun rises tomorrow," that is not an uncertain event; the sun will rise tomorrow, at a known time. If a donor pledges to give $10,000 to the Red Cross, "if there's an earthquake in California," that is very uncertain. (A geologist will say the eventual probability of an earthquake happening is 100 percent, but the timing is completely uncertain.) This latter pledge would be conditional upon an earthquake's occurring. Once an earthquake occurs, then the donor's pledge is unconditional (the condition has been removed), and the pledge is recorded by the Red Cross.

Another example of a condition is a matching pledge (also known as a challenge grant). A donor pledges to give an amount to a charity if the charity raises a matching amount from other sources. (The "match" need not be one for one; it can be in any ratio the donor specifies.) In this case, the charity is not entitled to receive the donor's gift until it has met the required match. Once it does, it will notify the donor that the pledge is now due.

A third type of donor stipulation sounds like a condition, but it may or may not actually be one. A donor pledges to contribute to a symphony orchestra "if they will perform my favorite piece of music [specified by name]. (A cynical person would call this a bribe.) Yes, this is an uncertain future event, since the piece of music has not yet been performed, but how uncertain is it? If the orchestra might very well have played the piece anyway, then the "condition" is really trivial, and the event would not be considered uncertain. However, if the piece were one that the orchestra would be very unlikely to perform without the incentive represented by the pledge in question, then the event would be considered uncertain and the pledge conditional. In this case, the condition is fulfilled when the orchestra formally places the music on its schedule and so informs the donor.

Note that the concept of a condition is quite different from that of a restriction. Conditions deal with events that must occur before a charity is entitled to receive a gift.

Restrictions limit how the charity can use the gift after receipt. Unconditional pledges can be either unrestricted or restricted; so can conditional pledges. Donor stipulations attached to a gift or pledge must be read carefully to discern which type of situation is being dealt with. For example, "I pledge $20,000 *if* you play my favorite music" is conditional but unrestricted (the donor has not said the gift must be used to pay for the performance), whereas "I pledge $20,000 *for* [the cost of] playing my favorite piece of music" is restricted but unconditional. In the latter case, the donor has said the pledge will be paid but can be used only for that performance. The difference in wording is small, but the accounting implications are great. The conditional pledge is not recorded at all until the condition is met; the unconditional restricted pledge is recorded as revenue (in the temporarily restricted class) upon receipt of notification of the pledge.

(iii) Discounted to Present Value

Prior to SFAS No. 116, pledges were recorded at the full amount that would ultimately be collected. None of the accounting literature for not-for-profit organizations talked about discounting pledges to reflect the time value of money. There had been for many years an accounting standard applicable to business transactions that did require such discounting, but not-for-profit organizations universally chose to treat this as not applicable to them, and accountants did not object.

SFAS No. 116 does require recipients (and donors) of pledges payable beyond the current accounting period to discount the pledges to their present value, using an appropriate rate of interest. Thus, the ability to receive $1,000 two years later is really only equivalent to receiving about $900 (assuming about a 5 percent rate of interest) now, because the $900 could be invested and earn $100 in interest over the two years. The higher the interest rate used, the lower will be the present value of the pledge, because the lower amount would earn more interest at the higher rate and still be worth the full $1,000 two years hence.

The appropriate rate of interest to use in discounting pledges is a matter of some judgment. In many cases, it is the average rate the organization is currently earning on its investments or its idle cash. If the organization is being forced to borrow money to keep going, then the borrowing rate should be used. Additional guidance is provided in SFAS No. 116 and APB (Accounting Principles Board) No. 21.

As time passes between the initial recording of a discounted pledge and its eventual collection, the present value increases because the time left before payment is shorter. Therefore, the discount element must be gradually "accreted" up to par (collection) value. This accretion should be recorded each year until the due date for the pledge arrives. The accretion is recorded as contribution income. (This treatment differs from that specified in APB No. 21 for business debts, for which the accretion is recorded as interest income.)

(iv) Pledges for Extended Periods

There is one limitation to the general rule that pledges be recorded as assets. Occasionally donors indicate that they will make an open-ended pledge of support for an extended period of time. For example, if a donor promises to pay $5,000 a year for 20 years, would it be appropriate to record as an asset the full 20 years' pledge? In most cases, no; this would distort the financial statements. Most organizations follow the practice of not recording pledges for future years' support beyond a fairly short period. They feel that long-term open-ended pledges are inherently conditional upon the donor's willingness to continue making payments and thus are harder to collect. These arguments have validity, and organizations should consider very carefully the likelihood of collection before recording pledges for support in future periods beyond five years.

(v) Allowance for Uncollectible Pledges

Not all pledges will be collected. People may lose interest in an organization; their personal financial circumstances may change; they may move out of town. This is as true for charities as for businesses, but businesses usually sue to collect unpaid debts; charities usually do not. Thus, another important question is how large the allowance for uncollectible pledges should be. Most organizations have past experience to help answer this question. If over the years, 10 percent of pledges are not collected, then unless the economic climate changes, 10 percent is probably the right figure to use. Care must be taken, however, because although an organization's past experience may have been good, times do change—as many organizations have discovered to their sorrow.

SFAS No. 116 and other existing accounting literature are silent about how to present the allowance in the financial statements. There is no question about the presentation in the balance sheet: It is an offset to the receivable amount. Thus, if the organization has outstanding pledges totaling $75,000 and it estimates that 10 percent of that amount will be uncollectible, the allowance of $7,500 is deducted from the $75,000 and the net amount of $67,500 is shown.

What is not clear is how to present the reduction in the amount recorded in the statement of income and expenses to reflect the fact that not all of the recorded revenue will actually ever become available to the organization. One obvious possibility is to reduce the reported revenue amount by the uncollectible percentage. Another is to report the full amount of the pledges as revenue and the uncollectible amount as an expense. Because expenses are deducted from revenue, either method of reporting results in the same net excess of revenue over expenses for the year.

The new AICPA audit guide uses the deduction-from-revenue method. The author believes that that method better reflects the reality of the way not-for-profit organizations manage pledges.

(vi) Recognition as Income

The second, and related, question is: When should a pledge be recognized as income? The answer is: immediately upon receipt of an unconditional pledge. This is the same rule that applies to all kinds of gifts under SFAS No. 116. Conditional pledges are not recorded until the condition is met, at which time they are effectively unconditional pledges. Footnote disclosure of unrecorded conditional pledges should be made.

Under the earlier audit guides/statement of position, pledges without purpose restrictions were recorded in the unrestricted class of net assets. Only if a pledge had a purpose restriction would it be recorded in a restricted class. Even pledges with explicit time restrictions were still recorded in the unrestricted class, to reflect the flexibility of use that would exist when the pledge was collected. Under SFAS No. 116, all pledges are considered implicitly time-restricted, by virtue of their being unavailable for use until collected. In addition, time-restricted gifts, including all pledges, are now reported in the temporarily restricted class of net assets. They are then reclassified to the unrestricted class when the specified time arrives.

This means that even a pledge not payable for 10 years, or a pledge payable in many installments, is recorded as revenue in full (less the discount to present value) in the temporarily restricted class in the year the pledge is first received. This is a major change from earlier practice, which generally deferred the pledge until the anticipated period of collection.

Sometimes a charity may not want to have to record a large pledge as immediate revenue; it may feel that its balance sheet is already healthy and recording more income would turn off other donors. If a pledge is unconditional, there is no choice: The pledge must be recorded. One way to mitigate this problem is to ask the donor to make the pledge conditional; then it is not recorded until some later time when the condition is met. Of course, there is a risk that the donor may not be as likely ever to pay a conditional pledge as one that is understood to be absolutely binding, so not-for-profit organizations should consider carefully before requesting that a pledge be made conditional.

SFAS No. 116 requires that donors follow the same rules for recognition of the expense of making a gift as recipients do for the income: that is, immediately upon payment or upon making an unconditional pledge. Sometimes a charity finds a donor reluctant to make a large unconditional pledge, but willing to make a conditional pledge. Fund raisers should be aware of the effect of the new accounting principles in SFAS No. 116 on donors' giving habits as well as on recipients' balance sheets.

(C) BEQUESTS

A bequest is a special kind of pledge. It is the ultimate conditional pledge: a very uncertain future event must occur for it to become payable. Accordingly, bequests should never be recorded before the donor dies—not because death is uncertain, but because a person can always change a will, and the charity may get nothing. (There is a special case: the pledge payable upon death. This is not really a bequest, it is just an ordinary pledge and should be recorded as such if it is unconditional.)

After a person dies, the beneficiary organization is informed that it is named in the will, but this notification may occur long before the estate is probated and distribution made. Should such a bequest be recorded at the time the organization first learns of the bequest or at the time of receipt? The question is one of sufficiency of assets in the estate to fulfill the bequest. Because there is often uncertainty about what other amounts may have to be paid to settle debts, taxes, other bequests, claims of disinherited relatives, and so on, a conservative, and recommended, approach is not to record anything until the probate court has accounted for the estate and the amount available for distribution can be accurately estimated. At that time, the amount should be recorded in the same manner as other gifts.

Thus, if an organization is informed that it will receive a bequest of a specific amount, $10,000, for instance, it should record this $10,000 as an asset. If instead the organization is informed that it will receive 10 percent of the estate, the total of which is not known, nothing is to be recorded yet, although footnote disclosure would likely be necessary if the amount could be sizeable. Still a third possibility exists if the organization is told that although the final amount of the 10 percent bequest is not known, it will be at least some stated amount. In that instance, the minimum amount is recorded with footnote disclosure of the contingent interest.

(D) SPLIT-INTEREST GIFTS

The term "split-interest gifts" is used to refer to irrevocable trusts and similar arrangements (also referred to as deferred gifts) whereby the interest in the gift is split between the donor (or another person specified by the donor) and the charity. These arrangements can be divided into two fundamentally different types of arrangements: lead interests and remainder interests. Lead interests are those in which the benefit to the charity "leads" or precedes the benefit to the donor (or other person designated by the donor). To put this into the terminology commonly used by trust lawyers, the charity is the "life tenant," and someone else is the "remainderman." The reverse situation is that of the "remainder" interest, whereby the donor (or the donor's designee) is the life tenant and the charity is the remainderman, that is, the entity to which the assets become available upon termination (often called the maturity) of the trust or other arrangement. There may or may not be further restrictions on the charity's use of the assets and/or the income therefrom after this maturity.

49.5 *Significance to Fund Raisers*

Accounting is important to fund raising for a variety of reasons. First, the results of fund raising—gifts—are reported in donees' (and sometimes in donors') financial reports. Second, those reports are used by many donors to help decide whether and how much to give, as well as by regulators and evaluation agencies to assess the performance of donees. Third, federal tax rules restrict (to some extent) what donors and donees can do.

Donors, as well as donees, should always be aware of the accounting, reporting, and tax rules affecting their activities. Donees will raise more money if they consider donors' concerns. Donors will have their gifts used more effectively if they structure the gifts with donees' constraints in mind. Both groups will more greatly benefit society if tax rules are observed. This section points out certain areas of accounting for contributions that are of particular interest to fund raisers.

(A) ACCOUNTING FOR CONTRIBUTIONS

Because the new accounting standard is that all unconditional gifts (including pledges) will be revenue when the gift or pledge is first received, many not-for-profits will record some of their revenue sooner than they do now. This means usually higher revenue, larger excess of revenue over expenses, and larger fund balances (net assets). These organizations will appear to be in better financial condition than heretofore and thus will sometimes present fund raisers with the additional challenge of convincing prospective donors that new gifts are truly needed. Fund raisers will have to be adept at pointing out to donors that parts of the resources of the donee are legally restricted and cannot be used for general operations.

Heretofore, not-for-profits have reported revenue and fund balances by funds: current unrestricted, current restricted, plant (fixed asset), endowment, and, sometimes, others. The new standards call for only three "classes": unrestricted, or resources with no donor-imposed restriction; temporarily restricted, or resources with a donor-imposed restriction that lapses with the passage of time or is fulfilled by action of the donee; and permanently restricted, or resources with a donor-imposed restriction that never lapses or is never fulfilled.

Included in the unrestricted class will be all board-designated funds (quasi-endowment, for special projects, or other purposes) and property, plant, and equipment purchased with unrestricted resources. The temporarily restricted class will comprise operating restricted funds, term endowments, annuity and life income (split-interest) funds, unspent gifts restricted for acquisition of fixed assets, and fixed assets donated or acquired with funds restricted for that purpose. Pledges payable in a future period are considered implicitly time-restricted until that period. In the permanently restricted class will be permanent endowment and revolving loan funds.

Because recording (or not recording) pledges can make a considerable difference in the apparent financial condition of the donee (and, perhaps, of the donor), fund raisers will find that sometimes management will very much want (or not want) to record some pledges. Especially with major fund drives and with very large single pledges, as soon as plans are made or evidence of the pledge becomes apparent, the fund raiser is advised to discuss with management of the donee, and with the donor, whether either has concerns about the way the pledge is to be accounted for. The fund raiser should be familiar with the different methods of accounting and the factors used in deciding which method is proper so that all alternatives can be discussed. For example, it may be that both the donor and the donee do not wish to record the pledge until a later period. In that case, if both agree, the language of the pledge can be written to make the pledge nonbinding or to include a condition that will not be met until the later period. Of course, there will be times in any fund raiser's career when one party wants to record the pledge and the other does not. Because the rules are the same for both, one of them will have to be flexible; maybe some inducement by one will convince the other. The fund raiser may be able to close the deal by facilitating such negotiation.

Fund raisers soliciting unrestricted gifts should call donors' attention to the financial data for the unrestricted class, and similarly for other types of gifts. A donee may have large amounts invested in fixed assets (property) or a large endowment or other restricted balance but still be genuinely in need of expendable unrestricted gifts because the fixed assets and the restricted resources are not available except for specific purposes. Fund raisers should not, however, attempt to gloss over quasi-endowment funds and mislead donors into believing that these cannot be spent. Quasi-endowments are legally unrestricted and thus can be spent at any time with approval of the board of the organization. Some boards may wish to pretend that they cannot use quasi-endowments, but because that is not the case, there is a risk of losing credibility with donors.

As with pledges, the fund raiser may be able to work with the donor to structure a gift so that accounting for it does not have adverse side effects for the donee. (In this case, the method of recording by the donee does not affect the accounting by the donor.) For example, a charity may receive support from a federated fund-raising organization whose policy is to deduct any unrestricted surplus as of year's end from the following year's allocation. An unexpected unrestricted gift received just before year's end can result in a surplus; the gift, in effect, ends up being turned over to the other funder next year. However, if approached with a proposal to restrict the gift to some specific anticipated need of the donee, the donor may be willing to comply, thereby retaining the gift for the charity. Fund raisers must always be up-to-date on the entire fund-raising and financial picture of an organization and alert for opportunities to plan gifts to achieve maximum benefit for both parties.

(B) PROGRAM EXPENSES

Another accounting issue of concern to fund raisers is when and how program expenses paid with restricted gifts are reported and how these expenses are "matched" in the financial statements with that revenue. Current principles are that when restricted resources are available for a particular activity, and money is spent to conduct that activity, it is presumed that the restricted resources were used, even though the entity may also have unrestricted resources available and may even have specifically used money identified as unrestricted. In the latter case, the restricted resources that remain are then considered unrestricted, by virtue of the donor's restriction having been fulfilled. An exception to all of this has been that colleges have had the option of specifying whether the resources used were unrestricted or restricted. FASB's new standards specify that restricted resources are always deemed to have been used first, thus removing the present flexibility enjoyed by colleges to "hold back" restricted gifts for future use even while fulfilling the donors' restrictions with other money.

An additional aspect of reporting program expenses is where they are shown in the statement of revenue and expenses. Under existing practices, expenses financed with restricted resources are reported in the restricted fund. FASB's new requirement is to report all expenses in the unrestricted class, with restricted resources being reclassified (transferred) to the unrestricted class to match the expenses incurred. Fund raisers will now have to be prepared to explain to donors how the donee reports the use of their gifts: At first, it will appear that no restricted gifts have been used. Because all expenses will be in the unrestricted class, the restricted class will show no expenses, which some donors will question. Also in computing the ratio of program expenses to contributions (an indicator used by some to evaluate a donee's performance), fund raisers will take the program expense number from the unrestricted class but have to add together unrestricted and restricted gifts to obtain the denominator of the ratio.

(C) AUDITING AND INTERNAL ACCOUNTING CONTROLS

Auditing and internal accounting controls, well covered in other literature, are mentioned briefly here to reinforce their importance. Primary responsibility for establishing sound controls and arranging for audits usually belongs to the organization's accounting staff, not the fund raiser. However, these matters are of concern to the fund raiser because of the close relationship among the functions of raising, controlling, and auditing gifts. If the fund raiser senses a lax attitude of management or the accounting staff about these matters, he or she is advised to bring the problem to the attention of someone in the organization. Not only can weak controls lead to a loss of assets by the organization, but also publicity about instances of loss will hurt the fund raiser's ability to attract gifts.

Contributions to charities are inherently the most difficult of all types of accounting transactions over which to establish strong internal controls and a thorough audit process. This is due to the nonreciprocal nature of the transaction: Cash comes in but no goods or services are provided in exchange. Thus, many of the checks and balances used in businesses to control sales and cash receipts are not available to a charity. This means that although management personnel should try to establish as strong a control environment as possible, the challenge to do so is great, and they must always be alert to weaknesses that could allow misappropriation of assets.

(D)   ACCOUNTING FOR FUND-RAISING EXPENSES

Reported fund-raising expenses figure prominently in many assessments of the efficiency and effectiveness of fund-raising efforts and of the charity overall. Whether this is really good or bad is left to others to discuss (see Chapter 6), although the author believes that too much importance is often ascribed to fund-raising expenses. Nevertheless, fund raisers must understand them to be able to discuss them intelligently.

Fund-raising expenses are those expenses incurred to induce donors to contribute to an organization. Such expenses must be reported separately in the financial statements of organizations that solicit significant amounts of gifts from the general public. The new FASB standards will require such disclosure by all not-for-profits (except where such costs are immaterial to an entity). Issues relating to these expenses include what types of expenses should be called fund-raising expenses, when they should be reported as expenses, and when and how to allocate multiple-purpose expenses.

(i)   Definition of Fund-raising Expenses

The short definition of fund-raising expenses given in the preceding paragraph requires elaboration to fully cover the various types of activities comprehended. These include planning fund-raising campaigns, managing the fund-raising process, actual public solicitation costs (mail, media, and so on), applying for foundation and government grants, training and supervising fund-raising volunteers, staff time required to participate in federated fund-raising campaigns, and other activities intended to advance the solicitation effort.

Some costs are usually not charged to fund raising, such as accounting for contributions received, which is considered for an administrative cost. Some consider the cost of recruitment of all volunteers to be a fund-raising expense, others consider it an administrative expense (akin to hiring paid staff), and still others would have the cost follow the duties of the volunteers being recruited. The new AICPA audit guide states that this is a fund-raising expense.

The subject of recording a value for the time of fund-raising volunteers was mentioned earlier in the discussion of non-cash gifts. Generally, as noted, such values are not recorded. Thus, comparison of fund-raising efficiency between two charities, one of which relies heavily on volunteers for fund raising and the other of which uses paid staff, is not very meaningful.

One other category of costs related to fund raising is usually not reported as fund-raising expense: costs directly benefiting participants in "special events" such as dinners, parties, games, athletic activities, and sales of items such as cookies and greeting cards. For example, at a dinner, costs of food, decorations, entertainment, and prizes are for items that benefit attendees, not the organization. On the other hand, costs of invitations, planning, and publicity do not directly benefit attendees. Costs benefiting attendees are reported as an offset to revenue from the event; other costs are reported as fund-raising expenses. So if one pays $500 a plate to attend a dinner and the costs to the organization of presenting it are $65 for food and entertainment and $20 for publicity, the financial statements would show $500 of gross revenue less $65 direct costs for net revenue of $435, and fund-raising expenses of $20.

(ii)   When to Report Fund-raising Expenses

Although fund-raising costs incurred in one period often result in contributions received in future periods, accountants generally require that these costs be expensed in the period incurred rather than partly deferred to future periods. This requirement is due largely to the inherent uncertainty of the response to any fund-raising activity, which leads to an inability to accurately assess the extent to which such expenses actually have any remaining value at the end of the year in which they were incurred. Even expenses incurred in one year to develop long-range giving programs, such as capital campaigns or deferred (split-interest) gifts and bequests, must be reported as expenses when incurred, not deferred until gifts are received. (One exception to this rule is that unused supplies of printed materials can be carried as inventories, so long as they are reasonably expected to be used in future periods.) Thus, comparison of fund-raising expenses reported in one accounting period with contributions reported in the same period may or may not accurately reflect the real cause-and-effect relationship of these items.

(iii)   Allocation of Expenses

The general question of allocation arises whenever an expense benefits more than one activity. For example, if office space is shared by two departments, the monthly rent is allocated to the departments, usually on the basis of amount of space occupied. Similar allocations are often required for salaries, utilities, supplies, and other expenses. In most cases, the basis of allocation can be readily determined: salaries by time spent, supplies by usage, or occupancy by space occupied. The allocation process does require additional record keeping: time sheets or effort reports by personnel, estimates of supply usage, or computation of space occupied. Then worksheet calculations produce the allocated amounts.

Once total fund-raising costs are determined, by adding directly charged and allocated amounts, it may be desired to subdivide these costs into components representing the costs of each separate fund-raising activity, for example, various separate mailings, television advertisements, door-to-door approaches, and solicitation of grants. The process is the same as before; however, the smaller the final pieces, the more difficult it becomes to be objective about the allocations and the less precise the outcome. That is, in attempting to subdivide fund-raising expenses, one must recognize that the result does not have the same level of accuracy as achieved with larger amounts.

One particular allocation problem requires separate discussion: allocation of "joint" costs. These occur when a cost item simultaneously benefits more than one function and there is no objective method available to decide how much of the cost to allocate to each function. In fund raising, this situation most often occurs with multiple-purpose mailings, such as those containing both educational material (e.g., the seven warning signs of cancer) and an appeal for donations. The printing costs of each component are not at issue here; those are charged directly to the respective functions. The issue is the joint costs: the outside envelope, mailing list rental, staff time to coordinate the mailing, and (usually the largest item) postage.

Two questions must be answered: Is it at all appropriate to allocate joint costs and, if so, on what basis? These questions may seem trivial, but they are not. If it were always true that such mailings had a bona fide educational purpose, then the question of whether to allocate would be moot. However, often such mailings are really just solicitations, and any educational component is an afterthought, added to take advantage of the mailing going out anyway. How does one distinguish the genuine program activity? State charity regulators are especially concerned about this issue.

The accounting profession has published guidance in the AICPA SOP 98-2, *Accounting for Costs of Activities of Not-for-Profit Organizations and State and Local Governmental Entities That Include Fund Raising*. This standard defines four requirements that must all be met in order to allocate joint costs to functions other than fund raising:

1. There must be verifiable evidence of the reasons for conducting the activity.
2. The content of the activity must include a bona fide purpose other than fund raising.
3. The audience targeted must have a legitimate interest in the non–fund-raising component of the activity.
4. The non–fund-raising component must include material designed to motivate its audience to action other than contributing to the organization.

Clearly, professional judgment is required in deciding whether these requirements are met. The first requirement is judged partly on the answers to the other three as well as on criteria such as written management plans and board resolutions and assignment of overall responsibility for the activity to persons other than fund raisers. The second requirement is judged on the inherent value of the material and its consistency with the stated purposes of the organization. The third requirement has two components: the assumed wealth of the audience (as measured by income statistics for the geographical areas targeted, under the assumption that a wealthier audience is more likely to have been targeted for its fund-raising potential) and the presumed benefit to the audience of receiving the information (measured by data such as epidemiological statistics for a disease, demographic data, or other methods). The fourth requirement is best illustrated by an example. If the "educational" material merely described the seven warning signs of cancer, that would not count. It must say "Here are the seven warning signs of cancer; if you notice any of them, *go to your doctor*." The action is "go to your doctor." The presumption is that learning about something is of real value only when one takes beneficial action based on that knowledge. The action called for must be fairly specific: "Don't pollute" is too vague, but "Don't dump used motor oil in a storm drain" would qualify. The action may benefit the person receiving the message, or it could also benefit other people ("Don't drink and drive") or the environment (the motor oil example).

When working with a charity to plan a fund-raising activity that will include an educational component, fund raisers should be aware of these requirements so they can help the charity comply with the accounting rules if allocation of some of the costs to program activities is desired.

The second allocation question is what and how to allocate. *What* to allocate was discussed earlier; *how* is often a difficult question. It may seem that one could merely measure the relative quantities of educational vs. fund-raising material (lines of print, square units of space, or some comparable measure). First, however, not all material is of equal value: How does one count photographs, for example, or blank space used for emphasis of surrounding material, or various sizes of type, or sweepstakes tickets? Second, if relative quantity were the sole measure, charities attempting to minimize fund-raising costs would simply use the technique well known to writers of school term papers: padding. Educational material would expand to find the desired outcome, likely with little or no additional benefit to readers; in fact, the benefit might decrease as the message drowns in a sea of fluff. As a result, judgment is significant to the question of how to allocate. Certainly content can be considered, but so too the relative impact and usefulness of the

material, the apparent intent of the activity, the need of the audience for the educational material, and other relevant factors.

(iv)   Assessing Fund-Raising Efficiency

Although the assessment of fund-raising efficiency is not an accounting matter, it does depend partly on accounting data. The use of accounting data to help assess fund-raising efficiency must be done carefully, owing to the interaction of various accounting principles that determine when and how contributions and fund-raising expenses are reported in financial statements.

Reading Internal Revenue Service Form 990

PETER D. SWORDS, LLB
Former Executive Director,
Nonprofit Coordinating Committee of New York

50.1 Introduction

This chapter is about how to read the Internal Revenue Service (IRS) Form 990. It is fair to conclude that many who look at an organization's Form 990 confine their attention to its first two pages. Here we help readers understand what is in these two important pages.

(A) WHAT IS FORM 990?

Form 990, entitled "Return of Organization Exempt From Income Tax," is a report that must be filed each year with the IRS by organizations exempt from taxes under Section 501 of the Internal Revenue Code (IRC) of 1986, as amended, whose annual receipts are normally more than $25,000 a year. Charitable organizations, those exempt from taxation under section 501(c)(3) of the IRC, must also file Schedule A to Form 990. (Schedule A need not be filed by most other organizations exempt under Section 501, such as trade associations, social clubs and the like.) Generally, organizations are exempt under Section 501(c)(3) if they pursue charitable, educational, or religious purposes. They will be referred to in this chapter as "charities." An organization normally receives more than $25,000 a year if its gross receipts for the immediately preceding three tax years average $25,000 or more. Organizations with gross receipts of less than $100,000 may file a short-form Form 990 called Form 990-EZ.

Today Form 990 is the basic component of the annual report that must be filed with various state offices that regulate charitable solicitation. (See Chapter 52.) A few states require annual reports not only from charities that solicit within their borders but also from those that are merely located there.

In brief, Form 990 is a six-page form (and Schedule A is another five pages) that elicits a great deal of financial information about the reporting organization, asks a number of questions that can be answered yes or no, and elicits some descriptive information as well as the names and addresses of the organization's directors and key employees. In addition to completing the form proper, the filer must append a number of schedules and attachments

(B) FUNCTIONS OF FORM 990

Form 990 serves three essential purposes. First, it provides information that helps government agencies (the IRS and state charity regulators) enforce their laws. For example, both the IRS and state regulators enforce what has been called the nondistribution constraint. This is a rule that holds that money and assets may not be transferred from the filing organization to those who control the organization (other than transfers for which the organization receives services whose value is equal to the transfers). Payments of excessive compensation and self-dealing transactions are examples. The current version of Form 990 has been so finely developed that if a violation of the nondistribution constraint has occurred during the period being accounted for and the return has been filled out honestly, the violation will be reported. In addition, the IRS is charged with ensuring that charities do not engage in improper political activity or conduct too much lobbying, and Form 990 elicits information on these activities. Information about unrelated business activities is also elicited by Form 990 to aid the IRS in overseeing these activities. Of particular interest to the states, Form 990 elicits certain information about fund raising.

Second, Form 990 elicits a great deal of financial information about the filing organization that enables the reader to learn about the organization's financial condition, make judgments about its financial strength or weakness, and find out such things as the sources of its income. This chapter concentrates on pages 1 and 2 of Form 990, where much of this financial information can be found.

Finally, at Part III, Statement of Program Service Accomplishments, Form 990 elicits some information about what the filing organization does and how much money it spends on its programs.

(C) IMPORTANCE OF KNOWING WHAT FORM 990 CONTAINS

Form 990 is a very public document and it is becoming more public. Today an organization's 990 forms for the past three years must be shown to anyone who wants to see them. In addition, copies of these forms must be given to anyone who requests them (either by person or in writing) for a reasonable fee—$1 for the first page and 15 cents for every page thereafter. (Copies of the organization's Form 1023, "Application for Exemption from Taxation," must also be provided if requested.) Furthermore, most 990 forms beginning with the year 1997 are being posted on the Internet by the National Center for Charitable Statistics and Guidestar, two not-for-profit groups in the Washington D.C., area. Finally, it is only a matter of time before all charities will be required to file their 990 forms electronically. Today, for example, all Securities and Exchange Commission (SEC) and Federal Election Commission (FEC) filings must be done electronically.

Thus, virtually every 990 form is or soon will be accessible by anyone in the world. That does not mean, however, that readers of the forms will understand their content.

(D) HOW TO READ THIS CHAPTER

This chapter aims to help readers of Form 990 to interpret what it means. What can readers learn about an organization by studying its Form 990? The first two pages of the form provide mostly financial information; here we will be asking what these numbers might mean. We will find they might mean a number of things and so all that can be done is to suggest the kinds of inferences that may be reasonably drawn from them. Obviously not all of the many possible inferences will be suggested here, and some of those offered may be more or less apt for particular Forms 990. The suggestions offered below should be taken as prompts to more reflective thinking about a Form 990 rather than as sure guides to interpretation. Ultimately, each Form 990 tells the unique story of the organization that files it, and only by looking at the whole form and determining how one part or line helps one understand other parts and lines can readers begin to piece together what the document means.

This chapter has been written with Section 501(c)(3) nonprofits in mind, namely, those charitable, educational, and religious groups described under that IRC section. It should be kept in mind, however, that a wide variety of other not-for-profits are required to file Form 990.

In reading Form 990, it is helpful to have at hand a copy of the IRS's instructions for Form 990 and Form 990-EZ. This document explains in very clear and easily understandable language exactly what is expected by each line and what the various terms used in the form mean. Developed carefully over a number of years by those who created Form 990, it also provides a great deal of useful context information about the form. It is authoritative and a high quality piece of work. The instructions can be downloaded from the IRS's Web site for forms: http://ftp.fedworld.gov/pub/irspdf/f990.pdf

50.2 *Form 990: Page 1*

(A) THE HEADING

The section comprising the eight or so lines above Part I is called the "Heading" and conveys some useful information. Line A indicates the organization's fiscal year if other than the calendar year. Line C gives the organization's address, which may be important for identification purposes, particularly if there are several organizations with similar names. Line D provides the organization's Employer Identification Number (EIN), which also can be important for identification purposes. And Line E gives the organization's telephone number, which can be useful in verifying information and the like. Line H indicates whether Form 990 is a group return for a number of affiliates or a separate return covered by a group ruling. Finally, Line J indicates whether the organization is on the cash or accrual basis for accounting. Today the huge majority of charities use the accrual accounting method. As will be seen later, this is important to keep in mind when interpreting the form.

(B) PART I: REVENUE, EXPENSES, AND CHANGES IN NET ASSETS OR FUND BALANCES

(i) *Revenue*

There are two important questions about an organization, the answers to which may be suggested by examining the Revenue section of Part I. First, is it likely that the organization will continue to receive financial support in the future and thus remain financially strong? Second, are there people and agencies that have concluded that the organization's activities and purposes merit support? The two themes suggested by these questions are sounded throughout what follows.

Before going through each line of the Revenue section, readers might want to go directly to Line 12, which indicates the total amount of income or revenue the organization received in the course of the year covered by the return. This information gives readers some idea of an organization's size. (Readers might also want to look at Line 90b near the bottom of page 5 to see how many people the organization employs.) This is obviously an important piece of context information. A large organization does not just emerge one day as a large organization. It must have generated considerable support over time to reach its current position. Lines 1 to 11 provide information about amounts and different sources of income the group received. This information is very suggestive and can only be interpreted confidently after taking into account the amount of an organization's total revenue.

A great deal more can be found about an organization by examining several years worth of forms. (Groups must make available forms from the last three years.) For example, if a source of income is reported at about the same level for three years running, there is a fair likelihood that it will continue coming in at this level. This inference could not be made with the same level of confidence on the basis of the information in just one Form 990.

Line 1 elicits data about contributions, gifts, and similar transfers for which the donor gets nothing back in return from the filing organization. This line is broken down into three sublines. Line 1a (direct public support) includes such transfers as contributions from individuals and foundation grants and dues from members where the members receive nothing or little of value back from the organization for their payments but rather make these contributions (dues payments) simply to support it.

Line 1b (indirect public support) includes contributions received from a federated fund-raising agency, such as the United Way. Line 1a elicits information about contributions received as a result of the organization's own efforts while Line 1b relates to contributions received as the results of another organization's efforts.

Line 1c (government grants) includes transfers from government agencies for which the agencies receive nothing in return. In that respect they are like grants from foundations and are quite different from government contracts. Government contracts, which are included on Line 2, involve the receipt of payments from a government agency for work performed by the organization for the agency.

Support from any source suggests that there are some who thought well of the group. If the return shows a good deal of revenue at Line 1a from direct public support (individual gifts and foundation grants, etc.), it may be inferred that many think well of it. There are, however, several cautionary points to keep in mind. First, check fund-raising expenses at Line 15. Significant fund-raising expenses might suggest that the gift revenue can be explained as much by the success of the fund-raising efforts as by favorable public opinion. On the other hand, if several years worth of forms show strong direct public support and relatively high fund-raising expenses, the organization probably has developed a solid means of supporting itself.

Line 1a also might include a foundation grant that is to be used over several years. Thus, only a part of the grant is properly attributable to the year being reported on. Looking at the amounts included on the line without knowing the size or length of the grant might lead one to make erroneous assumptions about the organization's income-generating efforts for that year. (Part IV, Balance Sheets, of Form 990 and particularly Line 68 (temporarily restricted assets) might provide some clues as to the existence of the multiyear grant. This problem is discussed below, although balance sheet analysis and Part IV are beyond the scope of this chapter.) Similarly, if the organization received a large bequest during the year reported, Line 1a may show a healthier amount of contributions than is usual, but there is no way of knowing from just one form. Therefore, it is important to look at the organization's 990 forms for several years.

Finally, Line 1a includes those amounts received from fund-raising events for which the contributor received nothing of value in return from the organization. For example, contributors to a fund-raising benefit pay $250 for a ticket to the event. The dinner they receive is worth $85 to them. Line 1a would list $165 ($250 – $85); and Line 9 would list $85. (See below.) Some organizations have regular fund-raising events, so this source of income may be expected to recur. Other fund-raising events are held relatively infrequently and should not be expected to be a recurring source of income. Examining Line 1a does not provide an answer to the source of funding.

Amounts listed at Line 1b as receipts from a federated fund-raising agency might reasonably be expected to be a reliable source of future income. On the other hand, if an organization lists contributions on Line 1b for two years but omits them in the third year, then perhaps the federated agency knows something about the group that is not evident from its Form 990.

Government grants (as distinguished from government contracts) are pretty rare for most groups, so it may be sensibly supposed that amounts included on Line 1c may not be recurring.

Line 2 (Program Services revenue including government fees and contracts) includes amounts received by an organization for charging for its services, such as tuition charged by a school or amounts received by a performing arts company from ticket sales. Furthermore, as suggested above, some not-for-profits receive fees for performing services for government agencies. Included in this latter group are some organizations that receive nearly all of their revenue from government contracts. Their 990 forms will show significant amounts at Line 2. However, to ascertain whether the amounts appearing on Line 2 are from government contracts, it will be necessary to look at Line 93 under Part VII on page 6. Line 93 breaks down program service revenue between fees, for example, charged to individual clients (Line 93a–e), Medicare or Medicaid payments (Line 93f), and revenues from government contracts (Line 93g column (e)). In understanding the nature of an organization, it may be considered significant that it receives nearly all of its revenue from a contract (or contracts) with a government agency (or agencies).

Line 3 (Membership dues and assessments) includes amounts received by an organization from its members from charging for services it provides to them. Note that the amounts included at Line 3 are payments for which the members receive more or less full consideration in services for their dues and not payments that are primarily ways of contributing support to an organization. These latter payments, as noted above, would be included on Line 1a. It is rare that charities have income on Line 3.

Lines 4 (Interest on savings and temporary cash investments), 5 ((Dividends and interest from securities), 6 (Rent), 7 (Other investment income), and 8 (Gross amount from sales of assets other than inventory—e.g., securities, real estate, etc.), cover what might be called "passive" income from investments. Groups with large endowments will receive substantial amounts of interest and dividend income, which will be shown on Lines 4 and 5. Line 8 for the most part will be receipts from the sales of securities and may also reflect the presence of endowments. Amounts on Line 6 (Rent) suggest the ownership or real property held for rental income. Line 7 (Other investment income) usually involves royalty income. Given the nature of the underlying holdings that produce these kinds of income, they may be expected to recur each year at about the same levels. On the other hand, income from temporary cash savings may not be a regularly recurring receipt as the savings may be soon exhausted.

Line 9 includes income from special fund-raising events (but only that part of income received for such events for which the contributor gets full value back for his or her payment; see comments and example accompanying the explanation of Line 1a above). Line 9 calls for the gross amounts from such receipts (Line 9a), the fund-raising expenses incurred in generating such amounts (Line 9b), and the net income received (Line 9c). Large and recurring net amounts at Line 9c may suggest that the organization spends a considerable amount of time and money producing events like trade fairs where a good deal of selling for value goes on. This may be relevant to the reader of a Form 990. (In the example given earlier regarding Line 1a, where each contributor paid $250 for attending and received in return a dinner worth $85, if we assume that 100 people attended the event and that each dinner cost the organization $55, Line 9a would show $[850] $8,500; Line 9b would show $[550] 5,550; and Line 9c would show $[300] 3,000.)

Line 10 includes income from the sale of inventory. This, while a significant source of income for some kinds of not-for-profits, is not likely to be a big item for charitable organizations.

Line 11 (Other revenue) includes items of income of a type that are not includable at Lines 1 through 10. Line 103 of Part VII explains what kinds of income are included.

Some organizations engage in unrelated business activities—activities that have nothing to do with achieving their exempt purpose conducted mostly to raise funds to support the organizations' exempt activities. An example would be a not-for-profit that published a journal that ran advertising for products having nothing to do with the organization's exempt purpose. Organizations with unrelated business income must file a Form 990-T; if such gross income is in excess of $1,000, they may have to pay an unrelated business income tax on such income. Revenue from such activities may be included on Line 2, 10, or 11. (In rare cases it may be included on some other revenue line.) By examining Part VII, readers can determine how much of the amounts included on those lines constitute unrelated business income. Depending on the "business," unrelated business income might be a constant and reliable source of income.

Now it is time to discuss what might reasonably be concluded by comparing the relative amounts included on the various lines on the Revenue section of Part I. To do so, it is helpful to think of a continuum, with groups that rely on donations for nearly all of their money at one end and those that receive most of their money from the sale of goods and services at the other end. The groups at the left end may be called "donative" groups. Since they engage in little commercial activity and rely heavily on contributions, they might be thought of by some as truly charitable. Those at the other end, which receive most of their income from charging for their services, may be called "commercial," although this term should be understood in the limited sense that fees are charged for services rendered and not in the ordinary sense of "commercial," which might suggest for-profit enterprises.

Keeping this continuum in mind, readers may think of groups with relatively large amounts on Line 1 (contributions) and relatively small sums on other lines to be truly charitable. Given the somewhat fickle nature of charitable giving, on the other hand, they may be thought to have a relatively unstable source of funding.

Groups with relatively large amounts on Line 2 (Program service revenue) and relatively small sums on other lines may be, for example, not-for-profit theaters, which derive much of their income from ticket sales. Or they may be groups that derive most of their money from government contracts. Here it would be useful to have some idea of what the group does. (See discussion of Part III below.) This source of income can be stable, although government funding may not be. In any event, the character of groups that receive little contribution income is quite different from those that get most of their income from contributions.

Groups with relatively large amounts on Line 3 (Membership dues and assessment) and relatively small sums on other lines are likely to be not-for-profits that finance themselves by providing services to their members and may not be of a charitable nature. In many cases the service fees will be a steady source of income.

Groups with large amounts of income listed on any or all of Lines 4 to 8, which indicate essentially investment-type income (or "passive" income), may be thought to have a fairly stable flow of income from these sources in the future. It might, however, be fairly concluded that the assets that produce this passive income were given to the organization in the past and the income generated from them does not indicate present support from outside sources for the organization.

A final point on sources of revenue. Many believe that it is desirable for an organization to receive income from a wide variety of sources. Whether an organization has been able to do this or not may be inferred from examining Lines 1 to 11.

(ii) Expenses

An organization's expenses are broken down into two sets of categories: functional expenses and object expenses. (Object expenses are discussed above.) The three functional expense categories are program services, management and general, and fund raising. The Expenses section of Part I of Form 990 gives the totals of an organization's functional expenses. These amounts are derived from Part II of the form on page 2. Part II contains about 25 lines (rows) at which are listed an organization's object expenses (e.g., salaries, supplies, etc.). These amounts are allocated among three columns for functional expenses, namely, Program services (column B), Management and general (column C), and Fund raising (column D). Column A lists the totals of each of the object expense lines. Totals of each functional expense column are entered on Line 44 (Total functional expenses). The totals from Line 44 that are carried back to the lines in the Expenses section of Part I. Thus, Line 44 column B, the total for Program services, is carried back to Line 13; Line 44 column C, the total for Management and general, to Line 14; and Line 44 column D, the total for Fund raising, to Line 15. The total of the total (i.e., the sum of Lines 13, 14, and 15) is entered on Line 17 (Total expenses). (Line 16 [Payments to affiliates] is for certain payments made by affiliates to their parents. These payments are extremely rare and the reader is unlikely to encounter them.)

Program services expenses are those incurred to carry out the organization's mission. Thus, expenses incurred by a social services organization in paying its social workers for delivering services to its clients would be program services expenses. By the same token, payments made by a performing arts organization to produce a play would be program services expenses. For a 501(c)(3) group, the activities that these expenses support usually are the basis of the organization's tax exemption.

Management and general expenses are those incurred in connection with providing overall administration to an organization. The instructions include as examples such things as preparing for and holding board meetings, working on office management and personnel problems, and accounting and investment activities. The Instructions also make clear that the expenses incurred in carrying out activities involving the supervision of program services or fund raising are not included under management and general. Thus, for example, preparing for and attending a development committee meeting would not be part of this category.

Fund-raising expenses are pretty much self-defining. The instructions define this category as "the total expenses incurred in soliciting contributions, gifts, grants, etc."

Not uncommonly, it is difficult to determine which functional category to assign a particular expense to. Another problem arises because some expenses may relate to more than one functional category (shared expenses). The subject of expense categorization and allocation is far beyond the scope of this chapter. By the time a reader examines a Form 990, these decisions have been made by those filling out Form 990, but careful readers should be aware that there is at least as much art as science (and sometimes a little spin) in assigning categories and will keep this in mind as they interpret the expense information contained in the form.

It is conventional wisdom that it is preferable for a group to spend most of its money on programs and relatively little on management and general fund raising. Thus, ratios are sometimes used for assessment purposes. It may be asked: Of a group's total spending, how much was made up by the three functional categories? The fund-raising ratio, for example, would consist of fund-raising expenses over total expenses. This ratio can be developed from the information found in the Expenses section of Part I, namely, the amounts found at Lines 15 (Fund raising) and 17 (Total expenses). For example, if Line 15 is $80,000 and Line 17 is $400,000, the fund-raising ratio would be 20 percent ($80,000/$400,000 = 20%). Similarly program services and management and general ratios can be developed from the data on Lines 13 (Program services), 14 (Management and general), and 17 (Total expenses).

A high program service ratio and relatively low management and general and fund-raising ratios might be thought to be desirable. Yet this wisdom is conventional and not necessarily sound. For example, groups that are young or are advancing unpopular causes may have to spend more on fund raising than well-established groups or those that provide services that everyone agrees are important. Furthermore, conventional wisdom is generally misinformed about the importance and realities of fund raising. For example, those who have never worked in a not-for-profit organization have little idea of how hard fund raising can be or how much time and effort are needed to do it successfully. Similar observations apply to management and general, except that the management and general ratios are usually fairly low (in part because a lot of what administrators do is fund-raise). As a final point on this subject, caution must be exercised in interpreting allocations of expenses among the three categories of functional expenses. Pressures of conventional wisdom, which insist that it is inappropriate to spend too much on fund raising, may in some cases induce people to underrepresent the amount of time and money actually spent on fund raising. A group that is "honest" (naive) in its reporting may be hurt when those who assess an organization follow the guidelines of conventional wisdom when interpreting spending ratios.

(iii) Net Assets

The Net Assets portion of Part I contains four lines that offer real grist for the interpretation mill. Line 18 (Excess or (deficit)) is the difference between Line 12 (Total revenue) and Line 17 (Total expenses) and shows whether the filer ended the year in the red or the black—a matter of some interest. Line 19 (Net assets or fund balances at beginning of the year) shows a figure taken from Part IV (Balance sheets) and generally represents the net worth of the filer at the start of its accounting period. It will be equal to a cognate line (Line 73 column A) on the filer's balance sheet (Part IV). Line 20 (Other changes to net assets or fund balances) is for certain adjustments, which are explained below. In many cases it will be left blank or the figure zero will be entered. And Line 21 (Net Assets or fund balances at end of year) shows a figure taken from Part IV (Balance sheets) and generally represents the net worth of the filer at the end of its accounting period. It will be equal to a cognate line (Line 73 column B) on the filer's balance sheet (Part IV). Where Line 20 is zero (which is usually the case), Line 21 is the result of combining Line 18, the organization's surplus or deficit for the year, and Line 19, the organization's net worth at the start of the year. (See below for information on Line 20.) To take a very simple case, suppose an organization had $100 at the start of the year and no outstanding liabilities. In these circumstances, Line 19 would show $100. If during the year it took in $200 and incurred expenses of $175, it would have a surplus (excess) of $25, and Line 18 would show $25. Combining Lines 18 and 19 would produce the amount of $125, which is the figure that would be entered at Line 21. (If the organization incurred expenses of $210 for the year, Line 18 would show a deficit of $10 and combining Lines 18 and 19 would result in a figure of $90, which would be entered at Line 21.)

Thus, from a financial standpoint, these lines in the Net Assets section of Part I provide significant information about an organization. Does it have solid financial resources behind it? Or is it getting by pretty much on what it brings in each year with little in reserve? The net worth lines (Lines 19 and 21) can provide information to help answer these questions. As noted, before any firm conclusion can be drawn, attention would also have to be paid to the balance sheet, since, for example, the filer might have all of its net worth tied up in real estate that might be difficult to liquidate.

It is of interest in itself to know whether the organization ended the year with a surplus (excess) or deficit. Of course, if 990 forms for the past three years are available, readers will be able to make more informed determinations about the organization's financial position than if only one year's form could be checked. An organization that has been running deficits three years in a row and has a constantly diminishing net worth is much different from one with only one year of deficit and an increase in net worth over three years.

Of course, few 990 forms are as simple as the one described here. Analysis is complicated by a fairly large number of special transactions with special accounting rules for their treatment. Only a few examples of these complications will be provided here.

We begin by considering a multiyear grant from a foundation. If, for example, an organization receives a grant that is to be spent in equal amounts over three years, the entire amount of the grant would be included on Line 1 and thus be part of total revenues on Line 12. Consequently, Line 18 (Excess or (deficit)) will reflect the full amount of the grant although only one-third of it was to be spent in the year covered by Form 990. Readers who look only at page 1 might conclude that the filer had a healthier financial performance for the year than if they knew that some if its revenue on Line 12 was to be spent in future years. Readers who know about the multiyear grant might discount an organization's excess at Line 18 somewhat; similarly, the readers might consider deficits at Line 18 somewhat understated. Readers would be alerted to the details of the revenue at Line 12 if they looked at the filer's Part IV and knew how to interpret Line 68. Line 68 shows temporarily restricted assets, and readers would learn from considering this line that some of the revenue included at Line 12 was to be used in future years. Thus they would be in a position to make a more informed judgment about Line 18 and generally about the Net Assets section of Part I.

As a second example, consider accounts receivable. Accounts receivable are amounts that the organization has earned for the year covered by Form 990 that have not yet been paid. For example, a group may have conducted workshops during the year and some of the participants may still owe the filer for attending the workshops. These (unpaid) amounts will be included as revenue at Line 2 (Program service revenue) and thus be a part of Line 12 (Total revenue) and, of course, ultimately be reflected in Line 18 (Excess or (deficit)). To readers of Form 990, it might be noteworthy if an organization's revenues included a fair amount of accounts receivable; readers would be able to know this only by referring to Line 47 (Accounts receivable) at Part IV (Balance Sheets) of the form.

There are many other such complications, both on the asset and the liability side. Consequently, to interpret with confidence the important Net Assets section of page 1, readers should know about these various accounting conventions and be able to read Part I in light of the information contained at Part IV.

A note on Line 20 (Other changes in net assets or fund balances). In rare instances, changes in an organization's net assets at the start and end of the year cannot be accounted for by the amount on Line 18. They would include such items as adjustments of earlier years' activities and unrealized gains on investments carried at market value. The net of these changes is entered at Line 20. (The complexities raised by Line 20 are beyond the scope of this chapter.)

50.3 Form 990: Page 2

(A) PART II: STATEMENT OF FUNCTIONAL EXPENSES

Part II (Statement of Functional Expenses) is where most of an organization's expenses are reported. As noted, it is structured in accordance with two types of expenses: object expenses and functional expenses. Object expenses include such things as compensation paid to staff, amounts paid for telephone, and travel. Functional expenses divide expenses by activity: amounts spent on program services, management and general, and fund-raising expenses. Functional expenses were considered in the last section. The relationship between program services expenses as reported at Part II and Part III in our discussion of Part III below. Here we concentrate on what can be concluded from studying an organization's object expenses.

A number of expenses do not appear on page 2's Part II but are listed on page 1. Thus, expenditures incurred in connection with rental income received from investment property are recorded at Line 6b; sales expenses incurred in connection with the sale of securities and the like at Line 8b; certain expenses incurred in connection with special events at Line 9b; and the cost of goods sold in connection with the sale of inventory at Line 10b. For the most part these expenses are incurred in connection with the production of income raised simply to support the organization and not in connection with any program of the filer. (Note, however, that the same could be said for general fund-raising expenses or expenses incurred in connection with the receipt of unrelated business income, which are reported in Part II of page 2.) It may be significant to know how much is expended on the production of these types of revenue. Knowing that an organization spends a substantial amount of money in producing rental income or in connection with the sale of securities rather than just the amount of net income from these sources may inform one's understanding of the filer. To complete the identification of non–page-2 expenses, certain kinds of payments made to affiliated organizations, such as dues paid by a local charity solely to support its state or national parent where nothing or little of value is received in return, are reported at Line 16. As noted above, this line is only rarely applicable and usually shows zero.

We now look at the expenses listed on Part II. The various object expenses listed at Lines 22 to 42 (salaries, postage, etc.) are fairly much self-defining and explanatory comment will be provided for only a few of them. (As suggested above, the Instructions to Form 990 are excellent in explaining these terms.) Line 22 (Grants and allocations) is where grants are listed. Many grantmaking organizations file Forms 990-PF, but some not-for-profits that are not private foundations nevertheless make grants and therefore file 990 forms. Such grants would be listed here. Line 23 (Specific assistance to individuals) is for direct payments to an organization's clients or patients, and Line 24 (Benefits paid to or for members) is for payments to members such as hospitalization or disability benefits. (Line 24 usually applies to non-501(c)(3) organizations.) As far as the categorization of functional expenses goes, Lines 22 to 24 must be allocated to Program services (column B). Amounts listed on these lines indicate how much an organization is spending on management and general or fund raising. (Of course, there is no assurance that the grants were intelligently or carefully made or that they accomplished their purposes. See generally the observations made below in discussing Part III on the utility of Form 990 for making substantive evaluations of a filing organization.)

Lines 25 to 29 have to do with payment of compensation to staff and (where applicable) board members. As there might be concern about salary levels (being too high or too low), these lines could be of particular interest. Line 25 is for compensation paid to officers, key employees, and (if applicable) board members and should equal the sum of the amounts listed at Part V (List of Officers, Directors, Trustees, and Key Employees). Part V lists the total compensation paid to directors and officers and each key employee. A key employee is defined as someone with authority to control the activities or finances of the organization and when there is an issue of excessive compensation, it frequently involves employees with such power. Thus, some close inspection may be paid to Part V. To avoid the disclosure of particular compensation payments that may be thought to raise awkward questions, unscrupulous organizations may hide these payments by including them at Line 26 (Other salaries and wages). However, when the amounts listed at Line 26 [24] are divided by the total number of employees as listed at Line 90b, if the average seems high, suspicious readers may want to probe deeper (particularly if they have information about compensation independent of the Form 990). Furthermore, Line 29 (Payroll taxes) includes amounts paid as the organization's share of social security and Medicare taxes and thus roughly reflects the level of its actual payments of compensation. As these amounts are reported to the IRS on other forms (e.g., Form 941) and to some extent can be cross-checked against employees' individual income tax returns, they are not likely to be falsified. At the other end of the question about salary levels, dividing the amount listed at Line 26 [24] by the number of employees listed at Line 90b may suggest that some salaries may be too low.

The only other specific lines on Part II that will be commented on are Line 30 (Professional fund-raising fees), Line 36 (Occupancy), and Line 43 (Other expenses). Line 30 is where payments to outside fund raisers for solicitation campaigns or for advising the organization on solicitation campaigns are put. Some groups may not want to disclose this kind of payment and choose instead to include it at Line 43 (Other expenses) as "professional services" or some such thing. Suspicious readers might cross-check Part II of Schedule A, where compensation paid to the five highest-paid independent contractors for professional services who are paid more than $50,000 should be listed. The instructions to Schedule A make clear that professional fund raisers are to be included here. Column a of Schedule A's Part II requires the filer to list the names and addresses of each independent contractor listed; column b requires that the type of service be noted. Thus, payments to professional fund raisers may be disclosed at Part II of Schedule A if not on Line 30 of Form 990 proper. The filing organization must file a Form 1096 with the IRS for every payment it makes to an independent contractor in excess of $600. Thus, the filer is likely to feel constrained to complete Part II of Schedule A accurately.

On Line 36 (Occupancy) should be put amounts paid for the use of space, heat, light, power, outside janitorial services, mortgage interest, property insurance, and similar expenses.

Finally, a word about line 43 (Other expenses) is merited. A large number of expenses are not included at Lines 22 to 42, such as payments for general liability and Directors and Officers (D&O) insurance, taxes for which the organization is not exempt, expenses incurred in connection with the production of workshops, purchase of food, computer services, and on and on. These expenses are listed at Line 43. In many cases filers will attach a schedule to their returns listing all these expenses; such schedules are well worth looking at. Certain payments may be listed here in ways that obscure their true nature.

What generally can be said about Part II? In connection with the Expense section of Part I on page 1, we have already discussed what might be made (or not made) of comparing the relative amounts spent on the three functional categories—program services, management and general, and fund-raising expenses. As far as evaluation of what object expenses might mean, perhaps some inferences might be drawn if the amounts listed on certain lines seem large as compared to other expenses (e.g., a large amount spent on legal fees or travel may raise questions), but extreme caution should be exercised in arriving at any such conclusion. A commonsense review of these expenses may offer some insight into a filer's activities (e.g., substantial amounts spent on printing and publication are consistent with an organization that publishes journals and reports while substantial amounts spent on travel are consistent with an organization that provides services in different places).

Just below the listing of object expenses is a question that asks whether the filer reported in column B (Program services) any joint costs from a combined educational campaign and fund-raising solicitation. For example, an organization may mail a pamphlet to its potential supporters that tells about the organization and the importance of its cause and solicits contributions. The costs of preparing and sending this pamphlet may be allocated between program services and fund raising. In this case the organization would answer the question "Yes" and in the space provided indicate the total amount of these joint costs and the amounts allocated to program services and fund raising. In interpreting these figures, readers should remember the art involved in making joint cost allocations. Perhaps the most relevant use that can be made of this segment of Form 990 comes up when readers know about activities to which it applies and find that the filer has answered the question "No." In these circumstances, some doubts may be raised about the accuracy of the filer's reporting of fund-raising expenses; caution should be used in making such an interpretation.[1]

(B) PART III: STATEMENT OF PROGRAM SERVICE ACCOMPLISHMENTS

In Part III of Form 990, a filer can indicate what it does. The filer is supposed to state the organization's primary purpose and then for each program describe its purpose and state the outputs of the program, such as number of clients served, publications issued, and students taught. The filer must then list the total of program expenses for each such program; the sum of all these expenses must be the same as the Line 44 (Total of functional expenses) total for Program services (column B). A creative filer may be able to provide a fair idea of its activities, but careful readers should not accept the statistics at face value. Site visits and interviews with those served are needed to assess the utility of a program. In any event we believe that this is a good place to start one's examination of a Form 990 since it is the only place that gives readers an idea of the activities an organization engages in; thus it provides an important context for interpreting the rest of the Form 990.

Suggested Readings

Sanders, Michael I., Celia Roady, and Andrew S. Lang. *Completing Your IRS Form 990: A Guide for Tax-Exempt Organizations.* American Society of Association Executives, 1990.
Swords, Peter D. "The Form 990 as an Accountability Tool for 501(c)(3) Nonprofits." *Tax Lawyer* 51 (1998).

---

[1] In 1998 the American Institute of Certified Public Accountants issued a Statement of Position on the subject of joint cost allocations that addresses this subject. See SOP 98-2 "Accounting for Costs of Activities of Not-for-Profit Organizations and State and Local Government Entities That Include Fund Raising," Mar. 11, 1998.

Federal Regulation of Fund Raising

BRUCE R. HOPKINS, JD, LLM
Polsinelli, White, Vardeman & Shalton

51.1 Introduction

The solicitation of charitable contributions constitutes practices that are recognized as being among the highest forms of free speech protected by federal and state constitutional law. This type of free speech may be regulated by only the narrowest of means. Thus, there are significant limitations on the extent to which fund raising for charitable, educational, scientific, religious, and like organizations can be regulated by government. Despite these constitutional law precepts, nonprofit organizations in the United States face considerable regulatory requirements at the federal and state levels when they solicit contributions for charitable purposes. The purpose of this chapter is to summarize this body of federal law.[1]

Some of the segments of this chapter are followed by a brief checklist, enabling an organization to review its status under and compliance with this body of law. An organization may wish to complete these checklists, and keep the information as part of its minute book or other document files. (See Checklists 51.1 through 51.9.)

51.2 *Private Inurement and the* United Cancer Council *Case*

The fund-raising charitable organization known as the United Cancer Council, Inc. (UCC) had its tax-exempt status revoked by the Internal Revenue Service (IRS) in 1990, on the grounds that its net earnings had inured to persons in their private capacity. The underlying rule of law is known as *private inurement;* the most common way to cause private inurement is to pay excessive compensation. For the private inurement doctrine to apply, the party to the transaction with the charitable organization must be an *insider.*

The UCC litigated the matter of its tax exemption in the U.S. Tax Court. The court's decision in the case, rendered by the court late in 1997, is one of the most significant judicial opinions shaping the law of fund raising.

The court found a fund-raising company to be an insider with respect to the UCC and concluded that private inurement took place because the firm was paid excessive compensation.

The UCC was established in 1963 and was recognized by the IRS as an exempt charitable organization in 1969. In 1984 the UCC entered into a direct mail contract with a fund-raising company by the name of Watson & Hughey (W&H). This contract—a version of the "no-risk" type of fund-raising arrangement—embraced a five-year period (1984 to 1989). While the UCC received about $2.25 million as a result of the fund raising, W&H obtained over $4 million in fees. Also, the parties had co-ownership rights in the UCC's mailing list, and W&H was able to exploit those rights to derive substantial income.

When the IRS revoked the exempt status of the UCC, it did so retroactively, to the date in 1984 when the contract relationship with the UCC began.

An organization cannot qualify as a tax-exempt charitable one when a portion of its net earnings inures to the benefit of a person who is considered an insider with respect to it. The term "insider" is borrowed from the securities laws and is not a technical term in the federal tax setting. The formal term is "private shareholder" or "private individual."

Prior to the UCC case, the law did not provide for an overarching definition of an insider; the then-existing cases involved individuals in the status of an organization's founder, its trustees, directors, and/or officers, and members of the family of individuals of this nature, along with controlled business entities.

The Tax Court, however, in the UCC case, wrote that an insider is a person who exercises "significant control" over the exempt organization's activities and finances. In a subsequent opinion, the court said that an insider includes an individual who has or had

---

[1]This body of law is summarized in greater detail in Bruce R. Hopkins, *The Law of Fund-Raising,* 2nd ed. (New York: John Wiley & Sons, 1996).

a "significant formal voice in . . . [a charitable organization's] activities generally and had substantial formal and practical control over most of [the organization's] income."

As noted, a charitable organization's paying excessive compensation to an insider constitutes private inurement. Whether compensation is excessive or unreasonable is a factual determination, made on the basis of all pertinent facts and circumstances.

The court evaluated the position that W&H occupied in relation to the UCC during the years at issue. It observed that the UCC was "heavily financed and kept in existence" by W&H by reason of the fund-raising arrangement they had. This relationship, wrote the court, "was in many ways analogous to that of a founder and major contributor to a new organization."

In general, the court concluded that W&H exercised substantial control over the UCC's finances and direct mail fund-raising campaigns over a period of several years. Thus, the court, also finding "extensive control" over the UCC by W&H, concluded that W&H was an insider with respect to UCC.

Having found the involvement of an insider, the court concluded that private inurement had occurred, in the form of excessive compensation to the UCC. The court conceded that the contract between the parties was bargained for but then found that that factor alone does not "by itself conclusively protect an arrangement from a determination that the compensation was unreasonable." The private inurement took place in the form of the fees paid by the UCC and W&H's improper use of the UCC mailing list.

This case thus involves a charity that became a captive of a fund-raising company. Although the facts are—to understate the matter—unique, the case illustrates the fundamental point that what may appear to be an independent vendor of services to a charitable organization can be an insider with respect to it. It is unfortunate for the development community that the first case to fully articulate this point had to arise in the fund-raising setting.

Critics of the opinion state that it is unfair, in that it penalizes a charity because of fund-raising results that turned out to be insufficient, including in relation to the money that was spent. This view, however, is not warranted or is at least understated. For one thing, the court specifically wrote: "We are not holding that an arm's-length arrangement that produces a poor result for an organization necessarily would cause the organization to lose its tax-exempt status."

This case involves more than the simple matter of payment of compensation that was deemed to be excessive. The charitable organization's mailing list—a valuable asset—and other of its resources were manipulated by the fund-raising company for its own private ends.

There are lessons to be learned from this unfortunate episode. First, a charitable organization should identify those who are insiders with respect to it. This is done by applying an encompassing definition of those who have or may have "substantial control" over its activities and/or finances. Second, the organization should be careful when engaging in transactions with insiders, being particularly thorough in determining whether any compensation paid is excessive. Third, this matter of private inurement goes beyond compensation: There are other ways in which an economic benefit can be accorded an insider. Charities should review their contractual relationships (e.g., management contracts, consultants' contracts, partnership agreements, and leases) and other aspects of their operations to see if somehow they are, inadvertently or otherwise, conferring unwarranted benefits on insiders.

There is one other aspect of all of this: the rules concerning *excess benefit transactions*. These rules, otherwise known as *intermediate sanctions* (summarized next), define the term "disqualified person" much the same way the law defines an insider. The statute defines disqualified person essentially to mean one who is in a position to exercise substantial influence over the affairs of the organization. Thus, one who is an insider is quite likely to be a disqualified person. This means that a set of facts such as those in the UCC case may give rise to some significant tax liabilities rather than (or in addition to) loss of the organization's tax-exempt status.

51.3 Intermediate Sanctions

(A) STATUTORY RULES

Intermediate sanctions rules were signed into law on July 30, 1996.[2] This is a historic development, bringing into the federal tax law one of the most significant bodies of regulation affecting charitable organizations ever enacted. The potential impact of this new tax law regime is enormous. This is due in part to the general effective date for this legislation: September 14, 1995.

The new sanctions are designed to curb abuses in the arena of private inurement using a mechanism other than revocation of the charitable organization's tax exemption. These sanctions are applicable with respect to all public charitable organizations and tax-exempt social welfare organizations. These two categories of organizations are termed *applicable tax-exempt organizations*.

In the past, revocation of an offending charitable organization's tax-exempt status has not solved the problem. The person receiving the undue benefit continued to retain it and the beneficiaries of the charitable organization's program were the ones who were hurt in the aftermath of loss of exemption. Intermediate sanctions are *intermediate* in the sense that they will be imposed on directors, officers, key employees, or other types of disqualified persons who engage in inappropriate private transactions.

The heart of this body of tax law is the *excess benefit transaction*. A transaction is an excess benefit transaction if an economic benefit is provided by an applicable tax-exempt organization directly or indirectly to or for the use of a disqualified person, if the value of the economic benefit provided exceeds the value of the consideration received by the exempt organization for providing the benefit. The immediate focus of intermediate sanctions will be unreasonable compensation—where a person's level of compensation is deemed to be in excess of the value of the economic benefit derived by the organization from the person's services. In that regard, an economic benefit may not be treated as compensation for the performance of services unless the organization clearly indicated its intent to so treat the benefit.

The concept of the excess benefit transaction includes any transaction in which the amount of any economic benefit provided to or for the use of a disqualified person is determined in whole or in part by the revenues of one or more activities of the organization, where the transaction is reflected in tax regulations and it results in private inurement.

---

[2]This body of law is the subject of Bruce R. Hopkins and D. Benson Tesdahl, *Intermediate Sanctions: Curbing Nonprofit Abuse* (New York: John Wiley & Sons, 1997).

A *disqualified person* is any person who was, at any time during the five-year period ending on the date of the transaction, in a position to exercise substantial influence over the affairs of the organization, as well as a member of the family of such an individual and certain controlled entities.

A disqualified person who benefited from an excess benefit transaction is subject to an initial tax equal to 25 percent of the amount of the excess benefit. Moreover, this person will be required to return the excess benefit amount to the tax-exempt organization. An *organization manager* (usually a director or officer) who participated in an excess benefit transaction, knowing that it was such a transaction, is subject to an initial tax of 10 percent of the excess benefit. An additional tax may be imposed on a disqualified person where the initial tax was imposed and the appropriate correction of the excess benefit transaction did not occur. In this situation, the disqualified person is subject to a tax equal to 200 percent of the excess benefit involved.

If a transaction creating a benefit was approved by an independent board, or an independent committee of the board, a presumption arises that the terms of the transaction are reasonable. The burden of proof would then shift to the IRS, who would then have to overcome (rebut) the presumption to prevail. This presumption may cause a restructuring of the boards of directors or trustees of many charitable organizations.

The concept of the excess benefit transaction could apply in the context of payments for fund-raising services. One circumstance would be where the recipient of the funds is an employee of the exempt organization. Another would be where the person paid is an independent contractor, such as an outside fund-raising company. The sanctions apply to disqualified persons, such as an individual who is in a position to exercise substantial influence over the affairs of the organization.

In many respects, the concept of the excess benefit transaction will be based on existing law concerning private inurement. However, the statute expressly states that an excess benefit transaction also includes any transaction in which the amount of any economic benefit provided to a disqualified person is determined at least in part by the revenues of the organization. These transactions are referenced in the legislative history of the intermediate sanctions as *revenue-sharing arrangements*.

The IRS and the courts have determined that a variety of revenue-sharing arrangements do not constitute private inurement. This includes arrangements where the compensation of a person is ascertained, in whole or in part, on the basis of the value of contributions generated. The legislative history of the sanctions states that the IRS is not bound by these prior determinations when interpreting and applying intermediate sanctions. The Department of the Treasury is developing guidance in this area, which will include revenue-sharing arrangements. Obviously, these developments should be of considerable concern to those in the field of fund raising.

(B) PROPOSED REGULATIONS

The proposed regulations expand upon the concept of *substantial influence*. An individual is in a position to exercise substantial influence over the affairs of an organization if he or she, individually or with others, serves as the president, chief executive officer, or chief operating officer of the organization. An individual serves in one of these capacities, regardless of title, if he or she has or shares ultimate responsibility for implementing the decisions of the governing body or supervising the management, administration, or operation of the organization.

An individual also is in this position if he or she, independently or with others, serves as treasurer or chief financial officer of the organization. An individual serves in one of these capacities, regardless of title, if he or she has or shares ultimate responsibility for managing the organization's financial assets and has or shares authority to sign drafts or direct the signing of drafts, or authorize electronic transfer of funds, from the organization's bank account(s).

There are some categories of persons who are deemed to *not* be in a position to exercise substantial influence. One, as noted above, is any other public charity. Another is an employee of an applicable tax-exempt organization who receives economic benefits of less than the amount of compensation referenced for a highly compensated employee, is not a member of the family of a disqualified person, is not an individual referenced above as considered to have this influence, and is not a substantial contributor to the organization.

A person who has managerial control over a discrete segment of an organization may be in a position to exercise substantial influence over the affairs of the entire organization.

Facts and circumstances that tend to show the requisite substantial influence include the fact that the person founded the organization; is a substantial contributor to the organization; receives compensation based on revenues derived from activities of the organization that the person controls; has authority to control or determine a significant portion of the organization's capital expenditures, operating budget, or compensation for employees; has managerial authority or serves as a key advisor to a person with managerial authority; or owns a controlling interest in a corporation, partnership, or trust that is a disqualified person.

Facts and circumstances that tend to show an absence of substantial influence are where the person has taken a bona fide vow of poverty as an employee, agent, or a representative of a religious organization; the person is an independent contractor (e.g., a lawyer, accountant, or investment manager or advisor), acting in that capacity, unless the person is acting in that capacity with respect to a transaction from which the person might economically benefit either directly or indirectly (aside from fees received for the professional services rendered); and any preferential treatment a person receives based on the size of that person's contribution is also offered to any other contributor making a comparable contribution as part of a solicitation intended to attract a substantial number of contributions.

There is a conflict between the legislative history of these rules and the proposed regulations. The legislative history states that an individual having the title of *trustee, director,* or *officer* does not automatically have status as a disqualified person. The proposed regulations, however, provide that persons having substantial influence include any individual who serves on the governing body of the organization and is entitled to vote.

One of the ways to be an *organization manager* is, as noted, to be an officer. An individual is considered an *officer* if he or she regularly exercises general authority to make administrative or policy decisions on behalf of the organization. An individual who has authority merely to recommend particular administrative or policy decisions, but not to implement them without approval of a superior, is not an officer. Independent contractors, acting in a capacity as lawyers, accountants, and investment managers and advisors, are not officers.

In a nice touch, the regulations provide that an individual who is not a trustee, director, or officer yet serves on a committee of the governing body of an applicable tax-exempt organization that is invoking the rebuttable presumption of reasonableness (see below) based on the committee's actions, is an organization manager.

The regulations restate the definition of the term "fair market value" to be used in ascertaining whether there is an excess benefit. The fair market value of property, including the right to use property, is the price at which property or the right to use it would change hands between a willing buyer and a willing seller, neither being under any compulsion to buy, sell, or transfer property or the right to use it, and both having reasonable knowledge of relevant facts.

A revenue-sharing transaction may constitute an excess benefit transaction regardless of whether the economic benefit provided to the disqualified person exceeds the fair market value of the consideration provided in return if, at any point, it permits a disqualified person to receive additional compensation without providing proportional benefits that contribute to the organization's accomplishment of its exempt purpose. If the economic benefit is provided as compensation for services, relevant facts and circumstances include the relationship between the size of the benefit provided and the quality and quantity of the services provided, as well as the ability of the party receiving the compensation to control the activities generating the revenues on which the compensation is based.

Some economic benefits are disregarded for this purpose. One set of these benefits is the payment of reasonable expenses for members of the governing body of an applicable tax-exempt organization to attend meetings of the governing body of the organization. This exclusion does not encompass luxury travel or spousal travel.

An economic benefit provided to a disqualified person that the person receives solely as a member of or volunteer for an organization is disregarded for these purposes, if the benefit is provided to members of the pubic in exchange for a membership fee of no more than $75 annually. For example, if a disqualified person is also a member of the organization and receives membership benefits such as advance ticket purchases and a discount at the organization's gift shop that would normally be provided in exchange for a membership fee of $75 or less per year, the membership benefit is disregarded.

An economic benefit provided to a disqualified person that the disqualified person receives solely as a member of a charitable class that the applicable tax-exempt organization intends to benefit as part of the accomplishment of the organization's exempt purposes is generally disregarded for these purposes.

The regulations detail the items that are included in determining the value of compensation. As to determining the reasonableness of compensation, however, the regulations merely extend this guidance: "Compensation for the performance of services is reasonable if it is only such amount as would ordinarily be paid for like services by like enterprises under like circumstances."

Some interesting rules are offered by the regulations as to what *circumstances* are to be taken into account, particularly in terms of moments in time. The general rule is that the circumstances to be taken into consideration are those existing at the date when the contract for services was made. Where reasonableness of compensation cannot be determined under these circumstances, however, the determination is to be based on all facts and circumstances, up to and including circumstances as of the date of payment. Here is the best rule of all in this regard: In no event shall circumstances existing at the date when the contract is questioned be considered in making a determination of the reasonableness of compensation.

The presumption is reflected in the regulations. (There were some who thought this presumption, not being in the statute, would be ignored by Treasury and the IRS.)

A small surprise: The IRS will allow the presumption to arise as the result of action by a committee, even if the committee is not composed wholly of board members. The committee must be permitted under state law. Nonboard members and nonofficers of these committees will, as noted, be considered organization managers.

When reviewing compensation arrangements, organizations with less than $1 million in gross receipts can rely on data as to compensation paid by five comparable organizations in the same or similar communities for similar services.

In determining the independence of a board or committee, the regulations prescribe a battery of conflict-of-interest rules.

Correction of an excess benefit occurs if the disqualified person repays the applicable tax-exempt organization an amount of money equal to the excess benefit, plus any additional amount needed to compensate the organization for the loss of the use of the money or other property during the period commencing on the date of the excess benefit transaction and ending on the date the excess benefit is corrected. The regulations also state that correction may be accomplished, in certain circumstances, by returning property to the organization and taking any additional steps necessary to make the organization whole. The proposal, however, does not indicate what these "certain circumstances" might be nor does it reveal what the "additional steps" might entail.

If the excess benefit transaction consists of the payment of compensation for services under a contract that has not been completed, termination of the employment or independent contractor relationship between the organization and the disqualified person is not required in order to correct.

(C) IMPACT ON FUND RAISING

One of the significant aspects of the proposed intermediate sanctions regulations is their impact on the law concerning charitable fund raising.

Clearly, a fund-raising company, or an individual undertaking fund raising as an employee or independent contractor, can be a disqualified person with respect to a charitable organization. This can occur when the person is in a position to exercise substantial influence over the affairs of the organization. An illustration as to how this can happen was provided in the *United Cancer Council* case. (See Section 51.2.)

The likelihood of this outcome is increased when the fund-raising person is being paid, in whole or in part, on the basis of the revenues of the charitable organization (commission-based or percentage-based fund raising). The proposed regulations state that facts and circumstances tending to show that a person has substantial influence over the affairs of an organization include the fact that the person's compensation is based on revenues derived from activities of the organization that the person controls.

Another element of the proposed regulations that bears on these considerations is the rule that a person "who has managerial control over a discrete segment of an organization may nonetheless be in a position to exercise substantial influence over the affairs of the entire organization." Thus, a fund-raising person need not control the charity as such to be a disqualified person. It is required only that the person control a "discrete segment" of the entity. This can happen, for example, in the context of fund raising by means of sales of services or special event fund raising.

The proposed regulations contain an illustration of this point. A charity enters into a contract with a company that manages bingo games. Under the contract, the company agrees to provide all of the staff and equipment necessary to carry out a bingo operation one night per week. The charity is to be paid, by the company, a percentage of the revenue from this activity; the company is to retain the balance of the proceeds. The charity does not provide any goods or services in connection with the bingo operation, other than the use of its hall for the bingo games. The annual gross revenue earned from the bingo operation represents more than one half of the charity's total annual revenue.

By reason of these facts, the bingo management company is a disqualified person with respect to the charity. The company controls the bingo game activity—a "discrete segment" of the operations of the charity, because it has "full managerial authority" over the charity's principal source of income. The company's compensation is based on revenues from an activity it controls. Consequently, the company is in a position to exercise substantial influence over the affairs of the charity.

A separate example makes the point that those who control a fund-raising company can also be disqualified persons with respect to a charity. In the illustration, the stock of the bingo game management company is wholly owned by an individual who is actively involved in managing the company. This individual is a disqualified person with respect to the charity.

It is thus critical that a charity (and perhaps a social welfare organization) review its fund-raising contracts, including general management agreements, to determine whether the other party to the contract is controlling a discrete segment of the organization and is therefore a disqualified person.

Note: This element of the law leads only to the conclusion that the person is a disqualified one. It does not mean that an excess benefit transaction is involved. Nonetheless, that outcome can be different when the compensation arrangement is a revenue-sharing transaction, as discussed next.

In general, an excess benefit transaction is one in which an economic benefit is provided by an applicable tax-exempt organization to a disqualified person, if the value of the benefit provided is in excess of the consideration received by the exempt organization. A simple example of this is an excessive fund-raising fee paid by a charitable organization to a fund-raising company that is a disqualified person (as happened in the *UCC* case).

Another form of excess benefit transaction is the revenue-sharing transaction. This is a transaction in which the amount of an economic benefit provided to or for the use of a disqualified person is determined, in whole or part, by the revenues of one or more activities of the organization, where private inurement results.

The proposed regulations make the point that a revenue-sharing transaction may be an excess benefit transaction regardless of whether the economic benefit provided to the disqualified person exceeds the fair market value of the consideration provided to the exempt organization. This can be the case if, at any point, the transaction permits a disqualified person to receive additional compensation without providing proportional benefits that contribute to the accomplishment of the organization's exempt purposes.

According to the proposed regulations, if this type of economic benefit is provided as compensation for services, the relevant facts and circumstances to take into account include the relationship between the size of the benefit provided and the quality and quantity of the services provided, as well as the ability of the party receiving the compensation to control the activities generating the revenues on which the compensation is based.

An example in the proposed regulations shows how a revenue-sharing transaction is not necessarily an excess benefit transaction. It concerns the manager of an investment portfolio of an applicable exempt organization. The manager and several other professional investment managers work exclusively for the organization in an office located in the organization's building. The manager's compensation consists of a flat base annual salary, health insurance, eligibility to participate in a retirement plan, and a bonus. This bonus is equal to a percentage of any increase in the value of the organization's portfolio over the year (net of expenses for investment management other than the in-house managers' compensation). The bonus gives the manager an incentive to provide the highest-quality service in order to maximize benefits and minimize expenses to the organization.

In this illustration, the manager has a "measure of control" over the activities generating the revenues on which the bonus is based. At the same time, however, the manager can increase his or her compensation only if the organization also receives a proportional benefit. Under these facts, this revenue-based bonus arrangement, while a revenue-sharing transaction, is not an excess benefit transaction.

Here is an example in the proposed regulations, illustrating how a revenue-sharing arrangement is an excess benefit transaction. A public charity enters into a contract with a company that manages charitable gaming activities for charities. This company is, because of the contract, a disqualified person (insider) with respect to the charity. The company agrees to provide all of the staff and equipment necessary to carry out the gaming activities for the charity, and to pay the charity a percentage of the net profits (calculated as the gross revenue less rental for the equipment, wages for the staff, prizes for the winners, and other specified operating expenses). The company retains the balance of the proceeds, after payment of the expenses and the charity's share of the profits.

The company controls the activities generating the revenue on which its compensation is based. Because the company owns the equipment and employs the staff, it controls what the charity is charged, including the profit the company makes in that connection. Thus, the company controls the net revenues relative to the gross revenues from the gaming activity.

This example emphasizes the fact that the company is not provided with an appropriate incentive to maximize benefits and minimize costs to the charity. The company benefits whether the expenses are high and net revenues low or whether expenses are low and the net revenues high. By contrast, the charity suffers if expenses for the gaming operation are high and the net revenues are low. All of the gross revenues generated by the gaming operation belong to the charity. This arrangement allows a portion of these revenues to inure to the company. Under these facts, there is a revenue-sharing transaction, private inurement, and therefore an excess benefit transaction. In fact, the *entire amount* paid to this company is an excess benefit.

It is essential for charities and social welfare organizations to review their contractual obligations to determine if a revenue-sharing feature lurks in any of them. If there is a revenue-sharing arrangement, the facts and circumstances need to be explored to see if the organization is receiving a proportional benefit as the result of the arrangement and if there is private inurement. If the corresponding benefit is lacking and there is private inurement, an excess benefit transaction is present.

51.4 Internal Revenue Service Audit Program

It is the perception of the IRS that some charitable organizations are misleading people, sometimes deliberately, into believing that a payment to a charitable organization is a deductible gift when in fact the transaction does not involve a gift at all or is only partially a gift. This is a matter that has concerned the IRS since 1967, when it issued guidelines directing charities to advise "donors" of circumstances in which their "gifts" are not deductible at all (when a payor receives something from the charity of approximately equal value for the payment) or are only partially deductible (when the donor receives something in return for the gift of a value that is less than the amount of the gift). The 1967 guidelines describe these rules in some detail and provide examples as to how the rules apply in common situations, such as theater parties and sports tournaments—special events. In 1988, a congressional committee expressed dismay over the continuation of, if not an increase in, the misleading practices of some charitable organizations and demanded that the IRS act to resolve the problem. Later in the year, the Commissioner of Internal Revenue sent a special message on this subject to the nation's charities.

This matter concerns a variety of practices. Some are relatively obvious and easy to resolve, such as those concerning tuition payments to schools and patient payments to hospitals. Although these are payments to "charitable" organizations, they are purchases of services and are not "gifts." Other payments to charitable organizations that are not gifts are payments for winning bids at auctions and purchases of tickets for games of chance (such as raffles and lotteries).

The IRS continues to believe that many charitable organizations are not adequately complying with the relevant disclosure rules, and so has further explored these types of fund-raising organizations and many others. Their explorations have led the IRS to conclude that charitable organizations are engaging in questionable fund-raising practices, with some solicitations appearing to mislead donors about the deductibility of their donations.

The IRS launched an attack on such fund-raising misperformance by inaugurating a Special Emphasis Program, which entailed a Charitable Solicitations Compliance Improvement (CSCI) Study. The program has two phases. This first, which nominally ended in 1990, was an educational phase whereby the IRS endeavored to disseminate information about the law in regard to the nation's public charities. This was accomplished by means of speeches, review of the practices of a variety of charitable organizations, and the establishment of a special telephone number so that people could call the IRS for advice and interpretations on the subject.

The intent of Phase I of the CSCI Study was to determine the extent to which charities furnished accurate and sufficient information to their donors concerning the deductibility of their contributions. The IRS sought to assess the voluntary compliance level. It also attempted to learn the amount of the "revenue loss" caused by the taking of erroneous charitable deductions. The IRS consistently asserts that there is a presumption that the total amount paid by the "donor" in these circumstances represents the fair market value of substantial benefits received in return. Thus, the presumption is that there is no charitable contribution deduction in such cases.

The second phase of the program is the examination phase. Agents of the IRS examine the fund-raising practices of public charities, using an 82-question checksheet entitled "Exempt Organizations Charitable Solicitations Compliance Improvement Program Checksheet" (IRS Form 9215). The IRS is intent on ferreting out instances of what it terms "abusive" fund raising. The National Office of the IRS has sent to its examining agents across the country instructions and guidance as to the CSCI Study. It has told these agents that "there is evidence to suggest that taxpayers, in the absence of clear disclosure of the deductible amount by the charities, claim a deduction for their donation in excess of the amount permitted by law." Indeed, it is the fundamental assertion of the IRS that the "charities have an obligation to both know the rules and to properly inform donors about the deductibility of their donations."

In using the term "abusive fund raising," the IRS includes the following:

- Misleading statements in solicitations literature that imply deductibility of contributions, where none probably exists
- Contracts with professional for-profit fund raisers, who themselves use questionable fund-raising methods to solicit funds from the general public
- Situations in which other expenses, such as administrative and fund-raising costs, constitute an unusually high portion of the solicited funds or noncash contributions; and
- Fund-raising activities that result in other tax consequences (i.e., generating taxable income, resulting in additional filing requirements, etc.)

The check sheet, which is at the heart of Phase II, explores all forms of fund raising: annual solicitations; membership drives; awards ceremonies; bingo and other forms of gambling; charity balls; sporting events; raffles, lotteries, and sweepstakes; luncheons, dinners, and banquets; and cultural exhibitions.

The check sheet searches for information about property gifts, use of professional fund raisers, use of games of chance, travel tours, thrift stores and like activities, provision of goods or services in exchange for "gifts," and noncash contributions. It suggests a battery of penalties that might be assessed against a charity for failure to comply with the rules, such as through the promotion of abusive tax shelters, aiding and abetting understatements of tax liability, and failure to file certain returns.

The IRS Exempt Organizations Division is referring returns of donors for examination where the records of a charity indicate that an individual taxpayer made a donation meeting certain (unstated) dollar threshold criteria and that he or she received goods, services, or benefits in exchange for the donation.

The IRS National Office has cautioned its agents that the "scope and depth of the examination should be sufficient to fully disclose the nature of abusive situations involving fund-raising activities that mislead donors to claim the incorrect charitable contribution deduction; misrepresent the use of the solicited funds; engage in questionable fund-raising practices or techniques, etc." The instructions state that "workpapers and responses to checksheet items must fully describe these abuses and provide copies of supporting evidence of the abuse."

The results of the CSCI Study are being used to accumulate case-oriented statistical data and other data on the fund-raising methods and practices conducted by charitable organizations. It is believed that this information has been provided to the Department of the Treasury and to Congress. Because of this end use of the Study results, the IRS guidance states that it is "essential that the examinations be thorough." The examiner is importuned to "pursue the examination to the point where he or she can conclude that all areas and data concerning fund-raising activities have been considered."

The IRS has conceded that it cannot impose any sanctions for violation of these disclosure rules. Thus, these rules are less "law" and more in the nature of "cajoling." The IRS has advised its examining agents that "the charities have an *obligation* to both know the rules and to properly inform donors about the deductibility of their donations."

This, then, is a form of fund-raising regulation that, as law, is murky at best. The IRS stated its hope that its activities under the Special Emphasis Program would spur charitable organizations into "voluntary compliance"—to, in effect, act on their own without benefit of statutory legal sanctions. Regrettably, this approach failed, causing Congress to write more stringent rules into law, as discussed in the next two sections.

Checklist 51.1

Was the organization contacted by the IRS during Phase I?	Yes____	No____
Was the organization contacted by the IRS during Phase II?	Yes____	No____
Identify outcome(s) of either contact.		_____

51.5 *Gift Substantiation Rules*

The federal tax law contains charitable gift substantiation rules. Under this body of law, donors who make a separate charitable contribution of $250 or more in a year, for which they claim a charitable contribution deduction, must obtain written substantiation from the donee charitable organization.

More specifically, the rule is that the charitable deduction is not allowed for a separate contribution of $250 or more unless the donor has written substantiation from the charitable donee of the contribution in the form of a contemporaneous written acknowledgment. Thus, donors cannot rely solely on a canceled check as substantiation for a gift of $250 or more. However, canceled checks will suffice as substantiation for gifts of less than $250.

An acknowledgment meets this requirement if it includes the following information: (1) the amount of money and a description (but not value) of any property other than money that was contributed; (2) whether the donee organization provided any goods or services in consideration, in whole or in part, for any money or property contributed; and (3) a description and good-faith estimate of the value of any goods or services involved or, if the goods or services consist solely of intangible religious benefits, a statement to that effect. The phrase "intangible religious benefit" means "any intangible religious benefit which is provided by an organization organized exclusively for religious purposes and which generally is not sold in a commercial transaction outside the donative context." An acknowledgment is considered to be *contemporaneous* if the contributor obtains the acknowledgment on or before the earlier of (1) the date on which the donor filed a tax return for the taxable year in which the contribution was made or (2) the due date (including extensions) for filing the return.

There are other defined terms. The phrase "goods or services" means money, property, services, benefits, and privileges. However, certain goods or services are disregarded for these purposes: those that have insubstantial value and certain annual membership benefits offered to an individual in exchange for a payment of $75 or less per year. A charitable organization provides goods or services *in consideration* for a donor's transfer if, at the time the donor makes the payment to the charity, the donor receives or expects to receive goods or services in exchange for the payment. Goods or services a charitable organization provides in consideration for a payment by a donor include goods or services provided in a year other than the year in which the payment was made. A *good-faith estimate* means a charitable organization's estimate of the fair market value of any goods or services, without regard to the manner in which the organization in fact made the estimate.

As noted, the substantiation rule applies in respect to separate payments. Separate payments are generally treated as separate contributions and are not aggregated for the purpose of applying the $250 threshold. In cases of contributions paid by withholding from wages, the deduction from each paycheck is treated as a separate payment. It is to be anticipated that the IRS will issue antiabuse rules in this area (addressing practices such as the writing of multiple checks on the same date).

The written acknowledgment of a separate gift is not required to take any particular form. Thus, acknowledgments may be made by letter, postcard, or computer-generated form. A donee charitable organization may prepare a separate acknowledgment for each contribution or may provide donors with periodic (such as annual) acknowledgments that set forth the required information for each contribution of $250 or more made by the donor during the period.

It is the responsibility of a donor to obtain the substantiation and maintain it in his or her records. (Again, the charitable contribution deduction is dependent on compliance with these rules.) A charitable organization that knowingly provides a false written substantiation to a donor may be subject to a penalty for aiding and abetting an understatement of tax liability.

The substantiation rules do not impose on charitable organizations any requirement as to the reporting of gift information to the IRS. Nonetheless, the law states that charitable organizations have the option to avoid these rules by filing an information return with the IRS, reporting information sufficient to substantiate the amount of the deductible contribution. As of late 2000, however, the IRS had not implemented this approach.

There are special refinements of these rules for substantiation of payments to a college or university for the right to purchase tickets to athletic events, substantiation of charitable contributions made by a partnership or small business corporation, the establishment of a charitable gift annuity, gifts to distributing organizations, and substantiation of out-of-pocket expenses.

These substantiation rules do not apply to transfers of property to charitable remainder trusts or to charitable lead trusts. The requirements are, however, applicable to transfers to pooled income funds. In the case of these funds, the contemporaneous written acknowledgment must state that the contribution was transferred to the charitable organization's pooled fund and indicate whether any goods or services (in addition to the income interest) were provided in exchange for the transfer. However, the contemporaneous written acknowledgment need not include a good faith estimate of the income interest.

The substantiation procedure must be observed in addition to the following:

- Rules that require the provision of certain information if the amount of the claimed charitable deduction for all noncash contributions exceeds $500
- Rules that apply to noncash gifts exceeding $5,000 per item or group of similar items (other than certain publicly traded securities), where the services of a qualified appraiser are required, and the charitable donee must acknowledge receipt of the gift and provide certain other information.

Checklist 51.2

Does the organization receive gifts of $250 or more?	Yes____	No____
If so, does the organization provide the requisite substantiation to its donors?	Yes____	No____
Is the organization providing any goods or services in consideration for gifts?	Yes____	No____
If so, is the organization having any difficulties in ascertaining the value of the goods or services?	Yes____	No____
If yes, what steps are being taken to resolve the problem?		_____
State any problems in identifying separate payments.		_____
Has the organization received any complaints from donors as to (alleged) noncompliance with these substantiation requirements?	Yes____	No____
If so, identify the steps that are being taken to resolve this problem.		_____

51.6 Quid Pro Quo Contributions

As discussed, among the practices that entail payments that are partially gifts and partially payments for goods or services, are special event programs, whereby the patron receives something of value (i.e., a ticket to a theater performance or a dinner, the opportunity to play in a sports tournament, and auctions), yet makes a payment in excess of that value amount. In these circumstances, the amount paid that is in excess of the value received is a deductible charitable gift. Thus, for example, the IRS ruled that contributions to athletic scholarship programs are not deductible as charitable gifts where the donors are provided the preferential opportunity to purchase tickets to athletic events hosted by the educational institution providing the scholarships. (This ruling was largely overruled by Congress, however, when it wrote a tax law providing that 80 percent of the value of this type of "gift" is deductible as a charitable contribution.)

The IRS also held that payments by corporate sponsors of college and university bowl games are not charitable gifts to the bowl game associations, but must be treated by the association as forms of unrelated business income because the corporate sponsors received a valuable package of advertising services. This position led to IRS and congressional hearings, proposed regulations, and finally legislation (enacted in 1997). This legislation shields from taxation *qualified sponsorship payments*. A payment of this nature is one made by a person engaged in a trade or business, from which the person received no substantial return benefit other than the use or acknowledgment of the name or logo (or product lines) of the person's trade or business in connection with the organization's activities. This use or acknowledgment does not include advertising of the person's products or services. *Advertising* entails qualitative or comparative language, price information or other indications of savings or value, or an endorsement or other inducement to purchase, sell, or use the products or services.

The federal tax law imposes certain disclosure requirements on charitable organizations that receive *quid pro quo contributions*.

A quid pro quo contribution is a payment made partly as a contribution and partly in consideration for goods or services provided to the payor by the donee organization. The term does not include a payment made to an organization, operated exclusively for religious purposes, in return for which the donor receives solely an intangible religious benefit that generally is not sold in a commercial transaction outside the donative context.

Specifically, if a charitable organization (other than a state, possession of the United States, a political subdivision of a state or possession, the United States, and the District of Columbia) receives a quid pro quo contribution in excess of $75, the organization must, in connection with the solicitation or receipt of the contribution, provide a written statement that (1) informs the donor that the amount of the contribution that is deductible for federal income tax purposes is limited to the excess of the amount of any money and the value of any property other than money contributed by the donor over the value of the goods or services provided by the organization, and (2) provides the donor with a good faith estimate of the value of the goods or services.

In other words, this law is designed to cause a donor/patron to know that the only amount deductible in these circumstances as a charitable gift (if any) is the amount paid to the charity in excess of any benefits provided by the charity. A charitable organization may use any reasonable methodology in making this good faith estimate as long as it applies the methodology in good faith. A good faith estimate of the value of goods or services that are not generally available in a commercial transaction may be determined by reference to the fair market value of similar or comparable goods or services. Goods or services may be similar or comparable even though they do not have the unique qualities of the goods or services that are being valued. Of course, where the goods or services are available on a commercial basis, the commercial value is used.

It is intended that this disclosure be made in a manner that is reasonably likely to come to the attention of the donor. Therefore, immersing the disclosure in fine print in a larger document is inadequate. It is the fair market value of the good or service that triggers this rule; it is not the cost of the item to the charity.

For purposes of the $75 threshold, separate payments made at different times of the year with respect to separate fund-raising events generally will not be aggregated. The IRS may issue anti-abuse rules in this area (addressing such practices as the writing of multiple checks for the same transaction).

These rules do not apply where only *de minimis,* token goods or services (i.e., key chains and bumper stickers) are provided to the donor. In defining these terms, prior IRS pronouncements are followed. These rules also do not apply to transactions that do not have a donative element (such as the charging of tuition by a school, the charging of health care fees by a hospital, or the sale of items by a museum).

The law in this area is vague on the matter of *celebrity presence.* If a celebrity is present at an event and does nothing, or does something that is different from that for which he or she is celebrated, the value of the presence is zero. (An example of the latter is a tour of a museum conducted by an artist whose works are on display.) Presumably, if the celebrity performs as such, the charitable organization must utilize the commercial value of the performance.

No part of a payment can be considered a contribution unless the payor intended to make a payment in an amount that is in excess of the fair market value of the goods or services received. This requirement of *donative intent* has particular application in the instance of auctions conducted by charitable organizations. The procedure preferred by the law is that a charity holding an auction will publish a catalog that meets the requirements for a written disclosure statement, including the charity's good faith estimate of the value of items that will be available for bidding.

A penalty is imposed on charitable organizations that do not satisfy these disclosure requirements. For failure to make the required disclosure in connection with a quid pro quo contribution of more than $75, there is a penalty of $10 per contribution, not to exceed $5,000 per fund-raising event or mailing. An organization may be able to avoid this penalty if it can show that the failure to comply was due to reasonable cause.

In general, a person can rely on a contemporaneous written acknowledgment provided in the substantiation context (described above) or a written disclosure statement provided in the quid pro quo transaction setting. However, an individual may not treat an estimate of the value of goods or services as their fair market value if he or she knows, or has reason to know, that the treatment is unreasonable.

Checklist 51.3

Does the organization solicit payments in excess of the $75 threshold that are partially deductible gifts?	Yes____	No____
Does the organization solicit payments in excess of the $75 threshold, none of which are deductible gifts?	Yes____	No____
If either answer is yes, is the organization in compliance with the quid pro quo contribution rules?	Yes____	No____
Is the organization in compliance with the IRS donor recognition guidelines (for smaller gifts)?	Yes____	No____
Has the organization paid any penalties under these rules?	Yes____	No____
If yes, identify the steps being taken to resolve this problem.	_____	

51.7 Gift Property Appraisal Rules

There are additional requirements in the law relating to the substantiation of deductions claimed by an individual, a small business corporation, and certain other entities for charitable contributions of certain property. These requirements must be complied with if the charitable deduction is to be allowed.

Affected by this body of law are gifts of all types of property (other than money and publicly traded securities) if the aggregate value of the property (and similar items of property), for which deductions for charitable contributions are claimed by the same donor for the same year, is in excess of $5,000. This is the case irrespective of whether the property is donated to the same charity.

The phrase "similar items of property" refers to property of the same generic category or type. Such property includes nonpublicly traded securities, books, clothing, jewelry, furniture, stamp and coin collections, paintings, photographs, lithographs, china, crystal, and silver.

For gifts of this type, the donor must obtain a qualified appraisal and attach an appraisal summary to the tax return. A *qualified appraisal* must relate to an appraisal made not earlier than 60 days prior to the date of contribution, is prepared by a qualified appraiser, contains the requisite information, and does not involve a prohibited type of appraisal fee. The information that must be contained in this appraisal document includes a sufficient description of the property, the date of the contribution, a statement as to any restrictions on the charity's use of the property, the appraised fair market value of the property, the date(s) of appraisal, the method of valuation used, and the qualifications of the appraiser.

The *appraisal summary* must appear on the requisite IRS form (Form 8283, Section B), signed and dated by the charity and the appraiser, and attached to the appropriate tax return of the donor. The information in the appraisal summary must include a description of the property and its physical condition, the manner of acquisition of the property by the donor, the cost basis of the property, a statement as to whether the charity provided anything of value to the donor in consideration for the gift, and the appraised value of the property.

The appraisal summary form (Form 8283, Section A) must be filed by contributors where the total value of all noncash contributions exceeds $500 and is less than $5,000. This portion of the form must also be used to report contributions of publicly traded securities, even where their value is in excess of $5,000.

A *qualified appraiser* is an individual who holds him- or herself out to the public as an appraiser, or performs appraisals on a regular basis, and is qualified to make appraisals of the type of property being valued. The appraiser must express an understanding that an intentionally false overstatement of the value of the property may subject him or her to a civil penalty for aiding and abetting an understatement of tax liability.

An individual cannot be deemed a qualified appraiser if the donor had knowledge of facts that would cause a reasonable person to expect the appraiser to falsely overstate the value of the donated property. Moreover, neither the donor, managers of the donee, nor certain other related persons can be qualified appraisers of the property involved in the gift transaction. Generally, no part of the fee arrangement for a qualified appraisal can be based on a percentage of the appraised value of the property.

A separate set of rules applies to appraisal requirements to regular corporations (other than those mentioned earlier). These rules, in general, require such corporations to obtain a qualified independent appraisal to validly claim a charitable contribution deduction for gifts of most nonmoney property having a value in excess of $5,000.

This body of law is subject to the *doctrine of substantial compliance*. That is, these requirements are not *mandatory*, but *directory*. Where the donor meets all of the elements required to establish the substance or essence of a charitable contribution but fails to satisfy a technical requirement, the charitable contribution deduction will be preserved.

Checklist 51.4

Does the organization receive gifts of property having a value in excess of $5,000?	Yes____	No____
If so, does the organization inform the donors of these rules?	Yes____	No____
Does the organization work with its donors to obtain the qualified appraisals and appraisal summaries?	Yes____	No____
Are steps taken to ensure that the appraisers are qualified?	Yes____	No____

51.8 Procedure for Valuing Gifts of Art

Individual and corporate donors and other transferors can obtain from the IRS, in Washington, D.C., a statement of value to be used to substantiate the fair market value of art for income, estate, or gift tax purposes, including charitable giving.

These procedures generally apply to an item of art that has been appraised at $50,000 or more and has been transferred as a charitable contribution for income tax purposes, by reason of a decedent's death, or by an inter vivos (lifetime) gift. However, the IRS may issue a statement of value for items appraised at less than $50,000 if (1) the request for the statement includes a request for appraisal review of at least one item appraised at $50,000 or more, and (2) the IRS determines that issuance of this type of statement would be in the best interest of efficient tax administration.

For this purpose, *art* includes paintings, sculpture, watercolors, prints, drawings, ceramics, antique furniture, decorative arts, textiles, carpets, silver, rare manuscripts, and historical memorabilia.

To request this statement of value for income tax purposes, the submission must be prior to filing the income tax return that first reports the charitable contribution. This request must include (1) a copy of the appraisal of the item of art; (2) a check or money order payable to the IRS in the amount of $2,500 as a user fee for a request for a statement of value for up to three items of art, plus $250 for each additional item of art; (3) a completed appraisal summary (Form 8283, Section B) (see the preceding description of this form); and (4) the location of the IRS district office that has or will have examination jurisdiction over the tax return.

A request for a statement of value may be withdrawn at any time prior to its issuance. When this happens, however, the IRS will retain the user fee and notify the appropriate IRS district director.

This appraisal must meet the requirements for a qualified appraisal under existing law and must also include (1) a complete description of the item of art, including the name of the artist or culture, the title or subject matter, the medium (such as oil on canvas), the date created, the size, any signatures or labels (or marks) on the item of art (or on its back or frame), the history of the item (including any proof of authenticity), a record of any exhibition at which the item was displayed, any reference source citing the item, and the physical condition of the item; (2) a professional-quality photograph of a size and quality fully showing the item, preferably an 8- by 10-inch color photograph or a color transparency not smaller than 4 by 5 inches; and (3) the specific basis for the valuation.

The appraisal must be made no earlier than 60 days prior to the date of the contribution of the item of art. Contributors and their representatives are encouraged to include in the request any additional information that may affect the determination of the fair market value of the art.

Similar requirements apply in instances in which a person is seeking a statement of value from the IRS for an item of art transferred as part of an estate or as an inter vivos noncharitable gift. In this context, the procedures also state criteria for the appraisal and the appraiser. This is not done in the case of charitable gifts for income tax purposes, because the criteria are already in the tax regulations.

For a completed request for a statement of value received by the IRS after July 15, but on or before January 15, the IRS ordinarily issues the statement by the following June 30. As to a completed request for the statement received after January 15, but on or before

July 15, the IRS ordinarily issues the statement by the following December 31. It is the responsibility of the persons involved to obtain any necessary extensions of time to file tax returns.

If the IRS agrees with the value reported on an appraisal, it issues a statement of value approving it. If the IRS disagrees, it issues a statement of value with its determination of the value, as well as the basis for its disagreement with the appraisal.

A copy of the statement of value, regardless of whether the person involved agrees with it, must be attached to and filed with the appropriate income, estate, or gift tax return. If a person files a tax return reporting the transfer of an art item for which a statement of value was requested, before the statement is received, the person must indicate on the return that a statement has been requested and attach a copy of the request. Upon receipt of the statement, an amended or supplemental return must be filed with the statement of value attached.

If a person disagrees with a statement of value issued by the IRS, he or she may submit with the tax return additional information in support of a different value.

A person may rely on a statement of value received from the IRS for an item of art. However, a person may not rely on a statement of value issued to another person. Further, a person may not rely on a statement of value if the representations on which it was based are not accurate statements of the material facts.

Checklist 51.5

Does the organization receive gifts of art valued at $50,000 or more?	Yes____	No____
If so, does the organization notify donors of the availability of this procedure?	Yes____	No____
Has a donor made successful use of this procedure?	Yes____	No____

51.9   Unrelated Business Rules

The IRS applies certain rules to unrelated business income as a means of regulating the process of raising funds for charitable purposes.[3]

For an activity to be taxed as an *unrelated trade or business*, the general rule is that it must have these characteristics:

- It must be a *business*, that is, an activity that is carried on to produce revenue.
- The business must be *regularly carried on*.
- The activity must *not be substantially* related to the achievement of tax-exempt purposes.

Many fund-raising activities are "businesses" in this sense, particularly in respect to special event fund raising. Nearly all fund-raising activities are not inherently charitable or other tax-exempt undertakings. Thus, when a church sponsors a bingo game to gen-

---

[3]These rules are discussed in detail in Bruce R. Hopkins, *The Law of Tax-Exempt Organizations*, Part V, 7th ed. (New York: John Wiley & Sons, 1998).

erate funds for its programs, the bingo game is a business, not a religious activity. (An activity is not a related one solely because the net monies from it are applied to exempt purposes.)

If an activity is not conducted with a *profit motive*, it will not be regarded as a business. This is important where a loss from one unrelated business activity is used to offset the gain from another. Thus, for example, an activity that consistently, year in and year out, generates a loss is not likely to be regarded as a business.

Many fund-raising activities escape treatment as taxable businesses on the grounds that they are not regularly carried on. Thus, an annual charity ball, golf tournament, auction, car wash, bake sale, and the like are usually not taxable events because they are infrequently carried on and thus are not competitive with for-profit operations. However, it is the view of the IRS that, in determining regularity, the time expended by an organization in preparing for the event must also be taken into account. Also, time expended by another person, who is acting as agent for the charitable organization, is used in measuring whether an activity is regularly carried on.

There are some exceptions to unrelated income taxation that also help protect various fund-raising activities from tax:

- Businesses in which substantially all of the work is performed by volunteers
- Businesses carried on primarily for the convenience of the organization's members, students, patients, officers, or employees
- Businesses that consist of the sale of merchandise, substantially all of which has been received by the organization as gifts
- Certain bingo games
- Certain fairs and expositions
- Certain practices involving the rental to and exchanges of mailing lists with charitable organizations
- The offering of certain low-cost premiums as inducements to charitable giving

Nonetheless, a variety of fund-raising techniques and practices have been subject to litigation as to whether they are taxable business. Recent issues include the extent to which a revenue-producing activity can be structured so that the revenue to the tax-exempt organization can be regarded as a nontaxable royalty, whether the distribution of greeting cards is a sale of the cards to the public or a use of premiums to stimulate charitable giving, and the provision of group insurance policy coverage. Recent court cases involve instances where organizations have been successful in sheltering from taxation revenue derived from the rental of mailing lists on the ground that they are royalties.

Current popular fund-raising techniques that raise questions about application of the unrelated business rules are forms of *commercial coventuring* and *cause-related marketing*. The former involves situations in which a charitable organization consents to be a donee under circumstances where a commercial business agrees to make a payment to the charitable organization, with that agreement advertised, where the amount of the payment is predicated on the extent of products sold or services provided by the business to the public during a particular time period. The latter involves the public marketing of products or services by or on behalf of a tax-exempt organization, or similar use of an organization's resources.

A manifestation of the latter situation can be seen in the participation by exempt organizations in affinity card programs, in which an exempt organization is paid a portion of the revenues derived from the use of the cards by consumers who make up the affinity group. The position of the IRS is that the revenues from affinity card programs are taxable because they arise from the exploitation of mailing lists, and that the special exception for these lists is not available because the lists are provided to noncharitable organizations. The matter of the taxation of affinity card revenue is currently in litigation.

The dilemma in each of these situations for the fund-raising charitable organization is the extent to which it is actively involved in the activity which gives rise to the revenue. If it is passive, or relatively so, the income it receives is not likely to be taxed. By contrast, active participation in the underlying activity (i.e., advertisements or endorsements) will lead the IRS to assert that the organization is in a joint venture with the other party or parties, making the revenue taxable.

Checklist 51.6

Does the organization treat one or more fund-raising activities as unrelated businesses?	Yes____	No____
If yes, identify these activities.		
Does the organization rely on the royalty exception?	Yes____	No____

51.10 Exemption Application Process

A charitable organization generally must secure recognition of its tax-exempt status from the IRS. The application process requires the organization to reveal some information about its fund-raising program. The organization must describe its actual and planned fund-raising program. In this context, the applicant organization must summarize its actual use of, or plans to use, selective mailings, fund-raising committees, professional fund raisers, and the like (if any). The organization must identify, in order of size, its sources of financial support.

The application for recognition of tax exemption, if properly completed, amounts to a rather complete portrait of the programs, fund-raising plans, and other aspects of the applicant organization. It is a public document and thus, during the course of the organization's existence, it probably will be called upon to provide a copy of the application to interested persons. Inasmuch as those who inspect the document are likely to be prospective donors or grantors, it is particularly important that it be properly prepared.

51.11 Reporting Requirements

Nearly all tax-exempt organizations are required to file annual information returns with the IRS. These returns are open to public inspection.

An organization is required to report all amounts received as contributions or grants. It must attach a schedule listing contributors during the year who gave the organization, directly or indirectly, money or property worth at least $5,000. Separate reporting is required for program service revenue, membership dues and assessments, investment income, asset sales, revenue from special fund-raising events, and other revenue.

Revenue from special fund-raising activities generally is (as noted) separately reported; however, when the payment is partly a purchase for the event or activity and partly a contribution, the gift portion is reported separately from the purchase portion. Direct expenses associated with special fund-raising events are subtracted on the face of the return. A schedule must be attached to the return listing the three largest (in terms of gross receipts) special events conducted by the organization.

Revenue, for these purposes, does not include the value of services donated to an organization or the free use of materials, equipment, or facilities. However, these items may be reported elsewhere on the return.

In general, expenses must be totaled, as well as allocated to three categories: program, management, and fund raising. This is known as the *functional method* of accounting. Proper compliance with the requirements of the functional method obligates organizations to maintain detailed records as to their fund-raising and other expenses, because the fund-raising component of each line-item expenditure must be separately identified and reported.

51.12 Disclosure Requirements

The IRS issued proposed regulations detailing the rules by which tax-exempt organizations must disclose copies of their annual information returns (generally, Form 990) and application for recognition of exemption (Form 1023 or 1024). These regulations, issued on September 25, 1997, also spell out the criteria by which organizations may use one or both of the exceptions to the general disclosure rules, involving documents that are *widely available* or are being sought as part of a *harassment campaign*.

Under existing law, a tax-exempt organization must provide a copy of its application for recognition of exemption and its three most recent annual information returns to anyone who requests them. It is not necessary that copies be provided; the documents need only be provided for review. The request must be made during regular business hours.

In 1996 Congress revised this body of law, although the rules did not take effect until 1999. This law generally requires that anyone who requests the exemption application or annual returns, in person or in writing, must be provided a copy of the documents. These copies may be retained by the requestor.

If a request for these copies is made in person, the organization must provide them immediately. A request in writing must be responded to within 30 days. The only charge that can be imposed for these copies is a reasonable fee for photocopying and mailing costs.

This law contains two exceptions. That is, under two circumstances, the exempt organization is relieved of the obligation to provide copies of the application and returns. An exception is available where the organization has made the documents widely available. The other exception obtains where the IRS determines, following application by the organization, that the organization is subject to a harassment campaign and that a waiver of the disclosure obligation is in the public interest.

The regulations state the general rule that a tax-exempt organization must provide one who requests it a copy of the application for recognition of tax exemption. This requirement is applicable to private foundations.

This disclosure requirement embraces all supporting documents filed by the organization in support of its application. It also includes any letter or other document issued by the IRS in connection with the document. (If an organization filed its application before July 15, 1987, it is required to make a copy of its application available only if it had a copy of the application on that date.)

A tax-exempt organization must make its three most recent annual information returns available. Generally, this annual return is Form 990. For smaller organizations, it is Form 990-EZ.

The annual return disclosure requirement extends to all schedules and attachments filed with the IRS. For charitable organizations, this includes Schedule A. An organization is not required, however, to disclose the parts of the return that identify names and addresses of contributors to the organization. Also, a tax-exempt organization is not required to disclose its unrelated business income tax return (Form 990-T).

The regulations provide rules concerning the documents that must be made available by an organization that is recognized as tax-exempt under a group exemption.

These proposed regulations provide guidance to an individual denied inspection, or a copy, of an application or an annual return. Basically, the individual may provide the IRS with a statement that describes the reason why the individual believes the denial was in violation of legal requirements.

A tax-exempt organization must make the specified documents available for public inspection at its principal, regional, and district offices. The documents generally must be available for inspection on the day of the request during the organization's normal business hours. An office of an organization will be considered a regional or district office only if it has three or more paid full-time employees (or paid employees, whether part time or full time, whose aggregate number of paid hours per week is at least 120).

The regulations exclude certain sites where the organization's employees perform solely exempt function activities from being considered a regional or district office. The regulations prescribe how an organization that does not maintain a permanent office or whose office has very limited hours during certain times of the year can comply with the public inspection requirements.

A tax-exempt organization must accept requests for copies made in person at the same place and time that the information must be available for public inspection. The regulations generally require an organization to provide the copies on the day of the request. In unusual circumstances, an organization will be permitted to provide the requested copies on the next business day.

The regulations require that, where a request is made in writing, an exempt organization furnish the copies within 30 days from the date the request is received. If an organization requires advance payment of a reasonable fee for copying and mailing (see below), it may provide the copies within 30 days from the date it receives payment (rather than from the date of the request).

The regulations provide guidance as to what constitutes a *request*, when a request is considered *received*, and when copies are considered *provided*. The rules provide that, instead of requesting a copy of an entire exemption application or annual return, individuals may request a specific portion of either document. A principal, regional, or district office of an organization will be able to use an agent to process requests for copies.

The reasonable fee a tax-exempt organization is permitted to charge for copies may be no more than the fees charged by the IRS for copies of exempt organization returns and related documents. This currently is $1.00 for the first page and 15 cents for each subsequent page. Also, actual postage costs may be charged. An organization will be permitted to collect payment in advance of providing the requested copies.

If an organization receives a written request for copies with payment not enclosed, and the organization requires payment in advance, the organization must request payment within seven days from the date it receives the request. Payment will be deemed to occur on the day an organization receives the money, check (provided the check subsequently clears), or money order. An organization will be required to accept payment made in the form of money or money order, and, when the request is made in writing, accept payment by personal check. An organization will be permitted, though not required, to accept other forms of payment. To protect requestors from unexpected fees where an exempt organization does not require prepayment and where a requestor does not enclose prepayment with a request, an organization must receive consent from a requestor before providing copies for which the fee charged for copying and postage is in excess of $20.

As noted, a tax-exempt organization is not required to comply with requests for copies of its exemption application or annual returns if the organization has made them widely available. The regulations specify that an organization can make its application for recognition of tax exemption and/or an annual information return *widely available* by posting the document on its World Wide Web page on the Internet or by having the applicable document posted on another organization's Web page as part of a database of similar materials.

For this exception to be available, however, the following criteria must be followed:

- The entity maintaining the Web page must have procedures for ensuring the reliability and accuracy of the application or return that is posted.
- This entity must take reasonable precautions to prevent alteration, destruction, or accidental loss of the posted document.
- The application or return must be posted in the same format used by the IRS to post forms and publications on the IRS's Web page.
- The Web page that is used must clearly inform readers that the document is available and provide instructions for downloading it.
- When downloaded and printed in hard copy, the document must be in substantially the same form as the original application or return, and contain the same information as provided in the original document filed with the IRS (other than information that can be lawfully withheld)
- A person can access and download the document without payment of a fee to the organization maintaining the Web page.

The regulations provide that the IRS may prescribe, by revenue procedure or other guidance, other methods that an organization can use to make its application and/or return widely available.

An organization that makes its application and/or return widely available must inform individuals who request copies how and where to obtain the requested document.

The regulations provide guidance in determining whether a tax-exempt organization is the subject of a harassment campaign. Generally, a *harassment campaign* exists where an organization receives a group of requests, and the relevant facts and circumstances show that the purpose of the group of requests was to disrupt the operations of the exempt organization rather than to collect information.

These facts and circumstances include a sudden increase in the number of requests, an extraordinary number of requests made through form letters or similarly worded correspondence, evidence of a purpose to significantly deter the organization's employees or volunteers from pursuing the organization's exempt purpose, requests that contain language hostile to the organization, direct evidence of bad faith by organizers of the purported harassment campaign, evidence that the organization has already provided the requested documents to a member of the purported harassing group, and a demonstration by the exempt organization that it routinely provides copies of its documents upon request.

The regulations contain examples that evaluate whether particular situations constitute a harassment campaign and whether an organization has a reasonable basis for believing that a request is part of this type of campaign. For example, the IRS will not allow organizations to suspend compliance with a request for copies from a representative of the news media even though the organization believes that the request is part of a harassment campaign.

The regulations permit an organization to disregard requests in excess of two per 30-day period or four per year from the same individual or from the same address. There are procedures for requesting a determination that an organization is subject to a harassment campaign, the treatment of requests for copies while a request for a determination is pending, and the effect of this type of a determination.

These two exceptions are only exceptions from the rules concerning *distribution* of applications and returns. They are not exceptions from the *inspection* requirements.

51.13   Fund-raising Compensation Arrangements

Charitable organizations must be operated so that they do not cause any inurement of their net earnings to certain individuals in their private capacity or otherwise cause private benefit.[4] The private inurement and private benefit doctrines can be triggered when a charitable organization pays excessive or otherwise unreasonable compensation for services. Therefore, a charitable organization may not, without endangering its tax-exempt status, pay a fund-raising professional an amount that is excessive or unreasonable.

Questions about the propriety of compensation of a fund-raising professional may not have as much to do with the amount being paid as with the manner in which it is determined. This is particularly true with respect to compensation that is ascertained on the basis of a commission or percentage. Although the IRS is rather suspicious of fund-raising compensation that is based on percentages of contributions received, the courts have been rather tolerant of the practice.

Checklist 51.7

Does organization pay a fund raiser on a percentage
basis?   Yes____   No____
If yes, identify the arrangement.   _____

---

[4]*Ibid.*, Chapter 19.

51.14 Charitable Giving Rules

Much of the federal regulation of the process of charitable fund raising is accomplished by means of the laws relating to the charitable contribution deduction, principally those that are part of the income tax regime.[5]

The basic concept of the federal income tax charitable contribution deduction is that individuals who itemize deductions, and corporations, can deduct, subject to varying limitations, an amount equivalent to the value of a contribution made to a qualified donee. In general, a *gift* is a payment for which the donor does not expect anything in return. A *charitable gift* is a gift to or for the use of a qualified charitable entity.

The extent of the deduction may be dependent upon whether the charitable donee is a public charity or a private foundation. Another basic element in determining whether, or the extent to which, a contribution to charity is deductible is the nature of the property contributed: capital gain property or ordinary income property. Other distinctions may be made between current giving and planned giving, between gifts of money and gifts of property, and between outright gifts, partial interest gifts, and gifts by means of a trust. The value of a qualified charitable contribution of an item of property often is its fair market value.

The tax treatment of gifts of property is dependent upon whether the property is *long-term capital gain property,* which is a capital asset that has appreciated in value, which, if sold, would result in long-term capital gain. One feature of this type of property is that it is held by the owner for at least 12 months. Other types of property are *ordinary income property* and *short-term capital gain property.*

The deductibility of charitable contributions for a tax year can be restricted by percentage limitations, which in the case of individuals are a function of the donor's *contribution base.* For nearly all individuals, the contribution base is the same as adjusted gross income. These percentage limitations are (1) 50 percent of the contribution base for gifts of money and ordinary income property to public charities and certain operating foundations; (2) 30 percent of the contribution base for contributions of long-term capital gain property to public charities and certain foundations; (3) 30 percent of the contribution base for contributions of cash and ordinary income property to private foundations and certain other recipients; (4) 50 percent of the contribution base for contributions of capital gain property to public charities where the amount of the contribution is reduced by all of the unrealized appreciation in the value of the property; and (5) 20 percent of the contribution base for contributions of capital gain property to charitable organizations other than public charities and operating foundations, principally standard private foundations. Where an individual makes one or more charitable contributions and exceeds the percentage limitations, generally the excess may be carried forward and deducted in subsequent years, up to five years.

Deductible charitable contributions by corporations in a tax year may not exceed 10 percent of pretax net income. A corporation using the accrual method of accounting can elect to treat a charitable contribution as having been paid in a tax year if it is actually paid during the first two and one-half months of the following year. Special rules apply as to the deductibility of corporate gifts of inventory. The making of a charitable gift by

---

[5]These rules are discussed in detail in Bruce R. Hopkins, *The Tax Law of Charitable Giving* (New York: John Wiley & Sons, 1993).

a business corporation is not an act outside the entity's corporate powers as long as the general interests of the corporation and its shareholders are advanced.

A donor (individual or corporate) who makes a gift of long-term capital gain property to a public charity generally can compute the charitable deduction using the fair market value of the property at the time of the gift, with no taxation of the appreciation in the property. However, in the case of a contribution of ordinary income property to a charitable organization, the donor must reduce the deduction by the amount of any gain. A donor who makes a gift of long-term capital gain tangible personal property to a public charity must reduce the deduction by the amount of the gain that would have been recognized had the donor sold the property instead, where the use of the property by the charitable donee is not related to its tax-exempt purposes. In general, a donor who makes a gift of capital gain property to a private foundation must reduce the amount of the otherwise allowable charitable deduction by the appreciated element in the property.

Many itemized deductions, including the charitable contribution deduction, are subject to a floor of 3 percent of adjusted gross income in excess of $100,000 (with this amount adjusted for inflation). Total otherwise allowable deductions, however, need not be reduced by more than 80 percent.

A charitable deduction for a contribution of less than the donor's entire interest in the property—a gift of a *partial interest*—including the right to use property, generally is denied. There are exceptions for certain gifts of interests in trust, gifts of an outright remainder interest in a personal residence or farm, gifts of an undivided portion of one's entire interest in a property, gifts of easements with respect to real property granted in perpetuity to a public charity exclusively for contribution purposes, and a gift of a remainder interest in real property that is granted to a public charity exclusively for conservation purposes.

The general rule is that there is no charitable deduction for a contribution of a remainder interest in property unless it is in trust and the trust is a charitable remainder trust (annuity trust or unitrust) or pooled income fund. Defective charitable split-interest trusts may be reformed to preserve the charitable deduction. Other charitable gifts of remainder interests may be made by means of the charitable gift annuity. Contributions of income interests in property may be made by means of charitable lead trusts.

51.15 Sponsorship Payments

The term "unrelated trade or business" does not include the activity of soliciting and receiving *qualified sponsorship payments.*

A qualified sponsorship payment is any payment made by any person engaged in a trade or business, with respect to which there is no arrangement or expectation that the payor will receive any substantial return benefit other than the use or acknowledgment of the name or logo (or product lines) of the payor's trade or business in connection with the activities of the tax-exempt organization that receives the payment. For example, if in return for receiving a sponsorship payment an exempt organization promises to use the sponsor's name or logo in acknowledging the sponsor's support for an educational or fund-raising event conducted by the organization, the payment would not be subject to the unrelated business income tax.

There are three exceptions to this definition.

1. This use or acknowledgment may not include advertising the payor's products or services (including messages containing qualitative or comparative language, price information, or other indications of savings or value, an endorsement, or an inducement to purchase, sell, or use the products or services).

2. *Qualified sponsorship payment* does not include any payment if the amount of the payment is contingent upon the level of attendance at one or more events, broadcast ratings, or other factors indicating the degree of public exposure to one or more events. (The fact that a sponsorship payment is contingent upon an event actually taking place or being broadcast, in and of itself, does not cause the payment to fail to be a qualified sponsorship payment.)

3. The term does not include any payment that entitles the payor to an acknowledgment or advertising in regularly scheduled and printed material published by or on behalf of the payee organization that is not related to and primarily distributed in connection with a specific event conducted by the payee organization (i.e., periodicals).

To the extent that a portion of a payment would (if made as a separate payment) be a qualified sponsorship payment, that portion of the payment and the other portion of the payment are treated as separate payments (in other words, an allocation is allowed). That is, if a sponsorship payment made to an exempt organization entitles the sponsor to both product advertising and use or acknowledgment of the sponsor's name or logo by the organization, the unrelated business income tax would not apply to the amount of the payment that exceeds the fair market value of the product advertising provided to the sponsor.

Mere distribution or display of a sponsor's products by the sponsor or the exempt organization to the general public at a sponsored event, whether for free or for remuneration, is considered to be *use or acknowledgment* of the sponsor's product lines (as opposed to advertising). The provision of facilities, services, or other privileges by an exempt organization to a sponsor or the sponsor's designees (e.g., complimentary tickets, pro-am playing spots in golf tournaments, or receptions for major donors in connection with a sponsorship payment) will not affect the determination of whether the payment is a qualified sponsorship payment. Rather, the provision of such goods or services is to be evaluated as a separate transaction in determining whether the organization has unrelated business taxable income from the event. In general, if the services or facilities do not constitute a substantial return benefit or if the provision of the services or facilities is a related business activity, the payments attributable to the services or facilities will not be taxable. A sponsor's receipt of a license to use an intangible asset (e.g., a trademark, logo, or designation) of the exempt organization is to be treated as separate from the qualified sponsorship transaction in determining whether the organization has unrelated business taxable income.

In determining whether a payment is a qualified sponsorship payment, it is irrelevant whether the sponsored activity is related or unrelated to the organization's exempt purpose. This exemption is in addition to other present-law exceptions from the unrelated business income tax. This law applies to payments solicited or received after December 31, 1995. No inference is intended by enactment of this rule as to whether any sponsorship payment received prior to 1996 was subject to the unrelated business income tax.

51.16   Postal Laws

Fund raising for charitable purposes, when undertaken by means of the mail, is regulated by the federal postal laws. This is done by limiting the use of special, reduced bulk third-class mailing rates to qualified organizations when they are mailing eligible matter.

Qualified organizations that have received specific authorization from the U.S. Postal Service (USPS) may mail eligible matter at these third-class rates of postage. These organizations, which include charitable, educational, and religious entities, may not be organized for profit and none of their net income may accrue to the benefit of private persons.

In general, by statute, the special bulk third-class rates may not be used for the mailing of material that advertises, promotes, offers, or, for a fee or consideration, recommends, describes, or announces the availability of:

- Any credit, debit, or charge card or similar financial instrument or account, provided by or through an arrangement with any person or organization not authorized to mail at the special third-class rates at the entry post office. These are generally known as affinity cards.
- Any insurance policy, unless the organization promoting the purchase of the policy is authorized to mail at the special rates at the entry post office; the policy is designed for and primarily promoted to the members, donors, supporters, or beneficiaries of the organization; and the coverage provided by the policy is not generally otherwise commercially available.
- Any travel arrangement, unless the organization promoting the arrangement is authorized to mail at the special rates at the entry post office; the travel contributes substantially (aside from the cultivation of members, donors, or supporters, or the acquisition of funds) to one or more of the purposes that constitute the basis for the organization's authorization to mail at the special rates; and the arrangement is designed for and primarily promoted to the members, donors, supporters, and beneficiaries of that organization.

According to the *Domestic Mail Manual*, the phrase "not generally otherwise commercially available" applies to the actual coverage stated in an insurance policy, without regard to the amount of the premiums, the underwriting practices, or the financial condition of the insurer. When comparisons with other policies are made, consideration is given by the USPS to policy coverage benefits, limitations, and exclusions, and to the availability of coverage to the targeted category of recipients. When insurance policy coverages are compared in determining whether coverage in a policy offered by an organization is not generally otherwise commercially available, the comparison is based on the specific characteristics of the recipients of the piece in question (e.g., geographic location or demographic characteristics).

The types of insurance considered generally commercially available include homeowners', property, casualty, marine, professional liability (including malpractice), travel, health, life, airplane, automobile, truck, motor home, motorbike, motorcycle, boat, accidental death and dismemberment, Medicare supplement (Medigap), catastrophic care, nursing home, and hospital indemnity insurance.

An authorized nonprofit organization's material is not disqualified from being mailed at the special rates solely because that material contains, but is not primarily devoted to:

- Acknowledgments of organizations or individuals who have made donations to the authorized organization
- References to and a response card or other instructions for making inquiries about services or benefits available as a result of membership in the authorized organization, and if advertising, promotional, or application materials specifically concerning the services or benefits are not included

Additional content-based statutory restrictions on the use of the special bulk third-class postage rates by qualified organizations apply, in that certain types of advertisements, promotions, and offers, as well as some products, are ineligible to be mailed at the special rates. For material that advertises, promotes, offers, or for a fee or consideration recommends, describes, or announces the availability of any product or service to qualify for mailing at the special bulk third-class rates, the sale of the product or the provision of the service must be substantially related to the exercise or performance by the organization of one or more of the purposes constituting the basis for the organization's authorization to mail at the special rates. (This rule does not apply to the products and services listed earlier in this section.)

The determination as to what is and is not unrelated business activity or income is made in accordance with federal tax standards. The fact that an organization does not pay unrelated business income tax on an item of revenue does not necessarily establish that the activity is a related business, but reflects the statutory exemptions for certain activities or forms of income.

The rules allow the mailing of low-cost items and items contributed to the organization at the special rates. (The exception for low-cost items parallels that in the federal tax law.) However, advertisements mailed at the special rates do not have to meet the "substantially related" test if the material of which the advertisement is a part meets the content requirements of a periodical publication.

The USPS has developed rules concerning the treatment of mail matter that solicits contributions or membership dues and offers low-cost premium items. The material can now qualify for the not-for-profit mailing rates. The requested contribution or dues payment will have to be at least five times the total cost of the premium to the organization. The requested contribution or other payment will have to be at least three times the represented value, in the mail piece, of the premium.

51.17 Securities Laws

The applicability of federal and state securities laws to the activities of charitable organizations in connection with the maintenance of certain *charitable income funds* is limited. These funds are not investment companies subject to the registration and other requirements of the Investment Company Act of 1940. There are exemptions under the federal securities laws for charitable organizations that maintain these funds.

A charitable income fund is a fund maintained by a charitable organization exclusively for the collective investment and reinvestment of one or more assets of a charitable remainder or similar trust, of a pooled income fund, contributed in exchange for the issuance of charitable gift annuities, of a charitable lead trust, of the general endowment fund or other funds of one or more charitable organizations, or of certain other trusts of which the remainder interests are revocably dedicated to or for the benefit of one or more charitable organizations. The Securities and Exchange Commission (SEC) has the authority to expand the scope of the exemptive provisions of the legislation to include funds that may include assets not expressly defined.

A fund that is excluded from the definition of an investment company must provide, to each donor to a charity by means of the fund, written information describing the material terms of operation of the fund. However, this disclosure requirement is not a condition of exemption from the Investment Company Act. Thus, a charitable income fund that fails to provide the requisite information is not subject to the securities laws, although the fund may be subject to an enforcement or other action by the SEC. Charitable organizations have flexibility in determining the contents of the required disclosure.

This exemption in the Investment Company Act is also grafted onto the Securities Act of 1933, although charitable income funds are not exempted from that law's antifraud provisions. A similar rule operates in respect to the Securities Exchange Act of 1934.

The Securities Exchange Act also provides that a charitable organization is not subject to the Act's broker-dealer regulation solely because the organization trades in securities on its behalf, or on behalf of a charitable income fund, or the settlors, potential settlors, or beneficiaries of either. This protection is also extended to trustees, directors, officers, employees, and volunteers of a charitable organization, acting within the scope of their employment or duties with the organization. Similar exemptions are provided for charitable organizations, and certain persons associated with them, in connection with the provision of advice, analyses, and reports, from the reach of the Investment Advisors Act of 1940 (other than in regard to its antifraud elements).

Interests in charitable income funds excluded from the definition of an investment company, and any offer or sale of these interests, are exempt from any state law that requires registration or qualification of securities. No charitable organization or trustee, director, officer, employee, or volunteer of a charity (acting within the scope of his or her employment or duties) is subject to regulation as a dealer, broker, agent, or investment advisor under any state securities law because the organization or person trades in securities on behalf of a charity, charitable income fund, or the settlors, potential settlors, or beneficiaries of either. These rules do not, however, alter the reach or scope of state antifraud laws.

There is an opt-out provision in regard to state law. That is, a state can timely enact a statute that specifically states that these newly enacted laws shall not prospectively preempt the laws of the state.

Prior to the time this matter was made the subject of statutory law, the applicability of the Securities Act, the Securities Exchange Act, and the Investment Company Act to charitable income funds was addressed by the staff of the SEC. This administrative approach can be traced back to 1972, when a "no-action letter" as to pooled income funds was issued, which was predicated on the fact that these entities are the subject of federal tax law and are subject to the oversight of the IRS. One of the principal conditions of this no-action assurance was that all prospective donors receive written disclosures fully and fairly describing the fund's operations. (In addition, the SEC staff has consistently maintained that the antifraud provisions of the securities laws apply to the activities of these funds and their associated persons.) This no-action position has always

been rationalized by the view that the primary purpose of those who transfer money and property to these funds is to make a charitable gift, rather than to make an investment.

A favorable letter from the SEC staff does not insulate its recipient from liability asserted by a private litigant who alleges that a transaction violates the securities laws. For the most part, the codification of these rules embodies the approach taken over the past two and one-half decades by the staff of the SEC.

Checklist 51.8

Does the organization maintain one or more charitable income funds?	Yes____	No____
Does the organization provide adequate written information about these funds?	Yes____	No____

51.18   Antitrust Laws

The antitrust laws contain an exemption, stating that agreeing to use, or using, the same annuity rate for the purpose of issuing one or more charitable gift annuities is not unlawful under any of the antitrust laws. This exemption extends to both federal and state law. The protection is not confined to charities: it extends to lawyers, accountants, actuaries, consultants, and others retained or employed by a charitable organization when assisting in the issuance of a charitable gift annuity or the setting of charitable annuity rates. This legislation defines *charitable gift annuity* by cross-reference to the federal tax law.

Moreover, this antitrust exemption also sweeps within its ambit the act of publishing suggested annuity rates. Thus, organizations—most notably, the American Council on Gift Annuities—cannot be in violation of the antitrust laws owing to its publication of actuarial tables or annuity rates for use in issuing gift annuities.

There is an opportunity for a state to override this legislation in regard to its antitrust laws. To do this, the state would have to, on a timely basis, enact a law which expressly provides that the antitrust exemption does not apply in respect to the otherwise protected conduct.

The antitrust laws generally apply to a charitable organization when such an organization is engaged in a "commercial transaction" with a "public service aspect." Prior to the amendment of statutory law on the point, there was uncertainty as to whether charitable gift annuities involve these types of transactions or are "pure charity." Nonetheless, Congress concluded that giving by means of these annuities is "legitimate," particularly inasmuch as the IRS "approves and regulates" these instruments.

Checklist 51.9

Does the organization issue charitable gift annuity contracts?	Yes____	No____
Does the organization adhere to suggested annuity rates?	Yes____	No____
Does applicable state law contain an exception to the federal exemption?	Yes____	No____

51.19 *Federal Trade Commission Telemarketing Rules*

The Federal Trade Commission (FTC) has developed rules prohibiting deceptive and other abusive telemarketing practices. These rules do not directly pertain to charitable organizations, but apply to for-profit companies that raise funds or provide similar services to charitable and other tax-exempt organizations.

Even though these rules generally are not applicable in the charitable fund-raising setting, they nonetheless serve as useful guidelines for proper telemarketing practices. In this regard, they:

1. Define the term "telemarketing."
2. Require clear and conspicuous disclosures of specified material information, orally or in writing, before a customer pays for goods or services offered.
3. Prohibit misrepresenting, directly or by implication, specified material information relating to the goods or services that are the subject of a sales offer as well as any other material aspects of a telemarketing transaction.
4. Require express verifiable authorization before submitting for payment a check, draft, or other form of negotiable paper drawn on a person's account.
5. Prohibit false or otherwise misleading statements to induce payment for goods or services.
6. Prohibit any person from assisting and facilitating certain deceptive or abusive telemarketing acts or practices.
7. Prohibit credit card laundering.
8. Prohibit specified abusive acts or practices.
9. Impose calling time restrictions.
10. Require specified information to be disclosed truthfully, promptly, and in a clear and conspicuous manner, in an outbound telephone call.
11. Require that specified records be kept.
12. Specify certain acts or practices that are exempt from the requirements.

51.20 *Conclusion*

The giving public is deserving of protection against fraud and other abuse in charitable giving. At the same time, the process of raising money for charitable purposes has become heavily weighed down with a plethora of federal regulatory procedures and other burdens.

For a nation that has a tradition of a healthy and productive not-for-profit sector, this slow but steady imposition of additional burdens on the good works of not-for-profit organizations is becoming a drain on charitable resources. One of the challenges for the nonprofit community in the years ahead will be to minimize these impediments while simultaneously protecting the charitable giving public.

52 ▾ State Regulation of Fund Raising

SETH PERLMAN, ESQ
Perlman & Perlman

52.1 A Brief History of State Fund-raising Regulation

In the 45 years states have been regulating fund raising, there have been few new approaches by the states to protect the public interest and charitable assets while recognizing not-for-profit organizations' special needs and limitations. The only constant, it seems, is the continuing growth of paperwork.

Until the 1950s, charities were governed by Charitable Trust statutes, whereby trustees were held accountable for properly discharging their fiduciary duties. Modern fund-raising regulation first appeared in New York with the establishment of the Secretary of State's Office of Charities Registration in Albany in 1955. Legislation modeled on the emerging consumer protection statutes was the basis for fund-raising regulation. The "consumer protection" theory of regulation would eventually espouse the types of provisions deemed unconstitutional in 1988 by the Supreme Court. Those provisions required disclosure of fund-raising costs in the course of solicitation, limits on fund-raising costs, and disapproval of solicitation licenses to groups not meeting these or other criteria.

The regulation of *fund raising*, rather than of the charities themselves, developed as fund-raising practices became more mechanized in the 1950s and 1960s with the advent of the computer, as applied to direct mail and telephone solicitation.

An intriguing hypothesis that would explain the growing interest of the states in fund-raising regulation has been proposed by University of Arizona law professor Leslie Espinoza, a former regulator in the State of Massachusetts. According to her research, a number of well-established organizations saw themselves threatened by a new crop of not-for-profits that could use the techniques of direct mail to their advantage. As a way of countering these new organizations' success in fund raising, a group convened by the Rockefeller Foundation, known as the Hamlin Committee, recommended regulatory strategies that would emphasize fund-raising costs as a measure of general effectiveness. This approach benefited larger groups with an established funding base and placed the smaller, newer organizations at a disadvantage.

A memorable excerpt from the Hamlin Committee report of 1958 declared: "It does not take over 100,000 voluntary agencies in the opinion of many, to provide private health and welfare services in the United States. A better job could be done by a smaller number, and a greater joint effort." Such a view is anathema to many people today, because they recognize the value of diversity in the not-for-profit sector and the fundamental role that freedom of association plays in a democratic society. The Supreme Court has recognized, in three decisions of this past decade, known collectively as *Schaumburg, Munson,* and *Riley,* that fund-raising activities are inseparable from the protected speech used to advocate ideas and express viewpoints. Fund raising is *not* commercial speech, such as advertising, and cannot be regulated in the same way as product advertising—This was the basis for changing the consumer protection–type regulation of the past 45 years.

But what are the principles that will replace them? The Hamlin Committee, among many others, found fund-raising costs to be a legitimate means of separating the worthy from the unworthy. Yet focusing on fund raising ignores other potential abuses in not-for-profit operations, such as overcompensation of staff or directors, self-dealing, use of charitable assets for lavish offices and furnishings, and other inappropriate uses of funds.

It is significant that the most recent allegations of impropriety in the not-for-profit field, exemplified by the case of the Foundation for New Era Philanthropy and the conviction of United Way of America president William J. Aramony, did not involve fund raising but were about the use (and abuse) of funds raised.

52.2 Regulatory Trends

Recent legislation is attempting to keep pace with the ever-changing field of fund raising. New technology, such as telephone solicitation, the Internet, the growth of the direct mail industry, and new marketing arrangements between not-for-profits and corporations, have state officials concerned that their current laws are insufficient to regulate these activities. These new methods of fund raising, coupled with a widely held and unsubstantiated belief that fraudulent fund raising is increasing, have brought about a number of new state laws. These new laws go beyond traditional regulation to stipulate:

- Written disclosures on all appeals mailed to residents of the regulating state.
- Provisions in contracts between not-for-profits and fund-raising counsel or professional solicitors.
- The manner in which contributions must be distributed.
- Fewer exemptions from registration.

Enforcement of registration compliance has increased, leading at least one state to fine organizations that register voluntarily, if the state determines such organizations have solicited in that state prior to registration. The state is also pursuing organizations that it has determined are soliciting without registering, and levying heavy fines.

As a result of these new policies, not-for-profit and fund-raising executives' knowledge of filing requirements has become important. Registration is among the few tools left to regulators that courts have not substantially limited. The Supreme Court's decision in *Riley v. North Carolina Federation of the Blind*, and the *Munson* and *Schaumburg* cases that preceded it, ruled that states cannot require not-for-profits or fund raisers to disclose how much of a particular donation will go to fund-raising costs or limit the amount a not-for-profit may spend on fund raising. These provisions were found by the Court to violate the not-for-profit organization's First Amendment right of free speech.

In the post-*Riley* world of fund-raising regulation, the registration and filing of contracts, financial reports, and (in some states) samples of fund-raising materials take the place of limits on fund-raising costs and mandated cost disclosures. States are monitoring filings and registration closely. In one precedent-setting case, state officials sued and won the return of $58,000 in contributions donated by New York State residents to a not-for-profit that was not properly registered in New York.

Recently the National Association of State Charity Officers ("NASCO") issued a set of principles for states to use in regulating the activities of charities and other 501(c) organizations on the Internet. The principles known as "The Charleston Principles" require regulation of those organizations which purposely direct their Internet activities at the citizens of a particular state. As of this writing, the definition and parameters of "purposely direct" are under discussion by regulators, charities and legal practitioners.

(A) REQUIRED DISCLOSURES

As noted earlier, the states have been severely restricted in fund-raising regulation by Supreme Court decisions involving free speech rights. Because the Court has ruled that fund raising is protected speech, states cannot require not-for-profits to disclose their fund-raising costs at the time of an appeal. Such mandated disclosure is as much a violation of the First Amendment right of free speech as a denial of the right to speak. The courts have also concluded that this type of mandated cost disclosure is inherently misleading and often gives little information about how effectively or prudently a not-for-profit is operated.

States have been allowed other, less intrusive, mandated disclosure techniques. They require a pre-solicitation disclosure of whether the individual making the appeal is a professional solicitor and mandate statements telling donors that further financial information is available from the not-for-profit or from state officials. The latter disclosure technique is becoming increasingly popular with states, which view public education as an effective regulatory tool. By encouraging the general public to obtain background information on the charities seeking their support, the states hope donors will become more discerning. Many states publish list of charities soliciting within their borders along with the financial information about their solicitation campaigns. Charities with high administrative and fund-raising costs, it is assumed by state authorities, will lose out on contributions, for states can require this type of breakdown in state financial reporting forms but not in a point-of-solicitation disclosure (which cannot be mandated). Their belief is that an informed public can make a wise choice in giving to organizations with lower fund-raising costs because more of their funds will be used for charitable purposes.

A list of the states requiring these disclosures, and the contents of these disclosures, is included in Exhibit 52.1.

There are also disclosure requirements for commercial co-venturer/charitable sales promotions, such as the amount of a purchase that will benefit the charity. These disclosures may be mandatory, even if registration of commercial co-venturers is not required.

(B)   COMMERCIAL CO-VENTURERS

A commercial co-venturer is a company normally engaged in trade or commerce other than the solicitation of contributions, which conducts a "charitable sales promotion" involving the sale of a product or service, of which a portion of the proceeds will in some way benefit a not-for-profit organization. This relatively new fund-raising technique was first recognized and defined in the Charitable Solicitation Model Law produced by the National Association of Attorneys General 1986. In response to a growing number of cause-marketing arrangements, a small number of states have enacted specific legislation to regulate commercial co-venturers. In 1999, sixteen states signed onto a report entitled "What is in a Charity's Name", setting forth an outline of proposed rules of conduct for charities involved in commercial cause marketing relationships.

Several of these states do not require commercial co-venturers to register, only to keep records of their promotions for several years. Other states, such as Maine, Washington, Alabama, and Massachusetts, require registration of the company as a commercial co-venturer and in certain cases the filing of a bond. A number of states do not require such a company to register at all, but assume the charity will register and file annual reports covering the charitable sales promotion. Connecticut requires only the filing of a formal contract between the co-venturer and the not-for-profit. Many states require that a contract be executed, although no filing or registration is actually necessary.

However, an even greater number of states may insist that the company register as a professional fund raiser or commercial solicitor, depending on the nature of the promotion and the agreement between the charity and the co-venturer. For example, a company that advertises that it will give 5 cents for every product sold may not have to register in many states, because it is making a contribution. On the other hand, a company promoting a program whereby the consumer may donate funds to a charity through the purchase of a product may be setting itself up as a professional solicitor, in the states' view, because it is acting as a conduit for donated funds. Registration as a professional solicitor involves filling out forms, filing bonds, and filing financial reports in at least two dozen states.

It is difficult to generalize about the states' view of commercial co-venturer arrangements when their definitions of professional fund raiser or solicitor vary—or are interpreted—so widely. In states in which a professional fund raiser works for "financial *or*

EXHIBIT 52.1 Charitable Solicitation Disclosures

The following states require certain information to be included in all charitable solicitations mailed to residents in these states.

Florida

The following verbatim disclosure must be conspicuously displayed, in capital letters, and included on all fund-raising materials sent to Florida residents:

A COPY OF THE OFFICIAL REGISTRATION AND FINANCIAL INFORMATION MAY BE OBTAINED FROM THE DIVISION OF CONSUMER SERVICES BY CALLING TOLL-FREE, WITHIN THE STATE, 1-800-HELP-FLA. REGISTRATION DOES NOT IMPLY ENDORSE-MENT, APPROVAL, OR RECOMMENDATION BY THE STATE.

The statute states that when a solicitation consists of more than one piece, "the statement must be displayed prominently" in the materials.

Maryland

Solicitations must state that, for the cost of postage and copying, documents and informa-tion filed under the Maryland charitable organizations laws can be obtained from the Secre-tary of State.

According to the statute, the statement must be "conspicuously displayed on any written or printed solicitation." If there is more than one piece in the solicitation package, the state-ment must be displayed on a "prominent part of the solicitation materials."

Michigan

Michigan law does not require a disclosure statement. However, the state Attorney General's office strongly encourages inclusion of the organization's Michigan registration number in all solicitations.

Mississippi

The following statement must be reproduced verbatim on written solicitations, confirma-tions, receipts, and reminders of oral solicitations:

"The official registration and financial information of (insert the legal name of the charity as registered with the Secretary of State) may be obtained from the Missis-sippi Secretary of State's office by calling 1-888-236-6167. Registration by the Secre-tary of State does not imply endorsement."

New Jersey

The following disclosure must be "conspicuously printed" on any printed solicitation, writ-ten confirmation, receipt, or written reminder of a charitable organization, independent paid fund raiser, or solicitor:

INFORMATION FILED WITH THE ATTORNEY GENERAL CONCERNING THIS CHARI-TABLE SOLICITATION MAY BE OBTAINED FROM THE ATTORNEY GENERAL OF THE STATE OF NEW JERSEY BY CALLING 973-504-6215. REGISTRATION WITH THE ATTORNEY GENERAL DOES NOT IMPLY ENDORSEMENT.

EXHIBIT 52.1 (*Continued*)

New York

Solicitations must state that a copy of the latest annual report can be obtained from the organization or from the Attorney General by writing the Office of the Attorney General, Charities Bureau, 120 Broadway, New York, NY 10271.

The disclosure must be placed conspicuously in the materials, with print no smaller than 10-point boldface type or, alternatively, no smaller than the size print used for the most number of words in the solicitation.

North Carolina

Every charitable organization or sponsor that is required to obtain a license shall conspicuously display in capital letters, in bold type, of a minimum 9-point size, the following statement on every printed solicitation, written confirmation, receipt, or reminder of a contribution:

FINANCIAL INFORMATION ABOUT THE ORGANIZATION AND A COPY OF ITS LICENSE ARE AVAILABLE FROM THE STATE SOLICITATION LICENSING BRANCH AT (919) 807-2214. THE LICENSE IS NOT AN ENDORSEMENT BY THE STATE.

In addition, professional solicitors will be required to make the following disclosure pursuant to any oral or written solicitation, confirmation, receipt, or reminder:

FINANCIAL INFORMATION ABOUT THE SOLICITOR AND A COPY OF ITS LICENSE ARE AVAILABLE FROM THE STATE SOLICITATION LICENSING BRANCH AT (919) 807-2214. THE LICENSE IS NOT AN ENDORSEMENT BY THE STATE.

Pennsylvania

The following statement must be reproduced verbatim and "conspicuously printed":

The official registration and financial information of [insert the legal name of the charity as registered with the Department] may be obtained from the Pennsylvania Department of State by calling toll-free, within Pennsylvania, 1 (800) 732-0999. Registration does not imply endorsement.

Virginia

Although required by law only of professional solicitors, the Office of Consumer Affairs is requesting all not-for-profits to include a disclosure in their solicitations, stating that financial statements are available from the State Division of Consumer Affairs.

Washington

Solicitation must state if a charity is registered with the Secretary of State, that information relating to its financial affairs is available from the Secretary of State, and the toll-free number for Washington residents: 1-800-332-4483.

West Virginia

The following statement is required:

West Virginia residents may obtain a summary of the registration and financial documents from the Secretary of State, State Capitol, Charleston, WV 25305. Registration does not imply endorsement.

There are no placement requirements for this disclosure.

other consideration," the marketing benefit that comes from the pairing of the corporate name and logo with a not-for-profit may be enough to convince state officials that the company must register as a professional fund raiser. Other states may view co-venturers involved in promotions that require the purchase of a product to meet the definition of professional fund raiser and commercial solicitor. Hopefully, the efforts of the 16 state Attorneys General referred to above will bring some semblence of unity to the issue.

Registration and other requirements may be more trouble to a company, perhaps, than the promotion is worth. Proper planning and preparation before entering into a commercial co-venturer arrangement can save countless hours of staff time and legal fees.

(C) SANCTIONS

Executives of not-for-profits and professional fund raisers reviewing the list of requirements may be tempted to ask about the penalties for noncompliance. It is true that few people, if any, have gone to jail for violating charitable solicitation statutes, except, perhaps, for out-and-out theft or fraud.

In the past few years, however, criminal sanctions have been included in amendments and new statutes, making a violator of certain provisions guilty of a felony or an aggravated misdemeanor.

Many states look favorably on good-faith efforts by not-for-profits to comply with registration. Yet there has also been an increasing tendency of regulators to enforce deadlines and other process-oriented provisions that in the past have been overlooked and to fine those organizations or fund raisers that do not comply. This may be, in many cases, a revenue-raising technique. However, there can be more serious consequences to flagrant disregard of charitable solicitation statutes. Use of the media to publicly condemn noncompliers is becoming a favorite tool of regulators, particularly when an official is running for public office. The ultimate consequences may include auditing of books, a review of all solicitation in recent years, fines, and state oversight of the organization's operation for a period of time, or a court order to return donations to residents of a state in which the organization was not fully registered.

52.3 *Registration and Annual Reporting for Not-for-Profit Organizations*

Most regulation at the state level entails the filing of annual or one-time registration forms. Nearly 40 states presently require registration by charities soliciting within their borders. Soliciting (as defined in state statutes) can mean appeals by direct mail, telephone, and door to door (person to person) approaches as well as requests for contributions in the media or by advertisement. Many states requiring annual financial reports will accept a copy of the Form 990 tax return filed with the Internal Revenue Service (IRS), although they may also require a financial addendum of their own.

State registration forms for charities generally require information such as a list of directors, officers, and trustees; the individual responsible for distribution of funds; the charitable purpose of the organization; how funds are raised; and whether fund-raising counsel or solicitors are used. Some type of financial report is usually required; many states accept a copy of IRS Form 990. Most states also require an audited financial statement for charities if income is in excess of an amount raising from $100,000 to $250,000 (the exact amount varies among states).

Other requirements may include samples of fund-raising appeals; copies of contracts with fund-raising counsel, paid solicitors, or commercial co-venturers; articles of incorporation and by-laws.

(A) EXEMPTIONS FROM REGISTRATION

Practically every state requiring registration allows for specific exemptions. Not-for-profit organizations may be exempt from registration but must otherwise conform with the statute, or they may be exempt from the statute altogether. The state summaries specify which case is applicable. Fund-raising consultants and professional solicitors employed by exempt organizations must register and are not entitled to exemption by association, except in rare cases.

A few states require that an organization actually file an application for exemption from registration and annual reporting. Pennsylvania and New Jersey require short-form registration for some groups previously exempt from registration.

Although the list of exemptions varies widely among states, it generally includes these groups and circumstances:

- *Religious organizations* can be classified by the IRS in two ways: as 501(c)(3) organizations, which have to file 990 returns with the IRS, or as 501(c)(3) organization exempt from filing returns under paragraphs 6033(a)(2)(A)(i) and (iii) as "churches, their integrated auxiliaries, and conventions or associations of churches" and as "the exclusively religious activities of any religious order."

  Most states exempt from registration all religious groups, regardless of whether they are required to file 990 forms with the IRS. However, several states have recently passed new laws that tighten the exemption allowance for religious organizations, or have exemption filing requirements.

  The exact definition of each state's religious exemption is given in each state summary. It is recommended that religious organizations review these carefully to determine the states in which they must register.

- *Universities and other educational institutions* have almost universal registration exemption. (Massachusetts is the only state that does not exempt universities from registration.) The exemption may or may not extend to foundations and other organizations raising money on behalf of colleges or schools.

  However, many states define the exemption as applying only when solicitation takes place "among students, faculty, alumni, trustees and their families." There is no indication at this point whether states will begin to demand registration from institutions soliciting outside this definition.

- *Not-for-profit hospitals* are exempt in most states.

- *Small, community-based organizations* that raise amounts below $10,000 to $25,000 are allowed monetary exemptions. Most states require, however, that funds be raised by volunteers. Use of a paid fund raiser usually means revocation of any registration exemption.

- *Solicitation among an organization's members* may not require registration, but many states stipulate that an individual may not become a member simply by making a donation.
- *Other exemptions*, which vary widely among states, can include libraries, senior citizens centers, youth groups, parent-teacher associations, and similar organizations.
- *Public safety personnel organizations, associations of police, fire fighters, and ambulance personnel, and some veterans groups* may also be exempted in some states. Exemptions for veterans groups usually extend only to those organizations that are congressionally chartered. However, in recent years, fund raising on behalf of these groups, often by professional solicitors, has led to a number of abuses. States are concerned that professional solicitors may represent themselves either as actual police officers, or that the solicitation will imply that a donor will receive certain privileges. This area of fund raising most likely will continue to be the focus of regulatory efforts.

(B) FUND-RAISING COUNSEL AND PROFESSIONAL SOLICITORS

Fund-raising counsel and professional solicitors must register in 25 to 40 states, depending on the type of services they provide to not-for-profit clients. Most of these states require solicitors to file bonds in amounts ranging between $2,500 and $50,000 and to file detailed financial reports after each campaign. (See Exhibits 52.2 and 52.3.) Many of the states that define fund-raising counsel no longer require bonds, and some states have even dropped registration requirements.

For many years states grouped both types of professionals in the "professional fund raiser" category, treating consultants and solicitors alike. In the past decade, however, a growing number of states have recognized fund-raising counsel (consultants) as a group of professionals who do not solicit contributions, do not have custody or control of funds, or direct knowledge of campaign expenditures receipts.

For this reason, many states now have a separate definition of fund-raising counsel and do not require filing of bonds. Some states, such as Connecticut, Ohio, and Wisconsin, do not even require registration of counsel, unless such persons have custody of funds. Certainly this is a trend that should be encouraged, as more onerous registration for counsel only raises the cost of the service provided to not-for-profits. In the states' view, fund-raising counsel's services are preferable to those offered by professional solicitors, whose fees are often based on a percentage of the funds raised or who have custody of donated dollars. Recent court challenges in Utah and Florida have sought to limit the ability of states and counties to regulate out-of-state fund-raising counsel.

Professional solicitors have the most detailed registration and reporting requirements, because of their role as fiduciaries in receiving contributions. States are also concerned about the representations made to donors about the charity on whose behalf they are soliciting, as well as the payment of a commission or percentage of funds raised to outside solicitors.

The definition and registration requirements for professional fund raisers or solicitors, as found in many states, reflect the regulators' concerns about professional practice. Pennsylvania's statute, for example, defines fund-raising counsel, but also states that if counsel's compensation is based on the amount of money raised, that person or firm

EXHIBIT 52.2 Fund-Raising Counsel Fee and Bonding Requirements

State	Fee	Bond Amount	Registration Expires/Comments
Arkansas	$100	None	Registration anniversary date/annual report March 31
California	$200	None	January 15
Connecticut	None	None	File contracts only, no registration
Florida	$300	None	March 31
Hawaii	$60	$5,000	June 30
Illinois	None	None	Every two even years
Indiana	$1,000 initial; $50 renewal	None	July 1
Kansas	None	None	June 30; only counsels w/custody of funds must register
Kentucky	$50	None	December 31
Maine	$200	$25,000	November 30
Maryland	$200	None	Registration anniversary date
Massachusetts	$200	None	December 31
Michigan	None	$10,000	June 30
Minnesota	$200	None	April 30
Mississippi	$250	None	June 30
New Hampshire	$75	$10,000	Registration anniversary date
New Jersey	$250	$20,000	June 30; bond required only if counsel collects funds
New York	$800	None	August 31
North Carolina	$200	None	March 31
North Dakota	$100	None	September 1
Oklahoma	$50	$2,500	March 31
Oregon	$250	None	Registration anniversary date
Pennsylvania	$250	None	Registration anniversary date
Rhode Island	$200	None	June 30
South Carolina	$50	None	Registration anniversary date
Tennessee	$250	$25,000	December 31
Utah	$150	None	Registration anniversary date
Virginia	$100	None	Registration anniversary date
West Virginia	$100	$10,000	Registration anniversary date

Source: Excerpted from Fund-Raising Regulation: A State-By-State Handbook of Registration Forms, Requirements, and Procedures, *by Seth Perlman and Betsy Hills Bush. Copyright John Wiley & Sons, Inc., 1996. Used with permission.*

must register as a professional solicitor. Several other states define counsel as working on a "flat-fee" or "fixed-fee" basis, implying that commission-based compensation may mean the consultant will have to register as a professional solicitor.

(C) DIRECT MAIL FUND-RAISING COUNSEL

The regulation of consultants who help not-for-profits conduct direct mail appeals is fraught with ambiguity, misunderstandings, a lack of consensus on the nature of the ser-

EXHIBIT 52.3 Professional Solicitor Fee and Bonding Requirements

State	Fee	Bond Amount	Registration Expires/Comments
Alabama	$100.00	$10,000	September 30
Alaska	None	$10,000	Registration anniversary date
Arizona	$25.00	$25,000	Registration anniversary date
Arkansas	$200.00	$10,000	Registration anniversary date
California	$200.00	$25,000	January 15
Colorado	$62.50	None	Fee applies per campaign
Connecticut	$120.00	$20,000	Registration anniversary date
Florida	$300.00	$50,000	March 31
Georgia	$250.00/$100 renewal	$10,000	December 31; renewal fee $100
Hawaii	$60.00	$5,000	June 30
Illinois	$100 + $25/contract	$10,000	June 30
Indiana	$1,000 initial/$50.00	None	July 1
Iowa	$10.00	None	Registration anniversary date
Kansas	None	$5,000	June 30
Kentucky	$300.00	$25,000	December 31
Maine	$200.00	25,000	November 30
Maryland	$300.00	$25,000	Registration anniversary date
Massachusetts	$300.00	$10,000	December 31
Michigan	None	$10,000	June 30
Minnesota	$200.00	$20,000	April 30
Mississippi	$250.00	$10,000	June 30
Missouri	$50.00	None	Registration anniversary date
New Hampshire	$200.00	$20,000	Registration anniversary date
New Jersey	$250.00	$20,000	June 30. Bond required only if solicitor collects funds
New York	$800.00	$10,000	August 31
North Carolina	$200.00	$20,000–$50,000	March 31; bond amount based on funds received
North Dakota	$100.00	None	September 1
Ohio	$200.00	$25,000	March 31
Oklahoma	$50.00	$2,500	March 31
Oregon	$250.00	None	Registration anniversary date
Pennsylvania	$250.00	$25,000	Registration anniversary date
Rhode Island	$200.00	$10,000	Registration anniversary date
South Carolina	$50.00	$15,000	Registration anniversary date
South Dakota	$50.00	$10,000–$20,000	Registration anniversary date; bond based on custody
Tennessee	$800.00	$25,000	December 31
Texas	$500.00	$5,000–$25,000	January 15; police and veterans solicitors only
Utah	$250.00	None	Registration anniversary date
Vermont	None	$20,000	Registration anniversary date
Virginia	$500.00	$20,000	Bond expiration date
Washington	$250.00 initial/ $175 renewal	$15,000	Registration anniversary date; renewal fee $175
West Virginia	$100.00	$10,000	Registration anniversary date
Wisconsin	$50.00	$5,000–$20,000	August 31. Solicitor with custody files $20,000 bond

Source: Excerpted from Fund-Raising Regulation: A State-by-State Handbook of Registration Forms, Requirements, and Procedures *by Seth Perlman and Betsy Hills Bush. Copyright John Wiley & Sons, Inc., 1996. Used with permission.*

vices provided, and questions regarding who controls the process. The issue of costs, generally quite high in the early phases of a direct mail program, has states concerned that charitable donations are benefiting the fund raiser and vendors rather than the charitable cause. In 1991 Oregon became the first state to require registration of direct mail consultants, while traditional capital campaign consultants as well as special events and planned giving consultants remain exempt.

Although most states currently accept registration of direct mail consultants as fund-raising counsel, they can and do challenge the contract between the direct mail consultant and the not-for-profit if they think that the organization does not have proper control of funds or that the fund raiser should register as a professional solicitor. A state can challenge a contract even if the not-for-profit and the consultant are both located out of state, so long as the not-for-profit is soliciting in that state. Again, the regulation of out-of-state consultants is currently being challenged.

State regulators are becoming increasingly interested in contracts between not-for-profits and direct mail counsel, examining provisions regarding the collection of donations, relationships to subcontractors and, most important, ownership of lists.

The State of Maryland, among the most active states in this area, uses the following six criteria to distinguish between fund-raising counsel and a professional solicitor:

1. Is telemarketing involved in this campaign?
2. Are contributions received by fund-raising counsel or by the charity?
3. Is the charity given an opportunity to review or dispute bills from vendors?
4. Is the charity given an opportunity to choose vendors?
5. Is the charity given an opportunity to approve direct mail copy?
6. Are receipts deposited in a bank account of the charity; and, if so, is check-writing authority on that account limited to the charity?

(D) TELEPHONE SOLICITORS

A fund-raiser firm that is paid for telephone solicitation is generally regarded as a professional solicitor and must register as such. Some fund-raising counseling firms, which are not paid solicitors, may give training and direction to volunteer telephone solicitors, and generally are not considered professional solicitors. Although this fund-raising technique has always invited scrutiny from regulators because of the large number of complaints received from aggravated potential donors, it has continued to gain favor with not-for-profits and fund raisers. This trend should increase as direct mail becomes ever more expensive. As telephone solicitation grows, so will the demand for stricter regulation.

52.4 *Organizing for Registration*

Organizations and professionals registering in more than one state can take a number of steps to streamline the registration process:

- *List of states in which registered.* Most states will ask whether an organization "is authorized by any other governmental authority to solicit contributions." In other words, in which other states has the organization registered? Rather than listing each state on the actual form, keep a running list of states in which the organization or firm has already registered and include a copy as a separate document. Organizations filing 990 forms may be able to use the list of states filed with the IRS. However, be sure to include the regulatory agency and address of each state, rather than just the name of the state.

- *List of directors, trustees, partners, or corporate officers.* Not-for-profit organizations filing IRS 990 forms usually include a list of directors with that return. Use this list to respond to questions asking for a list of directors or trustees. State "See attached list" on the registration form.

Fund-raising counsel and solicitors may wish to provide the same type of separate list for ease in filling out the registration form. Bear in mind, however, that additional information may be required by the state such as "list of stockholders" and "percentage of ownership."

States may specifically request residence addresses, telephone numbers, Social Security numbers, and, as requested in one case, photocopies of drivers' licenses. Although these requirements may appear intrusive, there is little recourse available to professionals.

(A) FILING REGISTRATIONS

They may seem obvious, but be sure to take these four steps when registering, so as to keep files in order and to protect the organization:

1. *Copy the blank form.* Many states require the same form to be used annually. Although some states send new forms to an organization each year, others do not.
2. *Copy the completed form for the organization's records.* It will help in filing next year's registration, as much of the information remains the same from year to year. Copy the registration fee check, if any. A cashed check may be the only proof that the registration was received and processed.
3. *Include a cover letter with the registration, itemizing the documents and any filing fees.* Copy this letter and check off the documents as they are placed in the envelope.
4. *Check the state's registration requirements.* Filing fees at the time of registration vary by state, as do expiration dates. (See Exhibit 52.4.)

(B) FILING DURING THE REGISTRATION YEAR

Along with registration/annual reporting requirements, most states require the following be to filed during the year:

- *New fund-raising contracts.* Both the fund-raising firm and the not-for-profit organization should file new contracts with the states in which solicitation will be taking place, within 10 days of signing. Several states require a contract summary sheet be included with the contract; otherwise, the contract may be returned.
- *Solicitation notices.* These are forms that must be filed with state officials anywhere from 10 to 30 days prior to solicitation activities, usually by the profes-

EXHIBIT 52.4 Not-for-Profit Organization Registration Requirements

State	Fee	Expires/Comments
Alabama	$25.00	3 months after fiscal year end
Alaska	No fee	September 1
Arizona	No fee	January 31
Arkansas	No fee	Registration anniversary date; Final report due May 15
California	$25.00. Many municipalities require registration.	January 15
Colorado	$62.50	Register prior to campaign or annually
Connecticut	$20.00 initial, $25.00 renewal	5 months after fiscal year end
Florida	$10.00–$400.00, depending on receipts	Registration anniversary date
Georgia	$25.00 initial, $10.00 renewal	Registration anniversary date
Illinois	No fee	6 months after fiscal year end
Kansas	$20.00	6 months after fiscal year end
Kentucky	No fee	Fiscal year end
Louisiana	No fee	On anniversary date of campaign's commencement
Maine	$150.00	November 30
Maryland	$0.00–$200.00, depending on receipts	6 months after fiscal year end
Massachusetts	$35.00–$250.00, depending on receipts	4½ months after fiscal year end
Michigan	No fee	6 months after fiscal year end
Minnesota	$25.00	6 months after fiscal year end
Mississippi	$50.00	6 months after fiscal year end
Missouri	$15.00	75 days after close of fiscal year
Nebraska	$10.00	December 31
New Hampshire	$25.00 initial, $50.00 renewal	4½ months after fiscal year end
New Jersey	$30.00–$250.00, depending on receipts	6 months after fiscal year end
New Mexico	No fee	4½ months after fiscal year end
New York	$25.00	4½ months after fiscal year end
North Carolina	$50.00–$200.00, depending on receipts	4½ months after fiscal year end
North Dakota	$25.00 initial, $10.00 annual	September 1
Ohio	$0.00–$200.00, depending on receipts	4½ months after fiscal year end
Oklahoma	$15.00	Registration anniversary date
Oregon	$10.00–$200.00, depending on receipts	4½ months after fiscal year end
Pennsylvania	$15.00–$250.00, depending on receipts	4½ months after fiscal year end
Rhode Island	$75.00	Registration anniversary date
South Carolina	$50.00	July 1
Tennessee	$50 initial/$100.00–$300.00/ renewal, depending on receipts	6 months after fiscal year end
Texas	$150.00–$250.00	January 15; public safety and veterans groups only
Utah	$100.00	Approval anniversary date

EXHIBIT 52.4 *(Continued)*

Virginia	$30.00–$325.00 + $100 initial reg. surcharge	4½ months after fiscal year end
Washington	$20.00 initial/$10 renewal	4½ months after fiscal year end
West Virginia	$15.00–$50.00, depending on receipts	Registration anniversary date August 1/Financial reports due
Wisconsin	$15.00	6 months after fiscal year end

Source: Excerpted from Fund-Raising Regulation: A State-By-State Handbook of Registration Forms, Requirements, and Procedures *by Seth Perlman and Betsy Hill Bush. Copyright John Wiley & Sons, Inc., 1996. Used with permission.*

sional fund raiser. (See Exhibits 52.5 and 52.6 for lists of states.) Solicitation notices may have to be cosigned by the not-for-profit, so the fund raiser is advised to allow plenty of time to get these documents in order. Several states take seriously the waiting period between filing the Notice and commencement of solicitation activities.

- *Campaign financial reports.* Professional solicitors must file reports in a number of states within 90 days of a campaign's completion, or on the anniversary of a campaign lasting more than one year.
- *Changes to the registration statement.* Most states require that any changes in information filed with the original registration be submitted within 10 to 30 days.
- *Cancellation of contracts.* If the organization or fund-raising firm cancels a contract, the states in which it has registered should be notified as soon as possible. There is no form; a brief letter on the organization's letterhead will be sufficient.

52.5 *Uniform Registration Statement for Charitable Organizations*

The Uniform Registration Statement was developed as an attempt to ease the registration burden on charities. Because so many states ask for identical information, a "uni-form" was seen as the solution to this costly redundancy. The concept of the form was proposed by this author and his colleague Betsy Hills Bush at the 1990 National Association of State Charity Officials (NASCO) conference. Four years later, 21 states had, in principal, signed on to its use. Today, most states subscribe to the form's use. The most up to date information can be found at www.nonprofits.org/library/gov/urs/index.html.

However, allowance had to be made for the variations in state statutes and rules. Not all states appear able or willing to accept the form by itself. Many are requiring additional or supplemental forms of their own, minimizing the effectiveness of the uni-form.

52.6 *Working with the Regulators toward Improvement*

As tempting as it may seem to hope that the complicated issues of state regulation will go away, consider the more productive alternative of getting involved. Many develop-

EXHIBIT 52.5 Solicitation Notice and Related Filings for Fund-Raising Counsel

As a general rule, all new contracts between counsel and not-for-profits should be filed with every state in which solicitation will take place within 10 days of signing. (Both not-for-profits and counsel should be registered in all states in which registration is required.) The following states have special filing requirements.

Connecticut: Contracts must be filed with the state 15 days prior to commencement of services. (There are no registration requirements for fund-raising counsel in this state.)

Hawaii: Only contracts with percentage-based compensation must be filed within 10 days of execution.

Indiana: A Professional Fundraiser Consultant Checklist form is filed two weeks prior to solicitation.

Kentucky: A cover-sheet for Fund-Raising Consultant Contracts form is filed 14 days prior to solicitation

Michigan: A Contract Summary Sheet form is filed by the fund raiser 10 days prior to commencement of activities.

New Jersey: A contract, contract checklist, and $30 filing fee must be filed no later than 10 days prior to the commencement of any services in the state.

New York: A contract must have an addendum stating that the contract may be cancelled by the not-for-profit within 15 days without penalty. Addendum language may also be included in the body of the contract.

Oklahoma: A contract and $25.00 filing fee must be filed prior to the commencement of any services in the state.

Oregon: A Professional Fund Raiser Solicitation Campaign Notice form is signed by the fund raiser and filed 10 days prior to the campaign (applies to direct mail counsel classified as professional fund raising firms in the statute.)

Pennsylvania: Contracts must be filed ten days prior to the commencement of date of counseling services. Late filing of contracts may result in a fine.

---

ment executives, typically active in their Association of Fundraising Professionals (AFP) chapters, have found it surprisingly easy to make contact with state regulators and legislators and change current or proposed laws.

How to get involved? Many states have advisory councils that include industry representatives. AFP chapters can invite regulators and legislators to chapter functions, such as National Philanthropy Day celebrations; hold government affairs workshops

Many regulators and legislators do not have a clear understanding of how fund raising really works or the ethical standards upheld by thousands of development officers and consultants working with this country's best not-for-profit organizations. Many, if not most, lawmakers think of fund raisers as door-to-door solicitors, vendors selling tickets to circuses, and the like. Uniform legislation, assuming all fund raising involves these practices, snares fund-raising consultants and charities conducting their own fund-raising activities with a broadly cast net intended for paid solicitors. By being available to review draft legislation, a development officer will have a chance to see that new laws reflect standard practices and contain standard industry definitions.

EXHIBIT 52.6 Solicitation Notice and Related Filings for Professional Solicitors

As a general rule, all new contracts between professional solicitors and not-for-profits should be filed with every state in which the two parties intend to solicit within 10 days of signing. (Both the not-for-profit and the solicitor should be registered in these states as well.) The following states have special filing requirements.

Arizona: A Contracted Fund Raiser Solicitation Notice must be filed prior to the campaign.

Arkansas: A Notice of Entry into Contract is cosigned by the solicitor and the not-for-profit; filed 15 days prior to commencement of activities.

Colorado: A Solicitation Notice is signed by the charity and the solicitor; filed by either party prior to the campaign.

Connecticut: A Solicitation Notice is cosigned by the solicitor and the not-for-profit; filed with a copy of solicitation literature 20 days prior to solicitation.

Florida: A Solicitation Notice is signed by the solicitor; filed no less than 15 days prior to the campaign.

Georgia: A Solicitation Notice is signed by the solicitor; filed prior to the campaign; a $15 fee is required.

Indiana: A Professional Solicitor Notice Filing is signed by the solicitor; filed two weeks prior to solicitation.

Kentucky: A Professional Fundraiser Promotion Registration is filed two weeks prior to solicitation.

Maryland: A Fund Raising Notice is filed by the solicitor 10 days prior to solicitation.

Massachusetts: An Addendum to Registration Statement is filed by the solicitor for every new contract; cosigned by the not-for-profit.

Michigan: A Contract Summary Sheet is filed by the solicitor or the not-for-profit 10 days prior to commencement of activities.

Minnesota: A Solicitation Notice is signed by the solicitor and the not-for-profit; filed prior to solicitation.

Mississippi: A Solicitation Notice is signed by the solicitor and the not-for-profit; filed 10 days prior to the campaign.

New Hampshire: A Solicitation Notice is signed by the solicitor and the not-for-profit; filed 10 days prior to the campaign; a $75 fee is required.

New Jersey: A contract, contract checklist, and $30 fee are to be filed no later than 10 days prior to the performance of service within the state.

New York: A contract is to be filed within 10 days of signing. Scripts of any oral solicitation to be made must also be filed.

Ohio: A Solicitation Notice is signed by the solicitor and the not-for-profit; filed 10 days prior to the campaign.

Oregon: A Solicitation Campaign Notice is signed by the solicitor and the not-for-profit; filed prior to the campaign.

Pennsylvania: The contract and a Solicitation Notice, signed by the solicitor, are filed 10 days prior to campaign. The state may levy fines on late filing of these documents.

South Dakota: A Consent to Make Solicitation form, signed by the not-for-profit, and a Solicitation Notice, signed by the solicitor and the not-for-profit, are filed 30 days prior to the campaign.

EXHIBIT 52.6 (*Continued*)

Tennessee: An authorization to solicit, a Solicitation Notice signed by the professional solicitor and the not-for-profit, and any scripts and literature to be used or distributed are filed prior to the campaign.

Vermont: A Solicitation Notice is signed by the solicitor; filed 10 days prior to solicitation.

Virginia: A Consent to Solicit, signed by the not-for-profit, and a Solicitation Notice, signed by the solicitor and the not-for-profit, are filed 10 days prior to the campaign.

Washington: A Fundraiser Service Contract Registration Form, signed by the solicitor and the not-for-profit, is filed within five days of the execution of the form; a $10 fee is required.

---

featuring regulators as speakers; and establish government affairs committees that simply offer to review draft legislation.

The increasing burden of state regulation has been called one of the greatest crises facing fund raising today. Yet it can be ameliorated through involvement and coordinated action by not-for-profit professionals and volunteers. In addition, a group of not-for-profits have recently formed an organization called American Charities for Reasonable Fundraising Regulation with the express purpose of bringing challenges to state and local laws and regulations which are excessively burdensome or unreasonable.

52.7 *Other Regulatory Threats to Charitable Organizations: Payments in Lieu of Taxes (PILOT)*

As more and more local governments face budgetary difficulties, the tax payments forgone through not-for-profit institutions' property tax exemptions are seen as an increasingly attractive source of revenue. A number of municipalities are beginning to devise strategies to recoup some of the money they feel is owed to them. These attempts to tax not-for-profits are becoming a serious threat to these institutions' viability.

Many municipalities are facing fiscal crises. The cost of basic services, such as police and fire protection, is going up, yet there is tremendous resistance to property tax increases. Many cities with a large number of tax-exempt not-for-profit institutions are losing residents and businesses to suburbs made more attractive by lower taxes. Many government leaders think not-for-profits, particularly hospitals and universities, but also nursing homes and summer camps, among others, should pay for basic government services or pay a percentage of the tax a for-profit business would pay on a property.

The PILOT (payments in lieu of taxes) issue highlights the lack of understanding of the role of not-for-profit institutions in American life and why they deserve exemption from taxation.

All 50 states guarantee property tax exemption to organizations engaged in religious, charitable, and educational work. However, the definition of what is religious, charitable, and educational varies from state to state.

In Pennsylvania, where this debate has reached critical proportions, a state court actually ruled that the private Washington and Jefferson College did not qualify as tax exempt because students had to pay for their education. The court also ruled that the college did not meet the state's definition of a public charity because the institution does not relieve state government of a burden. The case was overturned by the Pennsylvania Supreme Court.

Many not-for-profit executives are working to head off PILOT efforts through documenting the services provided by their organizations to the community, especially free or highly subsidized services.

The Internet and the Regulation of the Not-for-Profit Sector

MICHAEL JOHNSTON, PRESIDENT
Hewitt and Johnston Consultants

Difficult to see. Always in motion is the future.

—Yoda, 800 year-old Jedi Master

53.1 A Tale of Two Cities: The Biosphere and the Bitsphere

While it is impossible to predict the exact direction of the Internet and its impact on the regulation of the not-for-profit sector (especially in the case of interstate solicitation), this chapter outlines how government, not-for-profit organizations, and citizens can try to anticipate, and control, the governance issues that surround this new technology.

When one studies the prospective impact of the Internet on regulation of not-for-profit organizations, one is reviewing the interface between two distinct yet deeply connected realms: the *biosphere* and what will be called here the *bitsphere*[1]—or the Internet. It

---

[1] A definition created by William J. Mitchell, *City of Bits: Space, Time, and the Infobahn* (Cambridge, MA.: MIT Press, 1995).

is called the bitsphere by a number of thinkers because this digital network or engi-neered, electronic world has a growing, organic complexity that some think eventually will rival the biosphere.

The *biosphere* is something most of us understand: Here it refers to all living creatures and the biological, physical, and mental systems that support them. The *bitsphere* is the sphere of "storage, display, and transmittal of information or data." This bitsphere is best represented by the network of computers that compose the Internet.

This chapter investigates the way in which these two spheres interact.

It is difficult to understand the impact of the Internet on the regulation of the not-for-profit sector due to:

- Insufficient historical analysis on the social impact of that technology
- Unwillingness of many citizens, governments, and private interests to accept the technology's unique impact on law
- Its regulation
- The technology's spillover effects
- Impact of the technology on nonusers
- Unfortunate acceptance by many citizens, governments, and private interests of technology as an autonomous, self-contained phenomena that is morally neutral

My colleagues and I are currently carrying out a study of current regulations concerning not-for-profit on-line. A comparative U.S./Canadian study, it will survey U.S. state regulation of the not-for-profit sector (see Appendix A) in 50 U.S. State Attorney General Offices and should provide theoretical underpinning and data for government, citizens, and the not-for-profit sector to use to make wise and effective decisions.

This chapter deals with the regulation of not-for-profit activity as it relates to on-line fund raising. The ideas presented here are also relevant to regulation issues regarding on-line access to any forms that not-for-profit organizations are bound by law (state or federal) to submit to maintain their not-for-profit access.

53.2 *Historical Background to Regulation*

To help us understand the struggle between the bitsphere (within which the Internet exists) and the biosphere (within which not-for-profit organizations and government exist), I borrow an analogy from Materials engineer, Professor Emeritus at the University of Toronto, and technology theorist Ursula Franklin that helps me illustrate wide scope and historical dimensions of the Internet regulation of not-for-profits by government.

The analogy offers the world as a delicious cake. Franklin describes it thus:

> *its wedge shaped slices are states or countries. As residents of a slice, we are closer to adjacent slices than to more distant ones. Within the slice we can picture social mobility as a vertical structuring, rearrangements of place between, say, the crumb of the bottom and the icing on top, with the raisins in between. Community, then, is locality, as is its representation. Democracy has local roots, its first practice is local. . . . Throughout history, language, law, and custom have been identified vertically in terms of locale: local has been slice dependent.*[2]

---

[2]Ursula Franklin, *The Real World of Technology* (Toronto, Canada: House of Anansi Press Limited, 1999), p. 158.

Of course, none of these slices has been completely isolated—there has always been trade and communication across any of the cuts. Likely communication and exchange have always been more common between adjacent slices, but common culture or language also has facilitated exchange between more distant slices.

Even before the advent of the Internet, people have traveled great distances to foreign lands and returned home with goods, knowledge, and impressions. This traffic of individuals can be understood as a horizontal slicing of the world cake.

In the past, historical barriers to this horizontal travel existed: through geography and by local, or vertical, laws. Passports, tariffs, and border surveillance protects vertical activities from the encroachment of horizontal endeavor. A wide range of technological innovations have pushed against the constraints of time and space and have facilitated horizontal movement. For example, navigational instruments, transportation vehicles, and telecommunication improvements have made an incredible impact on increasing cross-border, cross-boundary exchange.

In the last 10 years, there has been a new spurt of activities and participants that have put increasing pressure on governments to loosen vertical regulations. Free trade agreements have been undertaken, followed by an increase in the power and scope of multinational activity. The horizontal activities of these actors have also infused into the activities of the not-for-profit sector.[3]

But we did not get to this point quickly and easily. Government intervention has been necessary to monitor the growing amount of horizontal exchange. Governments have stepped in to facilitate and regulate horizontal activity. They began with customs unions, easing up on visa requirements, and making it easier for individuals to travel and take currency with them. All of this government facilitation of horizontal activity took place fairly slowly until the introduction of electronic communication.

The laws intended to regulate the effect of horizontal activities on the vertical patterns were made by state (provincial) or federal governments—that is, by the very states whose capacity to regulate and structure the vertical patterns would be impeded by the creation of autonomous horizontal patterns. Such processes usually result in a divestment of powers of the vertical in favor of the horizontal. This happens when governments surrender regulatory powers in certain areas to multinational corporations or when international trade agreements take precedence over national law.

The Internet may weaken state, provincial, or federal vertical authority to regulate not-for-profit fund-raising activities.[4] Conversely, it may strengthen government's ability to regulate not-for-profit organizations and their activity.

I believe that governments can create an effective regulatory environment for not-for-profit organizations only if there is a process that includes: a probation period, a consultation period, a period of study, and then implementation period.

Over the last 20 years, fund raising, like other fields, has seen major advances, including the increasing power and utility of computers, databases, and automated tele-

---

[3]A developing world-focused not-for-profit has hired security guards in East Asia to act as virtual nightwatchmen, using the Internet to watch a warehouse in New York.

[4]Internet service providers (ISPs) in North America are facilitating offshore gambling by accepting gambling licenses from offshore jurisdictions like Antigua and then running the back-end of on-line gambling that, for one ISP, has generated over $1 billion (*Toronto Star*, August 22, 1999). Will not-for-profits register offshore to conduct fund-raising activities in the future? How will governments regulate this?

phone banks. Now, with the rise of the Internet, many of these fund-raising advances have coalesced into the bitsphere, which is simply the interplay between new technologies (the Internet's HTML, Java, and other programming and communication protocols) and the application of older ones (databases, personalization, computers, etc).

53.3   Intent of Vertical Regulation

Not-for-profit organizations are structured and regulated with local requirements and shared values in mind. State regulations take this into account. They are there to protect local interests.

For many state and provincial governments, the fact that younger citizens in their constituency find on-line giving easy, quick, and a time-saver in their busy lives[5] is not the point. Their perspective is one of governance and responsibility to *all* local constituents.

The perspective of state governments regarding the regulation of the Internet fits into a pattern of disregard that is consistent with a social approach to much technology—one that is haphazard and does not treat technology as a force that needs to be regulated like other areas of social activity.

53.4   Technology as Law

Technology, as represented by the Internet, is not only impacting on the regulation of activities on a vertical level (state) and horizontal level (interstate and internation state) but may itself create something akin to law.

Technologies can often embody and express political or social choices that are binding on groups, whether such choices were made in political or legal settings. Richard E. Sclove, in *Democracy and Technology*, argues that "technological processes [in this case the Internet] have become the equivalent of a form of law—that is, an authoritative or binding expression of social norms and values from which the individual or a group may have no immediate recourse."[6]

In the case of the operation of many technologies, such as X-ray machines or automobiles, legal regulations provide citizens and governments with the ability to take recourse through socially enforced penalties. In the case of the Internet and not-for-profits (especially regarding interstate on-line solicitation), currently very few, or perhaps no, socially enforced penalties exist. If technology often creates its own form of law (a binding form of expression), then not-for-profit organizations, governments, and citizens need to review and study the social norms and values that are being created through on-line activities of the not-for-profits.

53.5   When We Need to Step In

If a particular technology plays only a small part in the lives of average citizens, or if the citizens are not conscious of the extent of its influence, then the issue of maintaining the

---

[5]Greenpeace Canada online donor survey conducted in the Spring of 1998.
[6]Richard E. Sclove, *Democracy and Technology* (New York: Guilford Press, 1995).

social, political, and economic conditions to keep the technology operating is not prominent in the public discourse. But as people and/or society grows dependent on a technology, or as they become more aware of their dependence, the necessary conditions of the operation of that technology loom as practical imperatives.[7]

Most not-for-profits and citizens do not use the Internet for fund raising or submitting to government regulatory requirements. The amount of money raised on-line as a proportion of total dollars raised in the United States is tiny.[8] However, if, as expected, more and more citizens begin to support organizations through the Internet and more and more citizens make the Internet their primary information tool to review public disclosure documents for a particular not-for-profit organization, then creating the necessary conditions (including regulation) for this technology's operation will become more important.

53.6   Spillover Effect

A particular technology can also exert significant effects on people who neither operate or interact with it directly. One clear example is found in what economists call "spillover effects" or "externalities." Take the example of a typical North American community that has state-sanctioned gambling establishments. People in that community may not ever gamble, but nevertheless part of their taxes may go toward state-funded gambling-addiction programs for local citizens hooked on the gambling establishments. Governments at many levels understand that some technologies can have a spillover effect.

On-line gambling may prove to be problematic for government regulation and not-for-profit fund raising. One future scenario could see not-for-profit organizations running highly profitable and highly addictive on-line gambling parlors that could create negative spillover effects for a state jurisdiction. How will states regulate this possibility?

The spillover effect can also be dynamic and transformative. For example, a person may not want to buy a lawnmower, but since all the neighbors have one and there is a lot of noise anyway, he may go and buy one. Similarly, with the Internet, next-door neighbors in a community may decide not to go to the yearly community-support street party to help a local charity because they feel they have done their part by making on-line donations to a particular charity. If enough people feel detached from local charities, then the end of local street party would be a negative spillover effect of a collective technology called the Internet.

---

[7]A recent, small fire in one building in downtown Toronto knocked out telephone, Internet, ATM, and cellular services for 400,000 customers. As citizens we are often subconsciously aware of how dependent we are on the technology around us, but when we lose temporary access to some of these technologies, we are upset. The author was standing in an ATM line-up during the Toronto communication blackout, and many citizens were visibly shaken by the event.

[8]Greenpeace International is a good example of the tiny proportion of total donations that on-line giving constitutes. Worldwide the organization raises close to a $100,000 in on-line donations; it raises over $100 million worldwide in all other areas of fund raising. However, strategic plans and current results show that the proportion of on-line donation will increase greatly over the next 10 years.

Currently, governments, citizens, and not-for-profit organizations do not have suffi-cient evidence to know if there are negative spillover (or direct) effects with on-line phil-anthropy and on-line not-for-profit activity. I believe that governments, not-for-profit organizations, and citizens need to study the impact of on-line not-for-profit activity to understand its influence and prospective negative or positive impact on vertical politi-cal and social structures.

53.7   Taking the Influence of Technology Even Further

To take the structural/social impact even further, it can be argued that the background needed to support a particular technology can have great impact on someone who does not use that technology.

For example, a citizen may not own a computer, let alone use the Internet, to visit a not-for-profit Web site. She is not connected to the Internet, but the texture of her world is influenced and impacted by the Net: by intense private and public investment in infor-mation infrastructure, electrical generating stations to run the computers, technology sector investments from private and public sources, cable and telephone companies lay-ing down communication conduits, and private and public investment in Internet tech-nology at the expense of other educational priorities (i.e., teacher-student ratios, physical plant, etc.).

This is what is meant by technology being a part of social structures. It means that our investment in Internet technology affects every member of our society, whether he or she uses it or not. While this may mean less or more government regulation of not-for-profit organizations and the Internet, it needs to be part of any discussion on regulation of the Internet.

53.8   The Bitsphere May Be Too Complex to Not Regulate

Interacting with not-for-profits on-line might help citizens define who they are and help them understand the world around them and how they fit into it. This idea runs counter to the Carnegie Mellon Study that found on-line use of just a few hours a week led to "increased levels of depression and loneliness."[9] Any way one slices it, the Internet seems to be an incredibly potent medium.

The Internet is fast becoming an incredibly influential, complex, and vital technol-ogy. Less influential technologies are regulated; perhaps this technology, as it impacts the not-for-profit sector, should be regulated as well.

53.9   Why There Are Few Laws Concerning the Internet
     and Not-for-Profits

Most people agree that laws are contingent social products. Societies tend to see laws as something that are a choice; laws could be different, there could be alternatives. With

---

[9]Sclove, Richard E., *Democracy & Technology* (New York: Guilford Publications, 1995).

technologies, society is prone to see an inevitability—that the direction of a particular technology is naturally predetermined rather than socially shaped and chosen. Perhaps it is this perspective that explains the lack of regulation from state governments and the lack of concern on the part of citizens.

Laws are commonly understood to function as social structures. Some laws can have unintended consequences—as Prohibition-era laws did—but for the most part, citizens expect legal statutes to shape social interaction and history with a particular purpose and intent. In contrast, many citizens believe that technology is structurally inconsequential and therefore tend not to put pressure on political and legal institutions to deal with technology.[10]

These collective misperceptions of technology often lead to a situation where the social impacts and dynamics of a particular technology are badly misunderstood or misinterpreted—a situation that is exacerbated by the double whammy of a lack of clear social impact studies on much technology and its introduction. As long as the Internet's impact on social structures (e.g., not-for-profit organizations and supporters) are little understood or ignored, then legal institutions will not be receptive to a legal strategy to sustain and support a healthy on-line regulatory environment—one that matches citizens' ideals, needs, and aspirations in their interactions with not-for-profits on-line.

53.10   Is Regulation of Technology Undemocratic?

There are those who argue that technological development and regulation are guided by market forces, economic self-interest, distant bureaucracies, or international rivalry and should be subordinated to democratic prerogatives.[11]

The process of developing technology regulation can thus encompass everything from the haphazard to the bitterly contested or the blatantly coercive. None of these is strongly democratic or particularly helpful to the not-for-profit sector.

This does not mean that Internet technology needs to be subjected to formal political review. That kind of legal scrutiny is inappropriate with on-line giving for the on-line donor. Similarly, it may be inappropriate for not-for-profit organizations to undergo onerous regulation with their on-line activities (especially around on-line fund raising).

A technology requires political scrutiny and rigorous approach that matches the degree to which it promises to fundamentally or enduringly affect social life. There needs to be a set of formal procedures for reviewing existing technology arrangements around the Internet and not-for-profits, including a monitoring and analysis of emerging trends by governments and not-for-profit organizations.

The Internet is often touted as a communications technology that can reinvorgate politics and democracy. That is why it is intriguing to note that there exists so little opportunity for citizens and citizen bodies to give their input into the direction of future regulation of the nonprofit sector. Such an opportunity for citizens to participate in this debate on the future regulation of not-for-profits and the Internet, through government and/or a nonprofit consultative process, is vital.

---

[10]As argued by Sclove, *ibid.*, chap. 2.
[11]As argued in *ibid.*

53.11 Internet Fund Raising and State Laws

With an Internet account, a computer, and a telephone line, a charitable organization can make inexpensive (virtually free) multistate, even multinational solicitations.

If a not-for-profit organization has its information residing on a computer (server) in one state, and an on-line visitor visits its Web page to make a donation, is this interstate commerce? It could be, according to a 1996 Federal Court of Appeals decision.

A postal inspector, working for the local U.S. Attorney's office in Tennessee, subscribed to a California-based bulletin board service (BBS) and then downloaded allegedly obscene materials. A Memphis jury found the images obscene. The couple operating the bulletin board in California were charged in Tennessee. On appeal, the Federal Appellate Court affirmed the conviction. A section of the ruling has relevance to charitable, interstate solicitations on the Internet. The court found that "the bulletin board service was set up so members located in other jurisdictions could access and order [obscene] files which would then be instantaneously transmitted in interstate commerce."[12]

If state courts agree with this federal decision regarding an Internet, interstate solicitation case—that communication via computer constitutes sufficient contact with the foreign U.S. state to subject the communicator to local law—then charitable organizations that solicit on-line also fall under the foreign charitable registration category.

Before the advent of the Internet, states constructed charitable fund-raising regulations regimes (statutes) that were designed to protect state citizens from solicitation fraud that were seen as stemming from multistate fund-raising drives backed by larger, more powerful organizations. Though these regulation regimes have been upheld in a number of states to apply to smaller organizations involved in multistate solicitations, many observers say applying these regulatory regimes to smaller organizations runs counter to the intent of these statutes. By applying these statutes to smaller organizations, most of which do not intend their Web sites to solicit out of state, many statutes will inadvertently force these smaller organizations to pay for the sometimes expensive process of obtaining state approval.

In other words, a smaller organization that simply wanted to communicate to its local constituency through a cheap, new medium is suddenly restricted from doing so because it cannot afford to fit into a regulatory regime that was originally designed to deal with large, out-of-state solicitors. These statutes and regimes, with their application to Internet solicitation, may be found to restrict the First Amendment rights of these smaller not-for-profit organizations that had no intention of multi-state solicitation.[13]

While it may be true that the intent of these laws was to restrict and control the larger, multistate organizations and protect state citizens from solicitation fraud, the Internet, with its low cost of publication and broad reach, may indeed allow small and large organizations to commit fraud more widely. The size of the soliciting organization has nothing to do with its inclination to commit fraud. In the past, state regulation regimes aimed at the largest organizations was the best way for the state to protect the greatest number of citizens from the greatest damage (in this case, solicitation fraud), with the understanding that the largest interstate solicitors had the greatest potential to rip off the most state citizens.

Furthermore, the First Amendment is not something the not-for-profit sector should

---

[12]Bruce Hopkins, *The Law of Fund-Raising*, 2nd ed. (New York: John Wiley & Sons, 1996).
[13]See Chapter 51, Bruce Hopkins, "Federal Regulation of Fund Raising."

rely on in defending itself from prospective state regulation. Instead, they should be proactive and take the initiative recommended by a number of not-for-profit thinkers, managers, and observers: call for a new registration service for all soliciting organizations, small and large, that would exist on-line. Why?

Currently, meeting the regulatory requirements for each state can be a difficult and prohibitively expensive proposition for smaller charitable organizations. Registration on-line, in a central registry, that government and the public could easily access, would be a low-cost and appropriate way for Internet solicitations to be controlled. Of course, there is the outstanding issue of who is going to run this central registry. Will it be the federal government, a voluntary organization, or a private company?

Whatever the choice, not-for-profit organizations should begin work now on that central registry, since nothing could be worse than letting things stand as there are. The current state of affairs is one of benign neglect by state officials. With very little money being raised on-line, there are very few public complaints about on-line fund raising; therefore, officials are content to let Internet fund raising alone for now.

However, as the efficacy and profitability of on-line fund raising grows, more organizations will be raising money—and that means there will be some that are unethical, commit solicitation fraud, and raise the ire of taxpayers/voters in various states. Inevitably there will be on-line solicitation fraud, somewhere, sometime. If not-for-profit organizations do not deal with the regulatory reactions to this kind of electronic fraud now, they will find themselves dealing with regulation regimes imposed from above that will be onerous on smaller organizations soliciting on the Internet.

The current vacuum in on-line regulation of not-for-profit organizations demands that all interested parties—government, not-for-profits, and citizens—push forward a more formal process of study, sharing, and planning for future regulation of the sector on-line.

53.12   Survey Results

The preliminary results of the survey of 50 state Attorney General Offices (or their affiliate offices responsible for regulation of not-for-profit activity (i.e., fund raising) indicate that most state governments are unaware, unconcerned, or proceeding cautiously with this new medium. A consistent answer on most questions included words like "unsure" and phrases like "who knows?" "haven't begun to look at those issues," "don't know," and "we'll do more when other states and the federal government does something."

Most government regulatory bodies seem to be taking a wait-and-see approach to the regulation of the Internet.

Such an approach will be confusing for many not-for-profit organizations. The Attorney General survey reveals that while 50 percent of Attorney General offices say a charity from another state would have to register its on-line fund raising in their state, 50 percent say the opposite. Obviously greater cooperation and coordination between states is necessary.

53.13   Understanding On-line Giving

There has been little study of the social impact of on-line giving. Ursula Franklin, in a recent lecture, mentioned the possibility that *"The Internet will make it easier to give to an earthquake victim halfway around the world, but it makes it easier to forget about the homeless person on our own street. Will the Internet dislocate time and space when it comes to our caring for others in our own community?"*[14]

I believe it would be a wise decision by state, provincial, and federal governments to fund studies of on-line givers to determine the positive or negative social impact of this new philanthropic endeavor. Studies in this area would help citizens, not-for-profits, and governments begin to understand the current and prospective social impacts of giving, caring, and sharing on-line.

53.14   Toward a Model of Regulation

The survey results indicate that state regulatory bodies have differing interpretations on how to regulate not-for-profit organizations on-line. Such a variety of interpretations is not helpful. For example, donors and not-for-profit organizations may not conduct on-line fund raising if they are unsure of the regulatory environment. Society may miss the opportunity to mature a new source of fund raising that may become terribly important in the future.

I recommend a probation period, with the agreement of state and federal governments, to not ask for solicitation registration related to Internet fund raising. During the probation period, government, not-for-profit, and citizen actors should collaborate to fund studies that investigate the negative and positive social impacts of on-line fund raising and other on-line activities by not-for-profit organizations.[15]

With studies in hand, government, not-for-profits, and citizens should conduct public input sessions to ensure that all participants affected by on-line activities get a chance to give their ideas and opinions on future regulation of nonprofits through the Internet. This stage may be called the consultation period.

Once the studies have been finished and after public consultation, a regulatory regime for the on-line regulation of not-for-profit could be implemented with the cooperation of all levels of government. This is the implementation period.

53.15   Conclusion

As Yoda stated, *"Difficult to see. Always in motion is the future."* The Internet is a technology that is difficult to predict because we have very little information on its social impact as it is used by citizens to make donations on-line and by not-for-profit organizations to do their work.

We as a society must choose how we want technologies to work for us and must create the rules that will make this happen.

The Internet is a radically different technology that demands careful analysis before society applies regulations because this bitsphere cuts across the biosphere horizontally,

---

[14]Ursula Franklin, lecture, "The Real World of Technology Revisited," Ursula Franklin High School, May 10, 1999.

[15]Mike Johnston, George Irish, and Alison Li have received funding from Queen's University in Kingston, Ontario, in conjunction with York University in Toronto, Ontario, to further flesh out the survey attached to this study. That study will be more effective with input from the participants of this conference. Please visit a copy of the study proposal at www.hjc.on.ca/netstudy. We would appreciate any comments and suggestions to help this study.

allowing interactions that our current laws were not set up to deal with particularly well. It will be an interesting challenge to find laws that can effectively deal with this cake-slicing technology as it relates to the not-for-profit sector.

Appendix A: Attorney General Office Questionnaire and Preliminary Results

1. In a chapter from the book *The Nonprofit Handbook*, 2nd edition, entitled "State Regulation of Fund Raising," Seth Perlman states that "recent legislation is attempting to keep pace with the ever changing field of fund raising. New technology, such as telephone solicitation and the Internet, have state officials concerned that their current laws are insufficient to regulate these activities."

   a. Do you believe your state's law adequately covers Internet fund raising?
   b. Do you have any legislation passed or pending that deals with fund raising and the Internet in your state?

   Interim Results
   a. 30%—yes, 30%—no, 40%—neither
   b. 100%—no

2. Do you see the Internet as an opportunity for state governments to reduce the paperwork/administrative requirements on nonprofits who must register with your office?

   Interim Results
   100%—yes, but only if states and the federal government cooperate in getting more information on-line, like all 990 information.

3. There are a number of states that require charitable solicitation disclosures. If your state is one of them, do you think that states will add (or perhaps they've already added) a new disclosure requirement that includes the Internet? Here is an example of how Florida's solicitation disclosure could look like if it included an Internet reference:

   A COPY OF THE OFFICIAL REGISTRATION AND FINANCIAL INFORMA-TION MAY BE OBTAINED FROM THE DIVISION OF CONSUMER SER-VICES BY CALLING TOLL FREE, WITHIN THE STATE, 1-800-HELP-FLA *OR VISIT WWW.HELPFLA.ORG.* REGISTRATION DOES NOT IMPLY ENDORSEMENT, APPROVAL, OR RECOMMENDATION BY THE STATE.

   Interim Results
   Of those with disclosure agreements, 100% were "unsure" if they would put in additional Internet-related information to their disclosure forms.

4. Do you think the Internet will lead to greater problems with commercial co-ventures? Will it be easier for commercial organizations to get away with improper cause-related marketing online? The Attorney General's Office of Connecticut makes reference to a case in which a child sponsorship Web site, with

commercial intent, had collected material from a child sponsorship not-for-profit and displayed that information on the Web site without the permission of the not-for-profit.

Will this happen more often? Is your Attorney General's Office aware of possible online abuses of cause related marketing?

Interim Results

80%—yes, there will be more cause-related marketing through the Internet.
80%—they are not prepared to judge the problems that will arise from this.

5. In your opinion, would your Attorney General's Office act against (fine or ask for registration of) an out-of-state not-for-profit, not currently registered within your state, if one of your citizens made an on-line gift to a charity's Web site that operates in another state? In addition, does there need to be an actual gift made or is the act of requesting funds on-line enough to warrant action by your office to ask for registration of the out-of-state charity?

For example, the Humane Society of Miami has a Web site that a New York State citizen visits on-line and makes an on-line credit card gift. Is that charity in Miami conducting fund raising in New York State, and would it have to submit fund-raising–related registration forms to the New York State Attorney General's Office? Are there cases like this before your office? How are you preparing to deal with them?

Interim Results

50%—yes, they'll have to register in our state
50%—no, they'll not have to register if they are not explicitly asking for a donation in that vertical jurisdiction

6. Are you putting (or planning to put) the Unified Registration Statement for fund raising in your state on-line? Can the "uni-form" be currently downloaded and/or submitted on-line in your state? Do you think the Internet will help move more states, including yours, to standardize more of their charity forms and put them online?

Interim Results

80%—haven't discussed these issues yet, haven't got own forms on-line
20%—beginning to put forms on-line

7. Do you think a central online registry (whether it is run by government, the not-for-profit sector, or a private enterprise) of charity forms could replace or reduce individual state filing requirements? If you answered yes, would it matter if the central registry was run by government, the nonprofit sector, or private enterprise? Finally, if a central on-line registry existed, would it empower or educate more citizens about the nonprofit sector and charitable giving?

Interim Results

80%—unsure of efficacy, effectiveness, or practicality of central registry; would not matter who was responsible for it and whether information submission was mandatory or voluntary

54 The Self-Renewing Organization

TRACY D. CONNORS, PRESIDENT
The BelleAire Institute, Inc.

Man's job is to govern the future, not simply be a victim of the wind blowing this way and that way. I know, the best plans are upset. But, without a plan there is no chance. Best efforts will not do it!

—*W. Edwards Deming*

The steady growth and expansion of the voluntary sector reflects the fact that contributions by not-for-profits are growing in response to the needs of our people. Demands are sharply on the increase for the myriad public services provided by not-for-profits. Competition is keen among not-for-profits for the human and financial resources needed to provide their essential public services. For many not-for-profits today, the search for always-scarce resources is not simply important, it is a matter of survival. For all not-for-profits, more effective, economical use of existing resources is essential. Constant attention must be paid to the tools and process improvement techniques needed to ensure organizational efficiency and resource conservation.

It has been 20 years since the first not-for-profit management handbook, *The Nonprofit Organization Handbook,* was published in late 1979. The "breakthrough" nature of that work lay in its recognition that regardless of the specific public purpose served by a not-for-profit organization, all had much in common when it came to management. Specifically, there were seven areas of management and leadership that, taken together, established that there was an emerging body of professional knowledge and new career fields in something called not-for-profit management. These seven management and leadership areas in which not-for-profits have such strong commonality include:

1. Organization and corporate principles
2. Leadership, management, and control
3. Volunteer administration
4. Sources of revenue
5. Communication and public relations

6. Financial management and administration
7. Legal and regulatory areas

Management of not-for-profit organizations has steadily become more professional. Information is shared through a growing number of associations; through print and electronic media that collectively enable sector leaders to adapt management principles, policies, and procedures to fulfill the various missions of their organizations. Approaches that work are steadily sorted out from those that generally do not. However, this process is often sporadic or subject to chance. The need for a convenient, comprehensive guide to the daily operation and management of not-for-profit organizations gave rise to the *Nonprofit Management Handbook*. Its primary objective was to compile the best of these proven approaches in an accessible, readily adaptable format.

The first edition of the volume was completed at the beginning of the 1990s and introduced a new management system called *quality management* as a tool to help improve management of not-for-profit organizations. Many of the contributors to the *Nonprofit Handbook: Fund Raising* were represented in the first edition of the management handbook, before fund raising became a separate handbook.

The first edition of the management handbook served as a comprehensive reference guide to the policies (guidelines, directives, rules, and courses of action) and procedures (established methods and proven best practices) now shared by a great majority of small and medium-size not-for-profit organizations. The second edition built on that solid foundation, even as it advanced additional key areas of management for not-for-profit organizations.

Operational policies and procedures are not static. They cannot be adopted and arbitrarily applied to a particular organization. If they are to be effective, they must be carefully *adapted* to the needs and realities of a specific organization. Also, internal and external environments change, just as the organization itself changes. Operational policies and procedures, once adapted and employed, must be reviewed regularly to ensure that they continue to fulfill the functions for which they were intended.

The dynamic, evolving nature of all areas of not-for-profit management policy and procedures requires constant review, assessment, renewal, and change. Outdated policies and procedures may become impediments to progress and the organization's ability to fulfill its mission. But how and where can changes be implemented? In what direction should the organization be moved? How do organizations organize for constant change and also bring about constant improvement in services, products, and processes? How do leaders know what they can and should do to fulfill their public services mission in the face of dwindling resources and a more competitive environment?

Timely, rational change is a major benefit gained by those organizations adopting continuous improvement techniques and philosophies. Therefore, a major objective for all of those dedicated to improving excellence in public service is to provide the foundation that not-for-profit organizations need to improve and sustain excellence.

Not-for-profit organizations, like their corporate counterparts, are affected by global systems of economics and production. Organizations from all sectors of the economy are trying to establish sustainable excellence as their "organizational culture." Not-for-profits, like business and government, must adopt the principles and best practices of excellence and continuous improvement, if they are to meet growing public service needs in the face of scarce resources. Because every element of our society is being forced to move in this new direction, excellence is not a trend likely to "fade away" when organizational leaders change or when press coverage wanes, as it inevitably will. Sustainable excellence must become the basic culture within nonprofit organizations, just as it must become the way all U.S. organizations do business, if they expect to be successful over time.

The *Nonprofit Handbook: Management, 2d edition,* built on the solid foundation established by the initial work, even as it advanced key areas of management for nonprofit organizations. The second edition for the first time used the Malcolm Baldrige Award/President's Quality Award Criteria as the basis to define and characterize quality performance and achievement in each of seven functional areas common to all organizations.

By adapting these national quality standards to the voluntary sector, readers gained the ability to benchmark their own organizations against established national criteria and standards. When readers determine where their organizations stand in relation to national standards, they can then prepare plans and strategies to help us overcome the "delta" between the next higher level of quality and the level at which we may now be performing.

The second edition of the handbook introduced *the excellence equation for self-renewing organizations* that identified the three fundamental elements necessary for not-for-profit organizations to achieve and sustain excellence: (1) effectiveness, (2) efficiency, and (3) organizational environment. This third edition expands coverage of management areas that most heavily contributed to organizational excellence. It organizes materials into three sections—(1) effectiveness, (2) efficiency, and (3) environment—each of which includes coverage of management topics reflecting national definitions of excellence. In addition, it emphasizes coverage of the following areas of growing importance for nongovernmental and/or not-for-profit leaders based on reader feedback:

- Identification of emerging management trends and better understanding of ever-changing leadership responsibilities and techniques
- Technology implications and applications for not-for-profits
- Understanding of the management context in which not-for-profits enter a competitive and challenging new millennium
- Successful governance structures, styles, and approaches within the ever-evolving public service organization
- What not-for-profits can and should do to fulfill their public services mission in the face of dwindling resources and a more competitive environment—from commercial ventures to strategic communications
- Second- and third-generation management, organizational excellence-enhancing practices that work
- Self-renewing strategies for achieving both mission effectiveness and efficiency
- Successful management approaches and models used by staff and volunteer managers
- Explanations and examples of proven operational techniques, from distance learning to emergency public affairs
- The importance of maintaining agency integrity to mission and purpose—core values
- Secrets of social entrepreneurism—generating resources while solving social problems
- Sample policies, procedures, reports, and forms designed specifically for not-for-profits

The "dynamic environment" in which most not-for-profits have to operate drives them toward proven approaches to create the self-renewing organization—one not only able to achieve but also to sustain high standards of excellence, including the ability to thrive under competitive pressures, using such management tools as: strategic planning, process improvement, change management, technology application, and resource conservation. Leaders of successful public service organizations find it important to develop a culture and organizational environment supportive of change. Leaders at all levels of the organization need all the help they can get to ensure that hard-won gains in productivity, effectiveness, mission readiness, and profitability are sustained.

54.1   *To Govern the Future*

Without ever having met you, I know we have at least one thing in common. Way back when we were young, someone important to us, someone dear to us, who cared about us and what we would become, gave us one of life's great lessons. "Do your best," they told us. It was, and is, good advice. In my case, it was my parents and grandparents. It was one of many terribly important, even vital, lessons in life and living that we learned as children. Simple, straightforward, not terribly complicated, but important and true—then as children and even more so now that we are adults.

Since we already know you remembered that good advice from your childhood and are doing your best, we can go on to some other important questions:

Do you take joy in your work?
If not, do you understand why not?
If you are already doing your best, but there is not enough joy in your work, what else should you be doing to add this vital feeling, to help you "govern" your future?

Robert Fulghum tells us "all I really need to know about how to live and what to do and how to be I learned in kindergarten."[1] Share everything, he reminds us.

> *Play fair. Don't hit people. Put things back where you found them. Clean up your own mess. Don't take things that aren't yours. Say you're sorry when you hurt somebody. Warm cookies and cold milk are good for you. Live a balanced life—learn some and think some and draw and paint and sing and dance and play and work every day some. When you go out into the world, watch out for traffic, hold hands, and stick together. Be aware of wonder. . . . And then remember the Dick-and-Jane books and the first word you learned—the biggest word of all—LOOK.*

Fulghum points out that everything you need to know is in there somewhere, from the Golden Rule to ecology, politics, equality, and sane living.

We should consider the lessons we learned the earliest as among the most important in our lives. Just because we learned them as kids does not mean they were trivial. Just because they were basic does not mean they were uncomplicated or even easy to put into

---

[1]Robert Fulghum, *All I Really Need to Know I Learned in Kindergarten* (New York: Villard Books, 1988), p. 6.

practice. "Playing fair" can be a real challenge in a highly competitive environment, as can "sharing everything." If I share, will they share back, or use my share against me?

Similarly, we should remember that basic truths about achieving excellence can be straightforward and uncomplicated—and yet be critically important. To understand and apply the fundamentals of organizational improvement does not require extensive training in quantitative analysis or statistical theory. It does, however, require an understanding of how excellence is defined within functional areas of management and knowledge of the basic definitions applied to levels of quality achievement.

"Man's job is to govern the future," Dr. W. Edwards Deming pointed out, "not simply be a victim of the wind blowing this way and that way."

The international authority on quality told hundreds of navy senior leaders 10 years ago at a convocation requested by the Chief of Naval Operation: "I know, the best plans are upset. But, without a plan there is no chance. Best efforts will not do it. Is anyone here not putting forth his best efforts? Let him stand." This was followed by silence, then a great deal of laughter.

"I've been inquiring for years, trying to find him who is not putting forth his best efforts," Deming said, with tongue firmly in cheek. "No one has stood up yet. That is our problem! Everyone is putting forth his best efforts—without knowledge, without understanding what his job is, just doing his best. He will not take joy in his work without understanding what his job is. He cannot do his work without understanding why, and who depends on him. Man is entitled to joy in his work."

With apologies to Mr. Fulghum, doing our best is *not* enough. For us to govern the future, we must do those things that give us knowledge, that bring us to a better understanding of what our jobs really are and how they contribute to the aims of the organization—the customer-focused mission.

Expressed as "great lessons," if we wish to govern our future and that of our organizations, we must:

- Know where we are going, why we are going, and how we plan to get there
- Improve constantly in everything we do
- Make change safe for ourselves and for those for whom we are responsible

54.2 Governing the Future and That of Organizations

Governing the future and putting joy in our work will take more than simply improving our processes, more than focusing on ever-greater efficiencies.

We have to *know where we're going*, to define our strategic vision, mission, and guiding principles.

We have to have a way as individuals and as organizations to *see where we're going*, even as we try to *get better at what we do*.

As Dr. Deming so wisely said, we have to have a plan, a "vision"—a desired future state—of what we desire for ourselves and our organization and a direction in which to travel. We need some "strategy."

The plan tells us what direction in which to move, and strategy gives us answers about what means we can use to get there. Moving from here to there, however, requires change, *doing some things differently*. When we were little kids, change was fun. We liked to take new routes home from school, to color the sun in the right-hand corner of the picture instead of the left. Before too long, however, we learned that change can be uncomfortable. In most organizations, change can be threatening to power, authority, position. Change, we learned, is suspect, perhaps even dangerous. Our path up the organization hierarchy was through "management." And managers allocated and coordinated. Most important, they controlled. Normally, they resist change unless it is their idea and to their personal advantage.

The essence of management is in its most vital function: dealing with the increased complexity in large organizations. Effective management enables increasingly complex, far-flung organizations to avoid chaos by helping impose order and consistency in key functions and operations. Management techniques taught in business schools stress controlling, planning, budgeting—setting goals and objectives for the future (usually a not-too-distant future). Detailed steps are determined to achieve targets, followed by the process of allocating resources—funds, people—to accomplish plans.

Management emphasizes those capabilities and processes needed to achieve *the plan*—organizing and staffing, creating an organizational structure: job descriptions and qualifications; communicating the plan down the "chain of command"; delegating responsibilities for implementing the plan; and then putting those systems in place that are needed to monitor implementation.

Accomplishing the plan is ensured by controlling and problem solving—comparing results against the plan in great detail—via reports, meetings, and inspections. Deviations from the plan are identified, then replanning and organization take place focused on solving the problem.

The essence of leadership, on the other hand, is coping with change. Leadership has become much more important to all organizations, particularly major U.S. corporations. The "world" has become much more volatile and competitive. Technological change on the order of exponential, international competition, rapidly fluctuating economic and political developments, and changing demographics are all having major a impact on organizations because they are all connected in some way to the "global marketplace."

The lesson we should take to heart about these global developments is that *change is not only necessary, it is inevitable—change is the only constant.* In addition, major change is increasingly necessary for any organization, large or small, if it is to survive and compete successfully in an always-evolving environment. More change inevitably requires and demands more effective leaders—the organization's change managers.

Until recently and in "normal" times, most organizations did a relatively good job of managing and administering their product lines, services, and their people—in "peacetime." However, the overall climate and environments in which most organizations must operate today more closely resembles that of "war"—from international competition to galloping technological change in the face of diminishing budgets. A "wartime" organization cannot be successful relying solely on management. A war-footing organization needs competent, effective leadership *at all levels.* Over 200 years of our country's military history have taught us repeatedly that soldiers and sailors cannot be managed in battle, *they must be led.* The same can be said for any of us and about almost any of our organizations. Management is important, but effective leaders are required at all levels in organizations.

The function of leadership is to produce change, not simply to react to forces and pressures at they occur. Intentionally determining and then setting the direction of that change or changes, then, is fundamental to effective leadership—and effective leaders are "change agents."

54.3   *Palingenesis: Birth Over Again*

Birth, growth, maturation, decline, and death—the cycle is ancient and universal. It is the subject of countless fables and myths. Finding out where the organization must go and how it should get there, constantly studying ways to improve its processes, changing outmoded concepts and approaches to ensure regeneration and growth—the life cycle never ends. If it does, death is the inevitable result. Only one thing holds death at bay—birth. Only birth can conquer death, not the old things (archaism) again but of some things new.

As with our bodies, *long-term organizational survival depends on a continuous recurrence of birth to nullify the unremitting partial deaths our organizations suffer from competition, technological advances, and market saturation.* From victories, the seeds of ruin can spring. Victorious countries continue to prepare for the last war. Organizations continue product lines or services long past their prime. Even organizations that have worked hard to become "quality managed" can and have fallen back from hard-gained high ground. When corporate death closes in, there is no salvation except dismemberment (acquisition) and rebirth as a reinvigorated component of another organization.

What is required to stave off inevitable decline or death is birth over again, regeneration, *palingenesis.* Organizational strategic planning is essential but not enough. Continuous improvement of all processes is essential, but leaders who are blind to other life-sustaining essentials can emphasize efficiency to the exclusion of other essential processes. And leaders can bring about change so disruptive or misguided that it destroys even as it breaks free from the outmoded past. Palingenesis requires a fertile organizational environment in which promising concepts and ideas can be conceived and nurtured to maturity. Even as processes and services are honed to ensure they make their strongest contribution to renewed organizational strength, their replacements are taking shape, form, and function behind them.

Old . . . new . . . These are two of the first words we ever learned. Mostly, we learned that *new* is good. *Old* is bad. *New* has potential, a future. *Old* is worthless, junk, irrelevant.

At the time, we did not realize that *new* and *old* are simply at opposite ends of a continuum matrix of two factors: *condition* and *time*.

The phrase "in mint condition" sums up the highest condition of *new*. Newly minted means, shiny, fresh, valuable. At this end "new" means fresh, recent, vigorous, changed for the better, or reinvented. The opposite end of the condition continuum brings to mind associations of stale, no longer needed, outmoded, antique, obsolete, and disposable—near death.

"With it," "in step," "cool," and "relevant" are terms we associate with things that are current, modern, and in sync with the times. This is the highest value of currency with whatever environment in which we may be operating or have as the center of interest. To be "dated" is to be totally out of sync. To be dated is to be considered irrelevant—extraneous and immaterial.

Organizational "newness" can also be understood in terms of *condition* and *surroundings*. For example, an organization's status or "condition" can be seen as its readiness to fulfill the *mission*(s) for which it exists. If an organization lacks purpose or is not meeting its public purpose, it is tottering on the lowest state of mission readiness. However, an organization that is customer focused and driven, and is meeting its public purposes, is fulfilling its mission.

Time and surroundings are closely linked as well. The complex circumstances and environment in which an organization operates are constantly changing—they are time-driven. Those organizations that are in synchronous rhythm with their operating environment(s) are seen to be relevant, modern, coping, fresh, and aware. If they are not, they are tuned out, unaware, and out of touch.

54.4　The Excellence Equation: Key to Sustainability

Organizations that are vigorously proactive in meeting their public purposes, in staying mission driven and customer focused, and that have synchronized their operations within their surroundings are prime candidates for excellence.

Organizations that can achieve and sustain excellence are rare. Some organizations have worked hard to achieve excellence only to see their hard-fought gains erode as they fall back from the pinnacle. They could not sustain their "newness."

For any organization to achieve and sustain excellence—to be self-renewing—it must understand and exploit the dynamic interdependent relationship between Effectiveness, Efficiency, and Environment—the **excellence equation.**

$N(ew) = E(nvironment) \times E(ffectiveness) \times E(fficiency)$

Self-renewing organizations have learned that they must operate at high levels of competence in both the condition (mission/effectiveness) and time (environment/efficiency) dimensions. In addition, they must create and sustain the enabling organizational environment needed to motivate, empower, and support the people on whom the services and customer satisfaction—results—depend.

Self-renewing organizations are effective. They use strategic planning to define and accomplish their customer-focused mission. They know they serve valid purposes. They *know* they are needed—and why. They know their public purpose is valid, and they continually adjust it, tune it to environmental conditions to achieve business results. Effective organizations use:

- *Customer focus and satisfaction* as the foundation for setting priorities and focusing improvement activities. Results and trends in this area offer a means to determine the appropriate direction for improvement activities and initiatives. Effective organizations listen to and learn from their customers on a continuous basis, then use that intelligence to determine their current and near-term requirements and expectations.
- *Strategic planning* to strengthen their customer-related, operational, and financial performance, to improve customer satisfaction. Planning is essential to help organization leaders use customer and operational requirements as inputs to setting strategic directions. Strategic planning guides ongoing decision making, resource allocation, and organization-wide management.
- *Business results* as the focus for all processes and process improvement activities to assess its progress toward superior value of its offerings as viewed by customers and the marketplace, and toward superior organization performance reflected in productivity and effectiveness.

Self-renewing organizations are efficient. They perform well and economically, with reduced waste of time, energy, and materials (at least in comparison with their competition). We applaud their use of process improvement, information and analysis techniques, and approaches to reduce waste, to streamline their operations, and to make economical use of all resources. They constantly reassess their processes, products, and services to ensure they meet customer needs while consuming the least amount of resources (money, time, and personnel). Efficient organizations use:

- *Process management* techniques to design and improve their customer/client service design, translating customer requirements into design requirements and into efficient and effective delivery processes. Efficient organizations also maintain process performance systems to ensure they are performing according to their design and are improved to achieve even better performance.
- *Information and analysis* to support overall organizational mission goals and to serve as the primary basis for key decision making.

Self-renewing organizations create and sustain a transformational organizational environment in both leadership and human resource development and management. They adapt to changing environmental conditions, manage change effectively, constantly transitioning to new states, turning as necessary in new directions. They are constantly evolving. Popularly we hear the term "they reinvented themselves." Organizations having a transformational environment use:

- *Visionary leadership* that establishes strategic directions implemented by a leadership system that fosters high performance, individual development, and organizational learning—a leadership that takes into account all stakeholders, customers, employees, staff, volunteers, suppliers, partners, the public, and the community. Leaders in the self-renewing organization set directions, create a customer focus, establish clear and visible values, and exemplify high expectations.

  Leaders focus their efforts to ensure the creation of strategies, systems, and methods for achieving excellence, stimulating innovation, and building knowledge and capabilities. The organization's values and strategies should help guide all activities and decisions made by leaders at every level. Senior leaders in the organization should inspire and motivate staff and volunteers while encouraging involvement, development and learning, innovation, and creativity by all members of the organization.

  Through their ethical behavior and exemplary personal roles in planning, communications, coaching, developing future leaders, review of organizational performance, and staff and volunteer recognition, senior leaders in the organization will serve as role models, reinforcing values and expectations and building leadership, commitment, and initiative throughout the organization.

  They use communications and dedicated commitment to "realize" the organization's values, expectations, and directions. Through transformational leadership, the organization's culture becomes one in which the self-fulfilled individual knows that change is not only "safe" but necessary to maintain effectiveness and efficiency.
- *Human resource focus—development and management*—practices directed toward the creation of a high-performance workplace, directly linking human resource

planning with the organization's strategic directions. Key human resource plans are derived from the organization's strategy and planning. The organization's job design, compensation, and recognition approaches enable and encourage all staff and volunteers to contribute effectively, operating within high-performance empowered work units or teams. In the self-renewing organization, employee and volunteer well-being, satisfaction, and growth potential are based on a more holistic view of them as key stakeholders.

Self-renewing organizations are effective, efficient, and evolutionary. We may find it increasingly difficult to point out future examples of organizations at the lower end of the "in accord with mission and environment" curve. Those that lack purpose are irrelevant, costly, wasteful, and slow to react to their environment; they are prime candidates for extinction.

Self-renewing organizations gain enthusiasm from their base of intrinsically motivated leadership, reinforcing their desire to excel at ever-higher levels of achievement and comparison with other organizations with reputations for excellence.

Self-renewing, palingenetic organizations have the visionary discipline in their senior leaders to plan and implement long-range strategies; an enlightened commitment to train, nourish, and foster intrinsically motivated "change agent" leaders at all levels of the organization; and the dedication to develop in their team-oriented work groups the tools and approaches needed to continuously improve all major organization processes.

Self-renewing organizations know where they are going. They constantly strive for excellence and improvement in all areas, and their leaders bring about nonthreatening change.

A self-renewing organization is the kind of organization we would all like to be a part of. It is the kind of organization we know would offer us the best opportunity for personal development and to make a meaningful contribution.

When we use the excellence equation, we establish a straightforward, easily understood "cognitive map" by which to understand the three fundamental elements necessary for organizations to achieve and sustain excellence. Further, the equation helps us understand the relationship of these three basic elements to the seven fundamental areas of organizational leadership and management, including:

- Effectiveness
  Strategic planning and development
  Customer focus and satisfaction
  Public service provider (business) results
- Efficiency
  Process management
  Information and analysis
- Environment
  Leadership
  Human resource development and management

In addition, by adapting the Baldrige Award/President's Quality Award Criteria as the basic definitions for these seven functional categories, we now have nationally defined descriptions and characteristics of organizational performance and achievement for each of these areas—and, with it, the ability to benchmark our own organizations against established national criteria and standards. When we are better able to determine where our organizations stand in relation to national standards, we then have the ability to outline plans and strategies to help us overcome the "delta"—or shortfall—between the next higher level of quality and the level at which we may now be performing.

The excellence equation is deliberately simplistic. It must be *adapted*, not *adopted*, to meet the assessment and planning needs of each individual organization. It is my hope that in explaining and outlining the approach to excellence in this way, we can encourage others in their efforts to achieve higher levels of quality—and to improve their ability to do so. In the public service, not-for-profit sector, success in quality management by thousands of organizations translates to an overall improvement of our national quality of life.

In addition, the excellence equation approach can encourage a deeper appreciation that sustained excellence is the goal we should be seeking—in our organizations and in our lives—and that requires the effective application of all three elements of the equation.

54.5 Description of Categories

The following discussion is adapted for not-for-profit organizations from the Presidents Quality Award criteria and guidelines. Each of the seven functional areas of excellence is explained and defined for not-for-profit organizations. It is doubtful that any single not-for-profit organization is currently able to assess itself as having reached these extraordinarily challenging levels of quality and excellence. However, the text does illustrate the current "ideal" level of achievement and integration between functional areas toward which not for-profit organizations should be striving. The extent to which these levels are achieved and *sustained* over time is the measure of the organization's overall health and viability. In addition, the assessment provides its leaders with some idea of the organization's survivability and sustainability in today's challenging, competitive, and fast-changing environment.

(A) EFFECTIVENESS

An effective organization, regardless of the sector in which it operates, has a valid purpose that is continually adjusted to its surroundings and context as it focuses on how to accomplish the customer-focused mission.

Management effectiveness includes the overall area of *strategic planning development* that deals with the organization's strategy development process. Strategic objectives, action plans, and related human resource plans that strengthen both organizational performance and help it achieve a self-sustaining position are included, as well as those approaches and techniques used to develop the organization's strategy deployment process, including key short- and longer-term action plans.

The *customer, client, and public service focus* includes the assessment processes needed to determine and target customer and client groups and/or market segments. As competition for finite resources sharpens, it is increasingly important to long-term survivability for not-for-profits to determine and project key client/customer requirements and their relative importance/value to customers in terms of marketing, service planning, and delivery. On the "back end" of that objective are the techniques and approaches used to determine customer satisfaction and build relationships, including: processes, measurements, and data used to determine client satisfaction and how to incorporate this information into strategic decision making.

Public service provider or business results are needed and used to determine and influence current levels and trends of customer/client satisfaction and key measures and/or indicators of service performance.

(i) Strategic Planning

The strategic planning functional area addresses strategic and business planning and deployment of plans, with a strong focus on client/customer and operational performance requirements. For self-renewing organization leaders, the emphasis here is that customer-driven quality and operational performance excellence are key strategic business issues that need to be an integral part of organization planning. Specifically:

- Customer-driven quality is a strategic view of quality. The focus is on the drivers of customer satisfaction—a key factor in business success.
- Operational performance improvement contributes to short-term and longer-term productivity growth and cost/price competitiveness. The focus on building operational capability—including speed, responsiveness, and flexibility—represents an investment in strengthening competitive fitness.

An important role for leaders is to ensure an effective focus for daily work, aligning it with the organization's strategic directions.

In particular, planning is needed to:

- Understand that key customer and operational requirements should serve as input to setting strategic directions; this will help ensure that ongoing process improvements will be aligned with the organization's strategic directions.
- Optimize the use of resources and ensure bridging between short-term and longer-term requirements that may entail capital expenditures, training, and the like.
- Ensure that deployment will be effective—that there are mechanisms to transmit requirements and achieve alignment on three basic levels: organization/executive level, the key process level, and the work unit/individual job level.

(ii) Strategy Development

Self-renewing organizations develop their view of the future, set strategic directions, and translate these directions into actionable key business drivers, including customer satisfaction. Effective leadership in fulfilling these functions is critical and determines the organization's operational effectiveness.

Every organization is impacted by key influences, challenges, and requirements that can affect its future opportunities and directions. Leaders of self-renewing organizations take as long a view as possible, emphasizing the importance of a thorough and realistic context for the development of a customer/client and market-focused strategy to guide ongoing decision making, resource allocation, and organization-wide management.

Strategy and plans are translated into actionable key business drivers, which serve as the basis for operationalizing and deploying plan requirements. This translation often includes a determination of those activities the organization should perform itself and those for which it might utilize partners or seek partners.

The self-renewing organization places a high priority on evaluating and improving its strategic planning and plan deployment processes. This can involve input from work units regarding key deployment factors—effective translation and communications of strategy and plans, adequacy of resources, and identification of key new needs by clients/customers. A list of strategic planning characteristics of self-renewing organizations follows.

- Sound, systematic, well-documented, effective processes are used throughout the organization to develop business strategies, business plans, and key business drivers for overall operational and financial performance.
- All appropriate staff, clients, customers, volunteers, and suppliers/partners participate fully in the planning process.
- Strategy development considers the organization's vision, customer-driven values and expectations; includes risk analysis, organization capabilities, and supplier/partner capabilities.
- Strategies and business plans are translated into actionable key business drivers used for deployment throughout organization, to key suppliers/partners; managers, staff, and volunteers are held accountable for attaining major targets throughout organization; staff know how their work unit contributes to overall business success.
- Systematic procedures are used to continuously evaluate strategic planning and plan deployment processes; improvements in processes are made on an ongoing basis.
- Specific business drivers are derived from strategic directions translated into an actionable plan throughout the organization. The plan includes: key performance requirements, operational performance measures, productivity improvement, cycle time reduction, waste reduction. Work unit and supplier/partner plans are fully aligned.
- Top priority is given to deployment of plans, improvement targets as evidenced by extensive resource commitment to ensuring plan success.
- Outstanding product/service quality and operational performance are projected for key business areas when compared with key benchmarks.

Self-renewing organization leaders are focused on developing a competitive strategy and on operationalizing this strategy. Operationalizing the strategy in the form of key public service/business drivers requires clear and measurable performance objectives. These objectives serve to guide the design and management of key processes. The objectives often serve to align organizational systems (e.g., communications, compensation, recognition) with performance objectives.

Leaders place high priority on the organization's key business drivers and how these drivers are translated into an action plan. This includes spelling out key performance requirements; aligning work unit, supplier, and/or partner plans; determining how productivity, cycle time, and waste reduction are addressed; and checking how the principal resources are committed to the accomplishment of plans.

(iii)   Customer Focus and Satisfaction

Customer focus and satisfaction is the functional area dealing with the need to understand in detail the voices of customers and the marketplace or operating environment. Much of the information needed to gain this understanding comes from measuring results and trends. Such results and trends provide hard, quantifiable information on customers' views and their "marketplace" behaviors. This knowledge then serves as a useful foundation on which self-renewing organization leaders can establish priorities and focus improvement activities. Subsequent results and trends offer the means to determine whether priorities and improvement activities are appropriately directed.

A quality-focused organization determines current *and* emerging customer requirements and expectations. This is not a one-time process. Many factors may affect customer/client preferences, needs, and loyalty, making it necessary to listen and learn on a continuous basis.

The self-renewing organization has established a process to determine current and near-term requirements and expectations of clients/customers. This includes the completeness of the client/customer pool, including recognition of segments and customers of competitors. There is sensitivity to specific product and service requirements and their relative importance to client/customer groups. Validity of the data should be confirmed by use of other data and information, such as complaints.

The self-renewing organization addresses future requirements and expectations of customers—its key listening and learning strategies. Such strategies depend significantly on the nature of the organization's services or products, the competitive environment, and relationships with clients/customers. The listening and learning strategies selected should provide timely and useful information for decision making. The strategies should take into account the organization's competitive strategy. For example, if the organization customizes its services, the listening and learning strategy needs to be backed by a responsive, capable information system—one that rapidly gathers information about customers and makes this information available where needed throughout the organization. Increasingly, Internet technologies will be used in this process, creating an organizational *intranet*.

Evaluating and improving processes to determine customer requirements and expectations is important. Such evaluation/improvement process could entail a variety of approaches, formal and informal, that seek to stay in close touch with customers and with issues that bear on customer preference. The purpose of these evaluations is to find reliable and cost-effective means to understand customer requirements and expectations on a continuous basis.

The self-renewing organization provides effective management of its responses and follow-ups with customers. Relationship management provides a potentially important means for organizations to gain understanding about, and to manage, customer expectations. Also, front-line staff or volunteers will provide vital information relating to building partnerships and other longer-term relationships with clients/customers. In addition, the organization provides easy access for customers specifically for purposes of seeking information or assistance and/or to comment and complain.

Complaints are resolved promptly and effectively, including recovery of customer confidence. In addition, the organization learns from complaints and ensures that production/delivery process employees receive information needed to eliminate the causes of complaints.

The self-renewing organization follows up with customers regarding products, services, and recent transactions to determine satisfaction, to resolve problems, and to gather information for improvement or for new services.

It evaluates and improves its customer response management with several types of improvements, including: improving service standards, such as complaint resolution time and resolution effectiveness, and improving the use of customer feedback to improve production/delivery processes, training, and hiring.

Satisfaction relative to competitors is determined. Such information can be derived from organization-based comparative studies or studies made by independent organizations. The purpose of this comparison is to develop information that can be used for improving performance.

The self-renewing organization evaluates and improves processes and measurement scales that it uses to determine customer satisfaction *and* satisfaction relative to competitors. This evaluation/improvement process draws on other indicators, such as customer dissatisfaction indicators (e.g., complaints). The evaluation also considers how well customer satisfaction information and data are used throughout the organization. Use by the leadership can be enhanced if data are presented in an actionable form that meets two key conditions: (1) survey responses are tied directly to key business processes and (2) survey responses are translated into cost/revenue implications.

Customer satisfaction and customer dissatisfaction are not the same and require different measures. Customer satisfaction measures can include information on customer retention and other appropriate evidence of current and recent past satisfaction with the organization's products and/or services, such as customer awards.

Customer dissatisfaction measures and/or indicators depend on the nature of the organization's services or products. For example, an organization's survey methods might include a scale that uses ratings such as "very dissatisfied" or "somewhat dissatisfied."

The reason for including measures of both satisfaction and dissatisfaction is that they usually provide different information. The factors in high levels of satisfaction may not be the same factors as those that relate to high levels of dissatisfaction. In addition, the effect of individual instances of dissatisfaction on overall satisfaction could vary widely depending on the effectiveness of the organization's resolution ("recovery") of a problem.

Customer satisfaction relative to similar providers should be measured and known where possible. A list of customer focus and satisfaction characteristics of self-renewing organizations follows.

- There exists a comprehensive, documented system for determining current, near-term customer requirements/expectations used throughout the organization.
- Methods used to obtain knowledge of customer requirements/expectations elicit a comprehensive set of quality features for products/services and the relative importance of these features. Other key data (e.g., complaints) are used to support determination of features' importance.
- Future customer requirements/expectations are addressed throughout the organization; listening/learning strategies are used to determine future requirements/expectations.
- Systems and processes for determining customer requirements/expectations are evaluated and improved on an ongoing basis.
- Information is readily accessible to all customers to enable them to seek assistance, comment, and/or complain.

- Most processes/transactions that bring employees in contact with customers are identified throughout the organization.
- Service standards are aimed at exceeding customer expectations; they are deployed to all employees needing such information and tracked throughout the organization.
- Effective feedback systems provide knowledge from customers about products/services and recent transactions.
- Formal and informal feedback/complaints received by all organization units are resolved effectively and promptly; the complaint management process ensures effective recovery of customer confidence, meets customer requirements for effective resolution, and eliminates causes of complaints.
- The organization consistently follows up with customers on products/services and transactions to determine satisfaction, resolve problems, seek feedback for improvement, and build relationships.
- Customer service standards, including access and complaint management, are reviewed and revised on an ongoing basis.
- Data from customer feedback systems are aggregated, evaluated, and used throughout the organization to improve customer relationship management.
- Feedback systems providing knowledge about customers are improved on an ongoing basis.
- A comprehensive set of approaches is used to determine customer satisfaction with products/services and their delivery throughout the organization.
- Comparisons of customer satisfaction for similar providers are determined for major products/services and some other products/services.
- Methods for determining customer satisfaction and customer satisfaction relative to similar providers are evaluated and improved on an ongoing basis.
- Key customer satisfaction results are sustained at a very high level, with consistent improvement each year for the last five years.
- Key customer dissatisfaction results are sustained at very low levels for the last five years.
- Customer satisfaction comparisons with similar providers are outstanding.

(iv) Public Service Provider Results

"Public service provider or business results" is the term used to describe another vitally important leadership responsibility in the self-renewing organization—ensuring a results focus for all processes and process improvement activities. The objective of this unrelenting focus is to maintain a dual purpose—superior value of offerings as viewed by customers and the public and superior organizational performance as reflected in productivity and effectiveness indicators. The initiatives included within business results provide "real-time" information (measures of progress or effectiveness) for evaluation and improvement of processes, aligned with overall business strategy.

Leaders of self-renewing organizations monitor current levels and trends in product and service quality using key measures and/or indicators of such quality. They select measures and/or indicators that relate to requirements of importance to the client/customer and to the public (marketplace).

Correlation between quality and customer indicators is a critical management tool—a device for focusing on key quality requirements. In addition, the correlation process may reveal emerging or changing market segments, changing importance of requirements, or even potential obsolescence of products and/or services.

Comparative information is developed to enable results reported to be evaluated against competitors or other relevant markers of performance.

Some information addresses factors that best reflect overall organization operational performance. Such factors are of two types: (1) generic—common to all organizations—and (2) business-specific. Generic factors include financial indicators, cycle time, and productivity, as reflected in use of labor, materials, energy, capital, and assets. Generic factors also include human resource indicators such as safety, absenteeism, and turnover. Productivity, cycle time, and other operational indicators should reflect aggregate organization performance.

Business- or organization-specific effectiveness indicators vary greatly throughout the sector. However, typical examples include rates of invention, environmental quality, percent of acceptance from recently introduced products or services, and shifts toward new segments.

Supplier performance results are important considerations. These address current levels and trends in key measures and/or indicators of supplier performance. Suppliers are external providers of materials and services, "upstream" and/or "downstream" from the organization. The focus should be on the most critical requirements from the organization's point of view—the buyer of the products and services. Data reported and assessed should reflect results by whatever means they occur—via improvements by suppliers within the supply base, through selection of better performing suppliers, or both.

Measures and indicators of supplier performance should relate to all key requirements—quality, delivery, and price. Self-renewing organization leaders also develop and use comparative information so that results reported can be evaluated against competitors or other relevant markers of performance. Public service provider results include the following:

- Key measures of service or product quality demonstrate exceptional results over the past five years.
- Current levels of service/product quality are comparable to recognized leaders for similar products/services.
- Key measures of operational/financial performance demonstrate exceptional results over the past five years.
- Current levels of operational/financial performance are comparable to recognized leaders for similar activities.
- Quality performance of major suppliers has been improving over the past five years; performance is comparable to recognized leaders

(B) EFFICIENCY

Efficient organizations perform well and economically, as evidenced by reduced waste of time, energy, and materials. These objectives are achieved through efficient resource development, process improvement, and resource conservation. Management areas that contribute to overall organizational efficiency include process management and information and analysis approaches.

Process management involves ensuring that the complex and interactive series of actions needed to develop and deliver public services do so in ways that conserve resources, satisfy clients and customers, and meet changing client/market requirements. *New technologies* must be continually evaluated. If validated for their contributions to increased efficiency, they need to be incorporated into services and systems in ways that improve customer satisfaction and/or efficiency. Throughout organizations, we need to be continually alert and proactive to assess, design, and improve processes that maximize quality, transfer of learning, cost control, productivity, and other efficiency/effectiveness factors.

Information and analysis approaches help us design and install performance measurement systems that help leaders understand, align, and improve organizational performance at all levels and throughout the organization. The challenge is to select measures and indicators that accurately track organizational performance. That information, in turn, helps us link the results of organizational-level analysis to improved client services delivery and other public service goals.

(i) Process Management and Improvement
Effective process management is a critical function for all self-renewing organizations, requiring effective design, a prevention orientation, evaluation and continuous improvement, linkage to suppliers, and overall high performance.

Virtually all organizations design and introduce products or services. Some do so with great frequency; others do so once in the proverbial "blue moon." How the organization goes about designing and introducing products and services says a lot about its "health" and future prospects in a highly competitive world.

For the self-renewing organization, a major focus in this functional area is the rapid and effective integration of production and delivery *early* in the design phase. This integration helps minimize downstream problems for clients or customers and reduces or eliminates the need for design changes that will be costly to the organization.

Leaders pay close attention to three important aspects of this process:

1. The translation of customer requirements into design requirements for products and services.
2. How these product and service design requirements are translated into efficient and effective production/delivery processes.
3. How all requirements associated with products, services, and production/delivery processes are addressed early in the design process by all appropriate organization units to ensure integration and coordination. Effective design must take into account all stakeholders in the value chain.

The design of products, services, and processes should meet customer requirements. However, truly effective design must also consider cycle time and productivity of production and delivery processes. This usually includes detailed mapping of service processes to achieve efficiency as well as to meet customer requirements.

Prior to full-scale operation, any product, service, production, or delivery process design should be reviewed and tested in detail. This ensures that all parts of the production/delivery system are capable of performing according to design. This stage is a crucial one. Positive or negative customer reactions and potentially high cost to the organization are virtually assured if pre-operation changes are significant.

Following initial process design, the process of designing the process should itself be evaluated and improved to progressively better quality and cycle time. This means that self-renewing organizations extract lessons learned to build capabilities for future designs. Their evaluation might take into account delays and problems experienced during design, feedback from those involved, and post-operation problems that might have been averted through better design. Evaluation and improvement should strive for a continuous flow of work in the key design and delivery processes.

Another important function is that of monitoring and evaluating process performance to ensure that processes perform according to their design. Leaders require a description of the key processes and their specific requirements and information on how performance relative to these requirements is known and maintained.

A process performance measurement plan requires the identification of critical points in processes for measurement or observation. Implied in this plan is that measurements or observations be made at the earliest points in processes to minimize problems that may result from variations from expected (design) performance. When measurements or observations reveal variations, a remedy—often called corrective action—is required to restore the performance of the process to its design performance.

Depending on the nature of the process, the correction could involve technical, human, or both factors. Proper action involves correcting at the source (root cause) of the variation. *Note:* In some cases, customers may directly witness or take part in the process and contribute to or be a determinant of process performance. In such cases, variations among customers must be taken into account in evaluating how well the process is performing. This is especially true of professional and personal services.

In the self-renewing organizations, processes are improved to achieve better performance—meaning not only better quality from the customer's perspective but also better operational performance (productivity) from the organization's perspective.

Key support service processes are based on the requirements of the organization's external customers and of other units ("internal customers") within the organization—those within the organization that use the output of the process. These processes are also measured, evaluated, and improved.

The performance of external providers of goods and services is another functional area that requires effective management. Such management is increasingly built around longer-term partnering relationships, particularly with key suppliers.

Certain basic information is required: on the organization's principal requirements for its key suppliers, on expected performance and measurements used to assess performance, on how the organization determines whether its requirements are being met, and on how performance information is fed back to suppliers.

Here leaders of self-renewing organizations evaluate and improve supplier management in three elemental areas:

1. Improving supplier abilities to meet requirements
2. Improving their own supplier management processes
3. Reducing costs associated with the verification of supplier performance

For many organizations, suppliers are increasingly important members of the complex team needed to achieve not only high performance and lower-cost objectives but also strategic objectives. For example, key suppliers might provide unique design, integration, and marketing capabilities. Exploiting these advantages requires joint planning and partner relationships to ensure longer-term planning horizons and customer-supplier teams. Process management characteristics of self-renewing organizations follow.

- New, improved products/services, processes are designed to exceed customer expectations.
- Measurement systems are designed to track process performance throughout the organization.
- Customer/quality requirements are reviewed by appropriate organizational units, suppliers, and partners to ensure integration/coordination/capability.
- Initial designs are reviewed and validated based on a variety of performance and capability considerations throughout the organization.
- Key designs/processes are evaluated to meet customer, quality, and operational performance requirements.
- Key production and delivery processes are managed throughout the organization to meet design plans; a measurement plan and measurements are used to maintain process performance.
- Appropriate analytic methods and measurements are used throughout the organization to identify and solve problems that disrupt production and delivery processes; corrections are systematically verified.
- Key production and delivery processes are improved throughout the organization to achieve better quality, cycle time, and operational performance; a wide range of techniques is used, including process simplification, process research/testing, benchmarking, customer information, and alternate technology.
- Key support service processes are designed and managed throughout the organization to meet customer, quality, and operational performance requirements; measurements are used to maintain process performance.
- Support design parameters are addressed early in the process by appropriate organizational units to ensure integration/coordination/capability.
- Appropriate analytic methods are used throughout the organization to identify and solve problems that disrupt support service processes; corrections are systematically verified.
- Key support service processes are improved throughout the organization to achieve better quality, cycle time, and operational performance requirements; a wide range of techniques is used, including process simplification, process research/testing, benchmarking, customer information, and alternate technology.
- Quality requirements defined throughout the organization for expected supplier performance; performance feedback is systematically communicated to suppliers.
- Quality is a primary consideration when selecting suppliers.
- Systematic approaches are used throughout the organization to evaluate and improve supplier performance; supplier abilities, procurement process, and inspection/audit costs are considered.

(ii) Information and Analysis
Information and analysis includes all key information needed to drive the improvement of overall performance. The objective of this functional area is to bring about the alignment of the organization's information system with its strategic directions. Performance can be improved, if key processes are analyzed and improved. This requires the identification and analysis of key information.

Leaders must ensure that the organization selects and manages key information and data that support overall business goals. Primary emphasis during this process must be on those actions and initiatives that support process management and performance improvement.

Information and data are selected for use based on their strategic importance; they are managed most effectively when they can be rapidly accessed and updated; in turn, these contribute strongly to their reliability.

Leaders of self-renewing organizations are concerned with how the organization evaluates and improves its selection, analysis, and management of information and data. They ensure an emphasis on alignment with business priorities, support of process management, and feedback from information and data users. Their evaluation should take into account factors such as paths of data use, extent and effectiveness of use, gaps, sharing, and organization of information and data.

Information and data are most frequently selected based on their utility to manage performance effectively. However, information, data, and information technology often have strategic significance as well. For example, information technology can be used to build and disseminate vital knowledge about customers and markets, creating the ability to operate more successfully.

Data and information related to competitive position and to best practices serve as external drivers of improvement, giving this information both operational and strategic importance. Of course, the organization should not only select and use this information but should consider how it evaluates and improves the processes it uses to do so.

The basic premises here recognize the fact that:

- Organizations need to "know where they stand" relative to competitors and to best practice performance for similar activities
- Comparative and benchmarking information provides impetus for significant ("breakthrough") improvement and alerts organizations to competitive threats and new practices
- Organizations need to understand their own processes and the processes of others before they compare performance levels

Carefully selected and analyzed benchmarking information may also be very helpful to support business analysis and decisions relating to core competencies, alliances, and outsourcing.

Organization-level analysis is the principal basis for guiding an organization's process management toward business results. Despite the importance of individual facts and data in the self-renewing organization, they do not usually provide a sound basis for actions or priorities.

Action should be undertaken only after an understanding has been achieved between cause/effect connections among processes and between processes and business results. Process actions often have many resource implications; results may have many cost and revenue implications as well. Because resources for improvement are limited and cause/effect connections are often unclear, most organizations face a critical need to provide a sound analytical basis for decisions.

Data and information from all parts of the organization must be aggregated and analyzed to support reviews, business decisions, and planning. Self-renewing organization leaders ensure the focus remains on two key areas of performance: customers and operational performance. Analyses use both nonfinancial and financial data, connected to provide a basis for action. For many not-for-profits, a particularly important analysis objective is that of linking customer data, improvements in product and service quality, and improvements in operational performance to improvement in financial indicators—guiding the selection of improvement efforts and strategies to achieve revenue growth and to reduce operating costs. Information and analysis characteristics of self-renewing organizations follow.

- Criteria for selecting data/information for use in quality and operational performance improvement are integrated and used throughout the organization.
- Key data/information relating to key public service/business drivers is used to improve quality and operational performance throughout the organization.
- Processes and technologies are used throughout the organization to assure that information collected is reliable, consistent, valid, and readily accessible in response to user needs.
- Processes are in place to evaluate and improve the information and data system supporting the improvement of organization performance; the processes are reviewed on an ongoing basis.
- A benchmarking process is established based on needs and priorities and aligned with the organization's overall improvement targets; data is used to establish stretch targets and/or support breakthrough approaches throughout the organization.
- Most organizational components use benchmark/comparison data, including: product and service quality, support service processes, staff, volunteer, and supplier-related activities.
- The organization evaluates and improves its benchmarking process on an ongoing basis.
- Performance and customer/client data is aggregated with other key data, then analyzed and translated into usable information to support reviews, business decisions, and planning throughout the organization.
- Performance data is aggregated with other key data, then analyzed and related to financial indicators of performance; the information is used to set priorities for improvement actions throughout the organization.

(C) EVOLUTIONARY ORGANIZATIONAL ENVIRONMENT

At times, effectiveness vs. efficiency initiatives create a push-pull within the organization that can create damaging, even destructive "currents." To keep this normal "give and take" from dividing the organization into "them and us" camps requires an overall organizational environment able to adapt to changing conditions, manage change effectively, transition to new states, and turn in new directions—in short, to constantly evolve. The management areas that deal with creating and sustaining the evolutionary environment include:

- *Leadership.* Leaders set, communicate, and deploy organizational values and expectations, including how senior leaders use organizational performance to improve effectiveness throughout the organization.

- *Human resource focus.* The organizational commitment encourages and motivates staff and volunteers to develop and use their full potential. It is enhanced by designing, organizing, and managing jobs and services to enhance cooperation, collaboration, individual initiative, innovation, and flexibility.
- *Staff and volunteer performance management.* Approaches are needed that support high performance. Staff and volunteers are recruited, oriented, and trained using key performance requirements, diversity, and fair work practices.
- *Education and training.* Approaches are needed that achieve organizational objectives; build staff/volunteer knowledge, skills, capabilities; and contribute to improved performance.
- *Organizational environment.* An organizational environment that contributes to the well-being, satisfaction, and motivation of all staff and volunteers must be created and maintained.

(i) Leadership

This excellence category includes the organization's leadership system, strategic directions, and expectations.

In any self-renewing organization, senior leaders fulfill key roles—those that cannot be delegated to others. These vital roles include setting the organization's strategic directions and building and maintaining a leadership system conducive to high performance, individual development, and organizational learning. Truly effective leaders at all levels of the organization, however, take into account all stakeholders, customers, employees, suppliers, partners, public, and the community.

Major aspects of leadership include: creating values and expectations, setting directions, developing and maintaining an effective leadership system, and building the organization's capabilities. Senior leaders need to reflect these values, and the leadership system needs to include teamwork at the executive level.

Senior leaders within the self-renewing organization devote significant time and attention to evaluating and improving the effectiveness of the organization and its leadership system. This function of leadership is crucial, due to the fast pace of competition. A major objective is to create organizations that are flexible and responsive—changing easily to adapt to new needs and opportunities. Both leadership and organization are crucial to high performance. Through their roles in strategy development and review of organization performance, senior leaders adapt leadership (creation and management of change) and the organization (vision, mission, customer focus) to changing opportunities and requirements.

In the self-renewing organization, the leadership system is translated into an effective overall organization structure and management system focused on performance.

The organization's management and work processes support its customer and performance objectives. Senior leaders are alert to identify functional or management barriers that could lead to losing sight of customers or create ineffective or slow decision paths. They take strong measures to ensure alignment of organization units.

The organization's values, expectations, and directions are "made real" throughout the organization via effective communications. Senior leader communications are necessary for effective overall communications. Making values, expectations, and directions real demands constant reinforcement and "truth testing," as employees observe whether stated values and expectations are actually the basis for organization actions and key decisions.

Senior leaders review organization and work unit performance and ensure that important work process assessments are included in these reviews. The information they assess addresses important aspects of reviews—types, frequency, content, uses, and who conducts them. Frequency, content, uses, and who conducts reviews will vary greatly, depending on many factors. Most commonly, the review system blends ongoing ("real-time") and periodic reviews.

As the Presidential Quality Award points out: "Reviews offer an effective means to communicate and reinforce what is really important, how performance is measured, and how well business objectives are being met. Important considerations in reviews are the content and organization of information to foster learning and to stimulate action. This means that reviews should include non-financial and financial information that together present a clear picture of status and trends relative to the organization's key business drivers. Reviews also provide an effective means to assist units that may not be performing according to expectations."

Public responsibility and corporate (organizational) citizenship are as important to not-for-profit organizations as they are to private sector organizations. This is measured by the extent to which the organization integrates its public responsibilities and corporate citizenship into its business planning and performance improvement practices.

Not-for-profits, like public and private sector organizations, should be concerned about three basic aspects of public responsibility:

1. Making risk and legal requirements an integral part of performance improvement
2. Sensitivity in planning products, services, and operations to issues of societal concern, whether these issues are currently embodied in law or not
3. Making legal and ethical conduct visible in the organization's values and performance improvement processes

Fulfilling public responsibilities means not only meeting all local, state, and federal laws and regulatory requirements but also treating these and related requirements as areas for improvement "beyond mere compliance." This means that all self-renewing organizations should maintain constant awareness of potential public impacts related to their products, services, and operations. Not-for-profits, often the target of legal or regulatory action by public regulators or private corporations, must be diligent in exceeding the "average" in each of these categories.

Self-renewing organizations serve as a "corporate citizen" in their key communities. They are productive, reputable, and involved as members of different types of communities and serve as a positive influence on other organizations. They work within and outside themselves to strengthen community services, education, healthcare, and the environment, and improve the practices of trade, business, and other community associations. A list of leadership characteristics of self-renewing organizations follows.

- All senior leaders are personally, visibly, proactively involved in a broad range of activities that substantially improve organizational excellence; they devote significant time to these activities.
- Senior leaders create a vision, core values, and a strong client/customer focus orientation.
- Senior leaders fully participate in establishing the organization's performance excellence goals through strategic business planning.

- Senior leaders devote extensive time to reviewing the organization's customer/client operational performance.
- The extent to which vision, core values, and a customer focus orientation have been adopted is evaluated and improved on an ongoing basis.
- All senior leaders use a variety of methods to communicate and reinforce vision, core values, and client/customer focus orientation to staff and volunteers; communication is two way, clear, and open, and covers all issues.
- Effective strategies involve leaders throughout the organization in core value-related activities; roles, responsibilities, and accountability are clearly defined; extensive cooperation among units is encouraged and evident.
- Senior leaders—staff and volunteer—actively participate in planning and attaining identified excellence-enhancing goals. Mutual support is visible throughout the organization and reinforced through communications and partnering.
- Partnering relationships exist with major client/stakeholder groups, suppliers, and others; the number of mutually supportive activities is expanding in support of excellence-related core value and performance goals.
- Vision, core values, and a client/customer focus orientation are effectively communicated inside and outside the organization.
- A documented review process of the organization's core values and operational improvement plans is used throughout organization; results are used to implement strategies to improve organization-wide performance.
- Core values/goals and objectives directly address (where appropriate) public health, safety, environmental protection, and ethical conduct. Accountability for achieving goals and objectives is clearly established; improvement efforts throughout the organization reflect this commitment. These core value goals and objectives go beyond minimum legal/community standards.
- The organization is recognized as an outstanding citizen in its key stakeholder communities; senior leaders, staff, and volunteers share talents/expertise with the community.

(ii) *Human Resource Development and Management*

Human resource development and management is the functional area and focal point within any organization for all-important human resource practices—those directed toward the creation and sustainability of a high-performance workplace. A vital objective for self-renewing organization leaders is to address human resource development and management in an integrated way—aligning them with the organization's strategic directions.

Strategic directions should address the development of all those involved in achieving the organization's mission and vision—staff and volunteers—in the context of a high-performance workplace. This requires a coordinated organizational strategy.

The overall human resource plan should be derived from the organization's strategic and business planning. Primary directions and resourcing must support its overall strategic directions. Senior leaders within the organization endeavor to develop a multi-year context and guide for human resource planning, management, and evaluation.

As in any values-centered organization, the human resource development area uses the Plan-Do-Check-Act cycle to evaluate and improve overall planning and management. Employee-related and organization performance data and information is tied to overall evaluation of the organization's strategy and business results.

Care is taken to go beyond broad strategy to the essential details of human resource effectiveness. The evaluation needs to provide the organization's senior leaders with information on strengths and weaknesses in human resource practices and development that might bear on the organization's abilities to achieve its short-term and longer-term business objectives. For example, the evaluation should take into account the development and progression of all categories and types of staff and volunteers, including those newly joining the organization.

The evaluation should also monitor the extent to which education and training is deployed throughout the organization and how well both support organization performance improvement. The overall evaluation will rely heavily on well-being and satisfaction factors.

Well-being considerations include the work environment and the work climate and how they are tailored to foster the well-being, satisfaction, and development of all employees. Long-term well-being and productivity (not to mention legal and regulatory requirements) require a safe and healthful work environment.

The approach of self-renewing organization leaders to enhancing staff and volunteer well-being, satisfaction, and growth potential is based on a more holistic view of the organization's human resources as key stakeholders. The leaders consider a wide variety of mechanisms to build well-being and satisfaction, from development, progression, employability, and external activities, to family or other community service activities.

Many factors might affect employee motivation. Although satisfaction with pay and promotion potential is important, these factors alone are not adequate to assess the overall climate for motivation, morale, and high performance. Therefore, the organization will consider a variety of factors relating to the work environment to determine the key elements of its culture and internal environment. Those factors identified that inhibit motivation will be prioritized and addressed. Additional understanding of these factors is developed through exit interviews with departing staff and volunteers.

In the self-renewing organization, job design, compensation, and recognition approaches enable and encourage all employees to contribute effectively, operating within high-performance work units. The latter requires effective work design and reinforcement. The basic intent of such work design approaches should be to enable staff and volunteers to exercise more discretion and decision making, leading to greater flexibility and more rapid response to the changing requirements of the marketplace; in short, they are "empowered" with a combination of authority, responsibility, resourcing, and accountability.

Effective job design and flexible work organizations are necessary but may not be sufficient, in and of themselves, to ensure high performance. Job and organization design needs to be backed by information systems, education, and appropriate training to ensure that information flow supports the job and work designs. Also important is effective communication across functions and work units to ensure focus on customer requirements.

Incentives need to be aligned with work systems. Compensation and recognition should be structured and implemented to reinforce high-performance job design, work organizations, and teamwork. These are important considerations because there should be consistency between the organization's compensation and recognition system and its work structures and processes. Compensation, benefits, and recognition may need to be based on demonstrated skills and evaluation by peers in teams and networks.

The self-renewing organization develops human resources via education, training, and on-the-job reinforcement of knowledge and skills. A major objective of "development" is meeting the needs of a high-performance workplace operating in a dynamic, highly competitive environment. Education and training need to be ongoing as well.

Education and training serve as key vehicles to build organization and people capabilities. These two capabilities are, in fact, investments the organization makes in its long-term future and the long-term future of people.

Leaders of self-renewing organizations pay particular attention to how education and training are designed, delivered, reinforced, and evaluated, with special emphasis on the on-the-job application of knowledge and skills. They recognize the importance of involving all levels and categories of people within the organization—staff, volunteers, and managers—in the design of training, including clear identification of specific needs. This involves job analysis—understanding the types and levels of the skills required and the timeliness of training.

Evaluation of education and training is vital and should take into account the supervisor's evaluation, employee/volunteer self-evaluation, and peer evaluation of value received through education and training relative to needs identified in design. The evaluation process could also address the effectiveness of education and training delivery, impact on work unit performance, and costs of delivery alternatives. A list of human resource development and management characteristics of self-renewing organizations follows.

- A systematic, integrated human resources plan is deployed throughout the organization to develop workforce potential; it is linked to core values and operational performance improvement plans.
- The human resources plan includes: redesign to improve flexibility, innovation, and rapid response to changing requirements; staff/volunteer development, education, training; and improvements in reward, recognition, and recruitment.
- Human resources planning is an integral, fully aligned part of the organization's planning process; it is systematically evaluated and improved on an ongoing basis.
- Employee-related (staff/volunteer) data and organization performance data are consistently analyzed and used to assess the development and well-being of all categories and types of employees and to assess the linkage of human resources practices to key business results.
- Reliable, complete human resources information is readily available for use in strategic and business planning.
- Stakeholder groups partner in the development and implementation of the human resources plan where appropriate.
- Work and job design promotes high performance throughout the organization by creating opportunities for initiative, self-directed responsibility, and flexibility.
- There is a rapid response to changing requirements.
- The working environment throughout the organization supports increased empowerment, personal responsibility, appropriate risk-taking, creativity, and innovation.
- Managers throughout the organization support employee contributions and teamwork; managers routinely exhibit coaching and facilitating behaviors and share authority.

- A variety of formal and/or informal reward or recognition mechanisms is used throughout the organization for all levels and types of employees. The mechanisms are developed in conjunction with employees. Emphasis is on recognition of teamwork.
- Employees throughout the organization are provided with feedback; they are evaluated, promoted, and provided with career opportunities based on personal development, contributions to quality, and operational performance goals.
- Systematic, documented education and training strategy deployed throughout the organization builds employee capabilities.
- Education and training consistently address key organization performance objectives and the motivation, progress, and development of all employees.
- Education and training is based on systematic needs assessment; employees and managers throughout the organization provide input.
- Special education and training is designed to enhance high-performance work units.
- Knowledge and skills are consistently reinforced through on-the-job application throughout the organization.
- Education and training are systematically evaluated and improved on ongoing basis using feedback from employees and customers.
- Extensive quality and skills training exists throughout the organization; all employees are trained in quality awareness; teams and work groups are trained in appropriate quality tools, techniques in support of customer service, and continuous improvement; cross-functional training is commonplace.
- The organization consistently maintains a safe, healthful work environment. Improvement efforts cover requirements and measures for all employee well-being factors (health, safety, ergonomics).
- Extensive services, facilities, activities, and opportunities are available to all employees to support overall well-being, to satisfy/enhance work experience, and to develop potential.
- A variety of measures is used to determine employee satisfaction, well-being, and motivation throughout organization; data is consistently used to improve employee satisfaction, well-being, and motivation on an ongoing basis.

Index

Printed in the USA/Agawam, MA
September 22, 2015